THE BOWL WITH ONE SPOON

Volume One

The American Empire and the Fourth World

Volume Two

Earth into Property: Colonization, Decolonization, and Capitalism

McGILL-QUEEN'S NATIVE AND NORTHERN SERIES
(IN MEMORY OF BRUCE G. TRIGGER)
SARAH CARTER AND ARTHUR J. RAY, EDITORS

Earth into Property

Colonization, Decolonization, and Capitalism

The Bowl with One Spoon
Volume Two

ANTHONY J. HALL

McGill-Queen's University Press
Montreal & Kingston • London • Ithaca

© McGill-Queen's University Press 2010
ISBN 978-0-7735-3121-5 (cloth)
ISBN 978-0-7735-3122-2 (pbk)

Legal deposit fourth quarter 2010
Bibliothèque nationale du Québec
Reprinted 2011

Printed in Canada on acid-free paper that is 100% ancient forest
free (100% post-consumer recycled), processed chlorine free

This book was first published with the help of a grant from the
University of Lethbridge.

McGill-Queen's University Press acknowledges the support of
the Canada Council for the Arts for our publishing program.
We also acknowledge the financial support of the Government
of Canada through the Book Publishing Industry Development
Program (BPIDP) for our publishing activities.

Library and Archives Canada Cataloguing in Publication

Hall, Tony, 1951–
    The bowl with one spoon / by Anthony J. Hall.

(McGill-Queen's native and northern series ; 34, 62)
Includes bibliographical references and index.
Contents: v. 1. The American empire and the fourth world –
v. 2. Earth into property : aboriginal history, human rights, law,
psychology, and politics in the making of global capitalism.
ISBN 978-0-7735-2332-6 (v. 1 : bound).
– ISBN 978-0-7735-3006-5 (v. 1 : pbk.)
ISBN 978-0-7735-3121-5 (v. 2 : bound).
– ISBN 978-0-7735-3122-2 (v. 2 : pbk.)

    1. Indians of North America – Government relations –
History. 2. America – Civilization – European influences.
3. Indians of North America – Land tenure – History.
4. United States – Territorial expansion – History. I. Title.
II. Title: The American empire and the fourth world. III. Title:
Earth into property. IV. Series: McGill-Queen's native and
northern series; 34, 62

E91.H34 2003   970.004'97   C2002-905551-2

This book was typeset by Jay Tee Graphics Ltd. in
10/12 Baskerville

To the late great

BRUCE G. TRIGGER

whose insights, vision, erudition, and encouragement are integral
to the intellectual archaeology of this project.

Contents

EARTH INTO PROPERTY

VOLUME TWO OF THE BOWL WITH ONE SPOON

The bowl with one spoon is an Aboriginal pictorial
representation of the principle that certain hunting territories
are to be held in common. In northeastern North America the
image appeared frequently in the design of many wampum
belts uesd to signify the terms of treaty agreements. In the era of
Tecumseh the image came to signify the need for federal unity
among Indigenous peoples if the shared Indian Country was ever to
achieve sovereign recognition in international law.

Memory and History in the Contest between Empire and Liberty

Not so very long ago, the earth numbered two thousand million inhabitants: five hundred million men, and one thousand five hundred million natives. The former had the Word; the others had the use of it. Between the two there were hired kinglets, overlords and a bourgeoisie, sham from beginning to end, which served as go-betweens. In the colonies the truth stood naked, but the citizens of the mother country preferred it with clothes on: the native had to love them, something in the way mothers are loved. The European élite undertook to manufacture a native élite. They picked out promising adolescents; they branded them, as with a red-hot iron, with the principles of western culture, they stuffed their mouths full with high-sounding phrases, grand glutinous words that stuck to the teeth. After a short stay in the mother country they were sent home, whitewashed. These walking lies had nothing left to say to their brothers; they only echoed.

Jean-Paul Sartre, Preface to Frantz Fanon's
Wretched of the Earth, 1961

MOTORCYCLE MEMOIRS

It is 1971. I have just turned twenty. The soles of my weathered Canadian boots are being hit from below by splashes of flying red mud. Then the road's texture changes from oozing muck to industrial-grade gravel as I chug along on my single-cylinder, British-made motorcycle – a BSA 250.

Since I left Nairobi, Kenya's capital, I have maintained a steady westward trajectory pointed at the Rwenzori Mountains. The melting snows flowing from the Rwenzoris feed the Great Lakes of equatorial Africa. Some of the runoff from the mountains descends northward to the Mediterranean through the Nile River. The peaks of this legendary range mark the imperial borderlands that historically divided British East Africa from the Belgian Congo. Two millennia ago the Greek geographer Ptolemy identified this striking feature in Africa's interior as the Mountains of the Moon.

Behind me lies the trauma of many falls from my vehicle during days of slippery travel. The dirt roads became especially soggy once I pushed beyond Kampala, Uganda's capital and main urban centre. I am badly bruised from my repeated tumbles, but none of my bones are broken. As I motor up a long gradual slope, the haze overhead burns away to reveal a shimmering sky of turquoise radiance. From the brow of the highest hill I can see an amazing alpine formation on the horizon rising from the wide expanse of hot African savannah. I rejoice at the sight. Deep down I know I have arrived at the promised land of my dreams and future reckonings.

The Rwenzoris provide the imposing backdrop of Uganda's Queen Elizabeth National Park. As I enter the zone of protected ecology I see elephants, lions, wart hogs, antelope, water buffalo, and hippopotami. But this area is not a zoo. There are no bars or barriers to separate me from one of the natural world's few remaining preserves of big predators and their game. The abundance, diversity, and curiosity of the aroused animal population invoke in me a mixture of trepidation and exhilaration. It is the people I am about to meet, however, whose insights, actions, and dilemmas will open my eyes to many of the major subjects and themes I address in *Earth into Property*, this second and culminating volume of *The Bowl with One Spoon*. Both volumes are self-contained, written to be read independently of the other. I hope, however, that the two books together constitute a literary oeuvre whose scale of significance is larger than the sum of its parts.

As I write these words, my coming-of-age pilgrimage is now almost four decades in the past. I have lived two-thirds of my life since those months when I ventured far beyond the frontiers of what was familiar, safe, and comfortable up to that point. Looking back, I can appreciate the way my experiences in that corner of the world fundamentally altered my conception of how the past connects to humanity's present conditions and future possibilities. During my African safari I was able to gain the necessary distance and perspective to picture myself as a member of a small but powerful colonizing culture amid a global majority of Indigenous peoples. I was able to picture my own North American society in its imperial relationship to the emerging civilization of global humanity. This global community of communities emerges from complex systems of cultural roots that infuse the nourishment of life into many intertwined traditions of Aboriginal history.

In 1971 the Indigenous peoples of East, Central, and West Africa were just beginning to emerge from the formal rule of imperial masters headquartered in Europe. Between 1962 and 1964 the citizens of Kenya, Uganda, and Tanzania were extended nominal independence by their departing British governors. In the vast region between the Rwenzoris and Africa's Atlantic coast, a similar transfer of power had taken place in 1960, when the government of Belgium withdrew its formal apparatus of imperial rule from the region drained by the Congo River.

I began to awaken to my own complicity in the continuing violence and oppressiveness of colonialism's harsh legacies as I travelled the Aboriginal soil of these supposedly liberated territories in the early years following their release from the formal hold of European empires. At its outer extremes the racial and ethnic severity of this ongoing violence goes far beyond anything I could have imagined growing up in York Mills, a suburb of class privilege in Toronto, Ontario. As I argue throughout this text, humanity is still a long way from realizing the egalitarian promise of genuine decolonization. The transformation of colonial empires into many dozens of nominally self-governing countries after the Second World War marks only the initial steps in the process of ending the exploitative subjugation of the largest plurality of global citizens by a small, disproportionately entitled minority.

I began *The American Empire and the Fourth World*, the first volume of *The Bowl with One Spoon*, with a description of a more recent road trip, one that took my son Sampson and me in 1992 from Charlottetown, Prince Edward Island, to Johnson Hall, just west of Albany, New York. In that narrative I identified the restored home of Sir William Johnson and his Mohawk partner, Molly Brant, as a major shrine commemorating a little-understood tradition of Anglo-American imperialism, one that I see as concurrently more conservative and more enlightened than the genre of empire building subsequently advanced by the United States of America. I traced the European-led movements of colonization initiated by Christopher Columbus in 1492 all the way across time and space to the US-led invasions of Afghanistan and Iraq in the early years of the twenty-first century. Here, in *Earth into Property*, I continue to elaborate and expand the scope of this narrative. As the title implies, this second volume of the *Bowl* project puts particular emphasis on the material aspect of interactions linking human beings with one another and the rest of nature. It places a spotlight on the complex and many-faceted trajectories of historical change that converge in the global pervasiveness of the system of political economy widely identified as capitalism.

I attempt throughout both volumes to balance my macroscopic consideration of the history of imperialism, capitalism, and decolonization with more detailed studies that illustrate various aspects of the human urge to break free from the onerous weight of repressive systems of foreign domination. As Karl Marx observed long ago, these harsh forces of subjugation have proven surprisingly adaptable and resilient over time. "In actual history," he wrote, "it is notorious that conquest, enslavement, robbery, murder, briefly force, play the greatest part."[1]

We live in a time when the cycles of imperial globalization that have been gathering force since 1492 find expression in the ongoing push to expand and totalize capitalism's pre-eminence as humanity's sole system of political economy. Never before in history have virtually all braches of humanity been subjected to so much pressure to conform to a single regime of material interaction. As I first began to apprehend during my circumnavigation of the Rwenzori Mountains, the greatest obstacle to the universalization of capitalism remains the collective propensity of Indigenous peoples the world over to resist both the appropriation of their Aboriginal lands and resources and the elimination of their diversity of languages, laws, and institutions.

From these deep wells of Aboriginal opposition to growing claims of colonialism emerge rivulets of resistance, which gradually merge to form a rising stream of anti-imperial globalization. I see this anti-imperial current as the other side of the massive imperial initiatives whose force became much more pronounced after Christopher Columbus began the modern era of globalization. In planting the cross of his Roman Catholic sponsors on the eastern shores of the Atlantic Ocean, Columbus pointed Western Europe towards history's most ambitious grab for new territories, plunder, and slaves. In Rome the Vatican sanctioned the imperial claims of Spain and Portugal as if the Pope was God's chosen lawgiver in the Western Hemisphere. The Protestant powers of Holland and England soon responded by pressing their own counterclaims of dominion to large portions of the so-called New World of America.

In their struggle to escape annihilation, subjugation, enslavement, and the theft of their ancestral lands and waters, many Indigenous peoples and their allies have tried to broaden the reach of their freedom struggles. As demonstrated in the complex alliances that coalesced around the anti-imperial mobilizations led, for instance, by Túpac Amaru, Tecumseh, Toussaint L'Overature, José Rizal, Mahatma Gandhi, Mao Zedong, Gamal Abdul Nasser, Kwame Nkrumah, W.E.B. Du Bois, Ho Chi Minh, Nelson Mandela, Patrice Lumumba, and Leonard Peltier, the world's colonized peoples have tried sporadically to draw unity from their Aboriginal diversity. To achieve this end, the natural enemies of imperialism have had to imagine themselves in larger and larger ways. They have bridged many divides of ethnicity, language, religion, and ideology in order to expand the scope of their confederacies of Aboriginal opposition to the oppressiveness of both colonial and neo-colonial rule.

This process of anti-imperial globalization did not end with the extension of independence to the citizens of former colonies. Rather, the agents of anti-imperial struggle have had to adjust to the transition from formal colonial rule to the informal imperialism based on imposed structures, such as rigged systems of manipulated debt. The necessity of continuing the anti-imperial struggle makes especially strong demands on the most self-aware component of humanity that Frantz Fanon once labelled the "wretched of the earth."[2] As long as cycles of anti-imperial globalization continue, humanity retains some access to strategic venues of escape from the tyranny of a single worldwide monoculture of economic exploitation.

Throughout both volumes of *The Bowl with One Spoon* I associate this diversity of decolonizing energies and strategies with the Fourth World. I attempt to widen and extend the meaning of this term, which was first popularized by George Manuel, the founder of the World Council of Indigenous Peoples. In the mid-1970s he advanced a vision of the Fourth World as the basis for non-aligned disengagement from the dual empires of the primary protagonists in the Cold War.[3] This Shuswap Indian leader from British

Columbia, the westernmost province of Canada, gave clear, straightforward expression to some of the underlying principles that were first articulated in 1955 at Bandung in Indonesia. There the leading representatives of the colonized peoples of Africa and Asia met to chart a non-aligned course aimed at evading the bipolar entanglements of the Cold War.

During the second half of the twentieth century, the Soviet and US-led antagonists in the Cold War sought to induce those just emerging from the formal colonialism of Europe to alter their societies in ways that adhered to externally derived models of change and development. Together, the competing superpowers promoted their mirrored and opposing systems of political economy as though these two options represented humanity's only available pathways to the future. This deceit was extended in the early 1990s, when the demise of the Soviet-led alternative was made to seem like the basis for reducing the number of options from two to only one. US-dominated capitalism was aggressively promoted as though this regime of political economy would inevitably assimilate all humanity at the end of history.[4] The rising economic power of China, India, and Brazil, together with the weakening position of the United States in the twenty-first century, has not reduced the pressure to eliminate all aspects of diversity that do not conform to the imperatives of making a single global market prevail over the human commonwealth of cultural inheritance, renewal, and creativity.

I explored the revelations that came my way in Africa first as an undergraduate, then as a graduate student, and, after 1982, in working my way through the ranks of the academy to full professorship. Throughout this process I attempted to add flesh, blood, and context to my core interests in empires, Indigenous peoples, and decolonization. I did so by investigating topics such as the fur trade of North America, the transatlantic slave trade, and the role of the Opium Wars in opening China to foreign domination. My pursuit of such lines of inquiry led me to expand the scope of my investigations across an increasingly broad array of topics, including mercantilism, Social Darwinism, European social democracy, the New Deal, the genesis of international law – and the striking failure to enforce it.

Any survey of the sparse and sporadic history of the enforcement of international law reveals that those individuals and agencies that have been most deeply involved in perpetrating the highest order of international crime have only infrequently been held accountable for their actions. In the rare instances where juridical processes have been instituted to try to punish those responsible for ordering and directing the highest level of international crime, these exercises almost invariably become show trials based on the brash claims of victors' justice. Those who give executive direction to war crimes and crimes against humanity have consistently been immunized from legal consequences for their actions as long as the outcome is to maintain the rule of the powerful over the vanquished, dispossessed, and marginalized portions of humanity. How much longer can the rule of law be subordinated to the culture of impunity that consistently protects a small, disproportionately entitled minority from the incursions of a massively disentitled global majority?

The thick weave of connections running throughout the wide array of interrelated topics explored in this text points consistently to the preeminence of economic factors in determining the outcome of many different types of political transaction. The consistency of this pattern became increasingly clear in the course of my detailed study of the history of warfare and treaty making with Indigenous peoples of North America in the genesis of the Dutch Empire, the French Empire, the Spanish Empire, the British Empire, Canada, Mexico, and the United States. Throughout *The Bowl with One Spoon* I locate the frontier expansions of Euro-America in the larger context of world history because of the importance of this saga in orienting the primary capitalist superpower during the twentieth century towards its myriad exercises of influence and control in the global community.

A key chapter in this volume emphasizes the fascist defence of capitalism's empire against the spread of Soviet-led communism, especially during the era when the Great Depression led to the rise of the Axis polities and those of its collaborators throughout much of Asia and most of continental Europe. The ascent of Adolf Hitler and his allies was supported by a worldwide network of industrialists and financiers, some of whom helped to engineer the extension of many US-based cartels into Germany. In this way a broad array of multinational companies, including Ford, GM, IBM, and Standard Oil of New Jersey, became key institutions in the fascist regime's military-industrial complex.

Beneath this saga of German-US relations lies a much deeper history linking the moving frontiers of Euro-America to the phenomenon of massive emigration from central Europe. The importance of German immigrants in the remaking of a continent helped to solidify the idea in the minds of some people that the westward expansion of the United States was a model for the eastward expansion of the German Empire for the purpose of obtaining *Lebensraum*. While the Old Testament authority for the spread of God's Chosen People was an essential element in the expansionary ethos of US Manifest Destiny, the secularization of imperial ideology was reflected in the core myth used to justify the expansion of the Hitlerian state into Eastern Europe and Russia.

For Hitler as for his fellow devotees of scientific racism, the elimination and subjugation of the "Red Indians" formed a prelude to the extension of the same process in the eastward expansion of imperial Germany through the conquest of the "Slavic races." Like the eugenic campaign to eliminate European Jewry, the effort to defeat, subjugate, and enslave Slavs was presented as the application of Darwinian conceptions of natural law. In this dark cosmology epitomizing the overlapping ideological terrain between the most aggressive varieties of imperialism and capitalism, human history is conceived as a theatre for the expression of evolutionary processes based on the struggle between competing organisms, races, corporations, and states. The other side of the Darwinian credo of the survival of the fittest is the elimination of the weak and the less fit. The leadership of the Hitlerian state set out to make its charter members instruments and agents of this process of historical progress through lethal competition, by implementing policies whose savagery became so ostentatious that they necessitated the invention of a new word. Coined by Raphael Lemkin in 1944, that word is "genocide."

After the Second World War, the United States took the lead in incorporating the defeated remnants of the military-industrial complex of Axis rule into its own ascendant military-industrial complex. The international fortunes of a favoured set of corporate patrons and clients were thereby advanced in the name of the quest to weaken and destroy international communism. In this fashion, some of the legacies of the fascist experiment in capitalist expansion were retained and injected into the mixed economy inherited from President Franklin Roosevelt's New Deal. This potent merger of two capitalist systems that had previously been at war introduced new energies into the effort to constrain humanity's diverse modes of material interaction. Old cycles of imperial globalization were rejuvenated with the application of updated techniques of command and control. In leading the process, agents of the US-led national security state pre-empted many initiatives in indigenous self-determination which might otherwise have filled the vacuum of authority that arose from the formal dismantling of European empires in Africa and Asia.

As formally empowered by Congress's enactment in 1947 of the *National Security Act,* the national security state extended the covert and overt interventions of the US executive branch to global proportions. Its functioning, as epitomized by the covert operations of the Central Intelligence Agency (CIA), was to pick up where the fascist powers had left off – as the primary shield and the spear in the campaign to defend and expand capitalism's empire of private property. These interventions went far beyond concerted assaults on any and all attempts to implement socialist and communist principles. They extended (and continue to extend) to steady incursions on any form of human interaction and organization whose effect is to constrain the growth of capitalism into new frontiers of privatization through the commodification of expanding orbits of mind, matter, and relationship.

A spotlight on the processes that converge in the Earth's transformation into property helps to illuminate the nature of the shift from mercantile imperialism to the subsequent era of capitalist neo-colonialism. An essential element in the maintenance of capitalism's hierarchy of material interactions resides in the policing functions carried out at the highest levels by operatives of the national security state. The invasive worldwide operations of the national security state and its attending military-industrial complex became increasingly difficult to justify and maintain following the demise of the Soviet Union. The end of the Cold War therefore necessitated the identification of a new global enemy to replace the role formerly assigned to communist internationalism.

Fortunately for those who have benefited most from the relationships of power cemented into place ever since the United States first adopted its permanent war economy in 1941, such an enemy was made to appear with considerable assistance from some of the national security state's own operatives. The new enemy was a coddled anti-communist ally of the United States. The same forces of radical Islamic jihad that had been organized, trained, financed, and armed by capitalism's Cold Warriors were now made to demonstrate the effectiveness of their hostility towards the Judeo-Christian West – just in time to pre-empt the changes that might have coalesced if the era of relative peace following the fall of the Berlin Wall had been allowed to continue. After September 11, 2001, the activities of the permanent war economy were accelerated and further privatized with a vengeance.

The effect of the Cold War, followed by the Global War on Terror, has been to hollow out much of the promise of decolonization that might otherwise have been realized after the dismantling of European empires. Some of the most oppressed and dispossessed branches of humanity remain as subjugated as ever. Those who are engaged in the continuing quest to decolonize a world polarized between rich and poor must continue to draw liberally on the deep heritage of anti-imperial activism even as they adapt to the altered motifs of military, psychological, political, and commercial control.

In the transition to the new forms of imperial globalization, the plight of the displaced and stateless Palestinians has provided a lightening rod and proxy for the grievances of colonized peoples the world over. Many of colonialism's core attributes have been replicated and extended in the imposition, beginning in 1947, of the Jewish state on the ancestral land of the Palestinians. The territory where Palestine and Israel overlap is situated on the eastern shores of the Mediterranean Sea, a strategic point of convergence between Europe, Asia, and Africa. The indigenous people of Palestine never consented to bear the huge human costs resulting from the international recognition of the sovereign Israeli state. This recognition was extended by some governments as an act of atonement for the long heritage of crimes against European Jewry which culminated in the horrors of the Nazi holocaust.

In *Culture and Imperialism* and a stream of other publications, the Palestinian-American scholar Edward Said has addressed some of "the big questions set by the grand narratives of emancipation and enlightenment."[5] In *The Bowl with One Spoon* I have attempted to continue Said's quest for synthetic understanding of both colonialism and the opposition responses that imperial domination invariably generates. Only by exploring the interface between the urge to build empires and the urge to decolonize humanity's most oppressed branches can we move effectively towards ending the destabilizing disequilibrium between imperial and anti-imperial globalization. By bringing forward telling examples and case studies that illuminate the Aboriginal history of both empire building and the resulting struggles for decolonization, new resources become available to inspire, inform, and orient those engaged in the contemporary struggle to advance the ideals of universal freedom, equality, and ecological sustainability.

In 1971 I saw real and compelling evidence of the failure to extend the formal end of European imperialism in Africa to genuine decolonization of its peoples. This failure was exemplified by the domestic repressions of Idi Amin's presidency in Uganda and Joseph-Désiré Mobuto's presidency in the Congo. Their respective military dictatorships governed the countries on both sides of the Rwenzoris during the time that I circumnavigated the Mountains of the Moon on my motorcycle. Both Amin and Mobutu had come to power by ascending the ranks of their respective armies. Both were installed through the connivance of outside intervention to protect the interests of international capital as part of the rivalry between the two superpowers and their allies in the Cold War. Similarly, both men were removed with the complicity of the same interests once they had outlived their usefulness to the main proprietors of imperial capital.

THE SECULAR FUNDAMENTALISM OF CHE VERSUS THE POSTMODERN MORAL RELATIVISM OF OBAMA

I have a clear picture in my mind of the moment in 1971 when four or five men carried my BSA motorcycle on their shoulders across the body of water marking the international border between Uganda and the Congo. Even at its deepest spot, the fast-flowing river emanating from the Rwenzoris' northeasterly slopes came only half way up the men's spines. The mental images on which I draw are more like still photographs than moving pictures. There are gaps in the sequence of scenes imprinted in my remembrances of things past. I can't recall, for instance, how I got across the river. Did I wade through the water, packsack over my head, or was I transported to the far shore in some kind of small vessel?

My difficulty in reconstructing the details of my journey across this divide between historical empires and contemporary nationalities illustrates the imperfect quality of relationships among memory, autobiography, and history. The uneven reliability and sometimes self-serving character of human recollection adds layers of complexity to the problems inherent in any literary representation of time's duration. This introduction forms a case in point. In it I want to convey a sense of how I viewed my world when I was twenty years old. But I am also incorporating information, reflections, and interpretations that have come to me at intervals over the years since my motorcycle safari. The paradoxes of applying contemporary analysis to various configurations of remembered, imagined, and reconstructed time do not end there. Like all authors, I am writing in a present that will slip into the past until the moment when, with luck, my prose begins to interact across a sea of time with the memories, experiences, and analytical capacities of you, the reader.

My non-linear approach to chronology throughout this text reflects my preoccupation with the many ways of measuring, marking, and imagining time's flow. I picture time as myriad spiraling cycles of change, all cascading down the fall lines of history's watersheds towards the levelling sea of humanity's commonalities. In much the same fashion that, say, an Olympic runner and a patient diagnosed with terminal cancer might understand and experience time in very different ways, so the same can be said of whole societies. The observation that time's movements are variable, elastic, and idiosyncratic was confirmed scientifically by Albert Einstein in his explanation of time's contingent relationship to the constant speed of light.

Einstein's theories of relativity helped to blast apart the false securities engendered by Newton's views of the cosmos as an ordered mechanical system operating with the linear and stable predictability of a well-oiled clock. If even time is not fixed and uniform, what else, then, is not as it seems? One need only gaze out at the stars in the night sky to see a mosaic of different moments in time displayed across the heavens. Each speck of light began its journey to our eyes at a different instant, perhaps only minutes ago or perhaps many thousands or millions of years in the past.

Edward Said has commented sagely on the importance of developing new narrative strategies to reflect the unprecedented proliferation of merging heritages, traditions, and systems of knowledge that meet in our changing orientations to the passage of time. "We are mixed in with one another," he observes, "in ways that most national systems of education have not dreamed of." He adds, "To match knowledge in the arts and sciences with these integrative realities is, I believe, the cultural challenge of the moment."[6]

In *The Bowl with One Spoon* I respond to Said's encouragement to make the social sciences more reflective of global patterns of mixture and métissage. "No one today is purely *one* thing," he famously declared.[7] Following Said's bold intellectual pursuits at the interface between scholarship and anti-colonial politics, I have tried to extend the frontiers of intercultural and interdisciplinary study with the goal of moving beyond the constraints of our ailing and often parochial systems of national education. This text, therefore, is more like an omnigraph than a monograph.

In this account of empire building and decolonization, I seek to renew and extend the project initiated by Denis Diderot and the other encyclopedists of the Century of Enlightenment. I draw on the primal wisdom of Aboriginal elders as well as the best inheritance of the *siècle des lumières* to survey the human condition from a multiplicity of vantage points. The result approaches that of an encyclopedic account of power's workings in an emerging global civilization encompassing many landscapes of inherited and contemporary knowledge. In moving beyond the confines of narrow and circumscribed academic specialization, I believe I have come up with a text that suggests the outlines for a new geography of global literature, a new genre of narrative in the social sciences that is more attuned to ecological and interactive models of globalization.

Enlightened models of globalization incorporate the democratic ideal of self-determination for both individuals and multitudes of groups, including peoples, nations, and transnational unions of workers. Democratic globalization would tie the ideal of multiple expressions of self-determination to the articulation of a global rule of law that could be arbitrated and enforced with consistency and uniformity, even on the most powerful members of society. Attention to the global enactment and enforcement of a universal code of conduct would have to be balanced with the Fourth World quest for ecological equilibrium through the cultivation of biocultural pluralism. The concept of biocultural pluralism emerges from the understanding that biological diversity in the plant and animal realms, and cultural diversity in the human realm, form different sides of the same ecological equation.[8] This emphasis on biocultural pluralism builds on themes and interpretations introduced by Richard Evans Schultes and his students in their pioneering studies of ethnobotany.[9]

In much the same style as in *The American Empire and the Fourth World*, in this volume I take the reader up and down many different representational watersheds of historical change. I leave the more predictable trails of specialized monographs in order to chart a freer and more far-ranging literary safari across broad kaleidoscopes of theory, ethnography, geography, politics, and ideology. This representational technique requires modes of explanation that delicately balance the subjective with the objective. It necessitates narrative strategies that reflect with sensitivity the subtle distinctions between what is relatively true, and therefore dependent on the context and orientation of the observer, and what, like the speed of light, is invariable and absolute. Unlike the dimensions of human experience and perception that involve subjectivity and relativity, the domain of absolute truth transcends the observers' changing orientations to time, place, and historical circumstance.

In the years since my motorcycle safari throughout Central Africa's Great Lakes region, I have come to associate the area with two pivotal figures – each of whom embodies a different relationship to the ongoing tension between imperial and anti-imperial globalization. One of these figures is Barack Obama, the current president of the United States; the other is Ernesto "Che" Guevara. Obama epitomizes moral relativism and the constantly shifting perspectives and orientations integral to postmodernism. Che was anchored in a posture of unflinching moral certainty reflecting an unbending interpretation of imperial capital as the major source of human exploitation.

As Barack Obama emphasizes in the culminating chapters of his autobiography, *Dreams from My Father*, he derives his paternal line of ancestry from the Luo tribe. The Kenyan-based Luo dominate the western shores of Lake Victoria. They are close ethnic and linguistic cousins of the Lango and Acholi peoples of Uganda. Barack Obama Sr visited his son only once, in 1971, when the boy was ten years old – the same year I toured Africa's Great Lakes region on my motorcycle. He had courted and married Ann Dunham, the future president's mother, when they were both students at the University of Hawaii.

Che's connection to Central Africa was that of a self-declared revolutionary freedom fighter who briefly entered the political and military fractiousness in that troubled corner of the world. When I crossed the river into eastern Congo, I had no idea that the iconographic Che Guevara had been in the region only six years before.

In the mid-1950s, Che and a handful of revolutionaries led by Fidel Castro had built a base of support among the poor peasantry of the Cuban countryside and, in 1959, they toppled the Mafia-backed regime of Fulgencio Batista. Then, after a tour of some of the newly independent countries in Africa, Che and a small group of Cuban soldiers tried to extend the spirit of the Cuban revolution to this strategic zone of Cold War conflict. As Che saw it, "neocolonialism has bared its claws in the Congo,"[10] to the point where "the Congo problem is a world problem."[11]

For several months Che's Cuban brigade attempted to train and inspire an indigenous opposition capable of pushing back the forces of international capital, as channelled most tellingly into the military actions of several hundred White mercenary soldiers from South Africa and Rhodesia. These mercenaries had been hired to root out the fighting forces of a number of factions, including Che's Cubans. All the opponents of the mercenaries and their backers claimed that their objective was to create military conditions conducive to bringing about various visions of African socialism.

The success of these well-financed mercenary forces in the air and on the ground highlighted the corresponding failure of Che and his men to replicate the success of the Cuban revolution in the biggest country of equatorial Africa. This outcome helped clear the way for the installation of the US-backed dictatorship of General Mobutu. Che had entered the African theatre of conflict at a time when the Congo was still reeling from the internal turmoil wrought by the CIA-ordered assassination of Patrice Lumumba – the first elected leader of the former Belgian Congo. Lumumba met his demise in 1960 after he declared that he intended to extend the self-government of his people to the nationalization of the country's great wealth in natural resources.

Che described his evolution as a soldier of revolutionary change in his *Motorcycle Dairies,* a text that inspired my own narrative of self-discovery in this introduction.[12] Setting out from his Argentine home in 1953 on his 500-cc Norton to discover the soul of South America, the young medical student confronted the reality of his own position of privilege as a middle-class Latino when he travelled among the poor but culturally vibrant Indian populations of Peru. Throughout the remaining years of his prematurely terminated life, this archetypal freedom fighter saw few shades of grey in his stark identification of "Yankee imperialism" as the epitome of capitalist evil to be defeated. With the heavy involvement of the CIA, Che was martyred in Bolivia in 1967 during a failed revolutionary campaign similar to the one he had attempted to lead in the eastern Congo.[13]

Although the Cuban military mission to the eastern Congo ended in failure, the government of Fidel Castro used this debacle to learn how to develop more effective and practical policies for constructive intervention in the turmoil of Africa south of the Saharan Desert. Cuba's commitment of doctors, teachers, agricultural experts, and soldiers to the liberation struggles of Africa's peoples proved more successful in Guinea-Bissau, Angola, and the other territories that had been shaped by the rise and fall of the Portuguese Empire.

This trajectory of involvement reached a climax in 1988–89, when the Cuban government committed more than 50,000 fully equipped soldiers to protect its allied government in Angola and to join the struggle for the political independence of Namibia. The decisive role of Cuban troops in the Battle of Cuito Cuanavale helped turn the military tide against the White minority regime and its proxy armies which were armed and financed to serve the US-led side of the Cold War. The retreat of the forces of White supremacy from the battlefields of the front-line states led to the release of Nelson Mandela from prison in 1990 and then to the South African government's abandonment of the most savage instruments of racial apartheid. With the now decriminalized African National Congress taking the lead, the principles of majority rule were allowed to prevail.

"The Cuban role in Africa is unprecedented," observed Piero Gleijeses. "What other Third World country has ever projected its power beyond its immediate neighborhood?"[14] Acting largely on their own, the Cuban people and their government proved to be key agents in tipping the scale of power against apartheid in its most notorious den.[15] In 1995 Nelson Mandela, the first president of post-apartheid South Africa and one of his continent's most revered icons in the struggle for human liberation, proclaimed, "Cubans came to our region as doctors, teachers, soldiers, agricultural experts, but never as colonizers." And he concluded: "They have shared the same trenches with us. We are deeply indebted to the Cuban people for the selfless contribution they made to the anti-colonial and anti-apartheid struggle in our region."[16]

As I motorcycled through the thick and verdant jungle on the Congolese side of the Ruwenzori Mountains, Mandela had been languishing inside South Africa's jail for seven years. As a leader of the military wing of the outlawed African National Congress, he would spend almost two more decades in Robben Island penitentiary before he was released to lead his country away from the era of White minority rule. Many of the international forces that combined to keep him criminalized and behind bars were the same ones that supported the Congolese government headed by Che's African nemesis, General Mobutu.

Che's foray into the eastern Congo acquired a different hue of meaning in light of Cuba's subsequent importance in disarming the forces of African apartheid. Similarly, Che's intervention in Bolivia took on heightened significance after the election in 2005 of Evo Morales as president of that country. Morales rose to power from humble origins in the complex of Andean Indian societies whose marginalized condition helped to radicalize Che during his motorcycle tour of Latin America. Soon after coming to power, Morales allied his left-leaning government with that of Cuba. By this time the Cuban Revolution had long outlived the careers of its former patrons in the defunct Soviet Union. The resilient determination of the Cuban Revolution's most committed cadres helped to inspire a new generation of socialist idealists and agitators who used the ballot box to gain a tenuous hold on political power in some South American countries. The Venezuelan president and firebrand Hugo Chavez became the leading figure in a more recent surge of anti-imperial activism that took hold in some of the oldest informal colonies of the American empire.

From 2004 to 2009, negotiations between the Castro brothers and Hugo Chavez became the seed of a diplomatic process that led the governments of Cuba, Venezuela, Bolivia, Honduras, Nicaragua, Ecuador, Dominica, Antigua, and Barbuda, as well as Saint Vincent and the Grenadines, to form the Bolivarian Alliance for the Americas (ALBA). In Spanish, *alba* means "dawn." In 2009 the ALBA allies moved to create a common currency, the sucre. In the course of these discussions, Honduras's membership in ALBA became problematic after Manuel Zelaya's presidency was targeted in a US-backed military coup, initiating a constitutional crisis.[17] In all the ALBA countries, Che has been adopted as a kind of secular patron saint. For many millions in Latin America and beyond, he continues to embody the spirit of uncompromising revolt against the corruption of ill-used power. Like Martin King Jr, Bobby Kennedy, and John Lennon, Che was murdered when he was still young, handsome, and extremely menacing to the most entrenched interests of the status quo.

Even in capitalism's most robust commercial metropolises, pictures capturing the earnest defiance of the gregarious Che have been replicated by the millions on T-shirts and other bric-à-brac. Che's stylish, avant-garde appeal continues to defy the grey stereotypes of stiff conformity and austerity colouring popular perceptions of Soviet-style communism. Like the qualities of fixedness epitomized by light's unchanging speed, Che's unbending hostility to the military force backing the imperial privilege of crony capitalism continues to exercise considerable allure across generations, ideologies, and cultures.

Those responsible for packaging Barack Obama drew unashamedly from the pictographic heritage of Che's legend as they mounted perhaps the world's most successful ever advertising campaign. As Naomi

Klein observed, "Obama beat out Nike, Coors, and Zappos to win the Association of National Advertisers top annual award, Marketer of the Year." She goes on to cite Desirée Rogers, the White House's social secretary, that "We have the best brand on earth: the Obama brand."[18] As Webster Tarpley has written, "Obama has unquestionably been the beneficiary of the biggest sustained effort of mass media manipulation since the events of September 11, 2001."[19]

The postmodern quality of brand Obama seems to go beyond the realm of public perception to permeate the man's inner life as well. The rapidly shifting vantage points and perspectives available to Obama is put on display in *Dreams from My Father*, the text he was commissioned to write in 1990 shortly after becoming the first African-American president of *The Harvard Law Review*. Like *The Biography of Malcolm X*, Obama's autobiography is at its core a story about an individual's quest for self-understanding and purpose. He relates his experiences of growing up in Hawaii, Indonesia, California, New York, Chicago, and Kenya, even as he muses at length about the abundant ethnic complexities of his family tree. He sees his youth and early manhood as a testament to the "fluid state of identity – the leaps through time, the collisions of culture – that mark our modern life."[20]

In *Dreams from My Father*, Obama often shifts his gaze from side to side of a lens of distorting stereotypes. He peers outward at the prejudices of others, then looks inward to observe and analyze his own foibles, blinkers, predispositions, potentials, and limitations. Raised by White grandparents from Kansas, a globetrotting mother with strong professional credentials in anthropology, a Muslim stepfather in Indonesia, and a mostly absent Luo father who nevertheless deeply affects his son's imaginative life, Obama is constantly marvelling at the dynamic quality of human attachments to community. Behind his maternal grandmother's façade of Whiteness, Obama finds a Cherokee ancestor who comes to hold a totemic importance in his American heritage. He confronts his own tendency as a Black man to generalize about the attributes of White people, even as he wonders what influence his own White ancestry exerts on the estimations of his Black friends and acquaintances. In Indonesia he adapts to the Islamic faith of his peers, whereas in Kenya he must deal with issues of class, clan, and tribe as he negotiates the complexities of an extended family derived from the polygamous relationships of his Luo father.

In an era when, as Said has declared, no one is any longer one thing, Barack Obama epitomizes the capacity of a single individual to encompass many identities simultaneously. This chameleon quality makes it possible for observers to see in him whatever they want. The positive twist on the "humpbacked, ugly," and even criminal connotations that, not long ago, attached to the concept of "miscegenation" has helped to give Obama's many-faceted political personae great popular currency.[21] It has also made it extremely hard to pin Obama down and to hold him accountable for the contradictions he regularly spins in weaving webs of high expectations along with illusions, delusions, deniability, and evasion. Often several different Obamas all seem to be residing within the corporal being of the same man.

The US president displayed one of his wise and conciliatory personalities at the Fifth Summit of the Americas in Trinidad and Tobago in April 2009. There he alluded to the high quality of the Cuban health-care system and its positive impact throughout Latin America. He referred to "the thousands of doctors from Cuba that are dispersed all throughout the region, and upon which many of these countries are heavily dependent." He spoke of the overdependence of his own government on military force and the importance of the Cuban example in highlighting the need to direct "development aid in more intelligent ways so that people can see practical, concrete improvements in their lives."[22]

President Obama's seemingly sensible approach to foreign policy was again on display in September 2009, when he addressed the General Assembly of the United Nations. One of the key passages in that speech could have been drawn from the ideals of the Fourth World and their expression in some of the principles and policies of the Non-Aligned Movement: "Democracy cannot be imposed on any nation from the outside," he said. "Each society must search for its own path, and no path is perfect. Each country must search for its own path rooted in the culture of its people and in its own past traditions."[23]

The Obama who spoke of his commitment to reconcile US power with the sovereign rights of the world's culturally diverse peoples was, however, sharply contradicted by the Obama who addressed an audience at the West Point Military Academy on December 1, 2009. This Obama revealed himself to be the servant of Wall Street's dominant clique, whose corporate extensions in the military-industrial complex form the great nexus of wealth and global influence in the American empire of monopoly capitalism.

The continuities linking the military policies of President George W. Bush to those of Barack Obama demonstrate persuasively the enormous power base of the axis of influence linking Wall Street, the Pentagon, and the worldwide networks of crony capitalists whose concentrated privileges flow from these centres of intertwined power.[24] Although subject to some internal jockeying among competing factions, this complex of interconnected insiders maintains sufficient coherence to control the financial nerve centre of the world's most well-equipped and massively mobilized military leviathan. The Obama administration gave this unaccountable plutocracy of bankers, war profiteers, and propagandists a green light to continue raiding the public treasury. He provided cover and support for the continued expansion of the national security apparatus of the US executive branch as the core agency in the emerging global police state of corporatist authoritarianism.

To keep sufficient public acquiescence for continuing this agenda of elite control, the substance or façade of a credible global enemy is essential if the ailing superpower is to justify and maintain the global operations of its permanent war economy. When he dutifully repeated the mythological mantra essential to the continued backing by taxpayers of the September 11 wars, President Obama renewed the psychology of fear that keeps viable and alive the reigning demonology of the military-industrial complex.

In announcing the addition of tens of thousands of extra US troops and mercenary forces to be deployed in Afghanistan and Pakistan, President Obama lent the weight of his electoral mandate to a set of objectives only slightly revised from those introduced by the Project for the New American Century.[25] In 2000, the think tank and war lobby PNAC proposed a massive augmentation in US military power. In laying out this program, PNAC's leadership recognized that the costly implementation of its far-reaching proposals to confirm, extend, and consolidate the coercive machinery of US global dominance would depend on a massive transformation in public opinion – through something akin to the surprise attacks on Pearl Harbor in 1941.[26]

In explaining the background of his government's decision, President Obama repeated President George W. Bush's core justifications for the Global War on Terror:

On September 11, 2001, 19 men hijacked four airplanes and used them to murder nearly 3,000 people. They struck at our military and economic nerve centers. They took the lives of innocent men, women, and children without regard to their faith or race or station. Were it not for the heroic actions of passengers onboard one of those flights, they could have also struck at one of the great symbols of our democracy in Washington, and killed many more.

As we know, these men belonged to al Qaeda – a group of extremists who have distorted and defiled Islam, one of the world's great religions, to justify the slaughter of innocents. Al Qaeda's base of operations was in Afghanistan, where they were harbored by the Taliban – a ruthless, repressive and radical movement that seized control of that country after it was ravaged by years of Soviet occupation and civil war, and after the attention of America and our friends had turned elsewhere.

Just days after 9/11, Congress authorized the use of force against al Qaeda and those who harbored them – an authorization that continues to this day.[27]

One of my tasks in the chapters ahead is to expose the contrived distortions, omissions, and outright lies in this short but extremely consequential interpretation of recent history. President Obama's presentation of this Bushite fable as fact signalled the emptiness of his promise that a partisan change of executive power in the United States would lead away from the imperial obsessions of the Republican Party's leadership. The speech and the many global responses it triggered revealed that the axis of influence between Wall Street and the Pentagon would continue to augment its unaccountable power – but faster, on a larger scale, and in a more devious and dishonest fashion.

What lay behind President Obama's commitment of increased high-tech killing power into those Eurasian territories where imperial conflicts between warring civilizations have been under way for millennia? The decision was mostly about the geopolitics of oil and gas extraction, pipeline construction, and the global distribution of commodified energy. It had much to do with a looming showdown between Euro-America, Russia, and China for control of huge reserves of the world's most strategic resource, one that has fuelled the ongoing Industrial Revolution ever since the oil magnate John David Rockefeller and the car maker Henry Ford altered the course of imperial globalization by creating new prototypes of corporate empire. It also had much to do with the strategy of Anglo-American power brokers seeking to balkanize yet further the world's oil-producing and -exporting heartland by inciting, funding, arming, and exploiting religious and ethnic civil wars in a part of the world where many of the international borders are inherited from earlier eras of imperial rule.[28]

Alternatively, President Obama's decision to send 30,000 more fighting forces into the Af-Pak battle zone had little to do with protection from international terrorism of those citizens who were obliged to pay for this military build-up with tax dollars. Indeed, much information is already in the public domain documenting in detail the role of key operatives of the national security state in helping to organize, augment, direct, and exploit the armed militance of hand-picked Islamic theocrats as proxy forces on the capitalist side of the Cold War, especially in Afghanistan and in the southern republics of the former Soviet Union. The overt and covert encouragement of the more aggressive branches of Islamic militance continued after the demise of the Soviet Empire and became a factor in the Balkan wars, the 9/11 attacks, and the 7/7 subway bombings in London in 2005.[29]

The transition from the Cold War to the 9/11 wars has given rise to a reversion to some of the same rationales that were used to justify the Indian wars – the wars by which the territorial outlines of the US Homeland were initially carved out. President Obama's reference in his West Point speech to an enemy that acts "without regard to the faith or race or station" of its victims is similar to the condemnation in the American Declaration of Independence of the "merciless Indian savages whose known rule of warfare is an undistinguished destruction of all ages, sexes and conditions." In 1776, 2001, and again in 2009, whole populations whose indigenous lands, polities, and persons were about to be hit by intensified attack were dehumanized and essentially criminalized in order to misrepresent wars of expansion as self-defence from terrorists.

Where the US cavalry and the vigilantism of settler populations did much of the ethnic cleansing of Indigenous peoples in the transcontinental expansion of the United States, in Pakistan much of the murder is being delivered with the robotic anonymity of unmanned drones. The cold methodology of this impersonal style of high-tech murder introduced heightened levels of bureaucratization into the command structure of crimes against humanity.

The deployment of preprogrammed drones to do the industrial dirty work of ethnic cleansing gave new expression to what Hannah Arendt once labelled "the banality of evil."[30]

In seeking the power of the presidency, Barack Obama appealed to the hopes of the US electorate. In his decision to continue the 9/11 wars as a central plank of his presidency, the commander-in-chief of the world's pre-eminent military-industrial complex fell back on the resort to fear. Hope and fear are the emotional twins most often stimulated and drawn on in the effort to manipulate and control masses of people in the task of governing them. Of the two emotions, hope is by far the more fragile sentiment. It can easily be trumped and extinguished when the stronger impetus of fear is invoked to mobilize public opinion against genuine, imagined, or manufactured enemies.

In *Dreams from My Father*, Obama refers to his understanding of the psychology of fear in describing his study of literature when he was a student at Occidental College in Los Angeles. He comments at some length on his impressions of Joseph Conrad's classic novel *Heart of Darkness* – a work of fiction based on a real voyage that brought the author up the Congo River in the late nineteenth century to witness the ruthlessness of King Leopold's reign of terror in his African proprietorship.[31] My own reading of *Heart of Darkness* so dumbfounded me when I first encountered the book in high school that the questions it aroused became significant factors in the series of decisions that put me in 1971 at the controls of my motorcycle as I sped through the rain forest on my way to the Congolese community of Beni.

In his account of his remarks to a college girlfriend, Obama agreed that, "the way Conrad sees it, Africa's a cesspool of the world, black folks are savages, and any contact with them breeds infection." The future US president then underlines what he sees as the novel's real importance:

... the book teaches me things ... about white people, I mean. See the book's not really about Africa. Or black people. It's about the man who wrote it. The European. The American. A particular way of looking at the world ... So I read the book to help me understand just what it is that makes white people so afraid. Their demons. The way things get twisted around. It helps me to understand how people learn to hate.[32]

As the new promoter-in-chief of the 9/11 wars, the US president seems to have drawn on his college studies of the mythological structures underlying the mass production of fear and hatred. In every era and every society, the ability of leaders to invoke and direct these most potent of emotions holds an essential key to political power. Like most imperial wars, the primary purpose of the augmented invasions in Eurasia is to seize, hold, and consolidate power through taking control of territory, resources, and people. The infusion of more US armed forces into Eurasia is part of the effort to prevent the emerging imperiums of China, Russia, Europe, and possibly India from asserting more power the region. In seeking to block public understanding of his imperial goals, President Obama repeated the lies of his predecessor with his spurious claims about the capacity of armed forces in Afghanistan to quash the all-purpose demon of terrorism through a massive resort to campaigns of high-tech violence. War *is* terror, not its antidote.

From the era of US wars to disarm and eliminate "merciless Indian savages," to the era of capitalist wars to contain and then vanquish red communism, to the current era of global police and military operations mounted in the name of opposing the largely manufactured demon of al-Qaeda, the American empire of material aggrandizement has always required an external enemy to give military support to the expansionary enterprises of its biggest engines of corporate profit. It has required pretexts to present wars of aggression as self-defence. No matter what identifying label is attached to the imperial campaigns of the twenty-first century, the 9/11 wars have more to do with favouring a regime of proprietary privilege for elites than with protecting civilians from arbitrary acts of violence.

Ernesto "Che" Guevaro was one of those killed because of his genuine attempt to block the expansionary course of an imperial juggernaut whose most extended frontiers now reside in the privatized terror economy. Because of the murder of Che and the maiming of the anti-capitalist forces he embodied, the operatives of the national security state had to conspire to help build up and publicize the real or imagined machinations of Osama bin Laden and his Islamic brotherhood of imperial theocrats.[33]

Without al-Qaeda, old Cold Warriors such as former vice president Richard Cheney and former defense secretary Donald Rumsfeld would have faced professional obsolescence rather than a vast augmentation in the powers of patronage available to them as strategists, generals, and paymasters of the Global War on Terror. They took charge of the switchover from engagement with the communist threat to engagement with the terrorist threat. Apparently the immense continuities of elite power held in place through this switchover from one enemy to the next escaped serious notice, let alone sustained study and debate, in the process of passing the torch of leadership to President Obama and his generation.

MY COMPLICITY IN THE VIOLENCE OF MOBUTU'S MEN

The rich cornucopia of natural resources available for exploitation in Congo's eastern region was perhaps a factor in the relatively high quality of the road ahead. As I continued my African safari, I covered the ground quickly. The farther west I travelled, the more concentrated the signs of human habitation became. As I approached the outskirts of a community known as Beni, I stopped for some refreshments at a roadside tavern. I entered to find myself in the midst of a lively mid-day party. Many of the male merrymakers wore pieces of military attire. I had the sense that some of them had guns and ammunition close at hand. Like numerous establishments of its kind in the region, the jukebox provided the central attraction of this little business.

I left the party as discreetly as I could and pointed my motorcycle into a trickle of traffic. I had painted the name "Mydreamfinder" onto the BSA just below the seat. The buzz of cars and scooters became more intense as I approached Beni's downtown district. When I arrived, I noticed that some of the shops were crammed with luxury items – Johnny Walker Scotch, Italian cashmere sweaters, and American cigarettes. This rich show of merchandise, I assumed, must be connected to lucrative mining operations in the area.

The Kivu region of eastern Congo is extremely rich in a wide array of minerals, including diamonds, gold, and copper. As I would later learn, the eastern Congo is also the world's largest-known source of columbite-tantalite, or coltan for short. Refined coltan forms a key ingredient in the gadgetry of wireless communications, linking networks of cell phones, laptop computers, and the like. In 1971, however, we were still years away from the point where the Internet, digitalized information, and cheap wireless telephones would become broadly available in ways that would seemingly accelerate time, compress space, and expand our collective capacity for interaction.

The concentration of so many recognizable brands in Beni's stores gave me the impression that I had arrived in a place with some of the safe banality of a North American shopping mall. How wrong I was! I had arrived at the edge of mayhem's abyss, and there was no guarantee that I would emerge unharmed from the events ahead. I began to notice that something was wrong when I failed repeatedly in my French-language attempts to elicit even rudimentary information about the underlying nature of the local economy. One person after another pretended not even to hear my most straightforward questions.

Gradually it dawned on me that most of Beni's inhabitants were probably loath to be seen conversing publicly with this bearded White stranger. Indeed, I began to suspect that I was perceived as some sort of spy sent from afar to report on activities whose character was apparently well known to everybody but me. My impression that I had fallen into some sort of snakes' pit multiplied once I checked into Beni's sole hotel. At first the establishment seemed like an oasis, and I changed some of my travellers cheques into Congolese currency at the reception desk.

After moving my gear into my room, I went to the hotel's dining room, where I ordered a dish of spice-fried matoke – a banana-like fruit that is a dietary staple throughout much of equatorial Africa. As I finished my meal, a stocky Congolese man in a plaid golf shirt stopped by my table. He introduced himself as Armel. After experiencing so much aloofness from Beni's inhabitants, I welcomed this individual's polite attentiveness. Armel mentioned that he had seen me riding my motorcycle days earlier when he

passed through Queen Elizabeth National Park on the Ugandan side of the
nearby border.

After Armel left, I realized I was the sole customer left in the dining room.
Even the staff seemed to have vacated the premises. Suddenly the silence
was broken by the sound of a locking mechanism being slammed shut on
the far side of the front door. Moments later I heard a similar sound at the
rear door. There was no way out. I responded at first by knocking politely
on one door, then on the other. Nobody answered. With a growing sense
of urgency I tried again and again to get some attention – all to no avail. I
rested my head in my hands and stewed in an internal mix of fear, anger,
and frustration. How had I become the unwilling captive of some unknown
jailer? Next I called for help out the barred windows of the dining room.
I managed to get the attention of some passersby, only to see them move
quickly away as if fleeing some sort of pestilence.

Then I marched to one of the locked doors and banged on it very aggressively, very self-righteously. In a firm tone of voice I insisted that I must be
set free from this indignity. Much to my surprise, someone responded – a
young woman opened the door. She said nothing, but calmly took me by
the hand and walked me into the African night away from the hotel. I felt I
had little choice but to accept her lead.

In the moments before we were engulfed by the black night, I noticed
that my guide's uniform was unusually well tailored. We continued along a
narrow pathway towards the buzz of an electrical generator. After several
minutes we reached a clearing dominated by a large two-storey house. We
went inside, and the girl deposited me at the door of a comfortable-looking
den. There in a large easy chair sat a rather emaciated White man, about
twice my age, sipping a pink cocktail. I assumed he was the proprietor of the
hotel. He turned up the dimmer switch controlling the overhead light as he
suspiciously eyed me up and down. I remained silent.

The man introduced himself in French as Andréas. He said he had been
raised in Cyprus, but had lived in the Congo for a number of years. He
began his interrogation by asking me how I had arrived in Beni. Where had
I come from? In the course of his questioning, he mentioned that he had
seen me bring a significant amount of camera equipment into the hotel,
including a Super 8 movie camera. Once the subject turned to photography, the coldness between us began to thaw. My inquisitor seemed to have
a genuine interest in photography. Andréas asked me about the kind of
subjects that attracted my attention. Was I an amateur or did I sell my pictures? What kinds of scenes had I filmed so far? What were my impressions
of Congo? When would I return to Canada? What would I tell Canadians
about what I had seen here.

I wondered if Andréas was some sort of investigator whose job it was
to question me, given that no border official had been posted at the spot
where I entered Congolese territory. Once I began speaking about my life
in Canada, he seemed to accept that I was a suitable guest for his hotel. I

returned to my room, where I slept peacefully. After so many nights in my pup tent and small sleeping bag, it was luxurious to spend the night on a comfortable mattress between clean sheets.

The next day I awoke well rested. I decided to explore my new neighbourhood by the morning light. When I returned to my room, I discovered that my Super 8 camera had disappeared. I realized I had forgotten to lock my door when I went for my walk. I dashed to the front desk, where I found Andréas, and blurted out what had happened. He did not seem surprised by my story – and I got the impression that he knew what had happened. Without any explanation, he ushered me outside, pointed me towards his baby blue Mercedes-Benz, and held the front door open for me. We drove along the main street and parked on a large square in front of an imposing public building – some combination of city hall, court, political party headquarters, police station, and armory rolled into one.

A group of onlookers was gathered around the man in the plaid golf shirt who had introduced himself to me as Armel the previous evening. Armel was making a spectacle of himself as he excitedly aimed my camera up and down, left and right. Taking the initiative, I stepped forward and publicly accused Armel of being a thief. The camera in his hands was mine. Armel responded by levelling his own barrage of accusations at me. He pronounced himself an investigator who had apprehended my camera because I was not authorized to use it in his country.

Things moved quickly after that as our private squabble assumed public importance. Within moments we were whisked into a large room on the ground floor of the public institution where the high walls were covered with unusual varieties of exotic wood. Many onlookers crowded into the space to observe the unfolding drama. A large and imposing individual in a brown safari suit appeared from an adjacent office and soon took control of the situation. From the obedience he nonchalantly commanded it was obvious that he was an influential figure in this community – a local strong man.

Several uniformed guards stood around the room's perimeter. Each of them sported a navy-blue baseball hard helmet. Each stood stoically at attention, a baseball bat firmly in hand. One of the guards approached Armel, took the camera from him, and deposited it on a table as a primary item of evidence. The headman dabbed sweat from his forehead, raised his voice to call the proceeding to order, and asked Armel to speak first.

My adversary made his case in a combination of French and a native dialect. Then it was my turn. Behind me stood Andréas, who by now was acting informally as my advocate. His advised me to be as direct, succinct, and polite as possible in addressing the magistrate. After hearing both arguments, the headman bowed his head in a moment of thoughtful reflection and then called Andréas to his side for a brief consultation. Onlookers went completely silent as he announced his decision – he pointed at Armel and declared him to be the guilty party.

On hearing this verdict, one of the guards came forward to retrieve the camera from the table and return it to me. Andréas put his hand on my shoulder and encouraged me to leave the premises quickly. As we moved outside into the sunlight, an assertive interloper approached us. He sported shorts, bare feet, a black sports jacket, and no shirt. He held out his hand and pushed it towards me repeatedly. I looked to Andréas for advice. He nodded his head in a way that indicated I must satisfy this request. I understood. I reached deep into my pocket and gave the interloper all my cash – the equivalent of perhaps two hundred dollars.

As I handed over the bribe, the decorum in the public square exploded into chaos, and the air reverberated with shock waves of violence. Terrible screams emanated from the man who had taken my camera. I saw him squirming in agony on the sidewalk. Crowding around him were the men wearing baseball hard helmets. They beat their prey mercilessly. They wielded their baseball bats expertly to inflict maximum damage. So gruesome was the spectacle that I did not even consider stepping forward to intervene between Armel and his attackers. The louder the victim's yelling became, the more heft went into each blow. In the moment before I slammed shut the door of the Mercedes-Benz, the victim's hearty screams decreased to a pathetic whimper. As we sped away in the luxury car, I caught a glimpse of Armel spitting blood into his golf shirt. I cannot say for sure whether he survived the ordeal. My guess is that he was killed on the spot. What mistake had he made to provoke these obedient loyalists of Mobutu's police state?

As Andréas and I departed, I wondered what would have happened if the roles had been reversed. How close had I come to being beaten to death myself? What were the chances I would find myself in a real Congolese jail if I stayed in this place much longer? It was too overwhelming for a twenty-year-old Torontonian. I had to seek safer ground. I had to exit this town and this country with all possible dispatch. When we got back to the hotel I cashed in some more travellers cheques, those magic bits of paper that privileged my mobility as one of capitalism's chosen people.

I assembled my gear and strapped it onto Mydreamfinder's rear rack. As I put Beni behind me, I gunned the BSA's throttle. My objective was to reach the border stations near the Ruwenzori's southern tip as soon as possible. My circumnavigation of the Mountains of the Moon continued. My biggest fear along the way was that the Congolese border authorities ahead might try to detain me. It was at the Ugandan border station, however, that I was questioned most harshly. My interrogators were members of a small military unit and about my age. They questioned me on how it was that I was entering Uganda without being able to show documentary proof that I had ever left it.

In my time in equatorial Africa I saw many such roving military units. Sometimes their members revelled too much in the power that grows from the barrel of a gun. My academic study of the ingredients that combine to form the chemistry of such violence lay years in the future. But as I entered Uganda I already began to theorize about the nature of the lethal episode I had just experienced and in which I felt I had some complicity. In the full brightness of Beni's public square, I had witnessed an expression of neo-colonialism's heart of darkness. From blood rubber to blood diamonds to the raw material of blood cell phones, genocide has consistently been the lubricant that has greased the foreign appropriation of indigenous wealth in this corner of the world.

THE CHANGING SYMBOLISM OF
THE BOWL WITH ONE SPOON

Chris Hedges lashes out at many sites of power in apportioning blame for the debacle in public consciousness that has given rise to the "Empire of Illusion." He is especially unrelenting in his criticism of professors in institutions of supposedly "higher learning" for their alleged role in "the end of literacy and the triumph of spectacle." Hedges accuses most academics of having abandoned their responsibility to engage in and generate deep critical thinking. Instead, he claims, they favour the more lucrative mass production of "hordes of competent systems managers." Rather than directing their energies to the timeless search for "the common good," professors stand accused of putting knowledge "in the service of developing weapons of destruction, surveillance and death."

Hedges reserves his most scathing condemnation for professors' alleged surrender to the forces that have "organized learning around minutely specialized disciplines, narrow answers, and rigid structures designed to produce such answers." He attributes the marshalling of these forces to "established corporate hierarchies" that impose "clear parameters, such as the primacy of an unfettered free market." The hallmark of this corporate assault on the generalist traditions of higher education is, he says, the "specialized vocabulary" that "thwarts universal understanding" and "keeps the uninitiated from asking unpleasant questions ... It dices disciplines, faculty, and students, and finally experts into tiny, specialized fragments. It allows students and faculty to retreat into these self-imposed fiefdoms and neglect the most pressing moral, political and cultural questions."[34]

Generally speaking I welcome Hedges's criticisms. His account of the pathetic failure of many professors to subject political expedience to the pre-eminence of truth, however inconvenient to the interests of power, affords me a platform to help explain my own rebellion against the balkanization of the academy into narrow enclaves of careerist privilege. I began the two volumes of the *Bowl with One Spoon* in 1994. The more I progressed in the early stages of this project, the more I realized that I wanted to transcend the domain of specialized monographs and begin the process of piecing together a coherent picture of the way many peoples, personalities, places, episodes, and time periods converge in the genesis of our emerging global civilization.

In developing this text over its formative phases, I learned from my own experience of teaching students. I applied to my writing my classroom tactic of coming back again and again to a few core themes, every time deepening the analysis by introducing new information as well as new conceptions of context, background, orientation, and relationship to other topics, themes, and interpretations. Perspective is everything. Only by examining the making of history from a variety of vantage points, in several different hues of light, and with various juxtapositions of topics assigned to foreground and background, can justice be done to the multidimensional quality of human experience and understanding.

The composition of the two volumes of *The Bowl with One Spoon* over fifteen of my most productive years in the academy embodies my best attempt to create a model of scholarship that eschews the seductions of power-point bullet phrases, sound-bite reductionism, and short executive summaries. The propensity to rush the processing, presentation, and assimilation of growing mountains of information occurs in an era when Attention Deficit Disorder (ADD) has assumed epidemic proportions. The other side of this same trend makes the ability to multitask and speed through research and writing a prerequisite of success in the best-remunerated fields of intellectual work. The mere act of holding the paper version of this big volume should be enough to suggest that my approach to the integration of knowledge over large spans of time, territory, ethnicity, character, and circumstances is not a task to be lightly delivered or received.

Continuing changes in the technology of books will probably contribute to alterations in the way this text will be used in the academy and by the general public in the future. Digital reading devices, connected to increasingly sophisticated search and reference mechanisms, will no doubt continue to replace the medium of paper and to transform institutions initially built to contain, organize, disseminate and preserve physical texts. As Marshall McLuhan observed, changes of media extend to the messages being communicated. The continuing digitalization of books and their content will continue to affect how literary production is conceived, implemented, consumed, and passed on to posterity. As a synthetic overview that combines the methodology of a detailed work of general reference with that of a very personal narrative presenting novel configurations of argument, setting, interpretation, and theme, this text, I hope, is well suited to sustain the ongoing revolution in information technologies that will continue to accelerate alterations in our ways of perceiving the world. I take it as a serious professional imperative, therefore, to contribute constructively to ongoing renovations in the architecture of knowledge during this time of rapid digitalization of information. I want to underline, however, how the scope and content of this work reflect my more conservative orientations to the responsibilities of serious scholarship and the rites of literary enterprise.

Human civilization would be impoverished without short and hard-hitting texts such as the American Declaration of Independence, the

Communist Manifesto by Karl Marx and Frederick Engels, or, for that matter, Chris Hedges's exposure of the empire of carefully engineered illusion. Certainly the formula of short, succinct, and sweet conforms better to the economics of modern book publishing as well as the exigencies of modern life on most fast tracks of material and professional success. The logistics of efficiency in time management will always favour synthesis and generalizations over the more belaboured subtleties of nuance and scope combined with careful attention to detail. But who knows? The attractions of distilled minimalism may yet take over my best efforts of authorship.

I have not yet, however, written my manifesto of the Fourth World. But I have been able to pay a tribute to the two volumes of *Das Kapital* with my completion of the second volume of *The Bowl with One Spoon*. In both texts I give broad latitude to the encyclopedist in me who has long been intent on chronicling the history of the encounter between Indigenous peoples and imperial proprietorships of many kinds. Who will join me and support the project of piecing back together a broader vision of the way the precious fruits of many academic specialties can be better combined, integrated, extended, and enhanced through the power of synergy? Who will contribute along with me to the challenge of concocting a recipe of twenty-first-century knowledge that nurtures, inspires, and empowers broad social criticism in the cause of the common good, even as it lures colleagues to move beyond the false security of the many narrow and postmodernist enclaves of fragmented overspecialization? As I see it, Hedges is generally correct in positing that the management of this machinery of scholarly production often reflects and advances corporatist agendas of monopoly capitalism.

In *Earth into Property* I continue my emphasis from volume one on the year 1492 as the beginning of the modern era of globalization. I devote the first chapter to the World's Columbian Exposition. This exuberant celebration of the 400th anniversary of Columbus's most transformative voyage took place in the summer of 1893 in Chicago, the emerging metropolis of the American Midwest. The public enthusiasms funnelled into this anniversary were not repeated a century later. Instead, in 1992 a revisionist view of history gained considerable ground. This anti-imperial interpretation of the quincentennary of 1492 highlighted the processes of oppression brought by Columbus to a whole hemisphere, one where the Aboriginal earth of Indigenous peoples would be reconstituted as proprietary frontiers of a New World civilization dominated by immigrants and their descendants. The European and Euro-American appropriation of the territories of Aboriginal America has long functioned as a great catalyst in the making of global capitalism.

While the period 1492–1992 frames a key temporal marker of this project, I trace the history of capitalism all the way to the financial debacle of 2008–9. I focus in chapter 15 on the relationship of General Motors and the insurance giant AIG to the genesis and breakdown of global capitalism.

In my investigation of the history of both corporate polities I find important indicators of what went wrong and what should be done in light of the
interventions by government which have dramatically altered the nature of
the world's political economy for all time.

The symbolism of the bowl with one spoon acquired added meanings
for me as I worked my way through the chapters between my survey of the
World's Columbian Exposition and my investigation of the Maiden Lane
companies. The Maiden Lane companies were created by the US Federal
Reserve system to take over the most dubious variety of financial instrument
retained from the era of maximum deregulation of the financial services
industry. The constitutional enigmas that permeate these polities named
after the address of the Federal Reserve system's New York headquarters
point to many of the tensions between the kind of accountability expected
from public institutions in a democracy and a financial system that privileges secret dealings among a small elite of wealthy insiders. Some of these
insiders have acquired various kinds of charters and franchises to exercise
disproportionate amounts of self-serving influence over the inner workings
of global capitalism.

One of the Maiden Lane companies was made to take over the most
secretive and notorious of AIG's insurance contracts on derivative bets – and
to reimburse the counterparties in AIG's most overzealous speculations. To
whom are the directors of the Maiden Lane companies accountable? Who
are the shareholders? Does the chain of accountability flow to citizens or to
those banks that are the chartered proprietors of the Federal Reserve system? In the United States as in many other countries, future tax payments
by regular citizens constitute the ultimate source of capital required to pay
interest on the mountains of debt incurred as a result of the handing over
of trillions of dollars in bailout monies to financial institutions, sometimes
through secretive polities such as the Maiden Lane companies. It remains
to be seen what political repercussions will flow from this single most substantial transfer of wealth ever from those at the bottom and middle of the
economic scale to those at the top of the pyramid of material entitlements.

The meanings to be drawn from this project's totem, the bowl with a
single spoon, highlight the problems entailed in a system of economic relations where liability and risk are often socialized even as profit is privatized.
The bowl with one spoon can be conceived as the antithesis of the thesis in
global capitalism which has put larger and larger proportions of the Earth's
store of property into the concentrated ownership of fewer and fewer individuals. The financial debacle of 2008 and 2009 epitomized the saddling of
working people with massive amounts of public debt so that a small number
of privileged individuals could continue to monopolize most of the profit
from risky investments and the kleptocratic bonuses often derived from the
secretive manipulations of money-like instruments known as derivatives.

The iconography of the bowl with one spoon began its career not as
a representation in the Marxist cosmology of dialectical materialism but

rather as an Aboriginal wampum symbol meant to signify shared hunting territory. The meaning of this symbol was further refined to signify the agreement of diverse indigenous nations in North America to join forces in the Indian Confederacy. The purpose of this pan-Indian polity was to develop a common front in order to oppose more effectively the trajectory of expansion that had created the United States as a vehicle to accelerate the privatization of lands on the western frontiers of Euro-North American settlements. The aggressiveness of this expansionary process helped to project a particularly ethnocentric version of possessive individualism towards the most extended frontiers of global capitalism.[35] As a community of communities facing the imminent prospect of their members being displaced, dispossessed, and exterminated by this trajectory of imperial privatization, the Indian Confederacy attempted through the agencies of both diplomacy and war to assert its members' collective rights of sovereign ownership and self-defence covering large hunting territories said to be held in common.

The metaphor of the bowl with one spoon can be usefully employed to illustrate principles and policies across a wide array of eras, frameworks, and contexts. The ideal of the common good is illustrated in the imagery of the whole Earth as a vessel of life-nourishing resources to be shared. The iconography of the bowl with one spoon speaks of an approach to governance that affords pre-eminence to the public interest even as it favours the values of public service. I develop this strategy of representation in chapter 15, where I relate the relationship of General Motors to the fundamental cycles of production and consumption in the global economy. Beginning with a pivotal labour relations contract in 1950 which was informally dubbed the Treaty of Detroit, General Motors was, for the next two decades, the vehicle of both great prosperity and relatively harmonious relations with members of the United Auto Workers' Union. This polity of collective bargaining emerged after the Second World War as a prime beneficiary of the legacy of the New Deal – the North American version of European social democracy.

The agreement to afford auto workers a substantial share of the wealth generated by one of capitalism's most successful companies allowed room for the principles of the bowl with one spoon to coexist with those of possessive individualism. The material basis of this coexistence began to break down in the 1980s, when the economic strategies of Ronald Reagan and Margaret Thatcher favoured the deregulation of the financial services industry, the movement of global manufacturing capacities away from North America and other high-wage areas, and the acceleration of covert interventions into the political economy of oil and gas development in Eurasia. The increasing emphasis on geopolitical interventions in Eurasia helped to drive the growth of the privatized terror economy, the vehicle for the continuing rise of the military-industrial complex following the end of the Cold War.

This combination of policies contributed to the dramatic failure of global capitalism in 2008 and 2009. A fully fledged depression was averted, temporarily at least, by the injections of huge quantities of public funds into the financial services sector and into segments of the automobile sector, including General Motors. GM was thus transformed in the general interest from a private company to the common property of taxpayers in the United States and Canada. In this way GM entered the symbolic terrain of the bowl with one spoon. As I propose in chapter 15, the finer spirit of the common good and enhanced public services could be expressed in the transformation of GM's Pontiac branch as a medium for significant improvements in the infrastructure of public transport. This initiative would ideally be accompanied by similar improvements in the global provision of public health, public broadcasting, and public education. In the United States the growth of all these modules of public interest would point some American dreams towards goals that are very different from those that have long stimulated the frontier expansions of the American empire of private property. As long as huge flows of taxpayers' money are funnelled into the series of imperial adventures extending from the Indian wars to the 9/11 wars, there will be insufficient resources to replenish the collectively held institutions of the bowl with one spoon.

Pontiac and Tecumseh were both visionaries of the Indian Confederacy whose policies were well expressed through the imagery of the bowl with one spoon. Both leaders were dealt the same sort of martyrdom extended to Che Guevara. As strategists and law givers, Pontiac and Tecumseh guided the policies of the Indian Confederacy during the era when those vying for control of North America sought to dominate the straits of Detroit in much the same fashion that imperial contestants vying for control of Eurasia have sought to dominate the cross-roads of Afghanistan.

The imperial history of empire building has been a major driving force in the transformation of Earth into property. Some of the most influential episodes of this imperial history of commodification have taken place in the Western Hemisphere, but most especially on the northern continent. Max Weber has outlined how, in New England and its offshoots, the elaboration of the Protestant work ethic did much to drive and enliven the spirit of capitalism. The resulting acceleration of the economic engines of industrial productivity helped to make the United States rich.[36] Much of this capitalist development was intensified by quick accumulation through the systematic dispossession of Indigenous peoples. The complexities of this process of invasion, conquest, and sporadic intercultural alliances have not, generally speaking, attracted the attention they deserve from capitalism's leading historians. From Karl Marx to Fernand Braudel, Karl Polanyi, Giovanni Arrighi, Immanuel Wallerstein, David Harvey, and Niall Ferguson, the scholarship of capitalism's rise and spread has been devoid of much serious reckoning with the transcontinental movement of Anglo-America into the Aboriginal lands and resources of Indigenous peoples.

It occurred to me only gradually that the making of global capitalism was profoundly affected by the many ways that the lands and resources of

Indigenous peoples have been incorporated into the world system of economic interaction. This impact arises not only from the magnitude of the material transfers from the societies of the colonized to those of the colonizers but also from the intellectual and institutional affects of the encounter between those on the expanding and imploding sides of moving frontiers. Again and again the treatment of Indigenous peoples gave expression to a range of colonial ideas about how best to privatize, register, and protect private property and how to organize commercial transactions among individuals, corporations, and governments. Similarly, debates about how North American Indians should be reformed, moved, or eliminated altogether frequently reflected disagreements among competing systems of belief about how capitalism should be conceived and constructed in the New Worlds of immigrants and their descendants.

One of the legacies that continue to flow from these competitive episodes of empire building and colonization is the complex heritage of Indian treaties in North America. As demonstrated with particular clarity in the Aboriginal history of British Columbia, these constitutional instruments of native-newcomer relations have posed, and continue to pose, significant challenges to prevailing systems of settler land tenure and jurisdiction. They continue to call attention to the need for balance between the ideals of the bowl with one spoon with those of possessive individualism.

The desire of North American governments to induce Native people to adopt Euro–North American concepts of property ownership were central to the *Act for the Gradual Civilization of the Indian Tribes in Canada* of 1857, the *Dawes Severalty Act* of 1887, and the federal termination policies advanced by the Bureau of Indian Affairs in the United States in the 1950s. In the midst of the most paranoid decade of Cold War confrontation, the US Supreme Court decided in 1955 in its *Hee-Hit-Ton* decision that the Indigenous peoples of Alaska did not have Aboriginal title to their ancestral lands because they had suffered the conquest of a more powerful polity. Decisions about how to conceive and administer the remaining estates of American Indians, however, were not all one-sided. In extending the New Deal to the Indians of the United States in the 1930s, John Collier, the executive in charge of the Bureau of Indian Affairs in Washington, DC, attempted to push back the encroachments of privatization. He introduced legislation in Congress to affirm the principle that Indian reservations should remain the collectively held property of the communities that inhabit them. The extension of the New Deal to Indians formed a prelude to the effort by the presidency of Franklin Delano Roosevelt to extend the US government's New Deal to all the world's peoples through the agencies of the United Nations.

This text can be seen as part of the emerging literature of so-called indigeneity, although I tend to apply the term, Indigenous peoples, in more broad-ranging ways than those who would reserve it for colonized minorities whose members lack access to the instruments of state power.[37] Some of the roots of my own effort to conceptualize Indigenous peoples as a particular category of humanity go back to a seminal parliamentary inquiry that took place in London, England, in 1836 and 1837. Its purpose was to survey the treatment, conditions, frustrations, and aspirations of Aborigines in British settlements.[38] This parliamentary inquiry emerged directly from the successful activities of the British anti-slavery lobby. The transformation of the movement to abolish slavery into a movement advocating justice for Indigenous peoples is part of the thick web of legal, political, and economic connections linking the history of human bondage and the history of colonial appropriation of Aboriginal lands.

The US State Department commissioned Alpheus Snow to write an analysis in 1918 that took up, extended, and applied more broadly many of the themes studied by the parliamentarians conducting the earlier inquiry into Aborigines in British settlements.[39] Snow's work was part of the preparation of the US government for entering into the negotiations of the Versailles Treaty in 1919. Snow introduced an astonishing array of connections, demonstrating, for instance, the importance of the Indian policies of the United States in setting precedents for the constitutional construction of the Congo Free State under the trusteeship of Belgium's King Leopold.

In using the term "Indigenous peoples" I draw on ideas that were first introduced to me in the preface written in 1961 by Jean-Paul Sartre to Frantz Fanon's *Les Damnés de la Terre*, or, in its English translation, *The Wretched of the Earth*.[40] Sartre began the preface by noting the distinction then drawn in the prevailing international system between "men" and "natives." The latter were said to outnumber the former by a ratio of three to one. I interpret Sartre's estimation of the mathematics of oppression as a guess at the comparative size of constituencies on the receiving and delivering end of imperialism. The so-called natives were transformed by the alchemy of colonial law into wards of the so-called men. The "men" referred to by Sartre were citizens who could vote, enter into contracts, and pursue justice through the courts. The "natives" were treated as savages under the tutelage of the civilized powers preparing for the day when they could be allowed limited powers of self-governance. How far have we yet to go before we break the hold of this appalling paradigm of human relations?

PART ONE

Accelerating Time, Shrinking Space, Privatizing the Commons

CHAPTER ONE

Looking Backwards and Forwards from the World's Columbian Exposition

The first condition for changing reality is to understand it.
Eduardo Galeano, *Open Veins of Latin America*, 1973

CHRISTOPHER COLUMBUS, THE AMERICAN FRONTIER, AND THE WORLD'S COLUMBIAN EXPOSITION IN CHICAGO, 1893

At the beginning of every story are mergers of memory and imagination that give life to Aboriginal history. The essence of Aboriginal history lies in the quest to describe those founding acts that infuse meaning and substance into new institutions, countries, cultures, religions, methodologies, motifs of encounter, and the like. This emphasis on starting points, inceptions, initiating enterprises, new departures, and rituals of birth offers analytic keys to fuller understanding of the dynamic relationship between the universal and the particular, the absolute and the relative, individual people and the groups to which we adhere. The study of Aboriginal history offers important windows of insight into the underlying structures and animating patterns of change. Hence the rewards are large for those with the ability to give sustained and detailed attention to those people, locations, and times that fate has placed at the headwaters of invention, destruction, and transcendence. Sometimes the sites of Aboriginal history are as hidden and obscure as an underground spring feeding a subterranean lake. In other instances they are as obvious as massive glaciers whose runoffs spew forth into the great rivers that define the landscape of whole continents. This story originates in relative obscurity in Madison, Wisconsin, as a young history professor, Frederick Jackson Turner, stepped purposefully into a departing train for Chicago – the site of the great fair known in 1893 as the World's Columbian Exposition.[1]

The dapper and self-confident Turner finally found his small, private compartment and closed the door behind him. He got right down to business. From his briefcase he pulled the draft of the paper he was preparing to deliver to his colleagues at the annual gathering of the

American Historical Association. The historians' conference was one of approximately two hundred special congresses hosted by the organizers of Chicago's international fair. The range of topics covered in these events was enormous. They included engineering, horticulture, journalism, women's rights, labour relations, banking, world religions, and intellectual property. Collectively, the delegates attending the congresses embodied key elements of many emerging configurations of business, science, culture, and politics. They personified the currents of thought, the institutional alliances, the professional associations, and the patterns of action, organization, and production that were converging to make the twentieth century an era like no other.

The large scale of the organizers' hopes and ambitions was evident in the fair's monumental architecture and its enticement of 27 million visitors. In marking out a site three times larger than any previous international fair, the organizers had signalled their intent to exceed the achievements of all those who, earlier in the century, had shaped such spectacles into vital vehicles of globalization. The most successful of the earlier world's fairs had been London's Crystal Palace Exposition in 1851, Philadelphia's Centennial Exposition in 1876, and Paris's Exposition Universelle in 1889. Together with Chicago's Columbian Exposition, these events would prove instrumental during the second half of the nineteenth century in imbuing the idea of imperialism with allure and prestige. They became venues to display and celebrate the concentration of the spoils of empire in the great metropolitan centres of Europe and North America.[2]

Visitors to the fair flocked to displays such as those featuring a 30,000-pound chocolate bar or a 22,000-pound chunk of Canadian cheese. Few could resist taking a ride on George Ferris's Bicycle-Wheel-in-the-Sky. Projecting 264 feet into the heavens, the world's premier Ferris wheel could carry an amazing 2,000 passengers at a time. Among the countless performers vying for attention at the fair's midway was the nineteen-year-old contortionist Ehrich Weiss. He would later achieve enormous fame as Harry Houdini. Of all the myriad shows, displays, presentations, and entertainments making up Chicago's Columbian Exposition, however, the little essay that Turner held on his lap would prove to be one of the most lasting and influential elements of the great event.[3]

Turner's paper, "The Significance of the Frontier in American History," reflected, in bold intellectual outlines, the sense of self-confident optimism that was making the Columbian Exposition such an important showcase. Like the World's Fair that provided its venue, Turner's essay gave notice of the industrial, scientific, ideological, and cultural capacities that were combining to render the United States such a mighty force of global transformation in the century ahead. His presentation would come to be described as "the most influential single piece of historical writing ever done in the United States." In Walter Prescott Webb's opinion, "it altered the whole course of American historical scholarship."[4]

As the train moved towards the outskirts of Madison, Turner looked up from the editing notes he was scratching at the margins of the typed text. He peered out the compartment window, glancing reverentially towards the stately home of Reuben Gold Thwaites, his mentor and teacher at the University of Wisconsin.[5] Turner had been one of Professor Thwaites's best students in his famed seminar on the history of Wisconsin. Before Wisconsin Territory became the thirtieth US state in 1848, it had been constituted as part of the North-West Territory in 1788, then of Indiana Territory in 1800, of Illinois Territory in 1809, and finally of Michigan Territory in 1818. Before the United States gained firm control of the Wisconsin area after the War of 1812, the region's Indigenous inhabitants had been deeply integrated into the Montreal-centred fur trade of French-Aboriginal Canada and then of British imperial Canada. In seeking to bring this Aboriginal history to light, Thwaites and his disciples were building up the State Historical Society of Wisconsin as a beehive of research and publication. This busy enterprise would result in later years in the Library of Congress's listing of over 170 entries under Thwaites's name. His edited publications range from the massive assembly of the reports of New France's Jesuit missionaries to the writings of baron de Lahontan and the journals of the US Corps of Discovery led by Meriwether Lewis and William Clark. As Fred Turner moved towards Chicago, his teacher, peers, and students were engaged in assembling, translating, and disseminating the primary literary sources for the indigenous historiography of a region then in the process of becoming the American Midwest. They were unearthing and interpreting the complex archaeology of encounter between Indigenous peoples and newcomers, imperial France and imperial Britain, Old World and New World empires, Canada and the United States.

Now Fred Turner was extending the Thwaites tradition of historical scholarship to the venue of the World's Columbian Exposition. As the ambitious young historian of the American Midwest rolled towards Chicago, he was intent on advancing his fame as well as the goals of his mentor. By articulating some sweeping generalizations about the larger significance of the history he had been teaching and studying in Madison, Turner sought to affirm the importance of the American West in shaping the past, present, and future course of US development. Like Thwaites, he sought to make his mark by challenging some of the arrogant assumptions he saw in the academic staff of older universities, but especially those in New England. In his view, those ensconced in the East's more entrenched pedagogical institutions were inclined to be self-satisfied and to presume that they held some sort of monopoly on intellectual discourse in the United States. Building on the legacy of scholarship created by Thwaites, Turner would devote his career to challenging this complacency. As he refined the academic paper on his lap, he was engaged in developing this critique into a full-fledged historical interpretation. With his "frontier thesis," Turner commented on the continuing force of westward-pointing colonization initially set in the geography of transatlantic relations by Christopher Columbus. There Turner emphasized the contrast he saw between the more inert, conservative East and the more innovative, vital, and individualistic resourcefulness of Euro-America's most westerly projections.

Turner's aspiration to boost the prestige of his region ran in parallel course to the process that had brought the World's Columbian Exposition to Chicago. When the town fathers first entered the contest to host the event, they were perceived as marginal figures residing on the geographical and political edges of American renown and influence. Nevertheless, those who favoured Chicago did not relent in challenging the apparent advantages enjoyed by promoters of New York, the United States' most important commercial and cultural centre. In the end the underdogs prevailed when, in 1889, the US Senate passed a resolution confirming Chicago as the site of the Columbian Exposition.

The central theme of the fair would prove to be a decisive factor in the decision to bestow the prize on the young urban centre. The event's primary purpose was to celebrate the 400th anniversary of Christopher Columbus's "discovery" of America. As a new city whose leaders were deeply engaged in harnessing, energizing, and directing the course of America's rapid frontier expansions, Chicago served as an apt symbol of how the United States itself was emerging as the primary expression of the forceful ascent of "the West" to global predominance.[6] The pace of this rise had accelerated dramatically following that most celebrated voyage. The course of history since 1492 seemed to demonstrate the importance of Columbus and all he represented in channelling the expansionary spirit of Western civilization. After the discoveries of this Italian explorer, the empire builders of Europe reoriented the aggressiveness of the Christian Crusades in the Middle East towards a saga of transatlantic colonization led initially by a procession of soldiers, priests, and merchants.

The honour of engaging the switch that sent electric power surging through the World's Columbian Exposition went to President Grover Cleveland. Like so many other aspects of the event, the placid exterior of the presidential ceremony disguised the bitter competitiveness of the contest that had led to this outcome. The "Battle of the Currents" had pitted the General Electric Company of famed inventor Thomas Edison against an upstart operation that combined the technological wizardry of Nikola Tesla with the financial and industrial knowhow of George Westinghouse. The Westinghouse Electric and Manufacturing Company seized the Columbian prize because of its success in demonstrating the superior attributes of industrialization through polyphase alternating current, or AC for short. In a desperate attempt to discredit the Westinghouse group, Edison had applied AC to constructing the first electric chair. His secret agenda was to turn public opinion against the competing system by associating it with criminality and lethal danger. The attempt failed.[7] When President Cleveland turned on the quarter-million lights illuminating the World's

Columbian Exposition, he signalled not only the direction for the future development of electrical power but also the way industrial decisions made in the United States would increasing set more general patterns of global transformation. The triumph of Tesla, Westinghouse, and the AC system signified the advancement of a trend that would see corporate winners in the United States move time and time again towards transnational frontiers of technological and commercial innovation.

In his speech, Cleveland masterfully manipulated the many metaphors of progress available to him on this auspicious occasion. He called attention to the fact that the fair's organizers had devoted a whole building to displaying the industrial applications of this powerful new source of energy, this medium for the formulation and distribution of information. Among the many electric devices displayed at the exposition was the Kinetograph, the parent of motion-picture projectors.[8] Once the president had initiated the opening ceremonies, other dignitaries took their turn in trying to illuminate the event's bigger meanings and possibilities. They were especially intent on showing the connections linking the United States, but especially the western portions of the ascendant republic, to the projection of westwardmoving progress that the voyage of Columbus was seen to epitomize and advance.

After celebrating "Columbus the Discoverer, Washington the Founder, Lincoln the Saviour," railway promoter and US senator Chauncey Depew referred to "the wise men" who "travelled from East to West under the Star of Bethlehem." As other biblical references followed, he identified Columbus as the key figure who transported across the Atlantic "the spirit of equality of all men before God and the law." "Under the Star of Bethlehem's guidance and inspiration," he asserted, Europe's immigrants to America "moved west and west again":

All hail Columbus, discoverer and dreamer, hero and apostle. We here of every race and country recognize the horizon which bounded his vision and the infinite scope of his genius. The voice of gratitude and praise for all the blessings which have showered upon mankind by his adventures is limited to no language but is uttered in every tongue. Neither marble nor brass can fitly form his statue. Continents are his monuments and unnumbered millions, past, present and future to come, who enjoy in their liberty and their happiness the fruits of his faith, will reverently guard and preserve from century to century his name and fame.[9]

In a similar vein Henry Watterson, a journalist who became one of Kentucky's most venerable patriarchs, called on the audience to reflect on the event's global significance "with a candor untinged by cynicism and a confidence having no air of assurance." He continued:

We meet this day to honour the memory of Christopher Columbus, to celebrate the four-hundredth annual return of the transcendent achievement, and, with fitting rites, to dedicate to America and the universe a concrete exposition of the world's progress between 1492 and 1892. No twenty centuries can be compared with this in its wide significance and reach; because since the advent of the Son of God, no event has had so great an influence upon human affairs as the discovery of the Western Hemisphere.[10]

In light of the awkward, almost tongue-tied response in 1992–93 to the 500th anniversary of Columbus's arrival in America, the extravagant language used at the 400th-anniversary ceremony serves as a telling marker of the unperplexed certainties that seemingly bound an ascendant United States in a moment of unselfconscious triumph. The spirit of exuberant triumphalism ran high in Chicago in spite of the pervasive class and ethnic schisms that lay beneath the unified surface of civic cooperation. It ran high despite the slowdown that plagued the US economy in 1893. This decline in commercial activity embodied the downside of the boom-and-bust cycles that characterized the emergence of capitalism's most important laboratory. It highlighted the sharpness of the tensions endemic to a new country engaged in rapid, sometimes violent transformations from a social organization based largely on rural agriculture to one founded primarily on urbanization and rapid industrialization.[11]

In such a society, it became increasingly difficult to sustain the imperfectly realized promise of Jeffersonian democracy, an ideal based on the mythology of a liberated polity grounded in the civic consensus of a rugged class of self-sufficient farmer proprietors. This founding agrarian myth, like many other related ideals of American liberty, was more and more confronted with the contradictory realities produced by a system of material relations in which large business corporations and their plutocrat proprietors monopolized the most privileged turf of political decision making and property entitlement in the United States. The tendency was manifest in the rendering of US political culture as, by and large, an extension, reflection, and instrument of the dominant business class.[12] The ascendant strength of corporate power was everywhere evident in the organization of Chicago's global exposition, an event that introduced a host of successful brand names and products, including Juicy Fruit Gum, Aunt Jemima Syrup, Shredded Wheat, Cream of Wheat, and Pabst Blue Ribbon Beer.[13]

The public spectacles used to introduce these brand names and their distinctive trademarks at the world's fair represented an early wave in the rapid development of the cult of American advertising. As Naomi Klein has observed, the development of the advertising industry would eventually culminate in making brand imagery as integral to the economy as the industrial processes entailed in manufacturing actual goods.[14] The rising importance of advertising and public relations in the political economy of the United States was foreshadowed in Edison's attempt to discredit AC power by connecting it in the public mind with the negative imagery of the electric chair. This manipulative PR campaign became a telling marker in

the genesis of a society where the means of manufacturing public perception were increasingly for sale in the marketplace of propaganda, myth, and
mass illusion. In 1893 at Chicago, the early signs of this trend were already
on display.

Accordingly, the Chicago exposition provided the launching pad for
many of those processes and techniques of production, marketing, and
public relations that would prove instrumental in making the United States
the most influential catalyst of globalization in the century ahead. Many of
the new products and new strategies of marketing were initially presented
in the Manufacturers and Liberal Arts Building. It was there that several of
the exposition's most ambitious corporate participants housed their displays. The sense of practical political economy, technical ingenuity, and
unrelenting salesmanship conveyed in these displays illustrated the forces
that continued to transform the United States into the world's primary testing ground for a new kind of corporate culture. The titans and architects of
this American corporate culture were developing that blend of commerce,
political influence, and coercive capacity that would force the planet's
diverse economies into the press of a single capitalist mould over the course
of the upcoming century.

In many instances the importance of the product innovations introduced
at Chicago remained latent and implicit rather than realized and complete.
For instance, the Chicago exposition first introduced many of its visitors to
hamburgers and carbonated soda – the tasty food and drinks that would
provide the strategic currency for the future growth of some of the United
States' most iconographic global corporate leviathans. In expanding the
field of the culture that would produce McDonald's and Coca-Cola, the
exposition helped to popularize and legitimize the mix of diet and political economy that were converging to transform the United States into
what Eric Schlosser has described as the "fast food nation."[15] The World's
Columbian Exposition helped to point the way towards that combination
of corporate showmanship and technological innovation that would later
congeal, for instance, in Disneyland of California, Disney World of Florida,
and Euro Disney of Paris.[16]

The one constant in this realm of juxtaposed fantasy and materialism
would be paradox. As the Earth's great polity of paradox, the United States
has been animated from its inception by an alchemy of power and imagination that defies simple, one-dimensional explanations. In 1893 the United
States continued to develop as a domain combining the extremes of both
Protestant fundamentalism and secular Enlightenment,[17] as a leading
opponent of Europe's colonialism as well as a prime protagonist and prototype of a new type of global commercial empire. As a country seemingly
custom-made to capture most of the internal contradictions vexing Western
civilization since at least the Renaissance,[18] the unrelenting crises of modernity were engulfed in the ongoing process of inventing the United States
and exporting, incorporating, or resisting its worldwide influences.

The World's Columbian Exposition provided a medium and a showcase to highlight the emerging strength of the world's future superpower. It provided a venue and an agency that gave the world a glimpse of the central role the United States was assuming in determining the fate of modernity and post-modernity in the global community. It signalled that the United States, but especially its business leadership, was moving into the vortex of history about to transform the planet from a realm of several competing imperialisms into a single commercial domain identified provocatively by Michael Hardt and Antonio Negri simply as "empire."[19] Myriad forces combined to influence this movement towards a new kind of global empire. As Schlosser emphasized in his case study highlighting the political economy of the American community of Colorado Springs, the culture that produced both fast food and the world's largest arsenal of weapons of mass destruction is based on innumerable connections between corporate interests, private wealth, and public policy. In Chicago in 1893 this facet of American innovation was illuminated clearly at the congress that brought together lobbyists and experts with a shared professional interest in the future of trademarks, copyright, and patents conveying monopoly power over the replication of registered inventions. Already this realm of activity had been identified as the domain of "intellectual property."

The leading figure guiding the course of these proceedings was Richard Jordan Gatling, the inventor of the famous automated gun bearing his name. Like Henry Colt and Benjamin Hotchkiss, Gatling was a significant innovator in the development of a global arms industry that the United States would later come to lead and dominate. Massive flows of public funds from the US Treasury would be devoted to the development of new weapons, a process that stimulated the creation of many new technologies with countless commercial spinoffs. The much mythologized violence characterizing the United States' westward-moving frontier created incentive as well as a lucrative laboratory for the development of increasingly lethal, compact, and reliable forms of weaponry. American arms merchants contributed significantly to a widening flow of products whose effect has consistently been to alter the balance of power on many edges of empire. The arms industry represented by R.J. Gatling in Chicago gave imperialists in Asia and Africa, as well as Indian fighters in the United States and throughout the Western Hemisphere, many new means of intensifying the four-century-old crusade aimed primarily at removing Indigenous peoples from the control of vast territories rich in natural resources. As president of the American Association of Inventors, Gatling pointed his audience in Chicago towards the amazing proliferation of patented inventions in the United States. His most telling statistic spoke emphatically about the rise of the United States as the world's leading centre of technological innovation.[20] He indicated that his own country was home to individuals and corporations that, collectively, were seeking and obtaining twice as many patents on new inventions as the rest of the world put together.[21]

The kind of opportunity extended to Gatling, Turner, and others in 1893 was replicated across all fields of endeavour as the best, the brightest, and the most ambitious made their way from many parts of the world to the shores of Lake Michigan. The Exposition, for instance, provided the venue for the Bohemian musician Antonin Dvořák to collaborate with the African-American performer Scott Joplin. Dvořák had come to the United States at the invitation of the National Conservatory of Music in New York. He was brought from the Czech capital of Prague, then part of the Austro-Hungarian empire, to develop and apply his theory that the key to formulating a unique and indigenous musical style in the United States must lie in finding classical roots in what the composer referred to as Negro melodies and Native American chants. "In the Negro melodies of America," Dvořák asserted, "I find all that is needed for a great and noble school of music. They are pathetic, tender, passionate, melancholy, bold, merry, gay or what you will ... I am satisfied that the future music of this country must be founded on what are called Negro melodies."[22] On August 12, Czech Day, Dvořák's musical prowess was highlighted at the Exposition, where he conducted a symphony orchestra whose performance featured many of his own compositions. Like the ancestral territory of the Poles, which was then divided between the imperial claims of Prussia, Russia, and Austria, the Czechs of that era formed a nationality without a nation state. This condition gave enhanced significance to setting aside a particular time for the celebration of Czech culture. The Poles too were given their own special day. This form of national recognition was interspersed with events like Stenographer's Day on July 22, or Maritime Transportation Day on October 25.

After his performance, Dvořák took time to sample the Exposition's rich array of musical offerings. He was especially impressed by the performance of Scott Joplin. Dvořák could easily see that the young pianist was an extraordinary composer and performer whose prolific musical experiments represented a unique blend of the new with older influences of African origin. When he showcased this blend before the large, receptive audiences at the Exposition, Joplin was well on his way to mastery of an American musical style that the world would come to know as ragtime. The exchange between Joplin and Dvořák was one of the factors that influenced Dvořák's most celebrated composition, the symphony entitled "From the New World." Dvořák completed this masterpiece at the Czech-American community of Spillville, Iowa.[23] The c``omposer's easy and adept collaboration with the makers of African-American music contrasted with the awkward efforts of the Exposition's organizers to deal with America's most notorious human divide. The organizers had designated August 25 as Colored People's Day. Their decision to hand out free pieces of watermelon to every "colored person" in attendance spoke eloquently of the often unconscious stereotypes and prejudices that characterized some aspects of the Columbian exposition and the society that mounted it.[24]

One of the most remarkable congresses at the Chicago exposition was the World's Parliament of Religions.[25] Looking back on the event years later, Washington Gladden, a leader of the Social Gospel movement, remembered it as "the most important religious gathering ever assembled." It was "an epoch in religious thought," observed another delegate.[26] The parliament's opening ceremonies took place in the Hall of Columbus on September 11. The Columbian Liberty Bell was sounded ten times to commemorate Hinduism, Jainism, Zoroastrianism, Taoism, Confucianism, Shintoism, Buddhism, Judaism, Christianity, and Islam. While Christians dominated most of the presentations, the spiritual superstar was undoubtedly India's Swami Vivekananda, a disciple of Sri Ramakrishna. With his graceful facility with English, his youthful good looks, his adept ecumenical diplomacy, and his masterful grasp of both the details and the broad outlines of his own Hindu heritage, Swami Vivekananda emerged at Chicago as one of the premier ambassadors of the Orient.[27] He found an especially devoted following among the many theosophists at the World's Parliament of Religions. The theosophist looked especially to the Hindu Vedas and to the teachings of a Madame Helena Blavatsky, a Russian aristocrat who claimed to have studied with an elite sect of religious seers in the Himalaya Mountains. Prominent among the theosophical delegation at Chicago was Annie Besant – the British Fabian socialist whose unique marriage of secular and religious politics would bring her in later years to the presidency of the Indian National Congress, the organization subsequently led by Gandhi.[28]

The importance of the theosophical delegation at the World's Parliament of Religions was part of a trend that saw a small but influential group of North Americans and Europeans look for spiritual enlightenment to the ancient learning of the Orient. This growing interest in Eastern religions was one small feature of a larger epistemological phenomenon famously identified by Edward Said and others as Orientalism. But, as Walter D. Mignolo has pointed out, it was not possible for the likes of Vivekananda to be seen as personifications of the "Orient" until the dominant groups in the Americas and Europe had collectively developed a shared sense of their own common orientation to global geography and world history. In Mignolo's view, the "discovery" and imaginative construction of "America" was the instrumental event in the evolving self-understanding of those who pictured their societies as part of the Occident and the so-called West. Indeed, the ritual of Chicago's Columbian Exposition was a strategic act in confirming and entrenching that imaginative construct. "There cannot be an Orient, as the other, without the Occident as the same ... America was perceived as the daughter of Europe and its promised future." Mignolo adds, "Asia and Africa were [conceived as] the past."[29]

The World's Parliament of Religions proved to be one of the exposition's premier venues for the process of cultural exchange and hybridization that today goes by the name of globalization. Its proceedings, however, were not universally embraced. Turkey's Sultan Abdul Hamid II, the theocratic emperor of the Ottoman Empire between 1876 and 1909, turned down the organizers' invitation to take part. This snub from the Islamic world's most influential leader hinted at the outlines of schisms to come in the relationship between the Judeo-Christian and Muslim branches of the broader religious community rooted in the Abrahamic tradition of monotheism. The Sultan's refusal to attend or even sanction the World's Parliament of Religions took place when the political influence of the Ottoman Empire was increasingly challenged in parts of the Middle East by France and Great Britain. Increasing the Ottoman Caliphate looked to Berlin to offset the incursions of the empires of London and Paris. Few Muslim delegations attended the Chicago religious parliament except for a few converts from the United States. Similarly, except for presentations by a few anthropologists, the vast diversity of spiritual traditions shaping the local cultures of many Indigenous peoples was left mostly unrepresented.

While the warm and enthusiastic reception extended to Swami Vivekananda epitomized the strength of the cross-cultural collaboration permeating most aspects of the parliament, the proceedings also included interventions highlighting the importance of religion as a rallying point for the as yet unfulfilled impetus of decolonization. In responding, for instance, to the missionary appeals of a number of Christian evangelists at the sessions, one Hindu delegate was reported to have remarked: "We look at England, the richest Christian nation in the world. Why is she rich and prosperous? Because she has her foot on the neck of 250,000,000 Asiatics. We read history and we see everywhere that Christianity has conquered prosperity by cutting the throat of its followers. At such a price the Hindoo will have none of it."[30]

This genre of criticism from within the Old World civilizations of Asia prompted a good deal of dialogue and serious introspection among some of the more thoughtful agents of Western civilization's missionary culture. And so the World's Parliament of Religions, like many other aspects of Chicago's Columbian Exposition, proved to be a fairly accurate barometer of future upheavals as the imperialism of the late Victorian era began to merge into the makings of a new century. The twentieth century would explode in a series of lethal combats among proponents of globalized communism, globalized fascism, and globalized capitalism. The developing storm clouds would profoundly colour the ongoing struggle of all the planet's peoples to share in the promise of a world order premised on a universal and unalienable right of life, liberty, and the pursuit of happiness – the democratic right and responsibility of all peoples to exercise self-determination.

TURNER AND THE MOVING FRONTIER

When he emerged from the passenger train in Chicago, Frederick Jackson Turner was poised to add his home-grown thoughts to an incredibly potent ideological blend being concocted in the world's newest major metropolitan centre. He was about to make his mark among numerous presenters on one of the most momentous global stages ever raised. He was joining the company of a significant set of thinkers, celebrities, and activists engaged in cultivating religious, artistic, technological, political, and scholarly turf as diverse as that nurtured by Scott Joplin, Antonin Dvořák, Harry Houdini, Swami Vivekananda, Annie Besant, R.J. Gatling, and Buffalo Bill Cody. An assembly of anarchists had even managed to congregate in Chicago in 1893. They met at the invitation of William Henry Jackson, who had taken to identifying himself as Major Honoré Joseph Jaxon during his years in the United States. This University of Toronto–educated Métis activist had served as Louis Riel's personal secretary throughout the tumultuous events of 1885 in the Canadian North-West.[31]

Turner's presentation, therefore, was one small part of an enormous cultural feast, with stimulation for every imaginable taste. The young historian from Madison was taking his place at a vast public ceremony introducing soda pop, hamburgers, and motion-picture projectors, all quintessential icons of a nascent global culture of corporate Americana. The historical conference at the Columbian Exposition attracted nothing like the media attention devoted to the World Parliament of Religions. In an era when specialization was already beginning to fragment the social sciences into many small enclaves of professional expertise, academic events such as those sponsored by the American Historical Association rarely attracted boisterous public involvement or the intense glare of supercharged publicity. When Turner's turn came to make his presentation, the response of his colleagues was polite but unremarkable. There was little in the respectful audience's reaction to suggest the excitement that the essay would generate in its published form.

Turner used the occasion to give succinct and lively expression to many of the animating principles that the Columbian Exposition had been created to celebrate, cultivate, and disseminate. "Since the days when the fleet of Columbus sailed into the waters of the New World," he declared, "America has been another name for opportunity, and the people of the United States have taken their tone from the incessant expansion which has not only been open but has even been forced on them."[32] At the heart of Turner's interpretation was the conviction that the single word "frontier" could be stretched in its meaning to comprehend and explain the entire saga of Euro-American expansion leading to the creation and the growth of the United States. Turner's breakthrough was, therefore, to go beyond the idea of the frontier as a place or even a series of places. He described the frontier more as a historical *process* that transformed human personality and human relationships even as it transformed the landscape.

As Turner presented it, the westward-moving frontier of Euro-American settlement was the most influential agency in making the United States the site of a very different kind of civilization from the one the immigrants to

North America had left behind in Europe. For Turner, the markers and the media of these different civilizations were the people who acquired distinct qualities of personality in responding to the environments distinguishing the New World from the Old. He defined the American frontier as "the meeting point between savagery and civilization" and as "the line of most rapid and effective Americanization." He began his reflections with a reference to a recent bulletin of the superintendent of the federal census and quoted the official's observation that "the unsettled area [of the US] has been so broken up by isolated bodies of settlement that there can hardly be said to be a frontier line."[33]

Having introduced the argument that the pre-eminent period of frontier expansion in the United States had run its course, Turner looked back to describe this transcontinental movement as a single monumental event whose meanings could be deciphered and synthesized into a few sweeping generalizations. As he saw it, the opening of each new frontier had the effect of removing the people and institutions of the United States yet farther away from their European origins towards the creation of a genuinely novel and distinct New World civilization. "American social development," Turner wrote, "has been continually beginning over again on the frontier." The effect of this repeating cycle of new beginnings lay in the extreme individualism and self-sufficiency of its citizens. This personal liberty was said to create the basis of a more robust democracy than the tradition-bound civilization of the Old World. Hence, "the advance of the frontier has meant a steady movement away from the influence of Europe, a steady growth of independence on American lines."[34]

These arguments led Turner to the conclusion that the moving frontier in the American West has consistently been the most prolific zone in the generation of the nation's intellectual dynamism as well as its political capital. A major factor contributing to the West's intellectual originality was that, "for a moment, at the frontier, the bonds of custom are broken." Thus he concluded that "each frontier did indeed furnish a new field of opportunity, a gate of escape from the bondage of the past; and freshness and confidence, and scorn of older society, impatience of its restraints and ideas, and indifference to its lessons, have accompanied the frontier."[35] Turner succeeded in encapsulating a range of convictions, attitudes, and aspirations that many other commentators had struggled with less precision to understand and articulate. The essay's contents served to celebrate and legitimate the process of US expansion in the secular language of the social sciences. From the era of the Puritans' founding of New England, the same process had most often been advanced in the name of a religious mission, a God-given Manifest Destiny to transform a savage wilderness into a Christian civilization, a New Jerusalem, a New Israel.

But what was to be said of the past, present, and future of the Indigenous peoples whose assigned function in the frontier thesis was to personify the savage antithesis of American civilization? How did the transformative process of the frontier appear from the perspective of those who experienced its movement as an implosion of space rather than as an expansion of geography, as a narrowing of life's horizons and possibilities rather than as an opening of opportunity?[36] And what prospects did the treatment of Indigenous peoples in capitalism's emergent laboratory and bastion hold out for diverse Aboriginal groups all over the world whose many distinct ecologies of relationship with their own native territories presented significant obstacles to the globalization of a single system of commercial interaction? Efforts to address various aspects of questions such as these have formed a major theme of much writing in the humanities and social sciences, especially since the era of the anti-war protests of the 1960s and early 1970s.

The protests against the large-scale US military intervention in Vietnam would significantly alter the climate of research, publication, and teaching in the academies of the West. The ideas emanating from this protest movement crept, for instance, into the interpretation of US expansion into Indian Country – the very name often applied to enemy territory by US soldiers in Vietnam. The zeal of the US government in taking over the imperial role from withdrawing French forces in Southeast Asia was widely interpreted as evidence that a new form of US-dominated neo-colonialism was moving into the power vacuum created by the dismantling of European empires.[37] The changed atmosphere of academic endeavour pointed its practitioners towards an altered range of issues and problems. Some of the revisionism challenged the ethnocentrism and unqualified Social Darwinism implicit in Turner's famous essay and in countless other works of its ilk. The conquest of Indian Country no longer seemed like a simple saga of civilization's ascent over savagery, but, rather, as a more complex human encounter representing an earlier phase of the same westward-pointing continuum of expansion that propelled US armed forces into an imperial role Southeast Asia.[38]

Turner's presentation at the World's Columbian Exposition, therefore, anticipated the emergence and intensification of many of the themes and tensions that would explode into global prominence, especially in the fateful year of 1968.[39] In 1893 Turner alluded to the possibility of further frontiers of extended US power when he observed: "He would be a rash prophet who should assert that the expansive character of American life has now entirely ceased ... Movement has been the dominant fact, and, unless this training has no effect upon a people, the American energy will continually demand a wider field for its exercise."[40] As Turner wrote those words, his country had embarked on an adventure that would culminate in the military overthrow of the Aboriginal Hawaiians' independent government – an outcome that would transform their islands into US federal territory. Furthermore, within five years of 1893, the US government would acquire formal imperial control of the Philippines, Puerto Rica, and a number of Pacific islands. In a closely related instance of appropriated anti-colonialism, the US government would also institute a regime of informal commercial and political control over Cuba.[41] Beginning especially with the Cuban Revolution of 1959, this neo-colonial project would generate an extremely resilient and widespread form of opposition to the incursions of a variant of global frontierism anticipated by Turner in his presentation at the World's Columbian Exposition.

The outcome of the US military adventures of 1898 were part of a well-established process that had long seen the United States push its expanding influence into the vacuum created by a shrinking Spanish Empire. In the era of the Chicago exposition, Rudyard Kipling, the bard of the British Empire, made a particularly evocative literary appeal to urge the US government to replace that of Spain as the imperial master of the diverse peoples indigenous to the Philippine Islands. With this objective in mind, Kipling poetically implored the Americans to "Take Up the White Man's Burden." Media mogul William Randolph Hearst returned to the same theme of race-based imperialism in the years ahead, urging the US government to adopt an expansive foreign policy based on the idea that "the Pacific Ocean is the white man's ocean."[42] The expansion of US power into the shrinking sphere of Spanish imperialism was one facet of a larger transformation in relationships of power. Portions of land on which the United States presently sit have been previously colonized not only by Spain but also by Sweden, the Netherlands, France, Russia, and Great Britain. Hence the global movement of US power into the vacuum of authority left by the dismantling of European empires after 1945 re-enacted a previous pattern reflected in the US incorporation of territory formerly colonized by a number of imperial regimes. Especially prominent in both successions was the pre-emption of the formal imperialism of Great Britain by US expansion, once in the course of the American Revolution and once again in the reordering of Anglo-America and the rest of the world following Europe's exhaustion in the Second World War.[43]

Frederick Jackson Turner was one of those at the Columbian Exposition who helped point the sense of Manifest Destiny in the United States beyond the Western Hemisphere towards more global fields of frontierism. As he looked from the past to the prospect of future surges of US expansion, Turner remained the optimist. He did not stop to reflect on what the experiences of Native Americans might portend for the future fate of countless other societies lying along the expansionary course of some as yet unrealized American empire. To the extent that he considered the effect of the United States' moving frontier on Indian peoples, he viewed the Aboriginal inhabitants of the United States as part of the primal environment to be absorbed and reconstituted in the process of remaking Old World Europeans into New World Americans.

Turner described the Indian role in the genesis of a distinct North American civilization as follows:

The wilderness masters the colonist. It finds him a European in dress, industries, modes of travel and thought. It takes him from the railway car and puts him in the birch canoe. It strips off the garments of civilization and arrays him in the hunting shirt and the moccasin. It puts him in the log cabin of the Cherokee and Iroquois and runs a palisade around him. Before long he has gone to planting Indian corn and plowing with a sharp stick; he shouts the war cry and takes the scalp in ortho-dox Indian fashion. In short, at the frontier the environment is at first too strong for the man. He must accept the conditions which it furnishes, or perish, and so he fits himself into the Indian clearings and follows the Indian trails. Little by little he transforms the wilderness, but the outcome is not the old Europe.[44]

With these few rhetorical flourishes, Turner was able to usher Native Americans to the margins of his historical narrative. Questions about the place of Indigenous peoples and people in the Columbian Exposition's overall staffing, organization, and imagery, however, presented a host of issues that proved far more perplexing than the content of Turner's lit-erary stereotypes and generalizations. Following in the tradition of the Philadelphia Centennial Exposition in 1876, Native American peoples were afforded significant roles in several aspects of the Chicago exposi-tion. In the exhibitions of the federal governments of both Canada and the United States, for instance, attention was directed to students in the Indian residential schools – institutions that figured prominently in the Indian pol-icies of both countries. The Canadian government sent different rotations of students to Chicago from eight of the residential schools that it was run-ning in conjunction with several Christian denominations. These student groups performed for the fair's visitors in a mock classroom where they made shoes, sewed, spun yarn, and operated a printing press. From that press emerged a pamphlet entitled *The Canadian Indian,* and copies were distributed to the onlookers. The pamphlet announced that the purpose of the Canadian Indian Department's display in Chicago was "to make known the steps by which the Canadian people have to a large extent succeeded in giving the aboriginal tribes their civilization with its advantages, in return for the lands they have received from them."[45]

The displays mounted by the federal administrations of Indian Affairs in both Canada and the United States conformed well to the imagery of North American history as an ascent from savagery to civilization – the paradigm that formed the basis of Turner's conception of the US frontier. These presentations, equating Indian policy with a civilizing mission, were put forward to complement more ambitious government exhibitions aimed at highlighting a host of technological achievements made over a range of industrial and agricultural fields. The intent behind many of the gov-ernment displays was to attract investment as well as to transform sparsely settled regions into thickly populated Euro–North American settlements. The resulting increase in real-estate values has consistently formed one of the most lucrative engines for the creation of new wealth in the United

States, a country that can be conceived as the most successful of the land speculations ever mounted by the monied interests of Europe. The key to maintaining the rise of land values was to attract a broadening stream of transatlantic immigration and to promote the westerly migration and non-Aboriginal settlement.

More generally, the goal of many of the displays at the Columbian Exposition was to arouse and to direct the ethos of expansive self-confidence – the most essential element in the many forms of empire building that characterized the era. The exposition's designers sought to instill and to edify those values of personal ambition, civil cooperation, scientific rigour, and religious conviction that made all of nature seem inviting of, and amenable to, human dominion.

SHOCK AND AWE, KWAKWAKA'WAKW STYLE

While the aims and objectives of the government displays were relatively clear and consistent, the same could not be said of a section of the World's Columbian Exposition known as the Midway Plaisance. As the name implied, that part of the fair was designed to integrate more overt varieties of entertainment into the overall weave of information and edifying public education. Visitors could choose from a range of amusement rides, cafés, and eateries. It was also the section that included, in the words of the exposition's own promoters, a "fantastically picturesque mosaic of odd bits of tribes and nationalities from every quarter of the globe." There was, for instance, a facsimile of a Cairo street and a Turkish village. And, at intervals, beating drums would attract spectators to witness "Cannibal and War Dances of South Sea Islanders."[46]

In a field near the Midway Plaisance, Buffalo Bill's legendary Wild West Show, which included many traditionally garbed Plains Indian warriors, did stupendous business during the course of the exposition. Among the Indian performers who had worked in previous years for William Cody was Sitting Bull, the Oglala leader who had achieved fame, or infamy, for his strategic leadership of the Indian fighting forces that emerged victorious in 1876 from the Battle of Little Bighorn. In 1893, however, this Indian victory over the United States' military establishment was downplayed in light of the fair's dominant message. In keeping with the overarching theme of the Columbian Exhibition, the promoters of Buffalo Bill's spectacle entitled their drama "How the West Was Won."[47]

During the warm summer months of 1893, there was a steady exchange between the residential encampment of the Wild West Show and the encampment of Native American performers employed by the Exposition's Ethnology Department. The work, rest, and play of these Aboriginal performers animated the live ethnographic exhibitions that were among the main attractions drawing visitors towards the Midway Plaisance. The musical presentations of these Native American performers proved especially popular. In fact, according to music historian Michael Broyles, "Native American music became the hit of the show." The enthusiastic public response to these renditions in the Indian villages gave rise to an entire "Indianist" musical movement in the United States. Arthur Farwell established the Wa-Wan Press specifically to publish many of the compositions heard there. The popularity and influence of this music persisted into the 1920s, when the emergence of jazz began to take American music in a different direction.

According to Broyles, in the 1890s the time was not yet ripe for African-American influences to rise to the level of musical prominence that Dvořák both anticipated and promoted. "The guilt and stigma of slavery and reconstruction were still too much on people's minds," he writes, whereas Native American music was considered "safe."[48] That sense of safety derived from the fact that, by 1893, most Indian people in the United States had been contained within the jurisdictional boundaries of reservations and within a particularly repressive genre of American law. The completeness of that containment had been confirmed in 1890, when members of the Seventh Cavalry Division of the United States Army had massacred Big Foot's band at Wounded Knee, largely in revenge for the unit's previous defeat at the Battle of Little Bighorn.

The Native American exhibitions at Chicago were organized as a series of small Aboriginal villages meant to represent the "traditional" cultures of Crees from Manitoba, Penobscots from Maine, Iroquois from New York, Chippewas from Minnesota, and Winnebagos from Wisconsin. A mixture of Sioux, Blackfeet, and Nez Perce people took on the job of representing the Indigenous peoples of North America's Far West. The display also included a section devoted to the Indians of South America. It ended with a ruin meant to depict the supposed demise of the Mayan civilization in the Yucatan region of Mexico.[49] Like most aspects of this ethnographic display, its ending with the depiction of an Aboriginal ruin was highly symbolic.

The most controversial group in the complex of Indian villages proved to be the eight Kwakwaka'wakw performers from British Columbia. The Kwakwaka'wakw have historically been identified in much of the anthropological literature as Kwakiutl.[50] The coastal region that is their Aboriginal home forms one part of Canada's westernmost province, a highly contested part of North America that has long sustained the continent's most elaborate and intense debate on the meaning of Aboriginal title.[51] The main intermediary who brought the Kwakwaka'wakw performers to Chicago's Columbian Exposition was the young Franz Boas, whose influence on the nascent discipline of anthropology would, in later years, prove as formidable as the influence of Frederick Jackson Turner on the historiography of the United States. The underlying assumptions of the two social scientists, however, were not compatible. Where Turner's view of American progress relegated Indian societies to savage obsolescence, Boas veered away from such ethnocentric judgments. In his work with the Kwakwaka'wakw and other Indian groups in the Pacific Northwest, Boas developed a more flexible estimation of the ability of Indigenous peoples to eschew assimilation while adapting themselves and their cultures to a changing world.[52]

In turning away from the Social Darwinism that was then the prevailing ethos in much of the transatlantic world, Boas's maverick approach to the nascent field of anthropology was seemingly pointed in a course parallel to the musical composition of Antonin Dvořák. It was permeated with the same inspirational perspective that prompted one of the academic delegates to the World's Parliament of Religions, a professor of Oriental languages named Charles D'Harlez, to underline the "necessity of penetrating oneself with the spirit of the people who form the object of particular research" – to attempt the imaginative feat "to think with their mind and to see with their eyes."[53]

Boas was afforded broad responsibilities in Chicago by his immediate supervisor, Frederick Ward Putnam, the director of the Peabody Museum of Archaeology and Ethnology at Harvard University. Boas's contributions as Putnam's main assistant in the Ethnology Department of the Columbian Exposition helped the German immigrant embark on an illustrious career that would help make the 500th anniversary of Columbus's transformative voyage a very different occasion from the 400th anniversary. With his many gifted students, Boas would elaborate a broad conception of culture that, in time, largely superseded the "scientific racism" of Social Darwinism. Turner and others who accepted Social Darwinism viewed human history as a simplistic extension of the evolutionary principles of natural history.[54]

At the time of the Columbian Exposition, Boas had just begun his long and extremely fruitful collaboration with his main Kwakwaka'wakw informant and colleague, George Hunt.[55] Hunt combined an agile mastery of the cultural heritage of his own people with formidable abilities as a translator and a mediator adept at negotiations on the middle ground of transcultural relations.[56] He embodied the balance between continuity and change, between adherence to tradition and embrace of the modern, that George Manuel, another Aboriginal innovator from British Columbia, would later describe as the animating feature of the Fourth World.[57] Hunt and the rest of the Kwakwaka'wakw delegation were not prepared to leave unchallenged the role assigned to them in Chicago as quaint icons of an obsolete culture. In their decision not to present a sanitized, folkloric image of themselves, the Kwakwaka'wakw delegation chose the course of shock and controversy. They mounted a spectacle that could not help but confirm in the minds of some onlookers their most base stereotypes of Aboriginal savagery.

The ceremony was strategically timed to achieve maximum international impact. While the Kwakwaka'wakw included traditional dances in their daily schedule of performances at Chicago, they tried something extraordinary on August 19, the eve of the exposition's "Great Britain Day." As a delegation from British North America, the group correctly calculated that they would be afforded extra attention by the public and by the press. In front of an audience of about 10,000, including reporters from the *New York Times* and the London *Times*, the Kwakwaka'wakw began their ritual. Near the climax of the ceremony, George Hunt removed a knife from his vest as he approached two of the male dancers. Calmly and deliberately he proceeded to cut long, deep incisions between the shoulder blades of two individuals described in the press as Two Bites and Strong Back. Then he reached into the bloody incisions, stretching linear bands of cut flesh away from the back muscles of the two men, and inserted ropes underneath the displaced skin.

The reporter for London's *Sunday Times* described what happened next:

During a pause Two Bites and Strong Back attached stout ropes to the end of the small ones passed through their backs, and throwing their weight upon them, tore them through their fleshy fastenings. By this time the expression of Two Bites was that of a famished wolf. His eyes glared like those of a furious wild animal, and, kneeling on the platform, he uttered hoarse cries. Two Indians sprang upon him and caught him by the shoulders. He turned on them, snapping and snarling like a mad dog, until George Hunt, the interpreter, walked over and extended him his bare arm. Two Bites gave a dismal howl, and fastened on it with his teeth, making them meet in the flesh. It was with difficulty, after being dragged half-way across the platform, that he could be induced to relinquish his hold, when it was discovered that a piece had been bitten off Hunt's arm as big as a silver dollar; but the inter-preter smiled and showed no signs of pain.[58]

The Kwakwaka'wakw performance was treated as a grave affront and as a matter of humiliation for many officials of church and state in the Dominion of Canada. They quickly circulated dire memos among them-selves about the episode's meaning and implications. Their communica-tions were rich in alarmed prognostications about the scandalous effect of the spectacle that had been presented in Chicago by George Hunt and company. The Kwakwaka'wakw display on one of the world's most public stages was seen to have completely overwhelmed the "civilized" imagery of Indian boarding-school life that had been so carefully cultivated by the Canadian government. In 1893 Canadian law makers were engaged in a process of extending the scope of the federal *Indian Act* to outlaw several forms of traditional dance and potlatch giveaways that were seen to counter the work of Christian evangelization on Indian missions. With abundant reports of the episode in Chicago before him, the deputy superintendent general of Indian affairs lamented, "the Department unfortunately cannot invoke the law to prevent or to put a stop to the disgraceful scenes referred to, as the law in Canada which prohibits the celebration of such orgies in British Columbia is of course inoperative while the Indians are in the United States."[59]

With the presentation of their shocking drama, the Kwakwaka'wakw illustrated that the World's Columbian Exposition really did bring together peoples with very different cosmologies and perceptions of how to express oneness with life's changing cycles. There, representatives of the colonizers and the colonized found ways to display, justify, and challenge their asymmetric relationships of power. The Kwakwaka'wakw protest found an echo in the presentation of Simon Pokagon, a Potawatomi intellectual from the Chicago area.[60] Having pointed out the failure of the exposition's organizers to include Indian presenters in the World Fair's opening ceremonies, Pokagon was invited to address the audience assembled for Chicago Day, an event scheduled near the conclusion. Pokagon declared that, for his people, the celebration of America's so-called discovery amid the graves of departed Indians amounted to a kind of funeral. He reminded the audience that the successes on display "had been at the sacrifice of *our* homes and a once happy race." This sole Indian on the speakers' podium ended with a haunting invocation: "And so we stand as upon a seashore, chained hand and foot, while the incoming tide of the great ocean of civilization rises slowly but surely to overwhelm us."[61]

The menacing rise of imperial power to which Pokagon alluded was in that era overwhelming the lives and well-being of many Indigenous peoples the world over. In 1893 the forces of Western expansion that had subjugated the Indians of the Americas were everywhere on the move. With its fast-growing naval power, the United States was reaching out across the Pacific to annex first Hawaii and then the Philippines. The European powers were in the process of carving up the remaining lands and peoples of Africa south of the Sahara. In this imperial competition, Belgium's King Leopold emerged as an unlikely winner. By making himself both a proxy of the United States and a recognized champion of the West's civilizing mission, Leopold gained a huge personal proprietorship in the drainage basin of the Congo River.[62] Throughout extensive reaches of the Middle East and Eurasia, agents of France and Britain conspired to discredit and replace the regime of the Ottomans. Czarist Russia continued to push its imperial frontiers southward, adding new territory at an average rate of 55 square miles a day.[63] The Portuguese, Spanish, Dutch, French, and British governments vied among themselves for advantage as colonial overlords throughout much of the Far East, even as the United States continued to muscle its way into the Chinese trade. Even Japan was starting to model itself for provisional membership in the White Man's imperial club. Its rulers were developing aspirations to expand their own colonial frontier throughout eastern region of the Pacific Rim.

The Columbian conquests, therefore, were in full swing as the 400th anniversary of Christopher Columbus's transatlantic voyage was celebrated. Simon Pokagon recorded his unease with the Columbian celebration in a very direct way. The Kwakwaka'wakw mounted a more unusual protest. Their provocative performance put the dissidence of the Aboriginal actors on public display. By enlivening the exposition with a performance that smashed complacency through the subversive deployment of the Victorian stereotypes of Aboriginal savagery, the Kwakwaka'wakw added an element of sensationalism to the Chicago exposition. Their shocking artistry helped highlight both the diversity and the commonalities of the human condition. The world's fair of 1893 portrayed, sometimes with crude audacity, sometimes with flair and imagination, the converging destinies of all human beings on a planet made to seem progressively smaller by various revolutions in communications technology; it served as an effective window on the reality that, ultimately, we humans share a single global home subject to the same laws of nature. At Chicago's international exposition, promised one of its promoters, "all people and all races here gain more than a day and more than a fortune in getting a more thorough idea of the habitable globe by coming west to Chicago."[64]

CHAPTER TWO

Imperialism and Its Enemies: From the Crusades to Enron

They stood to profit if they did not recognize the full humanity of
Aboriginal people.

Victoria Freeman, *Distant Relations*, 2000

HISTORY WITHOUT BORDERS

The promoters of the international expositions in the second half of the
nineteenth century hoped, as one of their goals, to present a macroscopic
vision of the entire planet in a single show. This ideal seems to have been
advanced in especially compelling ways at the Columbian Exposition
in Chicago in 1893. Its commemoration of the 400th anniversary of
Christopher Columbus's voyage served as a reminder that, before 1492,
there was no widely accessible understanding of the world as an orb that
could be circumnavigated; no accurate, widely available picture of the
shape and character of the one receptacle that contains all of humanity's
various parts. Even after four centuries, the character of the globe as the
common home of many thousands of linguistically distinct peoples and
many millions of diverse plant and animal species was still a relatively new
concept whose full meanings and requirements for humanity were unclear.
They remain so still.

Over the centuries following 1492, the idea has continued to grow that
the globe is a single environment encompassing the shared destiny not only
of all humanity but of all the living beings we know about. The growth of
that idea has been especially marked in recent decades as the Earth has
become the subject of photographs taken from platforms raised into outer
space through rocket science. It is no accident that the wide dissemination
of those photographs occurred around the same time that the term *globalization* began to pass into everyday currency in the English language. The
relatively sudden appearance at the end of the twentieth century of the
shape of our planet as a verb (to globalize) and as a process (globalization)
suggests that, more than five centuries after Columbus's voyage, the unitary
character of our shared terrestrial home is still being newly discovered.

While the word *globalization* is new, the complex of processes it describes
is not. In a general way, the process of globalization is as old as human

endeavours to widen our spheres of understanding and relationship.[1] In a more precise way, however, the modern era of globalization can be said to have started in 1492, when Christopher Columbus, acting under the patronage of Queen Isabella of Castile and King Ferdinand of Aragon, set out to test his theory that the world is round. On behalf of Spain's Roman Catholic monarchs, the Italian explorer sought a new route from Europe to the Far East's legendary riches in spices, silk, and hand-crafted finery. He sought to give his European sponsors better access to the inventiveness of Chinese civilization, one whose technologists had produced the world's first examples of, for instance, paper, printing, gunpowder, and compasses.[2] The new route was meant to provide an alternative to the arduous overland journey along the famed Silk Road. Marco Polo and his family of Venetian traders had exploited and publicized this route in the thirteenth century, when much of Eurasia, including China, was unified under Mongolian control.

By charting a westward pointing, oceanic highway to the Far East, Columbus sought to avoid antagonisms with shifting amalgams of Euroasian peoples, many of whom professed adherence to Islam. Of the three monotheistic religions whose sacred traditions go back to Abraham and his descendants, Islam is the most recent.[3] The rise of the Ottoman Empire in the fourteenth and fifteenth centuries had significantly strengthened and broadened the political base of Islam. Especially after Ottoman military forces captured Constantinople in 1453, direct overland contact between Europe and the Far East was made more difficult as Islamic peoples and polities exerted their increased capacities to oppose the incursions of Christians and other infidels in their territories.

In his effort to reach the Far East by heading west into the Atlantic Ocean, Columbus inadvertently stumbled on the vast land mass that subsequent generations would come to know as the Western Hemisphere.[4] The two continents – North and South America – that make up the Western Hemisphere were, in 1492, the site of almost unimaginable cultural pluralism. Scholars have estimated that 2,200 different languages were spoken in the territories that were soon baptized in Europe as both *Indias Occidentales* and as "America."[5] The monumental scope of this baptismal rite extended to naming as "Indians" most members of the Western Hemisphere's vast diversity of Indigenous peoples. Only "the Eskimos" of the Far North – or, according to their own language, the Inuit – were excluded from the new label imposed uniformly on the Aboriginal inhabitants of these continents as a result of Columbus's original miscalculation. At the basis of this error was his mistaken view that he and his men had landed in an outlying region of India – a name that described in the fifteenth century a far more extensive portion of the planet than it presently does. Columbus believed that he had arrived at one of the 13,000 fabulously rich islands of the so-called Indian Seas, which Marco Polo had described in his journals. More specifically, Columbus believed he had reached an outlying island of Zipango, the fabled realm that future generations would come to know as Japan.

Columbus's original mistake continues to extend from the misnamed peoples of the Americas to their Aboriginal lands. It continues in the axis of nomenclature between the East Indies and the West Indies.

The imposition of foreign names on the peoples and lands of the Western Hemisphere began a process of expansion and appropriation that drew heavily on the imperial heritage of the Greeks and Romans. The Greco-Roman legacy of empire building was dramatically renewed in 1493 with the Vatican's decision to assert its claims of universal sovereignty by "donating" all the newly discovered territories to the sponsors of Columbus's voyage. This enactment ranks prominently among the most consequential events in world history. It gave the seal of papal legitimacy to the beginning of a truly global process, one that would see the simultaneous integration and division of the world's land and peoples between subjugated colonies and privileged enclaves of military, commercial, and political dominance. The papal bull entitled *Inter Caetera* began with papal praise for the "recovery" of Granada from the "yoke of the *Saracens*," the term then used for Muslims. Pope Alexander VI went on to "give, grant and assign forever" to the Crown of Castile the region "hereto discovered ... and to be discovered ... together with all their dominions, cities, camps, places, villages, and all rights, jurisdictions, and appurtenances of the same." The only condition was that the Spanish government would "exalt, spread, and increase" the Christian religion and "that barbarous nations [would] be cared for and brought to the faith itself."[6] This papal donation was immediately challenged by the Crown of Portugal. Its representatives negotiated with the Crown of Castile a compromise in 1494 in the Treaty of Tordesillas. This treaty assigned the eastern extremity of South America – Brazil – to Portugal, a transaction confirmed by the Vatican in 1506 in the papal bull *Ea Quae.*

The treatment of parts of the Western Hemisphere as a colonial extensions of Spain, Portugal, and then of Western Europe's other sovereign powers dramatically shifted the tilt of world history throughout the subsequent era of globalization. Over many centuries before 1492, Western Europe's place in the world was consistent with its marginal location on the periphery of Eurasia, the planet's largest and most populated land mass. In the era of Imperial Rome, for instance, most of the Indigenous peoples of the northwestern extremes of the world's principal land mass were viewed as primitive tribesmen whose wild superstitions, untamed barbarism, and overall backwardness were to be feared and guarded against. While Western Europe was on the periphery, the zone where Europe merges with the Middle East, and where the Middle East blends into the rest of Asia, has served as the central nexus of interaction and human transformation. This massive realm hosting many of the world's oldest civilizations has been the site of especially complex and prolonged sagas of migration, merger, warfare, exchange, and invention.

William H. McNeil has attempted to account for the transformation of "the European Wild West" from "agrarian simplicity" during the Middle

Ages to its emergence as history's most "explosive" force of global trans-formation after 1492. "No other civilized society," he observes, "has ever approached such restless instability, nor exerted such drastic influence upon its fellows all over the world." He attributes this dynamism to the "tensions between the incompatible inseparables at the core of European culture." One such tension is derived, for instance, from "the collision and interaction of Renaissance and Reformation," the uneasy coexistence between reason and secular knowledge on the one hand and the conception of history as the outcome of God's will and intervention on the other. Such tensions have produced a society of "incessant and accelerating self-transformation, compounded from a welter of conflicting ideas, institutions, aspirations, and inventions ... a society eager to seize wealth, fame, and learning wherever they could be found."[7] This convergence of forces in Western Europe would result in a quick succession of intellectual, technological, military, commercial, and legal innovations whose cumulative effect would put the region at the metropolitan core of its own imperial systems after 1492. Paul Kennedy, author of *The Rise and Fall of the Great Powers*, describes the magnitude of the change that was initiated with the transatlantic extensions of Spain and Portugal: "Today, billions of people, descendants of the venturing nations and descendants of those who were invaded, still stand in the shadow of this epic transformation."[8]

The complex of peoples, polities, ideas, and actions identified simply as "the West" found a monumental site of expression, experimentation, consolidation, and expansion in the Americas. If the West is conceived as an artist, the Western Hemisphere is her largest and most revealing painting. If the West is conceived as a warrior, this same hemisphere is the scene of his most demanding and celebrated conquests. The role of the Americas as the primary medium, destination, prize, and propellant for the continuing current of history running through time and space from Mesopotamia to Egypt, Greece, Rome, and Western Europe is captured in the name given to the two continents that divide the Atlantic and Pacific oceans. It is captured in the designation of the last major body of land to enter the cartography of European knowledge as the Western Hemisphere. The Americas were found, invented, and transformed initially by Christian imperialists seeking to avert the rising power of Islam in their concurrent quest to convert souls and to gain improved commercial access to the wealth of the Far East. In the centuries following 1492, the Western Hemisphere would provide the Christian religion in all its proliferating theological diversity with its most fertile field of unchallenged evangelization and consolidation. The success of the Roman Catholic Church in establishing a new bastion for its religious empire is reflected in the emergence and entrenchment of a realm known to this day as Latin America.

The colonization of the Americas began more or less concurrently with a secessionist movement within Roman Catholicism that quickly gathered the force of mass protest. In 1517 Martin Luther responded to the corruption of the Roman Catholic hierarchy by posting his ninety-five theses on the entrance to the church in Wittenberg, Germany. Luther's protest rippled across time and space. It resulted in the division of Western Europe between imperial powers aligned with the Vatican and those aligned with the English, Dutch, and German proponents of a Protestant religion emphasizing the capacity of *individuals* to communicate directly with God. This split was expressed in the bitter competition in North America between largely English-speaking colonists, who tended to embody the most evangelical extremes of the Protestant Reformation, and those largely French-speaking populations whose Jesuit elites were leading champions of the Counter-Reformation. The competition between Roman Catholics and Protestants extended to a contest for the souls of the Indigenous peoples and for military alliances with their warring factions. Particularly on the Protestant side, this competition also extended to a concerted drive by God-fearing individualists to seize proprietary control away from the land's first inhabitants. The Protestant ascent in North America of the Netherlands, England, and, later, the United States merged with the transformation of a continent's material resources into capitalism's richest and most amenable frontiers of commodification. Hence the particular forms of extinguishment and subjugation imposed on the indigenous civilizations of Aboriginal North America invested the expansionary designs of the most Protestant of powers with a particularly distinctive capitalist character. The expansion to global proportions of the drive to homogenize and dominate the political economy of all humanity exceeded anything that Max Weber could have anticipated in his pioneering reflections of the commercial implications of the Protestant ethic.[9]

There were forces at work, therefore, far beyond those that could have been immediately apparent to Columbus and his men when they first made contact in October 1492 with the Taino Indians on Guanahani Island. Columbus eschewed the Indian place names to transform Guanahani Island into San Salvador. The sea-faring Taino were the Arawakan-speaking people indigenous to the Greater Antilles Islands. These include Cuba, Hispaniola (Haiti and the Dominican Republic), Puerto Rico, Jamaica, and the Bahamas. To the day of his death in 1506, Christopher Columbus remained convinced that the lands he had encountered in his three transatlantic voyages were the outlying islands of Asia – a continent sometimes referred to in those days simply as India. That view was one among several that influenced the papal bulls of demarcation in dividing the European title to North and South America between Spain and Portugal.

Columbus's understanding was rapidly pre-empted by the geographic calculations of other explorers, including those of Amerigo Vespucci. Between 1497 and 1504, Vespucci made four transatlantic explorations, two under the patronage of King Ferdinand of Spain and two under the patronage of King Manuel of Portugal. Because of Vespucci's growing appreciation that he was charting the coastal regions of whole continents rather than mere

islands off the coast of Asia, cartographers in 1507 introduced a variation
of the explorer's name on the first formal effort to represent the Western
Hemisphere in a map of the known world. In this fashion the scholars of
the Gymnasium Vosagense at St Die, a hamlet of Lorraine, introduced the
term *America* into the terminology of global geography.[10]

Transatlantic travel did not begin with Columbus. Certainly the Vikings
had frequently made the crossing, as had other European travellers, including, most likely, Basque fishermen. The achievements of these pre-Columbian navigators from Europe probably pale beside those of the admirals in
charge of the large Chinese fleet sponsored by the Chinese emperor, Zhu
Di. Between 1421 and 1423 this controversial embodiment of the Ming
Dynasty sent an armada of sophisticated vessels on a mission of global discovery that may well have infused Chinese influence into many coastal regions,
including those inhabited by the Mayan farmers of Central America and
the Algonkian-speaking peoples in the area of present-day Rhode Island.[11]
What differentiated these earlier initiatives from those of Christopher
Columbus was the willingness of the Italian explorer's sponsors to follow
up his discoveries with sustained initiatives of empire building. Columbus
first landed in 1492 on the Caribbean island he christened as San Salvador.
His decision to impose this Christian name signalled the intensity of his
imperial intent.[12] With this ritual of territorial baptism, Columbus helped
set in motion a concerted drive to Europeanize a whole hemisphere. His
initial transatlantic voyage, therefore, stands in a class of its own. In nudg-
ing humanity nearer to a more correct understanding of how our orb in
the heavens is actually constructed – in initiating the process of integrating
the planet's fourth and fifth continents into the realm of the Europeans,
the Africans, and the Asians – Columbus's exploration of 1492 acquired a
unique status as the instrumental act lying at the inception of the modern
era of globalization. The voyage began the epoch when it became possible
to conceive of a global community embracing all the world's peoples.

The arranged marriage in 1469 of Columbus's sponsors, Queen Isabella
of Castile and King Ferdinand of Aragon, brought unity from the competing factionalism of their ancestral jurisdictions in the Iberian Peninsula.
In joining themselves and their realms, Isabella and Ferdinand forged
the basis for a dramatic rise in Spanish power. An integral part of their
newly unified regime was the monarchs' embrace of Roman Catholicism
as a state religion. This move altered the Spanish propensity to accommodate, albeit with some bloody exceptions, the co-existence of Judaism,
Islam, and Christianity. The golden era of intercultural cooperation in the
Iberian Peninsula occurred after AD 711 when Islamic invaders from North
Africa defeated the Visigoths. The ascendant Moors began to build up their
Muslim Caliphate in Andalusia, making this jurisdiction the world's most
prolific site of exchange between the heritages of Europe, the Middle East,
and Northern Africa. Andalusia became a realm of relatively harmonious
relations on the frontiers between East and West – between increasingly

interwoven complexes of civilization as they converged and merged around the Mediterranean Sea. Much as in Venice and some of the other Italian city states, there flowed through Andalusia an especially creative blend of Arab arts and sciences that significantly enhanced the cultural resources of Europe. This infusion contributed significantly to those rising currents of knowledge and inspiration culminating in the phenomenon known as the European Renaissance.[13]

While Andalusia was for a time a beacon of skilful exchange and interaction on the borderlands of heritage and identity, the Crusades marked the intensification of the dark side of the relations bedevilling many elements of the encounter between adherents of Christianity and of Islam.[14] The Crusades began in AD 1095, when Pope Urban II called for a Christian war to seize Jerusalem from the holy city's Islamic occupants. Quite naturally, the unbounded zealotry expressed in repeated campaigns to convert or destroy the Islamic enemy was internalized within the Western heritage. The internalization of religious turmoil as a defining feature of Europe's Christian identity helped to transform that continent into a zone of increasingly lethal and divisive conflicts waged in the name of Jesus. The forces of religious antagonism found early expression in the emergence of a many-faceted Roman Catholic institution known as the Inquisition. Its practitioners aimed to identify and root out through conversion and torture, murder and expulsion, all forms of religious conviction deemed inconsistent with the universal dominion of Roman Catholicism as humanity's sole legitimate religion.

Ferdinand and Isabella attached their interests to the Inquisition with particular ferocity.[15] The religious zealotry of these monarchs culminated in 1492 in their conquest of the Emirate of Granada, the last remaining Islamic enclave on the Iberian Peninsula. Hence Columbus's transcendent voyage took place at precisely the moment when the excesses of the Crusades and the Inquisition merged with great theocratic force. This convergence was marked in the wording of the papal bull, *Inter Caetera*, which characterized the "donation" in 1493 of the newly discovered lands in the Americas as a reward for the Spanish extinguishment of the Islamic polity of Granada. The drive to vanquish all those who did not adhere to Roman Catholic orthodoxy had many targets. The intolerance extended, for instance, to the expulsion from Spain of indigenous Jews. In reflecting on the telling convergence of events at the dawning moment of the modern era of globalization, Mahmood Mamdani observed that "1492 stands as a gateway to two related endeavors: one the unification of the nation, the other the conquest of the world."[16] "This intensification of zeal, this new enthusiasm for conversion," notes J.H. Parry of Spain's imperial preoccupations, "quickly travelled to the New World, where it was to find new and more effective forms of expression."[17]

Christopher Columbus had grown up in Genoa. Along with Venice, Florence, and Milan, Genoa was a prominent northern Italian city state. These important centres of Renaissance learning spawned many of the early corporations that, through various experiments, contributed to the modern history of capitalism. The Italian banking institutions, including Florence's Peruzzi Corporation, helped facilitate the expansion of trade in wool, textiles, and grain, for example, even as they also provided the credit for the increasingly ambitious military campaigns of warring monarchs. Building on the commercial openings scouted by Marco Polo in his travels along the famed Spice Road, some of the Italian bankers helped to sponsor and organize Europe's long-distance trade with both the Middle and the Far East. When Columbus proposed to Queen Isabella and King Ferdinand the replacement of the difficult overland route to the Orient with the development of an ocean link pointing westward, the explorer's plan included the prospect of substantial financial backing from the bankers dominating his home community of Genoa. Much as the Medici banking house of Florence had become integral to the finances of the Vatican, so the bankers of Genoa would come to play a major role in the financial relationships accompanying the establishment and growth of the Spanish Empire in America.[18]

The Genoese financiers became especially active and well entrenched in the Spanish sea port of Seville, a community that drew on its Andalusian heritage in developing its new role at the nexus of transatlantic plunder and commerce. In establishing their role as financial facilitators of Spain's exploits in the Americas, the Genoese bankers found lucrative replacements in the West for the shrinking of commercial opportunities available to them in the East, especially in the Black Sea area. The growing assertiveness of the Ottomans increased the pressure not only on Genoa but on many of the emerging Christian powers of Western Europe to move decisively beyond their crusading obsession with the conquest and conversion of the Islamic inhabitants of the Middle East. The pressure increased even as the means became greater to colonize regions far beyond the Mediterranean world – to combine the expansionary tactics of imperial Rome with the religious zeal of the Crusades and the Inquisition in an unprecedented surge of imperial globalization.

The early stages of the modern era of globalization included some of its most cataclysmic episodes. The basis of this apocalypse was the murder, maiming, and enslavement of many millions of Aboriginal Americans. The death and destruction obliterated the integrity of whole civilizations even as it terminated or stunted the development of many hundreds of unique indigenous cultures. The most infamous phase of the Spanish conquest took place in Mexico, where several hundred mounted soldiers following Hernán Cortés overthrew the society at the pinnacle of Aztec civilization – a large pyramid composed of subject peoples and communities. The Spanish conquest took place in the wake of a previous phase of Aztec conquest that, in earlier decades, had placed a small, relatively insecure group at the royal summit of a society whose capital was Tenochtitlán. This Venice-like urban domain of islands and canals was located on the site of present-day Mexico

City. Bernal Díaz, one of the participants in and chroniclers of the conquest of Mexico, wrote of Tenochtitlán's "huge towers, temples, and buildings rising from the water, and all of masonry." He reported being "astounded" by Tlatelolco, the part of the Aztec capital that contained the city's great market. "We had never seen such a thing before," Díaz commented in describing "the number of people and the quantity of merchandise [Tlatelolco] contained, and the good order and control that was maintained."[19]

The Aztecs stood at the head of a very old and elaborate civilization that encompassed the heritage and contributions of many remarkable peoples. Many of these Mesoamerican groups thought of themselves as descendants of the legendary Toltecs. The Toltec feathered deity, Quetzalcoatl, retains a venerable place in the Aboriginal heraldry of Mexico until this day.[20] In the era of the Spanish conquest, the Aztec hierarchy had become so centralized and so coercively constructed that it was overthrown largely on the basis of Cortés's skill in channelling local resentments, rivalries, and jealousies into Indian-on-Indian violence. These divide-and-conquer techniques were to become increasingly important in the Columbian conquests as the perpetrators took control of one military or commercial frontier after the next. In pressing forward this seminal episode of imperial appropriation, privatization, and globalization the West's archetypical conquistador, Cortés, drew prolifically on the advice of Malinche, his Indian mistress, secretary, and translator. Throughout much of Latin America, Malinche is remembered as the original traitor, the comprador whose name remains synonymous with those who betray their own people through collaboration with oppressors.

Cortés's conquest of the Aztec Empire in the founding of New Spain established the basic model to be emulated by many warring conquistadors to come. These conquerors established the patterns of extinguishment or enslavement at the sharpest edge of the Columbian conquests' trajectory through history. Certainly Francisco Pizarro sought to replicate the conquest of Cortés when he set off from Panama in 1531 with the aim of winning glory and enrichment from the violent overthrow of the Inca civilization that was based in Peru. While the centralized militarism of the Aztecs and the Incas ironically made them particularly vulnerable to the imperial inroads of the Spanish conquistadors, the decentralized nature of the Mayan civilization in Guatemala and the Yucatan Peninsula made its people more difficult to dominate. "The Mayan civilization was less militaristic than the Aztec," writes Charles Gibson, "and for this very reason proved better prepared to withstand the warfare that the Spanish armies waged ... In Yucatan the routes of the conquistadors closed behind them in intermittent guerrilla forays. Towns were captured and lost, and no administrative capital compared with Tenochtitlán to determine the survival or loss of the entire civilization."[21]

The enticements of the Aztecs' and Incas' amazing treasure troves of gold and silver inflamed the acquisitive passions of many of Spain's most aggressive colonists. Their ruthlessness and their seemingly unquenchable lust for material enrichment imprinted the Iberian invasion with a notoriety known thereafter as the Black Legend. The pillage of Indian gold soon led to a preoccupation with mining as the quickest way to maintain and augment the flow of colonial wealth to the imperial capitals. Huge numbers of Indians in the colony were pressed into various forms of slavery in order to build up the human machinery of mineral extraction. This process of enslavement was transacted through legal innovations whereby the Spanish Crown issued charters known as *encomienda*. These documents authorized their holders to exploit Indian labour. A closely related legal device was the *repartimento*. It required Indians to devote long periods of work to the advancement of Spanish enterprise.

The Spanish mines in Central and South America quickly proliferated throughout the sixteenth and seventeenth centuries. As a result, writes Gibson, "the century from 1550 to 1650 was the great period of silver, and the prodigious import, far in excess of anything previously known in Europe, made Seville for a time the most prosperous and flourishing city of the entire continent."[22] Among the mines of Spain's American empire, the legendary Potosi stood in a class of its own. Situated in present-day Bolivia, Potosi was developed to exploit a veritable mountain of silver in the Andean realm of the Peruvian Inca. It became a site of incredible suffering, situated side by side with lavish ostentation on an outlandish scale. By the mid-seventeenth century the mountain city had given rise to legions of gambling houses, brothels, and theatres that proliferated amid a landscape dominated by thirty-six extravagantly decorated churches.

With its dense concentration of Iberian immigrants, native-born Creoles, and Indian slaves of diverse ethnic backgrounds, Potosi soon exceeded the populations of Madrid, Paris, and Rome in that era. In 1650 it had ten times the population of Boston. As described by Eduardo Galeano in his classic volume *Open Veins of Latin America*, the imperial system for extracting wealth from Potosi helped entrench patterns of foreign exploitation which have remained surprisingly consistent throughout most of Central and South America ever since. This exploitative continuum spans the era from the Spanish conquest of Mexico and Peru to more recent times, when the US government and its attending corporate and military agencies have systematically deployed instruments of state terror, often through paid intermediaries, to maintain the economic organization of Latin America in a mode that encourages huge economic disparities. This structure of class relations reserves the major share of the rewards for distant investors and their collaborating class of local Malinchists.[23]

As a symbol of the most ruthlessly exploitative features of the ongoing Columbian conquests, Potosi shines in the twenty-first century as a cautionary beacon signalling the determination of Fourth World activists not to allow the renewal of old cycles of injustice. It stands as an encouragement to replace the obsolete colonialism of a failing American empire with the grassroots urge felt all over the world to advance more ecologically sound models of globalization. This urge was eloquently expressed through the actions of a popular movement in Bolivia led by Indian peasants. The movement took form in 1999 to prevent the profit-driven privatization of fresh water by the US-based Bechtel Corporation. This mobilized force of anti-imperial resistance then turned to the task of stopping the foreign appropriation of the indigenous wealth emanating from new discoveries of oil and gas in Bolivia, a country where the stripped-out mines at Potosi serve as a constant reminder of the huge human cost of the failure to fend off the incursions of conquistadors, old and new.[24]

From its inception in 1492, the transatlantic machinery of imperial exploitation was integral not only to the structure of power between metropolis and hinterland but also to the emerging system of national and class relations within the colonizing continent. The wealth derived from Spain's violent plunder of the Americas was used to finance a vast increase of militarized violence within Europe and the Middle East. Seeking to assert and expand his claims as Holy Roman Emperor, King Charles v built up between 1519 and 1556 an extremely formidable army. He and his heir to the Spanish Crown, King Philip ii, then fought France five times. Over seven decades, the Spanish sovereigns maintained a concerted military opposition aimed at preventing Dutch Protestants from breaking away from the control of Madrid and Rome. A huge Spanish Armada was assembled to turn its aggressive guns against England, even as the riches of the Americas were deployed in a series of military campaigns directed at the Muslim polities of North Africa. This trend in warfare reached a climax in 1571, when Spain's navy fought in conjunction with other Roman Catholic powers to defeat the navy of the Ottoman Empire in the Battle of Lepanto. The increased aggression emanating from the Iberian Peninsula prompted many other powers to respond with their own policies of militarism on both land and sea. As chronicled by Fred Anderson and Andrew Cayton in *The Dominion of War*, one of the outcomes was that, "by the dawn of the eighteenth century, European navies could project force around the world and thus sustain imperial competition on a global scale."[25]

The huge cost of Spain's military engagements in and around Europe soon outstripped the rate of Spain's enrichment from the mineral wealth of the Americas. Spain's imperial government became so heavily mortgaged that it remained relatively low on the list of interests to benefit from the massive infusion of new capital derived from Potosi and the other Spanish-American mines. When the shipments of American silver arrived in Seville, most of the metal ended up in the vaults of Genose, Flemish, German, and Spanish bankers. As the imperial government's principal creditors, these financiers amassed personal fortunes even as they built up the institutional resources to help underwrite the next waves of colonial expansion, technological transformation, and intensification of warfare within Europe. The next four centuries were marked by increasingly brutal military rivalry among the European powers.

Another rich stream of silver, whose near-universal appeal provided a vital currency for the birth and growth of the global economy, was shipped westward to the Philippine trade emporium of Manila. From this Far Eastern port, which the Spanish seized as a vital metropolis in their global empire, much of the American silver found its way into China in the form of many hundreds of millions of coins. The massive infusion of this widely recognized form of money helped stimulate many new rounds of commercial activity in the world's largest, oldest, and most centralized polity.[26] The Chinese acquired American silver in exchange for their highly coveted textiles, tea, and porcelain objects. Chinese porcelain became especially popular in Holland and later in England, British North America, and the small enclaves of Creole privilege in Latin America. It was the forced labour provided by many millions of Indians that began the chain of transactions infusing the flood of silver onto the nascent global economy. The rates of death and disability became especially exorbitant after the addition of toxic mercury into Spanish procedures for extracting and refining pure silver. Who else but slaves, asks Fernand Braudel, "would have accepted to work in the Potosi mines and foundries, at the exhausting level of 13,000 feet in bitterly cold mountains lacking wood and food and even, sometimes, water?"[27]

The Jesuit *reducciones*, or missions, among the Guarani Indians of Paraguay formed a sharp contrast to the horrors of the American silver mines of the Spanish Empire. The Society of Jesus, known also as the Jesuit Order, emerged in the mid-sixteenth century from the vision of its founder, Ignatius Loyola. Under his guidance, the order leaped to prominence as elite educators, as key advisers to Roman Catholic sovereigns, and as one of the most disciplined and effective missionary orders ever to accompany European explorers and traders in their worldwide exploits. In the process of creating a worldwide network of missions spanning vast physical and cultural distances among, for instance, China, Japan, and the Western Hemisphere, the amazingly adaptable Jesuits quickly emerged as leading embodiments and instruments of Eurocentric globalization. Their animating goal was to check the rise of Protestantism and to lead a Counter-Reformation aimed at expanding the global domain of Roman Catholicism. As part of this work, the Jesuit leadership sought and gained exemptions for their Aboriginal converts from the regime of the *encomienda*. Instead of seeing Indians as a repository of cheap labour to be exploited, the Jesuits tended to view the Indigenous peoples they encountered as potential citizens for the Roman Catholic theocracies they sought to form. They went far in cultivating the establishment and growth under their own tutelage of several Roman Catholic states throughout the interior of South America. They achieved their most celebrated theocracy beyond Argentina's frontiers in the Parana and Uruguay valleys.

In the years before 1767, when the Jesuits were finally expelled from the region for their controversial defence of the Indigenous peoples, about 200,000 Guarani Indians in Paraguay were organized into the citizenry of one of the most successful theocracies the world has ever witnessed. This society was among the first on the planet to achieve universal literacy. It possessed schools, colleges, hospitals, and a sophisticated social safety net for the poor. After lengthy debate, its citizens outlawed capital punishment. The Guarani, however, eschewed pacifism for its own sake. For a time the officials of the Guarani state worked with their Jesuit advisers to constitute their own indigenous army. Its mission was to protect the territorial integrity of the Guarani polity and to defend its citizenry against the incursions of slave hunters. By the mid-eighteenth century, when the Portuguese Brazilians overseeing the Indian slave trade finally gained the upper hand, the Guarani Indians had built up herds of 725,000 cattle, 47,000 oxen, 99,000 horses, 14,000 mules, and 8,000 donkeys.[28]

The Jesuit reducciones of Paraguay helped inspire many other missionaries in their quest to achieve similar feats elsewhere in the Western Hemisphere. Certainly, several of the Jesuits of New France hoped to bring alive in northern North America something similar to the Indian theocracies that their colleagues had overseen in South America. This hope survived into the nineteenth century in the Great Lakes region, when French-speaking Jesuit missionaries sought to replicate many of the principles of the Paraguayan missions among the devoutly Roman Catholic Odawa at Wikwemikong on Manitoulin Island. So, too, the reducciones of Paraguay inspired a wave of Jesuit colonizers who moved among the diverse Indian societies of Oregon Country and Washington Territory before the US government set out to remake the region by promoting the building of railways and the immigration of predominantly Protestant, English-speaking settlers. The influence of the Paraguay example transcended even the domain of Roman Catholicism, inspiring, for instance, the successful Anglican Indian theocracy of Metlakalta in British Columbia. There, between 1862 and 1887, the Reverend William Duncan and his Tsimshian parishoners built up this model Christian community on the northwest coast.

The achievements of the Guarani Indians would be rivalled early in the nineteenth century by the elaborate civilization built up by Cherokee Indians in remnants of their ancestral territories in the southeastern portion of the United States. The fact that neither of these successful Indian adaptations to European colonization was permitted to hold ground or to integrate from positions of commercial and political strength into the surrounding society of newcomers is indicative of the extremely fragile quality of even the most enlightened applications of the European civilizing mission. In those instances where Indigenous peoples most deeply internalized the idealism of Christian civilization, expressing its principles in ways that creatively blended elements of their own Aboriginal heritages with imported elements of the newcomers' cultures, the converts were not permitted to bequeath their achievements to subsequent generations. Time and time again, Indians and their most beloved missionaries, who sometimes were themselves of Aboriginal ancestry, were pushed aside. The Indians of the Americas were extinguished, enslaved, displaced, or economically and legally marginalized even when they went far in achieving the goals in agriculture, industry, religious piety, and pedagogy that the Europeans and Euro-Americans frequently referred to in justifying their imperial enterprises.

The cruel inhumanity of the most genocidal thrust of the Spanish conquest began what David Stannard later labelled the "American Holocaust," a travesty of monumental proportions in which all the colonizing powers subsequently played some part.[29] The harshly invasive quality of most colonizing enterprises in the Americas combined with the infusion from Eurasia and Africa of hosts of new diseases for which the Western Hemisphere's Indigenous peoples lacked immunity. The outcome of these dual invasions, one human and the other viral and bacterial, led to monumental reductions in the Aboriginal population of Europe's and Africa's New World. Jared Diamond reports that in North America alone, the Aboriginal population of 1492 was reduced by as much as 95 per cent by 1900. In other words, the pre-Columbian population was reduced by colonization to about one-twentieth of its former size.[30]

One of the complicating factors in this kind of calculation, however, derives from the huge extent of intermarriage and population mixing that became especially prolific in those parts of the Americas where Roman Catholicism prevailed. Seen in this light, the relatively circumscribed European ancestry that characterized until recently the primarily Protestant and English-speaking populations of the United States and much of Canada represents more of an aberration than the rule in the Western Hemisphere, a domain where it could be postulated that a majority of individuals have at least some Indian branches on their family trees. Except for various islands of Latino predominance in, for instance, Argentina and Chile, the mestizo personality of most of Central and South America remains obvious to this day. The same pattern of hybridization between Europeans and Aboriginal Americans was well under way in the Roman Catholic domain of French-Aboriginal Canada before the British conquest of New France in 1759. Indeed, as long as the fur trade remained commercially viable in the northern part of North America, the exchange of goods produced an atmosphere conducive to intermarriage and the reciprocal blending of cultures on the middle ground of creative adaptation.[31]

DRUGS, PIRATES, AND PRIVATEERS IN THE RISE OF IMPERIAL EUROPE

In spite of the deep indebtedness of its imperial rulers, Spain rose through imperial enterprise to a kind of superpower status that had not been seen in Europe since the days of the Roman Empire. This development had many repercussions. The infusion of new wealth, for instance, offered added incentive, stimulation, and the means for further explorations. The most spectacular feat in this era of accelerated European exploration took place between 1519 and 1522, when Columbus's initiation of the modern era of globalization found more complete expression in the first circumnavigation of the planet. Using many of the maps and navigational skills he had acquired in his native Portugal, Ferao de Magalhães, known to the English as Magellan, set out on a mission to sail around the world on behalf of the Spanish monarchy. He crossed the huge expanse of ocean he labelled "the peaceful sea" – the Pacific – before he and some of his men were murdered in the Philippine Islands. The expedition was then taken over by Juan Sebastien del Cano. On his way home he and his remaining crew stopped at the famed Spice Islands to trade for cloves and nutmeg. The use of these items as medicines, preservatives, and taste enhancers became widespread in that era. Indeed, the Spice Islands, known also as the Moluccas, had attracted traders from China, India, and the Arab-speaking world long before this legendary archipelago became one of the Far East's strongest magnets of European exploration. Today the Spice Islands are part of Indonesia.

While the Portuguese were quick to stake their claims to the eastern part of South America, their most experienced navigators remained convinced that the best way to reach the Far East lay in opening an easterly route around Africa. Vasco da Gama proved the superiority of this route in 1498, when he reached Calcutta and returned from India with a shipment of pepper, cinnamon, ginger, and jewels that reportedly earned the expedition's funders 6,000 per cent profit on their investment.[32] The French and English sovereigns responded to this activity by sponsoring their own explorers, who headed westward along more northerly routes than those pioneered by Columbus and Vespucci. Between 1534 and 1542 Jacques Cartier oriented France to territory that he identified with the Iroquoian term for village, *Canada*. On August 10, 1535, Cartier christened a small bay on Canada's central river to honour the saint commemorated on that day. The term, St Lawrence, gradually came to designate the great river that the Iroquoian-speaking people of Canada identify to this day as *Kaniatarowanenneh*. Cartier described in his journals his encounters with the Iroquoian communities of Stadacona and Hochelaga, and he called the prominence above Hochelaga Mount Royal. This term gave Montreal its current name. While France entered the post-Columbian explorations rather late, King Henry VII of England was quick off the mark. In 1497 the English monarch sponsored the westward-bound journey from Bristol of another Italian, John Cabot. His voyage, although not resulting in the discovery of "townes, cities, and castles" as anticipated in the royal charter, helped establish an early axis of commercial involvement between the sailors of England and the rich cod fisheries of Newfoundland.[33] The Newfoundland fisheries were a magnet that helped pull England into a gradual process of colonial experimentation in North America. These trials and errors eventually resulted in the seventeenth century in planting a number of Anglo-American settlements on the continent.[34]

The resulting flood of new geographical and ethnological information entered Europe just as the printing press was invented. The wide dissemination of Johann Gutenberg's invention of movable type, an innovation that helped facilitate the spread of literacy and the reading of the Bible by many individuals, had a catalytic effect on the break from Roman Catholic universalism advanced by proponents of the Protestant Reformation. The Reformation, in turn, spawned the Counter-Reformation, a religious reaction whose most militant and strategically adept leadership was concentrated in the Jesuit Order. Martin Luther's quest for theological reform and John Calvin's litigious crusade against Roman Catholic privilege were part of a groundswell of revolt against the Vatican's ecclesiastical monopoly. The Reformation quickly transformed the religious culture of all of Europe, but especially northern Europe. The break with Rome was particularly dramatic in England, where, in 1534, King Henry VIII, with the *Act of Supremacy*, placed himself at the head of the Church of England after he failed to receive papal sanction for his divorce proceedings.

The developing antagonism between the Protestant powers and the Roman Catholic powers spread quickly to the high seas, as European monarchs experimented with new means of exercising, enforcing, and extending their claims of sovereignty. It was in this atmosphere that Henry VIII, and then his daughter Elizabeth I, the sovereign of England from 1559 to 1603, invested some of the most aggressive ocean-going adventurers of their realm with the legal powers of privateers. These privateers received royal authority to make war on the enemies of their home governments. They were granted royal certificates proclaiming that their holders were entitled to seize enemy cargoes, provided that the spoils of such seizures were shared with the privateers' monarchical sponsor, and sometimes with other public officials as well.[35] The royal empowerment of privateers proved to be a crucial step along the way to the chartering of imperial corporations. These joint-stock ventures were invested with an array of extensive authorities, which might include the power to attack and dispossess Indigenous peoples, to wage war on the agents of foreign sovereigns, to establish colonies, and to conduct trade with various parts of the non-European world. Some of these corporations, but especially the East India companies and the Hudson's Bay Company, proved to be extremely influential agencies in the development of European imperialism.

In the sixteenth century, several members of Plymouth's famous Hawkins family gave England some of its most successful privateers. Other prominent members of England's privateering guild included Sir John Gilbert, Sir George Somers, George Popham, William Parker, Ferdinando Gorges, Sir Francis Drake, and Sir Walter Raleigh. Drake's career was bound up closely with the early phases of the rise to global power of his small island country.[36] He initially followed his pirate kinsman, John Hawkins, into the transatlantic slave trade, which Portugal and Spain began to develop as a means of augmenting Indian labour in mining and initiating the development of sugar-cane plantations in Brazil and many of the Caribbean islands. After an exchange of fire with Spanish forces around the port of Vera Cruz in 1568, Drake took to raiding the ports and the vessels of Europe's richest and most powerful Roman Catholic realm. He concentrated particularly on plundering Spanish commerce along the Pacific coast of South America. Drake's voyage around the southern end of the Western Hemisphere led to his circumnavigation of the globe between 1577 and 1580 in his ship, the *Golden Hinde*.[37] This voyage was integral to the rise of Elizabethan England as a significant maritime power, a rise that culminated in the victory of the "English Sea Dogs" over King Phillip II's Spanish Armada in 1588. Drake had prepared the way for this conquest of Spanish sea power with a dramatic raid on the Port of Cardiz in 1587, a classic privateering operation where he and his men destroyed more than thirty vessels.

As John Maynard Keynes observed in his influential text *A Treatise on Money*, Drake's exploits were instrumental in bringing about the domestic prosperity that infused Elizabethan England with many varieties of creative energy in the final quarter of the sixteenth century. The expeditions of Drake and the other privateers, Keynes reminds us, "were financed by syndicates and companies and represented business speculations."[38] As Drake and the other English privateers were busy transforming the nature of naval power on the world's oceans, William Shakespeare and his theatrical associates began to conceive and stage those dramas that are still recognized as some of the most illuminating artistic explorations of human character. Many of these spectacles were first performed at the tellingly named Globe Theatre in London's Southwark district. The success of Shakespeare's theatrical work epitomized the convergence of cultural vibrancy and commercial creativity that came in the wake of the sudden infusion of new wealth into the island realm. Among the most significant innovations in Elizabethan England were advances in banking engineered by the Queen's economic adviser, Thomas Gresham. He began the process of investing England's money with the stability of fixed value that would eventually transform the currency into the primary medium of gold-backed exchange in the global economy.

The elevation by some European monarchs of pirates to privateers highlights the arbitrariness of operations inside and outside the law in the genesis of European imperialism. Indeed, from J.M. Barrie's children's story *Peter Pan* to Hollywood fables such as *Pirates of the Caribbean* starring Johnny Depp (2003), the plundering cutthroats of the high seas have enjoyed a remarkably benign reputation in the popular mythology of the West. This reputation glosses over the ethical complexities of operations based on the violent theft of rich cargoes, originating with Indian gold and silver. Sometimes pirate communities developed close and supportive relationships with those communities of escaped slaves whose plight is encapsulated in their being labelled as "maroons." The picture of pirates as rugged individualists operating beyond the frontiers of law resembles the academic imagery that Frederick Jackson Turner assigned at the World's Columbian Exposition to the individualistic agents of American frontierism. In the globalized culture of Americana, the mythological freedoms of the pirate and the cowboy have much in common.

Queen Elizabeth I became well known for her ability to walk a fine line in publicly distancing herself from the actions of her privateers even as she privately taxed and encouraged their incursions. In so doing, she cultivated a cunningly duplicitous form of foreign policy. The sovereign in a sense extended licences to private contractors which allowed them to exercise state violence at their discretion, even as she sought to evade the expense and official responsibility attending this form of coercive intervention. The privatizing warfare and imperial expansion that resulted established patterns that were replicated and refined in the chartering of mercantile companies. Many of these charters went far beyond investing the commercial polities they created with trade monopolies. As Janice E. Thomson explained in *Mercenaries, Pirates, and Sovereigns*, the charters of mercantile companies frequently included provisions authorizing their recipients to "raise an army or a navy, build forts, make treaties, make war, govern their fellow nationals, and coin their own money."[39] Edmund Burke attested to the extent of these wide powers. Referring specifically to the East India Company, which received its first charter in 1600, the British parliamentarian pointed out that it was much more than an agency of commerce. It was, rather, the receptacle of "a delegation of the whole power and sovereignty of this kingdom sent into the East."[40]

While Elizabeth chartered the first East India Company in the final years of her reign, the original powerhouse for this kind of corporate colonization was established in 1602 by the Dutch government. That company was the Dutch East India Company – the Verenigde Oost-Indische Compagnie (VOC) – which combined the force of several smaller Dutch enterprises. By the dawn of the seventeenth century the Netherlands was emerging as one of Europe's bastions of Protestantism and other forms of protest against the constraining limitations of the old feudal order. This development was one part of a gradual process that saw Holland and the other Dutch provinces join forces to break free politically from the oppressive jurisdiction of the Spanish Crown. After almost a century of movement in this direction, the Dutch state, referred to in the Treaty of Westphalia as the United Provinces of Holland, gained recognition in 1648 as an independent country with full sovereignty in international law. The violent emergence of the United Provinces from Spain's coercive embrace set one of the precedents for the emergence over a century later of the United States from the British Empire. The increasingly global reach of the combined complex of Dutch commercial, military, and political power quickly provided the laboratory for the extension of capitalism beyond the stage of sophistication formerly achieved in the city states of northern Italy.[41]

The port of Amsterdam was built up to the point where it became for a time the metropolis on the most extended edge of capitalist innovation and experimentation – the site, for instance, of many huge warehouses where the products of the world were gathered, stored, and re-exported when the time was deemed commercially advantageous. As one observer noted in 1728, the Dutch had become "Brokers of Europe ... They buy to sell again, take in to send out, and the greatest part of their vast Commerce consists in being supplied from All Parts of the World, that they may supply All the World again."[42] Alongside these activities grew up agencies for maritime insurance, currency exchange, the buying and selling of commodities, and speculation in the future prices of such goods. At the heart of these pro-liferating institutions was a permanent stock exchange, a venue of such importance that it attracted representatives and observers from most of the world's pre-eminent governments and businesses. In this milieu, great strides were made in the transformation of money into the ultimate com-modity of commodities.

The most important items bought and sold in the Amsterdam stock exchange were shares in the Dutch East India Company. The price of these shares fluctuated along with the profitability of the enterprise. According to Fernand Braudel, the VOC "remained for a long time the flagship of Western capitalism."[43] The agents of the VOC, along with those of the Dutch West India Company, chartered in 1621, pushed their way into many of the most lucrative commercial niches among the thickening web of trade links connecting Europe, Africa, America, India, the Levant, and the Far East. The representatives of the VOC were especially aggressive in replacing the agents of the Portuguese Empire in parts of Africa, the Middle East, and the Far East. In the sixteenth century it had been largely Portuguese adventurers who, following the lead of Vasco da Gama, extended the sea-borne trade of Europe into territory bordering on the Indian Ocean and the western Pacific.

In the seventeenth century, therefore, Dutch traders largely replaced the role formerly played in this region by the Portuguese.[44] Once the VOC achieved a position of dominance, especially over the lucrative spice trade in the area of present-day Indonesia and Malaysia, the company's agents tended to turn their hands, often coercively, to reorganizing Aboriginal political economies. In commenting on this process, whose main aim was usually to establish, protect, and widen the sphere of Dutch monopoly, Giovanni Arrighi writes: "The record of Dutch brutality in enslaving indig-enous peoples (literally and metaphorically) or in depriving them of their means of livelihood, and in using violence to break the resistance to the policies of the Company, matched or even surpassed the already abysmal standards established by the crusading Iberians throughout the extra-Euro-pean world."[45]

The Dutch role in the pushing European commerce into non-Euro-pean territories on both sides of the North and South Atlantic was far less substantial than its role in consolidating the linkages connecting the commercial orbits of Europe and the Far East. Nevertheless, Dutch traders played a significant part in expanding the globalized commerce of the West Indies, even as they helped to carry the information and ideas that stimulated the revolutionary atmosphere that would permeate societies on both sides of the Atlantic Ocean.[46] Dutch settlers and investors extended their activities to northeastern South America. They collaborated with Portuguese associates in Brazil in establishing some of the first major sugar plantations in the late sixteenth century. A number of Dutch settlers stayed on to establish a relatively small and troubled colony of the Netherlands on the northeast coast of South America.[47]

The rise of the political economy of sugar cane in the Caribbean area was the primary driving force in the growth of the transatlantic slave trade. The potent combination linking the economics of both sugar and the slave trade intensified the pace and complexity of colonialism.[48] This combination resulted in a huge increase in the profitability of European imperialism, even as the sale of millions of Africans and their descendants into bondage gradually split the citizenry of the West along the lines of a great moral divide.[49] This division would continue into the second half of the nineteenth century, when over 600,000 people eventually met their demise in an American Civil War – a conflict, essentially, between the advocates and the opponents of institutionalized slavery.

The expanding domain of sugar-cane plantations was most responsible for the rapid growth of the transatlantic slave trade. Sugar cane travelled westward, along with the process of its domestication, from India and China. Arab traders introduced sugar cane into Egypt and northern Africa. From there it passed into the agriculture of southern Europe on its way to the Americas. Processed sugar was embraced with particular extravagance by the citizens of England. They made sugar their country's largest import between 1750 and 1820, when the average consumption was about 20 pounds per person – ten times the amount consumed by the average individual in France.[50] The stimulation of many millions of "sweet-tooths" in Europe and throughout its expanding sphere of influence helped clear the way for the acceptance by consumers of tea and coffee. These drinks, which provided liquid vehicles for the addition of sugar, joined a range of mildly or heavily addictive substances, including alcohol, opium, and tobacco, as major commodities whose systems of production and distribution helped to kick start the reach and intensity of global commerce.

On many Caribbean Islands, the cultivation of sugar cane replaced that of tobacco, a family of plant domesticated for ceremonial purposes by Indigenous peoples throughout the Americas. The practice of smoking tobacco for recreation developed first among sailors and then more generally among European populations. It was one of the first colonial products to be seen as a luxury item that even individuals of modest income could afford. The growth of the English colony of Virginia was driven by the

commercial cultivation of tobacco on both small farms and large plantations. The viability of the plantations depended on the work of indentured
servants, convict labour, or, increasingly, Black slaves brought involuntarily
from West Africa. Some of the plantation owners of Virginia began to prosper when they replaced the native strain of the plant, *Nicotina rustica*, with
one imported from South America. The imported variety, *Nicotina tabacum*,
appealed much more to European tastes.

The globalization of cross-cultural trade after 1492 originally depended
on the extraction of gold and silver primarily from Central and South
America. The near universal fascination with the unique properties of these
metals was instrumental in helping to give the increasingly interconnected
societies within the emerging global trade system a widely acceptable currency of exchange. Access to rich new supplies of gold and silver helped
merchants in Europe and the Western Hemisphere to supply their domestic customers with the highly coveted spices, silk, porcelain, and other finery uniquely available from the Far East. From the perspective of those
outside the Orient, however, one of the great weaknesses of this emerging
global system was the difficulty in procuring trade items with a ready market
in the world's oldest and most highly self-sufficient society. Other than the
large Chinese demand for otter skins from the northwest coast of North
America, consumers in China coveted few products from either Europe
or the Western Hemisphere. European merchants were forced to pay for
the Chinese trade items with precious metals. In an era of mercantilism,
the attending school of economic orthodoxy increasingly interpreted this
net outflow of precious metals as fatal to the internal commercial health of
imperial systems of commerce.

This problem was eventually addressed between 1840 and 1842 by the
British navy. In the first Opium War, British gun ships blasted aside a zealously enforced prohibition on the domestic importation and consumption
of this notorious drug. The main agent of this Chinese version of the War
on Drugs was Lin Zexu, whose name is sometimes also rendered as Lin
Tse-hsu. Lin Zexu brought on the wrath of the British government when
he confiscated about 20,000 chests of smuggled opium. The importance
of the Opium War and the opium trade in the rise of the British Empire to
commercial dominance helps to demonstrate the instrumental role played
by the imperial exploitation of human addictions in spreading and consolidating global capitalism. Addictive substances can be especially lucrative
items of trade because increased supply tends to heighten rather than ease
demand. The addictions of consumers to sugar, alcohol, tobacco, and, later,
tea, coffee, opium, heroine, cocaine, and scores of prescription drugs have
helped to stimulate appetites and raise demands in ways that break down
local barriers to global commerce. To this day, the huge worldwide commerce in both legal and illegal drugs remains a powerful force in the politics, economics, and transnational culture of globalization.[51] No less than
in the era of the Opium Wars, control of the movement of the enormous

pools of capital attached to the commercial distribution especially of illegal and addictive drugs remains an instrumental tool of imperial power.

THE IMPORTANCE OF THE FUR TRADE IN THE IMPERIAL AND COMMERCIAL HISTORY OF NORTH AMERICA

The Dutch played a significant role in the early stages of the development of another important item of transoceanic trade – fur. Historically, furs had moved into the European market from Russia and from some of the other countries on the Baltic Sea. They were used in the making of warm clothing, and they frequently adorned the ceremonial vestments of royalty, the judiciary, and the clergy. The hair from some species, most notably beaver, is well suited for the making of felt. Felt from beaver pelts has often been in high demand for the manufacture of many styles of hats. As an item that transcended the realm of mere utility to make a variety of cultural statements about the wearers' status, rank, wealth, and taste, hats acquired a central role in the genesis of the lucrative European fashion industry. The fur that went into the making of felt hats and other garments became a medium for the development of surprisingly complex and many-layered alignments of commerce and power in the genesis of North American history.

The trade of fur for manufactured items in a closed system of imperial exchange embodied mercantilism in its most classical form. The exchange served the interests of the imperial centre by creating increased demand for the products of its industry without the prospect of bringing new factories on line that would compete with those of the colonizing power. On the Aboriginal side, this exchange provided the basis for mutually beneficial forms of intercultural trade, a phenomenon that was all too rare in the colonization of the Americas, Australasia, and Africa. Where mining and imported regimes of agriculture stripped Indigenous peoples of their lands and sometimes even of ownership of their own persons through the institution of slavery, the fur trade could not be viable economically without the willing participation of Aboriginal groups and individuals. It required forms of land tenure that left Aboriginal societies collectively in charge of most aspects of life in their own ancestral areas.

While this form of commerce was by no means an ideal activity either for the ecology of wildlife or for the economic and social stability of those societies whose leading members devoted themselves to gathering, preparing, transporting, and exchanging the fur trade's principal commodity, it represented a far more gentle manifestation of colonization than, say, the experiences of most Aboriginal Mexicans during the severe stages of the Spanish conquest. Moreover, involvement in the fur trade on the part of Europeans and Euro-Americans tended to make them opponents of the spread of imported styles of agriculture into those territories whose ecological cycles supported the reproduction of large numbers of wild animals. It also tended to make them proponents, within limits, of the principle that Indigenous peoples should retain certain rights, freedoms, and imperatives within the framework of imperial rule. This propensity of fur-trade officials to support some expressions of Aboriginal self-determination frequently made them distrustful of Christian missionaries, but especially of those evangelists whose zeal to win converts extended beyond the goal of transforming Aboriginal belief systems. There were sound business reasons for fur-trade officials to block systematically the incursion of missionaries whose objective was to persuade Indian converts to leave the yearly cycle of hunting animals and making trade excursions in order to devote themselves to becoming full-time farmers in the style of many Euro-American settlers.

The fact that the expansion of the fur trade often led to the decimation of whole animal populations induced the industry's directors to promote a constant search for new frontiers to exploit. Fur-trade agents sought to discover new areas where game populations were still large and where the availability of manufactured items, such as guns and ammunition, was minimal enough that the Indigenous peoples could be persuaded to part with large quantities of animal pelts at relatively low prices. As the fur trade expanded into new regions, it invariably had significant effects on the balance of power among different Aboriginal groups and individuals, among competing and allied trade consortiums, and among various imperial powers. It also affected the relative reach and power of local governments that developed either as extensions or opponents of imperial rule. Accordingly, the North American fur trade rapidly acquired a geopolitical importance out of proportion to its economic size. At the same time, it provided financial incentive for representatives of corporations and governments to engage in the expensive activity of inland exploration. While changing configurations of commerce and politics in the fur trade affected the advance or retreat of various imperial and national claims in the continent's interior, much still depended on the exercise of sea power – on the ability of traders in the interior to coordinate their activities with those of navies and with the movement of commercial vessels throughout the world's oceans.

One of the richest areas of the North American fur trade until the end of the War of 1812 was the vast region surrounding the Great Lakes. These five inland seas flow to the Atlantic Ocean along a course that includes Niagara Falls and the St Lawrence River. Montreal would become the key point of exchange along this route. Canada's first major metropolitan centre took its place in the global economy as the main port on the "River of Canada," where European imports were unloaded and exchanged for exports from the interior of North America.[52] Under certain conditions, however, a significant proportion of the commerce between Europe and the Great Lakes basin could be directed away from the St Lawrence system and through the Hudson River system. By the mid-seventeenth century, officials of the Dutch West Indies Company began to accomplish just that.

They began attracting significant quantities of fur away from New France, a colony whose expansionary career began once Samuel de Champlain established the settlement of Quebec in 1608 below the cliffs guarding the Plains of Abraham. In taking control of this promontory, the French Empire was able to command one of the most strategic entry points into North America's inland waterways.

The Dutch traders funnelled commercial activity away from the nascent commercial empire of the St Lawrence by allying their interests with those of the Aboriginal confederacy inhabiting the strategic territory between Lakes Ontario and Erie and the upper reaches of the Hudson River. At the head point of the navigable section of the Hudson, a site that bordered on the eastern frontier of the Five Nations' Iroquois heartland, the Dutch traders built Fort Orange. It stood on the site of present-day Albany. From Fort Orange, the Dutch shipped the valuable pelts down the Hudson River to the small oceanic port of New Amsterdam. This settlement, along with other Dutch hamlets such as Haarlem and Breukelen, provided the colonial seeds from which the metropolis of New York would subsequently grow. A trickle of Dutch settlers began to colonize the fledgling New Netherlands after 1609, when, on behalf of the voc, Henry Hudson charted the river that subsequently carried his name. In the tradition of Columbus, Cabot, and Cartier, Hudson's explorations continued the European quest for a western water route to the Far East.

The strategic geography of the future "Empire State" immediately began to be exploited. The Dutch fostered their relationship in particular with the formidable Five Nations Iroquois, whose Longhouse League dominated the strategically vital passage between Fort Orange and the lower Great Lakes. The interests of New Netherlands were best served when Dutch negotiators carefully assimilated the ceremonial and diplomatic motifs of the Longhouse, and when the agents of the colony exchanged wampum belts with Longhouse spokesmen to formalize the terms of negotiated settlements. Treaty wampums were most often woven from certain types of shell beads to form pictographic designs signifying the content of common understandings achieved through intense diplomacy between different groups. For a brief time the wampum shells used to make such belts doubled as currency for some of the cash-poor inhabitants of the Swedish, Dutch, and English settlements in the area.[53]

The importance of the Longhouse Confederacy's heartland in the rise of the Hudson River empire would be demonstrated again and again in the decades and centuries ahead – as, for instance, after 1823, when the completion of the Erie Canal further consolidated the transportation link between the Great Lakes and the Hudson River. The Erie Canal created the conditions for the early growth of urban centres along the shores of the Great Lakes. It enabled communities such as Chicago, Milwaukee, and Toronto, all predominately non-Aboriginal towns with Aboriginal names, to begin their metropolitan ascent in the first half of the nineteenth century.

In turn, the expansion of regional centres in the interior, each with its own agricultural hinterland, generated huge surges of commercial growth for New York City as the central metropolis for many dependent regional centres. According to John Steele Gordon in *An Empire of Wealth*, "the Erie Canal would prove the most consequential public works project in American history." It was, he writes, "the first of the long and continuing list of megaprojects – the Atlantic cable, the transcontinental railway, the Brooklyn Bridge, the Panama Canal, the Hoover Dam system, the Apollo project."[54]

The commercial importance of the Erie Canal after its completion suggests the strategic significance of the heartland of the Longhouse Confederacy in earlier times. The history of the foreign policy of this most legendary of all Aboriginal confederacies is deeply tied up with the early history of New York City, a metropolis that began its rise to global prominence as the capital of Dutch empire building in North America. From its inception, the founders of New Amsterdam, the forerunner of New York, set their sights on the quest to colonize a vast hinterland. In the seventeenth century the Dutch outflanked their more cautious Puritan neighbours in New England by reaching deeply into the Aboriginal political economy of the vast North American continent through trade and diplomacy with Indian allies. In this fashion the merchants of New Netherlands gained a vital point of entry into the North American fur trade. This transoceanic commerce tended to be built on the elaboration of pre-existing networks of political and economic relationships among the culturally diverse peoples of Indian Country.[55] The negotiation of treaty alliances with the members of the Longhouse League and other Aboriginal groups was also useful in other ways. It produced an array of documented evidence that supported the territorial claims of Dutch settlers in North America against the sometimes competing claims of Swedish and English colonists in the vicinity of New Netherlands.

The continuing importance of the fur trade in the rise of New York until well into the nineteenth century is best illustrated through the career of John Jacob Astor.[56] When he died in 1848, Astor was the richest man in America, the founder of a family dynasty that epitomized "Knickerboker" elitism. This Dutch-German immigrant began his career in 1786 as the proprietor of a small New York fur shop. There Astor met Sarah Todd, whose mother was a Brevoort. The Brevoorts were one of New York's old Dutch families, with deep roots in the fur-trade heritage of New Netherlands. The marriage helped the ambitious husband to widen his scope of associations in New York's top circles of business and government.

Astor's major breakthrough resulted from the close association of his business interests with the mission of Meriwether Lewis and William Clark. As authorized by President Thomas Jefferson, the Lewis and Clark Corps of Discovery was to add territory to the lands already obtained from France in the Louisiana Purchase of 1803. The aim was to extend the United States to the Pacific Ocean, based on claims of "discovery" to be derived from a successful expedition. Lewis and Clark moved towards this objective by ascending the Missouri River, crossing the Rockies, and securing a base on the continent's West Coast. The goal of establishing a window of access on the Pacific Ocean for the United States was advanced when Astor extended the success of Lewis and Clark in 1808 by exporting to China a cargo of West Coast sea-otter furs. In the era before the Opium War, otter furs – one of the few European or North American products coveted by a large number of buyers in China – acquired a unique importance in the trans-Pacific trade. By obtaining Chinese products through trade in otter skins rather than through direct purchase with gold or silver, Astor made a significant breakthrough in international finance. In that era, the expenditure of gold and silver, or hard currency, to secure trade items was considered to be a violation of the most fundamental principles of mercantilistic commerce.

Astor made a small fortune from this business bonanza. His breakthrough helped open the way for the subsequent systemization of a form of smuggling that, in the years before the Opium Wars, produced great wealth for the seafaring traders of Great Britain and New England. On their fast schooners they transported opium from India to the dope dens of China. This stream of commerce significantly increased once the force of British arms was deployed to overpower Lin Zexu's crackdown on illicit drugs. Hence the geopolitical significance of the transaction of 1808 involved much more than the acquisition of new wealth by one New York businessman. Not since the days of Marco Polo or the era when large quantities of Spanish-American silver found their way into China had such a strategically significant new trade connection with the Far East's most important polity been achieved. Through cooperation with one of its most dynamic entrepreneurs, the US government began to realize the trade objectives going back to the days of Columbus, Cabot, Cartier, and Hudson. All these European explorers and many others had sought to open a westward-oriented trade route with China. Some of the main geopolitical imperatives of imperial globalization had thus been significantly advanced. With his entry into the Chinese market from the transcontinental platform of his New York–centred trade network, Astor helped to open the way towards greater participation by the United States in global commerce. A coordinated effort linking the government of the future superpower with its emerging community of international traders had succeeded in injecting a New World twist into the Occident's old quest to establish trade links with China. When he realized the larger economic objectives of Lewis and Clark's expedition with his successful trans-Pacific trade mission, Astor anticipated the era when the US empire of commercial capital would acquire a far more global personality.[57]

In all his transactions in the North American fur trade, Astor's financial dealings were closely connected to his ability to exploit and affect the changing balance of geopolitical power between the US, British, Spanish, and Mexican governments and the continent's diverse Aboriginal societies. Astor operated through a number of fur-trade corporations, entities that he frequently founded, purchased, merged, or dissolved as changing circumstances opened or closed business opportunities. Among his leading ventures were the American Fur Company, the Pacific Fur Company, and the Southwest Fur Company. In his financial and political dealings, Astor became very skilful in incorporating the pre-existing trade systems of the older imperial powers into the expanding fur-trade domain of the United States. In developing this skill from his base in New York, he refined some of the commercial techniques of imperial Britain, whose entrepreneurs had ingested into their own commercial systems the fur-trade empires of the Dutch (after 1664) and of the French (after the conquest of Canada in 1759–60). In refining this technique during a formative phase of US expansion, Astor helped to establish basic patterns that would culminate in some of the most important geopolitical transformations on the planet after the Second World War. During this period, the emergent capitalist superpower absorbed and refined into its expanding sphere of transnational interests many of the most profitable facets of the old imperial systems that had developed during the course of European colonialism.

As attested by the names on many New York landmarks, Astor became active in the hotel trade and real-estate market of his home city. In transferring his energies and investments from the fur trade to land speculation, he continued well-established patterns that had contributed significantly to the emergence of the United States from the British Empire. The fur traders of pre-revolutionary Philadelphia, for instance, but especially those in the firm of Bayton, Wharton, and Morgan, increased the pressure for geopolitical change in North America when they shifted their business priorities from buying furs in the Ohio Valley to transforming the rich, arable lands in this region into titled private property. Astor's skill in driving, directing, and exploiting the course of US expansion, both geographically and financially, led the way for the creation of the next wave of American dynasties. These commercial and familial empires were led by the likes of John D. Rockefeller, Andrew Carnegie, Andrew Mellon, J.P. Morgan, and Cornelius Vanderbelt.

Long before the power of the Empire State was globalized, the Dutch founders of colonial New Netherlands set in place somewhat feudal forms of land tenure along the Hudson River. They set up *patroons* to link tenants and aristocrats in much the same way that the *seigneuries* of New France and the *haciendas* of Spanish America were created to transplant old forms of European land tenure and social organization to outposts of empire. Who would have thought that from these patroons, and from the Dutch-Iroquois fur trade, would emerge one of the planet's most powerful urban centres? Who would have anticipated that the flow of furs from Five Nations territory to Fort Orange, to New Amsterdam, to Amsterdam, and then to other European centres would initiate the development of a huge metropolis hosting the headquarters of some of the Earth's richest and most globally engaged financial institutions? And yet, that is what happened. The New York Stock Exchange and its attending agencies would become inheritors of the Amsterdam stock market. The barons of Wall Street would draw many commercial inheritances from London, an imperial capital that began gradually, in the late seventeenth century, to replace Amsterdam as the planet's most influential centre in the genesis of global capitalism.

Nowhere did the sometimes complementary and sometimes antagonistic influences of the empires of the Dutch and the British mix and blend so prolifically as in New York. That process of blending cultures and imperial strategies was integral in the early stages of the still-continuing process that elevated the metropolitan influence of New York from regional, to national, to hemispheric, and then to global proportions. A number of transnational forces converged in the rise of New York to the point where it became the heir of the experiments in capitalist expansion started by the northern Italian city states and carried on by the financiers of Amsterdam and then London. This rise depended also on the rapid western expansion of the United States within North America through a process that resembled the imperial expansion of the major European powers. Commenting on this similarity, Gareth Stedman Jones has written, "American historians who speak complacently of the absence of the settler-type colonialism characteristic of the European powers merely conceal the fact that the whole internal history of United States imperialism was one vast process of territorial seizure and occupation."[58] Henry Cabot Lodge made a similar observation, noting that, within the Western Hemisphere, the United States had "a record of conquest, colonization, and territorial expansion unequalled by any people in the nineteenth century." [59]

Accordingly, many keys to better understanding of the history of globalization, capitalism, and the growth of the informal American empire lie in the local history of the metropolis of New York. It is more than coincidental that the most prominent empire of the seventeenth century and the dominant empire of the nineteenth century both invested imperial capital in the growth of the metropolis that today hosts many of the world's most important financial agencies, including the New York Stock Exchange. This exchange, where the shares of most of the world's largest global companies are traded, works as a magnet, drawing capital for speculation and investment from every corner of the planet. This flow of money would become a force to counterbalance the trade deficits that beginning in the mid-1980s transformed the United States from a creditor nation into a debtor nation. As the twenty-first century progressed, this descent into debt accelerated into a freefall.

The role of New York as a site for the interplay of a vast array of local, regional, and global influences began with the mixing of Dutch, English, and Mohawk styles of empire building in the years following the reconstitution of New Netherlands as New York in 1664. This mixing of empires was particularly evident in the way imperial continuity was maintained in retaining collaborative relations with the members of the Longhouse League. Rather than eject the Dutch, the colony's new English governors constructively used Dutch expertise in the conduct of fur-trade diplomacy with the Five Nations Iroquois, but especially with the largest nationality in the Longhouse Confederacy, the Mohawks. The outcome of this imperial strategy established the vital precedent for the British to incorporate both the fur-trade expertise of the *canadiens* following the conquest of New France in 1759 and the Dutch Afrikaners' techniques for exploiting native labour following the Boer War in 1902. It was a pattern the British repeated many times in the growth of their empire. In colonizing India, for instance, the British built their system of imperial power by incorporating the tactics that the Islamic builders of the Mughal Empire had used. "The British absorbed not only Mughal Territory but Moghul practices," observed Karl Meyer and Shareen Brysac in *Tournament of Shadows*.[60]

The advice rendered by the old Dutch settlers of New Netherlands to the early builders of New York was one of several significant factors to converge in the late seventeenth century in the complex of diplomatic relations known as the Covenant Chain. This web of diplomatic protocols governed the process of ongoing negotiations linking the English colonies on the eastern seaboard with a number of Aboriginal polities in the northeastern portion of North America. At the strategic centre of the Covenant Chain was the dynamic relationship between the governor of New York at Albany and the leadership of the Mohawk Nation, the most easterly polity in the Longhouse League. In this way, some of the federal principles of the Longhouse League were extended into the imperial realm of the English colonies.

The constitution of the Longhouse League is often described as the Great Law, a term, significantly, that is identical in Mohawk to the term for the Great Peace.[61] This Great Law, the *Kayanerenhkowa*, is said to create the conditions for the Great Peace. From the earliest days of Dutch, French, and English colonization in northeastern North America until the present day, the *Kayanerenhkowa* has remained one of the most celebrated, influential, and carefully studied institutions of Aboriginal America.[62] The story of Deganaweda and Hiawatha's difficulties in winning acceptance for the *Kayanerenhkowa*, a code for achieving harmony and equilibrium in human relations, has been related in numerous narratives published in many languages. While the Great Law was initially accepted by the Longhouse League's five founding nations, the *Kayanerenhkowa* was proclaimed by its prophetic messengers as a universal system applicable to the governance of all human beings situated in the four sacred quadrants of the four sacred directions. On accepting the Great Law, the leaders of the original Five Nations ceremonially buried their weapons under the Great White Pine of Peace at the Confederacy's new capital at Onondaga. The federalism of the Five Nations – the Mohawk, Onondaga, Seneca, Oneida, and Cayuga – and later the Six Nations after the Tuscorora joined them in 1721, was acknowledged by joint resolution of both the House of Representatives and the Senate in 1987. To commemorate the 200th anniversary of the US Constitution, Congress officially recognized "the historical debt which the

Republic of the United States of America owes to the Iroquois Confederacy and other Indian nations for their demonstration of enlightened democratic principles of Government and their example of a free association of independent Indian nations."[63]

The classic 1851 text *League of the Ho-de-no-sau-nee*, where Lewis Henry Morgan outlined the workings of the Longhouse constitution, is generally viewed as one of the seminal works in the intellectual genesis of anthropology.[64] Morgan built on the contents of this volume to construct a more general theory of human evolution,[65] one seized upon by Karl Marx and Frederick Engels as proof of the validity of their sweeping theories. These theories were subsequently used by the founders of the Soviet Union and other communist governments to justify their regimes. In *The Origins of the Family, Private Property and the State*, Engels explained the importance of the stream of thought and inspiration going back to Morgan's research on the Longhouse League.[66] But the heritage of the league did more than figure prominently in the intellectual genesis of the two superpowers that came to dominate much of the second half of the twentieth century. In his *White Roots of Peace*, Paul Wallace portrays the establishment of the *Kayanerenhkowa* at Onondaga around 1450 as the beginning of the tradition of transnational law making which led to the establishment of the United Nations in 1945.[67] While this notion represents a big stretch of interpretation with little supporting evidence, there is, nevertheless, much poetry in the idealization of UN negotiations in New York as an extension of Longhouse and Covenant Chain negotiations. The very idea of such a stream of intercultural continuity running through the history of the planet's most internally complex and influential metropolitan centre is highly suggestive of a vision of globalization much more in line with the thinking of Franz Boas than with that of Frederick Jackson Turner.

EXTENDING SOVEREIGNTY THROUGH CORPORATE VEHICLES OF IMPERIAL EXPANSION: ROYAL CHARTERS AS MEDIA OF EMPIRE

The English took New Netherlands through the force of arms, although the Dutch did not systematically resist the incursions of the initial occupying forces. The transformation of the Dutch colony into the English colony of New York took place in 1664 under the direction of King Charles II. In being elevated to the throne of England in 1660, the new king and his backers restored the duality embodied in the evolutionary relationship linking the monarch and Parliament. They made changes to one of the most enduring, adaptive, and archetypal systems of governance in human history. Their constitutional reforms were set in place after two decades of turmoil, a period that saw the military strongman Oliver Cromwell emerge victorious from a period of civil war to reorganize England first as a Puritan republic and then as a dictatorship.

With the monarchy's restoration in 1660, Charles II began reorienting English foreign policy towards the goal of overcoming Dutch pre-eminence in commerce. The Dutch regime favoured a less-regulated, more free-flowing system of global commerce. In moving away from the Dutch example, the English moved closer to the French monarch's system of imposing mercantile boundaries on imperial commerce. With their overlapping commitments to the expansion of self-contained systems of imperial aggrandizement, England and France entered an era of increased competition for colonial holdings. They clashed in a struggle that was not resolved until the second half of the eighteenth century, when the imperial government of Great Britain decisively overpowered that of France in the Seven Years' War. This war, which is remembered as the French and Indian War in the United States, was fought especially in North America, India, and on the oceanic corridors that more and more provided the lifelines for a growing portion of the world's inhabitants.

The English conquest of New Netherlands expressed many features of this change in England's domestic and imperial policies. Charles II granted his brother, James, extensive titles to the new addition to the English Empire. As Duke of York and Albany, James made sure that his credentials were well reflected in the naming of the colony and its future capital. He transferred part of his new estate to his friends, Lord Berkeley and Sir George Carteret, thereby providing the legal and territorial basis for the founding of New Jersey. The establishment of New York during the Restoration as a royalist stronghold reinforced older patterns that had placed the conservative Dutch patroons in positions of strength in the organization of New Netherlands. Reflecting on this aspect of New York's history, Samuel Eliot Morison observed that patroon privileges "came nearer to pure feudalism than any other land system in the future United States." He continued by noting that this conservative orientation "continued under English rule and even outlasted the Revolution, ending only with the Rent Wars of the 1840s. This legacy helps explain why New York became the most aristocratic of the English colonies, not excepting Virginia, and the leading Tory colony in the Revolution."[68]

The royalist conquest of the Dutch New Netherlands in the founding of English New York was one part of a very extensive array of imperial changes ushered in by Charles and his inner circle during the Restoration. When the Convention Parliament of 1660 brought back the institution of monarchy by accepting the Declaration of Breda, King Charles faced somewhat more checks on his power than those that had adhered to his father, Charles I, before he was executed in one of history's most famous episodes of regicide. It was not, however, until the Glorious Revolution of 1688, when William and Mary of Orange left Holland to have English Crowns placed on their most Protestant of royal heads, that the principle of parliamentary supremacy was fully entrenched in England's largely unwritten constitution. During the period between 1660 and 1688, therefore, the English monarch still retained extensive powers to express the king-dom's sovereignty through personal grants of imperial authority. It was an era when Charles and then his imperial successor, James, continued their religious affiliation, sometimes covertly and sometimes openly, to Roman Catholicism.

The Restoration was a time when those in control of the English gov-ernment flexed the imperial attributes of their royal power. In the bitter process of losing state power and in witnessing subsequently the ruthless-ness of Cromwellian expansion in Ireland and the Caribbean, the royalists had learned valuable lessons about the art and science of expanding their own influence along with that of England. They lost no time in exploiting their restored grip on state power by extending the sovereign authority of the monarch to wider and more many-faceted frontiers. The early years of the Restoration, therefore, became a time when the English royal court experimented prolifically and expansively with various devices for empire building. In 1675, for instance, Charles established the royal observatory at Greenwich. Beginning with the appointment of John Flamsteed, royal astronomers were employed at Greenwich to measure and document the movement of stars in ways that would assist England's seaborne empire builders in navigating and mapping the world's geographical outlines. The Greenwich Observatory would continue as an important symbol and site of globalization, especially after this scientific research centre became the starting point of longitudinal calculations and, more recently, the site of the prime meridian establishing the basis for the world's universal system of Standard Time.[69]

Among the most important of the legal and political innovations made during the initial years of the Restoration in England were those connected to the chartering and operation of royal corporations. This emphasis on the law of corporate formation as a medium of imperial expansion drew on the principle of "the king as a corporation," a "conception" which, accord-ing to the authors of the ninth edition of the *Encyclopedia Britannica*, was "the key to many of his paradoxical attributes in constitutional theory – his invisibility, immortality etc."[70] During the reign of Charles II, who was replaced in 1685 by his brother, James, the king made extensive use of his power to generate new corporations from his own sovereign corporate per-son as a means of extending patronage to his favourite backers, supporters, and relatives. A primary prerequisite for those individuals seeking grants to participate in the overseas expansion of English royal authority was their willingness to group together with other favourites of the king as corpo-rate owners and directors. It fell on these corporate directors to raise and invest seed capital for imperial ventures and to provide the guidance for joint-stock companies.[71] The outcome of this approach to empire building was to intensify further the marriage between business and government. It produced a simultaneous emphasis on both privatization and monopoly on the most extended frontiers of globalized trade and military conflict. The imperial corporations at the forefront of this phase of English colonization created legacies that would be marked for centuries to come in the geographic and institutional shape of the British Empire and in that of its most important offspring – the United States of America.

In 1660, for instance, Charles II chartered the Company of Royal Adventurers Trading to Africa. Its main item of trade was African slaves. When this venture proved financially shaky, Charles granted it a monopoly in 1672 against other English enterprises in obtaining slaves in West Africa along with an absolute monopoly in supplying slaves to the English sugar islands. As a result, the Royal African Company, known colloquially as the Guinea Company, earned large returns for its shareholders. The profitability of this monopoly, which was broken up in 1698, infused sufficient wealth into the English shipping industry that it soon acquired the dubious distinction of being the most active agency in the transatlantic slave trade.

In 1661 the English East India Company, whose technical name was the Governor and Company of Merchants of London Trading in the East Indies, was granted a new charter. In it Charles II extended his sovereignty to invest the corporation with power to enforce criminal and civil jurisdiction over all inhabitants in key parts of India, as well as the authority to wage war or to negotiate peace treaties with non-Christian princes and people. The next year in North America, Governor John Winthrop of Connecticut obtained a charter from Charles which added new territory to his colony and elevated the status of its local government to make it equal to that of Massachusetts. In 1663 Dr John Clark obtained a similar charter securing Rhode Island from being divided by its neighbours. The charter also codified the extensive jurisdictional reach of its local government. Two years later Charles granted yet another royal charter creating the Carolinas. This valuable proprietorship was extended to key members of his inner circle. The recipients included Anthony Ashley Cooper (who became the Earl of Shaftsbury), Sir William Berkeley, and Sir John Colleton. A wealthy owner of sugar plantations in Barbados, Colleton conceived of the Carolinas as home for the overflowing white population of that island and other English colonies. The English political philosopher John Locke, secretary to the Earl of Shaftsbury, became deeply involved in the Carolinas project. He drafted a proposed constitution for the new jurisdiction, though it was never enacted. Locke's influence in North America, it turned out, would belong not so much to the final years of the seventeenth century as to the last half of the eighteenth century, when his writings made a strong impact on the founders of the United States. Thomas Jefferson, for instance, drew heavily on Locke's *Two Treatises of Government* for the initial draft of the American Declaration of Independence.

In 1682 Charles issued a charter to William Penn, the Quaker son of one of England's most celebrated admirals. The Penn name had become prominent in England after William Penn Senior led the naval expedition that seized Jamaica from Spanish control in 1655 as part of Oliver Cromwell's

"Western Design." To repay loans made by the senior Penn to the Duke of York and to memorialize the famous admiral's family name, the younger William Penn was granted a proprietorship to Pennsylvania. The recipient of this royal largesse turned his hand to making the new colony a refuge for Quaker immigrants from all over Europe. The Quakers were Christian dissenters who, unlike the more militant Puritans, were not implicated in the English Civil War. They believed that the deepest source of spirituality emanates from within the human spirit, and they emphasized hard work, frugality, peaceful co-existence, and the equality of all human beings. This focus on equality and brotherly love led them to identify themselves as the Society of Friends.

By far the most resilient of the corporate entities established by King Charles during this era was the Governor and Company of Adventurers Trading into Hudson Bay – a polity that came to be widely known as the Hudson's Bay Company (HBC). From 1670, when it was first chartered, until 1869–70, when the company's titles were purchased by the fledging government of the Dominion of Canada, the HBC remained one of the main instruments supporting the continuity of British claims to much of the northern portion of North America.[72] In the years following 1821, when the HBC finally absorbed the Montreal-based North West Company, its influence stretched over the Rocky Mountains to the West Coast as far south as the northern frontiers of Mexican California. The HBC charter went to many of the same individuals who were in the process of organizing the English colonization of New York, New Jersey, and the Carolinas. Prince Rupert, a cousin of the beheaded Charles I, was placed at the head of this consortium of empire builders. Given the broad involvement of its founders in many aspects of colonization, the HBC was, from its inception, but one part of more elaborate schemes to give England the edge over its imperial competition, but especially over French imperial enterprise in North America.

The plans for the HBC had resulted from proposals first advanced by two French citizens, Médart Chouart, sieur des Groseilliers, and his brother-in-law Pierre-Esprit Radisson. They had previously failed in their concerted efforts to arouse the interest of the French imperial government in colonizing the region around the huge northern sea named after Henry Hudson. The English colonization of the Hudson Bay region provided a major check against the forces of French imperialism in North America. In establishing the HBC in the northern region, the English gained an imperial base that enabled them to check French efforts to box in the Anglo-American colonies along the eastern seaboard. Following the lead of the explorer and geopolitical strategist Robert Cavelier, sieur de La Salle, French imperialists sought to achieve this geopolitical aim by linking Louisiana on the Mississippi River with the settlements of the *canadiens* on the St Lawrence River. They hoped to realize this expansion and consolidation of French power throughout the largest portion of North America by allying their own interests with those of the Indian groups in the strategically vital Ohio Valley.

The establishment of English posts on Hudson Bay held the possibility of pre-empting this French plan of encirclement. The French effort to cut off the westward expansion of the Anglo-Americans through the elaboration of trade, evangelization, and alliance building with the powerful Indian nations in the North American interior was countered by the rise of the English presence on Hudson Bay. While the French sought to limit the westward expansion of the Anglo-American colonists along the Atlantic coast, in the interior they found themselves outflanked by the English on their own northwesterly frontiers.

Like the charter of the East India Company, to which it has sometimes been compared, the charter of the Hudson's Bay Company was extremely comprehensive and sweeping in character. It set in place a legal structure that anticipated the growth of both trading and colonization ventures. The governors of the HBC were described by Charles II as "Lords and Proprietors" of "the land [to] be henceforward reckoned and reputed as one of our plantations or colonies in America, and to be called Rupert's Land." The Lords and Proprietors of this "one corporate body and politic" were declared possessors of the right to all fisheries and "also all mines royal of gold, silver, gems, and precious stones." While "sovereign dominion" was to remain vested in the English monarch, the land was "to be holden as of our manor of East Greenwich in free and common socage." The only requirement was to pay the Crown yearly two elks and two black beavers whenever the King, or his heirs and successors, should enter the territory so granted. The officers of the HBC were to make "laws, constitutions, orders and ordinances" for the good government of their forts, plantations, and factories. They could enforce these laws by imposing fines and other penalties on offenders.

The extent of the territory transferred was left vague, in large measure to accommodate the possibility that a water route to the Pacific Ocean and the Orient might yet be found. With this hope in mind, the drafters of the charter referred to a conveyance of "the sole trade and commerce of and to all seas, bays, streights, creeks, lakes, rivers, sounds, in whatsoever latitude they shall be, that lie within the entrance to the Streight commonly called Hudson's Streights; together with all the lands, and territories upon the countries, coasts, and confines of the said seas, bays, lakes, rivers, creeks and sounds aforesaid that are not now actually possessed by or granted to any of our subjects, or possessed by the subjects of any other Christian Prince or State." Elsewhere the document refers to the rights and titles of the governors and owners of the HBC in territories "which are not already possessed by any Christian potentate." Religious distinctions were highlighted also in the stipulation that the HBC may send "ships of war, ammunition ... and may erect forts in their territories, as well as towns; may make peace or war with any Prince or people not Christian; also may make reprisals on any others interrupting or wronging them; may seize on or send home all such English or other subjects sailing into Hudson's Bay without their license."[73]

The issuing and implementation of these charters represent one of the central sagas in the history of European imperialism. Many of humanity's most entrenched relationships of political economy go back to the relationships of power initiated when these potent legal instruments authorized their holders to take possession of foreign lands; to eliminate, control, or enslave foreign people and peoples; and to exercise monopoly jurisdiction over certain natural resources as well as the flow of particular kinds of trade between various overseas regions. The monarchs who granted these charters took their lead from the Vatican. Its papal head had "donated" all of the Americas to the crowns of Spain and Portugal in the years immediately following Columbus's transatlantic voyage of 1492. The creation and growth of enterprises like the VOC, the English East India Company, the Hudson's Bay Company, and the Royal African Company were, in some measure at least, imperial responses on the part of Europe's emerging Protestant powers to the claims and assertions embodied in the papal grants of the Americas to the Roman Catholic sovereigns of Spain and Portugal.

Prominent among the corporate descendants of the older organizations were the land-speculation companies in pre-revolutionary British North America. These corporate initiatives, in turn, pointed the way to the creation and operation of the railway companies, some of which became huge organizations that quickened the extension of the forces of globalization into the interior of several continents. The executives of the largest railway companies were instrumental in bringing together the huge concentrations of capital, technological expertise, labour, and political influence that helped prepare for the rise of the next generation of transnational and global corporation. This next generation of corporate leviathan has been spawned from the commercial applications of scientific and technological breakthroughs in chemical, electrical, and automotive engineering, with the oil and gas industry gaining huge influence over many of the most strategic intersections of business and government in the emerging global economy. Many of these commercial polities, whose logos and trademarks today form some of the most familiar and ubiquitous backdrops of daily life for much of humanity, drew their original founding charters from the state governments of the United States, but particularly from those of New York, New Jersey, and Delaware.[74]

The biotechnology industry's projection of property rights into the genetic composition of life's reproductive forces constitutes a key facet of the most recent extension of sovereign entitlement into new frontiers of mind and matter. Moreover, the push to invest the World Trade Organization and its attending agencies with the attributes of sovereign authority over the transnational constitution of global trade gave new life to very old processes originating in the imperial globalization initially advanced by the governments of Western Europe. The United States was born of a civil war within this imperial system. The emergence of the new republic from the British Empire replaced an old imperial sovereign with a new form of sovereign authority more geared to expedite the rapid transformation of a large part of a whole continent into personal and corporate capital. Just as the United States established the legal and political terrain conducive to the rise of a new type of transnational corporation, so now the World Trade Organization holds the seed of the sovereign capacity to extend new types of charters and new types of property rights, especially in the expanding field of intellectual property, to a new generation of global corporations.

EARLY RESISTANCE TO
THE ABUSES OF IMPERIAL POWER

Much of the discourse on human rights developed after the Second World War in light of the genocidal atrocities committed by Nazi agents and their sympathizers in Europe. The postwar efforts to create legal obstacles aimed at preventing the consolidation of any more savage tyrannies culminated in 1948 with the adoption by the General Assembly of the United Nations of the Universal Declaration of Human Rights. While this document gave contemporary language to the goal of rendering justice to all of humanity, the specific themes addressed by the declaration's authors have antecedents with very deep roots in history. The struggle to enforce a universal regime of human rights is thus much older than the Second World War. The human rights movement draws with particular strength on the vitality of old campaigns to eliminate slavery and to oppose the oppressiveness of empires imposed on the Indigenous peoples of colonized territory without their consent.

The struggle against imperial rule often developed through complex sets of relationships linking leading members of colonized groups to more progressive or even revolutionary factions in the colonizing societies. Benedict Anderson explores some of this complexity in *Under Three Flags*. He examines the interconnected movements that developed near the end of the nineteenth century in the quest to free Cuba and the Philippine Islands from Spanish control. The main focus of his book is Jose Rizal, whose first novel, *Noli me tangere*, became one of the primary inspirational texts in the indigenous struggle for Philippine liberation. Rizal was native-speaker of Tagalog, one of the Philippines many Aboriginal languages. He chose, however, to write for a larger audience in the language of his peoples' imperial masters. His literary quest took him to Madrid, Barcelona, and Paris, where he collaborated actively on a number of fronts with an engaging mix of anarchists, Marxists, and liberals. When Rizal returned to the Philippines, he faced increasingly hostile state actions until he was martyred in 1896 in a ritual that helped afford him, as Anderson's sees it, "the permanent status of Father of His Country and First Filipino."[75]

Anderson's study helps to illustrate the thesis that the anti-imperial struggle is rich with multicultural alliances, coalitions, confederacies, and associations among groups and individuals linked across large expanses of space and long intervals of time. Time is an especially significant dimension of anti-imperial struggle because of the propensity of many activists to draw examples and inspirations from earlier rounds of resistance to colonial rule. Several other cases will be briefly explored in this section in order to demonstrate further that the quest to express, protect, and enforce the universal human rights of all people is very old and extremely varied in its origins, inspirations, and manifestations. Roger Williams, for instance, the founder of Rhode Island, emerged in the first half of the seventeenth century as an outspoken critic of the unilateral extension of European sovereignty into alien territory without the consent of Indigenous peoples. As author of an early dictionary and grammar of the Algonkian-language dialects of the Massachusett and Narragansett Indians, Williams was one of the first advocates in Anglo-America of what future generations would come to call Aboriginal and treaty rights. He adopted this position in the process of condemning the imperial charters for granting titles to territory subject already to the proprietary and political control of Indigenous peoples. He was also very clear in his opposition to those who sought to use coercive methods in forcing Indigenous peoples to accept Christianity. Williams's position naturally aroused the ire of the autocratic leaders who ruled the Puritan theocracy of Massachusetts. This colony's paternalistic rulers not only saw themselves as primary agents of God's divine will but derived considerable authority from the royal charter granted to the shareholders of the Massachusetts Bay Company in 1629.[76]

In coming to these conclusions, Williams helped to introduce into the colonial discourse of the English Empire a host of ideas similar to those espoused in the Spanish Empire during the sixteenth century by a number of priests, most of whom were members of the Dominican or Franciscan orders. Prominent among them were Father Francisco de Vitoria and Brother Bartolomé de Las Casas. With their interventions, Vitoria and Las Casas sought to counter the most ruthless and arbitrary applications of Spanish rule over the Indigenous peoples in America. This tradition of activist scholarship within the Roman Catholic Church, certainly a formative chapter in the evolution of the ideal of universal human rights, sent political and ideological ripples through the Vatican and the Court of Castille. As in the famous court case at Valladolid in 1550–51, much of the growing body of Spanish litigation on the rights and titles of Indigenous peoples was derived from intensifying contentions over the legal status of Indian property rights. These contentions included a range of issues surrounding the question of whether it was legal to transform Indian people themselves into property through the institution of slavery.[77]

Roger Williams extended into New England key aspects of a discourse that was already well developed in Spain and New Spain by the end of the sixteenth century. Almost certainly, some of these ideas on the rights of Indigenous peoples flowed from Spain to New England through the Netherlands, where the Dutch jurist, Hugo Grotius, contributed prolifically to the intellectual quest for a law of nations to provide a regime of universal governance for all the world's peoples. The genesis of New England as a Puritan stronghold was deeply affected by the violent break of Holland and the other Dutch provinces away from both Roman Catholicism and the oppressive jurisdiction of the Spanish Crown. The strengthening independence of the Netherlands was finally formalized in the Treaty of Westphalia of 1648, a seminal instrument of international law advancing the principle that the sovereign autonomy of national governments formed the primary pillar of world order.

Williams traumatized New England's Puritan elites when he sought, in 1635, to establish a new colony, Rhode Island, based not on an English charter but on a grant of property from the Narragansett Indians. The idea of deriving the legitimacy for European expansion from the Aboriginal inhabitants of a colonized territory extended notions taking form in the fertile, intercultural atmosphere of the nascent fur trades of New Netherlands and New France. In making between 1682 and 1701 a series of Quaker treaties with the Lenni Lape, the Indigenous peoples of much of Pennsylvania, William Penn contributed to the idea that the charter he had received from the English sovereign was not on its own sufficient to justify taking the ancestral lands and resources away from the Aboriginal inhabitants of a newly created polity in the English Empire.[78]

The charges pressed against Warren Hastings provided another showcase highlighting the negative consequence for Indigenous peoples of that genre of imperialism which was rooted in the granting of corporate charters. The marathon litigation, which unfolded sporadically in Parliament's Westminster Hall between 1788 and 1795, grabbed the attention of both the British media and the public. It became one of the most spectacular show trials of the eighteenth century. Beginning in 1772, Hastings had served as the first governor general of that part of India dominated by the British East India Company. On taking office, Hastings used his power much as those who prepared the way for his governorship had done. He set to work forming, consolidating, and manipulating various indigenous puppet regimes. He aimed to secure commercial advantage by turning the East Indian Company's Indian allies and clients against those Indian groups that had been pulled into the commercial, political, and military orbits of French and Dutch traders in India.

In prosecuting Hastings on a number of charges, the British parliamentarian Edmund Burke used language that was clearly informed by the experiment in popular democracy under way in the nascent United States. While Burke applauded many of the constitutional arguments brought forward by the founders of the American republic, he passed harsh judgment on the revolutionary transformations in process in France.[79] He prosecuted the case against Hastings "in the name of the people of India, whose rights he has trodden under foot, and whose country he had turned into a desert." For setting Indian violently against Indian, without regard for any principle other than a narrow conception of commercial self-interest, Hastings was said to have undermined the reputation and integrity of his own country. "I impeach him," proclaimed Burke, "in the name of the English nation, whose ancient honour he has sullied."[80] The trial of Warren Hastings helped to cultivate the idea that obligations as well as commercial benefits were attached to the imperatives of imperial rule. These obligations included a duty to protect Indigenous peoples from the most vicious onslaughts and most aggressive incursions into their Aboriginal territories. The notion of bringing Indigenous peoples within the orbit of "imperial trusteeship" also extended to the perceived responsibility to share with subject populations the benefits of access to the wider world, but especially through the instrument of Christian education.[81]

In later years Sir Charles Metcalfe, a high-ranking official in the East India Company, added his voice to those arguing that Britain's imperial role in India could not be justified or even sustained without some respect for the Aboriginal rights of the Indigenous peoples. "Our dominion of India is by conquest," he wrote. "It is naturally disgusting to the inhabitants and can only be maintained by military force. It is our positive duty to render them justice, to respect and protect their rights, and to study their happiness. By performance of this duty, we may allay and keep dormant their innate disaffection." As provisional governor general of the East India Company, Metcalfe moved in 1835 to apply his philosophy of imperial governance by blocking an initiative to obstruct freedom of the press. "If India could only be preserved as part of the British Empire by keeping its inhabitants in a state of ignorance, our domination would be a curse ... and ought to cease," he wrote. Metcalfe's intervention almost certainly had significant long-term consequences. It contributed to the cultivation of an atmosphere that enabled India to become one of the few decolonized countries after the Second World War to develop and maintain a viable parliamentary democracy. In Metcalfe's own time, Thomas Babington Macaulay, who in later years would become one of Britain's most successful Whig historians, observed that India "was perhaps the only country in the world where the press is free while the Government is despotic."[82]

The elimination of the transatlantic slave trade and then of slavery itself constitutes one of the most important episodes in the centuries-old struggle to advance universal human rights. Like the push to eliminate the scourge of piracy from the high seas, the campaign to end slavery became one of the central subjects of international law in the nineteenth century. In its concerted effort to apply the explicit language of anti-slavery treaties on the high seas, Great Britain's Royal Navy did much to secure its reputation during that era as the world's premier law-enforcement agency.[83] Much of the credit for ending slavery has rightfully gone to the likes of William

Wilberforce in Great Britain and Abraham Lincoln in the United States. In the French Caribbean sugar colony of San Domingo, however, it was a former slave, Toussaint L'Overature, who provided the essential qualities of leadership that made it possible for about 500,000 slaves to free themselves from bondage. This monumental act of self-liberation continues to hold out a beacon of hope in a world where the largest masses of humanity remain subjugated to forms of oppression that give meaning to the concept of *virtual slavery.*

At the end of the eighteenth century, San Domingo was the site of such prolific productivity of sugar cane that it produced about two-thirds of France's colonial wealth. In 1789 the outbreak of the French Revolution began a series of transformations that would eventually give rise to the imperial career of Napoleon Bonaparte. Toussaint was pulled into the military conflicts that swept over his Caribbean Island once the French revolutionaries proclaimed their egalitarian ideals. In a series of battles, Toussaint led a disciplined army of former Black slaves who achieved victories over armies sent to the Caribbean by Spain, Great Britain, and France. In the course of this assertiveness, the island's enslaved majority were able to achieve a measure of liberation that they refused to give up in spite of Napoleon's efforts to return them to bondage. Toussaint himself was captured by Napoleon's forces and taken to France, where he died in prison of pneumonia in April 1803.

In spite of his death, the former slaves of San Domingo declared their sovereign existence in 1804 by asserting their identity as citizens of Haiti – the second independent republic of the Americas. They took as the name of their new country, the Indian word for their island. The transformation of San Domingo into Haiti became a powerful symbol of the convergence of issues raised by the institution of slavery and the dispossession of Indigenous peoples in the colonization of the Western Hemisphere. The life of Toussaint was compellingly chronicled by C.L.R. James in *The Black Jacobins.*[84] He wrote the text after authoring a successful stage play mounted in London in 1936, with Paul Robeson playing the title role of Toussaint. Like Frantz Fanon's *Wretched of the Earth,* James's study of Toussaint is widely viewed as one of the classic inspirational texts in the Fourth World movement that developed after the Second World War. The aim of this global liberation struggle has been to free oppressed peoples from the bondage of European rule, racism, sexism, and neo-colonial forms of exploitation.

In his goal of returning Toussaint's people to slavery, Napoleon found a strong ally in Thomas Jefferson, the Virginia slave owner who became president of the United States in 1801. His government refused to recognize the sovereign attributes of Haiti, and his successors continued this policy of non-recognition until 1862, when the US Civil War changed the international orientation of the first American republic. Inside the US government the fear was palpable that, if the success of the Haitian revolution was formally acknowledged, recognition might help to hearten the potential makers of a slave revolt inside the United States.[85]

France's loss of San Domingo, an important stopover point in the ocean journey to New Orleans, was one of the main motivations prompting Napoleon to transfer the huge region known as Louisiana to Jefferson's government for the nominal price of $15 million, or 3 cents an acre. The transfer of the European title to Louisiana from the government of Napoleon to that of Jefferson helped to reconfirm the importance of France as the first and most important ally of the United States. Both revolutionary regimes showed the limits of their liberalism in their common attachment to the institution of slavery. The link between the two polities found expression in the extension of the Napoleonic Wars to North America in the War of 1812. A crucial element of that clash was the alliance between the British imperial government and the Indian Confederacy of Canada, a polity that found its primary guidance in the gifted orator, general, and law giver Tecumseh. In seeking international recognition for an Aboriginal dominion within the British Empire, Tecumseh sought alterations in the structure of international relations similar to those envisaged by Toussaint L'Overture. Both men were martyred in their quest to win sovereign recognition for the dark-skinned constituencies they tried to represent at the highest level of international relations. Both met their death in the quest to break the monopoly of the European powers and their New World proxy, the United States, as the sole jurisdictions on earth capable of making treaties at the highest level of international law.

The issues raised for the international system by Toussaint and Tecumseh continued to challenge established institutions on a number of fronts. Some of their idealism was shared and absorbed by the powerful and effective anti-slavery lobby of the British Parliament. After outlawing the slave trade in 1807, this lobby, led by William Wilberforce, maintained its momentum to outlaw slavery itself in the British Empire in 1833. The activists then moved on from slavery to focus their attention on the plight of Indigenous peoples throughout Britain's expanding empire. Their work led, in 1836 and 1837, to the creation and then to the elaborate investigation of the British House of Commons Select Committee on Aborigines in British Settlements. This initiative represents to this day one of the most broad-ranging, comprehensive, and penetrating studies of the legal, constitutional, and political dynamics of the encounter between Indigenous peoples and empire builders. It presented a rare glimpse of how the most pervasive patterns of colonialism cut across many territories, creating common sets of dilemmas for many different Aboriginal societies. In the words of South African historian Noel Mostert, "The Aborigines Committee remains one of the most striking and impressive examples of public enquiry in nineteenth-century Britain, its massive report one of the most absorbing public documents of that century."[86]

The Aborigines Committee drew strongly on the advice of the Protestant missionary societies in Great Britain. Most of these societies were headquartered in and around London's Exeter Hall, where much of the behind-the-scenes lobbying occurred to influence the content and conclusions of this major parliamentary study. It is hardly surprising, therefore, that the Aborigines Committee gave a hearty endorsement in its report to the work of Christian evangelists as vital agents of British imperialism. They wrote, "It is not to be doubted that this country has been invested with wealth and power, with arts and knowledge, with the sway of different lands, and the mastery of restless waters, for some great and important purpose in the world. Can we suppose otherwise than that it is our office to carry civilization and humanity, peace and good government, and, above all, the knowledge of the true God, to the uttermost end of the earth?"

This embrace of a British and Protestant version of the European civilizing mission was qualified, however, with a bold if paternalistic emphasis on the need to integrate, within the machinery of empire building, strong constitutional and political mechanisms geared to both the recognition and protection of certain rights of Indigenous peoples. The report announced the arrival of "the moment for the nation to declare, that with all its desire to give encouragement to emigration, and to find a soil to which our surplus population may retreat, it will tolerate no scheme which implies violence or fraud in the taking of such territory: that it will no longer subject itself to the guilt of conniving at oppression, and that it will take on the task of defending those who are too ignorant to defend themselves."[87] Central among the committee's many recommendations was the stipulation that the executive branch of the imperial government should retain responsibility for the protection and arbitration of Aboriginal land rights. Under no circumstances, the report concluded, should this responsibility be left to the local governments, whose operations were often dominated by the interests and aspirations of land speculators. The local legislatures were too often "virtual parties" to Aboriginal land disputes, and their members would inevitably be in positions of conflict of interest if they were to become "the judge of such controversies."[88]

In raising this issue, the parliamentarians touched on one of the major points of contention that had contributed to the eruption of the American Revolution six decades earlier: the question of where to locate jurisdictional responsibility for the conduct of relations with Indigenous peoples. The conflict unfolded in British North America after 1763, when King George asserted in a Royal Proclamation the Crown's exclusive constitutional power to obtain the consent of the Indigenous peoples to transform their titles in their ancestral lands into other forms of non-Aboriginal title and jurisdiction. There were huge implications for the future course of colonization in this attempt to centralize imperial control over the process of westward expansion of non-Aboriginal settlements.

The Anglo-American settlers in the backcountry of North America quickly became irate that the authors of the Royal Proclamation seemed to be siding with Native people, the very enemies seemingly vanquished by the British victory in the French and Indian War.[89] A group from Paxton, Pennsylvania, registered their disgust that year by massacring about two dozen pacifist inhabitants of a Moravian Indian mission on the Susquehanna River. Some of the leaders of these Paxton Boys, including Matthew Smith, went on to become leading soldiers in the Continental Army of the nascent United States.[90] The negative response to the Royal Proclamation's qualified recognition of Aboriginal and treaty rights, therefore, helped to inflame the revolutionary zeal of those who plunged British North America into civil war in 1776. The irate response of the Paxton Boys in the genesis of the American Revolution repeated many of the same themes taken up by Nathaniel Bacon and his supporters in 1676. The rebellion led by Bacon started with his rejection of the principle that the government of Virginia should engage in friendly relations with Christian Indians in the region. According to Bacon and his followers, it was the responsibility of the colonial government to treat all Indians as Virginia's enemies, to be exterminated as quickly and completely as possible.[91]

The Royal Proclamation outlined a constitutional framework for the incorporation of Canada, Florida, and Grenada into the structures of British North America after the defeat of French imperialism in the Seven Years' War. The concluding paragraphs of the proclamation outlined the creation of a new kind of polity different from the corporate and governmental structures that had formed the organizational basis of the British Empire up to that time. After laying out the plan for the establishment of the province of Quebec in the St Lawrence River valley, King George designated the eastern half of the Mississippi River valley and the watershed of the Great Lakes as a giant Indian reserve under the shared jurisdiction of both its Aboriginal inhabitants and the imperial government. Under no circumstances would any private purchase of lands from the Indigenous peoples of this reserve be considered legal. Instead, the king established himself and his royal heirs as the sole authority capable of acquiring the Aboriginal title to these imperially protected territories. "If at any Time any of the said Indians should be inclined to dispose of the said Lands," he proclaimed, referring to his own person and his royal office in the first-person plural, "the same shall be Purchased only for Us, in our Name, at some public Meeting or Assembly of the said Indians, to be held for that Purpose."[92]

The qualified recognition of Indian rights in the Royal Proclamation represents the application of an extended imperial learning curve to the evolving constitution of the British Empire. The formulation of these rights drew on the Indian policies of New Netherlands and New France as well as on those of Roger Williams and the Pennsylvania Quakers. The codification of the principle that consent rather than coercion should govern Crown-Indian relations in the North American interior marked the apotheosis of the career of Sir William Johnson. He and his Tory allies in London had deftly taken advantage of the politics of an Aboriginal takeover of several British posts in the North American interior in 1763. This exercise in Aboriginal muscle flexing, which is usually associated with the tactics of an Aboriginal freedom fighter named Pontiac, helped to underline for drafters of the Royal Proclamation the wisdom of extending the diplomacy of the Covenant Chain as the optimal means of successfully integrating the fur-trade economy of French-Aboriginal Canada into British North America. In adopting Johnson's advice, King George began to come to grips, however imperfectly and incompletely, with the principle that the power of the British sovereign to charter new corporate and governmental polities needed to be balanced against other considerations – the need, for instance, to recognize and accommodate Aboriginal rights. Only thus could the Indigenous peoples be persuaded to integrate peacefully and voluntarily into the British Empire. These Aboriginal rights can be conceived as the pre-existing rights and titles of the indigenous inhabitants of newly annexed territories, and as the shared human rights of Aboriginal groups whose lands and societies had already been subjected to the foreign impositions of colonization.

Even this very limited recognition of Aboriginal rights and title by the British imperial Crown went much too far for some. On both sides of the Atlantic, the Royal Proclamation of 1763 became a symbol of Tory tyranny among those Whigs who tended to see King George's enactment as proof that the monarch was trying to undo the constitutional limitation on his powers as instituted in the Glorious Revolution of 1688. There were other more immediate causes, however, for the swelling rejection of the Royal Proclamation and all it represented by large segments of the Anglo-American population. The limits of their liberalism were tellingly displayed by their interpretation of the king's qualified recognition of Aboriginal rights. The dissidents saw the imperial commitment to obtain Indian consent for land cessions as an unjustifiable limitation on the imperative of Anglo-Americans to seize lands from Indigenous peoples and to push their settlements westward as fast as they could under the jurisdiction of their own local legislatures. This stance basically defined the position, for instance, of the Paxton Boys, who were never punished for the murder of so many pacifist Christian Indians. This vision of a decentralized empire, allowing maximum latitude for the expansionary pre-eminence of the Anglo-Americans, collided with the proclamation's goal of a more multicultural and centrally controlled imperial regime. The Royal Proclamation, therefore, was instrumental in establishing the basis at the end of the Seven Years' War of those divisions that would later clash in the American Revolution. It was a major source of the antagonisms that would eventually coalesce into a whole series of charges and accusations directed against George III in the Declaration of Independence.

Thomas Jefferson was one of the central figures who masterminded the channelling of colonial unease with the imperialism of Great Britain into a full-fledged revolution. He countered the Crown's recognition of Aboriginal title with a theory stating that Anglo-American settlers held their own form of native title. In a pamphlet published in 1774 entitled *A*

Summary View of the Rights of British America, Jefferson referred to the form of land ownership vested in the colonial population of British North America as "allodial title." He traced the notion of allodial title, his answer to the Royal Proclamation's recognition of Aboriginal title, back to the imagined rights of free Saxons in England before their liberties were supposedly constrained by an alien Crown in the Norman Conquest of 1066. In developing this theory, Jefferson was clearly preparing the ground for the day when his idealized constituency, the New World descendants of the Free Saxons, would throw off the weight of an illegitimate monarch. In liberating their own capacities to own and control North America, they would foil King George's plan to exploit alliances with the continent's Indigenous peoples as a way of asserting imperial title over one of the richest portions of the New World.[93]

In his theory of allodial title and in his authorship of large portions of the Declaration of Independence, Jefferson drew heavily on the writings of John Locke. In *Two Treatises of Government,* Locke had assigned North American Indians to the infant stage of humanity. He associated this imagined infancy with a state of undisturbed nature before the existence of money and before what he characterized as the improvement of North American lands through the investment of labour by transplanted English farmers.[94] This Lockean vision of the past combined with a Jeffersonian view of the future in the founding manifesto of the United States. The Declaration of Independence defined as criminal any resistance on the part of Indigenous peoples to the revolutionary polity's expansionary course. The "merciless Indian savages" referred to in the document were not to be permitted to exercise a right of self-defence, let alone the "inalienable rights" of "life, liberty, and the pursuit of happiness." In pioneering a form of racial profiling that sought to exclude a whole class of humanity from the rule of law and from the universal rights of equality cited as primary justifications for their revolutionary break with the past, the authors of the declaration anticipated the future outlines of the Global War on Terror. In direct response to George III's limited recognition of the inherent human rights of Indigenous peoples in the proclamation, the founding fathers of the United States of America charged that the British monarch "has endeavored to bring on the inhabitants of our frontiers the merciless Indian savages, whose known rule of warfare is an undistinguished destruction of all ages, sexes, and conditions."

The dissidence created by the contrast of ideologies in the Royal Proclamation of 1763 and the Declaration of Independence continued to fester for decades to come. It could not have been more clear that the Royal Proclamation was based on some measure of respect for the human rights of Indigenous peoples, whereas the Declaration of Independence held these same rights in utter contempt. Eventually this contrast extended to the Indian Country of Canada in the form of the Indian Confederacy's military alliance with the British imperial government during the War of

1812. That alliance was pointed against the expansionary exploits of the US Army. This Indian-fighting federal army was manned largely by volunteers from Kentucky who looked to Canada as the place where "the tomahawk of the savage has been moulded into its death-like form."[95] Like the effort to channel the slave revolt into a positive assertion of the human rights of the Haitian people, Tecumseh sought to transform the War of 1812 into a kind of American War of Aboriginal Liberation. In seeking admittance to the high tables of international diplomacy, where franchises to carve up, exploit, and govern the planet were regularly passed out and traded, both Toussaint L'Overture and Tecumseh embodied serious but failed bids to break the monopoly of the "White Nations" in the making of international law. They were both vital figures who provided continuity in the ongoing struggle to resist the genocidal incursions of slavery and imperial rule. This struggle for universal human rights extended from, for instance, the liberation movement led in the 1780s by the Peruvian aristocrat, Túpac Amaru, to the positions proclaimed in 1955 by leaders who assembled to oppose colonialism at the Bandung Conference in Indonesia in 1955. In the inspiration they provided for freedom movements spanning large expanses of space and long intervals of time, Tecumseh and Toussaint have both contributed significantly to stimulating forms of anti-imperial globalization as embodied particularly in the ideals of the Fourth World.

The course of human liberation for both Toussaint and Tecumseh lay not only in their quest to participate in the making of international law but also in their opposition to the regime of property law that served to bolster and perpetuate the supremacy of wealth and power vested in the White Nations. Accordingly, like the founding of Haiti, the fight during the War of 1812 to establish an Aboriginal Dominion in the interior of North America deserves far more serious scholarly recognition as a seminal episode in the history of activism to advance universal human rights. Both episodes were as decisive in their own way – albeit negatively – as the French and the American revolutions were in establishing the scope and limitations in the applications of Enlightenment thought to the geopolitical reorganization of the planet.

The issues raised about the domestic or international character of the title of Indigenous peoples in their own ancestral lands included and extended some of the same kind of contestations marking the debate over the nature of people's inherent right to title in their own persons. These contestations were paramount in determining whether the institution of slavery would be abolished. While the United States attempted to contain this debate within the framework of its own laws and institutions, it eventually exploded in 1861 in the American Civil War, a conflict characterized by C.A. Bayly as a truly "global event."[96] It remains to be seen when and how the question of Aboriginal title will burst similarly into the principal venues of international controversy. It also remains to be seen what forces will erode the domestic constraints within which many of the legal assertions of Indigenous peoples have been successfully bound by the successor states of those European empires that initiated and pressed forward the Columbian conquests.

REAPING FORTUNES ON THE FRONTIERS
OF FINANCIAL DEREGULATION

When he defined the American frontier as the meeting ground between savagery and civilization, Frederick Jackson Turner gave renewed expression in 1893 to many of the same notions that had inspired and motivated the authors of the Declaration of Independence. Implicit in Turner's interpretation was the expectation that his country would continue to move towards the centre of a coalition of nations dedicated to widening cycles of expansion and acquisition through liberating conquest. Those people and polities that failed to conform to the expansionary motifs of US-led frontierism could count on being eliminated or subordinated much as had already happened to many Aboriginal groups in North America. Turner's frontier thesis proved compelling in its time because it seemed to explain so much with such economy of expression. The argument was especially useful in an era when the United States was still busily engaged in disentangling itself from the complications of European empires in order to establish the distinct framework for its own empire, both formal and informal. Integrated into Turner's deceptively simple prose were metaphors invoking many of the most powerful themes in the mythological construction of the American Dream. Among the inheritances of belief and thought captured in the author's idealized frontiersman were Charles Darwin's evolutionary theory of "the survival of the fittest,"[97] John Lockes's political economy of "possessive individualism,"[98] and the United States' quasi-religious doctrine of "Manifest Destiny."[99] There was an element of genius in Turner's braiding together all these strands of inspiration into a single saga of idealized US conquest, democracy, and prosperity.

Turner's description failed, however, to address those processes that were already far advanced in making US corporate cartels the true inheritors of the American ethos of frontier expansion. Indeed, the extension of frontier liberties to corporate polities in North America would continue to be replicated even *within* the internal structures of these commercial entities. The dramatic fall beginning in 2002 of Enron, WorldCom, and Global Crossing, together with the business scandals ensnaring, for instance, Merck, Rite Aid, Bristol-Myers Squibb, Adelphia Communications, AOL Time Warner, Cendant, Tyco, Duke Energy, JP Morgan Chase, Citigroup, and Halliburton, all exposed to public view some of the implications of deregulation and the extreme centralization of corporate power in the hands of chief executive officers.[100] At the core of the revelations was news that some top business executives, including Enron's Kenneth Lay and Jeffrey Skilling, had resorted to fraudulent accounting practices in order to appropriate for themselves big chunks of the corporate capital belonging to shareholders.

In other words, the executive branch of business corporations had stolen significant portions of the assets of those who technically employed them to manage and direct their corporate property. An internal investigation of the media conglomerate Hollinger International referred in 2004 to this phenomenon as "corporate kleptocracy."[101] Many of the victimized shareholders were middle-class citizens of modest means who had invested significant portions of their life's savings in the vandalized companies through the medium of pension plans. According to J. Richard Finlay of the Centre for Corporate and Public Governance, these revelations precipitated "the greatest crisis of capitalism in our time."[102] But an even bigger crisis was to come in the years ahead.

A longer view of the unfolding crisis in capitalism demonstrates the continuing relevance of some of Turner's insights delivered at the World's Columbian Exposition. The business executives implicated in recent corporate scandals displayed many of the qualities of exuberant individualism attributed by Turner to his archetypal frontiersman. Similarly, the defrauded shareholders, who suffered the consequences of the executive aggrandizement on the frontiers of deregulation, assumed a role similar to that once assigned to dispossessed Indians. In the transcontinental expansion of the United States it was quite common for pioneer frontiersmen to travel beyond the reach of their own government's regulations in order to stake their own proprietary claims in the embattled Indian Country. In *Bad Money: Reckless Finance, Failed Politics, and the Global Crisis of American Capitalism*, Kevin Phillips extends and develops the imagery of the most deregulated frontiers of the US financial sector as a new version of the "Wild West." Phillips wrote the book in 2007 as the Great Housing and Credit Bubble initiated a global financial calamity.[103]

Phillips demonstrates how the manipulation of capital by banks and the so-called "shadow banking sector" overshadowed manufacturing to emerge in the 1980s as the largest and most influential sector of the US economy. This rise of a vast merchandising industry for the speculative buying and selling of credit and debt took place during an era when the market economy, but particularly transactions in stock markets, was aggressively promoted as *the* primary venue for the popular expression of democratic will.[104] Some of the biggest rewards went to those in the financial sector who packaged large bundles of debt supposedly secured by mortgages and the houses to which they adhere. These packages were then sold to other financial institutions around the world as part of a larger process that added all kinds of legally and economically complex derivatives to the global economy. In the prelude to the global financial breakdown, Enron was a major player in the Wild West breakaway from regulatory restraints that had initially been put in place during the New Deal when the Roosevelt administration intervened to save capitalism from its own worst excesses during the Great Depression. The creation of CDOs – collateralized debt obligations – was but one feature of a larger phenomena where unregulated "liquidity factories," including the secretive hedge funds, created the basis of "money-like debt instruments," "candyfloss money," or "money pyramids." Through such novel experiments, the financial sector's "twenty-first century digitalized nirvana" produced huge financial windfalls for some. For instance, the twenty highest-paid hedge fund managers in 2006 made an average of $657.5 million each.[105]

While the US government and the consortium of bankers represented on the Federal Reserve Board treated this activity as external to their regulatory responsibilities, these agencies were, in fact, instrumental in governing the regime of interest rates, currency creation, and other conditions that made such activities economically viable, at least for a while. The most important political decision entailed in this process was the federal determination to allow the amount of private debt individuals and corporations took on to multiply dramatically. Where domestic financial debt was 21 per cent of the Gross Domestic Product in 1979, by 2006 it had risen to over five times GDP.[106] At the same time, the rhetoric of free trade and free markets was contradicted by the frequent intervention of the Federal Reserve and Treasury Department in bailing out financial institutions and even national economies that failed.[107] These interventions include the federal response to the savings and loan fiasco between 1989 and 1992, the rescue of the Mexican peso in 1995, and the massive bailouts of the world's largest banking institutions in 2008 and 2009 to prevent the meltdown of the global economy. The public was told that the bailouts were to correct problems in financial instruments derived from sub-prime mortgages. Attention was thus diverted from the speculative breakdown of various schemes for deriving profit from the privatized terror economy of the post 9/11 world.

The federal intervention to save many Wall Street interests from the full effects of their overzealous opportunism was, it seems, part of a more general procedure whereby the US government and its Federal Reserve banking partners intervene quite often in the dealings of its favoured financial sector through the somewhat mysterious workings of the Plunge Protection Team, otherwise know as the President's Working Group on Financial Markets.[108] The core activity of this agency was the strategic creation and deployment of public funds to prop up US financial institutions and to inflate artificially the demand for shares in stock markets. As Martin Wolf commented in the *Financial Times*, "What we have is a risk-loving industry guaranteed as a public utility."[109]

Even as the scandals initially generated by the fall of Enron, WorldCom, and Global Crossing were still festering, a second wave of accounting fraud disclosed the frontiersmen in the US financial sector as descendants of those unrestrained Indian fighters described by Frederick Jackson Turner at the Columbian Exposition in 1893. Similarly, just as the violently acquired sections of Indian Country were generally recognized as lawful once federal authorities extended their presence into zones of proprietary lawlessness, so similar patterns seem to have taken hold as the huge distortions came to light of the manipulation of government as both the insurer and the deregulator of the coddled financial sector.

In the years before he became the disgraced former governor of New York State, Attorney General Eliot Spitzer made his name and fame as the Sheriff of Wall Street – as a gun-slinging investigator with an urge to prosecute some striking high-profile examples of executive criminality. Through his efforts and those of other law-enforcement agents, a few high-profile CEO's were eventually prosecuted for insider trading and for stealing corporate assets. The convicted included press baron Conrad Black and the media darling of American domesticity, Martha Stewart. While the public have been served up a few show trials, however, there is little doubt that much of the malfeasance in the Wild West financial sector remains uninvestigated and unprosecuted. Clearly the promises to clean things up after the Enron scandal were disingenuous or worse. As the *New York Times* proclaimed in a headline: "Enron's Other Legacy: The Idea That Anything Can Be Traded."[110]

The prospect of even larger political scandals coming from the Enron debacle may have been significantly diminished when, during the late afternoon of September 11, 2001, World Trade Center 7 (WTC 7) fell to the ground in a well-filmed episode still widely displayed on the Internet. The fall of WTC 7, reported by the BBC fully twenty minutes before it actually occurred, shows all the attributes of a controlled demolition. No airplanes crashed into WTC 7. The official explanation given for the instant destruction of the 600-foot structure is that the building had been damaged by fires caused earlier in the day when World Trade Centers 1 and 2 plunged to the ground. Interestingly, WTC 7 held the offices of the Security Exchange Commission that was then investigating Enron on a number of fronts, including its possible role in apparently manipulating supplies of electricity in California in order to advance its push to elevate profits through further deregulation and privatization of that lucrative energy market. Key records in Enron's investigation, along with those demonstrating possible infractions in the business activities of about 3,000 other companies, were destroyed in the destruction of WTC 7. This building also held the New York offices of the Internal Revenue Service, the CIA, the FBI, the US Secret Service, the Defense Department, as well as the New York Mayor's Office of Emergency Management.

The events of 9/11 seem to have been anticipated by some traders on the New York Stock Exchange.[111] While some corporations suffered heavily after that day, others benefited greatly. The heightened fear of terrorism, for instance, provided a bonanza for the global insurance industry. Moreover, the US government's quick declaration of a Global War on Terror significantly heightened the budgets and quickly advanced the further privatization of the world's largest military-industrial complex through vehicles such as the Blackwater Corporation.[112] Blackwater, also known as Xe corporation, is one of a whole generation of corporate entities whose operatives benefit enormously from the rapid development of the post–September 11 terror economy. The rapid increase in military budgets occurred even in the face of Defense Secretary Donald Rumsfeld's admission, made on September 10, 2001, that the Pentagon's accountants could not explain the disappearance of $2.3 trillion from the books of the US government's military spending.[113]

These suggestive facts, together with many more of their ilk, renew in a transformed context the validity of Frederick Jackson's Turner's insights on the importance of violence and lawlessness in those moving zones of frontier interaction where the political culture of the United States takes form. In the first decade of the twenty-first century, some of the leading frontiersmen of the capitalist superpower continued to move out in front of the law in order to avoid even minimal regulation. In the anything-goes atmosphere of New World fortune seeking, the frontiersmen of business deregulation staked their claims to new forms of wealth in a globalized Indian Country. There the attributes of the Wild West's new incarnation would extend to the quest to gain expanded ownership and control over the oil fields of the Middle East and Eurasia.[114]

CHAPTER THREE

Colonizing Time, Remaking Space, Shaping Opinions, Privatizing the Commons

The ground people walked on was no longer valued solely or even primarily in terms of shared experiences. It was no longer something people belonged to, but rather a commodity people possessed. Land was reduced to a quantitative status and measured by what it could be exchanged for. So, too, with people. Relationships were reorganized.

Jeremy Rifkin, *Biosphere Politics*, 1991

The history of the US is not the story of anti-imperial heretics. It is the account of the power of empire as a way of life, as a way of avoiding the fundamental challenge of creating a humane and equitable community or culture.

William Appleman Williams, *Empire as a Way of Life*, 1982

COUNTING TIME: FROM WOODHENGE TO THE OLYMPICS; FROM NEWTON TO EINSTEIN

The 400th anniversary of Christopher Columbus's initial transatlantic voyage implicitly emphasized the colonization of time as well as space. Indeed, the colonization of time was an integral, if more subtle, factor in the genre of globalization and imperial expansion that began with Europe's colonization of the Western Hemisphere after 1492. Among the many markers and facilitators of the imperial powers' growing capacity to colonize both time and space were increasingly sophisticated systems of navigation, map making, and surveying. Like the ability to calibrate and measure the passage of time, improvements in these means of representing and organizing geographical space were based on the ability to observe and predict with growing precision the cyclical changes in relationship between earthly locations and celestial bodies, including the Sun, Moon, planets, stars, and constellations.[1]

Accordingly, many layers of meaning were embedded in the presentation of a map of time, proclaiming the interval between 1492 and 1893 as pervasively significant for all the world's peoples and cultures. In interpreting global history within the matrix of a single chronological system, the organizers of the World's Columbian Exposition implicitly claimed a universal status for their own means of measuring and marking the flow of time. In affirming the worldwide importance not only of Columbus's initial transatlantic voyage but also of the temporal system used to date the event, the hosts of Chicago's exposition pressed forward, however unconsciously or inadvertently, the temporal frontiers of imperial globalization. Alternatively, they implicitly discounted the value of all means of explaining, organizing, and commemorating life's passages outside the tight scheme of time's measurement that has invested Western civilization with considerable resources of internal cohesion. The philosophical, technological, and sociological changes connected with the rise of a single regime of precise time keeping were integral to the growing influence of Europe and its satellites in America and elsewhere in the quick transformation of world order after 1492. "The invention of the mechanical clock," writes David S. Landes in *Revolution in Time*, "was one of a number of advances that turned Europe from a weak, peripheral, highly vulnerable outpost of Mediterranean civilization into a hegemonic aggressor. Time measurement was at once a sign of new-found creativity and an agent and catalyst in the use of knowledge for wealth and power."[2]

The central structures of temporal calculation binding Western civilization go back to the Egyptian calendar, which Julius Caesar adopted for the Roman Empire several decades before the birth of Christ. It took about five centuries after the life of Jesus until Dionysius Exiguus, a mathematically gifted Italian monk, proposed making the birth of Christ the marker for the central division in the Julian calendar during its subsequent career. In 1582 Pope Gregory XIII invested the calendar inherited from both Egypt and Rome with further mathematical precision. Like virtually all the competing systems of time measurement it encountered in accompanying the course of Western expansion, the Gregorian calendar combines a degree of scientific observation with elements of religious commemoration. While the Gregorian calendar is based on a year of 365¼ days, the Islamic calendar, the Hijri, is based on a year of 354 days. The Hijri takes as its starting point the date when the prophet Mohammed is said to have emigrated to Medina. The Jewish calendar adopted the main division of time of the Gregorian calendar, although it differentiates between BCE (Before the Common or Christian Era) and CE (Common or Christian Era) instead of BC (Before Christ) and AD (Anno Domini). The Chinese calendar uses the lunar cycle to establish the date of the Chinese New Year, an event recognized and celebrated by about one-quarter of the planet's total population.

Many of the world's systems for marking and measuring the passage of time have been based on the diverse life cycles of specific species and organisms used by Indigenous peoples as primary sources of food and medicine. On the prairies of North America, many Aboriginal groups kept detailed winter counts. Referred to as *waniyetu yawapi* by Dakota-speaking peoples, winter counts contain pictorial representations signifying important yearly events in the history of the groups that maintained them.[3] The most celebrated system of time measurement in Aboriginal America is that of the Maya, who developed two calendars, the *tzolkin* and the *haab*. The *tzolkin* is based on a sacred cycle of 260 days; the *haab*, on an annual round of 365 days, made up of eighteen months of twenty days each. The five extra days in the *haab* cycle are referred to as the *Uayeb*, which means nameless. The *Uayeb* days have been branded as inauspicious to mount any important venture or ceremony, such as marriage. The twenty-day month conforms with Mayan mathematics, a digital system that is organized around the number twenty rather than ten. Every 18,980 days, a period amounting to slightly less than 52 *haab* years, the two calendar cycles coincide in a moment of charged synchronicity.

Like the pyramids of Egypt, much of the monumental architecture of the Mayans and other Mesoamerican peoples was built to measure, mark, and commemorate the cyclical movements of stars, constellations, moons, and planets. This Mesoamerican culture extended far up the Mississippi Valley to include Cahokia, near the site of present-day St Louis. Cahokia was home to many tens of thousands of people until some unknown occurrence about twelve hundred years ago caused the demise of this centre of population, religious devotion, and Aboriginal science. Woodhenge is the name given by archaeologists to the elaborate astronomical observatory adjacent to the massive pyramid mound at Cahokia's core. Woodhenge is a classic example of an Aboriginal installation devoted to the study of mathematical relationships linking the passage of time to patterns of celestial change in the heavens.[4]

In Europe, the organization of civic spaces around the construction of large mechanical clocks symbolized the character of many of the internal renovations transforming that continent around the era of its great epoch of global exploration. Many changes looming on the horizons of European history were foreshadowed by the shifting gaze of curious eyes away from the architectural marvels of Christian cathedrals towards the construction and operation of a new array of monumental clocks. The shift signalled, for instance, the move from astrology to astronomy, from alchemy to chemistry, from religion to science in a period when various forms of secularization began to alter the content and rhythm of even the more pious branches of society.[5] This ascent of reason over revelation, of science over superstition, was instrumental in the realization of an expanding proliferation of philosophical, technological, and political breakthroughs. Taken together, these achievements helped to win wide public recognition that the 1700s were, indeed, the Century of Enlightenment. For some of the intellectual pioneers pointing the way to the Enlightenment, but especially for René Descartes, Francis Bacon, and Isaac Newton, the mathematical elegance manifest in the symmetrical movements of mechanical clocks became the master metaphor to explain the complex of relationships that was thought to govern the elements and forces comprising the entire universe.

The central idea stimulating the rise of scientific method in the West was the contention that human reason, as most powerfully expressed in the precision of mathematical calculation, held the key to unlocking and manipulating nature's secrets and enigmas. Inevitably, this turn of human development challenged some of the claims and assertions of organized religion. The historical shift also tended to edify the role of those centres of government whose councils, legislatures, and nascent bureaucracies often sat in the very buildings that housed the most famous instruments of standardized time keeping. The best-known of these monumental clocks is Big Ben, a symbol of Great Britain's parliamentary system. This legendary time piece, which became fully functional in 1862, has been dubbed "a direct descendant" of the King's Clock in the Palace of Westminster. The original time-keeping device was installed there in 1371 during the reign of Edward III.[6] Among the oldest and most celebrated of the other monumental clocks of Europe were those begun in Aragon in 1356, Salisbury in 1386, Rouen in 1389, Lyon in 1481, and Strasbourg in 1547. The widely celebrated Strasbourg structure, which was 25 feet in width, took twenty-seven years to complete. Its designer, Conrad Dasypodius, a professor of mathematics at the Strasbourg Academy, incorporated a number of displays to represent the rotations and cyclical migrations of various heavenly bodies throughout the circular skyscape known as the zodiac.[7]

The manufacturing of increasingly accurate clocks, both large and small, stimulated the further mechanization of many means of production in ways that would later give rise to the Industrial Revolution. Indeed, the growing regimentation of human interaction according to the movement of the clock was as instrumental as the harnessed power of James Watt's steam engines in initiating the massive experiments in technical and social engineering that would so dramatically alter the rhythms and faces of Western civilization. As the Industrial Revolution imposed patterns of manufactured uniformity on the vast diversity and pluralism of undomesticated nature, time itself became the ultimate currency of conformity, uniformity, standardization, and commodification. Among the most instrumental developments in the growing authority of the imperial clock were the construction in the second half of the nineteenth century of transcontinental railways and the spanning of the world's oceans with telegraph cables. The integration of vast portions of the world and its human inhabitants through the construction of interconnected grids of transportation and electronic communications heightened the need to encompass the entire planet with a universal system for measuring and marking the passage of time. The still unfolding process of interweaving a single system of standard time into the life patterns of different peoples and cultures was in its infancy in 1893, the year of Chicago's Columbian Exposition. That year, for instance, the US Nautical Almanac Office turned down a proposal emanating from Canada to unify three different systems for keeping track of the passage of single days. While the so-called civil day began with the stroke of midnight, the so-called astronomical and nautical days began at noon. It was not until 1925 that the US government rectified this inconsistency.[8]

Not surprisingly, it was a British North American promoter and engineer of railway construction, Sir Sandford Fleming, who emerged in the last three decades of the nineteenth century as the world's leading proponent of a single system of universal Standard Time.[9] Fleming advanced his plan by promoting the system before a wide array of scientific and professional associations, including the Canadian Institute, the American Metrological Society, the American Society of Civil Engineers, the Royal Society of England, and the Imperial Academy of Science at St Petersburg. He lobbied for the principle that "there should be only one reckoning of time common to all nations ... [with] one established zero and one common unit of measurement."[10] A major breakthrough in this quest occurred in 1884, when delegates from twenty-five countries converged at the International Prime Meridian Conference in Washington, DC. There the majority of delegates agreed that the Greenwich Observatory, long the widely acknowledged marker of zero longtitude, should become the new site of the "prime meridian." In this fashion, a heightened level of conformity was achieved in bringing the primary global system for measuring configurations of space into line with a universal means of measuring time's duration. Greenwich was recognized as the starting point for the organization of the entire planet into twenty-four time zones conforming to the division of the day into twenty-four hours. This system of measuring temporal duration was initially labelled as Greenwich Mean Time, and, after 1972, changed to Universal Coordinated Time. The Greenwich Observatory had, as already noted, been founded in 1675 by King Charles ii. The original building was designed by Christopher Wren as a research centre to assist in the expansion of English imperialism by placing advances in the science of astronomy at the service of global navigation and cartography.[11]

A number of voices of dissent were raised against designating Greenwich as the base point for the elaboration of a global system of time keeping. One line of disagreement was drawn by those who wanted to centre the world's time-keeping grid on the Great Pyramid at Giza, Egypt, rather than on an old English observatory. Other critics simply denied the need for a universal system transcending the traditions of their own localities. This position flowed naturally from the tendency of significant segments of most national communities to assume that their own centres of population, culture, and government were perfectly satisfactory points of reference when it came to the job of measuring time's passage. The astronomer royal for Scotland defended the imperatives of local tradition when he dismissed Fleming's scheme as being "convenient to no one." He claimed that Fleming was motivated by the misguided notion that "the grand object now of advanced civilization is to consult in everything the utmost development of internationality, or the breaking down of all ancient bounds which have hitherto divided one nation from another, and in fact formed them into nations."[12] With these comments on "internationality," Scotland's royal astronomer presented a succinct interpretation of what would come to be described as "globalization."

The establishment of a universal system for the calculation of Standard Time had implications that went far beyond the problem of instituting more sophisticated forms of temporal measurement and calculation. The experiment, rather, was a ground-breaking initiative pointing the way towards a range of possibilities for minimizing or eliminating all sorts of barriers dividing humanity, be they political, cultural, industrial, epistemological, or economic. Indeed, the standardization of industrial technology would prove to be an especially effective tactic for the generation of new wealth through efficiency and economies of scale in manufacturing. The same sorts of argument supporting the ideal of a single, worldwide regime of Standard Time could as easily be applied to a single, worldwide language, currency, system for calibrating weight and size, code of global law, or even government. While major obstacles were put in the way of such projects by two world wars followed by the Cold War, the decade following the fall of the Berlin Wall in 1989 witnessed a rush of initiatives aimed at making US-centred capitalism the basis of a more standardized regime of global integration. These initiatives sought to standardize transnational commerce, including, for instance, the global integration of systems of industrial production, property ownership, and transactions in trade, investment, and financial speculation. The end of the Cold War roughly coincided with the amazingly quick elaboration of the Internet, a new medium of human interaction that accelerated trends of globalization generated formerly by the circumnavigation of the planet; the construction of the transcontinental railways; the laying of communications cables across the world's oceans; the development of radio, telephones, and television; and the creation of worldwide networks of aviation.[13]

During the opening decades of the twentieth century, the ongoing revolution in science began to fracture some of the underlying assumptions supporting the introduction of a universal system of standardized time, an enactment that pointed towards more ambitious schemes of globalization. The nature of the eruption in knowledge and interpretation is suggested in the title of Stephen Hawking's *Brief History of Time*, one of the most popular scientific texts of the twentieth century. That volume, the author reported in 1996, has been translated into forty languages and has sold about one copy for every 750 men, women, and children in the world.[14] As he described the background of his own quest for a complete, unified theory of the forces governing the interplay between all elements in the universe, Hawking set his work in the evolving theoretical tradition of Aristotle, Copernicus, Galileo, Newton, Einstein, Hubble, and others. In recounting the history of thought on science's most advanced frontiers, he outlined how the Newtonian method of treating time and space as absolutes was overturned by Albert Einstein's general theory of relativity:

Up to the beginning of this [twentieth] century people believed in absolute time. That is, each event could be labeled by a number called "time" in a unique way, and all good clocks would agree on the time interval between events. However, the discovery that the speed of light appeared the same to every observer, no matter how he was moving, led to the theory of relativity – and in that one had to abandon the idea that there was a unique absolute time. Instead, each observer would have his own measure of time as recorded by a clock that he carried: clocks carried by different observers would not necessarily agree. Thus time became a more personal concept, relative to the observer who measured it.[15]

Many ways of conceiving and negotiating life's passages in the twentieth century were affected by the discovery that time and space, two apparent fixed elements of human experience, could be stretched or compressed according to the observer's trajectory of motion in the universe. Although this finding did not necessitate immediate changes in the manner of keeping Standard Time on Earth, the shift towards a very different way of conceiving the universe and our relationship to its elements gave widened currency in many fields to the terms *relativity* or *relativism*. Indeed, over the course of the twentieth century, the growing power of the idea of relativity challenged a host of orthodoxies on many fronts. It undermined the perceived legitimacy and role of many establishments that had coalesced around particular notions of how reality is constructed. The cultural relativism of Franz Boas and his students, for instance, would eventually reorient much of the social sciences away from their preoccupation with absolutist notions of racial hierarchy. This reorientation in the social sciences was part of the same intellectual current energizing Albert Einstein as he moved to the revolutionary conclusion that energy equals mass times the speed of light squared.[16] The enormous consequences of this equation for the future of human relationships were chillingly suggested in 1945, when the US government dropped two atomic bombs on the Japanese cities of Hiroshima and Nagasaki. This act, one of history's most succinct examples of a crime against humanity, brought the Second World War to a quick close.

I think we are only just beginning to apprehend the extent of the disorienting crisis of consciousness emanating from the discovery that the flow of time varies according to the trajectory of one's relationship with the speed of light. This disorienting revelation introduced a rush of further discoveries, theories, and paradigms that exploded into the twentieth century primarily from the scientific discipline of physics.[17] Many of those on the most extended frontiers of physics have tended to favour theories that emphasize, for instance, curves over straight lines in their explanations of light's trajectory. They have emphasized interpretations highlighting the chaotic relationship among subatomic strings or quantum surges of energy resulting from the convergence of waves as the most elemental components of mass and energy. This way of picturing the relationship of forces in the inner and outer spaces of our shared universe radically overturned Newtonian notions of nature as an orderly construct driven by forces similar to those expressed in the mechanical operation of clocks or in the steady movement of satellites rotating around fixed centres of gravity. In 1951 the Canadian literary critic Marshall McLuhan sought to set the revelations from physics in the broader context of intellectual and cultural movements. In his musings on "the folklore of industrial man," he observed:

Discontinuity is in different ways a basic concept of quantum and relativity physics. It is the way in which a Toynbee looks at civilization, or a Margaret Mead at human cultures. Notoriously, it is the visual technique of Picasso, or the literary technique of James Joyce ... Quantum and relativity physics is not a fad. They have provided new facts about the world, new intelligibility, new insights into the universal fabric. Practically speaking, they mean henceforth this planet is a single city.[18]

In this fashion McLuhan introduced his vision of the entire Earth as a global village. His analysis of the ascendance of electronic communications confirmed the view that the expanding domain of relativity challenged the dominance of many linear ways of thinking. McLuhan associated many older forms of linearity, such as the predominant method of surveying and apportioning square plots of private property, with the pre-eminence of print media before the advent of the telegraph and the telephone. If even the medium of time was not a constant, as Einstein and others postulated, what other aspects of lived experience would end up being revealed as more illusionary than real, more relative than absolute? The revelation that time and space were elastic rather than fixed encouraged the view that there was no such thing as absolute objectivity, no privileged vantage point, and no single trajectory of historical transformation offering superior access to truth, purpose, and meaning.[19] As illustrated, for instance, by the cubist art of Pablo Picasso and Georges Braque, postmodernism flowed naturally from relativism to express the notion that a variety of perspectives could simultaneously be embraced and presented, each one being indistinguishably close to, or far from, the truth. Indeed, as the age of relativity informed liberal pluralism, it seemed increasingly that the ability to discern truth depended on one's ability to consider a wide range of viewpoints, to look concurrently at people, things, events, issues, and concepts from a diverse array of perspectives.

By taking the position that no one group or individual, no one tradition or religion, no single institute or regime, no sole ideology or school could assert a valid monopoly on legitimacy, advocates of cultural relativism and postmodernism renewed the Enlightenment's heritage of anti-authoritarianism. They cast doubt on the status of many establishments, oligarchies and sites of entrenched power. This anti-authoritarian streak uniting relativism's adherents was inherent in the movement from its inception. As Lewis S. Feuer has argued in his study of the importance of the intellectual and social milieu in the Zurich-Berne region in helping to spur Einstein to challenge scientific orthodoxy, "the word 'relativity' [became] the emotive symbol of those in rebellion against the absolutes of the establishment in all fields."[20] Relativism's rapid infusion into society's myriad media of thought, attitude, and action increased resistance to many sites of established power, even those that had originally been thrown up from the revolutionary idealism and egalitarian rhetoric of the Century of Enlightenment. Among the most prominent of the institutions rooted in the revolutionary energy of the Enlightenment is the US government, whose federal sovereignty set the legal, commercial, and political stage for the rise of most of the world's largest transnational corporations. Indeed, the oligarchies that came to dominate the highest echelons of wealth and prestige in the military-industrial complex of the United States came to embody for many a close approximation of the same kind of unaccountable ruling class whose ostentatious privileges helped generate such revolutionary fervour in the eighteenth century.

At its outlying extremes, relativism sometimes gave way to the corrosive view that all knowledge is completely subjective and, ultimately, nothing more than an artificial and self-serving construct to maintain relationships of power.[21] This outlook was often accompanied by the slide from egotism to narcissism to outright nihilism. On the opposite extreme was the reactionary rejection of relativism and postmodernism to the point where this viewpoint sometimes merged into various forms of fundamentalist fanaticism. A common charge levelled at their opponents by more secular-minded fundamentalists was that, in advocating policies such as those affirming Aboriginal rights and official multiculturalism, relativists had turned away from the Enlightenment's quest to apply human reason to the identification and application of universal principles unifying all nature, including human nature. The charge that the resort to relativism represented an abandonment of the Enlightenment's most compelling assertions of universalism could be met with the claim that precisely the opposite had taken place. It was adherence to the best traditions of Enlightenment science that led Einstein and those who followed in his theoretical footsteps to postulate that the rate of time's passage varied according to one's speed of movement across the universe. Similarly, the embrace of moderate forms of cultural relativism can be seen to represent not a denial of the Enlightenment's emphasis on universal laws and equal human rights but, rather, an affirmation of those ideals. A more multicultural orientation to history and society, it could be argued, is better attuned to science's most significant revelations in the twentieth century, a period when humanity began to grapple with a radically altered picture of what is fixed and what is variable in the makeup of the universe. From the theory of relativity, it flowed that the cultural diversity of humanity, as expressed, for instance, in a vast array of unique relationships to the passage of time, was perfectly consistent with the findings of physics on its most advanced frontiers.

Of all the sites of conflict that littered the twentieth century with obscene arrays of killing fields and mass graves, none was so contested as the struggle to claim and control the prestige of science. Communists, socialists, capitalists, fascists – even anarchists – each advanced their utopian vision in scientific terms, in the terminology of "natural law." Even those opposed to the global monopoly of any one system of economic, political, or social organization could call upon the observations of science to argue that diversity and pluralism are consistently the hallmark of healthy ecological communities, including those that incorporate human beings.[22] For advocates of the principle that pluralism itself is one of the highest of all social goods, the heritage of science belongs to no single tradition of human evolution, no single stream of civilization. The heritage of science – the heritage of the application of human reason to identify and apply truth – is one that flows sporadically, and with varying degrees of intensity, through many branches of the human family, through countless traditions of culture, religion, and philosophy.

The transition from the imperial coherence of the Victorian era to the extreme militarism and economic pandemonium of the first half of the twentieth century was signalled by one seemingly isolated event. In retrospect, the loss of the *Titanic*, the world's largest and most advanced passenger ship, can be seen to announce the sinking viability of many tenets and assumptions supporting a tenuous world order. This system of global relations was based on the dubious claims of formal empire and on the obsolete view of the universe as a well-oiled machine displaying all the predictable attributes of a clock. The *Titanic* had been introduced with great fanfare in 1912 as a marvel of transoceanic transport. It seemed initially to encapsulate in a single industrial product the converging power of advanced technology, economies of scale, and high finance in the evolving culture of global capitalism.[23] As its name implies, the *Titanic* embodied in its own time many of the same symbols of manufactured gigantism and commercial triumphalism that the World Trade Center embodied in the era when the Twin Towers dominated New York's skyline. Similarly, the destruction of both, one in a collision with an iceberg and the other through an intricately coordinated act of premeditated sabotage, marked the onset of periods of rapid change and disequilibrium in the global community. The news that one of the greatest miracles of modern industrial production lay at the bottom of the north Atlantic was a spectacular story that helped feed the rise of the global media of mass communications.[24] Among the victims of the tragedy were members of some of the richest and most prominent families in the transatlantic world. The dead included the heir of the New York fur-trade, hotel, and real-estate magnate John Jacob Astor. Like the fall of New York's towering landmarks in the crash of September 11, 2001, the loss of the *Titanic* served unmistakable notice of the deep problems clouding the judgment of those charged to steer a safe passage of progress through the dangerous obstacles on globalization's most advanced frontiers.

The *Titanic* sunk on its maiden voyage as the ship's captain, Edward Smith, sought to squeeze the conquest of more space into less time by setting a record for a transatlantic crossing. The urge to pack more and more speed, acceleration, and productivity into shrinking packages of time would become one of the twentieth century's most characteristic obsessions. One of the most celebrated venues of this phenomenon was the Olympic Games, an ancient Greek sporting competition that was revived in 1896. As an international spectacle celebrating athletic achievement, the Olympics would prove to be a powerful venue and stimulant of globalization. Under the opportunistic auspices of the International Olympic Committee, the games would come to epitomize in sport the same unrelenting conquest of time, space, and efficiency that drove business activity on the most extended frontiers of commercialization. At the Stockholm Olympics in 1912, experiments were made with photographic-electric timers capable of clocking the passage of time in tenths of seconds. In the Paris Olympics of 1924 this same technology was refined to divide the second into a hundred parts.[25] The transformation of the Olympics from a spectacle of amateur athletics into a giant commercial for capitalism and corporate benevolence represented a gross misappropriation of the heritage of ancient Greece. It embodied the theft of an element of Aboriginal culture as blatant as Lord Elgin's infamous transfer of intricately carved sections of Athena's Parthenon Temple to the British Museum in the early nineteenth century. The sale of the Parthenon's sculpted treasures to Lord Elgin by officials of the Ottoman Empire signalled a telling trend in the culture of imperial rule. This pattern would see the rich material heritage of thousands of Aboriginal societies throughout the world frequently reduced to museum trophies, prizes, and artifacts symbolizing the ability of empires and superpowers to colonize the time, space, and artistry of subject peoples.

The increased precision in time's measurement at the Olympic games was part of a vast complex of transformations made possible by the expanding dissemination of AC electricity throughout growing portions of the Earth. The wide dissemination of AC electric power contributed dramatically to the changing pace, reach, and illuminated quality of human interaction. As James Gleick illustrates in *Faster*, electrical power helped advance "the acceleration of just about everything."[26] The changing relationship of most human beings to time and space has been influenced especially by the rapid transformation of money into yet another form of digital information amenable to instantaneous transmission on the Internet. Significantly, the digitalization of the world's money supply primarily in the 1980s and 1990s occurred just as the new orthodoxy of deregulation left businesses more and more free to conduct their transactions directly without the intervention of government. Hence the changing operations of markets in stocks, bonds, currencies, commodity futures, and such were part of more pervasive processes in the way that whole complexes of community, transaction, and jurisdiction were reconfigured along the silicon interchanges of the information highway.

Within the dominant motifs of capitalist political economy, stock markets and currency markets are by far the most volatile and influential centers of commercial activity. Stock markets are the venues where the prices of publicly traded shares in commercial corporations are determined in rushes of electrified business deals testing relationships of supply and demand. When demand for shares rises, so does the purchase price. The dissemination of news about inventions, patents, litigation, and the like can radically alter the market value of shares. When the market value of stocks fluctuates wildly, the commercial worth of strategic information about corporate conditions can change on a second-by-second basis. The same is true of strategic information about whole countries in venues where national currencies are bought and sold. Hence it can be said that stock markets and currency markets are, in a way, exchanges where the most valuable commodity is, ultimately, information. The changing value of certain kinds of commercial knowledge accelerates as networks of computer communications become faster, cheaper, and more extensive.[27] This acceleration in the movement of commercial information is being matched by acceleration in the movement of money itself. According to William Greider, at the end of the twentieth century the entire volume of publicly traded financial assets, or about $24 trillion, turned over every twenty-four days.[28]

As digital interactivity squeezes more and more transactions into less and less time, measurements of duration must keep pace. At one point, for instance, the rapid operations of new computing devices necessitated the division of the single second into a billion nanoseconds. From there the scientific division of time extended to femtoseconds and beyond. A femtosecond describes the unit resulting from the fragmentation of one billionth of a second into a million parts. The changing configurations of time and space on the moving frontiers of computerization and digitalization suggest that the most advanced media of globalization work in ways that are consistent with the theory of relativity. Time and space are apparently compressed and bent by networks of digital interaction that create new kinds of cyberspace community based on commonalities of interest, knowledge, professional association, and taste. From markets in stocks to chat groups, entertainment, research forums, and Google Earth, the Internet keeps expanding to incorporate expanding arrays of information, features, perspectives, systems, and networks. These processes transcend spatial divides to channel human perceptions into intimate webs of communicative interactivity that extend even to the expression of sexual urges. The sinews of digital connection linking the nervous systems of whole networks of wired humanity are suggestive of a new era of biological evolution, the onset of an unprecedented time in the natural history of our species. The most basic questions about what it means to be a human being are inescapably posed by the extension of our mental functions through the finger tip control of websurfing icons directed to create web content and to explore one another's cyberspace personalities as well as selected portions of the world's vast digital archives. At what point do virtual worlds and the "real world" merge? Access to the Internet can expand horizons of understanding even as it can also heighten prejudice and parochialism through blinkered contact with closed cybercommunities devoted to self-reinforcement.

On frontiers between real and virtual environments we struggle to maintain a sense of our place in a universe poised between the frequency of femtoseconds and the duration of eons whose measurement has long been the subject of particularly inspired interpretation by Mayan cosmologists. Like other astrologers of old, these masters in the merger of myth and science studied the complex of relationships between life's internal cycles and the cyclical orbits of the celestial bodies. They studied the transformative power of stars, seeds, and seasons, moods, moons, and memories on the transformative frontiers of time, space, and human perception.

AUTOMATION, COMMUNICATIONS, ATOMIC GLOBALIZATION, AND THE COLD WAR

In Detroit, Michigan, the famous car company of Henry Ford epitomized the optimization of productivity in the industrial sphere. The quick rise of Ford's business enterprise in the early twentieth century made it one of the most powerful embodiments of the emergent corporate culture that rendered the United States as capitalism's busiest laboratory in the decades following Chicago's Columbian Exposition. The system for manufacturing Ford's automobiles represented a full application of the time and motion studies described in 1911 by Frederick W. Taylor in his seminal text, *The Principles of Scientific Management*. As a result of his strides in increasing the productive efficiency of workers by harnessing their actions to repetitive cycles in the operation of Ford's mechanized assembly lines, thousands and then millions of relatively cheap, mass-produced automobiles moved from the factory to the market to the open road.[29] Ford's career is emblematic of an important stage in the revolution in commerce and communications that energized the rise of the American empire in the ongoing course of globalization. In applying Taylor's theories on a massive scale, Ford's name became synonymous with the means of industrial replication known as Fordism. In bringing the methodology of the assembly line to high levels of industrial efficiency and productivity, Ford's automobile company became the great prototype for a new type of manufacturing platform. From the operations of his suppliers at the open-pit iron mines in the Mesabi Range of Minnesota to the incessant experimentation at his sprawling factories on the Rouge River in Detroit, Ford's push to accelerate the pace of the Industrial Revolution pointed the way to vast extensions in the reach and pace of Earth's transformation into property.

Like the proliferation of train and airplane travel, the rapid infusion of both automobiles and automation into widening spheres of human interaction added enormous new forces to patterns of production, consumption, and transportation. Automation dramatically changed the rhythm, quality, and form of many environments. Whole landscapes of mind and matter were radically transformed. The expanding empire of the assembly line and the internal combustion engine accelerated the synchronization of human activity with the clocklike motion of engines. David S. Landes has succinctly described the essence of the industrial methodology pioneered on a gigantic scale by the Ford Motor Company. The US-led trend in technological replication and development consisted, he observed, "in the production of assembled objects from machine-made, standardized, interchangeable parts."[30] The replication of goods on an assembly line can be seen as a prototype for the legal and material reproduction of commercial corporations on a multinational basis. Accordingly, just as the full industrial potential of channeling scientific management into industrial production was first realized in the United States, so too did Ford's country provide the initial platform for the creation of standardized interchangeable business prototypes to be replicated and exported as multinational corporations.

As attested by the quick rise to commercial pre-eminence of John D. Rockefeller's oil empire, this fast proliferation of gas-powered vehicles quickly made the extraction, refinement, and distribution of fossil fuels a central fixture of the global economy.[31] The culture of the automobile changed forever the rate and quality of human interaction across many transformed landscapes of city, town, and country. The massive increase in personal mobility of those with access to cars introduced a dramatic new element in the revolution in communications that has been the great unifying theme of globalization since 1492. While the culture of automobiles helped integrate those societies where these vehicles were widely available, the car would emerge in the twenty-first century as a potent symbol of the division between the beneficiaries of imperial globalization and the poorer majority of humanity. The tensions of this division grew as it became increasingly apparent that Earth's atmosphere would be rendered inhospitable to many species, including humanity, if the gas-guzzling mobility of North American and European car owners was replicated in the economically ascendant regions of Asia.

Henry Ford's industrial breakthroughs in the corporate world provided him with a formidable base of wealth, organization, and prestige from which to project his ideas and will into the most contentious political struggles of the twentieth century. A determined opponent of the burgeoning trade-union movement, Ford achieved huge public fame in 1914 when he moved proactively to check the inroads among his assembly-line staff of radical labour organizations such as the Industrial Workers of the World. He fended off the trade unions by voluntarily doubling the pay of even his most junior employees to a minimum of five dollars a day.[32] He reasoned that, by compensating his workers at this level, they would then be in a position to purchase their own Model Ts – the basic and functional car that will always be remembered as the prototype of mass-produced transportation.

Ford's decision to pay his workers relatively well represented the brighter side of his ideology. As will be discussed in more detail in chapter 5, the darker side of Ford's politics was reflected in his instrumental role as a key ideological supporter, backer, and inspiration figure who infused his great influence into the seminal beginnings of the Nazi movement in Germany.[33] Ford's connections with the young Adolf Hitler can be seen as a direct extension of the Detroit industrialist's deeply held hostility to left-wing trade unionism. Like Hitler, Ford saw in the Bolshevists' takeover of state power in Russia a key element in a vast Jewish conspiracy. The protagonists of this conspiracy, both Ford and Hitler imagined, sought to inspire, finance, and exploit communist internationalism as a means of undermining Germany and dominating the world. As it turned out, Ford would have much company among leading US capitalists in his decision to offer support for the right-wing corporatism ushered into power first in Benito Mussolini's Italy and then in Hitler's Germany. European fascism, which offered ideological justification for the lodging of corporate governance into the most important mechanisms for the direction of national governance, seemingly afforded a shield and an alternative to communist internationalism. In 1938 William Dodd, then US ambassador to Germany, expressed his alarm at fascism's popularity among many of the richest members of US society. He observed, "Fascism is on the march today in America. Millionaires are marching to its tune. It will come in this country unless a strong defense is set up by all liberal and progressive forces ... A clique of U.S. industrialists is hell-bent to bring a fascist state to supplant our democratic government, and is working closely with the fascist regime in Germany and Italy."[34]

The need for a bastion of anti-communist, anti-socialist activism in Central Europe was felt especially strongly by many business elites on both sides of the Atlantic during the years of the Great Depression. The 1930s were a time when the future prospects of capitalism seemed menaced by rapid deterioration in the viability of open markets, prompting millions of marginalized and unemployed workers to explore the possibilities of alternative forms of political economy. In seeking to counter the enticements of socialism, Hitler was driven to co-opt its language with his promotion of the National Socialist German Workers Party. The organization's name betrayed its real nature, which was to give a broad array of non-Jewish capitalists a similar kind of union of shared protections, organization, and incentives to those that Karl Marx had so compellingly claimed decades earlier for the world's workers. Hitler's co-optation of socialist language and methods to advance the capitalist integration of business enterprise into the directing mechanisms of the Nazi state drew on Bismarck's earlier embrace of limited forms of social security as an expedient to broaden the popular appeal of a heavily militarized regime of German unification.

One of those caught up in this clash of ideologies was Henry H. Luce. He applied some of Ford's techniques in the making of automobiles to the reporting, replication, and sale of news as an item of mass production and consumption.[35] Luce, like Ford, was instrumental in realizing many of the business opportunities presented by the ongoing revolution in the technologies of communications, transformations epitomized by linking the information flows of whole continents through the laying of transoceanic cables.[36] This revolution, one based on the attainment of ever quicker and more efficient means of travel and dissemination of information, made trains, cars, airplanes, magazines, telephones, and other electronic media the vehicles of dramatically altered geographies of human interaction with space, time, and each other. In naming his new publication *Time*, the magazine's twenty-three-year-old founder staked a strategic claim to contested turf in the developing culture wars between relativism and absolutism, decolonization and imperial rule, liberalism and fundamentalism. Founded in 1923, *Time* explained world events in easily digestible bites of concentrated information. The new magazine was quickly incorporated into the busy schedules of millions of readers who collectively fell under the persuasive power of Luce's growing media empire, one that added *Fortune Magazine* in 1930, *Life Magazine* in 1936, and *Sports Illustrated* in 1954. In the mid-1930s the orientation of Luce's emerging media empire was decidedly hostile to President Franklin Roosevelt's left-leaning New Deal and friendly to the right-wing corporatism of the Italian dictator. Mussolini was featured five times on *Time*'s cover. In July 1934, when a special full edition of *Fortune* was devoted to coverage of Mussolini's regime, Laird Goldsborough wrote: "The good journalist must recognize in Fascism certain ancient virtues of race ... among these are Discipline, Duty, Courage, Glory, and Sacrifice."[37]

In expanding the communications industry's capacity to disseminate and popularize ideas and styles, Luce built on the techniques developed by earlier generations of press barons, including the most influential propagandist of the Spanish American War, William Randolph Hearst.[38] Indeed, Luce helped extend the commercial, cultural, and political influence of the United States along the same trajectory of commercial innovation pioneered earlier by John Jacob Astor in the fur trade and Henry Ford in the car trade. Astor, Ford, and Luce, in turn, stood on the shoulders of others whose earlier actions helped to widen the field and accelerate the pace of human interaction across time and space. Prominent among the most aggressive protagonists in the creation and consolidation of Eurocentric networks of global communications were Columbus, Magellan, Drake, the missionaries of the Jesuit Order, and the makers of the Dutch and British East India companies. These and many other frontiersmen of imperial expansion helped set in motion cycles of religiously and commercially driven globalization that prepared the ground for the emergence of the United States as the world's most influential agency of capitalist expansion, as the foremost inventor of weapons and consumer items, culture and ideas.[39]

Like many of Anglo-America's financial elites, Luce had been supportive of the rise of Italian and Germany fascism, but especially the former.
He sanctioned this trend as long as these experiments seemed to provide
capitalism with a shield against the spread of socialist internationalism, or
even the mild, liberal derivative of it as applied in the United States in the
name of President Roosevelt's New Deal. For some of those at the towering
heights of the US economy, Nazi devices for revving up capitalism after the
commercial debacle of 1929 seemed highly preferable to the regulatory
and democratizing thrust of the *Securities Exchange Act* of 1934 or the *Social
Security Act* of 1935.[40] The onset and early course of the Second World War,
however, began to change the landscape of opinions and practical politics.
In 1941, ten months before Japan's attack on Pearl Harbor, Luce came out
strongly for war against the Axis powers. His vision of the future, however,
remained at odds with that of the New Deal liberalism that had dominated
the executive branch of the US government for almost a decade.

In explaining his position, Luce introduced a phrase that would resonate
strongly in his own time and beyond, as, for instance, in the establishment
in Washington in the 1990s of the Project for the New American Century. In
a much reproduced editorial in *Life*, he argued in 1941 that the world was
already embarked on "the American Century," one that the United States
would come to dominate and shape to its own specifications. He celebrated
his conviction that United States was about to emerge as the Earth's dominant polity, as the heir of the Roman Empire, the Roman Catholic Church,
Genghis Kahn, the Ottoman Turks, the Chinese emperors, and the British
Empire. In terms that harkened back to an editorial in 1935 when *Time* had
praised Mussolini's invasion of Ethiopia as part of the "civilizing mission,"[41]
Luce encouraged his fellow Americans to join in the imperial tradition of
human history. He implored his readers "to accept wholeheartedly our duty
and our opportunity as the most powerful and vital nation in the world and
in consequence to exert upon the world the full impact of our influence,
for such purposes as we see fit and by such means as we see fit."[42]

Almost immediately, some sceptics pointed out that Luce's glorification
of the American Century seemed like a return to the national evangelism
of Manifest Destiny.[43] Theologist Reinhold Niebuhr called Luce's concept
"messianic."[44] The vice-president of the United States, Henry Wallace,
countered the publisher's call to global domination with a more egalitarian vision of the future, one that sought to extend the liberalism of the
New Deal to the international community. In hitting back at the power of
a media empire that had frequently sought to turn public opinion against
the liberal innovations of his administration, Wallace invited the American
people to mobilize militarily to bring about "the Century of the Common
Man." He called on the US citizenry to overwhelm the "slave world" of the
Axis powers with the force of the "free world." He posed this challenge
within the framework of a "Great Revolution" of the people, a continuing revolution extending from the American Revolution to the French

Revolution to the Latin American revolutions of the early 1800s, to the German revolution of 1848 and the Russian Revolution of 1917. In the world of the future, asserted Wallace, "no nation will have the God-given right to exploit other nations ... We ourselves in the United States are no more a master race than Nazis."[45]

The United States emerged from the Second World War as its most handsomely rewarded victor. One of its great prizes was control over the huge energy resources of the Arabian Peninsula. A consortium of US oil companies dominated the exploitation of this massive pool of oil once the US government agreed in 1945 to back militarily the compliant Wahabi clans whose interests were attached to the royal claims of Ibn Saud. State Department officials oozed about this oil reserve, characterizing it as "a stupendous source of strategic power, and one of the greatest material prizes in world history."[46] The Second World War can be seen as the culmination of several centuries of militarized acrimony between Europe's core polities.[47] These antagonisms among European empire builders began as dynastic and religious conflicts. Over time the politics of European wars acquired more complex economic, ideological, and ethnic features. The evolution of this heritage of military conflict changed instantly in August 1945 as news flashed around the world that the United States had detonated two atomic bombs over Hiroshima and Nagasaki in Japan. The horrendous destructive power of these devices forced on all peoples and nations a recognition that the complex abstractions surrounding Einstein's theories went far beyond mere speculation. After the instant incineration of hundreds of thousands of Japanese civilians in these two cities, the almost unfathomable intensity of atomic energy, multiplying mass by the speed of light squared, burst into global consciousness. This way of demonstrating the unprecedented power of the United States' new technology of mass destruction shook to their very foundations all institutions for the governance of human beings.[48] Many old configurations of power simply evaporated in light of the knowledge that a single polity had acquired such massive capacity to make life and death decisions affecting the destiny of all living beings on the planet.

What drove the US government not only to make atomic bombs but then to explode these lethal devices over the heads of dense urban populations? That fateful decision belonged ultimately to President Harry S. Truman, who had replaced President Roosevelt in April 1945 only weeks after the originator of the New Deal began his fourth term of high office. A compelling case can be made that Truman opted to destroy Hiroshima and Nagasaki primarily to demonstrate to the Soviet Union his government's determination to contain the revolutionary challenge of communist internationalism.[49] By ending the war with Japan in this way, the world received a very clear signal that Henry Luce's vision of the American Century would probably prevail over Henry Wallace's prediction that the Century of the Common Man lay just ahead. By annihilating a large civilian population with a new entirely new form of weaponry, Truman left little doubt about the determination of his government to assert the pre-eminent legacy in the global community of the American Revolution of 1776 over that of the Russian Revolution of 1917. Truman acted to direct the power of his government in the effort to maintain and advance the worldwide dominance of Western civilization under the military, commercial, and cultural leadership of his own country. Accordingly, the closing act of the Second World War can also be understood as the informal opening of the Cold War, even if its more formal beginning waited the enactment of the *National Security Act* in 1947.

Not since the modern era of globalization began in 1492 has there been any event that even remotely compared with the dawning of the age of atomic weaponry in terms of illustrating the intertwined destiny and interdependence of all human beings, and, indeed, all life on the planet. As President John F. Kennedy observed of the change in world order following the introduction of nuclear weaponry: "Today, every inhabitant of this planet must contemplate the day when this planet may no longer be habitable." He added: "Every man, woman and child lives under a nuclear sword of Damocles, hanging by the slenderest of threads, capable of being cut at any moment by accident or miscalculation or madness."[50] The prospect of an end to birth through universal death produced a profoundly altered condition in a global milieu pregnant with possibility as well as danger. It helped to bring more clearly into focus the necessity of forging the bonds of global security in an inclusive, worldwide polity sufficiently strong to subordinate all instruments of mass extermination beneath the democratic authority of a planetary rule of law.

Only gradually has the idea and imagery developed of a comprehensive system of global governance that would encompass both the diversity and the common attributes of all humanity. With recollections of its roots in the Roman Empire never absent from its institutional memory, the Roman Catholic Church long pictured itself as a polity of universal applicability whose destiny was eventually to integrate all branches of the human family under its theocratic wing. Indeed, in conceiving of a single God, a universal God reigning over all of heaven and Earth, the Abrahamic traditions – Judiasm, Christianity, and Islam – all advanced a form of global imagination. With a particular focus on the relationship of Indigenous peoples of the Western Hemisphere to the claims of his religion, theologians such as Father Francisco de Vitoria pictured a law of nations governing relations among all the planet's peoples. Starting with his quest for a legal code covering war and commerce on the high seas, Grotius contributed some of the essential abstractions that gave theoretical form to the field of international law. In the final years of the eighteenth century, Immanuel Kant identified "a universal civic society" as "the highest problem Nature assigns to the human race."[51] With *The Communist Manifesto* and *Das Kapital*, Karl Marx came up with his vision of a global alternative to the transnational reach and reign of high finance. Marx imagined a planet where a worldwide coalition of revolutionary workers would unite across state boundaries to usher in a new era of proletarian internationalism. This vision was advanced and elaborated by V.I. Lenin. On the eve of the creation of the Soviet Union, Lenin penned his commentary on *Imperialism as the Highest Stage of Capitalism.* President Woodrow Wilson responded to this challenge by advancing his own liberal vision of an inclusive world parliament to replace imperial rule. His vision gave rise to the League of Nations, a body the United States did not join.

After the Second World War, the founders of the United Nations attempted to realize many of the same ideals and principles of international law that animated the establishment of the League of Nations. In 1941 the state Senate in North Carolina anticipated the UN's founding by resolving: "It is better for the world to be ruled by an international sovereignty of reason, social justice, and peace than by diverse national sovereignties incapable of preventing their own dissolution by conquest."[52]At least one academic looked to the Aboriginal history of North America rather than the history of Europe as the main root source of the idea of universal law as espoused by some proponents of the UN. In *The White Roots of Peace,* Paul A.W. Wallace presented in 1946 a narrative of the founding of the Longhouse League. His text advanced Longhouse principles affirming the principle that human conduct as well as relations among nations must be governed by law rather than the coercive power of brute force. Like the founders of the Five Nations in what is now upper New York State, Wallace pictured the establishment in about 1450 of the Great Law animating North America's most celebrated Aboriginal confederacy as the beginning of a new era of enlightenment in the governance of all the world's peoples. He viewed the creation of the United Nations as the realization on a global scale of the principles of democratic unity in diversity that first inspired the warring five nations to bury their hatchets under the white roots of peace. The roots supporting the Great White Pine at Onondaga had the potential to grow to the four corners of the earth.[53] The idea of picturing the UN as an outgrowth of an old constitution indigenous to Aboriginal America points to the fact that no single tradition of culture, philosophy, or law can claim a monopoly on the idea of globalization and the universalization of human rights and responsibilities. There are many antecedents and roots to the notion that all humanity has the potential to form one collective polity with the entire planet as its domain. In such a world, the ultimate sovereignty of legitimate global governance would be derived from the democratic will of all the Earth's people and peoples.

The sudden onset of the age of atomic and nuclear weaponry injected a more intense sense of urgency into the old quest for a global rule of law. The prospect of universal annihilation helped underscore the possibilities inherent in affirmations of the universal attributes and requirements of healthy life. The destruction of Hiroshima and Nagasaki in 1945 gave humanity an enormous new incentive to unite in adhesion to the impera-

tives of life over the doom of mass extinction; to advance the ideals, for
instance, of a universal social safety net providing all humanity with at least
some access to health care, housing, and education as well as to freedom
from tyranny, genocide, starvation, and environmental degradation. While
the imagery of proliferating mushroom clouds had the ironic effect of helping to galvanize many constructive social forces, however, the bipolar division of humanity in the Cold War quickly blocked the way to any massive
convergence of global political will aimed at prohibiting militarism as a
means of aggrandizing the power of states and elites. Indeed, in the view
of some, the Cold War was largely engineered precisely to pre-empt the
possibilities of a new egalitarianism emerging from a more united global
community after the debacle of the Second World War. Whatever their personal and collective motivations for doing so, Cold Warriors on both sides
set to work to avert the threat of peace by mobilizing their own populations
through the wholesale manipulation of fear. Both sides hosted the development of concerted propaganda campaigns that elevated the arts and
sciences of psychological warfare to new heights of manipulative sophistication.[54] On the US side, the psychological warfare of the Cold War helped
to obscure the growing tensions between capitalism, with its propensity to
produce huge economic inequities, and liberalism, with its emphasis on the
equal worth, dignity, and rights adhering to every human life.

Throughout the Cold War, the United States publicly countered the policies of Moscow and Beijing by disseminating an image of its own revolutionary heritage as history's natural counterpoint and alternative to communist
internationalism. In the psychological warfare of that period, the United
States drew on the strength of its revolutionary background as the world's
first example of successful decolonization and as the planet's most dynamic
illustration of capitalism's huge capacity to combine Earth's elements with
investment, technology, and work in the generation of material abundance.
Especially between 1947 and 1989, when the Cold War dominated nearly
every aspect of global geopolitics, the appeal of the American way of life
depended heavily on communications strategies that equated the mythology of liberal capitalism with the aura of democratic rule in the Western
Hemisphere's first republic. "America from its beginning," wrote Arthur
M. Schlesinger Jr in 1949 in his manifesto of liberal anti-communism, "has
charted its history and its politics by the morning star of equality." [55]

The Cold War elevated to prominence for almost half a century the
iconography of a polarized struggle between two different yet profoundly
materialistic visions of how to organize humanity's political economy.[56] The
ideological warfare posed capitalist mythology against communist mythology, Marxist utopianism against the utopian idealization of market relations,
state-centred models of collectivization against corporate-centred models
of privatization. Even before public opinion turned against the US military
role in Vietnam, however, some argued that the optics of an all-encompassing rivalry between two superpowers, between two opposed systems of

political economy, was cynically manipulated to disguise the real interests being served by the imposition of a single false dichotomy on the human family's rich and complex diversity. In the view of Harry Elmer Barnes, C. Wright Mills, Arthur A. Ekirch, Mumford Jones, I.F. Stone, D.F. Fleming, Edmund Wilson, William Appleman Williams, A.J.P. Taylor, David Horowitz, Arnold Toynbee, Sidney Lens, Gore Vidal, and many others, the Cold War was set in motion primarily as an expedient to continue the commercial stimulus of the American war economy, to entrench the internal dominance of certain elites, and to give cover to a worldwide campaign aimed at widening and advancing the global interests of US business.[57] William Appleman Williams, a professor at the Madison history school pioneered by Reuben Gold Thwaites and Frederick Jackson Turner, was prominent among this group of revisionists. He extended Turner's frontier thesis into a diplomatic history of American empire. As Williams saw it, the transcontinental expansion of the United States formed the essential background in the continuing global drive to manipulate China and many other polities to maintain an open door of business relations with US enterprise. The Cold War embodied the most recent expression of this unbroken thrust of US policy.[58] As Senator Arthur Vandenburg advised President Harry Truman in 1947, once the decision had been made to maintain the United States on the footing of a permanent war economy, even though no other power even remotely approached its military and economic strength, "You had better learn to scare the hell out of the American people."[59]

"The detailed records ... show perhaps almost too emphatically," argued British historian A.J. P. Taylor in 1966, "that the Cold War was deliberately started by Truman and his advisers."[60] "An enemy had to be created," alleged Gore Vidal. "The dictator Stalin fit the bill. So did atheistic and godless communism as a rival religion."[61] According to Barnes, this "phony" and "synthetic" showdown with the Soviet Union and its satellites was engineered in a way that gave the Pentagon and its contractors in the United States a position of prestige greater than that ever enjoyed by the Prussian militarists in imperial Germany. The Cold War, Barnes asserted, justified "any amount of control over political and economic life, the most extensive invasion of civil liberties, the most extreme witch-hunting, and the most lavish expenditures."[62]

In the name of a global crusade to defeat communism, the US government actively intervened in the domestic politics of virtually every other country. The goal of these overt and covert interventions was to establish and assist client regimes whose leaders would sanction the establishment of US military bases and facilitate the transnational business operations of a favoured set of mostly US-based companies.[63] These interventions sometimes involved the US instigation of violent coups such as those in Iran, Guatemala, Congo, Chile, Indonesia, and other countries.[64] In the course of these operations, those most committed to US ascendancy were prone to label and counter as communist virtually every prominent proponent of the principle that natural resources should be used primarily to benefit Indigenous peoples, local institutions, and the collective ideals of national self-determination. In the waning days of European empires, therefore, the United States set itself fairly consistently in opposition to the power of most indigenous liberation struggles originating in convictions that had little to do with a conflict between economic abstractions championed by Adam Smith and Karl Marx. Historian Arnold J. Toynbee has underlined this point, arguing that the desire of Indigenous peoples to regain control over themselves, their territories, and their institutions was "a force stronger than either communism or capitalism." He saw it as a force emanating from "the majority of mankind's determination to recover equality with the Western minority."[65]

As Harry Barnes saw it, the propagandistic emphasis of the US government on its own history of revolutionary decolonization belied the reality of its aggressive moves to fill the vacuum of power created by the dismantling of old European empires after the Second World War.[66] The identification of the United States with the imperial heritage of its colonial predecessors and antecedents tended to bolster the image of the Soviet Union and Communist China as more sympathetic friends of the Fourth World movement to liberate the Indigenous peoples from the oppressions of empire and neo-colonialism. In taking over many of the expansionary methods and tactics of Czarist Russia, however, the Soviet Union also displayed imperialist attributes. Indeed, some Soviet strategists sought to replace the colonizing aggressions of the Columbian conquests with their own universalized version of proletarian globalization – their monocultural vision of history's culmination in a worldwide cult of communist conformity.[67] They presented their own secular vision of scientific materialism as the only viable alternative to capitalist materialism, as the only means of opposing the transnational tyranny of unmediated corporate rule.

The effects of the Cold War on the domestic and international politics of the United States were complex and often paradoxical, especially after the Soviet Union gained expanded geopolitical muscle with the acquisition of its own nuclear arsenal. On the one hand, the emphasis on real or imagined agents of internal subversion gave rise to a host of repressive excesses such as those flowing from Senator Joseph McCarthy's notorious witch hunt for communist activists and sympathizers. FBI director J. Edgar Hoover continued the radical traditions of McCarthyism by deploying federal agents to target and undermine the political activism of millions of US citizens who opposed racial segregation or US military involvement in Southeast Asia. The institutionalized antagonisms of the Cold War raised the prestige of the armed forces and its suppliers, contractors, and research scientists. It pushed some of the United States' most zealous anti-communists towards antagonism to virtually all forms of state enterprise except those associated with so-called national defence and national security. It turned such zealots towards the extremes of privatization, towards the goal of maximizing the role of commercial corporations in what Barnes has described as military state capitalism.

This agenda of extreme privatization and corporate deregulation, however, could not be activated immediately because of the checks imposed by the psychological warfare of the Cold War. As a result, the policies of the United States and its friends continued to support a mix of public and private enterprise near the middle of the political spectrum. The pull towards at least some measure of liberal moderation was energized by the international effectiveness of communist propaganda emphasizing the injustices experienced by marginalized minorities, but especially by poor Blacks in the United States. This aspect of the Cold War held especially serious implications for the capitalist superpower's efforts to steer the former colonies of Africa away from collaboration with the Soviet and Chinese spheres of interest, ideology, and politics. In this communist sphere, the makers of the Cuban revolution showed a surprising degree of independence in lending encouragement and strategic support especially to those liberation struggles targeted as enemies of the pro-capitalist, pro-apartheid regimes of South Africa, Rhodesia, and their notorious squadrons of White mercenaries for hire. As Piero Gleijeses observed of the period when, first, Algeria and then the former Belgian Congo were the sites of particularly bitter conflict between warring factions seeking to control the instruments of state power, "American racism was crippling American foreign policy." Gleijes cites the observations of several high-ranking US officials who confirmed that "the relationships you had with many Africans" was directly linked to "a barometric chart of how civil rights were going" in the US domestic realm. Because of the inability of the capitalist superpower to overcome the discriminatory legacy of US slavery, cautioned Dean Rusk in 1963, "Our voice is muted, our friends are embarrassed, our enemies are gleeful."[68]

The US need to counter such Soviet propaganda provided some protection for the fragile legacies of the social welfare state that had been introduced by President Franklin D. Roosevelt. He had applied some elements of social democracy to help save the overarching structures of the market economy from complete breakdown following the stock-market crash of 1929. Roosevelt swept to power in 1933 based on his promise to implement a New Deal geared to correcting the economic cataclysms of the Great Depression.[69] As Schlesinger observed, "the New Dealers [were] the most recent of a number of rescue parties which radicals have launched to save a beleaguered capitalism."[70] In 1936 British economist John Maynard Keynes provided a comprehensive analytic framework for Roosevelt's remedies in his *General Theory of Employment, Interest, and Money*. In that classic text, Keynes laid out a tight intellectual justification for modifying the role of the state in industrial capitalism. He argued that it was legitimate for national governments to run up deficits when economic downturns resulted in unacceptable levels of poverty and unemployment. For Keynes and his growing array of disciples, the state had an important role to play in regulating the pace of economic activity in order to moderate the extremity of capitalism's boom and bust cycles.

During the earlier stages of the Cold War, then, the leadership of the capitalist side of the conflict resisted the temptation to overturn the legacies of the New Deal and Keynsian economics. Because of the global challenge posed by the existence of an alternative world order conceived and organized in outright hostility to capitalism, even the most zealous of the right-wing anti-communists were inclined to moderate their antagonism towards liberalism. They compromised so as to lessen the capacity of communist propagandists to highlight and amplify in their own Cold War communications the huge disparities of wealth and opportunity that naturally arise whenever the law and ethos of capitalist privatization are allowed to run to extremes. The limited and often begrudging acceptance of somewhat liberal economic policies by even the most wealthy American plutocrats tended to translate into support for the type of relativist social and cultural relations espoused by Franz Boas and his students in anthropology. These Boasian policies were sometimes framed in the language of multiculturalism or affirmative action. Accordingly, it would not be until the mid-1980s, when the capitalist superpower moved decisively to eliminate altogether the state agencies of their weaker communist rivals, that the most highly orchestrated phase of the attack began on the whole complex of Keynsian economics and Boasian social policy. The push to retool even the public service functions of government into the profit-making activities of private businesses would epitomize the intensity of the drive to transform the welfare state into the stock-market state. This tendency gathered momentum in the 1990s and in the lead up to the Global War on Terror, when even the functions of waging war and gathering military intelligence were increasingly outsourced to private businesses set up to sell their services to governments and corporations.

Among the most gifted theorists and formulators of Boasian social policy had been Ruth Benedict. She had been a student of Franz Boas and a distinguished member of John Collier's esteemed group of anthropological practitioners who were hired by the federal government to help implement the Native American version of Roosevelt's New Deal. Benedict's *Patterns of Culture*, first published in 1934, would be elevated after the Second World War to the status of a standard university text as social scientists sought to bring an end to the racist application of Charles Darwin's ideas in many branches of the academy. Darwin's theory of evolutionary change through competitive struggle between organisms provided the rationale to justify all manner of hierarchical ordering, such as that expressed in imperialism, racism, and the illiberal version of capitalism generated by hyperprivatization.

During the Second World War, Benedict was recruited to help develop US war propaganda. Her work in both the academy and government celebrated the benevolent role of myth in shaping cultural personality. In her view, the twin dynamos of myth and culture combined to generate and sustain the positive ideal of diversity in the global community. Benedict's positive embrace of humanity's pluralism was deployed to counter the Nazi obsession with the idea of racial conquest as the highest ideal of human achievement and the major determinant of historical change.[71] For Hitler, Aryan and Teutonic mythology provided encouragement to denigrate, enslave, and, sometimes, to exterminate the foreign Other. For Benedict, humanity's rich store of myth and culture offered important keys to answering the conundrum of how to reconcile the exercise of equality with the celebration of difference. Where both thinkers agreed, however, was in their shared recognition of the unparalleled power of mythology to mobilize social and political action.

PROPAGANDA, HYPERPRIVATIZATION, AND THE MILITARY-INDUSTRIAL COMPLEX

In January 1961 as he was leaving the office of president of the United States, Dwight D. Eisenhower publicly pointed to the dangers that the Cold War posed for the quality of government within the United States. He feared that the adoption of a permanent wartime economy after 1945 was pulling his country away from political pluralism towards a new kind of tyranny by concentrating too much power in too few hands. In his retirement speech, this top US general and two-term commander-in-chief warned his compatriots of the monopoly of authority being amassed by "an immense military establishment and a large arms industry." He explained that its "total influence – economic, political, even spiritual – is felt in every city, every statehouse, every office of the federal government." He went farther, cautioning that "public policy could itself become the captive of a scientific-technological elite." This elite worked at the core of a mixture of domineering government departments and profit-making companies that Eisenhower labelled "the military-industrial complex."

In thus describing the amalgam of research scientists, arms manufacturers, energy cartels, media companies, and government employees in the Pentagon and other federal agencies, Eisenhower introduced an evocative phrase into the English language. "The military-industrial complex," the US president warned in one of the most significant speeches of the twentieth century, was a vehicle with a huge "potential for the disastrous rise of misplaced power."[72] When he uttered these words, Eisenhower was in the best possible position to recognize the onset of an insidious form of creeping totalitarianism capable of subverting the checks and balances of the US political system. In spite of the seriousness of this warning from America's most celebrated soldier, however, it was not until the rise of the anti-war movement in the mid-1960s that a significant constituency emerged that rallied to avert the outcome Eisenhower had warned against. That liberal challenge, however, proved short lived. By the end of the twentieth century, any serious opposition to the rising influence of the military-industrial complex had been largely neutralized. Indeed, following the debacle in Vietnam, a well-orchestrated and richly financed series of initiatives was mounted to edify and extend those branches of the military-industrial complex devoted to public indoctrination. The aims of this initiative went far beyond maintaining a high level of public support for massive spending on the US military. Rather, the goal was to turn public opinion against the liberal legacy of the New Deal by actively promoting more absolutist alternatives on the right-wing extremes of the political spectrum.

Federally backed propaganda in the United States goes back at least as far the First World War, when President Woodrow Wilson appointed journalist George Creel in 1917 to head up the US Committee on Public Education.[73] More recent surges of activity to manipulate public opinion have been built on the foundation of the US Central Intelligence Agency's very broad and deep infiltration of the domestic and international mass media to promote anti-communist messages as part of the psychological warfare of the Cold War.[74] The CIA's covert intervention in the workings of the news and information business expanded rapidly to become a central feature of its overall operations. Some elements of the print and broadcast media in many countries, including the United States, were manipulated with varying levels of intensity to serve as vehicles of US-sponsored attempts at thought control. Much of the CIA money earmarked for this purpose was funnelled through the US Information Agency and a front organization known as the Congress for Cultural Freedom. One of the coordinating arms of this work was code-named Project Mockingbird. By the late 1950s the CIA devoted over a third of its budget to media-related operations, with approximately three thousand journalists around the world on its payroll. These journalist /agents both gathered intelligence and planted stories. Sometimes their stories were merely distortions of reality; other times they were based on outright disinformation. The amount spent by the CIA on its media-related activities, about $265 million a year, was greater than the combined expenditures of Reuters, United Press International, and Associated Press. The FBI also developed its own network of collaborating journalists who worked with the federal police force in efforts to smear and discredit those voices of internal dissent that had been targeted by COINTELPRO operatives.

Henry Luce and some of his staff were active participants in building up the US government's elaborate institutions of propaganda and psychological warfare, a facet of statecraft whose importance the Nazis had powerfully demonstrated under the studious direction of Joseph Goebbels. Charles Douglas Jackson, for instance, went from being managing director of Time-Life International in 1945 and then publisher of *Fortune* to work in a variety of Cold War capacities, including as Eisenhower's special assistant for psychological warfare. In 1960 Jackson moved back into the corporate sector of the military-industrial complex as publisher of *Life*. The deployment of the Luce publishing empire to disseminate Cold War propaganda and to gather intelligence throughout the world established patterns that were replicated by other major US media outlets. William Paley of CBS, Arthur Hays Sulzberger of the *New York Times*, and Katherine and Philip Graham of the *Washington Post*, for instance, were deeply involved in the mobilization of the commercial mass media to serve the public indoctrination functions of the military-industrial complex. Indeed, almost every major media organization in the United States was involved in some way in CIA operations. The CIA had agents in ABC, NBC, Reuters, *Newsweek, Reader's Digest*, the *Christian Science Monitor*, Scripps-Howard, *Saturday Evening Post, Miami Herald*, the Mutual Broadcasting System, and Copley News, to name but some.[75]

The subversion of key parts of the mass media to serve the Cold War agenda of the United States was noted by W.E.B. Du Bois, the great social scientist and intellectual guiding light of the civil rights movement throughout much of the twentieth century. In 1958 DuBois observed in the *Monthly Review*: "From the use of psychology to spread truth has come the organized gathering of news to guide public opinion, then deliberately to mislead it by scientific advertising and propaganda ... Mass capitalistic control of books and periodicals, news gathering and distribution, radio, cinema, and television has made the throttling of democracy possible and the distortion of education and failure of justice widespread."[76]

The most influential branches of the US media, therefore, have been deeply integrated into the structure of the military-industrial complex since the United States was placed on the basis of its permanent wartime economy. The limits of the US government's capacity to control public discourse became evident, however, as controversy grew over the military role of the United States in Vietnam. Even among those staffing the news desks of commercial media outlets, deep schisms developed about the appropriate course of US foreign policy in Southeast Asia. The effectiveness of the anti-war movement was bolstered by the many-faceted cultural creativity of what became known as the New Left. The music of social protest, showcased as never before in the summer of 1969 at Woodstock, New York, epitomized both the innovative best and the self-indulgent worst of the youth-driven quest for anti-imperial alternatives to the status quo. At its best, this quest for alternatives was a struggle to express some of the insights of cultural relativism through identification with the liberation struggles of the world's most chronically oppressed populations. The New Left sought to extend the old search for more egalitarian forms of world order by emphasizing the ideal of self-determination as a universal human right cutting across all boundaries of gender, nationality, race, and ethnicity. Some of the movement's members pointed these traditions of struggle towards new frontiers, seeking ecological modes of being that eschewed the imperatives of conquest in human interaction but also in human relations with the rest of nature.

The success of the New Left in challenging the old orthodoxies and absolutes entailed in racial segregation, patriarchy, conspicuous consumption, religious intolerance, and American exceptionalism signalled to the super-power's increasingly embattled elites that they would have to employ their own experts in the arts and science of manipulating public opinion. They would have to go beyond the level of intervention engineered by the CIA and related agencies in the name of the Cold War quest to contain and defeat those deemed unfriendly to US-centered capitalism. They would have to counter the culture and style of the New Left by directly financing the creation of their own networks of think tanks, media outlets, and trend-setting commentators. And they would have to intervene more aggressively in public discourse in order to harness public opinion to the overlapping agendas of the very wealthy, the religious right, corporate libertarians, and the complex networks of interests at home and abroad that benefit most from the central place of the US military-industrial complex in domestic and global relationships of power.

Lewis Lapham has chronicled the history of this privately financed effort to pull US politics rightward, away from even the limited forms of liberal-ism apparently permitted and sometimes even promoted by the CIA in its media-related interventions. He labelled this newer generation of would-be thought police "the Republican propaganda mill," a set of interconnected initiatives aimed at eliminating the legacy of the New Deal and advanc-ing, instead, the agenda first laid before the US public by Senator Barry Goldwater in his failed presidential campaign in 1964. The purpose has been, argues Lapham, to turn public opinion against almost all forms of state enterprise, except its increasingly aggressive control of policing, spy-ing, and military activity, and to expand the frontiers of corporate privatiza-tion through the containment and elimination of as many public domains as possible. Lapham ends on a satiric note: the purpose has been to repeat in as many different contexts as possible the same "abiding lesson ... money ennobles the rich people, making them strong as well as wise; money cor-rupts poor people, making them stupid as well as weak."[77]

The presidency of Ronald Reagan between 1981 and 1989 marked a decisive stage in the move away from liberalism in the United States. Reagan's initiatives duplicated and advanced many of the policies intro-duced by Margaret Thatcher, prime minister of the United Kingdom from 1979 to 1990. Like the alliance between Franklin Roosevelt and Winston Churchill or George W. Bush and Tony Blair, the close relation-ship between Reagan and Thatcher restored many of the associations that have long given Anglo-America an internal coherence that survived the split of 1776. In Reagan, the think tanks and media commentators of the New Right found an ideal embodiment and spokesperson. The New Right imitators of the New Left had in the actor president an experienced script reader capable of giving simple yet dramatic coherence to an array of poli-cies all aimed at diminishing the legacy of both the New Deal and the anti-war movement through hyperprivatization, union busting, the wholesale deregulation of business, and large spending increases on the police, the "national security" apparatus, and the Armed Forces. The dismantling of the Berlin Wall in 1989 was widely perceived on the right as a vindication of Reagan's policies and as a fulfillment of the militant brand of anti-communism that had thrived in the United States at least since the formation of the Soviet Union in 1917.

The implosion of Soviet communism's bastion near the end of the twentieth century produced a rush of capitalist globalization. No longer did it seem necessary to balance the privileges enjoyed by capitalism's winners with the provision of social safety nets for those left behind in capitalism's sharp division of society into rich and poor. Many forms of public property were broken up and apportioned at cut-rate prices to the favourite cronies of governing parties. The inclination of those so enriched was to see as victory bonds the new capital they acquired in the breakup of many forms of shared public property. This same pattern extended outward to the territories previously subject to Soviet rule and inward to new frontiers of intellectual property. The project of widening private property's domain extended from the rapid commodification of fresh water and to the commercialization of the genetic blueprints at the basis of life's organic designs.

For the elites who already owned a large share of the world's pool of capital, the demise of the Soviet Union signalled that there were no more major bastions of organized state resistance to prevent the transformation of transnational companies into global companies. There were no large engines of communist collectivization to stop the spread of privatization into almost every recess of the remaining global commons. Even the inner operations of national governments became prime sites for the commercial expansion of private business. The push to privatize the design and delivery of government services contained within it an attack on the negotiating power of public service unions. The post–Cold War assault on trade unionism of all kinds was part of an ideologically driven campaign to weaken the collective bonds of virtually any kind of group whose bonds of shared identification present obstacles to the expansion of market relations into every facet of society. Only the relationships in business corporations between share holders, executives, managers, workers, and customers conformed with the ideological preoccupations of those who sought to treat all social interaction as nothing more than a series of transactions between buyers and sellers, law-abiding citizens and criminals, free nations and evil axes.

The close of the Cold War, therefore, removed a host of fragile protections for the liberal legacies of the New Deal, Keynsian economics, and Boasian social policy. It helped bring to the surface many issues whose severity could no longer be disguised by the often artificial dichotomies of superpower rivalry. The worsening predicament of disadvantaged children in an era of increasing polarization between rich and poor helps highlight the growing gap between liberalism and capitalism in an era of hyperprivatization. According to UNICEF, the United Nations Children's Fund, 30,000 children die every day of poverty-related causes. More than two million children die every year because they are not immunized. About two million a year die of simple diarrhoea.[78] Since 1990 child poverty has grown in the United States, the industrialized country with the highest and fastest-growing divide between rich and poor. The entrenchment of these patterns amounts to the hardening of a new caste system that might be pictured as hereditary capitalism.[79] Hereditary capitalism places humans at life's starting point in dramatically different positions. When a spotlight is placed on the life prospects of newborns, the idealization of free-market relations runs strongly against the liberal idealization of equal opportunity.

Some of the most severe contradictions between liberalism and capitalism have grown from the globalization of US models of corporate and property law, which, since the late nineteenth century, have gradually universalized the treatment of commercial corporations as "persons" in venues of contract making, jurisprudence, and many theatres of political decision making. The legal term *person* generally signifies what is known in plain language as a citizen. The fact that increasingly human "persons" cannot perform on a level playing field with corporate "persons" makes a growing farce of the liberal proposition that individuals should be treated equally before the law. Human persons must age and eventually die. Alternatively, as long as corporate persons remain profitable, they can be immortal. Furthermore, the vast wealth of some corporations gives them levels of influence with public officials that is far beyond the capacity of all but a few human persons to shape the laws, policies, and judicial decisions that determine the kind of society in which we all live. Accordingly, there can be no genuine equality of rights, legal status, and opportunity between corporate persons and human persons.

The contrasting treatment of human and corporate rights is especially apparent when it is remembered that the colonial expansion of European empires in Asia, Africa, and the Western Hemisphere and the territorial expansion of settler states such as Canada, Australia, the United States, and South Africa all proceeded by defining Indigenous peoples outside the legal framework of citizenship. Indeed, until the era of the First World War, even women within the core polities of the industrialized West were placed outside the complex of rights and responsibilities attached to legal personhood. Accordingly, in the very era when business corporations acquired the legal personality of persons, colonized peoples, including women in the colonizing societies, were precluded from exercising the most basic expressions of political, legal, and economic self-determination. Humanity has yet to overcome the general patterns of relationship that found evocative expression in Rudyard Kipling's poetic plea to the United States in the late nineteenth century to "Take Up the White Man's Burden." Humanity has yet to overcome the legacy of a period when all the world's people were divided in venues of international affairs between those categorized as civilized trustees and as uncivilized wards, between law-giving parents and law-receiving children. Where Christian missionaries and Christian boarding schools were once empowered by various colonial powers to tutor Indigenous peoples in the name of the West's civilizing mission, today a more secular version of this role has been perpetuated by agencies such as the International Monetary Fund and the World Bank. Through their oversight of the accumulated credits and debts inherited from many generations of imperialism and neo-imperialism, such agencies continue the role of institutional parents. They retain means of controlling the finances and politics of subject populations held, because of their indebted status, in perpetual conditions of wardship. Where the subordination of many Aboriginal groups was formerly explained in the language of Christian condemnation of pagan savagery, the new governors of global finance look down on their wards as the inhabitants of "failed states."

The World Trade Organization emerged in 1995 from one of the Bretton Woods agencies, the General Agreement on Tariffs and Trade. The emergence of the WTO from the GATT following the demise of Soviet communism epitomized the triumphalist urge by the Cold War's apparent winners to treat the whole planet as the site of a single regime of capitalist market relations. Like the North American Free Trade Agreement, the WTO helped spawn a new generation of transnational trade court. The narrow franchise of those entitled to gain standing in these media of arbitration illustrates the growing inconsistencies between capitalism and liberalism. In WTO courts, corporate persons can gain access to forms of arbitration that are unavailable to human persons. Moreover, these new judicial venues have rules that enable corporate persons to sue sovereign governments and, in some instances, to strike down their national laws and policies. In this fashion, global corporations are gaining forms of transnational sovereignty that can trump the collective capacity of human citizens to exercise sovereign self-determination through the agency of national governments. The most basic principles of responsible government, collective self-determination, and national sovereignty are thus turned on their head. The citizenship of human persons is contained within the domestic framework of nation-states, whereas some corporate persons have gained more privileged access to a new genre of supranational citizenship within the framework of an emerging network of supranational trade agencies.[80]

MAKING THE CONNECTIONS BETWEEN SCIENTIFIC MANAGEMENT, THE VIETNAM WAR, AND THE WORLD BANK

Shortly after the lethal demonstration of US military might at Hiroshima and Nagasaki, George Orwell looked with trepidation at the prospects of a planet dominated by a very small circle of people who would probably monopolize control of the next generation of atomic weaponry. In 1945 he anticipated some of the ironies that would, in later years, infuse both the Cold War and the so-called War on Terror. He predicted that the concentration of the technological basis of so much coercive terror in so few hands would "rob exploited classes and peoples of all power to revolt." He believed that the introduction of the atomic bomb would probably not result in further episodes of mass extermination but anticipated, rather, that humanity would probably be apportioned among two or three superpowers – polities that would become "horribly stable ... slave empires."[81]

In 1948 Orwell poured his fears and gloomy prognostications into his masterpiece, *Nineteen Eighty-Four*, a novel that pictures the outlines of a future dominated by dark, totalitarian forces. In this prophetic text, he describes a host of weird social malformations, some of which would prove remarkably similar to the maladies that deformed both sides throughout the Cold War.[82] In imagining the stifling and soul-destroying stalemate of a time when the propaganda of "perpetual war" would be promoted as the key to "perpetual peace," he drew heavily on the work of James Burnham. Like Orwell, Burnham had briefly flirted with the ideas of Stalin's communist nemesis, Leon Trotsky. Burnham then swerved sharply to the right wing of the political spectrum and published *The Managerial Revolution* in 1941. Its content helped Orwell imagine the dominant role of a new type of technocratic elite whose managerial power would be based on its members' ability to combine expedient lies with the mass application of selective elements of scientific rationality.[83]

After the Second World War the prestige of science, but also its dark and menacing mystique, continued to grow. Science confirmed and enhanced its reputation as Western civilization's most characteristic hallmark, achievement, and threat. At the pinnacle of science's deployment in the cause of informal empire was the emergent military-industrial complex of the United States. The managers in charge of this complex of agencies became expert at transforming the technology of warfare into the political economy of mass production and consumption, as in the creation of a vast new arsenal of consumer items such as industrial-strength weed killer, styrofoam packaging, computers, and satellite dishes.[84] All these items and many thousands more were developed largely as commercial spinoffs from the research and development conducted in many corporate and university laboratories sponsored by the US Defense Department.[85] The distribution of so-called defence contracts came to dominate the domestic politics and national economy of the United States in much the same way that the politics of railways had dominated the politics of patronage and urbanization in the nineteenth century. Similarly, the rough outlines of the informal American empire were heavily shaped by patterns of sales and prohibitions governing the distribution of the powerful weaponry emerging from the busy laboratories and assembly lines at the strategic core of the military-industrial complex.

In this New World order, the armed forces of the United States became the ultimate police force charged to oversee and expand the field of monopoly capitalism, a realm where time was declared to be money, and money was treated as the equivalent of canned time. Robert S. McNamara was one of the brightest, most complex, and, in his later years, most thoughtfully introspective figures to emerge from the managerial echelons of the military-industrial complex.[86] With his Harvard Business School background, the suave McNamara moved boldly into the nexus between US corporate and public governance with the efficient ambition that James Burnham and George Orwell had attributed to the dominant managerial class of the future. A prodigious producer and interpreter of statistical data, McNamara rose quickly through the ranks of the Ford Motor Company to become briefly its president. Then, in 1961, he was conscripted into the War Cabinet of President John F. Kennedy and appointed defense secretary. McNamara's primary function in this capacity was to build up and manage the American fighting machine deployed in Southeast Asia. In 1968 he was moved by the US government from the military to the financial frontiers of the informal American empire. He served until 1981 as the head of the World Bank, one of the financial institutions created in 1944 at the United Nations Monetary and Financial Conference at Bretton Woods, New Hampshire.

At the World Bank, McNamara's primary duty was to help continue the commercial transition from the formal imperialism of Europe to the informal colonialism of the United States. His mandate was to inject the power of a major US-dominated financial institution to help fill the vacuum of power brought about by the dismantling of European empires. "We stepped into the role left vacant by the departed European powers," wrote the former US diplomat Ronald Steel in outlining what he referred to in 1970 in *Pax Americana* as the United States' "Cold War empire."[87] Accordingly, an essential part of the work assigned to McNamara was to use the World Bank to affect an orderly transfer of wealth and power inherited from earlier rounds of empire building. His task was twofold: to help bring the largest part of the planet under the control of the new lords and masters of the US-centred system of international credit and debt; and to further the integration of the new, nominally independent polities formerly colonized by Europe into an increasingly integrated structure of global property relations and transnational production. He advanced these goals by favouring the transfer of control over natural resources in former colonies to the complex of transnational agencies near the strategic core of the capitalist side in the Cold War.[88]

The push to privatize and consolidate the corporate ownership and control of natural resources on a worldwide basis renewed old patterns of imperial globalization. It continued an entrenched pattern of world history expressed most dramatically in recent times by the deep intrusion of foreign corporations, often with the backing of the US military, in the exploitation of the black gold of oil in, for instance, Indonesia, Nigeria, and the Persian Gulf. This privatizing thrust of industrialization has often run contrary to the Fourth World desire prevalent in most of the newly decolonized countries to nationalize resource wealth under public ownership and control. The promotion of the ideals of corporate privatization assumed the aura almost of religious zealotry, especially among the Washington-based crusaders leading the US side in the Cold War. This constituency found a particularly articulate and capable manager in McNamara, a late-twentieth-century personification of certain streams of Enlightenment rationality.

During McNamara's time at its helm, the World Bank was involved in a broad range of initiatives, including the effort to stem population growth in Third World countries, the building of large hydroelectric and irrigation dams, and the replacement of Aboriginal methods of agriculture with the industrial techniques of the so-called Green Revolution. One persistent pattern of change promoted by the World Bank, the International Monetary Fund, and the many corporate entities operating under their geopolitical umbrella has been supplanting local and Aboriginal systems of political economy. In the place of this Aboriginal diversity in systems of economic relations – systems that reflect, at their best, the investment of many thousands of years of careful Aboriginal adaptation to the particular attributes of bioregions and their delicate local ecologies[89] – the World Bank and its related institutions promoted more centralized methods of monocultural production.

The effect of these changes has been to narrow biocultural diversity and to polarize the division between rich and poor, both within regions and on a global basis. The consequences of the Green Revolution have been especially dire for the cultivation of rice in Vietnam, China, and Malaysia. In these countries and others, the massive overuse of herbicides and pesticides killed off all natural predators of the brown planthopper insect population, causing infestations that devastated crops and contributed to the skyrocketing of food prices in 2008. The drive to globalize the reach of the Green Revolution has also caused the world to lose its natural inheritance of fertile soil at an accelerating rate.[90] As Alex Roslin has written, "the US-backed Green Revolution did to farming what the Model T did to auto production." He adds, "It subsidized peasants in developing countries to abandon centuries-old, small-scale farming techniques that used diverse, locally adapted crops and instead plant vast fields of single crops specially bred for [export and] high yields."[91] No rhetoric of band-aid reform from the World Bank and the IMF can contradict the enormous body of evidence that the effect of their policies since the Second World War has been to replace biocultural diversity with monocultures of matter and mind and to widen the gap of economic inequality, not only between North and South but also within many client countries. The gap has contributed to the intensification of material divisions within and among national communities, no matter where they are situated on the scale said to distinguish development from underdevelopment.[92]

McNarmara was quoted at length in *Le Defi Americain* (*The American Challenge*) by Jean-Jacques Servan-Schreiber. In this volume, a bestseller in

France in the late 1960s, the author presents McNamara as the quintessential embodiment of the Enlightenment's heritage of rationality – as a primary representative of the superior techniques of US business said then to be subjugating the rest of the world, including Western Europe, under a kind of "technological colonialism." In a speech delivered at Jackson, Mississippi, in 1967, McNamara is reported to have said:

God is clearly democratic. He distributes brain power universally. But he quite justifiably expects us to do something efficient and constructive with this priceless gift. That is what management is all about. Management is, in the end, the most creative of all arts – for its medium is human talent itself. What, in the end, is management's fundamental task? It is to deal with change. Management is the gate through which social, political, and technological change – indeed, change in every dimension – is rationally and effectively spread throughout society ... The under-organization, the under-management of society is not the respect of liberty. It is simply to let some force other than reason shape reality.[93]

McNamara's attempt to achieve greater levels of efficiency through the application of scientific management in industrial production, warfare, and high finance bogged down most notoriously in the quagmire engulfing US troops in their failed effort to maintain the power of a puppet regime in Vietnam. In *Facing West*, Richard Drinnon characterized the US involvement in the Vietnam conflict in the 1960s and early 1970s as the climax of the same expansionary push that began with the Indian wars and continued with, for example, the forced assertion at the end of the nineteenth century of US sovereignty over Hawaii and then the Philippines. Seen in this light, the US intervention in Vietnam marked the continuation of a very old type of aggression whose roots predate the American Revolution.[94] Like the US role on the offensive side of the Indian wars, the clash in Vietnam renewed patterns of history, putting the United States in the vanguard of the Columbian conquests. In the long continuum of conflict aimed at seizing the lands of Indigenous peoples or subjugating them to various forms of economic, military, and political control, the United States fought for reasons that were very different from those that guided its military interventions in the Second World War.

The classic mistake made by McNamara and the other formulators and managers of US military intervention in Vietnam lay in their narrow perception that the resistance they faced was a one-dimensional manifestation of an international communist conspiracy. Their Cold War blinkers prevented them from seeing the full depth of the desire held by most Vietnamese to assert their Aboriginal rights and title against the incursions and claims of a foreign colonizer. The resistance of Indigenous peoples to the inroads of foreign imperialism has been the most consistent theme of Aboriginal history in Vietnam and throughout much of Indochina over the course of the sometimes overlapping efforts by Portuguese, Dutch, British, French,

Japanese, and American empire builders to dominate all or parts of the region both economically and politically. A powerful expression of the determination of Aboriginal Vietnamese to retain and exercise a degree of autonomy in their occupied lands lay in their construction of elaborate tunnel networks in strategic war zones. By burrowing far into the ground to maintain their presence even in areas dominated on the surface by enemy troops, Ho Chi Minh's Vietcong demonstrated the depth of their resistance and the strength of their determination to express and defend indigenous self-determination.

In their Cold War obsession with the real and imagined machinations of the communist superpowers, McNamara and those of his ilk failed to apprehend the true character of the opposition they faced in Indochina. In their propensity to interpret and manage all conflict in the region as the outcome of bipolar tensions centred on antagonisms between the capitalist United States and the Marxist governments of China and the Soviet Union, McNamara and his fellow hawks were diverted from understanding the Aboriginal sources of the convictions animating many of their Vietcong enemies. They were prevented from coming to grips with the intensity of the psychology of resistance that motivated the Indigenous peoples of Vietnam and many of the world's other Aboriginal groups who have suffered under the oppressive weight of colonialism and neo-colonialism. As Arnold J. Toynbee wrote in 1968 in the introduction to *Struggle against History*, the US "is being opposed in Vietnam not by 'world Communism,' but by the determination of the great non-Western majority of mankind to shake off Western domination at whatever cost."[95]

PRIVATIZATION IN ITS PARTICULARS: CAPITALISM VERSUS LIBERALISM

The attachment of the US government and its largest corporations to the monocultural ideal of a world enclosed in a universal system of capitalist property relations continues to run contrary to the philosophies and possibilities that arise naturally from an era when the theory of relativity has become scientific orthodoxy. Just as the theory of relativity highlights the concurrent legitimacy of different ways of thinking about, and adapting to, the passage of time, so this same approach to scientific analysis points towards diversity as the essential element of ecological health in the ongoing course of globalization. This emphasis on diversity in the pursuit of ecological globalization means moving beyond the imposed conformities of universalized capitalism.[96] It means transcending the machismo drive to penetrate and privatize the totality of relationships linking human beings with each other and with the rest of nature, as if unlimited commercialization and commodification represents an end and a fulfilment of history.

There have been many stages in the genesis of the current means of conveying proprietary interests in ideas, inventions, designs, names, logos, drugs, seeds, and many other extractions and ingredients of the natural world. The first patent for a new mechanical invention was issued in Florence in 1421. By 1886 the governments of many countries entered into the Berne Convention for the Protection of Literary and Artistic Work. The aim of this international treaty was to provide a consistent regime of copyright protection enabling authors, musicians, and visual artists to receive royalties through the exercise of control over the reproduction of their creative work. The busy proceedings of the congress on trademarks, patents, and inventions at the World's Columbian Exposition in Chicago in 1893 were a marker of things to come in the expanding realm of intellectual property. By 1893 there were already two times as many patent applications being sought in the United States as in the rest of the world put together. In 1967 the responsibility to administer the terms of the Berne Union, the outgrowth of the 1886 treaty, was transferred to the World Intellectual Property Organization, a new agency of the United Nations.

As new platforms of interaction took shape in the political economy of globalization, the US Congress intervened repeatedly to maintain and extend the worldwide advantages of US-based corporations in the area of intellectual property. As the Disney Corporation's seventy-year period of copyright control over the images of Donald Duck and Mickey Mouse approached an end, for instance, the *Sonny Bono Copyright Term Extension Act* of 1998 added another twenty-five years to the period before such privately owned representations passed into the public domain. In 1998 Congress passed the *Digital Millennium Copyright Act* in order to adapt the laws of copyright to the new media of computer interactivity. The European Union joined this initiative in 2001 with its own Copyright Directive. At the global level, the World Trade Organization absorbed under its auspices the operation of the WIPO and the sweeping terms of a new transnational agreement on "trade-related intellectual property."

There are huge social and ecological ramifications in the rush to privatize and enclose large new portions of the intellectual and biological commons. One marker of this accelerated urge lay in the increase in worldwide patent applications from 885,000 in 1985 to 1.600,000 in 2005.[97] This surge in the privatization of the remaining intellectual commons engendered opposition at many levels.[98] Critics argued, for instance, that without a good measure of free and unfettered exchange of ideas, discoveries, and inventions, the development of many of the world's most powerful technologies could never have taken place. A good example lies in the development of computers, devices that emerged only gradually from long accumulations of innovation done in large measure in the public domain.[99] Why stifle, some asked, the fluidity of intellectual exchange in pursuit of technical innovation? Why enact and enforce a particularly restrictive genre of intellectual property law whose effect in many cases would be to appropriate for a few the intellectual contributions of many generations of innovators?

Many difficult legal and ethical issues were raised by the concept of treating the genetic design of DNA much like the digital design of computer microchips – as patentable inventions subject to copyright law. Individual life forms have emerged from many millions of years of evolutionary adaptation and competition. Moreover, many of the world's most important vegetable, fruit, and fibre crops have developed from thousands of years of human intervention in the reproductive cycles of plants. The attributes of many thousands of varieties of potatoes, corn, beans, tomatoes, and coco, for instance, have resulted from the careful selective breeding and hybridization performed by many, many generations of patient Central American farmers.[100] This injection of intellect, experimentation, and Aboriginal science into agriculture over thousands of years represents a huge gift to humanity by the Western Hemisphere's Indigenous peoples. It represents a contribution marked year after year in the monetary, nutritional, and aesthetic value of the world's agricultural output. By what right can any human or corporate "person" claim the fruits of all this evolution, with or without the help of human intervention, by merely adding slight genetic modifications? It would make as much sense to proclaim that the designers of, say, a particular chair could claim the title to all buildings housing that chair.

Ever since the revolutionary vanguard of the Century of Enlightenment sought to pull down the structure of superstition supporting the divine right of kings, the liberal emphasis on the equality of individuals has provided legal constructs that can be co-opted to edify a system of property rights that entitles the few at the expense of the many. In too many cases the high-sounding language of national constitutions and international treaties ends up being interpreted by judges in ways that advance the privilege of those with the wealth to purchase the best legal representation in expensive litigation. Indeed, corporate assets, investments, and trade are generally afforded much higher levels of domestic and international protection than are many of the world's most menaced populations. The language deployed to outlaw various forms of discrimination sometimes ends up being turned, for instance, to the goal of preventing national governments from favouring their own local businesses in the awarding of contracts. Constitutional affirmations such as those proclaiming freedom of expression end up being exploited to counter restrictions on, say, the advertising campaigns of tobacco companies.

There is virtually no realm of geography, no function of biology, no form of human association or creativity that is safely off limits when it comes to the propensity of capital and capitalists to commodify and commercialize every facet of nature susceptible to privatization. The overwhelming preoccupation of those on the most advanced frontiers of this process is to seek the subordination of almost all types of relationship to the most privileged set of relationships connecting buyers and sellers. The breakdown of the Soviet system under the weight of superpower rivalry was received in some circles as a signal that capitalism, much like the United States itself, had been vindicated as the ultimate synthesis of religious zeal and Enlightenment rationality, as the ultimate marriage of providential will with history's most successful scientific application of natural law to human relations.[101] In this scheme the disappearance of the Soviet system was interpreted as the attainment of Henry Luce's vision of the American Century, even as it simultaneously signalled the defeat of Henry Wallace's more liberal premonitions of the New Deal's extension to the whole world. Sovietologist Condoleezza Rice suggested the extent of this extravagant optimism when, in 2000, as President Bush's top adviser on national security, she argued that "American values are universal."[102] There was enormous synergy, therefore, in the series of events linking the end of the Cold War with the push to create and expand the realm of both the World Trade Organization and that of so-called trade-related intellectual property rights (TRIPS).

The expansion of the value of shares traded on the New York stock exchange by about 700 per cent between 1990 and 2006 helped to reflect, propel, and justify the changes entailed in an era of hyperprivatization.[103] Prominent among the driving forces behind this growth was the transformation of much of the state-controlled property of the former Soviet Empire into new pools of capital that could be leveraged through mortgages and other instruments of credit. This rapid privatization was executed in ways that created a few instant billionaires rather than millions of modestly enriched property holders. Another source of value added to the price of corporate shares was the wholesale transfer of wealth from unionized workers to investors and speculators as low-wage economies took over the major share of business in the manufacturing of consumer goods for the global economy. In *The New Imperialism*, David Harvey referred to this process as accumulation by dispossession.[104] This accumulation of capital through appropriation from discarded and underpaid workers built on earlier cycles of capital accumulation through the dispossession of Indigenous peoples and the exploitation of slaves.

The apparent multilateralism of the superpower in the 1990s in the extension and elaboration of the transnational imperatives of property and corporations contrasted starkly with the militant unilateralism of the United States in the opening years of the first decade of the twenty-first century. Beginning with invasions of Afghanistan and Iraq, and with the heightened US backing of the Israeli government's increasingly repressive treatment of the Palestinians, the core agencies of the superpower's military-industrial complex deepened their penetration of Eurasia. In the name of the Global War on Terror, capitalism's ultimate police force turned against some of its former Cold War clients and allies. The instruments of coercive force were mobilized in ways that deepened the US role in a region that has long hosted some of humanity's oldest and most robust civilizations. As the British had done before them in the course of their imperial "great game" with Russia, the United States intensified its military role in Eurasia, but especially in those regions of the Caspian Sea area and the

Persian Gulf that are rich with oil or strategically important for pipelines or ports. As the Cold War's self-declared winner of an expanded imperative for global domination, the US government turned the operation of capitalism's military-industrial complex towards the corporate privatization of the resource wealth on the long-contested frontiers of the arena where the empires of Britain, Russia, and China have historically clashed.[105]

The end of the Soviet Empire removed ideological as well as military and political constraints to opening all available frontiers of privatization to the conquest of international capital. The rapid extension of the institution of private property through many corporate variations on some of the old themes of the enclosure movement helped to feed and nurture capital's unrelenting appetite to reproduce itself. Where capitalism's internal drive to replicate itself has long depended on imperialism's incorporation of new lands and resources within international systems of property relations, the end of the most classical form colonialism necessitated new motifs of material conquest and commercial empire building in order to create the new streams of added financial value that constitute a key to satisfying and encouraging speculators, creditors, and investors. The transition from the old imperialism to new forms of empire building was especially apparent in the effort to construct the necessary framework of law, politics, and mythology to facilitate the proprietary colonization of DNA and those many new provinces of mind and matter that, henceforth, were to be governed under the expanding, transnational gambit of intellectual property.[106]

This colonizing surge of proprietary globalization on a variety of fronts has helped to shape and energize the resistance of eclectic bands of activists who share in the conviction expressed by Lewis Henry Morgan that "a mere career of property is not the final destiny of mankind."[107] The worldwide coalition of Zapatistas was prominent among the groups who attempted to join forces in order to oppose the hyperprivatization of the planet's resources. The Zapatistas rallied around a Mexican-centred stand for Aboriginal rights and against the kind of economic integration conceived by the authors of the North American Free Trade Agreement.[108] The new genre of activism was integrally connected to the Internet's unparalleled effectiveness as a medium for the quick generation of new networks of collaboration across many former barriers of geography and politics. The cyberspace networks linking Fourth World activists formed some of the essential sinews of collaboration that resulted in the massive demonstrations in, for instance, Seattle, Washington, Prague, Quebec City, and Genoa between 1999 and 2001.[109] The aim of this movement was to draw attention to the democratic deficit implicit in the massive handover of power from the public sector to the modern-day corporate incarnations of the privateers who have tended to dominate globalization's high seas since the days of Francis Drake.[110] This mobilization of popular resistance to the dominating interests of corporate capitalism resembled the muscle flexing of the Progressive Movement in the United States in the early years of the twentieth century. In calling for legislation to break up the country's huge "trusts," the Progressives placed a spotlight of public scrutiny on the concentration of enormous economic and political power in the hands of a tiny oligarchy who controlled that country's biggest monopolies and cartels.[111]

The expanding frontiers of privatization, therefore, have been closely connected to the widening range of power and wealth vested in commercial corporations. While the division of the Earth into narrower and narrower enclaves of private property continues the fragmenting force of the enclosure movement, the architects of large corporations have been able to mediate this pattern by bringing extremely large concentrations of capital to the profit-driven mobilization of complex configurations of technology, expertise, raw materials, labour, distribution, advertising, and public relations. The move of manufacturing operations from high-wage areas to low-wage areas accelerated near the end of the twentieth century, becoming a prevalent tactic in the generation of substantially increased profits for investors. Typically, this strategy meant laying off relatively well-paid unionized workers in North America and Europe and transferring jobs to factories in Latin America, India, China, or Southeast Asia, where regulation is minimal and collective bargaining is frequently outlawed or discouraged.[112]

One of the paradoxes in this trend in the transformation of the global economy is the emergence of the People's Republic of China as capitalism's great factory, where a huge and growing proportion of the world's consumer items are manufactured.[113] The speed of China's commercial rise was undoubtedly one of the most dramatic and surprising developments during the opening years of the twenty-first century. There are clearly vast yet unpredictable ramifications in China's ascent to the status of the world's richest creditor nation, accompanied by the rapid decline of the United States into various forms of chronic indebtedness and imperial overstretch. China's rise drew on many forces, including the Aboriginal inventiveness and sophistication of the world's largest and oldest continually organized civilization. Mao Zedong had a major hand in making the changes that helped put China in a position to regain its old status as a superpower capable of changing the face of world order. Mao's sometimes ruthless efforts between 1949 and 1976 to industrialize, modernize, and unify China helped to prepare the ground for the emergence of corporate capitalism's new power house of productivity. In drawing on one of the most challenging traditions of Western thought and action – Marxism – Mao helped the diverse amalgam of societies encompassed by China to regain their pride. He helped create the conditions that enabled the citizens of his country in the years following his death to claim their central role in the world on the basis of an indigenized ideology pointed against the corrosive legacies of European, Japanese, and American imperialism. There are few ironies on the planet as potentially consequential as China's reconstitution of the framework of global capitalism by an authoritarian regime that continues to deploy the image and reputation of one of communism's most determined and iconographic leaders.

CONTRACTORS WITH GUNS AND THE MAKING OF THE TERROR ECONOMY

By 2001 the transnational expansion of the corporate sector resulted in many of the world's largest companies dwarfing the size of the vast majority of nominally sovereign governments on the planet. Only the United States, Germany, the United Kingdom, Italy, France, China, and Japan had governments whose budgets were larger than those of the biggest corporations. This development made the economy of Exxon Mobil almost twice as large as that of the Canadian government, the economy of Wal-Mart over twice the size of the Australian government's, and the combined economy of Ford and General Motors well over four times the magnitude of the money taken in and spent by the Norwegian government.[114] Especially after the demise of the Soviet Union, the push to enlarge the field of property falling under the private governance of the corporate sector was directly connected to the drive to shrink the size of the public sector through downsizing, downloading, deregulation, decentralization, and contracting-out activities formerly performed by state agencies. This view of government would limit the function of state bureaucracies to the role of making and enforcing contracts with the private sector for the delivery of government services. The public sector inhabits the administrative and legislative heartland of sovereign governments as well as the territories, institutions, and resources under their jurisdiction.[115] The idea of the public sector is closely connected to the idea of the commons and the ideals of the Bowl with One Spoon. The commons refers to the remaining realm of land, water, and life forms not enclosed by, or subject to, the laws of private property.

As highlighted in the 1980s in the rhetoric and policies of US president Ronald Reagan and UK prime minister Margaret Thatcher, the coalition of business libertarians and evangelical Christians who joined forces during the final stages of the Cold War succeeded in elevating the ideal of privatization almost to the level of a holy crusade in their anti-communist jihad.[116] For Reagan, this preoccupation coincided with the strategic problem of how to exercise US military might when vivid memories of the Vietnam fiasco kept public opinion solidly hostile to the deployment of significant numbers of US troops to foreign conflicts. His administration responded by funding and assisting private armies, sometimes through intermediaries. These Cold War proxies included the anti-Sandinista Contras in Central America, REMANO and UNITA in the former Portuguese colonies of Mozambique and Angola, and the Mujahadeen in Afghanistan. Not only did these armed proxies attack government forces but they also committed acts of random terror with the objective of demoralizing civilian populations and thereby turning them against their socialist or communist governors.[117] Building on tactics developed by the CIA and the US military in the covert infiltration of Laos during the height of the Vietnam conflict, agencies of the US government sometimes cooperated with their anti-communist allies by lending cover to their proxies' frequent involvement in the preparation, distribution, and sale of illegal drugs. By participating as partners in the worldwide trade in illegal narcotics, some of the most covert branches of the US government sought to maintain and heighten their secrecy by privatizing their means of obtaining funds.[118]

The pattern of merger in the relationship between privatization and militarization on the contested frontiers of the US empire became especially clear in the US-led invasion and occupation of Iraq beginning in 2003. The Third Squadron of the Seventh Cavalry Regiment was strategically located at the "spearhead" of that invasion along the valley of the Euphrates River. Under the doomed leadership of General George Armstrong Custer, the Seventh Cavalry was the US military unit that had been decimated through the military prowess of the Indian fighting forces at the Battle of Little Bighorn in Montana Territory in 1876. It was this same Seventh Cavalry that later sought revenge for its defeat through its infamous slaughter of Big Foot's band at Wounded Knee in 1890. There were echoes of this slaughter of Sioux women, children, and elders at Wounded Knee in the lead role afforded to the Second Battalion of the Seventh Cavalry in the notorious destruction of Fallujah in 2004.[119]

Accordingly, the Anglo-American invasion of Iraq renewed many old patterns of US conduct in the Indian wars. Similarly, the US delegation of broad military, economic, and political powers to private corporations in occupied Iraq was reminiscent of some features of the corporatist organization on the fascist side of the Second World War. The integration of state violence with an expanded regime of corporate influence throughout Nazi-controlled Europe was epitomized by the slave-based operations of the privately owned synthetic fuel factory that formed the initial basis for the creation of the Auschwitz concentration camp in Poland. The owner of that notorious industrial facility was the IG Farben Company, a conglomerate of petrochemical and pharmaceutical enterprises that was closely affiliated with many major US-based corporations, but especially the Standard Oil Company of New Jersey. This type of public-private partnership was conceived and implemented in the fascist Axis as a means of countering the international expansion of Bolshevist trade unionism. As Zeev Sternhell, Mario Sznajder, and Maria Asheri have argued, the European fascists and their supporters in the United States, Great Britain, and elsewhere "adopted the economic aspect of liberalism but completely denied its philosophical principles."[120]

The effort to privatize and hand over as much of Iraq as possible to the corporate sector renewed on a larger scale many similar cycles of economic experimentation that took place after the military regime of General Augusto Pinochet overthrew the elected government of Salvador Allende in 1973 in a US-backed coup. In the aftermath of this intervention, General Pinochet and his advisers gave a free hand to economist Milton Friedman and his disciples in the Economics Department at the University of Chicago. As Naomi Klein has compelling argued, Friedman's radical surgery eliminated all elements of socialism or social democracy from the Chilean economy to begin a more comprehensive drive directed at transforming the global political economy. The aim of the "Chicago Boys," together with that of their patrons, agents, and supporters, was to remake the structure of the global economy by eliminating the fragile legacies of Keysian liberalism and instituting in their place very extreme models of business deregulation and hyperprivatization. In Chile this transformation involved efforts to privatize the national pension plan and more than two hundred state-owned enterprises, including the largest part of the country's rich copper mines. It also included massive reductions in the civil service, the virtual elimination of the laws of collective bargaining, and the abolition of both minimum wages and taxes on wealth and business profits.[121]

After ousting the discarded former client regime of Saddam Hussein, the US government rushed to put in place an economic plan more sweeping in scope than that promoted for Chile. In September 2003 Paul Bremer, the US government's top man in Iraq, issued Order 39, which called for sweeping changes to Iraq's constitution aimed at making that country the most privatized society on Earth. Some critics responded immediately. They argued that the US push to entrench the most fundamental laws of property relations, during the brief period before the promised return of sovereignty to friendly locals, effectively robbed the Iraqi people of their right to decide democratically key aspects of their own future. Moreover, legal opinions were marshalled alleging that Order 39 violated many provisions of the international law of armed occupation, including the Hague Regulations of 1907 as appended to the Geneva Convention of 1949.[122]

"Privatization in Iraq Is Out of Control," proclaimed the headline of a column written by Princeton economist Paul Krugman.[123] Naomi Klein reinforced and expanded Krugman's analysis. She developed the case that not only Iraqi oil but also Iraqi water, roads, cell phones, trains, ports, health care, and many other elements of the country's basic infrastructure were slated to be privatized as instruments of profit for the corporate allies of President George W. Bush. "Iraq," Klein argued, "is being treated as a blank slate on which the ideological neoliberals can design their dream economy: fully privatized, foreign owned and open for business."[124] Details of the scheme to place Iraq on the frontiers of new innovations in corporate and property law emerged in the form of a leaked secret document prepared jointly by the US Agency for International Development and the Treasury Department. It styled itself as an outline for a "Mass Privatization Program" emphasizing "private sector involvement in strategic sectors, including privatization, asset sales, concessions, leases and management contracts, especially in oil and supporting industries." The document's authors proposed a consumption-based tax regime and the creation of a major stock market in Baghdad to facilitate the buying and selling of shares in all the newly privatized entities.[125]

As the occupying forces met growing levels of resistance in the fall of 2003 from the Iraqi people, the US government put on hold the plans for immediate privatization of the oil fields. Indeed, it was forced to back away, temporarily at least, from many aspects of its plans once it became clear that the superpower could not bring about a sufficient level of civil order to attract private-sector investment and that Iraq's organized labour would aggressively resist any wholesale selloff of the country's nationalized businesses.[126] The early failure of the major occupying power to realize its goal of making Iraqi's political economy a showpiece of illiberal hyperprivatization, however, did nothing to negate the underlying power of the principal enticements that drew the armed forces of the United States into that part of the world. An ongoing goal of the occupation was to advance the process of eliminating all nationally owned and operated companies from the global system of oil production and distribution. Ironically, however, the international hostility to the US invasion of Iraq only reinforced the determination of many oil-exporting countries and their citizens to advance and extend schemes of control over their own fossil fuels through nationalized companies. Their aim was to exclude the Seven Sisters conglomerates that were essential instruments of US geopolitical power for much of the twentieth century.[127]

Beginning with a successful popular revolution in 1958, the people and government of Iraq have historically been important proponents of the principle that Aboriginal oil resources should be harnessed to the national objectives of the countries where oil originates. The association that initially embodied this ideal, the Organization of Petroleum Exporting Countries (OPEC), was founded at a meeting in Baghdad in 1960. In 1962 the government of Abdul Karim Kassem created an Iraqi national oil company to assert some measure of indigenous control over the country's most lucrative natural resource. A year later, Kassem was removed from office and executed in a US-backed coup that cleared the way in subsequent years for the Iraqi government of Saddam Hussein. For many years Saddam was an important client and agent of US interests, but especially after the control of neighbouring Iran was seized in the name of an Islamic revolution in 1979. The Iraqi government's pioneering efforts to assert some measure of indigenous ownership and control over the country's oil resources was duplicated in whole or in part by many of the world's oil-producing countries. Moreover, the nationalization of Iraqi oil was a significant factor in the success of the Arab Oil Embargo of 1973, an event that dramatically elevated the market price of the black gold of modern industrialization even as it traumatized key interests in the United States and most of the other oil-consuming polities.[128]

By using the hammer of military force rather than more covert forms of "regime change," a US specialty during the Cold War, the superpower's government embarked on an overtly imperial course of action in Iraq. Among its objectives was the establishment of a prototype of hyperprivatization in an oil-rich Middle Eastern country that the Bush regime hoped to make a model of Arab adaptation to the New American Century.[129] The effort to privatize the ownership of Iraq's infrastructure went far beyond the enormous contracts given to Bechtel and Halliburton, giant US corporations poised strategically in the military-industrial complex between the rich oil and gas sector and the US Armed Forces. The US intervention in Iraq advanced the privatization of many military functions that had previously been treated as the exclusive domain of government forces. The guarding of Paul Bremer, for instance, was one of the responsibilities contracted out to the armed mercenaries employed by the US firm of Blackwater Security Consulting.

In 2004 the retired Special Forces operatives who made up the core of Blackwater's employees were prominent among the 20,000 private security contractors doing business in Iraq.[130] By 2007 the number of private individuals working on contract for the US government had grown to 180,000, a larger contingent than the 160,000 US soldiers deployed in occupying the country where OPEC had been founded. These contractors were drawn from the national populations of about one hundred countries. They worked on the staff of approximately 630 military corporations.[131] Some of these hired guns had done part of the dirty work in "disappearing" critics of the government in Chile after the US-backed coup installed the right-wing dictatorship of General Augusto Pinochet.[132] Others were White South Africans coming from long lines of mercenary soldiers who had a notorious history of selling their services throughout Africa in many violent conflicts, such as those that had brought General Mobutu to power in the Congo. Indeed, the intimate experience of Black South Africans with the role of mercenary armies has made the post-apartheid government of their country the most informed and persistent critic of the broad new functions assigned to commercial armies in the era of privatized militarism.[133]

The activities of these contractors with guns included the interrogation and torture of Iraqi prisoners in operations such as those that came to light in the spring of 2004 with the publication of shocking pictures taken at the Abu Ghraib prison in Baghdad. This story acquired prominence largely as a result of the investigative journalism of Seymour Hersh, the same reporter who publicly introduced the details of US state terrorism in the My Lai Massacre in 1969 in Vietnam.[134] Employees of the Titan Corporation and CAIC International ranked prominently among those most deeply implicated in the Abu Ghraib scandal.[135] Meanwhile, Aegis Corporation handled some of the darker and more covert aspects of the British government's role in the occupation of Iraq.[136]

The US government's delegation to private contractors of some of the dirtiest jobs of invasion, occupation, and intelligence gathering in Iraq built on well-documented patterns in the privatization of state terror, especially during the post-Vietnam phase of the Cold War. The transfer to private businesses of responsibility for some of the government's most covert and murky operations helped to shield these activities from outside scrutiny. It helped to hide these operations behind laws, policies, and conventions giving the private sector much broader capacities than the public sector to maintain confidentiality and secrecy. The rush to transform the work of espionage and counterinsurgency into the activity of profit-driven businesses recast the role of the Central Intelligence Agency. The CIA became the main recruiting centre for many US security corporations, including Booz Allen Hamilton, Northrop Grumman, and the Abraxis Corporation. The amount spent by the US government on private intelligence agencies increased from about $18 billion in 2000 to $42 billion in 2007, or about 70 per cent of all federal monies spent on this kind of activity.[137] In commenting in the *New York Times* on "the privatization of our spies," James Bamford referred to the role of contractors in the Abu Ghraib scandal. "The potential for disaster only grows," he wrote, "when not just the agents on the ground, but their supervisors and controllers back at headquarters too, are working for some private company."[138]

Some of the US government's apparent disregard for the rule of law in its waging of the War on Terror drew on patterns of conduct established during the Cold War.[139] At the School of the Americas in Fort Benning, Georgia, for instance, training in techniques of torture and other means of waging physical and psychological warfare were regularly taught to the military staffs of those Latin America regimes that were friendly participants in the informal US empire. The preparation of military and paramilitary soldiers at Fort Benning was consistent with the techniques taught to the jailers in the big US incarceration facilities at Guantanamo Bay in Cuba, Abu Ghraib in Iraq, and Bagram air base in Afghanistan. When the brutal and illegal treatment heaped on inmates at these notorious installations began to come to light, the US government opted to evade the scrutiny by opening an undisclosed number of secret US jails around the world. These facilities became known generically as dark sites, places prone to become virtual "law-free zones" where the lack of accountability allowed state-sponsored murder and torture to run rampant. In some instances US officials sent their "detainees," most often held without charge, to jails in countries known for the ruthlessness of their interrogation techniques. The publicity surrounding the case of Maher Arar, a Canadian telecommunications expert sent to Syria for interrogation and torture, helped highlight patterns of "extraordinary rendition" taking place globally in name of the Global War on Terror.[140]

Many legal challenges were contemplated or mounted as jurists such as Philippe Sands documented in detail the failure of the US executive branch to adhere to instruments such as the Geneva Conventions prohibiting the infliction of any form of torture on prisoners of war.[141] As part of this process, the Supreme Court of the United States in June 2008, in the case of *Boumediene et. al. versus Bush*, upheld the right of inmates held at Guantanamo Bay to invoke the principles of habeus corpus in seeking fair trials. Even the military commission appointed to rule on the charges brought in 2006 against two Gantanamo inmates, Canadian citizen Omar Khadr and Yemeni citizen Salim Ahmed Hamden, refused to accept jurisdiction in the prosecutions because of the failure of federal authorities to have properly categorized the accused as unlawful enemy combatants. "Unlawful enemy combatants" is an Orwellian phrase specially created by the War on Terror's official wordsmiths to describe the status of individuals targeted anywhere in the world through the US president's unilateral decree.[142] In the name of the US-led Global War on Terror, the president of the United States sought to equip his office with a form of global jurisdiction not subject to the will of other sovereign polities or to the checks entailed in international treaties and US domestic law.

Because of Khadr's Canadian citizenship and because he was only fifteen years old when he was alleged to have taken part in an armed encounter with US soldiers in Afghanistan in 2002, this young man's case proved to be particularly controversial. In the spring of 2008 Canadian general Romeo Dallaire made international headlines when he chastized the governments of both Canada and the United States for their shared roles in Khadr's incarceration. Dallaire alleged that both governments had wrongfully criminalized Khadr in ways that directly violated domestic laws and international treaties prohibiting the maltreatment of child soldiers.[143] Dallaire earned his understanding of the tragedies attending the military exploitation of children during the agony of Central Africa in the 1990s, when he commanded the badly understaffed United Nations force that proved too weak to hold back a terrible outburst of ethnically motivated genocide in Rwanda in 1994.[144] The genocide in Rwanda was integral to even more lethal episodes of ethnic violence in neighbouring districts of eastern Congo, where competing mining interests helped sponsor fighting between rival militias vying for control of lucrative mineral deposits.

The failure of international institutions to afford human rights anywhere near the same level of protection afforded corporate rights is compellingly illustrated by both the genocidal outbursts in the eastern Congo and the failure to prevent the proliferation of illegal renditions, incarceration, torture, abuse of child soldiers, persecution of legitimate dissent, and outright executions done in the name of the Global War on Terror. As private companies line up to take advantage of government and corporate willingness to pay for their military services, a new form of terror economy is taking form. The terror economy thrives on the intensification of feelings of fear and insecurity in the post-9/11 world. The importance of the privatization and corporatization of coercive power in the terror economy is suggested by the text of an advertisement promoting a subsidiary of the Blackwater Corporation. That advertisement advances the theory that the "Fortune 500 companies are especially attractive targets as governments continue to emphasize Homeland Security." In light of this threat against business, Blackwater officials declare, "We seek to anticipate and defeat the next terrorist tactic –disruptions of supply chains, coordinated attacks on key assets or customers, or even assassination of top executives. Corporations are the most vulnerable targets. It's our job to keep them safe."[145]

The expanding domain of corporate privatization in the terror economy of the post-9/11 world calls attention to the connections between intelligence gathering and insider trading on stock markets where the essential currency is information about what to expect in the future. Indeed, while shares are bought and sold in stock markets, these venues of exchange make knowledge pertaining to the future price of shares the real commodity of highest worth. In this commercial milieu, those corporate operatives who gain access to restricted intelligence obviously gain significant advantages in making decisions about how to invest money. The importance of this kind of insider knowledge is multiplied in those situations where private mercenary armies such as those organized and overseen by Blackwater Corporation intervene with armed force to bring about preordained outcomes in political struggles for the control of state power. Indeed, a Blackwater subsidiary known as Total Intelligence had no qualms about advertising that its spies-for-hire also provide timely advice on "investment strategies."[146] Again, privileged access to secret information available to a favoured few has huge monetary worth in a capitalist society where the identity of winners and losers is largely decided through trajectories of changing value affixed to corporate shares in stock markets.[147]

As more and more of the fastest-growing areas in the economy depend on the willingness of governments, corporations, and wealthy individuals to purchase what appears to be protection and security, the market price for attaining these conditions increases. Hence, the laws of supply and demand in a terror economy create an incentive for business to maintain and even elevate those forms of suspicion and uncertainty that breed the most readily exploitable forms of fear. The propensity of profit-making enterprises in capitalism's military-industrial complex to advance their interests in the terror economy raises deep and serious questions about what really transpired on September 11, 2001, a day when, we are told, an enormous failure of military intelligence allowed a few Saudi plotters with box cutters to cut through all obstacles in an concerted attack on key symbols of the military and commercial might of the capitalist superpower. Why was no one directly held accountable for the alleged failures in military intelligence? Why were those directly responsible, such as General Richard Myers, the acting head of the Joint Chiefs of Staff, or General Ralph Eberhart, the officer in charge of NORAD (North American Areospace Defense), promoted rather than fired for their roles in the events of 9/11? What is wrong with this picture? In spite of the transformative importance of what transpired on that fateful day, no credible investigation of the background and events of 9/11 has ever taken place. The commission appointed by the US president to assess the genesis of the events of 9/11 was so lacking in rigour and credibility that it was has been described by Benjamin DeMott in *Harper's Magazine* as a "cheat and a fraud" – as an exercise in "artful dodging" that "infantilizes" it audiences even as it "conceals realities that demand immediate inspection and confrontation."[148]

The accelerating commercialization and privatization of the instruments of state terror in the post-9/11 world have permeated attitudes in ways that have helped instill the view that the global role of the United States is akin to a property right that needs to be aggressively enforced. In *American Power and World Order*, Christian Reus-Smith examines this phenomenon. He argues that the cult of hyperprivatization became so marked during the presidency of George W. Bush that even the idea of power came to be viewed more as a function of ownership rather than a relationship between polities. The "commodification of power," Reus-Smith writes, leads to the notion that "it is *possessive* ... something an actor owns, a tangible resource that he or she commands individually." The radical unilateralism of the Bush regime flowed from the perception that "power is primarily material," the outcome of "a standard catalogue of America's power resources, giving pride of place to military, economic, and technological pre-eminence, guns and money."[149]

The policy of emphasizing the hard power of militarism over other expressions of US influence was actively promoted by a tight circle of politicians, bureaucrats, and academics that would come to be known informally as the Vulcans.[150] This group would dominate the War Cabinet of President George W. Bush during his first term of office from 2000 to 2004. In the 1990s the Vulcans, whose leading members and associates included Richard Cheney, Paul Wolfowitz, Donald Rumsfeld, Condoleezza Rice, Richard Pearle, Richard Armitage, William Kristol, Doug Feith, and Zalmay Khalilzad, assertively placed themselves in the tradition of Henry Luce and his conception of the American Century. They did so in close association with a number of the US oil and weapons companies including Halliburton, Lockheed-Martin, Boeing, Bechtel, Raytheon, Chevron Texaco, Union Oil of California, and Exxon Mobil. The participants in the Project for the New American Century set to work to "exert upon the world" the "full impact" of US influence, for such "purposes" and "means" as its government saw fit. In 2000, for instance, the directors produced a rationale for the invasion of Iraq. The mobilization of public support, the authors acknowledged, would require some "catastrophic and catalyzing event, like a new Pearl Harbor."[151]

The Vulcans' positions formed the primary basis for the release by the White House in September 2002 of the report entitled *The National Security Strategy of the United States of America*. Although the new polices were presented as responses to the events of September 11, 2001, the document gave formal status to many positions already well developed within the Vulcans' own circle long before the Twin Towers exploded into fine particles blanketing Manhatten with an asbestos-laden carpet.[152] This trajectory of planning within the military establishment's bureaucracy went back at least to the work of Wolfowitz and Khalilzad in the Policy Planning Office at the State Department in the early 1990s. There they worked for President George Bush Senior's defense secretary, Richard Cheney, as this larger-than-life personification of the military-industrial complex began his quest for new justifications for increased federal expenditures on high-tech weaponry after the demise of the Soviet Union. Cheney continued to work on this big-picture planning when he left the US executive branch to become the chief executive office of the Halliburton Company between 1995 and 2000. *The National Security Strategy* formalized the case for the superpower's abandonment of even the fiction that the US government was committed to subjecting the rule of force to the supremacy of law through the agency of the United Nations. In the Orwellian language of perpetual war for perpetual peace, the policy statement anticipated a series of "preventive wars" in the name of "anticipatory self-defense." Moreover, it asserted the intention of the Bush regime to maintain the coercive capacity of US fighting forces at such massive levels that "potential adversaries" will be "dissuaded ... from pursuing a military build-up in hopes of surpassing, or equaling, the power of the United States."[153]

The authors of this unabashedly imperialist strategy clearly perceived the basis of US power on the planet as being more like a thing than a relationship, more like an object than a process, more like a proprietary interest than a democratic right. In emphasizing its hard power, the US government sacrificed much of its capacity to exercise "soft power" through the medium, for instance, of international diplomacy.[154] For some, the subsequent decision of the US government to apply its policy through the invasion and occupation of Iraq without regard to the will of its allies, the UN Security Council, and international public opinion served as a marker of weakness rather than strength, as a sign of desperation more than a signal of unflappable resolve.[155] While the Bush regime undertook the mission with the hope of vanquishing the ghosts of the US failure in Vietnam, Iraq became a new theatre of conflict to remind the world of the internal contradictions, ironies, and limitations of American power.

As Kevin Phillips has written, "the botched occupation of Iraq boiled up into a local insurgency, destroying Washington's private dream of throwing open Iraqi oil spigots, driving down oil prices, and breaking the power of OPEC and its state-owned oil companies."[156] In fact these nationalized oil companies, the most important of which are Saudi Arabia's Aramco,

Russia's Gazprom, PetroChina, the National Iranian Oil Company, Brazil's Petrobas, Malaysia's Petronas, and Petroleos de Venezuala, grew in wealth and popular support just as the expansionary plans of the likes of Exxon Mobil, Chevron, BP, and Shell were checked along with the setbacks suffered by US military forces. As a result, the national oil companies came collectively to control about three-quarters of the world's remaining reserves. The other side of this equation puts enormous importance on the energy resources of Canada, currently the largest source of US oil and gas imports.[157] Indeed, according to the *International Herald Tribune,* the tar sands of northern Alberta represented in 2007 about 50 to 70 per cent of the reserves not barred to international oil companies because of government prohibitions.[158]

There are many other forces at work, however, in the transformed political economy of oil and gas. When oil prices quadrupled after OPEC's oil embargo in 1973–74, the *quid pro quo* negotiated between US president Richard Nixon and Saudi Arabian officials was that all future purchases of OPEC's main export would have to be paid for in US dollars. In this fashion, US money was restored to its former role as the world's primary medium of commercial transaction. US dollars became Saudi-American petrodollars. Those governments exporting large quantities of oil tended to build up particularly large quantities of US cash in their national reserves. This pattern accelerated as the United States moved from being a creditor nation to the world's biggest debtor nation. With the invasion of Iraq, however, attitudes towards the US dollar soured, especially in Muslim countries. Before 2003, Saddam Hussein had made himself a target when he defied the dictate that his country's oil must be sold in American currency. Saddam attempted to demean the dollar by elevating the Euro to a more important role in the world of international oil transactions. Other OPEC leaders such as Hugo Chavez followed this lead. As national treasuries shifted their reserves from dollars to a more varied array of currencies, downward pressures on the value of US money grew. This trend quickened as the Great Housing and Credit Bubble began to burst in 2007. As *Financial Times* investment editor John Authers observed in 2007, "A high oil price used to mean a strong dollar. But now we have record crude prices and the weakest dollar in decades."[159]

With two million Iraqis having fled the conflagration and two million more citizens being internally displaced, the huge consequences of the muscle flexing by the US government's military forces continued to mount. The fiasco placed huge pressures on the internal cohesion of the Republican Party and the Bush White House. Indeed, it pointed a spotlight of worldwide scrutiny at the military-industrial complex, an inheritance from the Second World War and the Cold War whose gas-guzzling, nuclear-energized capacity for destruction on a truly monumental scale seemed increasingly discordant with the real needs and priorities of humanity in the twenty-first century. While this complex of agencies had acquired almost unimaginable power to kill, the chaos in Iraq demonstrated its incapacity to reconstruct shattered societies. There were few ideological resources on which to draw to replicate the kind of mobilized liberalism, however self-serving, that had energized the reconstruction of Japan and of Western Europe following the US adoption of the Marshall Plan after the Second World War.

The failure of the US government to investigate credibly the events of 9/11 before rushing ahead with a very controversial set of pre-existing military and domestic plans added significantly to the huge currents of suspicion and dismay in the international community. In the name of waging a Global War on Terror, the primary victors of the Cold War attempted to continue their domination of key relationships of power and property in the twenty-first century. A new enemy was needed to justify heightened military expenditures, and a new enemy was identified to embody the necessary threat for the elaboration of a terror economy in the twenty-first century. This terror economy continues to centralize global power in the executive branch of the US government. It gives the US commander-in-chief expanded powers of patronage as the primary purchaser of war-oriented goods and services from a vast host of suppliers. These suppliers include those corporations that assemble and logistically support mercenary armies whose largely secret and unaccountable activities give new meaning to the concept of hyperprivatization. In the era of the Global War on Terror, enterprises such as Blackwater Corporation performed services for their paymasters that replicated in an altered environment many similar functions to those performed by the privateers and mercantile companies that colonized new frontiers in the rise of imperial Europe.

By hitching the machinery of imperial privatization to its first major deployment of its own armed forces since the Vietnam fiasco, the US government highlighted the continuing nature of its own unbroken tradition of experimentation with the apparatus of corporate and property law. The United States itself was born from an earlier phase in this continuum of experimentation in the legal and political means of transforming major expanses of the Earth into registered private property. The United States emerged from the laboratory of British imperialism as the new polity's founders implemented a novel form of federal sovereignty capable of accelerating the corporate colonization and commodification of the material resources throughout the better part of a whole continent. This continuing tradition of experimentation in the development of capitalism's constitution continues to be devoted to inculcating new strains of corporate formation through modifications in the methodology of war, the biotechnology of seeds, the commercialization of death, and the privatization of life.

Visions of Self-Determination in Eras of Imperial Rule, Apartheid, the Cold War, the War on Terror, and Late Consumer Capitalism

Gazing from afar at the ghastly heaps of dead and the hosts of the mutilated, at science turned into devilry and ever inventing new tortures for rending and slaying, Asia may be forgiven for thinking that, on the whole, she prefers her own religions and civilizations.

Annie Besant, Presidential Address to the Indian National Congress, 1917

Here we are in our tragedy.
Security has gone but danger remains.

Osama bin Laden, 2002

VANDALIZING THE BOWL WITH ONE SPOON: PERSISTENT PATTERNS OF DESTRUCTION AND RESTORATION

The single most powerful force to emerge from world history since 1492 is the complex of legal, commercial, psychological, and political relationships that goes by the name of capitalism. The ongoing globalization of an increasingly homogenous system of capitalist interaction continues to extend the boundaries of private property towards new frontiers of matter, mind, and relationship. The expansion of capitalist transactions into ever more facets of life has been so steady and unrelenting that the process is made to seem normal, even inevitable. It is made to seem like a realization of natural law. Changes in stock-market indexes, currency values, and commodity prices are disseminated in the media with the matter-of-fact regularity of weather reports. Hence the culture of capitalist privatization has become as much a fixture of our environment as the wind and the rain. As Immanuel Wallerstein has written, "the historical development of capitalism has involved the thrust towards the commodification of everything."[1]

A focus on the history of Indigenous peoples before the imposition of capitalism helps to clarify the great range of possible ways that material relationships can be organized. In their varied adaptation to local ecologies, Indigenous peoples developed a vast array of distinct political economies. In the rich abundance of North America's West Coast, the famous potlach came to express and renew many of the core ideals of a sophisticated Aboriginal civilization. The West Coast Indians' potlach can serve as a symbol signifying the existence of a great variety of systems for conducting material relations among and within Aboriginal groups. Almost none of these systems are culturally consistent with the type of market-driven transactions epitomized by the operation of stock markets. In societies organized around the potlach, the great motivation for accumulating wealth is to give it away in eleborate ceremonies that confirmed the prestige of the host as well as relationships of power linking the guests.[2] Today, the organization of large portions of the Internet essentially as a kind of gift economy duplicates some features of the potlach. It demonstrates the viability of models of exchange that do not conform with the capitalist systems of commercial transaction between buyers and sellers. The Internet radically alters ways of picturing and configuring both private and public property, private and public personalities. Much is freely given and taken on the Internet without the incentive of profit. As Matt Mason oberves in his study of capitalism's "reinvention" in this era of digital interactivity, the use of the Internet as a medium for sharing artful communications proves again and again the wrongness of all "abstract economic constructs [that] have long told us we are governed by nothing but self-interest."[3] The idea of the Internet as the site of a great potlach of digital creativity gives credence to the contemporary possibilities of the Fourth World as a realm of free and open exchange informed by Aboriginal traditions of sharing.

The ideals of the Fourth World continue to call into question the view that the universal adoption of capitalist hyperprivatization is the inevitable outcome of the ending of the Cold War. The vision of Indigenous self-determination in the Fourth World continues to expose the Cold War's lie that all humanity faced a single choice between capitalism and communism and that the demise of the primary state symbol of the latter necessitates the adoption of the former as the sole means of organizing the planet's political economy. The idealization of capitalist privatization as the great engine of human progress starts with the conviction that large portions of the Earth must be surveyed, registered, apportioned, and enclosed as the private property of individuals. From the idea of privatizing land flows naturally the idea of transforming minerals, forests, and even water, air, and the life forms they support into the private property of human and corporate "persons."[4] The rush in the 1990s to transform fresh water into a commercial frontier of corporate privatization represents a significant aspect of the post–Cold War drive to expand the scope of imperial globalization, to remove one of life's most essential elements from the collective domain of the bowl with one spoon.

Although over 70 per cent of the Earth's surface is covered by water, the world's supply of fresh water represents less than half of 1 per cent of the total amount. The consumption of life's primary element has been doubling every twenty years, a rate twice that of human population growth on Earth. Toxic pollution has rendered many water bodies unfit for both healthy aquatic life and human consumption. The potent chemistry of the Industrial Revolution has been the primary ingredient in the deteriorating quality of water. The sources of increased water pollution include human sewage, aquatic dumps, the runoff from heavy applications of agricultural fertilizers, insecticides, and herbicides, as well as the radioactive byproducts generated by various types of uranium mining and nuclear power plants. The quick runoff of soil resulting from rapid deforestation has radically damaged the ecological health of many aquatic systems. Even the industrial base underlying the most recent phase of the revolution in global communications is having an effect through the use of massive amounts of deionized water to make the raw material for silicon microchips.

The evidence is overwhelming that the availability of clean drinking water and healthy aquatic ecology is being sacrificed in many thousands of ways to the rush to expand the frontiers of capitalist privatization. The consistent pattern in this system of prioritization is that healthy ecology is to be sacrificed to the rapid replication of capital through maximization of corporate profits. Commercial corporations and their shareholders reap an unfair share of the capital to be derived from the transformation of natural resources into commodities, while the public takes most of the environment costs and liabilities resulting from this kind of exploitation. The subordination of the health of ecological systems to the commercial and political imperatives of the fossil fuel indusry has been especially dramatic.

One of most serious consequences of the massive burning of oil and gas is to warm the global climate and thereby raise the levels of oceans through the rapid melting of polar ice caps. Moreover, in the oil-rich districts of Russia and Alberta, for instance, vast quantities of fresh water are being contaminated in dirty industrial techniques aimed at flushing out oil and gas from deep within the Earth to more accessible levels. Great quantities of fresh water are also contaminated in the energy-intensive process of separating the oil from the Albertan tar sands, where it takes seven barrels of fresh water to produce one barrel of oil.[5] As fresh water becomes increasingly scarce, the incentives grow for commercial corporations to commodify life's most essential liquid. Indeed, those who stand to derive enhanced profits from the growth of markets in fresh water have a vested interest in the proliferation of all processes that pollute water and limit the free supply of this precious resource in its most uncontaminated state. The diminishing supply of pure water is thereby providing a new currency of capitalist privatization, a new frontier of commodified liquidity.

"Water," writes Johan Bastin of the European Bank for Reconstruction and Development, "is the last infrastructure frontier for private investors."

On a darker note, World Bank vice-president Ismail Serageldin has famously prophesied that the wars of the twenty-first century will be largely about the control of fresh water.[6] The biggest companies leading the push to privatize the world's supply of fresh water are based in France. In 2005 Vivendi Environement operated in one hundred countries; Suez Lyonnaise, the commercial descendant of the same company that built Egypt's Suez Canal in the 1860s, had investments in forty-one. This progression is suggestive of the many trajectories of continuity linking older forms of imperialism with newer techniques of capitalist empire building.

In the small, landlocked South American country of Bolivia, the politics of the struggle to resist the corporate privatization of water has combined with growing hostility to the US-led dominance of the oil and gas sector. Bolivia forms one small part of the larger territory of the Incan civilization. In the days of the Spanish American Empire, the Incas' Aboriginal domain in the Andes Mountains formed the basis of the Viceroyalty of Peru. Present-day Bolivia contains the stripped-out silver mines of Potosi, once the world's richest source of mineral wealth as well as the Spanish Empire's most notorious centre of Indian slavery. The presence in Bolivia of Potosi, one of the Earth's most telling symbols of the profound inequities generated by imperial globalization, helps inject a larger-than-life element of drama into the clash of political visions in Simón Bolívar's national namesake.

In Bolivia in 1999, a people's movement dominated by the Aymara- and Quechua-speaking communities renewed the spirit of the eighteenth-century protest movement against foreign exploitation led by the Incan aristocrat Túpac Amaru. The more recent campaign opposed the effort by Bechtel Corporation to take over a significant part of Bolivia's aquatic resources. The Indian-led resistance to the corporate privatization of water grew into a broader revolt against the exploitation by US companies of new discoveries of indigenous oil and gas. Evo Morales was one of the most determined and innovative leaders to emerge from this upsurge of popular protest. With his own deep roots in the Indian heritage of resistance to the Columbian conquests, he was strongly opposed to all aspects of the so-called Washington consensus. In the presidential elections of 2002, Morales argued that this plan for subordinating the public powers of the Bolivian government to the privatizing agenda of foreign capital had little to offer the majority of his fellow citizens but deeper poverty and heightened inequality. He surprised many observers with the strength of his second-place finish in a multi-party field. He attracted even more attention when he became Bolivia's president in 2006. Shortly following his ascent to the presidency, Morales committed his own government to work with those of Cuba, Venezuala, and Ecuador to institue as socialist trade block emphasizing the freedom of peoples to exercise economic self-determination. His original constituency was Indian coca farmers, many of whom he characterized as ex-miners "on the run from neoliberalism."[7] According to Felipe Quispe, an Aymara speaker who has emerged along with Morales as one of the leading Aboriginal voices to condemn the foreign pillaging of his country: "We are no longer servants. We are Indians of the post-modern era, even though some find that difficult to understand."[8]

The forces of international capital fought back in 2008 by advocating more local autonomy for regional governors in Bolivia's oil-rich districts such as Santa Cruz, Pando, Beni, and Tarija. The strategy was to weaken the movement for fundamental changes to Bolivia's constitution, including land reforms, by wearing down and exhausting those movements aligned with Morales. The main tactic was to force his supporters into a rapid-fire series of referenda. The growing reaction of the wealthier class to Bolivia's induction into the ongoing Bolivarian revolution led by Hugo Chevez helped mobilize the workings of the Ponchos Rojas, a militia that draws in membership primarily from Bolivia's Indian communities.

The convergence of the politics of water and of energy in Bolivia is rich with premonitions about the nature of the struggles ahead on the frontiers of globalization in the twenty-first century. Unlike fossil fuels, water is a renewable resource. While the unprocessed byproducts of burned oil and gas cause significant damage to the environment in the form of smog, acid rain, and climate change, water, by its nature, is the ultimate embodiment of constant movement, of life's cycles of ceaseless transformation. The qualities that make water life's most vital constituent part also make this primal liquid an extremely controversial currency of capitalist privatization. For idealists of capitalism, water's constant circulation provides the perfect metaphor for the workings of the money system. Just as the same water keeps moving through its transformative cycles, renewing life as it goes, so money shifts from pay cheque to pocket to store to bank to factory to pay cheque, generating livelihoods and economic well-being as it travels.

For those who emphasize the pre-eminence of human rights over property rights, however, the transformation of water into capital is a travesty that violates the most fundamental principles of natural and international law. The right of access to clean water can be characterized as a human right because, without this access, neither human life nor any other kind of life can be sustained and renewed. The tension between those who see access to clean water as a property right to be purchased and sold and those who view it as an inherent human right mirrors the debate over the provision of health care on a global basis. Like questions pertaining to the provision of medical services for the poor, questions about the provision of clean water tend to pit those who would limit the recognition of human rights to political and civil rights against those who situate human rights in the broader context of social and economic rights. The latter group tend to see Article 25 of the UN's Universal Declaration of Human Rights as a central text: "Everyone has the right to a standard of living adequate for the health and well-being of himself and his family, including food, clothing, housing, and medical care and necessary social services, and the right to security in the event of unemployment, sickness, disability, widowhood, old age, or other lack of livelihood in circumstances beyond his control."9

The problems raised by the commodification of water go on and on. How, for instance, can water be legitimately possessed when its very essence is perpetual movement, when it continually migrates between frozen atmospheric and liquid states, between the Earth's surfaces and its depths? Since every living organism, including human beings, is largely made up of water, the idea of privatizing the main constituent part of our own bodies resonates with some of the same themes that made property of slaves. The privatization of the aquatic commons extends the reach of the Columbian conquests into new frontiers of matter and life. This development helps to illustrate the continuing power of the idea and institution of private property in shaping the course of imperial globalization. The processes of capitalist privatization extend from mountain peaks to the depths of the oceans, from the content of microchips to the design of genes. In an era when there are no more huge hemispheres to claim, colonize, and render as apportioned private property, there is a need to open new territories of mind and matter in order to provide capital with the expanded space it needs to replicate and expand itself.

The huge and almost instant expansion of the domain granted for monopoly patents in the abstract realm of "intellectual property" helped to fill capitalism's need for new fields of proprietary interest. Ironically, this expansion took place with the claim that it was part of a process of diminishing the scope of state jurisdiction. The real dynamic, however, was quite different. Just as the extension of charters to colonizing companies in the seventeenth century entailed enormous expansions in the reach of the sovereign claims asserted by European powers, so the expansion of claims to new realms of intellectual property meant massive extensions of the sovereign assertions of nation-states and their corporate extensions. As John C. Weaver has observed, "property rights cannot exist without governments, because they are the creation of governments and require enforcement."10

The elaboration of the empire of possessive corporatism through the rapid expansion of the proprietary domain of intellectual property further diversified the enormous complexity of capitalism's apparatus of ownership. By the late nineteenth century, Lewis Henry Morgan was already marvelling at the intricate genius embodied in this system's increasingly international apparatus of proprietorship. His pioneering ethnographic work stood prominently in the continuum of social analysis running between that of Jean Jacques Rousseau and Karl Marx. "The outgrowth of property has been so immense," Morgan mused, "its forms so diversified, its uses so expanding and its management so intelligent in the interests of its owners, that it has become, on the part of people, an unmanageable power." He added, "the human mind stands bewildered in the presence of its own creation."11

The type of imperialism that gathered force after 1492 helped to drive, accelerate, and extend the progess of Europe's enclosure movement.

Enclosure helped facilitate and express the transformation of shared feudal property into individually owned plots. The growing complexity of material relations attending this privitization of the land was closely connected to the rise of urbanization, the elaboration of a more finely calibrated class system, and the migration of displaced peasant farmers away from Europe to colonial holdings in the Americas, Australasia, and parts of Africa. At its most basic level, enclosure involves the surveying, registration, and, often, fencing of individual plots to keep human trespassers out and to keep animal livestock in. This surge in the growth of fenced private property made possible the primitive beginnings of biotechnology through the selective breeding of animals. The essence of selective breeding is to assert human control over the procreative process rather than leaving to chance the pollination of domesticated plants and the sexual liasons of commodified animals. As the financiers, industrialists, traders, adminstrators, and assorted journeymen in the vanguard of capitalism struggled to break free from the collectivist weight of feudal institutions, the enticements of overseas empire proved increasingly attractive. Colonial expansion presented whole continents whose raw matter could seemingly be privatized more easily, efficiently, and extravagantly than was the case at home.

The urge to expand the boundaries of imperial ownership extended the institution of private property into the bodies of many millions of Black Africans who were sold into the slaving plantations that proliferated, especially in the tropical zones of the Americas.[12] Moreover, the emigration from Europe of wave after wave of fortune-seeking colonists vastly accelerated the pace of the imperial drive to impose alien regimes of property apportionment on wider and wider sections of the Earth.[13] As Paul Johnson explains in his monumental study of *The Birth of the Modern,* the years following the Napoleonic Wars witnessed the displacement and extinguishment of Indigenous peoples outside Europe on an unprecedented scale. This assault on some of humanity's most deeply rooted societies helped established the necessary conditions for the greatest surge of migration in all human history. Part of this outward explosion of European migrants was expressed in Russia's rapid colonization of southern Siberia and south-central Asia. The worldwide spread of European people, together with their languages, laws, and prorietary institutions, saw the pricing of land at rates "cheaper than at any time in history, before or since." In Johnson's words, this saga of material and political expansion occurred during "a unique moment, which could never conceivably occur again."[14] The growth and exodus of Europe's surplus populations was partially fuelled by the changes that had occurred after European farmers began cultivating plants first domesticated in the Americas by Indian horticulturalists. The adoption of corn and potatoes was especially instrumental in increasing Europe's domestic food production and, with it, the number of mouths that could be fed from agricultural output of fixed areas of land.[15] The mass migration to the New World was anticipated and accompanied by the founding of the United States and the Latin American republics. These polities were designed to combine the expansionary thrust of commercial empire build-ing with a means of appeasing the desire of transplanted Europeans and their Creole descendants to bring widening spheres of proprietary relations under their own local control. Why, asked many of those who demanded sovereign status for their New World countries, should they expand the pro-prietary claims of imperial masters when they could declare independence in order to seize, control, and build up their own indigenous empires of private property?[16]

The circumstances attending the birth of the United States combined with the abundance of its resources and the attributes of its entrepreneurs to make the future superpower the world's emerging dynamo of capitalist privatization. Christian religiosity has been an essential ingredient of the material culture that has long ruled the political economy of capitalism's most busy laboratory. This connection between American capitalism and Christian fundamentalism became absolutely clear in 1956 at the height of the Cold War, when the US system of paper currency was transformed into a religious symbol. Through an Act of Congress, the phrase, "In God We Trust," was introduced onto the written text of paper money in the United States in order to emphasize the contrast between the Christian origins of the capitalist superpower and the atheistic communism at the ideologi-cal basis of the Soviet Union. In arguing for the marriage of church and state in the wording applied to US money, President Dwight Eisenhower maintained: "In this way we are affirming the transcendence of religious faith in America's heritage and future; in this way we constantly strengthen those spiritual weapons which forever will be our country's most powerful resource in peace and war."[17]

The direct linkage between the Christian deity and American money was first made in 1864. The phrase "In God We Trust" was inserted on American two-cent pieces in a moment of great turmoil during the height of the Civil War.[18] That terrible confrontation, which consumed the lives of 600,000 victims, came down ultimately to a lethal conflict between the property rights of slave owners and the human rights of slaves. The intensity of the war to resolve this fundamental issue points to the potential volatility of the intensifying contemporary dispute over the role of religion in the law and politics of the superpower. It points to the profound and growing schism between those who adhere to the separation between church and state in the US Constitution and the powerful lobby on the religious right who want to remake American institutions to reflect the theocratic prin-ciple that the United States is the Christian God's primary instrument of divine power on Earth.[19]

The privatization of one frontier after the next created enormous incen-tives for those eligible to own rather than to be owned, for those eligible to claim or purchase title to the new living spaces on the moving edge of the expanding empire of global capital. The conditions of imperial capitalism's charter group contrasted dramatically with the circumstances of those Indigenous peoples who often saw their Aboriginal territories transformed beneath their feet into someone else's property.[20] The imposition of standardized grids of privatized property relations on widening expanses of life, land, and resources generated huge conformities within the framework of capitalism's intermittent rounds of boom and bust, competition and monopolization. The production of Olympic champions, Model T Fords, or big-breasted chickens, for example, presented winning prototypes to be emulated by competitors with only slight modifications. The act of replicating again and again the commercial design of capitalism's winners pushed humanity into narrowing enclosures of conformity, into motifs of life where eclecticism and diversity were frequently sacrificed to inflexible prescriptions for the maximization of profit through the achievement of industrial efficiency.

The extension of commercialization to broader expanses of matter, mind, and relationship enormously increased the range of commodified sevices and manufactured products even as the unrelenting privatization of nature pressed the process of capital's replication into narrower channels of monoculture. This propensity to replace diversity with expanding conformities was marked especially in the accelerating industrialization of forestry, agriculture, and animal husbandry. The hardiness and adaptability of bananas, chickens, wheat, and spruce trees, for instance, was dramatically undermined by commercialized regimes of breeding and genetic manipulation aimed at replicating sameness. The impoverishment of genetic diversity within industrialized life forms is but one aspect of a larger phenomenon that is fast eliminating both the space and complexity of habitat for the renewal of many millions of life forms that have not been domesticated and transformed into the raw material of food, fibre, drugs, and other merchandisable products.

The same industrial and economic forces resulting in the rapid loss of biological diversity extend also to the institutions, cultures, and minds of human beings. For many generations the ascendant populations on the moving frontiers of the Columbian conquests have been rolling over and pushing aside many peoples whose evolutionary development occurred over very long cycles of Aboriginal history. One result has been the replacement in many parts of the world of the languages of the colonized with the languages of the colonizers. This shrinking of humanity's commonwealth of languages narrows our collective range of expressive capacity for thinking, discussing, and writing about many subjects. As Peter Kulchyski observes, "it is a 'highly developed' culture indeed when we systematically destroy the world only marginally faster than we destroy every remaining capacity within ourselves to appreciate what is being destroyed."[21]

The rapid loss of the vast majority of the world's Aboriginal languages is integral to a global epidemic of amnesia that is fast extinguishing our capacity to connect with many of humanity's oldest and most ecologically strategic heritages of memory, experience, and reflection. The shrinking base of linguistic pluralism diminishes especially our capacity to draw on the accumulated insights and observations of Indigenous peoples. Their shared polities have often embodied some of humanity's most successful adaptations over thousands of years to the unique ecological attributes of specific bio-regions. The potential economic and environmental utility of this Indigenous ecological knowledge, as embedded most securely and authentically in the structures and vocabularies of Aboriginal languages, is almost incalculable.[22] From Amazonia to Borneo to the northwest coast of North America, the contemporary industrial plundering of biocultural diversity tends to be especially severe in the Earth's remaining tropical and temperate rain forests. These sites of ecological abundance constitute some of the Earth's greatest reservoirs of biological diversity in the plant and animal worlds as well as in the linguistic and cultural pluralism of the human realm.[23]

The inroads of monoculture are especially evident in the sameness of the shopping malls and the intensively branded urban sprawls that increasingly define the world's cityscapes. The fast expansion of the worldwide culture of malls is projecting deep inroads of privatization into what remains of the urban commons. Although these malls are often promoted as welcoming centres of community life, they are usually owned by companies whose officers are unafraid to exercise their organizations' imperatives of private property. They do so, for instance, by treating unwanted visitors as trespassers to be forcefully removed by the private police forces that closely monitor and control these emporiums of commerce and popular culture. The big chains that tend to dominate these privatized public spaces, including, for instance, Wal-Mart, McDonald's, Burger King, or the Gap, depend for survival and growth on their corporate capacities to generate and exploit massive conformities of taste and consumption. The iconography of mass tastes, desires, and imagination draws heavily on the mythological constructs manufactured by the info-entertainment industry. This complex of closely interwoven media businesses was built up by the likes of William Randolph Hearst, Henry Luce, Walt Disney, Akio Morita, Rupert Murdoch, and the moguls of both Madison Avenue and the Hollywood Dream Machine. Through the process of merger and convergence, a small number of giant media conglomerates have come to monopolize the largest and most influential global platforms of commercial communications. In the words of Edward S. Herman and Robert W. McChesney, these giants of commercial communications have become "the new missionaries of global capitalism."[24]

This complex of show business, production, marketing, and consumption excludes a growing and increasingly resentful portion of humanity who collectively lack the economic means to take part in most rituals of market relations. The results of this exclusion are to be seen in the rapid growth of homelessness and shanty towns in many of the world's cities. The forces underlying the intensification of urban poverty are re-enacted again and again in China, Mexico, Peru, Russia, Indonesia, India, Canada, Australia, and other countries. The effects of mining and hydroelectric flooding, for instance, have combined with disruptions from the rapid industrialization of vegetable and fruit farming, livestock breeding, and forestry to uproot and destroy scores of Aboriginal communities. Many of their members have responded by swelling the ranks of the urban poor.

The rapid destruction of many of the world's remaining hunting cultures forms an integral element of the forces driving the massive migration of human beings from rural regions to overcrowded cities. This process is weakening and killing the very communities whose members have collectively kept alive some of humanity's oldest and richest stores of insight into the puzzle of how animals and plants, drainage basins and climate systems, spiritual rituals and other forms of human intervention are interconnected in the web of life. The death of much of the strategic ecological knowledge held by hunting communities fractures the integrity of the Bowl with One Spoon. As genocide combines with the severed or fading memories of Aboriginal history's increasingly displaced and disoriented survivors, the way is cleared for the accelerated transformation of Earth into property. These changes go far beyond the set of phenomena usually associated with urbanization. They illustrate well the intense antagonism between the mobile individualism required by capitalism and the deep ties of time and community linking most members of hunting societies to the unique ecologies of the territories of their ancestors.

This heritage of antagonism draws heavily on John Locke's influential theory of capitalist property relationships where he alleges in *Two Treatises of Government* that the English farmers of Devonshire are about a thousand times more productive in their use of land than the Indian hunters of North America.[25] Putting aside the reality that many Aboriginal societies throughout the Western Hemisphere were based primarily on farming rather than on the taking of wild animals, Locke's relegation of hunting to the realm of primitive obsolescence echoes across the generations right up to the present. The assumption that progress demands the imposition of a death sentence on all hunting societies has been challenged in recent years by a growing array of voices from the social sciences, including those of Marshall Sahlins, Hugh Brody, Peter Kulchyski, Harvey Feit, Paul Nadasdy, Colin Scott, and Julie Cruikshank.[26]

While the history of capitalist economies is to be measured in hundreds of years and the history of agriculture in thousands of years, the history of human hunting cultures goes back perhaps a hundred thousand years. Much as the efficient anatomy of sharks demonstrates their success over long periods of evolutionary adaptation, so the most resilient Aboriginal hunting societies encapsulate systems of social and ecological organization whose sustainable viability is demonstrated by the duration of their survival. The precious ecological knowledge of Aboriginal hunting societies has many contemporary applications to the great tasks facing the generations who must shoulder the immense responsibility of facing and reversing the accelerating degradation of the environment in our time. While there must be no constraints preventing those who grow up in hunting societies from leaving this way of life to pursue other options, so, too, is it in the interest of all humanity that the necessary measures be set in place nationally and internationally to encourage the continuation of some Aboriginal hunting traditions throughout broad zones of protected territory.[27]

In his condemnation of Canadian officialdom for its persisting unwillingness to accept the unbroken viability of Aboriginal hunting cultures throughout large parts of northern North America, Peter Kulchyski has written:

In Canada, for over a hundred years a whole trajectory of social, political and economic policies has been developed to assimilate hunters. The cumulative effects of these policies have been nothing short of tragic for northern Aboriginal communities. It is the modernizers, those who think they can build northern suburbs that will replicate southern realities in the subarctic and arctic, who are the true paternalists and romantics here: they still have a naïve faith that sporadic wage work on projects that will last one or two decades offers a future for Aboriginal communities.[28]

In *The Other Side of Eden*, Hugh Brody also addresses the many prejudices against Indigenous peoples who have retained their hunting cultures. He highlights, for instance, the representational reversals that made "nomads" of the "natives," even as the so-called sedentary settlers drew many of their members from those jumping on and off the migratory highways of global colonialism.[29] The easy persistence even today in the assignment of "native" identity to such a diverse array of the planet's peoples says much about the nomadism animating the psychology of that portion of the Earth's population that does not consider itself to be "native" or Aboriginal.

In *Like the Sound of the Drum*, Kulchyski observes that the historical tension between farmers and hunters extends more recently to the tension between family farmers and agribusinesses that operate according to the industrial principles of capitalist privatization.[30] This tension is particularly pronounced in Latin America. Like Aboriginal hunters, traditional Indian farmers throughout this region have faced an imposed death sentence on their ways of life. This dictate of modernity and of the Green Revolution is illustrated by the government implementation of "fumigation" in Columbia. This intervention was carried out in the 1990s in the name of the US-sponsored War on Drugs. In spraying huge quantities of toxic chemicals on the lands of peasant farmers, government operatives destroyed the viability of whole communities whose diverse array of crops went far beyond poppies and coca. The use of coca as the major ingredient in cocaine represents a recent use of a traditional crop long cultivated and used in a variety of fashions by Indigenous peoples throughout large areas of the Americas.

Noam Chomsky has noted that war-torn Colombia combines the distinction of having one of the world's worst human rights records with being concurrently one of the planet's most generously rewarded recipients of US military aid. The toxic poisoning of some of Colombia's oldest and most thickly populated agricultural regions, argues Chomsky, is destroying "some of the richest biodiversity in the world." He adds: "Campesinos, indigenous people, and Afro-Colombians are now joining the millions in rotting slums and camps. And with the people gone, multinationals can strip the mountains for coal, extract oil and other resources, and probably convert what is left of the land to ranching by the rich or agroexport in an environment torn of its treasures and variety." The fumigation process, Chomsky concludes, is "another stage in the historical process of driving poor peasants from the land for the benefit of foreign investors and Colombian elites."[31] In commenting on efforts to extend the same destructive process to Bolivia, Evo Morales observed, "Zero coca means zero Quechua and Aymara."[32]

The destruction of rural political economies to meet the needs of agribusiness, industrial resource extraction, and employers seeking pools of cheap, easily exploitable workers form elements in an equation of injustice that some have dubbed "global apartheid."[33] Building on the metaphors of South African history as a representation in miniature of larger patterns of imperial expansion and rule, the term refers to the persisting divisions between those centres that gave rise to the expansion of empires and those regions that experienced colonization as a process of subordination, as a continuum of dispossession, disenfranchisement, and, sometimes, genocide. As Eduardo Galeano observes of our world of "powerful centers and subjugated outposts, there is no wealth that must not be held in some suspicion." He continues: "The underdevelopment in Latin America is a consequence of development elsewhere."[34] The idea of global apartheid can also highlight the growing inequities *within* most societies, the increasingly acrimonious class divisions often resulting in the withdrawal of the entitled minority, no matter what their skin colour, into tightly guarded enclaves of walled privilege.

The polarization of economic classes puts severe stress on the liberal principle that every human life is invested with equal dignity and worth. How can even the fiction of liberal equality be maintained in a world that rewards the work of some at many millions of times the rate of others; when three people have a net worth equal to the gross domestic product generated by all the citizens of forty-eight countries; when about 250 of the planet's richest individuals control assets equivalent to the annual income of about half of humanity; when the richest one-fifth of the world's people consumes almost 90 per cent of all goods and services and when the bottom fifth must make do on about 1 per cent of the global economy's output?[35] How can this fiction hold when almost half the world's children live in poverty; when 1.6 billion people lack adequate access to fresh water; when 2.6 billion lack basic sanitation; and when 1 per cent of what is annually spent on weapons could give all the world's poor children at least some access to rudimentary schooling?[36] These vast and widening disparities form the backdrop against which many members of the world's disproportionately entitled minority are increasingly prone to purchase their protection from privatized police forces.

The privatization of the capacity to inflict violence represents a recent expression of an old phenomenon. Some European sovereigns such as England's Queen Elizabeth I secretly delegated the delivery of overseas violence to privateers. The more recent privatization of the means of violence flows from the process whereby some government agencies in the United State, Israel, and the largest of the formal imperial powers have downloaded the exercise of state terror to proxy regimes, for-profit agencies, and non-state groups and individuals. Peter Dale Scott has devoted much energy to describing this process. In particular he emphasizes the "deep politics" of close associations between those who specialize in the covert production, distribution, and sales of illegal drugs and those who specialize in the manipulation of government policies to advance the economic interests of oil and gas cartels.[37] Since at least the first half of the nineteenth century, when British merchants penetrated Chinese commerce through the Royal Navy's military onslaught in the Opium Wars, the manipulation of trade in addictive drugs has been an essential pillar of imperial governance on a global scale. The willingness of US authorities to become active or passive participants in the intertwined networks of transaction linking the trade in drugs and oil is an essential factor in the process of outsourcing control over the deployment of lethal violence to a widening array of state actors (as in Pakistan and Saudi Arabia), non-state groups, and even individuals. This process is complicated by the acceleration of technological breakthroughs that make weaponry cheaper, more desructive, and more compact as time progresses.

An important development in the corporate privatization of the public sector occurred in 1913, when the US Congress created the Federal Reserve system. With the *Federal Reserve Banking Act*, the structure of the US economy was made to conform more thoroughly with the banking system that had evolved in Europe. Indeed, many of the twelve banking consortiums that owned and controlled the new agency were European entities that had profited greatly from their speculative bets on the rising value of lands, first in British North America and then in the United States. The Act transferred substantial powers from the government to the corporate sector by extending to the favoured banking consortium strategic monopoly powers in the issuing and distribution of paper currency and in the selling of credit to finance and service the US national debt. The reorganization of the US economy around a single central financial institution was the culmination of a long struggle within the rising capitalist superpower about about who should control the power to issue money and finance the national debt. The creation of the Federal Reserve system epitomized the success of the monopoly forces against which Thomas Jefferson and Andrew Jackson had fought in their presidencies. They had vehemently opposed any form of special charter for a national bank because it would concentrate too much control over politics and the economy in too few hands.

The Federal Reserve system was closely connected to creation, also in 1913, of the still-contested federal power to tax the income of American citizens. Moreover, a significant body of historical literature directly connects the major banking figures who gained enormous new privileges from the Federal Reserve system to the US decision to enter the first World War and to the financing of the main protagonists behind the creation of the Soviet Union in 1917. Jacob Schiff of the Wall Street firm of Kuhn, Loeb and Company was the largest financial backer of the revolutionary forces led by Leon Trotsky and Vladimir Ilych Lenin. Kuhn, Loeb was one of those favoured entities that derived enormous competitive advantages from the federal charter granted to the banking consortium that acquired proprietary control of the Federal Reserve system. Although it is important to bring a sceptical eye to the abundant literature on the role of international bankers as actors who have played a disproportionately large role in the unfolding of these events, we cannot discount the pervasive influence emanating from the highest echelons of global finance. Wall Street's involvement in helping to finance the genesis of the regimes led by both Lenin and Hitler is indisputable. The waging of war in all its manifestations has always offered an excellent platform for profiteering. Wall Street power brokers in the twentieth century proved adept at developing the skill of their European forerunners, teachers, and partners in hedging their bets by situating their investments on both sides of key conflicts.[38]

As the empire of private property has grown, its units of exchange have been more and more divorced from the material realm they are meant to represent. This process was reflected in the abandonment of the gold standard by Great Britain in 1931 and by the United States in 1971. The growing abstractions in the existential essence of money reached ridiculous extremes in the creation of all sorts of legally and economically complex derivatives whose proliferating importance in the US and global economy came to light in the deflation of the Great Housing and Credit bubble beginning in 2007. The move from money backed by gold reserves and fixed rates of exchange to a system of massive speculation in the buying and selling of floating-value currencies introduced vast new vulnerabilities into the worldwide system of financial transactions. This change helped prepare the way for the transformation of much of the global economy into a network of commercial transaction whose main media of interactivity are mere bits and bites of electronic data sent hurtling along information highways. Breakthroughs in the technology of global communications helped hasten the conditions for the formation of a single worldwide regime of digitalized property relations, one that has enabled creditors and debtors, investors and speculators to move capital in all its profusely variegated formats throughout the planet at rates approaching the speed of light. The enormous transformations entailed in the digitalization of money took place just as the regimes of Ronald Reagan and Margaret Thatcher took charge of the process of dramatically dismantling many forms of direct government involvement in the regulation of business. The concurrence of new forms of business transaction on the Internet together with the deregulation of business and the privatization of many functions formerly performed by public government is having results whose full implications remain unclear.

In the spring of 2008 Thomas Homer-Dixon reflected on these trends in the wake of the demise of the Bear Stearns Investment Bank, one of many corporate lenders that grossly overextended lines of credit to feed speculation on endlessly rising real estate prices. He observed that "enormously powerful computers and software, along with fibre-optic communication, have allowed financial wizards to conduct transactions in a blink of an eye around the world and to create financial instruments – derivatives, swaps, structured investments and the like – of mind-boggling complexity. For all intents and purposes these new instruments have blurred the boundaries of what we call money." He concluded, "What counts as money isn't at all clear, and many things that look and behave like money can't be regulated."[39]

GANDHI, MANDELA, THE AFRICAN NATIONAL CONGRESS, 9/11, AND THE ANTI-POLITICS OF LATE CONSUMER CAPITALISM

In September of 2001 in the days leading up to the attacks on the Pentagon and the Twin Towers, an important international conference took place in Durban, South Africa. This UN-sponsored event was entitled the World Conference against Racism, Racial Discrimination, Xenophobia, and Related Intolerance. The topics spotlighted at this assembly could all be linked to the officially sanctioned version of what happened on 9/11, the event used by the administration of President George W. Bush to push ahead a broad array of expansionary and authoritarian policies that were justified in the name of the Global War on Terror. Might the so-called war have been averted if the warnings signals sent before and during the Durban Conference been more seriously heeded? The central message sent by many of the delegations at Durban was that the racial, economic, and political inequities which continue to divide humanity deny the global community any real chance of achieving peaceful equilibrium. The international dilemma of the stateless Palestinians became a flash point of division highlighting the most recent manifestation of a very old and enduring schism. Where the future of apartheid in South Africa had only years earlier been at the centre of contention dividing progressive forces from those of reaction, so disagreements about the condition of the displaced Palestinians assumed a broader symbolic significance for most of the delegations. This interpretive turn caused Irwin Cotler, a Canadian professor and politician, to dub the Durban gathering as "the conference against racism that became a racist conference against Jews."[40]

Cotler was far from alone in his criticism. The barrage of allegations directed at Israel and its US sponsors was met in Durban, Washington, Tel Aviv, and other world centres with elaborate arguments accusing the critics of being anti-Semitic, of perpetuating forms of persecution and conspiracy mongering that have plagued Jews for generations. Many of those in the forefront of this line of argument pointed to the striking hypocrisy of some individuals and groups who heaped accusations on Israel, Zionism, and the United States while remaining silent on the racism and ethnic warfare that was tearing apart Zimbabwe, for instance. To complicate the Durban Conference, its South African hosts attempted to introduce into the agenda a resolution calling for reparations for the transatlantic slave trade and the colonial oppression that contained it. "There is no doubt that slavery, colonialism and apartheid were crimes against humanity," proclaimed the resolution's authors. They continued, "The nature of the damage caused by slavery and colonialism is complex and manifold: It involves the wholesale destruction of peoples and groups, the erosion and in some cases theft, of social, economic and human capital and the destruction of the social fabric of entire peoples. In recent years, there has been a growing demand that some form of satisfaction be provided for these serious and grievous wrongs."[41]

The South African government's controversial motion helped to shed light on the deep-rooted inequities that remain embedded in the world's political economy. An improved understanding of some forms of institutionalized discrimination emerged from the effort to sort out the legacies of a system of international relations that had been based on divisions of the world's peoples between civilized and savage, masters and slaves, Christians and infidels, wards and trustees. At Durban considerable attention was devoted to mechanisms that create forms of debt slavery, even as disproportionately entitled minorities continue to control large concentrations of wealth in ways that perpetuate the material basis of global apartheid.[42] In a world of such deeply entrenched and heavily enforced injustices it is inevitable that some of the alienated will occasionally resort to random acts of violence in vain attempts to even the score. In other instances, such as when the main political organization of the South African hosts was outlawed by the proponents of apartheid, oppressed groups might opt to take up arms in self-defence and in the hope of unseating tyranny. Typically, however, the economic issues underlying such acts of public violence get lost in the reporting. The economic disparities underpinning outbursts of murder and mayhem are frequently ignored or downplayed, whereas the ethnic and religious character of violent disruptions are reported in lurid detail. This bias in the commercial media is not accidental but, rather, deep and systematic.

The Durban Conference highlighted issues that would be swept from the headlines days later when the events of September 11, 2001, changed history. There is a growing body of theory, some of it serious and well informed and some spurious, that the events of 9/11 were a false flag operation.[43] Although uneven in substance, the lively citizens' investigations into these matters cannot be categorically dismissed. In false flag operations, acts of violence are perpetrated or purposely misinterpreted through the covert activity of governments, corporations, and their agents in order to turn public opinion against a previously targeted group. Acts of violence are engineered and portrayed in the media in ways that cause the public to look to their own authorities for protection from groups that those in control want demonized and attacked. The bombing of the Reichstag in 1933, for instance, is now generally understood as a false flag operation to prepare public opinion in Germany for Adolf Hitler's totalitarian rule as initially justified in the name of waging an internal war against a phantom conspiracy of communist Jews. Many media outlets inside and outside Germany, including Lord Beaverbrook's *Daily Express*, helped to repress any alternative interpretations of the fire's causes. Operation Gladio was a similar covert operation where right-wing operatives planted bombs to blame and demonize left-wing groups in Italy. False flag operation like Operation Gladio or the Tonkin incident in Vietnam took place fairly frequently throughout the Cold War to justify various forms of intervention and aggression.

Regardless of the identity of the true protagonists behind the events of 9/11 –regardless of whether it was a false flag operation or not – that episode provided the primary justification for significant changes in the world's political economy in the name of the Global War on Terror. This war has been used to explain many intiatives, including military invasions, the curtailing of civil liberties, and the further elevation of the national security state and its corporate extensions to positions far above the laws that most common folk are compelled to follow. The psychological dimension of this strange war without end has been mythologically constructed to focus attention on religious and ethnic antagonisms even as it draws attention away from those forms of inequality that regularly materialize in the economic violence that permeates global capitalism. While Arab and Muslim people globally suffer most obviously from the kind of profiling and targeting that flows naturally from the theory that the world is engulfed in an inevitable clash between discordant civilizations, the prejudices do not end there.[44] The Global War on Terror helps to protect the claims of the rich to large concentrations of property even as it helps to downplay the plight of those whose marginalized socioeconomic status gives them the greatest reason to reject the proprietary status quo. For all these reasons, the Global War on Terror is first and foremost the most concerted and most broadly cast campaign of psychological warfare ever attempted in the global community. The aim of this war is to perpetuate oligarical governance rooted in popular fears and counter the possibility of anti-authoritarian governance rooted in popular hopes.

The main *modus operendi* of this dubious campaign of control through fear is to manufacture consent for continued global domination as policed through the instruments of the national security state and its attending military-industrial complex. The War on Terror's propganda, as epitomized by the work of David Frum and Richard Perle, lends legitimacy to entrenched plutrocacies everywhere, even as it arouses suspicion that those who question authority are outright evil.[45] This pretext for aggression gives cover to the propensity of ruling elites to repress rivals and dissenters through the denial of civil liberties and suppression of the rule of law. It gives credence to the erroneous assumption that history is approaching an end, and that there can be no basis for any legitimate revolutionary challenges to the proprietary advantages enjoyed by those who have gained disproportionate amounts of influence over the dominant means of political, economic, military, and technological exploitation in today's world.[46]

It makes no sense to try to vanquish terror from the world through increased warfare, more systematic and broadly applied methods of torture, or the militarization of space. In the long run, global security through peace is attainable only through concerted efforts to ease the maladies identified at gatherings such as the World Conference against Racism, Racial Discrimination, Xenophobia, and Related Intolerance. The host of the Durban Conference was the government of South Africa. Since 1994, when White minority rule was finally replaced by an electoral regime of universal adult suffrage, that government has been dominated by the political wing of the African National Congress. Since its inception in the early twentieth century, the ANC has served as a rallying point in the movement of colonized peoples to liberate themselves from the bondage of imperialism, racism, and commercial exploitation. Even before the founding of the ANC, the struggle against the South African state's racist institutions engaged the concerted activism of a great oracle of decolonization. In 1893, the year of Chicago's Columbian Exposition, India's Mohandas Gandhi relocated his family to Durban. Ever since he centred the seminal phase of his work of liberation in this important urban centre, Durban has been closely identified with the struggle to overcome the intertwined forces of racism and imperialism. The ANC and UN organizers of the anti-racist conference of September 2001 had this association in mind when they located the event in Durban.

In the course of his two decades of activism in South Africa, Gandhi achieved his first surge of prominence as the most determined legal and political advocate of the local East Indian population. During these years, Gandhi began developing the techniques of passive resistance and civil disobedience which he later applied in mobilizing a mass movement aimed at pushing the imperial government of Great Britain to "Quit India."[47] More than any other figure in the twentieth century, Gandhi elevated the struggle against the oppression of imperial rule to the level of a global movement. As South Africa's Nelson Mandela observed, "Gandhi is the archetypal anti-colonial revolutionary ... his non-violent resistance inspired anti-colonial and anti-racist movements internationally."[48] Ghandi absorbed many influences to form the tough sinew of his own unbreakable resolve to oppose wrongfully imposed authority through principled non-cooperation. He drew sustenance from the Hindu sacred texts such as the *Bhagawad Gita*, the philosophical musings of Henry David Thoreau and Leo Tolstoy, the poetry and personal friendship of Rabindranath Tagore, as well as aspects of both Christianity and the British Constitution. As Gandhi saw it, his quest to transcend the exploitation of colonialism was based on a rejection of all forms of corrupt domination. His non-violent protests were directed not only at the external forces of oppression but also at the internal tyrannies of the spirit that often prevent us from realizing our full potential as liberated and truly self-conscious human beings.

Based on his early experiences in South Africa, Gandhi promoted the principles of *satyagraha*, a Hindi word signifying the force of truth. These ideals were adopted by the Indian National Congress in 1930 when India's most powerful indigenous organization formally embraced a policy of *Purna Swaraj* – independent self-governance. In order to dramatize this stance, Gandhi led a march to Dandi on the Indian Ocean. His strategy for drawing broad attention to the injustice of foreign rule was to challenge the British monopoly on the production and taxation of sea salt. The news of Gandhi defying British law simply by taking salt from a beach on the Indian Ocean was reported around the world. With this single dramatic act Gandhi greatly widened the scope and effectiveness of the movement he came to embody. His violation of Crown laws governing the extraction of salt led to his being incarcerated along with about 80,000 others who copied his example. Philip Glass, the author of the opera *Satyagraha*, has obseerved that Gandhi understood the importance of the media. "He understood the power that holding up his dhoti drenched with seawater would have around the world ... The salt march always strikes me as the most ingenious piece of street theater ever conceived."[49]

Gandhi's unrelenting campaigns of peaceful defiance cast growing doubts not only on the legitimacy of British rule in India but also on the forced imposition of imperial domination over all colonized peoples. His example of non-violent protest has been drawn on again and again, even after he was assassinated in 1948 by a militant Hindu nationalist angry at the dismemberment of India the previous year. Gandhi's teachings proved particularly influential in giving strength to the pacifist wing of the civil-rights movement in the United States led by Martin Luther King Jr. During the boycott of the segregated bus service in Montgomery, Alabama, in 1956, King declared, "Christ gave us the goals and Gandhi gave us the tactics."[50] More recently, Tibet's Dalai Lama and the Burmese Nobel Laureate, Aung San Suu Kyi, have met the authoritarian suppression of indigenous self-determination in their home countries with Gandhi's methods of satyagraha. His insistence that the force of truth can overcome the force of violence continues to inspire hope even in times dominated by fear.

In much the same fashion that Adolf Hitler has been cast as the incarnation of ultimate evil in the twentieth century, Gandhi has emerged in the popular mind as the outstanding saint of the era he inhabited. Such depictions, however, do an injustice to the importance of average people in moulding the mental, political, and social environments that contain the lives of history's most lionized figures. As James Shaheen has noted in his introduction of a Buddhist publication providing an array of perspectives on the continuing importance of Gandhi's legacy, "While telling history through the stories of heroic [or diabolical] individuals makes for compelling drama, it does grave harm to our ability to appreciate the complex shaping of events that give birth to change."[51]

When Gandhi is viewed as a man rather than a saint, it becomes clear that he tempered his ascetic idealism with the pragmatic compromises necessary to attract and build up the networks of allies he needed to achieve at least some of his goals in an imperfect world. Like Thomas Jefferson, Gandhi was notorious for coming down on both sides of many of the big issues confronting him. This ambivalence in relationship to industrialization, for instance, is revealing. Gandhi was outspoken in condemning the evils of centralized production even as he extolled the values of self-sufficiency as displayed in India's vast number of small agricultural villages. His spinning of his own cloth on a totemic spinning wheel – a *charkha* – was meant to symbolize Gandi's promotion of India's indigenous forms of artisanship and political economy. Even as he espoused these principles in public, however, Gandhi and his close associates were handsomely financed in their political campaigns by the Indian industrialist Ghanshyam Das Birla.

Birla built up several large enterprises as he replaced British imports with products manufactured domestically in India's own factories. Gandhi's acceptance of Birla's patronage may have been a factor in the fact that his criticism of capitalist excesses did not extend to an outright rejection of capitalism itself. Indeed, Gandhi's view of the rights and responsibilities of extremely wealthly people were close to those of Andrew Carnegie, one of the richest men in the United States in an era closely associated with the power and ostentation of financial elites. Gandhi adopted the principle that the rich should see themselves as *trustees* rather than outright owners of their personal fortunes. They should recycle their wealth to help the needy and other good causes through their philanthropy. Carnegie first published his much reprinted article on this subject in 1889. Carnegie's "Gospel of Wealth" seems to have influenced Gandhi even as in more recent times it has informed the financial philosophy of many well known financiers, industrialists, and media personalities, including Bill Gates, the founder of the Microsoft Corporation.[52]

In a tribute to Gandhi, Nelson Mandela explained, "The South African A.N.C. remained implacably opposed to violence for most of its existence." He added, "I followed the Gandhian tradition for as long as I could, but then there came a point in the struggle in the 1960s when the brute force of the oppressor could no longer be countered through passive resistance alone."[53] The pacifist roots of the ANC go back to the founding of the South African Native National Congress in 1912. The organization changed its name to its current designation in 1923. The older political entity was initially the brainchild of Pixley ka Isaka Seme, a well-educated Zulu man who was moved to action by the exclusion of Indigenous peoples from the rights of citizenship in the Union of South Africa. The Union was established in 1910 as a so-called White dominion by Great Britain's Westminster Parliament. At the Congress's founding meeting two years later, Seme called together a representative group of Black South Africans at Bloemfontein in order to address the underlying injustice of a polity founded on principles of racial exclusiveness. "We have discovered," he told the covention, "that in the land of their birth, Africans are to be treated as hewers of wood and drawers of water." He added, "The White people of this country have formed what is known as the Union of South Africa, a union in which we have no voice in the making of the laws and no part in their administration."[54]

In his quest to remake South Africa as an inclusive polity, Seme was unrelenting in his desire to point the new organization in a direction that would draw unity from the ethnic and cultural diversity of his country. The failure to rise above ethnic differences, he believed, is "the cause of our woes and all our backwardness and ignorance today." He proposed that the new organization transcend "the demon of racialism, the abberations of the Xhosa-Fingo feud, the animosity that exists between Zulus and Tongaas, between the Basutos and every other Native." He insisted that these divisions "must be buried and forgotten; it has shed among us sufficient blood. We are one people."[55]

With his contempt for unnecessary antagonisms among local Aboriginal groups, Seme presents a classic example of the propensity of many colonized peoples to seek larger confederacies and coalitions in order to defend their lands, their nations, their polities, their families, and their individual lives. This same pattern has been re-enacted repeatedly in a variety of contexts as those on the receiving end of imperial expansion have explored ways to broaden their networks of self-defence through resistance, adaptation, and positive affirmations of their own rights, titles, and interests. This urge to draw unity from diversity permeated, for instance, the resistance movements led by Túpac Amaru in Peru in the late eighteenth century and by Tecumseh in the interior of North America in the early nineteenth century. Many opponents and would-be reformers of British imperial rule in India have sought to instill similar sentiments of shared identity among the wide array of religious communities, ethnic groups, and castes governed by the Raj.

Along with Bal Gangadhar Tilak, one of the instrumental figures in helping to prepare the ground for Gandhi's drive to unite his fellow Indians in the cause of *Purna Swaraj* –independence – was the Fabian socialist Annie Besant. Around the turn of the century she emerged as one of Great Britain's most devoted theosophists. She became a leading figure in this influential movement, emphasizing the universal qualities animating most of the world's major religions. Besant moved to India to deepen her understanding of the sacred origins of humanity's oldest spiritual traditions. In the process of seeking to identify her own quest for spiritual enlightenment with the political aspirations of her hosts, this pioneer of applied anthropology became a key figure in the Indian National Congress. The Congress had been founded in 1885 by a British civil servant with the goal of opening up dialogue with educated Indians on civic and political issues.[56] As part of her presidential address in Calcutta in 1917, Besant promoted the principle of "home-rule" for India. She sought fundamental reforms within the British Empire that would enable India's multitudes to express greater degrees of local autonomy. In advancing this plan, she attempted to impress on the members of her audience a sense of how their shared stake in India's past translated into a shared responsibility to realize the full potential of India's national destiny. In advancing this concep, Besant referred to the words of Swami Vivekananda, a religious sage whom she had met in 1893 when she attended the World's Parliament of Religions in Chicago. Besant quoted Vivekanada's words: "Of the past is built the future. Look back, therefore, as far as you can, drink deep of the eternal fountains that are behind, and after that look forward, march forward and make India brighter, greater, much higher than she ever was."[57]

Sometimes the effort to create wider confederacies of more effective resistance to imperial expansion involved some dramatic remaking of identies. New mythologies and self-understandings emerged to help open the way for the development of more inclusive coalitions that transcended older divisions of culture and ethnicity. The broadening networks of resistance to the inroads of empire builders formed a distinct dynamic in the process of globalization. A clear demonstration of the growing involvement of the African National Congress in the process of anti-imperial globalization took place in 1943. In that year an assembly was organized to respond to the terms of the Atlantic Charter, a succinct document laying out the underlying principles for the Allied fight against the fascist axis linking Germany, Italy, and Japan. The Atlantic Charter was initially signed by President Franklin Delano Roosevelt and Prime Minister Winston Churchill. Among its several provisions is a section referring to "the right of all peoples to choose the form of government under which they will live." The ANC responded to this provision by noting the "demands of the Africans for full citizenship rights and direct participation in all the councils of the state." This imperative, the organization declared, "is most urgent in the Union of South Africa." The members of the ANC declared that "Africans are in full agreement with the aim of destroying Nazi tyranny, but they desire to see all forms of racial domination in all lands, including the Allied countries, completely destroyed."[58]

The ANC's response to the Atlantic Charter was instrumental in helping to catapult the organization towards the vanguard of the global movement for decolonization. Like the Indian National Congress as it was nearing the culminating phase of its campaign to remove India from the imperial impositions of war-ravaged Great Britain, the ANC confirmed its reputation as a nexus of global transformation. It did so during an era when fascism brought to the heart of Europe many of the same bestial incursions long inflicted on brown-skinned peoples on the frontiers of imperial expansion. The ANC's responses to the Atlantic Charter contained the seeds of many principles that were given fuller democratic expression at an assembly in June 1955 at Kliptown, where thousands of ANC members enthusiatically adopted a Freedom Charter.[59] Nelson Mandela remembers the public reading of the provisions in English, Sesotho, and Xhosa. "After each section the crowd shouted its approval with the cries of *Afrika* and *Mayibuye*."[60] This seminal manifesto not only affirmed the importance of transforming South Africa by the removal of colour barriers to political equality but also affirmed the necessity of extending the principles of equality and self-determination into the structure of South Africa's economy. The key sections on the subject of economic self-determination are as follows:

The People Shall Share in the Country's Wealth!
The national wealth of our country, the heritage of South Africans, shall be restored to the people;
   The mineral wealth beneath the soil, the Banks and monopoly industry shall be transferred to the ownership of the people as a whole;
   All other industry and trade shall be controlled to assist the wellbeing of the people;
   All people shall have equal rights to trade where they choose, to manufacture and to enter all trades, crafts and professions.

The Land Shall Be Shared among Those Who Work It!
Restrictions of land ownership on a racial basis shall be ended, and all the land redivided amongst those who work it to banish famine and land hunger;
   The state shall help the peasants with implements, seed, tractors and dams to save the soil and assist the tillers;
   Freedom of movement shall be guaranteed to all who work on the land;
   All shall have the right to occupy land wherever they choose;
   People shall not be robbed of their cattle, and forced labour and farm prisons shall be abolished.[61]

In *The Shock Doctrine*, Naomi Klein uses the example of post-apartheid South Africa to illustrate the extent of the global shrinking of the jurisdictional sphere left to electoral politics. The result of this diminished role for legislators in a world of increasingly universalized capitalism has been to prevent popular movements from realizing the kind of egalitarian economic policies called for in the Kliptown Freedom Charter. In the period of transition between the White minority regime's release of Nelson Mandela from prison in 1990 and the first national election based on universal adult suffrage in 1994, many key instruments of economic policy, including South Africa's central bank, were placed beyond the reach of the law-making powers of elected officials. Indeed, in the behind-the-scenes preparations for the end of White minority rule, agents of international capital intervened aggressively to assure a large degree of continuity in the economic sphere between the old regime and post-apartheid South Africa. Hence the dramatic expansion of the right to vote was accompanied by the imposition of significant constraints on what citizens could decide by casting their ballots. In the name of keeping South Africa as attractive as possible to foreign investors, this regime of corporate deregulation and hyperprivatization was overseen by the country's long-serving president Thabo Mbeki.[62] As Klein says of this controversial ANC leader, in the 1980s when many of his people were "flooded" with tear gas, Mbeki was in London "breathing in the fumes of Thatcherism."[63] This failure to realize the promise of economic democracy in South Africa has placed severe obstacles in the way of achieving what Madela has referred to as a "deracialized economy."[64] Since apartheid came to an end, the economic polarization of the country has significantly widened. Unemployment has doubled and life expectancy has dropped.[65] According to Klein, "South Africa has surpassed even Brazil as the most unequal society in the world."[66]

Klein refers to the collective disempowerment of the newly franchised majority in South Africa's economic sphere as "a process of infantilization." The phenomenon, she writes, "is common to so-called transitional countries – new governments are, in effect, given the keys to the house but not the combination to the safe."[67] As Benjamin R. Barber observes in *Consumed*, this process of infantilization is not unique to countries just emerging from imperial governance or White minority rule. Indeed, the more prosperous classes in the richer countries are particularly prone to be infantilized in a milieu where laissez-faire ideologues have contributed to the devaluation of collective participation in the public sphere even as they have inflated the importance of individual choices in the marketplace. As many businesses give up on the hope of deriving profits from the economic provisioning and elevation of poorer classes, the impetus grows to concentrate marketing energies on exploiting the whims and self-indulgences of those with the means to engage in conspicuous consumption. In what Benjamin Barber refers to as "late consumer capitalism," individuals with significant disposable income are encouraged to see the activities of public government as the enemy of their personal liberty. They are encouraged to enter "an anarchic commercial playground" where "the ethos of infantilism and the ideology of privatization privilege the consumer in us over the citizen in us." Barber laments the dismantling of "the civic commons." In his view, "political freedom is defined by participation in government rather than freedom from its reach."[68]

A movement aimed at developing the substance and theory of what it calls post-autistic economics has helped to call into question the mystique of those who deployed the language of hard science to support the materialist and infantilizing fantasy that the only social interaction worthy of sustained attention occurs in some imagined state of perfect self-interest.[69] The call on college campuses for more nuanced and authentic academic accounts of how people relate to one another and the rest of nature in the world's real political economy, not the idealized academic representation of it, is part of a larger movement that is breaking down old paradigms. The positive response of many professors to their students' insistence that they move beyond the autistic dysfunction of neoclassical economics is part of a process that is redefining intergenerational relations in an era when the power of youth culture and of the Internet converge to break down many barriers.

THE BANDUNG CONFERENCE OF 1955 AND THE POLITICS OF NON-ALIGNMENT

As the ink was drying in 1955 on the Kliptown Freedom Charter, the printing presses were just beginning to roll on two other publishing projects of considerable consequence. In 1955 William F. Buckley Jr issued the premier edition of the *National Review*, a bi-weekly vehicle of right-wing opinion in the United States. Many of the policies that would later coalesce during the presidency of Ronald Reagan found seminal expression in the magazine's early issues. The *National Review* gave voice to Buckley's unique brand of anti-communist zealotry together with his sneering contempt for most of the legacies of the New Deal.[70] Buckley situated himself and his new publication well to the right of Henry Luce, the driving force of the *Time-Life* media empire. As Buckley was staking out intellectual turf in New York and Washington, Alioune Diop was engaged in a very different kind of media venture in Paris. In 1955 Diop's left-wing publishing house, Présence Africaine, issued an iconographic work – the revised French edition and a new English translation of Aimé Césaire's *Discourse on Colonialism*. The work quickly became an essential text among a rising array of writings that were part of what Malcolm X identified as "a tidal wave of color." In the literature of Marxist-inspired protest, Césaire's contribution marked a shift away from concentration on the exploitation of industrial workers towards an emphasis on the encounter between those on the delivering and the receiving end of colonization.[71] As Césaire saw it, the phenomenon of Nazi fascism had flowed consistently from the barbarism accompanying the treatment of Indigenous peoples under imperial rule.

In the same year that Buckley and Césaire established markers on the right and left branches of political contention in an increasingly bipolar world, many of the acknowledged leaders of the decolonization movement met in Bandung, Indonesia. These leaders affirmed in an international context many of the same principles adopted several months earlier by the ANC at Kliptown. Although an assembly of diverse delegations had met in Brussels in 1927 to form a League against Imperialism,[72] the Bandung

Conference can be conceived as the first major assembly of its type in world history.[73] Never before had there been such a significant constituent assembly whose members could make a credible claim that they represented a broad cross-section of those who had lived, or who were still living, under the imperial weight of formal colonial rule. The gathering can be seen as the first organized global response by the world's colonized majority to centuries of White minority rule on the planet. Historically this exercise of colour-coded power was qualified only by the inclusion of the Ottoman Turks and the brief and provisional acceptance of the Japanese at the high tables of international diplomacy, where huge pieces of the Earth had been carved up and passed out like so many morsels to appease the imperial powers' appetite for colonies and commercial spheres of interest. Now the representatives of those whose Aboriginal lands and polities had been devoured were assembling to oppose such glutonny.

The assembly at Bandung occurred just as the dismantling of Europe's overseas empires was getting seriously under way. India, Pakistan, and Indonesia were already independent. Malaysia was about to become so, as soon as the British government completed the military task of ensuring that its imperial power would not be passed to Chinese communists. Egypt had recently escaped the indirect rule of its British puppeteers. The formal decolonization of much of Africa, however, would not come until the 1960s. The White settlers in South Africa were just beginning to seek protection in police-state hostility to the extension of the vote and, with it, the acquistion of state power by the Black Aboriginal majority in their region. France's eight-year war to hold onto parts of Indochina had recently ended, and agents of the US government were just beginning to pick up where the French imperialists had left off in Vietnam. Although the French government had withdrawn its colonial governors from the Far East, in 1955 it still intended to hold onto Algeria, the site of a protracted and particularly bitter conflict to come. Portugal was still two decades away from giving up its colonies in Angola and Mozambique in Africa and in East Timor in Asia.[74]

The freedom fighters of Africa, but especially those of Algeria, Congo, Angola, and South Africa, would in the years ahead receive significant backing from the Cuban government led by Fidel Castro.[75] In 1955, however, the makers of the Cuban revolution, including Ernesto "Che" Guevara, the iconographic personification of anti-capitalist guerrilla warfare, were gathering strength aimed at overthrowing the US-backed puppet regime of Fulgencio Batiste. The US-backed removal of the democratically elected government of Jacabo Abenz in Guatemala in 1954 had served to radicalize those whose goal it became to remove Cuba from the orbit of the United States' informal empire in Central America. The ruthless removal of the Arbenz government, together with a similar US-backed overthrow in 1953 of the Iranian leader Mohammed Mossedeq, underlined the fact that a new form of imperial rule was already in the ascent even before the formal dismantling of European empires had been completed.

Against this background, the representatives of the Indigenous peoples in twenty-nine African and Asian polities assembled at Bandung, even though many of them were still the receptacles of imperial rule. They met with the objective of charting a mutually supportive course. Their primary goal was to cooperate on initiatives that would enable the world's newly emerging governments to exercise true independence in both domestic affairs and the international arena.[76] The delegates worked to formulate a shared strategy aimed at releasing the colonized portion of humanity from the formal controls of imperialism as well as from the mounting domination of Cold War bipolarism. "The despised, the insulted, the dispossessed – in short the underdogs of the human race were meeting," wrote Richard Wright, a prominent African-American writer who attended and chronicled the Bandung gathering. "Here was class and racial and religious consciousness on a global scale ... The meeting of the rejected was itself a kind of judgment upon the Western world."[77]

As at Durban almost a half century later, there was considerable discussion at Bandung on the subject of Israel and the Palestinians as instruments and symbols of larger global patterns. One of the delegates from Iraq labelled the Zionist founders of the Israeli state as authors of "one of the blackest most somber chapters in human history." A resolution was passed characterizing Israel as a base for imperialism and a threat to world peace.[78] The Bandung delegates could readily see that the Palestinian-Israeli conflict reflected the new face of superpower colonialism in the Cold War. So too the Cold War's first hot conflict in Korea between 1950 and 1953 demonstrated that the natural wealth indigenous to the Bandung delegations' Aboriginal territories had become prizes to be acquired in a new contest between the superpowers. These two nations were able to monopolize much power by insisting on the global pre-eminence of their mutual antagonisms. They could intermittently fight or cooperate as they held the whole world to ransom through their monopolization of nuclear weapons.

As they explored their shared aspirations and dilemmas as well as the lines of division within their own ranks, the Bandung delegates were able to confirm the existence of a shared hostility towards the replacement of the imperialism of Western Europe with an even more invidious system of subordination under the false dichotomy of two alien regimes, two competing systems of governance vying for global supremacy. As H.W. Brands observed in his study of US relations with the Third World over the 1950s: "To those in attendance and those watching, Bandung signaled a refusal to accept the bipolar scheme, to join the superpower competition, or to subscribe to either of the mutually exclusive ideologies on which that competition rested ... Bandung symbolized a resistance to this trend, a denial that the Cold War applied to the world at large."[79]

Most of the delegations agreed that the indigenous genius rooted in their own peoples' diverse heritages of culture, religion, and political economy should not be sacrificed to make way for the false constraints and artificial limitations of a bipolar world. The victims of colonialism should not be corralled into the false option of a single, all-embracing choice, as if capitalism and communism comprised the totality of options available to all of humanity. They should not be entrapped by the lie that the only viable models of progress lay in traditions foreign to their own Aboriginal histories of innovation and achievement. Having confirmed the scope and intensity of their shared trepidations, the delegates left Bandung with added resolve to resist the entrapments of the new categories, institutions, motifs, and arrangements of international relations. They correctly predicted that the new instruments for their peoples' integration into global systems would give the appearance of positive, egalitarian reform without really eliminating imperialism's false division of humanity between civilization's agents and the savage wards of colonial masters. They correctly predicted that the new imperialism would be largely enacted in the language of economics rather than race, in the language of the bottom line rather than philanthropy, noblesse oblige, or Christian mission.

The Bandung gathering brought together a number of the most controversial figures of the twentieth century. The conference's host, Achmed Sukarno, had been instrumental in steering Indonesia towards independence from Dutch rule. In his welcoming speech he emphasized points of agreement that all the delegations shared. "We are united by a common detestation of colonialism in whatever form it appears," he declared. "We are united by a common detastation of racialism. And we are united by a common determination to preserve and stabilize peace in the world"[80] These ideals would help establish the platform for the future establishment of the Non-Aligned Movement. Jawaharlal Nehru, the first prime minister of an independent India and Gandhi's principal understudy, was intensely aware of his image and larger responsibilities as perhaps the best-placed international statesman for all the world's colonized peoples. He would come to epitomize the effort to point the global movement for decolonization away from bipolar entanglements and towards true independence. He came to this non-aligned position gradually after flirting earlier in his career with Soviet models of development. In 1936 he had declared, "I see no way of ending the poverty, the vast unemployent, the degradation and subjugation of th Indian people except through socialism." He added, "That involves vast and revolutionary changes in our social structure, the ending of vested interests in land and industry ... that means ending private property, except in a restricted sense, and the replacement of the present profit system by a higher ideal of cooperative service."[81]

Ghana's Kwame Nkrumah emerged at Bandung as one of the most assertive voices of pan-Africanism. He was a disciple of W.E.B. Du Bois, the American pioneer of pan-African scholarship and diplomacy who had been instrumental in 1909 in founding in the United States the National Association for the Advancement of Colored People. Nkrumah would go on one decade later to write *Neo-Colonialism: The Last Stage of Imperialism*, a text that captured the essence of the concerns that dominated the Bandung proceedings.[82] The attendance of Harlem's Black Congressman Adam Clayton Powell symbolized a begrudging recognition within the dominant superpower's government that the legacy of slavery gave a colonial dimension to race relations within the United States.

The gathering's historic importance was elevated further by the attendance of Egypt's Gamal Abdel Nasser, Vietnam's Ho Chi Minh, Algeria's Ahmed Ben Bella, and Burma's U Nu. As the leader of the delegation representing the world's most heavily populated country, China's Zhou En Lai was something of an anomaly at the meeting. Many remarked that this master diplomat succeeded in keeping his government's communist orientation in the background of the proceedings. Certainly the presence of the Chinese delegation enhanced the gathering's credibility as an authentic expression of pan-Asian solidarity. Indeed, by commemorating the Bandung Conference almost fifty years later with the production of a dramatic motion picture entitled *Zhou Enlai at Bandung*, the Chinese government under Jiang Zemin's leadership signalled the importance it attached to its own participation in a meeting that has been described as "the most emotional and visionary conference of non-aligned countries ever to be held."[83]

Taken in their totality, the delegations at Bandung collectively advanced the principles articulated by Pixley ka Isaka Seme in his founding of the South African Native National Congress, the root organization of the ANC. The Bandung assembly epitomized the transcendance of ethnic and national barriers to achieve a common front in the struggle to achieve anti-imperial forms of globalization. The common front, however, covered over some of the divisions that were already beginning to coalesce in those polities that had gained formal independence. In his chronicle of the event, Wright was alive to the many inconsistencies between the words and the actions of some of the leaders who gathered at Bandung. In spite of the inspirational eloquence of Sukarno, for instance, he was inclined to resort to police-state tactics when it came to the exercise of his own power. The ironies went on and on. The greatest of these was that most of the delegations at Bandung seemed prepared to work largely within the same territorial and institutional configurations that had been put in place by the imperial masters they were seeking to replace.

As the light of future history would confirm, the internalization in many national liberation struggles of some of colonialism's worst attributes would severely limit the capacity of these campaigns to deliver on their promise of democratic self-determination. The failure to follow up the replacement of colonial governors with a thoroughgoing replacement of many of imperialism's methods would have grave consequences. That failure would substantially broaden the base of responsibility for the fact that the promise of decolonization still remains largely unrealized. Some would go further, arguing that promises of human liberation that were supposed to flow from the dismantling of Europe's empires turned out to be fraudulent. In the place of the imperial rule of foreign governors, a large part of the world's colonized majority would suffer the injustices of Aboriginal dictators who, in defiance of the Bandung principles, would align the repressive corruption of their own regimes with the military and commercial priorities of distant patrons. While the citizens of former colonies share some responsibility for this outcome, it is primarily the result of decisions made in the new capitals of the neo-colonial empire to oppose the agenda of global pluralism that was clearly put forward by the Bandung delegations.

The proof of the liberating potential of the ideas animating the Bandung leadership lies in what subsequently happened to them and to others of their ilk such as Congo's Patrice Lumumba[84] – and in the huge amount of energy, resources, and political capital that the agents of the powerful, the custodians of the status quo, would expend in overt and covert campaigns to obstruct the plans, platforms, and policies of the Bandung alumni. It is also revealed in the ruthlessness of the tactics (from incarceration to media smear to assassination to coups to invasions) that would be deployed to remove from government the most committed proponents of economic decolonization – the principles consistent with those expressed by the ANC in its Freedom Charter in 1955. In place of Lumumba or Sukarno and their ilk, those leading the charge on the capitalist side of the Cold War installed more compliant and easily corruptible Aboriginal puppet regimes such as those led by General Mobutu in Congo or General Suharto in Indonesia. The ruthlessness of the blood bath in Indonesia accompanying the removal of President Sukarno from power in 1966–67 is highly suggestive of how much the principles expressed in the 1955 gathering were seen as a menace. The murder of almost a million Indonesians in this debacle exposes the harsh realities of genocide as a means of ideological cleansing in the second half of the twentieth century.[85] Ideological cleansing can be pictured as the cousin of the ethnic cleansing that would infect the politics of Sudan and Rwanda, for instance, in spite of the prohibitions spelt out at the Nuremberg trials.

At Bandung, the aspiring strategists of the worldwide movement to eliminate the bane of colonialism from the human condition advanced their own agendas of Fourth World globalization. The policies and plans of the likes of Sukarno, Nehru, Nasser, Ho Chi Minh, and Nkrumah drew on long inheritances of resistance to imperial globalization. Over many generations the wisest leaders of colonized peoples tried to craft larger conceptions of shared identity. The increasingly pan-Aboriginal nature of resistance to colonialism developed because of the expanding appreciation that isolated, sporadic struggles in the face of expanding empire are almost always doomed. It developed from Aboriginal recognition that, without confederacies of resistance, Indigenous peoples were almost totally vulnerable to the often lethal, divide-and-conquer tactics of the likes of Cortés and the many conquistadors to follow, no matter whether the aggressors wore armour, red tunics, blue cavalry uniforms, or business suits.

The Bandung delegations joined forces to resist the diversion of all humanity into a contest between capitalism and communism. They would counter this diversion with a global vision of their own. From the various visions of decolonization articulated at Bandung there emerged the picture of a world order where the political leverage of the former imperial powers would be balanced against the influence and interests of the liberated citizens of pluralistic pan-African, pan-Arab, pan-Asian, an pan-Islamic polities. Underlying the whole regime of governance would be the principle that the universal human rights of all the world's citizens must be recognized, exercised, and, if necessary, arbitrated and enforced. The quest to build up increasingly inclusive confederacies of Aboriginal resistance to colonialism would subsequently give rise to alternative visions of globalization aimed at reflecting, cultivating, and enhancing humanity's rich inheritances of indigenous cultures in the ongoing invention of the Fourth World.

The ideals emerging from the Bandung Conference were simple yet eloquent. They appear on the wall of the Savoy Hotel, where the conference took place. There the Bandung Principles are described as follows:

1 Respect for fundamental human rights and the principles of the United Nations Charter.
2 Respect for the sovereignty and territorial integrity of all nations.
3 The recognition of the equality of all peoples.
4 The settlement of disputes by peaceful means.[86]

The world's dominant powers have complex histories of interaction with various forms of pan-Aboriginal resistance. The imperial powers have both supported and opposed these movements depending on the context of time, place, and metropolitan interest. The British government, for instance, backed a pan-Indian Confederacy in North America as a strategy for opposing US aggression in the era of War of 1812. A century later the same imperial power, through the activities of Lieutenant-Colonel T.E. Lawrence (Lawrence of Arabia), encouraged pan-Arab unity as long as it undermined the viability of the Ottoman Empire in the Middle East. In the era of the Bandung gathering, however, pan-African, pan-Arab, or pan-Asian visions of unity were received unsympathetically in Washington and in the old imperial capitals of Western Europe. Indeed, the US "disgust" for almost every aspect of the Bandung gathering was palpable. Its foreign policy was based on the view that "there could be no such thing as an unaligned nation ... that countries not for the United States were against it."[87] Still, the promoters of pan-Islamic unity did attract some backing from the capitalist superpower. As demonstrated by the recruitment of US-backed jihadists from throughout the Muslim world to overthrow the Soviet-backed regime in Afghanistan in the 1980s, the national security state within the US government sponsored radical forms of pan-Islamic activism in its Cold War attacks on atheistic Marxism. In fact, the US Cold

Warriors secretly financed and helped the endeavours of many different kinds of religious activists, all of whom were guided by theocratic principles that were necessarily anti-communist in practice. In 1955 Indonesia's former prime minister, Dr Mohammed Natsir, had already anticipated the basic outlines of this pattern. He was paraphrased by one of the Bandung Conference's chroniclers as having "predicted that the West would collaborate with what the media now calls Muslim 'fundamentalism' as a lesser evil against communism."[88]

It would be going much too far to argue that all the delegations at Bandung were perfectly united among themselves. Nasser, for instance, had very complex and ambivalent relationships with the colonized peoples of Black Africa south of the Sahara. On one level he championed their quest for decolonization. His identification with their cause was prominently displayed in his close friendship with Ghana's first prime minister, Kwame Nkrumah. On Nkrumah's request, Nasser would choose an Egyptian wife for his fellow African leader in 1957.[89] In spite of his closeness to the ideals of pan-African liberation, however, the Egyptian champion of pan-Arab unity shared some of the same prejudices towards the diverse peoples of sub-Saharan Africa that had long coloured the perceptions of that continent's most zealous colonizers. Nasser pictured himself and his constituents as bearers of something like an Arab version of the White Man's Burden. As he expressed it: "We certainly cannot, under any conditions, relinquish our responsibility to help spread the light of knowledge and civilization up to the very depth of the virgin jungles of the [African] Continent."[90]

Nasser and the members of his secular Ba'ath Socialist Party were, in 1955, already being pulled into a bitter struggle for state power with the theocrats of Egypt's Muslim Brotherhood. In spite of the hostility between them, however, future history would demonstrate that both antagonists could agree on the superior imperatives of the pan-Arabic cause over the rights of Black Africans. This Arab variation on the major themes of American Manifest Destiny or the German quest for *Lebensraum* became especially clear in the expansionary and genocidal policies of an offshoot of Egypt's Muslim Brotherhood. With US backing, members of this theocratic movement came to dominate the government of Sudan over the course of a decades-long civil war. The Islamic activists in charge of the Sudanese government would one day play host to Osama bin Laden.[91] They would demonstrate their mounting extremism by displacing, enslaving, and killing Christian and traditionalist Black Africans in preparation for the Arab takeover of lands south of the Sahara. The Aboriginal lands of Sudan's Black Indigenous peoples include the cattle-grazing zones of Darfur and the oil-rich zones concentrated mostly in the south.[92]

While the alumni of the Bandung Conference objected to the subordination of the rights and interests of their constituencies to the imperatives of the Cold War, they were not individually or collectively powerful enough to halt the superpowers' domination of international affairs. A year after the historic meeting at Bandung, Nasser sparked one of the Cold War's most telling episodes when he nationalized the Suez Canal in retaliation for the withdrawal of the World Bank's support for his pet project of the Aswan Dam, to regulate the Nile River's flow. The rapid succession of military and diplomatic responses to this Aboriginal seizure of such a prized imperial asset demonstrated that the historical power of France and Britain in the Middle East had become thoroughly subordinate to that of the United States. The Suez crisis also signalled to the new and old imperial powers the negative repercussions of allowing their internal divisions to explode into public view.

In 1961 Nasser was instrumental in revisiting many of the principles of the Bandung Conference by helping to institute at meetings in Cairo and Belgrade a permanent basis for the Non-Aligned Movement. Yugoslavia's president, Josip Broz Tito, brought an especially strategic element of balance to the politics of non-alignment by using NAM as a means of resisting Moscow's control. Tito's ability to balance the interests and rights of several Balkan nations within the constitutional framework of a single Yugoslavian federation provided a classic display of the kind of unity in diversity revered by proponents of the Fourth World. The complex axis of ideas and interests linking Tito, Nasser, Sukarno, and Nehru dominated the politics of the Non-aligned Movement in its early years. Among the most gifted of the many leaders of new African governments to join NAM were Julius Nyerere of Tanzania and Kenneth Kuanda of Zambia.[93]

By the early twenty-first century, the Non-Aligned Movement had attracted the membership of 115 countries. A Jamaican official described its goals in the following terms: "The fundamental principles of NAM are a commitment to peace and disarmament, independence, economic equality, cultural equality, and universalism and multiculturalism through strong support for the United Nations system. Originally political in perspective with a sharp anti-imperialist focus, the Movement is becoming more and more concerned with economic and social issues." In looking back from the perspective of NAM's thirty-fifth anniversary, Tanzania's Julius Nyerere observed in 1996: "It was started by countries which had gained their independence from colonial rule who objected to the assumption that they had to belong to, or at least support, one of those [Cold War] Blocs – that they had to be 'aligned' one way or the other. They were determined to assert that they had an identity of their own, and that they had a right to make their decisions on the basis of their own opinions on international and also on national issues. In forming the Non-Aligned Movement they were refusing to be shadows of other nations or creatures of other Powers."[94]

GEORGE MANUEL, THE FOURTH WORLD, AND THE SPIRIT OF ABORIGINAL NON-ALIGNMENT

One of the most engaging and accessible personal accounts of the philosophy of non-alignment was co-written by George Manuel, a Canadian Aboriginal man. Manuel's own Aboriginal nation had not been represented at Bandung in 1955, nor would it gain representation in the General Assembly of the United Nations as the imperial powers of Europe dismantled their empires and extended sovereign standing to their former colonies. What was true of Manuel's Aboriginal nationality applies also to all the Indigenous peoples of the Western Hemisphere. Their exclusion to this day from most of the central venues of international relations highlights the ironic character of the Americas as Europe's most intensively colonized extension.

George Manuel was a Shuswap Indian from the interior of southern British Columbia. His reflections were published in a book entitled *The Fourth World: An Indian Reality*.[95] That text captured many of the major themes of the Non-Aligned Movement in its insistence that Indians in the Americas, like other colonized peoples the world over, could go forward by applying their own indigenious traditions of philosophy and political economy. They need not accept the Cold War's dictate that they must choose between two competing systems of political economy in their internal dealing and in their relations with the rest of the world.

The text of *The Fourth World* was based on interviews that Michael Posluns conducted with the Shuswap sage. Posluns taped, transcribed, and edited the Aboriginal leader's words just as Manuel was embarking on the most creative and ambitious phase of his international work. Born in 1921 at the Adam's Lake reserve amid the mountainous splendour of Canada's westernmost province, Manuel was a true freedom fighter. He gained his initial insights into the forces oppressing much of humanity by wrestling with the colonial institutions of Canada's Indian administration – he moved from a brief experience in boarding school to various forms of manual labour and finally to his life's calling. That calling would be to give political representation to progressively broader coalitions of Indigenous peoples provincially, federally, hemispherically, and globally.

As Manuel initially explained it and as others have subsequently interpreted it, the Fourth World presents an alternative to the assumptions underlying the idea of the Third World.[96] The term "the Third World" had been popularized in the reporting of the Bandung Conference in 1955 and seized upon by journalists as it became clear that the then-prevalent term "people of colour" did not capture the essence of the forces drawing together the likes of Nehru, Nasser, Sukarno, and Ho Chi Minh. The First World signified those committed to the US-led, capitalist side in the Cold War, whereas the Second World signified the complex of powers, particularly in Asia, Eurasia, and Eastern Europe, which were integrated into the socialist orbit of the Soviet Union and China. It can be said that Cuba under Fidel Castro kept alive the collectivist vision of the Second World long after the demise of the Soviet Union.

While the phrase the Third World began its life as an identifier of non-alignment, it soon assumed connotations more connected to images of poverty, backwardness, and underdevelopment. It conjures up images similar to those once invoked by words like "savage," "primitive," or "tribal." The

Third World is often used in ways that suggest its members are devoid of "development"; that being "undeveloped" or "underdeveloped," they have to choose between external models of progress based on imported dualities like capitalism and communism; or right-wing and left-wing politics. An emphasis on externally generated dichotomies such as these seemed an anathema to a movement whose proponents found common purpose in the goal of throwing off the impositions of their colonizers. The shift from the conception of the Third World to that of the Fourth World suggests, as Nyerere indicated, the "refusal" of the decolonizing peoples "to be shadows of other nations or creatures of other Powers." The shift announces the unwillingness to accept the relegation of Aboriginal identities to the realm of obsolescence, quaint folklore, dead artifacts, frozen culture, antiquarian ethnography, or backward-looking museology. It invokes instead a sense of confidence in the capacity of living Aboriginal cultures to contribute actively to the betterment of all humanity, to generate adaptive strategies for indigenous, national, transnational, and global progress.

The idea of the Fourth World emerged from the struggle of Indigenous peoples to avoid the subordination of their own diverse identities beneath the ongoing imperialism of the Columbian conquests and the bipolar impositions of the Cold War. The term persists with broader and more inclusive meaning to describe an approach to relationships, a motif of creative adaptation in meeting the contingencies of an uncertain future with foresight, imagination, and prudence. In the Fourth World, people and peoples refuse to become alienated from their own pasts. Instead, all are encouraged to draw on the nutritive energy of humanity's diverse inheritances of language and culture, on our complex and often intertwined stories of migration and indigeneity.[97] The ethos of balance and ecological equilibrium are central to the Fourth World. This quest for balance is expressed in the need to combine the natural conservatism of tradition, inheritance, and organic community with the revolutionary energy inherent in all struggles for decolonization.

In the Fourth World, the biocultural diversity of life is celebrated, cultivated, and, if necessary, protected. The dynamic interdependence of the global community is concurrently recognized and affirmed through prolific exchange and multifaceted translation. In the Fourth World there is clear understanding that the shared attributes of the human spirit and the human condition far outweigh the necessary differences we proclaim and encourage for the common good. By upholding universal human rights and adhering to the attending ideal of the universal sanctity of the rule of law, the citizens of the Fourth World provide humanity with the necessary keys to achieve a higher global destiny. They open the way to greater equilibrium between what we share in common and what is unique to each individual person, community, nation, and bioregion. This system of universal rights and universal responsibilities to protect, for instance, the ecology of biodiversity must extend to the use of law to promote concurrently a wide array of different political economies. The colonization of law to bring about a universal capitalist monoculture of inequitable property relations represents a betrayal of the Fourth World.

As Manuel used the term, the Fourth World carries connotations of completeness and transcendence. Many Aboriginal traditions identify the centrality of the four sacred directions in orienting humanity to our place on the Earth and in the cosmos. Even the Christian symbol of the cross has this implication. The idea of the Fourth World, therefore, draws on this multiplicity of heritages. It points to the fulfillment of history in the realization of forms of globalization that embrace the ecology of biodiversity as the most conducive environment for healthy human relationships with one another and with the rest of nature.

Manuel first heard the term the Fourth World from a Tanzanian diplomat stationed in Canada. His name was Mbuto Milando. "When Native peoples come into their own, on the basis of their own cultures and traditions," Milando told Manuel, "that will be the Fourth World." Manuel mulled over this concept as he travelled. Almost everywhere he went he found the same legacies of imperial, national, and corporate rule and the same aspirations of colonized peoples seeking to draw on the adaptive strength of their own Aboriginal heritages to break free from the instruments of their oppression. These instruments of repression, it was fast becoming apparent, were flexible and resilient enough to withstand many of the political realignments that came in those ceremonies, conducted mostly in the 1960s, when elements of state power were passed from colonial officials to a new class of indigenous politician.

It was in Tanzania, East Africa, in 1974 on the tenth anniversary of one such ceremony that George Manuel encountered Jules Nyerere. In the years before Manuel's visit, Nyerere's Tanzania had given refuge to a host of leaders representing some of Africa's most important anti-imperial movements. As Gordon Hyden has written, "Tanzania became a political Mecca for liberal and socialist progressives from all over the world, anxious to see a challenge to neo-capitalism."[98] As one of the most determined, experienced, and thoughtful members of the Non-Aligned Movement, Nyerere is the most obvious direct connection between the Bandung tradition and the political philosophy of the North American founder of the World Council of Indigenous Peoples. Nyerere described the form of Aboriginal socialism he attempted to cultivate as *ujaama*.[99] He outlined the importance of rooting the policies of his government in the indigenous cultures of Tanzania's citizens in 1967 in the Arusha Declaration. Manuel conferred with Nyerere for several days as the two men moved with their associates around the Tanzanian countryside. From this experience Manuel concluded, "Tanzania is such a good example of the difference between the Third and the Fourth World because neither the people nor their leaders have been content to produce a new society that is merely a darker imitation of the world of their colonial masters."[100]

How is it that George Manuel's own Aboriginal polity or others like it were not represented in the proceedings at Bandung in 1955? Why was the Aboriginal nationality of the *The Fourth World*'s author not extended direct representation at the United Nations even as the membership of the General Assembly roughly quadrupled throughout the 1960s and the 1970s? There are important hints of an answer to those questions in the name of the provincial jurisdiction that, since the mid-nineteenth century, has claimed title to the Aboriginal territory of the Shuswap Nation and to that of many other Indigenous peoples. There could be no clearer marker of this province's non-Aboriginal origins and genesis than the name, British Columbia – no more telling nomenclature to suggest that the Columbian conquests continue through the design of many of our institutions and the colonial principles and ideologies they mirror, uphold, and perpetuate. Just as questions about Tibet's relationship to China permeated the politics of the 2008 Beijing Olympics, so similar issues reared their head as Aboriginal leaders in British Columbia contemplated disrupting the 2010 Winter Olympic Games at Vancouver and Whistler Montain in order to call attention to the marginalized condition of their constituents.[101]

In the same way that the Olympic protests highlighted the international dimension of Tibet's colonized status, so the problems that Manuel tried to address had implications that go far beyond the specific relationship between his own Shuswap people and one Canadian province. The Shuswaps' diilemma in British Columbia is deeply embedded within a broader exclusion of Indigenous peoples throughout the entire Western Hemisphere from almost any sovereign representation whatsoever in venues where international relations are conducted and where treaties and other instruments of international law are ushered into existence. How is it that there is not one delegation representing an Aboriginal polity in the Americas in the two hundred or so delegations in the UN General Assembly? Regardless of the size of their surviving Indian populations, there is not one country in North, Central, or South America that can truly be said to derive its laws and institutions from those whose heritage is rooted primarily on the Aboriginal side of the colonial schism that cut through the Western Hemisphere's history after the transformative events of 1492. The government of Mexico has probably gone the farthest in terms of incorporating the iconography of the Indian civilizations of Mesoamerica into its national heraldry. But those kinds of reform, important and innovative as they may be, are still a long way from transforming the legacy of the conquest of Aboriginal America into a Fourth World dynamic of indigenous and popular liberation.

The exclusion of the Indians and the Inuit of the Americas from the highest venues where the principles of international sovereignty are expressed speaks eloquently of the intergenerational continuity of what David Stannard has described as the "American Holocaust."[102] The near total exclusion of Aboriginal America in all its diversity from official venues of international affairs is indicative of the extreme intensity of colonial enterprise in the Western Hemisphere in general and, in particular, in the United States. The exclusion constitutes strong evidence that America is Europe's most intensively transformed frontier, its most lucrative land speculation, and the primary demonstration of Western Civilization's power to change the course of world history. There is much symmetry, therefore, in the emergence of the United States as Europe's agent, critic, and, after the Second World War, primary rebuilder. There is historical logic in the emergence of the United States as the most forceful agency of "the West's" more expansionistic attributes.

The repeated failure to incorporate the Indigenous peoples into leading roles in the national liberation struggles that gave rise to the formation of the Western Hemisphere's Spanish and Portuguese speaking republics is evidence of the Eurocentric preoccupations that permeated those movements.[103] Nevertheless, some of the Latin American revolutions did include provisions for the theoretical extension of legal equality to Indians. As a rule, however, Indigenous peoples in the Americas looked not to their non-Aboriginal neighbours for recognition and protection but, rather, to imperial governments as natural opponents of the most expansionary forms of settler self-aggrandizement. New strategies became necessary, however, once the creation of sovereign settler nation-states severed the ability of Indigenous peoples in the Americas to appeal to Old World centres of European power to protect their Old World societies in the Western Hemisphere. The formation, first, of the League of Nations and then of the United Nations presented new sites of decision making to fill the imperial void left by the withdrawal of European powers from a direct role in the governance of the Americas. As expressed in the politics of the World Council of Indigenous Peoples and other Aboriginal organizations of that ilk, the leadership of many of the planet's most chronically dispossessed constituencies opted to transfer their quest for the protection of law to the United Nations.[104] They tried to escape the complete domestication of their Aboriginal polities within the sovereign rule of settler states by seeking recognition and representation in venues where international relations are transacted. One such venue capable of extending membership and other recognition to the Indigenous peoples of the Western Hemisphere is the Non-Aligned Movement itself. That organization is uniquely placed to expand its framework to include places for representatives of peoples as well as of nation-states.

ASSESSING THE EVIDENCE, COMPARING INTERPRETATIONS

The application of relativity's pluralistic meanings to expanding frontiers of human interaction points at the effort to impose a single system of universalized property relations on all branches of the human family. The intensity of the thrust to privatize as many frontiers of mind, matter, and relationships as possible has planted the seeds of a new totalitarianism. It has anointed the apostles of a new creed of monotheistic materialism. In the church of market fundamentalism, capitalism is conceived as the outcome of some mystical union of providential will and universal natural law, the global fulfilment of Manifest Destiny in the stock market's marriage of myth and rationality, rumour and hard information.

Hannah Arendt's classic study of totalitarianism has important light to shed on the prospects of a new plunge into heavily policed conformity. Echoing themes already introduced by Aimé Césaire, Arendt argued that the expansionary policies of the fascist regimes of the 1930s and early 1940s emerged from the determination of their leaders to replicate within Europe the imperial aggressions deployed in the expansion of overseas empires and in the transcontinental growth of the United States.[105] The fascist regimes gained power in the hope they would defend capitalism from the incursions of communism. They sought to defeat their enemies and expand the scope of their dictatorships by inflicting on Europeans some of the same sorts of ruthlessly applied control that had long been visited on colonized non-Caucasians. The zeal of many transnational businesses in advancing the fascist responses to communist internationalism demonstrates conclusively that corporate capitalism can be completely unhinged from the liberal values of democracy and individual rights.

The deeper the penetration of capitalist privatization into the shared domain of any society, the less common ground is left for the liberal expression of the people's democratic will. In other words, the more the arena of privatization is expanded, the smaller becomes the arena for the expression of public will. Accordingly, once officials are elected to serve in government, they face a constant conflict of interest because of their dual accountability both to their local constituents and to distant money traders whose speculative activities amount to minute-by-minute referenda on the worth of all national currencies. These speculators have frequently pulled the rug from beneath the governments and the peoples who depend on the purchasing power of, for instance, the Mexican and Argentinian peso, the Indonesian rupiah, the Russian ruble, or the Thai baht. Money speculators have sucked power and effective jurisdiction away from people and their elected representatives in much the same fashion as have the World Bank and the International Monetary Fund. The IMF exercises especially great power over many of the poorer countries by playing a significant role in setting interest rates on national debts.

This uploading of power away from people and towards the realm of transnational agencies has become even more severe with the expanding power of a new form of judiciary that operates within, for instance, the WTO and the North American Free Trade Authority. The powers of these supranational bodies to arbitrate and dictate the terms of material relations among people has drawn economic jurisdiction away from lower levels of government. The effect has been to deprive whole societies and their elected officials of vital levers of self-determination and to advance the impressment of all the world's peoples and governments into straightjackets of economic monoculture. As attested by Naomi Klein's description of the shrinking base of economic democracy in post-apartheid South Africa, the trend has been to place obstacles in the way of all forms of economic self-expression that do not conform to the zealously policed contours of globalized capitalism. The diminished jurisdiction of elected assemblies everywhere demonstrates the darker side of the finding made in 2001 by Freedom House. According to this US-based agency, the number of countries it deemed to be democracies had jumped from 30 to 121 during the previous thirty years.[106] This growth in the number of officials who derive their authority to govern from the ballot box fails to take into account the increased restrictions on what elected politicians can actually do with their electoral mandates.[107] These limitations gut the rituals of democracy of much of their substance in a process that might be referred to as ballot-box colonialism.

The penalties directed at peoples who fail to fall in line with the pre-conceived scenarios have been demonstrated in Haiti by the two interventions of the governments of the United States, France, and Canada in 1991 and again in 2004 to remove the democratically elected governments led by Jean-Bertrand Aristide.[108] Like Haiti's founder, Toussaint L'Overature, Aristide was a devout Roman Catholic. His governing philosophy was heavily influenced by the ideals of liberation theology as professed and taught by members of Roman Catholic Church throughout Latin America. A number of these priests, including Bishop Oscar Romera, who was murdered in 1980 in El Salvador by US-backed paramilitaries, payed with their lives for their identification with the liberation struggles of the poor in their region.[109]

The chilling message from such developments announces in no uncertain terms the sovereign omnipotence of capital. The other side of this same process is to perpetuate colonialism by intensifying the disenfranchised and dispossessed condition of the disentitled majority of people on the planet. Peruvian economist Hernando de Soto illuminated this process plainly when he argued in 2000 in *The Mystery of Capital* that "the economic reforms underway open doors only for small and globalized elites and leave out most of humanity."[110] Rather than interpreting this persistent inequity as the outcome of the ongoing Columbian conquests, however, he proposed a further acceleration of capitalist privatization as the panacea for global poverty. De Soto's ideas were shaped in a country whose economy retained many elements of the old system of property relations rooted in thousands of years of Incan history. As he saw it, the undocumented and unregistered nature of several traditional property interests rooted in Aboriginal custom prevented many citizens of his country from being able to lever the full financial value of what they owned. It prevented them from being able to use their property as collateral to borrow money in order to expand and diversify their businesses. De Soto's recipe for improvement was to eliminate the last vestiges of customary property relations. He proposed transforming unwritten systems of Aboriginal proprietorship into systems of registered private property capable of being fully integrated into domestic and international regimes of capitalist transaction.[111]

De Soto's proposals seem uninformed by the knowledge that his suggested remedy has much historical precedent. There has been episode after episode where efforts have been made to break up the traditional Aboriginal property regimes and integrate individual Indians into the process of privatizing their lands under the laws of their colonizers. From John Locke's proposal in the seventeenth century to integrate individual Indians into the private property system of Carolina colony, to the distribution of title deeds in the form of scrip to the Métis of Manitoba and the North-West Territories in the 1870s, to Senator Henry L. Dawes Congressional initiative in the 1880s to privatize, apportion, and sell large parts of US Indian reservations, such initiatives have time and time again ended up enriching non-Aboriginal speculators and accelerating the dispossession of Indigenous peoples. These processes actually widen the divide between rich and poor, between colonizers and the colonized, between peasants and urban elites.

In *The Unconquerable World*, Jonathan Schell articulates the growing conflict between democracy and universalized capitalism in the following terms: "The paradox of the global market system is that while it offers a wide choice of goods to many consumers within the system, it closes off choice among systems. Countries going shopping for economic systems will find only one product on the shelf."[112] This monopolistic outcome violates ideals espoused by F.A. Hayek, whose economic theories were drawn upon by Milton Friedman and others to provide justification for Reaganomics and Thatcherism. Hayek's scholarship was comandeered to help legitimize the push during the final stages of the Cold War to expand the range of corporate privatization and to diminish the size and reach of public government. A critic since the 1930s of both Keynes and Keynesian economics, Hayek's most accessible publication is *The Road to Serfdom*. He published this volume in 1944 in the shadow of the totalitarian experiments of the 1930s and 1940s, and he proposed strategies there for preventing governments from becoming captive to monopolies of ideology and power of any kind. In seeking ways to avoid the kind of tyranny embodied by both Hitler and Stalin, Hayek brought to his analysis preoccupations similar to those of Arendt and Karl Popper.[113] If from very different perspectives, all three of these thinkers sought to liberate the forces of democratic pluralism as a permanent check against the return of totalitarian repression.

With the fall of the Berlin Wall, however, the way was opened for the globalization of capitalist monoculture. After the demise of the Soviet Union, the agenda of hyperprivatization was promoted with great zeal by the triumphant governors of the capitalist superpower and its military-industrial complex. Their aim was full-spectrum domination – to eliminate all remaining space for the cultivation of any alternative systems of political economy. This agenda went dramatically against the pluralistic ideals outlined by Hayek as the Second World War was coming to a close. His critique of totalitarianism had been deployed to justify an approach to governance that held the seed of a new form of global totalitarianism. As Schell observed, "the theoretical enemy of monopoly had itself become a global monopoly."[114]

The spirit of non-alignment and of the Fourth World offers a basis for the transformation of the historical struggle against colonialism into a broader resistance aimed at countering the monopolizing force of universalized capitalism and superpower rule. The rise of Zapatismo in opposition to the terms of the North American Free Trade Agreement linking Canada, the United States, and Mexico in 1994 presented an especially rich example of the transformation of pan-Aboriginal resistance into a broader, more inclusive coalition.[115] The Fourth World embraces many of the philosophies informing those activists of decolonization who have drawn on the Bandung tradition to develop the case that the colder and richer countries of "the North" have exploited the poorer and hotter countries of "the South."[116] The Fourth World is a vessel that holds ideas and inspirational traditions similar to some of those that animate the analysis of Michael Hardt and Antonio Negri. These Marxist theorists have explored many of the new structures of supranational sovereignty and the new possibilities of global democracy through the revolutionary networking of "cultures, races, ethnicities, genders, and sexual orientations, different forms of labor, different ways of living, different desires." Hardt and Negri describe this churning cauldron of agitated identity politics as "multitude."[117]

While the Fourth World contains the revolutionary heritage of the decolonization movement, it is concurrently conservative in ways that do not conform to the theoretical geography of Hardt and Negri's map identifying their recommended fast track to global democracy. The Fourth World embraces not only human attachments to the Aboriginal ecologies of particular places but also their integration. It celebrates the continuing capacities of some of the oldest surviving human polities on Earth to inspire loyalties, attract and assimilate new adherents, and inform adaptive strategies amid the uncertain contingencies of a changing world. It looks to the histories of Indigenous peoples, but also to those of empires and nation-states, as media of human creativity that have produced some legacies which must not be entirely extinguished. Accordingly, activists of the Fourth World's are not prepared to demolish entire philosophical inheritances of culture and tradition in the name of some idealized "democracy of the multitude."[118] For instance, the constitutional heritage of the Royal Proclamation of 1763 offers strategic ground from which to challenge internationally the doctrine of empire building through conquest.

Where Hardt and Negri treat efforts to excavate, renovate, and renew old polities as "primordialism,"[119] as nostalgic detours away from the fast track of dialectical progress, the Fourth World is more geared to the vital necessity of achieving balance between the old and the new, change and continuity. It is more attuned to the potential of creative tension between the need to conserve and the need to innovate. Sensitivity to the strategic interplay between the power of precedent and the force of invention has been the consistent hallmark of the most enlightened leadership in the quest to advance the decolonization of minds, matter, and political relationships. The ability to look beyond the Lockean and Darwinian ideals of linear progress to more complex movements of cyclical transformation permeates the thought, for instance, of Rousseau, Túpac Amaru, Tecumseh, Toussaint L'Overture, Louis Riel, Ho Chi Minh, Gandhi, Nkrumah, Nyerere, and Rigoberta Menchú.

LATIN AMERICA AND THE PROSPECTS
OF GLOBAL DECOLONIZATION

With its resort to military adventurism in Eurasia and with the attempt by its armed forces to achieve "full spectrum dominance," the United States heightened its image among a significant portion of humanity as the site of a concentrated imperial brew, one that represented the mixing and distillation of many older vintages of Western colonialism.[120] The rush of the military-industrial complex to dominate and weaponize space added to the imagery of the whole planet as a single encircled property, as the captive orb of a technology-based empire. By 2002 the funding directed by the US government towards so-called missile defence outstripped that of the entire State Department.[121] Vividly televised displays highlighting the dexterity of "smart" bombs blasting into Belgrade and Baghdad hinted at the spectacle of shock-and-awe extravaganzas to come under the electronic Big Top of Star Wars.[122]

The weaknesses of this aggressive approach to empire building became especially evident in the oldest hinterland of the informal US empire. The imperial overreach of the United States in Eurasia was accompanied by a rising tide of protest against the inequities of wealth and power in Latin America. This part of the world has been tied especially closely to US-centred systems of command and control ever since 1823, when President James Monroe issued his famous doctrine declaring the Western Hemisphere as a zone where all European empires except that of Great Britain were prohibited from claiming territory. The mass mobilization of many groups in Latin America, but especially of Indian peoples and their mestizo relatives, therefore suggests the beginnings of a more inclusive movement to decolonize a global regime of material oppression. This upsurge of protest, led by two self-identifying Indians elected to lead two important South American countries, presented the rudimentary outlines of a worldwide plan to oppose the global incursions of an imperial trajectory of monopoly capitalism that began in 1492 with a monumental overturning of a vast and diverse indigenous civilization.

At different times, Central and South America have been strategically situated at the nexus of interaction between the three main superpowers intent on seizing the initiative in the globalization of the Columbian conquests. The empire of Spain gave way to that of Great Britain in the eighteenth and nineteenth centuries, just as the empire of Great Britain gave way to that of the United States in the twentieth century. In *Open Veins of Latin America*, Eduardo Galeano explores the competition and cooperation between US and British interests in the nineteenth century in renewing the thrust of Spain's empire building in the Western Hemisphere. The interests of the Union Jack adapted to the Monroe Doctrine, which expressed US antagonism to any formal projects of European colonization in the Western Hemisphere apart from those already in place in British North America. Undeterred, British manufacturers, importers, exporters, engineers, transporters, insurers, bankers, and financiers went to work to build up their informal empire of free trade in Latin America. The other side of their success, which depended on many interventions to secure and maintain the political dominance of a local class of Malinchist collaborators, was what Galeano referred to as the "industrial infanticide" of the most self-directed and technologically sophisticated means of creating added economic value locally.[123] In the process of keeping Latin America under foreign domination in spite of the region's nominal independence, the British imperial superpower helped to guide and prepare the future superpower, the United States, for its own global career of informal and formal empire building.

The most recent variation on the imperial philosophy of the Monroe Doctrine was delivered to Latin America in a set of directives labelled the Washington consensus. These directives presented the peoples and governments of Central and South America with the usual post–Cold War mantra of government austerity, deregulation, open markets, and hyperprivatization. In 2001 Argentina experienced a devastating financial meltdown even though its government had conformed religiously to the Washington consensus as administered under the pontifical authority of the IMF. The episode sent shock waves throughout the whole region, and many responded with a determination to try other options. They sought to return to the struggle for economic self-determination by asserting some measure of Aboriginal control over the organization of labour and the use of indigenous natural resources.[124]

In Venezuela, a country long governed essentially as a resource colony of the big US energy consortiums, Hugo Chavez survived a US-backed coup attempt and then a recall referendum in August 2004 to press forward reforms aimed, in part, at redistributing oil wealth to the more disadvantaged sectors of Venezuelan society. His social activism even extended in 2005 to help the poor of New York during a whirlwind visit to the city. The Venezuelan leaders's most loyal constituency was the country's urban and rural poor. An open friend and ally of Cuba's Fidel Castro, Chavez saw himself as the inheritor and champion of the pan-American revolution initiated by Simón Bolívar. Like Evo Morales in Bolivia, Chavez embraced his Indian and mestizo heritage, identifying himself with the cultures of those who, in the vast majority of cases, have remained trapped at the bottom of most of Latin America's socioeconomic hierarchies. In his foreign policy, Chavez worked hard to resuscitate OPEC, the Organization of the Petroleum Exporting Countries. Its origins were rooted largely in the efforts in the late 1950s of the Venezualan oil minister Perez Alfonzo.[125]

Chavez has been credited with carrying on Dr Martin Luther King's struggle to deflate the forces of war and aggression and to elevate the poor through a systematic redistribution of wealth. The comparison has been made by William F. Pepper, the lawyer for the King family who effectively proved in a Memphis trial in 1999 that US officials in a number of agencies, including the army, played a significant role in the assassination of Dr King in 1968. In 2008 Pepper wrote:

I have become close to Hugo Chavez, a charismatic revolutionary leader who invites a comparison with Martin King. Chavez, more than anyone drawing breath, carries on and expands King's struggle on behalf of the wretched of the earth. He is a revolutionary deeply commited, as was King, to liberating the poor from impoverishment, physical deprivation, and exclusion that denies all life in the face of the challenge to survive. Chavez has chosen to attain power and use the assets and legitimacy of an elected government, while King remained outside government, seeing himself as an independent force applying pressure to elected officials to do the right thing ... I see the Venezualan Bolivarian Revolution and its commitment to the poor as the most important movement on the planet ... Corporate media will continue to distort and misrepresent what is going on there, as it will to every non-capitalist, cooperative effort.[126]

An upsurge of popular resistance similar to that of Venezuela transformed the political landscape of Bolivia and Brazil. In Brazil, Luiz Inacio Lula da Silva took over the country's top job in 2003 and swept to victory on behalf of the Workers' Party. He replaced Fernando Henrique Cardoso, who, in 2002, was already giving the winds of change clear articulation. Referring to a meeting of the leaders of the G8 countries, Cardosa alleged that they met only "to validate what a single power has decided." He added, "This isn't the world we prepared ourselves for over so many decades. This is a world of unilateralism."[127] While the priority of the Lula government was to attract international investment to Brazil, his unwillingness to criminalize those committed to more radical ways of remaking the Brazilian economy helped to embolden the more assertive critics of capitalist globalization. Much of this agitation for a fundamental reordering of material relationships moved in and around the Landless Peasants' Movement, or the Landless Workers' Movement as it is sometimes known. Often this group is referred to simply as the MST, a short form for the Portuguese name, Movimento dos Trabalhadores Rurais Sem Terra. This organization began in 1984 as Brazil was emerging from a period of direct military rule. The MST was initially devoted to changing the system of land distribution in Brazil in order to enable landless peasants to acquire title deeds.

Like the system of *latifundias* and *haciendas* and in the Spanish-speaking parts of Latin America and the seigneurial system that took form in the French Roman Catholic colonization of Canada, Brazil's organization of property ownership has deep roots in feudal institutions. The Brazilian equivalent of Spanish haciendas and French seigneuries is the *fazendas*. While the laws of property ownership in Brazil have changed over the years, they have continued to favour the concentration of land ownership in very few hands. The MST challenged the system through direct acts of occupying unused farm land. In doing so the occupiers sometimes faced violent opposition from the police and the hired guns of absentee land owners. Nevertheless, the MST persevered to the point where its members began organizing thousands of cooperatives in reconstituted districts. According to the MST's own statistics, by 2008 about 350,000 families had acquired titles to land in 2,000 agricultural settlements, even as about 180,000 families lived in encampments awaiting the issuing of legal documents that would confirm the legitimacy of the way they have organized their lives. The MST has refused to participate in government policies that displace Indians from the traditional territories through the destruction of the Amazonian rain forest.[128]

In recent years, the quest for the redistribution of land has been updated to emphasize the concept of food sovereignty.[129] The basic ideals of food sovereignty place an emphasis on local production and consumption of the food staples that all human beings need to live. Indeed, a central tenet of food sovereignty is that food, like clean water, housing, basic education, and health care, is a fundamental human right. The proponents of food sovereignty stand opposed to most aspects of the Green Revolution, but especially to the allocation of large areas of agricultural land for the massive production of monocultures cultivated primarily for export to global markets. The apportionment of large plots for cultivating the ingredients of biofuels is especially repellant to the proponents of food sovereignty. As an alternative to the present regime, where a few global companies control a large part of humanity's food supply, the MST and its allies suggest that local communities be empowered to fill the vacuum – that the small-scale operations of farmers, pastoralists, and fisherfolk apply the science emerging from the practical application of the best attributes of their traditional cultures. The goal is to continue making pragmatic reforms that provide for the nourishment of human beings in ways that are ecologically sound and consistent with the Fourth World ideals of biocultural diversity.

The MST has developed these principles in association with the growth of a global organization known as Via Campesina. The mandate of Via Campesina is to assist in the transnational networking of peasant, indigenous, youth, and workers' groups seeking to bring about locally based solutions in an approach that has been described as globalization from below. In 2003, activists of the MST began occupying corporate installations such as the Brazilian branch of the Monsanto Corporation, a leader in the production of genetically modified foods. In the summer of 2008 the MST crossed a new threshhold of militance by occupying the facilities of many other large global conglomerates that do business in Brazil. Among the commercial operations targeted by many thousands of MST activists was a railway run by a mining corporation known as Vale, a supermarket group owned by Wal-Mart, the facilities of the France-based Suez Corporation, and a US fertilizer manufacturer known as Bunge Ltd.[130]

DICTATING THE TERMS OF THE CONNECTION BETWEEN THE OLD WORLD AND THE NEW WORLD

The cyclical movement of Aboriginal history seems to have come full circle with the imagery of a new cycle of globalization from below: it began with Aboriginal farmers in the Americas pointing the way to a remaking of the world's political economy by replacing the unsustainable replication of monocultures with a life-enhancing proliferation of biocultural diversity. But can the root polities of English-speaking empire be drawn along in the process? From the days of the Elizabethan colonization of Virginia until today, the dual-headed giant of the North Atlantic – Anglo-America – has proven amazingly adept at moulding the human family, however crudely and incompletely, to its changing specifications. In the four-and-a-half centuries between the reign of Elizabeth I and Elizabeth II, the whole world has been affected by myriad struggles to oppose, resist, subvert, replicate, borrow from, adapt to, or join what Kevin Phillips has described as "the triumph of Anglo-America."[131] The division of Anglo-America into two core sovereignties in the eighteenth century raises many questions. What, for instance, caused the split? What are the continuities and lines of fracture marking the relationship between the old and the new superpowers? Have the dynamics of this division stimulated the dialectical energies of anglobalization? Is the level of global security better or worse than it would have been if the British Empire had not been divided to make way for the formation and rise of the United States?

To address questions such as these conscientiously, we must revisit the Aboriginal history of some of the most contentious problems of our time. The need for deeper understanding of our current dilemmas inevitably brings us to examine the forces that converged in the creation of the most powerful country on Earth. The founding of the United States set many forces in motion which have rippled across space and time to influence the most basic structures of relationship throughout the global community. Even in the years leading up to the revolutionary break of 1776, when disagreements between competing camps of imperialists escalated towards civil war, there was a sense that whichever side won would gain turf of such enormous strategic consequence that its influence would eventually extend to all humanity. As observed by Alexander Hamilton, the most influential architect of the laws of property relations in the nascent United States, the acquisition of control over the richest part of the former British North America conferred on its recipients "all trans-Atlantic force of influence," the power to be "able to dictate the terms of connection between the Old and New World."[132]

Hamilton's insight proved prophetic. But the success of the United States in fulfilling his prediction has compounded rather than resolved the ironies and contradictions embedded in the superpower's underlying constitution. It has only heightened the necessity of some reckoning with the complex of myth, politics, finance, and law which invested the world's first settler sovereignty with a title for expansion, with a mandate to act as the primary intermediary between the sovereignties of the Old World and the vaguely defined geography in the imperial imagination that came to be known as the New World. A civil war in British North America opened the way for the creation of the new polity, which drew simultaneously on the energy of imperialism and decolonization.

The genesis of the revolutionary divide in Anglo-America cannot be reduced to the dichotomous categories of a mythological contest between democracy and repression, liberty and tyranny, good and evil. As Arthur Schlesinger observed, "the revolutionary movement was the product of a complexity of forces, governmental and personal, British and colonial, social, economic, geographical, and religious."[133] Since the time when Schlesinger wrote these words, literally thousands of studies, some of them thick and erudite, have been devoted to exploring various aspects of the American Revolution.[134] With varying degrees of skill, authority, and literary finesse, the authors of these works have assessed, for instance, the role in the conflict of the interconnected controversies over taxation and representation in the British Parliament, disagreements over who was going to command and pay for the army and militia in British North America, and various contentions concerning shipping laws, trade regulations, and the like.

As significant as all these aspects of the revolutionary break prove to be, however, they are secondary or derivative compared with the importance of one central controversy driving all the other forces of division in Anglo-America. The heart of the contention came down to the question of who was going to exploit, govern, and *own* the lands and resources of the North American continent. Who in the English-speaking, predominantly Protestant world was going to control the process of immigration from Europe and the attending expansion of non-Aboriginal settlements on the moving western frontiers of the North Atlantic community? What agency, what sovereign, what government was going to make the decisions about the rate and form of the westward expansion of predominantly Euro-American communities? What authority would be empowered to give out the licences and title deeds conveying rights to lands so similar in climate and fertility to those inhabited by the quickly replicating masses in Europe? Would an Old World sovereign prevail or would history be directed to create a new type of sovereign, one geared to extending the boundaries of global capitalism in the rush to privatize the richest treasure trove of new lands and resources ever to be transferred from Indigenous peoples to a mix of immigrants and their descendants?

Beginning with R.G. Thwaites and Frederick Jackson Turner, the frontier historians of the United States have been especially well equipped to appreciate the importance of the break with the British Empire as the prelude to the most aggressive phase of Anglo-America's transcontinental expansion. Although Charles A. Beard was never formally part of the history faculty at the University of Wisconsin, his investigations into the role of economic elites in the genesis of the United States have been consistently popular with the teachers and students at Madison. In 1913 he made his intial mark on US historiography with his text, *An Economic Interpretation of the Constitution of the United States.* The US Constitution, he asserted, "was essentially an economic document based upon the concept that the fundamental rights of property are anterior to government and morally beyond the reach of popular majorities."[135] As Beard saw it, the central dichotomy driving US decision making repeatedly came down to "a question of commercial expansion or stagnation and decay; world power or economic decline."[136] The result was a form of "mechanical" expansion whose agents were inclined to be unattentive to "the exclusion of national cultures – ideas, loyalties, passions, political traditions, the development and clash of races and nations."[137] William Appleman Williams helped to project the preoccupations of Turner and Beard into the era of the Cold War. In Williams's view, the US government was the primary aggressor in the contest between capitalism and communism. Williams's hope was that the United States would join much of the rest of the world in striving to achieve a "true human community based far more on social property than on private property."[138] The cost of continuing the journey from transcontinental expansion to the imposition of open door policies on the rest of the world could be catastrophic, for "the frontier was now the rim of hell, and the inferno was radioactive."[139]

In his own work on the geopolitical strategy of the US government during the post–Cold War era, Andrew J. Bracevich draws on the studies of both Beard and Williams. He uses their observations to help bebunk the self-serving myth that the United States is a "reluctant superpower." Instead, he argues, the US government has consistently coooperated with its indigenous producers to open up and protect foreign markets. "The challenge confronting American leaders," he writes, "was to formulate policies that provided the benefits of empire without its burdens. In that regard, what mattered was not ownership or even administrative control but commercial access."[140] In beginning his analysis of contemporary US diplomacy with insights derived from the frontier school of US historiography,

Bacevich would have been well served if he had gone on to consider the work of Clarence Walworth Alvord. Focusing on the nexus of cooperation between the European and the American branches of business lobbies that attempted without much success to create colonization companies capable of opening and privatizing the backcountry lands obtained from France in the Seven Years' War, Alvord went on to investigate the complex of inter-connected Anglo-American interests linking Benjamin Franklin and his network of land speculators with the circle of politicians and financiers sur-rounding Lord Shelburne in Great Britain. As Alvord argued persuasively nearly a century ago, the politics of the American Revolution were, at their deepest level, the politics of land speculation. Who was going to exercise ownership and control of the richest portion of North America? Would the Indigenous peoples be included in the enterprise of remaking their conti-nent or would they be pushed aside and exterminated? Much depended on the outcome of this controversy. Many cycles of Aboriginal history in our interdependent world would turn on the answer to these questions.

In conducting his research, Alvord simply applied the core investigative technique of the most credible forms of intelligence gathering, police work, and journalism. He followed the money.[141] Others have taken Alvord's pio-neering investigations further,[142] but not in ways that challenge any of the Turnerian historian's original insights about the centrality of land specula-tion in the clash of imperialisms culminating in the founding of the United States. These frustrated land speculations eventually found fulfilment in the creation of a new republic that secured the capital for the mother of all mortgages. The transfer to the US government of title to much of Anglo-America was integral to the structure of assets and debt, the written and unwritten contracts whose cumulative effect was to invest the success-ful secessionists with an internationally recognized charter to conjur into existence the world's first New World sovereign. That sovereign investment would be leveraged again and again in increasingly ambitious pyramid schemes underlying the rise and rule of a superpower whose global domi-nation seemed almost complete and invincible during the first few years of the post–Cold War era.

Accordingly, the creation of the United States culminated the first stage of imperial globalization. Its establishment opened the way to a more mediated and locally directed phase of Euro-American colonization in the Western Hemisphere. The United States would eventually turn the table on its former patrons by re-engineering Western Europe according to its own specifications in the Marshall Plan and by moving into the vacuum of power created by the dismantling of European empires. Beginning in the 1970s, first Japan and then China began penetrating capitalism's main bastion, symbol, and laboratory by exporting massive quantities of consumer items to the United States and using the attending financial leverage to purchase large portions of the superpower's rapidly escalating debts.[143] The resulting changes in the global balance of power suggested that the United States could itself become the site of a renewed struggle between an increasingly outward-looking China and an increasingly factionalized West.[144] It remains far from clear, therefore, who will ultimately benefit and who will lose from the great gamble involved in the investment of international recognition in a new type of sovereign. As the outgrowth of one of the most radical experiments in political science ever attempted, the United States has from its inception been geared to the technological mastery of nature and to the conquest of new frontiers of territory, culture, commerce, and consciousness.

CHAPTER FIVE

Hitler or Roosevelt?
Finding Third Ways to the
Fourth World

Far in the east the light-god Quetzalcoaltl, born of a virgin, arose
and set about recovering and making his own again the land of
which the gods of the Aztecs had dispossessed him.

Paul Herrmann, *Conquest by Man*, 1954

CAPITALISM, COMMUNISM, RACISM,
SOCIAL DEMOCRACY, AND TRADE UNIONISM

During the twentieth century, the criticism and defence of capitalism animated domestic politics, international affairs, and world public opinion on
a scale that transcended all other issues. In the course of the struggle to
determine capitalism's place in humanity's future, the United States moved
towards the centre of global geopolitics. The transformation of a single
country into the pre-eminent symbol and living laboratory of capitalism
flowed naturally from US history. It emerged in stages from the transformation of Western civilization's most piercing projectile of transatlantic expansion into the worldwide command structure governing the superpower's
military-industrial complex. In claiming and remaking a transcontinental
territory, the people, government, and corporations of the United States
established patterns of conquest and procedures of privatization that prepared some for positions of leadership on capitalism's most extended frontiers. As the militarized Manifest Destiny of religious mission merged into
that of commercial domination, the United States came to embody Stalin's
notion of "a capitalist center, drawing to itself the countries that incline
towards capitalism." In 1927 Stalin predicted that such a capitalist centre
would "do battle" with a mirror-image centre of socialist countries in the
contest "for command of the world economy."[1]

The close identification of capitalism with class exploitation, the imperialism of Europe, and the rise of US corporate and military power helped to
generate a tradition of social science that would cast a long shadow of criticism over the world's pre-eminent system of political economy. This continuum of analytical commentary includes the work of Jean-Jacques Rousseau,

Lewis Henry Morgan, J.A. Hobson, Friedrich Engels, Vladimir Ilyich Lenin, E.P. Thompson, Eric Hobsbawm, V.G. Kiernan, Antonio Negri, and Michael Hardt. This tradition of anti-imperialist, anti-capitalist scholarship found its strongest centre of ideological gravity in the prolific commentaries of Karl Marx. His insights into the causes, character, and consequences of the Industrial Revolution provided the essential analysis deployed to inform and justify the founding of the Soviet state. In 1917, in the October Revolution, the Bolshevik Party led by Lenin and Leon Trotsky seized control of a popular eruption directed against the autocratic monarchy of Czarist Russia.[2] Between 1918 and 1921 the Bolsheviks fought a bitter civil war to secure and broaden their power. The US military intervened in this conflict, offering sporadic support to the anti-Bolshevik White Russians.[3] In responding to the October Revolution, US president Woodrow Wilson had referred to the "poison" of Bolshevism as "the negation of everything that is American."[4] In this conflict, the Reds prevailed over the Whites. The victory of the Red Army confirmed, entrenched, and extended the grip of Lenin's Bolsheviks on the government of the world's largest country. This dominance was formalized in 1922 with the creation of the Union of Soviet Socialist Republics.

In the communist scheme of ideology and politics, the main engine of historical change lies in the material conflict among various classes of humanity. The essential element of class conflict is rooted in the human quest to control, manipulate, and *own* increasingly intricate assemblages of natural and manufactured environments. The competition entailed in the drive to transform the Earth into property has divided humanity between slaves and slave owners, tenants and landlords, labourers and capitalists, colonizers and the colonized. For communists, therefore, the primary dynamo of historical transformation is the instability of material relationships linking human beings with one another and with the rest of nature. Many human institutions, including the governing mechanisms of capitalist states, were thought to have emerged from this history of conflict on the moving frontiers of private property. As Marx and the other proponents of historical materialism saw it, the primary purpose of capitalist states was to extend the appearance of sovereign legitimacy to elites whose privileges were derived from the ownership and control of disproportionately large concentrations of property. From this stance, it seemed axiomatic that only a revolutionary remaking of the primary institutions governing most facets of human interaction could provide the necessary corrective to the imagined theft of property from those who labour in the mills, malls, and other media of capitalist exploitation.

Like the United States, the USSR was designed for expansion. The Soviet Union's founders pictured their new polity as the core jurisdiction in an expanding federation of workers' republics. The term *soviet* referred, in the Bolshevik terminology of proletarian internationalism, to a council of workers in any given area. The worldwide proliferation of soviets was portrayed by Bolshevik propagandists as a key to achieving a global coalition of oppressed classes capable of throwing off the repressions of those who owned and controlled the instruments of imperial capital. The Marxian interpretation of dialectical materialism was derived from the philosophy of Georg Wilhelm Hegel. Francis Fukuyama would, in turn, draw on Hegelian theory after the demise of the Soviet Union to picture an unbounded vista of capitalist market relations at the end of history. His use of Hegel marked an ironic counterpoint to the ideas of those who were inspired by Marx to believe that history would culminate in an era when workers would unite to transcend the limitations of an inequitable social order structured to entrench and extend those class privileges derived from ownership and control of private property.

Woodrow Wilson brought his own sense of history's dialectical trajectory to his definition of Bolshevism as the very antithesis of "everything that is American." His response to the Russian Revolution helped define for the United States a new frontier of ideological savagery, a new evil empire to be repelled, conquered, and eliminated in the course of universalizing capitalism as the ultimate fulfilment of the West's civilizing mission. Indeed, it was Marx and his adherents who were most instrumental in giving capitalism its name. Alternatively, capitalism's defenders found common ground in opposing communist principles. Even though some Wall Street bankers were perfectly prepared to do business with the new Soviet regime, the most committed anti-communists embraced the institution of American private property as a sacred bastion poised against the official atheism of Marxist ideology.[5] The insertion of the reference to God on US money nicely encapsulates how the defence of capitalism from communism was permeated with the zeal of religious mission. With the rise of the Soviet Union, the acquisition of wealth was no longer a matter of mere self-interest. It became, rather, the means of advancing a political agenda whose most extreme proponents openly associated their empire of fortune with the crusader ideal of holy war.

The religious materialism of the anti-communists helped to intensify the secular materialism of the anti-capitalists. For the activists and ideologues who sought to make Marxism the basis of worldwide revolution, the capitalist ruling classes and their bourgeois collaborators were robbers whose ill-gotten power was based on the legalized theft of labour and Aboriginal resources. Where capitalism's defenders sought to advance the appropriation and privatization of the commons, the communists sought to push history in a different direction. They sought to construct the collectivist alternatives to those institutions that justify themselves with the capitalist mythology of individual self-realization through individual ownership. Sometimes with coercion, sometimes by persuasion, the frequently disputatious deputies and disciples of Marx and Lenin pressed forward policies proclaimed in the name of communism's promise to obliterate all expressions of capitalist entitlement. They favoured policies permeated with the rhetoric of sharing, equality, and scientific planning as the essential ingre-dients of social harmony. By attempting to extend the frontiers of trade unionism towards truly global dimensions, the self-declared vanguard of the "commonwealth of toil" endeavoured to alter the international land-scape of belief, culture, and politics. They sought to change society in order to help many coalitions of workers seize control of national and transna-tional economies from the proprietary privateers of corporate capitalism.

In turning the analytical rays of Enlightenment rationality towards the interpretation of the changing alignments of power and interest permeat-ing the Industrial Revolution, Karl Marx had looked to the future as well as the past. The bearded prophet of capitalism's demise had predicted that the most technologically advanced societies of Western Europe held the ripest conditions for the organized revolt of workers against their capital-ist task masters. As it turned out, however, it was the rural peasantries of Russia, China, and Cambodia rather than the urban factory workers of, for instance, Glasgow, Dusseldorf, Cologne, Chicago, Detroit, or Genoa who would provide the primary human grist for the sometimes violent mills of communist experimentation. Nevertheless, few societies on Earth were immune to the effects of the outcome of the Russian Revolution. In country after country the expanding aura of Soviet power emboldened a growing body of workers, intellectuals, and politicians to experiment with expanded roles for government as the main media for widened fields of coopera-tively controlled and collectively held property. Indeed, especially after the onset of the Great Depression, the Bosheviks' real or imagined successes prompted even liberals at least to contemplate theories of social better-ment involving various formulae for the nationalization of land, utilities, and many of the other instruments of industrial/biological reproduction.

The dramatic entry onto the world stage of an alternative model of state formation further polarized relations between employers and work-ers locally and between empire builders and colonized groups globally. Throughout large areas of India, China, the Middle East, Southeast Asia, Latin America, and Africa, for instance, news of the founding of the Soviet Union encouraged some activists of decolonization to expand and intensify their quests for indigenous liberation. The introduction of a new type of polity in Eurasia's core had an especially pervasive impact on the nations to the west of the Soviet giant. Many of Europe's commercial and political capitals would become principal sites and prizes of the contest between the two prevalent systems of political economy that dominated much of the twentieth century. Indeed, some of these metropolises, including London and Zurich, were the very locales where communist ideology had initially been conceived and cultivated in the process of extending the European Enlightenment's most aggressively secular traditions. The coming to power of fascist governments in Italy and Germany represented the right-wing extreme of capitalism's defence in Europe. The exercise of political influ-ence by a number of social democratic parties, however, embodied a more

moderate approach to the problem of countering the radical anti-capitalism of the far left.

The cosmology of both social democracy and Marxist revolution drew
heavily on European traditions of popular resistance to the most extravagant assertions of monarchy, clergy, and aristocracy. It also drew on the heritage of the French Revolution and the violent tremors of 1848 that swept
through the political culture of much of Europe. Like the appearance of
Adam Smith's *Wealth of Nations* in 1776, the publication of *The Communist
Manifesto* in 1848 highlighted a moment of significant change in history's
flow. But how far would the rejection of the old regimes go? Once feudal
elites lost much of their power, who would come to dominate the strategic high ground of legitimacy, authority, and control? Would the liberalism
of free trade predominate or would the liberalism of self-determination
give rise to new paradigms and institutions of popular democracy? Would
reforms emphasizing political equality in the electoral arena be sufficient
to satisfy the public's desire for change or would the mobilized masses
demand more revolutionary expressions of economic equality as the real
prerequisite for viable regimes based on the universality of human rights?

Many of the tensions implicit in these questions were briefly brought
to the surface during the First World War. Beneath the clash of empires
and armies simmered an ideological disagreement whose effect was to pull
social democrats away from the more uncompromising internationalism of
Europe's more extreme socialists and communists. The social democrats
let their nationalism prevail over the ideal of a borderless world founded
on workers' solidarity. Instead of ascribing to Lenin's view of the war as
a capitalist conspiracy cynically orchestrated by a nationless tribe of war
profiteers, the founders and early practitioners of social democracy joined
the military campaigns of their own home governments. In doing so they
helped to locate the strategic fault lines between radicals and progressives.
In distancing themselves from the idealists and zealots of class-based revolution, the social democrats signalled their intent to restrict their politics
to parliamentary means of reforming capitalist society from within. Many
of the more moderate social reformers drew on communitarian strands
of Christian belief and organization. This religious orientation created yet
another wedge of division separating Christian social democrats from those
on the left who adhered to the atheistic tenets of Marxist materialism.

Social democrats were first voted into power in Sweden and Norway.
Then, in 1923, the electoral victory of Prime Minister Ramsay Macdonald's
Labour Party in Britain injected the influence of moderate social democracy directly into the main artery of parliamentary governance in the imperial capital of the British Empire. Although John Maynard Keynes's own
attachment was to the British Liberal Party, the strength of the Labour Party
proved instrumental in the genesis of the political culture where this prolific pioneer of Third Way strategies could thrive. Keynes and his disciples
formulated much of the theoretical framework used to justify relatively

deep intervention by government in the ebb and flow of market relations.[6] In 1936 Keynes published his most detailed commentary on the economic role of the state in *The General Theory of Employment, Interest and Money.* He saw his work as a defence of capitalism against both Marxism and laissez-faire extremism. In the view of Samir Amin in *Obsolete Capitalism,* Keynes and Marx together defined the main outlines of the political landscape inhabited by much of humanity. They became "the two major inspirations for the social thought and the dominant economic, sociological and political theories that legitimated ... the welfare state in the West, Sovietism in the East, and populism in the South."[7]

The influence of Keynes and the Keynsians helped give cohesion to the design and implementation of President Roosevelt's New Deal in the United States. France also embraced a variation of social democracy. The Popular Front government of Léon Blum took power in 1936. His "Third Way" politics, both before and after the Second World War, anticipated in the heart of the industrialized world some principles similar to those that would animate the proponents of the Non-Aligned Movement and the Fourth World in the era following the Bandung Conference of 1955. In the eyes of some, however, the reforms of the Third Way were in large measure a defence of propertied interests. By adapting government finances to the goal of providing broader public access to education and health care and by putting in place the rudimentary beginnings of social welfare systems, proponents of social democracy, the New Deal, and the Popular Front effectively defended the overarching culture and institutions of capitalism. They did so by making concessions to fend off the radical agendas of their more extreme opponents whose goal it was to pre-empt various forms of market relations through the exercise of workers' rights and state-controlled central planning. It was the Prussian autocrat, Otto von Bismarck, who pioneered this strategy of co-opting the socialist option through widened state involvement in social planning. Chancellor Bismarck is best remembered as the primary navigator of the project to unify the complex of jurisdictions that came to compose the modern German state in the final decades of the nineteenth century. He offered ordinary Germans access to a widened array of social programs in the effort to help engage their loyal attachments to the heavily militarized apparatus of the newly consolidated German nation.[8]

Just as it was the rural peasantry of Russia and China rather than Europe's high-tech factory workers who provided the primary human material for the most ambitious experiments in revolutionary communism, so too in North America expectations that capitalism would face its most serious opposition in the areas of highest industrialization were defied. It was the miners, loggers, and agricultural workers scattered throughout the continent's western frontiers rather than the more highly skilled labourers in the urbanized East who were most inclined to back the call for revolutionary transformation of the prevailing system of governance and property relations.[9] Indeed, in the United States, a country which never produced an equivalent to Britain's Labour Party or Canada's New Democratic Party, the trade union movement was itself the site of particularly bitter contention among the forces of capitalism, socialism, and communism. At the left-wing extreme of this spectrum lay the Industrial Workers of the World,[10] whose members were sometimes referred to as Wobblies. The IWW had been founded in the atmosphere generated by the Russian General Strike in 1905, an episode that is generally interpreted as an important prelude to the Russian Revolution.[11] The famous preamble to the IWW's constitution left no doubt that the organization was born from the womb of class warfare. "The working class and employing class have nothing in common," asserted the founders. "There can be no peace so long as hunger and want are found among millions of working people and the few, who make up the employing class, have all the good things of life. Between these two classes, a struggle must go on until the workers of the world organize as a class, take possession of the earth and the machinery of production, and abolish the wage system ... By organizing industrially we are forming the structure of the new society within the shell of the old."[12]

In the worst of the labour strife accompanying the rapid industrialization and urbanization of the US economy, the most committed agents of the IWW and its related organizations faced various forms of martyrdom through lynchings, execution, and lengthy incarceration. The aura of secular sainthood descended on some of those who faced the most severe forms of persecution for their efforts to represent some of the real underdogs of US society during the most visceral phase of open confrontation between the forces of labour and of capital. Prominent among the persecuted pioneers of the US labour movement were Frank Little, Wesley Everest, Joe Hill, Bill Haywood, Eugene Debs, Daniel De Leon, Vincent St John, and Mary Harris. Harris, who came to be known simply as Mother Jones, was the irrepressible organizer of the United Mine Workers. Those who felt most menaced by the radicalization of a small but vital component of the US workforce developed many tactics and networks of allies to counter socialism and thereby safeguard their interests. This mobilization of various types of pressure and force to pre-empt any major redistribution of American wealth occurred both inside and outside government, the political parties, and the formal structures of trade unionism. The quest to defend the status quo from socialism or from even more radical currents of political and economic change involved methods of outright repression as well as more subtle forms of co-option. It involved very elaborate schemes whose viability ultimately came down to the success or failure of strategies to defuse the potential for revolutionary change by inducting enough of the North American working class into the relative comfort and safety of the middle class.

At the other end of the political spectrum from the IWW was the American Federation of Labor. Samuel Gompers, an ambitious New York cigar maker turned union organizer, prevailed as the AFL's most influential leader for almost half a century before his death in 1925. The AFL was formed as a crafts union that generally upheld and defended the dominance of the most highly skilled and highly paid elites among US workers. In restricting itself to minor tinkering with prevailing economic orthodoxies – bargaining for better pay and benefits for its members – the AFL turned its back on those who saw trade unionism as the vehicle for a radical transformation of the American way of life. Indeed, the AFL was tightly bound to the popular expectation that the engine of capitalism should continue to drive the US economy in perpetuity. It would be hard to overestimate the broad allure of the Jeffersonian mystique making the ownership of private property the key to achieving personal independence and, with it, the successful realization of a distinct American brand of democracy. The AFL and the majority of its members were intimately caught up with the attractions of this most American of mythologies. While the pioneer politics of war and peace with Indian nations may have created some of the oldest and most seminal motifs of indigenous US law, the most solemn commitments at the basis of the US system of contracts resided elsewhere. The deepest covenant binding the core elements of American society lay not in some problematic chain of relationships with the continent's Indigenous peoples but, rather, in the conviction that capitalism must prevail in the United States for as long as the sun shines, the grass grows, and the rivers flow. That promise, insisted the Great Polity's most influential leaders, must never be broken.

In bowing to the influence of the most widely revered elements of the American Dream, the AFL accommodated the legend that the culture of US business should serve as the natural receptacle for the unregulated freedoms captured in the conquest of the American frontier. The AFL's identification with the competitive ethos of capitalism translated into an array of policies reflecting many of the prevailing orthodoxies held by groups seeking to maintain their positions of privilege within US society. The AFL, for instance, was generally hostile to the integration of Blacks into better-paying jobs and into the membership and leadership of trade unionism's main agencies of collective bargaining. This reactionary stance extended also to antagonistic attitudes towards women's rights, the plight of the poor, and large-scale immigration. In its hostility to new influxes of foreigners into the United States, the AFL mirrored attitudes that were concentrated especially among the descendants of North America's White, Protestant Creoles. These native-born descendants of European immigrants tended to combine idealized perceptions of their racial and religious roots in Western civilization with the potent delusion that they had been granted a special entitlement by God to dominate the New World's most dynamic country. Clearly the "nativism" of this self-declared charter group was antagonistic to the orientation to history of most Aboriginal Americans, the original victims of the appropriation by Euro-Americans of a whole hemisphere's destiny.

The nationalism of White, Protestant exceptionalism drew on the legacy of slavery and on the ethos of dominance and exclusion generated through the often violent elimination, enclosure, and marginalization of Aboriginal Americans.[13] The nationalism of US exceptionalism was expressed and edified by many expressions in US popular culture which drew on the Calvinist myth that the makers of the United States were acting with providential sanction as God's Chosen People. As Edmund S. Morgan observed, the Puritan aspect of this patriotic perception has tended to induce attempts to "reform the world in the image of God's holy kingdom" even as it promotes the opinion that "the evil of the world is incurable and inevitable."[14] The consciousness emerging from these concurrent yet contradictory ideals has tended to coalesce in xenophobic and isolationist attitudes that became especially pervasive in the decades between the two world wars. A telling feature of this xenophobia was the distrust of both immigration and immigrants, as reflected especially in the federal government's preoccupation with "enemy aliens." The AFL shared this distrust of outsiders. As Gompers and his associates reasoned, the introduction of large numbers of immigrants into the United States would undermine pay levels and working conditions even as it would expose domestic populations to a host of foreign and potentially subversive ideas.

The distance between the IWW and the AFL was matched and exceeded by the extreme polarization characterizing the larger terrain of US society in the early years of the twentieth century. In 1914 the Ludlow massacre illustrated the extent of the polarization on the outer frontiers of class antagonism. Like the sinking of the *Titanic* two years earlier, the Ludlow massacre drew attention to an array of lethal forces threatening whole systems of industrialization. During the climax of the episode, federally sanctioned agents of John D. Rockefeller's energy consortium murdered about two dozen strikers and their family members during a labour dispute in the coal mines of Colorado, a prime nurturing ground for the defiant brand of trade unionism cultivated by Mother Jones, the United Mine Workers, and the IWW. Some miners took revenge and killed soldiers on the other side of the dispute. This tragic episode in the history of industrial relations would acquire the mystique of legend as artists of the American left, including Upton Sinclair and Woody Guthrie, mined the event for its deeper social and psychological meanings. "You pulled the trigger of your Gatling guns," wrote Guthrie in his 1946 folk song "Ludlow Massacre." "I made a run for the children but the fire wall stopped me. Thirteen children died from your guns."[15]

The labour unrest continued and in some ways intensified after the First World War, when returning soldiers faced many hardships in their efforts to reintegrate themselves viably into the civilian economy. The unrest reached a crescendo in 1919, the year of the "Red Scare."[16] During this seminal episode of many red scares to come in capitalism's emerging bastion, North America was shaken by a rash of labour disputes. They included a steel workers' strike, a miners' strike in West Virginia, a police strike in Boston, and general strikes in both Seattle and the Canadian frontier metropolis of Winnipeg. The atmosphere of increasing polarization led to several terrorist bombings and the forced expulsion of socialist representatives from Congress and from the New York State Legislature. Predictably, the politics of class division were accompanied by the politics of racial division. The racial character of class conflict was especially apparent in an accelerated surge of lynchings and in the convulsions of violence that swept over Washington, Chicago, and Philips County in Arkansas. In an episode sometimes referred to as the Arkansas pogrom, White vigilantes murdered nearly two hundred Black share-croppers who dared protest the terms of their economic oppression. This wave of race-related violence extended in 1921 to Tulsa, Oklahoma, where scores of White vigilantes uprooted an entire Black community from forty-four city blocks in its downtown neighbourhood. The vigilantes were representative of a significant constituency, centred especially in the American South, who sought to push back even the modest gains made by the Black workers during the brief period when the wartime economy opened relatively well-paying jobs for the descendants of slaves.

The resurgence of the Ku Klux Klan after the First World War marked a more militant manifestation of the reactionary upsurge in White, Protestant hostility to those deemed alien to the charmed inner circle of US identity. By 1925 the unabashedly racist, anti-Semitic, and anti-communist KKK boasted 4 million members under the leadership of Grand Wizard Hiram W. Evan.[17] The renewal of the most militant forms of racism in the United States was opposed on a number of fronts. Among the most tenacious critics of the KKK and all it represented was W.E.B. Du Bois – by far the most erudite, articulate, and persistent voice of the American civil rights movement over a prolific career that stretched from the end of the nineteenth century to the middle years of the twentieth century. For much of this period, Du Bois provided the most public face and the busiest pen of the National Association for the Advancement of Colored People (NAACP). In his seemingly tireless rounds of writing, speaking, and organizing, he condemned the urge to structure the United States around principles of racial segregation. This urge animated not only significant sections of the White population but also some portions of his own Black community. Indeed, Du Bois himself flirted briefly with the enticements of segregation after he witnessed again and again the depth of hostility to the broad integration of coloured Americans into the political, economic, and institutional facets of US culture.

Like most of the social democrats of Europe, Du Bois had supported the participation of his home government in the First World War. He saw the participation of Black soldiers in the conflict as a means of promoting the wider acceptance and integration of Blacks generally. Du Bois set his quest for a more just regime of race relations in the United States in the context of an international campaign to correct the racial inequities of imperialism. His work was permeated with the desire to demonstrate that the intertwined ills of colonial oppression and racial inequality went far beyond the level of local or even national problems. The issues to be addressed, rather, were international and even global in scope. This prophet and practitioner of the globalization of the anti-imperial struggle counselled that the maltreatment of dark-skinned people was "a great world-wide problem to be viewed and considered as a whole."[18]

One of the main media promoted by Du Bois in his efforts to elevate, coordinate, and internationalize the struggle of all those opposed to the racist oppression of coloured people and peoples was a series of "pan-African" congresses. Du Bois was one of the main organizers of these elaborate cross-cultural events, which took place intermittently over a period of several decades in a number of European and North American venues. In the course of this work, Du Bois looked to the League of Nations and its International Labor Organization as bodies that might help bring a measure of democratic fairness to the apportionment of political and economic power.[19] He sought further help from the London-based Anti-Slavery and Aborigines' Protection Society, an organization that effectively embodied the convergence of the movements to abolish slavery and to put limits on the theft of Aboriginal lands, work, and resources. These dual goals met most seamlessly in the quest to terminate the gross exploitation of "native labour" throughout large parts of Africa. In advancing these causes, Du Bois went to considerable lengths to distance his own more elitist variety of pan-African activism from the more populist version promoted by the Jamaican orator Marcus Garvey. The flamboyant Garvey, a segregationist who was frequently accused by his critics of collaborating opportunistically with White segregationists, called for a massive migration of Blacks from the United States and the West Indies to the African country of Liberia. Garvey established a shipping enterprise, the Black Star Line, with the aim of facilitating the return of his followers to Mother Africa.

In seeking to ease injustice by exposing and combatting racism's most brutal manifestations, Du Bois continued and elaborated the long tradition of Fourth World activism. All his endeavours, but especially his advocacy of pan-African ideals, stand poised between the indigenous liberation struggles of, for instance, Túpac Amaru, Pontiac, Tecumseh, and Toussaint L'Ouverture and the politics of decolonization and non-alignment as expressed by the Bandung delegates and in George Manuel's writings. Although Du Bois was drawn increasingly to Marxism over the course of his long career, he eschewed revolutionary violence as a means of taking political power. As he wrote as the editor of the NAACP magazine, *The Crisis*, "We expect revolutionary changes to come mainly through reason, human sympathy and the education of children, and not by murder."[20] Du Bois was increasingly pulled towards Marxist thought as he identified a growing web of connections linking exploitation on the basis of race with exploitation on the basis of class. Referring to the regime of racial segregation supported by the AFL and other branches of the US trade union movement, he observed in 1926: "Unless white labor recognizes the brotherhood of man it becomes the helpless tool of modern industrial capitalism." Du Bois wrote these words shortly after a visit to the Soviet Union, a transformative event that caused him to remark on his return: "Letting a few of our capitalists share with the whites in the exploitation of our masses would never be the solution to our problem."[21]

FROM PROGRESSIVISM TO FASCISM ON THE CONTESTED FRONTIERS OF THE EMPIRE OF PRIVATE PROPERTY

Business and government worked closely together to pre-empt any radical departures from the status quo during the period in which the KKK and the NAACP competed to direct the future course of US history. In those years the domestic policies of the government anticipated many features of US foreign policy during the Cold War. Throughout the twentieth century, many of the country's leaders would find common cause in the quest to contain and push back any challenges to the hegemony of private property in capitalism's emerging imperial heartland. Efforts to fend off or co-opt any significant changes to the prevailing order of material relations emanated from a variety of points on the political compass. President Woodrow Wilson's decision to commit US troops to fight in the First World War, for instance, was almost certainly influenced by the opening this initiative presented to repress domestic opposition at home. Citing the need for emergency measures in a time of war, the US government passed the *Espionage Act* and then the *Sedition Act* in 1918. These bills and the administrative structures to which they gave rise helped to establish many features of "the national security state" – a regime of centralized police powers whose methodology remains deeply embedded in the superpower's hegemonic arsenals to this day.[22]

The wartime laws invested many formal and informal deputies of the federal government with extensive new authorities to spy on their fellow citizens and to bulldoze aside the basic civil liberties of those deemed hostile to the dominant system of apportioning influence and wealth in the United States. The targeted groups' rights of freedom of speech, freedom of assembly, and freedom from unreasonable search were unilaterally sacrificed to serve the interests of those in a position to twist the politics of wartime emergency to advance their own agendas. By 1920, dossiers had been put together documenting the personal lives of about 200,000 individuals considered prone to "un-American" activity. As head of the Enemy Aliens Registration Section of the General Intelligence Division of the Department of Justice, J. Edgar Hoover was the functionary charged with the task of compiling these files. He had come to the attention of his employers as a result a university term paper he had written entitled "Radicalism and Sedition among Negroes as Reflected in Their Publications." In *Gag Rule,* Lewis Lapham observed that the major idea linking those caught in the net of Hoover's investigations was that they were all "suspected of having an illicit relationship with the ideas of Karl Marx."[23]

Hoover was one of the deputies to Attorney General A. Mitchell Palmer. Over the Christmas holiday season of 1919–20, Palmer directed the arrest and incarceration of about six thousand "enemy aliens" who were thought to be spreading the subversive contamination of left-wing ideas. Approximately five hundred of those taken into custody were deported. A disproportionate number of the targeted individuals were Jews with family roots in Eastern Europe. In his effort to justify the exercise of such sweeping police powers, the primary instigator of the Palmer raids used language similar to that employed by the authors of the Declaration of Independence when they pointed to the alleged propensity of "merciless Indian savages" to inflict "undistinguished destruction" on "all ages, sexes, and conditions." As Palmer viewed it, "the Reds" were political and ideological arsonists who collectively menaced the American way of life. These agents and allies of communist savagery were proliferating "like a prairie-fire." He warned that "the blaze of revolution was sweeping over every American institution of law and order ... It was eating its way into the homes of the American workman, its sharp tongues of revolutionary heat were licking the altars of the churches, leaping into the belfry of the school bell, crawling into the sacred corners of American homes, seeking to replace marriage vows with libertine laws, burning up the foundations of society."[24] The Palmer raids represented the most dramatic betrayal of the liberal ideals espoused by President Wilson as he took office. The episode, however, was not an aberration. It was, rather, the predictable extension of a number of policies and enactments all designed with the goal of breaking the momentum of those seeking to point the United States towards a major redistribution of wealth.

Wilson's betrayal of the promise of American liberalism at home anticipated a similar betrayal at the international level. The Treaty of Versailles emphasized the punishment of Germany by the victors rather than the principles of democratic anti-imperialism Wilson had emphasized in bringing the US Armed Forces into the First World War. John Maynard Keynes wrote a text in 1919 predicting many of the problems that would arise from placing such a heavy burden of war reparations on Germany.[25] Wilson's policies were formulated with a close eye towards Theodore Roosevelt, a former US president who changed his party affiliation in his quest to regain the nation's top job in the federal election of 1912. As the vigorous and charismatic leader of the Progressive Party, or the Bull Moose Party as it was sometimes labelled, Roosevelt took hold of a large surge of popular protest aimed at countering the abuses of wealth and power by a small clique who dominated America's huge industrial conglomerates. He courted this constituency with a populist flair displaying flourishes of what Arthur M.

Schlesinger Jr referred to as "rhetorical radicalism." At the basis of this approach was a strategy that effectively defended the dominant system of political economy by characterizing some of the richest men in the United States as capitalism's worst abusers.

Roosevelt took aim at the propensity of US businesses to merge into larger and larger units known as cartels or trusts. A primary aim of this consolidation of capital was quite clearly to limit competition among enterprises and maximize profits for those industrialists and financiers who gained the capacity to fix prices with their monopoly control over large sectors of the economy. This way of undermining the competitive dynamic of market forces can be conceived as monopoly capitalism.[26] Roosevelt proposed that the federal authorities should be invested with new powers to break up the giant industrial monopolies, those corporate conglomerates that are sometimes referred to as trusts. After intervening in this way, the federal government should play a more assertive role in regulating the new commercial configurations of corporate transaction. According to Schlesinger, "Roosevelt transfixed the imagination of the American middle class as did no other figure of his time … He gathered into himself the mounting discontent with which Americans were contemplating business rule. By offering that discontent release in melodrama, he no doubt reduced the pressure behind it for accomplishment." Paraphrasing the criticism of one of Roosevelt's left-wing opponents, Schlesinger writes, "Cannonading back and forth, [Roosevelt] filled the air with noise and smoke, but when the cloud drifted by, little had been achieved."[27] By occupying so much political space at such a strategic moment in US history, Roosevelt prevented the proponents of other possible remedies from gaining ground. His management of the trust-busting movement, for instance, helped divert attention away from the considerable attractions of Eugene Debs and his presidential campaigns as head of the Socialist Party of the United States.

In spite of the concerted and many-pronged efforts to contain support for both socialism and communism in the United States, these systems of political economy continued to attract proponents. The attractions of these alternative approaches to organizing society's material relations grew considerably after the Great Depression dramatically undermined confidence in capitalism's ultimate viability. Under the strain of the apparent breakdown of capitalism following the stock market crash of 1929, even prominent liberals such as John Dewey could proclaim: "The people will rule when they have power in the degree they own and control the lands, banks, the producing and distributing agencies of the nation. Ravings about Bolshevism, communism, socialism are irrelevant to the axiomatic truth of that statement."[28] Similarly, the literary critic Edmund Wilson surveyed the economic wreckage around him and observed: "If the American radicals and progressives who repudiate the Marxist dogma and the strategy of the Communist Party hope to accomplish anything valuable, they must take Communism away from Communists, and take it without ambiguities or reservations, asserting emphatically that the ultimate goal is the ownership of the means of production by the government." In another commentary, Wilson asserted that the Soviet Union remained "the moral top of the world where the light never goes out."[29]

Such articulate and influential endorsements for the installation of dramatically expanded regimes of state ownership and intervention helped fortify the resolve of those who were most strongly opposed to the nationalization of industry and land. They helped radicalize some of the strategies of those who championed more aggressive motifs of privatization, including the corporatist integration of business organizations into the directing mechanisms of national governance. The desire for drastic action on the part of some of capitalism's most zealous protectors was stimulated by the quick spread of the theory following the First World War that some broad but covert coalition of conspiring Jews had engineered the rise of Soviet power and the spread of communist ideology to advance their own dark designs of global domination. In 1920 Winston Churchill contributed to the web of rumour and speculation which gave a new twist to the old prejudices that have historically made scapegoats of the Jews for all manner of imagined ills and dilemmas. Referring to the Soviet Union's founders and founding ideology, he commented: "With the notable exception of Lenin, the majority of leading figures are Jews. Moreover," he added, "the principal inspiration and driving power comes from Jews."[30]

Soon after the formation of the Soviet state, therefore, an axis of collaboration developed around the view that communist internationalism was best understood as a key element in a plot to expand the power of an evil network of prominently placed Jews. In its initial phase, this axis of anti-Semitic conspiracy mongering was especially active along a channel of collaboration linking Munich and Detroit.[31] The main protagonist at the German end of this axis was the young politician, Adolf Hitler.[32] The austere face of Henry Ford, the dominant figure at the Detroit end of the connection, stared out from the large portrait in Hitler's Munich office. Beginning with the conviction that the Treaty of Versailles was profoundly unjust to his people, Hitler sought to continue Bismarck's quest to advance pan-German unity. He sought to further the linkage and empowerment of the entire German people by expanding the scope of their national government to the point where it could dominate all of Europe. One of Hitler's main platforms in his agenda for Germany's imperial conquest of *Lebensraum* – living space – was the goal of ridding Europe of what he saw as the dual and intertwined contaminants of Jews and Bolshevism.[33] He viewed Bolshevist trade unions as a menace to the convergence of capitalist and Social Darwinist ideals emphasizing the survival of the fittest. The Nazi leader pictured the Jewish infiltration of the European power structure as a check on the ability of his imagined master race to exercise its imagined competitive advantage in governing the planet.

Because the Nazi regime expressed in a radical and unambiguous way the emergence of a number of new forces in the genesis of capitalist globalization, the Third Reich merits analysis through the lens of Aboriginal history.

Hitler's government provided a laboratory in which to work through the implications of a number of novel theories about how to order a society founded on militant anti-communism. In forming his vision of a world order structured to reflect an imagined hierarchy of superior and inferior peoples, Hitler drew heavily on many decades of work in the social sciences. He became an outspoken proponent of racial interpretations that had long been promoted by many of Darwin's disciples as keys to understanding the forward progress of human evolution. As Hitler's first deputy, Rudolf Hess, observed, "National Socialism is nothing but applied biology."[34]

Hitler drew on a wide infatuation throughout the Western world with the emerging science of eugenics.[35] The eugenic approach to "public health" sought to apply to human procreation many of the same principles of selective breeding that had long been seen as essential to the achievement of improved productivity in agriculture and animal husbandry. The initial Nazi policies promoting the political ascendance of Nordic peoples through the forced elimination of those deemed genetically inferior drew strongly on eugenic research and models of legislation and jurisprudence originating in the United States. In his *War against the Weak*, Edwin Black highlights the US origins of the eugenic philosophies and methodologies that were adopted and dramatically extended by Nazi Germany. He chronicles how the campaign to study, publicize, and apply eugenics through the forced sterilization of those deemed genetically "unfit" involved the support of some of "America's finest universities, most reputable scientists, most trusted professional and charitable organizations, and most revered corporate foundations."[36] In particular, the Carnegie Institution, the Rockefeller Foundation, and the estate of the railway magnate E.H. Harriman backed the diverse activities of the richly funded Eugenics Record Office and the related enterprises headquartered at the Cold Spring Harbor research facility at Long Island, New York. When Germany's Nazi government instituted its first law in 1933 authorizing the forced sterilization of groups and individuals, Charles Davenport, the American founder and driving force of the Cold Spring Harbor facility, praised the development. He boasted in *Eugenical News* that the German law replicated some aspects of the legislation on forced sterilization already enacted in twenty-seven US states. The German law, he claimed, "reads almost like the 'American model sterilization law.'"[37]

The initial sterilization law of 1933 was extended to the anti-Jewish Nuremberg Laws in 1935. The application of the Nuremberg laws became, in turn, a prelude to the state-sanctioned vigilantism of *Kristallnacht*, when in 1938 over a hundred synagogues were burned to the ground and thousands of Jews were violently pulled from their homes and transported to concentration camps. Ultimately, the Nazi obsession with eugenics as a means of implementing their master-race fantasies led to an orgy of forced labour and industrialized genocide on such a massive scale that the Nazi regime would forever be held synonymous with the emerging concept in international law of crimes against humanity. In spite of news of the growing cycles of internal violence in the prelude to the Second World War, the application of concepts of "racial hygiene" to the widening populations under Nazi control continued to receive the enthusiastic support of the most committed eugenicists in the United States. "No matter how dismal the plight of Jews in Germany," writes Black, "no matter how horrifying the headlines, no matter how close Europe came to all-out war, no matter how often German troops poured across another border, American eugenicists stood fast by their eugenic hero, Adolf Hitler."[38] One such admirer was Clarence Campbell, the president of the Eugenics Research Office. In 1935 in Berlin, at the World Population Congress, he declared: "Guided by [Germany's] anthropologists, eugenicists and social philosophers, [Adolf Hitler] has been able to construct a comprehensive racial policy of population development and improvement that promises to be epochal in racial history. It sets a pattern which other nations and other racial groups must follow if they do not wish to fall behind in their racial quality, in their racial accomplishments and in their prospects for survival."[39]

Once Hitler and his deputies assumed near omnipotent authority over the machinery of the German state in the mid-1930s, their reintroduction of slavery would become an important means of integrating the Nazi defence of capitalism with the regime's racist preoccupations. As the military-industrial complex of Hitlerian Germany gathered momentum in its bid for global dominance, a host of Nazi decrees began the process of making slaves of many millions of Jews, Slavs, gypsies, and others. It is estimated that the Nazi regime enslaved between 8 million and 12 million individuals.[40] These slaves provided cheap labour for literally thousands of companies. Some of these enterprises continue as integral components of the superpower's military-industrial complex. The corporate exploiters of Hitlerian slavery included Volkswagen, Ford Werke, Siemens, and Diamler-Benz. The most notorious exploiter of slave labour was the consortium of chemical enterprises known as IG Farben. This amalgam of interrelated businesses has been described as "the corporate headquarters of the industrial force behind Hitler's Third Reich."[41] IG Auschwitz was prominent among IG Farben's many commercial enterprises in the military-industrial complex that briefly dominated Europe during the apogee of Hitler's career.[42] Auschwitz got its name from the Germanified pronunciation of Oswiecem. The small Polish town of Oswiecem was strategically located in a region rich with coal mines, railway links, and ample resources of fresh water. It became the nexus for one of the most notorious displays of industrialized ruthlessness in all recorded history.

The IG Farben conglomerate has a prominent place in the history of capitalism's expansion on the commercial, technological, political, and military frontiers of globalization. As the basis of a case study, this international enterprise stands in a class of its own for the light it sheds on the ascendance of the world's dominant military-industrial complex. IG Fraben's origins go back to 1903, when Carl Duisberg travelled from Germany to New York to establish a US subsidiary of the Bayer corporation. While in the United States, he studied the workings of industrial cartels. These commercial monopolies maximized profits by minimizing competition. Duisberg devoted most of his attention to an evaluation of John D. Rockefeller's Standard Oil Company, an enterprise renowned for its ability to fix prices by destroying or ingesting competitors. When he returned to Germany, Duisberg sought to extend and replicate Standard Oil's business model by negotiating a merger of six enterprises, all of them makers of chemicals or drugs. The businesses were consolidated to form a community of interests, a *Interessengemeinschaft,* or "IG" for short.[43] Building from a monopoly in the domestic manufacturing of military explosives, the IG Farben consortium was consolidated in 1925. In subsequent years this enterprise would extend its network of business connections to ninety-three countries. In the process, the directors of IG Farben established cartel agreements to minimize competition and enhance cooperation with about two thousand firms worldwide. Among IG Farben's business partners were Imperial Chemical and Shell Oil in Great Britain and, in the United States, Ford, General Motors, Du Pont, Union Carbide, Dow Chemical, and Texaco. The main axis of business collaboration linked IG Farben with Standard Oil of New Jersey and the network of financial institutions whose core of capital lay in the merged interests of the Rockefellers and J.P. Morgan and Company. Standard Oil of New Jersey formed the basis for Exxon Mobil, which is currently the world's richest and most thoroughly globalized corporate entity.

The axis of cooperation linking IG Farben and Standard Oil had as its primary business the fuelling and provisioning of the war machine of the Third Reich. At Auschwitz, for instance, factories went up to house complexes of potent new technology designed to transform coal into aviation fuel and the main ingredients of synthetic rubber. Like the steel and electricity cartels integral to the structure of the Third Reich, the institutional shape of IG Farben was heavily influenced by the leading figures in a number of Wall Street firms who succeeded in privatizing the scheme of war reparations owed by Germany according to the most controversial provisions of the Treaty of Versailles. With their creative accounting, the Wall Street bankers were able to re-engineer in their own interests the masses of credit and debt inherited from the First World War. They constructed institutional relationships in ways that served the commercial interests of their own elaborate networks of corporate partnership.[44] The Wall Street agents of Standard Oil and J.P. Morgan and Company worked closely with IG Farben's chairman, Herman Schmitz, and Hitler's most gifted economic adviser, Hjalmar Horace Greely Schact.[45] Schmitz was especially effective in using the secretive Swiss banking establishment to broaden the scope of IG Farben's and Nazi Germany's international involvements. Included among the diverse operations of the petro-chemical and pharmaceutical giant were the activities of an international network of spies whose job it was to supply the German government with military, industrial, and economic intelligence. As Senator Homer T. Bone saw it, "Farben was Hitler and Hitler was Farben." A US War Department study of the conglomerate would later conclude: "Without IG's immense productive facilities, its intense research, and vast international affiliations, Germany's prosecution of the war would have been impossible."[46]

IG Farben's Auschwitz factories covered about 12 square miles. The German government created four concentration camps surrounding the huge private facility in order to supply this core institution of the Third Reich's military-industrial complex with a steady supply of slave labour. SS boss Heinreich Himmler was responsible for rounding up Jews from throughout Europe and Slavs from the Eastern front to supply the Third Reich's military contractors with unpaid workers. As time passed, Auschwitz was less and less devoted to housing slave labour and more and more to hastening the pace of the industrialized extermination of European Jewry. A sign displayed on the arch over the entrance to IG Auschwitz infamously proclaimed *Arbeit Macht Frei* – work makes one free. Among IG Farben's vast array of valuable patents, it held exclusive rights to Zyclon B, the gas used at Auschwitz and other Nazi death camps to exterminate inmates not selected as slaves. The life expectancy of the Third Reich's unpaid workers decreased over the course of the war to the point where the cycle of lethal exploitation was dubbed Extermination by Labour. One of the major killing fields besides Auschwitz was the V-2 missile facility at Dora. There, vast numbers of slaves died in the process of tunnelling their way into a mountain. The reintegration of the institution of slavery into the political economy of a sophisticated state apparatus in the middle years of the twentieth century was an expedient that was well calculated to enrich stockholders and to undermine the collective bargaining power of those labourers in the Third Reich whose work was purchased rather than appropriated.

Hitler could not have established such a comfortable grip on power if his theories and actions had not resonated with meaning and purpose for many admirers. Nor could he have dramatically mobilized so many millions of people at every level of society.[47] Clearly, this embodiment of forces far larger than himself was able to connect his personae and his regime to some of the most compelling currents of culture and style permeating his time. With his uncompromising preoccupation with extreme anti-communism and extreme anti-Semitism, Hitler provided a powerful centre of political gravity globally for many constituencies, both large and small, nascent and mature. His emphasis on the idea of race as the primary criterion of human worth as well as the main catalyst of historical destiny held broad attractions in an era when the science of eugenics attracted many admirers on the left, right, and centre of the political spectrum.

With his slogan "Race First," the Black Jamaican activist Marcus Garvey, for instance, derived political capital from currents of attitude that extended to people on both sides of the imposed divisions of colour. Garvey's populist version of North American pan-Africanism demonstrates the versatility of interpretations stressing racial difference as the springboard for political action. The Ku Klux Klan of the United States was a more obvious embodiment of the principles espoused by Germany's fascist leader.[48] Closely connected to the KKK was the Black Legion, a well-funded terrorist organization that specialized in violently opposing all efforts to unionize the highly contested turf of industrial relations in Detroit's automobile factories. Like other pro-Nazi organizations in the United States, the Black Legion received backing from Irénée Du Pont, a major shareholder in General Motors and in the chemical company bearing his family name.[49] Du Pont also played a prominent role in the American Liberty League, one of the right-wing groups whose leadership was deeply implicated in a failed attempt to overthrow the regime of Franklin D. Roosevelt in 1933.[50]

The international Axis of fascist power linked Germany, Italy, and Japan in the Second World War. This Axis, but especially the core regime that coalesced around Adolf Hitler, drew on many new sources of social, ideological, technological, and economic energy in the genesis of global capitalism. While the Hitlerian regime took form near the aboriginal sources of many new currents of thought and action in world history, this polity also internalized many old patterns of external conquest in "the West's" history of imperial expansionism. Many of the Third Reich's policies represented extensions, refinements, and expansions of procedures and tactics developed by European and North American empire builders over many generations. Where previous expansionists had reserved their most ruthless incursions for brown-skinned people on the frontiers of empire, Hitler did not hesitate to direct the unrestrained ruthlessness of his machinery of genocide, enslavement, and theft towards targeted groups of fair-skinned Europeans.

The military defeat of fascism's strongholds required an enormous sacrifice of lives and resources. It involved the most concerted mobilization of people, arms, and ideas that the world had ever witnessed until that point. Without doubt, the defeat of the Axis powers represents a huge achievement in the defence of the principles of human decency and human rights. Posterity owes an enormous debt of gratitude to those who gave so much to check the Nazi quest for global domination. There are, however, many trajectories of continuity running through the Nazi regime connecting developments after the Second World War to European and imperial history before the incursions of the Axis powers. Much depends now on our ability to understand that, although the fascist Axis was defeated, those authoritarian regimes served as conduits and laboratories for many elements of the world we presently inhabit. The institution of colonialism, for instance, was forever affected by the Nazi importation into the European heartland of many tactics of repression developed since 1492 on the imperial frontiers of globalization. This redirection of imperialism's most lethal attributes towards the exercise of power *within* Europe and *among* Europeans helped to illuminate for many millions the enormous inhumanity attending the most aggressive forms of empire building. No doubt the Nazi imposition of such a massive crash course in the dark side of applied Social Darwinism helped turn European public opinion against the idea and practice of imperialism after 1945. Nevertheless, the imperial project rooted in the expansion of European empires survived the Second World War to assume new forms and configurations in the context of the Cold War.

The US-led side of the rivalry between the Cold War's dual superpowers drew especially on the anti-communist and pro-capitalist legacies of Hitler's military-industrial complex. In this way, the short-lived but intensely busy fascist empire proved to be a major testing ground for many material, legal, and psychological facets of the world's ascendant military-industrial complex. The Third Reich provided an especially rich field of invention in the arts and sciences of propaganda, psychological warfare, public/private partnerships, highway and automobile development, petro-chemicals, pharmaceuticals, rocket technology, and espionage. The continuity manifest in this evolving complex of relationships linking government and big business in the shared defence of capitalism is best expressed in the smooth replacement after 1945 of Germany by the United States as the primary shield and wedge against the spread of Soviet communism to Europe and the rest of the world. The continuing hold of anti-communism throughout much of Asia after the Second World War was similarly enforced by the decision of the region's US conquerors to allow the family dynasties responsible for the military mobilization of imperial Japan to maintain their wealth, prestige, and authority.

The demise of the Soviet Union after 1989 also rests on the lasting effects of Nazi aggression. It took the sacrifice of approximately 30 million Russian lives, including both soldiers and civilians, to halt Operation Barbarossa and turn back Hitler's push towards the east.[51] The turning point proved to be the Battle of Kursk in 1943.[52] The ratio of Soviet to US soldiers killed in the Second World War is 60 to 1.[53] The enormity of this loss on the Soviet side had a huge effect on that polity's long-term viability, including the Soviet experiment in militant anti-capitalism. The regime's architects and managers were not able to overcome the vast internal contradictions embedded in such a massive machinery of technocratic, centrally controlled governance. But the Soviet Union failed also because of the severe one-two punch inflicted first by Nazi Germany and then by the increasingly elaborate military-industrial complex of the United States over a period of half a century. Throughout much of the twentieth century the enemy of Soviet-centred communism gave coherence to the shape and form of the world's ascendant military-industrial complex. The metropolitan core of capitalism's bulwark shifted very quickly from Berlin to Washington once the Third Reich went as far as it could at Kursk in inflicting damage on the state apparatus formed with the explicit goal of applying and exporting Marxist principles to all the world's peoples.

WARS ON INDIANS, SLAVS, JEWS, COMMUNISTS, AND
TRUTH IN THE GENESIS OF THE MILITARY-INDUSTRIAL
COMPLEX

For much of the nineteenth century, the United States played the role of a kind of protégée or understudy of the British imperial government. The British government, for instance, moved aside when it allowed the United States to take control of the Oregon Country in 1846 or of Hawaii in the 1890s. In return, the US government afforded British enterprises a number of concessions, including a wide latitude to do business throughout the Spanish- and Portuguese-speaking portions of the Western Hemisphere. As early as 1823 in the Monroe Doctrine, the US government had staked out Latin America as the primary sphere of influence for the exercise of power through the instruments of informal empire. By the beginning of the twentieth century, new forces began to come into play. The industrial and economic power of the United States began to rise so quickly that the global dominance of the British Empire no longer seemed assured. The industrial ascent of the United States was matched by that of Germany. The old order began to come unglued as German and US businesses increasingly vied with those of Great Britain for commercial dominance in international markets. Would Germany and the United States vie with each other to replace the British Empire as the world's dominant polity? Would Germany team up with Great Britain to rejuvenate some expanded and revised version of British imperialism? Or would Germany and the United States combine forces, possibly with Japan, to create some new alliance capable of global hegemony?

These questions were pushed to the forefront of international affairs in the 1930s as the effects of the Great Depression set in. While Germany initially suffered more from its effects, the crisis cleared the way for Hitler's radical centralization of authority. Hitler's system of control linked a populist version of Teutonic Manifest Destiny with an especially sophisticated platform of high-tech militarism. Following the lead of Mussolini's Italy,[54] Hitler's regime took shape as a kind of mirror image of Bolshivik totalitarianism.[55] The National Socialists broke the back of most workers' organizations even as they integrated many local and transnational businesses into the cartels installed at the core of the German system of political economy. The regime was constructed as a haven for monopoly capitalism. The resources of the state were channelled through the privately owned corporate sector to create the material, organizational, and psychological conditions for the most modern and effective military-industrial complex of its day. Competition among corporations and between employers and employees was minimized so that power could be centralized and directed coercively outwards.[56]

The Nazi ideal combined the defence of capitalism with a race-based variation on the conception of the West's civilizing mission. One of the most effective agents of this worldview was the famous US aviator Charles Lindbergh. He had achieved enormous prominence in 1927 when he became the first pilot to cross the Atlantic in his legendary airplane, *The Spirit of St. Louis.* In the late 1930s Lindbergh moved easily between the air ministries of Germany, Great Britain, and the United States and, in November 1939, drew on this experience in an article he published in *Reader's Digest* entitled "Aviation, Race, and Geography." It was part of his work for the America First Committee, one of the primary agencies with the goal of shaping public opinion to prevent the United States from joining the fight against the fascist takeover of Europe. Lindbergh encouraged his readers to see the invention and proliferation of airplanes as "one of those priceless possessions which permit the White race to live at all in a pressing sea of Yellow, Black, and Brown." For him, air power represented nothing less than a "Western Wall of race and arms," an innovation that should be used to hold back "the infiltration of inferior blood."

With this thought as his introduction, Lindbergh proceeded to warn against the folly of US participation in a war that he alleged would divide and weaken the White race. We must not "commit racial suicide by internal conflict," he proclaimed. "We, the heirs of European culture, are on the verge of a disastrous war, a war within our own family of nations, a war which would reduce the strength and destroy the treasures of the White race ... the White race is bound to lose, and the others bound to gain, a war which may easily lead our civilization through more Dark Ages if it survives at all." For Lindbergh, the alternative to war with the Nazis was a grand alliance of Western nations to preserve the ruling imperatives of the White race. He proposed an "English Fleet, a German Air Force, a French Army, an American nation, standing together as guardians of our common heritage."[57]

Reader's Digest was part of the media empire owned and controlled by William Randolph Hearst. After meeting Hitler in 1934, Hearst used his publications to present fascist Germany to his readers in a positive light. Lindbergh's contribution reflected many of the prevailing orthodoxies among leading eugenicists on both sides of the Atlantic. His emphasis on the need to prevent the "White race" from being overwhelmed by "inferior blood," for instance, is quite consistent with the writings of Lothrop Stoddard. Edwin Black describes Stoddard's *Rising Tide of Color against White Supremacy* as a "eugenic gospel." First published in 1926, this volume is said to have influenced the policies of Adolf Hitler. During his tour of Germany's Eugenic Courts in 1939, Stoddard actually met with Hitler.[58] In words that echo the ethnocentric alarmism of Lindbergh, Stoddard asserted: "If white civilization goes down, the white race is irretrievably ruined. It will be swamped by the triumphant colored races, who will obliterate the white man by elimination or absorption ... Just as we isolate bacterial invasions, and starve out bacteria, so we can compel an inferior race to remain in its native habitat."[59]

Lindbergh's Nazi connections are chronicled by Max Wallace in his contribution to the growing body of literature exploring the many-faceted roles of a number of prominent US citizens and corporations in the rise and spread of European fascism. The US auto maker, Henry Ford, is the other major figure whose role in the ascent of German fascism is chronicled by Wallace in his study *The American Axis*. Where Lindbergh assisted the Third Reich by using his celebrity to help prevent the United States from joining the opening phase of the Second World War, Ford's role went much deeper.[60] He helped Hitler at the very beginning of the Nazi leader's political career by using the prestige of the Ford name as well as an extremely well-funded Ford publishing network to articulate, publicize, and legitimate some of the ideas at the ideological base of the Nazi movement. In cooperation with a shady collection of German spies and disgruntled émigrés from Czarist Russia, Ford advanced his wildly anti-Semitic theories between 1919 and 1927 in a complex of publications starting with his Detroit-area newspaper, the *Dearborn Independent*, which was subtitled *The Ford International Weekly*. The articles in this newspaper were collected and repackaged as pamphlets and books that were distributed wherever Ford products were sold, including throughout much of Germany. Its staff's main assignment was to create the impression that the covert actions of an elite cabal of Jews lay at the basis of many of the world's most severe woes. "Ford started the Jew-hatred snowball rolling," writes Albert Lee.[61]

Ford's packaging of his newspaper's anti-Semitic articles into a number of edited texts, including in 1921 *The International Jew: The World's Foremost Problem*, would play a significant role in facilitating the contest of ideas and interests culminating in the Second World War.[62] *Der International Jude*, the German translation of some of the most virulent of the *Dearborn Independent* articles, was given especially wide distribution by Nazi and Ford agents in Europe. Samuel Untermeyer, an American Jew travelling in Europe in 1923, left a vivid account of the role of this Ford publication in preparing the ground for the rise of Hitlerism. "Wherever there is a Ford car," he wrote, "there is a Ford agency not far away, and wherever there is a Ford agency, those vile libelous books in the language of the country are to be found." Utermeyer added that the European-language translations of *The International Jew*, "coupled with the name of Ford, have done more than could be undone in a century to sow, spread and ripen the poisonous seeds of anti-Semitism and race hatred."[63]

In 1946, during the war-crimes proceedings at Nuremberg, one of the accused, Baldur von Schirach, left vivid testimony about the important role of Henry Ford's initiatives in inspiring and legitimizing Nazi policies. The German Führer's governor of Vienna and a leader of the Hitler Youth Movement, Von Schirach explained:

The decisive anti-Semitic book which I read at the time, and the book which influenced my comrades, was Henry Ford's book, *The International Jew*. I read it and became anti-Semitic. This book made in those days a great impression on my friends and myself because we saw in Henry Ford the representative of success, also the representative of successful social policy. In the poverty-stricken and wretched Germany of the time, youth looked towards America, and, apart from the great benefactor Herbert Hoover, it was Henry Ford who, to us, represented America ... If he said Jews were to blame, naturally we believed him.[64]

In the early years of his political rise from relative obscurity, Adolf Hitler kept multiple copies of *The International Jew* in his Munich bureau, an office dominated conspicuously by a large portrait depicting Henry Ford. Ford is thought by some to have contributed funds as well as the huge prestige vested in his name, reputation, and ideas to Hitler's political party.[65] In his autobiography, Hitler paid a tribute to Ford, calling him the "single great man" able to maintain "full independence" in spite of the alleged propensity of Jews to be "the controlling masters of [US] producers" as well as the dominant governors of "the stock exchange forces of the American Union."[66] Ford and Hitler both saw themselves as leaders in Western civilization's crusade to defend the freedoms of capitalist business enterprise from the dark Jewish schemes they saw permeating Soviet socialism and communist trade unionism. Throughout most of his career, Ford maintained his stance of harsh antagonism towards the inroads of organized labour into his industry. Even his much-hailed decision in 1914 to raise his company's minimum wage to five dollars a day was largely motivated by his desire to fend off labour organizers, but especially those representing the Industrial Workers of the World. "Labor organizations," Ford declared, "are the worst things that ever struck this earth ... We'll never recognize the United Automobile Workers Union or any other union."[67] He did not relent from this position even after the institution of the New Deal. Ford refused to sign the automobile code of the Roosevelt government's National Recovery Administration which stipulated that employees had the right to organize and to bargain collectively.

Ford's determination to fend off labour organizers became so extreme during the 1930s that his company has been described by Wallace as "a totalitarian state in miniature." Ford's anti-union operatives in the notorious Ford Service Department, the "Ford Gestapo," maintained an atmosphere of "violence, espionage, and lawlessness" in their repressive oversight of the motor company's workers.[68] This department included among its spies and goons over two thousand Ukrainian immigrants known for their pro-fascist and anti-communist politics. Their leader, Ford employee John Koos, was appointed minister of internal affairs of the Ukraine once it was placed under Nazi rule in the course of the Second World War. Generally speaking, the Ford Motor Company was known to be one of the most active hot beds of Nazi sympathizers and agents in the United States. As an official of the US Military Intelligence Division wrote in 1937, "Henry Ford and his subordinates Ernest G. Liebold, W.J. Cameron, and others have turned the Ford Motor Company Chemical Division into the headquarters of the Nazis here."[69] The Nazi agents at Ford collaborated closely with the populist, pro-Hitler preacher/broadcaster Father Charles Coughlin, who regularly reached as many as 40 million listeners on the CBS network from the Detroit area headquarters of what he called the Radio League of the Little Flower. A strong proponent of the theory that Jews were the main driving force behind communism, Father Coughlin attempted in 1937 to help Ford establish a sham union entitled the Workers Council for Social Justice.[70]

Ford was a pioneer among those American industrialists and financiers who offered a broadening stream of support for European fascists in helping them to move from the fringes towards places of prominence in European politics. After 1927, Ford was pressured by boycotts and negative publicity to back away from his extreme, anti-Semitic positions. But both Ford and his famous automobile enterprise continued their special relationship with the German National Socialists, a relationship entirely consistent with the "big push" by what was then "the world's most famous company" to dominate European and global markets.[71] In 1938 Hitler's government honoured Ford, as it did Lindbergh, with major Nazi awards. This recognition came with the deep integration of Ford Werke AG, a subsidiary at least half owned by the US-based head office, into Germany's military-industrial complex. The role of the Ford Motor Company in the growth and operation of the Hitlerian war machine was one aspect of a far larger project with many influential proponents on both sides of the Atlantic. One of their key strategies was to link the marketing and manufacturing strength of the United States with the legendary German prowess in science and technology. Hitler's plan for the unification of Europe presented Ford and many other US capitalists with the enticing prospect of a huge new unitary and militantly anti-communist market peopled by hundreds of millions of consumers with the combined capacity to purchase a vast array of American goods, services, and patents.

The convergent thinking of Henry Ford and Adolf Hitler is clearly marked in the striking similarities linking the simple, functional designs of the great prototypes of cheap functional cars, the Model T Ford and the Volkswagen bug. Hitler himself did the first sketch of Volkswagen's original car. This design was handed to Hitler's designate, Ferdinand Porsche, who initially developed the Volkswagen Company primarily to serve the German war machine rather than to provide common folk with economical cars. As he developed his plans for Volkswagen, Porsche visited the main Ford factory in Detroit several times. Moreover, he recruited a number of German-American engineers from Ford's US operations. Porsche paid special attention to Ford's elaborate system for spying on the actions and words of Ford employees. Most of Volkswagen's first wave of production was directed to the manufacturing of military vehicles geared to the technique of lightening-quick ground attacks known in German as *Blitzkreig*. The effectiveness of this method of warfare depended on Hitler's development of a massive system of European autobahns. These autobahns provided the primary model for the rapid expansion of North America's extensive system of highways after the Second World War.[72]

This saga of transportation history, a key facet of globalization's apparent bending of time and space, would have huge implications for the future. It would, for instance, help elevate the oil industry yet higher into the strategic stratosphere of global geopolitics and geo-economics. Indeed, the popularization of the automobile as a key medium of mass transport in the West helped give many millions of average people a major stake in a system of political economy whose overarching features remain those of the military-industrial complex. The ecological catastrophe arising from the worldwide spread of automobile culture, but especially as it is integrated into the quickly proliferating middle classes of China and India, highlights the unsustainability of a whole system of production and consumption derived largely from military models of industrial reproduction.

The shared preoccupation of Ford and Hitler with the mobility of the car had beneath it a common body of assumptions about the availability of large areas for unobstructed motor travel. Hitler's quest to conquer *Lebensraum* comparable in size to Ford's own country was almost certainly a factor in the German leader's interest in the history of US transcontinental expansion. The main focus of Hitler's attraction to this facet of US history was the overpowering of Aboriginal resistance to the westward movement of the dominant population, which then built up the property base of the rising capitalist superpower. One of Hitler's biographers, John Toland, has explained his subject's concentration on the US treatment of North America's Indians as follows:

Hitler's concept of concentration camps as well as the practicality of genocide owed much, so he claimed, to his studies of English and United States history. He admired the camps for Boer prisoners in South Africa and for the Indians in the Wild West, and often praised to his inner circle the efficiency of America's extermination – by starvation and uneven combat – of the red savages who could not be tamed by captivity. Hitler frequently referred to the Russians as Redskins.[73]

In his text *Hitler and His Secret Partners*, James Pool makes observations similar to those of Toland. Pool attributes some of Hitler's fascination with Indians and their fate to his early reading of Karl May's children's fables about Native American exploits. He quotes Hitler as having said, "I don't see a German who eats a piece of bread torment himself with the idea that the soil that produces this bread has been won by the sword. When we eat from Canada we don't think about the despoiled Indians." According to Pool, Hitler looked for antecedents of his genocidal policies in the Turkish slaughter of Armenians, in the Red Terror during the Russian Revolution, and in the Japanese butchery at Nanking. Apparently, however, the warehousing and elimination of American Indians stimulated his imagination like no other historical precedent for the kind of treatment he would extend to Jews, Gypsies, and Russians. Of Hitler, Pool writes:

He was very interested in the way the Indian population had rapidly declined due to epidemics and starvation when the United States government forced them to live on reservations. He thought the American government's forced migration of the Indians over great distances to barren reservation land was a deliberate policy of extermination ... For some time Hitler considered deporting Jews to a large "reservation" in the Lubin area where their numbers would be reduced through starvation and disease.[74]

Hitler's reference to Russians as Redskins anticipated the frequent labelling by US soldiers of enemy territory in Vietnam as "Indian Country." What meanings lie embedded in this pattern of metaphor to describe relations of power on capitalism's most extended frontiers? Why have the terms employed in the conquest and colonization of North America translated so easily into the language of capitalism's most concerted military attacks on communism? One of the most ruthless of these genocidal assaults on the real or imagined Red enemies of capitalism took place in Indonesia in 1965. In this murderous episode of ideological cleansing, many hundreds of thousands of communists and suspected communists were systematically eliminated as part of the US- and British-backed coup that installed the government of General Suharto. The importance of making the germane connections between the history of transcontinental expansion in North America and the most infamous episodes of genocide in the Third Reich is emphasized by Lilian Friedberg. She writes: "The American Holocaust might be viewed as the prototype for the extermination of the Jews in Europe. At the very least, the event must be seen as a predecessor of the Nazi Holocaust."[75]

HITLER OR ROOSEVELT?

Adolf Hitler and Franklin D. Roosevelt were leaders whose regimes embodied two competing systems of capitalism. The fight between these two systems of capitalist business culture formed an important element of conflict in the Second World War.[76] Many of the commercial forces that coalesced around the leadership of Hitler and Roosevelt continue to do battle in the struggle to determine the future shape of both the global economy and the military-industrial complex.

Hitler and Roosevelt shared some attributes even as they also personified profoundly different approaches to the governance of humanity. They both came to power in 1933 at the height of the Great Depression, and they both died in 1945. In their time in high office, both leaders sought ways of defending capitalism from communism. Hitler and his supporters waged open warfare on their Marxist enemies. Roosevelt sought to defuse the revolutionary potential of communist extremism by incorporating the social democracy of the New Deal into the political economy of the United States. The practitioners of the New Deal hoped to achieve a degree of balanced equilibrium in the relationship between capital and labour. They wanted to incorporate Boasian policies of respect for cultural pluralism into the fabric of a mixed economy. Roosevelt's liberalism can be equated with rational relativism. In contrast, Hitler's fascist policies epitomized the absolutism inherent in a centralized regime of totalitarian rule.

The blueprint for the global extension of the US-centred New Deal was drafted in August 1941 at a meeting between President Roosevelt and Prime Minister Winston Churchill. Together with an array of military advisers, the two leaders met on naval vessels anchored in Placentia Bay off the coast of Newfoundland. At this point in the Second World War, the US government theoretically remained neutral. Because of the influence on public opinion of Charles Lindbergh, William Randolph Hearst, and others of their ilk, the forces of isolationism prevented Roosevelt from officially joining Great Britain in its war with the fascist Axis. Nevertheless, the ground was being prepared for the US government to move beyond the provision of material support for the British war effort. In anticipating the entry of the United States into the war as a military ally of Great Britain, Roosevelt returned to some of the larger themes that had been raised by President Woodrow Wilson when he outlined his famous Fourteen Points as justification for bringing his government into the First World War. Like Wilson, Roosevelt presented himself as an opponent of imperialism. He pressured Churchill to put his signature on a document which strongly suggested that the British Empire – indeed, all the European empires – would be dismantled once the fascist Axis was defeated. Much like Wilson, Roosevelt advanced a vision of a new regime of international security based on "the right of all peoples to choose the form of government under which they will live."

Although Churchill was a strong proponent of a continuing British Empire, the conditions of his besieged country were sufficiently dire in the late summer of 1941 that this pugnacious English aristocrat had little choice but to bend to Roosevelt's will.[77] In this fashion, the Atlantic Charter came into being.[78] The animating spirit of that document infused the content of the address delivered the following year by US vice-president Henry Wallace when this New Dealer countered Henry Luce's promotion of the American Century. Wallace's vision called for the continuation of a "people's revolution" in the Century of the Common Man. From West Africa to India, the Atlantic Charter immediately infused new hope into the struggle by colonized peoples to escape the weight of imperial rule. The document anticipated the fuller consolidation in 1945 of the United Nations and the attempt at Nuremberg to elaborate and enforce a regime of international law to punish and prevent war crimes. Over the signatures of Roosevelt and Churchill, the Atlantic Charter proclaimed:

First, their countries seek no aggrandizement, territorial or other;

Second, they desire to see no territorial changes that do not accord with the freely expressed wishes of the peoples concerned;

Third, they respect the right of all peoples to choose the form of government under which they will live; and they wish to see sovereign rights and self- government restored to those who have been forcibly deprived of them;

Fourth, they will endeavor, with due respect for their existing obligations, to further the enjoyment by all States, great or small, victor or vanquished, of access, on equal terms, to the trade and to the raw materials of the world which are needed for their economic prosperity;

Fifth, they desire to bring about the fullest collaboration between all nations in the economic field with the object of securing, for all, improved labor standards, economic advancement and social security;

Sixth, after the final destruction of the Nazi tyranny, they hope to see established a peace which will afford to all nations the means of dwelling in safety within their own boundaries, and which will afford assurance that all the men in all the lands may live out their lives in freedom from fear and want;

Seventh, such a peace should enable all men to traverse the high seas and oceans without hindrance;

Eighth, they believe that all of the nations of the world, for realistic as well as spiritual reasons, must come to the abandonment of the use of force. Since no future peace can be maintained if land, sea or air armaments continue to be employed by nations which threaten, or may threaten, aggression outside of their frontiers, they believe, pending the establishment of a wider and permanent system of general security, that the disarmament of such nations is essential. They will likewise aid and encourage all other practicable measures which will lighten for peace-loving peoples the crushing burden of armaments.[79]

The Atlantic Charter has been sometimes dismissed as little more than a rhetorical flourish designed to paper over the divisions and real aims of the signatories to the agreement. J.F.C. Fuller, for instance, referred to it as "first-class propaganda and probably the biggest hoax in history."[80] His cynicism speaks to the reality that many of the principles of the Atlantic Charter were indeed sabotaged by the anti-communist zealotry of "the national security state." Nevertheless, the strategic nature of the circumstances surrounding the birth of the Atlantic Charter makes it a major landmark of our times. Its drafters created a beacon of enlightenment in the quest for an ideal of globalization that would emphasize international law and universal human rights rather than empire building, religious mission, and the appropriation of land, resources, and labour. The Atlantic Charter formed the basis for the shared principles affirmed by a broader representation of allied forces in the United Nations. In January 1942, representatives of twenty-six polities, including the Soviet Union, China, Greece, Belgium, South Africa, Czechoslovakia, and Norway, put their signature on the Joint Declaration of the United Nations. This initial statement by the UN referred to the allies' shared endorsement of the Atlantic Charter and added new language to their affirmation of basic principles. The members of the UN agreed in 1942, for instance, "to preserve human rights and justice in their own lands as well as other lands." The signatories sought "victory over Hitlerism" through "common struggle against savage and brutal forces seeking to subjugate the world."[81]

The Atlantic Charter aroused considerable attention among the emerging leadership of the anti-colonial movement. It was referred to often, for instance, by the likes of George Padmore and W.E.B. Du Bois in the discussions in and around the pan-African Congress that took place in Manchester in 1945.[82] Nelson Mandela has referred to the Atlantic Charter and its powerful influence in infusing new energy and inspiration into the African National Congress. In his autobiography, *Long Walk to Freedom*, Mandela writes: "Some in the West saw the charter as empty promises, but not those of us in Africa. Inspired by the Atlantic Charter and the fight of the Allies against tyranny and aggression, the ANC created its own Charter, called African Claims, which called for the full citizenship of all Africans, the right to buy land and the repeal of all discriminating legislation."[83] The Atlantic Charter extended and expanded the same traditions of Anglo-American constitution making which earlier gave rise to the Royal Proclamation of 1763. Like the Royal Proclamation, the Atlantic Charter effectively outlawed conquest as a legitimate means of imperial expansion and state formation. Both documents emphasized the necessity of obtaining the consent of Indigenous peoples for any change in the status of their Aboriginal lands. The drafters recognized the need for the edification of a central authority to protect weaker parties from the incursions and dictates of stronger neighbours. Both instruments codified the principle that the most acquisitive forces of capital expansion would have to be regulated in ways that outlawed genocide, the theft of land, and various forms of enslavement. While the Royal Proclamation recognized the right of Indigenous peoples not to be molested or disturbed in the exercise of their own self-government, the Atlantic Charter looked beyond the political rights of colonized peoples to the legal and economic dimension of universal human rights. The more recent document broke new ground in envisaging a world community where global citizens would be universally provided with improved labour standards, economic advancement, and social security together with an "assurance that all the men in all the lands may live out their lives in freedom from fear and want."

The Atlantic Charter renewed the sense of Anglo-America as a single polity whose unity of origins and purpose transcended the division of sovereignty formalized in the Treaty of Paris in 1783. When Anglo-America is conceived of as a single polity in the global community, it is easier to identify the direct line of thought and action linking King George and Sir William Johnson with Franklin Roosevelt and John Collier. Johnson was the British King's main superintendent of Indian affairs in North America. John Collier performed a similar function for President Franklin Roosevelt. Where Johnson's advice was instrumental in the formulation of the Royal Proclamation, Collier was the main architect of the Indian New Deal instituted in 1934. This Indian New Deal stands poised between the principles outlined in the Royal Proclamation and in the Atlantic Charter. The main purpose of the Indian New Deal was to put a halt to the assimilationist and colonial policies permeating federal governance of Indian reserves and Native American peoples in the United States.

Like the Royal Proclamation, the Indian New Deal had faults and limitations. Both initiatives, however, should be viewed in the context of their times as highly significant steps aimed at easing the injustice directed at Indigenous peoples on the very continent where the formal imperialism of the British Empire gave way to the informal empire building of the New World superpower. On a planet where the Anglo-American community has long exercised a disproportionate amount of power, the experience of Aboriginal North Americans has tended to foreshadow that of many other constituencies in the ongoing process of globalization. As Part Two of this volume will illustrate, this pattern of interactivity in Aboriginal and world history suggests the broader significance of encounters between Indigenous peoples and the colonizing societies in places like Georgia, Missouri, California, Washington, and especially British Columbia. The tactics employed to transform the legal status of Aboriginal lands in such places tend to reveal earlier stages in the development of the different streams of capitalism that would eventually clash on a global scale in the Hitler-Roosevelt confrontation.

John Collier was a visionary whose conception of the role of Indian societies in the United States, the Western Hemisphere, and the entire planet adds depth and substance to the conception of the Fourth World. He pictured the Indian reserves under federal authority in his country as test tubes of ethnic relations. He self-consciously styled the Indian New Deal as a laboratory for the creation of Aboriginal regimes that would replace the structures of colonial administration once the empires of Europe had been dismantled. The Atlantic Charter was one of the key instruments that projected the ideals of the New Deal generally, but the Indian New Deal more specifically, onto a larger canvas during a period when many of the world's people still lived under the imposed constraints of colonial governors. With its vision of a global community organized around principles of universal justice, the Atlantic Charter helped identify Third Ways to the Fourth World. It gave clear articulation to anti-colonial principles that would be revisited and more fully elaborated at the Bandung Conference in Indonesia in 1955.

The Atlantic Charter would generate much opposition. Hitler is said to have seen the document as a prime indicator of a developing Jewish plot to block the progress of his regime. He responded by accelerating the industrialized pace of his bid to exterminate European Jewry. In Japan, the Atlantic Charter helped to stimulate plans to attack the US naval base at Pearl Harbor. In the longer term, Cold War anti-communism provided the means of pre-empting the promise in the Atlantic Charter that "the sovereign rights" of all the world's peoples would be recognized and respected. President Harry Truman's institution of the *National Security Act* of 1947 helped to initiate the Cold War. This Act was rooted in the belief that Marxist ideology and the Soviet Union were, in Woodrow Wilson's words, "the negation of everything that is American." The implementation of the *National Security Act* did much to subvert the system of international law and multilateralism envisaged first in the Atlantic Charter and then in the UN's joint declaration in 1942, the UN Charter of 1945, and the Universal Declaration of Human Rights of 1948. The *National Security Act* centralized yet more power in the imperial presidency of the United States even as it attacked the principle that all peoples have the inherent right and responsibility to govern themselves free from foreign meddling in their internal affairs. Continuing a policy trend expressed earlier in Wilson's zealous enforcement of the *Espionage Act* and *Sedition Act* of 1918, the NSA brought the National Security Council into existence. The NSA also formalized the reconstitution of the Office of Strategic Services as the Central Intelligence Agency.[84]

Accordingly, the fear of communist subversion was fanned and exploited over much of the twentieth century, first domestically and then internationally, to build up a "national security" apparatus within the directing mechanism of the emerging superpower's military-industrial complex. After 1945 that national security state drew heavily on the anti-communist brain trusts developed under the rule of Nazi Germany, fascist Italy, and imperial Japan. The defence of capitalism and privately held capital from the collectivization of wealth forms a key element in the genesis of the United States from its inception as Europe's most successful land speculation. This fear of communist collectivization entered a new phase of intensity with the "Red Scare" of 1919. Since that time, but especially after the Second World War, those who have operated within the framework of the national security state have been largely unconstrained by the rule of law and the requirements of a fair, free, balanced, and accurate press. With the immense resources of the United States behind them, the agents of the national security state intervened, often covertly and illegally, in the internal political affairs of many countries, including their own. They have done so in ways that have systematically violated the sovereign right of all peoples to choose their own form of government and to influence the decisions of their own representatives and legislative bodies.

Just as Cold War anti-communism provided the means of averting the kind of law-abiding, equitable human relations that might have flowed from the global implementation of the Atlantic Charter, the American Revolution earlier provided a route of escape from adherence to the terms of the Royal Proclamation of 1763. The division of Anglo-America by civil war and secession provided a means of averting forms of development that might have included the Indigenous peoples as partners, collaborators, and substantial stake holders in British North America. The national security apparatus of the future superpower really began in 1776 with the charge that King George was giving assistance to the Red terrorists labelled by the Declaration of Independence as merciless Indian savages.

For a time, Hitler's regime served many interests during a period when the expansiveness of imperial globalization tended to turn inwards. Economic historian Robert Skidelsky has described some of the economic dimensions of this change. He pointed to the "contrast between the nineteenth-century world of small private firms operating in a continually expanding economy and the twentieth-century world of ... great businesses of vast scale, salaried management and diffused ownership." This tendency "towards cartel, merger, and monopoly was driven not only by the technical conditions of production and the financial advantages of large-scale industry in raising money from the Stock Exchange, but by the menace of surplus capacity."[85] From the time of his emergence as a local politician in Bavaria to the period where his military juggernaut cut most deeply into the vital organs of the Soviet Union, Hitler operated at the vortex where many new forces in industrial capitalism met. His quest to unite Europe engendered the support and collaboration of many who shared an avowed interest in distancing the ownership and control of private wealth from the myriad sovereign constraints imposed on capital by a multiplicity of European governments. Hitler's regime offered a right-wing alternative to the liberal social democracy that dominated Europe's national polities after the First World War, and the United States after the election of Franklin Roosevelt. Borrowing from Leon Trotsky's concept of permanent revolution, Hitler looked to the military function of government as the highest field for the synthesis of conquest and laissez-faire competition among races, technologies, ideologies, and capitalist enterprises.

The onus of war reparations provided Hitler with the ultimate grievance, together with the unique set of financial circumstances that made his Third Reich the world's main laboratory for the development of a new kind of military-industrial complex. The organization of German business and the German fighting machine around a few privately owned industrial cartels was largely the product of the financial engineering performed through a few key institutions, including the Bank of England, Germany's Reichsbank, and those Wall Street enterprises centred on the investment house of J.P. Morgan.[86] As demonstrated by the connection between IG Farben and Standard Oil of New Jersey, Germany's industrial cartels were modelled on, or developed as outright extensions of, the industrial cartels that came to dominate the political economy of the United States during the Guilded Age. The important role of Wall Street investment bankers and the US cartels in determining the form of German industry before the Second World War can be seen in Owen D. Young's role in the transactions. A leading executive of the General Electric Corporation, Young was instrumental in the formulation of the Young Plan to consolidate the structure of borrowing and repayment attending the war reparations imposed by the Treaty of Versailles.[87] A key element of this plan involved the establishment in Basle, Switzerland, in 1930 of the Bank for International Settlements as a kind of ultimate central banker to the world's central banks.[88] The growth of the cartel system into a global network of financial institutions operating at arm's length from all national governments raised the process of privatizing the commons to new heights of financial wizardry. It foreshadowed forms of denationalized privatization that would be pressed forward with great intensity once the demise of the Soviet Union cleared the way for the totalitarian globalization of universalized capitalism.

When Hitler came to power, his government fulfilled his political promise to terminate the reparations symbolizing Germany's humiliation in the First World War. The politics of Hitler, his party, his country, and his empire were very much an outgrowth of the Treaty of Versailles. His rise to authority was helped along by many influential parties who shared the conviction that the punishment imposed on Germany in 1919 was detrimental to building up the edifice of German capitalism as a bulwark against Soviet-based communism. The most consistent propellant of Hitler's rise from obscurity to global prominence was the widespread fear that Bolshevism would take deep root in the industrial heartland of Europe. His natural audience, therefore, was the worldwide community who welcomed the image of Christian Nazis pushing back the rising tide of communism near the godless doctrine's Soviet stronghold. This group encompassed the opponents of the view that Karl Marx, Vladimir Illich Lenin, Leon Trotsky, and Josef Stalin were primary guides in an expanding human procession marching towards a workers' paradise at the end of history. This anti-communist, pro-Christian, pro-capitalist perspective informed the judgment, for instance, of those in the Vatican's papal precinct who had to decide whether Hitler's state-run Jew hunting would be tolerated or religiously condemned.[89] It influenced the positions of many throughout Europe who were seeking ways of escaping the polarization of capital and labour during the 1920s and early 1930s, a period that saw many uneasy coalitions of German social democrats with Communist Party stalwarts.

Hitler started his political career as part of the process of retaking control of Bavaria, a province briefly governed in 1919 by a workers' soviet led by Kurt Eisner. Hitler began to be noticed as a significant contributor to a growing anti-communist, anti-Jewish movement centred in Munich. He drew on the esoteric occultism of the Thule Society as well as the union-busting fervour of Bavaria's White Guards of Capitalism. A former British prime minister, David Lloyd George, articulated succinctly the widely held orthodoxy that German fascism was the necessary antidote to a more serious malady. In 1934 he quoted approvingly in the House of Commons "a very distinguished German statesman" who apparently said, "I am not afraid of Nazism, but Communism." Lloyd George continued as follows: "If Germany is seized by the Communists, Europe will follow; because the German could make a better job of it than any other country. Do not be in a hurry to condemn Germany. We shall be welcoming Germany as our friend."[90] This assessment was cited to support the interpretation of R. Palme Dutt, the British editor of *The Labour Monthly*. In 1936 Dutt observed: "Continuously since Versailles, Britain has given general support to the restoration of German power in order to counterbalance French power in Europe, and has sought at the same time to draw Germany into a Western orientation in opposition to the Soviet Union. The advent of Hitler to power was seen as the opportunity to press this line forward."[91]

Dutt makes reference to the "continuously close" relations between Montagu Norman, the governor of the Bank of England between 1920 and 1944, and Hjalmar Schact, the financial genius who served in several capacities as Hitler's main economic deal maker.[92] The ties of friendship and professional association linking Norman and Schact were integral to a complex network of connections orienting a significant body of elite opinion in Great Britain towards either sympathy with, or outright support of, European fascism. This positive regard for many facets of Hitler's policies, but especially his unrelenting anti-communism, is generally associated with Clivedon, the home where Lord and Lady Astor entertained a well-placed circle of aristocratic friends associated with the movement to "appease" German demands.[93] The British Astors were direct descendants of John Jacob Astor, the New York–based fur trader and real-estate speculator who established one of Anglo-America's truly legendary transatlantic dynasties.[94] Among those entertained by the Astors of Clivedon were Henry Ford, Charles Lindbergh, Lord Londonderry, and Winston Churchill. Churchill had been one of the first in Great Britain to condemn Nazi policies forthrightly as Hitler tightened his grip on power. He cherished that part of his family lore connecting him to the Indian Country of North America. Much to Roosevelt's delight, Churchill proudly identified himself as part Iroquois through one branch of the family tree of his famous American mother, Jenny Jerome. "We Churchills take great pride in our Native American heritage," declared Winston Churchill the younger in introducing his grandfather's text *The Great Republic*.[95]

Churchill's uncompromising attack on Nazi policies made him a lonely voice among British elites in the mid-1930s. The backing given Hitler's regime in Great Britain extended across the Atlantic to some of the world's most important centres of economic decision making in the United States. Britain's heavy borrowing during the First World War had accelerated the eclipse of "the City," London's financial district, as the banking interests of New York rapidly overtook those of the British imperial metropolis. John Maynard Keynes was an attentive observer of this trend. In 1917 he wrote to his mother, remarking that "in another year's time we shall have forfeited the claim we staked out in the New World and in exchange this country will be mortgaged to America."[96] The American mortgage holders of Europe's growing debts included a number of powerful figures who much preferred the anti-union policies of European fascism to the union-friendly attributes of Roosevelt's New Deal. Prominent among the many rich and influential Americans who favoured Hitler's regime over Roosevelt's New Deal were Ford, Hearst, Andrew Mellon, Irénée Du Pont, and many leading figures in the Harriman, Rockefeller, and Morgan clans.

These money masters of the growing US empire of proprietorship set patterns of attitude, ownership, and political association that permeated the activities of broad networks of lawyers, brokers, managers, and public relations consultants who helped to construct the financial, industrial, and political infrastructure of European fascism. These facilitators included the likes of Prescott Bush, George Herbert Walker, Ivy Lee, William Farish, William H. Draper, John J. McCloy, Allen Dulles and his brother, John Foster Dulles.[97] The Dulles brothers were especially instrumental in creating bridges between German and US capitalists through a variety of agencies, including the Wall Street legal firm of Sullivan and Cromwell.[98] They and a number of their Ivy League colleagues were instrumental in constructing the legal arrangements to facilitate the flow of investments, loans, trade, and technology bringing many elements of US business and industry into the increasingly militarized political economy of fascist Germany.

The importance in this saga of Prescott Bush and his father-in-law, George Herbert Walker, is especially interesting, given the fact that two future US presidents would emerge from this family liaison.[99] One of the most engaging tales in the family lore of the Walker-Bush clan invokes the ghost of Geronimo, America's most legendary Apache resister. In 1918 at Fort Still, Oklahoma, Prescott Bush is reported to have taken part in robbing the famous Apache's grave. The skull of Geronimo, or possibly that of some other Indian thought by the grave robbers to be Geronimo, was snatched and whisked east. In New Haven, Connecticut, this dubious trophy became an object for display and ritual at Yale University's most notorious secret society, the Order of the Skull and Bones. George Herbert Walker, Prescott Bush, and their presidential progeny were all initiated as Bonesmen. This association linking some of Yale's most influential alumni has been the subject of both wild speculation and temperate argument about the role of secrecy, elitism, and the lack of accountability in what Peter Dale Scott has described as "deep politics."[100]

Not surprisingly, the role of the Bush clan and their Wall Street associates in building up the military-industrial complex of both Nazi Germany and the United States has attracted comment. As Kevin Phillips notes in *American Dynasty: Aristocracy, Fortune, and Deceit in the House of Bush*, "the men who managed most of the high-level financial and corporate relations between the United States and Nazi Germany in the period from 1933 to 1941 developed an unusual kind of information and expertise that made them important to the war effort in general and the U.S. intelligence community in particular." He continues: "As a result, after World War II was over, with the Soviet Union soon becoming an enemy and Germany being transformed into a U.S. ally, the new American national security state formed around a new establishment in which Prescott Bush and many of his friends were prominent and honored members."[101] A key link in "the high-level financial and corporate relations" linking Wall Street and Nazi Germany in the 1930s was the axis between the Union Bank of New York and the Bank voor Handel en Scheepvart in Rotterdam, Holland. The officials connected to both institutions enriched themselves and their associates by moving around large portions of the Thyssen clan's wealth. By his own free admission, Fritz Thyssen was one of the first and richest of Hitler's financial patrons.[102] In due course, this same man was confirmed as the presiding mogul of the nascent Nazi empire's pre-eminent coal and steel cartel. The Thyssen clan had constructed their financial affairs to straddle the Atlantic in a way that would enable them to protect their interests no matter what course a future war might take. Brown Bothers Harriman, Dillon Read and Company, Kuhn Loeb Bank, and National City Bank (which later spawned Citibank, Chase National Bank, Chase Manhattan Bank, and JP Morgan Chase and Company) were other significant Wall Street players in the integration of US business with the forces of fascist anti-communism.

FROM THE WARS ON COMMUNISM TO THE GLOBAL WAR ON TERROR

The saga of involvement by many large US enterprises in the rise of the Third Reich forms a vital part of the history of the world's pre-eminent military-industrial complex.[103] It forms an integral aspect of the thick web of connections linking Germany and the United States, two nationalities connected by a long history of migration from the former to the latter. As William Dodd, US ambassador to Germany, reported in 1937: "I have had plenty of opportunity in Berlin to witness how close some of our American ruling families are to the Nazi regime."[104] "Hitler's Germany," Kevin Phillips has observed, "was the European country in which U.S. investment grew most rapidly in the 1930s even as it declined on the Continent as a whole. Rearmament was the growth sector and the high-profit stock ticket."[105] Wall Street provided a major portal through which some of the richest and most influential figures in the United States could participate in the construction of the most massive and technologically sophisticated machinery of military conquest ever assembled up until that point. While this war machine took shape under the auspices of the German government, it derived much of its broader direction from a transatlantic coalition of power brokers who decided that Nazi anti-communism was both good for business and a strategic check on Soviet power. The creation of the financial, industrial, scientific, and cultural infrastructure of fascist Europe opened new frontiers of experimentation and expansion for some on the vanguard of the American empire of private property.

All the major US auto makers participated fully in the rise of the German military-industrial complex. Their operations included GM's Opel plant, where slave labour was employed to manufacture trucks and airplanes for Germany's armed forces.[106] A special place of honour in the National Socialist constellation of industrial greatness was reserved for Henry Ford and the machinery of automated conquest provided by his fabled car company. With Owen Young's help and advice, General Electric's global grid of business and technology extended to Germany's electricity cartel. American GE cooperated closely with Germany's Krupp Industries in dividing up the global market for titanium compounds used in the manufacturing of hard metal products. The axis of cooperation between Standard Oil of New Jersey and the IG Farben was massive in both scope and consequence. The effectiveness of this partnership in influencing the course of world politics added enormously to the body of evidence demonstrating that control of the world's dominant military-industrial complex would rest on dominion over oil, gas, and coal resources for both energy and petrochemical products.[107] An early interpreter of IG Farben's role in Hitler's Germany, Richard Sasuly, referred to this cartel as the core operation in "a dictatorship of monopoly capitalism." He added: "Its fascism is that of business enterprise on a monopoly basis in full control of all the military, police, legal, and propaganda power of the state."[108]

Throughout most of the twentieth century, the growing partnership between German and US cartels engendered huge wealth together with a monumental weight of political influence. This pattern of US-centred capitalist consolidation was expanded by the reconstitution after 1945 of Japan's family-based *zaibatsu* cartels as six major Keirestu conglomerates. *Zaibatsu* translates roughly as financial cliques. The story of the growth and integration of these cartels to form some of today's largest global corporations is deeply intertwined with the course of history leading to, through, and beyond the militarization of both sides in the Second World War. The transnational collaborations linking German and US enterprise in the construction of the world's dominant military-industrial complex has been an especially rich bonanza of inventions and patents in plastics, synthetic rubber, pharmaceutical products, and aviation. Much of the industrial technology reflected in these patents remains foundational in the industrial construction of the global economy. Some of the richest technological rewards for close collaboration with the German war machine fell to IBM and the chemical company of Irénée Du Pont. As Edwin Black has chronicled in great detail, the German subsidiary of the New York–based IBM Company developed the data-processing system used in Hitler's attempt to isolate and eliminate European Jewry.[109] Irénée Du Pont was a major shareholder in General Motors. He was extremely clear about his preference for Hitler's model of capitalism over that of Roosevelt. Andrew Mellon's Aluminum Corporation of America supplied much of the light metal that built up the German air force. Similarly Coke, Kodak, International Harvester, and ITT would not be excluded from the fascist business action. The list goes on and on. The domain of fascist business enterprise expanded with the proliferation of Nazi puppet regimes in occupied Europe. For instance, the fascist government of Henri-Philippe Pétain in Vichy France and the Christian Falangist regime of Francisco Franco in Spain provided wide latitude for transatlantic business transactions supporting the Axis side of the Second World War. Similar patterns developed in parts of South America and the rich oil fields of the Middle East, where the commercial ambitions of US business and the expansionary enterprise of Hitler's empire sometimes coincided.[110]

General George S. Patton was prominent among those in the US government who wanted to continue the war in Europe in 1945 by invading territory controlled by the Red Army in Eastern Europe. He proposed raising divisions of Nazi soldiers to "lead them against the reds." "What do we care about those goddamned bolshies?" he proclaimed. "We're going to have to fight them sooner or later. Why not now while our army is intact and we can kick the Red Army back into Russia? We can do it with my Germans ... they hate those red bastards."[111] Patton was deemed by his superiors to be too outspoken, and his days in the US military were numbered. His ideas, however, figured prominently in internal discussions about the US role in Europe after Franklin Roosevelt's death in April 1945 catapulted Harry Truman into the superpower's top job. The supreme command of the US Armed Forces in Europe was initially composed of General Eisenhower and his staff, who took over the IG Farben headquarters in Frankfurt. In the years ahead, this classic Bauhaus structure was known informally as the European Pentagon, and formally as the General Creighton W. Abrams Building Complex. It housed everything from the offices of those charged to implement the Marshall Plan to the West German headquarters of the CIA. This transformation of the IG Farben headquarters into the European Pentagon serves to illustrate the direct way that the US government took over from Hitler's Nazi government in providing the capitalist world with its primary bulwark against communism. The symbolism of the transformed use of the IG Farben headquarters would find an eerie equivalent decades later when the US government took over Abu Ghraib prison in 2003 for its own violent sessions of interrogation through torture. Abu Ghraib was initially made notorious as the facility where the regime of Saddam Hussein conducted many of its terrible bouts of torture and murder.[112]

The scope and intensity of the links between Nazi Germany and the key elements of the business community in the United States both before and during the Second World War were effectively shielded from public scrutiny by a host of strategically placed operatives. Prominent among them were General William H. Draper, head of the Economics Division of the US Control Council for Germany in 1945 and 1946, and John J. McCloy, US military governor and high commissioner of Germany from 1949 to 1952. Draper had been an agent of the Thyssen banking complex and a champion of the eugenic policies developed in the United States and Germany in the years leading up to the Second World War. While in charge of the US occupation of Germany, McCloy intervened to release from jail a number of convicted war criminals, including Alfred Krupp and several directors of Krupp's company. Eleanor Roosevelt wrote McCloy to ask, "Why are we freeing so many Nazis?" "Wittingly or not," Nuremberg prosecutor Telford Taylor commented, "Mr. McCloy has dealt a blow to the principles of international law and concepts of humanity for which we fought the war."[113] McCloy embodied many facets of the continuity linking elite support for Nazi anti-communism before 1941 with the fast integration of German assets into the capitalist side of the Cold War after the defeat of the Axis. Before the war he served as legal council for Germany's IG Farben conglomerate. Like Draper, Walker, and Prescott Bush, McCloy was also deeply involved with Thyssen's Union Bank in New York. In 1936 at the Berlin Olympics, McCloy sat in Hitler's box at the invitation of Rudolph Hess and Herman Goring. McCloy encouraged the US government to adopt, adapt, and refine German techniques of psychological warfare.[114] In later years he would serve as president of the World Bank and president of the Chase Manhattan Bank. He was a leading member of the Council on Foreign Relations, and he gave legal advice to the Seven Sister oil consortium.[115]

The New York–based Council on Foreign Relations has been a major source of political and academic influence on the policies of the United States since its founding in 1921. From the Dulles brothers to Robert McNamara to Franklin Roosevelt and to Jack Kennedy, Richard Nixon, and Henry Kissinger, to name only a few, the CFR has counted among its members many of the key decision makers in determining the orientation of the United States to the rest of the world. The CFR has been the subject of considerable investigation and speculation by those in the tradition of Antony Sutton and Carroll Quigley, who have characterized much of the history of international affairs in the twentieth century as the emanations of deals reached by the world's most powerful bankers. One application of this approach to historical interpretation would make the major policies of Franklin Roosevelt, but especially his determination to create the United Nations, the outcome of a bankers' conspiracy to create a "one-world" system of governance they could control. In this extravagant scenario and others of its ilk, the CFR is often portrayed as one of the main agencies for the legitimization and delivery of Wall Street's policy preferences to the federal government, but especially to the US State Department. The essentialism implicit in this kind of narrative makes mere pawns of far too many who can and do act on history to defy the imposed will of even the most cunning cabal of conspirators. On the other hand, there is often much to be learned from the writing of those who attempt to look beyond the official record of the formulation of policy to understand how power is exercised in fact. Analysis based on narratives that essentially "follow the money" is frequently informative no matter how far a given author might overreach his or her evidence in drawing conclusions.[116]

A number of factors facilitated the surprisingly high degree of continuity maintained after the Second World War in the investment portfolios, research agendas, political networks, and professional associations of many who financed, commanded, designed, and administered various elements of the Axis war machine. One strategic ingredient in this phenomenon was the decision in Washington to cancel all but a circumscribed prosecution at Nuremberg of Nazi industrialists. On the advice of General Douglas MacArthur, the US government refrained also from pressing charges on Emperor Hirohito and many of the *zaibatsu* aristocrats who used their wealth, prestige, and knowhow to build up the military capacity of imperial Japan. The decisions making it possible for many of the Nazi industrialists to become pillars of capitalist enterprise in postwar West Germany were replicated with some minor modifications in Japan. Much of the wealth of German and Japanese financiers had been expertly hidden, transformed, and dispersed through expert manipulations of Switzerland's secretive banking operations. Martin Bormann is reputed to have played a decisive role in shepherding much of the core capital of Nazi enterprise through to safety and renewed profitability in the postwar world. He began his rise in the Third Reich as an understudy of Rudolf Hess and of IG Farben's legendary money wizard, Herman Schmitz.

In Japan, a considerable portion of the wealth used to kick start Japanese industry after 1945 came from the treasure in gold that had been amassed and then hidden in the course of the imperial army's Asian conquests. Emperor Hirohito and his top aid, Koichi Kido, helped to protect and redirect some of the capital used in replacing, within a relatively short period, Japan's military empire with an empire of commerce. The retention of Hirohito as emperor was considered by General Douglas MacArthur, the head of the US army of occupation, as a key to helping the Japanese people adjust themselves to their new situation in the postwar world. While MacArthur briefly flirted with initiatives to break up the family cartels of the *zaibatsus*, the pressures of Cold War anti-communism proved too overwhelming. The result was that the *zaibatsus* of imperial Japan were permitted to reconstitute themselves as the Keirestu conglomerates, such as those rooted in the wealth and prestige of the Mitsubishi and Mitsui clans. The quick ascent of the American empire of corporate capitalism after the Second World War can be partially explained, therefore, by the willing effectiveness of business and government in integrating the wealth, skill, and militant anti-communism of a representative sample of the surviving elites from Nazi Germany, fascist Italy, and imperial Japan into the increasingly global operations of their military-industrial complex.[117]

Allen Dulles was one of the most effective front-line operatives in overseeing the orderly transition from the anti-communism of the fascist Axis to the anti-communism of the US-led side in the Cold War.[118] He was especially instrumental in administering the redeployment of whole complexes of Nazi spies, financiers, and scientists after 1945. From his days as a lawyer at Sullivan and Cromwell to his role in 1953 and 1954 as CIA director in charge of the covert removal of the government leadership in Iran and Guatemala, the career of Allen Dulles serves as a striking symbol of many of the same patterns of continuity embodied in the transformation of the IG Farben building into the European Pentagon of the US government. Dulles's work epitomizes the extent of the licence for lawlessness and insider dealing granted to some representatives of America's ruling dynasties in the name of national security – an all-purpose alibi employed to justify the abuse of power by elites.[119]

Once it became inevitable that the Roosevelt government would wage war on the Axis, Dulles went to work as an operative of William Donovan's Office of Strategic Services.[120] His base was Switzerland, the main surviving seat of European neutrality where agents of the world's leading cartels, financiers, and governments secretly bargained among themselves in preparation for the postwar era. In 1945 Dulles recruited Reinhard Gehlen, the man who had built his career as Hitler's spy master in Eastern Europe, to work for the US government. With Gehlen as his guide, Dulles went on to hire many more former Nazis to staff the US government's increasingly elaborate espionage networks.[121] This covert network of US operatives conspired to limit the success of anti-fascist activism throughout postwar Europe, but especially in northern Italy, where workers had mobilized to take over factories.[122] The employment of fascists to counter the inroads of socialism was particularly blatant in Greece.

Dulles was instrumental in bringing some of the best of the Nazi scientists into the research and development establishment of capitalism's military-industrial complex. Two of the operations to expedite this process were dubbed Project Paperclip and Operation National Interest. Another CIA operation distributed funds through a front organization known as the Congress for Cultural Freedom. That agency richly financed all sorts of publications, conferences, and think tanks with the objective of drawing intellectuals in Western Europe away from the option of communism.[123] This initiative was one small part of a whole complex of CIA-funded attempts to manipulate public opinion in ways that severely undermined the independence of both the media and the academy in the United States and many other countries.

The induction of the Nazis' v-2 rocket scientists to form the core of the US space program forms another aspect of the integration of Nazi expertise into the capitalist side of the Cold War.[124] Wernher von Braun was one of the most public faces of the effort to make German innovation in rocket technology serve the new US space program. He worked closely with the Walt Disney Company in the 1950s to promote the goal of US space exploration. In this way, the former Nazi scientist became the poster boy for a major infusion of intelligence, talent, expertise, and methods from the failed superpower into the organizational matrix of the ascendant superpower. The Soviet Union mirrored this effort in its own attempt to recruit and integrate some of the top personnel of the Nazi regime into its own Cold War machinery.

The division of Europe in 1945 between the informal empires of the United States and the Soviet Union established the core dichotomy of the Cold War. In 1961 the East German government built a wall across Berlin to prevent its citizens from migrating across what Churchill had dubbed the Iron Curtain. Between 1949 and 1961, about 2.5 million of 17 million East Germany citizens escaped their communist polity to seek brighter opportunities in the capitalist West. The Berlin Wall became the Cold War's most evocative symbol. The maintenance of the peace in a divided Europe, however, took much more than a wall. The balance of power was expensively maintained by a huge mirrored build up of military armament on the part the capitalist and the communist superpowers. While a degree of equilibrium prevailed in Europe, Japan, the Soviet Union, and North America, the Cold War spawned military confrontations between competing armies in China, Korea, Indochina, Angola, Mozambique, Afghanistan, and other countries.

Some elements of the New Deal liberalism made a lasting imprint on Cold War America, extending even into the national security state. Indeed, the liberalism of the civil-rights movement was for a time nurtured by the requirements of Cold War propaganda once the United States took over from Germany the role of capitalism's chief anti-communist bulwark. Certainly, significant strides were made in exposing the moral and scientific corruption permeating Hitler's degrading brand of race-based statecraft. The intense ant-Semitism of Nazi anti-communism was properly condemned once the US government seized the leadership of the anti-Soviet crusade from the defeated Axis powers. The effort to purge the anti-Semitic demons, however, had paradoxical outcomes. Many in the Arab and Muslim worlds saw the muscle flexing demonstrated in the establishment and backing of Israel by public and private agencies in the United States as a continuation of the imperialism of the Occident towards the Orient.

There was very little that was liberal and tolerant about the postwar treatment afforded the people of Guatemala, El Salvador, Iran, Congo, Indonesia, Chile, Argentina, and Nicaragua. The national security state installed puppet regimes in all these polities to take the place of the leadership quelling up from indigenous political cultures. The primary duty relegated to the imposed military dictators has been to repress by any means necessary the local opposition to the transnational activities of the same complex of US-based firms that participated in building up Nazi Germany's military-industrial complex. The Atlantic Charter must have seemed like a hoax to those who identified with the policies of indigenous self-determination espoused by the likes of Guatemala's Jacobo Arbentz Guzman, Iran's Mohammed Mossedeq, Congo's Patrice Lumumba, Vietnam's Ho Chi Minh, Indonesia's Akmed Sukarno, Iraq's Abdul Karim Kassem, Ghana's Kwame Nkrumah, Chile's Salvador Allende, and Haiti's Father Jean-Bertrand Aristide. To many of those denied the leadership of these icons of decolonization, it must have seemed clear that the world's dominant military-industrial complex has drawn many ideas and tactics from the fascist side of the Second World War. The influence of Nazi anti-communism was to be felt in the broad array of tactics used and the wide range of targets hit in the name of Cold War anti-communism.

The skull of Geronimo, apparently now at Yale, is a very significant skeleton in the imperial closet of the United States. The involvement of the Walker/Bush patriarchy with the Skull and Bones, Nazis, the CIA, Wahabis, arms dealers, Big Oil, the Bank of Credit and Commerce International, 9/11, Saddam Hussein, and Iran is now legendary. But the process of sorting out fact from disinformation has only just begun. The alleged treatment of Geronimo's remains by Prescott Bush and his fellow Yale grave robbers may be significant for the clues it might give about patterns of attitude and action that would be re-enacted again and again in the rise of the national security state. Geronimo's ghost would inhabit with especially serious effect the Asian, African, and Latin American frontiers of the US empire of direct and indirect rule. The internal and external displacement of four million Iraqis, together with the death of hundreds of thousands more, is only a sign of the growing dangers facing the whole region – indeed, the whole world – as the price of oil fluctuates, global warming accelerates, and the full implications of the superpower's eroding foundation of civil, financial, and moral capital become increasingly clear.

The dubious official conspiracy theory to explain the events of 9/11 gave the Republican Party of George W. Bush and the bipartisan leadership of the military-industrial complex some evocative, yet conveniently vague and elastic imagery of an ethnically and religiously defined enemy. Conveniently absent from day one was even a hint from the official sources that there might be some sort of domestic and/or economic motivation woven within the complex texture of an extremely elaborate and multifaceted crime. As with the Kennedy assassination, the "culprits" were identified almost immediately, forming the basis of an explanation that was quickly reified in report after report. The enemy appeared just when it was needed to give the US president a rallying cry and the US executive branch a justification for continuing the enormous military expenditures that have grown ever since the United States adopted its permanent wartime economy after the Japanese government attacked the US naval base at Pearl Harbor. The mythology of 9/11 gave the United States yet another savage *Other* against which to develop its self-understanding of its own civilization's superiority.[125] As Richard Cizak of the National Association of Evangelicals saw it, many of his constituents responded to the official explanation of 9/11 by substituting Islam for the Soviet Union. "The Muslims have become the modern-day equivalent of the Evil Empire," he declared. One poll of right-wing Christian leaders found that two-thirds of those questioned agreed that Islam is "dedicated to world domination." They agreed that Islam is "a religion of violence."[126]

The official interpretation of the events of 9/11 created a perfect basis to renew the alliance between Christian fundamentalists and Cheney-style business hawks. It was the dawning of this alliance that had ushered in the era of corporate deregulation as promoted by the anti–New Deal presidency of Ronald Reagan. In ways that were completely antagonistic to the social democracy of Roosevelt and Keynes, the Global War on Terror opened the door to ratcheting up right-wing tactics for the expanded reach of government into every facet of human interaction. Patterns were repeated that had earlier developed when the fascist Axis had first been fashioned as an anti-communist laboratory of totalitarian capitalism.[127] Now terrorism replaced communism as the all-purpose demon to be manipulated as deemed necessary in order to protect the power of finance capital and those who control it. Terror capitalism thus gave new life to the military command economy that grew from the wars on communism led first by Nazi Germany and then by the United States. Even more than the wars on communism, the Global War on Terror evoked the mythological encounter between savagery and civilization that Frederick Jackson Turner had identified at the World's Columbian Exposition as the formative interaction in shaping his country's political culture.

As in both the Nazi-led and US-led versions of the war on communism, in the Global War on Terror business cartels were once again dealt lucrative licences to derive large profits from their expanded function as privatized agents of the state's expanding claims to police, propaganda, and military powers. The *Patriot Act* of 2001, the *Homeland Security Act* of 2002, the *Military Commissions Act* of 2006, and the amendments of 2008 to the *Foreign Intelligence Surveillance Act* are prominent projectiles in the legislative arsenal aimed at piercing the fragile protections of universal human rights both inside and outside the United States.[128]

Plans to eliminate *habeas corpus* – the basis of the principle that individuals are innocent until proven guilty – were already well advanced before the events of 9/11 created the necessary psychological environment to trigger military invasions abroad and police state transformations at home. The invocation of the ideals of Homeland Security conjured up the same language used by the White minority regime during the height of South African apartheid even as it exposed the outward orientation of so-called national security. In the United States, national security has always meant going outside the so-called Homeland to meddle in other people's sovereign business. The remarkably quick enactment of the *Patriot Act* barely a month after the events of 9/11 suggests that its drafting was already well in the works even before the Twin Towers were instantly pulverized as if in a controlled demolition energized by the coordinated explosions of many thousands of thermite charges. Similarly, the growth of the apparatus of so-called Homeland Security applied principles already outlined in January 2001 in the reports of the United States Commission on National Security co-chaired by Gary Hart and Warren D. Rudman.[129]

The technological engines of capitalism have changed significantly since the era when the German subsidiary of IBM Corporation handled the data processing for the Nazi assault on European Jewry. Since the early 1980s much of the most sophisticated intelligence gathering has been done with computer software such as PROMIS and Echelon. These and other programs have enabled spy agencies and banking institutions secretly to observe each other's data bases, current communications, and ongoing transactions through myriad forms of back-door access.[130] High-tech spying can also extend to outright manipulation of digital traffic. Indeed, software companies such as Ptech, Mitre, and AMDOCS have been well positioned to enhance, disrupt, or monitor the flow of communications among core agencies in the military-industrial complex. Ultimately it all comes down to who possesses the computer codes or access to technology powerful enough to obtain or break through these codes. This transformation of the so-called intelligence industry in the era of the Internet developed simultaneously with the digitalization of financial transaction in stock markets, venues of buying and selling that make *information* about what to expect in the future the most valuable of all commodities. Technological transformations such as these have dramatically altered the nature of economic relations during this era of ascendant terror capitalism. The workings of terror capitalism afford tremendous financial advantages to those who possess insiders' knowledge about the inner workings of the global police state that is being constructed in the name of the Global War on Terror. Indeed, transactions on stock markets are key sites for the gathering of crucial intelligence about the identity of those interests that sponsor, promote, or exploit major changes in the alignment of geopolitical power.

The core elements of terror capitalism informed the compelling script of *A Few Days in September*. Written and directed in 2006 by Santiago Amigorena, this dramatic feature film focuses on the intrigues swirling around an imaginary cartel of investors who seek to exploit their prior knowledge about how the pretext for the Global War on Terror would be created. Why has there been no serious public investigation into the activity of the New York stock market to identify those who may have exploited prior knowledge about the global transformations that would be set in motion after the events of September 11, 2001? What insights do Wall Street insiders have about the events of 9/11? Why did Eliot Spitzer, the former New York state attorney general who clearly enjoyed his persona as the Sheriff of Wall Street, not seriously investigate the 9/11 crime scene, the site of a terrible mass murder that decimated the lives and destroyed the morale of thousands of functionaries who inhabit the very core of the commercial capital's financial district?

Rather than demonstrate due diligence by ordering a thorough investigation of the scene of the crime, Spitzer forfeited his claim as a disinterested law-enforcement officer by submitting an amicus brief to a New York court arguing that Larry Silverstein, the lease holder of the World Trade Center buildings, should receive a $4.5 billion settlement from insurance companies for two separate terrorist attacks rather than one. Silverstein's finances were deeply integrated into a complex set of legal and financial arrangements confused by the fact that the Twin Towers, which were initially nicknamed David and Nelson after their Rockefeller brother builders,[131] had become giant liabilities because they were infested with industrial asbestos that would have cost a fortune to remove.[132] The evidence at the crime scene was removed as quickly as possible after 9/11 by operatives of the Federal Emergency Management Agency whose agents began arriving in New York on September 10 for a drill named Tripod II on how to respond to a biochemical terrorist attack.[133] The failure of the US Air Force to identify and intercept the attackers was similarly explained by the supposed coincidence of several drills on September 11 involving mock responses to terrorist attacks.[134] In the months after 9/11, Silverstein appeared on a PBS documentary where he seemed to refer to the decision to "pull" a mechanism triggering the quick fall of World Trade Center building number 7 in a fashion that epitomized all the attributes of a controlled demolition. This demolition required the insertion of explosives within the structure *before* its demise.[135]

The genocide of North American Indians helped clear the way for those who sought to erase the past in their rush to achieve a New World Order. There are striking elements of continuity linking the westward expansion of the United States into Indian Country and the Hitlerian drive to acquire *Lebensraum* at the expanse of the Slavic nations and the Soviet Union. Similarly, there are some undeniable threads of continuity linking the financial and industrial backers of the fascist Axis's rise and those with the largest interest in promoting the national security state's so-called Global War on Terror. The national security state points humanity away from the Fourth World principles of people's security, environmental security, health security, educational security, and global security. The citizens of the Fourth World seek a Third Way between those who would idealize or obliterate the past. The Atlantic Charter and the international institutions and covenants to which it gave rise still point towards the possibility of a world governed by law rather than force. They still point to the possibility of a planetary regime of biocultural diversity governed democratically by a confederacy of many sovereigns. They point towards extensions of the vision of Roosevelt and away from the heritage of Hitler.

PART TWO

Indian Country, the Industrial Revolution, and the Making of the Military-Industrial Complex

Encounters with Indigenous Peoples in the Making of Two Transcontinental Polities in North America

> The military-industrial complex is the love match of capital and conquest first brokered during the Civil War. It is no accident that the "wild" Indian of the West is attacked soon after the rebel South is vanquished; that the communist boogeyman appears soon after the last Indian is confined on a reservation; that the Muslim fanatic is inflated to the level of a worldwide conspiracy soon after the Red Menace gives up and starts dining at Moscow McDonald's.
>
> Ronald Wright, *What Is America? A Short History of the New World Order*, 2007

> NATO is fighting this war against Yugoslavia to outlaw ethnic cleansing, massacre and pillage as an instrument of domestic policy by any state.
>
> Michael Ignatieff, *National Post*, 1999

FROM THE INDIAN WARS TO STAR WARS

The world's pre-eminent military-industrial complex acquired much of its character during the Second World War. The clash between two different types of capitalism embodied by Hitler and Roosevelt initiated the rise of a permanent wartime economy in the United States that continues to this day. The national security state can be conceived as the directing mechanism of the military-industrial complex. The national security state began to take form after 1917 when the US government entered the First World War just as the Czarist Russia was violently reconstituted as the founding and core polity of the Soviet Union. The US government's domestic response to the Red Scare of 1919 anticipated the fuller expression of Cold War anti-communism that dominated US relations with the rest of the world throughout much of the second half of the twentieth century.

The military-industrial complex and the national security state built on patterns of conquest and domination that developed in the transcontinental expansion in North America, first of European empires and then of the United States. Where the United States was born of a revolutionary break with the British Empire, Canada, North America's other transcontinental polity, emerged gradually from the genesis of the fur trade as well as from constitutional reforms within the British Empire and the Commonwealth. Between 1776 and 1814 Great Britain and the makers of the United States clashed in sporadic rounds of North American warfare. Thereafter the two governments largely cooperated in their dual enterprises of westward expansion much as they collaborated in their shared exploitation of Latin America.

The US Armed Forces were deeply involved in the process of westward expansion. Between 1789 and 1895 the US Army built 475 military posts to subdue the resistance of hostile Indians. The location of these forts has been mapped by Father Francis Prucha, one of the most prolific chroniclers of US Indian policy. In describing the purpose of the superpower's original military installations, Prucha writes: "The United States army through the nineteenth century was frequently an Indian-fighting army ... Most of the military installations (aside from coastal fortifications) owed their existence to the presence of Indian tribes on the frontiers."[1]

The construction of these armed outposts of military rule in the transcontinental expansion of the United States created and reflected patterns of perception, behaviour, and relationship that would be replicated and extended in the years ahead. The commitment of substantial government resources to this proliferation of military bases demonstrates that the American frontier was not quite the zone of unfettered individualism that Frederick Jackson Turner described in his famous commentary on the westward expansion of the United States. From its inception until the time of Chicago's World Columbian Exposition, where Turner announced the completion of his country's transcontinental expansion, the US Armed Forces have been integrally involved in the territorial growth of the United States.[2]

The construction of forts to keep Indians out was followed by the establishment of reserves to keep Indians in. The building of military forts to keep hostile Indians at bay anticipated a day when property relations would become so polarized that many of the wealthiest Americans would decide to withdraw behind the gates of their walled and heavily guarded communities. These flips in the territorial configuration of personal and national security form telling episodes in the genesis of a society that, by the early years of the twenty-first century, would incarcerate a far greater percentage of its own people than almost any other nation on earth. A striking feature of this process saw young Black males locked up at a rate about ten times the level of the general population in a privatized system that has been described as the prison-industrial complex.[3] In an era when the US government devotes massive resources to the effort to constitute the whole of North America as a military camp surrounded by Star Wars palisades, who can say any longer who are the incarcerated and who are the jailers in the military-industrial complex's armed occupation of Earth?

The Indian wars in the United States were particularly emblematic episodes in a more global phenomenon marked by the removal of Indigenous peoples from many fertile and mineral-rich regions in order to make way for millions of transplanted Europeans together with the extractive activities of their corporate extensions. Only now is it becoming clear that the treatment of Indians in the transcontinental expansion of the United States signalled the fate that would befall many other groups on the frontiers of capitalist expansion. From the contested lands of Vietnam to those of Soviet Russia during the Second World War, the imagery of Indian Country's conquest acquired many larger iconographic meanings in the history of both imperial and anti-imperial globalization.

The westward expansion of the United States into Indian Country was advanced through the deployment of increasingly sophisticated systems of weaponry whose invention, refinement, mass production, and deployment form essential elements in the constant technological transformation of industrial civilization. The US wars on the Indian Country moved into a new phase of industrial efficiency after the US Civil War. The outcome of that conflict eliminated the problem of how to balance the increase of slave-owning states with the increase of US states where slavery was outlawed. The military ascendance of the federal government over the defeated secessionist confederacy in the south was quickly redirected after 1865 to subduing those Indian people who refused to submit without a fight to the imposition of US hegemony. In the period after the Civil War the US government, now militarily invincible within North America, threw off the legal obligations entailed in treaty relations with Indigenous peoples. Instead, the emergent superpower developed a greater dependence on the methods and legal theories of military conquest as it moved towards its career as capitalism's most aggressive agent in the globalized Indian Country colonized by the national security state and the military-industrial complex.

"THE UNITED STATES RECEIVES YOU UNDER THE PROTECTING WING OF HER EAGLE"

Indigenous peoples were excluded from direct representation in US federalism as a result of the wording of several key provisions in the US Constitution. Article I of that document, which was adopted in 1787, refers to "Indians not taxed," a phrase that is repeated in the Fourteenth Amendment. This provision effectively placed Indian people outside the framework of US citizenship, an exclusion that was eventually repealed by legislation in 1924. The most substantial mention of Indians in the new republic's Constitution was the article authorizing Congress "to regulate Commerce with foreign Nations, and the several States, and with the Indian Tribes." The inclusion of Indian tribes on a list with foreign and state governments was supplemented by Article VI, which reaffirmed previously negotiated treaties. At the time the Constitution was adopted, most US treaties with other polities were with Indian groups. These pre-1787 Indian treaties, together with those negotiated between 1787 and 1871, were afforded the same treatment as treaties with foreign governments insofar as they required ratification by a two-thirds majority vote of the US Senate. Moreover, the Constitution stipulated that these federally ratified treaties, including Indian treaties, were superior to state laws. In Article VI, treaties are identified along with the US Constitution itself as "the supreme law of the land."[4]

The Constitution of 1787 laid out the ground rules for the creation of a single, uniform regime of property relations in the United States. The markers and media for this monocultural commercial domain included a single currency as well as a single legal regimen for interstate commerce, for the making and enforcement of contracts, for patents and copyright, and for weights and measures. According to Edward Countryman, this constitutional blueprint for the creation of a large common market represented a drastically altered vision of society from the ones that had sustained the resistance of many against the authority of Crown rule during the revolutionary era. "The bundle of uneven, specific, community-based 'liberties' that most colonials set out to defend against the British onslaught," he writes, "was radically different from the 'blessings' of undifferentiated political and economic 'liberty' that the Constitution proposed to secure 'for the people of the United States' and their 'posterity' in 1787."[5]

Certainly, the narrow franchise of those entitled to participate as citizens and proprietors, together with the pronounced trend towards monoculture implicit in the uniform structures of the new republic's common market, boded ominously for the continent's Indigenous peoples. Their own diverse domestic economies supported a complex of Aboriginal nationalities that collectively constituted the primary obstacles blocking the transformation of the western frontiers into private property under US law – a transformation on which the future viability of the new republic would depend. The formulation in 1787 of the Northwest Ordinance, legislation that vested the federal government with primary responsibility for the westward expansion of the United States, was closely connected to the negotiations resulting in the creation that same year of the new Constitution. The statute was meant to hold out the promise to those US citizens living beyond the boundaries of the organized states that they would soon acquire equal status with those living farther to the east. The westerners would gain access to the local instruments of democratic governance once the population of their federal territories rose sufficiently to allow for the admission of their jurisdictions into the federal union as full-fledged states. This promise was meant to neutralize the local independence movements that arose relatively frequently from within those non-Aboriginal populations on the western extremities of Anglo-American settlement both before and after the American Revolution. The failed effort of local residents in 1784 to establish the state of Franklin on the western frontiers of North Carolina is indicative of the kind of pressures brought to bear on Congress to orchestrate quickly some regular procedures for western expansion. The most immediate catalyst leading to the creation of the Northwest Ordinance, however, was the pressure brought to bear by a consortium of politicians and financiers who organized a formidable vehicle of land speculation known as the Ohio Company. According to Ray Allen Billington, a frontier historian in the Turner mode, this entity was "one of the most important land companies in history."[6]

The core business plan of the Ohio Company was similar to the speculative schemes put together by George Washington after the Seven Years' War. The idea was to amass the devalued Continental Certificates issued to pay many veterans of the revolutionary war. The Ohio Company's agents would assemble these certificates and use them to purchase large quantities of unorganized federal territory from the central government in Washington. The key to the transformation of this speculative enterprise into living Euro-American settlements was the willingness of Congress to sell title at the cost of a few pennies per acre and then to provide organized federal governance beyond the Ohio River. Congress expressed its willingness to do exactly that by extending legislative approval in the famous Northwest Ordinance of 1787. The sister enterprise of the successful Ohio Company was the Scioto Company, or the Compagnie de Scioto, a speculative venture whose zealous promoters sold many forms of fraudulent titles in the frontier lands of the United States primarily to individuals in France. This fraud culminated in huge disappointments for hundreds of new settlers who came to America to face a wreck of broken dreams.[7] Their misfortunes contributed to the dark shadows that almost invariably accompanied the brighter saga of legal and economic innovation on the moving frontiers of Euro-American settlement in the nascent republic. Under the auspices of the United States, the method of moving this frontier westward enabled a powerful few to acquire huge fortunes and mobilized many to extract modest gains.

The suffering caused in the East from the too-zealous stimulation of unrealistic and overinflated hopes was closely connected to the determination of Indigenous peoples in the West not to give up their homes and their lives without a fight. Clearly, the architects of the Ohio Company understood the deadly seriousness of this continuing challenge to the viability of their colonizing venture in their decision to give free "Donation Lands" in strategic and vulnerable locations to individuals they called "Warlike Christian Men."[8] These icons of the American way of life, with both gun and Bible firmly in hand, were charged to protect their fellow White settlers against the anticipated attacks of those Aboriginal patriots who retained the conviction that the banks of the Ohio River had been guaranteed to them in the Fort Stanwix Treaty of 1768 as the fixed southeastern boundary of their inviolate Indian Country.

It is doubtful that the new federal government could have long survived if it had not quickly given into the enormous pressures to privatize and deliver into the real-estate market significant quantities of land beyond the western boundaries of the original states. After all, the western lands were in a sense the major reward for having prevailed as victors in the American Revolution. If the national government had held back from distributing to its citizens the territorial fruits of victory, the authorities in Washington, DC, could anticipated a fate similar to that of the British government following the Seven Years' War. The British imperial government's effort to impede and closely regulate the westward expansion of non-Aboriginal settlements fired the flames of secessionist desire among many Anglo-Americans. But even though the architects of federal authority in the United States sought to push aside the legacies of the Royal Proclamation of 1763, there still remained many deep and strategic constitutional questions about how to conduct of relations with North America's Indigenous peoples.

In the first years following the Treaty of Paris in 1783, the federal government in the United States conducted an Indian policy that can only be described as deeply schizophrenic. Technically, the federal government viewed Indian peoples as having been conquered and, therefore, as subject to the authority of the United States whether or not they agreed to this relationship. Nevertheless, federal authorities used forceful tactics to gain, under duress, the appearance of some Aboriginal sanction for land-ceding treaties in order to enhance the aura of legitimacy of the new Anglo-American settlements in a few districts north of the Ohio River. This duplicitous position, treating Aboriginal groups as conquered peoples while advancing the fiction that they were willing agents of their own diminished status, was illustrated in the making of the "treaties" of Fort Stanwix, Fort McIntosh, and Fort Finney between 1784 and 1786. The Northwest Ordinance in 1787 theoretically changed the nature of constitutional relations between the US government and Indians in the newly created internal colony of federal authority known as the Northwest Territory. In replicating many of the principles of the Royal Proclamation of 1763, the Northwest Ordinance consolidated federal control over the process of westward expansion, especially by asserting an exclusive federal jurisdiction over trade, war, or the making of peace treaties with Indian peoples. Neither the Northwest Ordinance nor the US Constitution of 1787 received any sanction whatsoever from Indigenous peoples themselves. Indeed, the demonstration that most Indian peoples in the West completely rejected any view of themselves as conquered or subject peoples was left for the proof of two successful battles waged against the fledgling US federal army by the fighting forces of the Indian Confederacy.[9]

There was a tangible sense of *déjà vu* in the reaction in the US capital to the victories of the Indian Confederacy over the federal army in 1790 and 1791. These military victories demonstrated the continuing vitality of the uncontained spirit of Aboriginal independence that continued to animate the citizens of the Indian Country beyond the Ohio River in spite of the Eurocentric peace settlement in 1783. This display of first peoples' armed determination to retain their ancestral lands and to exercise their Aboriginal self-determination signalled to the leaders of the nascent republic a message similar to the one sent by Pontiac and the other Aboriginal freedom fighters who had demonstrated their will to resist the British Empire in 1763. For a time it seemed that the US government would respond to its military setbacks on its western frontiers in 1790 and 1791 much as the British sovereign responded in 1763 to the military assertions of the Indian Confederacy, which briefly found leadership in the person of the Odawa strategist Pontiac. Through his representatives, President George Washington announced the federal government's decision in 1793 to integrate the legal principle of Aboriginal title into the constitutional framework of US law.

Washington's determination was conveyed during the summer of 1793 to a council meeting organized south of Lake Erie. It brought together one delegation representing the US head of state and a second one described as "the Deputies of the Confederate Indian Nations." At this assembly, the US delegation announced a change in its government's constitutional position vis-à-vis Indian peoples north of the Ohio. The federal representatives declared the decision of the US government to recognize "the right to the soil" of Indigenous peoples in their ancestral lands.[10] All subsequent westward expansion of non-Aboriginal settlements in the new republic would henceforth be made to conform with the constitutional recognition of Aboriginal title. This recognition amounted to a return to many of the same legal principles outlined for British North America by King George III in October 1763. In his fateful Royal Proclamation, King George had detailed the basic terms for his government's recognition of Aboriginal title as well as the procedures, protocols, and requirements for its purchase. The new federal position of 1793 renewed many of the same legal recognitions first outlined when the British sovereign had laid out the constitutional terms for the integration of French-Aboriginal Canada into a vastly expanded British North America. Now Washington's agents were formalizing their government's intention to incorporate much of the substance of the Royal Proclamation into the constitutional makeup of the new republic. Henceforth Aboriginal title could not be unilaterally extinguished. The Indian policies of the United States required explicit Aboriginal *consent* through formal treaty negotiations before any transfer of Aboriginal title to federal authorities could take place. Hence, the US government declared its intention to incorporate the law of Aboriginal and treaty rights into its own domestic legal framework.

Although the negotiations with the delegates of the Confederate Indian Nations represented one facet of the imperial personality of the new US government, other factions were determined that no niceties of law or policy should stand in the way of the imperative of westward expansion. From the earliest days of the United States, many of its citizens insisted that *conquest* would be the ultimate means of either eliminating the Aboriginal presence altogether or forcing Native people to bend to the sovereign authority of a superior power. Thus, while US officials held out an olive branch to the assembled delegates in 1793, the next year the US government chose to clarify its now-qualified assertion of authority over Indians with a decisive military victory over Aboriginal fighting forces north of the Ohio River. While the army of US General "Mad Anthony" Wayne failed to obtain a truly decisive military conquest of Indian Country in 1794, the display of US military prowess in the Battle of Fallen Timbers was sufficiently effective to persuade a significant constituency of Indigenous peoples to refrain from further warfare directed at the United States.

The Battle of Fallen Timbers, followed by the negotiation of the Treaty of Greenville in 1795, began a pattern in the federal conduct of US Indian policy whereby the central government preferred not to commence formal land negotiations with Indigenous peoples until they were at least partially humbled in battle. Echoes of this approach could be apprehended roughly two centuries later in the Israeli-US insistence that Palestinian resistance fighters must be militarily overwhelmed, disarmed, and rendered subordinate as a precondition to treaty negotiations on the powers and territories to be afforded some sort of Palestinian pseudo-state. The treaty of 1795 was negotiated with great pomp and ceremony. The observance of this ceremony was calculated to make a show of bringing Indian policy into line with key provisions of the Northwest Ordinance of 1787. It had affirmed that "the utmost good faith shall always be observed towards the Indians; their land and property shall never be taken from them without their consent; and in their property, rights, and liberty, they shall never be invaded or disturbed, unless in just and lawful wars authorized by Congress."[11] The document negotiated at Greenville seemingly fulfilled the requirements of the ordinance by stipulating:

The Tribes who have a right to those [unceded] lands, are quietly to enjoy them, hunting, planting, and dwelling thereon, so long as they please, without any molestation from the United States; but when those tribes, or any of them, shall be disposed to sell their lands, or any part of them, they are to be sold only to the United States; and until such sale, the United States will protect all the said Indian tribes in the quiet enjoyment of their lands, against all citizens of the United States, and against all other white persons who intrude upon the same. And the said Indian tribes again acknowledge themselves to be under the protection of the said United States, and no other Power whatever.[12]

The most famous Indian leader on the Greenville Treaty council grounds was the Miami war chief Little Turtle.[13] Having led the fighting forces of the Indian Confederacy that, in 1790 and 1791, defeated the federal army, Little

Turtle was ready to consider a peace agreement with the US government. In negotiating the terms of peace, as in leading his people in war, Little Turtle was consistent in his quest for strategic advantage. In the months leading up to the agreement's ratification, he pressed General Anthony Wayne to widen the territory set aside for the Miami and sought to use the treaty to retain the means of economic self-sufficiency for his people. He therefore proposed that the United States and the Miami together might exercise a shared jurisdiction over a strategic transport site on the Little River. In council he explained: "This carrying place has heretofore provided in a great degree the subsistence of your younger brothers [the Miami]. That place has brought us in the course of one day the amount of one hundred dollars. Let us both own this place and enjoy in common the advantages it affords."[14]

When Little Turtle found himself increasingly isolated in his hard-line approach, he backed down. Not only did he sign the treaty but, in the years ahead, he used his influence to advance an awkward integration of his people into the US republic. The Delaware spokesperson, Tetabokshke, and the Potawatomi representative, New Corn, were also prominent among those Indians on the Greenville treaty grounds who wanted cooperation and friendship with the United States. Another advocate of peace with the American Long Knives – the *k'chi mokomanuk* – was the Shawnee leader Black Hoof, or Catahesca. He encouraged his small band to accept federal offers of assistance in its efforts to adopt the Euro-American style of settlement and farming. Some officials in the US government extolled a new regime of federal trusteeship for Indigenous peoples, promising that it held the key to achieving a more secure way of life. In the negotiations of 1795, General Wayne had explained the concept of federal trusteeship as the United States' adoption of Indigenous peoples "under the protecting wing of her eagle."[15] Secretary of War Timothy Pickering revealed another motivation when he advocated including yearly annuities in the treaty offer as a means of generating "*dependence* on our yearly bounty" and as a way to "create an obligation of which [the Indians] would feel the force."[16]

The negotiation of the Treaty of Greenville was one of the most conspicuous dramatizations in the entire history of the United States of the ritualized determination to make law the instrumental principle in the conduct of relations with Indigenous peoples. Essential to that ideal was the concept that Indigenous peoples must willingly give consent to subordinate themselves as groups and individuals under the republic's higher authority. Andrew Cayton has reflected on the strange psychology generated by the need felt by some officials to gain Aboriginal sanction for the American republic's imposition of power over the persons, nations, and ancestral lands of the continent's Aboriginal societies. "American officials genuinely believed that their triumph was incomplete without the defeated tribes' public acknowledgment of its essential justice," he wrote. "They required the Indians' acceptance of their new republican order as a pre-requisite for their right to govern the territory they took from them in the Treaty of Greenville. The acquiescence of peoples excluded from the exercise of power was a critical ratification of their sense of legitimacy as leaders."[17]

More was at stake, however, than the quality of a psycho-drama exposing the personality traits of the leadership of the new society. Rather, the viability of the Treaty of Greenville and others like it would become a harbinger of whether the United States would develop on the basis of the rule of law or on the basis of the rule of force. Efforts to make good on the promises set out in the Northwest Ordinance of 1787 were sporadically channelled into negotiations that presented Indigenous peoples with some small openings, real or illusory, to a say in defining the institutional format of their future relations with the society of newcomers. In return, various assemblies of Indigenous peoples were expected to give recorded sanction to the sovereign claims of their counterparts in treaty talks. As a rule, the newcomers did not go as far as allowing the claims to legal sovereignty of their own polities to become contingent on grants of legitimacy from the First Nations.

The pre-eminence of European rather than Aboriginal sources of legal legitimacy was reiterated by the Supreme Court of the United States in 1823 in the case of *Johnson v. McIntosh*. In that decision, Chief Justice Marshall ruled that the right of the United States to jurisdiction in, and ownership of, its territory was "subject to" the rights retained by Indigenous peoples. Marshall stated further that the underlying title of the United States was derived from Great Britain through the Treaty of Paris rather than from land purchases directly from Indigenous peoples. Marshall's ruling has retained a provisional quality, especially in light of the changing constructs of the international law on the rights of peoples' self-determination. Indeed, questions surrounding the source and the locus of legal legitimacy for European empires and their successor states remain very much alive to this day.[18] The principle that some polities in the so-called New World acquired their original charters not from European sources but rather from Aboriginal sources is illustrated in the history of Rhode Island. That jurisdiction was established by refugees fleeing the strict theocratic rule of Massachusetts. Lacking a charter from the English monarch, the settler group following Roger Williams went to the Narragansett Indians to obtain legal sanction from them, in the form of a treaty authorizing them to establish the Rhode Island colony on Narragansett territory.[19]

FROM REPUBLIC TO EMPIRE: THE ROLE OF INDIAN AFFAIRS IN ORIENTING THE UNITED STATES TO THE GLOBAL COMMUNITY

The decisions made by Little Turtle and the other Indian signatories of the Treaty of Greenville foreshadowed many similar choices made in the years ahead by a great many other prominent Aboriginal leaders. Their decisions were sometimes reflective of federal efforts to cultivate friendships and collaboration with hand-picked Indian men who, for personal rewards, could be persuaded to sanction the assertion of US authority over Indian people. Accordingly, the United States followed the lead of older imperial powers in developing its own colonial system of indirect rule over subjugated peoples. This approach to informal empire building in Indian Country would be applied to wider vistas of US foreign policy, especially through the propping up of comprador regimes throughout much of Latin America and, more recently, in the oil-rich sheikdoms of the Middle East.[20] The extension of US influence into Indian Country was a complex process involving all manner of bribery, cajolery, persuasion, intimidation, and, frequently, outright violence. The Aboriginal leaders on the receiving end of this range of treatments by and large faced only a poor range of options in meeting the growing power of the future superpower. The diverse images of many of the Aboriginal men who came to represent, often begrudgingly, the authority of the United States in Indian Country are displayed almost as trophies of colonization in a portfolio of engravings put together in the early decades of the nineteenth century by Thomas Loraine McKenney – the longstanding federal superintendent of Indian Affairs during the presidencies of James Madison, James Monroe, John Quincey Adams, and Andrew Jackson.

Typically, McKenney would engage Washington artist Charles Bird King to paint the portraits of the principal men in those many Aboriginal delegations who came to the nation's capital to plead their grievances to various officials, from the president on down. As a rule, these delegations were accommodated as guests at the luxurious Indian Queen Hotel on Pennsylvania Avenue. There they were generally treated to sumptuous and unlimited offerings of food and drink as officials endeavoured to impress on them the dire consequences for their people of resisting the military, technological, and economic strength of the United States. The portrait gallery created by McKenney in this way was later published to become one of the richest and most authentic documents we have recording the pluralistic array of dress, style, and personality that characterized the diverse citizenship of Indian Country during the generation before the light-catching magic of photography.[21]

The rise of Tecumseh was stimulated by a grassroots revulsion among many Indians who revolted against the early stages of this co-optation. The resistance of Tecumseh and his supporters to the United States was also a stand against a class of Indian collaborators willing to undermine, for personal gain, the shared rights and titles of their own peoples. Tecumseh's advancement of the principles of the Bowl with One Spoon formed the constitutional basis of the Indian Confederacy as a sovereign polity capable of full participation in the international community of nations. The key to exercising this sovereign self-determination lay in asserting the shared jurisdiction of all the Confederated Indian Nations in the territories they held in common. It lay in Tecumseh's understanding that the universal solvent of Indian Country was the newcomers' legal alchemy that divided, privatized, and reapportioned the former Indian domain. In the prelude to the War of 1812, Tecumseh refused to accept as legitimate the signature of any Indian men professing to sanction in ceding treaties the "extinguishment" or "termination" or "surrender" of Indian rights and titles. On behalf of a growing constituency who began to heed his call for Indian unity, Tecumseh rejected the very process of dividing territory under Aboriginal control into fragmented pieces of real estate. The privatization of the former Indian Country under the alien, non-Aboriginal law of possessive individualism effectively crippled the jurisdictional vitality of a confederated Indian realm, both as a sovereign law maker or even as a cohesive object of US law.

The meaning of the wampum symbol of the Bowl with One Spoon was therefore expanded by the Indian Confederacy to represent something more than shared hunting territory. The symbol came, in fact, to represent an Aboriginal response to the emphasis on private property as the primary object and fulfillment of the American Dream. In the American Declaration of Independence, the pursuit of happiness was emphasized along with life and liberty as fundamental to the "inalienable rights" of "all men." Clearly, in 1776 the category of "all men" did not include Indians any more than the Black slaves who lived within the United States but outside the laws of citizenship. The defence of the principles of the Bowl with One Spoon was given urgency by the undeniable reality that the future acquisition and breakup of Indian Country formed the key to supplying the private property essential to the form of happiness pursued by most US citizens. The image of the Bowl with One Spoon presented a simple yet evocative picture of the political economy of Indian unity and the strategy of elevating their treaty making with non-Indian sovereigns beyond the level of domestic politics to the status of international law and international relations.[22]

Accordingly, for Tecumseh, the collaboration with US officials of Little Turtle, Black Hoof, and those of their ilk amounted to virtual treason against the sovereign integrity of the Indian Confederacy. In making such charges, Tecumseh both expressed and generated a virtually revolutionary determination among many of his own peoples, a revolutionary dynamism that in many ways amounted to an Indian mirror-image of the forces that had converged in the American War of Independence. In thus renewing and elaborating in a new context the constitutional principles of the Indian Confederacy, Tecumseh aimed to mobilize, organize, and strengthen the diverse citizenry of an Aboriginal Dominion capable of opposing the hostile forces which he believed had been strengthened by the creation of the United States. As he correctly perceived, the Anglo-American preoccupation with the extinguishment of Indian Country remained fundamental to the revolutionary spirit of the new republic in spite of the principles articulated in the Northwest Ordinance of 1787 and the Treaty of Greenville in 1795. Tecumseh's visions were not realized. He became a martyr to his cause when he was killed in battle in 1813. Nevertheless, his mobilization of the fighting forces of the Indian Confederacy in the War of 1812 saved the largest part of Canada from annexation by the United States. It remains to be seen if the Canadian people can accept Tecumseh as being as instrumental in the development of their polity as, for instance, John A. Macdonald or Wilfrid Laurier.

The apparently unrelenting character of the US war on Indian Country aroused considerable unease, angst, and condemnation among some men and women of conscience in Great Britain. These individuals tended to feel a palpable sense of guilt and worry about seeing their own government abandon most of the Indian peoples who had fought in alliance with the British imperial government during the American Revolution and especially during the War of 1812. They feared the inhumane or even murderous treatment that might damn the fate of their former allies and comrades in arms under the government of the United States. In the 1820s Lewis Cass, the governor of Michigan Territory, tried to convince the British public that the United States was not a country governed by the animosities and predilections of vicious Indian fighters. A veteran of the War of 1812 and the probable author of a famous proclamation urging Upper Canadians to join the United States,[23] Cass played a role in the formulation and conduct of Indian policy south of the Great Lakes much like that of Thomas Gummersall Anderson in the remaining Crown domain to the north.[24] Both Cass and Anderson came of age in a place and time intimately shaped by the culture of the fur trade. Both men played significant roles in the transition from an era when Indigenous peoples were strategically crucial to the geopolitical balance of power in North America to one when Indians began to be treated as wards of the state in the name of the civilizing mission.[25] In his arguments in defence of US Indian policy and in his corresponding criticism of the management of Indian Affairs in Canada, Cass revealed a great deal about the psychology of US relations with Europe.[26]

Lewis Cass used the pages of the *North American Review*, which was widely distributed in Great Britain, to counter the barrage of criticisms directed at US Indian policy in the years following the War of 1812. He began his crusade with a strategic attack on the worth and authenticity of the writings of John Dunn Hunter, a controversial "White Indian" embraced by many important figures in Great Britain. Among Hunter's well-placed admirers was Robert Owen, the celebrated industrialist who shared in the broad fascination engendered by this White Indian's published account of his experience growing up as a captive and then as an adopted member of the Osage nation.[27] In 1827 Cass broadened his volley to oppose allegations that appeared in the *London Quarterly Review*. Among the published criticisms that most aroused Cass was the charge that "the outsettlers of Kentucky, Ohio and the other back states" were "utterly abandoned to vice and crime – so devoid of all fear of God and regard towards man." According to this critic of US Indian policy, the British nation, like the Indians of North America, had incurred the hostile wrath of these Godless outsettlers. Thus, the *London Quarterly* correspondent would allege, "our cause was common with that of the Indian nations." He added, "Against them, as against us, the Americans have been the real aggressors."[28]

In answering these charges, many countercharges were pressed by Cass, who later received a Doctor of Laws degree from Harvard University in recognition of his assumed authority as "the best informed man in the United States on Indian Affairs."[29] In addressing what had transpired in the War of 1812, Cass denied that Indian peoples had fought to protect their lands on "the southern coast of Lake Superior and the table land of the Mississippi." He found it altogether laughable that "these improvident human beings, with whom the past is forgotten and the future condemned, and whose whole life is absorbed in the present," would ever have been motivated to protect militarily their interest in territory. In Cass's estimation, this region would not in any case be sought by the United States for purchase from the Indians and for settlement by Euro-Americans for several more centuries.

Cass accused Tenskwatawa, Tecumseh's brother, of being a "dupe" and a puppet of the British imperial policy. In the opening years of the nineteenth century, Tenskwatawa had started what is sometimes remembered as the Brothers' Movement, when he achieved fame among many Indian people for the power of his visions and prophecy. After Aboriginal men and women of many nationalities began to gather around Tenskwatawa and follow his spiritual teachings, Tecumseh proceeded to direct and mobilize the religiously driven enthusiasm towards more secular objectives – the promotion of an elaborate Indian Confederacy as the basis for an Aboriginal Dominion that would be recognized in international law.[30] In the view of Cass and many other US patriots, members of the British Imperial Indian Department had a significant covert role in directing the course of the Brothers' Movement from its inception. Cass charged the British with employing the prophet to turn the "phrenzy" and the "fanatical spirit" of his followers against the US government in a manipulative and ruthless fashion.[31] Moreover, Cass tried to dismiss, marginalize, and discredit the resistance movement associated with Tecumseh in language that would become almost a standard feature of the continuing psychological warfare directed at the most aggressive, pan-Indian expressions of Aboriginal sovereignty. Officials deployed this same language of demonization, for instance, in an effort to discredit those activists who gathered at Wounded Knee in South Dakata in 1973; at Anicinabe Park in Kenora, Ontario, in 1974; at Oka in the Ottawa Valley area of Quebec in 1990; and at Gustafsen Lake, BC, and at Ipperwash, Ontario, in 1995.

Cass described those Aboriginal patriots who fought to defend their country in the War of 1812 as "deserters from a few tribes." He continued: "The acknowledged government of each tribe disavowed any participation in their projects. And they were in fact a lawless predatory band, obeying no common authority, and seeking no common authority, and seeking no rational object."[32] Cass attempted to defend the United States in Great Britain's court of public opinion by describing the terms of a treaty he had been instrumental in negotiating at Prairie du Chien in 1825. He boasted that the power of the United States had been humanely invoked to bring about peace between two old enemies – the Sioux and the Chippewa.[33] Having thus attempted to exonerate the United States of allegations that it made cruel and unjust wars on Indian Country and that it had abused its expanding jurisdictions in the conduct of relations with the Aboriginal inhabitants of its territory, the Michigan governor presented his case that neither the people nor the government of Great Britain were in a position to claim any moral high ground with respect to the treatment of Indigenous peoples. He reminded his readers, for instance, that as the ruling authority of the Anglo-American colonies before 1776, Great Britain held ultimate responsibility for much of the violence directed at Indian Country since the earliest beginnings of English colonization. He also pointed to the harsh and sometimes murderous treatment directed at the Aborigines in the British colony of Australia and presented this indictment as evidence of the alleged hypocrisy and double standards practised by those subjects of the Crown who tried to demonize the United States for its Indian policies.[34]

In advancing this line of argument, Cass produced a lengthy condemnation of Indian policy in Upper Canada, a quickly expanding jurisdiction that later provided the basis for the province of Ontario. According to Cass, Crown officials in that British colony were in the process of removing the Aboriginal inhabitants from large tracts, offering only small reserves to replace what was being lost. He charged that, unlike in the United States, where the harmful trade in alcohol to Indian people was said to have been sharply restricted, in Upper Canada there were no prohibitions at all against selling liquor to the Indigenous inhabitants. Nor were there any laws protecting the remaining Indian hunting grounds from encroachment by non-Indians.[35]

Cass reserved some of his harshest criticisms for the activities of both the North West Company and the Hudson's Bay Company, two major instruments of Crown policy in North America. These two fur-trade enterprises had merged in 1821, marking the decline of Montreal and the ascendance of ports on the coast of Hudson Bay as the major exchange points linking Indian Country and Europe in ever more globalized networks of economic and political exchange. Cass was especially outspoken in his characterization of Lord Selkirk's HBC-sanctioned effort to establish a colony in the Red River area. In the final analysis, he argued, this initiative amounted to nothing more than a giant "land speculation" whose ambition made any similar schemes in the United States look puny by comparison.[36] Cass also expressed consternation at early news of a British plan to establish an Indian territory "to become a living bastion on the flank of Canadian defences." He anticipated the scheme that would coalesce a decade later to make Manitoulin Island into a supposedly permanent Indian Territory. In pointing to yet another experiment aimed at creating an Indian barrier zone between the United States and British North America, Cass feigned empathetic concern for those Aboriginal individuals who would take part in this plan. Writing as if he were addressing the future residents of this Indian Territory, he exclaimed, "Hapless people! Still destined to fight the battles of others, after your own are fought and lost!"[37]

Lewis Cass became one of the key operatives in both justifying and implementing the Indian removal policy of President Andrew Jackson.[38] On the basis of this support for a controversial federal initiative, Cass was appointed Jackson's secretary of war in 1831. In 1848 the former governor of Michigan became a candidate for president of the United States, a demonstration of the importance of "Indian Affairs" in the mix of governmental activities at the heart of presidential politics during the era of the American republic's most rapid westward expansion. His bid did not meet with success. Having already served a term as US ambassador to France, Cass culminated his career as President James Buchanan's secretary of state, a diplomatic post entrusted to him largely in light of his long service defending, expressing, and implementing, both at home and abroad, the United States' assumed right to assert power over Indians.

Cass completed his plea to the British public in 1827 by appealing to their sentiments as a kindred people with deep, familial bonds of shared history, values, and experience. His comments do much to clarify the nature of the connections linking US relations to Indigenous peoples on its western frontiers to US diplomatic relations with European powers. Basically, Cass asked the British for some show of trust that the United States would uphold what was best in the legacy inherited from the birthplace and heartland of the English language. He framed this declaration of the United States' honorable intentions towards Indian people by appealing to the British public to see the republic as the most substantial and worthy expression of its own genius.

How much more honorable would it be, and we cheerfully add, how much more becoming the British character, to cherish kindly feelings; to look back on the little band of pilgrims, who sought liberty of action and conscience beyond the ocean, and who carried with them the spirit of those institutions which, in their native land and in their newly sought home, have secured so much national prosperity and private happiness; and to look forward to the United States as the great depository of English literature and science and arts, and the living evidence of English intelligence and principles.[39]

Cass's analysis illustrates well the American propensity to identify with the prestige, authority, and genius of the heritage of Western civilization while, simultaneously, putting strategic and diplomatic distance between the United States and Europe. That posture towards Europe was made especially clear in the formulation of the Monroe Doctrine. In 1823 President James Monroe sought partially to disentangle the affairs of North and

South America from the involvement of European empires. He declared that both "the American continents" would "henceforth not be considered as subjects for future colonization by European powers."[40] In this fashion, the president of the United States essentially staked out the entire Western Hemisphere, excepting the British provinces together with the domain of the Hudson's Bay Company, as the exclusive realm of US influence (as the holdings and hinterland of the informal American empire). A twist to what became known as the Monroe Doctrine was the president's last message to Congress. In 1825 Monroe added his voice to those promoting the scheme of relocating all Indians in close proximity to Euro-American settlements to new enclaves west of the Mississippi River. This most ambitious scheme of US apartheid would be implemented in the years ahead through a range of political and military initiatives that later generations would come to identify as "ethnic cleansing."

Monroe's interrelated statements of 1823 and 1825 extended and elaborated forms of US isolationism that were anything but non-interventionist for Indigenous peoples east of the Mississippi and for all the inhabitants of the Americas outside the United States and British North America. All the citizens of the hemisphere, including the Indian or mestizo majorities in much of Latin America, were served notice that their relations with the outside world were henceforth to be under the imperial dominance and oversight of officials in either Washington, DC, or London, England. In *Facing West: The Metaphysics of Indian-Hating and Empire-Building*, Richard Drinnon comments on Monroe's pronouncements: "One of the curiosities of American scholarship has been the failure of historians to explore the connections between Monroe's doctrines on foreign policy and on Indians. They were mirror images of each other. Indian removal at home reflected a policy abroad addressed to 'natives' (and potential European colonizers) throughout the world ... Both [policies] provided prospective justification for the rapid multiplication of the citizens of the United States and for their expansion into the lands of nonwhites."[41]

Different aspects of Monroe's strategy found strong embodiment in the career of Lewis Cass. As part of his wide involvement in foreign policy, Cass sought to confirm and finalize the withdrawal of Great Britain from the jurisdictional domain of Indian Affairs in the United States. He later participated in the physical removal of Indian peoples from territory east of the Mississippi River to territory initially acquired from Napoleon, without Indian consent, in the Louisiana Purchase of 1803. The effort to make westward expansion a matter of exclusively domestic concern for Washington foreshadowed the development of patterns that would repeatedly colour the relationship of the United States to the international community. Time and again the US leadership has resisted any role in making or enforcing international law if this involvement included the empowerment of international institutions to intervene in matters considered internal to the domestic affairs of the United States. The failure after the First World War of the United States to join the League of Nations, an international institution that a US president had envisaged and promoted, represents the outstanding example of this very marked, ongoing phenomenon of US unilateralism.

Throughout much of the nineteenth century the two areas where the United States remained most vulnerable to international condemnation were in its treatment of Indigenous peoples and in its treatment of Black slaves and their descendants. Both are areas of public policy that lie at the crucible of human rights issues with broad implications for the international community. Both involve matters that are obvious subjects of international law. The intervention of Lewis Cass in Great Britain illustrates how one of these areas of public policy was shielded from outside intervention, how Indian Affairs was removed from the arena of international politics to become a matter of exclusively domestic concern. The US government has repeatedly been hostile to the empowerment of international agencies capable of intervening for the protection of human rights within the United States.

COMPETITION BETWEEN THE UNITED STATES AND BRITISH IMPERIAL CANADA FOR COMMERCIAL HEGEMONY IN THE INDIAN COUNTRY OF OREGON

Throughout much of the colonial history of the Western Hemisphere, many disagreements brewed about the extent of various territorial claims. Some of these disputes remain unresolved to this day. The government of Quebec, for instance, maintains that Labrador properly belongs to it rather than to the province of Newfoundland. Disputes over competing title to territory could sometimes burst into major battles of empire, as happened in the Seven Years' War. More often the European powers simply agreed to disagree. Who, for instance, could say in the first half of the eighteenth century where France's claims to western North America ended and where Spain's claims started? And what was to be made of Virginia's charter that theoretically extended that polity's territory into the Northwest as far as the Pacific Ocean? The charter extended to the Hudson's Bay Company was based on similar ignorance combined with extravagance. Like Virginia's charter of 1609, the HBC charter of 1670 was issued by an English sovereign who lacked precise knowledge of the Aboriginal geography of the lands he was claiming and granting with his royal imprimatur.

While the imperial powers boasted in Europe about the inflated extent of their New World empires, the Indigenous peoples had their own ideas about who belonged where and who could properly claim what. The agents of European empires in Indian Country often had little choice but to accommodate Aboriginal assertions of sovereign self-interest. The agents of New France, whose main media of commerce and diplomacy with Indigenous peoples was the fur trade, learned the importance of reassuring Indian people that they remained secure in the possession of their own Aboriginal territories. They often paid rent to host communities for the small posts they maintained throughout vast reaches of the interior of North America. This payment symbolized to their Aboriginal recipients that their own form of land tenure was recognized and respected by their European ally and trading partner. The agents of the British Empire responded to the effectiveness of French Indian policy by building up the Six Nations Iroquois, but especially the Mohawks, as a kind of Aboriginal extension of the imperial claims and assertions of the British Empire. The emergence of the United States from the British Empire simply added a new republican element to an old heritage of disagreement and dispute over the nature and extent of imperial land claims in North America.

In 1783 the diplomats who met in Paris agreed that the United States could with legitimacy enter the community of nations recognized as sovereign in international law. In 1818 this tradition of elaborating in Europe the geopolitical map of North America was continued. According to the convention of that year, the forty-ninth parallel was established as the border between the United States and British North America from the Lake of the Woods to the Rocky Mountains. This line was meant to correspond roughly with the southern limits of the Hudson's Bay Company Charter – in other words, with the height of land dividing the Arctic watershed from the western portion of the Mississippi drainage basin. The territorial division of 1818, therefore, had some authentic basis in geography and previous history, although the new border cut directly across the northward flowing Red River, whose origins lie deep in western Minnesota.

The 1818 convention left unresolved the location of the international border west of the continental divide along the Rocky Mountains. As elsewhere on the continent, the Indigenous peoples had virtually no formal say in how European and Euro–North American officials would apportion sovereign jurisdiction among themselves in the vast, rich region that today forms the basis for the province of British Columbia and the states of Oregon, Idaho, Washington, and part of Montana. The clash of claims to control of this domain tested in the late eighteenth century the assertions of naval power on the Pacific coast by Great Britain, Spain, the United States, and Russia. Integral to this contest for maritime control on the Pacific coast north of Mexican California was the trade in otter skins. The west-coast trappers and traders who specialized in this item included the coastal Salish, the Kwakiutl, the Tlingit, the Tsimshian, the Haida, and the Nootka. The otter skins their hunters and traders offered for exchange had special importance in the developing economy of the Pacific rim. This commodity constituted one of the few trade items from Europe or the Americas for which a significant demand existed in China in the era before that country was coercively pried open to the penetration of Western commerce through the Opium War of 1840.[42]

The competition to control what became known as Oregon Country pitted two systems of jurisdiction and political economy against each other.

Each pushed its way westward along one of two natural thoroughfares of east-west water communication. The architects of the US system sought to use the Missouri River as the major supply link to provision its outposts on the far side of the Rocky Mountains, while those of the Canadian system, who met annually at Grand Portage and then at Fort William on the present site of Thunder Bay, Ontario, sought to use the fur-trade infrastructure along the Saskatchewan, Athabaska, Fraser, and Columbia rivers to extend the hinterland of Montreal into the complex geography west of the continental divide. A decisive moment in the effort to broaden the influence of the United Sates into Oregon occurred when Meriwether Lewis and William Clark explored the lands beyond the headwaters of the Missouri and Yellowstone rivers all the way to the Pacific. Their travels, which took place between 1804 and 1806, were commissioned by President Thomas Jefferson in the expectation that his government's purchase of Louisiana from France in 1803 opened the way for the transcontinental extension of US claims all the way to the continent's west coast.[43] The explorations of Lewis and Clark were followed up in 1811, when the Pacific Fur Company, owned by New York entrepreneur John Jacob Astor, established the post of Astoria at the mouth of the Columbia River west of present-day Portland.[44] Astor turned the geopolitical strategies pioneered by Sir William Johnson, the British imperial superintendent of Indian affairs, to serve his own commercial interests together with the territorial ambitions of the United States.

The efforts of those who sought to extend the territorial base of the United States to transcontinental proportions were initially outflanked and overshadowed by the carefully orchestrated campaign to extend the fur-trade domain of British imperial Canada beyond the Rockies and southwards towards Mexico.[45] In those times, Mexico included most of what is now the southwestern quarter of the United States, including California. The primary institutional instrument of this extension of Montreal's influence was the North West Company, an extremely flexible commercial partnership whose principal shareholders included several Scots entrepreneurs schooled in the multicultural dealings of Johnson Hall. Together these Montreal-based entrepreneurs embodied a formidable convergence of capital, expertise, and raw ambition. Heather Divine has chronicled the importance of the busy intercultural milieu surrounding Sir William Johnson's mansion near Albany in cultivating the attitudes and expertise before the American Revolution that later coalesced in the success of the North West Company.[46]

As the founding Tory patriarch of the northern division of the British Imperial Indian Department, Johnson was an important empire builder whose later career was aimed at extending the Covenant Chain of Crown influence beyond the Mohawk Valley towards the larger Indian Country and fur-trade preserve of Canada. Johnson can be viewed as a prototypical personification of Red Toryism in North America. The Red Tories embodied a more conservative yet socialist tradition of governance than those

Anglo-Americans who sought independence from the British Empire. The North West Company enlarged the commercial hinterland of British imperial Canada by projecting the transcultural ethos of Johnson Manor to transcontinental proportions. After the American War of Independence, the North West Company became the key corporation in the expansion of what Donald Creighton has famously characterized as the commercial empire of the St Lawrence.[47] It provided the prototypical network of east-west communications that would later be built upon through the creation, expansion, and federal elaboration of the Dominion of Canada. The viability of this northern polity would be secured through the completion in 1885 of the Canadian Pacific Railway.

The most renowned Nor'Wester was Alexander Mackenzie.[48] Not only was he a trail blazer and skilled geographer but his entrepreneurial imperialism extended to lobbying the British government to coordinate its immense naval power with Crown control of the transcontinental transportation network of the Montreal fur traders.[49] Mackenzie's book to promote this adjustment in imperial policy found one of its most avid readers in Thomas Jefferson, who, as president of the United States, was developing ambitious transcontinental ambitions of his own for the Imperial Republic. Mackenzie's ambitions had required that he explore and chart from *within* North America the river routes leading to the remaining two of the continent's three ocean perimeters – the Arctic and the Pacific. After charting in 1789 the great northward-flowing river that would subsequently bear his name, Mackenzie pointed his own exploratory efforts towards finding a route to the Pacific Ocean through the Rocky Mountains. He succeeded in 1793. Mackenzie's achievements as a geographer were soon built upon by Simon Fraser, David Thompson, and a host of lesser-known individuals including John Clarke, Alexander Ross, Peter Skene Ogden, and John George McTavish. By 1813 the commercial dominance of the Canadian Nor'Westers west of the continental divide was confirmed when their company's agents purchased the post of Astoria shortly before the arrival of a British war sloop. After this transfer, Astoria was renamed Fort George.[50] When the North West Company merged with the Hudson's Bay Company in 1821, many of the Nor'Westers, including a number of Mohawk men from the Roman Catholic Indian missions in Lower Canada, continued to work in the southwesternmost districts of the British imperial Crown's fur-trade empire.[51] That sphere of British influence through the fur-trade activities of the Hudson's Bay Company extended south into the Sacramento Valley of Mexican California by the mid-1830s.[52]

In his classic text *The Course of Empire*, Bernard DeVoto reflected on the importance of the idea of continentalism in the genesis of the United States. He wrote that "the American people have always had a feeling that they must become what they have become, a single society occupying the continental unit. That feeling was a powerful force in the creation of the American nation and the American empire."[53] These urgings found a parallel in the transcontinental aspirations that were eventually coalesced in the Dominion of Canada, even though it was rooted in very different orientations to the land and to the peoples indigenous to North America. As a new country and a nascent empire founded in a revolutionary rejection of the hereditary titles of the monarchs and aristocrats of Europe, the makers of the United States were less inclined to recognize the hereditary titles of North America's Indigenous peoples. Moreover, they were more inclined to oppose with military force any overt defence of those Aboriginal rights and titles by either Native people or by their imperial allies and trading partners.

Alternatively, the conservative orientation of the founders and shapers of British imperial Canada was more readily aligned with the recognition of the Aboriginal titles and human rights of the Indigenous peoples. Indeed, recognition of that Aboriginal title is still working its way through the political culture of Canada, however sporadically and imperfectly, in the negotiation of many modern-day treaties with a number of Aboriginal communities. Among the Aboriginal groups who have participated in the new round of Crown-Aboriginal treaty making that began in 1973 are the James Bay Cree, the Inuvialuit of the Beaufort Sea area, the Nisga'a of British Columbia, and the Inuit of the eastern Arctic jurisdiction of Nunavut that was created in 1999. Loyalist rejection of the American republic's revolutionary break with the past, together with Canadians' continuing constitutional ties with Great Britain, was more conducive to the creation of lasting accommodations of the Old World cultures of Indians, Inuit, and, more ambivalently, the Métis. While the greater and longer dependence of Canada on the economics of the fur trade offers one clue to the more conservative style of colonization in the northern half of North America, that fact alone is insufficient to explain the differing character of the two transcontinental polities dominated by English-speaking North Americans. The prototypical pathfinders of these differing traditions of continentalism were Lewis and Clark on the one hand and Alexander Mackenzie on the other. The differing nature of the polities supporting their enterprises suggests much about the contrasting characteristics of the nascent New World empire and the resurgent Old World empire they respectively represented.

EXPLORATION, DISCOVERY, OR ENCOUNTER? GENDER AND INTELLECTUAL PROPERTY IN THE COLONIZATION OF NORTH AMERICA

The accomplishments of the pathfinders and map makers in the last great era of North American "exploration" need to be subjected to the same kind of reflection and commentary directed at the legacy of Christopher Columbus during the 500th anniversary of his famous transatlantic voyage in 1492. Indeed, we need to revise how we understand and describe the achievements of a host of "explorers" of the continent, including Hernando de Soto, Samuel de Champlain, Pierre-Esprit Radisson, Médard Chouart des Groseilliers, Henry Hudson, Henry Kelsey, Robert Cavelier de La Salle, La Vérendrye, Samuel Hearne, Peter Pond, and Zebulon Pike together with Meriwether Lewis and William Clark, David Thompson, Simon Fraser, and, of course, Alexander Mackenzie. These men no more discovered new territories than Christopher Columbus discovered America. What they did do, however, was widen the fund of geographical knowledge available in Europe and in those societies derived primarily from Europe. They transferred knowledge across large cultural and linguistic divides separating those who saw America as a New World from those Indigenous peoples who were very much at home in their own Old Worlds. The intellectual basis for this transfer of knowledge was as much ethnographic as geographic in character. Not only did the non-Aboriginal route finders of North America need to be able to locate precisely the rivers, lakes, heights of land, mountain passes, portages, and other natural features but, to get this knowledge, they also needed to learn about the foods, poisons, and medicines in the territory through which they passed. Most of all they needed to know enough about the Indigenous peoples of various regions to be able to negotiate with them for, at the very least, permission to cross their lands.

Almost invariably, the primary sources of this vital ecological and ethnographic information were those Aboriginal guides and advisers whose cooperation was crucial to the success of the early stages of European reconnaissance of the interior of North America. By replacing narratives of discovery with narratives of encounters between different peoples, the way is gradually being opened to a wider understanding of the crucial role of Aboriginal groups and individuals in the transformation of the continent throughout the post-Columbian era. A key part of the prelude to the imperial taking and colonization of Indian Country was the gathering of intelligence from Aboriginal informants and collaborators about the myriad details constituting the human and physical geography of particular regions. In the contemporary language of possessive individualism, this gathering of intelligence might be described as a massive transfer of intellectual property from the Indigenous peoples. The commercial value of this original transfer of knowledge to the pathfinders of Western civilization is so immense as to be beyond calculation. Its worth is becoming especially controversial in an era when property rights to seeds and to the genetic blueprints of other living organisms are being patented as the next great frontier in the privatization and replication of capital. Where is the legitimacy in a process that would see large biotechnology companies claim as their own the intellectual property resulting from the careful breeding by many generations of Indian horticulturalists of diverse strains of corn, potatoes, tomatoes, squash, and other crops?

Gender has been an important factor in the movement of intellectual property across cultural, scientific, and philosophical watersheds between peoples. In many instances this movement of interpretation and information has been based on a process of Aboriginal women educating European and Euro-American men. The predominance of this pattern is derived largely from the reality that it was mostly men who undertook the naval, military, commercial, and evangelical aspects of European colonial expansion, especially during the earlier phases. This tendency was especially pronounced in the Indian Country beyond the frontiers of concentrated Euro-North American settlement. It was rare, for instance, for many Aboriginal people throughout much of present-day Canada to see a White woman until well into the twentieth century – even though the country's Indigenous peoples have been dealing extensively with European and Euro-Canadian fur traders, sometimes since the seventeenth century. Indeed, in some areas of northern Canada where resource-extraction industries bring in large numbers of non-Aboriginal working men who are either single or who live away from their families for extended periods, the gender imbalance between Indigenous peoples and newcomers continues to this day.

There are many celebrated or reviled instances where Aboriginal women changed history through the guidance, help, and information they extended to European or Euro-American partners. An Indigenous woman named Malinche, or sometimes Marina, became the translator, secretary, and mistress of Hernando Cortéz and provided him with strategic information used in the Spanish conquest of the Aztec Empire of Mexico.[54] The real or imagined assistance rendered by Pocahontas saved Captain John Smith from being murdered during the founding episodes of Virginia. This drama, the basis of an archetypal legend in America's most primal folk culture, presented many generations of writers and readers with "a popular and sentimental myth of reconciliation between Red and White."[55] Aboriginal women played a significant role in many episodes that were central to the contest between the North American empires of Britain and France. An instrumental figure in the Roman Catholic transformation of the Indian Country of New France was Kateri Tekakwitha, whose dramatic conversion in 1676 was instrumental in the consolidation of Jesuit influence among the Indigenous peoples of the St Lawrence Valley.[56] In 1934 the Vatican declared her venerable, and in 1980 she was beatified by Pope John Paul II in a ceremony that signalled a major initiative within the Roman Catholic Church in North America to establish and consolidate a locus of Aboriginal self-governance. The life and legacy of this woman formed the central story line in Leonard Cohen's classic free-form novel, *Beautiful Losers.*[57]

The intense relationship between Tekakwitha and the Jesuit priesthood in New France was integral to the genesis of that colony's fur-trade relations with Indian Country. Similarly, the intimate relationship between Sir William Johnson and the Six Nations matron Molly Brant, or Kionwatsi'tsiaienne, was equally central to the security of British North America. That connection was especially crucial to the most strategic link of British-Indian relations in the era of the French and Indian War. Accordingly, the love and friendship between Sir William and Molly extended to the most basic issues of war or peace; their exchange of commitments helped in the metaphorical polishing of the silver Covenant Chain, a medium of intercultural diplomacy that facilitated the gradual merger between the Indian Country of Canada and British imperial Canada. This Covenant Chain provided the stories and protocol to connect in theory and in practice a hierarchically organized complex of Indian nations with a loose confederacy of Anglo-American colonies in the decades leading up to the American Revolution.[58]

In fur-trade society, some Indian women became important power brokers and intermediaries. In 1715–16, for instance, the Chipewyan woman Thanadelthur led the negotiation on behalf of her close associates in the Hudson's Bay Company of a major treaty of friendship between her own people and the Cree as a necessary prelude to the founding of the strategically placed fur-trade post of Fort Churchill.[59] Similarly, a powerful Chinook woman named Lady Calpo warned the Nor'Westers of imminent Indian attacks on their Oregon Country stronghold in the period shortly after agents of the North West Company took over Astoria and changed its name to Fort George.[60] Indian women proved equally influential on the expanding frontiers of the American empire. The Shoshone woman Sacajawea travelled with the Lewis and Clark expedition all the way to the Pacific, conducting important negotiations with Native groups and individuals along the route. These negotiations included talks that resulted in the purchase of horses, without which the expedition could not have succeeded.[61]

In the United States, particular importance has been attached to the memories of Sacajawea and Pocahontas. Both have been cast again and again in all manner of plays, novels, films, and other depictions. The role of both women in helping the founders and trail blazers of Anglo-American patriarchy has been emphasized with such insistence that their images have become powerful redemptive symbols. Just to invoke their names is to call upon an elaborate New World mythology of self-justification suggesting that Aboriginal women both sanctioned and helped facilitate the subordination of the Indigenous peoples to a superior Euro-American civilization manifestly empowered to claim as its own the destiny of "the West." Where Pocahontas became an animated Disney character, the image of Sacagawea found its way onto the first US one-dollar coin in 2000. The Sacagawea dollar thus joined the famous Indian-head nickel. This nickel, depicting the profile of an Indian man with a very strong, patrician-like nose, became one of the most iconographic representations on US currency throughout much of the twentieth century. In contrast, one of the most famous coins ever issued by the Canadian Mint has been the nickel graced by the image of a lone beaver, the animal whose hide became the primary medium of exchange in the development of the fur-trade society of Canada. This emphasis on the medium of commerce rather than the human participants in the intercultural exchange conformed to the preoccupations of Harold Innis, the author of a pioneering work in economic history entitled *The Fur*

Trade in Canada.[62] Innis's emphasis on beaver pelts as a medium of exchange in the formation of the first empire of transcontinental communications in northern North America helped to inform the thinking of communications guru Marshall McLuhan. In looking from his vantage point in a sparsely populated transcontinental country, where exchanges over large distances and across wide divergences of culture have been integral to the process of national growth and consolidation, McLuhan explained in one of his best-known texts that "the medium is the message."[63]

Throughout large areas of the world colonized by Europe, empire building was an intensely gendered enterprise because it was almost uniformly men far from their homes who staffed the exploratory, military, commercial, administrative, and religious agencies of empire. Still, it is risky to impose overly sweeping generalizations. As attested, for instance, by the homosexual relationships of Oblate Father Émile Petitot with a number of Indian boys and young Indian men, there were many possible variations in the type of cross-cultural relations that facilitated the transfer of strategic information across cultural divides. No doubt information from some of Petitot's male Aboriginal partners contributed to the development during the second half of the nineteenth century of his achievements as "one of Canada's greatest amateur geographers, ethnographers, and map-makers."[64] In spite of these nuances, however, there can be no doubt that the politics of gender and colonization often put Aboriginal women in extremely influential positions as translators, interpreters, and intermediaries between their non-Aboriginal lovers, friends, confidants, or husbands and their own Indian families, bands, nations, and confederacies.[65] As Alexander Mackenzie observed of the Athapaskan-speaking region of Canada where the Dene Indians prevail, Aboriginal women often possessed "a very considerable influence in the traffic with Europeans."[66] In many cases, Indian women were able to translate their preferred access to European trade items such as guns and ammunition into strategic advantages for their clans and nations. It would be difficult, therefore, to underestimate the importance of intercultural friendship, love, eroticism, marriage, and procreation in the colonial history of capitalism's empire.

The first waves of European or Euro-American explorers were almost entirely ignorant of the Aboriginal geographies, Native languages, and complex of alliances and antagonisms among the diverse clans, bands, nations, and confederacies of the Indigenous peoples. George Simpson, the powerful governor of the Hudson's Bay Company, left a telling suggestion of the importance of the intelligence he secured from at least one Aboriginal woman. In his comments on the state of Fort George in 1824, he revealed that the Chinook matron Lady Calpo was his indispensable source of information on the local intrigues of the Oregon Country. From her, Simpson learned "more of the Scandals, Secrets, and politics both of the out and inside of the Fort than from Any other source."[67]

The children of the formal and informal unions between non-Aboriginal men and Indian women introduced new complexities and nuances into the relationships of Indian Country with the colonial societies of North America. One of the results was the growing tendency of White fur traders to choose Métis marriage partners over Indian wives, a significant step in the evolution of the elaborately calibrated racism that would come to characterize dramatically the social structure of the newcomers, especially after the arrival of significant numbers of European or Euro-North American women in a given region.[68] As some of the old intercultural intimacy from fur-trade marriages was lost, intermarriage, or miscegenation as this practice was sometimes described, presented increasingly complex legal and sociological problems for those inside and outside the families created by this form of union.[69]

"WHO WILL DARE TO ADVOCATE THE MONSTROUS DOCTRINE, THAT THE PEOPLE OF A WHOLE CONTINENT MAY BE DESTROYED, FOR THE BENEFIT OF THE PEOPLE OF ANOTHER CONTINENT?"

The conclusion of the War of 1812 can be seen as the final chapter of a long civil war that erupted following the integration of Aboriginal–French Canada into British North America. The peace settlement formulated in the Flemish city of Ghent in 1814 confirmed the sovereign independence of the United States just as it also clarified the likelihood that the new American republic would continue its rapid westward expansion fed by massive waves of emigration from Europe. Between 1763 and 1814, disagreements about the appropriate status of Aboriginal North Americans presented major points of contention in the genesis of the crisis that divided the sovereignty of Anglo-America in two. Underlying the hostility between Anglo-American factions lurks a fundamental disagreement about the constitutional existence of Aboriginal and treaty rights. Section 35 of the current constitutional law of Canada, the polity that emerged from the Tory side of the American War of secession, both recognizes and affirms the existence of Aboriginal and treaty rights. This affirmation flows naturally from the history of the North American polity whose deepest legal, political, and cultural roots lie in the fur trade of French–Aboriginal Canada and British imperial Canada. It flows naturally from the polity that would not now exist as a constitutional monarchy and as a sovereign dominion in the British Commonwealth if its core territory had not been defended by the Indian Confederacy mobilized into military action by Tecumseh. Section 35 of the Canadian constitution reflects the history of a polity sustained through a military alliance with Tecumseh's Indian Confederacy in the War of 1812. Alternatively, those on the republican side of the American Revolution announced themselves to the world in a document that denied and negated the existence of the human rights of Indigenous peoples. The one reference to Indians in the Declaration of Independence of 1776 can be seen as a seminal instance of racial profiling. It demonized them as terrorists – "as merciless Indian savages whose known means of warfare is an undistinguished destruction of all ages, sexes, and conditions."

The contrasting characterization of Indians in the Royal Proclamation of 1763 and in the Declaration of Independence of 1776 constitutes a powerful code signifying its authors very different orientations to whole complexes of political and economic relationship in the global community. The difference between the characterization of Indians as allies or as criminalized Others is no mere footnote to history. Instead, this contrast points to unresolved contentions whose outcome remains central to the kind of world our posterity will inherit. Disagreements among Anglo-Americans about the status and rights of the continent's Aboriginal societies were closely connected to a host of other questions concerning the legal quality of land tenure, the nature and location of sovereignty, the power to tax, and the ability to control and direct the deployment of armed forces. The contrast between the manifestos of 1763 and 1776 would project across expanding frontiers of time, space, and the human condition. John Collier, Franklin Roosevelt, the Indian New Deal, and the Atlantic Charter embodied the affirmative view that all people, including Indigenous peoples, are invested with the inherent right not to be unilaterally dispossessed of their Aboriginal lands. Alternatively, many of the industrialists and financiers of who invested heavily in the rise of the Third Reich, the Nazification of Europe, and the globalized operations of the national security state emerged from a tradition of history whose roots go back to the demonization of savage Indians in the Declaration of Independence. The paired criminalization of King George and "the merciless Indian savages" anticipated the dehumanization of many other groups and individuals who blocked the expansion of monopoly capitalism. The continuation of this self-serving conduct in the Cold War and then the War on Terror re-enacted patterns established in 1776 with the characterization of North America's original title holders as merciless savages. This way of condemning those societies lying in the way of the United States' territorial expansion helped secure a licence for empire for those who displaced and eliminated Indians in the name of American liberty.

Just as contentions over the treatment of Indigenous peoples helped to shape the geopolitical milieu of the long civil war among Anglo-Americans between 1763 and 1814, in the same way some of the major issues of the American Civil War of the 1860s found early expression on the physical and ideological borderlands of the remaining Indian Country. The developing acrimony between advocates of states rights and those who favoured a strong central government found expression in the controversy testing the status of Cherokee lands in US federalism and in the question of whether Georgia's state government would be allowed to displace the Cherokee Nation and assume sovereign jurisdiction over territory that had been guaranteed to it through several treaties with the federal government. This clash, in turn, was integral to the larger controversy over whether the territorial organization of the United States would be made to conform to one of the most ambitious plans of apartheid ever conceived.

The outcome of the War of 1812 helped to create the conditions for those who favoured the removal of all Indians from east of the Mississippi River to territories on the western side of that aquatic divide. The Supreme Court of the United States was drawn into the process of determining whether to proceed with this plan. It became prominent among those agencies seeking to affirm the pre-eminence of federal authority over state authority in efforts to prevent the outcome sought most zealously by the citizens and government of Georgia. While the proponents of Indian removal, including Lewis Cass, ultimately prevailed, they had first to face not only a major court challenge but also a highly organized evangelical lobby that expertly advanced the legal and ethical arguments for recognizing the existence of Aboriginal and treaty rights. In making that case, the critics of Indian removal drew on important currents of opinion that have historically identified the reputation of the United States and even the republic's very legitimacy with its treatment of Indigenous peoples within its borders.

Those who advanced a more humane embrace of the first peoples within the territorial and constitutional edifice of American freedom could point to a number of US laws and precedents to buttress their positions. Among those legal instruments proclaiming a relatively expansive federal recognition of the existence of Aboriginal and treaty rights were the Northwest Ordinance of 1787 and the Treaty of Greenville of 1795. Both these documents seemingly opened the prospect that the United States could be made to accommodate a place of dignity and security for Indigenous peoples. The career of Lewis Cass in the federal government pointed in the opposite direction. His ideas and actions embodied many of the forces that made Indian removal an attractive option for many powerful constituencies in the United States. One of Cass's most outspoken critics was the Reverend Jeremiah Evarts. This determined clergyman and lawyer proved to be the single individual most responsible for elevating the public debate over Indian removal to the towering heights of political controversy. His vision of the treatment of Indians as the primary test of the integrity of the rule of law in the United States anticipated the development of the ideals that would be given further expression by John Collier and the Indian New Deal. Evarts was a seminal voice giving eloquent articulation to ideals that in subsequent generations would find expression in the Atlantic Charter, the United Nations Charter, and the Universal Declaration of Human Rights.

In responding to an 1830 article in the *North American Review* where Cass supported President Andrew Jackson's plan to clear the United States of Aboriginal communities east of the Mississippi River, Evarts referred to his opponent as being "distinguished for servility and sycophancy," as a man who "wishes to trim his sails in such a manner as to catch the breeze of government favor and patronage."[70] Cass's advocacy of Indian removal came in the form of a review of a pamphlet published by the New York Board for the Emigration, Preservation, and Improvement of the Aborigines of America. That organization brought together Christian leaders supportive of Jackson's controversial Indian policy. The decision to give clergymen a prominent voice in the defence of this policy was deemed necessary because of the growing effectiveness of the anti-removal lobby centred in the American Board of Commissioners for Foreign Missions. As an agent and officer of the board, Evarts put that organization at the centre of the most contested political dispute on Indian policy in the entire history of the United States. In leading and mobilizing the very broadly based crusade to oppose one of the planet's most sweeping plans ever for ethnic cleansing, Evarts emerged as a visionary and an erudite champion of Aboriginal and treaty rights.

To Evarts, the decision of whether to uproot the Cherokee Nation from their prosperous agricultural settlements in the region of present-day southeastern United States presented the American people with one of the most momentous decisions they would ever face about the kind of country they would bequeath to posterity. Would the US government adhere to its own laws? Or would federal authorities violate treaties made by some of its most venerated law givers, including President George Washington? Would the US government effectively "tear out sheets from every volume of our national statute-book and scatter them to the winds?"[71] What was ultimately at issue in the Indian removal question, therefore, was whether the United States would develop as a nation governed by law or by force. If it chose the latter by making strength "the only rule for action," then "the sentence of an indignant world will be uttered in thunders, which will roll and reverberate for ages after the present actors in world affairs have passed away."[72] Evarts continued: "An indelible stigma will be fixed upon us [that] will ultimately be understood by the whole civilized world. No subject, not even war, slavery, nor the nature of free institutions, will be more thoroughly canvassed."[73]

These secular considerations, he argued, were secondary to the religious questions at stake. What was ultimately at issue for him was whether the United States would live up to what he saw as its providential mission to serve as an exemplary beacon for the rest of the world in the inspired application of Protestant Christianity to statecraft. Would the rulers of the United States commit such a heinous act of criminal and sinful injustice against the Cherokee, as well as against "the doctrine of the law of nations," that they would "expose themselves and their country to the curses of Almighty God?"[74] "No sophistry can elude his scrutiny," he warned; "no array of plausible arguments, or of smooth but hollow expressions, can bias his judgment."[75] A series of twenty-four essays, originally published in 1829 between August 5 and December 19 in the *National Intelligencer*, contained the analytic core of Evarts's case outlining the many wrongs entailed in the plan of Indian removal. The articles were republished in different journals and as pamphlets, and they were abundantly quoted in speeches made in Congress and at the large public meetings in many US cities where memorials and petitions were introduced condemning the offending statute then working its way through the machinery of Congress.

While Evarts was universally known to be the author of the articles, he submitted them under the signature of William Penn. There was much historical logic in the decision to associate the anti-removal cause with the name of Pennsylvania's Quaker founder. Penn had established his Quaker colony while making of a series of treaties with the Indigenous peoples of the territory. The philosophical basis of these agreements was outlined in three letters written in 1681 and 1682 which were addressed in the first instance to the colony's Delaware neighbours.[76] There Penn recorded his wish for the establishment of relations with the Indigenous peoples based on "brotherly love, friendship and fundamental justice." His dealing with the Indians soon entered the mythology of the British Empire and the United States as an example of the benefits to be derived from fair treatment of the continent's first peoples. In 1772, in *William Penn's Treaty with the Indians*, for instance, the British Empire's most celebrated iconographer, Benjamin West, painted his tribute. He wanted, he explained, "to express savages brought into harmony and peace by justice," to show "conquest over native people without sword or Dagger."[77] Along with the treaty with the Narragansett people secured by Roger Williams to establish the legitimacy of the Rhode Island colony, Penn's dealings with the Delaware were widely perceived among many evangelical Protestants in the nineteenth century as the epitome of the most advanced conception of Aboriginal and treaty rights.[78] This evangelical constituency, one that was coming to form the core of the anti-slavery coalition as well, is precisely the group that Evarts was most intent on mobilizing with his series of articles aimed at turning public opinion against the objective of Cherokee removal.

President Jackson's Indian removal scheme was directed not only at the Cherokee but at all Indigenous peoples living in identifiable Aboriginal communities east of the Mississippi River. While the sweep of the plan was truly continental, the fate of the 25,000 Cherokee blocking Georgia's plans to extend its sovereign claims westward became the primary test case for the outcome of the larger project. There were a number of reasons why Evarts and others placed so much emphasis on the Cherokee. One was that most Cherokee families had embraced the Christian teachings of missionaries, including those in the employment of Evart's own institutional anchor, the influential American Board of Commissioners for Foreign Missions. The willingness of many Cherokee to enter and influence the Protestant denominations that dominated the religious affairs of the United States is illustrative of a more general Cherokee disposition. Many Cherokee adopted a broad array of innovations and attributes from Euro-American society, but they often turned these importations to serve a range of their own Cherokee national interests, objectives, procedures, and institutions.

The decision of a significant portion of Cherokee people to practise or condone intermarriage with Europeans and Euro-Americans both reflected and elaborated this pattern. Cherokee society was prone to esteem highly those among its own people who could combine deep loyalties to their own Aboriginal nationality with strategically vital, transcultural connections with the outside world. As a result, the Cherokee had many friends and even family connections throughout Euro-American society, including among its elites. Their main lawyer, for instance, William Wirt, was a former attorney general of the United States. Another reason for the centrality of the Cherokee in determining the larger issues of Indian removal was that they had succeeded in agriculture and in many of the other arts and sciences most esteemed in Western civilization. Hence, the main legal, political, and moral issues had to be faced on their own terms and could not be evaded with the specious resort to allegations that the Cherokee were too "uncivilized" to use scientifically what remained of their ancestral lands in order to achieve maximum economic output. There could be no invocation of the old rationales outlined, for instance, by John Locke in his famous commentaries on government, a text that proved extremely influential in helping the founders of the United States to rationalize Anglo-American appropriation of the supposedly "unimproved" Indian Country.[79]

Evarts made this consideration explicit in one of the William Penn essays, explaining that the Cherokee "are at present neither savages nor hunters":

From about the commencement of the present century, [the Cherokee] have addicted themselves more and more to agriculture, till they now derive their support from the soil, as truly and entirely as do the inhabitants of Pennsylvania or Virginia. For many years they have had their herds, and their large cultivated fields. They now have in addition their schools, a regular civil government, and places of regular Christian worship. They earn their bread by the labor of their own hands, applied to the tillage of their own farms; and they clothe themselves with fabrics made at their own looms, from cotton grown in their own fields.[80]

Details of the recent history of the relationship among the Cherokee, the state of Georgia, and the federal administration of President Andrew Jackson added to the convergence of forces making this one Indian nation in the United States the receptacle and the vehicle for the destiny of so many others during these years. In July 1827 the Cherokee drafted and ratified their own national constitution. It asserted Cherokee jurisdiction over the remaining Cherokee territory. That territory amounted to about 8 million acres, or about one-quarter of their ancestral lands. The other three-quarters of their ancestral territory had been given up in earlier ceding treaties. About 5 million acres of this remaining Cherokee heartland lay within what the Georgia government claimed were that state's own borders, touching Alabama, Tennessee, and North Carolina.

President Andrew Jackson's ascent to the White House was based in part on the reputation he had gained for himself as a general who had fought with the assistance of some Cherokee soldiers against the imperial forces of Great Britain and also against the Creek Red Sticks. These Red Sticks had answered Tecumseh's call to join the cause of Indian unity in the War of 1812. In later years General Jackson was also involved in the opening stages of a prolonged military conflict with the Seminole freedom fighters in Florida. This Seminole stand would in later years give rise to the emergence of Oceola, one of the most renowned of the Aboriginal resistance leaders. The Seminoles successfully incorporated many runaway African-American slaves into their prolonged Aboriginal resistance to the expansion of US authority into Florida. Given this background, Jackson came to the American presidency as a veteran and as a primary beneficiary of Indian removal before that policy was formalized through Congressional statute.[81] When he was first elected president in 1828, Jackson encouraged the government of Georgia in its increasingly aggressive efforts to pass and enforce laws covering lands that the Cherokee considered their own sovereign territory, guaranteed to them by a number of treaties with the US federal government.

Jackson resisted all interventions by the Cherokee and their friends aimed at persuading his administration to live up to federal obligations to protect Cherokee lands and citizens from the wrongful imposition of state jurisdiction. Indeed, Jackson secured his political base in the South by taking Georgia's side in the dispute. Indian removal was the proposed remedy that he introduced in his speech to Congress in December 1829, just as the last of the William Penn essays appeared in the *National Intelligencer*. In advancing the plan, Jackson rendered explicit a concept that had already been discussed both privately and publicly in Washington, DC, most recently by President Monroe in a speech in 1825. The idea of using the Mississippi as a fixed border for an entrenched Indian Country repeated the theme that had earlier been envisaged in 1768, when the Ohio River was first identified in the Treaty of Fort Stanwix as the southeastern marker for a permanent Aboriginal jurisdiction in North America. That geopolitical conception of the Ohio River as a fixed boundary for an Aboriginal Indiana remained alive until it was finally killed through the martyrdom of Tecumseh in the War of 1812.

In a bid to make conceptions of race and configurations of territory conform to each other, much of the top leadership of the United States embraced the idea of the Mississippi as the main geographic marker in a system of transcontinental apartheid. The US government stood poised to adopt both apartheid and ethnic cleansing in what was then viewed as the ultimate solution to its Indian question. Large parts of Evarts's William Penn essays were devoted to presenting the arguments of the proponents of Cherokee removal and then showing the flaws, inaccuracies, and internal contradictions that undermined their case. Having countered the arguments of those in favour of Jackson's Indian policy, Evarts went on to present clear descriptions of the history of constitutional relations among the Cherokee, the British Empire, the United States, and Georgia. These discussions included learned commentaries in non-specialist language on a host of key terms and concepts, including original title, treaties, and the delicate vulnerability of the rule of law. In developing the case for the anti-removal cause, Evarts made ample comparative references to European examples and even to the Roman Empire. These comparisons were calculated to illustrate the viability of small nationalities that retain attributes of sovereignty even as they develop alliances with, and dependencies on, larger and more powerful sovereign entities. What emerged from the William Penn essays, therefore, was a vision of a US future with a more inclusive approach to democracy and respect for human rights, including those rights vested in distinct peoples as well as in individuals. What Evarts advocated was a republic that eschewed ethnocentrism and embraced a more pluralistic and intercultural paradigm of human relationships. Time and time again, Evarts emphasized that the issue of Indian removal was not merely one question among many in the normal ebb and flow of the republic's political existence. So fundamental were the constitutional and ethical dimensions of this issue that they touched the essence of all that the United States had been and all that it would become, not only for its own people but as a force in the world either for good or for evil.

By the time of Evarts's campaign, the republic had entered into more than one hundred treaties with Indigenous peoples. All these treaties, which were identified in the US Constitution as part of "the supreme law of the land," had passed through the same constitutional procedures as treaties with foreign nations. They had been approved by the president and sanctioned by two-thirds of the sitting members of the US Senate. The prospect that so many of the nation's law makers seemed poised to relegate treaties with the country's Indigenous peoples to the status of "mere waste paper" filled the Protestant clergyman with dismay and consternation, and, in his effort to convey a sense of the gravity of the crisis in national legitimacy facing the United States at this crossroad, he wrote:

Government has arrived at the bank of the Rubicon. If our rulers now stop, they may save the country from the charge of bad faith. If they proceed, it will be known by all men, that in a plain case, without any plausible plea of necessity, and for very weak and unsatisfactory reasons, the great and boasting Republic of the United States of North America incurred the guilt of violating treaties; and this guilt was incurred when the subject was fairly before the eyes of the American community, and had attracted more attention than any other measure since the close of the last war.[82]

With an eye to the future, Evarts added: "If the Indians are to be removed, let it be said, in an open and manly tone, that they are removed because we have the power to remove them, and there is a political reason for doing it; and that they will be removed again, whenever the whites demand their removal, in a style sufficiently clamorous and imperious for the government."[83] Evarts then outlined the germane details in sixteen treaties with the Cherokee ratified by the US Senate and by five different US presidents between 1785 and 1819. Of all these instruments, he identified the Treaty of Holston of 1791, negotiated when Washington was president, as the one with the most bearing on the issue of Indian removal. Article 7 stipulated: "The United States solemnly guaranty to the Cherokee nation all their lands not hereby ceded."[84] To Evarts, these words signified an unambiguous constitutional commitment – a "guaranty" – on the part of the US government:

The United States solemnly engaged to preserve and defend the Cherokee against all foreign powers (a colony of Spain being then in the neighborhood) against the States of Georgia and North Carolina ... against all whites who should threaten to commit aggression upon the Cherokees. The word guaranty can mean no less, unless limited by the subject or context. If Bonaparte guarantees the integrity of Switzerland, he engages to defend and protect Switzerland from aggression and invasion, whether the danger arises from Austria, Prussia, Holland or even France itself. It is the chosen and appropriate word to express the utmost security, which can be pledged to one party by the power and good faith of another.[85]

Evarts presented one of the most succinct and transparent accounts of the meaning of federal treaties with Indian nations ever directed at a wide US audience. In seeking to answer the question "What is a treaty?" he responded: "It is a compact between independent communities, each party acting through the medium of its government. No instrument, which does not come within this definition, can be sent to the Senate of the United States, to be acted upon as within the scope of the treaty-making power." He went on to note that unlike Indian nations, state governments do not have the power to enter into treaty agreements:

One of the confederated States is not an independent community; nor can it make a treaty, either with the nation at large, or with any foreign power. But the Indian tribes and nations have made treaties with the United States during the last forty years, till the whole number of treaties thus made far exceeds a hundred, every one of which was ratified by the Senate before it became obligatory. Every instance of this kind implies that Indian communities had governments of their own; that the Indians, thus living in communities, were not subject to the laws of the United States; and that they had rights and interests distinct from the rights and interests of the people of the United States, and, in the fullest sense, public and national. All this is in accordance with facts; and the whole is implied in the single word treaty.[86]

The subject of title to territory was central in most of the federal government's treaty negotiations with the Cherokee. Like other Aboriginal groups in the vicinity of Anglo-American settlements, the Cherokee had something their treaty opposites wanted – land. Little by little, the remaining Cherokee lands were narrowed through the cession of title to portions of their ancestral territories. As the policy of Indian removal became imminent, questions arose about the nature of Cherokee's title to their remaining lands. Were the Cherokee "tenants at will," with nothing to support their legal connection to their settlements other than a tenuous, delegated form of land tenure susceptible to being terminated at any time by the agent that had given it, the government of Georgia? Or did the Cherokee retain an "original title" to their remaining lands – a title that "cannot be affected by the charter of kings, nor by acts of provincial legislatures, nor by the Compacts of neighboring states, nor by the mandates of the executive branch of our national government." Those who promoted Cherokee removal often argued the former. Like Evarts, the Cherokee themselves consistently argued the latter.

Evarts outlined the conceptions of the Cherokee people with regard to their collective jurisdiction over themselves and their settlements:

The Cherokee contend that their nation has been in possession of their present territory from time immemorial; that neither the King of Great Britain, nor the early settlers of Georgia, nor the State of Georgia after the revolution, nor the United States since the adoption of the federal constitution, have acquired any title to the soil and sovereignty over the territory; and that the title to the soil and sovereignty over the territory have repeatedly been guaranteed to the Cherokees, as a nation, by the United States, in treaties that are now binding on both parties.[87]

In the sixteenth William Penn essay, Evarts directly addressed the argument that the underlying title to the United States and, by implication, to the rest of the so-called New World as well was rooted ultimately in extensions of the right of "discovery" claimed by European monarchs. Chief Justice John Marshall had reiterated this most ethnocentric of all legal interpretations as recently as 1823 in the case of *Johnson v. McIntosh*. To this day the legal doctrines of "discovery" and of the "infidel" character of non-Christian nations remain integral to the line of legal precedents going back to *Calvin's Case* of 1608 – a line of precedents drawn on again and again to counter arguments for the broad existence of Aboriginal and treaty rights in many successor states of European empire, including Australia, Canada, and the United States.[88] Not surprisingly, the convergence of many vested interests has prevented any serious political grappling with basic questions about the originating source of the titles on which the legitimacy of many of the world's governments, borders, and territorial proprietorships are founded. As we have seen, even after the revolutionary departures aimed at decolonization were initiated with the Declaration of Independence, the independence of the United States was ultimately based on a grant from the European powers that used their treaty-making authority to extend legitimacy to the jurisdictional and territorial claims of the new republic.

The Indigenous peoples of many territories have been denied any role whatsoever in the international deal making to legitimate the independence of former colonies. The process of cutting the United States loose from the constitutional structures of the British Empire epitomized the exclusion of Indigenous peoples from the world's precedent-setting instance of what future generations would call decolonization. Indigenous peoples had no representation at the assemblies where the constitutional shape of the new republic was decided, nor did they have any seat in the negotiations with Great Britain and the other European powers that formalized US independence with the Treaty of Paris of 1783. The ethnocentrism inherent in these procedures remains integral to the shape of world order to this day. The other side of the extension of self-governance to liberated colonials has often been a heavy increase in the weight of repressive colonialism experienced by Indigenous peoples. At the very least, enhanced powers of self-governance seized by, or extended to, colonial populations have been directly connected to a sharp decline in the capacities of self-governance available to Indigenous peoples. Integral to this process of deterioration has been the litany of violations and infractions of the original agreements wherein the imperial powers sometimes gained their licences for overseas empire from the Indigenous peoples on the expanding frontiers of European claims to jurisdiction and sovereignty.[89]

To this day, however, such questions are rarely the subject of public controversy and debate. Only at moments when the most fundamental characteristics of empires and their successor nation-states are exposed and challenged are the underlying issues of Aboriginal history seriously addressed. Only then are the fundamental questions about the nature of the starting point – the Aboriginal source – of jurisdiction and title likely to come to the surface. Only then do the wider implications of the relationship of Aboriginal title to all other forms of title find their way into more public venues of overt argument and litigation in the struggle for control of state power.[90] In the eyes of Jeremiah Evarts, the prospect of Indian removal presented a moment of such sweeping significance for the future of the United States that it was necessary to face the most fundamental issues of Aboriginal history in the genesis of the first American republic. The prospect of applying such a vast scheme of ethnic cleansing to the territorial organization of the United States called for a political campaign that would confront the deepest legal and ethical questions concerning the root source of the country's claims to sovereignty, jurisdiction, title, and legitimacy. In the world's emerging laboratory of capitalism, what political questions could have broader implications than those testing antagonistic interpretations about the originating point of the right to own and control property, and the right to transform large portions of the Old World Indian Country into a New World mecca for the proprietorships of immigrants, their descendants, and their corporate extensions?

Evarts challenged the doctrine that the Aboriginal rights and titles of Indigenous peoples to their ancestral lands had been somehow extinguished by the initiating acts of English colonization:

Not even a king can grant what he does not possess. And how is it possible that he should possess vast tracts of country, which neither he, nor any European, had ever seen; but which were in fact inhabited by numerous independent nations, of whose character, rights, or even existence he knew nothing? Many grants to American colonists were bounded by lines running from the Atlantic to the Pacific oceans. This was particularly the case with the charters of Georgia. Will it be seriously contended that a royal grant of this kind conferred any rightful authority to dispossess of their territory the original occupants of the soil? From such a principle it would follow that all the aboriginal inhabitants might be lawfully driven into the ocean, and literally and utterly exterminated at once; for the European powers, by their proclamations and charters, divided the whole American continent among themselves. But who will dare to advocate the monstrous doctrine, that the people of a whole continent may be destroyed, for the benefit of the people of another continent?[91]

The Indian removal question did indeed render the Mississippi River as a kind of North American equivalent of Julius Caesar's Rubicon River. Once the decision was made to relocate whole Indian nations against their will and in direct contravention of their treaties with the federal government, the people and government of the United States moved beyond the point of no return in shaping their national destiny. The decision to proceed in this way went forward in the face not only of the powerful arguments marshalled by Evarts and his many supporters but of the most clear prohibitions on this course of action issued by the Supreme Court of the United States. At no time before or since did the basic political, ethical, and legal questions concerning the place of Indigenous peoples so permeate the consciousness of the larger citizenry in the United States. This politicization of the most basic questions in the conduct of Indian affairs greatly intensified the forces of public opinion brought to bear on the country's elected officials. The polarization of opinion was in large measure a function of the great distance between the different outcomes produced by the decision to proceed or not to proceed with Indian removal. At no time since has the division of options offered the people of the United States ever been quite so great, in terms not only of charting the rules of relationship with Indigenous peoples but also of establishing the constitutional groundwork for apportioning titles and rights to large portions of the country's most basic resources of land, air, and water.

Through his prodigious efforts to disseminate all relevant information on the Indian removal question, Evarts played a major role in helping to democratize the debate among non-Aboriginals. In politicizing the issue, he ensured that the outcome was based on shared public responsibility. There could be no sound alibi for citizens seeking to distance themselves from the decision with claims that "we didn't know what was being done." Accordingly, accountability for Indian removal at this time was spread widely throughout the entire citizenry of the United States. Responsibility for the decision fell broadly on the nation as a whole, with the greatest burden of accountability resting on those officials who designed, enacted, and implemented the plan.

Evarts contributed significantly to opening up for wider scrutiny and debate one aspect of government activity that was notoriously subject to elitist control by small circles of political insiders. Often these insiders derived great personal advantage for themselves and their political patronage networks by placing themselves and their cronies at those crossroads of power where the process of extinguishing Indian Country met the procedures for distributing private titles to those lands and resources being added to the individual, corporate, state, and federal patrimonies of the United States. A recurrent theme that was either explicit or implicit in many of Evarts's arguments was that the treatment of Indigenous peoples by the US government would have profound implications in shaping the republic's relationships with the world beyond its borders. In other words, his commentaries were very clear in their identification of Indian affairs with matters of international as well as domestic concern. The decision of whether to violate the treaties at the basis of the US nation's own legal claims to territorial integrity – treaties defined in the US Constitution as part of the "supreme law of the land" – would inevitably figure prominently in determining the republic's future role in making and enforcing international law. In the 1830s the realm of jurisdiction involving relations among sovereign entities in the global community was still often described as the law of nations.

Evarts's prophecies have become manifest in the ambiguities of the relationship of the US government to international law, international institutions, and the prospect of enforcing universal standards for the protection of human rights throughout the Americas and the rest of the world – and even *within* the United States itself. As the United States grew in power, its government tended to view its own military apparatus as the ultimate police force in the global community. The growing preoccupation of the government with its own status as a superpower has been instrumental in pointing the world away from the development of a genuine global rule of law in spheres other than commercial relations. The development of a global rule of law attuned to the protection of human rights on a par with the investment rights of transnational corporations would require the elaboration of properly resourced agencies with the democratic capacity to provide due process, consistent and binding arbitration, and the means of holding violators of international conventions and treaties accountable for their criminal transgressions. It would require universal adherence to, rather than the national security state's denigration of, principles that, after the Second World War, briefly coalesced in the case against the accused at Nuremberg. The alternative to some global rule of law, however rudimentary, is incarnate in the present status quo. Without any provisions to enforce with some consistency the content of international law, relations in the international community are ultimately governed by little more than ad hoc political arrangements based on nothing more than what is politically expedient for the powerful.

In this international arena, there is as yet no consistency in determining when the doctrine of national sovereignty is to be upheld or transgressed in the face of gross human rights violations. In 1999 that inconsistency was dramatically clarified in the complex politics surrounding the decision of the US-dominated North Atlantic Treaty Organization to violate international law through the conduct of a bombing campaign on the strategic infrastructures of Yugoslavia. Like the US invasion of Iraq four years later, NATO's bombing campaign involved clear violations of the international law vesting the UN Security Council with the final power to authorize legal warfare. NATO's bombing campaign went forward with the promise that this military campaign was to advance the application of some higher law. Michael Ignatieff, a parliamentarian and former Harvard professor who has sought the job of Canadian prime minister, was one prominent voice among those who sought to justify the illegal bombing as a necessary expedient to counter the incursions directed largely by Christian Serbs against Muslim Albanians settled in Kosovo.[92] Ignatieff and many others justified this stance as a necessary action to counter violence that many described as "ethnic cleansing." The term, "ethnic cleansing" emerged from the conflicts in the Balkans during the 1990s. While this combination of words is new, the activities they describe are very old. They point to a genre of crime against humanity that finds one of its most classic examples in the US government's implementation in the late 1830s of Indian removal, ultimately through the force of federal arms. Indian removal was pressed forward by the US government in direct contravention of its own treaties with America's original title holders as well as a very explicit ruling of its own Supreme Court.

Evarts has acquired the aura of a prophet for foreseeing that there would be large and longstanding implications in the decision to allow politics to dominate law in the implementation of Indian removal. Subsequent developments on the planet have seemingly fulfilled his prediction. He anticipated that "violating the most solemn engagement which it is in the power of the [US] government to make" would indeed contribute significantly to the confirmation of "force" as the ultimate "arbiter" in the making of future history.[93] To simplify a very complex series of episodes, there is a clear line of consistency linking Indian removal and the Trail of Tears in the late 1830s to NATO's bombing of Yugoslavia in 1999, to the US invasion and occupation of Iraq, and to the incarceration of an unknown number of individuals in a worldwide network of ghost prisons. There is no doubt, moreover, that Adolf Hitler was an avid student of Indian removal, an episode that provided him with an example and a precedent for the onslaught of state terror directed at Jews, Slavs, and others in the debacle that has come to be known as the Holocaust.

The debate over Indian removal raised many of the same issues that arose in the earlier debate conducted in the sixteenth century in the metropolitan centres of the Spanish Empire over whether the Indigenous peoples could with legitimacy be unilaterally dispossessed, not only of their ancestral lands but also of control over their very persons through the institution of slavery. Accordingly, the internal debate within the United States on Indian removal at this formative moment in the genesis of the informal American empire had a comparable significance in world history to the elaborate trial at Valladolid in 1550–51. What place would be afforded to the human rights of Indigenous peoples of the Americas as Western civilization secured a new bastion of power through its transatlantic leap?[94] In his eloquent defence of the rights of Indigenous peoples, Evarts played a role within Protestant America that was similar to that of the Roman Catholic priest Bartolome de Las Casas in the proceedings at Valladolid. Evarts became the voice of conscience and human rights at this most significant moment in the imperial republic's reckoning with the great ethical, political, and legal questions that had first arisen for Christendom and the Occident in the light of Christopher Columbus's "discovery" of 1492. His failure to win the day with his arguments constitutes a significant episode in the Aboriginal history of the United States of America.

There is great irony in how so much of the most spirited, non-Aboriginal defence of the principles of Aboriginal and treaty rights has emanated from the mouths and pens of Christian clergymen. That irony attends the complexities surrounding the theology of the specific Protestant tradition both embraced and embodied by Evarts. In the early years, the Calvinistic beliefs of New England's Puritan founders often translated into interpretations of the providential mission assigned to God's Chosen People. The Puritan founders of New England frequently interpreted their view of themselves as God's "elect," selected to perform a special task in the world, as the basis of a divinely sanctioned charter to dispossess and push aside the country's Indigenous peoples. That Puritan conviction helped to establish the philosophical basis of what would later come to be known as Manifest Destiny, the national creed that drew the nation westwards and outwards towards new frontiers of mind, matter, and relationship.[95]

Evarts devised and advanced an entirely different interpretation of Protestant principles. In his theology, the special favour granted by God to the United States gave the country special responsibilities to live up a higher moral standard than the rest of humanity. Again and again Evarts predicted that God's Elect would experience a terrible fall from His grace if they failed to live up to the unique responsibilities they had inherited from the way the founders of the United States had entered the main currents of global history. In his evangelical estimation, the providential character of the American nation's unique calling imposed a divinely mandated require-ment to render justice to the country's Indigenous peoples. This national mission was pictured as integral to the Creator's plan to make the people of the United States become instruments of a global dominion of Christian benevolence. Indeed, as the country that most fully embodied the marriage of the Reformation's spirit with the Enlightenment's revolutionary zeal, the United States faced in the question of Indian removal its most profound test. Could the young republic live up to the great ideals of democracy and human rights with which the nation's makers had so extravagantly identi-fied in their founding rhetoric?

In staking out the principled high ground, Evarts saw himself as defend-ing not only the Cherokee but also the reputation and actions of the found-ers of the American nation. He was particularly offended by the arguments of those who sought to "dishonor Washington" – those seeking to justify Indian removal through advancing positions that treated as law breakers and liars all those law makers involved in formulating and ratifying federal treaties with Indigenous peoples. As he saw it, "Washington was neither a usurper, nor an oppressor," just as all those US senators who had ratified treaties with Indian nations were not "novices or cheats." Instead, asserted Evarts, the "eminent men" who had established the rules for the recogni-tion of Indian title and for the negotiation of federal Indian treaties had "labored to make every part of their political system harmonize with every other part."[96]

THE TRAIL OF TEARS, INTERNATIONAL LAW, AND THE CRISIS OF AMERICAN FEDERALISM

The complexity of the religious politics surrounding the Indian removal question increased after 1831. That year the Reverend Samuel A. Worcester, a missionary in the employment of the American Board of Commissioners for Foreign Missions, was arrested in the Cherokee Nation's territory. Worcester's alleged crime was that he had refused to obtain a licence from the state government of Georgia to live and work among the Cherokee. He believed that the Georgia government did not have the constitutional authority to impose state jurisdiction on Cherokee people and lands. The imprisonment by the state of Georgia of a dedicated Christian missionary temporarily created some conflicts for those Christian activists aligned in support of Indian removal. The state of Georgia had already asserted its jurisdiction by trying and executing a Cherokee man named Corn Tassel for the crime of murder. The fact that officials in the Georgia government had now attempted to criminalize a non-Aboriginal missionary to demonstrate the scope of their assumed power over the Cherokee and their remaining lands gave pause to clerics, such as Isaac McCoy, who were publicly in favour of moving Indigenous peoples from their homes east of the Mississippi.

Georgia's attempt to criminalize Worcester provided the major test case on whether there was any genuine constitutional basis for Indian removal. The verdict given in *Worcester v. Georgia* in 1832 by Chief Justice John Marshall left no doubt about where the US Supreme Court stood on this matter. Marshall ruled that the state of Georgia had absolutely no power to impose its authority between the Cherokee and the federal government. Such an intervention by a state government was deemed to be "repugnant to the Constitution, laws, and treaties of the United States." Here Marshall attempted to make a definition of the legal status of Aboriginal polities in North America. He described them as "distinct people, divided into separate nations, independent of each other, and the rest of the world, having institutions of their own, and governing themselves by their own laws." In explaining the pre-eminence of federal treaties with Indigenous peoples over the claims and assertions made by the government of Georgia, Marshall seems to have adopted the basic principles outlined by Jeremiah Evarts in the William Penn essays. The chief jurist explained: "The Constitution by declaring treaties already made, as well as those to be made, to be the supreme law of the land, has adopted and sanctioned the previous treaties with the Indian nations, and consequently admits their rank among those powers capable of making treaties." The act on the Aboriginal side of entering into a treaty relationship "was that of a nation claiming and receiving the protection of one more powerful, not that of individuals abandoning their national character, and submitting as subjects to the laws of a master." Like Evarts, Chief Justice Marshall drew on European examples to illustrate the point. "A weak State in order to provide for its safety," said the ruling, "may place itself under the protection of one more powerful without stripping itself of the right of government, and ceasing to be a State."[97]

The response that President Andrew Jackson is reputed to have made to *Worcester v. Georgia* dramatizes his concerted determination to afford preference to the politics rather than the law of Indian affairs: "Well, John Marshall has made his decision, now let him enforce it."[98] The Jackson administration proved unrelenting in its zeal to enforce the Indian removal law passed by Congress in spite of the judiciary's clear indication that such action was inconsistent with both the Constitution and the Indian treaties of the United States. In pressing forward their illegal but politically expedient policies, federal officials sought to identify those Aboriginal groups and individuals who would accept money payments to put their signatures on treaty documents that gave the appearance of Indian sanction to the implementation of Indian removal.[99] As early as 1825 federal authorities made a cash-for-land exchange with a small Creek faction already resolved to pick up stakes and move beyond the Mississippi. The leader of this faction was William McIntosh, a slave owner and US soldier who had fought under General Andrew Jackson in the War of 1812. As retribution for his role in sanctioning a very dubious ceding treaty made at his own Indian Springs resort hotel, McIntosh was sentenced to death and assassinated by Creek patriots. A similar fate was visited on John Ridge, who had led the small Cherokee minority willing to cooperate with the federal government on Indian removal. In 1835 the Ridge faction negotiated the Treaty of New Echota, an act that carried with it a death sentence for its principal Indian proponent.

The largest Cherokee group, led by John Ross, held tenaciously to their homes until they were forced from them by authorities of both the state and the federal governments. These families faced the added humiliation of being displaced by those Georgia citizens who had been awarded in a state lottery with ownership of the Cherokee farms in freehold tenure. The displacement of the Cherokee, as well as of the other "Civilized Tribes" – the Creek, Choctaw, Chickasaw, and Seminole – was part of a larger process involving all manner of forced and voluntary relocations.[100] While some Aboriginal groups and individuals in the Old Northwest sought new homes in the area of present-day Oklahoma and Kansas, others fled north of the Great Lakes, where most sought refuge in the scattered Anishinabek communities of Upper Canada. In 1836 British authorities designated Manitoulin Island as a large Indian reserve that, it was anticipated, would receive several thousand Indian refugees from the United States. In designating Manitoulin Island as a place of asylum, especially for the families of the Indian veterans of the War of 1812, imperial authorities served the Indigenous peoples of the northern Mississippi Valley notice that they would have to move to what remained of British North America in order to continue to receive their annual tribute of "presents" from the Crown's Indian Department. These presents can be conceived of as a kind of military pension delivered by the Crown to its Indian allies. The fact that these presents included guns and ammunition provided the basis for especially volatile exchanges of diplomatic correspondence between the foreign affairs offices of Great Britain and the United States. In that era, both governments tended to share a common determination not to allow their Indian policies to become sources of international tension.

As the geopolitical upheavals that characterized eastern North America between the French and Indian War and the War of 1812 subsided and as the border between the United States and British North America became increasingly stable and calm, the governments of both regimes settled into new patterns of relations with the continent's Indigenous peoples. Both regimes were increasingly less preoccupied with the treatment of Indigenous peoples as either military allies or enemies of their respective governments and were ever more prone to treat Indians as wards of their federal polities. As "Indian affairs" became identified as an area of domestic rather than international concern, the Indigenous peoples in close contact with Euro-American settlements were treated as non-voting subjects of US or British law – even though this tendency conflicted constitutionally with the continuing practice of entering into treaty covenants with them. The treaty-making act, even if only to obtain Indian sanction for Indian removal, formally continued the international personality of both federal and Crown relations with the peoples and governments of North America's remaining Indian Country. Accordingly, the conduct of Indian affairs moved yet more deeply into a constitutional twilight zone between international and domestic jurisdiction, between the competing orbits of regional and central authority, between law and politics.[101]

The Monroe Doctrine helped to cloak the implementation of the Indian removal policies of the 1830s in the claim that the United States was acting within the framework of its own domestic sphere. Even at the time, however, Jeremiah Evarts and others pointed out that a national crime of this enormity could not help but have wide and longstanding consequences in determining the character of the United States' relations with the international community. There could not help but be unforeseen ramifications from the execution of such a consequential policy that so clearly violated both the US Constitution and international law. A new light is shed on the history of Indian removal in the United States by the growing recognition internationally that the doctrine of national sovereignty must be subordinated to the enforcement of a higher law of human rights, especially when it comes to the crimes of genocide and ethnic cleansing. With crimes against humanity of this magnitude, what statutes of limitations should apply? How can African or Asian perpetrators of genocide and ethnic cleansing be brought to justice in an evolving system of international law without any formal process of reckoning with the ethnic cleansing that is so integral to the history and present geopolitical shape of the Americas generally and of the United States specifically?

The Trail of Tears is the name given to the central drama that took place as the culminating act of one of the most sweeping acts of territorial reorganization ever attempted at any time on any continent. The forced march in 1838 of the largest part of the displaced Cherokee was but one element of a complex saga of ethnic cleansing that unfolded at intervals over the first half of the nineteenth century. The Indian removal policies of the United States eventually uprooted over 100,000 Native people from their Aboriginal lands. At least thirty distinct nationalities were displaced in this way. In the 1830s and 1840s Native Americans left about 100 million acres of their reserved lands east of the Mississippi. The land they received as compensation in the West was, of course, already the Aboriginal territory of other Indigenous peoples. Indians west of the Mississippi had no formal part in instituting the policy of Indian removal, which made the reapportionment of their own home regions the key to the plan. At one point, 13,000 men, women, and children from the Five Civilized Tribes waited together at Memphis under the authority of federal removal agents for steamboat transportation across the Mississippi.[102]

The controversies embodied in the genesis of, and federal non-compliance with, the case of *Worcester v. Georgia* clarify the pivotal character of Indian affairs in determining the balance of power between state and federal authorities in the United States. Clearly, the federal government had gained a pre-eminence over state governments largely through the constitutional powers it had acquired in the Northwest Ordinance of 1787 to acquire Aboriginal title through treaty or by waging war on Indigenous peoples on the new republic's western frontiers. The imploding frontiers of Indian Country thus became zones of federal rather than state aggrandizement. This centralization of authority over Indian affairs had deep roots in the Aboriginal history of British North America. One of the main reasons behind the American Revolution had been the determination to take the power to govern western expansion away from the British king and to redeposit it in a new sovereign authority indigenous to the continent. The capacity to govern the westward movement of Euro-American settlements over broad swaths of North America's temperate zone was a rich vehicle of economic clout and a powerful source of political patronage. The resulting investment of centralized authority in imperial Washington held an important key to deciding the future role in the world of the United States – a polity that developed a distilled, high-octane version of the expansionary energy of its British imperial parent.

Because constitutional control over the conduct of relations with Indigenous peoples represents a touchstone in the ascendance of federal authority over state authority, the insistence of the government of Georgia that it possessed the jurisdiction to extinguish Cherokee land tenure was aimed ultimately at constraining the power of Washington. The Georgia government's assault on the constitutional constructs linking the continent's original title holders directly to the institutions of imperial Washington was one part of a more broadly based attack on the central organs of US federalism. The goal of the states' rights movement was to limit, reduce, neutralize, or destroy all obstacles to the expanded expression of state sovereignty. Georgia's assertions were aimed particularly at the jurisdiction of the Supreme Court, a national institution whose very existence implicitly checked the principle of unlimited state sovereignty. This hostility to the Supreme Court became manifest in a political campaign to eliminate it through the enactment of a constitutional amendment. This most radical project of the states' rights movement was centred in, but not limited to, those jurisdictions in the American South whose laws sanctioned slavery.

The lobby to eliminate the Supreme Court gave rise to a lobby to defend it. During the most intense phase of the conflict between the Cherokee and the state of Georgia, the court's defenders purchased advertising space to assert, "Once deprive the Court of power of determining constitutional questions, and the Legislatures of the States will be let loose from all control, and as interest or passion may influence them, will reduce the National Government to a state of dependence and decrepitude, which would be more characteristic of a feeble colony than that of a large, powerful, independent nation."[103] In his decision to ignore the ruling of the Supreme Court in the case of *Worcester v. Georgia*, President Andrew Jackson, the top official of the national government, seemed to be siding with the proponents of states' rights. The apparent weakness at the centre of the US federal system drove Chief Justice Marshall to pessimism. He privately mused: "I yield slowly and reluctantly to the conviction that the Constitution cannot last. I had supposed that North of the Potomack a firm and solid government competent to the security of rational liberty might be preserved. Even that now seems doubtful. The case of the South seems to me to be desperate. Our opinions are incompatible with a united government even among ourselves. The Union has been prolonged thus far by miracles. I fear they cannot continue."[104]

The crisis over the human and constitutional rights of the Cherokee anticipated how the crisis over the human and constitutional rights of African-American slaves would lead to a violent fracture in the United States' federal system in 1861. In exposing some of the basic schisms that would eventually break into open conflict between the North and the South, the split over Cherokee rights in the 1830s anticipated the coming US Civil War. Conflicts over the status to be afforded Indian peoples and their Aboriginal lands have historically been extremely divisive in Anglo-America. Disputes over the relationship among the Cherokee, Georgia, and the US government, for instance, were driven by disagreements similar to those that provoked Bacon's Rebellion against the colonial government of Virginia. Where the makers of this rebellion in 1675–76 rejected even the Crown's very limited protections of Aboriginal rights, similar objections motivated the Anglo-American rebels to reject imperial policy in the lead up to the American Revolution. The Royal Proclamation of 1763 and the *Quebec Act* of 1774 were provocations that found a response in the linkage of anti-Indian and anti-imperial language in the Declaration of Independence.

The negative response to the Royal Proclamation is best embodied in the violent actions of the Paxton Boys. In December 1763, just as news of the proclamation was spreading in the backcountry of the Thirteen Colonies, a group of vigilantes from Paxton, Pennsylvania, swept down on the Moravian Indian mission at Conestoga Manor on the Susquehanna River. There they killed six innocent victims in their opening act of terror. The Paxton Boys then broke into a workhouse in Lancaster to murder fourteen more Moravian Indians who had been given refuge there. On the basis of these actions, the Paxton Boys gained both fame and notoriety. With their numbers swelling, they marched on Philadelphia, where they demanded the removal of Indians from the backcountry and greater representation in the local assembly. They were treated by Benjamin Franklin, Joseph Galloway, and other officials not as murderers but as a legitimate delegation presenting a legitimate petition. The Paxton Boys and many Scots-Irish frontiersmen of their ilk would be well represented in General

George Washington's Continental Army. Their revolt against the Royal Proclamation and the British government between 1763 and 1765 antici- pated the outbreak of a more general civil war in British North America.[105] They were animated by many of the same hostilities that caused Bacon's Rebellion in Virginia in 1676. From Bacon's Rebellion to the Paxton Boys' rejection of the Royal Proclamation of 1763 to President Andrew Jackson's revolt against the authority of the Supreme Court and its ruling on the case of *Worcester v. Georgia*, the pattern of resistance is clear. Until the era of John Collier's Indian New Deal, any initiative on the part of government to entrench and enforce the protection of Indian rights was met with hostility in that portion of Anglo-America that gave rise to the creation and west- ward expansion of the United States.

In an address in 1830 to the people of the United States, the General Council of the Cherokee Nation left a poignant protest against the injustice the people faced as the pressure grew to eject them from their homes. The council members anticipated that the Cherokee would not be well received by the Indigenous peoples of their adopted territory. "They would regard us intruders," the authors predicted, "and look upon us with an evil eye." The new land would contain "neither the scenes of our childhood, nor the graves of our fathers." The Cherokee Council concluded the message by pointing out the ironic parallels linking their own plight and the epi- sodes in history that first led the Puritans to cross the Atlantic in search of freedom. Referring to the citizens of the American nation, the Cherokee implored: "We pray them to remember that, for the sake of principle, their forefathers were *compelled* to leave, therefore *driven* from the old world, and that the winds of persecution wafted them over the great waters, and landed them on the shores of the new world, when the Indian was the sole lord and proprietor of these extensive domains." The course of history had reversed the roles. The Indigenous peoples were now persecuted by the descendants of those who had come to America to escape persecution. The Indigenous peoples were humbled to the point where it seemed all that was left for them was to plead for "a spot of earth, a portion of our own patrimonial possessions, on which to live and die in peace."[106]

CHAPTER SEVEN

Pushing Westward

Just as Islam needs to be understood in its complexity, so does US
power, which is at least as complex ... We must not repeat the follies
of Napoleon and Hitler in the heartlands of Eurasia.
> Peter Dale Scott, *Drugs, Oil, and War: The United States
> in Afghanistan, Colombia, and Indochina, 2003*

CONQUEST AND CAPITAL IN THE MAKING OF
THE US EMPIRE

Imagine a filmic dissolve from the 475 forts built over the course of the
superpower's transcontinental expansion to the 725 acknowledged US
military bases in 130 countries around the world. This blending of images
goes a long way to suggest the nature of the links of Aboriginal history connecting the US conquest of Indian Country to the US government's more
recent quest in the international arena for Full Spectrum Dominance and
Total Information Awareness. In *The Sorrows of Empire*, Chalmers A. Johnson
points to this global network of US military bases, together with the golf
courses and soldiers' pleasure palaces that surround them, as key embodiments of the current state of US imperialism.[1] As he sees it, "the military
base is today's equivalent of the colony in the past."[2] The number, 725,
leaves out many military installations, such as the secret bases in Uzbekistan
and Kyrgystan, that are integral to US plans to dominate the vast reserves
of the Caspian Sea area in the heart of Eurasia.[3] It omits US installations in
England disguised as Royal Air Force bases, along with the unknown number of "ghost prisons" all over the world, including some on US war ships,
where "ghost prisoners" are incarcerated, usually without charge.

The merger of the massive US system of privatized prisons with the
War on Terror was advanced in November 2001 when George W. Bush
announced the US government's intention to disregard the principles governing national sovereignty since the Treaty of Westphalia in 1648. Under
Military Order No. 1, the US president formalized the position that the
sovereign status of all countries would henceforth be subordinate to the
global jurisdiction of the United States. As Isabel Hilton reported in *The
Guardian*, President Bush "gave himself the right, in defiance of national
and international law, to detain indefinitely any non-US citizen anywhere in
the world."[4] In announcing this position and then aggressively acting on it,

President Bush advanced the claim that the power of his office extended to the combined functions of the world's chief prosecutor, judge, jury, executioner, and prison warden.

In blurring the lines between the US president's domestic authority in the so-called Homeland and his or her global role, George Bush re-enacted some of the same patterns of policy that were earlier manifest in federal efforts to negate the international character of North America's Indian wars. The effects of the Indian wars on the genesis of the US military establishment have been indirect as well as direct. As we have seen, the treatment of Indians in the transcontinental expansion of the United States formed one of the models Adolf Hitler drew on in his regime's military push into the vast expanses of Russia. Hitler often compared Slavs, but especially Russians, to the "Red Indians" of North America. Similarly, he justified the eastward expansion of his own regime as an extension of the same sort of imperative that the US government had used in its transcontinental expansion. As Hitler and many of his advisers saw it, the Red Communist Slavs and the Red Indians were both inferior peoples whose destiny was ultimately to be pushed aside and eliminated to make way for the expansionary enterprises of the world's dominant race. With the aim of pushing history along in order to realize the imagined Manifest Destiny of the Nordic master race, the Third Reich was organized with the involvement of many US-based companies as a military-industrial complex. This cooperation evolved as a living laboratory in the organization of the state and a favoured group of corporate cartels as a vehicle of conquest. The attempt to minimize competition through monopoly capitalism was seen as a way of channelling competitive energy away from internal economic contestation and towards the quest for a centrally controlled regime of domination over expanding realms of subject peoples and territories.

This trajectory of experimentation continues to this day to be reflected in the power alignments, shape, and activities of the world's dominant military-industrial complex. As Kevin Phillips observes, this polity has become increasingly more elaborate and more oriented to advancing the interests of the private parties who have integrated their businesses into the rise of the terror economy and the national security state. Phillips argues that "the revitalized national security state that resurged in the 1980s, and then again after 2001, transcended Eisenhower's definition of the military-industrial complex, which had not mentioned the intelligence agencies." In its more recent manifestation, the national security state eschewed the balance between capital and labour that was integral to the New Deal and to Vice-President Henry Wallace's proposal for a Century of the Common Man. Instead, the national security state favoured "Sun Belt bases, non-unionized high-tech workforces, de facto private armies, and every kind of subcontractor possible." Phillips highlights the subordination of the ideals of public service to the values of private interest by noting that the 4,000 intelligence analysts at the CIA's Northern Virginia headquarters are "dwarfed" by 40,000 analysts who work in the region for businesses that have government intelligence contracts.

In "the huge honeypot" where the conduct of the Global War on Terror is planned and implemented, the massive Halliburton cartel has assumed a logistical centrality similar to that of the IG Farben Company in the Axis of fascism before 1945.[5] And the expanding contingents of mercenary soldiers employed by Blackwater have become shock troops in the push to further energize and privatize the violent operations of the military-industrial complex. Halliburton's former CEO, Richard Cheney, became the vice-president of the United States in 2001. Blackwater's founder, Erik Prince, drew much of the inspiration for the corporatized militarism of his enterprises from his own deep involvement in the religious politics that infused the US government's resort to more fundamentalist motifs of empire building with the aura of Christian evangelism.[6] One of the many hundreds of federal contracts awarded since September 11 to Halliburton went to its former subsidiary Kellog Brown and Root (KBR). In January 2006 KBR was given $400 million to begin the process of establishing new military detention camps within the United States. In a press release, KBR officials referred to their project as preparation for "an emergency influx of immigrants or to support the rapid development of new programs."[7]

The proliferation of ghost prisons, now possibly inside as well as outside the United States, forms one element in the expanding operations of the world's dominant military-industrial complex. William Rosenau, former policy adviser at the State Department, has commented on the hidden character of much US military intervention in the twenty-first century. He claimed that the US operations in Afghanistan and Iraq after 9/11 constitute only the "tip of the iceberg" compared with many hundreds of more covert operations pressed forward in the name of the War on Terror in places such as Uzbekistan, Azerbaijan, Colombia, Chad, Niger, Mali, Malaysia, Indonesia, the Philippines, Bulgaria, Romania, Djibouti in northeastern Africa, and the Pankisi Gorge in the border region between Georgia and Chechnya. Developments in Djibouti illustrate more general patterns. According to Doug Saunders of the *Globe and Mail*, over 100,000 people were expelled from Djibouti in order to secure the ground for a major US military spy installation and to solidify the political turf of the US puppet regime of President Ismael Omar Guelleh. Similarly, the superpower provided the cover for Mauritian president, Maaouya Ould Ahmed Taya, "to ban the opposition" and to "torture some leaders to death in prison, with full US support." Saunders continues, "All across Southeast Asia, this pattern is being repeated: fragile democracy movements ... are being menaced by armies and governments emboldened by the War on Terrorism." He concludes that this web of "stealth, spy craft, diplomacy and dirty tricks ... is more like the Cold War, which the CIA types like to consider World War Three."

Those engaged in the more recent mobilization of US global power in the name of "counterterrorism" have often referred to their missions as elements of yet another world war. "We are in the midst of World War Four," General Tommy Franks is reported to have announced in 2003 to an Addis Ababa audience before "imploring them to arrest local Islamist leaders in exchange for $100-million in aid." As Steven Simon, a former US National Security Council director who has worked as a private consultant for the Pentagon and the RAND Corporation, observed, one of the "main griev-ances" of these "terrorist groups" is that "the United States is consorting with evil regimes that repress their people." Simon compared the Cold War to the much more volatile and unpredictable nature of the War on Terror, one where the enemy is less "tangible" and where there is no upward limit to the escalation of conflict such as that which had previously been imposed by the system of mirrored nuclear weaponry configured to create "mutually assured destruction."[8]

The North American roots of the superpower's imperial adventurism in the Global War on Terror go far deeper than the expedition of the US Army's Corps of Discovery led by Lewis and Clark[9] or even the events of 1776. Beneath the morphology of US history lies the experience of almost three centuries in the Western Hemisphere where the encounter between colonists and Indigenous peoples was absolutely central to the course of European empire building. In *The Dominion of War: Empire and Liberty in North America, 1500–2000,* Fred Anderson and Andrew Cayton attempt to integrate five centuries of the history of imperial relations with Indigenous peoples into the matrix of more recent US history. With particular empha-sis on the Indian wars, the Seven Years' War, the Mexican-American War, and the Spanish-American War, the authors endeavour to demonstrate the importance of military conquest in shaping the ethos, psychology, and global orientation of the United States. With the reality of the contentious US inva-sion and occupation of Iraq in the background of their literary effort, these authors exclaimed in 2005, "Now, we think, is a proper occasion to con-template the possibility that the United States was conceived in empire as well as liberty." As Anderson and Cayton see it, this relationship between liberty and empire is complex, given that "the power-abhorring ideology of resistance, republicanism, formed the basis of political culture in what soon proved one of the most dynamically expansionist territorial empires in world history." Only by coming to grips with the idea of their country as an "Imperial Republic" can citizens of the United States properly orient them-selves to how they are viewed by many observers in the rest of the world. To help this process of self-reflection along, Anderson and Cayton seek "to rear-range the landscape of historical memory and meaning by emphasizing the importance of the wars Americans have fought less to preserve liberty than to extend the power of the United States *in the name* of liberty."[10]

The interpretations advanced in *Dominion of War* stand in stark contrast to the theories outlined by Niall Ferguson in *Colossus: The Price of America's Empire.* With a single sentence, Ferguson waves away the whole imperial history underlying the future superpower's most formative episode of territorial expansion. "The Indian Wars," he writes, "were doubtless cruel but they were small wars."[11] To Anderson and Cayton there was nothing small or insignificant about "the two-and-a-half-century-long era during which native peoples played a determining role in American historical development."[12] Beginning with a study of Samuel de Champlain's entry into the military alliance linking the Hurons, Algonquins, and Abenaki against the "Imperial Iroquois," Anderson and Cayton argue that the "success" of France "as an imperial power in North America depended on accommodation with, not dominion over, the native peoples."[13] The authors go on to demonstrate in considerable detail that the French-Aboriginal alliances at the basis of Canada's political economy were duplicated in different ways by the Dutch, Spanish, and Pennsylvanian governments. The leadership of each of these polities sought to incorporate different alignments of Aboriginal allies and trading partners into their respective colonial projects. The Indigenous peoples of North America were not pawns in these schemes. Instead, Aboriginal groups and individuals were active participants in the making of North American history. In advancing this case, Anderson and Cayton add their voices to those of Bruce Trigger, Francis Jennings, and Richard White, to name only a few. Many Aboriginal groups and individuals sought to shape events and to advance their own interests and enterprises with full consciousness of their own powers of agency, their own inherent rights of self-determination.

The phase of North American history when Aboriginal-imperial wars and alliances figured most prominently reached a climax between 1754 and 1765. The imperial conflict that unfolded over this period placed the balance of power in the hands of the Indigenous peoples of the Ohio Valley and Great Lakes area. This Aboriginal group was at the strategic core of a major military contest pitting Britain against France. The conflagration is often remembered in the United States as the French and Indian War; otherwise, it is generally described as the Seven Years' War, followed by the series of events associated with Pontiac and the Indian Confederacy of Canada. The British defeat of the French Empire removed a fundamental division that had previously blocked the achievement of confederated unity in the Indian Country of North America's interior. Very soon, however, fresh schisms appeared among the non-Aboriginals because of the new policies of imperial Britain as formalized in the Royal Proclamation of 1763. One of its purposes was to persuade the Indigenous peoples formerly aligned with the French to abandon their resistance and to integrate into an expanded British North America on the basis of law and consent. The disagreement between Anglo-America's divergent imperial factions would culminate in the revolutionary reconstitution of the most expansionary side in the conflict as the founding citizens of United States of America. In their conclusion, Anderson and Cayton attempt to characterize the importance of Indian affairs in the period leading up to the creation of the Imperial Republic. They write:

For two and a half centuries after Europeans arrived in North America, empire was a fact of life on a continent where relations between peoples were continually shaped and reshaped by warfare. Native attempts to survive and prosper by manipulating the colonizers and maneuvering between powers seeking to extend their imperial sway knit together the story of those centuries and their forgotten wars. They are of enormous importance ... Through the first half of North America's history it remained unclear that any one empire would dominate the continent or that Indians were doomed to subordination. Two of the three colonial regimes that survived to the middle of the eighteenth century depended on native peoples for their survival; the Indians themselves demonstrated extraordinary resourcefulness and skill in adapting to the demands of life in an imperial world. At the close of the Age of Colonization and Conflict, Britain's subjects were unique among European colonists in that they cared less about trading with the Indians, exploiting their labor, or saving their souls than appropriating their lands.[14]

The final sentence of this commentary neglects the actions and attitudes of those "British subjects" who organized their political economy around the fur trade of British imperial Canada. This elaborate commercial system was taken over from the voyageurs, coureurs de bois, military men, and priests connected to the elaborate fur trade of New France. With the collaboration of the British Imperial Indian Department, a key division of the British military establishment in North America, the fur trade of British imperial Canada was edified and extended after the Seven Years' War and again after the American Revolution. In particular, Anderson and Cayton fail to take proper account of the importance of the Montreal-based North West Company and the London-based Hudson's Bay Company in creating the coast-to-coast-to-coast network of British imperial commerce and communications throughout vast parts of the continent's still vibrant Indian and Inuit Country. The Euro-American fur traders and their Aboriginal families and trading partners tended overwhelmingly to line up against the Imperial Republic during the American Revolution and the War of 1812. They were instrumental in the defence of British North America and the Indian Country of Canada. Because of their actions in business, war, and cross-cultural exchange and adaptation, the British Crown was able to retain some jurisdiction in a number of territories that were stitched together during the second half of the nineteenth century to form the transcontinental Dominion of Canada.

This criticism aside, however, *The Dominion of War* sheds much informative light on the relationship of US history to earlier imperial history. The authors' narrative helps to illuminate the importance and character of Aboriginal history in the emergence of the United States from the imperial colonization of Indian Country over many generations of European empire building. Much Aboriginal history deals directly with the history of Indigenous peoples. Aboriginal history, however, need not be limited to the past experiences of peoples who are indigenous to particular places. It can, instead, encompass episodes, events, and themes that cut broadly across the experiences of all kinds of people. Seen in this broader context, Aboriginal history emphasizes the original sources of change, the founding acts of creation. It assumes that it is extremely important to understand the convergence of energies creating the origins of new institutions, systems, societies, or technologies. Aboriginal history is important because originating forces tend to establish trends, traditions, patterns, paradigms, and propensities that are re-enacted again and again in different contexts over the passage of time.

An excellent illustration of a formative episode of Aboriginal history lies in the emergence of the United States from a disagreement among British imperialists over how to incorporate Indigenous peoples and their ancestral territories into the constitutional and economic fabric of British North America. The United States resulted from the triumphant rebellion by one side in a conflict that came down ultimately to a power struggle over who was going to govern westward expansion and who was going to profit most richly from the transformation of earth into property. To the founders of the United States, it was a violation of common sense to treat the interior of North America as a British imperial Indian reserve and as a fur-trade hinterland of the mercantilistic metropolis of Montreal. In the Thirteen Anglo-American colonies along the Atlantic seaboard, the sovereignty of the British imperial Crown was replaced by a new type of sovereign, a new type of Imperial Republic that would facilitate more rapid Euro-American expansion, accompanied by an accelerated pace of territorial privatization to increase the new polity's seed capital. The ramifications of this act of inventing something original are still ricocheting across the planet. The forces that converged in the birth of the United States have been continually renewed in patterns of expansionism that replicate in different environments the dynamics of the superpower's Aboriginal beginnings. As Reginald Horsman has affirmed in *Race and Manifest Destiny*: "In dealing with the Indians the United States began to formulate a rationale of expansion which was readily adaptable to the needs of an advance over other peoples and to a world role."[15]

Like Anderson and Cayton, Horsman considers the treatment of Indigenous peoples as an integral feature in the process that has helped to orient the United States to the rest of the world. Other commentators, including Richard Drinnon and Jack Forbes, have similarly transcended the constraints that limit the scope of much writing on US Indian policy. Forbes in particular has directed his transcendent scholarship against those nervous impulses of reactionary parochialism that would enclose Native American Studies within narrow enclaves of intellectual domesticity. He has observed that the study of the treatment of Indian peoples provides "a looking-glass into the souls of Anglo-Americans." As he sees it, the treatment of Indigenous peoples constitutes "the most valid weather vane" in anticipating how the US government and citizenry will negotiate all sorts of transitions, both at home and internationally. "Just as meteorologists study storms out in the Pacific to predict weather patterns for the Pacific coast,"

Forbes writes, "social scientists and lay people should study Indian policy to predict political patterns for the United States."[16]

Observations similar to those of Forbes have been made by Felix S. Cohen, the legal historian whose *Handbook of Federal Indian Law*, published in 1942, is still indispensable.[17] "The Indian," he wrote, "plays much the same role in our American society that Jews played in Germany. Like the miner's canary, the Indian marks the shifts from fresh air to poison gas in our political atmosphere; and our treatment of Indians even more than our treatment of other minorities, reflects the rise and fall of our democratic faith."[18] Cohen was a pillar in the administration of the Indian New Deal of the 1930s, and, in his work as the Indian New Deal's leading legal strategist, he worked under John Collier. The sometimes messianic reflections made by Collier on the role in world civilization of the Aboriginal civilization of the Americas anticipated many of the major themes in the debate about globalization that became more intense with the demise of the Soviet Union. In 1945 Collier wrote of US Indian policy as "a laboratory of ethnic relations." He pictured the New Deal's extension of "ethnic democracy" to Indian communities as part of the quest for alternative models to replace Eurocentric systems of colonial rule.[19] Collier's vision represents a seminal critique of assimilation and the ideals of an imaginary melting pot as the pre-eminent metaphors of US cultural policy. He questioned the imperial and monocultural assumptions underlying the ideals of US Manifest Destiny. Rather, his Indian policies pointed towards the vision of a global regime based on the multicultural self-determination of peoples. They anticipated the ideals of the Atlantic Charter and the array of international instruments that were subsequently instituted to advance the ideals broached in this seminal articulation of global juridical principles.

Collier's contribution to Roosevelt's vision of the Fourth World was largely subordinated by the empowerment during the Cold War of the national security state as the primary antidote to communist internationalism. In *Indians of the Americas*, Roxanne Dunbar Ortiz grappled with this phenomenon. She characterized the relationship of the United States to Indigenous peoples as the possible Achilles' heel of the US-centred system of global dominance that arose with the rise of the national security state following the Second World War. In 1984 she wrote: "Indians hold national territories within the US, and these unliberated nations seek self-determination. The potential for the disintegration of US power, based in part on fragmentation starting with these scattered enclaves, should not be underestimated." As Ortiz saw it, the territorial integrity of the United States was put in question by the anomalous position of Native Americans. Moreover, she added, "the mobilization of Indian peoples throughout the hemisphere challenges the artificial state entities that are the links in US political, economic and military control of the hemisphere." Ortiz concluded her volume by observing, "The US was the first and perhaps only state ever formed for the sole purpose of capital accumulation."[20]

Ortiz's conception of the centrality of capital accumulation in the genesis of the United States is consistent with the observations of Patricia Limerick. In her survey text depicting US western expansion, Limerick writes:

White Americans saw the acquisition of property as a cultural imperative, manifestly the right way to go about things. There was one appropriate way to treat the land – divide it, distribute it, register it. This relationship to physical matter seems to us so commonplace that we must struggle to avoid taking it for granted, to grasp instead the vastness of the continent and the enormous project of measuring, allocating, and record keeping involved in turning the open expanses of North America into transferable parcels of real estate. Like the settlers themselves we steadfastly believe in the social fiction that lines on the map and signatures on a deed legitimately divide the earth. Of all the persistent qualities in American history, the values attached to property retain the most power.[21]

One of the classic themes of Aboriginal history puts a spotlight of attention on encounters between Indigenous peoples and the agents of imperial societies. These encounters are rich with the possibility of creativity as well as destruction. Something new can emerge from the blending of peoples, cultures, and political economies. Taken collectively, these surges of reconfiguration in the matrix of human relations form essential elements in the process of globalization. The phenomena of first encounter tends to be reenacted as new history is made where first peoples experience the inroads of empires, successor states, and the transnational corporations whose agents operate in both the imperial cores as well as the outlying frontiers of capitalism's empire. Key aspects of this process are encompassed by the genesis of the United States, a polity whose Aboriginal history has circumscribed or, in some instances, completely terminated the Aboriginal histories of some Aboriginal societies.

The European Union represents another orientation to Aboriginal history. While much of the history of Europe was shaped by that continent's imperial enterprises, the more recent preoccupation of the European Union's architects is with forms of internal federation. It remains to be seen if the European Union will become a base of genuine opposition to the informal American empire or whether it will continue to be organized commercially and militarily as an adjunct of a US-based system of command and control.[22]

PROPRIETORSHIPS OF WHITE SUPREMACY: FROM SLAVERY, TO INDIAN REMOVAL, TO LIBERIA, TO THE GLOBALIZATION OF THE PRISON INDUSTRIAL COMPLEX

During the formative stages in the colonization of the Western Hemisphere, but particularly in the remaking of territory claimed by the United States, many of the most remarkable episodes of capitalist expansion occurred where the institution of slavery converged with the process of removing land and resources from the control of Indigenous peoples. Indeed, the genesis of slavery and the history of Aboriginal dispossession were closely intertwined throughout much of the Americas as interrelated aspects of the same process of economic transformation. During the early phases of the Columbian conquests, the means of reconstituting the ownership of land and of persons were made synonymous in a series of campaigns directed at enslaving Indians. With varying degrees of intensity, efforts to impose the shackles of human bondage on Indian people took place in the genesis of many of the Spanish, Portuguese, Dutch, French, and British colonies in the Western Hemisphere.

The enslavement of many Aboriginal groups led to their rapid decline in numbers. It also helped stimulate concerted Indian resistance to the prospect of their own extermination. A particularly rapid pace of Aboriginal genocide resulted from Spain's notorious system of forced labour in the rich silver mines of Mexico. The combined affect of Aboriginal depopulation and resistance led in due course to increases in the importation of Black slaves from West Africa. The transatlantic slave trade linking Europe, Africa, and the Americas was increasingly intertwined with the rise of the plantation economies devoted to the cultivation of sugar, cotton, and tobacco in the Western Hemisphere's more tropical regions. The cultivation of these monocultures formed the basis for systems of property entitlement and social control that emerged from this triangular pattern of international trade. So large and lucrative did the importation of African slaves become that, between 1500 and 1800, more Africans than Europeans were transported to the Americas.[23]

The Anglo-American colony of Virginia was the main site where many of the procedures, laws, and customs developed that would dominate the slave-owning jurisdictions in the United States for almost a century following the American Revolution. According to Theodore Allen, it was not until the early eighteenth century that Virginians invented the concept of "race" as the main conceptual category to govern the economic, legal, and political hierarchies of their society. To support this contention, Allen points to the history of the rebellion against the imperial government led in Virginia by Nathaniel Bacon in 1676 and 1677. Bacon's Rebellion presents an example where the interests and rights of Indians were posed against those of slaves and indentured servants in the developing political economy of Virginia's tobacco monoculture. In its later stages the revolt evolved into one expressing a degree of unity between "the English and Negroes in Arms."[24] What united a number of the rebels was their common experience of subjugation under laws that transformed their work and their persons into property entitlements of their masters. In the era of Bacon's Rebellion, both African-American slaves and Euro-American indentured servants were categorized as "bond-labourers." These exploited workers sought reforms that would not only free them from the oppression of their masters but also break up the huge holdings of the plantation owners in order to open space for their own transformation and that of their progeny into land-owning farmers.[25]

In describing the successful repression of this failed effort on the part of bond-labourers to transcend their different backgrounds in order to assert class solidarity, Allen emphasizes a statute passed in 1723 by the Virginia Assembly. That law stipulated that "no free negro, mulatto, or Indian whatsoever, shall have any vote at the election of burgesses, or any other election whatsoever."[26] The wide net thrown by this instrument of disenfranchisement helped introduce the idea of skin complexion – the concept of "race" – as a primary criteria for the apportionment of legal status in a society bringing together members whose ancestry was rooted in three different continents. Increasingly, those of European ancestry developed an exclusive, race-based idea of themselves as "whites." The racial abstraction of *whiteness* was not the same as the invented *Creole* identity. The latter was be made to apply to native-born but non-Indian populations in the Portuguese and Spanish-speaking colonies. The Creole identity could be made to apply to those of African as well as European ancestry in the genesis of Latin America.

In the English-speaking colonies, a very circumscribed identity was thus developed by those who sought to distance themselves from both Indians and African-Americans, whether nominally "free" or legally enslaved. The development of that identity was bolstered through the passage of laws and the development of theory defining "whites" as a distinct and uniquely entitled category of North American human being.[27] As the United States developed throughout the first half of the nineteenth century, many of the arguments over the legal status of slavery and of African-Americans were cloaked in the language of debate over the character of federalism. In that controversy the polemics of states' rights and state sovereignty were frequently invoked by those seeking to secure and to widen slavery's hold over a significant segment of the US political economy. Alternatively, many opponents of the United States' most peculiar institution framed their arguments in terms of the need for a strong federal authority capable of overriding the southern states' jurisdiction over slavery's legal apparatus. Even the politics of the national government, however, gave slave-owning interests an advantage in determining the outcome of federal elections. Although slaves could not vote, the constitutional negotiations of 1787 required that three-fifths of the adult male slave population must be included in the formula for counting federal ballots and apportioning tax revenues. This strange arithmetic of colour-coded gerrymandering gave added clout to non-slaves in slave-owning jurisdictions who generally used their disproportionately enlarged franchise to defend their proprietorships of White supremacy.

Nevertheless, many of slavery's fiercest opponents had little choice but to look to the federal government to advance the abolitionist cause. The US government was also seen by the opponents of Indian removal, including the likes of the Reverend Jeremiah Evarts, as the most strategic political ground for their activism. The Northwest Ordinance of 1787 as well as Indian treaties and section 8.3 of the Constitution provided the primary basis of the federal government's legal responsibility to protect the rights and titles of Indigenous peoples from state incursion. In large measure the ability of Indigenous peoples to exercise even a truncated version of their rights depended on federal recognition of Aboriginal title as well as on the federal willingness to implement those treaties that some Indian nations had contracted with the US government. The close constitutional identification of Indian peoples with federal power made the whole concept of Indian rights seem doubly menacing to champions of state sovereignty or states' rights. Prominent among them was Thomas Hart Benton, one of the first two senators elected to represent Missouri after it became a pro-slavery state in 1821. In this role Benton articulated political positions linking support of slavery with a vehement opposition to the existence of Indian rights. As a representative of what was then the United States' westernmost state, Benton candidly observed that "extending the area of slavery" required "converting Indian soil into slave soil." As he saw it, the capacity to "remove Indians" in order to make room "for the spread of slaves" required that the citizens of Missouri must "make a fair and regular stand against the encroachment of Congress upon the Sovereignty of the States."[28]

Thomas Hart Benton's life spanned a huge sweep in the history of western expansion in the United States. The "Far West" of Benton's childhood stretched towards the Blue Hills of Kentucky. His father, Jesse Benton, had participated in the land speculations of Judge Richard Henderson and Daniel Boone. In the years before the American Revolution, these initiatives involved a direct purchase of Aboriginal title from Cherokee Indians in blatant contravention of the principles of the Royal Proclamation of 1763. This illegal transaction helped clear the way for the later establishment of Kentucky.[29] The hot-blooded Benton personified much of the triumphant swagger characterizing the US bid to "win" the West. In 1813, on the eve of a Creek Red Stick attack on the US military base at Fort Mims in Mississippi Territory, Benton and his brother Jesse engaged in a gun fight with General Andrew Jackson. This showdown amid the bars and brothels of Nashville left Jackson with a wound in his left shoulder, and Benton narrowly escaped being lynched by Jackson's friends. "I'm literally in hell here," Benton wrote before escaping Nashville.[30] The repeated and much-embellished telling of the episode ended up investing the emerging politician with a gun-slinging mystique that served him well as a US senator representing voters pushing the edges of Anglo-America's settlement frontier across the Mississippi River. Benton's role in this process was to translate for imperial Washington the local politics of a slave-owning portion of the Wild West. Benton's son-in-law, John Charles Fremont, led much-publicized surveying expeditions that helped point the consciousness of the rising American nation towards Oregon, California, and the Pacific Rim.[31] In 1822 Senator

Benton represented his friends in the fur-trade conglomerate led by John Jacob Astor. The politician's aim was to persuade the federal government to abandon its own fur-trading posts throughout the vast expanses beyond Euro-American settlement. Benton promoted this agenda to advance his vision of unfettered commerce as a pre-eminent ideal that must be made to override the interventions of government in the conduct of Indian affairs.[32]

In his early years as a politician, Benton's developing sense of Manifest Destiny drew from his visits with the aging Thomas Jefferson. Jefferson had first pointed the Imperial Republic towards its transcontinental destiny with the Louisiana Purchase in 1803, followed by his sponsorship of the Lewis and Clark expedition. Unlike the studied ambivalence of his political mentor, Benton's politics favouring slavery and Indian removal were completely straightforward. The fervour of his Puritan zeal was unmistakable when he promoted "armed occupation" and "conquest" as the proper fashion to take control of Florida. In justifying this position he asserted: "The children of Israel entered the promised land, with the implements of husbandry in one hand, and the weapons of war in the other."[33] In extending these Old Testament principles to the expansion of the United States, Benton renewed the ideological heritage of the Virginian revolutionary Nathaniel Bacon. In his manifesto initiating the rebellion of 1676, Bacon had declared that all Indians were "wholly unqualified for the benefitt and Protection of the law." He maintained that even "the protected and Darling Indians" were "Robbers and Theeves and Invaders of ... our Interest and Estates."[34] The Aboriginal population that Benton was intent on uprooting from Missouri was composed of people and peoples of extremely diverse backgrounds. The families living along the western shores of the Mississippi River included Shawnee migrants who had withdrawn first from the area of Kentucky and then from the contested lands north of the Ohio River. Unlike most of the other Algonkian-speaking peoples of the eastern woodlands who had fought with Tecumseh in alliance with the British during the War of 1812, some of the Missouri Shawnee claimed they had sided with US forces.

The Indian and Métis population living around the juncture of the Mississippi and Missouri river were widely recognized for their industriousness. "These Indians," wrote Missouri's territorial delegate to Congress in 1820, "have their Houses, Towns, and farms ... Their Animals are domesticated to the place – and all their property there."[35] From Benton's perspective, this property and the Aboriginal people who held it provided a possible opening for the federal government to assert its jurisdiction within Missouri, and the continued presence of Indians and Métis on the riverfront lands threatened his ideal of state sovereignty. While Benton's antagonism towards Indians was saturated with the usual racist prejudice typical of many who shared his background, his hostility went further. He believed that the elimination of Indians from Missouri would pre-empt the possibility that the federal officials might intervene at some future date in fulfilling their legal role as trustees of Indian interests in lands and resources.

Accordingly, the politics of slavery were, as Benton frequently declared, deeply integrated with the politics of Indian removal.[36] The notion of using the Mississippi as the boundary for a transcontinental system of apartheid began working its way into the political discourse of the United States from the time of the Louisiana Purchase. As a politician representing a new US jurisdiction west of the great river, Benton took on the task of lobbying for an even more circumscribed outline of Indian Territory. That territory was to incorporate among its influx of migrants the displaced Native Americans from Benton's home jurisdiction in the trans-Mississippi West. From the early days of its statehood, therefore, Missouri became the site of an informal campaign of Indian removal that anticipated the more large-scale removals in the late 1830s. As John Mack Faragher observed of Missouri: "With impunity the state allowed squatters to steal Indian farms and appropriate their improvements." The resulting transformation in the region's character he described as a transition "from ethic mixing to ethnic cleansing ... as the brutal stick of American policy."[37]

The experience of the Native American population of Missouri epitomized the general lack of protection for Indian lives and Indian property in the United States. As William Christie MacLeod asserted in 1928 in his seminal *American Indian Frontier*, "the nastiness of the frontiersman was an actual problem for the Indian." But the "vanished ghosts of innumerable Indians" were not in a position to comment on the "cruel ... vicious ... villainy" they had experienced in the course of their termination.[38] A few Aboriginal groups were in a position to stand their ground temporarily, most notably the Cherokee with their strong connections to the powerful missionary societies. But in the end even the Cherokee had to submit. As Thomas D. Clark has noted, it came to be understood on both sides of the moving frontier "that the only course of appeal in cases of [Indian] treaty violations was with arms."[39] Brigadier-General George Crook shared this view of the realities of power governing transactions on the frontiers of western expansion. He was seen by many of his contemporaries in the late nineteenth century as "the greatest Indian fighter in American history"[40] and took the pragmatic view that "the American Indian commands respect for his rights only so long as he inspires terror from his rifle."[41]

The experiences of African-Americans and Indigenous peoples have intersected at many points in American history.[42] Often, for instance, the Indian Country beyond the frontiers of the Anglo-American settlements offered refuge for runaway slaves. Many of the early treaties between Indian groups and the Anglo-American colonies included provision aimed at averting this outcome. A treaty made in 1700 between the colony of Maryland and the Piscataway people exemplifies this pattern. It detailed, "in case any servants or slaves runaway from their masters" and thereby arrive a Piscataway town, "the Indians shall be bound to apprehend them and bring them to the next English Plantation."[43] According to William S. Willis, the fear of Black-Indian alliances was a major factor in the gradual decision to desist from enslaving Indigenous peoples in the American Southeast.[44] In spite of all the obstacles placed in the way of Indian-Black partnerships, however, many real and metaphorical marriages of Native Americans and African-Americans took place in the course of American history. These marriages became especially important in the genesis of the Seminole resistance movement. Under the leadership of Osceola and others, an intermarried complex of Native people, Black runaway slaves, and their mixed-ancestry descendants opposed through guerrilla warfare the imposition of US jurisdiction on Florida until the early 1840s.[45]

The history of Indian removal found strong parallels in the effort to encourage free Blacks in the United States to migrate eastward to the West African polity of Liberia. The dual movements to push Indians westward and to encourage Blacks to migrate eastward across the Atlantic Ocean points to the power of the propensity on the part of dominant elites to promote, maintain, and widen divisions between the two groups whose experiences most dramatically contradicted the imagery of the United States as the land of the free. These dual movements demonstrate the strength of the urge to develop the Imperial Republic as a realm of segregated spaces. The effort to encourage Black Americans who were not slaves to migrate voluntarily to West Africa gathered momentum in 1816 with the creation of the American Colonization Society (ACS). From Thomas Jefferson to James Madison, James Monroe, John Marshall, Andrew Jackson, Abraham Lincoln, and many other pillars of US governance, the ACS garnered much elite support before slavery's abolition in the American Civil War. The main force driving the ACS's policies was the perception that free Blacks might directly or inadvertently encourage Black slaves to revolt against their masters. This fear was reinforced by the powerful example posed by the founders of Haiti, who had fought to liberate themselves and their descendants from the shackles of slavery.[46] In the words of W.E.B. Du Bois, "the colonization schemes were a device to rid America of free Africans so as to fasten slavery more firmly to support the cotton kingdom."[47]

The goals of the ACS were advanced dramatically in 1857, when Liberia became an independent republic with a constitution patterned after that of the United States. The idea of Liberia as a new home for free Blacks from the United States was connected to the history of neighbouring Sierra Leone. Since the time of the American Revolution, Sierra Leone had become a destination for free Blacks from throughout the British Empire. An early surge of migration came from Black Loyalists who had sided with the Crown against the Anglo-American rebels in the American War of Independence. After they experienced injustice and disappointment in their efforts to make new homes in the British colony of Nova Scotia, Granville Sharp and others pointed these former slaves towards Sierra Leone.[48] This West African territory was constituted as a British Crown colony in 1808. Among the Black immigrants who settled in Sierra Leone were maroons from the settlements of escaped slaves in Jamaica and some of the survivors of slave ships captured by the British navy after the British Parliament outlawed the trade in human chattel.

The lack of confidence in the potential of the United States to become a zone of comfortable integration passed from the White founders of the American Colonization Society to Black activists such as Paul Cuffe, Martin Delaney, Bishop Henry M. Turner, and Marcus Garvey. These individuals adopted the view of Liberia as a venue of escape from the harshness of race relations in the United States. The politics of this segregationist alternative to integration became especially heated in the 1920s and 1930s. The populist Black leader Marcus Garvey and the social scientist W.E.B. Du Bois both figured prominently in the controversy.[49] Garvey characterized Black migration from the Americas to Liberia as a pan-African equivalent to the Jewish Zionist movement to recover Palestine. He saw Liberia as the New Jerusalem, as the City on the Hill, for the descendants of the slaves. He looked to Liberia as a beachhead from which his people could begin the process of reclaiming the African continent from the clutches of White colonialism. Garvey's quest to build up the Black Star Shipping Line as a major venue of commerce and communications in the Back-to-Africa movement advanced his efforts to stimulate Black pride and to promote the ideals of Black entrepreneurship during an era when the Black penetration of the political economy of the United States was blocked in many places by high walls of institutionalized and informal segregation.[50]

Du Bois's approach to pan-Africanism was far more intellectual, elitist, and persistent than the flash of populist enthusiasm sparked by the more flamboyant Marcus Garvey and his Universal Negro Improvement Association. Both leaders competed for the allegiance of the same Black constituency whose spiritual and cultural capital in those years was centred in New York City among the makers of the Harlem Renaissance. In 1924 Du Bois travelled to Liberia as a representative of the US government. In the years that followed, he became embroiled in a controversy involving the alleged abuse of African labour by the local ruling class and the Liberian operations of the Firestone Rubber Company.[51] As the formulator of the idea of the Black community's "talented tenth" being obliged to provide leadership to African-Americans, Du Bois was inclined to identify with the Americo-Liberian elites who dominated the West African country. But the mass migration to Liberia by the descendants of the Western Hemisphere's Black slaves never materialized, and, as in Sierra Leone, the migration at every stage was more of a trickle than a flood. This trickle was interspersed with small surges of immigration to be counted in the hundreds or sometimes in the thousands rather than in the hundreds of thousands. The Black immigrants and their descendants in both countries tended to hive themselves off from the Indigenous peoples. As Du Bois indicated, "the immigrants to Liberia found that Africans did not regard them as Africans."[52] The Americo-Liberians tended to dominate and exploit their countries' Aboriginal groups.

The broader significance of the envisaged mass migration of Black Americans to Africa lies more in the realm of perception and political activism than in the fulfillment of preconceived plans. The prospect of an African-American exodus to Liberia represented at every stage the conviction that the United States could never be shaped to accommodate the genuine integration that would transcend the colour line dividing the descendants of masters and slaves. Some have seen in the Black complexions of the largest group of incarcerees in US prisons a stark demonstration of the persistence of racial segregation in the superpower's motifs of social, political, and economic organization. The power of American apartheid was briefly lessened after the Second World War when a significant number of Black Americans and other marginalized minorities found reasonably well-paying work in industries governed by the desegregated trade unionism that was largely a legacy of Roosevelt's New Deal.

Beginning in the Reagan-Thatcher years of the 1980s, the entitlements of investors were dramatically globalized at the expense of North American workers. The openings for workers in unionized factories were dramatically reduced by the rapid export of manufacturing infrastructures to low-wage countries where trade unionism is either limited or absolutely prohibited. At the same time the spaces available in American jails were quickly doubled, tripled, and then more than quadrupled under the auspices of business enterprises such as Wackenhut and the Correctional Corporation of America. Where in 1980 there were 500,000 prisoners, by 2006 the number had grown to 2.25 million. With only 5 per cent of the world's population, the United States thereby came to house fully a quarter of the world's total number of prisoners. A disproportionately large number of the new spaces was filled by unemployed young Black males often convicted on drug-related offences. While Blacks represent about an eighth of the overall population of the capitalist superpower, they make up about one-half of the US prison population. Approximately one-third of young Black males in the United States are presently either incarcerated or under some sort of supervision by the US criminal justice system.[53] "The scandalous truth," writes Glenn C. Loury, "is that the police and penal apparatus are now the primary contact between adult Black men and the American state."[54]

Hence the increasingly privatized precincts of the US Police State replaced Martin Luther King's civil rights movement at the strategic nexus of relations with the descendants of America's slaves. In the process, new proprietorships of White supremacy were apportioned in the retooling of the criminal justice system to become the primary medium in a new version of American apartheid. The privatized prison system of the United States is thus becoming a commercial heir to the transatlantic slave trade, with Black bodies again forming a major currency for private enrichment through the resurgence of a new form of human bondage. A big part of this process of criminalizing and locking up such a disproportionately large percentage of the Black population results from the War on Drugs, a deeply flawed enterprise pitting different agencies of the US government against one another as both agents and opponents of the worldwide increase in the production, distribution, and sale of illicit narcotics.[55]

One of the few areas where the disproportionately Black underclass had a reasonable chance of finding paid employment was in the US Armed Forces and in that establishment's rapidly proliferating networks of private contractors and subcontractors. In the era of the Global War on Terror, Black Americans could easily find work as soldiers of occupation, jailers, interrogators, and torturers in the worldwide operations of the military-industrial complex. These operations include the oversight and operation of US-directed ghost prisons, where thick covers of secrecy were added to lessen public scrutiny of the worldwide spread and intensification of state terror that wrote the names of Guantanamo Bay, Abu Ghraib, and Bhagram into everlasting infamy. Seen in this light, the War on Terror signifies what Philippe Sands has characterized as "a war on law." Under the dual leadership of George W. Bush and Tony Blair, Anglo-America provided a study in the "systematic disregard of established international rules on human rights, the treatment of prisoners and the use of military force around the world."[56]

The penal warehousing of such a large proportion of America's most impoverished and marginalized population marks a domestic expression of some of the same forces that have been advanced globally in the name of the Global War on Terror. The intersection between the domestic and international branches of the US-centred prison industrial complex is evidenced by the role of Erik Prince, the founder of Blackwater Corporation, in efforts to make US jails the sites of faith-based efforts to win Christian converts.[57] This initiative was promoted as part of the work of the Council for National Policy (CNP), a secretive organization formed to counter the influence of the Council on Foreign Relations (CFR). The CNP grew from the right's profound distrust of the CFR's role in creating the rhetoric of One World idealism that permeates the United Nations in spite of all that organization's many problems and limitations. The New Deal's equalizing thrust was thereby further subordinated to policies of evangelical hyper-privatization. The renewal of American apartheid in the prison-industrial complex continues the legacy of slavery and Indian removal in a changed context. The assertion of so-called law and order through the incarceration of so many disadvantaged Americans reveals the inner dynamics of a political culture becoming increasingly disconnected from genuine adherence to the rule of law.

FROM AN INDIAN CANAAN TO FREDONIA: CHRISTIANITY AND ENLIGHTENMENT IN THE EVOLUTION OF INDIAN COUNTRY AFTER TECUMSEH

There is much paradox in Christianity's ongoing role in the production of "the West's" most aggressive machinery of imperial globalization. While some Christian evangelists demanded a total cultural transformation of those societies they sought to convert, other missionaries called on their own governments to recognize and affirm the existence of Aboriginal and treaty rights. This collaborative approach helped give rise to the syncretism of some branches of Christianity with indigenous spiritual traditions throughout the West in much the same way that Islam was integrated with the Aboriginal ways of many Indigenous peoples in, for instance, Indonesia and the large Philippine island of Mindanao.

The importance of religion in "the West's" expansion was demonstrated in the process leading to the formal amalgamation in 1801 of England, Scotland, Wales, and Ireland into the United Kingdom of Great Britain and Ireland. The Scots Highlanders and the indigenous Irish were often viewed by their initial colonizers as savages to be conquered and, if possible, assimilated into the expanding orbit of English-speaking Protestant civilization. This saga of Aboriginal history set patterns of expansion that were re-enacted on the western frontiers of Anglo-America. It is tempting, for instance, to situate one of the main antecedents of US Indian removal in the assault on Ireland's Aboriginal Roman Catholics by Oliver Cromwell and the Protestant army of the English Parliament. Under Cromwell's leadership, Parliament passed the *Act for the Settlement of Ireland* in 1652. That statute sought to clear much of Ireland east of the Shannon River of its Native Roman Catholics. The aim was to extinguish the Aboriginal title of the land's indigenous inhabitants so that this same territory could be reapportioned to Protestant settlers. It would be given as payment to the veterans of Parliament's wars with the vanquished defenders of the Roman Catholic monarchy.

In order to clear the Native Irish from possession of their ancestral lands, Cromwell's Puritan regime sought to push the Indigenous peoples of the conquered Irish districts westward across the Shannon into Connacht.[58] Given the obvious parallels between the revolutionary origins of American independence and the revolt of Cromwell and his Puritan army against the forces of the English monarchy, it is not too much of a stretch to imagine this episode as a prototype in the minds of some proponents of Indian removal, with the Mississippi standing in for Ireland's Shannon River and Indian Territory taking the place of Connacht.

The power of the historical parallel was almost certainly buttressed by the experiences of many influential Americans, not least of whom was Andrew Jackson. Jackson rose to the top job in the United States largely on the basis of the fame he gained fighting Indian and British soldiers in the War of 1812 and, later, Seminole-maroon warriors on the frontiers of Spanish-Aboriginal Florida. In pressing Indian removal forward, Jackson faced the formidable opposition of the Reverend Jeremiah Evarts, who embodied a dimension of the Christian heritage that stood for the spirited defence of Aboriginal and treaty rights within certain limitations. Many varieties of Christian theology were drawn upon to make the opposite case. This dark side of the Christian heritage renewed patterns that were earlier expressed in the twelfth and thirteenth centuries during the violent Crusades of European Christendom in the Islamic Middle East. The Crusades helped give rise to the Roman Catholic Inquisition and an elaborate body of anti-infidel legal theory that was used sporadically over several centuries to provide juridical justification for the dispossession and colonization of Indigenous peoples on many frontiers of empire.[59]

The legal principles and precedents that grew from the Crusades were renewed in 1608 in English-speaking jurisprudence through the vehicle of *Calvin's* case, a ruling handed down by the English Lord Chief Justice Edward Coke. This decision was informed by the jurist's identification with the religious principle that Christian kings possess some divine rights to govern and expand the realm of Jesus Christ. This continuum of crusader law extended through English law all the way to the principles put forward by the government of Ontario between 1885 and 1888, when it convinced the highest constitutional court in the British Empire to accept most of its legal arguments in the *St Catherine's Milling* case. The ruling in this case helped slant the balance of power in Canadian federalism towards the position that provincial governments hold the power to control and apportion the rights of the Crown to Canadian lands and natural resources. *Calvin's* case held that the laws of all "infidel" nations – all non-Christian peoples – were immediately extinguished once subjected to the higher order of legal authority vested in Christian sovereigns. In their defence of their client's proprietary claims, the lawyers for Ontario paraphrased the line of precedent flowing from the Crusades and *Calvin's* case as follows: "At the time of the discovery of the Americas, and long after, it was an accepted rule that heathen and infidel nations were perpetual enemies, and that the Christian prince or people first discovering and taking possession of the country became its absolute proprietor, and could deal with the land as such."[60] The view of Indians as "perpetual enemies" was expressed in the revolt led by Nathaniel Bacon against the imperial governor of Virginia. In 1676 Bacon generated considerable popular support for his contention that all Indians, both inside and outside the frontiers of the Crown colony, must be treated as "Robbers and Theeves and Invaders of His Majesty's Right and our Interest and Estates."[61]

In taking their stand against Indian removal, Jeremiah Evarts and the American Board of Commissioners for Foreign Missions were going against the grain of much Protestant theology, but especially Puritan theology, as this body of religious philosophy had been developed, interpreted, and used in the course of English colonization. Without a doubt there was a richer tradition of defence for the existence of Aboriginal and treaty rights in the Roman Catholic heritage going right back to the formative stances taken by Brother Bartolome de Las Casas. In his defence of the Indians of Mexico, Las Casa was acting affirmatively on the principles outlined by Pope Paul III in 1537. In *Sublimus deus sic dilexit,* Pope Paul issued a papal pronouncement that constitutes one of the seminal statements in the Aboriginal history of universal human rights. The author of this instrument of papal rule articulated the idea of international law in identifying the shared humanity of the Indigenous peoples of the Western Hemisphere. The Chief Vicar of the Roman Catholic Church declared from the Vatican that "the said Indians, and other people who may be discovered by the Christians, are by no means to be deprived of their liberty or the possession of their property, even though they be outside the faith of Jesus Christ ... nor should they be in any way enslaved."[62]

The most concerted pressure of colonization in North America north of Mexico came from Protestants, most of whom spoke English as their first or second language. As the settlements and influence of English-speaking Protestants spread across increasingly broad expanses of the continent, they created the conditions for alliances of non-Protestants, who often were made to feel alien from the emerging majority culture. One facet of this alliance resulted in a synthesis of some Aboriginal resistance movements with the forces of Roman Catholicism. The Roman Catholic heritage was woven into the Aboriginal heritage of much of the Western Hemisphere largely through the syncretistic styles of evangelization used by many of the missionaries of New Spain, New France, and the Portuguese colony of Brazil. The vitality of these missionary movements was not broken by Britain's defeat of French imperialism in the Seven Years' War or by the withdrawal in the early nineteenth century of Spanish and Portuguese claims to sovereignty in Central and South America. Moreover, since Lord Baltimore's founding of the largely Roman Catholic colony of Maryland in 1634, Roman Catholics have been present, if not always comfortably so, within the societies that created and built up the United States and English-speaking Canada. The power of North American Roman Catholicism has been strengthened by influxes of immigration, particularly from Ireland, Germany, Poland, and the largely Roman Catholic countries of southern Europe.[63]

In a variety of instances throughout the course of North American history, Roman Catholic missionaries encouraged the spirit of Aboriginal defiance, even if the priests and nuns stopped short of actively joining in armed struggles. There were strong elements of Roman Catholicism in the Aboriginal resistance movements that animated, for instance, the Sioux of Minnesota as well as the ethnically diverse Indigenous peoples of Washington and Oregon Territories in the 1850s and 1860s. A similar pattern was re-enacted in the Aboriginal resistance to the expansion of the Protestant, Anglo-Canadian presence on Manitoulin Island in 1862[64] and into the Métis stronghold of the Red River between 1869 and 1871. The Red River settlement developed around the confluence joining the Red and Assiniboine rivers in what is now the province of Manitoba. This Métis community became a major centre of the fur-trade culture that thrived in the northwestern quarter of North America from the founding of the Hudson's

Bay Company in 1670 until well into the nineteenth century.[65] The merger of Roman Catholic and Aboriginal assertiveness found renewed expression in the mid-1970s when the Oblate priest, Father René Fumoleau, brought forward scholarship whose strategic effect was to help the Dene Indians oppose a Mackenzie Valley pipeline and reopen treaty negotiations with the Canadian government. These negotiations extended the tradition of Crown-Aboriginal treaty making towards the possibility of reconstituting a portion of the Northwest Territories as Denendeh.[66]

In Minnesota, Washington, Oregon, Red River, Manitoulin Island, and Denendeh, Roman Catholic clergy intervened with Protestant-dominated officials to advance various actions and prohibitions whose effect was to recognize and affirm the existence of Aboriginal and treaty rights. High Church Anglicanism also can boast of a strong tradition of defence for the existence of these same rights. The positioning of the British monarch at the theological pinnacle of the Church of England has been a factor in this heritage. The geopolitical use of the marriage of church and state in the person of the British imperial sovereign was demonstrated clearly in the famous alliance between the British Crown and the Mohawk Loyalists who opposed militarily both French imperialism and the revolutionary movement of secessionists that broke from the British Empire to create the United States.[67] This Anglican tradition of defending the existence of Aboriginal and treaty rights was renewed by the activism of the Reverend E.F. Wilson, who, in the 1890s, was outspoken in his lonely condemnation of the cultural genocide implicit in the assimilation objectives of Canadian Indian policy.[68] A similar pattern became manifest in the legal advice and monetary backing given by some Anglican missionaries, including the Reverend Arthur O'Meara, to help those Aboriginal activists most responsible for keeping alive the struggle for the recognition of Indian land title in British Columbia.[69]

The multifaceted character of Christianity in the Indian Country of the Americas permeated the politics of many aspects of Christian involvement in Jacksonian Indian policy in the late 1820s and 1830s. Not all clerical support for Indian removal was based on the vile theological interpretations flowing from *Calvin's* case. Some religious leaders who advocated Indian removal did so out of the sincere conviction that Indigenous peoples east of the Mississippi were doomed unless they withdrew farther into the continent to regroup and consolidate their collective strength in a protected Indian Territory. Some of those who envisaged such a course looked forward to the creation of different kinds of religious theocracy. These evangelists anticipated the time when the relocated people would become the primary citizens of utopian communities operating according to prescribed religious principles. The quest to transform parts of Indian Country into Christian theocracies runs strongly through the evangelical history of the Jesuit and Oblate orders in North America. In their wide travels, many of these Roman Catholic missionaries were inspired and sustained by the theocratic hope of duplicating in North America the kind of Christian dominion that their predecessors had cultivated among some Aboriginal societies in South America. The most famous of these theocratic transformations lay in the creation of the Roman Catholic Indian state of Paraguay, where many of the Indian towns were identified as "reductions." Whether in Oregon Territory, Canada's Mackenzie Valley, or at Wikwemikong on Manitoulin Island, Roman Catholic missionaries were frequently among the most dedicated soldiers of Christian evangelization in their efforts to re-enact the transformative saga of the Paraguayian reductions.

The prospect of Indian removal generated many similar theocratic urgings among some Protestant missionaries. One of them was the Reverend Isaac McCoy, a Baptist preacher whose evangelical mission was directed at Indigenous peoples south of the Great Lakes in the decades following the War of 1812.[70] These peoples, including many Ottawas, Chippewas, Potawatomi, and other Anishinabek, had risen up against the United States with powerful military force. The republic's most recent war with Britain provided the opening for a kind of Indian equivalent to the movement for American independence as advanced in the American Revolution. The largely Algonkian-speaking Confederacy of Indigenous peoples led by Tecumseh sought to defend and secure with Crown backing an Aboriginal Dominion with permanent, fixed borders in the North American interior. The united stand of the Indian Confederacy's fighting forces in the War of 1812 represented the most concerted Aboriginal resistance ever faced by the armies of the United States on the republic's moving western frontiers.

The failure of the government of Great Britain to stand firm in its support of the Indian Confederacy in the peace treaty concluding the War of 1812 meant that the Aboriginal strongholds south of the Great Lakes were doomed. Like the Cherokee of the South, the Aboriginal inhabitants of what is known in the United States as the Old Northwest were targeted to be eliminated or displaced in the name of Indian removal and US Manifest Destiny. McCoy worked closely with those Aboriginal groups who decided to escape the wrath and intolerance of many of their increasingly numerous non-Aboriginal neighbours and opted voluntarily to move to the federally designated Indian Territory west of the Mississippi. It was in this milieu that McCoy developed his elaborate theories of "Indian colonization." This vision pictured Indigenous peoples as pioneer settlers who would collectively establish an Indian colony rooted in the legal authority of the federal government. The colony would incorporate a sufficient legal basis to give certainty to those Aboriginal colonists willing to apply themselves to creating all sorts of Aboriginal institutions in both the public and the private spheres. McCoy anticipated that this form of colonization would eventually give rise to an Indian state, a jurisdictional concept that had first been raised in 1778 in the context of federal treaty negotiations with the Delaware.

Inevitably, the religious visions of McCoy and some of the other proponents of Indian removal were integrated into the planning for the new jurisdiction. Hence, the Indian Territory was prone to become for some of its evangelical enthusiasts a kind of Indian Canaan – a North American promised land to provide refuge from the distracting and destructive influences that limited the capacity of missionaries to cultivate their religious ideals among Aboriginal converts. These expectations were part of a phenomenon in which many aspiring architects of imagined polities struggled to see hope beyond the Aboriginal Dominion that Tecumseh and the mobilized soldiers of the Indian Confederacy had fought to secure in the heart of North America. The military defeat of Tecumseh's great campaign for Aboriginal unity and collective sovereignty necessitated the development of new paradigms and survival strategies. The most practical of these would have to include some pragmatic reckoning with the reality that the United States was no longer a tenuous geopolitical experiment whose viability remained uncertain. After the War of 1812, it began developing instead into a seemingly permanent and powerful expansionary country in which Aboriginal groups and individuals would have to learn to live.

Some, including the Reverend Eleazar Williams, looked to the Wisconsin area as a rallying site for a renewed Indian Confederacy. This part-Oneida evangelist declared himself to be the adopted son of Louis XVI and Marie Antoinette. He was a prominent figure among a number of migrating Indian groups who settled on the shores of Wisconsin's Fox River. Among the new Indian settlers were several Stockbridge clans and a band of Oneida from the New York state area. Both the Stockbridge and the Oneida people were among the few Aboriginal communities that had sided with the revolutionaries in the American War of Independence.[71] Farther south, the area of present-day east Texas became an especially fertile territory for the genesis of various geopolitical schemes. In this zone of contested jurisdiction, the aspirations of the people and the government of Mexico, newly independent of Spain's imperial authority, rubbed up against the expansionism of the United States. Between these two powers were the Indigenous peoples, including a number of Cherokee who were in the process of pushing westward in the search for new territories where they could hope to set down new roots with some permanent security of land tenure.

Out of this mixture grew the vision of a new country, called Fredonia, and in 1826 its founders issued their own Declaration of Independence. The flag of the Fredonian republic had two vertical stripes, one red and one white, symbolizing an enduring union of Indian peoples and White settlers, along with the inscription "Independence, Freedom and Justice." These words were reflected in Fredonia's internal boundaries, apportioning large portions of territory to "the United Nations of Indians."[72] Fredonia's Declaration of Independence drew heavily on the document of the same name that provided the United States with its founding manifesto. The essence of the plan was a commitment to freedom and the "inalienable rights" of all its citizens, including Indigenous peoples. Its goal was to bring a "League and Confederation" of Indigenous peoples together with non-Aboriginal citizens through a shared recognition of "the ligaments of reciprocal interests and obligations."[73] It hoped to transcend the racial divides that prevented the United States from realizing more consistently the responsibilities of its own democratic and egalitarian pronouncements.

John Dunn Hunter was one of the four principal architects and visionaries of Fredonia. He had been captured and taken as a child into Indian Country – a not unusual happening in an era when many Indian groups adopted captives to increase their dwindling numbers. He had passed through several Aboriginal clans and nationalities, becoming eventually the adopted son of an Osage band. At the age of about twenty he returned to Euro–North American society and acquired sufficient skills to write about his days among the Indian societies beyond the frontiers of Anglo-American settlement.[74] Hunter's book was well received, especially in Great Britain, and it won him a measure of fame. As a result, he was able to confer widely on the destiny of Indigenous peoples in the American West with many of England's most celebrated men, including the erudite and idealistic industrialist Robert Owen. In doing so, Hunter followed in the footsteps of Major John Norton, the Cherokee-Scots associate of those anti-slavery activists in the United Kingdom who went on to found the Aborigines' Protection Society.[75] In Hunter's view, the Aboriginal societies of the United States were doomed unless the republic radically reversed its policies of making itself "great and powerful as it were on the destruction of the Indians."[76]

A mark of the extent of Hunter's influence in Great Britain was the negative attention showered on him and his work by Lewis Cass. Cass was then in the process of taking control of the US government's efforts to remove the republic's expansion into Indian Country from the arena of European foreign policy. The practical extension of the Monroe Doctrine to Indian Affairs made it necessary to treat all relations with Indigenous peoples living along the Imperial Republic's expansionary course as the exclusive subject of domestic jurisdiction. Even warfare with Indigenous peoples along the frontiers of Anglo-American settlements was henceforth to be treated as the internal business of the US government. Cass's article in the *North American Review* attacking Hunter anticipated his more general literary assault on the Aboriginal policies of the British imperial Crown in its North American and Australian colonies and of the London-based Hudson's Bay Company in its expansive fur-trade enterprises.[77]

Hunter returned to the American West and the nascent republic of Fredonia in a quest to apply his strategies to save Indigenous peoples from the terrible fate he anticipated would be theirs unless some radical transformation took place in Anglo-American styles of colonization. His enemies wrongly feared that he had returned to North America as some sort of agent of the British government. They unrealistically believed that the imperial government was about to re-enact in Texas a role similar to the one it had played in encouraging the Indian Confederacy north of the Ohio River to create the basis of an Indian buffer state. The founding of Fredonia as an independent country based on a compact between Indian and non-Aboriginal settlers, therefore, encapsulated a contest of interests and ideas being fought on many fronts. The short-lived polity can be viewed as the expression of an effort to broaden the franchise of those eligible to share in the illumination and application of those great Enlightenment principles that were invoked in the founding of the United States.

In 1827 the Mexican army moved to block the establishment of Fredonia. Its soldiers killed the new polity by taking the lives of its founders, Richard Fields and John Dunn Hunter. One of Fredonia's most determined enemies was Stephen F. Austin, the governor of a Mexican settlement whose inhabitants were largely Anglo-Americans. Austin had written to Hunter to tell him that his vision for Fredonia was impossible; that neither the government of Mexico nor that of the United States would allow such a firm compact to take hold between Native peoples and non-Aboriginals. If necessary, predicted Austin, the Mexican government would cede the region to the United States to rid the country of potential Indian foes. Austin had no doubt about the outcome. "The U.S. would soon sweep the country of Indians and drive them as they always have driven them to ruin and extermination."[78]

The jurisdictional vacuum left by the quick fall of Fredonia was eventually met with the creation of the independent republic of Texas between 1836 and 1845. When that jurisdiction was annexed to the United States, the state government retained control of public lands, an arrangement that made for great constitutional uncertainty in the conduct of Indian affairs. A similar form of uncertainty would develop in British Columbia after 1871, when that jurisdiction entered the Dominion of Canada on much the same basis as Texas entered the US republic. Both jurisdictions had administered their own Indian policies before they entered the larger federal regimes of North America, and they both experienced considerable confusion with regard to which authority was now responsible for the protection of Aboriginal and treaty rights. Although Indian reservations were briefly established, Austin's prophecies proved to be all too accurate. The state of Texas became the site of the same policies and practices of ethnic cleansing that had already eliminated most distinct Aboriginal communities from US territory east of the Mississippi River.

The War of 1812 marked the culmination of the military resistance to US expansion mounted by Indigenous peoples in the eastern half of the present-day United States. Having tried and failed to oppose their dispossession in this way, many Native Americans east of the Mississippi had little choice but to give ground peacefully to the policy of Indian removal. The armed resistance in the Illinois area in 1832 by some Sac and Fox people represented an exception to this rule. The resisters found a leader in Black Hawk, a weathered veteran who had fought along with Tecumseh in the War of 1812.[79] In describing this conflict only three decades later as the nineteenth of twenty-two "Indian Wars of the United States," John Frost noted that Anglo-American settlers helped instigate the violence: "As they thought the proximity of the Indians was dangerous, the emigrants began to commit outrages intended to hasten their departure."[80] The group following Black Hawk was sometimes known as the British Band for its practice of continuing to visit the post of Fort Malden in British North America even after the termination of the War of 1812. At one point Black Hawk could boast two thousand followers. These numbers soon fell, however, leaving a small band of the most hard-core resisters. They clashed with members of the US Armed Forces and the Illinois militia at the Battle of Bad Axe River. Soon after, Black Hawk was captured by a group of Winnebagos and turned in to the Indian agents at Prairie du Chien.

After spending a short time in prison, Black Hawk and his eldest son were taken on a tour of eastern cities. The declared purpose was to impress on the warrior the futility of Indian resistance to the might and power of the United States. Black Hawk and his entourage aroused a good deal of excitement and fascination in the urban centres they visited – a pattern that became more prominent as the century progressed. It seems that the American people were willing to shower attention on those defeated Indian leaders who had put up a good fight. Indeed, the images of these warriors were quickly appropriated as virtual icons of America's fighting spirit. This celebrity treatment was particularly marked in the promotion of Sitting Bull as the star attraction of Buffalo Bill's Wild West Show after he was credited with the defeat of General George Custer at the Battle of Little Bighorn.

THE RISE OF "THE WEST" AND THE MAKING OF A NEW WORLD ORDER

The idea of "the West" as a distinct and dominant part of the global community emerged gradually from the process of transforming the Americas as an imperial extension of the Christian polities situated along the eastern shores of the North Atlantic. The colonization of Indigenous peoples in the making of, for instance, New Spain, New England, New France, New Netherlands, and New York helped to confirm and entrench the westward-pointing orientation of the world's most expansionary polities. The internal construction of the imperial West was significantly altered by the emergence of a new form of indigenous sovereign in North America. From its inception, "the West's" most distinctive yet characteristic polity, the United States of America, excluded Native people from the rights and responsibilities of citizenship. This telling exclusion helped to embed a very distinct form of hierarchical power within the West's mission to impose its own version of "civilization" on all the world's peoples and regions. The emergence of the United States from the British Empire thus forms a pivotal episode in Western civilization's Aboriginal history. Kerwin Lee Klein's assessment of a century of literature describing "the conquest of Native America" highlights how this body of representation reflects patterns of self-understanding among the most determined proponents, reformers, and antagonists of "the West's" expansionary career. In *Frontiers of Historical Imagination*, he writes: "Americans have imagined the West to have a special relation to American history. West, even as a particular arid region of the United States, also harks back to "the West" from ancient Greece to modern Europe. And since Americans have frequently claimed for themselves a privileged place in the course of history, 'the West' is crucial to understanding history in the abstract. The frontier was ... the ragged edge of history itself ... the very idea of 'America' balances on history's shifting frontiers."[81]

The idea of the West thus developed a dual personality. It could be both a distinct part of the global community as well as a portion of the Earth to be conquered, won, and transformed in the process of universalizing a civilization that began in Europe but was changed through the invention of America as the founding polity in a New World Order.[82] For those on the receiving end of these expansionary enterprises, the West became a bully that often acted in ways which completely contradicted the legal and ethical principles espoused by its primary polemicists. Allegations of hypocrisy and double dealing, for instance, permeate the text of Cheddi Jagan's *The West on Trial: My Fight for Guyana's Freedom.*[83] Jagan was descended from those families brought over from India as indentured labourers to work the sugar plantations of the British West Indies after the formal abolition of slavery in 1834.[84] After the Second World War, Jagan was widely acknowledged as the leader of the movement to liberate British Guiana from imperial rule. Because he openly embraced Marxist ideology, however, he and his supporters were targeted by the national security state as threats to capitalism's hegemony in Central America. With the help of the US-based trade unions, the CIA deliberately intervened to help build up the divisions between Blacks and East Indians in the political culture of a country that was not to be allowed to follow the example of the Cuban Revolution led by Fidel Castro.[85] The colony of British Guiana was reconstituted as the nominally independent state of Guyana in 1966 once the way was cleared for Forbes Burnham and his People's National Congress Party to form a government that could keep Cheddi Jagan and his People's Progressive Party in the opposition benches.

The idea of the West is closely connected to the concept of Western civilization, another intellectual construct more amenable to large generalizations and abstractions than to precise and detailed definitions. The spatial dimensions of Western civilization are especially problematic. What, for instance, is the geographic extent of Western civilization? How far towards "the east" does Western civilization extend? Norman Davies has been outspoken in his insistence that the Cold War's artificial division of Europe into eastern and western blocks has severely limited popular understanding of Western civilization's animating sources. By emphasizing in his own depiction of European history the importance of Poland and many other peoples and polities to the east of Germany, he seeks to remove barriers to fuller appreciation of the full extent of the linkages driving processes of change.[86] John Darwin has looked even farther towards the east in his ambitious overview of the global history of empire over the last six centuries. He sets the rise of Europe since 1492 in the context of the concurrent rounds of empire building that reorganized much of Asia and Eurasia when he writes: "It is salutary to remember that, contemporaneous with the triumphs of Vasco da Gama or Albuquerque in the Indian Ocean, or of Cortés and Pizarro in the Americas, were the consolidation of Ming absolutism [in China], the emergence of a new world power in the Ottoman Empire, the reunion of Iran under the Safavids, the expansion of Islam into South East Asia, and the creation of the new Islamic empire in North India after 1519."[87]

Darwin describes these histories with a view to explaining their role in helping to inform and propel the genesis of European imperialism in the so-called "Outer World" of the Americas, Australia, and Africa south of the Sahara. "We must set Europe's age of expansion," he writes, "firmly in its Eurasian context. That means recognizing the central importance of Europe's connections with other Old World civilizations and states in Asia, North Africa, and the Middle East." In making this case, Darwin advances the principle that "the centre of gravity in modern world history lies in Eurasia – in the troubled, conflicted, and intimate relations of its great cultures and states, strung out in a line from the European 'Far West' to the Asian 'Far East.'"[88]

Darwin's contribution to the imperial history of globalization helps debunk the idea of the West as a self-contained polity whose leadership independently imposed its identity on inert and stationary societies. While it is important to avoid the conceptual trap of too much emphasis on European exceptionalism, however, there is simply no escaping the unique role of the western portion of that region as the site of pioneering efforts in global exploration and conceptualization. After 1492 the emerging centres of commerce, scholarship, and government in Western Europe moved from the periphery of history towards the metropolitan core of a new saga of human imagination, understanding, and activity. The leading thinkers in these emerging sites of metropolitan rule could draw on the heritage of learning that they self-consciously identified with a continuum of civilization moving through space and time from Mesopotamia to Egypt, ancient Greece, the Roman Empire, and the Roman Catholic Church. The inheritors of this westward-moving tradition of knowledge and empire were faced after 1492 with the task of trying to adapt this cultural heritage to news flooding in from the worldwide explorations of da Gama, Vespucci, Magellan, Drake, Cook, and many others. The result of this meeting of old knowledge and mythology with infusions of new information and interpretation from all quarters of the planet gave rise to an unprecedented milieu. For the first time in history it became possible to picture the overall human condition in its true global context.

As Darwin emphasizes in his account of the global history of empire building, the European exploration of planet Earth was preceded by, and concurrent with, many other initiatives aimed at expanding spheres of dominance, trade, and human understanding. The peoples of China, Polynesia, India, and the Arab-speaking realm, for instance, all produced their own explorers who brought home bold interpretations of the larger environments surrounding their territories. All these non-Western societies engaged in forms of ocean-based transport and exchange that connected them with far-flung networks of human interaction. But the scope and scale of these non-Western reconnaissances and involvements simply do not compare with the explosion of worldwide interventions that were set in motion in the metropolitan centres of Western Europe. Those involvements reflected, applied, and advanced the proliferation of new insights about the shape, extent, and geographic features of our planet, together with its diversity of living organisms and inhabitants.

These developments made Western Europe the initial scene of a new kind of thinking where it became possible to picture the whole human species in all its similarities and variations. The ability to look outward at the totality of global conditions made the West the site of obsessive preoccupations with universal principles of all kinds and involved efforts to discover and apply these principles to all humanity, all living organisms, the whole planet, and all dimensions of the cosmos. This trend in human affairs was initially stimulated by the monotheism of European evangelists, who made it their mission to spread Christianity to the far corners of the world and reveal Jesus as the universal savior of all humankind. Soon the obsession with universal ideals and principles extended from the metaphysical to the material, from the religious realm to the secular domain in the quest to identify universal laws of nature, science, human conduct, and human rights. This thrust of ideas and actions led on the one hand to the great charters and proclamations of human freedom. It resulted, for instance, in the Declaration of the Rights of Man and Citizen in 1789 by the National Constituent Assembly of Revolutionary France. It extended to the wording of the Gettysburg Address in 1863, to the Atlantic Charter in 1941, and to the United Nations' articulation in 1948 of the Universal Declaration of Human Rights. But the same quest to identify and apply uniform laws of human relations could also attach the prestige of universal science to noxious theories of religious, racial, and civilizational hierarchy. The makers of the Third Reich had many precedents of European empire building on which to draw in writing their own imperial drama in their quest to carve out broader territories of German *Lebensraum* in Eastern Europe and Eurasia.

Indians in the Americas were very much part of the westward movement of peoples that made the rise of the West such a compelling facet of imperial globalization after 1492. Much as Aboriginal women often played significant roles as intermediaries and as power brokers in encounters with the newcomers, so too did Indian migrants from the East perform similar functions in their interactions with Indians indigenous to more westerly regions of the North America. The crest of this westward movement of Indians often materialized shortly before the arrival of wave upon wave of European and Euro-American settlers. Especially in the years immediately following the presidency of Andrew Jackson, much of this westward movement of Indian people was pressed forward through the US government's coercive uprooting of Indian communities east of the Mississippi River. The Trail of Tears was the dramatic culmination of this saga. The forced march of Indians under federal military control formed one element in a larger migration of Aboriginal groups and individuals. The biggest cause of the trend was the wholesale pre-emption of Indian lands in more easterly districts where the concentration of Euro-American settlement was higher. Another impetus to the westward migration of Native people was the fur trade, a commerce that demanded the continual exploration and opening of new districts where fur-bearing animals were plentiful and where the Aboriginal trappers had limited access to trade items. On their first entry into the new streams of global commerce, Aboriginal neophytes in the fur trade were prone to offer more animal pelts for smaller and less-valuable stores of trade items.

This westward migration of Indians was a significant factor in the devastating spread of diseases from Europe and Africa. These diseases severely undermined many Aboriginal societies – in some instances well before the non-Aboriginals arrived in significant numbers. The spread of micro-organisms from across the Atlantic often occurred through the medium of Aboriginal hosts, who sometimes carried the foreign diseases without themselves becoming ill. The introduction of foreign diseases was especially lethal because the Aboriginal people of the Western Hemisphere lacked immunity to many contagions such as measles, smallpox, and various strains of influenza.[89] The attack of alien viruses and bacteria on people indigenous to areas outside the world's main contiguous land mass of Europe, Asia, and Africa had an enormous impact on global relations of power. The inhabitants of hemispheres remote from the world's three connected continents tended to fall prey to forms of infection that severely dwindled their numbers. Their rapid population declines were instrumental in the rise of those European empires that accelerated the pace of imperial globalization after 1492.

The westward migration of Indian peoples, therefore, had substantial consequences for those Aboriginal societies on the receiving end of the influx. Sometimes the new arrivals brought with them hard-won lessons gained in the East about how best to deal with the seemingly limitless land hunger of the non-Aboriginal immigrants and their descendants. Certainly the Shawnee migrants from the Kentucky area, including the family of Tenskwatawa and his brother Tecumseh, carried vital information for those Indian peoples living beyond the frontiers of Anglo-American settlements. They brought news and insights about what could be expected from the *k'chimokoman* – the Algonkian term meaning "Long Knife" that is used to this day to identify the US republic and its non-Aboriginal citizens. Where some of the most experienced Shawnee became important guides and theorists of the Indian Confederacy after the American Revolution, the Ojibway-speaking Saulteaux tended to play similar roles among the Cree of the western prairies in their land transactions with the Canadian government in the 1870s.[90] The prominence of the Saulteaux in Crown-Aboriginal treaty making throughout the Canadian prairies is worthy of particular attention. The Saulteaux took their name from the French-Aboriginal community of Sault Ste Marie. The Saulteaux-Cree leader Big Bear was particularly prominent in questioning the motives and the methods of Crown officials seeking to obtain Aboriginal ratification of Treaty 6 in 1876 as a prelude to containing prairie Indians within confines of small and scattered Indian reserves.[91]

Christianity was one of the most influential cargoes of belief and devotion carried by Indian migrants entering the western portions of the continent. The active involvement of many Native people in the pioneering enterprises of Christian evangelization in North America is one of those largely unexplored legacies that tend to make Indian Country a place of such surprising ambiguities and paradox.[92] One of the most successful Aboriginal missionaries from the East was Ignace La Mousse, more often known as Old Ignace, a devout Roman Catholic from the Mohawk community of Kanewake near Montreal. Kanewake's Roman Catholic character drew strength form the legendary conversion about a century and a half earlier of Kateri Tekakwitha. The men of Kanewake, like those of the other Catholic missions in the St Lawrence Valley, tended to find work as voyageurs and as contracted hunters and trappers in the far-flung fur-trade enterprises emanating from Montreal.[93] The route Old Ignace used in his westward migration was already a well-beaten path for many of his people when he arrived in the Rockies sometime around 1820.

This Iroquois migration was part of a larger French-Canadian migration. The Roman Catholicism of many Indian, Métis, and *canadien* migrants was adopted in whole or in part by a number of the Aboriginal inhabitants of Oregon Country, and this early influence added an important ingredient to the Indian resistance to the integration of their ancestral lands into the United States after the Oregon Treaty of 1846. This region of the United States, now known as the Pacific Northwest, was the scene of an especially strong Aboriginal struggle aimed at curtailing the influx of predominantly Protestant, Anglo-American migrants who sought new lives for themselves by moving along the famous Oregon Trail. Old Ignace moved from Kanewake to the Bitterroot Valley area of Montana, where he settled among a group of Salish speakers who became fascinated with the Christian message their religious teacher preached. In at least two instances the Mohawk evangelist travelled to St Louis, hoping to attract some official commitment from his church to help him spread Roman Catholicism more broadly among the Nez Percé, the Flatheads, the Yakima, the Walla Walla, and the other Aboriginal groups of the Columbia Plateau area.[94]

Old Ignace's promotion of Roman Catholicism would converge with the agenda of several Jesuit missionaries. In 1825 twelve of them travelled from Maryland to St Louis. Since its founding in 1634, Maryland has been the most Roman Catholic of the thirteen original colonies that banded together to form the United States of America. The Jesuit missionaries had moved from Maryland to the trans-Mississippi West with the goal of founding "something like Paraguay."[95] These events gave rise to a series of episodes that led to the founding in 1841 by Jesuit Father Pierre Jean De Smet of St Mary's Indian Mission near present-day Stevensville, Montana. Father De Smet is generally identified as the evangelist at the root and foundation of the Roman Catholic Church in much of the northwestern portion of the United States. The success of his work, however, was largely based on the strong links through the Canadian fur trade between Oregon Country and the Roman Catholic stronghold along the St Lawrence Valley. Many Iroquois voyageurs, fur traders, and evangelists, including Old Ignace, played a role in forging this transcontinental axis of communications.[96]

Other Indian evangelists in the region included Spokan Gary and Kootenai Pelly, two Protestant converts who had briefly been students of the Hudson's Bay Company's school at Red River on the site of present-day Winnipeg.[97] In future years Spokan Gary became an advocate among his own peoples for the evangelical enterprises of Episcopalian and Presbyterian missionaries.[98] Spokan Gary was highly lauded by the non-Aboriginal community in the Pacific Northwest because of his quick and enthusiastic adoption of Anglicized ways. He cut his hair, adopted the dress of the Americans, and developed an easy command of the English language. The tensions between the Roman Catholic and the Protestant factions among the Aboriginal inhabitants of the Pacific Northwest was sometimes translated into references to the "French" and the "American" Indians. This division played a key role in the military clashes that shook the region and the republic in 1858. The linkages between Oregon Country and the French-Canadian heartland of the St Lawrence flourished especially in the years before 1821, when the Hudson's Bay Company absorbed the holdings of the North West Company, including the posts along the Columbia River system. Although Oregon was far outside the original charter of the HBC, the company's trading infrastructure in the 1820s and 1830s was so effective that the enterprise fended off all US competitors in the region. As D.W. Meinig observed of the era in his narrative of historical geography, *The Great Columbia Plain*, "American free enterprise proved decidedly inferior to the British monopoly."[99] Gradually, however, settlers from the more easterly regions of the Imperial Republic moved into the region,[100] and by 1845 about 5,000 of the 25,000 inhabitants of Oregon Country were US citizens. These numbers included a handful of Catholic and Protestant missionaries.

By this time most of these clergymen, including the Roman Catholics, were oriented towards the US branches of their Christian denominations.

These developments melded with the political pressure exerted by Pacific traders and US whaling interests seeking a secure foothold on the Puget Sound area. The result was the negotiation in 1846 of the Oregon Treaty.[101] This agreement between Great Britain and the United States extended the forty-ninth parallel from the continental divide to the Pacific coast. Some in the US government, including President James K. Polk, blustered politically about establishing the northwestern border of the United States immediately south of Russia's North American colony of Alaska at 54 degrees 40 minutes. This expansionist rhetoric, however, lacked the steel of true conviction. The Oregon Treaty was negotiated at a moment when the expansionary energies of the United States were directed largely towards the southwest. In 1845 the federal government annexed the republic of Texas as a prelude to war with Mexico. The outcome of this uneven contest between the US Army and the Armed Forces of Mexico was the Treaty of Guadalupe Hidalgo of 1848, a transaction that extended the territory of the United States southward to the Rio Grande and westward to the Pacific Ocean. By the mid-nineteenth century, therefore, the international boundaries of North America began to approximate their present shape even if the vastest part of the continent remained effectively an Indian Country interspersed with relatively small but densely settled pockets of non-Indian habitation.

The attachment of Louisiana, the Pacific Northwest, and then much of Mexico to the United States presented a set of problems similar to those raised for the British Empire after the incorporation of Canada during the Seven Years' War. Would the North American interior provide the basis for the extension of old states or the formation of new states? Would significant portions of the annexed territory be reserved for the Indians or would the land be devoted to providing living space and an expanded base of agriculture, resource extraction, and privatized capital for the nation of newcomers and their corporate extensions? The contentiousness of issues such as these led to a civil war in British North America in 1776. After 1848 the transformation of the northern portion of Mexico into the southwestern quarter of the United States accelerated the slide towards the next civil war in Anglo-America. The profound disagreement about slavery's future formed the festering core of the worsening crisis in US federalism. How could some sort of political equilibrium be maintained between the expanding range of national power and two antagonistic complexes of regional power that concurrently supported and opposed the institution of slavery? Could a degree of equality be maintained between the pro-slavery and the anti-slavery factions in Congress as new states were added to the union?

North of the international boundary between the United States and British North America, officials also struggled to make constitutional adjustments that would express the mounting pressure to transform earth into property. In 1849 the British government established a small colony primarily for non-Indian settlers on Vancouver Island. A subsequent influx of gold miners largely from California and elsewhere in the United States resulted in the decision in 1858 to establish a new British province. This mainland region had been previously known to non-Indians by a name given to the region by Simon Fraser in the early years of the nineteenth century. That name, New Caledonia, is one that Bernard DeVoto predicted would "shimmer forever in the annals of the fur trade."[102] In 1866 the union of Vancouver Island and the mainland colony was proclaimed. This new jurisdiction took its name from the Columbia River and, ultimately, from the individual who began the Columbian conquests. Hence the term British Columbia was added to the map of North America, the Western Hemisphere, and the world. The creation of British Columbia announced the transcontinental consolidation and renewal of British North America. With the full power of the British navy's Pacific fleet behind them, the founders of the new jurisdiction chose a name that proclaimed their enthusiastic embrace of the heritage of the European colonization of the Western Hemisphere that began in 1492.

CHAPTER EIGHT

Manipulating Law and Lawlessness in the Conquests of Anglo-America

We may have to decide whether to be the torturer or the tortured:
the horror of the one and the fear of the other drive us from one
decision to the other. Old memories awaken.

Jean-Paul Sartre, Introduction to Henry Alleg's
The Question, 1958

ACCUMULATING CAPITAL THROUGH THE OPIUM TRADE AND THE PRIVATIZATION OF INDIAN LANDS

The civil war that had erupted in British North America in 1776 ended with the Treaty of Ghent in 1814. The agreement terminating the War of 1812 was followed by the dramatic conclusion of the Napoleonic wars in the British victory over France at the Battle of Waterloo in 1815. These developments in the transatlantic world helped to clear the way for the accelerated rise of Anglo-America. John Jacob Astor stepped into the centre of one of the most important emerging fields of business between Great Britain and the United States in 1816 when he exported 10 tons of opium from Smyrna, Turkey, to Canton, China, under the banner of his American Fur Company.[1] With the success of this transaction, Astor was catapulted to a position of yet greater influence in the political economy of New York. With the military hostilities of France and the United States against Great Britain now a thing of the past, New York was poised to reassume its role as a major commercial agent, understudy, and competitor of imperial London. From its days as a Dutch fur-trading post on the frontiers of the empire of Iroquoia, New Amsterdam–New York has consistently been governed by an unusually creative convergence of imperial and indigenous imperatives. As such, it has long been a major site of interaction between the American empire and the Fourth World.

Astor was no stranger to bold commercial ventures on the frontiers of the US empire of capital.[2] In 1808 he had demonstrated the global implications of the overland expedition to the Pacific coast led by the US Army's Corps of Discovery under the commanding officers Meriwether Lewis and William Clark. Once these men realized their assignment of planting the US flag on the Pacific Rim, Astor took the process of imperial expansion one step further. He exported a large shipment of Pacific Northwest otter hides to Canton, a city known to the Chinese as Guangzhou – the South Gate of China. That gate would be rammed open with US help by the imperial navy of Great Britain.[3] In making the transition from the export of sea-otter hides to the export of opium, Astor was a key participant in a more general alteration in the content of global trade. At the core of the matter were changing motifs of enslavement in an era when mercantilist regulation was giving way to the adoption of more laissez-faire forms of capitalism.[4] The decisions in 1808 of both the British Parliament and the US Congress to prohibit the slave trade, if not slavery itself, created new pressures to exploit those forms of servitude that arise when human beings become dependent on addictive drugs and their suppliers.

The Anglo-American extension of the opium trade into China was driven by a complex array of forces. One of these arose from the growing taste throughout Europe and the Americas for Chinese tea. When mixed with boiling water, Chinese tea leaves provided an excellent medium for slave-grown Caribbean sugar. But the purchase of the produce of China's tea plantations with gold and silver, the only commodities acceptable to the sellers, offended the principles of mercantilist orthodoxy. The nature of the problem facing Westerners engaged in Chinese commerce was outlined in 1793 in a letter written to the British king by the Chinese emperor. Emperor Ch'ien Lung wrote "Our Celestial Empire possesses all things in prolific abundance and lacks no product within its borders." Hence he saw "no need to import the manufactures of outside barbarians in exchange for our own produce."[5] In the face of the Chinese unwillingness to part with indigenous products for anything other than gold or silver, the British East India Company orchestrated the violent drive to change market conditions. The company developed its own Calcutta-to-Canton drug connection as it attempted to feed and cultivate the Chinese demand for prohibited opium. In doing so, company officials made ample use of the renowned fleets of fast schooners sailing out of New England and New York under the direction of the likes of John Jacob Astor and James and Thomas H. Perkins. Warren Delano, the grandfather of President Franklin Delano Roosevelt, also figured prominently among those American frontiersmen in the Far East who seized large chunks of influence over capitalism's future when they successfully colluded with East India Company officials in Canton and London in concocting imperial drug deals.[6]

Like the Astor, Perkins, and Delano clans, the Cushings, Lowells, Higginsons, and Cabots also loomed large among those US family dynasties whose fortunes were built and consolidated by the smuggling of opium into China. Between 1839 and 1858 the First and Second Opium wars were directed at forcing the Chinese imperial government to join the West in treating the importation and consumption of opium as "legal" activities. In those times opium from India and Turkey was freely marketed throughout much of Europe and the Western Hemisphere with the sanction of the medical profession. Opium formed the basis for many pain-relieving products, including Laudanum.[7] China was not to be allowed to deviate from trade practices in the West: it was prohibited from making and enforcing its own laws based on its cultural sense of the appropriate boundaries between legitimate medicine and prohibited drugs. In the course of the Opium Wars the British colony of Hong Kong was established, and it soon became an Anglo-American base from which to police and expand the subordination of the Celestial Empire to the imperial dominance of Western transnational capital. The Opium Wars form the best evidence available for those who allege that the underlying basis of globalized markets lies in capitalism's violent promotion of addictions among rich and poor alike. While opium and heroine are among the most potent currencies of commercialized addiction, tobacco, sugar, tea, coffee, and alcohol are products with a similar propensity to generate expanded demand with increased supply.

A significant portion of the drug money extracted from China after the Napoleonic wars found its way into New England's Ivy League universities. John Cleve Green, for instance, drew on his earnings from the opium trade to help Princeton realize its ambitious building plans. Similarly, Abiel Abbot Low used a considerable portion of his profits from the sale of drugs in China to help Columbia University construct its New York campus. Opium profits also created the basis for the establishment by William Huntington Russell of the secretive trust at the basis of Yale University's notorious Skull and Bones society. He worked closely with his cousin, Samuel Russell, to build up Russell and Company, a firm whose fortune followed the lead of Astor in moving opium from Turkey to China.[8]

Gum from the type of poppies used to create opium was further refined to create morphine and, later, heroin. The Bayer Company in Germany first developed heroin as a prescription drug in 1895 and was one of the firms that joined to form the IG Farben conglomerate. The operation of many imperial systems, including those of the British Empire and the US Empire in Indochina, Central America, and Afghanistan, has been closely bound up with control over the production and distribution of the array of narcotics produced from cultivated poppies.[9] The drug trade has offered a means for empire builders to ally their interests with those of local strongmen and international crime syndicates. It has created streams of resources to bind patronage networks and to finance all sorts of covert operations in ways that do not require the approval of sanctimonious politicians, zealous accountants, or disgruntled taxpayers in imperial centres. The commerce in mind-altering drugs can be seen as an extreme expression of libertarian free trade on the outer frontiers of unrestrained capitalism. Control of the trade in illicit drugs implies the ability to protect and build up friends and to criminalize actual or potential foes. It speaks of the capacity to debauch and demoralize whole groups who may stand in the way of colonial expansion and commercial exploitation. The trade in rum, brandy, and whiskey to Indians played a similar role in the transcontinental expansion of

Anglo-America, as did the trade in opium in Anglo-America's push to subordinate China.

While some US fortunes took form in the opium dens of China, the rapid development of real-estate markets in North America offered more accessible horizons of opportunity for those eligible to buy and sell titles to land. Many struggled to get into the market, but the really big rewards for speculation in lands were reserved for a select few. One of the major requirements to join this inner circle of landed privilege was to possess the political and financial influence to mould to personal advantage the legal interface between governments and corporations on the frontiers where Indian Territory became registered private property. Robert Morris was ideally placed to find his way in the transformation of the richest part of British North America into the United States. This leader of the revolutionary forces within Anglo-America began innovations in public and private finance along lines that would subsequently render the US military-industrial complex a dominant instrument in the nation's political economy.[10] Morris embodied a combination of Robert McNamara's acumen as a manager with Allan Dulles's flair for skullduggery. Even before 1776 Morris had helped to smuggle arms from France into British North America, and he owned privateering vessels that seized British cargoes in order to help provision the Continental Army of General George Washington. Between 1781 and 1784 he was superintendent of finance of the United States. Morris acquired one of the country's largest fortunes, both as a war profiteer and as an intermediary between European investors and those responsible for opening new markets in the buying and selling of land on the moving frontiers of Indian Country.

Morris was prominent among those who speculated in the price and availability of land in western New York. Once independence has been achieved, the government of Massachusetts made extensive land claims against the Six Nations Iroquois. As a result of the Treaty of 1783, even this historic stronghold of Aboriginal sovereignty had been sacrificed by British negotiators in Paris to appease the land hunger of the Anglo-American revolutionaries and to draw them away from their attachments to France. In 1788 Massachusetts sold its claim of the right of pre-emption to about 6 million acres of New York land. The purchasers were Oliver Phelps and Nathaniel Gorman, who paid $1 million, or about sixteen cents an acre. The entrepreneurs then established a corporation, which paid a group of Seneca people $5,000 plus an annuity of $500 to clear the Aboriginal title from about half the area they had purchased from Massachusetts. When Phelps and Gorman failed to meet their schedule of payments to Massachusetts, much of the tract was resold to Robert Morris in 1791. He quickly flipped a large portion of it to the Holland Land Company, retaining a 500,000-acre tract for himself.[11]

Many common themes permeate the concurrent development of the Anglo-American opium trade in China and the process of privatizing

Indian lands in North America. While the two activities were geographically distant, they were both facilitated by closely related systems of ideology and commercial transaction. Both involved an enormous amount *of* ad hoc experimentation with the rules of trade, banking, and corporate formation. The creative engineering of corporate proprietorships became increasingly instrumental in the ongoing quest to universalize capitalism through the commercial, cultural, or military conquest of one frontier after the next.[12] More recent devices employed in what David Harvey has referred to as "accumulation through dispossession" include currency devaluations, asset stripping, hedge funds, and the manipulation of credit ratings and stock markets.[13] A persistent impetus in this complex of transactions is for the powerful to mould the law to protect their own interests, even as Indians, indigenous Chinese, and other colonized groups were stripped of their sovereign right and responsibility to protect their own properties, jurisdictions, and persons.

This pattern of selective application and enforcement of the rule of law is an essential feature of all empires. The inconsistencies become especially clear in a world where global corporations have been able to benefit from regimes of transnational law that protect their own assets and operations even as their agents are empowered to exploit many frontiers of cultivated lawlessness. It is these intersections of law and lawlessness where addictions, unprotected natural resources, and human desperation born of poverty form currencies of renewed enrichment for commercial empire builders in the modern-day extensions of the opium and the Indian wars.

RAILWAY CONNECTIONS TO AMERICAN DREAMS

In her article on "The Revolutionary Origins of the American Corporation," Pauline Maier argues that a new kind of corporate design emerged from the American War of Independence. She asserts that the founders of the American republic "rescued the corporation, an all-but-moribund institution in late eighteenth-century England, and utilized its capacity to empower individuals whose resources were unequal to their imaginations." The sovereign power to generate new corporations was acquired through the assertion of American independence, when the state governments acquired the constitutional authority to grant corporate charters. The government of Massachusetts generated a particularly diverse and prolific array of new corporations, covering all manner of civic, educational, religious, and commercial endeavours. Perhaps the activity of corporate creation was embraced so enthusiastically in the Puritans' old heartland because the state government's generation of charters played, in a secular way, on the religious notion of a *covenant* between a people and a higher authority.[14]

US innovations on the legal and institutional frontiers of corporate formation helped liberate the huge treasure troves of new capital derived from the privatization and mortgaging of vast portions of the North American continent. In order to move towards this formula for the generation of wealth, the founders of the new nation had to overcome the Aboriginal and mercantile obstacles that were strengthened by the British government's tendency to support the Canadian fur trade. And so, when the imperial Crown's support for the mercantile operations of the fur trade slowed the pace of the transformation of Indian Country into new capital and Anglo-American settlements, a new type of indigenous North American sovereign was invented to expedite more rapid and efficient processes of westward expansion. This new sovereign was constituted so as to give broad latitude to the expression of John Locke's seminal assertions that the primary purpose of government is to legitimize and protect the private property of its citizens. In the elaboration of these principles, corporations have gradually been able to acquire the legal personality of "persons" – that is, of citizens.[15]

The institutional vehicles for speculation in the price and availability of North American land have been important media for experimentation and innovation in the commercial rise of corporate America.[16] The transcontinental railway companies were the direct descendants of the North American land companies whose frustrated development before 1776 was, as Clarence Alvord and others have argued, so important in the genesis of the American Revolution.[17] The North American railway companies combined innovations in the law and politics of corporate design with technological advances in the harnessing of steam power and in the refining and shaping of hard metals. The result was a revolution in mobility that provided the practical means to implement and extend earlier colonization schemes. The expanding Armed Forces of the United States removed hostile Indians to help prepare the ground for the building and operation of the railways. The new railway lines provided openings for the expansion of telegraph networks. The use of electricity to transmit information transformed both the landscape of knowledge and the structure of relations between communities and nations.[18] It began the most intense phase of a revolution in communications that continues yet. Who could have predicted in the nineteenth century that the telegraph and Morse code would lead via the marvel of the telephone to the wired world of the Internet? The extension of telegraph cables inland led to the laying of transoceanic cables connecting the world's continents. As the networks of communications and human interdependencies grew, so too did the project of coordinating the activities of all societies into a single worldwide regime of Standard Time.

The expanding scope of railway development continued to accelerate the pace of industrialization, urbanization, and automation. As the railway companies spanned the continent, they built many bridges, both real and metaphoric. They formed the link between the America of John Jacob Astor and that of Henry Ford.[19] The same formula of using railways to exploit more fully the transcontinental character of the United States was later repeated with some modifications in the makeover of the largest part of British North America from an Indian reserve and fur-trade kingdom into a transcontinental dominion. In both instances the marriage of railway technology and corporate power depended on the aggressive intervention of federal authority. As the inheritors of the imperial role in the old British Empire, the federal governments of both Canada and the United States held important keys to deciding who would benefit the most from the communications revolution. And this revolution hastened the pace of Indian Country's transformation into new types of jurisdiction favouring the rapid integration of land and natural resources into currencies of capitalist transaction. This intensified commodification of the North American earth helped to provide the capital to construct some of the most ambitious engineering works ever attempted before or since.

Beginning in the 1840s, railways began to change radically the political economy of North America. Water routes into the interior lost some of their old importance as the growing efficiencies of overland transport created myriad new openings for more elaborate and sophisticated forms of industrialization, urbanization, and expansion on the continent's agricultural, ranching, mining, and forestry frontiers. Competition between railway enterprises increasingly dominated most spheres of public politics in the United States and, soon after, in British North America as well. This competition was centred on law-makers, as different consortiums of regional and financial interest fought each other for government charters and land grants.[20] Thus, the primary struggle among nineteenth-century North American business interests was political and juridical rather than commercial in nature. The most severe competition among those at the pinnacle of the business culture was to achieve favoured status in treatment by government.

Accordingly, entry into the competitive venue of the marketplace occurred only *after* the power of government was invoked to charter corporate entities and to reconstitute major portions of the so-called public domain – the former Indian domain – as corporate private property. Very often this corporate property was divided into multitudes of shares that could be purchased or sold in venues such as Wall Street's New York Stock and Exchange Board. The US system for the regulation of markets in stocks, bonds, and currencies was closely modelled on British innovations going back to the early eighteenth century.[21] As the leading engines of economic growth in North America, the railway companies established trends and prototypes of law, commerce, and the exercise of political influence.[22] Some of the biggest conglomerates of railway enterprise figured prominently among the original "trusts," as these commercial cartels concentrated greater and greater wealth and power in fewer and fewer hands. The movement to merge business enterprises to create large monopolies of commercial power reached something of a climax around the turn of the century. The primary aim of those who led this movement towards monopoly capitalism was to rationalize production and increase profits by reducing competition through price fixing.[23]

Major elements of the US cartel system were exported to Germany in the 1920s and 1930s, when Wall Street directed a large flow of US investment to help build up a country that was struggling to recover from the punishing weight of war reparations imposed by the Treaty of Versailles. The rise of the cartel system in North America resulted in a corresponding surge of both socialist and progressive agitation aimed at realizing a more equitable and democratic means of organizing the political economy of the United States. By these means, the influence of railway companies went far beyond the route of the train tracks they laid. These commercial institutions were primary instruments in the spread of the law and the ethos of a hierarchical organization of political influence and private property across great expanses of geographic and temporal space. The railways became a central symbol of the demise of Indian Country and the fur trade. The transcontinental railways became primary icons in the ascendance of increasingly ethnocentric paradigms of industrial progress as the culture of the Euro-American majority extended beyond the Appalachians and out onto the prairies, through Texas and into New Mexico and California,[24] through Missouri Territory and into the old fur-trade preserve of Oregon.[25]

Even before the United States fully confirmed its geopolitical status as a transcontinental country, promoters were lobbying to link the Atlantic with the Pacific through the culture of railways. Asa Whitney was by far the most committed and eloquent pioneering proponent of a transcontinental railway connection to capitalize on Lewis and Clark's explorations on behalf of the US government.[26] The child of a long line of New England farmers and merchants, Whitney was said to resemble Napoleon Bonaparte in size, appearance, demeanour, and ambition, and he soon amassed a personal fortune as part of the small group who were able to break into the China trade. This experience instilled in Whitney a modern version of the old dream that had inspired European pioneers since the time of Columbus: to seek a westward-pointing route to the Far East.[27]

In 1845 Whitney's personal crusade on behalf of an overland railway arrived on the floor of the US Congress. The proposal took the form of a report entitled *Railroad from Lake Michigan to the Pacific: Memorial of Asa Whitney, of New York City*. Not surprisingly, his scheme was at first dismissed as quixotic and unrealistic, but Whitney bolstered his lobbying efforts in the nation's capital with extensive public-speaking engagements, especially in the republic's westernmost urban centres of Pittsburgh, Cincinnati, Louisville, St Louis, Nashville, and Columbus. Typically, Whitney used a map of the world to illustrate his central arguments. At the core of his message was the view that the United States was well situated geographically to become the heartland of global commerce. With pointer in hand, he would emphasize the strategic character of the republic's positioning: "Here you see by this map that we are in the center of all," he declared, before taking his audiences through an imaginary journey that charted an expansive theory of globalization. "There is Europe on the one side, with 250 million of population, and all of Asia on the other side of us, with 700 million souls," he thundered. "The Atlantic separating us from Europe, the calm Pacific between us and Asia, and you will see that the population and commerce of all the world is on this belt of the globe – which makes a straight line across our continent."[28]

Whitney's plan became more feasible as the United States formalized its transcontinental status through a treaty with Great Britain in 1846 and, two years later, the acquisition of much of northern Mexico. In 1851 Whitney presented his proposal from the speaking rostrum of the House of Representatives in Washington. He used the occasion to caution the citizens and law makers of his country that, if the United States failed to capitalize on the advantages to be derived from a transcontinental rail route, then Great Britain might exploit its imperial holdings in North America to build such a project. Whitney failed to gain the corporate charter and land grants he needed to make his dream materialize, and his proposal once again foundered on the politics of sectionalism. Whitney responded to this setback by sailing to Great Britain to promote what his critics described as "a Canada and Pacific railway."[29] The political and commercial leadership of the old empire of Britain was even less prepared to take immediate action than the leadership of the nascent US empire and, disappointed, Whitney retired from public life. Nevertheless, his lobbying on both sides of the Atlantic stimulated debates and introduced conceptions that were instrumental in preparing public opinion for the building of several transcontinental railway lines in North America. The expansion and consolidation of two transcontinental empires in North America in the following decades through the massive application of railway technology was part of a worldwide phenomenon that intensified the pace and expanded the scope of imperial globalization.

For many generations after 1492, the process of globalization advanced gradually behind the ocean coastlines of the world. This process often involved the borrowing and adaptation of boats used by Indigenous peoples. The application of various kinds of canoes in the elaboration of the North American fur trade stands as the superlative example of the adoption of Aboriginal boat technology in expanding the web of European colonization and global communications. During the second half of the nineteenth century and early years of the twentieth century, the globalization of railway technology seemingly accelerated time and compressed space across many frontiers of human experience. The technology of the iron horse diminished the capacity of Indigenous peoples all over the planet to resist the subordination of their lands and themselves to the alien control of imperial regimes. The appropriated lands of Indigenous peoples in many parts of the world beyond Europe were often surveyed, commodified, and mortgaged to finance intensified cycles of globalization facilitated increasingly by the worldwide boom in railway construction.

In Africa south of the Sahara Desert, for instance, railways gave European empires a new way of flexing their imperial muscle throughout tropical regions long seen as too remote for the direct expression of colonial authority. On the Indian subcontinent, the makers of the British Empire used railways to broaden and strengthen their hold on the diverse multitudes of that vast region. At the end of the First World War, Czarist Russia gave way to the rise of the Soviet Union, Europe's last major empire. The Soviet regime was quick to take up the Czarist regime's exploitation of railway technology in reaching northward, eastward, and southward. One aim was to extend Moscow's metropolitan hold over the vast expanses of Siberia, home to many Indigenous peoples. Another was to increase the connections between Russia and the Eurasian nationalities in the south and east. In reaching towards China, India, and the faltering Ottoman Empire, the politics of Soviet railway construction vied with the politics of institutionalized religion in a region long dominated by Islam.[30]

In the United States, the decision of the US Congress to make the War Department responsible for exploring the possibilities for transcontinental railways made clear the imperial nature of that enterprise, one soon permeated with the ethos of American Manifest Destiny. The gathering of military intelligence about the trans-Mississippi West had started in 1804 with the expedition of US Corps of Discovery led by Lewis and Clark. This pattern continued after 1838 with the scientific studies conducted by the Army's Corps of Topographical Engineers. In 1853 Jefferson Davis, the secretary of war, created five separate expeditions to survey possible routes for a railway link to the Pacific Ocean. Its officers took on the assignment with an intensity fitting the factory-like rhythms that increasingly set the pace of development throughout the growing grids of metropolitan settlements in eastern North America. The local economies and cultures of these urban areas were increasingly integrated and homogenized through the expanding networks of railway communications.

The central role afforded the US Armed Forces in the transcontinental expansion of the United States belies Frederick Jackson Turner's vision of westward expansion as the preserve of isolated individual frontiersman. In charting the changing international boundaries of the United States or in looking for the overland route for a railway passage to the Pacific, military researchers interpreted their assignments in broad and comprehensive ways. In their wide-ranging explorations, they conducted studies that contributed substantially to the emergence of a host of scholarly disciplines, including botany, zoology, paleontology, and ethnography. A leading example of this genre of comprehensive exploration was the much-celebrated study conducted by the research team under Major William Hemsley Emory. Besides their survey work, Emory's men collected and documented more than 2,500 specimens of plants, mammals, birds, fish, and reptiles in the course of compiling the *Report on the United States and Mexican Boundary Survey* in 1857–59.[31] In method, scope, ambition, and purpose, the work of the army's researchers in the American West resembled that of the Institut d'Egypt, the army of scientists assembled by Napoleon in 1798 to bring the authority of scholarship to his extension of France's imperial aura over the ancient land of the pharaohs.[32] The transcontinental expansion of the United States generated a North American case reflecting themes similar to those described by Edward Said in his commentary on *Orientalism*. The militarization of scientific research in both Egypt and the American West was part of a larger process that would culminate in the second half of the twentieth century in what the retiring US president Dwight D. Eisenhower would describe as the "military-industrial complex."[33]

From its inception, the US Armed Forces has made a priority of the study of Indigenous peoples on the frontiers of Euro-American settlement. More than a century before Eisenhower warned of the dangers lurking behind the militarization of scientific enterprise, the Corps of Topographical Engineers developed the idea that the ethnographical study of the Indigenous peoples of the American West could be carried out as an extension of the study of rocks, hydrology, plants, and animals. Certainly the assumptions implicit in such groupings of subject matter edified already existing biases among many scientists poised on the cusp of the epistemological revolution that Charles Darwin was about to introduce into the natural and social sciences. This Darwinian revolution in scientific thought injected new confidence into the vision of imperialism and capitalism as human expressions of natural law. Darwinist social science added new elements into the search for conceptions of Indian policy in the United States which would transcend the dubious expediencies of Indian removal. The growing embrace of the transcontinental character of the United States began to undermine the assumption that the solution to antagonisms between Aboriginal and non-Aboriginal people was, perpetually, to push the weaker groups beyond successive western frontiers.

As Americans collectively gazed westward towards the Pacific Ocean and the Far East as the next frontiers of their expansionary ambitions, the old certainties driving the forced relocation of Indian groups began to be exposed as nothing but receding mirages. Increasingly it became clear that some modifications were needed to replace the old orthodoxies of Indian removal – a polite term for ethnic cleansing. The people and government of the United States would have to resolve either to complete the bloody business of outright genocide, with all that this terrible outcome would imply for the moral integrity and international imagery of the republic, or the citizens of the United States would have to resolve to transcend the illusion that there was some extensive part of the continent to which the Indigenous peoples could be permanently vanquished and rendered relatively invisible. The only alternative to Indian removal was to change the direction of public policy, to come up with a system of laws and institutions aimed at accommodating the co-existence of Indigenous peoples in the midst of non-Aboriginals.

The development of the United States as a transcontinental polity to be spanned by transcontinental railways set in motion a variety of powerful new forces. The comprehensiveness of the army's investigations to prepare the way for this commercial, industrial, and geopolitical transformation spoke of the broad expectations that accompanied this pioneering venture in government-sponsored research. In his account of the role of the US Army in directing and coordinating the gathering of such an eclectic array of data on the American West, William Goetzmann has emphasized the imperial or even conquistadorial nature of the exercise. "Not since Napoleon had taken his company of savants into Egypt had the world seen such an assemblage of scientists and technicians marshaled under one banner," he wrote. "And like Napoleon's own learned corps, the scientists, too, were an implement of conquest."[34]

"GOODS AND THE EARTH ARE NOT EQUAL": MAKING TREATIES AND WAR IN THE PACIFIC NORTHWEST

Much of Europe's early colonization of the Western Hemisphere was intimately bound up with the efforts of the Roman Catholic Church to win new converts as part of a more global strategy to counter the progress of the Protestant Reformation. This missionary strategy permeated the imperial policies of Spain and France in the Americas. The Roman Catholic Church made huge inroads among the Indian and mixed-ancestry populations of both these empires by incorporating aspects of Aboriginal spirituality into their strategies of Christian evangelism. Similarly, much of the expansionism of Dutch, British, and US Empire builders in the Western Hemisphere was permeated with Protestant theology. High Church Anglicanism, for instance, was an integral factor in the evolution of the Covenant Chain alliance whose main link connected the Crown's governor of Tory New York with the Six Nations Iroquois.

Throughout much of North America, Roman Catholic missionary work preceded Protestant evangelization. The resulting phenomena of Aboriginal Roman Catholics opposing the expansionary incursions of English-speaking Protestantism forms one element in an elaborate complex of factors animating various episodes of Aboriginal resistance to the takeover of their territories through the westward expansion of the United States. This pattern of Aboriginal religious history seems to colour the story of the Indian opposition to the US campaign to Americanize the Oregon Country in the years following the extension of the forty-ninth parallel to the Pacific coast, and it is one of several factors animating the Aboriginal resistance to the preparatory work by the US Armed Forces for North America's first transcontinental railway. One episode in this resistance involved the decision of a small band of Utah Indians to respond with lethal force to the incursions of one of the army's survey parties. Eight members of the targeted survey crew, including its commander, Lieutenant John W. Gunnison, were ambushed and killed in October 1853 by Aboriginal soldiers in their doomed attempt to defend their territory from encroachment and appropriation.[35]

Such skirmishes, together with the larger battles that have come to be known as the Indian wars, constitute some of the most heavily mythologized episodes in the expansion of the United States, Anglo-America, and Western civilization. As such, these conflicts constitute iconographic episodes in the Columbian conquests, a many-faceted complex of engagements among peoples, cultures, and economies that began in 1492 and that continues to this day. The military and quasi-religious character of these clashes was especially well defined in the northwestern extremity of the United States in the 1850s. During those years, the region was home to about 30,000 Native people. Their numbers far exceeded those of the Euro-American settlers in this former stronghold of the Montreal fur trade and then of the Hudson's Bay Company. The ethnic mix of these Aboriginal societies was extremely complex. There were at least thirty distinct Indian groups whose members spoke various combinations of dozens of distinct languages and dialects. This complexity, however, was balanced during much of the nineteenth century by the unifying influence that Roman Catholicism came to exert on many thousands of Native Americans in the Pacific Northwest. The influence of the Church of Rome had its origins in the region's historic attachments to the St Lawrence heartland of the French Canadians and the Red River heartland of the Métis fur traders, many of whom were also committed Roman Catholics.[36] This history provided the opening for Jesuit missionaries, the militants of the Counter Reformation, to continue their quest to establish North American equivalents of the Western Hemisphere's famous Indian theocracy in Paraguay. Indeed, when the most celebrated of these missionaries, Father Pierre De Smet, established several Catholic centres among the Indian peoples in Oregon Country, he patterned the church's new mission buildings on illustrations he found in the widely read histories of Jesuit evangelization in the "reductions" of Paraguay.[37]

Major Isaac Inglis Stevens was a striking personification of the US Army's many functions on the moving frontiers of the American empire, particularly in Indian Country. His military enterprise stands between the careers of Generals George Washington and Andrew Jackson before him and General William Tecumseh Sherman after him. A graduate of West Point Military Academy, Stevens was a thirty-five-year-old soldier when he was entrusted by the federal government with multiple executive functions in the United States' colonization of the Pacific Northwest. In 1853 this veteran of the recent US war with Mexico was appointed the first governor of the new federal territory of Washington, a jurisdiction that was created from the northern half of Oregon Territory, and assigned the dual jobs of superintendent of Indian Affairs and head of the northernmost survey party in the army's search for the best route for North America's first transcontinental railway. The key task of this survey work was to evaluate the feasibility of railway and road connections across the height of land separating the drainage basins of the Missouri and Columbia rivers.

As superintendent of Indian Affairs, Stevens moved quickly to organize assemblies where Aboriginal delegations were asked to sign pre-prepared treaty documents that would place them on reservations. Like his predecessors, Stevens briefly flirted with a scheme to relocate coastal peoples inland, but the coast Indians refused to leave their home terrain. This determination to hold their Aboriginal ground signalled the test of wills to come. Stevens's insistence on pushing ahead with a rapid-fire series of treaty talks was spurred by his reading of the legislative instrument that had brought Oregon Territory into existence in 1848. That Congressional statute affirmed the existence of the rights and titles of Oregon's Indigenous peoples, "so long as such rights shall remain unextinguished by treaty between the United States and such Indians."[38] Francis Paul Prucha has written that these treaty councils, many of which took place in 1854 and 1855, were "not to be negotiations between two political powers, but an imposition upon the Indians of the treaty provisions Stevens brought with him."[39] In order to gain a number of Aboriginal marks on the treaty documents, Stevens engaged in a litany of threats, intimidations, and extravagant unwritten promises he knew would never be met. He has also been accused of exploiting jealousies among Indian leaders and even of personally forging the x marks of chiefs who refused to sign.[40]

The records of these treaty councils contain ample evidence of abundant Indian unease and displeasure with the terms being offered. For instance, Owhi, a Yakima delegate at the Walla Walla Council held in the late spring of 1855, exclaimed: "What shall I do? Shall I give the lands that are a part of my body and leave myself poor and destitute? Shall I say I will give you my lands? I cannot say." At the same assembly, Walla Walla spokesman Peopeomoxmox looked at the items on offer for signing and asserted: "Goods and the Earth are not equal; goods are for using on the earth. I do not know where they have given land for goods." Even Spokan Gary seemed dismayed by the lack of flexibility on the federal side. A pioneer Aboriginal Protestant in the Pacific Northwest, he was regarded by Stevens as one of the most Anglicized and friendly Native Americans in the region. But he told the Washington Territory's governor, "When I speak you do not understand me. It is as if I have been talking for nothing." Chief Joseph, the Nez Perce leader who, two decades later, would lead one of the most legendary of the Aboriginal resistance movements, was unequivocal in his expression of distaste for what Stevens was proposing. "I will not sign your paper," he said. "You go where you please, so do I; you are not a child. I am no child; I can think for myself. No man can think for me. I have no other home than this. I will not give it up to any man. My people would have no home. Take away your paper. I will not touch it with my hand."[41]

One locus of overt Aboriginal resistance to American aggressiveness was Pugent Sound, where treaty opponents found a leader in the person of Chief Leschi of the Nisqually. An escalating cycle of violence in the region in 1854 and 1855 led to the declaration of martial law in Pierce County. As a result, nearly all non-Aboriginal adult males were inducted to take up arms to quell a possible Indian uprising. The conflicts generated the fear that a more widespread confrontation was brewing. As James Douglas, the governor of the Crown colony of Vancouver Island, observed, "The spirit of mischief may spread into our own territory, and weak and defenseless as we are, we shall have to stand the brunt of an Indian War. We are unfortunately quite unprepared."[42]

When Stevens sent an emissary from Olympia to Victoria, he got Douglas to agree to assign British arms and two British vessels, the *Otter* and the *Beaver,* to assist the US government in its military response. This willing cooperation between officials representing both the Crown and the republic on the Pacific coast dramatically curtailed the scope of strategic options available to the Indigenous peoples in their efforts to resist effectively their own extinguishment, subjugation, and dispossession. As long as the governments of Britain and the United States remained actively or potentially at war, there was always the chance that the animosity between them could be turned to the advantage of an Indian Confederacy, as had been attempted, for instance, in the War of 1812. That possibility sank from sight as the leaders of the continent's two transcontinental powers settled into a period of *Pax Anglo-Americana,* one that would be briefly but dramatically disrupted by the Civil War in the United States. In attempting to justify his assistance to the government of Washington Territory in helping to suppress Indian resistance to the jurisdictional claims of the United States, Governor Douglas gave voice to some of the underlying assumptions of this "peace." Most important was the development of a broadened and increasingly racialized conception of a shared Manifest Destiny among non-Aboriginals in North America. Douglas explained that "it was therefore clearly to our interest that the American cause should triumph, and that the natives be made to feel that they cannot successfully contend against the power and resources of the whites."[43]

All in all, Stevens and his predecessors in the Pacific Northwest sent nineteen treaty documents to Congress. For a time these documents failed to gain presidential sanction, together with the needed approval in Congress of two-thirds of the country's senators. This breakdown in the ratification process added to the atmosphere of unresolved animosities, especially as Euro-American settlers and miners continued to migrate into the region. Many of them were enticed to come by the terms of the Donation Land Law, which Congress had ratified in 1850. According to this enactment, American citizens or prospective citizens could perfect their title to 320 acres in the republic's most northwesterly jurisdictions so long as they cultivated some portion of their land grant over a four-year period. Those who took advantage of this offer frequently interpreted it to mean that they could establish homesteads wherever they wanted. The ad hoc nature of this arrangement was especially galling to the Indigenous peoples of the region, whose own Aboriginal title to the land remained from their perspective entirely uncompromised and unextinguished.

The flareups of violence between Indigenous peoples and incoming settlers continued to escalate in this volatile frontier zone. The temperature of antagonisms, however, reached a new threshold in the summer of 1858, when a major outburst of antagonism pitted a broad coalition of allied Aboriginal soldiers directly against the US Army. The decisive episode in the genesis of this Indian war is known as the Steptoe Disaster. Colonel Edward J. Steptoe, the officer in charge of Fort Walla Walla, met stiff Aboriginal opposition as he and his detachment marched across the Snake River with the intention of arresting some Palouses men for allegedly stealing cattle. The American soldiers were surprised to find themselves surrounded. As reports of their vulnerability flashed through the territory, the original antagonists on the Indian side were re-enforced by warriors from many different groups. Among the Aboriginal contingent described in the language of the US military as "hostiles" were some Coeur d'Alene, Spokan, Yakima, and Nez Perce people, together with members of the Flathead Confederacy. Along with those Indian people known as Kalispels, Kutenais, and Pend d'Oreille, the ethnically complex Flatheads included many strong Roman Catholic devotees who blended this faith with their continuing devotion to Aboriginal traditions of spirituality.

From the perspective of the Indigenous peoples, the Steptoe incident represented a significant victory. While the number of deaths on the US side was not great, Colonel Steptoe's unit had been humiliated. They had lost all their horses, totalling more than a hundred, and many of their soldiers had been touched by the sticks of their enemies in the famous ritual of Indian warfare known throughout much of the North American West as "counting coup." The US Army had clearly lost face in an outlying extremity of its authority. News of this episode resonated far and wide and was broadly interpreted as the beginning of a major Indian challenge to the still-tenuous authority of the US republic in the Pacific Northwest. In Washington, DC, the Steptoe Disaster made "a great sensation." In particular, it "made a very deep impression on the War Department" and demonstrated that something was profoundly "rotten" in the republic's capacity to control Indigenous peoples through military force.[44] Very quickly, wheels were set in motion to make a major show of force to tilt the balance of power back to a heavy disequilibrium favouring the army over the Indians. Indeed, the incident gave political leverage to those seeking to bolster the capacity of the US Armed Forces to fight Indians throughout the entire course of the republic's nascent transport system in the trans-Mississippi West. That road system linked the country's urban centres in the east with the growing pockets of Euro-American settlement in California and the Pacific Northwest.[45]

The ramifications of the Steptoe incident also extended north over the new international boundary. During the summer of 1858 the Indians north of the forty-ninth parallel were facing the first major influx of largely Californian miners who had flocked into the Fraser Valley in search of gold. The intensity and scope of this gold rush led the British government to create the new Crown colony of British Columbia that year to prevent a US takeover of the region. The Indigenous peoples of British Columbia were directly menaced by the alien miners' extraction of mineral wealth from their Aboriginal lands and waters, and the initial success of their relatives in challenging Steptoe's unit sent a signal about what could be done to fend off the predatory theft of Aboriginal lands and resources.[46]

This convergence of events led to an outburst of bloodshed in the Big Canyon region of the Fraser Valley about 20 miles upstream from Yale. While the Hudson's Bay Company had long operated relatively peacefully in the region, suddenly the Fraser erupted as Indian soldiers took the lives of several miners.[47] Some of the victims were decapitated and their bodies floated down the river. The miners responded in ways they had learned in the earlier gold rush that had triggered the extension of statehood to California. Not waiting for government to act, they constituted themselves into three armed units. One group declared war on the neighbouring Indians, killing, they claimed, about thirty of them. They also spoke of having burned several Native villages. Another contingent of miners set themselves up as a kind of peace contingent. They claimed to have made "peace treaties" with their antagonists, whose hostility subsided once the miners displayed the extent of their numbers and the strength of their firepower. By the time Governor Douglas arrived on the scene in HMS *Satellite*, a relative calm had settled on Big Canyon, and he satisfied himself with admonishing the miners for taking the law into their own hands, an act that he declared made some of them vulnerable to the charge of "high treason."[48]

The subsequent clashes south of the forty-ninth parallel between the US Army and the fighting forces of the Indian Confederacy of the Pacific Northwest are known as the Battle of Four Lakes and the Battle of Spokane Plains. The leading Jesuit historian of this saga, Father Robert Ignatius Burns, describes the confrontations as "the great Northern Indians' War of 1858." It came about, he wrote, as a result of "a general coalition of interior Indians centering on the mission tribes."[49] One of the central figures who inspired the pan-Indian unity essential to the genesis of such a multi-ethnic Aboriginal alliance was the Yakima leader Kamiakin. Roman Catholic Indians, including Kamiakin, formed the core of the resistance, and their Jesuit priests, especially Father Joseph Joset, intervened to draw an uneasy peace from the hostilities. The clerics' goal was to pressure the US government to recognize and affirm a relatively expansive regime of Aboriginal and treaty rights while stopping short of providing overt sanction for the Indian resort to armed aggression. The Jesuits' insertion of themselves as intermediaries between the US government and the Indian alliance surrounding Kamiakin anticipated a similar role for the church a decade later. In the winter of 1869–70, Roman Catholic officials became intermediaries between the Canadian government and the Red River Métis. Under the guidance of a former seminarian, Louis Riel, these predominantly Roman Catholic offspring of mixed Indian and Euro–North American parentage would aggressively resist the extension of the new dominion's jurisdiction into their home territory without fuller provisions to recognize their rights. Among these rights, ones that would be articulated in the founding instruments of the province of Manitoba, was the freedom to educate their children in the French language and the religious heritage of the Roman Catholic Church.

The end of the overt hostilities in 1858 opened the way for the ratification by the US Senate in 1859 of the backlog of treaties outlining the terms for the establishment of Indian reservations in the Pacific Northwest. Once again the pattern was renewed that treaties with the Indigenous peoples in the United States were most often instituted as a means to formalize the peace after a ritual conquest. Only rarely was the Canadian model followed where treaties were negotiated as the means to avert outright warfare. Many of the Indian treaties that were part of the early genesis of Washington state contained provisions entrenching the right of Indigenous peoples to continue their traditional fisheries. In the mid-1960s many Native Americans in the most northwesterly jurisdiction of the United States conducted "fish-ins" with the intention of calling attention to these treaties. The fish-ins generated public arrests, media attention, and, eventually, precedent-setting jurisprudence on the issue of treaty rights.

Among the Aboriginal groups who hosted these important events were the Yakima, Nisqually, Puyallup, and Muckleshoot peoples.[50] In the litigation flowing from the fish-ins, the federal government lived up to its constitutional obligations by defending Aboriginal and treaty rights against the contending arguments of lawyers representing the jurisdiction of Washington state. The result was a rare instance where the constitutional law of Aboriginal and treaty rights was upheld and enforced by the responsible parties within government. The result was a demonstration that the ideals of the Atlantic Charter, the UN Charter, and the Universal Declaration of Human Rights could be made to apply to the citizens of Aboriginal nationalities *within* the United States. The effect of the fish-ins helped give shape and energy to emerging centres of Aboriginal activism, including the National Indian Youth Council and the American Indian Movement.[51] The power of these spectacles extended beyond the United States to affect Indian communities throughout the Western Hemisphere. Certainly George Manuel, a Shuswap activist in neighbouring British Columbia, was inspired by what he learned from the fish-ins and from the leaders behind these events. One of these leaders was Robert Satiacum, who worked closely with the US film star Marlon Brando in drawing attention to the fish-ins as a test case to determine the quality of justice for Native people in the United

States. Satiacum helped Manuel to make the conceptual breakthroughs that led to his articulation of the principles of the Fourth World and to his founding of the World Council of Indigenous Peoples.

The Indian wars of the 1850s and the fish-ins of the 1960s are part of a long continuum of conflicts, antagonisms, and creative interventions that have made the Pacific Northwest and British Columbia a particularly significant region in the larger Indian Country of North America. The events of 1858 point to the complexity of a whole range of contributing elements affecting the alignment of allies and disputants in the struggle to shape North America's destiny. The conflicts pitting US settlers and the US Army against Indigenous peoples in the Pacific Northwest were first and foremost a fight for the control of land, water, and other natural resources. The Indian wars of the 1850s, however, also held elements of tension between Protestants and Roman Catholics and between the French-speaking and English-speaking heritages whose antagonisms form integral parts of the Aboriginal histories of both Canada and the United States.

In the clash of forces at Four Lakes and Spokane Plains, there were hints of many conflicts, some based in local conditions and some imported from other times and places. There were suggestions, for instance, of the ideological contentions of the Enlightenment, conflicts aligning the succinct certainties of Locke against the dreamy abstractions of Rousseau; of conflicts between the principles animating the Indian theocracies of Paraguay and those pushing forward the genocidal acts of conquistadors; of the tensions between those in the United States who drew from New England's Puritan founders a national conception of themselves as God's Chosen People and those who looked to the Vatican as the highest source of legitimacy. On the side of power were arrayed a number of different forces, including the notion of private property as a primary medium of freedom, zeal for the Protestant Reformation or for US Manifest Destiny, and what Kevin Phillips has described in *The Cousins' Wars* as "English, a Language of Victory."[52] Those embodying these ascendant forces clashed with Indigenous peoples whose complex traditions included the religious, cultural, and political legacies of New France – legacies invested with new means of transcontinental dissemination, adaptation, and renewal by the fur-trade enterprises of British imperial Canada.

GOLD, VIOLENCE, AND LAW IN THE MAKING OF
CALIFORNIA AND BRITISH COLUMBIA

The outburst of violence in the Big Canyon region of the Fraser Valley seems to have been connected to the aftermath of the Steptoe Disaster. Some Indian leaders sought to strengthen this link by exploring the possibility of expanding the Indian Confederacy among the Indigenous peoples north of the forty-ninth parallel in the new Crown colony of British Columbia. One of these leaders was Chief Tonsasket, the leader of a small Okanagan band in Washington Territory. He invited Chief Nkwala (Nicolas), a soldier, trader, and sage among the main body of Okanagan people, to join the resistance against the people and government of the United States. Chief Nkwala had acquired great influence as a principal intermediary between his own people and the Hudson's Bay Company officials at Fort Kamloops. He was reputed to have seventeen wives representing many different Aboriginal nationalities, a domestic arrangement that gave him an exceptionally broad scope of family contacts which he was adept at exploiting for commercial advantage to himself, his extended clan, and all those who looked to him for leadership.[53] But Chief Nkwala thought his own people had troubles enough locally and he declined the invitation to join in the Indian campaign to further humiliate and push back the US Army. The miners flooding into the Fraser and Thompson river valleys would have to be dealt with closer to home.[54] Although Chief Tonsasket would later marry one of the daughters of Chief Nkwala, there was no repeat of the broad military alliance that made the Indian Confederacy of Canada such a powerful geopolitical force in northeastern North America during the era of Tecumseh's greatest effectiveness.

In British Columbia, Indigenous peoples participated actively in many aspects of the region's transformation from a preserve of the fur trade to a region where mining, forestry, commercial fishing, and farming became mainstays of the economy. Many observers commented on the rapidity and scope of Aboriginal involvement in the new economic activities, not only as wage labourers in shipping, road building, and timber cutting but also in most aspects of mining, including prospecting and panning for gold. In a memorial from the London-based Aborigines' Protection Society to the British Colonial Office, secretary F.W. Cheeson commented in 1858 on his investigation into "matters affecting not only the rights and interests but the very existence of the numerous Indian population of the new Colony of British Columbia." He reported that many of the Native people of British North America's westernmost jurisdiction were "alive to the value of gold discoveries; no better proof of which could be furnished than the zest and activity with which large numbers of them have engaged in gold digging." Many Aboriginal individuals, he said, had "learnt the full value of their labour; in proof of which it is stated that they now charge five to eight dollars a day, instead of one dollar, for their services as boatmen in navigating the Thompson and Fraser Rivers."[55] Years later British Columbia's first judge, Matthew Baille Begbie, commented on the success of Indian people in maintaining their economic independence through a variety of means, including paid labour and entrepreneurship.[56] He made these observations in a decision rejecting the legal applicability in British Columbia of the dominion Parliament's *Indian Act.* Begbie maintained that Indian people in his province should not be entrapped legislatively as wards of the Canadian government. "All Indians in B.C. are self supported and self-supporting," he said; "clearly a code of laws [the *Indian Act*], which may suit a mass of state-fed paupers educated to habitual idleness, is not necessarily adapted for a race of laborious independent workers."[57]

The Aborigines' Protection Society, an outgrowth of Britain's great anti-slavery coalition, had the support of many of the British Empire's most important Protestant missionary societies. It had gained prestige for its important role in a major parliamentary investigation in 1837 into questions concerning the place of Indigenous peoples in Britain's overseas settlements. Accordingly, the intervention of this particular watchdog group, an ancestor of today's transnational non-governmental organizations, could hardly be ignored. The letter from Cheeson was part of a steady stream of communications that, for the most part, encouraged Crown officials to aspire to more humanitarian approaches in the design and implementation of Aboriginal policies in British North America and elsewhere in Great Britain's worldwide empire. In his 1858 intervention, Cheeson expressed deep concern that all the elements of a tragedy were fast converging: "The present danger of a collision between the settlers and the natives will soon ripen into a deadly war of races, which could not fail but terminate, as similar wars have done on the American continent, in the extermination of the red man." The source of conflict was the sudden intrusion of many thousands of miners from California into the southern valleys of the colony, and, the secretary warned: "The natives generally entertain ineradicable feelings of hostility towards the Americans, who are pouring into Fraser and Thompson Rivers by thousands, and who will probably value Indian life there as cheaply as they have, unfortunately, done in California."[58]

In California, the 1849 gold rush led to a genocidal assault on the Indian people once their Aboriginal lands were inundated by fortune hunters. This sudden influx created the basis for the reconstitution of California as the thirty-first state of the US federation in 1850.[59] The magnetic pull of this gold rush was strong enough to reduce temporarily the non-Aboriginal adult male population of Oregon Territory by about two-thirds.[60] Some estimates calculate that the Indian population was reduced from about 120,000 to 20,000 in the first years of the California gold rush. The Aboriginal population during the long interval when California was part of New Spain and then of Mexico had declined from a pre-contact number that has been estimated as high as a million, although about half that figure is probably a safer guess.[61] The vigilantism and frequent lynching directed at Indian people during the peak of the gold rush were often equated by local officials with progress. The first governor of California, for instance, is on record as predicting publicly, "A war of extermination will continue to be waged between the races until the Indian race becomes extinct."[62] In looking back on this history in the context of the 150th anniversary of California statehood, Edward D. Castillo wrote of the frontier warfare accompanying California's entry into the US federation as "a complete breakdown of all legal and moral constraints on American immigrants' civic and criminal behavior." He characterized the era as "the greatest orgy of land fraud, dispossession, slavery, and mass murder ever witnessed in North American history. The period from 1850 to 1868 was essentially a twisted Darwinian laboratory showcasing the triumph of brute force aided by the pathogenic and technological assault on a native people unparalleled in Western hemispheric history."[63]

The language of moral outrage and heavy irony that is frequently associated with the Aboriginal history of the United States' richest and most populous state permeated the intervention of the Aborigines' Protection Society. In informing the British government in 1858 about the need to discipline the anti-Indian proclivities of the flood of Californian fortune-seekers then entering British Columbia, Cheeson cited an article on the subject that had recently appeared in the *New York Times*. The author may have been aware of the aggressive stance of Aboriginal people that had led to the confrontations at Big Canyon, for he "rejoiced" at the fact that the Fraser River Indians were of a sufficiently "serious frame of mind" to strike back in self-defence after some of their members had been killed "in sport" by "so bad a set of men on the face of this fair earth." He referred to

the well-known injustice of the miner towards anything of the genus Indian or Chinamen ... [The miners] will get up a series of little amusements in the way of pistolling and scalping, quite edifying. It is the custom of miners generally to shoot an Indian as he would a dog; and it is considered a very good joke to shoot at one at long shot, to see him jump as the fatal bullet pierces his heart. And when, in the spirit of retaliation, some poor hunted relative watches his opportunity and attacks a straggling white man, the papers at once teem with accounts of Indian outrages. And yet the men that shoot down these poor Indians are not the ruffians we are led to suppose are always the authors of atrocities, but the respectable sovereign people, brought up in the fear of God by pious parents, in the most famed location for high moral character. The Indian and Chinese murders are frequently committed by men brought up in the quiet country villages of Eastern States, and who return looking as innocent as lambs.[64]

While the mining frontiers of British Columbia were places of considerable violence, the magnitude of the murder and mayhem between Indigenous peoples and non-Aboriginals never approached the scope of the race war that befell California during the height of its gold rush.[65] The self-image that was cultivated among most newcomers who identified positively with the colony's British connection was that, in British Columbia, the force of law would be made to prevail over the chaos of vigilantism in the conduct of relations with the land's original inhabitants. Judge Matthew Begbie conducted his arbitrations as though he was vested with full authority to exercise jurisdiction over the Native people. He maintained the view that "all men are on a level before the Courts of criminal justice ... That they are amenable to the same tribunals, for the same offences, triable by the same methods and ceremonies and liable to the same punishments as white men, exactly."[66] Only by taking considerable licence with the facts of history, however, could the fiction be maintained that Indigenous peoples in British Columbia had been engulfed in a regime of colour-blind law enforcement where equality of individuals before the law outweighed all other considerations.

The importance of the Royal Navy in the conduct of relations between the Crown and Indigenous peoples along the coastal regions exposed the persistence of another dynamic belonging more to the realm of international affairs than to domestic relations. Throughout the nineteenth century the imperial government of Great Britain depended heavily, in the words of the Admiralty, on its naval strength to "keep the Indians in awe."[67] The dependence of the local government on the British Empire's seagoing instruments of imperial might belied the myth of Indigenous peoples as willing agents of their own subordination to the laws and institutions of British Columbia.

With the transformation of New Caledonia into British Columbia in 1858, the British government heightened the deployment of a form of gunboat diplomacy along the coast to strengthen the prestige, might, and imperial authority of Crown claims to sovereign jurisdiction. From time to time the strength and accuracy of the fire power in these vessels was deliberately used and displayed to remove any doubt from the minds of coastal Indians about who would prevail in the advent of an all-out war. In 1860 three of these vessels, the HMS *Plumper, Termagant,* and *Alert,* visited all the major Indian villages on the west coast of Vancouver Island and northwards along the mainland up to the Russian colony of Alaska. The purpose of the visits was ostensibly to enforce a prohibition on the trade of alcohol to the Indigenous peoples and to enforce peace among the Tsimshian, Haida, Kwakiutl, Nootka, and Salish-speaking peoples along the coast. The raiding forays of these groups sometimes resulted in the enslavement of vanquished groups and individuals despite the fact that, since 1834, slavery had been outlawed throughout the British Empire.[68] The naval visits to the coastal Indians were treated on both sides as relatively friendly exchanges. A particularly interesting discussion took place at Skidegate, one of the largest Indian villages of Haida Gwaii, otherwise known as the Queen Charlotte Islands. The Haida were a renowned seagoing people sometimes identified as the Vikings of the north Pacific. Some of their best navigators, including the legendary Edenshaw, were much in demand as ship pilots to take trading vessels safely through Haida Gwaii's shoal-infested waters.

At Skidegate in 1860, Chief Nestecanna conferred with the commander of the *Alert* on recent changes in the imperial governance of the area. Nestacanna is reported to have said, "You tell me King George sends you to talk to all the Indians." But, he continued, "I am all the same as King George."[69] This reference to King George more than two decades into the reign of Queen Victoria is telling. It may indicate that, in 1860, King George's Royal Proclamation of 1763 was the subject of discussions between

Native people and naval officials up and down the BC coast. It may indicate that the Crown's representatives sought to reassure the Aboriginal leadership that recognition of their own peoples' Aboriginal rights and titles had long been entrenched in the constitution of British North America by a former imperial sovereign. From the earliest stages of colonization in the province there has been growing understanding among the Indigenous peoples that King George's Royal Proclamation established in Crown law a constitutional shield to protect some portion of the region's Aboriginal land, water, and jurisdiction from appropriation by the non-Aboriginal population.

The tenuous image of a benevolent imperial Crown with the will to protect Aboriginal peoples from the incursions of local non-Aboriginal settlers suffered a severe setback in 1863 when the Royal Navy's gunboat *Forward* opened fire on a Salish village on Kuper Island, east of Vancouver Island. The attack was motivated by the belief that the village harboured individuals who had assaulted non-Indians. Much to the dismay of the crew, the besieged coastal Salish responded by manning their war canoes and attacking the British vessel. This incident resulted in the largest display of Royal naval power in the history of British Columbia, when the imperial government made a show of strength that included the interrogation of Salish resisters under the torture of the lash.[70] The episode significantly belies the ideal presented by Judge Begbie of the integration of Native people as equals into the colonial system of criminal-law enforcement.

Between 1859 and 1870 Judge Begbie presided over cases that resulted in the hanging of twenty-six individuals, twenty-two of whom, or about 85 per cent, were Indian people. Only one was European, and the remaining three were of Chinese ancestry. This inequitable application of the criminal law seems to have continued a pattern started by Governor James Douglas, who sentenced seven Indian people to death in his oversight of the criminal justice system on Vancouver Island. In 1870–71 a second judge started work in the province and, in the initial months of his posting, he ordered the hanging of two more Indian people. In comparing these numbers with those of other jurisdictions, legal historian Sidney L. Harring has written: "There is no parallel to these executions anywhere in the hundred colonies that Britain founded, even in the penal colony of New South Wales; they make the founding of British Columbia a bloody colonial enterprise. But this violent history was 'legal,' with each of the executions ordered by a British judge."[71]

The number of Indian hangings in British Columbia, all of them conducted as public spectacles, was fairly high, even by comparison with US standards. For instance, fifteen Aboriginal men were publicly hanged by the US government for their part in the Washington Territory conflicts of 1858. In 1863 a larger public hanging of Sioux soldiers took place in Mankato, Minnesota.[72] Although a five-man military commission originally designated 300 individuals to be publicly hanged, President Abraham Lincoln intervened to reduce that number by about nine-tenths. Of the thirty-eight men executed, thirty-two requested baptism by Roman Catholic priests, an apparent indicator of the importance of religious politics in the resistance against an overwhelmingly Protestant foe.[73] There are many enduring reverberations arising from the thirty-one public hangings of Indian people that took place before the entry of British Columbia into the Dominion of Canada in 1871, and they continue to animate a wide array of questions about the nature of the relationship between Indigenous peoples there and the institutions of domestic and international law. The unresolved character of those questions permeates the uncertain status of about fifty ongoing Crown-Aboriginal treaty negotiations under way in British Columbia.[74]

Seen at their best, the current negotiation of Crown-Aboriginal treaties in British Columbia extend the Anglo-American traditions of enlightened law making which earlier gave rise to the Royal Proclamation and the Atlantic Charter. But the concerted effort by the governments of British Columbia and Canada to keep the BC land issue isolated from international venues of scrutiny, advice, and arbitration betrays the deeper dynamics of transformation inherent in the process. With an adequate investment of political will and imagination, this process of Crown-Aboriginal treaty negotiations could become a prototype of international relations in the tradition of the Fourth World. The city of Vancouver could become an especially important metropolis of the Fourth World if Indigenous peoples and non-Aboriginal citizens there could join together to demonstrate practical ways of *exercising* Aboriginal title even in urban settings. The innovative exercise of Aboriginal title in areas of shared jurisdiction and proprietorship would help advance the process of decolonization; it would help to pre-empt the violence bred from impositions of partition and segregation as the primary device for dealing with competing claims to the same land. In the language of the negotiations, the choice presented is one between "land-selection and co-jurisdiction."[75]

The negotiation of Crown-Aboriginal treaties in British Columbia presents a significant opening for Indigenous peoples to establish the precedent that they can exercise their human rights through the *exercise* of their Aboriginal title. Human rights can be recognized and affirmed or they can be denied and obstructed. They cannot, however, be extinguished with legitimacy. The goal of making treaties with Indigenous peoples which detail specific ways of *recognizing rather than extinguishing* Aboriginal title will advance the ideal of universal human rights. It furthers the principle that a fundamental feature of human rights lies in the ability of individuals and groups to express their differences and uniqueness within the larger framework of equality. Indeed, the great need of our times is to find ways of concurrently embracing the ideals of equality and biocultural diversity through media such as the negotiation and implementation of treaties with Indigenous peoples.[76]

It remains to be seen if some Tecumseh-like figure will emerge from the Indian Country of British Columbia to unify and internationalize the

Indian side of the negotiations. Certainly the celebration of the Winter Olympic Games in Vancouver and Whistler Mountain in 2010 gave rise to a global focus where the international personality of Indigenous peoples in British Columbia was highlighted, especially in the innovative opening ceremonies.

DOMESTICATING WARFARE: LITIGATION AND CRIMINAL LAW IN THE DENIAL AND NEGATION OF ABORIGINAL RIGHTS

The decades following the Second World War have sometimes been referred to as an era of *Pax Americana*.[77] This characterization of the era as a time of peace loosely conforms to the experiences over several decades of hundreds of millions of citizens in the hinterlands and metropolitan centres of North America, Europe, the Soviet Union, and Japan. The military power of the United States, combined with the proliferation of the agencies of international multilateralism flowing from New Deal, the Atlantic Charter, and the United Nations, shielded the citizens in many of the richest parts of the planet from invasion by hostile powers. The experience of those on the margins of wealth and geopolitical influence, however, has been very different. The Cold War was characterized by very hot wars for large masses of people in Indochina, Latin America, the Middle East, and Africa south of the Sahara. In a similar fashion, the century between the British victory at the Battle of Waterloo in 1815 and the onset of the First World War in 1914 has been described as an era of *Pax Britannica*.[78] This time of relative stability in the internal affairs of Europe gave rise to conditions facilitating the largest exodus in history to the Western Hemisphere and to many other colonized territories. Hence, the idea of a *Pax Britannica* is a complete non sequitur for the masses of Indigenous peoples who faced huge invasions of foreigners and alien influences into their Aboriginal lands and waters.

The time of so-called *Pax Britannica* was an era of literally thousands of wars and skirmishes on the formal and informal frontiers of European and Euro-American expansion.[79] Many of these skirmishes arose in the context of the sporadic resistance campaigns mounted by Indigenous peoples opposed to the eastward march of Russian colonization, an expansionary drive that continued to accelerate throughout the nineteenth century. As Paul Johnson affirms, "The Russian fur trappers would have gone right across North America had not the Western Europeans got there first and had not the Royal Navy been there to prevent them."[80] The violence deployed in opening China to the Anglo-American opium trade presents another example of the kind of conflict that made the era of *Pax Britannia* far less than peaceful for a large portion of humanity. Resentment by the indigenous Chinese to the foreign domination of their Aboriginal lands mounted throughout the nineteenth century, culminating in 1900 in the Boxer Uprising. This outburst of violence against foreigners, Christian

Chinese, and others stigmatized as local collaborators with the forces of Western imperialism began with the leadership of the Society of the Righteous and Harmonious Fists.[81] The growth of the Boxer resistance in China might be compared to the rise of the Ghost Dance religion in North America. The ghost dance, inspired by a messianic vision encouraging dancers to believe they could retake control of their territories and reverse the demise of the region's plundered buffalo herds, spread rapidly among many Aboriginal groups throughout western region in the 1880s. Occasionally the indigenous resistance movements met with temporary military success, as happened with the Indian vanquishment of General George Custer's forces at the Battle of Little Bighorn in 1876 or at the Zulu victory over the British soldiers at Islandlwana in South Africa in 1879.[82] In New Zealand the forces of British imperialism and Maori patriotism were for a time fairly evenly balanced. In 1864, however, British soldiers in the Waikato War finally overcame the considerable organized strength of the indigenous Maori King Movement.[83]

The Sand Creek Massacre in Colorado Territory stands as an example of a particularly vicious variety of military operation directed at the destruction of entire Indian communities, including children, women, and elders. Colonel John M. Chivington, a committed abolitionist and a former Methodist missionary to the Wyandot Indians, led a regiment of Colorado Volunteers who infamously slaughtered a band of Cheyenne and Arapahoe families.[84] The depredations of some US soldiers were mirrored in the actions of groups of civilians in the United States. Between 1882 and 1968, civilians are reported to have committed 4,742 documented lynchings of Indian individuals.[85] Almost inevitably the Aboriginal resistance struggles succumbed to the superior force of European and US weaponry, such as the rapid-fire Gatling Gun patented by the inventor Richard J. Gatling in 1862. Some of the worst episodes of imperial violence against Indigenous peoples took place in Africa. Millions were killed, maimed, or tortured in the drainage basin of the Congo River, for instance, by agents of the firms who derived licences to harvest rubber from the regime of Belgium's King Leopold. One of the clearest examples of outright genocide was directed against the Herero people indigenous to the area of South-West Africa that was colonized by Germany beginning in the late nineteenth century. It is estimated that about 85 per cent of the 80,000 Hereros were killed between 1904 and 1908 in a German military attempt to clear the land of present-day Namibia of its Aboriginal inhabitants. The crimes against the humanity of the Herero and the neighbouring Hamaka people included efforts to enslave them and contain them in the notorious concentration camp at Shark Island.[86]

In justifying these and many other frontier skirmishes and battles between Indigenous peoples and the imperial, national, and civilian shock troops of the ongoing Columbian conquests, the old archetypes of savagery versus civilization were enlivened by the infusion of new terminology giving the gloss of scholarly authority to new schools of scientific racism.[87] Edward Said has investigated many schools of social scientists who attached their research and publication to rationales for imperialism both before and after the Darwinian transition in the culture of empire building. He refers to "experts in legitimation" who were able to marshal a seemingly invincible array of "facts" to demonstrate that "the white races became scientifically different from reds, yellows, blacks, and browns, and consequently, territories occupied by those races became vacant, open to Western colonies, developments, plantations, and settlers." He cautioned that "imperialism ... cannot be blamed on science, but what needs to be seen is the relative ease with which science could be deformed into a rationalization for imperial domination." And, he continued, "the power to conquer territory is only in part a matter of physical force; there is the strong moral and intellectual component making the conquest itself secondary to an idea which dignifies (and indeed hastens) pure force with arguments drawn from science, morality, ethics, and general philosophy." In case after case "you get rid of the offending human and animal blight – whether it simply sprawls untidily all over the place or because it roams around unproductively and uncounted – and you confine the rest to reservations, compounds, native homelands, where you can count, tax, use them profitably, and you build a new society in the vacated space."[88]

These facts and observations establish the background and broader context of an outburst of violence generated by a road-building project in British Columbia in 1864. The incident was one of literally thousands of similar episodes of frontier violence that proliferated throughout the colonized world during the era of so-called *Pax Britannica*. These incidents, many of them unrecorded and now largely forgotten, made the nineteenth century and early years of the twentieth century a time of great turmoil and tragedy for multitudes of Indigenous peoples as they were incorporated, sometimes willingly and sometimes coercively, into what Immanuel Wallerstein has labelled the "modern world system."[89] The public hanging of five of the thirty-one Indians executed by BC's colonial government took place in Quesnelmouth in 1864. The multiple hanging culminated an episode that is remembered by a number of names, including the Chilcotin Uprising, the Bute Inlet Massacre, or the Waddington Massacre. The individuals who were hanged are sometimes referred to as the Chilcotin Five.

Edward Hewlett has described the Chilcotin Uprising as "the best documented instance of conflict between Indians and whites in British Columbia."[90] It involved the killing of twenty-one non-Aboriginals in a systematic assault carried out by a handful of Chilcotin men. The killing by Indian men of so many white road builders seemed to be the portent of a more widespread race war, a prospect that haunted the imagination of many newcomers in a jurisdiction where about 12,000 non-Aboriginal inhabitants lived in the midst of about 60,000 Aboriginal people. Indeed, the details of what happened are so loaded with a baggage of symbolic meaning that the event has taken on the status of a moral parable. It might be considered the mythological equivalent in the formation of British Columbia's identity to the role of King Philip's War of 1676 in the formation of New England's identity.[91] The Chilcotin Uprising was not only a seminal event in shaping the psychology of relations between Aboriginal and non-Aboriginal peoples but also a manipulated and supposed proof and illustration of the alleged distance between British and US approaches to the forging of new societies in North America.

The prelude to the killing was the imperial deployment of naval force in the attack on the Salish village on Kuper Island in 1863 and the smallpox epidemic that significantly reduced the Aboriginal population of British Columbia.[92] The plague is said to have befallen the Chilcotin with particular severity. One theory holds that the outburst of Chilcotin violence was related to this epidemiological tragedy, for it was not uncommon for Indian people to draw connections between their own sicknesses and close contact with Europeans and Euro-Americans.[93] Having noticed this pattern, Aboriginal groups or individuals would sometimes interpret the maladies befalling their people as having been purposely caused by non-Aboriginals, rather than inadvertently resulting from their very different immune systems. There was, therefore, some basis in the Chilcotin worldview ascribing to Whites the status of evil practitioners of bad medicine. The smallpox epidemic might well have been one of a number of factors in a complex of motivations prompting the decision of a Chilcotin group, whose leader was named Klatsassan, to fall on a crew of road builders. The construction project was a privately financed venture whose aim, as conceived by Alfred Penderall Waddington, was to create a shorter route to the site of a new gold rush in the Cariboo region of the interior. The projected road was to go from Bute Inlet on the Pacific coast directly through the prime hunting territory of the Chilcotin people.

News of the killings came to Victoria just as a new governor of British Columbia, Frederick Seymour, was taking office. The mood of hysteria that swept through the colony's non-Aboriginal population seemed likely to break out at any moment in indiscriminate vengeance killing. To avert this outcome, the government tried to apprehend the killers and make them accountable for their actions. A largely English contingent of former Royal Engineers went in pursuit of the offenders from Bute Inlet, while a largely American contingent of volunteers was put together in the Cariboo by a local mining official, William George Cox. It is said that the Cox contingent let it be known that if the killers did not give themselves up, the volunteers would go into the mountains and begin to "kill all the [Chilcotin] men, women and children."[94] The result was that Klatsassan presented himself in Cox's camp with the hope of saving his own wife and children. Cox reportedly gave tobacco to the hunted man. There was also some indication that the gold commissioner promised Klatsassan and the other hunted Indians amnesty if they would come voluntarily to see the colony's governor.

Whatever transpired, seven other Chilcotin men accompanied Klatsassan on his next visit to Cox's camp. Of the eight – Klatsassan, Telloot, Che-loot, Tahpit, Piel, Chessus, Chedekki, and Tananaki – five were subsequently hanged at Quesnelmouth.

Judge Begbie, who had presided over the trials of the condemned men, conferred with Klatsassan before the public hanging. Although an interpreter was present, it is said that the English law officer knew enough Chilcotin to conduct this interview largely in Klatsassan's own language. After this exchange, Begbie described Klatsassan as "the finest savage I have met yet."[95] The Reverend Lundin Brown, the Anglican minister who conducted the last rites for the Chilcotin Five before their death, had much the same reaction. His recollections in a text entitled *Klatsassan* form one of the episode's richest primary sources. With considerable literary acumen, the clergyman wove together the primordial elements of this striking saga of crime and punishment, resistance and repression. He described Klatsassan's visage in the following terms: "His strong face, piercing dark blue eyes, aquiline nose, and very powerful underjaw proclaimed the man of intelligence." In fact, he asserted, one could hardly lay eyes on this leader without feeling that "there was about the man something awful, and something winning – in fact, something *great*."[96]

Brown's and Begbie's superlatives were directed at the leader of an assault that came as close as colonial British Columbia ever got to a full-fledged Indian war. Their comments about Klatsassan suggest a thinly veiled official recognition that this outbreak of violence involved something larger than a few individuals acting in violation of the Crown's criminal code. Was it a question of law or an imperative of raw power that criminalized the Chilcotins' aggressive defence of their ancestral lands and waters from an encroachment as menacing as a road-building project pressed forward without their consent? Was it the rule of law or the rule of force that removed the Chilcotin from the law of international relations and entrapped them within the domestic confines of the colony's criminal code? There is much to recommend Judge Begbie's ideal of an egalitarian system of justice, however imperfectly implemented.

The central disparity between theory and practice in his scheme, however, was the reality that Indigenous peoples had not consented to the imposition of a foreign regime of authority and ownership on their Aboriginal lands. Unlike the immigrants to the jurisdiction, whose decision to take up residence in British Columbia implied voluntary acceptance of its governing institutions, most Native people in that colony had never been given the option, either as groups or as individuals, to embrace or reject by treaty the assertion of colonial jurisdiction on themselves and their Aboriginal lands and water. The failure to extend the principles of the Royal Proclamation of 1763 to most of British Columbia meant that the principles of equal rights and responsibilities were not implemented when it came to issues arising from the prior rights and titles of Indigenous peoples. The failure to attend to this aspect of the legal personality of the province's original inhabitants undermined the claim that Indigenous peoples had been incorporated into a legal regime based on the principles of equal treatment and democratic consent of the governed to the authority of governors. Because they were unilaterally deprived without their consent of legal jurisdiction in themselves, their Aboriginal territories, and their own Aboriginal polities, most Indigenous peoples in British Columbia were clearly not extended equal treatment by the agencies of law enforcement in colonial British Columbia.

Judge Begbie and the Reverend Brown could not have been totally inured to the ironies that make terrorists and criminals of some, and freedom fighters and patriots of others, who take up arms in defence of a cause, a people, a homeland, or all three. What makes the difference other than a balance of power that establishes the outcome? Given the absence of any forum of negotiation for the Chilcotin or other Aboriginal groups to bargain and compromise over some formula for the division of lands and resources in British Columbia, what seems surprising is how little violence there has been between Native and newcomer. In finding greatness in Klatsassan, it seems that Brown and Begbie were tacitly acknowledging the shared humanity of a man who had arguably responded in self-defence to a major incursion on the national rights of his people. Begbie's resort to the domestic criminal code could never entirely paper over the nuances of international warfare entailed in this incident or in many thousands like it that took place in the expansion of British North America, Anglo-America, the United States, Russia, Australia, South Africa, or the other battle zones of the Columbian conquests.

"The U.S. Courts never developed a consistent theory for the legal structuring of the Indian wars," Sidney Harring wrote. "International law was never applied, and Congress, with the sole power to declare war under the Constitution, never declared war on an Indian tribe." He added: "After these wars the tribes were often dealt with by military action that lacked any legal pretext at all; military trials and execution of Indians for murder and other offenses resulting from these wars occurred. Whole peoples were removed hundreds or thousands of miles from their homelands, held in concentration camps, and deprived of their lands without trial"[97] Legal historian Bruce Clark has made a number of similar observations, sharpened by his obstructed attempts to give legal representation to his Indian clients as they engaged in an Indian war involving the Canadian Army at Gustafsen Lake, BC, during the summer of 1995.[98] As Clark saw it, when the claims and assertions of Indigenous peoples rub up against the claims and assertions of the state, the judiciary in North America has steadfastly refused to look beyond the criminal code to the larger vistas of international and constitutional law:

The courts, whose duty it is to uphold the international and constitutional law, instead made it a practice to permit the starvation and hanging and imprisonment of protesting Indians, specifically by applying the domestic law in willful blindness to the international and constitutional law and the conflicts of law issue. The natives were caught and ground between the millstones constituted by the non-natives governments and courts. If and when the natives protested too vociferously, they were either shot by the military or arrested by the police and hung or imprisoned by the judges, all with a blind eye to the constitutional law. The key, the self-righteous genius of the genocidal mill, was that the shooting and hanging and imprisonment occurred under the proclaimed auspices of "just war" and the "rule of law."[99]

THE IDEA OF INDIAN RIGHTS AS A SYMBOL OF DIFFERENCE IN THE GENESIS OF TWO TRANSCONTINENTAL POLITIES

The violence underlying the events of 1864 brought to the surface many tensions in the colonial society of British Columbia. There was a growing acrimony among non-Aboriginals there over the future of the colony – whether it should remain part of the British Empire or throw in its lot with the United States. For those who remained attached to Great Britain's constitutional orbit, perhaps within the framework of some revised and expanded confederacy of Crown jurisdictions in North America, the prospects of a race war conjured up fears of being engulfed in a process identified as "Californiazation." John Robson and the other editors of New Westminster's *British Columbian*, a publication that would soon press for the incorporation of British Columbia into an expanded Canadian dominion, presented this specter as a kind of white savagery to be avoided at all costs.[100] The propensity of private citizens in the United States to engage in vigilante actions against Indian groups and individuals, as happened frequently on the mining frontiers of California, was contrasted with the presumed British preference for law and order as well as respect for properly constituted authority. As Robson wrote: "There are those among us who are disposed to ignore the rights of Indians and their claims upon us, who hold the American doctrine of 'manifest destiny' in its most fatal form. Under the shadow of this unchristian doctrine, the cry for 'extermination' is raised at every pretext. Very different, however, are the views and sentiments held ... by the British government."[101]

This passage, aimed at encouraging British Columbians to hold back from responding with violence to the killing of the road-builders, demonstrates how relations with Indigenous peoples served to mark differences among non-Aboriginals in their self-image and in their preferred means of taking control of their adopted continent. The imploding frontiers of Indian Country were not only physical places but zones for the production of myths with significant roles in the making of many forms of national identity. These places of encounter were realms of creative interaction vivifying flights of imagination about the expansion of old civilizations or the invention and elaboration of new ones.

Much was revealed in Robson's reference to American Manifest Destiny as an evil to be fended off through a generous accommodation of "the rights of Indians and their claims upon us." The comment serves to under-line the complex nature of the attractions and antagonisms linking the two North American polities engaged in constructing and consolidating claims of transcontinental hegemony. The constitutional empire of Great Britain had given rise to the commercial empire of the United States. From its inception, the leaders of the emergent US Empire conceived of themselves not only as nation-builders but also as the pioneer founders of a New World Order. From this perspective, the British imperial Crown's remaining Old World claims in North America were made to seem anachronistic and doomed – indeed, as anachronistic as the remaining Aboriginal titles of the Indigenous peoples. The conservative orientation of Indigenous peoples and British imperialists contrasted with the project of making the United States into what Frederick Jackson Turner would characterize at Chicago's Columbian Exposition "as a gate of escape from the bondage of the past."[102]

The US-led movement for continental integration held within it the urge to extinguish the conservative expressions of the Old World attachments of Indigenous peoples and British North America. Some of the most deter-mined proponents of US Manifest Destiny were still inclined to see two allied enemies, one imperial and one Aboriginal, in the persistence of the Indian Country of Canada as a bastion of resistance to their expansionary designs. The movement to absorb British Columbia and other parts of British North America into the United States reached heightened intensity in the years immediately following the US Civil War. This movement found many adher-ents both north and south of the forty-ninth parallel. Their fervour was stimulated by the reality that, before 1869, the only major vehicle for the Crown's continuing territorial claims from the region of Lake Superior to the Continental Divide along the Rocky Mountains was the ancient propri-etorship of a fur-trade monopoly vested in the Hudson's Bay Company.

The movement aimed at annexing the continent's northwesterly region to the United States was especially strong in the farms and communities scattered along the northward-flowing Red River, a body of water extend-ing deep into Minnesota. One of the few checks on the expansionistic ambitions centred in Minnesota was the harsh and bloody resistance of the Santee Sioux in that region. In 1862 and 1863 a group of militant freedom fighters including Little Crow and Medicine Bottle briefly broke free from the reservation culture that was beginning to entrap them. Their angry refusal to be boxed in by the laws and territorial constraints imposed on them initiated one of the bloodiest episodes of frontier war-fare in the trans-Mississippi conquest of the North American Indian Country.[103] And the military effort required to quell these two individuals and their followers helped to divert resources that might otherwise have been used in the US annexation of the western portion of what remained of British North America.

The power of the language employed by the movement to annex British North America in whole or in part helps to clarify one of the central ironies of Creole identity politics in the United States. That irony stems from the imperial quality of US expansionism in North America notwithstanding the reality that the United States emerged from the British Empire with a great barrage of rhetoric condemning European imperialism. Gareth Stedman Jones has commented on this irony, contrasting the policies of the United States within North America to the relative disinterest of the US government in acquiring overseas territory until the onset of the Spanish-American War at the end of the nineteenth century. "American historians who speak complacently of the absence of settler-type colonialism characteristic of the European powers," he writes, "merely conceal the fact that the whole *internal* history of United States imperialism was one vast process of territorial seizure and occupation. The absence of territorialism 'abroad' was founded on an unprecedented territorialism 'at home.'"[104]

By the end of the Civil War, this sense of so-called territorialism within the United States had already absorbed much of the lands formerly claimed by Canada and Mexico. James Wickes Taylor, who would serve as consul of the US government in Winnipeg, made himself a key figure among those who anticipated the absorption of the remaining Crown holdings in North America into the Imperial Republic. He envisaged the rise of St Paul, Minnesota, as the main metropolis of a vast hinterland, including the area of the present-day provinces of Manitoba, Saskatchewan, and Alberta. Among the other proponents of annexing all or part of the remaining British North America into the United States were William H. Seward (Abraham Lincoln's secretary of state), California's Senator William McKendree Gwin, and the publishers of the Chicago *Tribune* and the New York *Herald*.[105]

In November 1869 the British Columbians who favoured attaching their home jurisdiction to the United States issued a petition indicating their wish to be "united to a people of our own kindred, religion and tongue."[106] Their request was advertised and matched by Elwood Evans, a US lawyer who delivered an address before the Tacoma Library Association in Olympia, the capital of Washington Territory. His presentation carried forward many of the themes of Anglo-American Manifest Destiny that Thomas Jefferson had introduced and that Goldwin Smith would elaborate on from his perch in Toronto.[107] Evans described the United States' purchase of Alaska from Russia in 1867 as the prelude to that moment when "the whole Continent shall be one nation, with one sovereign government, one flag, one people."[108] Among the many authorities he cited for this prediction was John Quincy Adams, who, in 1827, had condemned the role of the Hudson's Bay Company on the continent. Where that enterprise was content to leave the land in "a savage and barbarous state," Adams claimed, the aim of the United States was "to make the wilderness blossom as a rose, to establish laws, to increase, multiply and subdue the earth, which we are commanded to do by the first behest of God Almighty."[109]

Evans invoked the authority of the Monroe Doctrine as a justification for his condemnation of "such a contradiction in terms as British America."[110] "American destiny," he proclaimed, "means the entire, exclusive, homogenous Americanization of North America, with but one nationality exercising sovereign powers, without the intervention, or right, or necessity, to intervene by any foreign power." With this as his idealized aim of history, "no reasonable excuse remains for European intervention in American affairs." Only by "the exclusion of England as a sovereign power from the American continent" will the day arrive when "we will have attained that true condition of national independence."[111] Clearly Evans's vision of "homogenous Americanization" left no room for the Aboriginal inhabitants of the continent to retain and renew their identities within a polity embracing cultural pluralism as one of its principles. The ideal to be achieved by the incorporation of British North America into the United States was monocultural rather than multicultural or intercultural. The imagery of society as a melting pot rather than a mosaic of distinct communities was to prevail. The ideal for Evans was the Darwinian absorption of the weak and the hegemonic domination of the strong as an expression of the Survival of the Fittest, as a manifestation of an evolutionary imperative to fulfill the outcome of natural selection among countries by holding sway over an entire continent. "We will indeed be *E Pluribus Unum*," predicted the orator.

Those who argued against Evans's vision of continental unity advocated the persistence of two transcontinental polities. The belief of those who sought to resist the draw towards the United States was built on the notion that British North America was different and in some ways superior to the republic to the south. The United Empire Loyalists and those who continued the tradition of attachment to the Crown of Great Britain believed that their form of citizenship sustained a way of life more conducive to the pre-eminence of the rule of law over the rule of strong men. As Robson's editorial in the *British Columbian* indicated, the conduct of Indian Affairs became a significant point of symbolic differentiation, the basis of a myth of national superiority in what would become the transcontinental Dominion of Canada. The course of North American history gave some genuine substance to this myth. The difference between the two systems of governance, one based on republican principles and the other on those of constitutional monarchy, was especially evident in the geography of Indian reserves and reservations in North America. The large number of Indian reserves in Lower and Upper Canada and in British North America's Maritime colonies contrasted dramatically with the near absence of Indian reservations in the United States east of the Mississippi. And that contrast embodied the outcome of two very different histories, one rooted in Indian removal and the other in a heritage of Crown-Aboriginal treaty alliances in shared defence of territory against the encroachments of US Manifest Destiny.

Again and again French imperialists and then British imperialists had joined forces with the Indigenous peoples to defend the Indian Country of

Canada and the domain of the Montreal fur trade against the acquisitive encroachments of the most land-hungry constituencies of Anglo-Americans. The United States took form in direct opposition to the more conservative yet socialistic array of groups who sought many dreams of liberty and justice in the northern half of North America. The Canadian community of communities was based on alliances linking the government of British North America with the Indian Confederacy, the Roman Catholic *canadiens*, many Black refugees seeking freedom from slavery, and a multicultural mosaic of vulnerable minorities who fled the intolerance of the new republic's tyranny of the majority.[112] The myth makers of US expansionism drew prolifically on the imagery created by the exploits of Daniel Boone, William Henry Harrison, Andrew Jackson, and others. Each of these individuals, two of whom became US presidents, fought against the Aboriginal-Crown alliances that gave the Indian Country of Canada a continuity that transcended the British conquest of New France.

The descendants of those who saw Indian fighting as a necessary duty of national aggrandizement were inclined to view the broader imperatives of US Manifest Destiny in a similar light. The speech of Elwood Evans on the "desirability" of the "re-annexation" of British Columbia clearly articulated the convictions of those who saw in the forces emanating from the whig side of the American Revolution a formula for an expanded field of *homogenized* individual liberty. That form of melting pot triumphalism was said to deserve continental, if not hemispheric and global, application. Accordingly, the seizure by the Anglo-American revolutionaries of the leadership in the ongoing war on Indian Country created a pattern re-enacted repeatedly in the push to expand US power against indigenous resistance in, for instance, Hawaii, the Philippines, Central America, Indochina, Afghanistan, Iraq, and Iran. The propensity to legitimate hot and cold wars on the real or imagined enemies of universalized capitalism renewed patterns established when the United States was founded in a Declaration of Independence defining all future conquests of Indian Country as ways to contain, pacify, or eliminate Aboriginal savagery. Beyond the frontiers of the merciless Indian savages awaited the frontiers of communism and terrorism. The Global War on Terror would complete the circle of aggression started with an Anglo-American revolt on King George and his Aboriginal allies, whom the US founders accused of "an undistinguished destruction of all ages, sexes, and conditions."

The fate of the Indians and the subordinate position of most Blacks in the United States served as a sobering caution for many Native people, French Canadians, and Anglo-Americans not to abandon their connection to the British Crown in order to widen the orbit of the continent's first republic. The aversion to the Californiazation of British Columbia resulted in the development of expectations that Crown officials would, in the words of John Robson, recognize "Indian rights and their claims upon us." This expectation, however, proved even less applicable to Canada's westernmost province than to other parts of the Dominion. Until the last years of the twentieth century, the BC government resisted any real reckoning with the tradition of Crown law that recognizes and affirms the existence of Aboriginal and treaty rights. That tradition runs from the Covenant Chain, through the Royal Proclamation of 1763, and then through the Crown-Aboriginal agreements that were extended in both the pre-Confederation treaties and the numbered treaties all the way to the eastern slopes of the Rocky Mountains. Except for three regions of British Columbia – the ancestral territory of the Nisga'a, a small area on Vancouver Island, and the northeasterly extremity of the province covered by Treaty 8 – the Aboriginal title in British Columbia remains uncompromised by the completed negotiation of Crown-Aboriginal treaties. The Crown of British Columbia thus lacks a regime of treaty relations with Indigenous peoples similar to that in the Canadian prairies or in neighbouring Washington state.

In more recent times, British Columbia has been the site of considerable tension between those who adhere to the expectation initially expressed by John Robson that the province will be brought within the rule of law and those who would dismiss the idea of Aboriginal title as an anachronistic remnant of British North America. Many of those on the neoliberal side of this contention, including the well-organized members of BC FIRE (Federation for Individual Rights and Equality), seemed to favour the Manifest Destiny of Anglo-America to obliterate all impediments to a regime of commercial relations based on the principle that all human and corporate "persons" are equal before the law.[113] Proponents of this interpretative school tend to refer frequently to their contempt for "race-based" policy and law. They rarely touch on the material requirements of biocultural diversity or the contemporary inequities that arise from the material discrimination which has disproportionately entitled a small minority of newcomers and their corporate extensions. This material enrichment remains directly connected to historic and ongoing dispossession of Aboriginal groups and individuals based on racist conceptions of who should inherit the future and who should be relegated to the past.

On the other side of the debate are those inclined to consider the origins of the present inequities in wealth and opportunity. Those with an openness to the ideals of the Fourth World tend to respect the continuum of imperial, international, and constitutional law expressed in the evolutionary genesis of ideas and actions connecting the Royal Proclamation of 1763, the Atlantic Charter, and the provisions in the Canadian *Constitution Act, 1982*, that recognize and affirm the existence of the Aboriginal and treaty rights of Aboriginal peoples. The most expansive versions of this outlook extend beyond British Columbia and the rest of Anglo-America to see Aboriginal title as a code for the right of Indigenous peoples globally not to be unilaterally dispossessed of their inherent jurisdiction in themselves, their Aboriginal polities, and their Aboriginal lands, waters, and attending resources.

LAW AND LAWLESSNESS IN BRITISH COLUMBIA

The publicity attending a showdown in the early 1980s between logging interests and Indigenous peoples in British Columbia drew attention to the movement to realize the ecological ideals of the Fourth World. That showdown took place in Haida Gwaii, the legendary archipelago also known as the Queen Charlotte Islands. The controversy attracted the attention of David Suzuki, who described his 1982 production of a Canadian Broadcasting Corporation documentary on the future of this island oasis as a turning point in his development as a scientist, broadcaster, and author. In making the film, Suzuki collaborated with a number of Aboriginal friends from the region, including Miles Richardson, Guujaaw, and Patricia Kelly, and he said, "Guujaaw changed the way I viewed the world and sent me on a radically different course of environmentalism."[114]

This breakthrough for the host of the CBC series *The Nature of Things* emerged from Suzuki's sudden appreciation of the thick web of connections linking the knowledge, culture, and philosophy of some Native people to the ecology of their ancestral lands and waters. Guujaaw's insights helped Suzuki to embrace Aboriginal wisdom, much as John Collier had done after his encounter with the ceremonies of the Tiwa people of New Mexico.[115] After this experience, Suzuki threw himself into the project of linking the principles of Aboriginal rights with environmental protection in British Columbia, Amazonia, Australia, Papua New Guinea, and the world. As he advanced this agenda, he developed the view that "most immigrants were incapable of learning from aboriginal people and the indigenous flora and fauna because they lacked the respect to watch, listen, and learn from them. Instead," he said, "they attempted to 'make over' the land to what is familiar, bringing their domesticated plants and animals, clearing the land of its native forests and prairies, draining the wetlands, straightening or damning rivers, and dumping wastes without a thought. And once they became established," he continued, "they attempted to remove indigenous people by killing them or forcing them to abandon their languages, culture, and values to become Canadians."[116]

The struggle to save large portions of Haida Gwaii from the inroads of loggers met with a reasonable measure of success. The campaign incorporated the idea of Aboriginal title into the work of a broad coalition of environmental activists and organizations, including the Sierra Club, the Valhalla Society, and the Western Canada Wilderness Committee.[117] This collaboration between Indigenous peoples, the environmental movement, and government resulted in the creation in the late 1980s of the Gwaii Haanas National Park Reserve and Haida Heritage Site, encompassing regions of abundant biodiversity and majestic geography.

As the pressure for conservation mounted, one of the anti-logging blockades was joined in 1985 by William (Bill) Reid. This well-known jewellery maker and sculptor is credited with inspiring and leading an international movement of ecological design that begins with the West Coast tradition of carving masks and totem poles and extends to the most advanced frontiers of contemporary artistic expression.[118] In the 1940s and 50s Reid spent much of his spare time studying the rich art forms of his mother's Haida people. Then he began to collaborate closely with the Museum of Anthropology at the University of British Columbia, assembling long houses, carving large totem poles, and making extensive studies and sketches of its collection of West Coast Aboriginal artifacts. With this institutional power behind him, it seemed as though Bill Reid had walked out of the Aboriginal past to point the way to a global future based on humanity's return to sustainable ways of combining both ecology and political economy. His 1990s masterpiece, the sculpture *Spirit of Haida Gwaii*, celebrates the Aboriginal mythology of life's renewal in a startling image of several life forms sharing their destiny in a single vessel. Here Noah's Arc meets the Fourth World and the Bowl with One Spoon. Versions of Reid's engaging icon of biocultural diversity sit prominently in the Canadian Embassy in Washington, the Vancouver International Airport, the Museum of Civilization in Hull, Quebec, and on the Canadian $20 bill. The application of Reid's design onto Canadian money adds an Aboriginal twist to Earth's transformation into property.

This successful bridging of many communities of interest helped to facilitate the kind of coalition building essential to the ecological conservation of Haida Gwaii. Reid's artistic and political leadership helped inspire many other West Coast Aboriginal artists, including Robert Davidson. Although the renaissance of Indian art on BC's West Coast highlights the reinvigoration of Aboriginal culture, the creative brightness of this movement must be pictured against the darker side of the human condition blighting the life and death of too many Native people. That darkness is sadly expressed in the human devastation that menaces the residents of Vancouver's Downtown Eastside. The disproportionately high number of Native people in this zone of violent urban anarchy forms a striking display of the consequences of BC's failure to recognize and affirm the existence of Aboriginal and treaty rights over several generations. Many of these people are homeless and even more of them face extremely high rates of addictions, poverty, street violence, and danger from the sex trade. In 2002 news reports began to circulate stories that a nearby pig farm contained the remains of possibly dozens of murdered young women from Vancouver's Downtown Eastside. Robert Picton's conviction five years later helped to draw attention to the unexplained and often uninvestigated disappearance of many hundreds of Native women throughout Canada. In 2006 it was reported that, on one stretch of highway in northern British Columbia alone, nine girls and women, most of them Aboriginal, have disappeared or are known to have been killed over a relatively short period.[119] Amnesty International and the Native Women's Association of Canada responded by working together on the *Stolen Sisters* report and by organizing the Sisters in Spirit campaign.[120] The aim of this activism has been to break through the walls of ignorance, prejudice, and stereotyping blocking the embrace of the shared humanity of those most exposed to the predators that feed, often with impunity, on the vulnerability of the traumatized victims of Indian Country's ongoing colonization.

There are complex cycles of history linking the legacy of sexual abuse in the Indian residential schools and horrors such as the epidemic of addictions plaguing some Aboriginal communities or the trafficking of children for the purposes of prostitution.[121] From the violent promotion of opium use in China in the nineteenth century to the flood of crystal meth into many reserves during the early years of the twenty-first century, colonialism new and old has frequently been facilitated, accompanied, and heralded by processes that chemically and psychologically enslave subject peoples. In British Columbia the legacy of the Indian residential schools merged seamlessly with persistent rumours and snippets of news suggesting that trafficking in drugs and the sexual exploitation of children, many of them Aboriginal, converged in corruption rings involving some high officials in the judiciary and the BC Law Society. In 1999 Jennifer Wade, a founder of Amnesty International in Vancouver, referred to this perception in a keynote presentation at the Global Conference on the Commercial Exploitation of Children and Youth. As part of her talk, she looked back at the seemingly surreal experiences in 1994 of Jack Cram and Renate Andres-Auger, two lawyers who made serious allegations about the involvement of top authorities in the sexual exploitation of children:

The sex trade in children is not a recent happening in Vancouver. While doing some research for this presentation, I came across the affidavit of a Cree lawyer named Renate Andres-Auger ... naming prominent legal personalities and the BC Law Society for destroying her legal practice and libeling and slandering her (I have a copy of that affidavit listing prominent plaintiffs with me). Renate Auger alleged this happened partly because of her knowledge of pedophile rings operating out of the Vancouver Club and out of resorts in Whistler. In a very bizarre scene as it was described in the papers, I discovered Ms. Auger and her lawyer, Jack Cram, were first not listened to in the court, and then were handcuffed and dragged out of the courtroom to a jail cell. When Cram eventually did speak, he put before the judge some of his allegations involving cover-ups by the head officers of the Law Society and the judiciary to aid and abet pedophiles and drug dealers. When he insisted on giving more details on radio, Cram was met by ten policemen upon his return from a radio station. He was then put into an ambulance and taken to the psychiatric ward of Vancouver General Hospital. He believes he was injected again and again with mind disorienting drugs.[122]

No public investigation into the treatment and accusations of Andres-Auger and Cram ever took place. We can only speculate, therefore, on the circumstances behind such a dramatic collapse of dignity and due process in the criminal justice system. Certainly it is made to seem probable that some highly placed group or individual believed that he, she, or they had a great deal to lose if Andres-Auger and Cram had been able to press their charges in the courts of law and public opinion. The accusations of the two lawyers merged with a powerful stream of allegations by critics who charged that rampant corruption and conflicts of interest permeated the entire proceedings of the $27 million federally funded test case to determine the legal status of Aboriginal title in the lands and water of British Columbia. The case would eventually emerge in 1997 as the basis of the Supreme Court of Canada's *Delgamuukw* ruling.[123] Jack Cram was deeply involved with various aspects of this controversial case. At the time he tried to represent Andres-Auger, he was also beginning to act for Gitskan Indian clients who charged that their own lawyers had committed fraud against them. The *Delgamuukw* case began with the initial assertion that the hereditary leaders of the Gitskan and Wet'suwet'en Indians continue to be the legitimate governors in a large area of the BC interior.[124] How, Cram's clients wanted to know, did a case beginning with allegations that the non-Aboriginal government has wrongfully pre-empted the jurisdiction of the Aboriginal government get remade to address issues of narrower consequence? Did those funding the lawyers on the Aboriginal side misuse public funds to assert inappropriate control over the matters to be decided?

Cram's rapid transformation from a successful and well-regarded Vancouver lawyer to an involuntarily institutionalized patient in the psychiatric ward of the Vancouver General Hospital resembled the treatment extended the following summer to lawyer Bruce Clark. It seems that the propensity is high in British Columbia to kill the messenger rather than to grapple with the content of difficult messages. Clark held that Crown institutions in Canada, including the courts, had wrongfully imposed their jurisdiction on the Indigenous peoples in British Columbia ever since Crown officials failed to obtain Indian consent for the province's development, as required by the Royal Proclamation of 1763. He alleged that the failure of the governments and courts in the province to adhere to the constitutional law of British North America and Canada as well as to the UN's international instruments made a number of Crown officials guilty of complicity in the crime of genocide. In 1995 Clark tried to bring these arguments forward on behalf of Aboriginal clients engaged in an armed standoff with the RCMP and the Canadian Army in Gustafsen Lake. In his effort to represent the self-styled Ts'peten Defenders, an incident transpired in a rural BC court similar to the one Andres-Auger and Cram experienced. While in the midst of attempting to present his legal arguments, Clark too was taken into custody and sent to an institution for a compulsory psychological examination.

The commercial media tend to misrepresent the substance of Bruce Clark's controversial legal practice. At its worst, this media depiction portrayed Clark as a nerd on LSD. There was huge emphasis on his shaved head, unorthodox designer glasses, and provocative sound bites. This approach left little room for balanced coverage of the serious and sweeping constitutional arguments he attempted to articulate for the public. Clark had been prominent among the first wave of lawyers to develop the field of Aboriginal land claims after the Supreme Court of Canada acknowledged the legal existence of Aboriginal title in an ambivalent ruling in 1973 in response to the legal arguments put forward by the Nisga'a Indians and their advocate, Thomas Berger.[125] Clark first devoted himself to developing the evidentiary base for an assertion of Aboriginal title by an Aboriginal group in Temagami, Ontario. His clients, many of whom lived on a small reserve on Bear Island, claimed they had been passed over in 1850 when William Benjamin Robinson negotiated two treaties on behalf of the British imperial Crown with the Aboriginal Anishinabek in territory north of the upper Great Lakes. When Clark failed to make headway in Ontario against a thick wall of judicial hostility to his constitutional interpretation, he continued to hone his arguments in MA and PhD theses, both of which have been published. These texts, together with a more recent book, many articles, and a large body of court reports and philosophical musings published digitally, form a rich record alleging that the judiciary, the law societies, and many elites of Canada's law profession have chosen the course of political expediency over genuine adherence to the rule of law in their interventions affecting Crown-Aboriginal relations.[126]

When Clark moved from Ontario to British Columbia, he specialized in representing Aboriginal clients such as William Jones Ignace. This Shuswap elder was typical of many of his Indian clients in that he found more legitimacy in his people's own traditions of Aboriginal governance than in the federally funded system of band council governance spawned by the *Indian Act*. As Clark and his clients saw it, the application of the *Indian Act* system in British Columbia was illegal and open to manipulation by Crown pay masters. Similarly, basing the organization of BC treaty negotiations on the system of political and legal representation rooted in the *Indian Act* was a real abomination. Clark's interpretation emphasized four dates – 1537, 1704, 1763, and 1948. The first corresponds with the Papal Bull recognizing the right of Indians in the Americas not to be enslaved or robbed of their liberty and property. The second date marks a constitutional ruling by Queen Anne's Privy Council in the case of *Mohegan vs Connecticut*.[127] A key facet of that ruling held that any future arbitration on the issue of Aboriginal title in the English colonies in North America would have to be done by independent jurists not connected to the contending jurisdictions – in other words, by third-party adjudication. In Clark's estimation, the precedent established in the *Mohegan* case applied in British Columbia and the rest of Canada; judges today are in no less of a conflict of interest when they decide on assertions of Aboriginal title, jurisdiction, and sovereignty than were the judges of Connecticut in 1704. How, Clark asks, could judges whose land titles, salaries, and judicial status come from the governments of colonies or their successor states fairly assess allegations against those same governments by Aboriginal litigants asserting that their own

Aboriginal jurisdictions have been wrongfully invaded? By what right or authority was a precedent set by the highest Crown court in the eighteenth century dispensed with by Crown courts in twentieth-century Canada?

Clark rounded out his interpretation by drawing heavily on the Royal Proclamation of 1763 and on the Convention for the Prevention and Punishment of the Crime of Genocide, an international instrument adopted by the UN General Assembly in 1948. The result was a reading of the law that must certainly rate as one of the most challenging ever brought forward by a legal advocate in Canada – or in any other jurisdiction. Employing the language of his key constitutional exhibits, Clark did not back away from accusing the judges he faced of treason, fraud, complicity in genocide, and the usurpation of jurisdiction. Not surprisingly, some jurists lost their composure when phrases such as these came their way. Chief Justice Antonio Lamar responded in 1995 in the Supreme Court of Canada, for instance, by calling Clark a "disgrace to the bar." The antagonism towards Clark did not stop with the judiciary but extended widely across the legal profession and many Aboriginal organizations. Again this antagonism is hardly surprising, given that Clark's interpretation put in question the use of the domestic courts to determine the extent and applicability over many fields of Aboriginal and treaty rights. If valid, Clark's interpretation stigmatizes this entire process as presently constituted. It calls into question the legitimacy of a system that generates good livelihoods for scores of experts, practitioners, consultants, elected politicians, and administrators willing to work within the framework of the agenda to confine Indigenous peoples and their Aboriginal polities within the constraints of municipal-type government, delegated authority, and corporate law. Clark's interpretation treats whole complexes of litigation as exercises in politics disguised as jurisprudence. In spite of his being disbarred from the Upper Canada Law Society in 1999, Clark remained unapologetically insistent that the rule of law is being violated by the domestic courts and by the regime of Crown-Aboriginal relations, including the BC treaty negotiations, based on the system of political and legal representation created by the federal *Indian Act.*

British Columbia continues to develop on the frontiers of Anglo-America's changing relationship to land, law, and liberty. Many flash points of controversy within Indian Country were ignited by the attempt of the US government beginning in 2003 to extradite John Graham from Vancouver to face the charge of murdering Anna Mae Pictou Aquash in South Dakota in 1975.[128] John Graham is a Southern Tutchone Indian from Canada's Yukon Territory. In the mid-1970s he was deeply involved in the American Indian Movement and its assertion of the international character of Aboriginal and treaty rights in North America and throughout the Western Hemisphere. Along with Russell Means, Dennis Banks, and Leonard Peltier, Anna Mae Pictou Aquash was one of the most high-profile AIM activists in the early 1970s. A young Micmac woman from Shubanacadie, Nova Scotia, she emerged as a prominent figure when AIM made an armed stand in

1973 at Wounded Knee, South Dakota, the scene of an infamous massacre of Native people in 1890 by the US Armed Forces. Gradually Pictou Aquash and her fellow AIM members, including John Graham, were drawn into a virtual civil war on the Pine Ridge Reservation in South Dakota through their efforts to oppose the corrupt leadership of the Indian community's federally backed tribal chairman, Dick Wilson. Dozens of AIM members and their sympathizers were murdered during the mid-1970s by paramilitary forces who were aided by the FBI, even as they took their direct orders from Wilson. One of those killed in this atmosphere of violent recriminations was Anna Mae Pictou Aquash.

The general assumption for many years was that Pictou Aquash had been murdered by the FBI or one of the federal police force's paid assassins. In the mid-1970s AIM was one of the prime targets of COINTELPRO, the so-called counter-intelligence division of the US federal police force. COINTELPRO's mission involved the planting of police collaborators, such as Douglas Durham, within AIM in order to confuse its members and to weaken, divide, and ultimately destroy the organization. Part of the technique of destabilizing AIM was through "snitch jacketing" – by creating as much suspicion as possible within a targeted organization through rumour mongering about who might be collaborating with the police. Pictou Aquash got caught within this web of suspicion. According to the authors of the charges brought forward in Rapid City, South Dakota, John Graham was assisted by Fritz Arlo Looking Cloud when they shot Pictou Aquash in the back of the head sometime between late December 1975 and February 1976. It is alleged that both were acting as enforcers on the orders of the security division of AIM's leadership. Graham denies that he killed Pictou Aquash and maintains he has been framed – much as AIM member Leonard Peltier is widely believed to have been wrongfully convicted for the killing two FBI agents in 1976. Peltier was extradited from Vancouver to face murder charges in South Dakota, and it is broadly recognized that his extradition proceedings in Canada were based on false evidence.[129] The memory of the FBI's submission of fraudulent evidence to Canadian authorities in the Peltier case has had a negative effect on the credibility of the agencies involved on the US side of these more recent extradition proceedings.

The background of the Graham case points to the ongoing character of the Indian wars in North America – to the ruthlessness of the effort to prevent Indigenous peoples from acting on the principle that their Aboriginal polities continue to draw sovereign jurisdiction from the unextinguished source of their Aboriginal and treaty rights. It reveals the severity of the sacrifices sometimes required of those who insist on asserting the imperative and right of Indian Country to survive even in the heartland of the American empire. After following the story of AIM for more than three decades, Ellen Klaver, a journalist for KGNU Radio in Colorado, observed: "Whoever was involved [in the murder of Anna Mae Pictou Aquash], the FBI was the architect. They either had her killed or tricked AIM into killing her."[130] The controversy swirling around John Graham touches on the quality of Canadian sovereignty in its relations with the United States. Both Graham and the woman he is accused of killing by officials of the US government are Native people from Canada. In December 2007 the Supreme Court of Canada refused to hear an appeal of a lower court ruling calling for Graham's extradition. As a result, the accused was transported across the international border and placed in the hands of US officials by members of the RCMP.[131] Graham's trial in Rapid City, South Dakota, gave renewed force and complexity to the litany of accusations and counter-accusations between AIM's founding leadership which proliferated in and around the legal proceedings leading to Looking Cloud's conviction for first-degree murder in 2004. The wild finger-pointing testimony from Kamook Banks and John Trudell proved especially inflammatory in illuminating the role of police, informants, and infiltrators in the undermining of one of America's most controversial warrior societies.

The controversies swirling in and around the criminal justice system in British Columbia extended to Judge David William Ramsay. In 2004 Judge Ramsay was convicted of sexually abusing a number of Aboriginal teenager girls who had appeared before him in court. Two years later some members of the RCMP were alleged to be involved in a cycle of sexual abuse as both the perpetrators and the investigators of those crimes. Do these cases have any connection to the accusations pressed years earlier by Jack Cram and Renate Andres-Auger? How broadly does this kind of behaviour extend within the core of BC's criminal justice system?[132] Janice Switlo, a lawyer who has traversed some of the same territory as Bruce Clark in her quest to affirm the international dimension of the rights and treaties of Indigenous peoples, wrote: "We have ignored the third- and fourth-hand rumours for too long. They were ignored for years before the warning was issued about ground-up remains of Indigenous women in BC's infamous Pickton pig farm. They were ignored for years before a surviving Indigenous man left for dead [by the police] in the bitter cold of a Saskatchewan winter found the courage to speak out."[133]

In her volume on the Battle of Gustafsen Lake, the Indian war waged in British Columbia in 1995, Switlo has given vital testimony suggesting the awkward discomfort flowing from the aftermath of the public execution of the Chilcotin Five. When she was working for the Canadian Department of Justice in the late 1980s, she visited Quesnel in the course of conducting some transactions with the local Indian band. Like many Aboriginal groups, this community had affirmed a basic right of self-determination by replacing the Anglicized version of its name with one more reflective of the sounds of its own language – Tsilhqot'in. During a coffee break, Switlo walked along the river by the Tsilhqot'in band office. She stopped and was casually informed by her Tsilqot'in colleague that the parking lot beside them held the buried remains of Klatsassin, Tellot, Tahpit, Piel, and Chessus. When she asked her hosts why no marker proclaimed the nature of what lay below, her informant shrugged and said, "I guess because they're an embarrassment."[134] How many other comparable "embarrassments" lie similarly concealed to hide the evidence of a very insidious form of genocide that began in 1492 and that never really ended?

CHAPTER NINE

Landscapes of Memory, Territories of Power

To characterize the Ts'peten Defenders as engaged in a mere land dispute or disagreement with government policy is to trivialize the nature of the controversy. Control over land is one of the primary reasons for government and is often the cause of war between nations. Given its substantial economic consequences, the Aboriginal title question in Canada clearly is a highly charged issue for both Native and non-Native people.

Judge Janice Stewart, ruling in the case of
United States of America v. James Pitawanakwat, 2000

The people who hold the clubs insist on historical amnesia.
Noam Chomsky, *What We Say Goes*, 2007

ABORIGINAL TITLE, THE COLUMBIAN CONQUESTS, AND THE MAKING OF TREATIES WITH INDIGENOUS PEOPLES AS THE MEANS OF OBTAINING LICENCES FOR EMPIRE

In *The Clash of Civilizations and the Remaking of World Order*, Samuel P. Huntington pictures the United States as the primary bastion, agent, champion, and defender of Western civilization. The attributes that helped make the United States the West's most influential polity have often been expressed through the reach of its compelling popular culture, its dazzling technological innovations, and its sometimes bold and adept diplomacy.[1] As Huntington reminds us, however, the rise of the so-called West, like the rise of the United States, has depended more on military force than on intellectual persuasion. "The West," he writes, "won the world not by the superiority of its ideas or values or religion (to which few members of other civilizations were converted) but rather by its superiority in applying organized violence. Westerners often forget this fact; non-Westerners never do."[2]

Few groups have been as directly confronted over a longer period of time by the West's methods of organized violence than those Indigenous peoples who lived along the course of the United States' transcontinental expansion. The imperial personality of the federal capital of the United States grew with every new conquest and pacification of Indian Country. Those appointed by the War Department in Washington, DC, to spearhead the westward movement of the United States were generally well trained military men. These soldiers included William Henry Harrison as governor of Indiana Territory and Isaac Stevens as governor of Washington Territory. Like many of the men sent to lead the American republic's western expansion during its initial century, Harrison and Stevens were both instructed by their commanders to combine warfare with treaty diplomacy so as to neutralize Aboriginal resistance to the assertion of US sovereignty. Between 1776 and 1871 the United States government made about four hundred treaties with Indigenous peoples. Then Congress renounced even the pretense that it recognized the Aboriginal title of Indigenous peoples within the boundaries of the United States and formally adopted instead the doctrine of conquest as the justification for American power over Indians and their ancestral lands.

The federal recognition of Aboriginal title before 1871 helped to bolster the power of the national government over state governments. This recognition was an integral feature of the arrangement that enabled officials in Washington, DC, to create federal territories on the western frontiers of Euro-American settlement as internal colonies of federal authority. During the most formative phase of the republic's western expansion, the federal territories embodied an intermediate stage in the process of transforming Indian Country into fully constituted states, where non-Aboriginal male Protestants who were not slaves and who owned property acquired substantial powers of local self-government. The federal territories thus embodied a half-way point along the imagined journey from savagery to civilization. Thomas Jefferson described this technique of asserting federal control over the creation of new territories and states in the former Indian Country as a core device in the machinery for expanding the new republic. In 1809 Jefferson wrote, "No Constitution was ever as well constituted for extensive empire and self-government."[3]

The Dominion of Canada copied the US approach to transcontinental expansion by creating federal territory as a prelude to creating new provinces, as happened in 1905 with the establishment, through federal statute, of Alberta and Saskatchewan. Before the formation of these provinces, eight numbered treaties were negotiated between officials representing Queen Victoria and Aboriginal groups east of the Rockies. The negotiation of the numbered treaties carried forward an evolving heritage of Crown-Aboriginal diplomacy with important antecedents in the Covenant Chain of relations linking the Anglo-American colonies to the Six Nations Iroquois and their orbit of allied Indians. The obtaining of licences for empire through treaty agreements with Indigenous peoples was not unique to North America.[4] This device was employed, for instance, in the British colonization of India and South Africa. The Treaty of Waitangi, which was negotiated with the Maori of New Zealand in 1840, embodies a particularly

significant example of this approach to colonization. Between1879 and
1884 Henry M. Stanley made many different treaties with about 450 so-
called Native chiefs as he helped prepare the way for his patron, King
Leopold of Belgium, to establish the Congo Free State in 1885.[5] All these
treaty agreements were premised on the principle that Indigenous peoples
held some sort of title to their ancestral lands which they could modify
through agreements with colonizing powers. This title might be described,
depending on the circumstances, as Native title, Indian title, Original title,
or, more specifically, as Zulu title, Maori title, Cree title, Nisga'a title, and
so on. In this text and many others, the umbrella term "Aboriginal title" is
employed to describe the type of Aboriginal interest and jurisdiction that
Indigenous peoples retain in their ancestral lands and waters.[6]

Aboriginal title is part of an array of terms used to explain aspects of the
human condition as they have developed since Christopher Columbus's
transatlantic voyages initiated the modern era of globalization in 1492.
Early in its history the US government defined Aboriginal title as "the property or the right of the soil" that Indian peoples held in the territory north of
the Ohio River in spite of US assertions of sovereignty over this region. This
definition was offered in 1793 by officials representing the US president to
the delegates of the "Confederate Indian Nations" at a treaty council south
of Lake Erie.[7] The Aboriginal delegates were told that the US government
would respect their right to the soil – in other words, their Aboriginal title
– until such time as they were ready to give their consent to sell it. If they
chose to sell, however, their Aboriginal title could be transferred only to
the federal government of the United States. The representatives of the US
president explained that the American republic had acquired the right to
prevent "other White Nations" from "purchasing or settling any part of the
[reserved Indian] country." This power, the commissioners explained, was
"a right which the King granted to the United States."[8]

This reference to White Nations is telling. The clear implication is that
the White Nations hold a higher form of sovereign authority than do
Indigenous peoples. While the White Nations can engage in international
relations and make treaties at the level of international law, the Indian
holders of Aboriginal title must constrain their relationships within more
limited fields. If an Aboriginal group chooses to sell its right of the soil,
only one White Nation is qualified to make the purchase. This right to purchase Aboriginal title from a territory's Aboriginal inhabitants is sometimes
described as "the right of pre-emption." The distinction made between
the legal personality of the White Nations and that of the Indigenous peoples outside Europe points to the reality that the inventors of the idea of
Aboriginal title sought to remove Aboriginal societies from venues of international relations and international law.

From its inception, the legal construct of Aboriginal title was part of an
effort to domesticate relations with Indigenous peoples in the imperial colonization of territory outside Europe. Over time, this process of domestication

moved through imperial, national, state, provincial, and even municipal phases as efforts were made to constrain Indigenous peoples within narrower tracts of territory and a lower orders of law. The idea of Aboriginal title, therefore, forms part of the same continuum of Aboriginal history that would transform many Indigenous peoples into inmates of reserves, wards of federal jurisdiction, or members of municipal entities capable of exercising only delegated authority extended to them by national, state, or provincial agencies. This trend of domestication has been consistently countered by many of the most outward-looking Aboriginal leaders, from Pontiac to Tecumseh, Levi General, Jules Sioui, Robert Satiacum, George Manuel, Art Solomon, Arthur Manuel, and the activists of both the World Council of Indigenous Peoples and the AIM-related International Indian Treaty Council. The main political agenda of this continuum of leadership has been to demonstrate and to exercise the international character of the Aboriginal and treaty rights adhering to Indigenous peoples. This quest for recognition and for liberty of action by Aboriginal individuals, groups, and polities in international arenas extends to members of the Non-Aligned Movement. From the era of this organization's founding at the Bandung Conference of 1955, its members have consistently struggled to avoid new forms of imperial domestication of their countries within bipolar, unipolar, or multipolar alignments of superpower rule.

The idea of Aboriginal title is closely connected to the "Columbian conquests." This simple phrase describes an extremely complex set of relationships of domination and subordination. While military aggression is their most obvious hallmark, the Columbian conquests have been pressed forward through myriad other media, including trade networks, financial arrangements for the calculation of credit and debt, and inequitable means of manipulating law and lawlessness. They originate in the imperial drive of the European powers to shape a world order constructed in their own image and in their own interests. The continuing global trajectories of this transformative process have tended to press all the planet's diverse peoples into replicated versions of institutions originally indigenous to Europe. The most influential and all-embracing of these institutional forms is the nation-state – sovereign entities that theoretically are the sole polities with the power to grant and enforce corporate charters and property entitlements. Except in Antarctica, nation-states have been replicated to cover almost the entire territorial surface of the Earth. Extending principles that were codified among the European powers in 1648 in the Treaty of Westphalia, individual nation-states assert sovereignty within their surveyed boundaries in a fashion that approximates at the international level many of the motifs of freehold land tenure as exercised by individual proprietors within sovereign countries.

The European empires that took shape after 1492 have been largely dismantled, especially during the second half of the twentieth century. The force of decolonization after the Second World War, however, was constrained or often pre-empted by the tight limitations placed on the instruments of sovereignty available to citizens of former colonies. As the delegates at the Bandung Conference could clearly see, the superpower rivalry of the Cold War would constrain the peoples of Africa and Asia in any attempt to exercise true self-determination drawing on the Aboriginal histories of their own indigenous polities. Instead, the institution of the nation-state was the only instrument of sovereign self-government put on offer to those peoples seeking liberation from their European governors. The nation-states that emerged from former colonies can be conceptualized as the successor states of European imperialism. Most often these successor states were built on the spatial, economic, and legal foundations of the European colonies they replaced rather than on the configurations of territory, ethnicity, culture, and political economy that prevailed among the Indigenous peoples before the Columbian conquests.[9]

A primary basis of Aboriginal title lies in the surviving trajectories of memory, law, political economy, and social organization that connect some of the planet's oldest communities with their histories before the onslaught of the Columbian conquests. Aboriginal title describes the continuing associations that link Indigenous peoples with their ancestral territories in spite of the imposition of non-Aboriginal claims, jurisdictions, and regimes for the privatization of land tenure. The survival of distinct Aboriginal groups, however much they may have been influenced or even radically transformed by colonialism, has often drawn heavily on the culture of shared resistance to the genocidal, enslaving, marginalizing, or assimilative forces of alien authority. Accordingly, the idea of Aboriginal title calls attention to those intergenerational continuities of family, community, language, and peoplehood that both antedate and survive imperial expansion and the subsequent establishment of successor states. The idea of Aboriginal title speaks with particular eloquence to the unfinished business of decolonization in many parts of the world, but particularly in those countries where constitutional powers from the old imperial sovereigns were transferred exclusively or primarily to non-Aboriginal settlers of primarily European descent.

The United States, Canada, Australia, New Zealand, and South Africa were all decolonized in ways that made the institutions of self-government the exclusive preserve of the liberated colonists and their descendants. In all these successor states of the British Empire, Aboriginal groups and individuals were explicitly excluded from the devolution of power from the imperial capital and transformed into wards of the government during the most formative periods of national development and expansion. The former colonists and their descendants consistently used their widened powers to undermine the autonomy and to hasten the dispossession of the Indigenous peoples on the expanding frontiers of national aggrandizement. In all five countries, there has been a direct relationship between the widening of freedoms available to immigrants and their descendants and the diminished space left for Aboriginal life, liberty, and pursuit of happiness. The transformation after the Second World War of most European colonies into what Robert Jackson has referred to as "quasi-states" was profoundly influenced by the desire of those who dominated the richer world to retain, extend, and simultaneously concentrate their global economic power.[10] As the twenty-first century unfolds, one of the most destabilizing forces in global geopolitics will probably continue to be the conflicts and antagonisms arising from the failure to fulfill the promise of decolonization.

The successor states of old European empires consist of about three-quarters of the world's two hundred or so countries. The territories on which most of these polities sit are sites of economic, political, legal, and ethnic relationships whose nature can be better understood through the interpretive lens of Aboriginal title. The idea of Aboriginal title can effectively be applied to countries like Fiji. There the Indigenous peoples have asserted their Aboriginal title not primarily against settlers of European ancestry but against the descendants of a population that emigrated from India as indentured labourers under the commercial laws of the British Empire.[11] In Zimbabwe the tables were turned when a corrupt, aging government sought to cling to power by exploiting the frustrated aspirations of an Aboriginal majority in the former Rhodesia. With the backing of the government of Robert Mugabe, some armed groups ejected a number of White Zimbabweans whose ownership of large plots of prime farm land was rooted in the institutional history of apartheid.[12] In 2008 the breakdown of civil order in Zimbabwe accelerated because of the failure of Mugabe and his henchmen to acknowledge their own electoral defeat to opposition forces led by Morgan Tsvangira and Simba Makoni. This controversy unfolded as a similar instance of electoral fraud by Kenya's ruling clique undermined the stability of this major African polity. Far to the east, Tibet under Chinese rule offers another clear example of the Aboriginal titles of Indigenous peoples being transgressed. Aboriginal Tibetans have been subordinated to a contemporary form of empire building not unlike that experienced by the Indigenous peoples in the Americas.[13] The common lineage of colonialism linking these three sites of recent unrest points to the existence of many forces of injustice which, as in Zimbabwe, can victimize the non-Aboriginal populations as well as the Indigenous peoples. Such injustice has been allowed to flourish for want of a global system capable of making and enforcing some universal standards that would balance the jurisdictional assertions of the imperial powers and their successor states with the Aboriginal titles, rights, interests, and political will of Indigenous peoples.

The Atlantic Charter of 1941 created the basis for the return of the principles of Aboriginal title to the realm of international law and international affairs. The principles of this charter were initially recognized, affirmed, and expanded in 1942 by the allied powers of the United Nations when they spoke of "the right of all peoples to choose the form of government under which they will live" and expressed the desire "to see sovereign rights and self-government restored to those who have been forcibly deprived of them." In language that extended the principles introduced into the constitutional law of Anglo-America by the Royal Proclamation of 1763, the Atlantic Charter expressed a strict prohibition on "territorial changes that do not accord with the freely expressed wishes of the peoples concerned." As much as the British government tried politically to limit and qualify these principles in the operation of its own empire, this anti-imperial manifesto of the Fourth World created a momentum that could not be stopped. It led to the elaboration of many future UN instruments, including the Declaration on Granting Independence to Colonial Countries and Peoples in 1960 – the beginning of the decade in which the decolonization movement in Africa and Asia peaked.[14] The first two provisions in that declaration, whose wording was integrated into future UN Covenants, asserted:

1. The subjection of peoples to alien subjugation, domination and exploitation constitutes a denial of fundamental human rights, is contrary to the Charter of the United Nations and is an impediment to the promotion of world peace and co-operation.
2. All peoples have the right to self-determination; by virtue of that right they freely determine their political status and freely pursue their economic, social and cultural development.[15]

The movement to dismantle European empires after the Second World War can be interpreted as an outcome of the international recognition of the Aboriginal titles and inherent human rights of all colonized peoples. Yet, while there was nothing in the wording of the international instruments of decolonization to prevent their application to the Aboriginal territories even of North America and the Soviet Union, the imperatives of the Cold War put severe limitations on the scope and depth of the juridical affirmation that "*all* peoples have the right to self-determination." A further example of the limitations that would be placed on the decolonization movement were signalled by one provision of the Atlantic Charter that referred to the goal of the "enjoyment by all States, great or small, victor or vanquished, of access, on equal terms, to the trade and to the raw materials of the world which are needed for their economic prosperity." The origins of this statement arguably lie in the desire by the government of President Franklin Roosevelt to remove British imperial obstacles to global trade and the global exploitation of natural resources by US-based companies. The terminology of this provision is different from that employed in many UN instruments. Beginning with the founding charter of the United Nations as a creation of "WE THE PEOPLES," many UN documents refer to peoples rather than states as the basic unit of political and legal interaction in the global community.

The ongoing crisis generated by the overlapping claims of Palestinians and Israelis highlights the volatile character of linkages among Aboriginal history, imperial history, and antagonistic constructions of Aboriginal title. The subordination of the rights of Palestinian self-determination to the priorities of superpower rule illustrate how the divisions of global apartheid become manifest in, for instance, the massive Israeli wall that partitions the Occupied Territory on the West Bank of the Jordan River. Just as the Berlin Wall became a symbol of the division of humanity in the Cold War, so the military imposition of the Israeli Wall on the Occupied Territory gives concrete expression to the renewed distinctions drawn in the name of the War on Terror between those classed as civilized Westerners and those relegated to the category of the savage Other. The unbroken imperial urge to partition humanity along the lines of self-serving hierarchies gives new expression to old patterns of empire building that once empowered members of some groups to *own* property even as members of other groups *became* property. As Edward Said has observed of the persistence of standard justifications for the perpetuation of various forms of apartheid, "natives already fit a more or less acceptable classificatory grid, which made them *sui generis* inferior to Western or white men."[16]

Harsh legal, political, and military battles have been fought between non-Aboriginal contestants seeking the constitutional power to acquire Aboriginal title and to control its transformation into other forms of title. Out of this process emerged two transcontinental polities in North America, both with sovereign federal authorities whose pre-eminent authority was frequently displayed and confirmed in the acquisition of Aboriginal title from the original inhabitants living along the moving frontiers of Euro–North American expansion. While the sovereignty of Canada is still vested in an evolved version of the same Crown that began the English colonization of North America in the seventeenth century, the sovereignty of the United States is said to have grown from a popular revolt against the British sovereign. A major cause of this revolt was the unwillingness by a significant part of Anglo-America's colonial population to permit the British imperial monarch to control the process of acquiring Aboriginal title and, with it, the capacity to reconstitute Indian land into Euro–North American proprietorships. After the Seven Years' War, conflicts over taxation and representation were peripheral to the more central question of how the ownership of a greatly expanded British North America would be regulated and apportioned. Who ultimately could hand out, sell, administer, and tax the new titles of possession in the vast Indian Country recently acquired by the British imperial government? Would the King's limited recognition of Aboriginal and treaty rights be allowed to constrain the assumed right of non-Aboriginals to acquire new holding of private property in the West? The answer lay in the success of the movement to secede from the British Empire and to create the United States of America. As David Dixon has observed in *Never Come to Peace Again*, "For these backcountry settlers, creation of a revolutionary fervor had more to do with hostility towards the Indians and disdain for an unresponsive and distant government than with British economic policies, parliamentary representation, or the social and class consciousness that instigated revolutionary unrest in the urban areas."[17]

In presenting his view of Aboriginal title before a US court in 1810, John Quincy Adams argued, "It is a right not to be transferred but extinguished."[18] Adams's view on the subject, however, need not be taken as the last word. There can be no real basis for the legitimacy of extinguishing Aboriginal title any more than there can be a basis for the legitimacy of extinguishing human rights. The requirements of evenhanded fairness, however, demand that Aboriginal title be expressed in ways that also respect the titles and rights of citizens who are not of Aboriginal background. In the context of the United States, Canada, and New Zealand, it makes considerable good sense to attach the exercise of Aboriginal title to the *implementation* of treaties with Indigenous peoples, based on positive interpretations of the best of these agreements as covenants meant to encourage co-existence, shared jurisdiction, and constructive reciprocity for as long as the sun shines and the waters flow. In the Australian context, the High Court's condemnation of the principles of *terra nullius* carries the obvious implication that the Aboriginal titles of Indigenous peoples must be recognized through the making of modern-day treaties, much as is presently happening, for instance, in British Columbia.

Projects of renovation such as these are required to reclaim some measure of the rule of law's integrity. The effort to live up to the promises formally made to the Indigenous peoples in the course of colonization, but especially in the world's most prosperous polities, would send a powerful signal to the global community that the genocidal displacement of one people to enrich another can never be countenanced. Indeed, the honouring of treaties to express rather than extinguish Aboriginal title would go a long way towards permanently ending the genocidal reverberations that continue to emanate from the ongoing Columbian conquests. The viability and credibility of all such processes would be enhanced rather that denigrated through the involvement of the United Nations. The ability to initiate and sustain such bold initiatives, combining the conservative urge to restore old traditions with the liberal embrace of pluralism, would have the best chance of success if it flowed from a popular determination of truly global proportions. Indeed, the power of international public opinion would have to be mobilized to force even superpowers and the elites they empower to favour the law of compromise and peace over the iron fist of military, commercial, and political conquest.

At the very least, a broader view of Aboriginal title, one that is oriented as much to the present and future as to the past, opens legal and political terrain for the cultural renewal of Indigenous peoples whose ancestral lands and waters have provided, even as they continue to provide, much of the enticement for imperial and neo-colonial expansion. The Royal Proclamation of 1763 forms a great monument in the formal prohibition of conquest as a legitimate means of expanding empires and adding to the territories of nation-states. The Royal Proclamation acknowledged that Indigenous peoples retain an Aboriginal title in their ancestral lands. Only by giving their consent to changes in the way their Aboriginal title would henceforth be expressed could new parts of Indian Country be transformed to allow the expansion of non-Aboriginal settlements. Without consent there is no democracy, only tyranny.

ANSWERING THE INDIAN LAND QUESTION: TREATY, CONQUEST, OR AMNESIA?

British Columbia encompasses an especially rich array of geographies hosting a broad diversity of plant and animal species. Like many parts of the world where biodiversity thrives, this pluralism of life extends to the human realm. There are more distinct linguistic communities among British Columbia's Indigenous peoples than in the rest of Canada combined.[19] Competition over the right to exploit the jurisdiction's abundant natural wealth has often been bitter and violent. These conflicts over the control of natural resources have included sharp contentions concerning the legal and political meaning of Aboriginal title. The concept of Aboriginal title acquired renewed currency with the Supreme Court of Canada's ruling on the Nisga'a case in 1973 and with the patriation of Canada's Constitution from Great Britain in 1982. Canada's indigenized Constitution contains a provision affirming the recognition of existing Aboriginal and treaty rights. Since 1982 the political and juridical controversies surrounding this provision have continued to mount. They test competing understandings of the appropriate structure of relations not only among peoples but also among legal principles pertaining to Aboriginal title, provincial jurisdiction, Canadian sovereignty, property entitlements, and the chartering of corporations. Although debates about these matters are frequently presented as if they are new, questions concerning the constitutional status of Aboriginal title go back to the era of British Columbia's founding. In Aboriginal representations to the colonial, provincial, national, and imperial governments, and more recently in local court cases, the same principles have been put forward again and again. Try as some of the province's most powerful interests might to close the book on uncertainty about who really owns the underlying title to the lands, waters, and natural resources of one of the world's most environmentally spectacular jurisdictions, the pages of that fascinating text keep flying open.

Contentions over the existence and character of Aboriginal title in British Columbia have resulted in factionalism among Native people and non-Aboriginals alike. Conversely, alliances across ethnic boundaries have been common.[20] Beginning in the early 1990s, some of the political tensions were channelled into a process of Crown treaty negotiations with about fifty distinct Aboriginal groups.[21] There is, therefore, a direct continuum of Aboriginal history leading from the Covenant Chain, to the Royal Proclamation of 1763, to various Crown treaties with Indigenous peoples east of the Rockies, and to the renewal of the tradition of Crown-Aboriginal treaty making in Canada's westernmost province.[22] These negotiations are extremely significant nationally, continentally, hemispherically, and globally. Because of a unique set of historical, legal, and political circumstances, no other jurisdiction on Earth has become so thoroughly implicated in the process of determining the meaning of Aboriginal title in the contemporary organization of industrialized society. Gradually British Columbia is becoming a testing ground for the Fourth World principle that Aboriginal title forms a fundamental and inextinguishable feature of Indigenous peoples' human rights. If British Columbia can be brought into the rule of law through innovations that recognize and affirm rather than deny and negate the existence of Aboriginal and treaty rights, then something of worth will be demonstrated to the world. For these and many other reasons, the history of relations with Indigenous peoples in British Columbia offers the basis for an illuminating case study on the frontiers between imperial and anti-imperial globalization. British Columbia is (or was) the home territory of George Manuel, David Suzuki, Bill Reid, and many other makers of Aboriginal history, including Andy Paull, Hollywood film star Chief Dan George, and the multitalented author, painter, dancer, and actor George Clutesi. It is a place where the citizenry is presented with clear choices between the option of building a political economy that conforms with the commercial monocultures of an imported civilization or one that embraces those indigenous expressions of biocultural diversity that are the Fourth World's true hallmark.

British Columbia was attached to the new Dominion of Canada as a province in 1871, based on the promise by the dominion government that a rail link with eastern Canada would be built. The year of its entry into Canada was also the year that the dominion government began negotiating a series of treaties with Indigenous peoples throughout the territory bounded by the Great Lakes, Hudson's Bay, and the eastern slopes of the Canadian Rockies. Between 1871 and 1877 Crown officials negotiated seven numbered treaties with the Cree, Ojibway, Siouian, and Dene inhabitants of this vast region, and in the years 1899 to 1929 the process was extended through the negotiation of adhesions to existing agreements and the addition of treaties eight to eleven. The negotiation of the first seven of the numbered treaties was meant to gain some degree of consent from Indian groups for their enclosure within a system of prairie Indian reserves. The establishment of the reserve system, in turn, was meant to clear the way for the form of privatized land tenure outside the reserves that was essential to the financing and operation of the Canadian Pacific Railway.

By connecting the Great Lakes–St Lawrence watershed to the Pacific coast, the CPR was meant to give the British Empire a rail link on the Pacific Rim, a region that, even in those years, was emerging as the dynamo of the global economy. It was also meant to make the Dominion of Canada a viable transcontinental polity within the larger framework of a modernized British Empire. Accordingly, the negotiation of the first of the numbered treaties and the integration of British Columbia into Canada were different facets of the same imperial strategy. By negotiating treaties with Indigenous peoples east of the Rockies, the dominion government and its imperial backers were fulfilling the Royal Proclamation's constitutional requirement that Aboriginal consent must be obtained for the expansion of Euro-American settlements into the "lands reserved for the Indians as their hunting grounds." The negotiation of these treaties signalled a more modest role for the fur trade and the coming of the era when the remaining Aboriginal freedoms would be supplanted by the laws of Indian wardship, Indian withdrawal into reserve enclaves, and the enclosure of Aboriginal youth in Christian residential schools.

Because British Columbia had developed as a distinct jurisdiction within the British Empire before it entered the Dominion of Canada, the province's local government already had its own Indian policies and administration. The local government was split on the issue of whether it was necessary to recognize Aboriginal title and purchase it, as was already happening east of the Rockies with the negotiation of the numbered treaties. Similarly, there was disagreement about whether it was the local or the imperial government that was responsible for paying the bill to acquire Aboriginal title. By 1875 the lines of disagreement began to harden. The BC provincial government became entrenched in its opposition to any recognition of the existence of an unceded Aboriginal title to the jurisdiction's lands and waters.

In 1875 the legislative committee studying the Indian land question issued a report – but it was quickly hidden from public view. Through procedural manipulations by Joseph Trutch and other officials, the report was not officially accepted and authorized by the local government of the day. The suppression proved temporary. In *Papers Connected with the Indian Land Question, 1850–1875*, posterity gained a very important primary source of Aboriginal history recording a flurry of agitation over Indian rights in the BC Legislature and in the executive branches of both the Canadian and the British imperial governments. The successful legislative motion to print this document was brought forward by William Tolmie, a former Hudson's Bay Company factor. Although the motion was opposed by the province's premier, G.A. Walkem, and although the documents submitted for reproduction were at one point conveniently lost by government administrators, the correspondence nevertheless was published under the imprimatur of the Queen's Printer in Victoria.[23]

The publication of the *Papers* contrary to the wishes of the executive branch of the BC government illustrates the contentiousness among non-Aboriginals towards the idea of Aboriginal title. The existence of the publication became a significant factor in widening public access to knowledge of the unresolved issues at the core of the BC land dispute. At different times, government officials, including Duncan Campbell Scott, the deputy minister of Indian affairs, conspired to keep the published document away from Indian activists in the province. Precisely this scenario came to pass during the proceedings of a parliamentary inquiry in 1927, when Andy Paull and the Reverend Peter Kelly, two of British Columbia's most important Indian leaders, made representations on the Aboriginal title question.[24] Government efforts to repress the circulation of this rich document more than half a century after its publication serve to highlight the volatile importance of its contents. The existence of this very detailed chronicle of the early genesis of disputes over title to land in British Columbia became an important factor in the extension of these same controversies in the twentieth and twenty-first centuries. This important primary source of Aboriginal history constitutes an authoritative starting point in any commentary on matters pertaining to the overlapping presence of Crown and Aboriginal title in one of North America's most ecologically diverse jurisdictions.

The consistency of efforts during the first half of the twentieth century to prevent the circulation of *Papers Connected with the Indian Land Question* points to the central role of memory and evidence in shaping how the oldest human rights issue in the Western Hemisphere is to be transacted. In many jurisdictions, the difficulties in coming to terms with violations of the rule of law in the appropriation of Aboriginal lands has been compounded by officials' propensity to manipulate, misrepresent, or conceal the public record pertaining to these matters. This pattern of manipulation serves to draw attention to the role of convenient forgetfulness or even willed amnesia in the process of making Indigenous peoples vanish from the process of transforming Earth into property. In spite of the efforts of some government officials to withhold the controversial document from circulation, enough copies were eventually released for its contents to work their way into the province's political discourse. Mastery of the contents of the *Papers* strengthened the bargaining hand as well as the organizational effectiveness of a number of key Indian activists, including George Manuel and his associate Len Marchand.[25]

The contrast between the treatment of Aboriginal title in British Columbia and in Ontario is striking. Situated north of the Great Lakes, the lands and waters of Ontario have been the site of the continent's most prolific and diverse array of Crown treaty agreements with Indigenous peoples. In the years during and after the American War of Independence, the principles of the Royal Proclamation were applied in about two dozen distinct negotiations to obtain Indian consent for opening parts of present-day southern Ontario to non-Aboriginal settlements. Then in 1836, 1850, 1854, 1862,

1873, 1905, 1923, and 1929, treaty relations with Indigenous peoples were further expanded, making Ontario one of the world's busiest laboratories for this form of cross-cultural negotiation. British Columbia stood poised, therefore, between Ontario's tradition of relatively peaceful treaty relations and the United States' tradition of combining warfare and ceding treaties as the preferred means of creating what Dorothy Jones has termed a "license for empire."[26] Where the pattern in Ontario and the prairie regions of Canada has been to depend on treaty negotiations as a means of averting warfare with Indigenous peoples, in the United States the more usual pattern was to engage in treaty negotiations only *after* a ritual defeat left the most determined Aboriginal freedom fighters either disarmed or dead.

THE IMPERIAL ABANDONMENT OF INDIGENOUS PEOPLES IN AN ERA OF DECENTRALIZATION, DEVOLUTION, AND LAISSEZ-FAIRE CAPITALISM

The question of how British Columbia's governing authorities would choose to treat the Indigenous peoples was a matter of some concern in the United States. For much of its history, the prevailing view of Canada in the United States has been of a land where the Indian enemies of the republic could find sanctuary and even arms, ammunition, and encouragement to continue their warring resistance. "Is it not in Canada that the tomahawk of the savage has been moulded into its death-like form?" asked the Kentucky politician Henry Clay in urging his compatriots to take the offensive in the prelude to the War of 1812.[27]

In the years before he became president of the United States, Theodore Roosevelt updated Clay's accusation in *The Winning of the West*. He referred to "the close alliance between the soldiers and the diplomatic agents of the old world powers" – Britain and Spain – "and the wild and squalid warriors of the wilderness." As the future American president saw it, "The kings and the peoples of the old world showed themselves the inveterate enemies of their own blood kin in the new; they always strove to delay the time when their own race should rise to well-neigh universal supremacy."[28] Roosevelt's view repeated Thomas Jefferson's opinion of the "unprincipled policy of England" to "seduce the greater part of the tribes within our neighborhood to take up the hatchet against us."[29] In 1828 a Kentucky judge named James Ballard reiterated this hostile view of British North America's Indian policy in his political endorsement of Andrew Jackson. Referring to the Indian wars in which Jackson was involved, Ballard alleged that "British instigation had been at the back of the red demons."[30] On the Crown side of this divide in Anglo-America, the merchants of Montreal were inclined in the era of the War of 1812 to equate "the protection of the Indian rights and the Security of the Canadas."[31] In the words of Montreal fur-trade entrepreneur James McGill, that strategy would enable both the Canadians and their Aboriginal allies to escape "American subjugation, if not extermination."[32]

The War of 1812 had been a significant event in the history of New Caledonia, Oregon Country, and the Pacific Northwest. In this vast region, the war translated into intensified rivalry between the British imperial North West Company and the fur-trade enterprises of New York–based John Jacob Astor. In 1811 Astor sent out an expedition on the *Tonquin*, and its passengers established a post near the Pacific coast at the mouth of the Columbia River. Astoria was set up as the base of the newly created Pacific Fur Company, a subsidiary of the American Fur Company. The following year, Astor's men established Fort Spokane near the North West Company's Spokane House. As the war became more intense, however, the Astorians realized that the viability of their enterprises was menaced by the superiority of the Royal Navy on the Pacific coast. In 1813 the US posts were sold to the North West Company.[33] The fur-trade enterprises of British imperial Canada continued to dominate the Columbia River basin until 1846, when the forty-ninth parallel was extended by treaty to the Pacific coast. By the time of the founding of British Columbia, therefore, the climate of antagonism between the two sovereign regimes of Anglo-America had eased off. There was less incentive or inclination on the part of the government of British imperial Canada to lean on military, commercial, and diplomatic alliances with Indian nations as a check against US expansion. And, as the old geopolitical importance of the fur trade of British imperial Canada began to decline, there was a growing resolve among Crown officials to accept the transcontinental personality of the United States.

The founding of British Columbia occurred at a time when the British government was trying to decentralize the organization of key portions of the British Empire. The goal was to lighten the weight of imperial governance and to move the colonial system closer to the philosophy of political economy expressed by Adam Smith in *The Wealth of Nations*. That volume, which first appeared during the fateful year of 1776, became closely associated with the concept of the "invisible hand" of self-interest as the greatest engine of economic progress. It came to symbolize the pressures to move much of the emerging global economy away from mercantile principles, where high tariffs were imposed on foreign imports to hold commerce within the jurisdictional framework of self-contained European empires.

The alternative to mercantilism was free-trade liberalism, emphasizing minimal tariffs and largely unregulated commerce among merchants located throughout a wide range of foreign and domestic jurisdictions. When officials in the imperial capital of London moved to institute an era of freer trade in the mid-nineteenth century, they attempted to download some of the expense of colonial government to Crown subjects, but especially those in colonies whose primary purpose was to receive White immigrants from Europe. In the name of responsible government, the colonial populations first of British North America and later of New Zealand, Australia, and South Africa tended to gain increased measures of local autonomy even as they lost preferred access to the rich British market. One

outcome of this change in British Columbia was the withdrawal of the imperial government from its role as intermediary between Indigenous peoples
and the local non-Aboriginal governments. This withdrawal has had serious consequences for those Indigenous peoples whose rights to land and
resources were stripped of even the minimal protections that had been
promised in the process of devolving powers to non-Aboriginal settlers.

Nevertheless, as the BC Legislature's *Papers Connected with the Indian Land
Question* make clear, there were many individuals both inside and outside of
government who sought continuity in the Crown's treatment of Indigenous
peoples as the devolution of imperial powers proceeded. Their expectation was that British Columbia would be founded and developed on the
basis of a clear recognition of the Indigenous peoples' Aboriginal title.
Such recognition would establish the basis for the negotiation of a series
of Crown-Aboriginal treaties to purchase the Indians' inherited interests
in their ancestral lands and waters. James Douglas, a seasoned hand in the
Hudson's Bay Company who was also the founding governor of both the
Vancouver Island colony and the mainland colony, was prominent among
the advocates of some sort of reckoning with the existence of Aboriginal
title. In 1861 he outlined for his superiors in Great Britain, on behalf
of Vancouver Island's House of Assembly, a request "for the aid of Her
Majesty's Government in extinguishing the Indian title to the public lands
in this Colony; and setting forth, with much force and truth, the evils that
may arise from the neglect of that very necessary precaution." In justifying his request for £3,000 to defray the expense of making ceding treaties, Douglas presented a characterization of the attitudes of at least some
Indian peoples towards their ancestral lands and waters. He wrote that "the
native Indian population of Vancouver Island have distinct ideas of property in land, and mutually recognize their several exclusive possessory rights
in certain districts. They would not fail to regard the occupation of such
portions of the Colony by white settlers, unless with the full consent of the
proprietary tribes, as national wrongs; and the sense of injury might produce a feeling of irritation against the settlers, and perhaps disaffection to
the Government that would endanger the peace of the country."[34]

The request of Douglas and the House of Assembly to the imperial government came several years after a brief flurry of negotiations dealing with
the land, hunting, and fishing rights of some of the Aboriginal inhabitants
of Vancouver Island. Between 1849 and 1854 Douglas negotiated fourteen
agreements with a few of the Aboriginal communities of Vancouver Island.
Collectively these transactions covered only 358 square miles, or a mere
3 per cent of the entire territorial extent of the Island. In composing the
wording of these so-called agreements, Douglas looked not to the treaties
flowing from the Royal Proclamation tradition but to the instruments sanctioning land purchases from the Maori by the New Zealand Company. This
company was an enterprise controlled by Edward Gibbon Wakefield. One
of the foremost theorists and promoters of emigration from the United

Kingdom, Wakefield developed theories on colonization that would provide Karl Marx with major points of departure in his major chapter on colonization in *Das Kapital*.[35] With the goal of moving British emigration policy beyond the transportation of British prisoners to penal colonies in Australia, Wakefield's objective, rather, was to replicate the British class system in Britain's colonial domain. He sought to maintain land prices at artificially high levels so that poorer immigrants would earn their livelihood as wage workers rather than as independent farmers.[36]

Wakefield's emphasis on the British colonization of New Zealand was part of a growing preoccupation in Europe with the Pacific Ocean as an inviting frontier of empire building. British Columbia's character as a Pacific polity was demonstrated by its use of the New Zealand model, rather than a Canadian one, in the making of Crown agreements with some of the Indigenous peoples of Vancouver Island. Among the Aboriginal groups identified in these transaction were the Teechamitsa, Kosampsom, Swengwhung, Chilcowitch, Whyomilth, Chekonein, Kakyaakan, Chewhaytsum, Sooke, Saanich, Quakeolth, Queckar, and Saalequun. Except for the specifics of references to geography, money, ethnicity, and time, the wording of all these agreements was based on the same template. In each case a single cash payment was offered, usually less than £100. The key paragraph of these short documents is as follows: "The condition of our understanding of this sale is this, that our village sites and enclosed fields are to be kept for our own use, for the use of our children, and for those who may follow after us; and this land shall be properly surveyed hereafter. It is understood, however, that the land itself, with these small exceptions, becomes the entire property of the white people for ever; it is also understood that we are at liberty to hunt over the unoccupied lands, and to carry on our fisheries as formerly."[37]

The Douglas transactions, which at the time were not described as treaties, ended up being isolated agreements establishing the beginning of a pattern of negotiation that was not continued. One of the major reasons for the termination of a process of negotiated settlements with the Indigenous peoples was the unwillingness on the part of both the local and the imperial governments to pay the expense of these transactions. In a letter to Governor Douglas in which he turned down a request for £3,000, Lord Newcastle, the secretary of state for the colonies, wrote: "The acquisition of the title is a purely colonial interest, and the Legislature must not entertain any expectation that the British taxpayer will be burdened to supply the funds or British credit pledged for the purpose." He proposed that the House of Assembly should either establish its own line of credit or find new sources of revenue to pay the cost of purchasing Aboriginal title locally. "Her Majesty's Government cannot undertake to supply the money requisite for an object which, while it is essential to the interests of the people of Vancouver Island, is at the same time purely Colonial in its character, and trifling in the charge that it would entail."[38] This refusal from the British

imperial capital was consistent with the general course of imperial governance after the termination of the mercantilistic Corn Laws and the extension of greater local autonomy to some British colonies. Lord Newcastle
proceeded in a way that was consistent with the prevalent themes of political
philosophy. From his post in the Colonial Office, he advanced the decentralization of imperial power, encouraging franchised British Columbians
to accept broader latitudes of self-government (or responsible government
as it was sometimes dubbed).

The position of the British government that the extinguishment of
Aboriginal title was a colonial as opposed to an imperial responsibility was
consistent with the devolution of responsibility for "Indian Affairs" which
had taken place in the province of Canada in 1857. That was the year when
the Legislature of the United Canadas passed the parent statute in the
complex of laws that would later become known as the Canadian Indian
Act. The seminal statute was entitled an *Act for the Gradual Civilization of
the Indian Tribes in Canada*.[39] The enactment of this law in the province of
Canada marked the transfer of *responsibility* over Indian Affairs from the
imperial government to the provincial legislature. The change had ramifications for many other parts of the British Empire, including the colonies
of Vancouver Island and British Columbia.

The jurisdictional shift was pressed forward without any Aboriginal consent whatsoever. In fact in Upper Canada, or Canada West as it was then
technically called, there had been an emergency meeting in 1858 at the Six
Nation reserve near Brantford to clarify Indian hostility to being handed
over to colonial control. Many Aboriginal delegations confirmed that "they
do not wish to be given over from the care of the Imperial Government to
the care of the Provincial one."[40] This stand was representative of a systemic
pattern of distrust among Indigenous peoples in many imperial settings,
including British Columbia, directed against any constitutional transformation that increased their subordination to the authority of local, non-Aboriginal government. Not only did the imperial downloading of responsibility
for Indian Affairs lack the sanction of the peoples most affected but it flew
in the face of one of the key recommendations of the report of a major
parliamentary inquiry completed in London in 1837. The mandate of this
committee had been to study the conditions as well as the imperial constitution and the local statutes affecting "Aborigines in British Settlements."[41]
The Committee's report specifically pointed to the conflict of interests that
arose whenever the local governments, whose citizens stood to benefit most
when the lands of Indigenous peoples were opened up for non-Aboriginal
ownership and exploitation, assumed the responsibility of safeguarding
Aboriginal rights and titles. How could the agency with the greatest interest
in appropriating the titles of Indigenous peoples also uphold the Crown's
constitutional responsibility to protect and enforce those titles? How could
the same party act as purchaser of Aboriginal title and as the fiduciary
guardian or trustee of Aboriginal rights?

The British parliamentary committee's recommendation called attention to a very old controversy in British imperialism, one based on a principle that had been pivotal in the contentions leading to the American Revolution: the central government, but especially its monarchical and executive branches, had an important role to play as trustee and protector of the rights of Indigenous peoples.[42] According to this principle, the imperial government was responsible for the conduct of relations with Indigenous peoples because the colonial government could not be counted on to treat them fairly. There were many factors contributing to the subordination of these old constitutional conventions, but the main force for change was the diminished strategic importance attached to Indian Affairs as a result of growing stability of Anglo-American governance. The extension in 1846 of the international boundary between British North America and the United States to the Pacific Ocean symbolized the growing stability of Anglo-America. This diminishing strategic importance of Indian Affairs in imperial governance helped to clear the way for the British government to act on its desire to enlist White colonists in sharing the expense of local administration. The quid pro quo of this arrangement was that a wider array of powers should be devolved to these same White colonists and their political representatives in the local legislatures. By placing responsibility for public lands within the jurisdictional domain of local government, for instance, the expectation in the imperial capital was that these valuable properties could be transformed into new sources of revenue to help pay the salaries and pensions of colonial personnel. This approach, however, failed to address the reality that public lands were also the Aboriginal territories of numerous Indigenous peoples. It failed to address a long history of monarchical promises to the Indigenous peoples that the central government of the British Empire would always protect the Crown's Aboriginal allies from the incursions of the Crown's subjects.

The same processes that expanded the powers of non-Aboriginal self-government in the New World generally limited the scope of Aboriginal self-government. While in 1871 the United States formalized this process of subjugation by resorting to the doctrine of "conquest" as the justification of its Indian policies, the government of British Columbia never went that far. It simply distributed proprietary titles and resource-extraction licences as though the Aboriginal title of the jurisdiction had never existed or it had already been extinguished. The position of the BC government was similar to that of the Australian government throughout much of the nineteenth and twentieth centuries. It is no accident that both these jurisdictions, whose interlinked histories are highlighted by the similar contents of the *Mabo* ruling of 1992 and the *Delagamuukw* ruling of 1997, have become sites where the contemporary role of Aboriginal title is highly politicized. Both jurisdictions have provided juridical test cases on the role of Aboriginal title as a factor in the political and economic organization of modern industrialized states. The linkage between these rulings and the legal controversies they address highlights the international dimension of issues that arise from the existence of Aboriginal title.

Lord Newcastle seems to have had little sense of the magnitude of the constitutional issues at stake when, with a few strokes of his pen, he withdrew the imperial government from any direct role in the process of determining the relationship among the Crown, Indigenous peoples, and Aboriginal title on Vancouver Island. The quiet exit of the imperial government from its constitutional obligations to Indigenous peoples would become a familiar theme in the devolution of powers to colonists in the British Empire. The theme of betrayal by the imperial government would arise, for instance, in the early 1980s, when Indigenous peoples challenged the legality of the transfer from Great Britain to Canada of extensive constitutional powers, including authority over the Crown's side of treaty relations with the First Nations. Newcastle's effort to extract the imperial government from its responsibilities violates the most fundamental terms of the licence for empire gained by the British government through the elaboration of treaty relations with Indigenous peoples in North America. This exit betrayed a heritage of trust developed over many generations when imperial officials repeatedly encouraged Indigenous peoples to see themselves as allies of the Crown under the protection of the British sovereign. It betrayed a whole tradition of British imperial promises that were codified in the Royal Proclamation of 1763, and subsequently renewed when Crown officials encouraged the Indian Confederacy of Canada to fight for its rights and to defend its Aboriginal lands from annexation by the United States. Put simply, Lord Newcastle was wrong, decidedly wrong. His mistake would have far-reaching implications to this day.

"A GREAT NATIONAL QUESTION": THE DOMINION OF CANADA TESTS THE POWER OF ITS IMPERIAL REACH

Even though the government of British Columbia refused to address the existence of Aboriginal title, Indian reserves were sporadically established by public officials in an ad hoc manner. The most notorious proponent of downsized Indian reserves was Joseph Trutch, who decided that these reserves should allow no more than 10 to 20 acres per family. Even this vague formula, however, was never applied in a consistent or systematic manner. The land set aside for Indian people in British Columbia was far less than the acreage apportioned through treaty for Indian reserves east of the Rocky Mountains, where the amount could be as high as 640 acres per adult Indian. Similarly, it was far less than that made available at nominal cost to non-Aboriginal settlers in British Columbia. The arbitrariness of this approach was characterized by Father C.J. Grandidier, a Roman Catholic missionary to the Shuswap people in the Kamloops area, as positively "illegal." His comment appeared in a letter of August 1874 to the editor of the *Victoria Standard* that was republished in the *Papers Connected with the Indian Land Question*.[43]

Like many commentators on the Indian land question, Father Grandidier premised his criticism with dire predictions of an Indian war. These predictions were often based on reminders of the conflict with the Chilcotin in 1864. He wrote: "If the Indians are persistently refused their demands, if they are deprived of their fathers' land without any hope of redress from the proper authorities, their dissatisfactions will increase ... We may have very serious disturbances, which it might be impossible to suppress except at the cost of human life and large expenditure of money, as our past experience has taught us with the Chilcotin Indians; and those were only a handful of men, whilst the present dissatisfaction pervades all the tribes living amongst the whites." In advancing the case for the importance of recognizing Aboriginal title, Father Grandidier contrasted British Columbia negatively with the United States: "Our American neighbours have recognized this [Aboriginal] title, since they have passed a treaty with all the tribes whose land they have come to occupy." The missionary added, "Whether they fulfilled that treaty or not is not the question; but they recognized the Indian title to the land, although those lands were in the same condition then as it was here when the whites came." In Father Grandidier's view, the Indigenous peoples in his territory were perfectly willing to live as neighbours to non-Aboriginal settlers. What they were not prepared to tolerate, however, was their complete dispossession. He observed that the Shuswap "are not unwilling to have the whites have the greater and the best portion of [the land], but not the whole or nearly so. Children and owners of the soil, they want a sufficient share of it to get a living from it. They do not think that when a man can pre-empt 320 acres and buy as much more, besides the facility of leasing more, that they are unreasonable in asking 80 acres of their own land per family; and that they are supported by the example of the Dominion Government's conduct towards the other Indians."[44]

The angst and unease among the Shuswap described by Father Grandidier was reflected in a petition brought forward in July 1874 by "the Chiefs of Douglas Portage, of Lower Fraser, and of the other tribes on the seashore of the mainland to Bute Inlet." Peter Ayessik, the head spokesperson of this assembly of Indian leaders from the region that now includes the urban heartland of British Columbia, identified himself as "Chief of Hope." The petition represented the continuing activism of a protest movement that, in 1872, had coalesced in a gathering of several hundred Coastal Salish people intent on seeking redress at the land registry office in New Westminster.[45] It explained how "our hearts have been wounded by the arbitrary way the Local Government of British Columbia have dealt with us in locating and dividing our Reserves." The petitioners presented a detailed analysis of the inconsistencies in the reserve lands: the people of Chamiel had been assigned 24 acres per family; the people of Yuk-Yuk-Y-Yoose on the Chilliwhack River, 5 acres per family; and the people of Cheam on the Fraser River, 13 acres per family. The seventeen families at Sumass collectively held only 43 acres of meadow for their hay and 32 acres of dry land. Keatsy, numbering more than 100 inhabitants, was allowed only 100 acres among them all. The Langely and Hope bands "have not yet got land secured to them, and white men were encroaching on them on all sides."

The spokespersons for these communities had, they claimed, tried to bring their complaints to the appropriate officials, but without satisfaction. They had been sent on pointless runarounds from one bureaucrat to the next. As a result, "we have felt like men trampled on, and are commencing to believe that the aim of the white men is to exterminate us as soon as they can, although we have always been quiet, obedient, kind, and friendly to the whites." The petitioners declared:

Discouragement and depression have come upon our people. Many of them have given up the cultivation of the land, because our gardens have not been protected from encroachment by the whites. Some of our best men have been deprived of the land they have broken and cultivated with long and hard labor, a white man enclosing it in his claim, and no compensation given. Some of our most enterprising men have lost part of their cattle, because white men had taken the place where those cattle were grazing, and no other place left but the thickly timbered land, where they die fast. Some of our people are now obliged to cut rushes along the bank of the river with their knives during the winter to feed their cattle. We are now obliged to clear heavy timbered land, all prairies having been taken from us by white men. We see our neighbours cultivate wheat, peas, etc. and raise large stocks of cattle on our pasture lands, and we are giving them our money to buy flour manufactured from the wheat they have grown on the same prairies.

This petition was one among many complaints brought by Aboriginal groups and individuals against the provincial government during this era. Ayessik concluded the group's statement by asking the recipient of the document, Dr Israel Wood Powell, "in case you cannot obtain from the Local Government the object of our petition, we humbly pray that this petition be forwarded to the Secretary of State for the Provinces in Ottawa."[46] The stream of complaints about the failure to resolve the Indian land question in British Columbia was collected and closely studied by Powell, who had been appointed by Prime Minister John A. Macdonald as the dominion's commissioner of Indian affairs in British Columbia. Powell's work, in turn, proved influential in shaping the policy of the new Liberal regime of Prime Minister Alexander Mackenzie, who unseated the Macdonald's Conservative government in 1873.

The Liberals had come to power fuelled by a scandal over the role of the Canadian Pacific Railway in financing Macdonald's Conservatives. This episode tended to confirm the Liberals in their antagonism towards the railway enterprise that had been promised to lure British Columbia into Confederation in 1871. The Mackenzie Liberals, therefore, were inclined to view most of the province's elites in much the same light as they viewed Macdonald's favoured railway enterprise. In the estimation of Mackenzie and his staunchest supporters, Canada's westernmost province was inclined to be "the spoilt child of Confederation,"[47] and the new government was sharply critical of the handling of the Indian land question there. This political schism developed against the background of the constitutional reality that, since 1867, the British statute outlining the federal division of powers in Canada made "Indians and lands reserved to the Indians" the legislative responsibility of the dominion parliament. This distribution of power was confirmed by the ironic wording of Article 13 of the *Terms of Union Act*, the legal instrument outlining British Columbia's integration into Canada: "The charge of the Indians, and the trusteeship and management of the lands reserved for their use and benefit, shall be assumed by the Dominion Government, and a policy as liberal as that hitherto pursued by the British Columbia Government shall be continued by the Dominion government after the Union."[48]

In March 1873 the federal Cabinet passed an order in council recommending that the government of British Columbia apportion 80 acres for every Indian family of five persons in British Columbia, and the next year federal authorities made a dramatic move to go from persuasion to coercion. When a provincial statute consolidated all the previous legislation concerning the lands of British Columbia into a single legal instrument – a farce given that the new provincial law made no reference whatsoever to Aboriginal title and rights – Mackenzie's government played its trump card and invoked the federal power of disallowance to cancel it.[49] Although the Mackenzie regime later backed down, this episode briefly suggested that Confederation's new central authority headquartered in Ottawa would indeed fill the vacuum left by the imperial government when it effectively vacated its constitutional responsibility to act as the protector of the rights and titles of Indigenous peoples. The Canadian government, it seemed, would safeguard a reasonable portion of the lands and resources of Indigenous peoples from the acquisitive appetites of local governments and the interests they represented.

Since the seventeenth century there has been a marked hostility by local authorities to any regime of centralized protection for the rights and titles of Indigenous peoples. In 1676 Bacon's Rebellion in Virginia provided an early example of the local rejection of imperial attempts to protect some Indigenous peoples;[50] in the early years of the twentieth century, Teddy Roosevelt criticized the Old World alliances with Indigenous peoples "against which the American settlers had always to make head in the course of their long march westward."[51] Simply put, the titles to land and resources of Indigenous peoples have repeatedly been a point of contention or a significant bargaining chip in the conduct of relations between imperial and colonial governments or between central authorities and state and provincial officials in North America's federal systems.

The Indian land question in British Columbia provided a major test case to determine the balance of jurisdictional authority between the governments of British Columbia and Canada in the new Confederation. Would the centre hold? Would Ottawa assert its pre-eminence over the provincial and territorial elements of a Canadian empire in much the same fashion that Washington, DC, developed the imperial personality of the nation's capital by asserting control over Indians and the exclusive federal authority to acquire Aboriginal title? Would the old alliance between the Crown and Indigenous peoples survive the consolidation of peace with the United States and the decline of Great Britain's fur-trade empire in North America? If this heritage of alliance was to survive in fact as well as in constitutional theory, who would take responsibility of upholding the commitments made to Indigenous peoples in British North America on behalf of the imperial sovereign over several generations? As minister of the interior in the new government of Prime Minister Mackenzie, David Laird was the key representative of the new dominion government's strategic defence of the fast-dwindling Indian Country in British Columbia. Against the tenuous alliance between the central government and the BC Indians, a constant stream of new immigrants joined the older non-Aboriginal settlers in looking primarily to the provincial government as the main facilitator and promoter of their local enrichment and aggrandizement. So hostile did this local conglomeration of non-Indians appear to the delegation of Native petitioners led by Peter Ayessik that they feared that these "white men" will "exterminate us as soon as they can."

In November 1874 Laird made copies of a letter available in British Columbia and London, England, that detailed and clarified the position of the government of Canada on the Indian land question in British Columbia. The letter was introduced by W.A. Himsworth, who, as clerk of the Privy Council, was also the top bureaucrat in the Canadian civil service. Himsworth attested that Laird's letter and the documents that supported it had been the subject of "attentive consideration" around the prime minister's cabinet table in Ottawa. This outreach by the dominion government to the imperial government was constitutionally significant. It indicated that, notwithstanding Newcastle's characterization of the Indian land question in 1861 as a purely local matter, from Ottawa's perspective the issues raised by the unextinguished and unaddressed quality of Aboriginal title in British Columbia was a major constitutional issue with significant implications for the imperial government. Himsworth further highlighted the importance of Laird's letter by referring to it as a key point of reference in "*the great national question* now seeking solution at the hands of the Dominion and British Columbia governments."[52]

Like the Reverend Jeremiah Evarts in the William Penn letters, Laird tried to define the Aboriginal land issue as one of such profound significance for the honour, reputation, and security of Canada that it should transcend the usual concerns of day-to-day politics:

In laying the foundation of an Indian policy in [British Columbia] on the same permanent and satisfactory basis as in the other portions of the Dominion, the Government of the Dominion feel they would not be justified in limiting their efforts to what, under the strict letter of the terms of Union, they were called upon to do. They feel that *a great national question* like this, a question involving possibly in the very near future an Indian War with all its horrors, should be approached in a very different spirit, and dealt with upon other and higher grounds ... the Government of the Dominion should make an earnest appeal to the government of British Columbia, if they value the peace and prosperity of their Province – if they desire that Canada as a whole should retain the high character she has earned for herself by her just and honourable treatment of the red men of the forest, to reconsider in a spirit of wisdom and patriotism the land Grievances of which the Indians of that province complain, apparently with good reason, and take such measures as may be necessary promptly and effectually to redress them.

In summarizing Indian "land grievances," Laird noted that even those lands cultivated by Indian peoples were taken from them without compensation. Similarly, their herds of horses and cattle were frequently pushed aside by new settlers who claimed leasing rights to the open country. These forms of "pre-emption" were said to have fallen especially hard on the Indigenous peoples "in the Interior of the Province, [who are] intelligent and industrious, and likely to turn to good account any farming lands which may be assigned to them." The pre-empted lands sometimes even included Indian burial grounds. In his effort to explain the growing sense of crisis surrounding these issues, Laird wrote:

All these several grievances have been, for many years past, the subjects of complaints among the Indians. But during the last two or three years they have assumed a more serious aspect than heretofore; partly from the fact that the Indians are now, for the first time, feeling practically the inconvenience of being hemmed in by the white settlers, and prevented from using the land for pastoral purposes; partly because the Indians are only now beginning to understand the value of agriculture and to desire the possession of the land for cultivation; and partly, it may be, because they have recently been made aware of the liberal land policy extended to the Indians of the North-West in recent Treaties, and naturally contrast this treatment with the policy meted out to themselves.

Laird underlined the urgency of coming to a resolution on the land question by referring to the prospects of an Indian War, a central topic featured in almost all commentaries on the issue during that period. He first cited dominion Indian agent Israel Wood Powell on this issue, noting, "If there has not been an Indian War, it is not because there has been no injustice to the Indians, but because the Indians have not been sufficiently united." Laird added:

All concur in the opinion that, until the land grievances of which the Indians complain are satisfactorily redressed, no treatment, however liberal or humane in the way of money grants or presents, will avail to secure peace or contentment among them. As an evidence of the strength of this feeling of dissatisfaction, Commissioner Powell states that the Indian bands at Nicola and Okanagan Lakes wholly declined to accept any presents from him last summer, lest, by doing so, they should be thought to waive their right for compensation for the injustice done them in relation to the Land Grants.

Laird left no doubt that he had been simultaneously shocked and impressed by the consistency of complaints emanating from both Native people and non-Aboriginal settlers in British Columbia about the destabilizing effects flowing from the lack of any resolution to the Indian land question. The resulting unease in the province, he reasoned, was deleterious to all inhabitants in the province, Aboriginal and non-Aboriginal. "To the Indian," he wrote, "the land question far transcends all others, and its satisfactory resolution will be the first step towards allaying the wide-spread and growing discontent now existing among the native tribes of the province." Referring to the array of correspondence whose bulk was about to create a large part of the *Papers Connected the Indian Land Question,* Liard concluded, "A cursory glance at these documents is enough to show the great discontent among the aboriginal tribes but also the serious alarm of the White settlers."[53]

In 1877 tension over the land question was ratcheted up yet another notch. Having replaced David Laird, David Mills, the new federal minister of the interior, suggested in a letter to a subordinate that, in the case of direct conflict, the dominion government would be duty bound to side with the Indians. He wrote, "Indian rights to the soil have never been extinguished. Should any difficulties occur, steps will be taken to maintain the Indian claims to all the country where rights have not been extinguished by treaty."[54]

CONSERVATISM, SOCIALISM, THE ROYAL PROCLAMATION, AND THE FOURTH WORLD

The initiative centred in Ottawa to change the size of Indian reserves was based on a formula of 80 acres per family of five. This proposal found some local support in the Legislative Committee formed in 1875 in Victoria, the provincial capital. Even those such as John Robson who pushed for a more generous apportionment of reserve lands, however, effectively sidestepped the deeper issues raised by Aboriginal title and the constitutional status of the Royal Proclamation of 1763. It states: "If at any time any of the said Indians should be inclined to dispose of the said Lands, the same shall be Purchased only for Us, in our Name, at some public Meeting or Assembly of the said Indians, to be held for the Purpose."[55] This reference to an Indian *inclination* to dispose of the said lands speaks very clearly to the necessity of obtaining voluntary agreement on the Aboriginal side in any transaction leading to a change in the status of land title. The proclamation, therefore, went some distance towards recognizing the democratic right of Indigenous peoples to express and exercise their collective will, at least during those occasions when the Crown sought to get treaty licences from different Indian groups to widen and deepen its own claims to sovereign title to the lands of North America.

Questions about the applicability of the Royal Proclamation to Canada's westernmost province have figured prominently in arguments about whether Aboriginal consent is required by law to legitimize the opening of large parts of British Columbia to exploitation by non-Aboriginal settlers and their corporate extensions.[56] These questions, which the Supreme Court of Canada has now answered unequivocally in the affirmative, remained contentious for more than a century following British Columbia's entry into Confederation. Those who denied that the imperial law of 1763 was part of the province's constitutional foundations pointed to the fact that the territory originally covered by the founding instrument of British imperial Canada explicitly excluded the domain of the Hudson's Bay Company. This exclusion, it was asserted, naturally extended also to those parts of British North America to the north and west of the Hudson's Bay watershed.

In contrast, others argued that although British Columbia was a long distance from the main metropolitan centres of British imperial Canada, the region had been very much a part of the domain of the Montreal fur traders and then of the fur-trade empire of the HBC. This history gave credence to the view that the principles outlined in the Royal Proclamation transcended the geographical configurations outlined in 1763 and became a law of more general application, enforceable throughout the full extent of British North America and its transcontinental outgrowth, the Dominion of Canada. The Canadian government apparently adhered to this larger view of the emerging law of Aboriginal and treaty rights by applying the principles of the Royal Proclamation to the former HBC lands in the form of the numbered treaties negotiated between 1871 and 1929. A more expansive interpretation would hold that the Royal Proclamation's prohibition on the unilateral dispossession of Indigenous peoples should have even broader application internationally as an emerging principle of global law

As bold and assertive as Laird's words were on behalf of the dominion government, his proposed solution was not in conformity with the Royal Proclamation of 1763. His was a unilateral approach, not one that went forward with Indian consent. While the offer of larger, protected reserves calculated on a formula of 80 acres per family might well have proven sufficient at that time to inspire Indian willingness to enter into treaty relations with the Crown, the constitutional principles governing the transformation of Aboriginal title into other kinds of title and jurisdiction were very clear.

The Royal Proclamation, together with the wording of section 91(24) of the *British North American Act* of 1867, created for the dominion government a major responsibility to help represent and *implement* the imperial sovereign's promises to safeguard the rights and titles of Indian peoples. The dominion government, however, was not constitutionally empowered to speak on behalf of Indian groups and to represent them directly in contracts. That, however, is precisely what happened with the *Indian Act*, legislation that violated Canada's deeper constitutional heritage by transforming Indigenous peoples from allies of the Crown into wards of the federal state. According to the specific words in the Royal Proclamation, Indigenous peoples had to be "inclined" to transfer their title. No negotiated settlement between the Dominion of Canada and the province of British Columbia could be binding until it was sanctioned by Indigenous peoples themselves.

One of the possible scenarios emanating from the Crown's recognition of Aboriginal title in 1763 was that the Indigenous peoples could use their bargaining leverage to reconstitute the Dominion of Canada as a tripartite federation, with Aboriginal government as one of three orders of Canadian government. In 1867 Canada's federal apparatus had been structured as in the United States to accommodate only a bipartite axis of relations between the central government and the regional governments of provinces. Indian people had been excluded from the process of shaping the Confederation pact of 1867 as surely as they had been excluded from the process of drafting the US Constitution in 1787. That exclusion remains entrenched to this day in the way the federal systems in North America have been conceived, designed, and operated.

Accordingly, the BC land question has from the beginning held within it the prospect that one or more North American jurisdictions might give expression to a new form of federalism that incorporates the principles of Aboriginal title as well as the right to self-determination of Indigenous peoples. In contemplating such an outcome in a reconstituted Canada, Michael Asch has proposed that such a polity "would locate Indigenous peoples at the centre rather than the periphery of the story of this place and it would understand the colonists as recent arrivals whose stories become added to, rather than radically depart from, the stories of this place."[57] This still-pending prospect would re-enact in a domestic way some of the same hopes and aspirations animated by the emergence of the Indian Confederacy onto the global stage during the era of the War of 1812. Tecumseh's vision and the quest of Haiti's Toussaint L'Overture pointed humanity towards the necessity of breaking the monopolistic hold of the "White Nations" in the making of international law. The constitutional requirement to *recognize* Aboriginal title – a recognition that most often has served as a mere prelude for non-Aboriginal acquisition of Aboriginal title and its transformation into other kinds of titles and jurisdictions – still holds out prospects for many kinds of political experimentation on the middle ground of an extended Covenant Chain of intercultural democracy. The movement towards the Fourth World would be advanced if evolving experiments in federalism, both within nation-states and among them, included innovative means for expressing Aboriginal title and implementing the inherent right of Indigenous peoples to self-determination.

In British Columbia and many other jurisdictions, the Royal Proclamation of 1763 has been the primary constitutional instrument necessitating some political reckoning with Indigenous peoples and their continuing connections to their ancestral lands. Such reckoning brings us face-to-face with one of Western civilization's most flawed abstractions – that the planet can be divided conceptually and legally between the Old and the New Worlds. Closely connected to this illusion has been the related idea that the Indigenous peoples and their Aboriginal polities in the New World could lawfully and rightfully be displaced, extinguished, or remade in the image of their colonizers, all in the name of human progress. In formalizing the principle that Aboriginal consent must be obtained in order to legitimize the Anglo-American colonization of Indian hunting grounds, King George III acted decisively on a major frontier of human rights. One of the underlying premises of his Royal Proclamation was the democratic notion that all *peoples* have a basic right to a voice in determining how their lands and resources will be developed and apportioned in the course of shaping the future. While the King's Proclamation recognized this right in a paternalistic and imperfect way, it nevertheless represented a vastly more nuanced and humanitarian approach to empire building than the genre of expansion advanced through the unrestrained triumphalism of Manifest Destiny. In *The Winning of the West*, Teddy Roosevelt presented a telling expression of this sense of Manifest Destiny by celebrating the expansion of Anglo-America "by right of conquest and armed occupation." The conquest of Indian Country demonstrated, in Roosevelt's estimation, the "universal supremacy" of the ascendant "race."[58]

CHRISTIAN MISSIONARIES AS AGENTS OF BOTH COLONIZATION AND DECOLONIZATION

The *Papers Connected with the Indian Land Question* contain indications of the scope and complexity of the discussions on Aboriginal title that took place in the imperial centre of London, the federal capital of Ottawa, and the colonial and provincial governments of British Columbia. This publication captures the essential features of the changing relations among these four kinds of government even as it documents the struggle of Indigenous peoples to adapt to rapid-fire transformations in the means of governing, apportioning, and exploiting their Aboriginal lands and waters. One of the most important letters is from F.W. Cheeson, on behalf of the Aborigines' Protection Society, to the imperial secretary of state, Sir Edward Bulwer Lytton. It begins with a long citation from the *New York Times* describing the propensity of the Californian gold miners in British Columbia to engage in race wars. Cheeson's letter represents the distilled essence of a process of memory and reflection rooted in the long history of British imperial expansion in overseas colonies. Its contents are especially representative of the positions of the Protestant missionary organizations that played a major role in the genesis of the British Empire.

Cheeson's intervention adds to the large body of evidence demonstrating that the existence of Aboriginal title in the lands and waters of British Columbia was broadly and explicitly recognized by virtually all the main actors who participated in discussions and negotiations leading to the imperial establishment of this Crown colony. Like the Reverend Jeremiah Evarts, Cheeson advanced his case by making specific reference to the example set by William Penn, the founder of Pennsylvania. "If British Columbia is to become an honourable and advantageous portion of the British Dominions," he wrote, "it would seem that a Treaty should be promptly made between the delegates of British authority and the chiefs and their people, as loyal, just and pacific as that between William Penn and the Indians of Pennsylvania." He recommended that "more stringent laws" be made "to ensure its provisions being maintained with better faith than was carried out on the part of the whites" and challenged the characterization of Indigenous peoples as "obstacles to the work of colonization." He maintained, rather, that "they might be made useful agents in peopling the wilderness with prosperous and civilized communities, of which one day they might form a part." The key to this genesis, however, was "that the English government should be prepared to deal with their claims in a broad spirit of justice and liberality."

It is certain that the Indians regard their rights as natives as giving them a greater title to enjoy the riches of the country than can possibly be possessed either by the English Government or by foreign adventurers. The recognition of native rights has latterly been a prominent feature of aboriginal policy of both England and the United States. Whenever this principle has been honestly acted upon, peace and amity have characterized the relations of the two races, but whenever a contrary policy has been carried out, wars of extermination have taken place; and great suffering and loss, both of life and property, have been sustained by both the settler and the Indian. We would beg, therefore, most respectfully to suggest that the Native title should be recognized in British Columbia, and that some reasonable adjustment of their claims should be made by the British government.

Cheeson's letter displays knowledge of the tactics that were frequently employed by European powers that sought to edify their claims in overseas territories by propping up and elevating those Aboriginal representatives who demonstrated a willingness to act with compliance and complicity as agents of empire. In words that anticipated the legal arguments of lawyer Bruce Clark, Cheeson warned: "No nominal protector of aborigines – no annuity to a petted chief – no elevation of one chief above another, will answer the purpose. Nothing short of justice in rendering payment for that which it may be necessary for us to acquire, and laws framed and administered in the spirit of justice and equality, can really avail." Cheeson touched on an old theme of imperial involvement in the Indian Country of North America when he referred to the need to make "allies" of Indigenous peoples. He proposed that responsible positions in the colonial administration be assigned to "well-selected men, more or less of Indian blood." Such a civil service, he predicted, would earn respect with the Native population and limit the propensity of the non-Aboriginal population to denigrate British Columbia's Indigenous peoples. The "recognized position among the whites" of Native public officials "would be some guarantee that the promised equality of the races would be realized." Cheeson pointed to the fur-trade heartland at the Red River settlement as an appropriate place to find the mixed-ancestry role models he sought for government service in British Columbia.[59]

Lytton forwarded Cheeson's letter to Governor James Douglas with the request that he attempt to secure for Indigenous peoples "the protection of Her Majesty's Government." At the same time, he said that he should not be understood as having "adopted the views of the Society as the means by which this may best be accomplished."[60] Although Cheeson had stipulated that, in the estimation of the Aborigines' Protection Society, the financial obligation to purchase Aboriginal title rested squarely with the British government, Lytton rejected this aspect of the advice. His preoccupation with matters of finance coloured a later letter to Douglas, dated December 30, 1858, in which he referred to what he saw as the admirable success of Native policy in South Africa, long a point of reference in the Colonial Office's oversight of Indian policy in British North America. Lytton proposed that British Columbia duplicate the system used in the Cape Colony of settling "the Kaffirs" in missionary villages, and he suggested that this initiative be paid for in part by "indirect taxation" on objects imported by Native people into the province. He even went so far as to suggest that Douglas seek consent from the Aboriginal inhabitants for "some light and simple form of direct taxation, the proceeds of which would be expended strictly and solely on their own wants and improvements."[61]

In 1871 the bishop responsible for the Roman Catholic Indian missions in British Columbia remarked on the duties that the local Legislature imposed on the price of items imported by the Indigenous people. In a letter to the secretary of state for the colonies, he estimated that the 50,000 or so Aboriginal inhabitants of the province contributed through their purchases at least a quarter of the overall revenues of the jurisdiction. He contrasted this estimate with the figures he cited from British Columbia's budget in 1869. Of the total expenditure of £122,250, the cleric observed that only one line in the list of government payments referred to "expenses connected with the Indian Tribes, £100." These figures provided the prelude for his request for government funds to subsidize Roman Catholic missions and schools in the province. He argued, "It will be advantageous to the Colony if, before the influx of Emigrants which is expected in connection with the Pacific Railroad, the Indian Tribes have been trained in the Christian principles and the arts of peace."[62] A persistent theme running throughout many of the documents included in the *Papers* is the important role of both Protestant and Roman Catholic missionaries in establishing the larger framework of government involvement in Aboriginal affairs. Large parts of British Columbia's vast interior and its more northerly coastal regions provided the space and the isolation that made it possible to form, temporarily at least, the kind of tight Christian theocracies that had been attempted by missionaries who had once looked to Oregon Country, New Caledonia, and Washington Territory as promising locales for their utopias. In the last decades of the nineteenth century, Father Paul Durieu laid the groundwork of an extremely detailed and elaborate scheme for the creation of model Roman Catholic communities where Native converts would zealously police one another in the oversight of their Christian devotions. As a member of the Oblate Order, Father's Durieu's "system" is said to have anticipated the behaviourist theories of B.F. Skinner.

One of those who inherited the methods and the converts of the Durieu system was Father Adrien G. Morice. He began his missionary work at Williams Lake in 1880 but soon moved northward to oversee Roman Catholic evangelization among the Athabaskan-speaking Carrier people.[63] Following in the footsteps of Father Emile Petitot, Father Morice achieved considerable fame as a pioneer ethnographer, historian, botanist, and linguist.[64] He also forged a reputation for himself as something of a local dictator within his Aboriginal and Roman Catholic domain. He expected, for instance, to be carried like a potentate on a throne-like contraption on his travels throughout the mountainous terrain of northeastern British Columbia.[65] Clearly, the memory of the Roman Catholic Indian reductions of Paraguay stimulated his imagination, and he also found inspiration in the evangelical work of some of the Oblates east of the Rockies and in the Jesuit missions of the Oregon and Washington territories.

Among the Tsimshian peoples of British Columbia's northern coast, the Reverend William Duncan led what might be viewed as a Protestant version of the Indian theocracy of Paraguay. Duncan worked for the Church of England's Church Missionary Society (CMS), which was active in Africa and New Zealand as well as parts of British North America.[66] The towering intellectual figure in the CMS in that era was Henry Venn, a veteran of the New Zealand missions, who hoped that Native-led churches would develop as the centres of a series of self-sufficient and self-governing Native communities. Venn's preoccupation with missionary reform helped to stimulate the desire for change within a faction of the imperial bureaucracy whose adherents sought a more decentralized British Empire by allowing greater latitude for local and indigenous self-governance.[67] With Venn's inspiration in the forefront, Duncan and a community of Tsimshian converts worked together to make the coastal community of Metlakalta a place of significant economic enterprise and theocratic order. Between 1862 and 1887 Metlakata was tightly policed and governed by its own Tsimshian citizens, with, of course, Duncan's help and oversight. At different times it was the site of a soap factory, a fish-canning business, carpenters' shops, blacksmith shops, a weaving consortium, and a famous brass band.[68]

The broad range of Metlakata's successful manufacturing enterprises, all based on Indian labour and artisanship, was reminiscent of New Helvetia, a community founded in the Sacramento Valley area of California by John A. Sutter in the years before that jurisdiction passed from Mexico to the United States.[69] Venn's approach to missionary work anticipated some aspects of the movement for decolonization that would prove such a powerful force for global change in the twentieth century. Another exponent of his ideas was the Reverend E.F. Wilson, who, along with members of the Shingwaukonse family of Sault Ste Marie, Ontario, founded the Anglican residential schools for Indian boys and girls in that district. In a series of articles published in 1891, Wilson extended Venn's thinking about autonomous Native churches to a broad proposal aimed at integrating a distinct order of Aboriginal government, with its own legislature, capital city, and Aboriginal lieutenant-governor, into the Canadian federal system.[70]

As part of the growing conflict between church and state, Duncan sided with the Tsimshian activists seeking recognition of their Aboriginal title. He accompanied three of their leaders – John Tait, Edward Mathers, and Herbert Wallace – to Ottawa in 1885 to meet Prime Minister Macdonald.[71] When their mission was not successful, Duncan and the citizens of Metlakalta moved their community to Alaska. The clergyman's direct intervention on the land issue contributed further to a growing pattern that made some Protestant missionaries along British Columbia's coast important allies in the struggle to gain recognition of Aboriginal title.[72] According to Paul Tennant, one branch of the Church of England in British Columbia was especially forceful in disseminating the teaching that the Christian God intended "that white authorities should acknowledge Indian title and negotiate its proper transfer." This view was especially pronounced in the High Church branch of Anglicanism, "since the British monarch was head of the Church, the fountain of British justice, and the author of the Royal Proclamation of 1763."[73]

The convergence of the religious and secular branches of British imperial governance in the Royal Proclamation of 1763 found an able and dedicated interpreter in Arthur O'Meara, a lawyer and an Anglican clergyman who participated integrally in the activism of the Allied Tribes of British Columbia.[74] The strategically vital work of the Allied Tribes began in 1916. The highest objective of its founders was to bring the issue of Aboriginal title in British Columbia before the highest court in the British Empire, the Judicial Committee of the Privy Council. That objective was ultimately placed out of reach by the Canada's Parliament when, in 1927, it amended the *Indian Act* to outlaw any unauthorized transfer of money in pursuit of a Native claim. O'Meara worked closely with the leading Indian politicians of his day and with James Teit, a remarkable Indianized Scots socialist who, along with George Hunt, had collaborated with Franz Boas in his anthropological studies of Indigenous communities on the west coast.[75] When the Allied Tribes of British Columbia was called into being at the Squamish reserve in northern Vancouver, sixteen Aboriginal groups were represented. Among those in attendance were Andy Paull, the future teacher and mentor of George Manuel,[76] as well as the Haida aristocrat, the Reverend Peter Kelly.[77] The Allied Tribes gave new organizational form to the old task of forcing some fundamental political and legal reckoning with the concept of Aboriginal title in British Columbia and the rest of Canada.

There is no contradiction in looking to the global enterprises of the Christian missionary societies for one of the sources of the decolonization movement that achieved some of its objectives, especially following the Second World War. After all, the Aboriginal activists who led this decolonization movement were in most instances the former students of Christian clerics who had travelled to the far corners of the world in an effort to spread and universalize the religious aspect of Western civilization. While Christian missionaries carried with them a great baggage of religious idealism, they also helped globalize, however inadvertently, some of the more secular facets of the Enlightenment's egalitarian spirit. By widening networks of literacy, language dissemination, and other media of worldwide communications, Christendom's evangelists helped to provide new channels of access for Indigenous peoples to the ideas of many Western thinkers. From Rousseau to Marx, Mary Wollstonecraft, Abraham Lincoln, Rosa Luxemburg, George Orwell, and W.E.B. Du Bois, many of these thinkers had proclaimed in their own distinct fashion the shared rights of all humanity to be free from political, economic, and psychological oppression.

The most violent features of the Columbian conquests have sometimes been eased by the interventions of a particular set of Christian missionary made up of individuals who were inclined to identify with the resistance struggles of Indigenous peoples among whom they laboured. Their interventions to protect Aboriginal rights combined with the activities of the more aggressive agents of missionary imperialism to form one of the most powerful and persistent forces of globalization. In this evangelical stream of globalization, members of the Jesuit Order have been particularly important in facilitating exchange and interpretation between different branches of humanity in widely separated geographic locations. Collectively the Christian missionaries, both Protestant and Roman Catholic, have figured prominently among the agents of empire who helped invent "the Native" as the universal object of their missions. The imperial invention of the generic Native helped to cover over and obscure almost countless cultural differences among Indigenous peoples. The global networks that often linked Christendom's native missions along transnational, denominational lines contributed to the bridging of some of the large distances between and among Aboriginal communities. This aspect of globalization has contributed to the emergence of the Fourth World as a realm where there has been enough shared consciousness to make it possible for different constituencies seeking various forms of decolonization to begin joining forces.[78]

The Christian orientation of Roman Catholic peasant farmers throughout the Mayan districts of southern Mexico was one of several factors in the rise of a protest movement named for Emiliano Zapata, an Indian leader who led the cause of land reform in the Mexican Revolution during the early years of the twentieth century.[79] The Zapatistas's stand resonated with meaning for many internationally. The international character of the activism instigated by Mexico's Zapatista movement helped demonstrate the inspirational power of the struggle by Indigenous peoples to transcend their colonized condition. It showed that many different kinds of constituencies seeking to resist the incursions of capitalist hyperprivatization were willing to take their lead from those who had been in the front line of resistance to the Columbian conquests since their inception in 1492. The campaign of the Zapatistas to resist the implementation in Mexico of the North American Free Trade Agreement was one of the first of its type to deploy in a broad and systemic way the enormous power of the Internet to disseminate information on a transnational basis. The connection of the Roman Catholic tradition of liberation theology to the Zapatista movement was personified in the mediating role of Father Samuel Ruiz Garcia in the early stages of the conflict. Ruiz was the bishop of San Cristobal do las Casas, where the Indian peasant revolt against Mexico's rulers began in January 1994. As a Roman Catholic official charged to administer to the needs of the inhabitants of a community named after the Bartolome de Las Casas, Ruiz was clearly aware of his special responsibilities to encourage respect for the Aboriginal titles and rights of Indigenous peoples in his home country. Las Casas is widely revered as New Spain's first non-Indian proponent of Aboriginal rights and the true founder of liberation theology in the Americas.[80]

Accordingly, the movement for Aboriginal decolonization is helping to mobilize broad coalitions of activists who join together in embracing the biocultural diversity of the Fourth World even as they reject the totalizing force of capitalist monocultures. The publication in 1974 of *The Fourth World* by Shuswap activist George Manuel and his founding the following year of the World Council of Indigenous Peoples marks a key moment in the globalization of the struggle for the recognition of Aboriginal and treaty rights, but especially those rights derived from the unextinguished existence of Aboriginal title. That moment in the mid-1970s was pivotal in the genesis of the conceptual linkages that helped bind together many struggles whose quest for liberation was sometimes more injured than helped by the proliferation of new nation-states during the second half of the twentieth century.[81] Like the brief existence of Fredonia or Tecumseh's hope that the Indian Confederacy of Canada could create an Aboriginal dominion within the British Empire, the twenty-five-year career of Metlakalta stands as a monument to yet another historical might-have-been in the process of inventing North American civilization on the frontiers of Indian Country.

CHAPTER TEN

Media of Power in the Construction (and Deconstruction) of America

We should, therefore, only treat with Sitting Bull by a force strong enough to compel him to accept such terms as our Government may see fit to dictate. Treaties with Indians are, at the best, worth little, and the fewer we have of them, the better it will be for all concerned.

The National Republican, August 30, 1877

Yet, in the absence of an effective source of central authority in the international sphere, the sovereign state is at once the source and possibly the violator of the law, controlled only by self-imposed mechanisms.

Madame Justice Louise Arbour, "Genesis of International Criminal Justice," 2000

SLAVES, INDIANS, AND CITIZENS IN THE UNIVERSAL HISTORY OF THE US CIVIL WAR

Social philosophers have showered much attention on identifying the connections linking the development of our personal senses of selfhood and our perceptions of those we relegate to the category of Otherness. This line of inquiry has figured, for instance, in the work of Friedrich Hegel, Jacques Lacan, Michel Foucault, Louis Althusser, Jacques Derrida, and Noam Chomsky. These and many other observers have helped to describe how our internal pictures of ourselves as individuals and as members of clans, nations, religious communities, and so on stem in large part from how we think about those whom we consider alien to our values, attributes, and way of life. We shape ourselves to distance our own personae from those whom we class as "the Other."

But as expanding conceptions of self and community emerge from our changing orientations to time and space, old conceptions of *us* and *them* begin to break down for some of us. Meanwhile, new frontiers of identity coalesce along networks of digital communications centred on the Internet. In an era when a growing constituency is reminded daily of the global framework of our merging political economies, one would imagine that it might become increasingly difficult to relegate any group of fellow human beings to the status of "the Other." In this accelerating globalization, the shrinking domain of Otherness is linked to the unstoppable attractions of the Enlightenment's core revelations. Many fountainheads of human culture and consciousness continue to cultivate the growing realization that all people and peoples have equal entitlements to the sense of dignity and hope that arises from sufficient access to nutritious food, clean water, good health care, progressive education, and the institutions of self-determination that we require in order to infuse our political choices as individuals into the collective will of larger constituencies. The other side of this same equation speaks of the equal right of all human beings to a reasonable measure of protection from the menaces of war, poverty, genocide, tyranny, illiteracy, commercial exploitation, and environmental holocaust.

The growing understanding of humanity's universal dependence on the health of a single biosphere has given rise to calls for more ecologically sensitive motifs of globalization. These calls have been expressed in many ways, including through the issuing of new declarations of environmental interdependence.[1] The pressure to formulate and apply truly global solutions to global problems is being significantly stimulated by a widening appreciation of the universal dangers posed by the way that the excessive burning of fossil fuels and other forms of toxic pollution are rapidly undermining the interconnected viability of some of life's main regenerative processes. The conditions of our growing interdependence transcend the human orbit to encompass every living organism within the Earth's delicate ecological cocoon. The expanding social imaginaries of life's shared attributes on a single planetary home form one of the most dynamic features in the accelerating process of globalization.[2] The most dynamic processes of globalization begin in the mind and spread outwards from the human imagination to affect changing configurations of conflict, oppression, culture, law, alliance, confederation, and exchange.

In the final analysis, we are all native to Mother Earth. We are all transient passengers in the intergenerational train of evolutionary transformation. Recognition of the commonalities that connect us across time and space should lead to the conclusion that all wars are civil wars. If all humanity is truly one, how can there be any such thing as war with or between foreigners? But we human beings are still far from having attained this level of shared self-understanding. We remain far from having achieved a level of global consciousness that would eliminate distinctions between international and civil wars. We have a long way to go collectively to reach the state where all military conflict is viewed as internal to the entire human family. Instead, we continue to draw sharp distinctions, placing warfare between nations in a very different category from warfare within nations. These distinctions must inevitably break down as conflicts between states and conglomerations of states give way to conflicts that place in the forefront militarized privateers operating along transnational lines for reasons of financial profit, religious conviction, addiction to violence, or various combinations of motives. In this sense, the War on Terror marks a watershed in the privatization of warfare and the triumph of mercenary motives as the core organizing principle of capitalism's military-industrial complex.

It is widely recognized that fraternal wars or "cousins' wars" within polities tend to be particularly vicious and cruel. When members of the same clan, tribe, nation, or state turn against one another through resort to organized violence, the opponents' familiarity with one another often leads to extreme forms of contempt. This heritage of ruthlessness in civil war has been especially instrumental in shaping the political culture of the English-speaking peoples of Europe and North America. As Kevin Phillips has written, the civil wars of Anglo-America form "an anvil on which some of the most lasting arrangements of English and American politics have been hammered out." They form "the most powerful convulsions, clarifications, and political watersheds of the Anglo-American global emergence and achievement."[3] Phillips bases these comments on his assessment of the English Civil War in the seventeenth century, the Anglo-American revolt against imperial Britain, and the conflict pitting the Confederate Army of the slave-owning South against the military forces of the US federal government in the North. Of these three conflagrations, the US Civil War was by far the most lethally destructive. It was the first North American conflagration to be fuelled by significant amounts of oil, the energy source that would propel the United States to global pre-eminence in the twentieth century's intervals of war and peace.[4] The fight to the death between Union and Confederate forces took the arts and sciences of military killing to new levels of industrial efficiency. The surge of military industrialization in the US Civil War edified patterns of institutionalized aggression that, in later decades, would be channelled into the ongoing repression of Indian Country and Latin America as well as the annexation of Hawaii and the imperial takeover of the Philippines.

The US Civil War provided the platform for the national government of the United States to affirm its federal pre-eminence. The war enabled central authorities in the United States finally to throw off the principle that they derived their powers from the sovereign states. President Abraham Lincoln assumed unprecedented authority as commander-in-chief. He imposed and enforced a military draft that compelled citizens to fight for their country. He granted the police many new powers to jail and harass without due process those deemed to be Confederate agents or sympathizers. Then Lincoln elevated the conflict to higher levels of ethical meaning when he invoked his executive authority in the Emancipation Proclamation of January 1, 1863, to abolish the institution of slavery in Confederate-held territory. In his presentation to Congress in December 1862, Lincoln affirmed that, by "giving freedom to the slave, we assure freedom to the free." By referring to the United States as "the last best hope of earth," Lincoln located the emancipation of his country's slaves in the context of world history.[5] He situated the freeing of the slaves in the United States in a continuum of events whose highlights include the abolition of slavery in the British Empire in 1833, in the French Empire in 1848, in Portugal's colonies in 1858, in the Spanish colony of Cuba in 1886, and in the constitutional monarchy of Brazil in 1888.[6] In acting so assertively to bring about one of history's most important milestones in the affirmation of universal human rights, Lincoln finally terminated a long legacy of federal complicity in the treatment of millions of Black Americans as objects to be bought and sold. This complicity had found one of its fullest expressions in 1857 in the US Supreme Court's notorious *Dred Scott* decision. That ruling defined slavery as an embodiment of the property rights of slave owners. Based on this theory, the US judiciary upheld the principle that slave owners could transport their human chattel anywhere in the United States without interference.

In 1863 at Gettysburg, Lincoln drew together several strands of US and world history in a brief address to commemorate those who had died in one of the Civil War's battles. In about three hundred words, he identified the moral purpose of his side in the conflict as the advancement of the ideals articulated in 1776 in the American Declaration of Independence. "Four score and seven years ago," Lincoln famously intoned, "our fathers brought forth on this continent a new nation, conceived in liberty, and dedicated to the proposition that all men are created equal." He completed the Gettysburg Address with an affirmation of both the supremacy of God and the republican ideal of popular sovereignty as the ultimate animator of national governance. "We here highly resolve that these dead shall not have died in vain," he declared, "that this nation under God shall have a new birth of freedom, and that the government of the people, by the people, and for the people shall not perish from the earth."[7] With the Gettysburg Address, Lincoln imbued one of the bloodiest civil wars in human history with a sense of higher purpose. Highlighting principles that would find fuller expression in the Fourth World ideals of the Atlantic Charter, he expressed a resolve to use US law as a force for universal justice. The Gettysburg Address gave powerful substance to his' earlier characterization of the United States as the last best hope of humanity. With his suggestion that the US Civil War was an event pointing the way to the emancipation of all human beings from all forms of slavery, Lincoln moved beyond the sphere of national politics to the arena of universal history.

Lincoln's words have been drawn on repeatedly to advance a diverse array of causes. In a particularly bizarre caricature of the Gettysburg Address, President George W. Bush had himself photographed on May 1, 2003, on the deck of the massive aircraft carrier *Abraham Lincoln* celebrating "the Battle of Iraq" as "Mission Accomplished." In this important speech, Bush pointed to the overthrow of the Iraqi government of Saddam Hussein as an extension of the same process that had led President Abraham Lincoln to free the slaves of the American South. He referred to the "enslavement" of Iraqis under Hussein and to the US intent to bring about a new regime in the oil-rich country that would be "of, by, and for the Iraqi people."[8] His invocation of this enduring phrase from the US Civil War became increasingly ironic as Iraq drifted towards its own civil war under the conditions of foreign occupation. The contrast between the quick military success of the invading forces and the subsequent incompetence of the US government in rebuilding the infrastructure and political economy of the Iraqi nation points to the ascent of the national security state over the heritage of the New Deal and the Atlantic Charter. While the reconstruction of Japan and Western Europe after the Second World War had drawn on the spirit of the New Deal, there was no similar vision of state-led nation building to inform the mission to remake Iraq. Rather, the conquest of Iraq was meant to expand the process of using national space to create more privatized space for the benefit of commercial corporations on the frontiers of capitalist globalization. Iraq was to be modelled as a Middle Eastern example of capitalist hyperprivatization, where the business of military occupation became the leading example of government outsourcing to the so-called private sector.

The resort in the US Civil War to the tactics of conquest to settle issues of such monumental consequence in the evolution of human relationships confirmed patterns of ideology and conduct that remain deeply entrenched in the military-industrial complex. In *The Dominion of War*, Fred Anderson and Andrew Cayton muse that "victory over Indians and Mexicans and what became, in a purely contingent way, a revolutionary war against human slavery affirmed the notion that the United States was something new under the sun, the very model of a society of independent individuals who accepted the responsibility to liberate other peoples so that they too could choose to embrace a superior way of life." By resorting to arms as the means of finally abolishing slavery, Americans "constructed their conquest of North America as a collective sacrifice in the service of humanity." The connections drawn between military solutions and "the cause of freedom led the citizens of the world's greatest imperial republic to understand any rejection of their nation as a rejection of liberty itself." The authors add that the US citizenry "thus freed themselves from any obligation to understand other people and places on their own terms and in their own contexts."[9]

Eventually, about 180,000 men of African ancestry served in the Union's armed forces. They constituted about 10 per cent of the entire federal force. Aboriginal soldiers were also present, but, unlike Black soldiers, they were well represented on both sides of the conflict. One of the most prominent Indian fighting men in the Union's army was a Seneca civil engineer named Ely S. Parker, who joined the staff of Union General Ulysses S. Grant. With great distinction, Parker served as Grant's secretary. Earlier in his career, Parker had acted as an informant and interpreter of Six Nations Longhouse traditions for pioneering ethnographers Henry Schoolcraft and Lewis Henry Morgan. Morgan's classic book on the subject of the

Longhouse Confederacy is widely regarded as one of the founding texts in the discipline of anthropology. It also holds a significant place in the core literature informing the genesis of communist ideology as developed by Karl Marx and Friedrich Engels. After the Civil War, Grant was elected as president of the United States, an event that would sweep Parker into the executive branch of the federal government. In Washington, Parker became the first Aboriginal person to fill the top administrative job at the Bureau of Indian Affairs.[10]

While some Cherokee and Creek men joined the Union forces, the largest weight of political and military support among the 100,000 inhabitants of Indian Territory rested with the Confederate states. The Chickasaws and Choctaws showed particularly strong support for the confederacy of pro-slavery states. This support was formalized in the making of several new Indian treaties. As has often been the case with those seeking to establish the sovereign jurisdiction of new polities in North America, the leadership of the Confederate states entered into these treaties with Indigenous peoples largely to affirm their assumed capacity to make international law. On the Indian side, the negotiation of these treaty alliances was part of a pragmatic adaptation to local circumstances. The treaty alliance embodied the legacy of a history that had seen the descendants of some Indian slaves become slave owners themselves.[11] Over several generations, the ownership of African-American slaves had become integrated into the domestic economies of the elite branches of the Five Civilized Tribes.

The legal and political position of the Five Civilized Tribes was significantly weakened by the federal victory in the Civil War. From the perspective of the federal government, many of the inhabitants of Indian Territory had effectively renounced their treaty relationships with the United States when they allied themselves with the Confederate states. The genesis of the US Civil War beginning in 1861 was similar to the genesis of the Anglo-American civil war of 1776. Both conflicts grew in significant measure from disputes over how to incorporate vast new territories into the legal and political systems of the conquering polities. The earlier war grew from a conflict over how best to incorporate the territorial spoils derived from the British conquest of Canada in 1759. The later war grew from a conflict over how best to incorporate the territories derived from the US conquest of much of Mexico in 1848. The Imperial Republic was pulled westward in the prelude to the Mexican-American War by the federal establishment of the new Indian Territory west of the Mississippi. The purpose of this territory was to receive the voluntary and involuntary migrants who left their Aboriginal homes because of President Andrew Jackson's Indian removal policy. The formulation and implementation of the policy had initiated a new chapter in the geopolitical organization of the United States.[12] In the prelude to the US Civil War, the project of imagining and imposing the geographical, political, and legal shape of this Indian Territory had figured importantly in the strategic thinking of proponents of both pro-slavery and anti-slavery constituencies. The continuing balance of power between the dual coalitions of states depended on the outcome of the process of creating new polities on the frontiers of US expansion.[13] This process was infused with memories of how the South's cotton-trade partners in Great Britain had deployed the concept of the Indian buffer state in their effort to check the expansion of the North's anti-slave territory after the American War of Independence. As a result, some pro-slavery strategists extended the idea of an entrenched Indian Country in the northwestern quarter of the United States to prevent the transformation of these lands into states controlled by anti-slavery constituencies. Alternatively, some northern politicians devised schemes of a permanent Indian Country in the southwest to check the extension of the slave-owning component of the American nation.[14]

Some of the migrants to Indian Territory had brought with them their own African-American slaves. Indeed, before the forced relocation in the Trail of Tears, many of the Five Civilized Tribes' most wealthy plantation owners were slave owners.[15] This adaptation to the local political economy of the US Southeast was one facet of a more sweeping pattern of transformation. The Cherokee were particularly adept at mixing their inherited traditions with the influences of Anglo-America to produce a prosperous and pluralistic society enriched by the activities of successful traders, entrepreneurs, legislators, and professionals of all sorts. The invention by Cherokee scholar Sequoyah of the Cherokee syllabic system of writing and the subsequent establishment of the *Cherokee Phoenix* as its principal medium of publication are often given as illustrations of Cherokee sophistication in blending their own Aboriginal heritage with that of the newcomers.[16] With their adoption in 1827 of a written Cherokee Constitution asserting exclusive Cherokee title and jurisdiction in their own lands, the Cherokee generated tremendous alarm among the people and government of Georgia. Those mounting tensions resulted in a flurry of litigation giving rise to some of Chief Justice John Marshall's most famous jurisprudence. His legal ruling on the nature of relations among Georgia, Indians, and the Cherokee treaties with the federal government highlighted many of the issues that would later flare up in slightly modified ways as points of constitutional conflict in the US Civil War.[17]

The relocated Cherokees, together with the relocated Creeks, Chickasaws, Choctaws, Seminoles, and other Aboriginal groups, combined their own ingenuity in Indian Territory with the available resources to build up a very elaborate complex of Indian public and private institutions – including Aboriginal courts, legislatures, schools, hospitals, ranches, plantations, food-processing plants, oil companies, and even a Choctaw railway company. The scope of these Indian innovations in business and parliamentary self-government resembled similar initiatives undertaken during the final decades of the twentieth century. These more recent innovations flowed from federal negotiations on Aboriginal title with Indigenous peoples in Alaska and northern Canada. In the mid-nineteenth century, the successful resettlement of many Indian groups in Indian Territory posed new problems for a number of railway promoters. The location of Indian Territory in the geographic centre of the United States became especially problematic once the building of transcontinental routes was technically feasible. Senator Stephen A. Douglas was instrumental in bringing about the passage through Congress in 1854 of the Kansas-Nebraska Bill. His main motivation as a senator from Illinois was to safeguard the importance of the growing metropolis of Chicago in westward expansion. The *Kansas-Nebraska Act* began the process of organizing as two federal territories the lands around Indian Territory in preparation for the eventual construction of transcontinental railways.[18] Uncertainties about the effects of the legislation on the balance of power between pro-slavery and anti-slavery constituencies effectively fanned the flames of acrimony. The *Kansas-Nebraska Act* resembled the so-called Missouri Compromise, when Missouri and Maine had both been elevated to full statehood in 1821 to maintain a degree of political equilibrium between those on the contending sides of the disagreement over the future of slavery in US federalism.

Senator Douglas and others expected that the principle of "popular sovereignty" would eventually lead to some sort of compromise, resulting in the positioning of Nebraska and Kansas on contending sides of the division over slavery. By 1854, however, it was increasingly difficult to postpone indefinitely some fundamental political reckoning with the legitimacy of America's most peculiar institution. The US Civil War marked the breakdown in the willingness of US citizens and their government representatives to compromise on one of the republic's two most basic issues of violated human rights. In 1865, with the end of the Civil War, the US federal government entered into a new round of treaty negotiations at Fort Smith with many leaders of the Cherokee, Choctaw, Chickasaw, Seminoles, and Creek nations. In the negotiations, the Indian leaders agreed to cease all hostilities with the US government and to outlaw slavery among their own people. They also agreed to negotiate the ceding of yet more land to allow the further expansion of non-Indian settlements pressing in on Indian Territory from Kansas and Nebraska.[19]

After the defeat of the Confederate states in 1865, the Indian Territory became a virtual laboratory for a broad range of experiments blending US laws of property relations with institutions designed to support and express the principles of limited Aboriginal sovereignty. An important contribution to the study of this fascinating episode in the history of US capitalism is H. Craig Miner's *The Corporation and the Indian: Tribal Sovereignty and Industrial Civilization in Indian Territory, 1865–1907*.[20] Miner's work details the process of breakup and atomization that occurred as Indian entrepreneurs within Indian Territory increasingly sought personal gain from the division and allotment of the collectively held tribal domain. The result was the demise of Indian Territory as a realm of practical Indian sovereignty, a development that helped clear the ground for the establishment of Oklahoma as a

regular US state in 1907. The prelude to the creation of Oklahoma constitutes a telling episode in the erosion of Indian Country. The process provides a revealing case study shedding light on how the growing force of US
corporate law shattered the integrity of a zone of shared Aboriginal jurisdiction to provide new media of privatized matter on the moving frontiers of
the US empire of capital accumulation.

INFLATING THE ROLE OF THE ARMED FORCES
IN THE CONQUEST OF INDIAN COUNTRY

The incorporation of Louisiana, Texas, Oregon Country, and northern
Mexico into the United States created the geopolitical context for the final
push to encircle, contain, pacify, and dominate what remained of the western Indian Country north of the Rio Grande and south of the forty-ninth
parallel. The Civil War hardly slowed down the pressures to transform
Indian Country into private property and non-Indian jurisdictions. In 1861,
for instance, mining discoveries led to the creation of Colorado and Nevada
Territories. In 1863, the same year as the Emancipation Proclamation and
the elimination of slavery in the Dutch West Indies, Arizona and Idaho territories were created. The following year the federal territory of Montana was
founded. Throughout this period and in the decades to follow, the diverse
Indian societies of California were subjected to an unrelenting onslaught
of murder and mayhem committed by local non-Indians. The prolonged
assault on the Indigenous people of this environmentally blessed region
amounts to one of the more clear-cut episodes of genocide on the face of
the planet.[21]

The military assertion of federal dominance to abolish the institution of
slavery and to pre-empt the sovereign claims of the Confederate states dramatically augmented the size, strength, and the organizational complexity
of the US Armed Forces. It was only natural that some of this expansion in
US military capacity was turned towards the project of quelling the remaining Indian resistance to the consolidation of the transcontinental character
of the United States. The US Army continued to conduct its operations in
the West in close cooperation and coordination with the activities of the railway companies. The form and purpose of the military-industrial complex
was effectively shaped by this partnership linking the US War Department
to the expansionary activities of the most dynamic transcontinental agencies of US corporate power. This alliance helped confirm patterns that
would continue in an era when the main challenge to the expansionary
operations of US corporate culture came not from Indians but from trade
unionists capable of organizing workers' opposition to the national, hemispheric, and worldwide ascent of capitalist property relations.

The use of railways to extend the hold of the United States on the
trans-Mississippi West initiated the final stage of the classic era of frontier expansion in the United States. The first transcontinental railway

came into existence in 1869, when the Union Pacific line was extended to meet the Central Pacific line at Promontory Summit, Utah. In 1883, three more transcontinental railway lines were completed – the Northern Pacific, the Sante Fe, and the Southern Pacific. Then, in 1893, the system was expanded, with the completion of the Great Northern line. The transcontinental railway companies were so favoured by the US government that they became by far the biggest landlords in the US West. In the second half of the nineteenth century, federal officials granted title to more than 180 million acres to the railway companies. According to Ray Allen Billington, federal authorities conveyed title to some 300 million acres of land to other corporate and state interests, whereas only 80 million acres were delivered as free grants to genuine homesteaders. In characterizing this comparison, one that completely contradicts the image of the US frontier as a domain of equal opportunity, Billington writes, "Half a billion acres were surrendered to monopolists in an era when orators boasted the United States was giving land free to its poverty-stricken masses."[22]

By taking over the leadership of the transcontinental expansion of the United States, the railway corporations moved towards the achievement of monopolistic and sovereign-like powers.[23] It was the lure of this type of outcome that had earlier inspired the promoters of the pre-revolutionary land speculation companies in British North America. Indeed, the lawyers for a transcontinental railway company gained the first decisive ruling in the courts enabling business corporations in the United States to assert the legal personality of "persons." The juridical use of the term *person* indicates that the individual described in this way is a rights-bearing citizen capable, for instance, of entering into contracts and of suing or being sued. The original case extending aspects of the concept of personhood to corporations is *Santa Clara County v. Southern Pacific Railway Company* – litigation that culminated in 1886 in a Supreme Court ruling based primarily on an interpretation of the applicability of the US Constitution's Fourteenth Amendment. In 1866 both houses of Congress had enacted the Fourteenth Amendment in order to protect freed slaves from abuses. This provision prohibits states from depriving "any person of life, liberty, and property without due process of law."[24]

By using the courts to claim for their own corporate vehicles some of the same rights and status residing in freed slaves, financial elites in the United States significantly enhanced their class interests, together with the potential worth of their members' own stock portfolios. Many examples could be cited right up to the present day of financial elites exploiting the medium of corporate law to turn to their own advantage the anti-discrimination provisions originating in legal instruments initially designed to recognize and affirm universal human rights. As exemplified by the history leading up to the Fourteenth Amendment, these anti-discrimination provisions tend to have especially deep roots in the egalitarian principles of Enlightenment thought. The corporate exploitation of the abolition movement's juridical legacy helped clear the way for new techniques of exploiting labour. These more recent trends have resulted in the institution of new forms of virtual enslavement through the aggressive manipulation of credit and debt as well as the mass transfer of manufacturing jobs away from heavily unionized sites to places with little or no legal protections for workers. In this scheme of capitalist globalization, national governments often face prohibitions preventing them from favouring their own national businesses on the grounds that such treatment would unfairly discriminate against corporations operating on a transnational basis.

The organization of capitalist society around the principle that corporate persons have rights similar to those of human persons has made a farce of the liberal ideal that all individuals should be treated equally before the law. It has rendered the whole construction of citizenship extremely problematic, especially when conflicts arise in the marketplace between human and corporate persons. While corporate and human persons are theoretically equal in many respects, the tendency in most capitalist countries has been for government officials to enforce corporate rights at the expense of human rights. This tendency becomes even more pronounced in the movement from national to transnational forms of governance. As a result, most human persons find themselves severely disadvantaged when their interests and rights clash with those of corporate persons, but especially those that operate on a global basis. The "unequal protections" afforded corporate and human persons informs Thom Hartmann's contention that "the rise of corporate dominance" is based on "the theft of human rights."[25]

The ruling on the Santa Clara County case was handed down the same year that the Supreme Court decided a legal case known as *United States v. Kagama*. In *Kagama*, a dispute involving a murder on the Hoopa reservation in northern California, the courts ruled that the plenary powers of Congress applied on Indian reservations. This decision directly negated the principle that US law afforded some qualified recognition of the sovereign existence of Indian nations within the territorial boundaries of the United States. The *Worcester v. Georgia* case in 1832 and the *Crow Dog* case in 1883 upheld the view of Indian nations as legal entities with their own internal means of making and enforcing laws. The *Kagama* ruling overturned this tradition of jurisprudence and advanced the legal view that Indians in the United States are wards of the government, entirely subject to federal laws not of their own making.[26] Much can be read into the concurrent rulings of the US Supreme Court in 1886 on the *Santa Clara County* and *Kagama* cases. At the very time that the US legal system was being retooled to enable corporations to act in many respects as "persons," the legal personality of the land's Indigenous peoples was reconfigured without their consent. Hence the same legal regime that defined corporations as persons defined Indians as non-persons – that is, as wards of federal authority without the ability to represent themselves in the courts, legislatures, and the making of contracts.

The treatment of Indians in North America as the uncivilized wards of a higher federal authority constituted one manifestation of a legal procedure that was becoming integral to various forms of empire building during an era when the imperial powers of Western Europe were reaching the zenith of their global claims and assertions. The rush of the European countries to divide up African territory among themselves, for instance, was all based on the theory that the Indigenous peoples of the colonized region could appropriately be treated as the uncivilized wards of the civilizing powers. Belgium's King Leopold would prove especially adept at the trick of legally infantilizing those on the receiving end of a particularly aggressive variant of colonization south of the Sahara Desert. As will be explored more fully in subsequent chapters, Leopold succeeded in setting himself up as a kind of trustee with claims that he represented the will of the civilized nations in his creation of the Congo Free State in the 1885. That exploitative polity came into existence just as the formal institutions of slavery were finally being brought to an end in Cuba and Brazil. The legal transformation of a significant portion of humanity into legal non-persons – as colonial wards under the legal tutorship of imperial trustees – gives yet further expression to the persistence of more subtle forms of enslavement long after the formal mechanisms of slavery were formally abolished.

This juridical slight of hand in the *Kagama* case had been preceded by a similar initiative in Congress. In 1871 the federal law makers decided simply to abandon through statute a long evolutionary process in the genesis of imperial, constitutional, national, and international law. The origins of this process of recognizing Aboriginal rights lay especially in papal decree – in the ecclesiastical scholarship of New Spain and in the Indian policies of New Netherlands. This legal tradition, one that weaved its way through the theory and thought of Vitoria, Las Casas, Grotius, Roger Williams, William Penn, and William Johnson, had gradually entered the jurisprudence of British colonization. Some elements of this tradition were effectively codified in the Royal Proclamation of 1763. Many Anglo-American dissidents were unwilling to accept the decision of the British government to offer some protections to Indigenous peoples. The hostility to the Royal Proclamation displayed by the Paxton Boys, Thomas Jefferson, and many other Anglo-American critics of imperial rule helped to generate the civil war in British North America whose outcome led to the creation and growth of the United States. In spite of the animosity of many Anglo-American settlers towards King George's efforts to make treaty alliances with Indians nations in North America's interior, however, the leadership of the new republic adopted principles that theoretically afforded Indigenous peoples protections similar to those outlined in the Royal Proclamation. Congress's ratification of about four hundred Indian treaties before 1871 stems from federal recognition that Indigenous peoples held the right of the soil in their Aboriginal lands until such time as they voluntarily agreed to cede it.[27] The underlying basis of the elaborate constitutional history signified in these treaties was overturned once Congress determined, in 1871, "Hereafter no Indian nation of tribe within the territory of the United States shall be acknowledged as an independent nation, tribe or power with whom the United States may contract by treaty."[28]

This legislative assault on the constitutional principles of Aboriginal and treaty rights was hidden in the Indian Bureau's annual appropriations bill. With this new enactment, the United States effectively renounced those aspects of the rule of law affording Aboriginal individuals and groups some say in the process of transforming the legal status of their ancestral lands. The decision not to continue the tradition of constitutional and international law expressed in treaties with Indigenous peoples found some surprising proponents – one being the Indian Affairs administrator Ely S. Parker. Referring to the tradition of Indian–US relations as transacted through treaties, this Seneca observed in 1869: "It is time that this idea should be dispelled, and the government cease the cruel farce of thus dealing with its helpless and ignorant wards."[29] The legislative prohibition on further treaty making with Indigenous peoples within US borders rendered explicit what had long been implicit in the process of western expansion. At every stage, that process of expansion depended more heavily on the assertion of military superiority over Indians than on the establishment of diplomatic relations with them. Very often the US government opted to engineer a military victory over an Indian group before negotiating the subject of land rights with its members.

The federal abandonment of the tradition of making treaties with Indigenous peoples implied a dependence on the rule of conquest over the rule of law as the main determinant of relations between stronger and weaker parties. The shift helped illustrate, develop, and reinforce patterns that would later be extended in the expansionary ascent of the lawless national security state over the rules-based international regime promoted by the authors of the Atlantic Charter and the founders of the United Nations. The shift helped renew, therefore, the personality of the United States as a revolutionary polity inclined to extinguish old constitutional traditions inherited from long durations of historical practice. As John R. Wunder has observed, "The Resolution of 1871 not only represented an end to pretense in Indian relations, but it also meant a serious modification and violation of international law and a threat to the diplomacy of the United States."[30]

The formal decision to rely on armed force rather than on treaty diplomacy with the Indigenous peoples of North America strengthened the role afforded to the US Army in the consolidation of transcontinental control by the federal government. The US Armed Forces had successfully disarmed the militant sovereignists of the Confederate states. The 1871 legislation made it clear that the same means of violent control enforced on the rebellious South would be extended to any Indian individual or group that failed to submit to the superior power of the United States. The military character of the final federal push to win the West after the Civil War was obvious, particularly in the region of the upper Missouri River. In this extended frontier zone, the US government built 110 forts manned by 20,000 troops to subdue Indian resistance to the taking and privatization of their lands.[31] The nature of these forts contrasted markedly with that of the British military posts retained by the Crown in the Indian Country south of the Great Lakes until 1796. After the fighting forces of Pontiac in 1763 had forced on imperial attention the need to respect Indian military capacity, the British posts in Indian Country continued as centres of trade and strategic planning between allies, much as they had been in the era when Canada grew from French-Aboriginal collaboration. While the British posts embodied one approach to imperialism, the US government's system of military operations in the trans-Mississippi West represented another. With the elevation in 1871 of the doctrine of conquest over the doctrine of consensual relations with Indigenous peoples, all ambivalence was stripped away from the imperial dynamic of US expansion. The mixing of the ethos of militarism, imperialism, and the corporate privatization of resources was further advanced in the process of asserting the territorial integrity of the polity that was fast emerging as global capitalism's most active laboratory.

CAPITALIZING ON THE IMAGERY OF THE INDIAN WARS

In 1904, one of many celebrations was mounted to mark the military, economic, and cultural triumphs of the United States in winning the West. That event was a parade to celebrate the inauguration of President Theodore Roosevelt in his first elected term as the nation's top public official. A major part of the parade presented two groups of Indian people. One group was chosen and dressed to represent Native Americans before they had been persuaded or coerced to bow before the power of the United States. The second group was chosen to represent how a portion of the Indian population in the United States had successfully integrated themselves into Roosevelt's idealized vision of the American way of life. This dramatic device was meant to portray the imagined transformation of the US Indian Country from savagery to civilization. The aim was to represent ritualistically Roosevelt's literary conceptualization of *The Winning of the West*, his multi-volume history dedicated to the memory of the Social Darwinist Francis Parkman.[32] From the content of the new president's historical writing, to his penchant for big-game hunting, to his promotion of national parks as an expression of environmental conservation, to his much-publicized role in the Spanish-American War as the officer in charge of the "Rough Riders," Roosevelt's rise to power was fuelled by a conscious strategy of identifying himself as an embodiment of the indomitable spirit of the US frontier.

There were other ideas that brought Roosevelt back to the White House in 1904.[33] In 1901 the assassination of President William McKinley had elevated Roosevelt from the US vice-presidency. Once at the executive helm of the Imperial Republic, Roosevelt moved in a limited way to challenge the monopoly powers then being actively asserted by the owners and officers of the corporate conglomerates engaged in expanding their influence over the broader landscape of the US political economy. Roosevelt chose to test the power of existing anti-trust laws by applying them to a single consortium named Northern Securities. This holding company dominated the ownership of a vast portion of the US rail system. In the decade ahead, Roosevelt's politics would focus increasingly on the idea that too much economic and political power was concentrated in too few hands. Just as this concept would animate the movement against corporate globalization a century later, so a growing abhorrence with the corporate subversion of democracy animated the rise of the Progressive Movement in the United States. Although Roosevelt would take the leading role in that movement in 1912, in 1904 he was still considered a safe bet for the presidency even by most leaders of Big Business. With his patrician connections and his populist bravado, Roosevelt had won the presidency in a land slide.

Besides the robust visage of Teddy Roosevelt, the most recognizable face in the inaugural parade was that of the renowned Apache guerrilla fighter Geronimo. Not surprisingly, Geronimo was placed among the group of Indians in the procession meant to represent the "before" phase in the imagined journey from savagery to civilization. Much to the surprise of the parade's planners, however, the audience did not respond to the comparison as they were expected to do. Rather than applauding the Indian group meant to represent assimilation into the American way of life, some of the biggest public cheers on Pennsylvania Avenue were reserved for Geronimo. Throwing their hats in the air, star-struck onlookers shouted, "Hooray for Geronimo! Public Hero No. 2!"[34] Geronimo had emerged as perhaps the leading celebrity from the most glamorized phase of North America's ongoing Indian wars. In the process of gaining this celebrity, he came to be seen as the quintessential guerrilla fighter of North America. At the peak of his exploits before his final capture in 1886, Geronimo led a tiny band of four dozen Apache raiders, only half of whom were full-grown men. To stop their marauding, a large force was raised comprised of about 5,000 regular and irregular US soldiers, 3,000 Mexican soldiers, and 1,000 vigilantes.[35]

A complex history lies behind Geronimo's mythologized last stand in the mountains and deserts of northeastern Mexico and the southwestern United States. Like the neighbouring Navajo, the Apaches are Dene speakers whose ancestors seem to have migrated from the Dene heartland in the Athabaska region of the Canadian North. From the sixteenth century on, the Apaches consistently resisted all Spanish encroachment into their territories and earned a reputation over many generations for being impervious to foreign domination. Their stamina and effectiveness as warriors became legendary. According to Brigadier-General George Crook, the Apache were "the tigers of the human species."[36] The superlatives flowed profusely in an era preoccupied with racial stereotypes and Darwinian notions of competitive advantage. The Apaches, wrote Britton Davis, "were the most perfect specimen of the racing type of athlete that one could hope to see."[37] Another commentator testified that the "military men have said that Apache warriors were the greatest fighting men who ever lived, in any period of history."[38] The congratulatory tone of this kind of recognition, however, tended to come only in retrospect. To many of their enemies during the era when the "renegade" Apaches stood in the way of the final US conquest of the West, the Apaches were nothing but murderous vermin requiring speedy extermination.

Geronimo belonged to one of seven divisions of the Apache. His own Chiricahua branch of the Apache people was widely seen as the centre of resistance to US and Mexican encroachments on Apacheria, a region about the size of France. The Chiricahua produced the most renowned Apache leaders, including Mangas Coloradas, Cochise, Victorio, Nana, and Geronimo himself. Geronimo was apparently given his famous name by a Mexican soldier who, after an Apache raid, pointed to its leader as he cried out to his patron saint, Hieronimo. Among his own people, Geronimo had entered the world as "Goyahkla," "the one who yawns." The heartland for Geronimo's Chiricahua people was the Sierra Madre Mountains in the Mexican region of Chihuahua. From their mountain hideaway, the Chiricahua guerrilla fighters would sweep down in raiding forays on small settlements in Chihuahua, Arizona, and New Mexico. As the murderous cycle of revenge and counter-revenge grew, seventy-year-old Mangas Colorado sought a meeting in 1863 with US military officials under a white flag. In spite of this promise of safety, Mangas was arrested and subsequently murdered while in custody.[39] His corpse was dismembered and apportioned as souvenirs.

Some US soldiers treated Mangas's dismembered head as a great prize. In the name of science, his brain was taken out, weighed, and reported to have "measured larger than that of Daniel Webster." It was subsequently taken to the Smithsonian Institution and placed on public display.[40] This treatment of Mangas's skull as a fetish anticipated the similar fate said to have been visited on Geronimo's skull. It was reportedly dug up in 1918 from the Christian graveyard at Fort Still, Oklahoma, by an elite contingent of Yale students who were receiving officers' training in the former Indian Territory. The grave robbers' leader was Prescott Bush, the father of one US president and grandfather of another. He is thought to have transported the macabre prize to New Haven, Connecticut. There Geronimo's skull was transformed into an object for display and ritual in the Tomb of the Order of the Skull and Bones on the Yale University campus. The Bush Bonesmen figured prominently among representatives of a number of rich and powerful US families that took part in the activities of a secret society notorious for the role of its initiates in the CIA and other key agencies of the national security state.[41]

Geronimo's rise to prominence began after he replaced Mangas as the leader of the Bedonkohe branch of the Chiricahua Apaches. The treachery involved in Mangas's murder while under the care of the US Army heightened the antagonisms between peoples. It began an era of accelerating conflict.[42] Between 1863 and 1872 it is estimated that the Apaches took 5,000 lives, compared with losing 100 of their own in battle. The amount spent by the US Army in this phase of the Apache wars was estimated to be $38 million.[43] At that point Brigadier-General Crook was sent into the losing side of this conflict. This innovative soldier soon transformed the army's method of tracking down the enemy in the daunting geography of Apacheria by using mule trains 'and also by hiring and integrating Apache scouts into military service.[44]

While Crook carried on the official part of the campaign, private citizens in Tuscon hired a group of Mexicans and Papago Indians to go after some Apache. In the Camp Grant massacre that followed in 1871, the mercenaries fell on an Apache camp while most of its men were away on a hunting expedition. The death toll on the Indian side was about 140, most of them women and children. Through a mixture of war and negotiation, Crook and Cochise established the beginnings of the reservation system to absorb the Apaches.[45] The main site for the "concentration" of the Apaches was the San Carlos Indian station in Arizona. For a time, even Geronimo submitted himself to the control of the civil and military authorities at San Carlos. Dominated by a business group known informally as the Tuscon Ring, these authorities became especially notorious for siphoning off large portions of the provisions and the resources allocated to support the Apache transition to "civilization."

Part of Geronimo's reputation for guile developed from his easy ability to evade the authorities as he moved on and off the San Carlos concentration camp. He joined the raiding band led by Victorio until the majority of this group were finally ambushed in 1880 at Tres Castillos in Mexico.[46] At about age seventy-five, Nana then rallied the few survivors as the core of yet another group identified by both the military and the press as "hostiles" or "renegades." After complex negotiations with the Mexican government, the US military force led by Crook finally tracked down the Chiricaua holdouts to their most secret hideaways in the Sierre Madre range. In 1883 Geronimo and his companions agreed to return to San Carlos. Once again, however, the pressures of subjugation were too much for the Apache leader. Passing repeatedly and seemingly invisibly under the noses of the soldiers at Fort Apache, Geronimo led a mass breakout from the Indian station. Once again he and his group headed for Mexico, spreading panic and outrage throughout Arizona and New Mexico as they went. Crook's forces tracked them down, this time to a place called Canyon de los Embudos. Accompanying Crook's contingent in 1886 was the photographer C.S. Fly, who captured some of the most famous images of Geronimo at the negotiations that followed. In the months, years, and decades ahead, these pictures would enter the psyche of the Western World as essential icons of the resisting spirit of North America's Indians.

The orderly proceedings at the Canyon de los Embudos were disrupted when an *agent provocateur* slipped the Indian captives several bottles of whiskey. After the leader regained his sobriety, Geronimo bolted again. When he was finally cornered by about 5,000 soldiers under the command of General Nelson Miles, "the last renegade" was tightly roped and freighted off by train to Florida. Among the Apache deportees with him were many of the same Apache scouts who had been employed by the US Army to capture the famed guerrilla fighter and his band of Chiricahua resisters. Anticipating Geronimo's magnetism as a powerful tourist attraction, the Florida town of Pensacola won a bidding war to host the celebrity warrior. Geronimo adapted to his new conditions. At Fort Pickens, he crafted souvenir items and sold autographs. He made himself available to the many curiosity seekers, some of whom came to gaze on the spectacle of the most lionized Indian in the Western Hemisphere as if they were viewing a caged animal in a zoo. In 1894 Geronimo and his small band of Chiricahua survivors were provided with a more permanent place of captivity in Fort Still, Oklahoma. There Geronimo and his people lived as "prisoners of war" until 1909. Even in his final years, Geronimo attracted scores of photographers seeking to capture on film his extraordinary self-composure.

Geronimo told the story of his life to S.M. Barrett, a school superintendent in Lawton, Oklahoma. His' military custodians at Fort Still originally prohibited the interview, but Barrett sought and received special permission from President Roosevelt. As Barrett saw it, his purpose was "to extend to Geronimo as a prisoner of war the courtesy due any captive, i. e. the right to state the cause which impelled him in his opposition to our civilization and laws."[47] One of his' most telling revelations was his account of a particular day in the early 1850s when he had returned as a young husband and father to his people's camp. He came to find his mother, his wife, Alope, and all their three children murdered by Mexican soldiers. "There were the decorations that Alope had made," he remembered, "and there were the play things of our little ones ... I had lost all."[48]

Although Geronimo was one of the major stars of President Roosevelt's inaugural parade in Washington in 1904, Quanah Parker also aroused considerable excitement from the audience. In a carriage seated beside several graduates of Pennsylvania's legendary Carlisle Indian Boarding School, he waved enthusiastically to the onlookers. His role in the festivities was intended to contrast with that of Geronimo. Where the Apache elder was meant to personify the "before" phase in the savagery-to-civilization continuum, Parker was probably the most recognizable icon of the "after" phase in the idealized saga of Indian transformation.[49] In the years before his thirtieth birthday, Quanah, as he was known then, was greatly feared by many Euro-Americans on the southern prairies. An accomplished horseman, this warring tribesman was recognized as one of the most ruthlessly hostile of the 20,000 Comanches. After 1875, however, Quanah eschewed further armed resistance to the imposition of US laws and institutions. He turned increasingly to the ranching business as the primary livelihood for his own people and for the neighbouring Kiowas. For a time these two groups were allowed to retain collective title to about 3 million acres.

Quanah's mother, Cynthia Ann Parker, was an Indianized White woman who had been taken captive by the Comanches as a child. Her son learned to make a living by charging Texas cattlemen for the right of passage of their longhorns through Comanche and Kiowa lands on their way to Kansas railway towns. As Quanah increasingly familiarized himself with the heritage and family of his mother, he entered into more complex leasing arrangements with Texas stockmen such as Dan Waggoner and Charles Goodnight. When news circulated that his mother was white by ancestry, he came to be known as Quanah Parker. The mixed nature of his family tree no doubt was a factor in his ready acceptance by the emerging aristocracy of the Texas cattle industry. Some of its members built a mansion for their Native associate, and it was soon tagged "the Comanche White House." In later years Quanah Parker, who gained a reputation as "the wealthiest Indian in America," became a fixture in the country's elite.[50] His inclusion in Theodore Roosevelt's inaugural parade was a significant mark of that prominence. In 1886, the year of the *Santa Clara County* and *Kagama* cases, the famous Comanche was made the chief judge of a newly instituted body known as the Court of Indian Offenses. Within a decade, however, most of the middle ground on which Quanah Parker endeavoured to stand was eliminated by the oligarchies that dominated the US government. Quanah Parker's function as a local magistrate was undermined by the transformation of US Indians into wards of federal authority even as the basis of his status and wealth was reduced by the subdivision and privatization of the Comanches's and Kiowas's shared domain. The famous old magistrate of the Comanche White House did not give in easily to the forces aligned against his peoples as he sought to defend the principles of the Bowl with One Spoon. In the end, however, Quanah Parker proved incapable of blocking those forces of subjugation and expropriation that he had temporarily held at bay through his ability to integrate into the upper echelons of the social and economic class system of the United States.

Quanah Parker had followed a course of accommodation similar to the one charted earlier in the nineteenth century by the Shawnee collaborator Little Turtle. This federally designated "chief" of the Comanches, however, found ways to mark his resistance to total assimilation into the culture and mores of those who came to dominate his people's lands. In the course of his life, for instance, Parker had eight wives – at one time, five simultaneously. His resistance to monogamy was part of his lifelong refusal to follow what many Indian people called the "Jesus road." Although he was always polite and respectful to those Christian missionaries who entered his orbit, he would never himself walk their evangelical path. Instead, this best-known Comanche spokesperson was influential in the movement that gave rise to the pan-Indian religion known as the Native American Church. The use of peyote in the rituals of this Aboriginal religion has made the Native American Church the focus of much controversy. The basis of that controversy lies in the overlap between two prominent features of US law: the constitutional recognition that people have the right to religious freedom, and the tough prohibitions against the distribution, possession, and ingestion of outlawed drugs.[51]

There was little room for irony in the inaugural parade's presentation of Geronimo and Quanah Parker as living embodiments of the before and after phases in the imagined transformation from Indian savagery to US civilization. Among the many paradoxes left mostly unexplored was the reality that a number of Indian people had joined the US Army to participate on the federal side of the recent Indian wars. In some instances the US Army inducted Indian scouts in ways that exploited the rivalries between hostile Aboriginal nationalities. The antagonisms of many Aboriginal groups towards the Siouian-speaking peoples, for instance, played a key role, particularly in the incorporation of Pawnee, Arikara, and Crow soldiers into the US Armed Forces. The intelligence work of the US Army was sometimes directed at exploiting or even stimulating ethnic and personal antagonisms among Aboriginal individuals and groups. Accordingly, just as the soldiers on the imperial frontiers of many European empires used divide-and-conquer tactics to weaken their opponents, so, too, the US military joined in the business of manipulating the internal schisms of Indigenous peoples standing in the way of Anglo-American expansion.

The main breakthrough on the US side in the Apache wars occurred once Brigadier-General George Crook succeeded in inducting Apache scouts into his contingent. In reflecting on the crucial importance of these scouts in his campaign of Apache pacification, Crook commented that, "to polish a diamond, there is nothing like its own dust."[52] Some of the Apache scouts had entered the US Army once they tired of the harsh life in a guerrilla war where their people could never ultimately prevail. They sought escape from an increasingly desperate and demanding resistance struggle, even as they also sought a way to avoid the stark oppressions of reservation life. This kind of tradeoff seems to have animated the decision of Tsoe, a young Apache who married into the Chiricahua band. Tsoe was the all-important guide who first led Crook's forces to Geronimo's camp in the Sierra Madre Mountains in 1883.

While the role of Apache scouts in the Apache wars is indicative of the loose character of the ties within this group, the US Army learned the hard way that there were limits to how far their scouts could be pushed in fighting their own people. In 1881 there arose from San Carlos a messianic visionary named Noch-ay-del-klinne. This shaman began preaching a message that inspired the hope for salvation among some of his audience. His teachings anticipated the rise of the ghost-dance religion that was about to sweep through many surviving Indian communities throughout the prairies. The effect of Noch-ay-del-klinne's words in reversing the demoralized state of his Apache listeners startled the Indian agent in charge of San Carlos, and the authorities decided to transport him away from his devotees. Before that could be arranged, however, some US soldiers tried to use the cover of night to kill him. His adherents surged to his rescue, including all but one of the Apache scouts. In the ensuing exchange of gun fire, there were a number of casualties on both sides. Among the dead were Noch-ay-del-klinne and several of the men who had tried to save him. Three of the Indian scouts who joined in his defence were subsequently hanged and two were incarcerated.[53]

The US Army's recruitment of Indian scouts in the Indian wars suggested the outlines of many future episodes in the rise of the informal American empire. Throughout Latin America, for instance, Indian recruits figured prominently among those military and para-military death squads who, in the name of anti-communism, killed scores of political activists and hundreds of thousands of traditional Indian horticulturalists. Similarly, at the beginning of the twenty-first century, US military forces were quickly drawn into the rivalries churning within and among the Indigenous peoples of Afghanistan and the surrounding regions. In the process of recruiting, arming, and financing the jihadists of the mujahideen, the US Armed Forces and the national security state became deeply immersed through the Inter-Services Intelligence Agency in Pakistan (ISI) in the internal controversies linking tribal and Islamic politics. In 1989 these agents of US interests in the Cold War overthrew the Soviet-backed puppet regime in Afghanistan. With the demise of the vanquished forces, the conquering Islamic groups tended to split along ethnic lines. The majority of the dominant Pushtan population supported the Taliban, who were opposed by a coalition of warlords and druglords, including those who governed many Persian-speaking Tajiks and conglomerations of Hazara, Uzbeks, and others who rallied against the Pushtan domination of their country. Together these opponents of Taliban rule formed the United Islamic Front for the Salvation of Afghanistan. The Western media dubbed this component of the former mujahideen as the Northern Alliance. As long as the Taliban seemed favourable to an oil pipeline planned through Afghanistan by the Union Oil Company of California (UNOCAL), they were allowed to govern Afghanistan. On September 9, 2001, however, the assassination of the Northern Alliance's most important leader, Ahmed Shah Massoud – the Lion of Panjshir – signalled that a fundamental shift in the geopolitical landscape of the region was about to take place. After the events of September 11, 2001, the US government and its NATO allies declared war on the Taliban and sided with the tribal warlords of the recently beheaded Northern Alliance. As a result of the Western powers' quick and decisive military intervention during this vacuum, the government of Hamid Karzai, a well-known CIA operative and former consultant to UNOCAL, was installed to secure the region on behalf of the interests that made the Global War on Terror their vehicle of self-aggrandizement.[54]

By intervening in the intrigues and tribal rivalries of Islamic groups in the oil-rich zones of Central Asia, the military apparatus of the national security state applied the lessons that first emerged for the US Armed Forces when its generals recruited Indian scouts to hunt down their own people in the Indian wars. The use of Apache scouts to disarm and contain Geronimo's raiding band of guerrilla fighters epitomized this process. By following this course of action in the American West, Afghanistan, and many other zones of contested sovereignty, the military-industrial complex of the United States attempted to incorporate the techniques of internal subversion and divide-and-conquer that had been so integral in the expansionary strategies of older European empires. While the supply lines considerably lengthened and the number of "hostiles" grew enormously in the early years of the twenty-first century, US military officials in Central Asia struggled to relearn lessons from the expansionary exploits of the US government in the conquest of the trans-Mississippi West.

FROM SITTING BULL TO APIKUNI AND GREY OWL: THE SHIFTING MARKERS OF INDIAN COUNTRY IN FACT AND IMAGINATION

The final push to consolidate the metropolitan hold of the US capital over its coast-to-coast empire resulted in the most universally recognized and widely commodified imagery of frontier conflict ever produced in the Western Hemisphere. Pictures and stories of Indian defiance were marketed and manipulated to justify the US conquest of its transcontinental territory as though this outcome was the realization of Western Civilization's Manifest Destiny to triumph over savagery. Almost immediately this last major series of military campaigns west of the Mississippi became the stuff of legend. Particular attention was showered on the apparently doomed heroism of Sitting Bull, Crazy Horse, Gall, Chief Joseph, Geronimo, Victorio, Cochise, Red Cloud, Roman Nose, Satank, Satana, and the other Aboriginal opponents of the consolidation of US control over the trans-Mississippi West. With electric speed, the new "talking wires" spanning North America buzzed with information about confrontations between fearless Indian warriors and the conquering forces of an emerging superpower. The Aboriginal resisters were quickly transformed into totems of America's fighting spirit. As in the days when Black Hawk's tour of US cities produced widespread fascination, the public was inclined to adopt the iconography of Indian defiance as though the courage shown by Aboriginal freedom fighters expressed the indigenous pride of the US nation.

The Indian wars heightened the prestige of the nascent military-industrial complex of the United States. Anticipating the day when the New World leviathan would produce Apache and Black Hawk helicopters as well as tomahawk cruise missiles, the makers of the Imperial Republic's transcontinental empire claimed the military legacy of both sides of the Indian wars. The array of heroes assembled in the drama of the winning of the American West required the inclusion of the original Tecumseh as well as a spotlight on William Tecumseh Sherman, the general who effectively served as the US Army's commanding officer in charge of westward expansion. The ability of the managers of the US military-industrial complex to draw on the military culture of their defeated enemies would be repeated after the conquest of the Axis powers. With the completion of the Second World War in 1945, the US government made ample use of Nazi advances in science, technology, espionage, propaganda, and psychological warfare. The anticommunist heritage of the Axis was deeply integrated into the strategic operations of the capitalist side in the Cold War. Patterns of conduct were established that would be extended and amplified with the ascent of the national security state in the course of the Global War on Terror.

Beginning in the final decades of the nineteenth century, the celebrity of the group that would come to be known as "the patriot chiefs" spread across time and space from news reports to other media of communication.[55] The imagery of the most mythologized showdown between "savagery and civilization" – this struggle to win the West for the empire of capitalist expansion – provided dramatic grist for a proliferation of dime novels, plays, and circus-like events such as the spectacularly successful Buffalo Bill's Wild West Show. In planning the spectacle to accompany Chicago's Columbian Exposition, the promoters and image makers behind Buffalo Bill borrowed from the title of Theodore Roosevelt's series of history books. The producers of the 1893 version of Buffalo Bill's Wild West Show entitled their extravaganza "How the West Was Won."[56] The Buffalo Bill Show and other similar spectacles provided some of the surviving Aboriginal veterans of the Indian wars with a means of earning livelihoods in an era when most Native people experienced great difficulty conforming to the conditions of their subjugation. These public events provided venues for former Indian enemies of the United States to trade on the ghoulish kind of celebrity they had acquired. Sitting Bull was the most famous and accomplished of these Indian war veterans. In 1884 he was put on exhibit in a tour of fifteen North American cities organized by showman Alvaren Allen.

As the primary promoter behind the success of the Buffalo Bill Show, Allen advertised his star attraction as "the Slayer of General Custer." The near obliteration of Custer's forces in 1876 at the Battle of Little Bighorn by Sioux, Cheyenne, and northern Arapahoe warriors is an episode in US history laden with an especially heavy baggage of symbolic meanings.[57] In the aftermath of their defeat of General George Custer's Seventh Cavalry Unit, the victorious Aboriginal forces of Sitting Bull sought permanent refuge in Canada's Northwest Territories. About four thousand Sioux set up camp amid the forested slopes of the prairie oasis of the Cypress Hills, just north of the international boundary running along the forty-ninth parallel.[58] The presence of Sitting Bull and his people in the federal territory of the Dominion of Canada created a major diplomatic controversy in relations between Great Britain and the United States.[59] In those days, the British imperial government retained constitutional responsibility for Canada's international relations. Sitting Bull's quest for a permanent sanctuary in Canada for himself and his diverse band of followers sparked a major debate among officials seeking to clarify the precise legal status of Indian refugees from the US Indian wars. As military allies of the Crown in the War of 1812, the Sioux had particularly strong claims that they were entitled to the protection of the British imperial government from their enemies in the United States. Some of the police and military officials responsible for overseeing Sitting Bull's band in the Cypress Hills clearly sympathized with the plight of its members. One of them, Colonel James Macleod, reported:

I think the principal cause of the difficulties which are continually embroiling the American Government in troubles with the Indians is the manner in which they are treated by the swarms of adventurers who have scattered themselves all over the Indian country in search of minerals, before any treaty is made giving up the title. These men always look upon the Indians as their natural enemies, and it is their rule to shoot them if they approach after being warned off.

In recounting his own dilemma, Sitting Bull explained to Colonel Macleod:

I tell you the truth; I have done nothing bad. The Americans tried to get our country from us.... They knew that the gold was there. I did not give them my land no more than you would have given it.... My people suffer from the Americans. I want to live in this country and be strong and well and happy.... The Americans kill ten or twenty of my children every day for nothing. I like to see my children alive. Soon you will see more of our tribe crossing the line.[60]

After elaborate and prolonged negotiations between the United States and Canada's imperial guardians in Great Britain, Sitting Bull and his followers were denied the sanctuary they sought in the territory of the Blackfoot, the Cree, and the Great White Mother. In 1881 Sitting Bull and his dwindling band were marched to the international border and delivered to the custody of US officers. Unlike in the era of the American Revolution and the War of 1812, Crown officials had determined that it was no longer expedient to encourage Indigenous peoples either to oppose the expansion of the United States or to seek protection in Canada from the hostility of US prospectors, settlers, and military forces.[61] As David Mills, Canada's minister of the interior, wrote of the victors of the Battle of Little Bighorn on their entry into the Crown's federal territories, "It is desirable that as wards of the United States they should return to that country, upon the

Government of which morally devolves the burden and the responsibility of their civilization."[62]

After being returned to the United States, Sitting Bull embarked on his short career in show business. His transition from the rigours of real frontier warfare to the play acting of feigned warfare took place even as Geronimo and his small band of Chiricahua resisters continued to elude the Mexican and US armies, the vigilantes, and the Tucson Ring's paid mercenaries. Along with American Horse, Rocky Bear, Flys Alone, Long Wolf, and several other Indian war veterans, Sitting Bull attracted huge business for Buffalo Bill Cody's Wild West extravaganza. Their employment as actors,portraying romanticized caricatures of themselves was part of a dramatic tradition reaching back long before George Catlin's travelling troupe of performing Indians and pointing towards the day when cinematic Westerns would help globalize the influence of Hollywood's empire of fantasy. Sitting Bull, however, soon tired of this life on display. He returned one last time to his own people to help them resist a major federal effort to diminish still further the extent of unceded Sioux lands in the Dakota and Nebraska areas.[63] His intervention made it considerably more difficult for the US government to coerce and bribe a sufficient number of Sioux to put their marks on a huge land-sales agreement. Those who resisted this pressure looked to their old war leader with renewed respect, admiration, and even veneration. Sitting Bull responded to his renewed position of influence by adopting the teachings and ceremonies of the Piaute mystic Wovoka. Like the movements generated by the Delaware prophet Neolin, by the Shawnee preacher Tenswatawa, or by the Apache visionary Noch-ay-del-klinne, Wovoka's ghost-dance religion empowered its devotees not to sink into despair. The dance ritual encouraged its initiates and devotees to dare to hope for a new beginning, where some revised version of the old ways would return to overpower the growing tide of newcomers in the American West.[64]

The ghost-dance religion renewed many old traditions in Indian Country even as it provided a new form of resistance during a time when armed opposition to the authority of the federal government was no longer possible or viable. For its adherents, this religion seemed to open the way for the hope of liberation through divine intervention.[65] In their obsession with bringing their own physical movements into conformity with the Creator's cosmic pulsations and harmonies, the ghost dancers sought to project themselves through the gateway of spiritual transcendence. They aspired to achieve a state where they would be freed from the choking constraints of reservation life, from the quick and devastating losses of so many loved ones, and from the ecological upheavals of an old world turned upside down by the self-proclaimed makers of a New World Order. This means of renewing the spirit of hope and resistance struck fear and even panic into the keepers of the reservations, whose purpose was to subdue, restrain, and concentrate the Aboriginal survivors of America's Indian wars. As we have seen, these concentration camps for Indians would in later years become a subject of study stimulating the imagination of the young Adolf Hitler.

The military custodians of the Sioux became especially alarmed by the seemingly ceaseless chanting and dancing of those Indians who believed in the mystical power of Wovoka's revelations. It was in this atmosphere of official dismay at the strength of the ghost-dance religion that one of its most influential practitioners, Sitting Bull, was killed in a botched attempt to apprehend him. His life was taken in his own home in 1890 by two Indian police officers employed by the federal government. The assault on the legendary Sioux leader proved to be the prelude to the subsequent massacre of Big Foot's band by a unit of the army's Seventh Cavalry.[66] This slaughter at Wounded Knee of about 350 unarmed Sioux helped to settle the score in the minds of those who saw revenge as the appropriate response to the last stand of General George Custer and his men of the Seventh Cavalry at the Battle of Little Bighorn. The unarmed victims in 1890 were mostly elders, women, and children. This episode is generally interpreted as the closing drama in the most overt military phase of the Indians wars of the United States.[67] It is often made to serve as a marker of the end of the aggressive, rambunctious, and intensively mythologized phase of the westward expansion of the Imperial Republic. Eight decades later, Dee Brown dramatically portrayed the events of the massacre as the tragic climax of his immensely popular volume *Bury My Heart at Wounded Knee.*[68] This book so moved and aroused many of its readers that it influenced as well as narrated key episodes in the Aboriginal history of the United States. There is little doubt that the unusual success of Brown's popularized account of western history was a factor in the decision of the American Indian Movement to return to Wounded Knee in 1973. AIM's stand on the site of the massacre of Big Foot's band gave rise to a federal military response. Thus, in 1973, the militant arm of an aroused Indian Country made one more display of resistance to the imposition of federal authority on the Aboriginal sovereignty of Indigenous peoples

The events of 1890 were psychologically and strategically decisive. The capture of Geronimo in 1886, followed by the US government's military massacre of Big Foot's band at Wounded Knee, marked the end of the most aggressive era in the consolidation of US transcontinental hegemony. Those events gave added weight to observations made in 1890 by the superintendent of the federal census. This federal official declared in a bulletin that the westward movement of an identifiable line of Euro-American frontier settlement had finally become a thing of the past. Frederick Jackson Turner would famously cite the superintendent's pronouncement in his presentation at the Columbian Exposition in Chicago in 1893. The Wisconsin historian used the news that the pioneer phase of US expansion was over to introduce his reflections on the role of frontierism in the development of the emergent superpower's political culture. Hence the transition from the nineteenth century to the twentieth century could be said to have started for the United States at the Wounded Knee massacre. The ruthless nature of the Seventh Cavalry's answer to its defeat at Little Bighorn announced the violent close of what Turner referred to as "the colonization of the Great West."[69] As Turner gazed westward towards Hawaii, the Philippines, and the immensity of the Pacific Rim, it seemed to him and to many others that the dramatic intensity of the colonization that had already taken place was a mere prelude to the conquest of new frontiers to come. Turner was far from alone when he looked optimistically towards the prospect of the United States continuing its conquering ways across wider expanses of geography, commerce, and culture in the global community.

In the deeper musings of some Americans, however, Manifest Destiny's bold optimism gave way to undercurrents of unease about the more profound implications of the Indian wars and Indian removal in the ethical and legal construction of the US nation. Those who harboured such doubts continued the intellectual traditions of Jeremiah Evarts and John Dunn Hunter. Both had interpreted the speed and character of the frontier expansions as being fraught with problems for future generations. They had warned of the dangers inherent in the United States making itself "great and powerful," based on "the destruction of the Indians."[70] As the US Army passed off its role in the subjugation of Indigenous peoples to missionaries, bureaucrats, police officers, and lawyers, the federal Indian reservations of the United States emerged as the new centres of Indian Country. Some challenged the orthodox view that the goal of federal Indian policy should be to assimilate Indian people into the dominant social structure defined by Christianity and capitalism. The alternative perspective pictured Indian reservations as sites where at least some aspects of Indian culture might be preserved and enhanced outside the assimilationist strategies favoured by the officialdom of church and state. The rise of the conservationist movement in the United States and Canada coincided with a shifting attitude towards the fate of Indigenous peoples in North America. Once the newcomers' domination of America's Aboriginal geography was no longer in doubt, a minority opinion began to coalesce aimed at integrating the continuing existence of Indian nations into the national mosaic of the North American society. The basic message was that the terrible genocidal thrust of the Indian wars, followed by the assimilationist Indian policies of church and state, must not be allowed to run their full, extinguishing course. They must not be allowed to culminate in the final termination of America's living Aboriginal heritage.

The revered Oglala philosopher Black Elk was one of those struck by the parallels between the movement for wildlife preservation and the consolidation of the reservation system during the early years of the twentieth century. He recognized that similar fates had been visited on Indigenous peoples in North America and on the game animals that had once been so integral to their political economy, and he observed that the federal government "made little islands for us and other little islands for the four-leggeds."

Every year these islands shrunk in size, so they were made to move farther and farther apart.[71] The main federal enclaves for the four-leggeds were, of course, the forest reserves and national parks that Teddy Roosevelt and others insisted must be set aside and protected for the enjoyment of future generations. The steps to disconnect the two-legged citizens of federal Indian reservations from the four-legged inhabitants of national parks had its mirror image. While one group of administrators sought to situate national parks beyond the legal limits of Aboriginal hunting and fishing rights, another group of activists sought to promote national parks by associating their image with idealized portrayals of Native American culture. The friction between these two approaches sheds light on the complex character of the identity politics of the dominant group once the West had seemingly been won. As foreshadowed by the quick transformation of Geronimo and Sitting Bull from hunted hostiles into sought-after celebrities, a groundswell of romantic nostalgia appeared in the post–Wounded Knee era both for what had been lost and how it had been taken. Accordingly, the range of psychic, emotional, and intellectual reactions to western conquest defies simple characterization. Behind the veneer of self-satisfaction on the part of the West's "winners," some supposedly situated on the dominant edge of history could not help but harbour tinges of regret, self-doubt, and even self-reproach. There were limits to the capacity of Manifest Destiny, Social Darwinism, and the operation of market forces to provide cover and sanction for the ongoing destruction and appropriation of such vast parts of a whole hemisphere's Aboriginal patrimony.

In the aftermath of the massacre of Wounded Knee, the need arose to invent a popular history of self-justification qualified with regret. This history would be peopled by desperados and justice-loving newcomers. It would include noble yet savage imaginary Indians who could be made to act as counterpoints to all that was seen as both glorious and evil in the new civilization of the conquerors.[72] The artist and naturalist George Catlin was one of the first US citizens to propose co-existence as an alternative to unqualified conquest as the basis of the relationship with the Indigenous peoples of the trans-Mississippi West. He recorded his proposal in the published journal chronicling his trip up the Missouri River in 1832. Like Paul Kane and Karl Bodmer, Catlin devoted himself to sketching and painting a pictorial record of North America's western Indian Country in the era when access to this vast domain was still largely controlled by the main fur-trade enterprises. Catlin hoped for some "great protecting policy of government" to preserve parts of the American West in "all its pristine beauty and wildness." He proposed the reservation of places "where the world could see for ages to come, the native Indian in his classic attire, galloping his horse ... amid the fleeing herds of elk and buffalo." In this spirit, Catlin arrived at the idea for a "*nation's Park* containing man and beast, in all the wild and freshness of their nature's beauty."[73] It would take several decades before even limited versions of Catlin's grand proposal found sufficient political backing to result, for instance, in the reservation of the Yosemite, Yellowstone, and Grand Canyon sites as federally protected shrines for the recreational, conservationist, and spiritual purposes they now so famously fulfill. Many of the connections between national parks and Indian peoples converged most clearly in the genesis of Glacier National Park, the "Crown of the Continent" in northern Montana adjacent to the large Indian reservation apportioned for Blackfeet people.

The creation in 1910 of Glacier National Park was largely the result of the commercial designs of the Great Northern Railway Company combined with the literary and lobbying efforts of George Bird Grinnell and James Willard Schultz. The eastern slopes of this famed mountain park were, from 1855 to 1895, part of the lands reserved by the US government for the southern Piegan branch of the Blackfeet Confederacy. The reservation was created through the provisions of the Lame Bull Treaty – part of the cycle of quick transactions pushed ahead by Major Isaac Stevens shortly after his appointment as Washington Territory's first governor and as one of the chief surveyors charged to identify the best pass through the Rockies for a transcontinental railway. The southern Piegan were pressured to hand over their mountain holdings to the federal government in 1895. The source of this pressure came from two competing factions: one set of promoters held that the ceded lands should give way to mining development; the other faction looked forward to forming a national park in this majestic Alpine region, one where a number of different watersheds meet in close proximity. When Piegan chief White Calf signed over the lands that subsequently became a federal forest reserve, he looked towards the most prominent peak in the transferred range and lamented, "Chief Mountain is my head. Now my head is cut off. The mountains have been my last refuge."[74]

The land cession was a complex transaction that included written acknowledgment that the Blackfeet people would retain certain logging rights together with the right "to hunt upon said lands and to fish in the streams thereof" for as long as "they remain the public lands of the United States."[75] The Blackfeet received $1.5 million for allowing the section in question to be severed from their reservation. James Schultz was part of the faction that had first lobbied for the land cession with the expectation of opening the region to mining development. George Bird Grinnell, one of the most effective pioneering conservationists in the United States, was intent on preserving the region as a national park. Grinnell was a man of considerable wealth with a wide network of strategic connections in the worlds of US politics, business, science, and culture.[76] He met Schultz when the latter had first guided him along the mountain trails that, in later years, would be opened to tens of thousand of wilderness-seeking pilgrims visiting Glacier Park. A guide to many a millionaire seeking big game in the High Rockies, Schultz had initially headed up the Missouri River in 1877 to seek his fortune.[77] Near the river's sources, Schultz had teamed up with some

Fort Benton traders who derived large profits exchanging whiskey for buffalo robes provided by Blackfeet Indians. The Blackfeet refer to themselves as Nitsitapi. The commercial exploits of the Fort Benton whiskey dealers had given rise to the legendary excesses of Whoop-Up Country on the chinook-swept expanses just north of the Canada-US border. Like his friend, painter Charles M. Russell, Schultz's wide reputation grew from his engaging portrayals of that brief era when Indians, mountain men, and cowboys mingled and clashed in the awe-inspiring scenery where the prairies, foothills, and Rockies converge.

Schultz and Grinnell were quick to realize that they would be more effective as allies than as adversaries. Schultz broke his connections with mining promoters to join Grinnell is his quest to create a new national park. Each man produced a flow of books and articles that helped to satisfy the insatiable appetite for interesting data and action-packed stories outlining the high drama of life on the western frontier.[78] One of their main goals was to give their readers an informed and sympathetic insight into the inspirations and actions of the peoples indigenous to the lands they both loved. Schultz used his Indian name, "Apikuni," on some of his publications. In his review of Apikuni's *My Life as an Indian*[79] Grinnell praised the work for penetrating "the veil of racial difference" and getting "close to the heart of the people about whom he writes."[80]

Both Grinnell and Schultz can be characterized as formative figures in a long line of writers from Long Lance to Hugh Dempsey to Adolf Hungry Wolf to Tom King. None of these men were born as Blackfeet, but they all tried to achieve authenticity in their literary work on the internal dynamics of Blackfeet life. As a friend and colleague of both John James Audubon and Theodore Roosevelt, Grinnell had originally come west as a paleontologist after graduating from Yale University. In the fateful year of 1876, George Custer invited the young naturalist to come along with his Seventh Cavalry unit to Montana Territory. Grinnell, however, declined. He used his position as editor of *Field and Stream* magazine to press for a number of conservationist objectives, including the creation of Glacier National Park, and seized on Schultz's early articles on Blackfeet Country. Grinnell published these essays prominently, with the objective of creating the right mystique to advance his political agenda. The key to gaining federal recognition for the creation of Glacier National Park in 1910 was the determination of the officers of the Great Northern Railway to develop the region as a tourist destination. Once the park was established and the visitors' accommodation set in place, the railway company exploited and expanded the imagery that Schultz and Grinnell had helped to generate.

Glacier Park's advertising, hotel interior design, and planned recreational activities all emphasized Blackfeet themes and motifs. As Robert H. Keller and Michael F. Turek described the new tourist attraction in their *American Indians and National Parks*:

Blackfeet in buckskin and feathers, once the most respected warriors on the northern plains, now greeted new arrivals at the park train depot, drove tourist buses, and welcomed guests to the hotels. At resorts decorated in quasi-Indian art, tourists shook hands with Blackfoot "chiefs" and flirted with "Indian door girls." The tribe drummed, danced, and signed postcards on the sprawling estate of a hotel, then conducted naming ceremonies in the crowded lobby. Indians "passed the tom-tom" for tips and sold miniature bows, arrows, and teepees. Between 1914 and 1919 hardier tourists slept in real teepees on the lawn of the East Glacier Hotel.[81]

This Indianization of the Glacier Park tourist trade stood in stark contrast to the tough stand taken by federal officials against the Blackfeet use of the federal land for hunting and fishing. This prohibition, which seemed to violate the written provisions of the land concession of 1895, quickly became the source of considerable legal and political acrimony. It remains so still. North of the international boundary, the land adjacent to Glacier National Park was transformed into Waterton Lakes National Park in 1911. In 1885 the Canadian government had created its first national park around the hot sulphur spring at Banff. In 1927 the Great Northern Rail Company created a Canadian subsidiary to raise the Prince of Wales Hotel in the northern park. That cross-border outreach proved instrumental in the creation in 1932 of an international peace park composed of the two national parks, one on each side of the forty-ninth parallel. On the urging of Canon S.H. Middleton, the Anglican clergyman in charge of the St Paul's Indian Residential School on the Blood reserve, the Rotary Clubs of both Alberta and Montana became the primary agencies in the process of lobbying for the peace park's creation. The Canadian Pacific Railway used almost identical strategies to the Great Northern Railway in promoting its new complex of Rocky Mountain tourist resorts. At the Banff Springs Hotel, for instance, "Indian Days" formed one of its greatest annual attractions over much of the twentieth century.

The National Parks branch of Canada's dominion government was instrumental in building up the public persona of Grey Owl, one of the most effective promoters of the conservationist ethic in the first half of the twentieth century. Grey Owl began his life in England as Archie Belaney. He emigrated to Ontario and, like thousands before him, he moved beyond the country's urban and agricultural zones to enter the surviving fur-trade preserve and unfenced Indian Country that persists even to this day throughout large parts of northern Canada. Belaney transformed himself into an Indianized bushman over many years in the north country of Ontario and Quebec. His Mohawk wife, Anahareo, from Oka, Quebec, persuaded him to put aside his life as a trapper and to devote himself instead to domesticating several beaver in their unusual wilderness retreat. In those years the voracious appetites of the fur trade had so weakened the beavers' legendary presence throughout Canada that the entire species was hovering close to extinction. This seminal experience as the beavers' friend formed the basis of Belaney's career as a writer and as a leading activist for wild-life conservation.[82] He added to these roles his reinvention of himself as Grey Owl, a Scots-Apache who lived as a traditional Indian in the wilds of the Canadian Shield. James Harken, the civil servant in charge of Canada's National Parks branch, first identified Grey Owl's potential. After hiring him, he transferred Grey Owl and Anahareo to Prince Albert National Park in Saskatchewan and authorized the filming of the couple at home with their beavers. The animals became virtual mascots of both wildlife conservation and Canada's national parks. With the synergy between his movies and his books, Grey Owl became a major celebrity in the transatlantic world before the Second World War. He was much in demand, especially in Great Britain as a public speaker. In seeking to explain Grey Owl's role, Harken asserted, "There is not the slightest doubt that we have secured for our Parks and for general conservation thousands of dollars of publicity through Grey Owl, his beaver, his books, his magazine articles, and the motion pictures we have secured of him and his beaver. As you know, these films have a worldwide distribution."[83]

It is easy from the perspective of the twenty-first century to belittle or deride the role of Grey Owl or Apikuni in helping to popularize a romanti-cized imagery of Indian lore as a key to mobilizing the conservationist ethos. It would be very short sighted, however, not to recognize in their celebrity the markers of an important shift in public opinion. Implicit in this shift was the beginning of a serious reconsideration of the conquistadorial heritage of Western Civilization. Grey Owl's message was especially rich in significance. During the years when the Nazis were pushing a racialized vision of Social Darwinism towards its hellish extremes, the counterpoint to these develop-ments lay in the flickering celluloid images of a lone Indian couple nursing back to life the survivors of North America's decimated beaver population. This imagery supported the mission to protect at least some representative samples of North America's Aboriginal geography.[84] The attention given to imaginary Indians such as Grey Owl and Apikuni highlight the failure to afford comparable attention to the activism of real Indians. The contrast puts in bold relief the very marginal role apportioned by the gate keepers of popular culture to those Aboriginal men and women who maintained against great odds the unbroken political struggle to secure for Indigenous peoples a more just place in North American society during the early decades of the twentieth century. Prominent among these leaders were Dr Carlos Montezuma, the great critic of the US Bureau of Indian Affairs;[85] Alice Lee Jemison, the outspoken proponent of Six Nations treaty rights;[86] Lieutenant Fred Loft, a leading advocate for the transformation of Indian wards into citizens;[87] John Tootoosis, a proponent of the need to respect and implement treaties with Indigenous peoples;[88] Andy Paull, a tireless witness of the unceded character of Aboriginal title throughout much of British Columbia;[89] and Clinton Rickard, a champion of the Aboriginal rights to move without restrictions across the Canada-US border.[90]

What is to be said of George Catlin's original vision of a vast protected area combining the functions of an Indian reserve with a national park? The Indianized tourism of Glacier National Park as it continued into the 1950s can be seen as a variation on what Catlin had in mind. The availability of teepee villages for hotel guests, however, represents a pale reflection of the kind of innovation that would have been necessary to retain, as Catlin first suggested, the continuity of the Blackfeet buffalo hunt. It is an open question whether Indian people would have cooperated with federal officials to the extent necessary to achieve the kind of conservation required for the realization of Catlin's proposal. Any effort to realize such a project would have run into legitimate allegations aimed at identifying the wrong-headedness of trying to hold Indigenous peoples within the constraints of some museum-like or even zoo-like niche of frozen stereotypes. In spite of its obvious shortcomings, however, Catlin's proposal entailed an imaginative effort to formulate a farsighted economic and cultural plan for the future of the trans-Mississippi West.

Two generations later, Big Bear took Catlin's idea one step further. In the 1870s and the early 1880s, Big Bear emerged as an influential leader in the Cree campaign to resist the physical and legal constraints of federally controlled Indian reserves. As a practical alternative to the subjugation of his peoples under an alien regime of forced assimilation, Big Bear proposed that the Indians of North America's Great Plains be invested with a special licence to protect, regulate, and harvest the continent's remaining buffalo herds. [91] This approach would have paralleled the practices that have developed in northern Scandinavia and parts of Russia, where Sami peoples have long exercised rights and responsibilities in tending to their partially domesticated reindeer herds.[92] Accordingly, both Catlin and Big Bear advanced visions that addressed the problem of how best to institute systems of human relations with other peoples and with nature which would sustain and express key facets of North America's biocultural diversity. Both proposals called for the positive intervention of government to place limitations on the capitalist tendency to impose monocultures on the interior geographies of imagination and on the exterior landscapes of commodified matter. A frequent outcome of this impoverishment of biocultural diversity through capitalist colonization has been to thin the populations of Indigenous peoples and to force their survivors into marginalized enclaves of poverty and dependency. Grey Owl also turned his mind to the Fourth World prospect of combining protection of endangered species with the goal of assisting in the positive self-renewal of Indian cultures. In a speech to the Empire Club of Canada in 1936, he said: "You give us education, give us recognition, and we will look after your north country for you. [Applause] ... I want to arouse in the Canadian people a sense of responsibility, the great responsibility they have for that north country and its inhabitants, human and animal."[93]

In more recent times, the Fourth World ethos combining the ethic of conservation with that of biocultural diversity has been advanced in pockets of enlightenment where the economic stimulation of tourism has been directed at assisting the protection of endangered peoples, geographies, and animal and plant species.[94] The creation in 1991 in Venezuela of the Alto Orinoco Biosphere Reserve, where several thousand Yanomani and Yekuana Indians have been afforded some measure of protection, is one of a number of initiatives worldwide that respond to the interconnected forces menacing both cultural and biological diversity.[95] These initiatives have all generated controversy on many fronts. For instance, Indigenous peoples and the national governments overseeing the creation of biosphere reserves have frequently disagreed over the forms of land tenure to be employed in securing these protected areas. Such disagreements invariably involve the most fundamental questions about Aboriginal title and the legal construction of power relationships. No matter how lofty the idealism of those who have sought to integrate the Aboriginal political economies of Indigenous peoples into biosphere reserves, inevitably some members of the threatened groups have opted to work in the very extractive industries that menace the ecological viability of their peoples' traditional ways.[96] Many other paradoxical implications for Indigenous peoples come with the rise of eco-tourism and cultural tourism.[97] In Kenya, for instance, the Maasai have traditionally been pastoralists who maintained large herds on grazing lands. These grazing lands, the basis of their traditional economies, have been increasingly pre-empted for the expansion of national parks to serve the country's booming tourist trade. According to Mark Cocker, some Maasai became deeply embittered at seeing their own Aboriginal way of life afforded less priority than wildlife and wildlife tourists. In response, some Maasai have protested by killing some of the rarest animals in their traditional lands. Cocker poignantly adds, "They have been forced to trade their warrior culture for Kenya shillings, putting on displays in fake villages and haggling with the Western visitor about the value of their dance routines once converted into video footage."[98]

THE *DAWES ACT*, TERMINATION, JOHN COLLIER, THE INDIAN NEW DEAL, THE ATLANTIC CHARTER, AND BETRAYAL BY THE NATIONAL SECURITY STATE

Officials in church and state viewed with great consternation the propensity of Native Americans to defy the principles and premises of possessive individualism even after the demise of their traditional economies and their containment on Indian reservations.[99] In the opinion of those charged to impose the ideals of US civilization on their Indian wards, the system of land tenure on collectively held reservations only confirmed and entrenched Aboriginal predispositions to favour the bonds of community over the aggrandizement of the individual, the ethos of sharing over the mores of private ownership and personal acquisition, the values of cooperation over those of competition, and the rhythms of transformation in nature over the more mechanical measurement of time as calculated by the clock. In 1887 – one year after the US judiciary defined corporations as persons and Indian people as legal non-persons completely subject to the plenary powers of US law makers – Congress passed the *General Allotment Act*, otherwise known as *Dawes Severalty Act*. The avowed purpose of the *Dawes Act* was to allot parcels of Indian reservations as private property. According to the statute's sponsors, the aim of the legislation was to generate the ethos and necessary attitudes for the integration of the federal government's Indian wards into the laws and institutions of possessive individualism and US citizenship.[100]

An underlying motivation for the passage of the allotment statute, however, was that most of the available arable grounds in the American West had already been distributed to railway companies, land speculators, and, increasingly, non-Indian settlers.[101] The Indian reservations of the United States, whose extent roughly equalled the size of California and Oregon together in 1870, thereby become the next major frontier for the territorial expansion of the American empire of private property. The *Dawes Act* was advanced through Congress with the strong support of many railway companies.[102] It created a procedure to survey and allot pieces of reservation land to individual Indians. The federal government was to hold the pieces of real estate in trust in preparation for the day when Indian individuals would receive full title to their land and, with it, the accompanying rights and responsibilities of US citizenship. In this fashion the collectively held domain of Indian groups would be broken up, privatized, and made subject to taxation.

According to the social engineers in charge of Indian policy, the territorial, legal, and social bonds of Aboriginal community would be broken while large and valuable areas of "surplus land" would be liberated for exploitation by non-Indian investors, farmers, and frontiersmen. This transfer would prolong the expansion of wealth through the transformation of earth into capital by God's chosen instrument of possessive individualism. The *Dawes Act* continued to operate until 1934. Through its large machinery, Indian people were separated from 86 million of the 138 million acres reserved to them when the legislation was first enacted.[103] The transfer of this land from the shared domain of Indigenous peoples to the personal wealth of individuals and corporations involved complex linkages of business and government which often made public officials informal agents of private entrepreneurs. As one historian has wryly observed, "Severality may not have civilized the Indian, but it definitely corrupted most of the white men who had any contact with it."[104] In the process of dividing up Indian Country and transferring title to non-Aboriginal entities, the public and private sectors, it seems, often merge with seamless precision.

In 1953 the US Congress passed further legislation aimed at renewing the atomizing principles of the *Dawes Act.* This statute, entitled Concurrent Resolution 108, was tellingly described as the basis of a termination policy. The major objective of this termination policy was to bring an end to the treaty relations with Indian nations entered into by the federal government before 1871. The aim of the bill's sponsors was to see the federal government unburdened of its trust responsibilities to provide services for Native Americans and to protect their remaining lands from encroachment.[105] Efforts to terminate the federal role in Indian Affairs and to privatize what remained of the collectively held Indian estate were accompanied by programs to relocate Native Americans from reservations to urban settings. The policy's makers sought to peel back the conditions and underlying assumptions of the Indian New Deal. The fires under the monocultural melting pot were thus rekindled. The old mission was renewed to de-Indianize Native Americans and to advance the process of their legal, cultural, and economic assimilation into the mainstream of Euro-American life.[106]

The ideas motivating the formulation of the termination law also animated the thinking of the judges of the US Supreme Court when they were asked to visit the legal theory attached to the Aboriginal titles of Indian and Inuit peoples in Alaska. As preparations moved towards the transformation of Alaska from a federal territory to a state in 1959, a test case was mounted to assess the legal argument that the Indigenous peoples could not be unilaterally dispossessed of their titles in their traditional lands. The Supreme Court disagreed with the Aboriginal position. In their ruling on the case of *Hee-Hit-Ton Indians v. The United States,* the judges decided in 1955 to renew the argument that the sovereign titles of the United States were founded on the conquest of the land's original peoples. The judges maintained, "Every American schoolboy knows that the savage tribes of this continent were deprived of their ancestral ranges by force." When treaties were made before 1871, according to the court, the transactions did not constitute a genuine "sale." Rather, it was "the conquerors' will that deprived [the Indians] of their land." Even the reservations that were sometimes provided "after the conquest" were said to be held on the basis of "a right of occupancy which the sovereign grants and protects against intrusion by third parties but which right of occupancy may be terminated and such lands fully disposed of by the sovereign itself without any legally enforceable obligation to compensate the Indians."[107]

The *Hee-Hit-Ton* decision can be seen as a return to some of the same issues dealt with at the Nuremberg Trials a decade earlier. The chief counsel for the United States had argued in 1945 that, to "persecute, oppress, or to do violence to individuals or minorities on political, racial, or religious grounds ... or to exterminate, enslave, or deport civilian populations, is an international crime."[108] In 1955 the highest court of the world's most powerful country declared that it was precisely this genre of violent incursion that had created the underlying basis of US claims to legitimacy. The world's pre-eminent superpower, the judges reiterated, was a regime conceived and consolidated in the course of conquest. The stark contrast between the positions of US jurists in 1945 and in 1955 speaks suggestively of the changing currents of opinion after the Second World War. The difference between the two legal interpretations illustrates the dramatic nature of the turn away from the principles of the Atlantic Charter, the UN Charter, and the Nuremberg Trials to the era when the zealous extremism generated by the Cold War permeated many institutions, including the highest echelons of the US judiciary. In rendering explicit the view of the United States as a polity founded in conquest, the *Hee-Hit-Ton* decision gave judicial sanction to the theory informing the decision of Congress in 1871 to end the making of federal treaties with Indian groups. The *Hee-Hit-Ton* decision had implications for the whole world, in the sense that it signalled the importance afforded even by judges to raw military power in determining the relationship of the capitalist superpower with weaker peoples and polities. The renewed drive to obliterate the remaining Indian Country, albeit by the manipulation of law rather than by the deployment of military force, became particularly aggressive during the era of Senator Joseph McCarthy's infamous crusade to rid the United States of "Un-American Activities."

The appointment in 1950 of Dillon S. Myer as head of the Bureau of Indian Affairs was a revealing sign of the Cold War climate. Myer came to this position from his former role as bureaucratic chief of Japanese internment during the Second World War. In *Keeper of Concentration Camps*, Richard Drinnon has written of Myer's racist cast of policy and mind as a manifestation of "the banality of evil, U.S. style."[109] Between 1942 and 1946, Myer led the War Relocation Authority (WRA), the federal agency that took custody of the many tens of thousands of Japanese Americans after they were classified as enemy aliens solely on the grounds of their ethnicity. Franklin Roosevelt's decision to press forward this policy of dispossessing and interning an ethnically defined category of people made up primarily of US citizens stands as his presidency's darkest blemish. As WRA head, Myer had many dealings with John Collier, the head of the Bureau of Indian Affairs (BIA). The original point of contact resulted from Collier's administrative oversight of the Poston Center on the Colorado River Indian reservation in southwestern Arizona. About 20,000 Japanese Americans were interned on this Indian reservation throughout the course of the war.

The shifting direction of the US federal government with the onset of the Cold War was clearly reflected in Myer's appointment to replace John Collier, the architect and primary administrator of the Indian New Deal. The contrast between the politics of the two men could hardly have been more stark. Collier was one of those social activists called in by President Franklin Delano Roosevelt during the Great Depression to help save capitalism from its own worst excesses. As chief commissioner of the Bureau of Indian Affairs, Collier finessed through Congress in 1934 a watered-down version of the *Indian Reorganization Act* (*IRA*). In spite of the many valid criticisms that have been directed at the *IRA*, this legislative package in its totality was arguably the most substantial single initiative ever undertaken by the federal government to fulfill its trust obligations to protect Indian lands and to provide appropriate services to Native American peoples. The Act brought an end to the process of allotment initiated by the *Dawes Act* and provided incentives for Indian peoples to reconsolidate their remaining holdings as the shared domain of their Indian nations. Moreover, it set in place procedures and budgets for Indian groups to develop their own written constitutions together with limited forms of self-government. This arrangement was a long way from the recognition of the full sovereignty that some Indian peoples see as the rightful inheritance of their Aboriginal polities. Nevertheless, the reform represented a major improvement over the dramatic forms of disempowerment and dispossession that Aboriginal groups and individuals had experienced during the decades when they were constrained almost completely within the legal straightjacket of wardship.

The Indian New Deal covered many fields of jurisdiction, from education to health care to economic development to the advancement of Indian arts and scholarship. What linked all these federal enterprises in Indian Country, however, was Collier's basic proposition that Aboriginal cultures are living, robust expressions of human creativity that have much to contribute to the United States and the world.[110] This position dramatically challenged prevailing orthodoxies advanced, for instance, by the likes of Diamond Jenness, the president of the American Anthropological Association and chief of the anthropological division of the National Museum of Canada. In 1932 this influential social scientist wrote of the Indians of Canada, "culturally they have already contributed everything that was valuable to our own civilization."[111] On the basis of this ethnocentric understanding, Jenness provided the Canadian government with an assimilationist plan in the mid-1940s on how to "liquidate Canada's Indian problem in 25 years."[112]

The contrast between the view advanced by Jenness and by Collier is indicative of how far the Indian New Deal went in pointing federal authority away from the notion that Aboriginal polities are obsolete remnants of an earlier era in human evolution. The contrast underlines the broader significance of Collier's efforts to move the United States away from policies reflecting the genocidal assumption that Indian nations are, and should be, terminal nations. Seen in a broader context, the institution of the Indian New Deal implied a move away from the metaphor of the United States as a melting pot. It implied a view of the rising superpower consistent with the higher ideals expressed in the Gettysburg Address and in the Wilsonian principles that infused the founding of the League of Nations.[113] By veering away from the principles of conquest and direct control to encourage instead a more egalitarian approach to Indian self-governance, the architects of the Indian New Deal presented a small window of hope for oppressed peoples everywhere. They gave early expression to some of the principles about to be articulated on a global platform when the leaders of Anglo-America outlined in the Atlantic Charter of 1941 the principles for combating fascism and founding the United Nations. The Charter would help convince members of the African National Congress and other colonized groups that they could anticipate a day when the empires that dominated their lives would fade into obsolescence.

Like the anthropology of Franz Boas, the Indian New Deal was based on a rejection of Social Darwinism and scientific racism as the rationale for a colour-coded ordering of human relationships. The continuum linking the Royal Proclamation of 1763, the abolition of slavery, the Indian New Deal, the Atlantic Charter, the UN Charter, and the Universal Declaration of Human Rights helped to build the momentum of the Fourth World movement for global decolonization. As Collier saw it, Aboriginal history belonged to the future as well as the past. Indian nations in North America should not be treated as terminal polities but as living nationalities with a great deal to contribute to the creation of a more just and vibrant world order. In bringing this position into the heart of the US federal government, Collier expanded currents of thought and action that had been part of the Mexican Revolution, especially during the 1920s. In seeking to incorporate and celebrate Mexico's Indian character as a fundamental characteristic of the Mexican state, educator Manuel Gamio and others had pointed the way towards the kind of ideals Collier attempted to cultivate with his version of *indigenismo*, US-style.[114]

The dual initiatives in Mexico and the United States were expanded and expressed institutionally in the founding of the Interamerican Indian Institute. This institute, which encouraged the establishment of national centres of Indian Studies in all countries of the Western Hemisphere, emerged from a conference organized in 1940 by the Pan-American Union and the Organization of American States. In helping to point the governments of the Western Hemisphere towards some kind of reckoning with the contemporary place of Indigenous peoples, John Collier's work clearly belongs within the heritage of thought and action leading to George Manuel's conceptualization of the Fourth World and his founding of the World Council of Indigenous Peoples. Collier's initial efforts to transform his theories into federal legislation and practice were often undermined and compromised by the biases and inertia of a large bureaucracy not known for its sensitivity to Indian aspirations. However imperfect the actual implementation of his concepts, however, Collier did effectively begin the long process of turning the direction of US statecraft away from blind faith in the merits of the melting pot towards a more realistic reckoning with the ideals of cultural pluralism.

What Collier saw in the Aboriginal societies of the Western Hemisphere were qualities of personality and community that he believed were fast disappearing from the increasingly urbanized, rootless, impersonal, machine-obsessed mass culture of the United States. In making this case, Collier became so outspoken that he tended to polarize his audiences. Depending on their biases, they regarded him either as a visionary or as a dangerously delusional messianic figure. In Collier's opinion, the future of the world depended on securing the conditions for the continuing communal orientation of Indigenous peoples. As he saw it, their ways of relating to each other and to the rest of the infinitely complex web of life provided necessary models crucial to the prospects of global survival.[115] Collier was recruited into his life's work by an erudite socialite from New York who found in the Indian societies of the US Southwest a guiding beacon of enlightenment. Mabel Dodge Luhan, a woman of means, attracted some of the leading cultural figures of her day to her Taos salon. Among them were D.H. Lawrence, Carl Jung, and Jaime de Angulo.[116] In the early 1920s Dodge Luhan correctly anticipated Collier's readiness to take part in the religious ceremonialism and political controversies of her husband, Tony Luhan's Tiwa people. The Tiwa's ancient but still-inhabited pueblo at Taos remains one of the most thriving symbols in the United States of the contemporary Aboriginal connection with pre-contact times.

Collier's belief in the regenerative power of Indian societies, not only for their own members but for others as well, developed from his critique of the prevailing trends of standardization, homogenization, and mechanization he saw all around him. "For more than a century," he wrote, "the best minds of the Occident have accepted as fundamental the isolation of the individual."[117] They took as axiomatic "the pulverizing uniformity of free-market operations."[118] In these words Collier summed up the monocultural presumption of those who envisaged the possessive individualism of capitalism as a universal system that affords market relationships pre-eminence over all other kinds of relationships linking human beings to each other and to the rest of nature:

The "free market" and laissez-faire doctrines and practices viewed the human world as an aggregation of persons – individuals – each of whom was controlled by a universal, and therefore interchangeable, rational or calculating economic self-interest. The law of the free market was considered to be the law of human life. The free market was lord of all; and if it wrought havoc upon societies, heritages, ethical and aesthetic values, family and community life and even the natural resources of earth itself, it remained the overriding principle; it dominated conduct and assured ultimate salvation. It would eventually heal every wound it inflicted.[119]

In Collier's opinion, the obsession with the individual, the corporation, and the market to the exclusion of all other facets of human organization and interaction was the cause of much alienation. What he saw was "the uprooting of populations, the disintegration of neighborhoods, the end of home and handicrafts, the supremacy of machine over man, the immense impoverishment of the age-old relationship between the generations, the increased mobility of the individual, the enormous expansion of commercialized recreation, [and] the quest by mass-circulating news-papers, the movies and radio for the lowest common denominators."[120] The antidote that Collier prescribed to rectify mass society's despoilment of human nature and the rest of nature was a return to respect for the importance of smaller societies as the essential starting point of sound and sustainable human organization. In Collier's experience, there were no human collectivities better suited to reflect and advance the ecological ideals derived from the interconnectivity of life than the ethnically diverse array of peoples known to the outside world as Indians. "They had what the world has lost," Collier wrote. "They have it still."[121]

As members of small nations who had withstood tremendous onslaughts on their lands, lives, and identities, many Native Americans retained a pro-found appreciation "that societies are living things, sources of power and values of their members; that to be and to function in a consciously living, aspiring, striving society is to be a personality fulfilled, is to be an energy delivered into communal joy."[122] Collier's most serious condemnation of mass society sprung from his observation that the borderless, standardized monoculture of unfettered laissez-faire could not produce the conditions for the shaping of healthy, well-balanced human personalities. Unmediated mass society could not produce human beings capable of integrating dis-ciplined exploration in the inner mysteries of human existence with joyful but reverential participation in the outer rhythms of the rest of nature. As Collier often recounted, he came to a thundering realization of the con-tinuing power of Aboriginal societies to shape and empower the personali-ties of their members when he participated in the sacred Tiwa Red Deer Dance. In that ceremony, a whole society of people "passed into ecstasy through a willed discipline, splendid and fierce, yet structural, an objec-tively impassioned discipline which was a thousand or ten thousand years old, and as near to the day of first creation as it had been at the prime."[123]

The first revelation was repeated and reinforced in many further meet-ings, episodes, and studies, where Collier gradually opened his mind to the living presence and the diverse scope of the Indian Country all around him.[124] This pioneer social worker and activist in the field of adult educa-tion had formerly experienced despair at what he saw as the apparent futil-ity of his earlier endeavours. Collier's new appreciation of the resilience, adaptability, and culturally rooted tenacity of Native American societies filled him with new hope – what he called "our *long* hope" that "the earth's natural resources and web of life would not be irrevocably wasted within the twentieth century." He affirmed this conviction with the belief that Aboriginal societies "were, and in representative samples still are, concen-trated on the attainment, through social ministration, of adequate human personalities, and upon the living, creative union of these personalities, with the earth and its web of life – with the universe and the God."[125]

Collier was asked to implement his ideas during an era when the Great Depression called into question many of the old orthodoxies of possessive individualism. The property base of the United States and much of the Western world had been over-mortgaged. Speculators had leveraged their assets so much in the stock market that the inflated price of shares lost all relationship to the real value of the corporate assets they were meant to represent. A financial bubble was inflated to the point where the expansionary pressure could not be contained.[126] The economy popped, and the confidence on which the whole structure depended drained away. The Depression called into question the faith that the surest route to human progress lay in the system of monopoly capitalism at the core of the US political economy. It instilled in some the conviction that market forces must be tempered with a more cooperative approach among citizens, communities, peoples, business enterprises, volunteer associations, and the state. John Collier was there to point out that the oldest societies on the continent offered some compelling examples of how to survive under conditions of crisis and hardship. As a social scientist, administrator, and author, Collier wrote about the encounter between Native Americans and newcomers in startlingly poignant and innovative ways. He outlined something radically different from the dusty old picture of Indian Country as a place of feathers and war whoops, dislocation and poverty. Where others had seen only dwindling enclaves of doomed humanity, Collier sketched out the literary outlines of a new kind of Indian Country as a place of psychic strength that very much belonged in the world of present and future. He went far beyond the cultural relativism of Boas to anticipate the Fourth World paradigms advanced by George Manuel, the Zapatistas, David Suzuki, and the imagery of Bill Reid's *Spirit of Haida Gwaii*.

Collier's vision extended from Aboriginal history to universal history. He encouraged his audience, whatever their background, to imagine a future where members would participate with various kinds of citizenship in the celebration, perpetuation, and institutional reform of Indian Country. This pluralistic Indian Country, he said, was one of humanity's great restorers of the social personality of groups and individuals. As a new kind of self-appointed citizen of the aboriginally oriented society he imagined, Collier exasperated some of his Native American associates with what they were inclined to see as his romanticism, his messianic complex, and even his meddling, intrusive, and overbearing ways. From the perspective of some on the reservations, here was one more outsider entrenched in Washington, DC, who thought he knew better than Indians themselves what was good for them. His opponents found a rallying point in the American Indian Federation and its president, a Creek politician named Joseph Bruner. Bruner gave voice to the attitudes of a number of Native Americans who had grown to prefer the system of individual rather than collective ownership of the remaining Indian estate. This right-wing faction believed that Collier was turning back the clock; that he was a communist blocking the progress of Indian capitalism. They believed that, knowingly or not, Collier had "unfurled the red flag of race-prejudice."[127]

Although Collier definitely had detractors, he also had a large network of Indian and non-Indian colleagues and admirers who recognized in his work the possibility of a new kind of social contract between individuals, groups, and governments. They saw in Collier the unwavering commitment of a seasoned social activist, that rare capacity to combine pragmatism with an uplifting idealism. As he himself expressed it: "The white conqueror, for reasons military, economic and religious, pronounced sentence of death on the Indian societies. Through century-long years of slavery, expropriation, physical decimation, and propaganda directed to the Indian against the Indian spirit, the conqueror worked hard to carry out the Indian's death sentence." Who could contradict this assessment that Indigenous peoples in North America have been subject to an especially pessimistic view of their capacity to survive as Indians, let alone to contribute actively as agents of positive change in the making of the future? Who could deny how the transformation of this death sentence into the assimilationist policies of church and state advanced the genocidal assault on the capacity of Indigenous peoples to renew and build up their communities? Collier asserted:

A broad view of history from 1492 until recent years shows a death hunt against Indian societies. To many of the societies, the death hunt brought annihilation, death everlasting. To others it brought wounds that seemed mortal; but with an astounding regenerative power they arose from the rubble. Harried into the wastes, secreted there for lifetimes, and starving, still Indian grouphoods, languages, religions, culture systems, symbolisms, mental and emotional attitudes towards the self and the world continued to live on. Not fossilized, unadaptive, not sealed into the past, but plastic, adaptive, assimilative, while yet faithful to the ancient values, these many societies somehow held their own. A few of them burgeoned right on through the centuries and entered our own day with the noise and shine of waters gushing from their ancient sources. More, many more, sustained only a life covert, indrawn; but they sustained the core and genius of their way of life. When so very, very late, and perhaps for only a brief term of years (none can be sure, as yet) some of the white man's societies lifted their sentences of death from these all but invisible Indian societies, the response was a rush of human energy, a creativity industrial, civic, aesthetic. How swiftly, with what flashing brilliance, with what terrible joy, these long-immured, suddenly reprieved little societies demonstrated the truth which our age has lost: that societies are living things, sources of the power of their members.[128]

John Collier reflected and advanced currents of thought rising from the increasingly professional discipline of anthropology. The genesis of Collier's school of anthropological thought took shape in, for instance, the minds of Lewis Henry Morgan, Horatio Hale, E.F. Wilson, Frank Hamilton Cushing, Paul Radin, and Franz Boas as well as his many talented students. All these thinkers developed interpretations that pointed towards the freeing of Indian societies from the verdict of obsolescence passed by the proponents of Social Darwinism and scientific racism. In 1934, the year that Congress adopted the *Indian Reorganization Act*, Ruth Benedict, a student of Franz Boas, published *Patterns of Culture*. This classic text advanced in Benedict's own language many ideas similar to those of Collier. Where Collier emphasized the word "society," for instance, Benedict widened the meanings and applications of the word "culture." In Benedict's text, the concept of culture is identified as the primary human construct that both shapes and reflects those connecting bonds of shared belief, manners, and conduct enabling individuals to integrate themselves into complex social systems.[129]

John Collier brought into the Bureau of Indian Affairs a stream of young social scientists, including Ruth Benedict. In 1935 they were organized as a unit of "applied anthropology."[130] Many of these intellectual workers entered "the field" where they worked with Indian communities on their reservations in drafting written constitutions and in creating the machinery for what was called, accurately or not, self-government. Among the most prominent of these inductees were Felix S. Cohen, Oliver LaFarge,[131] and D'Arcy McNickle.[132] A scholar of Canadian Métis extraction who had grown up on the Flathead reservation in northwestern Montana, McNickle's contributions to the federal government's Indian administration came to personify for some an image of the Indian New Deal at its best. The work of Collier and his entourage of applied anthropologists extended on an old tradition of thought where the changing frontiers of Western civilization were compellingly imagined and described on the frontiers of Indian Country.

Collier well understood that the legislative facets of the Indian New Deal served as a very imperfect substitution for the fuller elaboration of a regime of US-Indian relations based on the renewal, enforcement, and extension of treaties. In the United States, the door to extending that means of elaborating constitutional relations was slammed shut in 1871 and, except for the Indian New Deal, there has never been any serious effort to address the havoc thus wrought to the fragile integrity of the rule of law in the United States and the international arena. Although the judges on the US Supreme Court attempted in the *Hee-Hit-Ton* ruling of 1955 to incorporate the concept of conquest into their judicial interpretation, their ruling cannot disguise the ultimate lawlessness of any regime based on the credo that might is right. The *Hee-Hit-Ton* ruling has no more legitimacy than the *Dred Scott* ruling of 1857 upholding the right of slave owners to transport their human property throughout the full extent of the United States. Like the Indian removal policies of the 1830s, the prohibition of future treaty making in 1871, and the stunning consistency in the pattern of violating the four hundred or more treaties that were made in the process of seeking Indian consent for the expansion of the United States onto Aboriginal lands, the *Hee-Hit-Ton* ruling can be seen as part of the continuum of US history culminating in the ascendance of the national security state.

The national security state and the Indian New Deal embody antagonistic streams of action and ideology in the genesis of the United States.
The national security state extends the legacy of lawlessness frequently displayed in the treatment of North American Indians to the treatment of
citizens in many countries, including within the United States itself. By
promoting all manner of covert and illegal regime change and by coercively helping to prop up many corrupt oligarchies bound together in
the crony capitalism that thrives in the secretive inner sanctums of the
military-industrial complex, the national security state has systematically
violated the principle articulated in the Atlantic Charter affirming "the
right of all peoples to choose the form of government under which they
will live." The national security state has systematically undermined the
New Deal's international legacy.

The dubious official interpretation of the events of September 11 gave
the military-industrial complex the enemy it needed to justify and expand
the enormous federal commitment to military spending in the aftermath
of the Cold War. The Global War on Terror was exploited to extend further
the militaristic reach of the US executive branch into the political economy
of the entire world. It has provided the pretext for the extension of government involvement into every facet of human interaction. In the final
analysis, the War on Terror is meant to protect the inequitable regimes of
property ownership that are the hallmark of monopoly capitalism. To challenge the injustice of this way of apportioning the Earth's riches is to risk
becoming a target of an increasingly globalized police state.

Agents of the US executive branch's global police state are often privy
to insider information that comes to them from their unusual capacity to
employ state resources in order to obtain, gather, and deploy intelligence
not available in public venues. The currency of intelligence gathering in
the name of national security has enormous value on the stock market,
the institution at the core of the generation of new wealth in the terror
economy. Indeed, transactions on stock markets are key sites for the gathering of crucial intelligence about the identity of those interests that sponsor, promote, or exploit major shifts in the geopolitical alignment of global
power. The computerization of intelligence gathering at the same time that
transactions on stock markets were computerized created enormous new
openings for the garnering of windfall profits in an era when various forms
of spying and secret manipulation of current events are becoming the central activity of the privatized terror economy.

Just as the privatization of US prisons has given some corporate enterprises a financial stake in the rapid criminalization of a growing portion
of the domestic citizenry, so too the rapid expansion of the terror economy
has given some of the military-industrial complex's corporate privateers a
heightened financial interest in elevating the public's sense of anxiety that
they may become targets in random acts of violence. By these means the
growing commercialization of the terror economy increases incentives to

promote conditions where the political economy of fear overwhelms a more realistic sense of proportionality among the risks we encounter in our day-to-day lives. In these and many other ways the reigning cult of national security has sabotaged the goal of creating the "permanent system of general security" envisaged in the Atlantic Charter. The rise of the national security state points away from the principle of security for people, the environment, and the world. The most authentic basis for real global security lies in the replacement of the rule of conquest – might is right – with a viable rule of law based on applied principles of global democracy and global citizenship. In the final analysis, the rule of conquest represents the very antithesis of law as a medium for the cultivation of rules-based societies founded on the right of persons to be secure in their physical and social bodies.

CHAPTER ELEVEN

War and Peace

The Act requires that the Indian Nation be recognized on an equal
footing with any other nation in the world.

The North American Indian Constitution Act, 1945

THE UNITED NATIONS IN THE DIMENSION OF TIME

The two world wars of the twentieth century illustrated, extended, and
energized networks of cooperation and antagonism that bound an increasingly interconnected world. The fighting of both the wars and the planning, negotiation, and implementation of the post-war peace settlements
stimulated levels of interaction among individuals, peoples, governments,
corporations, and many other types of organization on an unprecedented
scale. Many new frontiers of globalization were reached and transcended in
the reconfiguration of empires, nations, communities, alliances, animosities, economies, and cultures.

In the Second World War especially the contest came down in large measure to a race to master the marriage of science and technology in the
production of new forms of weaponry, computation, and communications.
In the course of this inventiveness, the research laboratories in the interlinked military-industrial complexes on both sides of the war created new
moulds of industrialization. The emerging fighting machine of global capitalism created basic prototypes and manufacturing techniques for radar,
jet rockets, code-breaking computers, and atomic bombs, to mention only
a few of the innovations.[1] The diffusion of the new technologies from the
military orbit to the broader political economy of the whole planet accelerated the transformative processes that continue to change human relationships to space, time, and one another. The most consistent driving force
of globalization was once again demonstrated to be the human capacity
seemingly to speed up time and conflate space through the creation of
new technologies or the refinement and redeployment of old ones. The
evidence keeps mounting that Albert Einstein's theory of relativity and
Franz Boas's view of cultural relativism have sweeping implications for the
process of separating truth from falsehood, fact from hypothesis, across
many frontiers of human understanding.

The winds of political change drew power from the chemistry of convergence as science and technology merged in the industry of war. In two

grand military contests, the empire of Social Darwinism claimed the world as its test tube. During these wars, the theory of the Survival of the Fittest was applied on a global scale. The elevation of military competition to the level of total war seemingly prepared the ground for a new phase in humanity's history. The era of transition from the world wars to the post-war eras tended to be especially consequential periods when the latitude widened to make fundamental changes at the highest level of statecraft. In the final years of the First World War, for instance, the Czarist regime of Russia fell and the Soviet Union rose under a leader who had recently written a manifesto declaring that imperialism forms "the highest stage of capitalism."[2] In response to Lenin's revolutionary message, President Woodrow Wilson of the United States issued his liberal response. In his famous Fourteen Points, he boldly proposed a new architecture of global relations based on the ideal of a universal rule of law and the democratic right of all peoples to exercise self-determination both in their own internal affairs and through their representation in legislative venues of global governance. The war of rhetoric between Lenin and Wilson anticipated many of the main themes of the conflict in the Cold War's political, ideological, psychological, and propaganda battle zones.[3]

As the Second World War gathered momentum, the Atlantic Charter was formulated to embody the affirmative side of the anti-Axis position. With this short text as the basic manual for change, the United Nations evolved from an alliance to defeat the Axis into a nascent global parliament.[4] While Henry Cabot Lodge and others had intervened to prevent the United States from joining the League of Nations following its founding in 1919, the capitalist superpower after the Second World War played the leading role in launching an institution presenting humanity with the most elaborate working model yet achieved of what a legitimate agency of global governance might be. Representatives of the United States, Great Britain, the Soviet Union, and China met at Dumbarton Oaks in Washington in 1944 to plan for the reconstitution of the United Nations as a permanent instrument of collective security. Representatives of fifty-one nations attended the subsequent conference at San Francisco. It culminated in June 1945 in a signing ceremony to introduce the UN Charter. This document began with a statement affirming the "determination" of "We the Peoples of the United Nations ... to save succeeding generations from the scourge of war."

Many agendas converged in the process of creating the United Nations. The injection of Wall Street's interest in the project was largely funnelled through the New York–based Council on Foreign Relations (CFR).[5] This organization was founded as the US arm of an Anglo-American initiative whose British division is the Royal Institute of International Affairs. From the concluding years of the First World War, the CFR has been one of the most strategic centres for the coordinated blending of the public power of the US government with the increasingly global proprietorships of corporate America. It has been a nucleus of analysis, debate, and negotiation at the heart of this merger. Its members include a number of US presidents and many secretaries of state. The vast majority of CIA directors have belonged to the CFR. In both formal and informal ways, therefore, the CFR has been a key agency in the directing mechanisms of capitalism's military-industrial complex and the national security state. Seen from the perspective of the CFR's Wall Street patrons, the UN provided another instrument of US global power in the rapidly changing arena of international diplomacy. On a prime piece of New York real estate donated to the world body by John D. Rockefeller II, the United Nations provided the most powerful bankers in the world's richest commercial centre with an effective new means of monitoring and influencing many types of political alteration all over the world.

The creation of the United Nations did not immediately displace the theory going back to the Treaty of Westphalia that the governments of nation-states are sovereign within their own territory. The UN has no independent base of theoretical sovereignty, nor does it control in a centralized fashion its own independent police force with a mandate to enforce consistently a rules-based system of international relations. The peace-keeping forces of the UN are lent to the world body by the governments of nation-states, whose leaders negotiate the role of their soldiers on a case-by-case basis. Moreover, the UN is not a democratic institution. It was decided in 1944 that most of its power would be concentrated in the authority of a Security Council. In this agency, the four governments represented at Dumbarton Oaks, together with that of France, each exercise the capacity to veto the deployment of UN forces. The disparity remains enormous between the egalitarian idealism of the UN Charter and the way that power over the world body is actually exercised.

With all its problems and inadequacies, the UN has nevertheless provided a single venue where the process of bringing multilateral treaties, covenants, agencies, and conferences into existence has been facilitated and enhanced. In the form of its General Assembly, the UN has built up a legislative body that goes some way towards representing, however imperfectly and incompletely, the entire global community, in our diversity of language, religion, ethnicity, nationality, and other ways. To borrow a phrase from Abraham Lincoln, some see the UN as the last best hope on Earth. They rightfully see it as humanity's most legitimate venue to engender and organize international responses to the world's major crimes, dilemmas, and scourges. These problems include war, genocide, poverty, discrimination, the displacement of refugees, weapons proliferation, pollution, species depletion, climate change, enslavement and exploitation of labor, addictions, epidemics, homelessness, and illiteracy. In addition, a large constituency of global citizens see the UN as the best available agency to push for the implementation of the ideals of universal education, health care, and social security. The urge to situate these elements of decent human life in the context of the global community emerges from the same well of understanding and conviction that would treat all wars as civil wars. What body other than the UN is there to subordinate, on a worldwide basis, the rule of tyranny, war, and conquest to a democratically constituted and consistently enforced rule of law?

The importance of the United Nations lies as much in what the organization could become as in what it is. As long as the UN exists, it offers some glimmer of hope that a global consortium of peoples can someday combine forces to counter neo-colonialism and superpower rule through the instrument of law. With this Fourth World ideal as its inspiration, the Non-Aligned Movement has, from its inception, been a champion of a more empowered and democratic United Nations. The Non-Aligned Movement has given voice to the hopes of a broad array of oppressed constituencies that have sometimes looked to the world body as an agency where the wretched and betrayed of the Earth might someday achieve justice and vindication.

One of the most marginalized constituencies in the global community is composed of the broad array of peoples whose members have reason to see themselves as being unrepresented or actively oppressed by governments that have illegitimately asserted jurisdiction over their Aboriginal lands, waters, and resources. Given the history of most of the world's countries as former colonies whose boundaries and bureaucracies were initially imposed by the imperial powers, a very large proportion of the global community finds itself in polities that do not conform to their Aboriginal understandings of their own Aboriginal histories. Many Indigenous peoples the world over find themselves in successor states of empire whose laws, institutions, official languages, national mythologies, and territorial outlines do not reflect their own Aboriginal orientations to geography, culture, and time.[6]

The temporal dimension of many of the conflicts facing the UN is opaque, yet frequently deep and intractable. Conflicts over sovereignty and title to land often involve very different perceptions of how the past bears on the construction of the present and the possibilities of the future. In much of Africa, for instance, whole cycles of imperial appropriation and decolonization are little more than a century old. In the Western Hemisphere the cycle of European colonization and the creation of anti-Indian successor states is little more than five centuries old. In Palestine and Tibet the imposition of superpower control on Indigenous peoples and their Aboriginal lands is a process of only decades. Many Indigenous peoples, in contrast, often measure their Aboriginal histories in cycles of thousands and even tens of thousands of years. In order to assert the depth of their connection to their Aboriginal lands, many Indigenous peoples in the Western Hemisphere have had to counter the tendency of some social scientists to relegate their histories before 1492 to some lesser category of human experience. Until recently, for instance, the pre-Columbian past of the Americas was frequently described as "pre-history."[7] This way of dividing time has contributed to the division of humanity.

The opening chapters of humanity's Aboriginal history tend to merge with spiritual cosmologies describing the sacred origins of the Earth, the stars, and life's animating forces. This pattern is reflected in the Iroquoian legend of the beginning of the world on the back of a turtle, or in the Mayan narrative of humanity's divine creation from corn. It is reflected as much in the Aboriginal history outlined in the Book of Genesis narrating God's making of Heaven and Earth in seven days. The relationship between history and myth is no less striking when it comes to the movement through time of even the most secular processes and institutions. The genesis of global capitalism, for instance, has depended on the development of a mythology of disconnection highlighting the present and the risks of the future, even as the contemporary significance of the past is minimized and downgraded. Indeed, in the monoculture of capitalism, the ongoing reverberations of history tend to be muffled or diverted towards the oblivion of amnesia. The material basis of capitalist relations is particularly menaced by all interpretations that emphasize the function of imperial theft in determining present-day structures of wealth and poverty, empowerment and disempowerment, advantage and disadvantage, liberty, enslavement, and incarceration.

By treating the nation-state as the only acceptable receptacle of sovereignty, the United Nations has contributed to the recent erosion of whole complexes of Aboriginal law, leadership, and political economy emerging from extremely long durations of Aboriginal history.[8] The development of the UN system has helped to empower nation-states to undermine the ability of many Indigenous peoples to renew those Aboriginal polities, customs, conventions, and political economies that emerge from many thousands of years of human adaptation and invention. In making the replication of nation-states the only available process for the movement of colonized groups towards internationally recognized forms of sovereign self-governance, the UN system has diminished pluralism in the political economy of human interaction with one another and with the rest of nature. By contributing to the erosion of diversity in this way, the UN system has helped to stimulate the rise of the monoculture of monopoly capitalism. By pressing almost all of humanity into cookie-cutter containers of nationality, each with its own similar set of national institutions, the way was prepared for the creation of a global regime of universalized property and investment law. In failing to come to grips with the role of distinct peoples as well as nation-states in a world of about 6,000 languages and 200 countries, the UN has been less effective than it might otherwise have been in saving large portions of humanity from the scourge of war. It still has a long way to go to be true to the opening phrase of its charter – and before it can speak and act with credibility on behalf of "We the Peoples" of the entire world.

If the world body is ever to rise to the task of justly enforcing laws and standards of universal application, its courts must arbitrate the many conflicting interpretations of the past. The UN's arbiters must attempt to draw the ingredients of a universal history from many Aboriginal histories of peoples, constitutions, and institutions. Without the development at the world body of a sense of universal history, how can the ideals of universal human rights be effectively justified and advanced? By incorporating deeper layers of Aboriginal history into the evolution of its own constitution, the UN can begin to develop its personality as an embodiment of the political will of peoples as well as nation-states. For the United Nations to represent peoples as well as nation-states, it would have to broaden its criteria for membership and expand the nature of its franchise. It would have to help invest the global community with principles of law as well as venues of arbitration and negotiation, where the pitfalls of partition can give way to solutions encouraging peoples and nation-states to share jurisdiction and title in zones of contested sovereignty. Generally speaking, the UN must develop more sophisticated ways of helping two or more groups to exercise overlapping expressions of sovereignty – shared forms of jurisdiction and title – in the same soil. The histories of federalism and of Indian treaties both provide models for the sharing of jurisdiction in ways that could be built on by the UN to provide a richer repertoire of international responses to the assertions rooted in the Aboriginal histories and universal human rights of all peoples.[9]

To advance this agenda, the UN would have to be much more open to the existence of multiple types of political community. It would have to deal with the convergence of many different types of citizenship even in single individuals, and balance the rights of persons, peoples, and nations with the economic imperatives claimed by transnational corporations. If the UN were to move more fully in the direction of the Fourth World, it would become far more likely that aggrieved peoples could find justice through the juridical medium of genuine third-party adjudication aimed at resolving their disputes with nation-states and the commercial corporations generated from the chartering power of national sovereigns. It is common for Aboriginal people to allege that certain states, as well as their corporate extensions, have wrongfully appropriated control over both themselves and their lands, sometimes with genocidal consequences.

DESKAHE, W.E.B. DU BOIS, PAN-AFRICANISM, THE INTERNATIONAL LABOUR ORGANIZATION, AND THE RIGHTS OF INDIGENOUS PEOPLES

A very clear trajectory in the rise of US power is marked by the World's Columbian Exhibition in Chicago 1893, the dissemination of Woodrow Wilson's vision for global governance in his Fourteen Points, and the realization of some of the hopes for the League of Nations in the internationalization of the New Deal through the creation of the United Nations. The US intervention in the First World War marks the intermediate stage in the rise of the capitalist superpower. In her volume on the negotiations leading to the ratification of the Treaty of Versailles, Margaret MacMillan comments on the contrast between the stature of the United States at the end of the two wars: "In 1945 the United States was a superpower and the European powers were much weakened"; in 1919, however, "the United States was not significantly stronger than the other powers."

The focus of MacMillan's book is the negotiations that took place primarily in Paris in 1919 as the most powerful leaders on Earth sought to establish a new framework of global relations. She writes: "That spring and summer, Paris hummed with schemes for a Jewish homeland, a restored Poland, an independent Ukraine, a Kurdistan, an Armenia ... votes for women, rights for blacks, a charter of labor, freedom for Ireland ... The petitions poured in, from the Conference of Suffrage Societies, the Carpatho-Russian Committee in Paris, the Serbs of Banat, the anti-Bolshevik Russian Political Conference."[10] The Indians of North America were not to be excluded from this eclectic array of initiatives aimed at settling old wrongs through the stimulation of constitutional reform at the highest level of international relations. The most significant Indian intervention from the Western Hemisphere came from an Aboriginal government with a legendary tradition of sovereign involvement in some of the key events in the emergence of the United States and the Dominion of Canada from the imperial history of the Netherlands, France, and Great Britain. A Cayuga diplomat carrying the Christian name of Levi General and the Longhouse leadership title of Deskahe sought to make his mark by obtaining official standing for the League of the Six Nations Iroquois at the League of Nations. The Longhouse League's main seat of legislative authority was at that time the council house at Oshwegan on the Six Nations reserve near Brantford, Ontario.[11] In coming to Geneva in the early 1920s from the land of the Great Law, the Great White Pine, and the white roots of peace, the ambassador of the Six Nations sought to renew the international personality of one of the most widely cited and celebrated Aboriginal polities on Earth.

In the course of its own Aboriginal history, the Longhouse League of the Six Nations Iroquois has negotiated literally hundreds of treaties with the representatives of the governments of the Netherlands, Sweden, France, New York, Great Britain, and the United States.[12] The metaphors of the Covenant Chain treaties took shape during the zenith of this saga of intercultural diplomacy on the imaginative frontiers of Aboriginal America. By seeking an international remedy for the incursions of Canada into the jurisdiction of the Longhouse, Deskahe demonstrated the commitment of his constituents to retain their sovereign status, as it had repeatedly been recognized and affirmed by their British imperial allies in the Covenant Chain.[13] Deskahe's goal was to renew the principle that, in the words of a British colonial official reporting on the position of the Six Nations Iroquois during the era of the American Revolution, "the Indians are a free People Subject to no Power upon Earth, that they are faithful allies of the King of England, but not his Subjects."[14] Deskahe's initiative tested the willingness of those with official standing in the international system to apply Wilsonian ideals about the equality of small nations and the right of all peoples to self-determination. His quest to gain recognition as the legitimate Longhouse ambassador to the League of Nations had implications for colonized peoples globally. His short-lived ambassadorship in the world's primary venue for the negotiation of international law during the interwar years can be seen as a kind of proxy for many peoples and principles that were otherwise unrepresented in the League of Nations.

Deskahe's interventions at Geneva and other European capitals found a parallel in the international work of W.E.B. Du Bois, who was especially active in and around the institutions set in place by the Treaty of Versailles. The work of both Deskahe and Du Bois was consistent with many aspects of the Wilsonian ideal that the rule of colonial oppression must be replaced by a new structure of international relations expressing the inherent right of all peoples, including peoples of colour, to self-determination. Through transactions involving the International Labour Organization and the Anti-Slavery and Aborigines' Protection societies, Du Bois pressed forward an agenda that explicitly linked racism and colonialism as the dual driving forces behind the commission of many crimes against humanity. As the twentieth century's most unrelenting champion of pan-African unity, Du Bois stood at the nexus of many freedom struggles linking the plight of Indigenous peoples with that of "native labour."

Du Bois is widely regarded as the leading social scientist of the US civil-rights movement throughout much of the twentieth century. He stood up against the Ku Klux Klan even as he represented a more moderate approach to the Back-to-Africa movement led by the Jamaican populist Marcus Garvey. Du Bois's brilliance as an intellectual and activist rivalled that of Toussaint L'Overture. Both men were persecuted for their insistence that the egalitarian ideals of the Enlightenment applied as much to slaves and the descendants of slaves as to anyone else. With the establishment of the International Labour Organization (ILO) by the Treaty of Versailles in 1919, Du Bois was given an international vehicle with a mandate that could be made to serve his ideals. With his focus on the plight of exploited workers in some parts of Africa, he helped set in motion a trajectory of history whose outcomes include the International Labour Organization's Convention 169 on the rights of Indigenous peoples. The course of Du Bois's career therefore adds to the evidence of the many points of intersection connecting issues rooted in the transatlantic slave trade and in the dispossession, disempowerment, or outright elimination of Indigenous peoples throughout the colonized world, but especially in the Western Hemisphere. This connection is clearly revealed, for instance, in the relationship of Indian removal to the expanded domain of plantation slavery in the American South. It is illustrated in the emergence in the 1830s of the Aborigines' Protection Society from the movement in Great Britain for the abolition first of the slave trade and then of slavery itself.

A Harvard-trained sociologist, Du Bois played a significant role in the genesis of the National Association for the Advancement of Colored People in United States. He was a prolific author who combined journalism and scholarship to produce a steady stream of formidable articles and books, including in 1903 *The Souls of Black Folk*. As an activist, he realized the opportunities presented by the end of the First World War – a moment when myriad facets of the human condition were seemingly put on the table for negotiation. In keeping with the spirit of this moment, Du Bois was instrumental in assembling a worldwide assembly of Negro leaders and intellectuals in Paris in 1919 with the objective of influencing the peace settlement. To the dismay of the US State Department, he succeeded in enlisting the sanction of France's premier, Georges Clemenceau, for his Pan-African Congress.[15] In Paris, Du Bois and the other delegates at the Pan-African Congress added their proposals to the mix of suggestions for global geopolitical change.[16]

Du Bois came to Paris with the view that the clash of competing imperialisms in Africa was a significant factor in the genesis of First World War. At the Paris Congress he promoted the idea that Germany's African colonies should become the site of an international protectorate where the Indigenous peoples would gradually widen their powers of self-government under the guidance of educated Negros, recruited for the purpose from all parts of the planet. In its report of the Paris Pan-African Congress, the *Chicago Tribune* explained: "As 'self-determination' is one of the words to conjure with in Paris nowadays, the Negro leaders are seeking to have it applied, if possible, in a measure to their race in Africa." The reporter explained Du Bois's contention "that in settling what is to be done in the German colonies the Peace Conference might consider the wishes of the intelligent Negroes in the colonies themselves, the Negroes of the United States, and South Africa, and the West Indies, the Negro governments of Abyssinia, Liberia, and Haiti, the educated Negroes in French West Africa and Equatorial Africa and in British Uganda, Nigeria, Basutoland, Swaziland, Sierra Leone, Gold Coast, Gambia and Bechuanaland, and in the Union of South Africa."[17]

Du Bois was no devotee of cultural relativism. In making very clear distinctions between what he viewed as "civilized" and "uncivilized" people, he formed his ideas around the Darwinian assumptions that permeated his age. What incensed the educator, however, was his conviction that, "consciously or unconsciously there is in the world today a widespread and growing feeling that it is permissible to treat civilized men as uncivilized if they are colored and more especially of Negro descent." In identifying and recognizing this propensity, Du Bois sought to add volume to "the voice of Science, Religion and practical Politics ... in denying the God-appointed existence of super-races or of races naturally and inevitably inferior."[18] Du Bois's emphasis on the instrumental role of "the Talented Tenth" opened him to charges that he was elitist. His allegedly "aristocratic" ways, for instance, made him the object of constant derision from the more populist movement led by the Jamaican Marcus Garvey and his Universal Negro Improvement Association. While Du Bois distrusted Garvey's "dictatorial" ways, he nevertheless appreciated his success in orienting millions of Black people in the United States and the Caribbean towards a deeper identification with fate and role of Africa in the making of world history.[19]

The delegates to the Pan-African Congress passed a resolution that included the following provisions:

A. That the Allied and Associated Powers establish a code of law for the international protection of the natives of Africa, similar to the proposed international code for labor.
B. That the League of Nations establish a permanent Bureau charged with the special duty of overseeing the application of these laws to the political, social, and economic welfare of the natives ...

...

C.5. The State: the natives of Africa must have the right to participate in the government as fast as their development permits, in conformity with the principle that the government exists for the natives, and not the natives for the government. They shall at once be allowed to participate in local and tribal government, according to ancient usage, and this participation shall gradually be extended, as education and experience proceed, to the higher offices of State; to the end that, in time, Africa be ruled by consent of the Africans.[20]

In his efforts to enlist the help of possible allies in advancing the Pan-African agenda, Du Bois met in London with officials of the Aborigines' Protection Society.[21] The involvement of the APS in the Pan-African movement after the First World War illustrates yet again the tight connections linking the movement to abolish slavery, the movement to temper colonialism through measures to protect the Aboriginal rights and titles of Indigenous peoples, and the genesis of the movements that converged in the Bandung Conference of 1955. These movements can roughly be categorized as those seeking the decolonization of European empires, nonalignment in the Cold War, and the end of neo-colonialism through the realization of Fourth World ideals. Du Bois was dissatisfied with the position of the Aborigines' Protection Society on the restoration of African lands and on the issue of conscription in France's African colonies. Much more to his liking was his meeting with Albert Thomas, the head of the International Labour Organization. The ILO's early involvement with Du Bois's Pan-African movement was instrumental in making that body a pioneering champion of the international rights and titles of Indigenous peoples not only in Africa but elsewhere throughout the colonized world.[22] The importance that Du Bois attached to the work of the ILO is suggested by the resolution formulated in the proceedings of the second Pan-African Congress, which took place in London, Brussels, and Paris in 1921. Section

8 of that document called for "the establishment of an international section of the Labor Bureau of the League of Nations, charged with the protection of native labor."[23]

Like the leaders of the Pan-African movement, some of the leaders of the Pan-Indian movement in North America looked during the early decades of the twentieth century to the international trade-union movement as a model for, and as natural allies of, their struggle for decolonization. In *Indians at Work*, Rolf Knight has emphasized the importance of labour relations and trade unionism in the genesis of political organization among the Aboriginal peoples of British Columbia.[24] A Mohawk veteran of the First World War, Lieutenant Fred Loft from the Six Nations reserve in Ontario, expressed similar views about the importance of trade unionism as an example for Aboriginal organization as he sought to found and expand the League of Indians of Canada. Like many labour organizers of his generation, Loft faced much harassment from federal agencies in the course of his work. He explained: "Union is the outstanding impulse of men today, because it is the only way which the individual and the collective elements of society can wield a force and power to be heard and their demands recognized. Look at the force and power of all kinds of labour organization, because of their unions."[25]

The work of the ILO represents one of the clearest illustrations of the history of reciprocity between the trade-union movement and the Fourth World movement aimed at advancing the decolonization of Indigenous peoples. Trade unionists have looked to Aboriginal societies as a source of membership and as the object of particular categories of abusive exploitation requiring international as well as domestic remedies. The roots of this pattern of exploitation lie in relationships between capital and labour, colonizers and the colonized, the empowerment of some through the dispossession of others. This heritage of exploitation finds expression in, for instance, the violent coercion of Aboriginal workers forced to toil in the rubber plantations scattered throughout the jungles of the Congo Basin and Amazonia. In South Africa the system of laws and institutions known as apartheid was developed with an eye towards the imperative of extracting cheap labour from Indigenous peoples for the industrial mining of gold, diamonds, and other precious minerals.

Since the 1920s the ILO has devoted particular attention to the special circumstances of Aboriginal workers. Indeed, in developing that focus and expertise, the ILO pioneered the early use of the term "Indigenous peoples." In 1957 the ILO adopted Convention 107, one of the twentieth century's first international instruments formulated with the aim of ameliorating the lot of Indigenous peoples. The assimilationist bias of that earlier statement was altered in 1989 with the adoption of Convention 169, which breaks new ground in articulating an international standard for the treatment of Indigenous peoples.[26] Among the countries that have ratified this convention are Mexico, Norway, Columbia, Costa Rica, Paraguay, and Peru.

The governments of Canada and the United States entered the twenty-first century without sanctioning this important instrument of international law.[27] Convention 169 includes the following provisions:

7.1. The [Indigenous] peoples concerned shall have the right to decide their own priorities for the process of development as it affects their lives, beliefs, institutions and spiritual well-being and the lands they occupy or otherwise use, and to exercise control, to the extent possible, over their own economic, social and cultural development. In addition, they shall participate in the formulation, implementation and evaluation of plans and programs for national and regional development which may affect them directly ...

...

15. The rights of the peoples concerned to the natural resources pertaining to their lands shall be specially safeguarded. These rights include the right of these peoples to participate in the use, management and conservation of these resources ...

...

28. Children belonging to the peoples concerned shall, wherever practicable, be taught to read and write their own indigenous language most commonly used by the group to which they belong. When that is not practicable, the competent authorities shall undertake consultations with these people with a view to the adoption of measures to achieve this objective....

The ratification of the ILO's Convention 169 by several countries in the Americas, including Mexico, has significant implications for the initiative to expand the North American Free Trade Agreement to hemispheric proportions. That initiative began to encounter severe difficulties in the form of the mass protests that coalesced in April 2001 at Quebec City, where all the leaders of the thirty-five countries in the Western Hemisphere, except Cuba's Fidel Castro, converged to push forward the proposal for a Free Trade Area of the Americas. In the years ahead, this protest movement grew to form the basis of government policy in some South American countries. At a conference in Argentina to promote the trade deal, Venezuelan president Hugo Chavez promised in November 2005, "Here in Mar del Plata the FTAA will be buried. I brought my shovel."[28]

Without any direct representation in the development of transnational trade law such as that enacted in NAFTA, the World Trade Organization, the World Bank, or the International Monetary Fund, there is no way that Indigenous peoples can exercise "the right to decide their own priorities for the process of development as it affects their lives, beliefs, institutions and spiritual well-being and the lands they occupy or otherwise use." There is a deep legacy of precedent beneath the persistent exclusion of Indigenous peoples from the core processes of decision making that have given rise to the composition and operation of the more recent generation of transnational financial institutions. This heritage of exclusion goes back to the "donation" of the whole Western Hemisphere to the sovereign monarchy of Spain in 1493. From the Louisiana Purchase, to the sale of Alaska and the transfer without Indian consent of the Hudson's Bay Company lands, British Columbia, Prince Edward Island, the Arctic Islands, and Newfoundland to the Dominion of Canada, this legacy of exclusion permeates much of the history of colonization. Again and again the lands and persons of Aboriginal societies have been passed back and forth among the "White Nations" as if Indigenous peoples are disqualified from making decisions about their own future. This disqualification has repeatedly been justified through the resort to Eurocentric theories posing different models of religious, civilizational, and racial hierarchy. The distinction drawn between those considered eligible to colonize and those deemed suitable to be colonized depended ultimately on the power of a view of time that divided the polities of different peoples between those thought to be stuck in the past and those deemed deserving of a place in making the future.

We must revisit key episodes of the Aboriginal history of decolonization if we are to move beyond perceptions of time that have segregated humanity between those considered mature enough to shape the future and those who have been stigmatized as unwanted remnants of humanity's bygone childhood. The Indian Confederacy of Canada offered humanity a bridge to another way of negotiating the relationship between time and power. In the prelude to the War of 1812, Tecumseh sought to widen the alliance of the Bowl with One Spoon. He sought to build a coalition of diverse opposition to the imperial expansions of the American empire of private property. Facing the expanding intrusions of the United States into his peoples' Aboriginal lands, he travelled southward to gain the attachment to his cause of the Choctaws and Chickasaws. Like W.E.B. Du Bois, Mahatma Gandhi, and Nelson Mandela, Tecumseh sought to invoke symbols and principles capable of transcending many ethnic and cultural distinctions in order to instill a unified spirit of shared resistance to the continuing encroachments of the imperial foe. He told his listeners, "The annihilation of our race is at hand unless we unite in one common cause against the common foe. Think not, brave Choctaws and Chickasaws, that you can remain passive and indifferent to the common danger. Your people, too, will soon be as falling leaves and scattering clouds before the blighting breath. You, too, will be driven away from your native land and ancient domains as leaves are driven before wintry storms."

Looking to the past and casting a prophetic eye to the ethnic cleansing that would later be perpetrated in Georgia, Ohio, Indiana, Texas, California, Guatemala, Columbia, and many other jurisdictions throughout the Western Hemisphere, Tecumseh asked, "Where today are the Pequod? Where the Narrangansetts, the Mohawks, the Pacanokets and many other powerful tribes of our race?"[29] Tecumseh was posing these questions in the midst of a process that was pulling North America away from the continuity of tens of thousands of years of its Aboriginal history. This break with the past occurred in a more intense way than has ever taken place at any time on any continent. A New World civilization could not be cultivated without a genocidal purge directed at clearing aside the Aboriginal civilization of the Indigenous peoples. There can be no mistaking the fact that the marginalized condition of Indigenous peoples in their Aboriginal territories of North America makes this continent the scene of the most unrelenting and sweeping saga of ethnic cleansing ever perpetrated in history. The imperial remaking of space and reorientation of time finds its epicenter in North America, and especially in the United States.[30] Profound disagreements about the status to be afforded to Indigenous peoples and their Aboriginal titles were integral to the genesis of the violence that erupted in the rise of the American superpower from those rebellious elements that were hostile to the British superpower.

When Tecumseh asked his questions, the word *genocide* did not exist.[31] That word was not invented until the reckoning began with the war crimes and crimes against humanity of Nazi Germany. Nevertheless, the connection in Hitler's mind between the assault on the Indigenous peoples in North America and the Nazi assault on the Jews, Slavs, and gypsies of Europe and Eurasia is well established in the historical record. Tecumseh's words thus project far beyond the Choctaws and Chickasaws and his mission to expand, elaborate, and mobilize the Indian Confederacy of the Bowl with One Spoon. Indeed, Tecumseh's words have acquired expanded meanings over time because of the magnitude of events that came after him. With his quest to oppose ethnic cleansing, his determination at least to slow the pace of the displacement and elimination of his peoples, Tecumseh was helping to prepare the way for the proceedings at Nuremberg after the Second World War. At Nuremberg, the site of Hitler's most primal and pathological rallies, some top Nazi officials were tried for their crimes. Tecumseh was inadvertently helping to prepare the way for the activities of the International Criminal Court whose proponents seek to apply law uniformly throughout the global community to all those, no matter how powerful, who commit crimes against humanity.[32] Like Toussaint L'Overture, Deskahe, W.E.B. Du Bois, and George Manuel, Tecumseh was moving towards an expanded vision of international law, one extending towards the ideal of equal rights for all persons and peoples. His effort to unite Indigenous peoples throughout North America in a sovereign confederacy of unified diversity forms part of the Aboriginal history of humanity's quest for collective security – for global security. In attempting to move in this direction, Tecumseh led the Indian Confederacy of Canada in a just war of self-defence against the armed aggression of a new polity that would someday seek to justify its regime of global domination as a requirement of national security. Long before the existence of the League of Nations and its successor, Tecumseh was inadvertently helping to prepare the way for the day when the United Nations becomes sufficiently inclusive and democratic to act with true legitimacy in the name of "We the Peoples."

FROM THE *NORTH AMERICAN INDIAN CONSTITUTION ACT* TO THE INDIAN CLAIMS COMMISSION

President Franklin D. Roosevelt died in April 1945, just days before the gathering in San Francisco that resulted in the creation of the UN Charter. In its initial and most idealistic conception, the UN expressed Vice-President Henry Wallace's effort to usher in the Century of the Common Man. That vision of the future was based on the conviction that "no nation will have the God-given right to exploit other nations." It proposed a "free world" over the "slave world" of the Axis powers. In his speech delivered in 1942, Wallace hinted at the duplicitous role of corporations such as Ford, IBM, and Standard Oil which did business on both sides of the Second World War. "International cartels that serve American greed and the German will to power must go," he asserted. "Cartels in the peace to come must be subjected to international control for the common man, as well as being under adequate control by the respective home governments.... With international monopoly pools under control, it will be possible for inventions to serve all the people instead of only a few.[33]

The imagery of the Century of the Common Man was meant to counter Henry Luce's vision of the American Century. In an editorial he wrote in 1941 for *Life*, Luce proposed that the United States should enter the Second World War and forcefully project its status as "the most powerful and vital nation in the world." It should "exert upon the world the full impact of our influence, for such purposes as we see fit and such means as we see fit."[34] The philosophy of the American Century came to permeate the Cold War strategy of the United States. That strategy extended into the United Nations, whose diplomats succumbed, by and large, to the bipolar tensions of superpower rivalry. The application of the philosophy of the American Century to the US conduct of the Cold War was repeated in a different historical context with the application of the philosophy behind the Project for the New American Century to the US conduct of the so-called Global War on Terror.

Representatives of civil society were well represented at the founding sessions of the United Nations. One of those present, John Humphrey of McGill University, recounted the role of "the churches, trade unions, ethnic groups, peace groups etc." at the San Francisco meetings. He observed that there was "no parallel in the history of international relations." This experiment in inclusiveness was "largely responsible for the human rights provision in the [UN's] Charter," a document that Humphrey helped draft.[35] In much the same fashion as the era of transition following the First World War, there was a brief moment as the Second World War came to a close when it seemed possible to imagine and implement a major reconstruction of the international system to achieve a better, more just world. The UN's Charter and in its Universal Declaration of Human Rights were major reflections and instruments of that optimism. As Paul Wallace saw it, the Six Nations Longhouse Confederacy offered the United Nations a history where the new international agency could take over older urges to encourage the white roots of peace to grow to the four corners of the Earth.[36]

One of those who sought to exploit the potential for significant structural change in the mid-1940s was Jules Sioui, a Huron from a small Indian reserve just outside Quebec City. During this period, Sioui demonstrated a surprising genius for political organization and for the clear articulation of basic constitutional principles. Like Deskahe, he sought to use the transition from war to peace to insert Indigenous peoples into the conduct of international affairs. Sioui wanted to find a way out of the straightjacket of wardship and domestication preventing Indians from exercising sovereign self-determination in the global community. His mission gathered momentum when he assembled a number of Indian delegates in Ottawa in 1943 to present a petition to the Canadian government on conscription. Sioui's successful campaign against the Canadian government's conscription of Indians led him to attempt a more ambitious political gathering at the Ottawa YMCA in 1944. In spite of the steady hostility of the federal government's Indian Department to the event, Sioui attracted a broad representation of Indian leadership from across Canada. The minister of Indian affairs agreed to attend, but only if Sioui promised not to be present when the federal official spoke.[37]

This tactic split the convention. Sioui's more radical faction followed him to establish the League of the North America Indian Nation. The organization was founded on a fairly elaborate structure of chiefs, supreme chiefs, and assistant chiefs. Most of the League's French- and English-language correspondence, however, was written by Jules Sioui. His stamp identified him as secretary treasurer, National Indian Government. The year 1945 was a time when the League's National Indian Government established its political base, by-laws, and constitutional principles. That period of activity culminated in a communication sent from Detroit to Prime Minister Mackenzie King. In it, Sioui and Supreme Chief James Fox identified themselves as officers of the North American Indian Nation. They pointed to the fact that Canada had just ratified the Charter of the UN, a document that refers in its preamble to the need "to establish conditions under which justice and respect for obligations arising from treaties and other sources of international law can be maintained." Sioui and Fox indicated that, on behalf of their Indian government, "we formally accept the Provisions set out in the Preamble of the United Nations Charter in relations to treaty obligations, of which the Dominion Government has officially subscribed, and pledged formal obedience to the mandates thereof." With this introduction, Fox and Sioui asked that the dominion government recommend legislation to Parliament to fulfill the treaties with the Indians and to "expedite" full and complete settlement of all outstanding matters arising from the Crown's noncompliance with these agreements.[38]

In the process of preparing to intervene in this way, Sioui and the group around him generated a rich body of Aboriginal law in the tradition of the Indian Confederacy of Pontiac and Tecumseh.[39] Among the legal instruments they introduced into history was the *North American Indian Constitution Act.* Section 4 of that document proclaimed simply, "the Act requires that the Indian Nation be recognized as a Nation on an equal footing with any other nation of the world." This very simple yet eloquent plea for international recognition made reference to the need to respect Indian treaties and the Royal Proclamation of 1763. Section 8 asserted that "the Indian Government be entitled to enter into contracts with any Government regarding the natural resources of the country." While some of the provisions were grandiose in the extent of their claims, others were quite practical and pragmatic. Section 11, for instance, "requires that the Indian languages be practiced in Indian schools."[40]

From the other side of the split that occurred in 1944 emerged Andy Paull. He assumed the leadership of an organization known as the North American Indian Brotherhood.[41] The extension of that more moderate branch of the Indian rights movement would eventually begin to receive core funding in the late 1960s from the Canadian government under the leadership of Pierre Elliott Trudeau. Even without government funding, Sioui continued his political work until well into the 1980s on behalf of the League of the North American Indian Nation. He would never again achieve the level of political prominence that was briefly his between 1943 and 1945, though his contribution to the tradition of confederacy building in Aboriginal North America remains considerable. Although Sioui was a pacifist, many other Indian people of his generation were not. A significant number of young Indian men in both Canada and the United States volunteered to serve in the Second World War and then in Korea, Vietnam, and Iraq.[42] The ideological character of the Second World War was probably one of several factors prompting so many Native people in North America voluntarily to become soldiers. Their numbers included the now legendary Navajo code talkers who were able to take to the airwaves during major battles and to exchange strategic information in ways that confounded enemy efforts to comprehend.[43]

In reflecting on the decision of Native Americans to support the war effort overseas and on the home front, John Collier speculated optimistically, "It may be that they see in the victory of the democracies a guarantee that they too shall be permitted to live their own lives."[44] The inescapable links between the principles justifying the Nuremberg trials and the legacy of Western expansion in North America inspired some agitation for changes that might pre-empt the allegation that the United States is burdened with its own heritage of war crimes and crimes against humanity in its treatment of Indigenous peoples. After all, Adolph Hitler had not hidden the fact that one of his models for his racial and military policies – his quest for German *Lebensraum* – had been the frontier expansion of the United States into Indian Country.[45] With this strategic consideration simmering quietly in the background, the Indian Claims Commission was established in the United States in 1946.

Until it was replaced in 1978 with a Court of Claims, the Indian Claims Commission was entrusted to sort through numerous allegations that the appropriations, expropriations, and privatizations of the larger Indian Country of the United States were shot through with fraud and other forms of illegality.[46] Many individuals initially invested considerable hope in the ICC's work. Its operations, however, soon became bogged down in a thick quagmire of contradictory legal abstractions and petty professional rivalries, all set within the context of a larger process without the influence of substantial political will behind it. A few Indian groups did eventually derive cash settlements from the process.[47] As the dramatic actions of the Sioux Oyate would ultimately underline, however, the great flaw in the Indian claims system was that the only outcome on offer was financial compensation, not the return of land. The renewal at the end of the twentieth century of the old land-for-money formula in the continuing extinguishment of Indian Country stimulated much anguished debate, especially among Sioux Oyate citizens.[48] The debate intensified when the Sioux Oyate (Lakota / Nakota/ Dakota) ultimately refused a cash award of $105 million granted in 1980 to compensate them for the illegal seizure, contrary to the Fort Laramie Treaty of 1868, of the sacred Black Hills. As Sioux scholar Elizabeth Cook-Lynne mused on this refusal, it was "a significant tribal nation stance and an extraordinarily courageous thing to do."[49]

With all its liabilities, however, the work of the ICC helped to set in motion necessary debate about the way that cross-cultural interaction should be viewed in the writing of history and in the interpretation of law. The deliberations helped to stimulate many academics and jurists to draw from a variety of disciplines other than their own. Moreover, the work of the ICC also forced on some social scientists a heightened awareness of their need to question the nature of their professional interrogations of informants and colleagues of different ethnic backgrounds.

In 1954 the journal *Ethnohistory* was founded to address many of the new kinds of professional issues arising largely from the work of the ICC. It was one of a widening array of journals where social scientists began to work through some of the professional implications of the decolonization movement. Many of the scholarly journal's pages expressed the growing self-consciousness of a number of its contributors as they became attuned to the political implications of their efforts to characterize the changing circumstances of Indigenous people across North America and throughout the world. As usual, Iroquois Country proved to be particularly rich soil for the new intellectual developments. William N. Fenton, unofficial dean of an expanding school of Iroquoianists, laboured mightily along with his colleagues and students to break new ground on the expanding frontiers of interdisciplinary and, sometimes, cross-cultural scholarship.[50]

The rapid growth of North American anthropology after the Second World War caused considerable anxiety among some Indian people who felt imposed upon and misrepresented every summer by the influx of field-working "experts" on their communities.[51] To the apparent delight of many in his Native American audience, Vine Deloria Jr satirized the strange customs of this academic tribe of culture hunters in 1969,[52] articulating criticisms that George Manuel would echo several years later. Although Deloria's barbs found some conspicuous targets, the anthropological guild was quite capable of convicting some of its own for the intellectual crimes of unwarranted pretentiousness or misinformed pontification. "Now 'culture' has become our sacred cow," mused one disaffected anthropologist in 1970. "We keep it for ritual and display purposes," she remarked, noticing the unwillingness or inability of many of her colleagues to confront mounting rates of reservation poverty, illness, and overcrowding as developments well beyond folkloric constructions of "tribalism."[53]

A continuing source of controversy in the complex and often paradoxical relations between Indigenous peoples and the discipline of anthropology in the United States is the role of that profession in designing and implementing the machinery of the *Indian Reorganization Act*. The IRA was the primary legislative element in a broader array of initiatives that together formed the Indian New Deal. Taken in its totality, the Indian New Deal represents a remarkable reversal in the direction of government policy. In leading this reversal, John Collier confronted directly very old, entrenched, and broadly held opinions that Aboriginal societies in the Western Hemisphere are backward, primitive, and doomed to disappear in the course of progress. As reflected in the work of social philosophers from John Locke to Frederick Jackson Turner, this perception was deeply embedded in common assumptions about America's destiny. In imagining a strong Indian Country as a permanent feature in the US cultural landscape, Collier rejected the vision of America as a New World whose highest purpose is to provide a promised land to receive and remake immigrants. In making this stand, Collier took on some of the original assumptions at the foundation of the US sense of Manifest Destiny. While Collier drew some inspiration from the association of the Mexican Revolution with *indigenismo*, he basically was breaking new ground in his quest to replace assimilationist orthodoxy with something different. In this way, Collier's bold but imperfectly realized effort to strip colonialism and paternalism from the federal conduct of Indian Affairs promoted some of the Fourth World ideals that were given a far larger theatre in the process of negotiations leading to the Atlantic Charter and its outgrowths.

Collier's legacy, however, is complex. In his day, Collier was a leading theorist, promoter, and patron of applied anthropology. The work of applied anthropologists is generally associated with regimes of indirect rule, such as the system administered by British colonial authorities in Nigeria in the decades before it was granted independence in 1960.[54] Early practitioners of applied anthropology sometimes left the academy to work with a designated class of Aboriginal leaders in order to help them assert power in ways that were deemed consistent with both Aboriginal tradition and the overarching policies of colonial rule. As some saw it, Collier's federally funded practitioners of applied anthropology were, in reality, agents of federal indirect rule on US Indian reservations.

Moreover, the *Indian Reorganization Act*, which invested the power of Indian self-government in the officers of federally incorporated agencies, could easily be interpreted as an extension of federal authority into Indian Country. Seen in this light, the *IRA* can readily be viewed as a form of *institutional* assimilation even as it established important new tools for those Indian communities that adopted its provisions to enter into various legal and financial arrangements with all kinds of individuals, corporations, and public institutions.[55] The view of the *IRA* as yet one more effort to control Native Americans from Washington was advanced, for instance, by Rupert Costo, a Cahuilla Indian and president of the San Francisco–based American Indian Historical Society. At a Sun Valley conference to commemorate "Fifty Years under the Indian Reorganization Act," Costo argued, "The *IRA* was the last great drive to assimilate the American Indian." It was also, he said, a program to colonize Indian tribes through the legal organization of reservations as "communal enclaves subject to federal domination through the power of the Secretary of the Interior."[56]

Costo's understanding echoed the criticisms brought forward on the Pine Ridge reservation in the mid-1970s. That period was characterized by the armed return of the American Indian Movement to Wounded Knee, followed by a virtual civil war in the Sioux community of Pine Ridge.[57] AIM's leaders characterized the tribal administration of Chief Richard Wilson as an *IRA*-created extension and puppet of federal authority. For their criticisms, several dozen AIM members and sympathizers were killed by the federally backed paramilitary forces under the direction of the head of the Pine Ridge Tribal Administration. To this day the majority of these crimes have never received anything more than very selective and superficial investigations.[58] US law enforcement officials have showered attention on one of these cases, that of the murder of Anna Mae Pictou Aquash. The horror of the known and contested events surrounding her execution were brought to the surface in the court proceedings leading to the extradition from Canada to Rapid City South Dakota of AIM member John Graham. It is alleged that Graham murdered Anna Mae Pictou Aquash, thinking her to be a police informer in the FBI's COINTELPRO operations. The controversies surrounding Pictou Aquash's life and death point to the atmosphere of fear, violence, subversion, and recrimination generated in the federal assault on Aboriginal freedom struggles.

HOLLYWOOD'S INDIANS: THE MARKETING OF ABORIGINAL NAMES, MOTIFS, AND KNOWLEDGE, REAL OR IMAGINED

Once the largest part of the lands of the United States were patented, mortgaged, and generally entered into the marketplace of exchangeable commodities, the tremendous inventive energy spawned in the American empire of private property was turned towards many new enterprises. Quick fortunes were to be made in merchandising not only material commodities but also style, imagery, motifs, information, trademarks, advertising, celebrity, music, sports, stories, organizational systems, self-help programs – in short, all the less tangible currency of the modern culture of consumerism. Much of the added value in the new economy of intangibles is described as software, the service sector, intellectual property, advertising, public relations, and perceptions management.[59] Just as the transformation of Indian lands into property returned tremendous capital gains on original investments in ceding treaties and frontier warfare, so too did the imagery, nomenclature, and intellectual property of Native American peoples later become for some people a source of new wealth. By providing the brand names on everything from automobiles to sport teams, the inspiration for motifs on everything from wall paper to high-fashion clothing design, and intellectual capital for innovation in fields as diverse as food science, pharmacology, psychotherapy, political philosophy, literature, and ecology, Aboriginal knowledge and imagery have been, and remain, a lucrative source of both private profit and public wealth.[60]

The American film industry centred in Hollywood, California, became by far the most busy and successful packager and salesman of the dramatized imagery of Indian life. Indeed, the two-thousand or so Hollywood Westerns became almost ideal vehicles to express the Manifest Destiny of possessive individualism. Just as the Sioux or Apache or Cheyenne warriors who blocked the wagon train of American progress were doomed to subjugation, so too other groups and nations in the global market were sent the message that it was futile to resist participation in the dominant system of economic relationships. The emblems of this commercial dominance are trademarks such as those of IBM, Kodak, Coca-Cola, Nike, Xerox, Levi Strauss, McDonald's, Microsoft, Apple, Google, and Walt Disney. These global corporations provided the means not only for the winning of the West but for the West's winning of a dominant role in forging global markets for the consumption of goods, services, and cultural production. The frontier-devouring capacity of these global organizations of capital, technology, and human expertise is nowhere as starkly clear as in the Hollywood entertainment business. Its expansionary energy was long advanced, portrayed, and epitomized in a stream of celluloid re-enactments of wild, savage Indians giving way to the ascendant civilization of John Wayne and the other Marlboro men of the American West.

The Hollywood Western, a genre whose basic formula changed little until the 1960s, drew on symbols and attitudes already deep in the mythology of the American frontier. The directors of these dramas were bringing to the big screen a range of images and archetypes already well developed in the imaginative constructs of many people not only in the United States but the world over. The dramatic form of the Hollywood Western drew, for instance, on the fiction of James Fennimore Cooper, the visual art of George

Catlin, Charles Bird King, Paul Kane, Karl Bodmer, Charles M. Russell, and Frederic Remington, and the showmanship of William F. Cody and his Buffalo Bill's Wild West Show. The Hollywood versions of these older archetypes tended to be limited to a simplified and romanticized rendition of Plains Indian culture as representative of the cultures of all Indigenous peoples throughout North America. This case of severe cinematic over-representation of teepees, feathered headdresses, and horse-riding plains warriors has produced a limited public vocabulary of Indian imagery.[61] The result has contributed to the pervasiveness of a stereotypical way of thinking about Aboriginal identities and Aboriginal histories. The pervasiveness of these stereotypes has obscured appreciation of the tremendous scope and variety of different Aboriginal societies whose members have adapted in a multiplicity of ways to the extremely variable ecologies and geographies of North America.

Hollywood's renditions of Indian life, with a few notable exceptions such as the satirical film *Buffalo Bill and the Indians* (1976), have also dealt poorly with the blending of cultures. In the cinema of the US western expansion, there has been little careful exploration of the middle ground where family lines, along with modes of behaviour, styles, and convictions, mix to express hybrid combinations of New World and Old World orientations. This heritage of mixture and invention on the middle ground of trans-cultural adaptation is the true hallmark of the encounter between those who see North America as a new world and those who see in the same geography the old world of a changing but resilient Indian Country. By the 1970s, Hollywood's representation tended to shift away from images of Indians as hostiles to images of Indians as noble, pure, and empathetic witnesses of their own oppression. This shift in perspective continued the changes in popular culture that had been manifested earlier in the representations of Grey Owl, Apikuni, and George Grinnell. In their promotions of both national parks and the conservationist ethos, these entrepreneurs of Aboriginal imagery drew in turn on the earlier work of George Catlin or even Rousseau, Lahontan, and Lewis Henry Morgan.

Whether pictured as a place of warring reactionaries or as a home of spiritual seers, however, the Indian Country of the American cinema has remained a realm of walking stereotypes, a zone whose most frequent purpose is to provide a backdrop of dramatic tension for Euro-American lead actors to exploit. From Daniel Boone, to Davy Crockett, to Cooper's Leatherstocking, to Kit Carson, to Buffalo Bill, to the Lone Ranger, to the role played by Kevin Costner in *Dances with Wolves* (1990), the manufactured heroes of American frontierism, no matter how sensitive they might be to the plight of doomed Indians, have almost invariably come from the imperial side of the imagined contest between savagery and civilization. In print and broadcast media as well as in film, the old patterns continued of depicting Native Americans not as complex human beings beset with all the paradoxes and moral ambivalence that characterize the larger human condition but as points of contention on one side or the other of moral arguments. They are made to personify, for instance, either bravery or cowardice, independence or dependence, freedom or oppression, purity or degradation, childish innocence or elders' wisdom, spiritual sophistication or superstition, the urge to war or the instinct of peace. This limited and polarized imagery of Indian Country in popular culture has created major dilemmas for some Native men and women in the United States and Canada who seek to use the mass media to communicate with the larger public. The choice is often between being ignored or donning one of the roles expected of them in the stereotype-infested environment of popular culture.

Certainly some of the leading members of the American Indian Movement generated considerable unease and scepticism among some of their own people when they attracted attention to themselves and their ideas by consciously manipulating the stereotypical symbols of the imagined Indian Country of American popular culture.[62] For some of his critics, for instance, the appearance of Russell Means as Chingachgook in Michael Mann's Hollywood treatment in 1991 of James Fennimore Cooper's *Last of the Mohicans* illustrated a pattern where the mythology of Indian Country has been allowed to overwhelm, co-opt, and distort too much of its day-to-day substance.[63] The allegation that AIM's image had essentially been purchased by Hollywood for its romantic appeal was translated into the joke that the famous acronym had been reduced to a club name for the Association of Indian Moviestars.

At the same time, the international dissemination of the imagery of Indian Country, however ill-connected to reality, has given the liberation struggles of Native Americans a larger-than-life symbolic importance as a kind of beacon or precaution for oppressed peoples everywhere. As a realm of human experience that has so often been grist for the mill of the most prolific, flamboyant, and technologically advanced Dream Factory the world has ever seen, the mythology and substance of Indian Country are often so seamlessly interwoven that any attempt to explain one without reference to the other is highly problematic. Largely because of the awareness derived from the Civil Rights and Red Power movements, it became difficult in the 1970s for Hollywood to continue to cast Indians in their traditional roles as fierce warriors who, at once, opposed and epitomized the fighting spirit of American aggression. Nevertheless, the tried-if-not-true dramatic formula based on primal struggle between "savagery and civilization" continued to be relentlessly recycled, often in racially divided urban settings with a thousand different Hollywood detectives playing variations on the familiar old role of sheriff for the American empire of possessive individualism.

"INDIAN AFFAIRS" AND CONSTITUTIONAL POLITICS

In 1992 the leaders of the predominantly Cree communities of the Treaty 6 region assembled in Edmonton, Alberta. Their purpose was to meet with other chiefs, elders, and councilors representing most of the Indian groups in Canada who have treaties with the Crown. The lands and waters covered by Treaty 6 are roughly concurrent with the North Saskatchewan River basin. The terms of Treaty 6 were the outcome of many days of intense bargaining between the Cree leadership and Crown officials camped in and around Fort Pitt and Fort Carleton in 1876. Mistahimaskwa, or Big Bear in English, was leader of the large Cree faction opposed to making a treaty of the kind proposed by Crown officials. He and Poundmaker sought to hold the communal power of their people together by promoting the establishment of a large Cree national settlement in the region of either the Cypress Hills or North Battleford. The Canadian government, however, sought to divide the power of the Plains Cree. In 1885 Big Bear and Poundmaker were wrongfully criminalized and incarcerated to break the effectiveness of their leadership.[64] As a result, the Treaty 6 leaders who gathered in the provincial capital in 1992 came not from a large and cohesive Cree Territory but from a smattering of small Indian reserves sprinkled across the central region of Alberta and a smaller area in Saskatchewan. Oil was discovered in the Treaty 6 area at Leduc in 1947. Since that time, the oil and gas sector in Alberta has continued to expand to become the most powerful engine of rapid economic growth in Canada. In the process, a few Treaty 6 communities, but especially four reserves around the community of Wetaskiwin, have become quite wealthy. One of them, the Samson Cree Band, owns Peace Hills Trust, a company with assets well over a billion dollars.[65]

In their opening statement, some of the Treaty 6 chiefs pointed disapprovingly at the system of Indian administration in the United States. They stipulated that they did not want to see this same system reproduced in Canada:

A lot can be learned by us from the American experience and it is crucial we do not suffer the same fate as our relatives in the U.S.A. ... Our Treaties are international in nature and we cannot allow them to be domesticated as they have been unilaterally domesticated in the United States of America through a similar process called the *INDIAN REORGANIZATION ACT*. Through this Act the Chiefs and Councils of the American Indian reservations were made into legal entities incorporated under the laws of the United States. *They are no longer Chiefs and Councils but are referred to as tribal Chairmen and Business Committees, duly incorporated.*[66]

The meeting that drew Treaty 6 leaders to Edmonton was part of a process set in motion by the patriation of Canada's Constitution from Great Britain and the subsequent push to broaden its contents through the device of domestic amendment. As in the years leading up to the American Revolution, disagreements over the legal status and constitutional rights of the Indigenous peoples formed a major source of contention in the effort to domesticate and further define Canada's supreme law. The process of changing the legal quality of the Crown title to the northern half of North America during the final years of the twentieth century brought to the surface a range of old questions about the nature of sovereignty and Aboriginal rights in successor states of European empire – including fundamental issues about the nature of the rule of law as it has evolved in the colonized world since 1492.

For many reasons, Canada has been more open than the United States to political processes that at least address, if not resolve, some of the contentions emanating from the Fourth World. Indeed, the political deliberations to define the constitutional status of existing Aboriginal and treaty rights in Canada clearly had significant implications for a broad array of peoples and governments in the international arena, but especially for the United States. The very issues raised by Canada's invocation in 1982 of Aboriginal and treaty rights in its supreme law involved fundamental points of principle that, in the eighteenth century, exploded into the geopolitical split in North America between the constitutional monarchy in the north and the sovereign republic to the south. Beginning with the fur trade of New France, the recorded Aboriginal history of Canada long predates that of the United States. As the polity that grew from those portions of British North America which the British sovereign retained after the American Revolution, Canada constitutes that part of the continent where the Royal Proclamation of 1763 and the *Quebec Act* of 1774 continued to form the basis for imperial law even after the Treaty of Paris confirmed, in 1783, the independent status of the United States. As Francis Jennings has demonstrated in *Empire of Fortune*, it was the British imperial Crown's imposition of the Royal Proclamation at the end of the Seven Years' War that created the constitutional wedge that would break the unitary sovereignty of Anglo-America in two.[67]

Accordingly, when the Treaty 6 leaders travelled to Edmonton in 1992, they took part in an assembly whose participants revisited many of the big constitutional questions left over from the unresolved legacies of European colonialism generally and British imperial rule specifically.[68] They gave contemporary voice to legal interpretations that renewed some of the old debates of the era when uncertainties over the international status of Indian Country were integral to the emergence of the United States from the revolutionary schism in British North America.[69] The gathering in Edmonton was one episode in an elaborate and many-faceted process of constitutional negotiations that can roughly be said to have started with the election to office in 1968 of Prime Minister Pierre Elliott Trudeau. A constitutional lawyer by training, Trudeau sought to end the apparent anomaly residing in the reality that most of the major elements of the Canadian Constitution are enactments of the British government. Shortly after coming to office, he signalled his desire to remake the Canadian Constitution. Through Jean Chrétien, the young minister of Indian affairs, the Trudeau government announced in 1969 its intention of eliminating the entire federal apparatus of laws and institutions responding to the distinct constitutional status of Indian and Inuit persons and peoples. Trudeau advanced this initiative, soon dubbed the White Paper policy, in the name of his own classically liberal vision of Canada.[70]

Trudeau sought to redefine Canada in a way that would minimize and downplay its British imperial heritage. This heritage was reflected, for instance, in the country's transformation into a British Dominion in 1867 through an imperial statute known as the *British North America Act*. In advancing his own version of Canadian decolonization, Trudeau attempted to remake Canada as an officially multicultural land where the French and English languages are afforded equal status in the workings of the national government. Beyond that, he sought to express a conception of Canada as a liberal federation where each of the ten provinces and each citizen is afforded equal status and treatment before the law. Concerted Indian resistance to the White Paper policy by George Manuel, Harold Cardinal, Dave Courchene, and other Indian leaders caused Trudeau and Chrétien to back away, ostensibly at least, from their assimilationist initiative. Trudeau's halted effort to eliminate the institutional framework of distinct status for Indigenous peoples signalled his more ambitious intent to constrain the nationalist movement in Quebec. The White Paper proved to be only round one in Trudeau's fight to consolidate his regime in a way that would prepare the ground for the transformation of an imperial constitution into a domestic expression of Canadian sovereignty. At the core of his struggle to realize this vision was a prolonged showdown with the nationalist forces in Quebec. Under the leadership of René Lévesque, who became premier of Quebec in 1976, the anti-federalist aim of the nationalist movement was to remake Canada as a dualistic association supporting the development of an independent Québécois nation.

Trudeau succeeded in isolating his Parti Québécois opponents. Lévesque's party took control of the Quebec government in 1976, only to lose a provincial referendum on sovereignty-association in 1979. The Trudeau government responded to this outcome by moving decisively to patriate the Constitution from Great Britain. With the support of the nine English-speaking premiers, his government steered the *Canada Act* through a maze of legislative bodies at the provincial, national, and imperial levels. As the primary political organism representing the major concentration of French-speakers on the continent, the Quebec government has, until this day, refused to sanction Trudeau's constitutional transformation. The decision to patriate the Canadian Constitution without the approval of the Quebec government would prove to have very broad consequences for the subsequent course of Canadian history.[71] This exclusion remains one of the most formidable factors affecting the overarching shape of Canada's political culture. At every stage of the effort to formalize in law the existence of a "New Canada," the original constituents of the "First Canada" – the Indigenous peoples and the French Canadians – are inclined to seek reassurances that they will not be reduced constitutionally from founding peoples to mere fragments in Canada's multicultural mosaic.[72]

Although distinct Aboriginal constituencies were excluded from direct representation in the formal procedures of patriation, their leaders challenged the legitimacy of the process with sufficient effectiveness that they emerged as one of the most influential lobby groups in the course of the deal making. The Aboriginal leadership found particularly committed political allies in their interventions at the Westminster Parliament in Great Britain.[73] With all their experience in overseeing the legal dismantling of the world's foremost empire, some of the British jurists and politicians well understood the dilemmas created for Indigenous peoples in Canada by the imperial government's transfer of constitutional powers to federal and provincial authorities who derive their political mandates from predominately non-Aboriginal constituents. Those legislators and jurists who worked in Britain with Aboriginal lobbyists from Canada grappled with the deep constitutional legacies, some of them written and others, unwritten, derived from hundreds of years of close association between the British imperial government and the Indigenous peoples of North America. They grappled with the legacy of British imperial promises as frequently formalized in treaties. The cumulative import of these agreements has been to entrench the constitutional personality of the Crown's Aboriginal allies as members of polities whose distinct legal and political existence is to be recognized and affirmed rather than denied and negated for as long as the sun shines and the waters flow.

This British imperial tradition of cultivating alliances with Indigenous peoples drew on the diplomatic heritages of New Netherlands and New France. The architects of both these fur-trade polities had cultivated methods of colonization emphasizing commercial exchange and the making of treaties with Indigenous peoples. The Anglo-American colonists, in contrast, but especially those in the agricultural settlements of New England and Virginia, tended to fall back on wars of extermination as the basis of their Indian policies. The history of commercial and military alliances linking the Indigenous peoples of Canada to the imperial governments first of France, and then of Great Britain, created large openings for the elaboration of constitutional interpretations emphasizing the ideals of partnership, co-existence, and cultural pluralism.[74] This heritage of Aboriginal-Crown alliance encompasses the Covenant Chain and the Indian Confederacy's defence of Canada against US annexation in the War of 1812, just as it stands as a check against any resort to the *Hee-Hit-Ton* doctrine of conquest as a justification for the subjugation and retroactive extinguishment of Aboriginal title. It can truly be said that, far from being conquered peoples, the Indigenous peoples of Canada have defended their Aboriginal lands against the military invasion. In alliance with the British imperial government, they defended their land against the most serious attack ever mounted on the Indian Country of Canada. The Aboriginal defence of Canada has been re-enacted again and again through the high Aboriginal enlistment in the Canadian Armed Forces, but especially during the First and Second World wars. This pattern has been re-enacted in more modest ways as well. In 1985, for instance, Inuit people asserted the existence of Canadian sovereignty by dotting Canadian flags along the Arctic's contested Northwest Passage. The Inuit assertion of Canadian sovereignty came in response to the US government's decision to send one of its ice breakers, *The Polar Sea*, into the contested zone as a demonstration of Washington's view that the Northwest Passage is an international waterway.[75]

Many contemporary legal and political implications stem from the history of Crown-Aboriginal alliances forged in the cause of defending Canada from aggressors in the United States. The US invaders sought to combine the conquest of Indian Country with the termination of the remaining British imperial titles to the lands of North America. This heritage of shared resistance against the deep military incursions of the United States led to prolific inventiveness on the middle ground of cross-cultural negotiation;[76] it led to forms of transcultural diplomacy on many treaty council grounds where the heritage of the Covenant Chain was renewed, adapted, and extended westward to the eastern slopes of the Rocky Mountains. This saga of Crown-Aboriginal adherence to the constitutional principles outlined in the Royal Proclamation of 1763 helped to establish a North American polity with all the ingredients for treaty federalism.[77] In 1969 and again in his quest to patriate the Canadian Constitution, Trudeau encountered the legal and political legacy of this rich constitutional heritage of treaty alliances between the Crown and Indigenous peoples. In both 1970 and 1980–81, some opponents of Trudeau's constitutional vision drew on the Aboriginal history of conservative antagonism towards the revolutionary movement that divided Anglo-America into two sovereign components. The outcome of this clash of ideologies was a compromise. The Canadian Constitution was patriated in 1982 against the explicit objections of Aboriginal organizations. It included, however, a provision that recognized and affirmed the existence of the Aboriginal and treaty rights of the Aboriginal *peoples*.[78]

This provision, section 35 of the *Constitution Act, 1982*, created a bridge of continuity between Canada's domesticated Constitution and the inheritance of imperial and international law rooted especially in the Royal Proclamation of 1763. Moreover, this affirmation of the constitutional status of Crown-Aboriginal treaties significantly constrained Trudeau's effort to nudge the Dominion of Canada away from its legal personality as a constitutional monarchy towards a system of law closer to that of the US republic. The opposition to patriation was mounted by a coalition similar to that which had opposed Trudeau's White Paper in 1969. The opponents of patriation intervened so effectively that they forced some juridical and political reckoning in London, the old imperial capital of the British Empire, with the legal character of the Crown-Aboriginal treaties and the remaining Aboriginal titles of Indigenous peoples in northern

North America. One outcome of the Indian lobby's intervention in Great Britain was the requirement that a constitutional conference would have to take place within one year of patriation to clarify the legal place of Indians, Inuit, and Métis in the Canadian Federation.[79] This procedural opening was extended in 1983 to a series of four constitutional conferences over four years. The aim of the federal, provincial, and Aboriginal leaders who took part in these events was to come up with language to give greater definition to the constitutional affirmation of Aboriginal and treaty rights. One such amendment emerged from the first of these meetings in 1983. In the single time that the Canadian Constitution has ever been successfully amended within Canada, wording was added to section 35 to make explicit the equal status and rights of Aboriginal men and women.[80] As well, wording was inserted specifying that existing or future land claims agreements would acquire the force of "treaty rights" and become subject to constitutional protection.

Of the four constitutional conferences on Aboriginal matters, two took place under the chairmanship of Pierre Trudeau's Liberal government and two under the federal auspices of Prime Minister Brian Mulroney's Progressive Conservative government. In April 1987 the Mulroney government removed the Aboriginal peoples from the process of constitutional deliberations and thereafter redirected constitutional politics towards the subject of Quebec's role in Canada.[81] Between the summer of 1987 and the fall of 1992, Mulroney invested enormous political capital in two processes of political negotiation aimed at addressing the fact that Canada's *Constitution Act, 1982*, has not been ratified by the National Assembly of the Quebec. Under his guidance, a complex series of political compromises was negotiated with the aim of enabling Quebec's government to give its legislative approval to Canada's supreme law. At the heart of that series of compromises was a political accord given unanimous consent in 1987 by all of Canada's eleven first ministers, including Premier Robert Bourassa of Quebec, at a closed federal-provincial bargaining session at Meech Lake. But it was not to be. Building on the legacy of their intense involvement in Canadian constitutional politics up to that point, the Aboriginal leaders and their allies proved instrumental in blocking the process that would have given unanimous legislative approval to the Meech Lake Accord.

A complex series of developments put Elijah Harper, an Oji-Cree member of Manitoba's Legislative Assembly, in a position to take much of the credit for stopping the Meech Lake juggernaut in June 1990.[82] Within a matter of a few weeks, the tension between the Quebec government and Indian militants exploded into an armed confrontation between the Mohawk Warriors and the Canadian Army at Oka, Quebec. The dispute over the contested lands of an old Roman Catholic Indian mission soon spread to Aboriginal train blockades in northern Ontario, an armed stand-off over Aboriginal water rights in southern Alberta, and the Mohawk seizure of the Mercier Bridge across the St Lawrence River in Montreal.[83] The

Oka Crisis, together with the Aboriginal role in blocking the Meech Lake Accord, led to the decision by the government in Ottawa to integrate four Aboriginal organizations into a second constitutional process. When the Treaty 6 leadership addressed the forum of chiefs, elders, and councilors in Edmonton in 1992, then, they were reaching the climax of the second round of constitutional talks. They were responding to one more attempt by the Mulroney government to change the Canadian Constitution.

The Edmonton meeting was part of a whirlwind of consultations, negotiations, and conferences whose outcome in August 1992 was awkwardly labelled the Charlottetown Consensus Report on the Constitution.[84] The process leading to the production of that report was, without doubt, one of the most serious, high-level, and far-ranging deliberations ever held on the meaning of Aboriginal and treaty rights in the legal construction of a highly industrialized nation-state. In the effort to remake Canada's Constitution, an array of extremely innovative reforms were brought forward on how best to extend to Indigenous peoples and their Aboriginal polities a larger role in the exercise of government power. The package of constitutional proposals assembled at Charlottetown was perhaps the most substantial political embodiment of all the intense activism and historical revision stimulated by the 500th anniversary of 1492. The Charlottetown accord encapsulated politically the work of many individuals who had contributed to the project of deconstructing the idea of Columbus's "discovery" of America. The climate of opinion that gave rise to the Charlottetown Consensus Report had dramatically shifted away from the kind of imperial optimism generated by the 400th anniversary of Columbus's most famous voyage at the World's Columbian Exposition in Chicago.

The other side of this process of deconstruction was the need to *reconstruct* laws and institutions in ways aimed at breaking the colonizing momentum of the Columbian conquests. As some see it, this system of colonization has been so thoroughly incorporated and institutionalized into the predominant motifs of what is made to seem normal in day-to-day life that its continuing repressive force has been rendered invisible to the majority of those who are not on its receiving end. Fundamental to the discourse on the 500th anniversary of Columbus's arrival in the Western Hemisphere was the contention that the dismantling of European empires after the Second World War had only started rather than realized a more fundamental reckoning with the inequitable power structures inherited from colonialism. Those legacies of colonialism remain entrenched in myriad laws, institutions, and policies rooted in the fiction that humanity can be divided into men and natives, citizens and wards. They are manifest in a system of international relations giving new language to old paradigms of savagery and civilization, into divisions separating those in societies considered eligible to shape the future and those whose cultures are assumed to be archaic and obsolete. As was demonstrated in the Aboriginal rejection of Trudeau's White Paper policy, the language of liberalism and individual equality before the law can often disguise initiatives whose effect is to deny the legacies of history; to deny the existence of Aboriginal title and the distinct constitutional character of Indigenous peoples.

With the US termination policy of the 1950s, for instance, or Pierre Trudeau's White Paper policy of 1969, the attempts continued to abolish the remaining Indian Country and to fulfill the conquest of peoples, lands, and resources that had begun in 1492. The formulators of the Charlottetown Consensus Report genuinely sought to address the genocidal assumptions underlying that agenda – the termination of distinct Aboriginal societies through unbending adherence to the liberal principle of individual equality before the law.[85] The authors of the Charlottetown Accord had glimpsed the outlines of a North American nation-state embarked on a different trail of decolonization from the one pioneered by the United States. They had glimpsed the possibilities of a new kind of polity where Aboriginal titles and the titles derived from the process of colonization could be made to overlap and to co-exist. They had glimpsed an alternative to the model of imperial republicanism created by the United States when it broke free from the British Empire to construct its own commercial, cultural, and military empire of transcontinental, hemispheric, and global power.

The makers of the Charlottetown Accord decisively returned to the constitutional heritage of the Royal Proclamation and the international law of Aboriginal and treaty rights. Their document was far from perfect – it was a complex and patchy proposal that, in places, seemed more like an operating manual for technocrats than a bold statement of founding principles. Although many qualifications attended the deal's main provisions, its central principles were relatively straightforward. It envisaged Canada as a federation of three kinds of government – Aboriginal, provincial, and national. While Quebec was to be recognized as a "distinct society," all three orders of government would exercise sovereign powers within their own tightly defined fields of jurisdiction.[86] Rather than use the politically provocative language of sovereignty to describe the powers of Aboriginal governments, the Charlottetown accord described the Aboriginal right to self-government as an *inherent* right. This notion of inherency was a code to indicate that Aboriginal peoples and Aboriginal governments did not derive their rights and jurisdictions from any non-Aboriginal source. These rights and powers did not come by way of a grant from the national parliament, the provincial legislatures, the Crown, or the Canadian Constitution. Rather, they originated from cycles of Aboriginal history that long pre-date the existence of Canada. They came from sources that the people and governments of Canada could *recognize* but not create.

The most influential negotiator on the Aboriginal side was Ovide Mercredi, the national chief of the Assembly of First Nations.[87] One of the strategic problems Chief Mercredi faced in the negotiations was that he was in large measure lining up with provincial premiers in a joint raid on the constitutional powers of the central government. As illustrated by

Georgia's championing of Indian removal or by the Ontario government's anti-Indian arguments in the *St. Catherine's Milling* case, state and provincial authorities in North America are consistently the pre-eminent foes of Aboriginal and treaty rights. Alternatively, the protection of these rights and titles has depended from the days of the Royal Proclamation on the willingness and ability of imperial and federal officials to oppose those who promote decentralizing power towards colonial, state, or provincial governments. The Meech Lake Accord and the Charlottetown Consensus Report both diminished federal power in order to edify the role of provincial governments.

Mercredi's failure to oppose the further provincialization of Canadian governance was closely connected to his failure to grasp the fuller import of the critique presented in Edmonton. Like the Cree leaders from the Treaty 6 area, most of the delegates at the conference emphasized the international character of their treaties with the Crown. In their view, the nation-to-nation, sovereign-to-sovereign character of these treaties was confirmed by the historical reality that most of these transactions were negotiated on the non-Aboriginal side directly on behalf of the British monarch. Indeed, the Royal Proclamation makes it clear that the sovereign person of the monarch is the only authority capable of entering into treaty agreements with Indigenous peoples in Canada. As most of the delegations saw it, the bilateral and international character of their treaties with the British sovereign would be undermined by subjecting them to a trilateral process of constitutional amendment. In repeating a theme that remained consistent throughout the process of patriation, some of the more conservative treaty chiefs remained adamant that provincial premiers could have no legitimate say in defining treaty agreements that provincial governments had no part in formulating.[88] Indeed, Treaties 4, 6, and 7 were negotiated between the Crown and Indigenous peoples between 1874 and 1877, three decades before the provinces of Saskatchewan and Alberta were created on lands covered by these agreements.

The Treaty 6 leaders chose to highlight their perception of the international character of their treaty alliances with the British imperial sovereign by contrasting their own status with that of their counterparts in the United States. In their view the incorporated status of the agencies of Native American self-governance illustrated the heavily "domesticated" character of Indian groups south of the forth-ninth parallel. As proof of their contention, the Treaty 6 chiefs might well have pointed to a publication in 1984 of the American Indian National Bank. As that organization explained, "Tribes today can be viewed as ethnic land-owning communities and as quasi-corporations."[89] The Charlottetown Consensus Report included a great deal of language explaining that much would be done to implement their treaties within the domestic framework of a trilateral federal structure. Those assurances, however, proved insufficient to garner a solid body of Indian support for the report in the national referendum to which it was subjected. Of all the distinct constituencies measured in tabulating the national vote on the Charlottetown Accord, only the Inuit and the citizens of Ontario gave the Charlottetown document the sanction of a majority of "yes" vote.

The significant role of Aboriginal leaders in the constitutional politics of Canada from 1969 to 1992 highlights the absence of a similar role for Aboriginal leaders in the United States. Indeed, the United States has never entered into negotiations with Indigenous peoples with a view to changing the US Constitution. Like African-American slaves, Native Americans were not given a voice in those processes resulting in the creation and constitutional elaboration of the United States. That heritage of exclusions remains unaddressed to this day. The outcome of this heritage of exclusion was marked in the attitude of the Treaty 6 leaders in their presentation in Edmonton. Their self-assurance that their peoples were better off than most of their counterparts in the United States seemed, on the surface at least, inconsistent with the mathematical comparisons. In spite of all the territorial losses to Indigenous peoples in the United States through allotment and termination, at the end of the twentieth century they still retained control of far larger parcels of land than Indigenous peoples in Canada. According to some estimates, Native Americans constituted slightly more than 1 per cent of the total US population, and their reservations cover about 3.5 per cent of the forty-eight states south of the Canada-US border. The Aboriginal peoples in Canada constitute about 5 per cent of the Canadian population, yet Indian reserves cover collectively less than 1 per cent of all ten Canadian provinces. The 2,370 reserves scattered across all of Canada's provinces would not cover even half of the Navajo reservation in Arizona. The 298 Indian reservations in the forty-eight states, including the ninety-eight small "rancheria" settlements in California, are, on average, sixty-four times larger than the average reserve in the Canadian provinces. In British Columbia alone there are 1,600 tiny reserves with an average size of less than 250 hectares. The average reservation in the United States is 72,487 hectares.[90]

The insistence of the Treaty 6 leaders that their people were in a stronger political and legal position than Native Americans in the United States certainly conforms with the historical opinions of many clerics and administrators. As Hana Samek has documented, these officials of church and state regularly pronounced that the Indian policy of Canada was significantly superior to that of the US government.[91] In 1900, for instance, the Reverend Egerton Ryerson Young, a Methodist writer who achieved considerable fame in the United States lecturing as an evangelical frontiersman and a close observer of Indian life, made satisfied assurances to a gathering of self-described "Friends of the Indians." He addressed a group whose members gathered annually at a resort in Lake Mohonk, New York, to study and influence US Indian policy. "I come from Canada where we have no Indian question," he said. "We get along very nicely with our Indians."[92]

While the founding of the United States resulted from a decidedly different orientation to Indian Country than that of British imperial Canada, Indian policy in both polities has increasingly come to reflect the general movement towards continental integration. For instance, both the Bureau of Indian Affairs in the United States and the Department of Indian Affairs in Canada have developed centralized, relatively standardized procedures for the governance of the Aboriginal populations, including Inuit, within their borders.[93] The designation of "Indian Affairs" as the specific responsibility of the federal governments reflects the imperial history of both countries. Because Indian policy was so closely connected with westward expansion, or, in the case of Canada, with northward expansion as well, it was soon recognized that orderly development depended on the strict centralization of powers to deal with Indigenous peoples, whether through treaties, trade, warfare, legislation, or policy. As the application of this first principle became entrenched and institutionalized, the Indian Affairs branches of both federal governments increasingly reflected the colonizing ethos and method that was integral to the growth of the two nations. This feature of Indian administration was openly announced, for instance, by the name of one of the Canadian Indian Department's model agricultural communities, the File Hills Colony. This colony of federal authority was established near Indian Head, Saskatchewan, in 1901.[94] In the United States, too, the resemblance of Indian reservations to colonies of the federal authority was widely understood and sanctioned. As on official of the Indian Bureau commented in 1899, "Our Indian agents have a status very like that of British residents in the native states of India."[95]

While there are many similarities in the conduct of Indian Affairs in both Canada and the United States, there are also significant distinctions. In Canada there has been a far more concentrated degree of centralized control, standardization, and continuity in the way Indians have been governed. In the United States, however, there is no single body of legislation that applies as sweepingly to most Indian reservations as does the Canadian *Indian Act* to most Indian reserves. This contrast originates in the fact that there has been a far greater level of experimentation in the governance of Indians in the United States. The different "tribes" have been brought to conform to US federalism through a wider array of legislative, judicial, and administrative instruments. Moreover, the legacy of Indian removal in the eastern half of the nation has resulted in a wider range of gradations in the forms of recognition extended by federal and state authorities to different Indian groups. In the United States there is a far larger and more elaborate body of Indian Affairs case law than in Canada. Similarly, the federal Indian legislation in the United States is more likely than in Canada to apply to specific Native American tribes and communities than to all "Indians" generically. These more textured traditions of legislation, jurisprudence, and policy in the United States reflect the history of a more intensively colonized country whose population size has long been about ten times that of Canada. The larger scale of this colonizing endeavour in a country that is geographically smaller than Canada has resulted in more concerted, more elaborate, and more diverse drives to clear away the Aboriginal presence.

In the words of John Mack Faragher, the more intense phases of these drives can accurately be described as "ethnic cleansing."[96] Among the means used to clear the ground for the non-Aboriginal takeover were treaty negotiations, outright Indian wars, unpunished newcomer vigilantism, unregulated land theft by squatters, and the relocation of many Indian societies through the application of outright military force. The wider array of tactics employed in removing, constraining, and pacifying Indians has produced a more multi-faceted legal inheritance than in Canada, a country whose geopolitical origins lay largely in trade and military alliances *with* Indigenous peoples rather than in genocidal wars *against* them. More generally, the history of Indian policy in the United States has been played out in a theatre of national development founded in revolution.

That revolution led to the extinguishment of Crown title, a form of termination that made it more thinkable to embrace the idea of conquest and the extinguishment of Aboriginal title as an acceptable legal motif of national expansion. Even if the federalist inheritors of this revolution ended up restoring many features of Crown law to US law, the developments that flowed from the events of 1776 still render the US republic more prone than the constitutional monarchy of Canada to abrupt breaks with past practice. This propensity for discontinuity can be seen, for instance, in the contrast between the *Dawes Act* of 1887 and the *Indian Reorganization Act* of 1934. Where the former was aimed at privatizing Indian reservations, the latter sought to reintegrate the Indian domain as communally held territories. The IRA opened the way for limited forms of incorporated self-governance for some Indian groups that were described in the legislation as "tribes," though it was applied selectively and with various adaptations to local conditions.[97] Its influence, therefore, has been less pervasive in the Indian Country of the United States than has the *Indian Act* in the Indian Country of Canada.

In his opening address in 1939 to the participants of a conference entitled "The North American Indian Today," the Yale anthropologist Charles T. Loram tried to explain the distinctions between Indian policy in Canada and in the United States. He interpreted these differences primarily as a function of the differing political cultures in each country:

In the United States there is much more publicity regarding the present condition of the American Indians than in Canada. This may be due to a difference in tradition, for in the United States we seem to be more prone to wash our linen, clean or unclean, in public. Perhaps because of our restlessness, our willingness to experiment, our besetting sin in so often mistaking change for progress, our systems of education, all in the United States, officials as well as the general public have "views" on the Indian question which we are allowed and even encouraged to make public. In Canada, so it seems to me, the British tradition of reticence, of letting well enough alone, of hushing up "scandals," of trusting officials, are stronger, so there is apparently not so much interest on the part of the public in the so-called Indian Question.[98]

With the growing prominence after 1968 of constitutional politics in Canada, questions concerning the place of Indigenous people gradually acquired a far higher profile than in the United States. Loram's comparisons were therefore effectively reversed as the public debate heightened in Canada about how to conceptualize the place of Indigenous peoples in the changing institutional forms of a more fluid federation.[99] In this debate, elected representatives of Indian, Inuit, and Métis peoples added their proposals about what to retain from the British Empire and what to transform in the legal and geopolitical reconstitution of the northern half of North America. Their assertions stimulated a complex array of responses from all elements of the Canadian political spectrum as proponents of the left and the right, the Maritimes, Quebec, and the West, women and ethnocultural minorities, all made some references to Aboriginal rights in advancing their own visions of a less-colonized existence for their own constituents.[100]

Just as the rise of constitutional politics contributed significantly to elevating the politics of Aboriginality, so, too, was the political landscape altered by the reopening in 1973 of the issues connected to the existence of Aboriginal title. Although the tradition of treaty making in Canada was effectively shut down for almost a half a century after 1929, the litigious persistence, particularly of Indian politicians in British Columbia, finally forced a return to some political reckoning with the constitutional legacies of both 1763 and 1492. As a result of the Supreme Court's ambivalent response to the assertions of Frank Calder and the Nisga'a people, a new round of treaty negotiations with Indigenous peoples was initiated in Canada. That process continues until this day.

ABORIGINAL RIGHTS AND WRONGS

In the United States, Indigenous peoples have lacked significant venues of political negotiation to highlight how dramatically their histories and assertions touch on the fundamental characteristics of the world's most powerful nation. There has been no event giving Native Americans a platform comparable to that which was created in the effort to patriate and amend the Canadian Constitution. It is not for lack of trying, however, that the Indian leadership proved unable to ignite a serious discussion on the domestic and international implications for the United States of the prohibition by Congress in 1871 on further treaty making with Indigenous peoples. The effect of that legislation was to elevate the doctrine of conquest as the argument of last resort for US control of its home territory. How can the world's dominant superpower promote law rather than force as the foundation of international relations when it bases its own domestic self-justification on the principles of conquest?

One of the most concerted efforts to pressure the United States to renew its adherence to the international law of Aboriginal title took place in 1972 in the course of a caravan expedition entitled the Trail of Broken Treaties. At the outset of that campaign, Dennis Banks and Hank Adams issued a twenty-point plan in Minneapolis. Banks was one of the founders of the American Indian Movement, while Adams was the primary draftsman of the plan. At the time of its presentation, Adams was recovering from a gun-shot wound inflicted by vigilantes who correctly identified him as one of the chief strategists of the Washington state fish-ins. A Sioux theologian who had written *God Is Red* and many other formative texts supporting many of the positions of the American Indian Movement,[101] Vine Deloria Jr credited the twenty-point proposal as "the best summary document of reforms put forth this century." As he saw it, the provisions – especially those pertaining to treaties – "were extremely accurate in their assessment of the feelings of Indians around the nation."[102] Among the document's main points were the following:

1 The repeal of the 1871 federal statute that outlawed the making of further treaties with Indian nations.
2 The establishment of a commission to review past treaty violations and to propose structures and protocols for a new era of treaty relations.
3 The resubmission of unratified treaties, including those covering large areas of California, for ratification by a two-thirds vote of the American Senate.
4 Revisions in court procedures and in the apportionment of the burden of proof in litigation alleging treaty violations.
5 A change to allow the admission of the oral traditions of Indian elders in judicial proceedings involving treaty interpretation.[103]

The Trail of Broken Treaties ended in the occupation of the Bureau of Indian Affairs headquarters in Washington, DC. The building's occupiers hung out a banner declaring the existence of the Native American Embassy, a clear marker of the protestors' urge to throw off the constraints of domestication in favour of a more internationalized approach to Indian relations with the US government and the rest of the world. This episode become one of the key defining events during the intense period of activism framed by the Indians of All Tribes' occupation of Alcatraz Island in 1969 and AIM's return to Wounded Knee in 1973.[104]

President Richard Nixon responded to this upsurge in Indian activism in much the same way that he and his national security adviser, Henry Kissinger, responded internationally to the rise of regimes that they did not like. In Chile, for instance, a coup was manufactured by the US government in 1973 to replace the elected government of the socialist Salvador Allende with the authoritarian regime of General Augusto Pinochet. Within the United States, federal police and their networks of paid informants and collaborators covertly infiltrated the American Indian Movement. The Rapid City trial of John Graham beginning in 2009 helped bring to light the large scope of the infiltration and its corrosive effects on the relationships between AIM's leading members. It became extremely difficult to trust anyone in a milieu where there was good cause to suspect that somebody was working surreptitiously with the federal police. Many Indian activists targeted by the FBI's COINTELPRO, a forerunner of the policing functions now incorporated into Homeland Security, were subjected to various forms of injury, including wrongful criminalization and, in the dispute on the Pine Ridge reservation, outright murder. Meanwhile, Nixon cultivated through federal patronage a network of his own Indian friends and collaborators, particularly in the National Tribal Chairmen's Association. These associates of the US president worked cooperatively with the federal authorities to help marginalize and discredit the more militant wing of the Indian sovereignty movement as most fully expressed by AIM.[105]

In 1970 Nixon set in motion his own series of policies which he declared were intended to favour "cooperation rather than paternalism ... self-determination rather than termination."[106] Nixon's policy of "self-determination" could more accurately be described as one of self-administration. It was based on the principle of devolving powers and monies to tribal governments from the Bureau of Indian Affairs, a federal agency subject to increasingly embarrassing investigations and scandals. This devolution policy proceeded in an ad hoc fashion until it was provided with a legislative framework in 1975 through the *Indian Self-Determination and Education Act*. Nixon's announcement in 1970 of his government's renunciation of the termination policy of the 1950s came in the ceremony where he signed a bill returning the sacred Blue Lake to the Tiwa Indians of the Taos Pueblo. The return of this shrine, a ceremonial site where John Collier was once thunder stuck by the transcendant power of Aboriginal spirituality, was meant to symbolize the determination of the Nixon regime to restore justice to Indigenous peoples. Nixon's nod to Collier's legacy at Blue Lake suggests the resilience of the heritage of the Indian New Deal and the Atlantic Charter even among some Republican Party stalwarts of that era. With his presidential signature, Nixon put an end to a long-festering dispute that had its origins in the incorporation of Blue Lake without Indian consent in the Carson National Forest in 1906.[107]

The religious rationale cited for the return of Blue Lake reflects a continuing trend in the political discourse on Aboriginal rights in the United States. The basis of this trend lies in the frequency of the connections linking the constitutional protections afforded religious freedom with various positions on the appropriate place of Indigenous peoples in the US federation. In the 1930s, for instance, much of this controversy swirled around the Native American Church and its rituals involving the use of peyote. Like John Collier, ethnobotanist Richard Evans Schultes was one of those who advanced the principles of religious freedom to argue against a federal proposal to ban the use of peyote in Native American ceremonies.[108] Given the absence at the end of the twentieth century of any venues in the United States even remotely comparable to Canada's ongoing processes of treaty or constitutional negotiations, the issue of religious freedom was stretched even further to cover the central problem of how titles to lands and resources are to be conceived, constructed, and apportioned. The principle that Aboriginal titles form an integral part of the overall titles of the United States has frequently been implicit in those many legal challenges mounted to show that certain sacred sites are necessary environments for the exercise of Aboriginal religious freedoms.[109]

The channelling of contentions about the legal character of Aboriginal title into arguments over the legal quality of religious freedom is not surprising in a country that originates as much in the evangelism of the Protestant Reformation as in the dispassionate rationality of the European Enlightenment's most scientific expressions. New England's Puritan founders made their original transatlantic migrations in search of an oasis of asylum from the religious persecutions they had suffered in Europe. The importance of the First Great Awakening in the genesis of the American Revolution and of the Second and Third Great Awakenings in the reform of so many facets of law and governance throughout the nineteenth century demonstrates the importance of religious enthusiasm in shaping many aspects of North American political culture. In Robert Fogel's view, a Fourth Great Awakening began the 1970s. There is a huge difference, however, between the political exploitation of the most recent upsurge of Christian enthusiasm and the preoccupations of the Social Gospel movement with economic justice as reflected, for instance, in the socialist politics of Tommy Douglas, the Baptist minister who served as premier of Saskatchewan between 1944 and 1961. In *American Theocracy*, Kevin Phillips sees great peril in the trend towards increased integration of church and state in the United States.[110] This trend was powerfully illustrated in 1999 when the future attorney general, John Ashcroft, gave a speech while accepting an honorary degree from Bob Jones University in South Carolina: "Unique among nations, America recognized the source of our character as being godly and eternal, not being civic and temporal. And because we have understood that our source is eternal, America has been different. We have no king but Jesus."[111]

In the 1980s a group of Blackfeet elders brought forward a claim posed in the language of religious freedom, a claim that might have been channelled into the renewal of Blackfeet treaty relations with the federal government had Congress not been so forceful in shutting the door to this medium of negotiations in 1871. The Blackfeet claim covered a portion of southeast Glacier Park, an area described by the claimants as the Sacred Badger–Two

Medicine Wildlands. While this territory lay outside the boundaries of the Blackfeet reserve in Montana, the litigants pointed to an agreement made in 1896 that reserved some Indian rights to cut and remove timber. The Blackfeet position at the end of the twentieth century, however, emphasized not logging but the Wildlands' importance in the ceremonial life of those who adhere to a particular view of Blackfeet religion. Jay Vest played a role in putting forward the Blackfeet claim to the Sacred Badger–Two Medicine Wildlands. He concluded his submission by picturing the area as a place offering "the alienated and the lost a way back into traditional culture ... A reprieve from the demoralizing effects of alcoholism, racial abuse, and other acts of social injustice fostered by the dominant society."[112]

Vest's attachment of this list of grievances to his advocacy of the claimed spiritual character of the Sacred Badger–Two Medicine site illustrates the versatility of "religious freedom" as a code to highlight a broad range of alleged wrongs. The attachment of such serious allegations to an argument for religious freedom suggests the overworked character of this interpretive device, one that has been pressed into action many times as a substitute for a type of negotiation that should take place, but often does not for the lack of appropriate theatres of political interaction. It suggests the distorted nature of the discourse in the United States on Aboriginal rights in the absence of any serious transactions aimed at amending the US Constitution or at renewing and expanding treaty relationships with Indigenous peoples. A similar light can be cast on many legislative enactments acknowledging the existence of Aboriginal rights in a variety of jurisdictional fields except in the most fundamental and essential one – in the underlying title of the United States itself.

Museums have been important sites of contention for determining the place of Aboriginal culture and identity in public interpretations of American culture and identity. The passage in 1978 of the *American Indian Religious Freedom Act* drew attention to those museums where many tens of thousands of Indian skeletons have been collected over several generations. These collections had once been assembled in the name of scientific research. They had been put together to provide the evidence to prove or disprove various theories about the role of race in the evolutionary transformation of humanity, to test competing contentions about the relationship of, say, brain size to imagined hierarchies of human intelligence, or to advance Darwinian motifs of social science. The effort to interpret human attributes through the lens of racial difference quickly fell into disrepute after the Nazis effectively discredited this method of picturing and moulding society. The growing controversy over the fate of Indian burial sites – past, present, and future – was instrumental in the passage of the *Archaeological Resources Protection Act* in 1979, the *National Museum of the American Indian Act* in 1989, and the *Native American Graves Protection and Repatriation Act* in 1990. All these laws contributed to a process of returning Indian skeletons for reburial by those Indian clans and nations deemed to be closest to the lineage of the Aboriginal groups whose burial places had been raided. It remains to be seen if these laws will be implemented to return the skull reputed to be that of Geronimo from the Order of the Skull and Bones at Yale University in New Haven, Connecticut.

Arguments similar to those used to justify the repatriation of Aboriginal skeletons were employed to persuade the curators of museums to return sacred bundles, pipes, shields, and the like to those societies whose members initially produced them. This pattern of return has been part of the development of a number of Indian-run museums, institutions that often support the movement of Aboriginal communities to take over the responsibility of representing their own Aboriginal histories to the general public.[113] Although different forms of repatriation embody relatively coherent expressions of self-determination, it is difficult not to see this whole phenomenon as some sort of substitution or consolation for what is not being repatriated – the lands, jurisdiction, and appropriated wealth of the United States. It is difficult not to see the repatriation movement as a diversion away from more fundamental questions about how power is exercised and how property is legitimized and apportioned in the United States.[114]

What wedges of polarized inequity between rich and poor, the entitled and the disentitled, penetrate as deeply as those processes that rendered Indigenous peoples as dispossessed petitioners seeking alms and federal transfers from those now in control their Aboriginal territories? How did immigrants and their descendants move to the centre of American experience and effectively push Indigenous peoples to the margins of America's dominant political economy?

COMING TO THE CROSS-ROADS: INVENTING AMERICA AT DOUGLAS CREEK ESTATES

The United States forms one element of a broader and more abstract polity known as America. Although the term *America* has been appropriated to identify the most powerful country in Americas, it should be reclaimed so that it applies equally to all citizens of the Western Hemisphere. The idea of America remains as elastic and as subject to revision as ever. Throughout much of its history, America has been seen by many beyond its shores as a symbol of hope, as a promised land for those yearning to break free? But what is to be made of the experience of the Indigenous peoples who were pushed aside or eliminated to make room for wave after wave of immigrants? Will freedom for some in America continue to be purchased at the expense of others? Will America look outward to the world with confident humility, or is the idea of America to be associated with the corrosive xenophobia that brands all those who do not conform to imposed norms as deviants and possible terrorists?

A striking icon embodying some of the key choices to be made in the ongoing process of inventing America was the Six Nations' protest camp set up in 2006 on the site of a suburban real-estate project. The site's developers, Henco Industries, named their luxury housing project Douglas Creek Estates. This development at Caledonia, near Hamilton, Ontario, was to have been identical to many thousands of others of its type which proliferate around towns and cities all over North America. The contested development lies just outside the Six Nations Iroquois Reserve, but well within the territory six miles on either side of the Grand River which was transferred by the British imperial government to the King's most loyal Indian allies during the American Revolution. The transfer took place in 1784 to compensate its recipients for the loss of their Longhouse League's heartland. Without Indian consent, the British government transferred title to the US government of the Six Nations' Longhouse territory in what is now upper New York state. To compensate the Six Nations for what they had lost, Sir Frederick Haldimand, the top military commander in what remained of British imperial Canada, gave them the Grand River valley north of Lake Erie. The resulting Haldimand Deed is clear, succinct, and unequivocal. It can be cited in full:

Whereas His Majesty having been pleased to direct that in consideration of the early attachment to his cause manifested by the Mohawk Indians, and of the loss of their settlement which they thereby sustained – that a convenient tract of land under his protection should be chosen as a safe and comfortable retreat for them and others of the Six Nations, who have either lost their settlements within the Territory of the American States, or wish to retire from them to the British – I have at the earnest desire of many of these His Majesty's faithful Allies purchased a tract of land from the Indians situated between the Lakes Ontario, Erie and Huron and I do hereby in His Majesty's name authorize and permit the said Mohawk Nation and such others of the Six Nation Indians as wish to settle in that quarter to take possession of and settle upon the Banks of the River commonly called Ours [Ouse] or Grand River, running into Lake Erie, allotting to them for that purpose six miles deep from each side of the river beginning at Lake Erie and extending in that proportion to the head of the said river, which them and their posterity are to enjoy for ever.[115]

Throughout the nineteenth century, the Six Nation settlers in the Grand River valley were stripped of much of their lands through the usual array of unsavory and possibly illegal tactics. They were left with a reserve embodying only a small percentage of the territories transferred to them in the Haldimand Deed. The Six Nations community is in the midst of Ontario's urban and industrial heartland. The community's rich heritage of treaty making forms one part of the history that makes Ontario the North American jurisdiction with the most diverse array of treaty agreements with Indigenous peoples. The Six Nations community is the most heavily populated reserve in Canada, with slightly more than twenty thousand inhabitants. It has many Indian-run businesses, including a radio station and Grand River Enterprises, a cigarette manufacturing enterprise that exports its products globally. This tobacco company pays its full share of taxes to the provincial and federal governments. Many of the men in the community have worked as high steel workers, a Mohawk specialty. The Six Nations reserve is almost certainly the world's main nurturing ground for lacrosse players, an ancient Aboriginal game that at one time was Canada's national sport.

The Six Nations community is by no means a place of poverty and destitution, as are, tragically, many hundreds of other Indian reserves and reservations throughout Canada and the United States. Nevertheless, Six Nations citizens continue to be faced with constant pressures to give ground to the non-Indian society pressing in around them. In 2006 a group of concerned individuals took action in an attempt to prevent yet another round of dispossession. They set up their camp on the Douglas Creek Estates construction site in order to call attention to the continuing injustices they face as well as the unbroken force of the Haldimand Deed. They attempted to organize their protest in ways that reflected the structures of their clan system at the basis of their traditional Longhouse League. Until 1924 the Longhouse Council, the decision-making body of the Longhouse League, was recognized by Canadian officialdom as the functioning government of the Six Nations community. Then the Council was forcefully removed from the community's seat of government by the Royal Canadian Mounted Police.

The Mounties acted on the orders of Prime Minister William Lyon Mackenzie King. His decision to terminate the governing role of the Longhouse Council came in response to the embarrassment inflicted on the Canadian government by Levi General, also known as Deskahe. He had been sent to Europe by his Longhouse sponsors to inform the member governments of the League of Nations in Geneva that the Canadian government was not living up to the terms of the treaties made in the course of Great Britain's colonization of North America. King ordered that the Longhouse system be replaced by the regime of Indian rule created by federal legislation known as the *Indian Act*. Beginning in 1927, the Act was amended and then administered in a particularly repressive way, with a close eye to preventing Indians in British Columbia from bringing forward any legal case involving assertions of their Aboriginal title.

Earlier in his career, Mackenzie King had worked for the Rockefeller oil conglomerate in New York, giving his employer advice on how to undermine and co-opt trade unions in the era leading up to the so-called Red Scare. King's assault in 1924 on this significant embodiment of the history of treaty alliances between the Six Nations Longhouse government and the makers of British North America was entirely consistent with his general tendency as prime minister to nudge Canada away from its constitutional moorings in the British Empire. As his employment history with the Rockefellers suggests, he favoured Canada's deeper integration into the informal commercial, political, and cultural empire of the United States.

The role of the Longhouse League changed significantly after 1924, when it continued a sort of underground existence as a religious institution frequented by the more conservative members of community.[116] In the second half of the twentieth century it became clear that a substantial number of Six Nations people continue to see the Longhouse League and its attending Great Law, the *Kaianerekowa*, as the legitimate source and expression of their own unbroken sovereignty. This attitude was displayed in 1959, for instance, when a group of traditionalists tried to take back control of the Ohswegan Council House, the building where the Longhouse Council had conducted its meetings until 1924.[117] This same tenacity was displayed in the mid-1970s, when the Mohawk Warriors Society tried to express the sovereign character of the Longhouse League's Great Law by asserting jurisdiction over a territory in upper New York state known as Ganienkeh. The heritage of the Longhouse League's most militant branch was renewed when, in 1990, a dispute over the expansion of a golf course at Oka, Quebec, exploded into an armed standoff between the self-declared Mohawk Warriors and about 4,000 Canadian soldiers.[118]

This history informed the actions initiated by Janie Jamieson and Dawn Smith, two Six Nations women in their early twenties, as they began the process of mobilizing their clan mothers and other Longhouse adherents to express their opposition to the building of Douglas Creek Estates. In spite of their decision to eschew violence and to employ peaceful ways of making their case, the Indian stand generated serious outbursts of anger, fear, and dismay in the local non-Indian population. Many of the non-Indians organized politically and empowered their leaders to make impassioned pleas calling on the Ontario government and the Ontario Provincial Police (OPP) to enforce the law and remove the protestors. The developers sought and obtained an injunction from a local court, and the OPP made various shows of force, but season after season the protestors persisted. They refused to be bullied or intimidated into leaving the base they had established at the Estates.

Little by little the depth of the protestors' case pre-empted the mass of glib condemnations pointed their way. Who could disagree that the laws should be enforced? But what was the substance of the law in the Grand River valley? Is not the Haldimand Deed part of the rule of law that the police are professionally obligated to enforce? What is the status of this important legal instrument embedded into the proprietary structure of Canada at the crucial moment when its governors had to adapt to the establishment of the United States of America? The Indian stand at the Douglas Creek Estates began to force these deeper issues upward towards the light of day. Underlying much of the Ontario government's uncertain reaction was a genuine desire on the part of its leaders not to create the basis of a scandal similar to the one that had grown from an investigation into the killing of an unarmed Ojibwa protestor, Dudley George. An OPP officer shot George during an Ojibwa demonstration in 1995 involving the status of an Indian burial ground.[119]

The Six Nations stand led to negotiations with the governments of Ontario and Canada on the future of the contested lands. Significantly, the Six Nations side of the process is being led not by officials whose positions are derived from the Canadian *Indian Act* but by a council of elders who assert their identity as the contemporary extension of the Longhouse Council that was displaced from its governing role by Canadian authorities in 1924. With good faith on all sides, these negotiations held the potential for enlightened compromise. Such a compromise would have to recognize the continuing legal status of the Haldimand Deed and the Longhouse government, even as it recognized concurrently the legitimacy of the kind of land tenures and jurisdictional regimes that developed throughout the Grand River valley during the centuries since Joseph Brant first led his people across the Great Lakes to plant a new white pine of peace.[120] Such a compromise might be expressed in the sharing of local tax revenues as well as the responsibility to provide government services to all the citizens of the Grand River valley. Such compromises would require sufficient changes to give Six Nations citizens who do not adhere to the spiritual dimension of Longhouse traditions sufficient confidence that their own rights of religious freedom will be respected by their own representatives. Similarly, some specific adjustments might be required to acknowledge the special role of the Mohawks as referred to in the Haldimand Deed without undermining the egalitarian character of a multinational federation that has long made the civics of the Longhouse League and its Great Law the subject of much respectful international investigation and scholarship.

A contemporary treaty to make the Grand River lands the site of a new prototype of intercultural cooperation and combined jurisdiction could serve as a beacon in a world hungry for some signals of enlightened good sense in the sharing of Earth's abundance. Such an innovation might qualify as being both original and a conservative restoration of the ingenuity displayed in the making of both the Longhouse League and its extension in the Covenant Chain of treaty relations allying the Iroquoian nations with New York colony and some of the other Anglo-American jurisdictions. Here is a chance to build on the heritage of the teachings of the Peacemaker and Hiawatha, on the Royal Proclamation's prohibition on empire building through conquest, on the Indian New Deal's embrace of community building, and on the Atlantic Charter's promise to advance the rule of law as the basis of collective security in the international community. It is also an opportunity to move towards the Fourth World and away from the American empire. If it proves impossible to apply the principles of treaty federalism even in North America's Grand River valley, there is little hope of finding acceptable compromises among antagonists in many other parts of the world where sovereignty, jurisdiction, and ownership of natural resources are contested – in relations, for instance, between Russia and some of the Soviet Union's former republics, between ethnic groups and nation-states in Africa, between India and Pakistan, and between the Israeli state and the Palestinian people.

PART THREE

Empire and Multitude Meet the Fourth World

CHAPTER TWELVE

Indigenous Peoples in the Law and Practice of Nations

Europe applauded when the nations of the West sacrificed the lives of millions of *indios* in America, and definitely not to found other nations far more moral and peace loving. Yonder stands the North, with its egoistic liberty, its lynch law, its political manipulations; yonder stands the South with its turbulent republics, its barbarous revolutions, its civil wars, and its pronunciamientos, like its mother Spain.

José Rizal, *El Filibusterismo*, 1891

The flow of American business has turned westward. It is [in Indonesia] that the deep-rooted American concepts of free enterprise and Yankee ingenuity are finding new forms of expression. Moreover, the profit potential fairly staggers the imagination.

Copley Corporation special report, 1967

SOCIAL DARWINISM, IMPERIALISM, CAPITALISM, AND SCIENTIFIC RACISM

While the modern era of globalization began in 1492, the pace and intensity of imperial expansion entered a new phase during the second half of the nineteenth century when the language of Social Darwinism began to replace the mystique of Christian evangelism as the primary public justification for colonial expansion.[1] The chief literary marker of this epistemological transformation in the public mythology of imperial expansion came in 1859 with the publication of Charles Darwin's *On the Origin of Species by Means of Natural Selection, or the Preservation of Favoured Races in the Struggle for Life*. In this pivotal text Darwin put forward a sweeping theory of natural history that challenged the authority of most religious doctrines and establishments. Darwin advanced the thesis that only the fittest organisms in the struggle for survival are able to prevail long enough to pass on their superior genetic traits to subsequent generations. In emphasizing the importance of material factors over divine intervention in life's evolution from lower to higher forms, Darwin extended a particular facet of Enlightenment rationalism whose secular thrust remains heavily contested to this day.

Darwin's theory of the survival of the fittest was quickly seized upon, exploited, and reconfigured by many theorists whose efforts to systemize the study of human interaction were integral to the emergent social sciences. Among the most prominent of the Social Darwinists and scientific racists were Herbert Spencer, Francis Galton, Francis Parkman, Joseph Arthur Gobineau, Ernst Haeckl, John W. Burgess, Theodore Roosevelt, and Houston Stewart Chamberlain. Social Darwinism provided the authority of science to justify all manner of inequitable socioeconomic relationships. It allowed, for instance, promoters and apologists of imperial expansion to rationalize the process of colonization as an expression of natural law. It provided similar rationalizations to explain the competitive dynamics of capitalism, a system of material interaction that regularly sacrifices whole peoples, nations, and enterprises on the life-or-death alter of market relationships. Indeed, the merger of Adam Smith's philosophy of political economy with Darwin's natural history infused new ideological bravado into the interconnected drives to acquire colonies and to extend the frontiers of giant industrial and financial cartels. Darwin's reigning idea of biological improvement through the survival of the fittest complemented Smith's notion that some "invisible hand" maximizes collective abundance when individual producers are able to optimize their self-interest by concentrating their creative capacities on activities where they enjoy the greatest comparative advantage in the conduct of business.[2]

The imperial, racist, and capitalist exploitation of Social Darwinism tended to overwhelm and negate the fragile legacies emanating from the brief period when the most exuberant expressions of Enlightenment egalitarianism shook the foundations of Western civilization. The popularity of Social Darwinism, for instance, put obstacles in the way of the recognition of Aboriginal title and the requirement of obtaining Aboriginal consent for colonial expansion as codified, for instance, in the Indian provisions of the Royal Proclamation of 1763. Similarly, the rise of Social Darwinism helped to block broad popular embrace of the larger revolutionary meanings to be drawn from the courageous actions of those who followed the likes of Toussaint L'Overture and Tecumseh into armed engagement with their enemies. The leadership given to the anti-imperial struggle by both freedom fighters epitomizes the merger of the Enlightenment principles of egalitarianism with the innate desire of colonized peoples to liberate themselves. Both martyred generals were instrumental in giving organized military, legal, and geopolitical expression to the groundswell of indigenous resistance aimed at opposing the enslavement, dispossession, displacement, and extermination of dark-skinned peoples on imperialism's most expansionary and contested frontiers. Lamentably, the Aboriginal history of revolutionary movements such as these have not received the kind of attention showered on the upsurges of those First World protestors whose armed assault on the authority structures of their day have been dignified as the American and French revolutions. This bias is itself a reflection of Social Darwinism's continuing hold on the historical imagination. It reveals the continuing prejudices marked in the failure to elevate most Fourth World wars of attempted liberation to the prominence they deserve in the genesis of the global quest to recognize, realize, and protect universal human rights.[3]

The power of Social Darwinism was conspicuously manifest in the imperial division of much of Africa south of the Sahara during the final two decades of the nineteenth century.[4] Based on the theory that Aboriginal Africans were the untutored and uncivilized subjects of the civilized nations, the Aboriginal lands and waters of Indigenous peoples were appropriated and apportioned in the scramble by several European powers for new African colonies. The treatment of North American Indians as wards of federal authority was thereby extended across the Atlantic to the continent that had long provided the plantation owners of the Western Hemisphere with their primary supply of Black slaves. The consequences of such formative episodes of imperial appropriation continue to be deeply felt to this day. In Africa, North America, Australia, and many other parts of the world, the vast majority of those who descend from individuals and groups who have at one time or another been transformed into the colonized wards of some "civilized" power suffer disproportionately from high rates of poverty, mental and physical sickness, addictions, violence, and disempowerment.

The scientific authority of Social Darwinism seemed to know no bounds until the outcome of the Second World War demonstrated the tragic extent of the inhumanity generated by this system of belief and conduct. From the time of the richly funded eugenics research carried out at the Cold Harbor facilities on Long Island, New York, to the genocidal projects of Europe's Nazi conquerors during the Second World War, many were seduced by the conceptualization of history as a contest for supremacy among distinct races. The view of Aboriginal history as a competition among races for living space merged with capitalist notions of competition among producers as the best means of reaching the promised land of maximum human progress. At the extreme end of scientific racism was the idea that any effort to elevate the "inferior" races was doomed because of their biological limitations. The more liberal approach sought a renewal of the old civilizing mission so that "primitive" peoples could be made to merge with more advanced societies through education in Christianity, literacy, industrial trades, and scientific method. Supporters of both these views simply assumed that nothing in the Aboriginal heritage was valuable either to them or to others. Diamond Jenness was far from alone in his view that Aboriginal cultures were the obsolete relics of outmoded ways of life.

Naturally, many Aboriginal groups and individuals refused to accept the finality of this cultural death sentence. But their desire for survival as distinct peoples did not gain many adherents outside their own communities until the revolution in relativism began to break down the certainties attending imperial and capitalist interpretations of history as supported by

Darwinian theories of human evolution. With this transformation came the growth of the idea that Aboriginal identities could be transformative, self-renewing, and adaptable to change. With the revelation that neither time nor space was fixed came the conception that Aboriginal cultures might have a place in the future as well as in the past, and that this prospect represented something positive for the commonwealth of human understanding and interaction.

ABORIGINES, CIVILIZATION, AND CRIMES AGAINST HUMANITY

Social Darwinism found particularly fertile ideological soil in the United States.[5] This pseudo-science gave a secular dimension to many of the theocratic principles supporting the public mythology of America as the receptacle of a God-given Manifest Destiny to expand its territorial dominion and to bring about great transformations in humanity's constitution. The merger of Social Darwinism and Manifest Destiny gave renewed expression to the sense of US exceptionalism, which has its deepest and most enduring roots in the founding Puritan view of their colonial outpost as a New Jerusalem and a Promised Land for God's Chosen People.[6] The modern-day extensions of this theocratic vision continue to influence the US government's orientation towards the rest of the world, especially its relations with the state of Israel and the predominantly Islamic citizenries that dominate much of Eurasia.[7]

As chronicled by Reginald Horsman, Jack Forbes, Richard Slotkin, Felix S. Cohen, Richard Drinnon, Roxanne Dunbar-Ortiz, and many others, the treatment by the US government of Indigenous peoples within North America helped to create patterns and paradigms that affected the emerging superpower's relations with Aboriginal groups throughout the world. As the United States continued to extend its power westward into Hawaii and the Philippines in the 1890s, its justifications for the conquest were articulated increasingly in the language of Social Darwinism and the related terminology of scientific racism, wardship, and trusteeship. The taxonomy used by the US government to classify the Indigenous peoples of Hawaii and the Philippine Islands along imagined fault lines of religion, race, and civilizational hierarchy was similarly prominent in justifications for Europe's division of Africa south of the Sahara during the final decades of the nineteenth century.

As the First World War was ending, Alpheus Snow formally applied the intellectual constructs of Social Darwinism to his analysis of international law. Between April and December 1918 he compiled for the US State Department a sweeping survey of the historical treatment and juridical status of that class of human being he identified as Aborigines. In the course of his varied career, this Harvard-trained lawyer taught courses on colonial governance at George Washington University. In one of his major publications before writing *The Question of Aborigines in the Law and Practice of Nations* in 1918, Snow identified the British imperial origins of the United States as the key to understanding his own country's juridical personality as a "Federal Empire."[8] Throughout his body of work, he portrays the colonization of Indigenous people in Anglo-America both before and after the founding of the United States as an integral part of the extension of European imperial rule throughout large parts of the planet. It would be difficult to overstate the importance of this scholarly framework for the study of the rise of both the formal and the informal empire building of the nascent superpower during its transition from transcontinental to hemispheric to global forms of expansionary enterprise.

In *The Administration of Dependencies*, Snow emphasizes the importance of a Treaty Council in 1754 in Albany, where representatives of the Anglo-American colonies met with representatives of the Six Nations and other Indian groups to negotiate the future status of the Ohio River valley. The assembly gave rise to a Plan of Union aimed at creating a regime of colonial governance capable of conducting a coherent system of centrally coordinated relations with the Indigenous peoples in North America's interior. Snow calls attention to the importance of Benjamin Franklin in these formulations. In his description of Franklin's understanding of the envisaged polity, Snow writes, "The Plan of Union plainly provided for the establishment of an American empire, dependent on the imperial status of Great Britain, that is to say for the establishment of a *imperium in imperio*, or sub-Empire." He goes on to say that this scheme for creating a sub-empire was "annulled" by the Royal Proclamation of 1763, which created the constitutional framework for "only one Realm or Empire."[9] The clear implication is that the genesis of the secessionist movement leading to the founding of the United States was in large measure aimed at creating the American empire originally conceived by Franklin. In the period between 1754 and 1776, however, the plan of union was altered to make the Thirteen Colonies the basis not of a subordinate imperial system within the British Empire but of a unitary federal empire with its own indigenous claim to sovereign jurisdiction. This indigenous sovereignty, not the British imperial system, would become the legal source of land titles, corporate charters, and other commercial proprietorships.

In Snow's subsequent publication for the US State Department, he extends many of these themes, showing the strong links in the minds of policy makers connecting the treatment of Indigenous peoples in North America to slavery, the slave trade, and the culminating episodes in the colonial division of Africa south of the Sahara. As Snow saw it, the US government's termination in 1871 of treaty negotiations with Indigenous peoples within the United States was instrumental in effecting a general shift in the legal, political, and ideological construction of imperialism and colonization. Congress's decision in 1871 to prohibit further treaty making with Indigenous peoples and thereby disregard the continuing force of their Aboriginal titles in domestic, constitutional, and international law had global consequences. It helped clear the way for the fuller elaboration among the other colonizing powers of the notion that "Aborigines" throughout the planet are both collectively and individually wards of the "civilized States." By sending this signal to the other "civilized sovereignties," the US government helped prod the imperial powers of Europe towards adopting the rhetorical stance of civilized trustees who must make decisions for their uncivilized wards.[10] "The entrance of the United States into the work of colonization, with the fullest recognition and most complete application of the principles of guardianship and tutorship of aboriginal tribes," Snow wrote, "has profoundly stimulated the civilized States to a more and more complete acceptance and fulfillment of their international responsibilities in this respect."[11]

Snow's work helps to illustrate the dominance of Social Darwinism by the era of the First World War in deciding what was acceptable in colonization's expanding net of imperial control over a large proportion of the world's inhabitants. In one of his key definitions, Snow explains that "Aborigines are members of uncivilized tribes which inhabit a region at the time a civilized State extends its sovereignty over the region, and which have so inhabited from time immemorial; and also the uncivilized descendants of such persons dwelling in the region." Laws governing the treatment of "Aborigines" were "not strictly national or strictly international." "Aborigines," he insists, should be distinguished from "colonists," who were said to be "the citizens of civilized States who enter the region." The underlying principles governing "the relations of aborigines with each other, with the colonists, and with the colonizing State are necessarily subject to a special regime established by the colonizing State for the purpose of fitting the aborigines for civilization, and *opening the resources of the land to the civilized world*."[12] Snow makes repeated references to the lack of comprehensive studies on his subject. He identified the British parliamentary report of 1837 on Aborigines in British Settlements as the foundational investigation on which he drew. Closely connected to the work of the parliamentary committee were the activities of the British and Foreign Aborigines' Protection Society. In his view, the transformation of the anti-slavery movement into the aborigines' protection movement made perfect sense. Indeed, Snow's study provides perhaps the clearest account in the English language of the connections between anti-slavery arguments and those pertaining to the appropriate place of "Aborigines" in the global community.

Snow included sections covering how the governments of France, Italy, the Netherlands, Germany, Spain, Portugal, and Japan governed Aborigines under their rule, though he devoted his most detailed assessments to the colonial policies of Great Britain and the United States. In referring to the early years of US history, he noted that Presidents "Washington, Adams, and Jefferson had pursued a policy of dealing with the Indian tribes in the Northwest Territory on such an elevated plane that Indian 'treaties' came near to recognizing the tribes in so-called 'Indian country' as States." In the peace settlement ending the War of 1812, the British negotiators had pointed to these treaties, arguing without success that they could form the basis for "the recognition of the collective tribes as a native state."[13] Clearly this passage refers to the conception of Aboriginal Dominion sought by Tecumseh and some of his allies and like-minded officials in the colonial administration of Great Britain. It referred to the geopolitical view that motivated Tecumseh to mobilize the soldiers of the Indian Confederacy to defend Canada and the domain of the Bowl with One Spoon from annexation by the United States.

The policy of Indian removal, Snow explained, transformed the character of US relations with Indian peoples. The plan "to colonize the Indians in the Western Territory" was closely related to parallel initiatives aimed at freeing Negro slaves and sending them to settlements in western Africa.[14] Although the US government is said to have given some thought to sending its own colonial governors to oversee the settlements of former slaves, "on account of the Monroe Doctrine [the US government] denied itself sovereignty over them and asserted their independence under its patronage." The establishment of the African republic of Liberia, he mused, "is plainly not one of the relationship of a civilized state to aboriginal tribes, since the inhabitants, though of aboriginal descent, are civilized."[15]

This overview was not based on a desire to contribute to a dramatic remaking of world order consistent with the principles articulated by Woodrow Wilson in his contention that all *peoples* have the right of self-determination. Instead, Snow gave an approving nod to the continuation and extension of the underlying assumptions supporting the mode of imperial rule that had come into fashion during the culminating years of the Victorian era.[16] His text reported approvingly on the legal principles used to divide humanity into two classes. The "citizens" of "civilized States" constituted one side of the equation. Those deemed to be the members of "uncivilized aboriginal tribes" – the "merciless savages" referred to in the Declaration of Independence – constituted the other category. Snow's research seemed to point the United States towards an expanded role in the colonizing work of the "civilized sovereignties." His detailed discussions of the laws, policies, and jurisprudence emanating from the US government's relationship with Indigenous peoples within its own borders seems calculated to demonstrate that the United States had its own legacy to draw on as a colonial power. The underlying agenda seems geared to preparing the United States for more collaborative partnerships with the other imperial powers following the First World War.

Snow devoted particular attention to the role of the United States in bringing about the creation of the so-called Congo Free State as a sovereign polity that, between 1885 and 1908, was effectively run as a personal proprietorship belonging to King Leopold II of Belgium. According to Snow, Leopold's Congolese realm was founded on the principle that "the law of nations" could "recognize as a State a private association of civilized persons actually exercising a persuasive sovereignty over aboriginal tribes in Africa."[17] This private association emerged from the Brussels Geographical Conference of 1876. The meeting brought together an international array of diplomats and researchers who shared an interest in opening Central Africa to international trade and scientific investigation. The outcome was the organization of an umbrella committee whose political arm was the International Congo Association (ICA). The president of the ICA was King Leopold, who, according to Snow, essentially became the proxy of the United States in implementing its design to place the Indigenous peoples of the Congo River basin under the guardianship and tutelage of a new form of international trusteeship. In advancing this course, the US government sought to counter a competing initiative by the governments of Great Britain and Portugal. Snow highlighted the depth of the US government's conviction that it had compelling claims to control the course of colonial enterprise in much of Central and Western Africa. These claims were based on the extensive explorations and "discoveries" made in equatorial Africa in the mid-1870s by a US citizen of British ancestry, Henry M. Stanley.[18] By giving its support to the ICA as the legitimate government of the region, the US government believed it could expand its influence into this vast domain without violating the anti-imperial rhetoric of the Monroe Doctrine. The official aim of US authorities was to "avoid entangling alliances" and "interference in the affairs of other nations."

On behalf of King Leopold's ICA, Stanley negotiated a series of treaties with Indigenous peoples of the Congo Basin. The point of these treaties was to strengthen Leopold's claim that he had obtained the sanction of the Indigenous peoples to exercise his own jurisdiction in the region. In seeking to give these transactions some historical context, Snow pointed to earlier precedents set by the Northwest Ordinance. This enactment reproduced in 1787, in the context of US federalism, many principles similar to those first codified by King George in 1763 in his Royal Proclamation establishing the constitutional framework for the governance of a dramatically expanded British imperial America. The Congressional enactment of 1787 was a key instrument in the genesis of what Snow characterized elsewhere as the "Federal Empire" of the United States. The author emphasized the Ordinance's declaration that the US government would continue Europe's missionary drive to bring "civilization" to the Indigenous peoples residing in the US government's first federal colony.[19]

In September 1885, US president Grover Cleveland wrote to King Leopold: "I have the great satisfaction in congratulating your Majesty on being called to the chief magistracy of the newly formed Government ... of assuming the title of Sovereign of the Independent State of Congo." Leopold's status as the Congo's effective sovereign was viewed by the US government as being entirely separate from Leopold's role as sovereign of Belgium. His identity as the Congo's chief magistrate belonged to him in an "exclusively personal" capacity. "Under your majesty's good government," enthused Cleveland, "the peoples of the Congo Basin will advance in the paths of civilization."[20] According to the US president, Belgium "was not a colonizing power." This perception helped King Leopold put himself forward as a trustee of the "civilized States" who were united in their intention to provide a benevolent reign of domineering tutorship over a large confederacy of Indigenous peoples. "It was doubtless felt," wrote Snow, "that an international agency to civilize Africa would be more likely to appeal to the public as truly international if it had its foundation in Belgium, than if it were founded in one of the colonizing countries."[21]

Snow's text has nothing to say about the outcome of Leopold's role as the sovereign and chief magistrate of the Independent State of Congo. Under Leopold's rule, the Congo Basin became the site of what John H. Bodley has described as "some of the worst frontier violence in modern times."[22] The country was looted on a vast scale, especially by concessionaires whose corporate operations lay at the genocidal core of what became known as "the Leopoldian system." The central dynamo of this system was a regime of organized violence aimed at coercively extracting labour from the Congo's Indigenous peoples. Local populations were systematically terrorized into performing the many tasks aimed at extracting the lucrative sap from many millions of rubber trees indigenous to the area. A common method of punishment for real or imagined infractions in this brutal regime of forced labour involved executions or cutting off the hands of Congolese workers and their families. As US traveller Richard Harding Davis saw it in 1908, "the land and the people are [Leopold's] private property ... The natives he did not kill he made slaves."[23]

The Leopoldian system was closely connected to the dawning of the culture of the automobile in North America and Europe. The expanding market for tires led to an expansion in the demand for rubber, the main staple product that flowed in huge quantities from the concessionary companies' plantations. During the height of this reign of terror, a proverb was whispered throughout the Upper Congo Basin. It proclaimed, "Botofi bo le iwa" – rubber is death.[24] E.D. Morel, the English founder of the Congo Reform Movement, estimated that "ten million victims would be a very conservative estimate" of the number of lives lost under the Leopoldian system."[25] One of the first observers to chronicle the systemic violations of human rights in the Congo was the Black American journalist and historian George Washington Williams. He was at first taken in by King Leopold's propaganda about the great deeds being done to advance the civilization of the Indigenous peoples of the Congo River basin. When Williams wangled his way under Leopold's patronage to see the African country for himself, however, he quickly realized the extent of the tragedy before him. He called attention to a number of abuses in a short document he labelled, simply, *Open Letter*. It was widely reproduced, distributed, and published. Williams then expanded his account in a document entitled *A Report upon the Congo-State and Country to the President of the Republic of the United States*. In the *Letter*, Williams described what he saw in the Congo as "crimes against humanity."

With this comment, the African American missionary introduced this fundamental concept in international law. In observing first hand the crimes of colonialism in Central Africa, Williams put his finger on a concept that would become prominent in the trials of the Nazi war criminals at Nuremberg several decades later.[26] It is an idea whose full meaning is still being discovered as the scope as well as the lethal force and complexity of international crimes continues to grow in the twenty-first century.

The tragedy that befell the Indigenous peoples of Congo was re-enacted in the treatment of the Putumayo Indians in the Peruvian districts of the Amazon Basin. As in the Congo, the Aboriginal workers in Amazonia's rubber plantations were often subjected to horrendous brutalities whose terrible extent was proved by the subsequent discovery of mass graves. The brief intervention of the Peruvian judiciary, together with a British parliamentary investigation, led to some limits on the exploitation of Indian workers.[27] Similarly, in the Congo, the lobbying of E.D. Morel and others contributed to its reconstitution in 1908 as a colony of Belgium rather than as the personal fiefdom of King Leopold himself.

Snow's report demonstrates how many of the precedents in the exercise of colonialism in some parts of the world have been employed to justify imperial incursions in other parts of the world. For instance, Snow makes clear how the negotiation of treaties with the Indigenous peoples of North America was seen by Henry Stanley as a precedent for his negotiation of treaties with the Indigenous peoples of the Congo Basin. Similarly, Snow demonstrates how the abandonment of treaty making in US Indian policy in 1871 affected broader currents of understanding and practice in the international arena. The effort by the US Congress to abort legislatively the constitutional force in international law of the Royal Proclamation of 1763 and its own Northwest Ordinance of 1787 encouraged the other imperial powers to veer away from the principle that Indigenous peoples possess Aboriginal titles in their ancestral territories. Snow's *Question of Aborigines* is thus an important primary document in the Aboriginal history of the law, philosophy, and convenient fictions of colonialism. This publication, like Snow's earlier scholarly work, stands as a powerful contradiction to the myth that the United States was founded in opposition to imperialism. Snow's work demonstrates, rather, that the United States was first conceived as a sub-empire of its British imperial parent and subsequently as a federal empire based on the internalization of its own sovereign scheme for the territorial acquisition from, and governance of, Indigenous peoples.

FROM THE US ASSAULT ON THE REGIME OF QUEEN LILIUOKALANI TO THE RISE OF THE INTERNATIONAL NICKEL COMPANY

The pressure to absorb Hawaii into US territory developed quickly in the 1890s. This acquisitiveness contrasted sharply with the determination expressed by President John Tyler in 1842 that the United States desired "no peculiar advantage, no exclusive control over the Hawaiian government, but is content with its independent existence." The US government thereupon committed itself not "to take possession of the islands, colonize them, and subvert the native Government."[28]

The English explorer Captain James Cook had called the Hawaiian archipelago the Sandwich Islands. Given Cook's role in extending Europe's geographical knowledge to this realm, the same doctrine of "discovery" used to justify, for instance, the British colonization of Australia could have been invoked to make Hawaii a full-fledged British possession. The US determination in 1842 not to "subvert the native Government" needs to be understood in that light. By advocating local self-rule, the US government was declaring these strategically placed islands in the centre of the Pacific Ocean off bounds not only to its own ownership but also to that of Great Britain. As with Latin America, the United States chose to exercise its influence on the Sandwich Islands throughout most of the nineteenth century through a range of powerful but informal means. During most of this period the governance of Hawaiians citizens – the Kanaka Maoli, as they called themselves – was not vested in some Pacific version of those Creole regimes of Latin America which were dominated by groups who self-consciously situated their cultural and ancestral roots primarily in European heritage. After 1810 the Aboriginal Hawaiians found sufficient unity and political will among themselves to vest sovereign authority over their islands in their own version of monarchical government.

Puritan evangelists from the United States gained particularly strong influence over some of the Hawaiian monarchs. That rise in influence unfolded over the course of a century in which imported diseases foreign to the immune systems of the Kanaka Maoli decimated their populations. Like other immigrant communities in the colonized world, some of the Puritan newcomers to Hawaii exploited this disaster to expand and consolidate their positions of power and wealth. The children of the first wave of missionaries from New England, for instance, were inclined to exploit their growing influence at court in Honolulu to modify the land-tenure system. By these methods they gained extensive private holdings for the establishment of sugar cane and fruit plantations – and so established a number of family fortunes. Some of the resulting agricultural conglomerates, including the Castle and Cooke empire, went on to expand their operations into the Philippines and elsewhere throughout the Pacific islands. This expansion was one part of an elaborate process of military and corporate cooperation throughout the region that, in later years, would result in the Pacific Ocean being nicknamed "the American Lake."[29]

The last monarch of Hawaii was Queen Liliuokalani.[30] She took over the throne from her brother, King Kalakaua, in 1891. In her memoirs, Queen Liliuokalani described the workings of the Hawaiian royalty throughout a century of rapid transition, an era when Christianity, foreign commerce, and the growing commercial and military importance of the Pacific Ocean impinged on the lives of many Native Hawaiians. The monarchy seemed calculated to afford Hawaiians some degree of access to the high tables of international diplomacy during an era when access was difficult to obtain for any polity whose constituents were not of White European background. Queen Liliuokalani had personally befriended Queen Victoria and participated as a frequent guest and hostess in the life of the British royal family, with whom her British husband also had close connections. She devoted similar attentiveness to the high officialdom of the United States, including President Grover Cleveland and his wife, whom she visited at the White House. Queen Liliouokalani and her relatives walked a fine line between the government of the United States and the government of Great Britain, whose influence on her island nation was formidable during a century when Britannia was the unrivalled naval ruler of the world's sea lanes.

When the Hawaiian princess returned from Queen Victoria's Golden Jubilee in 1887, Queen Liliuokalani quickly became aware of what she deemed to be a conspiracy to overthrow the monarchy. It came in the form of a document soon dubbed "the Bayonet Constitution" which limited the power of the monarch. It disenfranchised many Native Hawaiians, even as it expanded the base of the executive power available to those Cabinet ministers whose family roots lay largely in the United States.[31] The wording of the preamble made clear the nature of the interests that the new law was intended to advance. Adapting the most famous phrase from the US Declaration of Independence, the Bayonet Constitution referred to "certain inalienable rights, among which are life, liberty, and the right of acquiring, possessing, and protecting property."[32] In looking back on these developments, Queen Liliuokalani wrote, "For many years our sovereigns had welcomed the advice of, and given full representations in their governments to American residents who had cast their lot with our people, and established industries on our island." With the passage of time, however, some of the wealthiest of these residents became greedy "with their love of power" as they "acquired titles to lands through the simplicity of our people and their ignorance of values of the new land laws." The wealthiest Americans in Hawaii, who made up what Queen Liliuokalani referred to as "the down-town party," had become preoccupied with schemes "for aggrandizing themselves still further, or avoiding the obligations they had incurred to us."[33]

When Queen Liliuokalani came to power in 1891, she attempted to reverse many of the decisions made by her predecessor, King Kalakaua, whom Stephen Kinzer has described as "the planters' puppet monarch."[34] The depth of Queen Liliuokalani's attachment to the interests and rights of the Kanaka Maoli alarmed the dominant group pf planters, but especially lawyer Lorrin A. Thurston. In 1892 he founded the Annexation Club and put himself at its head. Its purpose was to attach Hawaii to the United States. To advance this plan, the US ambassador to Hawaii, John L. Stevens, arranged for Thurston to meet in Washington with President Benjamin Harrison – the grandson of Tecumseh's nemesis, William Benjamin Harrison. On his return to Hawaii, Thurston accused Queen Liliuokalani of acting "illegally and unconstitutionally" to advance policies that were "revolutionary and treasonable in character."[35] This showdown culminated in a US-backed coup d'état in 1893. At the end of US guns, a self-declared provisional government was installed, led by Sanford Ballard Dole.[36] The power of the new regime was displayed through a show of US naval power and the landing of marines in Honolulu to overawe the Kanaka Maoli.

Without any sanction from the Indigenous people, Dole's US-backed provisional government arranged for the full incorporation of Hawaii into the United States as a federal territory – in other words, as a federal colony modelled on the status of Washington's first colonial extension, the North West Territory north of the Ohio River. Queen Liliuokalani's memoirs seethe with a sense of barely contained outrage that the Christian settlers with whom her people had generously shared their islands could have so ruthlessly betrayed their Hawaiian hosts:

It had not entered our hearts to believe these friends and allies from the United States, even with all their foreign affinities, would ever go so far as to absolutely overthrow our form of government, seize our nation by the throat, and pass it over to an alien power. And while we sought by peaceful means to maintain the dignity of the throne, and to advance national feeling among native people, we never sought to rob any citizen, wherever born, of either property, franchise, or social standing.[37]

Referring to the doctrine by which the United States to this very day justifies its claims to its territorial base on the mainland as well to Hawaii, the Queen reflected, "Perhaps there is a kind of right, depending upon the precedents of all ages, and known as the 'Right of Conquest,' under which robbers and marauders may establish themselves in possession of whatsoever they are strong enough to ravish from their fellows." She pointedly added, "I will not pretend to decide how far civilization and Christianity have outlawed it."[38] Appealing to the conscience especially of her readers in the United States, Queen Liliuokalani asked, "Is the American Republic of States to degenerate, and become a colonizer and a land-grabber? ... Is such an ambition laudable? Is such a departure from its established principles patriotic or politic?"[39] Although she suggested that the robbery of her people's country by right of conquest was a departure for the US government, she reversed this position when she exclaimed: "The people of the Islands have no voice in determining their future, but are virtually relegated to the condition of the aborigines of the American continent."[40]

The fate that befell the Aboriginal regime of the Sandwich Islands, long an ally of the British imperial government, is reminiscent of the fate experienced by the members of the Indian Confederacy of Canada shortly after the martyrdom of Tecumseh. In both instances, the British imperial government abandoned its Aboriginal allies and permitted the US government to place valuable new territories under its jurisdiction. In both cases, the transition of Indigenous peoples from a regime of alliance with the British to subjugation under US rule advanced the extinguishment of Aboriginal rights and titles. The outlines of many larger patterns of historical change are illustrated, encapsulated, or suggested in the transition of these islands from the exclusive domain of the Kanaka Maoli, to the Sandwich Islands, to a federal territory of the United States, to a full-fledged US state in 1959. Certainly one of these patterns finds its centre in the tensions and convergences linking the imperial history of Great Britain with the rise of the formal and informal American empire.

The British abandonment of the Crown's Aboriginal allies in Hawaii forms part of a prolonged and elaborate process in the transfer of power from Anglo-America's old empire to the new Imperial Republic. Beginning with the transfer of much of Canada to the United States in the Treaty of Paris in 1783, the world's pre-eminent imperial power gradually handed over parts of its territorial claims to feed and encourage the steady expansion of the new polity. The Indigenous peoples of Canada and their allies condemned the British government for its massive betrayal in 1783 of the Crown's Indian allies. This transfer to the US government of territory north of the Ohio River was of dubious legality because the region in question was part of the huge reserve created for the Indians by King George in the Royal Proclamation in 1763. The status of this land as a protected Indian Country had been reiterated in the terms of the treaty made at Fort Stanwix in 1768.

How could Great Britain transfer to the United States territories that were not fully its own to hand over? What was the legitimacy of this transfer between the "White nations" of Anglo-America without Aboriginal consent? This question would resonate for decades to come. It became a significant factor in an era of military instability among Great Britain, the United States, and the Indian Confederacy culminating in the War of 1812.[41] In that clash Washington's nascent war machine extended federal military support to the notorious Indian fighters of Kentucky and Tennessee to pursue their human prey into Canada. Washington's provision of military backing to the most ruthless class of Indian fighters in the United States can be seen as the final chapter of the civil war that divided British North America beginning in 1776. It applied with concerted lethal force the act of criminalizing the merciless Indian savages as described in the American Declaration of Independence.

In 1846 the British government continued to back away from its imperial role in North America by agreeing to cede the Oregon Country south of the forty-ninth parallel to the United States. The Crown claims to that contested region were based primarily on the prolific commercial activities in the region of North West Company and Hudson's Bay Company fur traders. Along with the influence of the predominantly Roman Catholic missionaries who sometimes accompanied them, the Canadian traders helped to set the predominant motifs of the initial surges of globalization in the Columbia River basin. For a generation after the withdrawal of the Crown's claim to an area covering present-day Washington and Oregon as well as much of Idaho and Montana, those influences continued to affect patterns of indigenous resistance to the sovereign assertions of the ascendant United States. It is no accident, for instance, that some of the leaders of the Aboriginal resistance movement in the region, including the Yakima freedom fighter Kamiakin, were committed Roman Catholics.

The willingness of the governors of the old British Empire to allow the governors of the US federal empire to take added geopolitical ground was similarly reflected in the former's tacit sanction of the internationally strategic transfer of Alaska from Russia to the United States in 1867. That unopposed transfer was interpreted in some circles as a signal that the British government was inclined to allow Canada to be absorbed over time into the US republic that henceforth boxed in what remained of British North America on both its southern and northwestern boundaries. Indeed, to some in Great Britain, it seemed that the continuing exercise of Crown sovereignty throughout the northern half of North America was misguided and that the Crown's on-going jurisdiction in Canada created the basis for many unnecessary irritants that negatively affected Britain's relations with the most important polity of the English-speaking people's real empire. This view was articulated, for instance, by Charles Wentworth Dilke, who argued, "In all history I see nothing stranger than the narrowness of mind that led us to see Canada as a piece of England and in America a hostile country ... For purposes of commerce and civilization, America is a truer colony of Britain than is Canada."

For Dilke, and for those whose viewpoints he shared or won over, the outcome of the civil war in British North America did not really alienate the United States from that society's fundamentally English character. In his widely read book outlining his reflections on a global tour in 1868 of English-speaking communities, Dilke commented, "America offers the English race the moral dictatorship of the globe, by ruling mankind through Saxon institutions and the English tongue." He continued:

In America the people of the world are being fused together, but they run into an English mould: Alfred's law and Chaucer's tongue are theirs, whether they would or no. There are men who say that Britain in her age will claim the glory of having planted greater Englands across the seas. They fail to perceive that she has done more than plantations of her own – that she has imposed her institutions upon off-shoots of Germany, of Ireland, of Scandinavia, and of Spain. Through America, England is speaking to the world.[42]

Dilke's imagery of "Greater Britain" reflects a vital aspect of the psychological landscape influencing the continuing expansionism of "Anglo-

America" from the era of the American Revolution right up to the present.[43] Although the issue of slavery and the contested rights and titles of Indigenous peoples were subjects of tension in the era of the emergence of the United States from the British Empire, the British imperial government, when put to the test, repeatedly chose political expediency over the defence of human rights as the animating principle in its relations with the emerging superpower. In return, the United States afforded British business a number of concessions, including the latitude to extend the free-trade empire of English commerce deeply into the political economy of Latin America over a long period of time.[44]

The change in the international status of the Hawaiian lands, therefore, was part of much broader patterns of geopolitical adjustment. Like the transfer of much of Canada, British North America, and Mexico to the United States in 1783, 1846, and 1848, the altered legal status of Hawaii signalled a willingness on the part of the British superpower to sanction and assist the rise of the federal empire of the United States. In annexing Hawaii, the United States obtained jurisdiction over territory with obvious global importance as the site of one of the planet's most strategically situated naval bases. To this day the US naval centre at Pearl Harbor in Hawaii is the command headquarters for the activities of the US fleet over almost half the oceanic waterways of the planet. The history of the US acquisition of Hawaii should be considered in connection with the Japanese attack on Pearl Harbor in 1941. The US colonization and annexation of Queen Liliuokalani's former realm also provides an important context for the events of September 11, 2001, and the proposal advanced a year earlier for the invasion of Iraq by the war hawks who joined forces in the Project for a New American Century. The authors of the PNAC report, *Rebuilding America's Defenses*, famously anticipated the difficulty in preparing public opinion in the United States for such an invasion in the Middle East, "absent some catastrophic and catalyzing event – like a new Pearl Harbor."[45]

It was no coincidence that the annexation of Hawaii coincided with the period when the US Navy began to join the navies of the other imperial powers in asserting military influence over the world's sea lanes. In the decades immediately following the US Civil War, the importance placed by the US government on sea power sharply declined. During this brief period the main military preoccupation of the United States was on fighting and pacifying Indians throughout its recently acquired territories in the western districts of North America. That land-bound orientation began to change in 1884, when Commodore Stephen B. Luce succeeded in his campaign to found a US Naval College. In 1886 Luce was replaced by Alfred Thayer Mahan, who, four years later, published *The Influence of Sea Power upon History*. That book, together with a steady stream of Mahan's subsequent publications, helped to initiate and sustain what became a formidable political campaign to build up the US Navy along with an effective merchant marine.[46] In following the lead of its British imperial parent by establishing a strong and effective navy, the conditions were being created for the US government to move into the vacuum of power that would, in future years, be left behind by the demise of European empires.

A key to securing the larger US role in the world of transoceanic commerce lay in the building of what became the Panama Canal.[47] As with the Suez Canal, a French company began the project. That company initially competed with a US initiative to build a shipping canal across Nicaragua. Under pressure from a campaign orchestrated by New York lawyer William Nelson Cromwell, the US government shifted its support to the French plan. Cromwell was a key figure in the rise of Sullivan and Cromwell, the Wall Street law firm that would prove adept in quietly administering the flow of investment, expertise, and technology to German industry from the top echelons of US capitalism in the era of Hitler's political ascent.[48] Once the US government purchased control of the Panama Canal project, it sent agents and money to assist a separatist movement in the northern reaches of what was then Colombia. President Theodore Roosevelt tipped the balance of power in favour of the separatist cause when he sent a US naval squadron to promote Panama's secession from Colombia in 1903. The new country of Panama emerged to serve the US objective of controlling the global flow of trade between the Atlantic and the Pacific oceans. Panama's leaders agreed to a ninety-nine-year lease giving the United States almost a century of near-absolute control over the new canal zone, which began its career as a shipping corridor in 1914.

The decision to build up the US Navy led to a number of changes in the further industrialization of the US political economy. The building of giant American war ships, for instance, created a large demand for nickel – the main ingredient in the alloys used to create hard metals. These hard metals were tooled to form the physical basis of armament, bullets, missiles, and, later, jet engines, space vehicles, and the like. As the strategic value of nickel increased, the planners of the rising military-industrial complex had to deal with the fact that there were no indigenous deposits of nickel in the United States. The world's main mine for this key mineral was discovered in the Canadian Shield during the construction of the Canadian Pacific Railway. The community of Sudbury, Ontario, developed to exploit first copper and then nickel. One theory holds that the abundant mineral wealth of the Sudbury Basin has its origins in a vast meteor that hit the region about two billion years ago. The increasing importance of Sudbury's nickel deposit led to the establishment of the International Nickel Company in Camden, New Jersey, in 1902. In 1916 the dominion government extended a corporate charter to the International Nickel Company of Canada, an innovation that was integral to the evolving complexities of transnational finance connected to the rising military-industrial complex of the United States. [49]

The trend towards the globalization of the informal American empire was not limited to mining operations. In the early twentieth century the Dominion of Canada provided one of the first frontiers where many US companies made their initial jump across an international boundary to set up manufacturing plants under the sovereign authority of foreign law. As part of Prime Minister John A. Macdonald's National Policy, the Canadian government had followed the US example by creating a tariff wall to protect the establishment of an indigenous industrial base. In Canada, much of that industrialization was undertaken by subsidiaries of US firms which exported their patents and manufacturing technology northward. In this fashion, the multinational careers of many US corporations began in the part of North America where Crown jurisdiction had not been severed by the outcome of the American Revolution. This trend developed to the point where Canada became the jumping-off point for the expansion of many US companies that moved their operations first into the British Empire and then into broader fields of international commerce. In this way Canada acquired a new role in mediating the continuing growth and informal coherence of Anglo-America.

Most of the US investments in the industrialization of the Canadian economy were directed at new technologies, including the production of industrial chemicals, automobiles, and all manner of electrical infrastructure and gadgetry. Although a heavy flow of British investment also rushed into Canada, most of it in the early twentieth century was conservatively directed at the overbuilding of the railway system, including the construction of a second transcontinental rail network.[50] The relegation of the most dynamic areas of future industrial growth in Canada largely to the industrial innovation of US enterprise had enormous implications for the future. Companies like Dow, Dupont, General Electric, Ford, and General Motors gained wider markets, enabling them to move even more decisively in developing the research, production, marketing, and distribution techniques for the mass replication of those technologies that would prove so influential in making the twentieth century into the American century. The managers and chief executives of these multinational firms had to learn how to infiltrate the political and legal cultures of diverse countries on the frontiers of their growing commercial empires. Most commonly the new generation of US-based multinational corporation moved outward into Canada and Latin America, and then to Europe and the worldwide colonial holdings of the European powers.

As in Hawaii, the treatment of Indigenous peoples in Canada represented a sensitive barometer of the shifting balance of power between the constitutionally centred empire of Great Britain and the commercially centred empire of the United States. Throughout much of Canada's earlier history, its defence against US annexation depended in large measure on the viability of the fur trade and the willingness of Indigenous peoples to oppose the absorption of their Aboriginal territories into the Imperial Republic. Accordingly, the remaining Crown titles on the North America mainland came to rest on the original titles of the Indigenous peoples. The innate conservatism of both kinds of Old World societies, one rooted in the

imperial title of the British Empire and the other in the Aboriginal title of
Indigenous peoples, was deeply challenged by the rise of the idea of the
United States and the Western Hemisphere as the launching site of a New
World Order.

During the era of the War of 1812, for instance, entrepreneurs of
the commercial empire of the St Lawrence equated "the protection of
Indian Rights and the Security of the Canadas."[51] They referred to "the
blended Interests of His Majesty's Canadian Subjects and His faithful
Indian Allies."[52] "The Indians are the Only Allies who can aught avail in
the defence of the Canadas," argued James McGill, a leading trader in
the North West Company whose contributions to Montreal's cultural life
are suggested in the name of that city's famous university. Referring to
Canada's Indian allies, McGill added, "They have the same interest as us,
and alike are objects of American subjugation, if not extermination."[53]
As the intercultural commerce and diplomacy of the mercantilistic fur
trade gave way to the capitalist culture of mining, railway development,
industrialization, urbanization, and the commercial cultivation of agricultural monocultures, Indigenous peoples were increasing characterized as
obstructions in the way of development rather than as allies of the Crown.
They were increasingly treated not as valued commercial and military partners but as wards of the government who should be contained and isolated
until they either disappeared or were assimilated legally and culturally
into the empire of possessive individualism.

A report describing a Crown treaty negotiation in 1850 with a number
of Ojibwa bands in the Canadian Shield is reflective of the ethos guiding the move away from the Old World constitutional empire of Great
Britain towards the New World commercial empire of the United States.
The Ojibwa are part of a larger complex of linguistically and culturally
related peoples who refer to themselves as Anishinabek. The negotiations
covered a vast region north of the upper Great Lakes, part of modern-day
northern Ontario. This region includes territory whose nickel resources
provided the crucial ingredient for the hard-steel weaponry at the technological core of the emerging superpower's military-industrial complex.
In asking the Indigenous peoples to accept very small payments to give up
their Aboriginal title to lands that would later host the operations of the
International Nickel Company, the Crown's treaty commissioner, William
Benjamin Robinson, observed: "The lands now ceded are notoriously barren and sterile, and in all probability will never be settled except in a few
localities by mining companies, whose establishment among the Indians,
instead of being prejudicial, would prove of great benefit as they would
afford a market for any things they may have to sell, and bring provisions
and stores of all kinds among them at reasonable prices."[54]

Variations on this argument, a forerunner of the trickle-down theory
of economics, were to be recycled frequently. Where Christian evangelization was formerly advanced as the primary justification of European

colonialism, the allure of "markets" and of "reasonable prices" provided all-purpose rationales for the neo-colonialism of the American empire. Robinson's explanation of his transaction with the Ojibwa embodies, therefore, a fairly typical statement of the main justification for the globalization of capitalism. The Indigenous peoples were told that their economic prospects would improve by ceding their Aboriginal title and handing over their rights to the region's abundant natural resources. Even those stripped of their Aboriginal inheritance would, it was claimed, be rendered more successful by moving aside to allow the privatized industrialization of their ancestral lands. Throughout the course of the Columbian conquests, few peoples in the colonized world have escaped some variation of the Faustian bargain presented to the Ojibwa in the negotiation of the Robinson treaties.

NEW VARIATIONS ON OLD FORMS OF IMPERIAL AND ANTI-IMPERIAL GLOBALIZATION

In 1898 the US government deployed its instruments of state violence to force Spain to end its imperial rule in Cuba, Puerto Rica, and the Philippine Islands. With the Spanish-American War, the United States continued the process of absorbing the territory and influence of the dwindling Spanish Empire. This process began in 1821 when the US government acquired formal control of Florida, a territory where the Indigenous peoples had fought a protracted campaign of resistance in alliance with the imperial forces of Spain. In 1845 the United States acquired Texas after its inhabitants had briefly declared their sovereign independence from Mexico. The US government then directed the full force of its federal army at the main bastions of Mexican military power, thereby securing formal jurisdiction over California and the accompanying regions north of the Rio Grande River. This incorporation of much of Mexico into the federal empire of the United States was confirmed in 1848 through the Treaty of Guadalupe Hidalgo.

In deploying its armed forces to acquire through conquest the northern portion of the former New Spain, the US government built on a process it had started in the opening years of the nineteenth century when it provided overt and covert support to those Creole resistance movements whose inspirational theorist and general was Simón Bolívar. Sometimes dubbed the George Washington of Latin America, Bolívar attempted to breathe unity and resolve into a larger constituency of Hispanic freedom fighters. With US support, the Latino forces of the Bolivarian revolution opposed the continuing reign of Spain and Portugal in Central and South America.

Not surprisingly, the United States ended up as a major beneficiary of the termination of Spanish rule in Mexico. US president James Monroe issued his self-named Doctrine in 1823 declaring that all the Western Hemisphere was henceforth closed to formal colonization by all European governments except that of Great Britain, the polity that had lent international legitimacy to the United States with its grant of sovereign authority in the Treaty of Paris of 1783. Without the continuation of the British imperial presence in northern North America as a check against the annexationist enthusiasms of US Manifest Destiny, Canada would not have survived as a polity with its own distinct system of federal sovereignty.

The expansion by the United States into the vacuum of authority left by the shrinking imperialism of Spain renewed a process that had its origins in British North America's earlier ingestions of New Sweden, New Netherlands, and New France. The emergence of the United States from the top end of this feeding chain of colonial powers continued after the Second World War, when the triumphant capitalist superpower globalized its imperial personality. With Japan in ruins and Europe fractured and bankrupt from its own indigenous version of continental civil war, the command structure of the informal American empire essentially took over the direction of much of Europe's worldwide system of colonies, protectorates, and zones of indirect rule. During the second half of the twentieth century, the Pentagon and the headquarters of the Central Intelligence Agency in Langley, Virginia, replaced the British Colonial Office in the minds of many as key symbols of imperial manipulation. The anti-communist doctrine governing the US-led side of the Cold War provided the propagandistic cover for the elaboration of a transnational empire of monopoly capitalism. The resulting US *imperium* appeared briefly to be unassailable during the decade bookmarked by the demise of the Soviet Union in 1992 and the Anglo-American invasion of Iraq in 2003

The Spanish-American War had its formal origins in the US response to the concerted efforts of Cuban freedom fighters to assert their nation's independence from Spain. The leader of this independence movement was José Martí, an inspirational figure in the genesis of the larger global movement for decolonization.[55] Stimulated by a jingoistic US media, and especially by those influential outlets controlled by press baron William Randoph Hearst, US forces intervened to "free Cuba." The sinking of the USS *Maine* in Havana Harbor, the event that initiated the Spanish-American War, is widely viewed today as a US-manufactured media event. The intent of this classic false-flag operation was to whip up public hostility towards the designated enemy. The US casualties incurred in confronting Spanish forces within Cuba were relatively light. As Stephen Kinzer observed, "Just 385 Americans had been killed in action, barely more than Sioux Indians had killed at Little Big Horn in the country's last military engagement, twenty-two years before."[56]

Theodore Roosevelt, the secretary of the US Navy, played a major role in preparing the US Asiatic Squadron, then based in Japan, for the conquest of the Philippine Islands once the US war with Spain began. In the weeks before the sinking of the USS *Maine*, which killed 260 US sailors, Roosevelt ordered Commodore George Dewey to move his ships to Hong Kong. Within hours of the formal beginning of the Spanish-American War, Dewey directed his war vessels to move southward in order to engage the antiquated Spanish fleet. That engagement took place in the waters around Manila Bay. The clash at sea gave the US Navy a major victory.[57] According to historian Samuel Eliot Morison, the attack on imperial Spain in both the Cuban and Philippine theatres made for a war "which America entered upon as lightheartedly as if it were with a tribe of Indians."[58]

After the victory at sea, the US government quickly acquired direct imperial control over the Philippines. The subsequent story of US relations with Cuba, however, is somewhat different. From the onset of the Spanish-American War, US officials declared that they had no intention of annexing their island neighbour. They had no clear plan to repeat in Cuba the same kind of scenario that led to their incorporation of Hawaii and northern Mexico into the territory of the United States. In its declaration of war, Congress stipulated, "The USA hereby disclaims any disposition or intention to exercise sovereignty, jurisdiction, or control of [Cuba] except for pacification thereof, and asserts its determination, when that is accomplished, to leave the government and control of the island to the people."[59] In spite of this statement of intent, however, the people and government of the United States soon faced in Cuba, as in virtually every other milieu where they have intervened militarily, the central contradiction embedded at the core of their federal polity.[60] This inconsistency involves the dual personality of the United States as an "Imperial Republic," to use the term coined by Fred Anderson and Andrew Cayton.[61] In orienting itself to the world in this paradoxical way, the United States became simultaneously the opponent and agent of that particular thrust of imperial conquest that began with Europe's "discovery" and subsequent invention of America.

The opponents of the Spanish-American War were characterized as "anti-imperialists."[62] Among them was pundit and novelist Mark Twain. He alleged that the United States had fought the Spanish Empire "to conquer, not to redeem."[63] Another anti-imperialist was Samuel Gompers, one of the founders of the association of national craft unions known as the American Federation of Labor. Gompers's opposition to the war was part of a whole series of policies that would place the AFL in league with some of the more reactionary elements of the US power structure. Gompers feared that the extension of US jurisdiction would result in the flooding of the labour market. He predicted that the annexation of the Philippines would result in a widening influx of immigration of "the Chinese, Negritos, and the Malays."[64] Those opposed to the military annexation of the Philippines used the classical argument that this assertion of US power contradicted the fundamental principles on which the US republic was founded. Among those who pointed to the American Declaration of Independence as a prohibition on the development of a US colonial policy was the Republican senator from Massachusetts, George Frisbie Hoar. He argued that any subordination of peoples under the authority of the United States without their consent marked a "trampling ... on our own great Charter, which recognizes alike the liberty and dignity of individual manhood."[65]

John W. Burgess, a founder of the School of Political Science at Columbia University in New York, is widely recognized as a Social Darwinists who helped prepare the intellectual climate in the United States for the Spanish-American War. Formerly a graduate student in Germany, Burgess became one of Theodore Roosevelt's professors.[66] Roosevelt's multi-volume history dramatizing the struggle of "the Germanic race" for supremacy over the Indigenous peoples of eastern North America displays the unmistakable mark of Burgess's identification of the "Teutonic nations" as the imagined vanguard of human progress. In his influential text, *Political Science and Comparative Constitutional Law*, Burgess cast in racist language some of the themes presented in slightly more liberal terms by Alpheus Henry Snow in *The Question of Aborigines in the Law and Practice of Nations*. Burgess argued that

the Teutonic nations are particularly endowed with the capacity for establishing nation states, and are especially called to that work; and, therefore, they are entrusted, in the general economy of history, with the mission of conducting the political civilization of the modern world ... by far the largest part of the surface of the globe is inhabited by populations who have not succeeded in establishing civilized states; which have, in fact, no capacity to accomplish such a work; and which must, therefore, remain, in a state of barbarism or semi-barbarism, unless the political nations undertake the work of state organization for them. This condition of things authorizes the political nations not only to answer the call of the unpolitical populations for aid and direction, but also to force organization upon them by any means necessary, in their honest judgment, to accomplish this result. There is no human right to the status of barbarism.[67]

Responding to both the indigenous movement for self-determination and to the exercise of US military force, the Spanish government gave up control of Cuba. At the same time it transferred Puerto Rica and the island of Guam to the colonial proprietorship of the United States. Then, at a peace conference in Paris in the autumn of 1898, the Philippine Islands were added to the war treasure gained by the US Armed Forces through conquest together with a cash payment to the Spanish government of $20 million. Once again, the US officials sat with representatives of the European powers to apportion proprietary control over a significant portion of the globe without any involvement whatsoever of those peoples indigenous to the territories being transferred. Although Cuba was afforded a degree of self-governance in the following years, the extent of informal US control over that island became notorious until the mafia-linked regime of Fulgencio Batista was overthrown in 1959. An indigenous revolutionary movement led by the new president, Fidel Castro, defied the Monroe Doctrine and allied his country with the Soviet Union. While Castro took charge of the Cuban government at home, Dr Ernesto "Che" Guevara moved throughout Africa and Latin America with the aim of infusing the spirit of the Cuban revolution into the liberation struggles of other colonized peoples.[68] Even in the face of unrelenting US animosity, Castro's government has proved incredibly tenacious, outliving its major ally, the Soviet Union.

In justifying the intervention in the Philippines, President William McKinley asserted that "the mission of the United States is one of benevolent assimilation."[69] That intent, however, shifted almost immediately to one of outright repression as the new occupiers faced resistance to their seizure of control over Spain's former colony. The novelist, poet, and doctor José Rizal is widely acknowledged as the primary founder of the indigenous movement for Filipino self-determination.[70] Born in 1861, he was a native speaker of Tagolog, one of many languages indigenous to the culturally diverse societies of the Philippine Islands. Rizal spent half his thirty-five years of life in Europe, where he studied, wrote, and travelled widely, learning about twenty languages in the process. His major literary contribution to the development of his people's sense of unified opposition to imperial rule came in the form of two Spanish-language novels, *Noli Me Tangere* [Don't Touch Me] and *El Filibusterismo*. In these works of introspection and satire, Rizal drew on his deep attachments to his indigenous roots in the Philippines. He was also deeply influenced by anti-imperial, anti-capitalist currents of activism – particularly anarchist idealizations of personal autonomy – that thrived in the major urban centres of Europe in the aftermath of the French crackdown on the Paris commune in 1871.[71]

In developing many of the ideals of Filipino nationalism in Europe's imperial capitals, Rizal followed a trajectory similar to that of José Martí. In preparing for his return to Cuba in 1895 as the leader of the anti-imperialist cause, Martí moved between the Latin-American communities in New York and Florida. Like Martí, Rizal was martyred by agents of imperial Spain. Rizal's execution in the Philippines in 1896 gave impetus to the rise of the Liga Filipina and its outgrowth, the Katipunan, an armed movement led by Andres Bonifacio and Emilio Aguinaldo. Rizal has a place of prominence in many anti-imperial traditions, including that of larger Asia. He was a contemporary of India's Rabindranath Tagore and China's Sun Yat Sen, both of whom shared with him a willingness to draw on the ideas of the West to help their own societies free themselves from the yoke of European domination.

Emilio Aguinaldo led the subsequent round of Filipino resistance to the US occupation of the Philippines. In January 1899 he proclaimed the free government of his people in a document known as the Malalos Constitution. Many of the US forces that opposed the Filipino freedom fighters were veterans of the US Indian wars. This experience coloured the way they saw their new enemy. One US soldier wrote home vowing to fight "until the niggers are killed off like the Indians."[72] The resistance struggle continued until 1902 near the capital, and until 1913 in the largely Muslim south. One of the most determined resistance struggles in the south was that mounted by the Bangsamoro people, the same community that would attract the intervention of US special forces acting in the name of the Global War on Terror. Many tens of thousands of Filipinos were killed by US forces in the early years of the twentieth century in the costly campaign to quell the nascent indigenous nationalism. A thousand American soldiers were killed in action, and another three thousand died from tropical diseases.[73]

The mobilization of US military power in the Philippines was followed by a flurry of US military intervention in Central America and the Caribbean.[74] In 1911 US troops entered Honduras. The following year US Marines intervened in a civil war in Nicaragua. In 1915 several thousands US troops occupied Haiti to quell a popular insurrection there, and the occupying force did not leave for twenty years.[75] In 1914 seven thousand members of US forces seized the port of Veracruz in the eastern coast of Mexico. The government of President Woodrow Wilson followed up this intervention in the Mexican revolution by sending a military contingent in 1916 under General John J. Pershing to quell the fighting forces of Francisco "Pancho" Villa. Like Geronimo's Apaches, Villa's forces had successfully attacked US targets on both sides of the Mexican-US border.[76] Between 1893 and 1916, therefore, a clear trajectory of US military adventurism extended from Hawaii to Cuba to the Philippines to Central America and the Caribbean. This military build-up culminated in the deployment of US troops in the main European theatre in the First World War. In the Second World War, the Philippines fell to Japanese occupation. After regaining jurisdiction over that archipelago, the United States moved it in 1946 from the domain of its formal empire to that of its informal empire. In the words of David Reynolds, "the Americans simply transferred power to the pro-American landed elite which would guarantee American economic rights and military bases."[77]

Along with Malaysia and Indonesia, the Philippines form part of the world's largest and most elaborate complex of islands. And, like them, the Philippines are the Aboriginal home of many diverse Indigenous peoples. On the northern part of the northern island of Luzon, the Igorots, Kalingas, and northern Luzon cultivated wet rice terraces. Elsewhere, the Indigenous peoples have been pushed from fertile lowlands into the more austere mountainous regions as their ancestral lands were pre-empted in favour of the large plantations integral to the economics of both the Spanish and the US regimes. This route of escape into the hill country often proved temporary, as logging operations such as that of the Cellophil Resources Corporation acquired massive concessions to cut trees after the Second World War. As in Central America, the success of the plantation culture in the Philippines has depended not only on forcing Indigenous peoples from their Aboriginal lands but on transforming them from self-sufficient farmers into wage labourers; on replacing production for local consumption with production geared to export; on the transformation of systems of land tenure from those based on communal expressions of Aboriginal title to proprietary regimes favouring corporate interests through private ownership. The system of privatization preferred in both the Spanish and the US empires has been overwhelmingly biased towards the concentration of wealth into tighter and tighter circles of imperial, neo-colonial, and comprador privilege and power.

The European enclosure movement, involving the displacement of many local peasantries to make way for more controlled methods of plant and animal breeding, has been replicated many times throughout the colonized world. Territorial enclosures, the cultivation of agricultural monocultures, and the privatization of land tenure have been reoccurring hallmarks of the empire of possessive individualism on the expanding frontiers of imperial globalization. The repetition of this process has seen Indigenous peoples variously extinguished, displaced, enslaved, or corralled on reservations or reserves. It has seen Indigenous peoples pushed from the ecological pluralism of their Aboriginal political economies to make way for the monocultures of plantations – to make way for mercantilism, capitalism, and agribusiness. On Mindanao and the surrounding islands of the south, the process of dispossession has fallen especially harshly on the Indigenous peoples, including the Manobo, Teduray, B'laan, Subanen, T'boli, Aruman, Sama, Yakan, and Kaulu.

The Islamic members of these and other Aboriginal groups in the region understand themselves to be part of the Bangsamoro people. Julian Burger has characterized the efforts to repress the independence movement of the two million or so in the Bangsamoro community as "one of Asia's most bloody secret wars."[78] In a country where the continuing strength of Roman Catholicism is probably the most lasting legacy of the Spanish Empire, the Filipino government's hostility to the Bangsamoro is old and deeply institutionalized. The pre-empted lands of the Bangsamoro and other Aboriginal inhabitants of Mindanao and the surrounding islands augmented the banana and pineapple empires of the Del Monte, Castle and Cook, and the United Fruit companies. The sugar plantations of the Bukidnon Corporation, the rubber plantations of the Firestone Corporation, and the logging operations of Boise-Cascade and Weyerhaeuser corporations expanded in similar proportion to the narrowed domain of Indigenous peoples.[79]

The independence movement among the Bangsamoro people of Mindanao has long been the target of reprisals emanating from the Roman Catholic empire of Spain, the capitalist empire of the United States, the Axis power of imperial Japan, and the national government of the Philippines. The Philippines government has been quick to respond with violence to the liberation struggles of many other groups, including the Kalinga and Bontoc of Luzon. In the 1970s these Indigenous peoples opposed the logging and the hydroelectric flooding of their Aboriginal lands. The military responses to their assertions of Aboriginal title had the effect of steering elements of the Aboriginal resistance movement towards support for the New People's Army, the armed wing of the Philippines Communist Party.

The radicalization of Aboriginal protest movements created many new dangers – for instance, those survey and construction crews seeking to dam the Chico River in the Aboriginal stronghold of northern Luzon – and the organized Aboriginal resistance to the dam was a factor in the World Bank's decision to withdraw its support from the ecologically unsound project.[80] In the Philippines, as in many other colonized territories, Fourth World politics have been complicated by the bipolar division of the Cold War, and sometimes by the religious divide between Christianity and Islam.

During the final decades of the twentieth century, the resistance movement of the Bangsamoro in the Philippines became increasingly integrated into a worldwide network of Islamic resistance to many real or imagined enemies. The *omma* – the worldwide society of believers in Islam – provided the basis of an elaborate mosaic of alternative perspectives and initiatives which put in question many fundamental tenets of capitalist universalism as policed by the self-interested oligarchs of the national security state and its military-industrial complex. A central drama in this ideological and geopolitical upheaval took place in 1979, when the populist theocracy of Shiite cleric Ayatolla Ruholla Khomeini overthrew the Western-backed regime of the Shah of Iran.[81] In referring to this event in his *Age of Extremes*, Eric Hobsbawm predicted that it "will enter history as one of the major social revolutions of the twentieth century."[82] The embrace of Islamic principles as the basis for the governance of one of the world's most important countries emboldened the Muslim citizens in many lands to heighten their efforts to turn back the tide of secularization. They were helped in this project by agents of the national security state during the period when the US-led side of the Cold War favoured theocracies of all kinds over godless communism. The capitalist Cold Warriors were especially anxious to arm and finance the militant extremism of jihadism in the Arab and Persian realms in order to keep in check the rise of more secular and sometimes socialist approaches to governance such as those attempted by Abdul Gamal Nasser of Egypt, General Abdul Karim Kassem of Iraq, and Mohammad Najibullah of Afghanistan.

This growing influence and zealotry of fundamentalist forces in all three of the major monotheistic religions – Judaism, Christianity, and Islam – confounded the expectations of many who had wrongly assumed that this movement of secularization had become an irreversible trend during the second half of the twentieth century. Inspired by the events in Iran, a maverick group of Islamic soldiers briefly seized control of the Grand Mosque in Mecca and proclaimed the overthrow of the US-backed House of Saud. Their revolution failed, but the signal had been sent that the royal descendants of Ibn Saud, the hand-picked custodians of the world's largest-known oil reserves, were not invincible. In 1981 the winds of religious revolution blew forcefully into Egypt. President Anwar Sadat was gunned down by his opponents as an extension of an old hostility between the Egyptian government and the Islamic Brotherhood.[83] Now the Islamic martyr Sayyid Qutb, one of the Arab world's most zealous opponents of the Western influence on the *omma*, was partnered with the more secular martyr Sadat.[84]

With its Islamic revolution, Iran joined Israel and Pakistan as nation-states that openly proclaim their avowedly theocratic purpose. Both Israel and Pakistan were established in 1947–48 with the specific purpose of creating national homes for religious communities. The United States initially backed the more or less secular regime of Iraq's Saddam Hussein in the fight to counter the Shiite revolution in Iran.[85] In much the same fashion that the US government had turned in 1989 on its former friend and agent in Panama, General Manuel Antonio Noriega, it began in 1991 a long process of demonizing, bombing, undermining, and finally conquering the regime of its former asset and ally, the secular Sunni dictator Saddam Hussein. One of Saddam's most serious infractions from the perspective of his former US allies was to have attempted to break the monopoly of Saudi-American petrodollars as the world's primary currency. Saddam promoted a shift to Euros as the favoured medium for buying and selling Iraqi oil.[86]

THE GREAT BETRAYAL OF DECOLONIZATION

In his classic historical study of Latin America since 1492, Eduardo Galeano demonstrates the limits of political decolonization in the absence of the means to defend the extension of indigenous self-determination to the economic sphere.[87] This same theme runs throughout Naomi Klein's study of "disaster capitalism," but especially her chapter on the sabotaging of the democratic potential of post-apartheid South Africa.[88] Both iconographic texts point to the fact that control of ever larger concentrations of capital in consistently fewer hands ran contrary to the decentralization of power that seemed to have occurred as formal systems of imperial rule were dismantled and the franchise was extended to larger and larger constituencies in a growing number of polities. In this era when more people than ever before can vote in electing public officials, the jurisdictional sphere of the ballot box has been squeezed into tighter enclaves of public administration. When, for instance, major changes in economic policies took place in response to the cataclysmic financial meltdown of 2008 and the early months of 2009, the alterations happened mostly through closed-door negotiations among elites rather than through elections offering well-informed voters a clear range of choices. In the United States the transition from the presidency of George W. Bush to that of Barack Obama did not disrupt the system of bailouts to the financial services sector, as consistently overseen by top federal executives of the US Treasury and Federal Reserve system recruited from the Wall Street *uberfirm* of Goldman Sachs.[89]

Ellen Meiksins Wood describes this phenomenon as one where "political rights" have come to be seen "as essentially passive, and citizenship as a passive, individual, even private identity, which may express itself by voting from time to time but which has no active, collective or social meaning."

She continues, "the whole point of this strategy is to put formal political rights in place of any social rights, and to put as much of social life as possible out of the reach of democratic accountability."[90]

Questions about the relationship of political rights to social life, such as those pertaining to the nature of the material relationships linking human beings to one another and the rest of nature, have always been at the core of controversies over the meaning of democracy. The evolution of a society where a handful of people can each command commercial resources worth literally hundreds of billions of times more than those of individuals at the bottom of global pyramids of wealth and worldly power, signifies the extreme nature of this controversy's outcome to date. What does it mean in such a world to repeat the mantras of human equality and one-person-one-vote?

The limitations placed on formal grants of independence to the citizens of many former colonies after the Second World War constitutes an important chapter in the process of divorcing the political rights of individuals from the possibility of expressing collective rights and responsibilities in the core social field of economic interactions. The menace of the Cold War's institutionalized Red Scare created the pretext for the national security state to intervene in order to prevent the citizens of the new, nominally independent countries from using their franchise to assert collective ownership and control over the indigenous wealth invested in their lands, waters, and collective creativity. They were blocked in their movement towards socialist, social democratic, or Fourth World models of self-determination and, instead, were forced into the alternative paths leading towards various combinations of kleptocracy, theocracy, and dictatorship favoured by the handful of plutocrats seeking to globalize the commercial reach of their corporate extensions in the name of winning the Cold War. To label this process as neo-colonialism, neo-imperialism, neo-liberalism, or neo-conservatism hardly captures the extent of this great betrayal of humanity's democratic promise – this great denigration of the West's most redeeming inheritance emanating from the Enlightenment's egalitarian ideals.

There were two basic routes for those in colonies to attain forms of governance outside the formal structures of imperialism. One of these prevailed in imperial territories where most of the lands and resources were devoted to attracting immigrants and enriching their descendants. In the British Empire these polities came to be known as the White Dominions – Canada, Australia, New Zealand, and South Africa. The development of the United States and many of the Latin American republics, but especially Chile and Argentina, represent modifications of this same model, ones that indigenized the course of European expansion. In the White Dominions, power was devolved to non-Aboriginal colonists through the expanded range of jurisdiction granted to their local parliaments and legislatures. The tradeoff was that the local governments, where the Indigenous peoples were in most instances entirely unrepresented, would pick up the expense of self-administration. Alpheus Henry Snow discussed this pattern in his published report for the US State Department in 1918. Commenting on the treatment of Indigenous peoples in those polities designed to receive large influxes of immigration, he wrote, "Where aboriginal tribes are located in a country suitable for settlement by citizens of civilized States, the modern practice is to discourage tribal organization and to deal with the aborigines as individuals under guardianship."[91]

The other route to decolonization evolved primarily in equatorial regions such as India, Nigeria, and Indonesia. The imperial rulers of these polities did not anticipate large influxes of European settlers; rather, they expected the Indigenous peoples to continue to form the majority populations for the foreseeable future. These innovators of imperialism attempted to dominate their subject peoples by collaborating with local elites who could benefit personally by governing on behalf of the colonial masters. This move towards indirect rule was accelerated as the imperial powers encountered more and more violent freedom struggles of subject peoples no longer willing to accept their subordinate status. The full extent and scope of these anti-colonial stands have yet to be fully recovered in memory and documentation. Some of the most broadly publicized of these armed stands by Aboriginal freedom fighters included the revolt against the East Indian Company in 1857, the Morat Bay Uprising in Jamaica in 1865, the Anglo-Zulu War of 1879, and the assault by members of the Society of the Righteous and Harmonious Fists who sought to rid China of Christian missionaries and foreign embassies in 1899–1900.

In Africa the indigenous agents of indirect rule were sometimes referred to as native kings or chiefs. In India the colonial administration depended on the assistance of assorted maharajas, nawabs, nizams, and jagirdhars. These indigenous intermediaries of empire were encouraged to align their own family fortunes with the interests of the colonizing power. This means of expressing imperial power through the cultivation of an indigenous class of compradors formed a central feature not only of the British Empire but of virtually all systems of colonial rule. Túpac Amaru, Tecumseh, Gandhi, Du Bois, Fanon, Nkrumah, Padmore, Mandela, and Jagan are among the many leaders who have criticized this corrupt method for nominally indigenizing the machinery of foreign control. In 1894 Sir H.H. Johnston, the commissioner in charge of the British Protectorate of Uganda, added his voice to the critique. "Even here," he wrote, "we are striving to induce the members of one homogenous tribe to recognize a single chief as their supreme ruler so far as native administration is concerned." He proposed, instead, a more laissez-faire approach to empire where Indigenous peoples "should be assisted and encouraged to govern themselves as far as possible without too much interference on the part of European officials."[92]

Even among some Christian missionaries, but especially in the High Church tradition of Anglicanism, a movement developed to moderate the assimilationist preoccupations of evangelization with a more tolerant and pluralistic approach. Increasingly, the evangelical proponents of indirect rule questioned the wisdom of encouraging Indigenous peoples to abandon the cultures of their ancestors in favour of the new religion. The ethos of relativism was making inroads even within Christian institutions. In applying to Western Africa the same currents of thinking that inspired the Reverend E.F. Wilson in Canada or Henry Venn in New Zealand, the Reverend Edwin W. Smith contemplated the excesses of religious proselytization. Smith wrote, "Our ideal is not a Christian world made of a uniform pattern throughout, but one that preserves within its unity all the diversities that the Almighty has given to the individual peoples."[93]

This Christian conception of imperial pluralism found a more secular expression in the theories of indirect rule developed initially by Sir Frederick Lugard in his capacity as high commissioner of the protectorate of Northern Nigeria in the early years of the twentieth century. Lugard was the author and implementer of theories and policies aimed at putting limitations on pressures both to Westernize and to Christianize the Afro-Islamic communities within the scope of his imperial jurisdiction. Rather than rule the Indigenous peoples of his district directly in a top-down fashion, he sought to govern through the vehicle of native institutions and native authorities. In Northern Nigeria these authorities were the Faluni emirs and the Sokoto Caliphate. As governor of a newly amalgamated Nigeria in 1914, Lugard widened the reach of his applied theories and attempted to explain his actions in an influential report written in 1919.[94] Three years later he extended his reputation as a leading intellectual of colonial administration yet further with a study entitled *The Dual Mandate in British Tropical Africa*. His ideal was to structure the British Empire to serve concurrently the Indigenous peoples of the colonies and the working people in the imperial heartland. The essence of "the dual mandate" was, therefore, to organize colonial administration in such a way that it served "the mutual benefit of [Britain's] own industrial classes and of the native races in their progress to a higher plane."[95]

To the critics of indirect rule, the system put an Aboriginal face on a system of repression whose true character was revealed by the fact that the appointment of native intermediaries was left entirely to the discretion of colonial administrators and not at all to the local communities.[96] In assessing the role of the chiefs in the Nigerian system, George Padmore alleged in 1936, "No oriental despot ever had greater power than these black tyrants, thanks to the support they receive from the white officials who quietly keep in the background."[97] Like John Collier in his role as federal director of the Indian New Deal, Lord Lugard's ideas and actions helped to stimulate professional development in the field of applied anthropology. As in Collier's federal Bureau of Indian Affairs, new opportunities arose for practitioners of the social sciences in the bureaucracy of the British colonial service as it became increasingly committed to the formal methodology of indirect rule throughout much of colonial Africa.[98]

The effort to develop a jurisprudence of indirect rule had significant implications for the practice of colonial, international, and religious law. In particular, the attempt to rule through indirect means necessitated the development of juridical theory to address the nature of Aboriginal title in lands where Indigenous peoples were encouraged to maintain their customs and traditions. The British secretary of state for the colonies appointed a special committee of jurists to investigate how Aboriginal systems of law in southern Nigeria connected groups and individuals to land and resources. In 1910 the findings of this committee upheld the principle that the Indigenous peoples all shared systems which emphasized collective approaches to land tenure and intergenerational inheritance – that "the use of the land by the inhabitants throughout the Protectorate could be, and was by custom, transferred and inherited, but it was the use of the land, and not the land itself, which was dealt with."[99]

This view of Aboriginal title was reaffirmed in 1921 in a decision by the Judicial Committee of the Privy Council (JCPC) in Great Britain, then the highest court in the British Empire. In the case of *Amodu Tijani v. The Secretary, Southern Nigeria*, the deciding jurists referred to the unextinguished survival of "native title" throughout large parts of the imperial Crown's remaining realm. On behalf of his fellow judges, Viscount Haldane penned the decision:

In interpreting the native title to land, not only in Southern Nigeria, but other parts of the British empire, much caution is essential. There is a tendency, operating at times unconsciously, to render that title conceptually in terms which are appropriate only to the systems which have grown up under English law. But this tendency has to be held in check closely ... The title, such as it is, may be that of a community ... The original native right was a communal right, and it must be presumed to have continued to exist unless the contrary is established by the context or the circumstances.[100]

The JCPC's decision affirming the existence of native title was regarded with particular alarm by some in British Columbia, a jurisdiction where, as in Australia, the newcomers' society has been allowed to expand and grow as if Indigenous peoples had no legal interests or claims in their Aboriginal lands. The worry that Indigenous peoples and their Anglican allies in British Columbia might use the *Tijani* decision to advance their constitutional arguments was a factor in the decision to amend the Canadian *Indian Act* in 1927. A new section was added with the aim of pre-empting judicial recognition of Aboriginal title. The new provision, section 141, outlawed any transfer of money to pursue an Indian claim.[101] That prohibition cast a wide net. The effect was essentially to outlaw political organization and lobbying on the part of Canada's registered Indians – to criminalize Indian political work and drive much of it underground. In Snow's words, the policy was "to discourage tribal organization and to deal with the aborigines as individuals under guardianship."

By the mid-1940s the Canadian government began to back away informally from its blanket criminalization of all efforts to represent Aboriginal political will at the national level. It began to accept the legitimacy of some political organizing among Indians. But there were extreme limitations on the willingness by dominion officials to let Indians decide for themselves how far to go with their political demands and legal arguments. The practice continued of deploying law enforcement agents and the flow of federal funding to keep the more militant organizations, such as Jules Sioui's League of the North American Indian Nation, outside the sphere of federally recognized agencies for the expression of Aboriginal political will.[102]

Nevertheless, the emergence of the allied powers from the violence of the Second World War translated into an initial boost for the forces of decolonization almost everywhere. The United Nations Charter of 1945 and the UN's Universal Declaration of Human Rights of 1948 were of enormous symbolic significance in removing legitimacy from the proponents of Social Darwinism, scientific racism, and imperial rule. These instruments of international law gave fuller and carefully negotiated articulation to the quick sketch of a better world as penned by the authors of the Atlantic Charter in 1941. The amendments to Canada's *Indian Act* in 1951 were one small expression of the larger ideological transformations as they eased or removed some the most repressive features of this legislative monument to colonialism. Henceforth Indians in Canada could embrace their Aboriginal spiritual traditions, including the potlatch, and their own forms of dance without fear of being criminalized. For the first time since 1927 they could raise money to advance their claims, although it was not until the 1960s that they were allowed to vote in federal elections, run for public office, purchase alcohol legally, or bring civil litigation to court.[103]

In 1955 the promise of true decolonization attracted to Bandung the leading representatives of those who had been treated as the wretched of the earth. The decolonization movement reached a climax between 1960 and 1964, when twenty-five former colonies, mostly in Africa, were reconstituted as nominally independent nation states.[104] In 1947 some of the basic patterns were set when the government of Great Britain pulled the *raj* out of a newly partitioned Indian subcontinent. The withdrawal of imperial authority from this jewel of the British Empire left the citizens of India and the newly created, predominantly Muslim country of Pakistan to work through the violent trauma of bringing their human geography into rough conformity with their new international borders.

The pressure for decolonization increased after Great Britain and France displayed their imperial weakness in 1956 when they tried unsuccessfully to use military force to prevent Abdel Nasser from seizing control of the Suez Canal.[105] As the dynamic new leader of Egypt, a country that has acted since the days of the Roman Empire as both a civilizational centre of resistance to European expansion and as a conduit to Europe's widened imperial hegemony, Nasser quickly became a rising star in the firmament of Arab nationalism. His successes in fighting the imperial grip of a diminished Europe were balanced by his military losses to the new state of Israel, a country born in 1947–48 largely as an act of atonement for the barbarism of Nazism's genocidal war against the Jews. Meanwhile, the Jewish state's systematic displacement of most of the Palestinians from their homes came to represent for many in the Arab and Muslim worlds a further extension of Judeo-Christian aggressions towards their communities – hostility that is at least as old as the Crusades.[106]

The Suez Crisis probably accelerated the pace of the United Kingdom's withdrawal from empire. As the cry of freedom was heard in many African and Asian languages – as the Kikuyu of Kenya, for example, continued to idealize the goal of *uhuru* that some of them had advanced with their Mau resistance[107] – British authorities handed over power to many local governors. Acting in accordance with what Prime Minister Harold Macmillan described as "the winds of change," the British government negotiated transfers of power in, for instance, Sudan in 1956, Ghana in 1957, Nigeria in 1960, Uganda in 1962, Kenya in 1963, and Zambia in 1964. A federation was briefly tried in Britain's West Indian colonies as a transitional instrument of decolonization, but in 1962 Jamaica peacefully left this association. The inhabitants of some localities hosting Great Britain's main naval bases were given formal independence too. These polities included Cyprus in 1960, Malta in 1964, and Aden in 1967. The transfers of power at these sites involved considerable manoeuvring to make certain that the military stations they harboured would not become part of the Soviet Union's imperial system.[108]

In Central Africa the vast colonial holding around the Congo River gave rise to a violent surge of nationalist assertiveness. The Belgian government responded in 1959 with a quick evacuation, leaving behind the new republic of Congo. As Che Guevara well understood, the history of the resource-rich Congo River basin has epitomized many of the most sordid features, first of colonialism and then of capitalist neo-colonialism and neo-imperialism. Where the region was once organized as the personal fiefdom of King Leopold, it emerged in the mid-1960s in spite of Che's intervention as a kleptocracy to be run in the interests of international capital by General Joseph Mobutu. Like many of the CIA-sanctioned dictators whose rise to power was backed by the covert operations of the US government, Mobutu derived huge personal wealth from his domination of his country's politics. With his invocation of "African authenticity," Mobutu changed the name of the Congo to Zaire, even as he also renamed himself Sese Seko, or "all-powerful warrior."[109]

The formal dismantling of France's global empire proceeded in a pace and style that reflected the unique characteristics of that imperial regime.

The French withdrew relatively quickly and willingly from their colonial holdings in Indochina in 1954. In contrast, the withdrawal of France from Algeria over the subsequent eight years was slow, extremely violent, and cataclysmic in its effects on domestic morale and politics. In the interval between 1954 and 1962, the government of France changed its constitutional relationship with fourteen African territories that had entered the post–World War II period as members of a polity known as the Union Française. Over several generations, the French imperial system had cultivated a small elite group of Black Africans who identified themselves closely with the *mission civilatrice* of France. The leading embodiments of this approach to empire building were Leopold Senghor of Senegal and Felix Houphouet-Boigny of Côte d'Ivoire. Both of them had emerged from the French system of higher learning with excellent credentials. Both men were integrated into the government of France as representatives of their African constituents, and they remained convinced that the peoples of the French polities in Africa would be best served by building up their local political economies within the broader jurisdictional sphere of the mother country.

Beginning in 1958, however, the winds of change quickly swept aside these fragile principles. The pivotal event was a referendum where the citizens of the African polities in the Union Française were asked to decide whether they wanted a future inside or outside the jurisdiction sphere of France. Only the citizens of Guinea, led by a committed trade unionist named Ahmed Sékou Touré, voted to sever their attachment to France. Nevertheless, the genie was out of the bottle. Spurred by developments in Algeria and the example set by British moves to dismantle its empire, the government of France conducted a quick series of independence ceremonies in 1960. In August, Dahomey (later Benin), Niger, Upper Volta (later Burkina Faso), Côte d'Ivoire, Chad, the Central African Republic, the French Congo, Gabon, and Senegal all received their formal political independence. Similar ceremonies took place in Mali in September and in Mauritania in November.[110] The opening rounds of violence accompanying the rapid decolonization in some parts of Africa south of the Sahara, including the former Belgian Congo, pointed to yet more cataclysmic conflicts on the horizons of the continent's future.

INDIRECT RULE, INDIGENOUS RESISTANCE, AND CAPITALIST NEO-COLONIALISM IN INDONESIA AND MALAYSIA

As suggested by the rapid intensification of the US intervention in Indochina after the French withdrawal in 1954, Southeast Asia was held to be the most strategic contested zone in the Cold War where the future of global capitalism would be decided. The great fear was that the successful Communist Revolution in China would set off a "domino" effect in the region. The fear was that the Indigenous peoples of Southeast Asia would be drawn away from the American empire of possessive individualism and, in response to the dismantling of European empires, would enter that revolutionary current of world history initiated in 1917 with the communist takeover in Russia.

Many of the big currents of global history came together in Indonesia. This convergence extended and intensified old patterns of imperial globalization. One of the big enticements that had energized the modern era of imperial globalization after 1492 had been the lucrative attractions of European traders to spices derived from the rich diversity of plant life domesticated by a broad array of culturally distinct peoples indigenous to the huge archipelago now known as Indonesia and Malaysia. As in Amazonia, the ecological marriage between the biological diversity of plants and animals and the cultural pluralism of human beings is integral to this region's complex geography. European traders could make spectacular profits by bringing home from the islands of Java and Sumatra large quantities of pepper, ginger, and cinnamon. Similarly, European traders could make themselves and their patrons rich by importing from the Moluccas, sometimes known as the Spice Islands, great quantities of cloves.

The Dutch East Indian Company ultimately prevailed in controlling the trade in these commodities – a major saga in the rise of Amsterdam as an instrumental staging point and laboratory in the rise of capitalism, especially during the seventeenth century.[111] The empires of Holland and England would meet and merge in the rise of New York as the main inheritor of the capitalist legacies of both Amsterdam and London. Although the Dutch fought briefly with British and US assistance after the Second World War to regain control of their large and lucrative colony, they faced heavy indigenous resistance.

By 1949 this resistance wrested Indonesia away from the control of its former imperial master,[112] as Achmed Sukarno led the culminating phase of the movement for the decolonization of Indonesian. His role as a mentor and role model for other anti-colonial movements was reflected in his effectiveness as the main sponsor and host of the Bandung Conference of 1955. John Pilger has observed that this conference "alarmed the western powers, especially as the vision and idealism of non-alignment represented a potentially popular force that might seriously challenge neo-colonialism."[113] In the era of Sukarno, the PKI, the local Communist party, grew to become one of the more influential political parties in the country: with three million members, it was the largest nationally based Communist organization in the world outside China and the Soviet Union. As one of the world's leading proponents of non-alignment, Sukarno had to maintain some distance from the PKI. He used the party as a hedge against the power of the army, which did eventually remove him from office.[114]

Sukarno was violently displaced from power in 1966. Marshall Green, the US ambassador in Jakarta, is generally recognized as the episode's "coupmaster" as he worked closely with British operatives who were experts in media manipulation.[115] They planned first to support the Indonesian army's installation of General Suharto and then to create a deluge of international propaganda that would give both cover and licence for the new regime to decimate the PKI and all its attending support systems through a concerted campaign of mass murder. The result was a terrible blood bath. Gabriel Kolko has described it as "one of the most barbaric acts of inhumanity in a century that has seen a great deal of it." He highlighted the US involvement in this debacle, emphasizing that it "did everything in its power to encourage Suharto, including equipping his killers, to see that the physical liquidation of the PKI was carried through to its culmination."[116]

The violent replacement of the Sukarno regime with that of General Suharto cleared the way for the handover of one of the world's most ethnically diverse and resource-rich countries to the capitalist enterprise of the planet's biggest transnational corporations. The new arrangements were put in place at a conference in Geneva in 1967. Planned in large measure by the Ford Foundation, the meeting was entitled "To Aid in the Rebuilding of a Nation." The event's main sponsor was Time-Life Corporation. Its founder, Henry Luce, had pointed the way to the American Century in 1941. As his plans began to be realized, many prominent employees of the Time-Life media empire had double careers as agents of the psychological warfare on the capitalist side of the Cold War. David Rockefeller of the Chase Manhatten Bank was a key figure on the corporate side of the negotiations in Geneva. Hamengku Buwono, the sultan of Jogjakarta, led the negotiators on the side of the puppet regime. The companies with representatives in attendance included most of the world's major oil conglomerates, General Motors, Imperial Chemical Industries, British Leyland, British Imperial Tobacco, American Express, Siemens, Goodyear, and the International Paper Company.

The heart of the negotiations detailed the nature and extent of corporate rights to be apportioned over five sectors of the Indonesian economy. The Freeport Company came away with rights to the massive copper and gold deposits in West Papua. Alcoa got the biggest slice of the polity's abundant bauxite, and a group of US, Japanese, and French companies gained access to the largest part of the country's forest resources.[117] James Linen, the president of Time-Life, tried to capture the essence of the conference in a published tribute to General Suharto. In a statement that anticipated much of the enthusiasm of capitalist globalization following the Cold War, Linen explained: "We are trying to create a new climate in which private enterprise and developing countries work together ... for the greater profit of the free world. This world of international enterprise is more than governments ... It is the seamless web of enterprise, which has been shaping the global environment at revolutionary speed."[118]

In the aftermath of Sukarno's regime, the new US-backed strong man organized his government much as did Zaire's Mobutu – almost as a personal proprietorship. A pioneer and prototype of this form of kleptocracy was King Leopold, the Belgian monarch who used the power of the proxy granted him primarily by the US government to construct the machinery of appropriation in the blood-soaked rubber plantations throughout the watershed of the Congo River. Between 1970 and 1980 Indonesian debt went from $2.4 billion to $14.9 billion, much of it to grease Suharto's personal patronage network. By 2001 the Indonesian debt stood at $262 billion, almost twice the amount of the country's annual gross domestic product. The World Bank and the International Monetary Fund extended much of the credit that created this debt as Suharto enriched himself and his cronies.[119] Though the main US priority was to secure concessions for its oil companies, its overall goal was to integrate Indonesia and its raw materials into what Kolko described as "a United States–led world economy."[120]

The murder spree following the change of regimes in Indonesia demonstrated how far the national security state and its corporate partners were willing to go in encouraging and aiding the systematic violation of international law in one of the Cold War's most contested and strategic zones. The installation of General Suharto's regime to erase the PKI from Indonesia's political landscape represents a capitalist variation on the themes of ethnic cleansing and the final solution. What *Kristallnacht* was in 1938 for European anti-Semitism, the annihilation of Indonesia's PKI was for Cold War anti-communism. The executed members of the PKI, together with the other victims of the politically motivated onslaught, can be conceived as the symbolic descendants of the merciless Indian savages who were targeted for elimination as a race of terrorists in the American Declaration of Independence. From the Paxton Boys' massacre of Indians on the frontiers of revolt against the Royal Proclamation to the massacre of Indonesia's real or imagined communists, the makers of the US empire have always reserved the right to suspend the operations of law in order to eliminate those standing in the way of their own assumed Manifest Destiny to own, control, and exploit large portions of the earth.

The resort to regime change, combined with massive crimes against humanity to remake Indonesia as a prototype of capitalist globalization, continued the same US push into the Asian Pacific that began with John Jacob Astor's export of sea otters and opium to China following the transcontinental mission of the Lewis and Clark expedition. It brought a higher level of coordination to the same expansionist energies expressed in earlier decades by the US acquisition of northern Mexico, Hawaii, and the Philippines. The massacre of hundreds of thousands of real or imagined socialists through the actions of a well-armed client regime, rather than through the direct action of US troops, confirmed a pattern of operation that became increasingly integral to the tactic of US empire building. The ruthlessness of Suharto, like that of Mobutu in the Congo, demonstrated how far the tactics of indirect rule had been extended since Lord Lugard developed his relatively benign theories during the imperial governance of Nigeria.

Suharto's regime extended the structure, reach, and sophistication of the military-industrial complex centred in the United States. It also extended a long history of dominance by the Javanese over the rest of the country. In spite of this domination, however, many of Indonesia's 13,000 islands continued to provide some amount of refuge for a prolific diversity of Indigenous peoples. Collectively, these peoples have kept alive about 250 Aboriginal languages. This miracle of cultural survival was achieved notwithstanding the violent expressions of a tight partnership between business and the Indonesian armed forces. The incursions on the Aboriginal rights and titles of Indonesia's Indigenous peoples during the reign of General Suharto took place within the framework of a more general assault on the civil liberties and human rights of large portions of the population in a polity where the army's role was not so much self-defence as the repression of entire sections of Indonesia's domestic population.

The Indigenous peoples of West Papua faced a particularly harsh barrage of assaults from the Suharto regime on their lands, persons, and Aboriginal institutions. These pressures emanated from the operations of resource-extraction enterprises, including those of Shell, Conoco, Texaco, and Chevron as well as the huge copper and gold mine at Freeport. This mine displaced the Amungme, Dani, Komoro, and Ekari peoples without compensation. Their Aboriginal economies were undermined along with the ecology of the Aykwa River, which was transformed into a virtual waste sewer. Some Aboriginal groups experienced conditions of virtual slavery. The Asmat people, for instance, were compelled to log and transport trees from their region with the understanding that, if they refused, they would likely be tortured or killed by government agents as communist subversives.[121] In many other parts of the country the Indigenous peoples were pushed further to the margins by a massive policy of "transmigration." The aim of this policy was to overwhelm the Indigenous peoples with the settlement of hundreds of thousands of settlers from Java, the site of the Indonesian capital. In commenting on the implications of this influx of Javanese settlers, one former governor of West Papua observed, "Papuans will become like the Aborigines of Australia, the Indians in America or the Maoris in New Zealand. All pushed out by newcomers."[122]

Like the governing authorities of Indonesia, Malaysia's indigenous leaders took over an imperial realm of great cultural pluralism and biological diversity. Much of Malaysia was part of the British Crown colony of Malaya. The prelude to its decolonization was especially contentious. The British government was determined not to give up power there until it was satisfied that it had sufficiently undermined the strength of communism in the region. Communist convictions were most intense among a portion of the resident Chinese population who sought to extend the revolution that was taking place in the Chinese motherland under the regime of Mao Zedong. In 1957 Malaya was formally granted decolonized status. The Crown colonies of Sahba, Sarawak, and Singapore were then folded into this culturally and constitutionally complex polity to form Malaysia in 1963. Two years later, Singapore withdrew from Malaysia to become a modern-day city state.

In Malaysia a special ministry was established for the governance of Indigenous peoples, who are identified collectively as the Dayaks and sometimes also as the Orang Asli. Much of the pressure on the Orang Asli has been centred in Sarawak, where the regional government has overseen extensive logging operations, especially in the legendary rainforests of Borneo. The rate of commercial deforestation in Sarawak was calculated in the mid-1980s as 2,100 acres a day, with most of the timber going to Japan.

This activity effectively ruined the Aboriginal political economies of many peoples of the forest, including the Iban, Kayan, Kelabit, Kenyah, Kejaman, Punan Bah, Tanjong, Sekapan, Lahanan, and Penan. Some Penan people led a concerted resistance by organizing road blocks and other group actions. When the Malaysian government responded with harsh punishments, the Penan resistance obtained the backing of a number of influential groups, including Survival International and the European Parliament. The lead organization in pulling together this international response was Sahabat Alam Malaysia (Friends of the Earth, Malaysia). The coordinated, transnational response to the violation of Aboriginal rights and titles in Sarawak was part of a growing merger of environmental organizations with the activism of Indigenous peoples.[123]

The stresses on the culturally diverse polities of Malaysia and Indonesia point to the tension inherent in a process that combined the rhetoric of decolonization even as it violated the principle of self-determination. Indeed, in the twenty-first century, one of the most consistent, reoccurring themes of ethnic conflict is rooted in the poor fit between the inheritance of Aboriginality that survived European imperialism and the institutional and geographical shape of the new nations that were recognized after the Second World War. Most often these new polities were built on the foundations of European colonies rather than on the configurations of territory, culture, memory, and law of surviving Aboriginal societies whose origins predate the European empires.

The failure to address these deeper inheritances of Aboriginal history at the time of decolonization created the seed of much ethnic conflict to come. Especially in Africa and parts of Asia, it put in place the outlines of a host of national sovereignties that did not reflect the orientation to language, identity, and space integral to the sense of self-determination harboured by a great many of the world's peoples. A large portion of humanity therefore lives in nation-states whose laws, institutions, and boundaries do not conform to their diverse senses of Aboriginal history, culture, and territory. An index of this tension is expressed by the difference between a world of approximately two hundred sovereign nation-states and about 6,000 distinct languages. Seen in this light, the experiences of Indians in North America reflect those of a large constituency on the planet. Where Indians seem by their marginalized status in North America to be in an aberrant category all their own, their condition in fact mirrors many elements of the dominant experience of most citizens on Earth. The basis of that experience is to have felt the expansion of European and Euro-American empires as a force of aggression and dislocation rather than as a force that widened horizons of opportunities for work, recreation, and the acquisition of new wealth.

To enter the Fourth World is to combine the sovereignty of nation-states with the self-determination of older polities more attuned to deeper configurations of human relationship with one another and the rest of nature. It is to combine conservatism with a revolutionary openness to a future of sustainable and democratic life based on diverse motifs of ecological globalization. In the Fourth World, Indigenous peoples are encouraged to renew rather than renounce their adaptation to the distinct character of their Aboriginal bio-regions. As Gandhi prophesied, the key to realizing this more comprehensive approach to decolonization depends on transcending imperialism in all its manifestations. In the era when the informal structure of the American empire replaced the more formal structures of European empires, the self-determination of peoples was often denied through the forced imposition of an economic regime that centred increasing concentrations of power in global corporations, but especially in those most deeply integrated into the operations of the national security state and the military-industrial complex.

The tension between the peoples and the state of Indonesia became evident as early as 1950, when the Aboriginal inhabitants of the South Moluccas tried to declare independence from Djakarta. The South Moluccan independence movement was crushed, foreshadowing the vicious repressions that would be visited by the Suharto regime on the Indigenous peoples of West Papua and East Timor. The primary international vehicle of resistance in West Papua has been the Free Papua Movement. In East Timor the indigenous inhabitants opted to become independent after the Portuguese government finally withdrew its colonial rulers in 1974. Acting with the explicit sanction of the administration of US president Gerald Ford, the Suharto government intervened militarily, beginning a long reign of terror aimed at forcing the peoples of East Timor to submit to Indonesian rule.[124] After the genocidal killings of around 200,000 people in a country of only about 700,000 inhabitants, the limits of Indonesian tyranny began to be reached as the United Nations finally intervened at the end of the twentieth century to assist the East Timorese in the design and implementation of national self-governance.

The violence in East Timor was mirrored in the violence following the withdrawal in 1975 of the government of Portugal from its imperial role in Angola and Mozambique. This violence was permeated with the instabilities of South African apartheid, the zeal of the Cuban revolution, and superpower politics in the Cold War.[125] It was part of the machinations of the international arms trade that has made much of Africa, including, for instance, Sudan, Liberia, and Sierra Leone, the dumping ground for vast stockpiles of small arms. As demonstrated by the huge death toll from African civil wars, this mass of small arms collectively forms an arsenal of such lethal capacity that it can be conceived in its entirety as the world's most murderous weapon of mass destruction. Much of this weaponry finds its way into the hands of child soldiers, a preventable tragedy that plagues parts of Africa as surely as the disproportionately high concentration of AIDS in that troubled continent.[126]

In the course of the dismantling of European empires after the Second World War, the number of nation-states on the planet jumped from 74 in 1946 to 192 in 1995.[127] There was much unevenness, however, in the outcomes from this process of decolonization. Indeed, the evidence is overwhelming that the frontier expansions of global corporations, along with the exercise of coercive authority centred in the military-industrial complex of the United States, intensified the disparities of wealth and power that continue to reside at the very core of colonialism in its most essential sense. Class exploitation and colonial exploitation are two sides of the same coin of injustice. As Masao Miyoshi concluded from her reflections on these outcomes, "Ours is not an age of post-colonialism but of intensified colonialism, even though in an unfamiliar guise."[128] The transfer of jurisdiction from imperial capitals to new centres of national governance tended, therefore, to favour the interests of small, local oligarchies rather than to deliver on the ideals of broad-ranging liberation that the winds of change seemed initially to promise.[129]

ALGERIA, VIETNAM, ATTICA, AND GUSTAFSEN LAKE

Beginning in the autumn of 2005, a firestorm of violent protest swept throughout many urban regions in France. Most of the rioters were young Franco-Arab men of Islamic background whose family origins lay in the former French colonies along the Mediterranean coast of northern Africa.[130] That region is known as the Maghreb. Beginning in the ghetto-like milieu of the poorest Parisian suburbs, the rioters discharged small weapons, torched thousands of cars, and set fire to police stations and schools. The disorder spread from districts such as Raincy and Savigny-sur-Orge to other French cities including Lille, Toulouse, and Orléon. The protestors' resort to violence drew global attention to the schisms of religion, culture, and economics dividing the citizens of France into zones of indigenous privilege and enclaves of immigrant Arab underemployment, marginalization, and unrest.

The upheavals dramatized the increasingly volatile state of ethnic relations that has developed in many of Europe's old imperial capitals. In the process of globalization, many of these cities became magnets for immigrants who left their Aboriginal territories to seek new lives in Europe. This process is part of a larger, worldwide phenomenon.[131] A near universal pattern in the world's richest countries has seen economic success translate into birth rates so low that they do not even replace the populations of prosperous societies. The capitalist response to this demographic reality of shrinking and aging populations has been to bring in significant numbers of immigrants, many of whom undertake the most unpleasant and poorly paid types of jobs. Often these immigrants have difficulty obtaining full-fledged citizenship in their adopted countries. The implementation of these expedients to maintain economic growth in the rich world has created fertile ground for racial discrimination and the proliferation of resentments of all kinds in increasingly polarized societies.

Many shuddered in November 2005 when the French government responded to the crisis by imposing the same emergency measures act that had been crafted in 1955 during the fight for the decolonization of Algeria. For instance, the Paris-based Human Rights League charged that this renewal of the old law constituted a "disastrous symbol" of a particularly harsh phase of French colonialism.[132] The reference to the Algerian War served as a clear marker that the riots had deep roots in France's heritage as a major imperial power. Between 1954 and 1962 the Algerian War rocked France to its foundations. It turned factions of French people against one another in much the same way that the US military intervention in Vietnam, Laos, and Cambodia split the citizenry of the United States into bitterly opposed camps during the late 1960s and early 1970s.

The dogged persistence of European imperialism into the second half of the twentieth century was dramatically illustrated by the coercive campaign to maintain French military control over Algeria in the face of a concerted independence struggle. The coercive techniques deployed by the French armed forces included ample use of torture. The FLN, the Front de Libération Nationale, spearheaded the Algerian drive for indigenous self-determination. Like the international support adhering to Gandhi's decolonization campaign in India in the years before 1948, the FLN's military, political, and ideological struggle provided a major focus for anti-colonial activists throughout many parts of the world. The example of the FLN proved especially inspirational for those who would spearhead the Cuban revolution. The heightened levels of awareness, exchange, and organization that developed in and around the cause of Algerian liberation helped to stimulate new surges of anti-imperial globalization.

The French government had abandoned its formal imperial role in Southeast Asia without significant internal acrimony once Ho Chi Minh's Viet Minh army of national liberation decisively defeated French forces in 1954 in the Battle of Dien Bien Phu.[133] Like the decisive defeat in 1876 of the US Armed Force's Seventh Cavalry by an Aboriginal fighting force at the Battle of Little Bighorn, the vanquishing of a sophisticated European military unit by an indigenous band of freedom fighters challenged many assumptions.[134] It was one thing, however, to dismantle the machinery of French imperial rule in the Far East. It was quite another to challenge's

France's old and elaborate relationship with Algeria. Many in both polities saw Algeria as an extension of France. They could no more conceive of it as a colony than as an independent country. Increasingly French actions against the FLN were justified with the slogan "Algeria is France, or France is at home in Algeria."[135]

The resistance of some French citizens to the prospect of losing Algeria was buttressed by the way the laws and systems of political representation of the North African polity were integrated with those of France. The French attachment to nearby Algeria was rooted in many rich complexes of familial, social, cultural, and economic relations that had developed over many generations. The hardliners in the conflict on the French side were known as *pied noir* – French citizens of French and Christian heritage whose families had lived in Algeria sometimes for many generations. Ahmed Ben Bella emerged as the leading figure on the other side of the conflict. With an eye towards extending the decolonization movement to pan-African dimensions, he worked closely with Egyptian president Gamal Abdel Nasser in establishing the organizational foundations of the FLN. Both leaders were committed to moving along more secular, materialistic paths towards the goal of human liberation. Both had to contend with some indigenous opposition to their policies from Islamic theocrats who were often covertly helped and encouraged by Cold Warriors on the capitalist side of the global conflict. In 1955 Nasser and Ben Bella advanced their agenda at the Bandung Conference, where most of the delegations rallied to show support for the FLN's armed struggle. The next year Ben Bella was apprehended and incarcerated by French officials, who did not release him from prison until the peace negotiations of 1962.[136]

The ideological shock troops of the Algerian War did battle largely in Paris, the famed City of Light. Since the Century of Enlightenment, Paris has been the scene of repeated intellectual combats between the forces of empire and of human liberation. Many of the Parisian advocates of Algerian independence gathered in and around a publishing house known as Présence Africaine. This publishing initiative built on the literary traditions pioneered by Martinican native Aimé Césaire. During the Second World War, Césaire had edited the journal *Tropiques*. The nature of colonialism was rendered absolutely clear to him when he was governed in the French Caribbean by the Vichy regime of Nazi collaborators. This experience confirmed his understanding that European fascism emerged as a direct outgrowth of imperialism and the racism that facilitates this system of political, economic and cultural oppression.

In Paris, Césaire collaborated with other Black sojourners from France's African colonies. One of the most prominent of them was Léopold Senghor, the poet and literary critic who would return to Senegal in West Africa to become its president between 1960 and 1979. Césaire, Senghor, Léon Damas, and others were instrumental in the rise of different aspects of a movement known as *negritude*. The negritude movement drew on a number of influences, including the earlier cultural achievements of the Harlem Renaissance in the United States.[137] The idea of negritude extended the effort by colonized peoples to push aside the dehumanizing categories of savagery and primitiveness that had been assigned to them by imperialism's social scientists. The elaboration of this idea helped to energize the rise of a more broadly based movement for decolonization across a wide array of human relationships.[138] It helped open the way for the transition from the Cold War category of the Third World to the post-colonial notion of the Fourth World, as advanced in North America by George Manuel or in sub-Saharan Africa by Tanzania's Julius Nyerere and Zambia's Kenneth Kuanda.

The Algerian Revolution's catalytic effect on left-wing militance in France was helped along by Albert Memmi, a Tunisian Jew who, in 1957, published the French-language text of *The Colonizers and the Colonized*.[139] France's most prominent public intellectual, Jean-Paul Sartre, was not to be left behind, and he joined in the swirl of ideological agitation in and around the Parisian publishing house of Présence Africaine. In 1958 Sartre contributed a preface to Henri Alleg's text, *La Question*. Alleg, a member of the French Communist Party, published a left-wing newspaper in Algeria and, in 1957, he was taken into custody and jailed without charge at El-Biar prison. There members of the French army systematically tortured him. His published account of this experience created a major scandal in France. The French people were forced to confront the reality that the most grue-some forms of torture were inflicted even on French citizens in attempts to garner intelligence about the identity, plans, and intentions of FLN mem-bers and their supporters.[140]

The French government responded to the furor by banning Alleg's book. It was quickly republished, however, in Switzerland, and, in an English translation, in London. Sartre characterized France's resort to torture as an expression and illustration of the repressiveness of colonial relation-ships of power. He observed, "Hitler was only the forerunner ... Torture is neither civilian or military, nor is it specifically French; it is plaguing our whole era ... Torture is imposed by the circumstances and required by racial hatred; in some ways it is the essence of the conflict and expresses its deepest truths."[141]

The realization that the government of France was resorting to this noto-rious form of international crime helped to polarize the French nation almost to the point of civil war. At a moment when the government of France had committed about 500,000 soldiers to hold Algeria for France, Charles de Gaulle was handed the reigns of power by activists of the far right.[142] De Gaulle, however, could not contain the impetus for change. Like the move-ment for decolonization throughout sub-Saharan Africa, the Algerian inde-pendence movement had advanced too far to be turned back. In March 1962 the FLN and the French government signed the Évian accords, calling for commercial and political cooperation between two sovereign countries.

Factions of the French army and elements of *pied noir* in Algeria perceived the Évian accords as a capitulation on the part of their own government. In spite of the violent effort by the proponents of French Algeria to sabotage the deal through an attempted coup, an assassination attempt, and a variety of terrorist bombings, the division of France and Algeria established broader patterns in the dismantling of European empires.

The transition of France from a major imperial power to a more modest role in Europe and the rest of the world was part of the same process that saw the global growth of US influence.[143] The turmoil over the role of the US Armed Forces in the undeclared war in Southeast Asia was anticipated when the Algerian conflict brought to the heartland of the European Enlightenment the basic contradictions in France's relationship to liberty and empire. The fight over Algeria's future forced on the French people a fundamental reckoning with the contradictions between imperial rule and the egalitarian ideals frequently associated with their country's revolutionary heritage. France's gift to the United States of the Statue of Liberty in 1876 was meant to commemorate the centennial of the American Declaration of Independence – to give tangible representation to over a century of shared development as two revolutionary polities allied in the advancement of universal justice and freedom. It was difficult to reconcile these elevating principles, however, with the interconnected roles of United States and France in the genesis of the tragedy engulfing Vietnam, Cambodia, and Laos during the peak of the Cold War.

In the name of anti-communism, the US government moved to fill the vacuum of power left in Indochina after the French withdrawal. The transition in South Vietnam from the formal imperialism of France to the elaborate machinery of US dominance renewed a pattern that had been instrumental in shaping the geopolitical map of North American in the early nineteenth century. In 1803 Napoleon had authorized the sale to the US government of France's vast but ill-defined imperial claims to Louisiana. The Louisiana Purchase was transacted between parties that simply ignored the rights, titles, and political will of the Indigenous peoples west of the Mississippi. A similar disregard for the Aboriginal rights and titles of the peoples of Southeast Asia was evident in the shift from the imperial oversight of France to the informal empire building of the United States and its military-industrial complex.

Like Geronimo, Che Guevera, or Mao Zedong, the Vietnamese freedom fighter Ho Chi Minh favoured guerrilla warfare as the most strategic way of empowering those who would otherwise have limited ability to exercise political power.[144] Ho Chi Minh took this classic tactic of anti-imperial warfare to new frontiers of effectiveness. This student of many Asian and European languages was sufficiently flexible in his ideology to admire concurrently the insights of Karl Marx, Marcus Garvey, and Thomas Jefferson. As an admirer of Jefferson, he once looked to the United States as a potential ally in his quest to free his peoples from the shackles of imperial rule. His effort to gain recognition from the United States for the sovereign Aboriginal rights and titles of the Vietnamese was strengthened by the moral authority he and his Viet Minh associates had achieved in opposing with covert US support the imperial force of Japanese occupation during the Second World War.

The US government chose not to back Ho Chi Minh's opposition to French imperialism or his call for the unification of North and South Vietnam after its division at a conference in Geneva in July 1954. Rather, it attempted to build up South Vietnam as a shield against the spread of communism throughout Southeast Asia. This strategy was reminiscent of the effort by leading financiers and corporations in the United States to back the rise of German fascism, in order to make it a bastion of anti-Soviet power and agitation in the heart of central Europe. The unwillingness of the Truman administration to sanction the form of political self-determination sought by Ho Chi Minh forced the Aboriginal leader to reach out for assistance to China and the Soviet Union. This history forms the background for one of the Cold War's most violent and lethal conflagrations. The assumption by the United States of the French imperial role in Vietnam specifically and in Indochina more generally helps to clarify the connections linking the expansion of US influence to the dismantling of several European empires after the Second World War.

The mounting controversy within the United States over the role of its military-industrial complex in Vietnam reflected and extended controversies that had coalesced in France about a decade earlier. This contention stimulated the search for historical antecedents to help explain the genesis of the capitalist superpower's imperial role. The quest for broad explanations of the rise of imperial America was epitomized by the panoramic study *Facing West: The Metaphysics of Indian-Hating and Empire Building*, in which Richard Drinnon presents a series of episodes that identify a single, coherent westward push undertaken in the name of Western civilization's expansionary ascent over Aboriginal savagery. That push westward, one whose meanings and metaphors Frederick Jackson Turner had earlier explored in his presentation at the World's Columbian Exposition, extended all the way from the Puritans' Indian wars in New England to the assault by the US Armed Forces on the peoples indigenous to Southeast Asia.

What Drinnon made explicit was left as an implicit subtext in much of the historical research and interpretation accompanying the surge of popular protest against the US military role in Indochina. That surge of scholarly energy, inspired largely by the convergence of the anti-war movement with the civil-rights movement as well as the movement for decolonization, women's rights, and environmental protection, shifted the emphasis in many fields of academic inquiry. It contributed, for example, to an elaborate reconsideration of US triumphalism and exceptionalism as epitomized particularly by the writings of Francis Parkman, Theodore Roosevelt, and the Turnerian school of frontier historians.

Like the work of Richard Drinnon, that of Francis Jennings, Richard Slotkin, and Michael Paul Rogin became representative of a larger revisionist school. Underlying the efforts to build up a new historiography of western expansion was the idea that the treatment of Indigenous peoples in North America provided a key to understanding the genesis of US political and economic orientation towards much of the rest of the world. This leftward shift in the political culture of the academy extended also to the content of popular culture. The anti-war movement was a major factor in, for instance, the demise of Hollywood Westerns. No longer could the mythological ascent of conquering cowboys over vanquished Indians be celebrated unabashedly.

As the phenomenon of anti-imperial globalization grew in influence, Kwame Nkrumah's *Neo-Colonialism: The Last Stage of Imperialism* (1965) found an audience far beyond the author's home country of Ghana in West Africa. Under the mentorship of George Padmore and W.E.B. Du Bois, Nkrumah had emerged as a prominent member of the brain trust in the movements for decolonization and pan-African unity.[145] A virtual refugee from the intense red baiting of Cold War America, Du Bois moved to Ghana in the final years of his life to help counsel and advise the African leader. Another admirer of Nkrumah was the Black Muslim leader Malcolm X, who correctly identified in 1964 the existence of a covert campaign centred in the CIA to overthrow the Nkrumah regime. The main objective of that campaign was realized in 1966.[146]

Nkrumah's *Neo-Colonialism* discomforted those who were determined that, despite the restructuring of political institutions in Europe's former colonies, there should be no radical remaking of existing patterns of economic relations. The book's seminal arguments proved influential in bringing some of Nkrumah's readers to an appreciation of the global power of corporate capitalism. For those who practised neo-colonialism, Nkrumah wrote, "it means power without responsibility and for those who suffer from it, it means exploitation without redress."[147] In elaborating and illustrating his arguments about how neo-colonialism was imposed and enforced after formal decolonization, Nkrumah included among his examples abundant reference to the US-backed puppet regime in South Vietnam.

Nkrumah's assessment of neo-colonialism was one small part of a growing tide of international criticism directed at the global role of the capitalist superpower. This surge of global criticism coincided with growing opposition within the United States to the incursions of the military-industrial complex and its overseers in the national security state. In 1968 the literary critic Leslie Fidler tried to explain the culture of some North Americans who rebelled against the empire building of their elders. "Into what exactly is the transplanted European converted by the Western encounter when he resists resolving it by genocide?" he asked, and replied:

We are tempted to say that it is the woodsman which the ex-European becomes beside his red companion: the hunter, the trapper, the frontiersman, the pioneer, at last the cowboy – or maybe only next to last, for after him comes the beatnik, the hippie, one more wild man seeking the last West of Haight-Ashbury in high-heeled boots and blue jeans. But even as he ceases to be beatnik and becomes fully hippie, the ultimate Westerner ceases to be White at all and turns back into the Indian, his boots becoming moccasins, his hair bound in an Indian headband, and a string of beads around his neck – to declare he has fallen not merely out of Europe, but out of the Europeanized West, into an Aboriginal and archaic America.[148]

At their best, the emergent "hippies" expressed the animating ideals of a broader surge of opposition to colonization in all its manifestations. The brief domination by the hippies of a significant facet of popular culture culminated in a huge musical pow wow organized in 1969 at Woodstock in up-state New York. This ritual announced the coming of age of the "Woodstock Generation." The festival was followed two years later by an intense expression of underclass solidarity at a nearby penitentiary also in up-state New York. In their brief takeover, the Attica prison inmates called attention to the continuing oppressiveness of racism and class exploitation essential to the colonialism *within* the United States. The prisoners seized control of Attica in September 1971 in an act that initiated the most lethal episode in US penal history. It grew from the politicization of prisoners in ways that momentarily invested in them a shared sense that they could collectively overcome the deep antagonisms that would otherwise have divided this representative sample of America's most marginalized groups. Hostages were taken, negotiations took place, and, before the episode was over, forty-three people had been killed, most of them prisoners shot in the violent attack mounted by New York State Troopers to retake control of the institution.

Robert B. McKay chaired the official investigation into the debacle at Attica. In highlighting an episode that took place in the weeks leading up to the prison's takeover, the report outlined how the "worst fears" of the prison guards were confirmed, how "the officers' apprehensions soared" when they witnessed a number of inmates engaged in a ceremony to greet a prominent Muslim inmate as he joined the prison population: "Standing in a line along one side of the yard, arms folded across their chests, was a group of inmates recognized as Muslims. Facing them was another group, similarly stationed, and recognized as [Black] Panthers. Seated and standing around a table between them were leaders of both groups and a number of [Puerto Rican] Young Lords, apparently serving as intermediaries." The Attica staff feared that the stately diplomacy of this ceremony pointed to "the prospects of an inmate population unified in its hostility and capable of speaking with a single voice."[149]

Sam Melville was prominent among those inmates recognized as instigators of the jail's takeover. A resident of New York City, he had made the transition from peaceful activism to violent protest after he provided cover and shelter for two refugees from Canada who were members of the FLQ, the Front for the Liberation of Quebec. Following the FLQ's violent example, Melville embarked on a short career as a self-styled revolutionary, planting bombs in several locations including the New York Harbor pier of the United Fruit Company. Pleading guilty to the charges against him, Melville ended up as a prisoner in Attica. There he embarked on a campaign to draw attention to conditions inside one of the most notorious jails in the United States. In Attica, he claimed, "the mortality rate rivals that of Bengla Desh."[150]

Melville brought on the ire of the authorities, especially for his campaign to identify as unconstitutional many elements of the regulations governing Attica. He identified as illegal, for instance, the policy that made prison officials the arbiters of what published materials the inmates could or could not read. Many in the prison population gave Melville high levels of respect because of his willingness to accept severe punishments for defying those aspects of the penal regime he considered wrong. Especially among the African-American prisoners, Melville's reputation helped him to transcend some of the unwritten codes that might otherwise have prevented this White man from exercising influence across the prison's colour lines. Melville's letters were published after his death, and his writings constitute a telling record of the politics and psychology of violent protest on the most radical fringes of the decolonization movement within the United States.[151] In his view, the criminal actions for which he had been jailed were directed towards "salvation from meaningless annihilation."[152]

Among Melville's published writings is the first edition of the newsletter that he secretly wrote and distributed throughout Attica during the prelude to the uprising. Entitled *The Iced Pig*, the newsletter encouraged inmates to think of the crimes that had landed them in prison as based on "doing in a crude way what the Rockefellers and Fords have been doing since they stole this land from the Indians 200 years ago."[153] Old copies of *The Iced Pig* may have made a significant impact on a new inmate at Attica, nineteen-year-old John Boncore. He arrived at the notorious penitentiary just days before the riot that would radically alter his life forever. According to his account of his childhood, his mother, Joan Hill, was born on the Six Nations reserve near Brantford, Ontario, and he was taken from her by child welfare authorities in New York when he was seven years old. Twelve years later he would face a murder charge for allegedly killing a prison guard during the inmates' takeover of Attica. Two and a half decades later he would again be at the centre of controversy for the role he played in the genesis of a modern-day Indian war in British Columbia. An essential element of this conflict pivoted on Boncore's close relationship with lawyer Bruce Clark, a legal advocate who sought to identify the "theft" of the lands of British Columbia from the Indigenous peoples as an international crime.

Boncore's narrative of the background of the Attica uprising, like Melville's, places considerable emphasis on the impact on the inmates of the news that George Jackson, an author, member of the Black Panther Party, and a jailed champion of prisoners' rights, had been murdered in San Quentin penitentiary in August 1971.[154] Jackson's many admirers inside and outside the US penal system suspected that the government was directly or indirectly behind his violent assassination. As Boncore saw it, "there were a lot coming into prison who were challenging issues about racism and sexism and taking part in the anti-imperial, anti-colonial move-ment. They were bringing these issues in with them to the joint ... It seemed like most of us that had that sort of attitude ended up in Attica and it all made for a very explosive situation."[155]

On September 13, 1971, the government moved to reclaim jurisdiction over the Attica facility and its inmates. As Boncore describes it, the action began with the firing of tear gas canisters in the prison yard:

Thousands of bullets were flying everywhere. Screams of agonizing pain and horror echoed against the bullet-riddled walls. Troopers stormed the prison afoot. They were yelling out people's names they intended to kill, like Sam Melville whose chest was blown to pieces and Elliot Barkley, whose whole back was blown away. Brothers' faces were blown from their brains, others were holding guts that were sagging to the ground. Cops were systematically killing in a blood rage like a thirst that could not be quenched.... Many were tortured. Some brothers had Xs marked on their back for executions that were carried out late into the evening even after we were all re-caged and posing no threat. To this day, not one single cop has been tried and convicted for these blatent murders.

Looking back on these events, Boncore reflected: "Attica was certainly the operation that figuratively lifted the cataract off my internal vision as the illusions of freedom, justice and equality in this so-called democracy dis-sipated forever. Physically my corneas were permanently damaged by CN-4 gases [tear gas]. I certainly understood the grief, pain, and horror of the countless massacres of my people. The killing hasn't stopped to this day."[156] As news of this episode began to circulate, the word *Attica* passed into the realm of popular imagination and folklore. For many, the term became syn-onymous with the resistance of the underclass to the violent imposition of unjust authority. The allegation of murder pressed on Boncore was part of a series of high-profile prosecutions that helped steer the American Indian Movement (AIM) along a trajectory of internal divisions and acrimony simi-lar to that suffered by the activists of the Black Panther Party. Boncore's own journey from the care of child welfare authorities, to orphanages, to reform schools, to the mean streets, to jail, and finally to penitentiary embodied larger patterns of oppression that permeate many relationships of caste and class in North America. His experiences were representative of those of many others in a society where the most marginalized groups provide a disproportionately large part of North America's prison popula-tion. This phenomenon helps to explain how it was that AIM first coalesced in the prisons and urban ghettos of North America's Mid-West. It began in initiatives to help urban Indians and to raise levels of education and self-awareness among Aboriginal inmates. This process sometimes included efforts to advance the cause of religious freedom in North America's jails by bringing in Aboriginal elders to conduct ceremonies that reflect and renew the land's oldest spiritual traditions.

Boncore's growing embrace of his Native American heritage both led and mirrored the genesis of the American Indian Movement. In the course of this journey the Attica veteran was given the Mohawk name Dacajeweiah, which translates in English as Splitting the Sky. In 1995 he emerged as a key figure in the Battle of Gustafsen Lake, a modern-day Indian war in the interior of British Columbia. This battle renewed some of the turbulence that, historically, has injected considerable violence into the relationship between Indigenous peoples and non-Aboriginal governments in Canada's westernmost province. It drew on some of the same sources of acrimony that led the Royal Navy to bombard the Salish village on Kuper Island in 1863 or that culminated in the Crown's hanging of the Chilcotin Five in 1864. This violence serves as a reminder of the tumultuous history that has made British Columbia the home territory of a particularly determined array of advocates who have championed the cause of Aboriginal rights, including the likes of John Robson, Andy Paull, the Reverends Arthur O'Meara and Peter Kelly, Frank Calder, Senator Len Marchand, James Gosnell, Thomas Berger, David Suzuki, Arthur Manuel, Miles Richardson, Jack Cram, and Janice Switlo.

In calling attention internationally to the plight of Indigenous peoples in the province, Joseph Stiglitz, the former chief economist of the World Bank, gave an updated version of the defence of Aboriginal rights advanced by F.W. Cheeson in 1858 when he intervened in the *New York Times* on behalf of the London-based Aborigines' Protection Society.[157] Stiglitz helped an Aboriginal intervention into a trade dispute at the World Trade Organization by pointing out that the failure to pay royalties to Indigenous peoples in British Columbia for trees cut on their traditional lands amounts to a kind of Aboriginal subsidy to the local forestry industry.[158]

The Battle of Gustafsen Lake took place during the decade of transition from the era of the Cold War to that of the Global War on Terror. Seen in the broader context of imperial globalization since 1492, both wars provided cover for episodes of theft in the ongoing appropriation of lands and resources from Indigenous peoples. The government's priority in the Battle of Gustafsen Lake was to avoid any public reckoning with the unresolved controversies swirling around the unceded status of Aboriginal title in British Columbia. It was to confine media attention to allegations of the protestors' criminality and thereby point public attention away from the possibility that Indigenous peoples in British Columbia have suffered for generations from the onslaughts of international crimes. In the terminology of the Royal Canadian Mounted Police (RCMP), the government orchestrated a campaign of "disinformation and smear" to depict the targeted group as terrorists rather than as principled militants seeking to force the appropriate authorities to face legal consequences for their infractions of constitutional and international law.

Arrayed on one side of this conflict was a contingent of modern-day Indian fighters employed by the governments of Canada and British Columbia. The Crown's Indian fighters operated out of Camp Zulu, a secret military base in BC's interior near 100 Mile House. Government troops were equipped with armored personnel carriers provided by the Canadian Armed Forces. Among the Canadian soldiers assigned by the federal Cabinet to serve in the operation were members of the elite unit Joint Task Force Two. Camp Zulu was also the headquarters for a contingent of about four hundred members of the Royal Canadian Mounted Police. The Canadian government admitted that Crown agents fired some 77,000 rounds of live ammunition into the Aboriginal camp. Moreover, the federal and provincial ordinance experts on the site employed trip-wired explosive devices that some have described as land mines. While the governments of Canada and BC deployed overwhelming force on the ground, state officials reserved their most concerted efforts for the media campaign to turn public opinion against the targeted group. In a behind-the-scenes strategy session caught on video and available on You Tube, one of the RCMP's media liaison officers boasts, "Smear campaigns are our specialty."[159]

The core group on the other side of the dispute consisted of about twenty members of the self-declared Defenders of the Shuswap Nation, also known as the Ts'peten Defenders. They and their international network of allies and supporters embodied a blending of AIM-inspired traditionalists, constitutional experts, Internet activists, and New Age idealists who drew hope and inspiration from their interpretation of some prophetic elements of Aboriginal spirituality. Those who would become the Ts'peten Defenders began the summer of 1995 as participants in a sun dance. This Aboriginal religious ceremony took place on a privately owned ranch near Gustafsen Lake. Some of the dancers restyled themselves as freedom fighters after local ranch hands attempted to evict the Native ceremonialists as trespassers. According to Splitting the Sky, the protagonists referred to his group as "red niggers." Not all the Ts'peten Defenders were of Aboriginal ancestry. The non-Aboriginal activists included Shelagh Franklin, a committed activist convinced that the Canadian government was not living up to its legal responsibility to recognize and affirm the constitutional existence of Aboriginal and treaty rights. Throughout her trial she never deviated from her position that the Crown's actions at Gustafsen Lake ran contrary to the rule of law. Another prominent visitor to join the stand was Suniva Bronson, a member of a prominent US banking family and an environmentalist with strong ties to Robert Hunter and Paul Watson, the founders of Greenpeace.[160]

The Ts'peten Defenders sought to force into the spotlight of public attention the connection between the BC land question and the international crime of genocide. Closely connected to the allegation of genocide was the charge that the Indigenous peoples of Canada's westernmost province had been robbed of their lands and resources in ways that violated even the imperial and constitutional law of British North America. The provincial government's decision in the 1990s to reverse its old hostility to the recognition of Aboriginal title still did not address the problem of how to structure negotiations to resolve the outstanding issues in a fair and conscientious manner. As the Ts'peten Defenders saw it, the system for transacting the fifty or so Crown-Aboriginal treaties in BC is deeply corrupted by funding mechanisms that involve conflicts of interest as institutionalized by Canada's *Indian Act*. This Act is an elaborate body of Canadian legislation that treats the elected officials of Indian bands as administrators of Crown law. It places the Aboriginal administrators of federal Indian policy under the higher powers of the federal minister of Indian affairs, a figure of authority not elected by Indigenous peoples or directly accountable to them in any way. The outcome is a system of negotiations that puts Indian representatives of the Crown across the table from provincial and federal representatives of the Crown. By its very nature this format for bargaining undermines the sovereign-to-sovereign, nation-to-nation ideals that some see as the essence of viable Crown-Aboriginal treaties.

As the Ts'peten Defenders lawyer, Bruce Clark argued with great zeal and determination that the problems connected to the placement of Crown officials on all sides of the issue are made more extreme when the venues of transaction include the Crown's courts. In order for the chiefs and band councillors to receive federal or provincial funding to advance their positions through litigation, they effectively have to limit their choice of lawyers to those who adhere to the principle that the Aboriginal and treaty rights can only be exercised within the framework of municipal and domestic law. There is no latitude on the federal and provincial sides to allow for negotiations on the recognition of Aboriginal and treaty rights in venues of international relations or to recognize the need for vehicles of international jurisprudence in order to achieve neutral and disinterested third-party adjudication in disputes involving contested assertions of sovereignty. [161]

In their shift of focus from the spiritual expression of the sun dance to the legal status of title to land and resources in British Columbia, the Ts'peten Defenders based their actions on the principle that they were engaged in a legitimate act of self-defence. They saw themselves as protectors of Aboriginal territory subject to a regime of private ownership that does not conform to the regime of imperial, constitutional, and international law associated with the Royal Proclamation of 1763. The Battle of Gustafsen Lake can thus be viewed as part of a long continuum of North American Indian wars that has never really ended. The confrontation and the different court actions to flow from it are recognized by some of those who have looked most closely at the affair as a serious stain on the reputation of law-enforcement agencies in Canada. As one BC columnist wrote in

The Province, the "RCMP took reporters for a ride." Most of what they fed journalists covering the confrontation "was a crock."[162]

Indeed, a US court that subsequently investigated the episode characterized it as a simmering civil war in which Crown officials undermined the rule of law by favouring an agenda that politicized the criminal justice system. One former RCMP agent who acted as a lawyer for some of the defendants indicated that it was "a police constructed event ... probably 100% ... the police didn't go into this thing as an impartial group, attempting to gather evidence of a crime. They went in as a large media campaign, to first create these [Ts'peten Defender] people as 'bad,' as 'terrorists."[163] The media dissemination of RCMP lies worked to counteract the efforts of the Ts'peten Defenders and Bruce Clark to present the episode as the basis of a constitutional test case. Clark had devoted about twenty-five years of concerted study to his specialty in the law of Aboriginal title. In the course of his efforts he added a master's degree and a doctorate to his law degree.[164]

The maverick lawyer inspired intense acrimony when he attempted to link the confrontation at Gustafsen Lake to the UN's Genocide Convention. He attracted further ire when he argued that domestic courts in British Columbia lack jurisdictional legitimacy as disinterested third-party arbiters on questions concerning the legal framework of Crown-Aboriginal relations. Instead of addressing the constitutional arguments put forward by Clark, the local judge arbitrating the facts of the confrontation sent the unorthodox lawyer for a mental examination. Another key figure in the Gustafsen Lake conflict was William Jones Ignace, a Shuswap-speaking elder who, at the time of the standoff, was in his late sixties. Ignace resided on the Adams Lake Reserve near Chase, BC, the same community that was home to the Fourth World visionary George Manuel. During the confrontation, Ignace infuriated Ovide Mercredi, a lawyer and national chief of the Assembly of First Nations (AFN). The national chief is chosen by the elected Indian chiefs of Canada's 633 federally constituted Indian bands. Their favoured access to federal recognition and funding is based ultimately on the willingness of these elected chiefs to adhere to the relationships of power and accountability put in place by the Parliament of Canada in the *Indian Act.*

Mercredi entered the fray at Gustafsen Lake as a mediator between the RCMP and the Ts'peten Defenders. His interest in this intervention was to defend his core constituency from the kind of pointed criticisms directed by the Aboriginal militants at those Native elites who build careers as both administrators and beneficiaries of federal Indian policy. In one of their discussions, Ignace asked Mercredi to put his signature on a document outlining the Indian sovereignists' stand. When the chief refused, the elder referred derisively to the AFN's Cree lawyer as a water boy for the federal government. In subsequent court proceedings Ignace, or "the Wolverine" as he was widely identified in the media, turned aside all attempts to make him abandon his constitutional position. He refused to compromise his contention that the regime of property relations in the lands and waters of much of British Columbia does not conform to the requirements of the rule of law, or that the uncompromised character of Aboriginal title throughout most of the province flows from Aboriginal law, British imperial law, Canadian constitutional law, and international law. To him and the Ts'peten Defenders, Aboriginal title grows from principles recognized in the Covenant Chain tradition of Crown-Indian diplomacy, the Royal Proclamation of 1763, and section 35 of Canada's *Constitution Act, 1982*.

Ignace's stance, together with his unwavering attachment to his legal advocate Bruce Clark, was almost certainly a factor in the heavy prison sentence imposed on the Shuswap elder for his role in the Battle of Gustafsen Lake. Suniva Bronson and some of the other accused engaged in plea bargaining with the Crown, though not all the accused gave up their principles to succumb to the enticements of lighter sentences. Throughout the court proceedings, the pregnant Shelagh Franklin refused to abandon her contention that BC and Canadian courts lack proper jurisdiction to adjudicate cases involving issues such as those that arose from the her defence of Aboriginal title and of Indian sovereignty at Gustafsen Lake .

Ignace's teachers included Robert Satiacum, whose legal interpretations and political tactics helped inform the positions of the Ts'peten Defenders. Satiacum was one the most effective Native American strategists to emerge in the late 1960s during the course of the Washington state fish-ins. A close associate of the movie star and Aboriginal rights activist Marlon Brando, Satiacum became a leading figure in the quest to expand the applications of the reference in section 2.3 of the US Constitution to "Indians not taxed." As Ignace saw it, the criminal justice system was improperly deployed to undermine Satiacum's ability to advance constitutional positions that held the potential to create the basis for more viable Indian economies. Satiacum acquired powerful new enemies, however, once he pressed his legal arguments beyond Indian gaming and the tax-free sales of tobacco and alcohol to attempt a fundamental reordering of the tax structure of the US oil and gas industry.[165]

Ramsay Clark was another key figure who intervened in the legal and political proceedings arising from the Battle of Gustafsen Lake. He had been attorney general of the United States during the administration of President Lyndon Johnson and, in the course of his ascent within the federal government, he and his predecessor, Robert Kennedy, began to collaborate in the quest for positive outcomes to Indian land claims (at the same time as they criticized the US role in Vietnam).[166] When Clark left the federal government, he became Splitting the Sky's lawyer in the aftermath of the Attica debacle and, in the years that followed, he took part on the side of the defence in a number of highly politicized show trials – including the prosecution and conviction in 2006 of the Iraqi leader Saddam Hussein.[167] In his quest to use the institutions of law to draw attention to the alleged crimes against humanity even on the part of his own government,

Ramsay Clark would come to personify over a number of decades the irrepressible ideals of the movement for decolonization arising from *within* the superpower's own citizenry.

In his comments published on the book cover of Splitting the Sky's autobiography, *From Attica to Gustafsen Lake*, Clark refers to the author as an "emerging leader in a worldwide movement, observer, strategist and chosen Sundance Chief at the time of the Gustafsen Lake confrontation in British Columbia ... In the course of this standoff Canada employed all the violence, deception, wiles and corruption learned from five hundred years of experience in crushing Indian peoples."[168] The autobiography ends on a hopeful note based on the US judiciary's granting political asylum in November 2000 to James Pitawanakwat, an Odawa veteran of the Battle of Gustafsen Lake. The Pitawanakwats are a prominent Indian family centred at the Wikwemikong Reserve (unceded) on Manitoulin Island in Ontario. In overruling the extradition request of the US State Department, Judge Janice Stewart wrote a decision with broad implications for the conduct of both Canadian Indian policy and US foreign policy. She drew on an expert's report prepared for the court (by this author) at the request of Pitawanakwat's lawyer, who worked for the Federal Public Defenders Office in Portland, Oregon. Judge Stewart determined that the political offenses exception clause of the extradition treaty between Canada and the United States applied to the circumstances surrounding the criminalization of James Pitawanakwat in Canada and concluded that the criminal justice system in Canada was subjected to political interference in a dispute manifesting some attributes of a civil war. The US government was therefore not allowed to proceed with the delivery of the Aboriginal dissident to Canadian authorities.

In overruling the executive branch of the US government, Judge Stewart stated that "the Gustafsen incident involved an organized group of native people rising up in their homeland against the occupation by the government of Canada of their sacred and unceded tribal land." She referred to the Canadian government's "disinformation and smear campaign" to cover up the constitutional and international issues permeating the conflict.[169] In arriving at this position, she drew on the existing case law of extradition proceedings involving, for instance, Palestinian soldiers, the Tamils of Sri Lanka, and members of the IRA. The effect of Judge Stewart's decision was to advance the internationalization of the BC land question. Indeed, the moment that the Canadian government committed elements of the Canadian Armed Forces to intervene in the dispute over the constitutional status of the BC lands, it confirmed that the issues advanced by the Ts'peten Defenders transcend the bounds of domestic law enforcement.

The effectiveness of the disinformation and smear campaign in the Canadian media helped to pre-empt any broadly based political movement to demand some sort of public inquiry to investigate how a US judge had arrived at such significant conclusions about Crown violations of international law. Generally speaking, the misapprehension was allowed to continue that the only transgressions, if any, that had taken place on the Crown side of the Battle of Gustafsen Lake involved an infringement on the rights of a few radical Indians. Few men and women of influence were ready to face up to Bruce Clark's unrelenting contention that the true victim of the Crown's role was the integrity of the rule of law itself. Editorialists at the *Vancouver Sun* helped to defend the imperative of governments to break their own laws with their response to the ruling on the Pitawanakwat case: "If Judge Stewart's ruling stands it could potentially undermine the effectiveness of the Canada-US extradition treaty in the future," Tthey asserted. And just as importantly, it puts a U.S. judge in the position of shaping Canada's national policy on one of the most pressing matters facing the country." On the basis of these arguments, the representatives of the *Vancouver Sun* concluded that the Canada's Ministry of Justice should appeal the ruling.[170] The Canadian government declined this advice. Judge Stewart's judicial interpretation of the extradition treaty between Canada and the United States still stands.

Interestingly, Splitting the Sky would become in future years an outspoken advocate of the position that the official explanation of the cause of the disintegration of the World Trade Center's three towers and the attack on the Pentagon on September 11, 2001, do not meet even the most basic tests of truth. In taking this stand, he called on his knowledge of how the criminal justice system and the media had conspired to misrepresent the nature of the confrontation in the Battle of Gustafsen Lake and its attending processes of litigation. This example of a smear campaign to demonize as terrorism a position advocating adherence to the rule of law presents in microcosm a telling illustration of the abuses that would become rampant during the era of the so-called Global War on Terror. Splitting the Sky (STS) sought to address these abuses when, in March 2009, he attempted a citizen's arrest of George W. Bush for war crimes and crimes against humanity when the former US president visited Calgary, Alberta, to give a public lecture. STS's intervention embodied the assertiveness of a growing global movement whose adherents are no longer willing to see the highest level of authority responsible for international crimes such as torture, illegal renditions, political assassinations, and mass murder remain above the law and therefore immune to criminal charges. STS's stance has received support from a number of public figures, including Ramsay Clark and Cynthia McKinney, the African-American former Congresswoman from Georgia. When in Congress, McKinney formally questioned the official explanation of September 11. She has spent time in an Israeli prison for her efforts to bring humanitarian aid to the victims of the Isreali government's bombing and chemical attacks on the people of the Palestinian ghetto of Gaza during the period of transition from the presidency of George W. Bush to that of Barack Obama.[171]

ON THE DESTRUCTION OF PEOPLES THROUGH THE CRIMINALIZATION, INCAPACITATION, AND KILLING OF THEIR NATURAL LEADERSHIP

History has been repeated many times when the rich and wealthy are immunized from legal accountability for their crimes, whereas those who have been most effective in calling into question the legitimacy of imperial rule, slavery, apartheid, and the unilateral extinguishment of Aboriginal rights and titles have again and again been unjustly criminalized. Such episodes of victimization extend, for instance, from the death in a French jail of Toussaint L'Overture, to the forced removal by the US Armed Forces of Cherokee patriots in the Trail of Tears, to the wrongful incarceration of Big Bear and Poundmaker in Stony Mountain Penitentiary in Manitoba,[172] to the FBI's covert war on the Black Panthers and the American Indian Movement, and to the lengthy incarceration of Nelson Mandela by the White minority regime in South Africa. From Pontiac to Sitting Bull, José Rizal, Gandhi, Patrice Lumumba, Martin Luther King Jr, Robert Kennedy, Salvador Allende, and many more, a disproportionately high number of those who oppose the oppressive relationships of power meet their deaths through execution or assassination. In the course of the Cold War, the process of criminalizing the leadership of many indigenous movements advocating economic decolonization resulted in the installation of dictators such as the Shah of Iran, or Generals Mobutu, Suharto, and Pinochet. The primary function assigned to such coddled agents of monopoly capitalism has been to repress their local dissidents in order to make their countries safe and profitable for the activities of transnational corporations.

Tecumseh was one of those martyred by the US Armed Forces in the course of his campaign to achieve international recognition for a sovereign polity that would afford a degree of national security for Indigenous peoples in North America. Lewis Cass heaped contempt on the memory of the resistance movement led by Tecumseh in language similar to that employed by those authorities who dismissed the stand of the Ts'peten Defenders and their lawyer, Bruce Clark. Cass was a former Michigan governor and presidential candidate who went on to become one of the White House's key apologists for the so-called Indian removal policies of President Andrew Jackson. As the top official responsible for the Trail of Tears, Jackson had broad political backing for his scheme to move Indians east of the Mississippi to an Indian Territory farther west. Cass described those Aboriginal patriots who fought with Tecumseh to defend their country in the War of 1812 as "deserters from a few tribes." He continued: "The acknowledged government of each tribe disavowed any participation in their projects. And they were in fact a lawless predatory band, obeying no common authority, and seeking no common authority, and seeking no rational object."[173]

Similar allegations were pressed against Louis Riel.[174] He was criminalized and executed for treason in 1885 for the stand he took in assisting his fellow Métis in the region of the Saskatchewan River to defend themselves from being dispossessed by the builders of the Canadian Pacific Railway Company. It was not until Canada's assembly of an Indian fighting army at Camp Zulu in British Columbia in 1995 that the Crown forces resorted to anything like their assault on Riel's small band of resisters over a century earlier. In 1869 and 1870 Riel first attracted the attention of the authorities in Ottawa when he challenged the right of the Dominion of Canada to annex the vast territories of the Hudson's Bay Company without any negotiations whatsoever with the Indigenous peoples of the region. As a result of his interventions, the province of Manitoba was created and the Aboriginal provisions of the Royal Proclamation of 1763 were extended into much of the newly annexed territories in the form of eleven Crown-Aboriginal treaties.

At his trial in 1885, Riel explained that his own experience of having been criminalized was part of a larger pattern of colonization. Referring to the Aboriginal communities of the Canadian West, he asserted, "When they began by treating the leaders of the small communities as bandits, as outlaws, leaving them without protection, they disorganized the community."[175] In the context of the Western Hemisphere, but particularly in North America, this disorganization is manifest in appallingly high levels of Aboriginal incarceration, suicide, domestic violence, addictions, fetal alcohol syndrome, and unemployment. The extreme marginalization of many Native people in North America serves as a marker for the continuing power of a global system originating in the colonization of much of the planet by the major powers of Western Europe. It is a basic denial of the right of self-determination to criminalize and thereby remove the natural leaders of indigenous communities in order to replace them with authorities whose primary job is to safeguard and enforce capitalism's monopoly of material relations.

Such assaults on the resourcefulness of indigenous leadership violate many international laws, including the provision in the Atlantic Charter that refers to "the right of all peoples to choose the form of government under which they shall live." For a community to undergo the criminalization and consequent disabling of its natural leadership is to lose its capacity to organize in order to assert indigenous control and jurisdiction over Aboriginal lands and resources. The impoverishment that accompanies this process has grave consequences in a world where the realm of the Bowl with One Spoon is in retreat. To be dispossessed and poor in this era most often means the loss of sufficient good food, clean water, sanitation, health care, education, and access to the vital flows of information available on the Internet. To deprive the largest part of whole groups of these basic necessities is to advance genocidal processes.

Riel proposed placing a great emphasis on the making and implementing of treaties as an enlightened means of instituting equality and respect between collectivities. In his final address to the Canadian court, he referred to the process of negotiation that had taken place between the Métis and the Dominion of Canada in their founding of Manitoba. Riel considered these negotiations as the prelude to the treaty that created the constitutional foundation of Manitoba: "There were two societies who treated together," he said; "one was small but in its smallness it had rights. The other was great but by its greatness it had no greater rights than the rights of the small, because the rights are the same for everyone."[176] Riel's line of thought leads to the conception of a global federation of polities great and small, all bound together by the integrity of a law capable of being enforced with equality and consistency on all global citizens.

Colonialism Incorporated: International Finance, Treaties, Crimes, and the Law during the Age of Impunity

I see in the near future a crisis approaching that unnerves me and causes me to tremble for the safety of my country ... Corporations have been enthroned and an era of corruption in high places will follow, and the money power of the country will endeavor to prolong its reign by working with the prejudices of the people until all wealth is aggregated in a few hands and the Republic is destroyed.

US President Abraham Lincoln to
Colonel William F. Elkins, 1864

Truth is treason in the empire of lies.

Ron Paul, *The Revolution: A Manifesto*, 2008

THE LEGAL AND POLITICAL FRAMEWORK OF CORPORATE POWER IN CAPITAL'S EMPIRE

During the last four centuries, for-profit corporations have given concerted expression to some of the West's most deep impulses to dominate all nature, including human nature. From the business navigations of the East India companies to those of Google, for-profit corporations have long resided at the core of the most basic processes where technological, financial, legal, political, and psychological manipulations converge in the transformation of matter, invention, and organized work into privately owned objects, spaces, and ideas. So widespread and pervasive did this pattern of corporate commercial enterprise become that, by the mid-1950s, it was embedded as much in the interior landscapes of imagination as in the external structures of economic interaction. In 1957 William T. Gossett, a former general council for Ford Corporation, outlined how large companies and the culture that surrounds them had moved to the forefront of an increasingly pervasive Americanism then being disseminated throughout much of the world. "The modern stock corporation is a social and economic institution that touches every aspect of our lives," he explained; "in many ways, it is an institutionalized expression of our way of life. During the past 50 years, industry in corporate form has moved from the periphery to the very center of our social and economic existence. Indeed, it is not inaccurate to say that we live in a corporate society."[1]

The growth of this corporate society to truly global proportions has depended on the success of the expansionary drive to atomize and reconfigure realms of mind and matter as property. In this fashion, significant elements of nature have been isolated, deconstructed, and reconstituted as receptacles of proprietorship whose adherence to human and institutional possessors is often represented in patents, deeds, shares, receipts, and other certificates of proprietary entitlement. The primary driving force animating capitalist strategies for the organization of time and space, credit and debt, consumption and production – even war and peace – is the promise of profit, but especially corporate profit. Through the medium of profit, capital replicates itself as it must in order to deliver a financial return to those who invest their wealth in commercial enterprises. How much more can the conditions of biocultural diversity be diminished in the capitalist production and replication of commodified monocultures? At what point are nature's ecological laws so irredeemably transgressed that life's healthy renewal can no longer be sustained?

The unrelenting efforts of capital's owners to increase their material entitlements by privatizing the commons pulls ever more of the earth away from the narrowing domain of the Bowl with One Spoon. It denigrates the complex of forces described by John Story in 1953 in his "first book of ecology" as *The Web of Life*.[2] Where the web of life favours pluralism and biodiversity as hallmarks of ecological health, the web of global capitalism favours the mass production of sameness as the primary condition for profit through economies of scale. The process of mass marketing begins with the creation of monocultures of the mind and extends to the replication of the manufactured world through industrial processes that impose uniformity on nature's infinite capacity for variety.

Canadian philosophy professor John McMurtry has introduced his own categories to explain the destructive outcomes of the "values wars" that pit the imperatives of "the global market" against the needs of "the life economy."[3] In illustrating his thesis, McMurtry refers to the major corporate-led military invasions of the twenty-first century as being dependent on a very "blinkered" interpretation of the events of September 11. He describes this response as an outgrowth of "the corporate market structure of consciousness," as the product of "a ruling group-mind led by a corporate America harnessed to the US military juggernaut." He continues:

There is a clear pattern to the madness that expresses this ruling group-mind. What is selected to remove or destroy always advances the corporate order's subjugation of formerly independent societies and resources, however false the justifications and however defenseless the victims may be. One form of Other is always selected for attack and appropriation – any autonomous, public or civil sector that can be privatized for profit, and any individuals, movements, or societies obstructing this conversion. All who oppose are "communists," "terrorists," or their "sympathizers," and are therefore subject to threats, torture, or death. When the global marketization of peoples happens by "peaceful means" it works by strategic electoral marketing and fiat trade treaties. When it proceeds by armed force, it is preceded by a *casus belli* for Armed Crusade against the Enemy. This was 9/11's function.[4]

Many historical factors converged to make the United States the launching site for the majority of the world's major transnational corporations. Most of the biggest of these enterprises would become well integrated into the military-industrial complex and the national security state. A root explanation of the aggressive vigour of this corporate culture lies in the reality that most of the original English colonies in North America began their life as corporate entities. The jurisdiction of Virginia, for instance, entered the world as a grant conveyed in 1606 by the English King to the London Company and the Plymouth Company. The New England Company obtained a royal charter in 1629 as the Governor and Company of Massachusetts Bay. The legal existence of Maryland began in 1632 with a corporate grant to Baron Baltimore. Carolina's distinct existence has its origins in a corporate grant in 1663 to eight Lords Proprietor. The origins of Pennsylvania lie in a corporate charter granted to William Penn in 1682. Georgia began with a corporate charter extended to James Oglethorpe in 1732.

This method of corporate colonization in the Western Hemisphere was very different from the imperialism of Spain. The Spanish government had obtained its charter to own and govern vast portions of the Americas directly from the Vatican. With this papal "donation' as their point of departure, Spain's sovereigns organized their holdings in the Americas as direct, unmediated extensions of their imperial jurisdiction. These two streams of colonial history produced very different types of empire. Unlike the centralized system of Roman Catholic dominion in the Americas, the main thrust of Protestant colonialism allowed for wider latitudes of formal local autonomy. The corporate structure of English governance in North America effectively inserted a mediating legal distinction between the colonial and the imperial branches of a more decentralized empire. While the ideals of Protestant liberty and evangelization were emphasized in all the English Crown's chartering instruments, Edward Winslow noted as early as 1624 that, in Anglo-America, "religion and profit jump together."[5]

The English companies in charge of colonizing North America and East India applied on land many of the lessons and principles acquired from the earliest stages of empire building when Queen Elizabeth authorized the seafaring exploits of privateers such as Sir Francis Drake. The rise of the English East India Company was closely connected to the rise the Dutch

East India Company, an enterprise whose proprietorship was based in publicly traded shares that were the primary medium of transaction in the Amsterdam stock market. While stock markets had previously existed in some of the Italian city states, the Dutch capital quickly acquired a reputation in the early seventeenth century as the site of the world's most prominent bourse. Attending the rise of the Amsterdam Bourse was an impressive array of complementary agencies of business, including those devoted to currency exchange, maritime insurance, and markets for speculation in the future price of commodities.[6] The convergence of Dutch and English business practices in New York, the site of the former New Amsterdam, was an important factor in the rise of a New World mecca of corporate culture. The core of that business culture developed along the legendary street where the Dutch had built a wall between the Hudson and East rivers to protect against the intrusion of unwanted Indians. Wall Street's future would depend on the success of its financiers in aligning their commercial interests with those of agencies whose exploitation, extermination, cooptation, or repression of Indigenous peoples the world over extended strategies originally developed in the treatment of Indians during the transcontinental expansion of the United States.

The growth of the slave trade often involved the extension of monopolies of trade to corporate agencies of imperial power such as the Guinea Company and the Company of Royal Adventurers Trading to Africa. The extension of lucrative corporate charters continued in the nineteenth century as Aleksandr Baranov consolidated his country's claims to Alaska through the agency of the Russian American Company. Barnov's advances in the commercial colonization of western North America through the fur trade helped to stimulate the competing activities of John Jacob Astor's American Fur Company and the London-based Hudson's Bay Company (HBC). Under George Simpson's energetic governance, the most enduring of England's old mercantile companies expanded its trading territory and modernized its methods during the decades before the HBC's extensive titles in Rupert's Land and the North-West Territory were sold to the Dominion of Canada in 1870.[7]

The growth of the English-speaking empire of imperial Britain continued into the late nineteenth century with the establishment of the British North Borneo Company in 1881, the Royal Niger Company in 1886, and Cecil Rhodes's British South African Company in 1889. The style of colonization advanced by these agencies of corporate globalization varied significantly from the style of commercial expansion that, by the beginning of the twenty-first century, had rendered the economies of Exxon Mobil, Wal-Mart, General Motors, Royal Dutch Shell, General Electric, and Mitsubishi much larger than the national economies of most countries on earth.[8] What transpired in the United States to make commercial institutions such as Wal-Mart, the huge oil and gas conglomerates, and the prescription drug companies such massive agencies in the world's political economy? How is it that the internal structures of commercial corporations became preeminent models for the organization of so many other kinds of institution, from universities to non-governmental organizations to national governments? What are the forces that have so dramatically altered the relationship of power between business companies and national governments that are the sovereign source of the authority invested in corporate charters? How did the corporate progeny of sovereign governments so effectively devour their parents? How is it that, even after the huge taxpayer-backed bailouts of 2008 and 2009, the fictions of corporate pre-eminence retained sufficient mystique to enable top executives of the financial sector to continue treating officials of elected governments as subordinates?

According to Charles Derber, the idea of "corporate privatism" has helped to give ideological justification to the withdrawal of many corporations from any sense of direct accountability to the sovereign states and peoples who gave them their legal charters.[9] As he explains in *Corporation Nation*, proponents of corporate privatism advanced the case that commercial companies inhabit a private sphere that must be shielded from direct state control and regulation as much as possible. Similarly, the case was made that the capital assets of commercial corporations should constitute private property under the same laws governing the assets owned by private individuals.

The combination of private rights and public privilege gained by chartered corporations cut against some of the idealism invested in the American Revolution. The United States was founded in opposition to the alleged tyranny of British imperial governance in North America. It was founded with a loud burst of Anglo-American protest condemning the British Empire as a royal bastion of monopoly and privilege. The Bank of England was seen as an especially oppressive imperial agency, one that had intervened politically to prohibit the Anglo-American colonies from continuing to issue their own debt-free local currencies often described as scrip. To some in the founding generation of the United States, the very idea of chartering corporations seemed like the extension of monopoly powers to a new class of favoured elites. Others in the new polity were content to retain those features of British law that treated corporate enterprises as contingent polities that could be terminated when their operations tended "to the common grievance, prejudice, and inconvenience of His Majesty's subjects."[10]

In the United States it was the legislatures of the sovereign states rather than the national government that first took from the British sovereign the constitutional capacity to grant corporate charters.[11] Except in Massachusetts, however, these powers were used sparingly. Broader debates about the appropriate legal relationship between citizens, corporate entities, and state power found a flash point in the first half of the nineteenth century in controversies over whether the United States should institute its own national bank. With memories still fresh of the monopolistic powers claimed in the Anglo-American colonies by the Bank of England, the answer to this question was at first a resounding no! Presidents Thomas Jefferson and Andrew Jackson both identified themselves as committed opponents of the invocation of federal authority to charter such an institution. These populist leaders both advanced the case that the concentration of so much centralized control over the financial future of the United States would be bound to concentrate power in a way that favoured the special privileges of the few over the equal rights of the many.

When state governments did create corporate charters before the Civil War, they generally followed the British model of having precise and stringent conditions attached. Moreover, the officers of the new corporate entities were expected to seek periodic renewals of their charters. The assumptions underlying these practices were that corporations should serve the public good, that corporate charters could be revoked when the public interest was no longer served, and that corporations and their officers were ultimately accountable for their actions to the governments that had granted them their charters.[12] In this sense all corporations were viewed as public institutions – as extensions of the legislatures that created them. These assumptions animated, for instance, a decision of the Supreme Court of Virginia in 1809 when it ruled: if the motivations of those seeking a corporate charter were "merely private or selfish; if detrimental to, nor not promotive of, the public good, they have no adequate claim upon the legislature for the privileges."[13] In 1834 the Pennsylvania legislature elaborated this conception, entrenching in statute the principle that "a corporation in law ... may be molded to any shape or for any purpose that the Legislature may deem most conducive for the general good."[14]

The idea that all corporations represented extensions of the sovereign public sector was dramatically transformed during the final decades of the nineteenth century, a period dominated by the vast expansions in the territory of railway enterprise together with massive industrialization stimulated by the US Civil War. During this time of rapid growth in the property base of the United States there was a return to many of those principles first expressed in the quest of the pre-revolutionary British North American land companies to control the pace as well the legal form of westward expansion. Unlike their pre-revolutionary predecessors, the new champions of expanded corporate power succeeded in infiltrating the deepest recesses of the executive, legislative, and judicial branches of government. The aim of many of these "frontiersmen" of "corporate society" was to make the corporate vehicles of their own personal wealth and influence the legal extensions of both the public power derived from legislatures and the private rights vested in US citizens. The goal was to combine rights derived from the sovereign personality of government with the constitutional guarantees and protections reserved for private persons.

The US Supreme Court's ruling in 1886 in the case *of Santa Clara County versus the Southern Pacific Company* represented a major leap forward in the realization of these goals. The jurists decided that corporations qualified as "natural persons." This interpretation arose from a consideration of the Fourteenth Amendment of the US Constitution, a provision added in 1868 to protect former slaves from being deprived of "life, liberty or property without due process of law." With this change the primary engines of business development in the United States were able, both metaphorically and actually, to suck up more public oxygen by burning greater quantities of privatized fuel. The leaders of commercial expansion were able to advance the agenda of corporate privatism while extending simultaneously their influence on public policy. The business activity of corporations was thus provided with an extremely broad zone for economic, legal, and political manoeuvres. Multiple share owners in a given corporation could pool their capital in increasingly complex and profitable ways in order to expand their private accumulations of wealth. The marriage of private gain with the collective enterprise entailed in the complex organization of giant corporations did not end with share owners but extended to directors, executives, managers, scientists, technicians, machine operators, sales personnel, public relations specialists, political lobbyists, distributors, franchisers, and the like.

The proliferating mechanisms of corporate capitalism transformed the earth into property at accelerating rates. The sometimes brutal incursions of this capitalist revolution laid the groundwork for opposition to the inequities of *laissez-faire* commercialism. Capitalist expansion gave rise to anti-capitalist resistance movements as institutionalized most elaborately in the state machinery of the Soviet block and Maoist China. On the middle ground between these two revolutionary wings of privatized and collectivized materialism developed European social democracy, the US New Deal, Keynesian economics, and the Non-Aligned Movement. With the fall of the Berlin Wall in 1989, the social welfare state was increasingly challenged and belittled by the imperatives of the shareholder state.

The totalization of capitalism as an all-encompassing system of global material relations cast new light on the growing tension between rich and poor, creditor and debtor, jailer and inmate, drug lord, drug dealer, and junkie. This growing force of polarization was expressed by the raising of many walls and fences to protect the enclaves of the rich, to isolate and incarcerate the poor, and to separate Israeli power and privilege from the recriminations of dispossessed Palestinians. The deployment of authoritarian tactics to protect the entitled minority from the anguish of a disentitled majority found expression in China, a country where capitalist hyper-privatization flourished under the authoritarian auspices of a one-party state. The frontier expansion of capitalism in the one-party regime of China symbolized a larger phenomenon where the globalization of a comprehensive system of material relationships is being policed by the authoritarian workings of the world's pre-eminent military-industrial complex.

The tension between the idea of the corporation as a vehicle of individual entrepreneurship and the idea of the corporation as a vehicle for collective cooperation among its suppliers, officers, employees, and customers was reflected in a more generalized tension over the direction of US growth. Would the United States live up to the eloquence of Lincoln's Gettysburg Address by expanding at home and abroad the principles of government of the people, by the people, and for the people? Or would this unique polity on the frontiers of so many human hopes and expectations give itself over to the autocracy of unilateral executive rule as epitomized in the hierarchical and centralized organization of corporate governance? Would US corporatism and militarism converge in a new axis of authoritarian rule? Clearly the egalitarian principles embodied in the ideals of one-person-one-vote were contradicted by the concentration of such disproportionately large amounts of political power in the hands of the super rich and their agents, those who do their bidding in board rooms and executive suites of large corporations. This concentration of control intensified as the executive branch of most commercial corporations was increasingly cut off from the proprietary authority theoretically vested in large masses of share holders, many of them middle-class rather than rich, many of them owners of corporate property through the vehicle of their pension plans.

After detailing the extensive powers allowed by a submissive judiciary to modern-day chief executive officers, Robert Monks observed that the "accountability" of CEOs to the largest mass of shareholders is "only a polite fiction."[15] The plutocracy of wealth and executive privilege increasingly dominated not only the back rooms of political intrigue but also the public debating chambers in the storefronts of government. The merger of public- and private-sector governance through the domination of both by the same circles of power brokers depended increasingly on the manipulation of public opinion by media conglomerates. The owners, managers, and content producers of these media cartels thereby increased their influence over the careers of public officials and the content of public discourse.

In the era when corporate communications were allowed to monopolize most venues for the shaping of public opinion, much of the commercial media became a non-stop infomercial for conspicuous consumption, celebrity, and aggressive wars.[16] It was made to seem that only the likes of Saddam Hussein or Osama bin Laden were guilty of crimes at the highest international level, whereas crimes at the local level, but especially those committed by members of poor racial minorities, were highlighted with consistent urgency. In this agenda of diversion, distraction, and pumped-up fear of the Other, public attention was directed away from most serious economic topics, the exceptions being the quest for low consumer prices and an emphasis on public antipathy to taxes. Alternatively, the cultural wars, emphasizing subjects such as gay marriage, were afforded disproportionately large amounts of media ink and air time.

The financial crisis beginning in 2008 was the direct outcome of repeated rounds of deregulation and hyperprivatization that began with the domination of Anglo-America's core governments by Ronald Reagan and Margaret

Thatcher. The dramatic plunges in 2008 and 2009 in the value of corporate shares, the demise and near demise of major financial institutions, and the massive bailout packages directed by governments to the ailing financial services and automobile sector helped, at last, to draw considerable public attention away from the cultural wars towards the more basic structures of material interdependence in the increasingly integrated global economy. On the libertarian right wing of the US political spectrum, Ron Paul began to amplify his long emphasis on the lack of accountability characterizing the secretive Federal Reserve Board's monopoly control over both the creation of US currency and the US national debt. A Congressman from Texas, Paul has been a perennial candidate in races to become the Republican nominee for the US presidency.

Ron Paul achieved the status of a working-class hero for millions with his blunt condemnations of the US banking system and the imperial policies of the US executive branch.[17] He made major headway in advancing his political agenda in November 2009, when he, along with the Florida Congressman Alan Grayson, sponsored an amendment to the *Financial Stability Improvement Act* to empower Congress to audit the transactions of the Federal Reserve Board. These audits would extend to the Federal Reserve's Maiden Lane companies, the secretive polities where many of the most toxic derivative instruments were transferred in order to keep the insurance giant AIG, together its worldwide array of so-called counterparties, from going bankrupt.[18] A Bloomberg News reporter, Mark Pittman, helped build the momentum of the movement to hold the Federal Reserve more accountable. It was Pittman's investigative reporting that culminated in a court ruling in August 2009 that the Federal Reserve must disclose information about its bailout loans.[19] Widely recognized as the "most fearless, most trusted" financial reporter in America, Pittman died a few months later of unspecified causes at the age of fifty-two.[20]

Joe Bageant added his ironic voice to the chorus of commentators alleging in 2008 that Wall Street had betrayed Main Street, the shrinking middle class, and the working poor. His unique brand of humorous yet pointed analysis on the role of race, class, and ideology in US political culture has been celebrated by the acclaimed Spokan Indian poet and screenwriter Sherman Alexie as "a love song to the great American redneck."[21] In *Deer Hunting with Jesus*, Bageant hammers home his trenchant assessment of the illusions that finally dissolved along with the Great Housing and Credit Bubble.

Every time a bank made a mortgage loan of say, $400,000, even though the debtor had never even made a payment yet, the loan was declared a bank asset and another $400,000 was loaned against it. Meanwhile, the Federal Reserve Bank yelled whoopee and printed another $800,000 in currency. Of course at some point the country had to run out of customers, so the loans got easier and easier. No matter that debt is not wealth. Wink and call it that and most folks won't even look up from their new big screen high resolution digital TVs.

Problem was that all the jobs to pay for this stuff were stampeding off toward places in China with names containing a lot of Xs, Zs and praying for a vowel. It was becoming clear that the entire economy was running on fumes. In fact less than fumes. It was running on the odor of paper. Mountains of the stuff. Bundles of mortgages and very strange securities and derivatives of unknown origin and value. Paper that stated its own worth and signed by some mystic hand no one could quite identify through the blurry signatures.[22]

CHARTERING THE MEANS OF EXPANDED CORPORATE LIBERTIES

One of the most effective means of opening legal, political, and economic space for the growth of corporations and corporate culture has been the ability of commercial organizations to have sovereign governments and their constituents compete for their business activity. In commenting on this phenomenon, William F. Pepper has written, "In effect all countries, localities, and their workers become competitors for corporate favors. As a result, wages and social and employment conditions sink to the level that desperation requires."[23] This slide towards the regulatory bottom comes about primarily from the effort of politicians to outdo their counterparts in other jurisdictions in lowering the bar on environmental standards, labour relations, and tax rates. This type of competition in the global arena began in the Imperial Republic as a competition between states. Some of the largest US companies achieved their initial successes by turning different state governments against one another as political leaders struggled to attract corporate head offices and corporate investment. This pattern found its initial focus in battles pitting legislators in New Jersey, New York, and Delaware against one another. The competition of these three governments was instrumental in establishing prototypes of government-corporate relations within the United States. Later, this competition among US states was exported into the arena of international relations in the process of globalizing the extent of the informal US empire.

The state governments of New Jersey, New York, and Delaware sought to outdo each other in removing from the laws of incorporation all those provisions originating in the principle that commercial corporations exist to serve the "public good." Restrictions limiting the lifespan of corporate charters, for instance, were removed. Moreover, the idea developed that the applicants for corporate charters, rather than government officials, should draft the terms and provisions of the instruments of incorporation. This process culminated in the state of Delaware enacting in 1899 the General Incorporation Law – a statute that has been identified as "the Magna Carta of modern corporate sovereignty."[24] It stipulated that Delaware's procedure for granting corporate charters would allow "the incorporators" to formulate all major provisions for "creating, defining, limiting, and regulating the powers of the corporation, the directors, and shareholders." The effect of this provision was to empower those seeking corporate charters to become law makers and self-regulators with but one restriction: the content of corporate charters could not be contrary to the specific laws of Delaware. With a few words, therefore, Delaware's General Incorporation Law turned on its head the old relationships between corporation and state. Variations of this potent legal language would soon be exported to other US states and then to other countries along with the expanding influence of US corporate culture. Where the US federation began with the principle of state sovereignty over all fields of jurisdiction not granted specifically to the federal government, the Delaware Legislature introduced a new proposition. The effect of the General Incorporation Law was that corporations could henceforth acquire their pick of commercial controls over all jurisdictional fields not specifically reserved and staked out in the specifics of state statute.

Over time this single legal innovation significantly altered the apportionment of power in the United States and much of the rest of the world. The activists and architects of corporate autonomy had effectively seized a kind of residual authority for commercial corporations, a class of legal edifice that was not even mentioned in the American Declaration of Independence or the US Constitution. As Derber and others see it, the elevation of corporations to the heights of juridical privilege in the emerging superpower represents a significant contradiction of much of the revolutionary spirit accompanying the founding of the United States. For Derber, Delaware's General Incorporation Law marks the real beginnings of the "Corporation Nation." As I see it, however, Delaware's bow to the rise of corporate autonomy was not a reversal but rather an expression and fulfillment of old tendencies in a national polity composed of constituent parts, many of which began their constitutional existence in England's emerging empire *as* corporations.

Delaware's General Incorporation Law brought to fruition some of the ideals of the promoters of the colonization companies that had competed for political backing before the constitutional structure of British North America was severed through the military application of the secessionist principles articulated in the Declaration of Independence. The civil war that divided the Anglo-American branch of the British Empire might have been averted if the powerful transatlantic lobby of land speculators had not been so severely checked in realizing the ambitions of its members. These land speculators promoted their favoured agendas for the expansion of Euro-American settlements through vehicles with names such as the Ohio Company, the Indiana Company, the Illinois Company, the Transylvania Company, and the Mississippi Company. The Philadelphia-based firm Baynton, Wharton, and Morgan holds an especially important place among the corporations devoted to the transformation of "lands reserved to the Indians" into the private property of non-Indian settlers. It began by specializing in the purchase of furs from the Indians of the Ohio Valley. With the encouragement of Philadelphia's political godfather Benjamin Franklin, the company's executives gradually shifted orientation to concentrate on the promotion of various political schemes for the transformation of various parts of Indian Country into Anglo-American real estate.

Many land speculators became leading advocates of transatlantic colonization. They were innovators seeking corporate profits on the proprietary frontiers of America through the blending of the public power of government with the private power of business. In spite of their repeated efforts to make political breakthroughs, the land speculators were frustrated again and again in their attempts to gain from the British government green lights for their plans of corporate colonization. They were frustrated in their efforts to dip their own corporate vessels deeply into the great flows of profit that would surely arise from future floods of transatlantic emigration – floods that would create conditions for tidal waves of transcontinental migration. The patronage networks of this lobby of land speculators extended from the Thirteen Colonies into the imperial business cultures of London and Paris. If the colonization companies of British North America, but especially Baynton, Wharton, and Morgan, had been able to secure more profit or promise of profit from the capital to be derived from Earth's transformation into the private property of settler populations, the frustrated ambitions of the land speculators might not have been channelled into support for the revolt of the armed secessionists who founded the United States.[25]

With a focus on the deep and intimate working relationship between Benjamin Franklin and Lord Shelburne as guardians of the continuing bond of Anglo-American cooperation, Clarence Alvord highlighted almost a century ago the geopolitical importance of the colonization companies in his ground-breaking "study of trade, land speculation, and experiments in imperialism culminating in the American Revolution."[26] In the course of their War of Independence, the most expansionary elements of Anglo-America defied the principles of the Royal Proclamation of 1763 to establish the foundations of their own laissez-faire empire.[27] Where the British imperial government attempted to govern an expanded British North America through the force of laws that afforded some protections for the continent's Aboriginal inhabitants, the founding manifesto of the United States characterized all Aboriginal peoples as "merciless Indian savages," as terrorists and illegal enemy combatants whose "known means of warfare is an undistinguished destruction of all ages, sexes, and conditions."

The inclusion of these words in the world's most consequential political manifesto signalled that the most revolutionary component of Anglo-America would over time also be its most aggressively expansionistic element. A basic pattern of material expansion was set by placing the Indigenous peoples situated along the course of Anglo-America's expansion outside the sphere of law. The corporate heirs of the British North American colonization companies were instrumental in setting the pace and form of this expansion as it extended from transcontinental to hemispheric to global proportions. As extensions of the sovereign authority of the United States, these corporate vehicles renewed old patterns of expansion in a New World version of the trajectories of imperialism pioneered by the East Indian companies, the slaving companies, the fur-trade companies and the colonization companies. The corporate agencies of the informal US empire were afforded maximum latitude for unbounded expansion with a minimum of government constraint.

New frontiers of capitalism were thus colonized as the activities of the land-speculation companies gave way to the pursuits of the railway companies. These railway enterprises became the main vehicles for the commercial application of many revolutionary technologies that fundamentally altered human relationships with time, space, and each other as well as the rest of nature. The seed money for one new enterprise after the next was derived from the success of the railway companies in speeding flows of profit through the quick transformation of vast new territories into capital accumulations. The extension of the US railway system into Central America, for instance, gave rise to the activities of the United Fruit Company. The shift from the political economy of railways to that of automobiles and the internal combustion engine helped secure the commercial empire of John D. Rockefeller's Standard Oil Company of New Jersey and its many interlinked corporate progeny, including Germany's chemical and pharmaceutical giant IG Farben.

Again and again the same patterns of proprietary interaction were reenacted, extended, and reinforced with the rise, for instance, of Ford, GM, Du Pont, GE, IBM, Halliburton, Bechtel, Lockheed Martin, and the new generation of "private" military contractors whose main lobbying agency bears the Orwellian title of the International Peace Operations Association.[28] The old intrigues of Baynton, Wharton, and Morgan thus found new life in the activities of huge commercial polities such as the Science Applications International Corporation (SAIC). Its many highly secretive functions at the lucrative nexus of the national security state and the military-industrial complex are aimed at transforming many global extensions of Indian Country into the private property of corporate investors. While the energy cartels, weapons manufacturers, and mercenary companies have become key agencies in channelling imperial capital into the rising terror economy, the media conglomerates specialize in the psychological warfare that creates the public mythology necessary for perpetuating the 9/11 wars. By virtue of their roles in sponsoring many of the advertisements that fund the media conglomerates, iconographic companies such as Coco-Cola, McDonald's, and Wal-Mart are also integrated into the global economic workings of the national security state and its attending military-industrial complex.

Collectively these corporate enterprises grew to become the main constituency, driving force, and beneficiary of the thrust of empire building which began with the revolutionary rejection in 1776 of the British imperial attempt to colonize Anglo-America on the basis of constitutional provisions requiring the lawful consent of Indigenous peoples to any change in the status of their Aboriginal lands. The rejection of the Royal Proclamation of 1763 gave rise to the founding of a republic that introduced itself to the world in a paradoxical document. The Declaration of Independence affirmed the ideals of democracy and human equality even as it also condemned Aboriginal North Americans uniformly as merciless Indian terrorists. From British Red Coats to Red Indians to Red Communists to those targeted as the Global War on Terror's Islamic savages, the growth of the US empire has been energized by a series of real, imagined, or constructed enemies always conveniently located on the material frontiers of corporate expansion.[29] No matter whether the material to be run through the mill of corporate privatization might be, for instance, bananas from Central America, oil and gas from the Middle East, or supplies of Congolese columbite-tantalite for the manufacture of cell-phones, the political milieu surrounding the extraction of such resources has often been permeated with violence and with variations on the rhetoric of capitalist civilization's assumed right to prevail over those defined as primitive, savages, socialists, and citizens of failed states.[30]

While the Civil War of the United States was fought to determine how labour would be provided in the US economy, the Second World War was in part a civil war among capitalists with conflicting views on how business and government should interact. When the administration of President George W. Bush attempted to end the legacy of the New Deal during the opening decade of the twenty-first century, the resulting controversies echoed many elements of the clash that earlier pitted Rooseveltian capitalism against Hitlerian capitalism. In the name of the Ownership Society, the Bush government attempted to push through changes that would have privatized social security and further privatized the delivery of health care. The limits to the viability of the Ownership Society became apparent when the crisis resulting from Wall's Street's abuses in the marketing and leveraging of subprime mortgages helped to burst a huge credit bubble. This crisis, a direct outgrowth of too much deregulatory codling of the financial sector, instigated a dramatic shrinkage in the constituency of potential homeowners in the United States. It precipitated a breakdown in the overheated engines of capitalist hyperprivatization.

By drawing on the heritage of the political economies on both sides of the Second World War, the world's pre-eminent military-industrial complex transcended the legacy of the conflict between competing versions of capitalism espoused by Roosevelt and Hitler. Anti-communism was the essential glue binding the financiers and industrialists who built up the war machines of both sides in the conflagration of the Second World War. The remarkable speed with which the US government was able to integrate the assets, expertise, and corporate structures of German and Japanese business into the capitalist side of the Cold War clearly illustrates the strong trajectories of continuity linking the anti-communist politics of Hitler's Third Reich and the convergence of military and corporate rule in the United States as facilitated in 1947 by the *National Security Act*.

The adept reconfiguration of international business in the transition from the Second World War to the Cold War suggests that capitalism's all-important corporate sector has developed largely on the basis of a law unto itself. Commercial corporations developed as largely self-regulating agencies whose global career of laissez-faire commercial conquest was foreshadowed and facilitated by Delaware's General Incorporation Law. The result has been the expansionary career of a global system of political economy that is largely of, by, and for corporate "persons" rather than human persons. While the United States has played a crucial role in enlarging space for the corporate sector in the political economy of many countries, the propensity has been for large companies to attempt to free themselves from as many national moorings and restrictions as possible. This trend was clearly described in 1972 by Carl A. Gerstacker, chairman of the Board of Dow Chemical Company. He told a reporter for the *New York Times*, "We appear to be moving strongly in the direction of what will not be really multinational or international companies as we know them today, but what we call anational companies – companies without nationality, belonging to all nationalities."[31]

Companies like Dow Chemical were empowered to become global in character because they were the primary recipients and beneficiaries of the expanded freedoms resulting from the rejection of British imperial authority by the revolutionary secessionists of Anglo-America. The primary impetus energizing the expanding domain of corporate autonomy has been to assert commercial domination over as many facets as possible of nature, including human nature. The governing propensity has been to privatize and commercialize as many kinds of interaction as possible – interactions linking human beings not only to each other but to our plant and animal relatives as well as to the habitats we share with them in our common interdependence in the web of life. In linking the recent rush by business and government to create and enforce a new genre of intellectual property rights, John C. Weaver draws attention to the similarities connecting this recent rush to expand the empire of proprietorship with earlier episodes in the history of Earth's transformation into property. In 2003 Weaver wrote: "The recent relentless expansion of intellectual property rights displays the same irrepressible momentum, haste, and global scope as the great land rush. In common with the older frenzy to engross property, the current mad scramble may also shrink the public domain, placing amazing riches in private hands in the name of improvement."[32]

The clashes between Indigenous peoples and commercial corporations consistently present some of the most revealing illustrations of the inner dynamics of capitalism's frontier expansions. As demonstrated, for instance, in the cooperation between corporations and the US military in the westward expansion of the country's railway system, the process of removing Indians and containing them on reservations provided a basis for corporate and state cooperation in preparing the soil for its incorporation into the empire of capital. This collaborative approach to expanding the commercial reach of US corporate culture would prove increasingly integral to the rise of capitalism's military-industrial complex. It proved important especially after the military-industrial complex of Anglo-America absorbed the legacies of corporate-state integration developed throughout the expansionary course of Axis rule in Europe, Eurasia, and Asia. The German effort to conquer *Lebensraum* and dominate the Aboriginal lands of the Slavs took some of its most basic queues from Anglo-America's history of transcontinental expansion.

The activities of the railway companies were often followed by the operations of forestry companies, mining companies, factory farms, energy consortiums, and the like. The damming of rivers, as frequently backed by international financial agencies such as the World Bank, has played an especially persistent role in the displacement and destruction of many cohesive Aboriginal communities the world over.[33] This genre of industrial activity has been decisive in destroying the Aboriginal political economies of many Indigenous peoples. The industrial destruction of the material basis for their collective survival has often led to the complete destruction of Aboriginal societies and to the extreme marginalization of survivors as wards of the colonizing power.

The tremendous legal weight attending the legal institution of incorporation is well illustrated by the different order of treatment consistently afforded by government to Indigenous peoples and to commercial companies when their claims clash. As demonstrated by the priority given to the enforcement of corporate title over Aboriginal title, commercial companies and their executive officers have effectively been able to combine both the public power derived from the sovereign source of their business charters and the extensive private rights vested in the institution of private property. The strength of this hybrid constitution of corporate power is underscored by the frequent treatment of Aboriginal people as legal non-persons, especially during the era of their most quick and dramatic dispossession. In identifying a "person" as "an individual other than an Indian," the Canadian *Indian Act* made explicit in 1876 a more general condition of colonialism that often categorized Indigenous peoples as wards of government in many jurisdictions, including the United States, Australia, and, as Alpheus Snow has documented, large parts of Africa.[34] The members of many Aboriginal societies were often incapable of gaining access to courts as *persons*, just as the companies taking control of their Aboriginal territories were afforded the status of *persons* qualified to make contracts and to defend and advance their interests through civil litigation. Accordingly, the distinction between "men" and "savages" codified in the American Declaration of Independence has been replicated and amplified on one commercial frontier after the next.

With much of Europe and Japan in ruins, the United States emerged from the Second World War as the most powerful polity on earth. How would it use its pre-eminence? Would the US government opt to live up to the egalitarian principles of the Atlantic Charter or would it turn its energies towards the goals proposed in Henry Luce's promotion of the American Century? George F. Kennan famously advanced the case for choosing for the latter. This State Department official tried to limit the idealism associated with the founding of the United Nations. Kennan is widely recognized as the main author of the policy to contain Soviet influence through heavy US investment in building up Japan and Western Europe. In 1948 Kennan observed that the United States possessed 50 per cent of the world's wealth with only 6.3 per cent of the world's population. "Our real job in the coming period," he advised his colleagues in the US government, "is to devise a pattern of relationships which will permit us to maintain this position of disparity." He added, "To do so we have to dispense of all sentimentality... we should cease thinking about human rights, the raising of living standards and democratization."[35] Until the financial crisis of 2008 and 2009, the global structure of corporate power, including its dependence on the US dollar, has helped to uphold this formula of disparity. But given changing patterns of business and work, credit and debt, the people and government of the United States have little choice but to be less voracious in consuming the world's wealth.

FROM COLD WAR BIPOLARISM TO THE EXPANSION AND CONSOLIDATION OF THE EUROPEAN UNION

The movement of US power into the vacuum left by the rapid exhaustion and decline of European imperialism was characterized in many ways. In 1967 in *Pax Americana*, Ronald Steel described the animating force of the informal US empire as "welfare imperialism." Depicting US power as a benevolent force in the world, Steel continued: "We engaged in empire-building for noble ends rather than for such base motives as profit and influence ... We have not exploited our empire ... Have we not been generous with our clients and allies?"[36] As Steel was defending the US empire from within, many of those on the receiving end of the imperial intrusions sought words to describe their own perceptions of the new colonialism. That same year, Jean-Jacques Servan-Schreiber wrote in his best-selling *Le Défi Américain* (translated as *The American Challenge*) of the transformative power of large US corporations on the economy, politics, and culture of Western Europe. "American industry has gauged the terrain and is now rolling from Naples to Amsterdam with the ease and speed of an Israeli tank in the Sinai desert," he noted. "We see a foreign challenger breaking down the political and psychological framework of our societies."[37] He outlined how US companies brought with them superior management techniques, vast technological know how, and the attitudes and access to capital needed to exploit all of

Western Europe as a single market. A key to the technological and organizational strengths of the largest US companies was "the systematic and organized assistance the U.S. government gives to key industries through its contracts and research grants": the US electronics industry, for instance, did 63 per cent of its business with the US government. Europe's electronics firms, in contrast, did only 12 percent with their own governments.[38]

Servan-Schreiber's text illustrates the extent to which the power of the United States replaced the power of Western Europe, not only in its colonies but in its inner, metropolitan cores as well. The small peoples and nations on the planet, therefore, were not the only polities profoundly affected by the assimilationist pressures emanating primarily from the United States. Even in France there were growing concerns that European civilization was being colonized by an economic and cultural force beyond its ability to harness. Servan-Schreiber's volume was written to encourage Europeans to accept and replicate many of the techniques of US corporate culture as the necessary strategy to compete and thereby regain some degree of economic self-determination, however imitative. The ironic message was clear: integrate into the technocratic order epitomized in the corporate extensions of the capitalist superpower or be resolved to accept "a subsidiary role ... the position of a satellite."[39]

In dramatizing the paradox that "American firms ... already form the framework of a real 'Europeanization,'" Servan-Schreiber made reference to the European Economic Community – a federation for European countries that had its origins in the European Coal and Steel Community established in 1951. This nascent polity, at first uniting Germany, France, Italy, the Netherlands, Belgium, and Luxenbourg, entered a new phase in 1957 with the Treaty of Rome. While the prospect of a United States of Europe remained a distant possibility for most Europeans, Servan-Schreiber argued that large US corporations were leading the way in giving substantive economic expression to this newly invented polity. The European Community's common market, the author exclaimed, "has become the New Frontier of American industry ... it has become a new Far West for American businessmen."[40]

This comment deserves to be taken more seriously than the author may have realized at the time. The westward expansion of commercial enterprise on the moving frontiers of Euro-American settlements did indeed establish many of the primal patterns of US enterprise. In their initial transcontinental expansion, the corporate agencies of US business acquired many of the attributes that would enable them to reproduce in markets beyond the Western Hemisphere the political, psychological, and legal environments friendly to their mode of invention, industrial production, advertising, labour relations, distribution, and consumption. Hence for the French, no less than for Kenya's Maasai or for the Indigenous peoples of Polynesia, layer upon layer of cultural baggage was heaped on the adoption of Marlboro cigarettes, Levi jeans, Scotch tape, Kodak cameras, Coca-Cola,

Tupperware, Tampax, and the like. The vast majority of the world's peoples and nationalities were deeply affected by the wide proliferation of this genre of US-designed consumer item, even where the supply of such goods was relatively scarce and the purchasing power of potential consumers was low. The import of such items into new markets was generally accompanied by an onslaught of political and ideological pressures aimed at forcing those governments and peoples on the consuming end of the American empire to adopt financial arrangements and military orientations deemed conducive to the interests of capitalism's core polity.

In *The American Challenge*, Servan-Schreiber presented himself as an indigenous proponent and champion of this kind of US-driven change. The push to remove barriers to the transnational operations of US-centred business was one element of a larger process whose main frontiers lie ultimately in the internal landscapes of human perception, imagination, and desire. The spread of US consumer culture, along with the corporate culture that feeds it and helps to manufacture it, depended ultimately on the generation of attitudes and mythologies that support the values of possessive individualism, the replication of patterns of human belief and behaviour that uphold capitalist constructions of family, work, education, agriculture, extraction, production, investment, exchange, and law enforcement. It has also depended on the subordination through persuasion or coercion of the power of public governance to the proprietary pre-eminence of markets and the still-higher power of commercial monopolies.

In the decades following Servan-Schreiber's bow to American business as the primary model and impetus for European capitalism, the European Community has grown to the point where it has become one of the largest and most diverse polities in the world. By 2008 it encompassed twenty-seven countries with a total population almost twice that of the United States. The precedent-setting quality of this striking act of integration must be viewed against the historical background of a war-torn continent divided between the Roman Catholic West and the Byzantine East, a powerful religious establishment and the polities of the Protestant Reformation, monarchists and republicans. This embattled region has been home to competing imperial heartlands of antagonistic worldwide empires, the primary battle zone between Stalinist and Hitlerian totalitarianism, and two opposing systems of political economy. Given this heritage of violent conflict, one that repeatedly brought new levels of industrial efficiency to the arts and science of mass murder, the emergence of European cohesion from the deforming debacle of the Cold War is little short of miraculous. The European Union has the makings of a new type of superpower emphasizing the rule of law over the rule of force.

The EU developed its own currency even as it continues to experiment with the elaboration of new forms of federal integration and citizenship. In 1970 Denmark, Ireland, and the United Kingdom became members. Greece joined in 1981, followed by Spain and Portugal in 1986. In 1995

Austria, Finland, and Sweden cast their lot with the growing polity. In 1999 the Euro was introduced in ten EU countries. Between 1997 and 2007 EU negotiations took place with a host of countries, most of which had emerged either from within the now-defunct Soviet Union or from Soviet-dominated territory in Eastern Europe. In 2004 the Czech Republic, Estonia, Latvia, Lithuania, Hungary, Poland, Slovenia and Slovakia, as well as Cyprus and Malta met all the financial, legal, and political criteria that gave them EU status. In 2007 the EU added Bulgaria and Romania to its membership.

In exploring the attractions that made many former subjects of Soviet rule attach their personal and national destinies to the rise of a Greater Europe, Croatian author Slavenka Drakulić reflected on what she saw as the drab structures of communist conformity. This perception caused Drakulić and others of her ilk to look with optimistic hope towards the culture of Western Europe. For us, she writes, "Europe is plentitude: food, cars, light, everything – a kind of festival of colours, diversity, opulence, beauty. It offers choice: from shampoo to political parties. It represents freedom of expression. It is a promised land, a new Utopia, a lollipop."[41]

The forces that converged in ending the Cold War, a conflict whose strategic beginnings and core contestations lay in the division of Europe after the Second World War, opened the way to the rise of a Greater Europe. Europe's release from the remote-control manipulations of the mirrored superpowers was long in the making, As early as 1968 it began to appear that the bipolar division of Europe was starting to break down under the force of popular expectations encouraged by the spread of television and the growing reach and effectiveness of satellite communications. Imperial systems of all kind were beginning to be challenged by the spread of new electronic technologies whose effect is to make the dissemination of information increasing difficult to manage through instruments of centralized control. During the Prague Spring, the government of Czechoslovakia sent shock waves far and wide when its leader, Alexander Dubcek, opened his country's airwaves, borders, and the machinery of print to the operations of a free press. Soviet forces did eventually intervene in an effort to shut down this new openness, but the genie of expanded consciousness and awareness was out of the bottle in Eastern Europe and beyond. The Prague Spring was one episode in a tumultuous year of anti-establishment demonstrations that rattled entrenched oligarchies on both sides of the Cold War. Whether it was the massive student protests in Paris, the rioting in Black ghettos throughout the United States following the state-incited assassination of Martin Luther King Jr, or the beginnings of social unrest in Poland, the heavily televised events of 1968 highlighted the growing interconnectivity of all humanity together with the fragility of the status quo in many different contexts.[42]

The growing pervasiveness of global communications provided the venue for heightening transnational unease with the organization of the entire world into two heavily armed camps, each with the capacity to annihilate life as we know it on the planet. In this climate, the Non-Aligned Movement's emphasis on peace and pluralism continued to spread even into some elite circles in the imperial capitals of the mirrored superpowers. In the 1970s the Cold War's protagonists in both Washington and Moscow felt compelled to extend their good will across the barrier known as the Iron Curtain. The coalescing force of global public opinion pointed to the need to slow down the competitive development and amassment of the technology of mass death. This popular effort to put some rudimentary regulations on the arms race helped unleash forces that were integral to the end of the Cold War.[43] The movement for détente resulted in the negotiation of the Anti-Ballistic Missile Treaty in 1972 and the Helsinki Accords in 1975. The Helsinki agreements would prove instrumental in integrating the discourse of human rights into the agenda of dissident activism in Eastern Europe.

This surge of activism reached a new threshold of effectiveness in Poland beginning in 1979. An alliance between the Polish Pope, John Paul II, and an association of workers in and around the famed ship-building facilities of Gdansk helped to embolden an upsurge of resistance to the imperial hold of the Soviet government over its own citizens and its satellite regimes. This revolt was fuelled by the long-simmering contention that the life possibilities of the largest mass of people dominated by the Soviet empire had been diminished when President Roosevelt and Prime Minister Churchill effectively ceded Eastern European to their ally, Josef Stalin, at the Yalta Conference in February 1945.[44]

The inheritances of Polish history helped to make the alliance between the Vatican and the workers association led by Lech Walesa so effective. Over long sweeps of time the Roman Catholic Church effectively embodied and defended the Polish nation when its lands and peoples were entirely subject to the competing imperial claims of Russia, Prussia, and Austria. The Roman Catholic Church in Poland helped funnel resources of the US Central Intelligence Agency to the workers' association known as Solidarność – Solidarity. The Polish agents of Soviet domination responded to the mass uprising by declaring martial law and incarcerating many of Solidarność's leaders. This form of repression, however, ultimately failed not only in Poland but throughout Eastern Europe. In Czechoslovakia a playwrite named Václav Havel gave expression to an anti-Soviet movement whose success was realized in the Velvet Revolution.[45] Havel's leadership drew on his own history in the Czechoslovakian resistance to Soviet domination – his involvement in the articulation of Charter 77, a statement that arose in response to the banning in 1977 of the Plastic People of the Universe, a Prague-based band modelled on Frank Zappa's Mothers of Invention. The authors of Charter 77 emphasized how the prohibitions on the band's psychedelic performances illustrated the repressiveness of many state actions that violated the Helsinki Accords and UN covenants on political, civil, economic, and cultural rights.

The upsurge of popular resistance in Eastern Europe occurred concurrently with a period of major reforms within the Soviet Union led by the general secretary of the Soviet Communist Party, Mikhail Gorbachev, who promoted economic reforms in the name of *Perestroika* and a more open, transparent society in the name of *glasnost.* This convergence of ideas and activism became a factor in the decision in East Germany to allow emigration to West Germany, thereby negating the original purpose of the Berlin Wall. The citizens' dismantling of the wall in 1989 was a manifestation of an array of forces that smashed apart the authoritarian cohesion of the Soviet empire. The resulting realignment of loyalty and power led to the reunification of Germany in 1990 and to the subsequent demise of the Soviet Union. These developments formed the prelude to the making of the Maastricht Treaty in 1992. This international agreement was devised with an idea of radically expanding the scope as well as enriching the economic, juridical, cultural, and educational content of a post–Cold War, post–Berlin Wall European Union.

In his masterful account of the deep politics that created *The Road to 9/11*, Peter Dale Scott recognized the lead role of Henry Kissinger in negotiating the moves towards détente that "helped set the stage for Solidarność and the Velvet Revolution in Eastern Europe." These mass expressions of popular resistance to empire, Scott hopes, may some day be "emulated in America."[46] This Canadian poet, diplomat, and professor documents how the movement to moderate the worst excesses of the Cold War helped to stimulate a reactionary coalition within government, the academy, the commercial media, and key military contractors of the United States to intensify the arms race and ultimately to push for unassailable global dominance. During the presidency of Ronald Reagan the push to expand military budgets and intensify the pace of military interventions, often through the deployment of US-backed proxy forces, was countered by a concerted drive to merge the peace movement based in Western Europe with the rise of dissidence in the portion of Europe dominated by the Soviet Union. The celebrated English historian E.P. Thompson emerged as a particularly effective proponent, philosopher, and technician of this strategy. While the movement fell far short of obtaining its ultimate objectives, global disarmament, it did contribute to giving Europe, East and West, some relief from the Cold War protagonists' obsession with the intimidating force of nuclear brinksmanship – what Thompson described as "exterminism." As Thompson saw it, the lethal ideology of those most committed to "winning" the Cold War so menaced humanity's future that the quest for disarmament trumped all other issues, including the old preoccupations of his left-wing associates with class conflict.[47]

The legacy of this most influential phase of the movement for global peace lives on in the underlying assumptions enabling the European Union to incorporate so many of the polities that, for so long, made warfare their primary purpose and activity. In this way some of the most war-prone portions of humanity tried something different. This is not to say that the European Union is devoid of internal contradictions and its own imperial attributes. For instance, some old themes of empire building can be read into efforts by agents of the European Union to expand their role in the political economy of Latin America and the Caribbean. Similarly, there is a lively debate within the European Union among constituencies seeking deeper federal integration and other factions seeking a looser coalition of sovereign countries. The desire to slow down or halt altogether the push for a more cohesive integration of the EU countries was marked by the negative votes in referenda in France, Holland, and Ireland on the Lisbon Treaty. The financial crisis, however, was enough to undermine the opposition to greater integration. The Lisbon Treaty was therefore ratified and came into force on December 1, 2009.

Much of the debate within Europe about the delegation of powers to a European Parliament and an executive branch known as the European Commission involves consideration of the general propensity of this kind of mass polity to extend the political and economic entitlements of the rich and to further disenfranchise and marginalize the poor as well as the lower middle class.[48] In this way some aspects of the EU's internal politics reflect and extend controversies over the functioning of the North American Free Trade Area or the possibility of an even larger trade association throughout the Western Hemisphere. The criticisms of expanded corporate capitalism within the European Union, however, must be balanced against the stark spectacle of a whole continent emerging from centuries of the most bitter and concerted forms of warfare to pursue integration through trade, cultural exchange, social welfare, and a strong commitment to the force of compromise and negotiation over the force of armaments and coercion.

Like the richest and most powerful of its member states, the EU poured hundred of billions of Euros into its constituents' own domestic economies following the international spread of the "contagion" that began with the initial bursting in the United States of the Great Housing and Credit Bubble.[49] This form of European response to the workings of the business culture in the ailing capitalist superpower represents a dramatic reversal of the strategies for success proposed by Servan-Schreiber in *The American Challenge*.

FROM NUREMBERG TO ABU GHRAIB

Much of the initial expression of hope for a world ruled by law rather than force was channelled into the chartering of the United Nations in 1945. The UN Charter came into force in October, one month before the initiation of the proceedings of the International Military Tribunal established at Nuremberg.[50] There a global audience was presented with a glimpse of the kind of court procedures that are needed if humanity is ever to transcend the scourge of war. The public was given a preview of the kind of judicial interventions the UN seemed poised to deliver on a sustained basis early in its career. Like the idealism expressed in Woodrow Wilson's Fourteen Points, the Nuremberg process at its best established a monument pointing to the enticements of a world governed as a federation of free peoples whose collective security would be uniformly guaranteed through an inclusive approach to the enforcement of international criminal law.

The Nuremberg process began with the decision of the victorious US government to set up an international court capable of prosecuting, defending, judging, and sentencing the top Nazi leadership for crimes that violated the well-being of all humanity. For the optimists, the Nuremberg trials would create a new juridical space for the development of universal jurisdiction, a concept whose origins go back to the broad international effort first to prevent piracy and then to outlaw the slave trade. Many hoped that the Nuremberg trials would initiate a process that would, in due course, lead to the elimination of all sanctuaries for the perpetrators of the highest order of international crime. In such a world there would be no escape from legal accountability even for those at the top of regimes that commit atrocities against their own citizens or against the populations of foreign countries.

But for those of a more sceptical turn of mind, the Nuremberg trials, like the similar proceedings in Tokyo, were little more than highly politicized show trials – displays of the victors' justice towards the vanquished. This view was initially given articulate expression by Radhabinod Pal, a jurist from India who was one of eleven judges in the International Military Tribunal for the Far East. In his dissenting ruling, Judge Pal acquitted all the defendants because he saw the overall proceedings as illegitimate – the prosecutors were dealing exclusively with the alleged crimes of perpetrators on only the defeated side of the conflict. The atomic attacks by the victors on the civilian populations of Hiroshima and Nagasaki, for instance, were ignored. The result, Pal claimed, was more a demonstration of the triumphant powers' capacity to dominate than a genuine display of the applied principles of universal jurisdiction. US and British officials conspired to prevent the immediate publication of Pal's 1,235-page opinion.[51]

Robert H. Jackson, the chief council for the United States government in the Nuremberg trials, believed he was standing at the beginning of a new era in the evolution of a shared rule of law to govern all humanity. In trying to record for posterity the importance of the legal proceedings at Nuremberg, he declared: "The wrongs which we seek to condemn have been so calculated, so malignant, and so devastating that civilization cannot tolerate their being ignored, because it cannot survive their being repeated."[52] His goal, he informed President Harry Truman in his report, was to render "explicit and unambiguous" what he believed was already "implicit" in international law. The basis of that law was the principle "that to prepare, incite, or wage a war of aggression, or to conspire with others to do so, is a crime against international society, and that to persecute, oppress, or to do violence to individuals or minorities on political, racial, or religious grounds in connection with such a war, or to exterminate, enslave, or deport civilian populations, is an international crime, and that for the commission of such crimes *individuals are responsible.*"[53]

From the Trail of Tears to the German genocide of the Herero and Namaqua peoples of Namibia, and the British slaughter of hundreds of peaceful protestors in Amritsar India in 1919, the treatment of Indigenous peoples in the imperial governance of many colonies and states fulfilled Jackson's definition of crimes against international society. Indeed, the saga of rapid Euro-American expansion in North America was identified by Hitler as one of his models for his own ruthless quest to eliminate Jews and gypsies and to subordinate the Slavs of Eastern Europe and Russia so as to gain wider fields of *Lebensraum* for German civilization. As Norman Rich detailed in *Hitler's War Aims*, the fascist leader believed "neither Spain nor Britain should be models of German expansion" but, rather, "the Nordics of North America." They "had ruthlessly pushed aside" "an inferior race" in order "to win for themselves soil and territory for the future." According to Rich, "this was Hitler's version of the White Man's Burden."[54] Hitler is reported to have told his underlings in 1941 that he intended "to treat the original inhabitants [of Russia] like Indians." As he explained: "Never have I heard a German who has bread to eat express concern that the ground where the grain was grown had to be conquered by the sword. We eat Canadian wheat and never think of the Indians."[55]

There was little inclination at the Nuremberg trials to identify European fascism as a trajectory of history emerging from a deeper continuum of European imperialism[56] or to picture the obsessive biological determinism of the Nazis as an extreme application of eugenics. The pseudo-science of eugenics was a theory of "public health," of applied "racial hygiene" and "mental hygiene," that developed a broad constituency of experts and proponents in Britain, the United States, Canada, Australia, and most European countries before the Second World War.[57] The unwillingness to situate the crimes of the Nazis in the context of imperial expansion and Darwinian social and medical science extended to a clear political decision not to indict the vast majority of those industrialists and financiers who had built up the Axis machinery of war and genocide. Many of these captains of industry saw their leading roles in the edification of the military-industrial complex of the Axis powers as an imperative of the anti-communist struggle and as an expression of the merger of capitalist and Darwinian ideals that meet in the imagery of the survival of the fittest. But Jackson's views never changed and, in a radio interview, he declared that he viewed the German industrialists as "one of the chief causes of the war" and fretted about the decision not to include them in the original trial. "I feared failure to include them would mean they would never be tried," he said.[58]

Jackson's fear proved prophetic. The full plans for a subsequent trial to deal in a comprehensive manner with the financiers and industrialists of Nazi Germany did not come to fruition. A rapidly changing political climate in the months and years following the Second World War prompted a decision to narrow and truncate the scope of the proceedings at Nuremberg as the United States moved to take over from Nazi Germany its former role as the primary shield against the spread of revolutionary communism centred in the Soviet Union. With the hasty incorporation into its own Cold War machinery of many of the anti-communist methods and agents of the Axis powers, the US government pulled away from the positions advanced by its chief prosecutor at Nuremberg. In transforming the Soviet Union from a war ally into the pre-eminent enemy of the United States, the Truman administration pulled back from the determination to champion the equitable enforcement of international law against all those individuals believed culpable of committing crimes against humanity.

If the US government had conscientiously continued the process of exposing and criminalizing the industrialists and financiers in charge of the political economy of the Axis powers, the charges would have extended to some of the richest and most influential figures in the United States (see chapter 5). The process of bringing to light the importance of US business relations with the government of Adolf Hitler began during the Second World War, when the administration of Franklin D. Roosevelt enforced the *Trading with the Enemies Act* against the Union Banking Corporation, the Silesian-American Corporation, and the other agencies involved in the extensive economic networks connecting Wall Street and the Third Reich. This process of exposure has been advanced by a number of scholars, such as Max Wallace in *The American Axis* and Edwin Black in *IBM and the Holocaust*.[59] Generally speaking, however, the discussion about the broad extent of the transnational collaboration to build up a centre of anti-communist fascism in Europe remains on the periphery of professional historical discourse. When the subject of North American, British, and French involvement in the rise of European fascism does get addressed in venues of mainstream scholarship, it is most often presented with an emphasis on the "appeasement" of the Axis rather than on the active role of US financiers and enterprises in building up the Axis war machine.

Hjalmar Horace Greeley Schact was in a good position to expose the role of US companies and individual investors in augmenting the capacities of Germany's military-industrial complex. An economist of considerable renown, he was a primary participant in the domestic and international negotiations that brought together the political and economic facets of the fascist form of capitalism that would briefly dominate Europe. Before 1939 he had been president of the Reichsbank and briefly Hitler's minister of economics. In the 1930s he travelled and spoke widely throughout the United States in an effort to improve German-US relations. As part of this initiative, he personally decorated on behalf of the German Führer IBM's president, Thomas J. Watson. When Watson received this award in 1937, his company was in the process of bringing its data-processing technology to the service of the Nazi quest to identify, trace, cage, enslave, and destroy European Jewry.[60]

Schact was deeply influenced by the theoretical and applied work of both John Maynard Keynes and the US New Deal, and he brought these influences from the moderate left of the Anglo-American political spectrum to his promotion of extensive public works in Germany. Hitler applied Schact's advice to the rapid development of the autobahn system, an initiative that helped advance the integration of the political economy of car transport into the infrastructure of capitalism's military-industrial complex. Schact eventually fell into disfavor in Hitler's regime for criticizing the diversion of large amounts of government money to the development and purchase of arms. He was gradually stripped of his public offices and, in 1944, incarcerated on the basis of an accusation that he had participated in a plot to assassinate Hitler. Schact's transformation from a leader to a jailed enemy of the Nazi state did not sway Robert Jackson's opinion of him as one of Germany's most influential behind-the-scenes financial power brokers.[61] He saw in Schact a personification of the power of the industrial interests that had proved so influential in the genesis of the Second World War. Like his colleague Telford Taylor, Jackson became frustrated in his attempt as a prosecutor to penetrate the veneer of the Nazi political leadership to the deeper alignments of commercial interest that, he contented, had elevated Hitler and his associates to power. He saw in Schact a "façade of starched respectability" a representative embodiment of those merged forces of wealth and aggression that had financed and facilitated the Nazi quest for global domination. At Nuremberg he characterized Schact as "the most dangerous and reprehensible type of all opportunists, someone who would use a Hitler for his own ends, and then claim, after Hitler was defeated, to have been against him all the time."[62]

Schact answered Jackson's accusations with self-assured composure, aware, no doubt, that he could implicate many US businesses in war crimes and crimes against humanity before the International Military Tribunal.[63] G.M. Gilbert, the prison psychiatrist during the trial, referred to this leading financier of the Third Reich as follows: "Schact, the only confident one, was being interrogated for information on the German industrialists to be indicted in the next trial. He laughed about it in his cell. 'If you want to indict industrialists who helped to rearm Germany, you will have to indict your own too. The *Opel Werke*, for instance, who did nothing but war production, was owned by General Motors. No. That is not the way to go about it. You cannot indict industrialists.'"[64]

Schact was one of twenty-four defendants in the first and most famous of the Nuremberg trials – and one of three in this initial group to be acquitted. Nine of his Nazi associates were imprisoned, and twelve others were sentenced to be executed. The subsequent set of proceedings at Nuremberg involved charges against 185 individuals, including judges, military leaders, and doctors.[65] In the Justices Cases, charges were pressed against Judge Josef Alstotter and fifteen other senior law officers of the Third Reich. The prosecutors endeavoured to call attention to the important role of jurists in giving the appearance of legitimacy to the international crimes of the Nazi regime. The Alstotter case established important precedents that may yet have significant application to the future trials of those jurists whose legal opinions, advice, and judgments have given a green light to acts of state criminality in the conduct of the Global War on Terror.[66] Similarly, the Doctors Trial had consequences that continue to be felt to this day. It created a factual basis for prohibitions against harmful or lethal forms of medical experiment on human subjects, such as those conducted by the notorious Josef Mengele at Auschwitz.[67] These medical principles are known as the Nuremberg Code.

In spite of the good intentions expressed in the Nuremberg Code, the Cold War created conditions conducive to the testing of many new procedures and theories on unwitting human guinea pigs. Dr Ewen Cameron, one of the world's most recognized psychiatrists of his day, sought between 1957 and 1964 to develop methodologies of brainwashing and behaviour modification by using LSD, electric shocks, sleep deprivation, and other intrusive techniques. The CIA funded Ewen's secret military research at McGill University as part of the national security state's MKULTRA program.[68] The US government similarly used uninformed human subjects, including prison inmates and hospitalized children, in an array of studies to test the effects of radiation. Some of those tested were fed plutonium or purposely exposed to atmospheric releases of radiation. This testing took place within the larger context of more than 1,000 trial explosions of atomic and nuclear weapons primarily in Nevada. The long-term effects of these detonations on human health still remain a subject of scientific, political, and legal controversy.[69]

At Nuremberg a few industrialists did come before the International Military Tribunal, but Schact's advice was more or less followed by the political figures ultimately in charge of the persecutions. Some charges were ineffectively pressed against the directors of the IG Farben petrochemical empire and some principal figures in the Krupp family empire.[70] The main proceedings on the financial aspect of the Nazis' international crimes, however, never took place. There was no serious and sustained focus on the role of leading capitalists in planning, constructing, and mobilizing the Nazi war machine.

A ruling in 1948 dismissed most of the major charges against the officers of IG Farben Corporation, a commercial organization whose directors were shown "quite clearly to have favored a dictatorship long before Hitler came to power."[71] The ruling handed down by the three US judges basically elaborated the principle that war profiteers enjoy extensive immunities from conviction when it comes to apportioning legal responsibility for the involvement of their corporations in war crimes and international crimes against humanity. The tribunal in this case was reported to be "less concerned with the leading business figures and other industrial leaders" than with persons "actually carrying out orders ... or with political leaders with the power to control government policies." Moreover, it ruled "that spoliation or plunder was not a war crime."[72]

The failure of the International Military Tribunal to hold the directors of IG Farben fully accountable for their part in Nazi atrocities angered many, starting with those who had developed the case for the prosecution. One of them was Josiah Ellis Du Bois, deputy chief prosecutor in the IG Farben case. He attempted to set the record straight by authoring a detailed study of the role the IG Farben cartel and its worldwide network of corporate clients, customers, and allies played in instigating and exploiting the Second World War. Du Bois moved on several fronts to bring truth to light. He helped Charles Higham, for instance, to chronicle the role of US business in advancing the Nazi cause. Robert Jackson's replacement, Brigadier General Telford Taylor, also put his pen to the task of illuminating the central importance of the IG Farben cartel in the rise and operations of the Third Reich.[73] Du Bois and Taylor were joined by many other authors who argued, as did Victor Bernstein, that the Farben organization was known to have played a "Protean part" as "propagandist, espionage agents, international banker and political wire puller" for Germany's Nazi government.[74]

The Nuremberg trials gave rise to the Nuremberg Principles, an instrument of international law ratified by the UN General Assembly in 1950. The UN's International Law Commission drafted this legal instrument based on its studies of the court's proceedings.[75] The Nuremberg Principles include legal definitions of crimes against peace, war crimes, and crimes against humanity. Crimes against humanity include "murder, extermination, enslavement, deportation and other inhumane acts done against any civilian population, or persecutions on political, racial, or religious grounds." The text sets out six basic principles whose intent is to clarify that no legal immunity is available to individuals involved in perpetrating international crimes. Principle III affirms: "The fact that a person who committed an act which constitutes a crime under international law [has] acted as Head of State or responsible government official does not relieve him from responsibility under international law." The best-known provision stipulates: "The fact that a person acted pursuant to order of his Government or of a superior does not relieve him from responsibility under international law, provided a moral choice was in fact possible to him." Like the Convention on the Prevention and Punishment of the Crime of Genocide, the Nuremberg Principles outlaw "complicity" in the commission of international crimes. The legal notion of complicity attaches criminal responsibility to those individuals who are aware that international crimes are taking place but neglect even to call attention to the infractions.

The proceedings of the International Military Tribunal at Nuremberg represent a blending of the ethos of the Atlantic Charter and the national security state. The Nuremberg Principles put forward a vision of a global rule of law that applies uniformly to everyone, prince or pauper, lord or serf, capitalist or communist, Christian or Muslim. This crucial principle of law was contravened, however, by the serious errors of omission at Nuremberg. The imperatives of the looming Cold War were allowed to intervene in a fashion that exempted most financiers and industrialists from legal accountability for their part in the war crimes and crimes against humanity committed during the era of fascist rule in Europe. When issues concerning corporate involvement in international crimes were addressed in the Krupp and IG Farben cases, the judges' rulings suggest that commercial enterprises and their officers partake in a kind of legal immunity reserved for capitalism's leading figures and agencies. These dual legacies of the Nuremberg proceedings cast a long shadow over subsequent events right up to the present day. The imagery of Nuremberg was invoked, for instance, at the court martial of Charles Graner, the man who faced charges in January 2005 for his role in the torturing of prisoners at Abu Ghraib prison in Baghdad, Iraq. In his closing statements, Graner's lawyer, Guy Womack, asserted: "In Nuremberg it was generals being prosecuted. We were going after the order-givers. Here the government is going after the order-takers."[76]

The revelations of torture at Guantanamo Bay in Cuba, Abu Ghraib in Iraq, Bagram in Afghanistan, and at many so-called Black Sites extended to disclosures about techniques of interrogation involving "forced group masturbation, electric shock, rape committed with a phosphorescent stick, the burning of cigarettes in prisoners' ears, involuntary enemas, and beatings that ended in death." It extended to revelations about some detainees being made to eat their food from toilets or to face interrogation techniques designed to create the impression that they were being drowned to death. It involved "sensory deprivation, isolation, sleep deprivation, forced nudity, the use of military working dogs to instill fear, cultural and sexual humiliation, mock executions, and the threat of violence or death toward detainees or their loved ones."[77] Clearly this type of treatment embodied systematic violations of the Nuremberg Principles outlawing "inhumane acts." It involved clear violations of a whole complex of prohibitions on torture developed since the era of the Nuremberg trials.

The passage by the UN General Assembly in 1984 of the Convention against Torture and Other Cruel, Inhuman or Degrading Treatment or Punishment brought together a substantial body of pre-existing law in a single juridical instrument. Most countries of the world have since signed, ratified or acceded to the convention. The UN received the agreement of the United States to become a party to the instrument in 1994.[78] It incorporates elements of the four Geneva Conventions on the treatment of civilians and prisoners of war adopted in 1949. The preamble of the 1984 Convention refers to prohibitions on torture in Article 55 of the UN Charter, Article 5 of the Universal Declaration of Human Rights, Article 7 of the International Covenant on Civil and Political Rights. It refers to the UN General Assembly's Declaration on the Protection of All Persons from Being Subjected to Torture. The 1984 Convention is clear in defining torture as "any act by which severe pain or suffering, whether mental or physical, is intentionally inflicted on a person." It goes on to stipulate that "no exceptional circumstances whatsoever, whether a state of war or a threat of war, internal political instability or any other public emergency, may be invoked as a justification of torture."[79]

The systematic violations of these clear and succinct rules on the international crime of torture by agents and contractors of the US government help put in perspective the growing disparity between the rule of law and the deeds done in the name of the Global War on Terror. It helps put in perspective the fact that the accelerated growth of the national security state since 2001 runs counter to the trajectory of institutional and juridical development flowing from the Atlantic Charter of 1941, the Nuremberg Principles, and the UN's subsequent elaboration of the substance and applicability of international criminal law.

THE AGE OF IMPUNITY

The Nuremberg trials and the Nuremberg Principles were part of a larger complex of events and enactments that coalesced in an era when there was a genuine determination throughout the global community never to allow a repeat of the barbarities that had culminated in the Second World War. This mood translated into a surge of confidence that a better, more just world could be collectively willed into existence. The passage in 1948 by the UN General Assembly of the Universal Declaration of Human Rights was that era's boldest expression of this worldwide surge of political will to improve some of the most fundamental aspects of the human condition for everyone. This remarkable document arose from the work of a committee chaired by Eleanor Roosevelt. The efforts of this former First Lady between 1945 and 1948 epitomized the drive to infuse the finer spirit of the New Deal into the workings of the international community. Where the Universal Declaration presented the positive vision of a world where justice and equality would prevail, the UN Convention on the Prevention and Punishment of the Crime of Genocide spoke to the need to outlaw and punish the most heinous acts of international crime.

While it was one thing to make stirring declarations about the attributes of a better world or to prohibit genocide, colonialism, racist oppression, and sexual discrimination, it would prove to be quite another matter to enforce the juridical instruments that define and outlaw international crime. Important precedents grew from the decision not to hold most of the industrialists and financiers legally accountable for their role in facilitating the brutalities of the Nazi war machine. Moreover, the enactment in 1947 of the *National Security Act* by the Truman government established a legislative framework that gave the colour of law to the litanies of international criminality that would be committed in the name of Cold War anti-communism. Lisa Hajjar has described this schizophrenic character of the decades following the Second World War as "the age of impunity." Throughout this period an elaborate regime of international legislation on human rights was developed, although it was only rarely enforced and never with uniformity and consistency. Hajjar writes, "From the close of the Nuremberg and Tokyo tribunals to the end of the Cold War, international laws pertaining to the rights of human beings functioned not as law but as moral rhetoric framed in legal language." She adds, "During these decades, more people were killed and harmed by practices that had come to be characterized as international crimes than in any previous period. The politics of sovereignty held sway over any meaningful commitment to legality, evidenced by active refusal to authorize international action to stop or prevent grotesque abuses. It was an age of impunity."[80]

The evidence is overwhelming that the era of the Cold War was indeed an age of impunity – and this impunity continues, more or less, to this day. Obviously, however, the problem goes back centuries, not decades. Indeed, only very rarely over the entire sweep of human history has the rule of law been enforced against those who commit the highest order of crime. When law is invoked to punish perpetrators of international crimes, it is virtually always to inflict further humiliation on those who have been stripped of power by losing at warfare. Seen in this light, the massive over-representation of the poorest and most disempowered communities in the prison systems of the United States, Canada, Australia, and New Zealand, for instance, serve as a metaphor for larger patterns of punishment and privilege that divide the global community between those with and without the protections of law. Indeed, those lacking this protection have often been rendered victims of law. As the legal regime of corporate America has expanded to become more transnational in character, the proprietary interests of a heavily entitled few have received enormous safeguards, whereas the Aboriginal titles of the many continue to be denied, extinguished, and stolen. The unbroken persistence of colonialism is reflected in the way law is often manipulated to entrench and edify the powerful at the expense and further disempowerment of the marginalized. In environments dominated by the trappings of formal and informal colonialism, the coercive appropriation of indigenous wealth is often disguised through the cover of laws that do not conform to prohibitions on international crime.

Human rights were systematically violated by the perpetrators of international crime on both sides of the Cold War. On the communist side, most of the state terror was directed by totalitarian regimes against their own citizens.[81] In the Soviet Union the vast system of repressive isolation and incarceration of millions in an elaborate "archipelago" of detention centres and forced labour camps outlived Josef Stalin, the primary architect of these gulags. Stalin retained power until his death in 1953.[82] The Stalinist legacy infused the governing style of various regimes throughout the Soviet block, including that of Romania's dictator Nicolae Ceauşescu. He and his influential wife, Elana, ruled through the violence and intimidation of the

Romanian secret police, the Securitate. Ceaușescu's schemes to augment the number of Romanian citizens by forceful means were integral to a cycle of increasingly severe human-rights violations. His narcissistic preoccupation with the cult of his own personality together with his desire to control Romanians' thought and behaviour led to a situation where it was necessary to obtain a licence even to possess a typewriter.[83]

Albania was dominated by a regime of communist totalitarianism that drew on the ideology of Mao's Great Proletarian Cultural Revolution. In 1967, when Enver Hoxha declared Albania to be the world's first officially atheist state, his government closed more than two thousand churches, mosques, monasteries, and other religious institutions.[84] The extent of the violations of human rights in China during Mao's regime is a source of serious contention. Much of the controversy pits opposing interpretations about the responsibility of the Chinese state in the death through famine of many millions of people in the years 1958–61 – the period of forced collectivization and industrialization known as the Great Leap Forward.[85]

The flagrant oppressiveness of acts such as these appalled one of the most eloquent anti-communists the United States has ever produced. In his text describing the boycott in 1955 of the segregated bus system of Montgomery, Alabama, Martin Luther King Jr. outlined his view of the distortions linking the individual and the state in countries dominated by Marxist regimes. King observed that "man is an end because he is a child of God," and continued: "Man is not made for the state, the state is made for man. To deprive man of freedom is to relegate him to the status of a thing, rather than to elevate him to the status of a person. Man must never be treated as a means to an end of the state, but always as an end within himself." As King saw it, Marxist governments were prone to treat "man only as a means to an end ... if any man's so-called rights or liberties stand in the way of that end, they are simply swept aside. His liberties of expression, his freedom to vote, his freedom to listen to what news he likes or to choose his books are all restricted. Man becomes hardly more, in communism, than a depersonalized cog in the turning wheel of the state."[86]

The view of people as a means to an end rather than as ends in themselves found horrific expression in the communist regime of Pol Pot in Cambodia. In 1975 his Khmer Rouge swept into the vacuum of power left by the hasty US retreat from Indochina.[87] The journey of the Khmer Rouge to power followed a number of paths, some set deeply in the local culture and geography of Indochina and some heavily intertwined with the superpower rivalry of the Cold War.[88] The power of the Khmer Rouge was bolstered by the initial support of Prince Norodom Sihanouk, Cambodia's leader from the time of formal decolonization in 1953 until his removal from power in 1970. Between 1970 and 1975 the country was subject to the kleptocracy of Marshal Lon Nol, an anti-communist puppet installed by the US government.

Sihanouk had attended the Bandung Conference in 1955. There he conferred closely with Mao's foreign minister, Chou Enlai. As a founding member of the Non-Aligned Movement, Sihanouk sought to exploit the antagonism between the United States and the Soviet Union through flirtations with China. Much changed, however, once the US government intensified its military campaign in Indochina by dropping 500,000 tons of bombs on Cambodia, killing, maiming, and uprooting millions.[89] In this era of chaos, Sihanouk joined the displaced multitudes seeking refuge from the bombs and toxic chemicals showered on them by the US Air Force. Some portion of these displaced masses was recruited to help build up the backcountry strongholds of the Khmer Rouge.

A number of its leaders had immersed themselves in structuralist theories of Marxism as developed with particular zeal in France by Louis Althusser and others.[90] Most leading figures in this school of hard-line communists had been ardent supporters and students of Mao Zedong's Cultural Revolution. Pol Pot and his comrades brought from this experience an uncompromising determination to apply the theories of dialectical materialism through a radical remaking of every facet of Cambodian society. Pol Pot became Brother Number One even as 1975 was transformed into Year One. This transformation of time extended to the reconstitution of space as Cambodia became Democratic Kampuchea.

The core mission adopted by the revolution's leaders was to remake the country's largely urban population as rural peasants. In Pol Pot's view, urban life was a major root cause of capitalist decadence. Alternatively, the ideal of an indigenous rural peasantry was romanticized as the model of a society where classlessness and the subordination of the individual to the collective will could thrive. Working from this understanding, the leadership of the Khmer Rouge justified its actions as ones where former Cambodians would be liberated from the corrupting force of religion, money, and the institution of private property. The government's violent means of forcing adherence to these principles led to increasing repression and death on a vast scale. The notorious killing fields of Kampuchea swallowed the lives of about two million victims during a three-year reign of state terror. Cambodia lost about a fifth of its citizens. As with the slaughters embodying Stalin's worst international crimes, some of the most psychopathic ruthlessness fell on those who had made the Kampuchean revolution and thereby gained places for themselves in the inner circles of state power. The scene of much of this internal purging took place at a site called as s-21, a notorious torture chamber situated in an abandoned high school in suburban Phnom Penh. In the years following the vanquishment of the Khmer Rouge by Vietnamese invaders, s-21 was transformed into the Tuol Sleng Genocide Museum.

The invasion of Cambodia in 1979 by the Vietnamese armed forces altered US strategy in the region. Agents of the national security state found ways to intervene through intermediaries to help the Khmer Rouge maintain sufficient military strength to oppose a puppet Cambodian government backed by the Soviet Union through the country's Vietnamese occupiers. China's pragmatic new leader, Deng Xiaoping, also gave advice and support to Pol Pot and the military leadership of the Khmer Rouge. The emergence of Cambodia as a battle ground between competing proxy armies, one allied with China and the other with the Soviet Union, illustrated the increasingly triangular shape of the Cold War's superpower rivalries. The continuing US hostility to communist Vietnam made the national security state a supporter of the Khmer Rouge's surviving military wing, and the US government favoured Pol Pot's surviving government in many ways. It applied international pressure, for instance, to ensure that the Khmer Rouge retained its control over Cambodia's seat at the United Nations until well into the 1980s.[91]

Most of the international crimes committed on the anti-communist side of the Cold War were inflicted on populations outside North America, Western Europe, and Japan. Nevertheless, there have been many clear violations of international conventions and treaties by the national security state's domestic branch – that realm of governance currently identified as "Homeland Security." As with the global discussion of Czechoslovakia's Prague Spring, intense controversy was aroused by the concurrent news that Dr Martin Luther King Jr. had been assassinated in Memphis, Tennessee, at 6:01 pm on April 4, 1968. His murder constitutes a vivid illustration of the existence of an elaborate system of state terror within the domestic confines of the United States. The operatives of this system have been caught in the spotlight on a number of occasions, as, for instance, in 1969 in the publicity surrounding the FBI-directed assassination in a barrage of police fire of Fred Hampton, the eloquent rising young star of the Chicago branch of the Black Panther movement.[92]

Where Hampton was killed just as he was beginning to make his mark, King was approaching the peak of his power when he was eliminated in an act of state. By 1968 this Christian sage and seer was well known for his peaceful opposition to racial segregation. In his quest to achieve racial integration in America, King inspired millions to move along the same strategic path of passive resistance and civil disobedience that Gandhi had travelled in his campaign to free oppressed people from the repressions of colonialism in all its many manifestations. As he approached the time of his assassination, however, King was looking well beyond the goal of racial integration to key issues in the global community. Especially after he won the Nobel Peace Prize in 1964, the Baptist minister turned his attention to the crime of economic exploitation and its devastating consequences for the poor. Moreover, King had expanded the subject matter of his well-reported speeches to include a devastating critique of the US military assault on Indochina's people. As King saw it, this aggressive war was being perpetrated by many of the same corporate and class culprits who were responsible for depriving the American underclass of the basics of food, shelter, decent education, and rudimentary health care – all items of necessity referred to in the Universal Declaration of Human Rights.

The Nobel laureate had come to Memphis to help the city's Black garbage men with their strike. In the early spring of 1968 King was deeply engaged in the project of organizing a procession of poor people that would descend on Washington to set up a tent city. The intent was to make the plight of the poor in America fully visible to the nation's media and lawmakers and to pressure politicians to support policies that would diminish economic inequality through a redistribution of wealth. In the period before he was killed, therefore, King was connecting the dots linking militarism, racial oppression, the persistence of economic colonialism, and the machinery of plunder that relegates a huge portion of humanity to poverty, illiteracy, ill health, and political powerlessness. This understanding was marked in his words and in his organizational work during a period when he was beginning to challenge the legitimacy of the military-command economy that has dominated monopoly capitalism in the United States ever since its government entered the Second World War in 1941.

James Earl Ray was initially charged and convicted with shooting King dead while the civil rights leader was standing on the balcony of the Lorraine Motel. But the real nature of Ray's involvement in the assassination, if any, remains unclear. This uncertainty came to public light due to the investigative and legal work conducted over several decades by William F. Pepper, who represented Ray and then the King family as their lawyer. Pepper's untiring determination to expose the truth culminated in a civil trial in Memphis that concluded in 2000. After four weeks of testimony involving seventy witnesses, a jury found that "government agencies were parties to this conspiracy," which culminated in King's murder. The US Army was one of many government units shown to have been involved in the assassination. Pepper points out the uniqueness of the case of *King v. Jowers et al.*, an official response to a political assassination where "the detailed evidence of what had occurred and why it took place was tested and confirmed under oath in a formal judicial proceeding." The evidence was deemed by a jury to have demonstrated that "the blame for the initiation, planning, conspiracy, and execution of the killing should be laid squarely on the shoulders of agents of the government of the United States in collaboration with Memphis operatives of the Marcello criminal organization."[93] Pepper attributes the successful cover-up of the facts surrounding King's assassination to episodes of "murder, solicitation of murder, attempted bribery, suppression of evidence, alteration of the crime scene, and the control, manipulation, and use of the media for propaganda purposes."[94]

What insights can be derived from the contrast between the massive news coverage showered on the murder trial in the mid-1990s of ex-football star O.J. Simpson and the virtual media blackout over the court proceedings in Memphis where the US government was convicted of playing a role in the assassination of one of the most revered social reformers of the twentieth century? Does this contrast point to the role of the mainstream media as a corrupt instrument of propaganda that often diverts attention away from those episodes where truth is most effectively spoken to power? Does it present the mainstream media as censor rather than as advocate and facilitator of the public's right to have reliable access to the strategic information we need to illuminate our true conditions?

How much did the elimination of King at the age of thirty-nine diminish the moral stature of the United States as well as the chances of achieving the principles of economic justice and peaceful coexistence for which he stood? Two months after King was killed, Robert F. Kennedy was murdered in California. He was shot just as he achieved an electoral breakthrough in his quest to attain the presidential post that his brother, John Fitzgerald Kennedy, had held until being gunned down in Dallas in November 1963. The outspoken Black Islamic nationalist, Malcolm X, was the fourth victim in this slew of political assassinations that dramatically redirected the course of future history.[95] Over time the evidence has continued to mount indicating that the domestic apparatus of the national security state is implicated, one way or another, in various aspects of the intrigues swirling around all four murders. Did the orders to kill King, or Fred Hampton for that matter, emanate from the same circles of privilege that called for the political assassination of, for instance, the Congolese nationalist Patrice Lumumba? If the operatives of the national security state could so readily eliminate foreign leaders identified as obstacles to the global growth of the military-command economy sometimes equated with capitalism, what would prevent the same strategy of lethal intervention from being applied to the management of domestic politics? How might the world be a different place if, say, John F. Kennedy had been able to govern for a second term, or if King had become Robert Kennedy's pick for US representative to the United Nations? What would be different in the world today if the Kennedy brothers, Martin Luther King, and Malcolm X had not been executed?

The FBI's Counterintelligence Program, COINTELPRO, was one of the central agencies in the national security state's domestic assault on political agitation deemed menacing to the survival of the established order.[96] Its operatives infiltrated a number of left-wing organizations such as the American Indian Movement and the Socialist Workers Party. In the process they secretly investigated many tens of thousands of US citizens suspected of holding subversive ideas. In their effort to destabilize and cripple the organized pursuit of significant social, political, and economic change, the FBI's counter-intelligence unit hired infiltrators, informers, agents provocateurs, and assassins. In order to advance and cover up their operations, COINTELPRO officials used forgery, perjury, and illegal surveillance, as well as the dissemination through the media of disinformation and smear campaigns. They fabricated evidence and engineered other abuses of the criminal justice system.[97] The disproportionately high amount of state terror reserved for the domestic proponents of Red Power and Black Power was closely connected to the great depth and severity of the injustices directed against Indigenous peoples and the descendants of Black slaves. In order to avoid a fundamental reckoning with this heritage of injustice and its continuing consequences, authorities have been prone to keep re-enacting variations of the Imperial Republic's original sins. This propensity points to the need to emphasize the concept of international crimes and universal human rights, along with both international arbitration and law enforcement, in responding to the treatment of those Americans who have been subjected to the harshest forms of racial discrimination, repression, exploitation, and demonization.

From the time of the original Red Scare in the early twentieth century, the fear of communism has frequently extended to officialdom's hostile suspicion of all ideas generated by Black intellectuals. This phenomenon is epitomized in the career of the FBI's longest-serving director, J. Edgar Hoover, who was first recruited into the Justice Department to help prepare the groundwork for the anti-communist purges of 1919. Hoover initially impressed his employers with a college essay he parlayed with the help of others into a government publication entitled *Radicalism and Sedition among Negroes as Reflected in Their Publications*. In the era of the Cold War, Hoover's old prejudices were renewed and reinforced.[98] He ordered his COINTEL-PRO agents to do everything in their power "to prevent the rise of a messiah who could unify and electrify the black nationalist movement." No effort should be spared to discredit, incapacitate, and otherwise neutralize potential Black messiahs, but particularly his personal nemesis, Dr Martin Luther King.[99] Whether in the streets of Chicago or on the Pine Ridge Reservation in South Dakota, many murders resulted from COINTELPRO's efforts to instigate divisions, jealousies, and violence among rival groups, to frame targeted individuals for crimes they did not commit, and to fund and encourage those willing to destroy or discredit the condemned activists. Among those known to have been subjected to the FBI's tactics of "neutralization" were Black Panther leaders Stokely Carmichael, H. Rapp Brown, Bobby Seale, Geronimo Pratt, Kathleen Cleaver, Angela Davis, and Huey Newton. The lengthy and complex legal proceedings associated with this era of bitter tumult continues to this day, as in the prosecution of John Graham, who is accused of murdering Anna Mae Pictou Aquash in 1976 because of his alleged belief that she was secretly informing the police on the internal politics of the American Indian Movement.

Outside the United States, the age of impunity drew on the reality that allied forces faced no legal repercussions for their devastating attacks in 1945 on civilian populations through the firebombing of Dresden and the detonation of atomic devices over Hiroshima and Nagasaki. The scale of the combined deaths and injuries perpetrated on these three cities was probably exceeded by the onslaught of US carpet and cluster bombing directed in the late 1960s and early 1970s at Laos and Cambodia. It is estimated that the quantity of explosives dropped there amounted to twice the tonnage used in the course of the entire Second World War. About a million people died immediately from these attacks aimed at destroying the supply lines of the Vietcong. Several times that number were transformed by the violence into refugees. Moreover, there were huge affects to public health, including high rates of cancer and birth defects, stemming from the toxic defoliants used in this "pacification" campaign. The defoliants included the notorious the Agent Orange. The effects of this chemical contamination continue to this day, as do the lethal and crippling effects of the lands mines left by the US forces in the course of the hostilities.[100]

Even before the worst of the bombing raids in Indochina, Teleford Taylor drew on his experience as a prosecutor at Nuremberg to point out that the direct US military intervention in Vietnam represented a clear violation of the Nuremberg Principles. In his text, *Nuremberg and Vietnam*, Taylor quoted from a report by an assistant secretary of defense who wrote in 1967: "We seem to be proceeding on the assumption that the way to eradicate the Vietcong is to destroy all the village structures, defoliate all the jungles, and then cover the entire south Vietnam with asphalt."[101]

The history of direct US military intervention during the Cold War forms only one aspect of the capitalist superpower's many-faceted role as an agent, patron of, and collaborator in state terror. Throughout Latin America and in most African and Asian polities emerging from formal imperial rule, the national security state intervened repeatedly to remove regimes deemed unfriendly to the transnational interests of large business corporations headquartered primarily in the United States but also in Japan and Western Europe. The regimes installed in this way did much of the dirty work to silence, eliminate, and disable those representatives of Indigenous peoples seeking to extend the principles of collective self-determination to the realm of the economy. The pre-eminent example of the contracting out of international crime took place when the regime of General Suharto slaughtered in the name of anti-communism close to a million Indonesians following the British- and US-directed removal of President Achmed Sukarno. Sukarno sealed his fate when he revealed his unwillingness to endorse fully the military and commercial agenda of the capitalist superpower by hosting the Bandung Conference in 1955 and by asserting leadership in the founding of the Non-Aligned Movement.

The importance of the culture of impunity in the rise of global capitalism is epitomized by the unaddressed nature of the massive crime spree that created the basis for the governance of Indonesia as it operates up to this day. The infatuation of the operatives of the national security state with regime change as a primary means of edifying its corporate empire of monopoly capitalism began in the early 1950s in response to the efforts of Iran's elected leader, Mohammed Mossedegh, to indigenize control and ownership of his country's oil and gas reserves. Mossedegh was typical of his generation of native leadership in the movement for decolonization in that he attempted to realize the full potential of economic self-determination by nationalizing ownership of his country's abundant natural resources.[102] William Blum has commented on the consistency of US intervention either directly or through proxies to prevent the consolidation of any regimes supporting systems of political economy that do not conform with the requirements of monopoly capitalism. As he asserts, "every socialist experiment of any significance in the twentieth century – without exception – has either been crushed, overthrown, or invaded, or corrupted, perverted, subverted, or destabilized, or otherwise had life made impossible for it, by the United States."[103]

In 1999 Walter J. Rockler emerged as an outspoken critic of the regime of international lawlessness promoted in the age of impunity by the national security state and by capitalism's military-industrial complex. Like Teleford Taylor, Rockler was a former prosecutor of the Nazi regime who raised his voice against the violation of the Nuremberg Principles by his own government. He took aim especially at NATO's US-led bombing invasion of Serbian Yugoslavia without the sanction of the UN Security Council. In a much-reproduced letter to the *Chicago Tribune* in May of that year, Rockler drew attention to the hypocrisy entailed in presenting the bombing missions as media for the advancement and protection of human rights:

Our alleged concern with human rights borders on the ridiculous. We dropped twice as many bombs on Vietnam as all the countries involved in World War II dropped on each other. We killed hundreds of thousands of civilians in the course of that war. Very recently in Central America we sponsored, trained and endorsed local armies – Guatemalan, Salvadoran, and Nicuarguan Contras – in the killing of at least 200,000 people. We encouraged the Pinochet coup in Chile with the killing of another few thousand or so people, including the democratically elected president. We saw nothing wrong with the Croat slaughter and expulsion of 200,000 Serbs from the Krajina area. We have taken very little stand in the monumental killing of hundreds of thousands, if not millions of people in Africa. We have restrained the Iraqis from attacking Kurds but see nothing wrong in Turks attacking Kurds. We cannot even agree to abandon the use of land mines.[104]

Rockler's sketch of US involvement in violations of universal human rights touches only the surface of the international crimes committed on the capitalist side of the Cold War during the age of impunity. Many of the violations have their origins in episodes of so-called regime change. From Jacobo Arbenz of Guatemala, to Mohammad Mossadegh of Iran, to Achmed Sukarno of Indonesia, to Kwame Nkrumah of Ghana, to Patrice Lumumba of Congo, to Cheddi Jagan of British Guiana, to Salvador Allende of Chile, to Jean-Bertrand Aristide of Haiti virtually every national leader seeking to deepen indigenous ownership and control of Aboriginal resources has been overthrown or killed with the backing or assistance of US agents. In virtually every polity where regimes advocating economic decolonization have been eliminated, the puppet governors made to replace the terminated leaderships have engaged in wholesale repression of their own citizens. The cumulative result was a transnational reign of state terror through murder, intimidation, torture, and unlawful incarceration. Such activities were over time institutionalized as a regular part of the global operations of the executive branch of the US government.

The extensive and systemic character of these illegal interventions contradicts any notion that the expansion of capitalism following the Second World War took place primarily through the natural workings of self-regulating markets. In 1944 in *The Great Transformation*, Karl Polanyi anticipated the importance of coercive intervention in eliminating or crippling resistance to the globalization of capitalism.[105] His text foreshadowed the growing importance of state and corporate terror in eliminating all cultural, political, ideological, and legal barriers to the worldwide integration of market economies. As Polanyi implicitly predicted through his analysis of major trends in economic history, the transnational growth of increasingly uniform motifs of market interaction would take place during the second half of the twentieth century not so much because of some invisible hand quietly knitting together the political economies of the world's nations and peoples. It would happen, rather, largely because of the illegal intervention into the sovereign affairs of many countries by agents of the CIA, the US Armed Forces, and other corporate divisions of the national security state. These for-profit polities include the Science Applications International Corporation and the Blackwater Corporation. Blackwater officials reconstituted their mercenary polity as Xe Corporation in the early months of 2009. This change may have come about because the company executives' desire to distance themselves from the bad publicity arising from its soldiers' random execution in 2007 of many civilians in Baghdad's Nisor Square. It may also have been an expedient to help retool the corporate polity politically for the Democratic presidency of Commander-in-Chief Barack Obama.

US president Richard Nixon engaged in a very different kind of intervention in his secret negotiations with representatives of the government of Saudi Arabia. Beneath the public façade of the Arab Oil Embargoes of 1973–74 lay a secret agreement giving the sanction of the US executive branch to a quadrupling of the price of oil on the condition that the black gold of industrialization could only be purchased from its suppliers only in US currency. This single deal dramatically affected the entire global economy as it significantly strengthened the status and value of the US dollar. It enabled the US-based oil conglomerates and their Wall Street bankers to shake off recession and move towards higher profits. But for the wretched of the Earth, however, the consequences were disastrous.

The enormity of the consequences arising from Nixon's secret deal with the Saudis started to become clear in the mid-1970s, when the citizens, businesses, and governments of many countries were forced to import their fossil fuels and to pay for this resource with artificially expensive US dollars.

As one national economy after another sputtered into depression as a result of this manipulation of the energy market, the quality of life was severely undermined for hundreds of millions, if not billions, of people. Levels of unemployment, sickness, illiteracy, and morbidity increased dramatically, but especially in the world's poorest countries where governments lost much of their already limited capacities to deliver health care, education, and social services to their most impoverished constituents.[106]

The political imperative that linked the value of petrodollars to the price of oil had nothing to do with movements of an invisible hand in self-regulating markets. The decision of President Nixon to exploit the combination of US military might together with the dominant position of its corporations in the oil industry was consistent with George F. Kennan's insistence that his government must "dispense of all sentimentality ... [and] cease thinking about human rights, the raising of living standards and democratization." The resulting transfer of wealth from the disentitled many to the massively entitled few renewed and accelerated processes of imperial appropriation as they have continued since the modern era of globalization began in 1492. This single intervention, which rearranged the exercise of power in many key agencies of the national security state, has produced more lethal and broadly felt harm than all the murder and torture conducted by a host of US-supported death squads in Indonesia, Central America, sub-Saharan Africa, and elsewhere. It remains to be seen if this kind of expression of monopoly capitalism's inner dynamics meets the current criteria of those international crimes that violate the universal human rights of a large percentage of the global community. If such commercial manipulations do not qualify as international crimes, perhaps the international prohibitions on economic crimes against humanity should be expanded and strengthened.

THE LIES AND CRIMES OF EDWARD BERNAYS, ALLEN DULLES, AUGUSTO PINOCHET, AND RIOS MONTT

The role of the national security state in the transformation of Guatemala from a democracy into a military dictatorship constitutes a good case study on the subject of international crime on the capitalist side of the Cold War during the age of impunity. As revealed in the text *I Rigoberta Menchú, an Indian Woman from Guatemala,* the history of the Indian wars and the Cold War converged most seamlessly in the violence of this small Central American country.[107] Much of the history of international crime in Guatemala has swirled around the operations of the United Fruit Company (UFC), a US corporation rooted deep in the historical bowels of the national security state. United Fruits' historic position in the genesis of corporate capitalism stands poised in time between the growth of the old railway empires and the subsequent rise of US oil and gas conglomerates in the Middle East. In much the same way that Indigenous peoples had to be "pacified" by the army to make way for the transcontinental railways in North America, so the

Indians of Central America had to be made to accept their role as landless peasants subordinate to the monopoly powers of a giant US food company.

The corporate subordination of the local population was placed in jeopardy by the actions of Guatemala's elected president, Jacobo Arbenz Guzman. As Piero Gleijeses has wriiten of Arbenz's brief period in office, "for the first time in the history of Guatemala, the Indians were offered land rather than being robbed of it."[108] Arbenz's policies of land redistribution prompted the United Fruit Company and the CIA to join forces in orchestrating a coup. This violent intervention replaced a slightly left-of-centre elected government with a string of military dictatorships that would exterminate hundreds of thousands of Guatemalans – Indian , Meztiso, and Latino – in the name of anti-communism.

The US government went far towards developing its overall strategy of public relations and psychological warfare in the Cold War through selling the American people a mythological account of what took place in Guatemala in 1954. Much of the dirty work of regime change was done under the cover of this myth. Edward Bernays was the key figure hired initially by the United Fruit Company to present the US-backed coup in Guatemala as if it were the expression of a large popular movement aimed at preventing Soviet-backed communists from gaining a beachhead in the Western Hemisphere. A nephew of Sigmund Freud, Bernays is widely recognized as the father of public relations, a phrase he invented to replace the term "propaganda."[109] He has also been dubbed the father of spin. A student of his uncle's preoccupation with the role of the subconscious in influencing human actions, Bernays introduced the term "public relations" to disguise his preoccupation with the arts and science of propaganda. He made history in his chosen field in 1929 when he engineered a successful media campaign equating female smoking of cigarettes, or "Torches of Freedom," with the ideals animating the quest by many women for equal rights. After significantly increasing cigarette sales for the American Tobacco Company, Bernays went on to work for many other large conglomerates, including the Hearst publishing empire. His assignments included helping the Hearst corporation design and launch an array of women's magazines.

In a larger sense, Bernays's job as the pioneer of public relations was to help change attitudes in order to accelerate the growth of mass consumption. His job was to design the tools of mass persuasion that would stimulate the psychology of conspicuous consumption without which capitalism cannot flourish. His work in promoting the sale of goods through the manipulation of imagery and mythology led to his expanding involvement in promoting the ideals of patriotism and the American Way. The original spin doctor's techniques for shaping public opinion merged increasingly with the more hard-edged techniques of propaganda employed, for instance, by the right-wing National Association of Manufacturers.[110] Bernays crossed the line into full-fledged psychological warfare when he marketed a myth of freedom's triumph over tyranny in Guatemala. The apparent success of this marketing job, where he applied his techniques for "the engineering of consent," helped to tighten the partnership between Madison Avenue, the US Armed Forces, and the corporate constituents of the national security state.[111] Together the technocratic staffs of these interlinked agencies sought to disseminate more secular versions of the myth of Manifest Destiny through the idealization of global capitalism as the key to achieving universal liberties and freedoms. They equated the freedom to buy and sell in open markets with religion freedom and freedom of expression.

The role of Allen Dulles in overseeing the US-backed coup in Guatemala is telling. So too is his succession of jobs, assignments, and involvements both before and after the CIA's illegal replacement of the Arbenz government with a military dictatorship. Dulles was the CIA's executive at the time of the Guatemalan coup. The previous year he had overseen the CIA's removal from office of the Iranian nationalist, Mohammed Mossedegh. Dulles began his career in the 1920s with the Wall Street legal firm of Sullivan and Cromwell. This company was deeply involved in channelling US investment to Germany to build up the anti-communist infrastructure of Adolf Hitler's war and propaganda machine. Dulles participated at intervals in the corporate governance of Germany's IG Farben Company, the Rockefeller's Standard Oil conglomerate, and the United Fruit Company. He was a US intelligence officer in Switzerland during the Second World War. His series of involvements in the business dealings of both sides during the war embodies a trend in the deep politics of the national security state that would be renewed with a vengeance during the Global War on Terror. The consistency of Dulles's role on the front lines of both German and US anti-communism is suggestive of the source of the fascist intensity that often permeated the violently imposed puppet regimes that would govern with US backing much of Central and South America throughout most of the Cold War.[112] In the name of anti-communism, those regimes often empowered military or paramilitary death squads whose victims have included tens of thousands of social activists and hundreds of thousands of traditional Indian horticulturalists.

The military personnel attached to these right-wing regimes received much of their military training in the US Army's notorious School of the Americas in Fort Benning, Georgia.[113] This school is well known for inculcating in its students expert knowledge in the dark arts of torture, assassination, and other techniques of state terror. In 2001 it changed its name to become the Western Hemisphere Institute for Security Cooperation. The military academy's graduates were prominent among those who carried out the ethnic cleansing of Indians ordered by General Efrian Rios Montt in Guatemala during the most intense phase of Reagan's anti-communist crusade. Mayan farmers accounted for the majority of the 200,000 people murdered during the 1980s when Montt's government was in power.

The UN-sponsored Commission on Historical Clarification reported in 1999 that the US government's training of the Guatemalan military in "counter-insurgency techniques" was a "key factor" in the "genocide." The report's authors explained, "Entire Mayan villages were attacked and burned and their inhabitants were slaughtered in an effort to deny the guerrillas protection."[114]

The US role in the overthrow of the Arbenz government was instrumental in radicalizing the politics of Fidel Castro and Ernesto "Che" Guevera as they moved towards taking control of the Cuban government in 1959. "President Arbenz and his group in the country's leadership," said Castro in an interview with the British Broadcasting Corporation, "were a team of very progressive people who wanted to work for the Guatemalan people – for the most part very poor, indigenous people." The CIA's role, Castro continued, "made a deep impression on all the progressive forces of the hemisphere and on Latin American public opinion, because it was perceived as an interventionist action and a violation of the Guatemalan people's sovereignty. A government that had wanted to work for the people had been overthrown."[115]

The covert interventions of the US government in Central America on behalf of the United Fruit Company provided a prep school and a launching pad for yet wider and more aggressive interventions, especially on behalf of US-based oil and gas conglomerates. The shifting of concessions to exploit fossil fuels in, for instance, the former Dutch East Indies, Iran, the Arabian Peninsula, and West Africa formed a key element in the movement of the informal American empire into the vacuum of influence left by the waning viability of European empires. As Middle Eastern oil grew in importance in the global economy, the US government increasingly looked to Israel as a front-line military ally in the region. As the dismantling of European empires opened the way for the expansion of US influence in Asia and Africa, the local factions most likely to gain the favour of the capitalist superpower were the ones that accepted the mores of possessive individualism tied to the values of conspicuous consumption. In manipulating access to arms exports, intelligence reports, military training, and foreign aid, the operatives of the national security state helped their client regimes to fend off local opposition.

The term "foreign internal defense" became the euphemism sometimes employed to describe the work of the US military and intelligence establishment in training client regimes to kill, cripple, smear, or otherwise silence local dissidents. As the killing of Martin Luther King and the covert activities of COINTELPRO demonstrate, there was plenty of experience with this kind of internal suppression of ideals and idealists within the United States. Some facets of foreign internal defense proceeded under the auspices of the Joint Combined Exchange Training Program authorized by Congress in 1991. A more recent trend has witnessed veterans of US special operations forces creating private companies for the purpose of exporting instruction and expertise in state terrorism. That expedient is seen to hold the advantage of shielding secret operations from the scrutiny of the public and the workings of the *United States' Freedom of Information Act*. Those responsible for the US government's increasingly privatized "counter-insurgency" operations in foreign lands can make the claim that these activities are governed by the corporate laws of "proprietary information" rather than those of public disclosure.[116]

The aims of the US national security establishment, therefore, have included initiatives to counter the extension of the principles of Aboriginal title to the fuller exercise of sovereign jurisdiction by Indigenous peoples over property law and property relationships. Its goals have included pre-empting the leadership of those with the capacity to inspire Aboriginal resistance across a wide range of indigenous ethnicities and cultures. In this way the process of decolonization can be held within the limits of narrow political reform, thereby preventing sweeping economic transformations that would negatively affect transnational profit cycles of large corporations. The mission has been to form a world order based on the cookie-cutter replication of nation-states, however ill adapted these polities might be to Fourth World configurations of political association, culture, language, and ecology. All this political, economic, and social engineering has been sold to those paying for it through their tax dollars with barrages of propaganda extolling the promotion of "freedom" and "democracy." Meanwhile, there has been no fundamental reckoning at the United Nations or elsewhere with the basic principle of international law – that all *peoples* have an inherent right to self-determination. In the words of Chalmers Johnson, the aim has been "to compel every significant economy on earth to remodel itself along American lines."[117]

In the years immediately following the dismantling of the Berlin Wall and the demise of the Soviet Union, it appeared that the age of impunity might be coming to an end. In 1993, for instance, the UN Security Council established the International Tribunal for the punishment of those accused of committing international crimes in the former Yugoslavia. In November of the following year a similar process was established to bring to justice the perpetrators of genocide in the small African country of Rwanda. Similar processes have begun tentatively to address international crimes in Sierra Leone, East Timor, and Cambodia (see chapter 14 for information on all these episodes).

In 1998 more indications arose that the age of impunity might be coming to an end even for those who have committed international crimes on the stronger side of the Cold War. One development was the creation of the International Criminal Court after the approval by 121 states of the Rome Statute. The ICC was established to apply the Nuremberg Principles and other instruments of international law to those who commit war crimes and crimes against humanity. The other development had its beginnings in the work of a young Spanish judge, Baltasar Garzon, whose efforts were part of a broader initiative leading in 1998 to the apprehension in London, England, of the former Chilean dictator, Augusto Pinochet.[118] Pinochet had come to power in 1973 in a US-backed coup aimed at removing the socialist regime of Dr Salvador Allende.[119] Allende's most serious infraction in the eyes of the coup masters had been to nationalize in 1970 the lucrative extraction of copper in mines developed by the Anaconda and Kennecott conglomerates. Pinochet sought to secure the base for his fascist campaign of anti-socialism by overseeing the "disappearances" of thousands of dissidents as part of a reactionary upsurge in his region that made both Chile and Argentina major centres for this kind of international crime.

These episodes of state terror formed the background of the London proceedings against Pinochet. The case involved efforts to extradite Pinochet to Spain to face charges involving the crimes of genocide and terror. There was also the possibility of using this process to initiative a more elaborate complex of prosecutions extending to the perpetrators of Operation Condor, a transnational system of state-sanctioned murder that brought together military leaders representing US-backed puppet regimes in Argentina, Bolivia, Chile, Paraguay, Uruguay, and Brazil.[120] Operation Condor, in turn, was just one of the litany of covert and overt actions on both sides of the Cold War that violated core principles of common morality and international law.

These complex proceedings led to a hearing before the Judicial Committee of the House of Lords, a venue of arbitration whose historic personality was once that of the highest court in the British Empire. The British jurists were obliged to choose between heavily contested legal theories. One of these treated foreign heads of state as being constitutionally immune from criminal prosecution for acts committed in their home jurisdictions. The competing theory was based on the view that international law has developed to the point that the age of impunity is no more. There is no such thing in law as automatic immunity for those who commit crimes, but especially for those who commit the highest order of international crime. In their first proceeding the jurists opted for the latter argument, prompting Hugo Young in *The Guardian* to describe the judges' ruling as "bold and principled, taking a stand on behalf of the globalization of fundamental human rights."[121] The validity of this ruling was then called into question because one of the Law Lords was seen to have had too close a relationship with Amnesty International, an organization that had intervened in the proceedings. After sixteen months it was deemed that Pinochet was unfit to be extradited to Spain for reasons of health. Nevertheless, he was allowed to return to Chile. While the former Chilean dictator ultimately escaped the formal punishment of international criminal law, the episode showed that the political will was building in some influential circles to apply the Nuremberg Principles even to former heads of state.

EXTENDING THE LEGAL IMPUNITY OF ELITES INTO THE ERA OF THE 9/11 WARS

The age of elite impunity was extended when President George W. Bush responded to the attacks of September 11, 2001, not by ordering a careful and thorough investigation of the crime scene but rather by declaring immediately that the United States would launch a Global War on Terror. From the earliest reports following the attacks, the alleged enemy was presented through the mythological veil of concerted media spin. With an intensity befitting the popular myth making of Edward Bernays, we were informed that a secret brotherhood of Arab terrorists had made the Twin Towers plus World Trade Center 7 crash to the ground. We were instructed that the kamikaze pilots of the four doomed aircrafts were operating under the hypnotic spell of Osama bin Laden. There could be no avoiding the media's unrelenting message that bin Laden's demonic persona epitomized the dark perversity of radical Islam. We were reassured that the same complex of agencies that had failed to repel the attacks was prepared to mount a counter-attack immediately in Afghanistan and later in Iraq.

Without any opportunity for reflection or thoughtful public debate, the bipolar divide of the Cold War was reconfigured to reflect a new kind of division said to pit *our* Judeo-Christian civilization against Muslim zealots devoted to inflicting savage acts of terror on innocent civilians. Where the Berlin Wall had once symbolized the central division of the Cold War, the core dichotomy of the new conflict was vividly expressed in a hastily erected barrier to protect Jewish Israel from the angry recriminations of Palestinians penned into small enclaves in Gaza and the Occupied Territories west of the Jordan River. Where Ronald Reagan had fought the evil empire, George Bush would do battle with al-Qaeda or any other group, regime, or individual said to be linked to it. In the 1980s al-Qaeda had been born as a "base" of communications among the guerrilla warriors known as *mujahadeen*. On the basis of advice given to President Jimmy Carter in 1979 by his national security adviser, Zbigniew Brzezinski, the US government began, with Saudi assistance, to recruit, train, and arm the mujahadeen with the aim of destabilizing the Soviet-backed regime in Afghanistan.[122]

According to Peter Dale Scott, it remains unclear to this day if the events of 9/11 prompted President Bush secretly to suspend some features of the US Constitution by invoking a pre-prepared plan of emergency measures known as Directive 51 for the Continuity of Government.[123] Indeed, the US executive branch had a surprisingly wide array of pre-prepared plans that it introduced in the days, weeks, months, and years following the events of 9/11. The military command economy of the United States was extended to form the basis of terror capitalism. The growth of the terror economy depended on changing domestic laws, widening police powers, undertaking foreign invasions, developing a global network of gulags, and pressuring allies to accept the thuggery of a US-led global police state. These developments provided a bonanza of new government spending directed largely at private contractors in the business of procuring mercenary armies, weapons systems, military infrastructures, and strategic intelligence, as well as the covert violence and psychological operations done in the name of counter-intelligence and counter-insurgency.

Not surprisingly, the leading corporate and government operatives of the national security state had no intention whatsoever of allowing international treaties, conventions, or laws to stand in the way of their zeal to globalize new forms of militarized Manifest Destiny. The quick reversal of the US government's relationship with the International Criminal Court (ICC) signalled the intention of the Bush White House to deploy the 9/11 wars as a legal shield to protect the agents of the national security state from persecution for past or future international crimes. Where the government of President Bill Clinton had given qualified approval to the ICC, the administration of President George W. Bush "unsigned" the Rome Statute in May 2002. "The jurisdiction [of the ICC] does not extend to Americans," Bush asserted when he announced his government's plan to increase the size and the power of the national security state.[124]

The murder of about three thousand civilians on September 11, 2001 was itself an international crime. Are the guilty parties responsible for planning and implementing this international crime the same individuals who have been incarcerated, tortured, or killed in the name of the Global War on Terror? Who was actually responsible for committing various aspects of this elaborate international crime? Did senior executives in charge of corporate media cartels play a role in misrepresenting the true nature of this international crime? Who would be held legally accountable if it could be conclusively demonstrated in an international court of law that some officials in the US government had prior knowledge of the imminent attacks but failed to act proactively to prevent this tragedy? What would the nature of the international crime be if the attacks could be shown to have originated in the plans of some conspiring faction within the corporate and government branches of the national security state in the expectation that benefits were to be garnered from the accelerated growth of the terror economy? If this scenario of internal responsibility could be demonstrated, would the guilt of the culprits most responsible for planning and directing the 9/11 attacks also extend to culpability for the broad array of international crimes committed in the name of the Global War on Terror?

As with the assassination of President John F. Kennedy, the media was offered an elaborate explanation of the 9/11 attacks in the first few hours following the most violent phase of the event. Rather than interrogate the hastily produced interpretation of the crime, the government's explanation was amplified in the echo chambers of global communications. As the mainstream media embellished the Global War on Terror's psychological landscape of fear and apprehension, a sufficient if uneven level of consent was manufactured for the litany of invasions, assaults, illegal renditions, and other intrusive acts that have been justified in the name of a very explicit demonology of 9/11. In the atmosphere of shock and awe aroused by the spectacle, even an aging Noam Chomsky, once one of the world's most unrelenting unmaskers of media spin, censorship, and lies, sanctioned the official account. "There is no serious doubt that the attack was 'external,'" he announced. In spite of mounting evidence to the contrary, this icon of American dissent went as far as to proclaim that the attack "was surely an enormous shock and surprise to the intelligence services of the West, including those of the United States."[125] Whose interests did Chomsky serve with these unsubstantiated statements?[126]

As the terror economy was pressed forward domestically, internationally, and through the further militarization of space, a small but important constituency began to question the official story used to justify the slide towards a new form of global police state. In July 2002 a new periodical was launched in Toronto entitled *Global Outlook: The Magazine of 9/11 Truth*. Another major challenge arose in France. Thierry Meyssan's *Effroyable Imposture* presented a French view of the United States very different from that provided by Jean-Jacques Servan-Schreiber in 1967 in *Le Défi Américain*.[127] Meyssan's book has been translated into twenty-eight languages, and the English version is titled *9/11: The Big Lie*.[128] That same year Nafeez Mossadeq Ahmed produced a third major counter narrative published in Great Britain: *The War on Freedom* directly connects the events of 9/11 to those factions within the national security state that played a guiding role in assembling, funding, training, and directing al-Qaeda.[129] Then, with his seminal volume, *The Terror Timeline*, Paul Thompson gave this developing thrust of investigative scholarship a still more solid grounding in documented fact and precise chronology. His text has been repeatedly updated since it was published in 2002 as new information becomes available.[130]

As the years passed, many public figures came forward to help pierce the public mythology of 9/11 with their sceptical interpretations and insights. They include former Italian president Francesco Cossiga, the former British environment minister Michael Meacher, the former British MI5 agent Annie Machon, the politician and functionary in the German security apparatus, Andreas von Bulow, the former US Congresswoman and presidential candidate, Cynthia McKinney, the former US assistant treasury secretary, Paul Craig Roberts, the former CIA analysts Ray McGovern and Bill Christison, the former chief of staff of the Russian armed forces, General Leonid Ivashov, and the former head of the Pakistan's Inter-Services Intelligence agency, General Hamid Gul. The whistle blowers also include Japanese parliamentarian Yukihisa Fujita, the architect Richard Gage, New York University Media Studies professor Mark Crispin Miller, and, from Canada, the economist Michel Chossudovsky, the political philosopher John McMurtry, the journalist Barry Zwicker, the literary critic and English professor Michael Keefer, as well as the Berkeley professor emeritus and

former diplomat Peter Dale Scott. In 2004 and 2005 anthropology professor Richard B. Lee, a Fellow of the Royal Society of Canada, made pedagogical history by teaching a course at the University of Toronto looking at
the disparity between the existing evidence and the official account of what
happened on 9/11.[131]

The organizational form and intellectual approach of the 9/11 Truth
movement began to coalesce at early conferences, such as those conceived
and planned by Nicolas Levis in Berlin, Carol Brouillet in San Francisco,
Barry Zwicker and Ian Woods in Toronto, and Kevin Barrett in Madison,
Wisconsin. As the movement gathered momentum in the digital interactivity of the Internet, talk-show host Alex Jones and the makers of the video
hit *Loose Change* gave the growing network of truth seekers a populist twist.
These innovators of New Media production inspired many emulators and
emulations. Some of this activity went forward in the name of a network of
activist communities entitled *We Are Change*. In their signature videos that
appear by the hundreds on the Internet, agents of *We Are Change* confront
public officials on camera with probing questions concentrating on the
9/11 wars' origins, character, and course. In the more cautious, conservative, and orthodox branches of the movement, many thousands of professional people in various fields have added their contributions to the quest
for the 9/11 Truth. These experts chose to put their reputations on the line,
as evidenced by the contents of websites such as Patriots Question 9/11,[132]
Scholars for 9/11 Truth and Justice,[133] and Architects and Engineers for
9/11 Truth.[134]

With his steady production of a stream of consistently well-researched
and argued books, retired theology professor David Ray Griffin gradually
emerged as the effective dean of the emerging interdisciplinary investigation that some have labelled 9/11 Studies. Griffin's body of work on the
events of 9/11 is based on his careful analysis of the incomplete but extensive primary sources as well as the relevant secondary literature. Among the
questions addressed in this literature is the following partial list: How could
the impact of two jet crashes have caused the complete obliteration of three
steel-framed towers? How was it that all three structures plunged into their
own footprint through the path of maximum resistance roughly at the
speed of free falls in events displaying all the classic characteristics of controlled demolitions? What was the source of the massive amount of energy
required to vaporize and pulverize the largest of the World Trade Centers
into huge billows of toxic gases and talcum powder–like dust? How could it
be that alleged hijacker Mohammed Atta's passport miraculously survived
the debacle to be found in pristine condition at Ground Zero whereas the
black box cockpit voice recorders and data recorders from the two airliners
were never recovered? How could nineteen Saudi men said to be armed
with nothing but box cutters, a smattering of flight training, and intense
jihadist zeal cut through every element of the world's most elaborate intelligence and defence apparatus in order to hit their targets?

Carrying on, Why did the whole system of North American air defence fail so spectacularly on that day? If the events of 9/11 really did include an enormous failure in the operations of the military-industrial complex, why was it that not one official in the whole chain of command was fired for negligence, misfeasance, or malfeasance? Why was FEMA, the Federal Emergency Measures Agency, in such a hurry to cart away and dispose of the major physical evidence at the crime scene? How can President Bush's peculiar actions throughout the day of 9/11 be explained? When did Vice President Richard Cheney enter the White House's bunker to take control of the national security state's response to the attacks on the morning of September 11, 2001? What orders did he give? Did Dick Cheney preempt the powers of the president of the United States on the morning of September 11, 2001? What kind of flying machine was it that made such a deep but narrow penetration of the Pentagon's thick walls, and why has the US government not released its own extensive video records of the event? Why was the supposed crash site of Flight 93 in Pennsylvania so bereft of physical wreckage? Who had the means to plan, coordinate, and execute all facets of the international crimes committed on September 11, 2001? Who had the motives? Who benefited?

Efforts to investigate and answer any one of these questions point to the fault lines where fact and fiction meet in the 9/11 wars' mythological construction. With some few exceptions, the mainstream corporate media avoided any serious reckoning with research and publications introducing new information that cast doubt on the original story. The consequence of this convenient lack of attentiveness left the analysis of the empirically verifiable data concerning the events of 9/11 primarily to the investigative enterprise of independent citizen journalists whose research and publication take place largely on noncommercial Internet sites. The disparity in worldviews presented by the centrally controlled info-entertainment conglomerates and the decentralized interactivity of the New Media could not be made more clear than in the stark contrast between discordant interpretations of 9/11. Even before 9/11 the info-entertainment industry's propensity simply to stonewall new truths that are inconvenient to power was classically demonstrated in its failure in the winter of 2000 to inform the public on the findings of the Memphis court that had agreed with the legal contentions of the late Martin Luther King's family that there was deep involvement by several government agencies in the conspiracy to assassinate America's most celebrated civil-rights leader. If the info-entertainment cartels could disregard key courtroom revelations about the government's role in King's assassination, what other exposures of strategic truths have they prevented through their studied inattention?

Before the Internet emerged as a major network of communications, the leadership of the info-entertainment cartels could maintain a fairly tight but invisible hold on the content of news reporting and widely disseminated political discourse. Accordingly, the oligarchs of information control faced few repercussions for subjugating the content of their media empires to the imperatives of advertising, public-relations spin, imperial disinformation, and psychological warfare. The advent of the worldwide web, however, enabled some of its more astute navigators to bypass more recent versions of what George Orwell identified as "the most flagrant violations of reality" in his fictionalized reflections on society's imagined oversight by Big Brother and his thought police.[135] In the decades since 1984, but especially since the rise of the widely accessible Internet in the mid-1990s, the politics of propaganda and thought control became much more complex and nuanced than Orwell once predicted. In the relativist culture of capitalist post-modernism, Multiplethink has replaced the Orwellian conception of Doublethink. But some reckoning with the absolute requirements of truth cannot indefinitely be delayed. Either explosives were, or were not, implanted and detonated in the three steel-framed towers. Were the three towers brought down by controlled demolition or were they obliterated, as we have been instructed to believe, by the impact of two airliner crashes, fire, and the weight of gravity? Was it a jet passenger plane or a missile that struck the Pentagon?

By far the largest weight of evidence points away from the official story towards controlled demolitions and a missile strike. As the evidence supporting these conclusions mounts, the most grave sorts of issue arise about power's relationship with truth. What happens when truth is spoken to power? Is truth for the many or only for the few? Is truth relative or absolute? What is the relationship between democracy and truth, capitalism and truth? What happens to society when the appearance of truth is fabricated for the masses through advertising, public relations, perceptions management, and psychological warfare? Do we see reality through the lens of our own wandering eyes? Or do we maintain a steady, hypnotic gaze on TV illusions presented as high-definition plasma truths by the public-relations branches of the military-industrial complex? Do we trust that the commodified imagery of the big media brands coincides with objectively verifiable truth, especially when it comes to determining how questions of war and peace will be answered?

The quest for 9/11 truth, therefore, has more to do with the nature of truth itself than with the minutiae of debate over what happened to make the Twin Towers and WTC 7 fall. But why has this particular episode emerged as such a strategic test case in evaluating truth's artifice, substance, and capacity for being covered up? There are, after all, many scores of episodes in the terrible annals of international crime that far exceed the magnitude of 9/11 in terms of the mathematics of murder and mayhem. But such calculations fail to take into account the number of subsequent international crimes, including the "supreme crime" of unprovoked foreign invasions, which have been pressed on humanity because of an unproven interpretation of the 9/11 attacks. They fail to take into account the strategic importance of the events of 9/11 in creating the psychological landscape on which the primary beneficiaries of the terror economy depend. Hence the stakes are large in this particular struggle to sort out fact from fiction. The struggle to determine the actual content of 9/11 truth involves the most profound issues concerning the credibility and legitimacy of our governors. This contentiousness extends beyond the details of a specific instance of disinformation towards the need for some broader reckoning with the whole history of vandalism done to public perceptions and public institutions as a result of the national security state's subversion of corporate capitalism's commercial media venues.

In North America especially, the history of capitalism and the history of the commercial media's role in advertising, public relations, and psychological warfare are deeply intertwined. The political economy of this interaction between mind and matter has been closely linked to the capacity of corporate capitalism's media monopolies to dominate venues of public discourse by privatizing control over airwaves that technically are owned by the public. Already in 1893 in Chicago some of these patterns of commercialized communications were acquiring their present shape. At the World's Columbian Exposition, new means of marketing products, ideas, and mythologies were starting to develop, but especially through the creation of brand names, brand logos, and brand loyalties. As capitalism developed in its American bastion and laboratory, advertising and public relations became increasingly more integral to the process of constructing the perceptual machinery of accelerated commercial interaction.

The important business of creating public mythologies was headquartered on New York's Madison Avenue, where the executive suites and board rooms were dominated by the likes of Edward Bernays, Henry Luce, and William Randolph Hearst. The empires of communication that these men messaged and dominated blended fantasy and reality to create whole mythological systems of symbolic meaning through the application of much the same marketing techniques as were used to advertise and promote products, companies, politicians, styles, and ideas. At the extreme end of this continuum of mass persuasion lies the project of channelling the consciousness of whole populations into the violent psychology of war. In a society capable of throwing up a global empire of merchandised celebrity, sport, Disneyworld escapism, and Hollywood spectacle, the campaign to sell the American people a revised agenda of religious and ethnic warfare was bound to reach new frontiers of manipulative audacity.

Those in charge of mainstream corporate media in the United States made one concerted attempt to fend off revelations that the Global War on Terror's origins rest on a bogus interpretation of the events of 9/11. In 2005 the executives overseeing the media empire founded by William Randolph Hearst made their magazine, *Popular Mechanics*, the site of a concerted counter-offensive. After a dramatic changing of the guard in the editorial offices of this publication, its staff produced an article entitled "9/11: Debunking the Myths."[136] In 2006 that article became the basis of a book, *Debunking 9/11 Myths: Why Conspiracy Theories Can't Stand Up to the Facts.*[137] This Hearst publication began with a forward written by Senator John McCain. The publications of *Popular Mechanics* are frequently cited to bolster the official explanation of the events of 9/11. Guy Smith's BBC documentary *The Conspiracy Files: 9/11,* for instance, treats the *Popular Mechanics* publications as the most authoritative source on the subject.

The contents of the Hearst corporation's interpretation has been countered by many authors, such as David Ray Griffin. His books include *Debunking 9/11 Debunking: An Answer to Popular Mechanics and Other Defenders of the Official Conspiracy Theory.* Griffin's treatment of the subject leads him to the conclusion that "*Popular Mechanics* owes its readers an apology for publishing such a massively flawed article on such an important subject."[138] This controversy unfolds against a background pointing to repeated instances when the power of the Hearst media empire was deployed to manipulate public attitudes and opinions on the most fundamental issues of war and peace. The founder of the Hearst media empire is widely seen as the father of yellow journalism in the United States. In 1898 the publisher William Randolph Hearst played an instrumental role in building up public support for a US war with Spain by portraying the sinking in Havana Harbor of the US battleship *Maine* as a justification for invading Cuba and the Philippines. Like the Reichstag fire of 1933, the sinking of the *Maine* is widely seen as a classic false-flag operation – an act of violence perpetrated by authorities with the conscious intent of preparing public opinion for pre-planned attacks on demonized enemies falsely blamed for the highly publicized occurrences.[139]

In the interval between his success in marketing cigarettes to women and his authorship of a fraudulent myth to disguise the US-orchestrated coup in Guatemala, Edward Bernays included the Hearst corporation among his clients. In 1933 Bernays learned from a Heart correspondent covering Germany that the Third Reich's chief propagandist, Joseph Goebbels, was an avid student of his methods of public persuasion.[140] The following year, William Randolph Hearst travelled to Germany to negotiate a business deal directly with Adolf Hitler. Hearst and Hitler agreed that the Reich Ministry of Public Enlightenment and Propaganda would purchase content from the American media conglomerate's International News Service. Like Henry Ford and many other US plutocrats of his day, Hearst clearly preferred the Third Reich's ultra-right form of capitalism to the more mediated form of capitalism advanced in the name of the New Deal.

Hearst's newspapers ran syndicated columns by the Nazi leaders Hermann Goering and Dr Alfred Rosenberg.[141] The media baron's desire to keep US public opinion hostile to any intervention in Hitler's takeover of Western Europe was expressed very clearly in an article published by *Reader's Digest* in November 1939. The editors of this Hearst publication featured an article by the celebrated aviator Charles Lindbergh, who argued that the United States should not go to war with Germany but rather join forces with Hitler's regime to enable the "White race" to maintain its technological superiority over the "pressing sea of Yellow, Black and Brown."[142] Will the Hearst publications addressing the 9/11 wars' originating episode someday appear as darkly manipulative as Hearst's jingoist news coverage of the Spanish-American War or Lindbergh's appeal in *Reader's Digest* to support the supremacy of the White race by eschewing war with Hitler's Third Reich?

While William Hearst advanced many of his own personal and class agendas through the content generated by his media empire, many of the publisher's campaigns, like those of the other major media cartels in the United States, were expressions of the US government's covert efforts to manipulate public opinion. This US government's quest to shape attitudes and opinions began seriously between 1917 and 1919 with the work of the Committee for Public Information. The PCI was chaired by George Creel, who boasted about the success of his mission to carry "the Gospel of Americanism to every corner of the Globe."[143] The Creel Committee worked with Hollywood filmmakers in the production of propaganda movies aimed at shaping public opinion to bolster US objectives in the First World War. The committee's work involved the spawning of many "patriotic organizations," together with the hiring of spies to uncover any evidence of pacifist resistance to the US war effort in Europe. The public side of the work included the voluntary efforts of thousands of "four-minute men," who gave almost a million public speeches. The journalist Walter Lippman, the author in 1922 of *Public Opinion*, was an adviser to the Creel Committee.[144] So too was Edward Bernays. His work with the PCI helped him identify the importance of propaganda, or public relations as he would later call it. In 1928 in a work entitled *Propaganda*, Bernays wrote: "The conscious and intelligent manipulation of the organized habits and opinions of the masses is an important element in democratic society. Those who manipulate this unseen mechanism constitute an invisible government which is the true ruling power of our government." He added, "We are governed, our tastes formed, our ideas suggested, largely by men we have never heard of."[145]

After the Second World War the staff of most mainstream media venues, like many of the most high-profile faculty members in the major US universities, were secretly recruited to design, implement, and monitor a broad range of psychological operations on the capitalist side of the Cold War. The global extent of the national security state's lethal, illegal, and disruptive interventions in the sovereign affairs of many polities, including those of the United States itself, came briefly to light after the Watergate scandal of 1974. Reports of executive wrongdoing cast a spotlight of public attention on President Richard Nixon's political abuses of federal government's intelligence agencies and their offshoots. Among the litany of shocking exposures was news about the national security state's secret infiltration of the big info-entertainment conglomerates. The Congressional investigations led by Senator Frank Church revealed how far the CIA and the FBI had gone to subvert the functions of public education that are required of mainstream media if its communications are to facilitate and safeguard free and democratic societies.

For democracy to function properly, those who run networks of communications must be invested with sufficient honesty and integrity to make sure that media coverage of the human condition is sufficiently balanced and truthful to enable citizens to make informed political decisions. But what happens when truth becomes a threat or an impediment to the exercise of power by the ruling elites? Will facsimiles of truth – call them pseudo-truths – be fabricated as an expedient of public relations? Will distortions, disinformation, or diversions be concocted to steer public attention away from those facets of reality that call into question the very legitimacy of the most fundamental relationships of power and social control? To those who direct the operations of the national security state, the answer to questions such as these has often been a resounding yes. Their preference for politically palatable pseudo-truths showed clearly in the covert hiring of many thousands of journalists, experts, authors, media managers, and media owners with the goal of distorting truth, twisting it, or replacing it altogether with fiction disguised as fact. The CIA's Project Mockingbird involved particularly outlandish efforts to transform many major media brands into venues for the delivery of calculated obfuscations, cover-ups, and outright lies in the psychological operations of the Cold War.

There is every reason to expect that the same kind of covert interventions that took place during the Cold War have been accelerated, intensified, and diversified in the era of the Global War on Terror. This pattern of covert intervention almost certainly extends, as it did during the Cold War, to the manipulation of the content even of progressive, left-of-centre news venues. Historically the CIA has established front operations disguised as philanthropic organizations as one means of holding in check those media venues and personalities with the greatest potential to turn public opinion against the agendas of the national security state.[146] More and more this tactic for containing the scope of progressive politics has been reinforced by the way funding is distributed by family foundations such as those set up in the names of Ford, Rockefeller, Carnegie, Mellon, Kellogg, and others. The ample stream of funding directed to supposedly progressive venues of antiwar activism and alternative media by the wealthy philanthropist George Soros is often cited as a possible explanation for the concerted efforts of leftist gatekeeping that held the quest for the truth of what happened on 9/11 on the edges of mainstream political debate.[147]

Henry Luce first articulated the expansionary goals of the national security state with his advocacy in 1941 of the American Century. His ideas were renewed and updated in 1998 by the war hawks who combined to form the Project for the New American Century (PNAC). The authors of the infamous PNAC report of 2000 called for a massive build-up of the military-industrial complex. They devoted considerable attention to making the case for the invasion and domination of Iraq. In preparing their wish list, the PNAC group recognized that US public opinion would probably not readily support their plans for the future "absent some catastrophic and catalyzing event, like a new Pearl Harbor."[148] Philip Zelikow was one of those technocrats of the national security state whose job it was to make sure that public perceptions of 9/11 were managed and channelled in ways that promoted the political viability of PNAC's blueprint for action. Through his deep involvement in the Aspen Strategy group, Zelikow had worked closely with a number of PNAC activists, including the future US vice-president Richard Cheney and the future US deputy secretary of defense Paul Wolfowitz. Zelikow's main political ally and mentor among the war hawks was Condoleezza Rice, who served first as national security advisor and then as secretary of state in the administration of President George W. Bush.

A professor of international law and diplomatic history, Zelikow developed particular expertise in the applied field of constructing and manipulating public mythologies to achieve political objectives. A member of the president's Foreign Intelligence Advisory Group, Zelikow was appointed by his White House friends as executive director of the heavily politicized 9/11 Commission.[149] Only belatedly and begrudgingly did the Bush White House set up this under-funded investigative body, known formally as the National Commission on the Terrorist Attacks upon the United States. The main political purpose of this tawdry exercise in obfuscation was to placate the demand by many of the victims' relatives for an official investigation into how their family members had been killed. Given the centrality of the executive director's role in the 9/11 Commission's work, its concluding statement can most accurately be characterized as the Zelikow report. The many strategic omissions and gross distortions of truth in this document have been widely noted.[150] In *Harper's Magazine*, for instance, Benjamin DeMott labelled the Zelikow report as a "whitewash" and "fraud" that "dangerously reenergizes a national relish for fantasy."[151]

Gradually the members and staff of the 9/11 Commission have come forward to condemn all or parts of their own investigation. The chair of the commission, Thomas H. Kean, asserted that it was "set up to fail." "We didn't have enough money, we didn't have enough time, and we were appointed by the most partisan people in Washington," he commented.[152] Former Democratic senator Max Clelland, a disabled veteran of the Vietnam conflagration, resigned from the commission, calling it a "a national scandal," an example of President Bush's "Nixonian stonewalling" where he "cherry picked" information that was put on record.[153] The 9/11 Commission's own legal counsel, former New Jersey attorney general and Rutger's Law School dean John Farmer, wrote a book in 2009 about the work of the inquiry. Focusing particularly on the failure of air defense, he asserted, "At some level of the government, at some point in time ... there was an agreement not to tell the truth about the national response to the attacks on the morning of 9/11."[154]

After his stint with the 9/11 Commission, Zelikow was promoted to the job of counselor in the US State Department, a position once held by George Kennan. There Zelikow went to work to help fashion the public mythology necessary to build up public support for an invasion of Iran. He characterized Iran as "the most active state sponsor of terrorism in 2004" and even suggested that control of Tehran should be seized because "at least one of those in Iranian custody helped plan the September 11 attacks."[155] Years before the events of 9/11, Zelikow extended some of the ideas pioneered by Edward Bernays to his own study of the relationship between "catastrophic terrorism" and public perceptions. In 1998 in the journal *Foreign Affairs*, Zelikow addressed with two other colleagues the various scenarios that might have developed if the bombing in 1993 of the World Trade Center towers had been successful:

If the device that exploded in 1993 under the World Trade Center had been nuclear, or had effectively dispersed a deadly pathogen, the resulting horror and chaos would have exceeded our ability to describe it. Such an act of catastrophic terrorism would be a watershed event in American history. It could involve loss of life and property unprecedented in peacetime and undermine America's fundamental sense of security, as did the Soviet atomic bomb test in 1949. Like Pearl Harbor, this event would divide our past and future into a before and after. The United States might respond with draconian measures, scaling back civil liberties, allowing wider surveillance of citizens, detention of suspects, and use of deadly force.[156]

The connection that Zelikow drew between an imagined attack on the World Trade Center and the bombing of Pearl Harbor found an echo in the most frequently cited phrase in the PNAC report. Indeed, Zelikow anticipated many elements of the Global War on Terror as they would develop after some key features of his hypothetical scenario were rendered actual by the events of 9/11. In imagining the content and outcomes of a future crisis, Zelikow took part in the kind of planning exercise through war games that has long formed a major part of the work assigned to the national security state. But while it is one thing to picture a hypothetical sequence of events leading to war, it is quite another thing for powerful interests to conspire in ways that cause or permit a version of the imagined scenario to take place with the specific object of transforming public consciousness.

The possibility that the attacks of 9/11 were engineered in some fashion to assure the continued build-up of the military-industrial complex in the post–Cold War era must be considered in the context of a political culture where the discipline required for truth's pursuit has frequently been subordinated to the imperatives of popular myth making through the media's manipulation of evocative images and symbols. This possibility needs to be considered in the context of the historic role of the info-entertainment cartels as polities susceptible to the direction from what Edward Bernays long ago identified as an "invisible government which is the true ruling power of our government." It needs to be considered in the context of a psychological environment where "we are governed, our tastes formed, our ideas suggested, largely by men we have never heard of." The contest to exercise power in such a milieu, where the biggest of all businesses is the industrial tweaking of attitudes, opinions, and perceptions, is clearly more dependent on what the public can be made to believe rather than on what can be shown to be true through careful consideration of all the relevant evidence.

This distortion of truth to serve the interests of power replicates in a new context some epistemological features of old mythologies supporting the divine rights of kings in the era before the Century of Enlightenment gave emphasis to reason, objectivity, and proof. In the new assault on the power of reason and secular rationality, the major pharmaceutical companies and conservative religions join Madison Avenue and the big info-entertainment cartels as major players in the politics of manufacturing consciousness. Meanwhile, the oversight of drug lords and the global distribution of illicit substances such as heroin and cocaine has largely been taken over by elements of the national security state, whose agents further privatize their operations even as they avoid any public accountability for their actions.

Accordingly, it is the large and growing distance between publicly perceived pseudo-truths and empirically verifiable truths that informs the quest for 9/11 Truth. The 9/11 Truth movement points to the terrible possibility that the Twin Towers were felled in order to provide the central spectacle in the most audacious and dramatic psychological operation of all time. Were the events of 9/11 and their aftermath actually driven more by divisions, factionalism, and internal competitions within the national security state rather than by the religious extremism of radical Islam? Did the events of 9/11 embody the outcome of the massive privatization and deregulation of the national security state, in much the same fashion as the economic meltdown in 2008 and 2009 embodied the outcome of the massive deregulation of financial markets? Whoever they are, the authors of this devastatingly effective Black Op that took place in the heart of the New York's financial district handed the national security state a potent new weapon in its psychological arsenals. On 9/11 the shock doctrine's application to the transformative workings of disaster capitalism – terror capitalism – breached new frontiers of social impact.

In the post-9/11 atmosphere of the terror economy, "everything was being securitized, repackaged and traded" in a an orgy of fantasy accounting that continued in spite of the early warning signals sent by the corporate implosion of Enron.[157] How might history have been different if the evidentiary basis of the deeper investigations into the business dealings of Enron and other corporate cheaters had not been destroyed in the demolition of World Trade Center 7? What happened to the $2.3 trillion that Donald Rumsfeld announced on September 10, 2001, had gone missing from the Pentagon's books? Who are the beneficiaries of these missing public funds?

Has this figure grown since the events of 9/11 conveniently prevented the story of the missing trillions at the Pentagon from becoming the subject of subsequent media coverage?

Like the events of 9/11, the ensuing 9/11 wars helped divert attention away from rampant manipulations and frauds in financial markets such as those that enabled Wall Street's Bernard L. Madoff to manipulate tens of billions of dollars of other people's money in a giant pyramid scheme disguised as a legitimate investment business. Indeed, the heavy emphasis on the requirements of "national security" pointed the political agenda away from many other areas of importance, such as our worldwide need for collective security as well as security in the environment, in education, and in health. All these pressing needs can be achieved only after enforced prohibitions on the international crimes that have proliferated in the age of impunity.

ORTHODOXY AND HERESY

In his book review "The Lies They Told," Jacob Heilbrunn lauds John Farmer's *The Ground Truth.* "Farmer's accomplishment is to throw 9/11 into fresh relief," writes Heilbrunn in the *New York Times.* The reviewer quotes the contention of the former senior counsel of the 9/11 Commission that "whether through unprecedented administrative incompetence or orchestrated mendacity, the American people were misled about the nation's response to the 9/11 attacks." The reviewer concludes by asserting that Farmer's work fills a void on the events of 9/11 because "a precise and reliable accounting has been absent until now."[158]

There was nothing in President Obama's West Point speech of December 1, 2009, to reflect the convergence of judgment between Farmer and the *New York Times'* book reviewer that officials of the US government have systematically lied about what transpired on September 11. In his announcement that tens of thousands more US troops and mercenaries would be committed to add to the violent turmoil of Afghanistan and Pakistan, Obama repeated an unrevised account of how "19 men hijacked four airplanes and used them to murder nearly 3,000 people ... As we know, these men belonged to al Qaeda ... Al Qaeda's base of operations was in Afghanistan, where they were harbored by the Taliban – a ruthless, repressive and radical movement that seized control of that country after it was ravaged by years of Soviet occupation and civil war, and after the attention of America and our friends had turned elsewhere."[159]

Farmer appoints himself as a judge to decide through his powers of intuition the limits of officialdom's lies to the 9/11 Commission and the world. Rather than demanding that the perjury be revisited and punished, he puts himself above the law by favouring his own theory of what happened as a substitute for a credible investigation demanding honest answers from witnesses. He puts his own pet theories before the still unfulfilled need for a genuine inquiry conducted by esteemed jurists empowered by some international agency to look into the full array of possible scenarios for the planning and implementing of this complex and many-faceted crime against humanity. Farmer does not let all the fibbing of officialdom get in the way of his adding of his own voice to the unproven theory that the attacks originated in the actions of an entirely external enemy whose members were motivated by radical interpretations of Islamic texts.

There is no suggestion in Farmer's interpretation that all the lying and covering up might have beneath it some official complicity, or event direct involvement, in the attacks. Accordingly, Farmer's work does not deviate from the verdict delivered very quickly after 9/11 by Noam Chomsky. Without any reference to supporting evidence, the oracle of critical anarchism joined with the administration of George W. Bush and the corporate media in simply pronouncing that all the perpetrators were entirely "external" and that "this attack was surely an enormous shock and surprise to the intelligence services of the West."[160]

From Noam Chomsky to Glenn Beck, Naomi Klein, Barack Obama, Amy Goodman, or Richard Cheney, the view of 9/11 as the outcome of a huge failure of intelligence and defence preparedness has been made to prevail as a kind of orthodoxy of the state widely sanctioned by most dedicated careerists across many partisan and ideological lines. To transgress this line of interpretation is to invite ridicule or serious recriminations. Nevertheless, many thousands of professional people, some of whom have much to lose, have chosen to veer away from the path of the official interpretation in spite of the possibility of negative repercussions. One of them is whistle blower Kevin Ryan. Because of the high-stakes nature of the quest for 9/11 truth, he was fired from his job as the site manager of a subsidiary of Underwriters Laboratories (UL), a giant of consumer product safety testing. The employment of this highly respected professional was terminated after Ryan accused his employer of systematically violating good scientific principles in its work with the National Institute for Standards and Technology. NIST is the federal agency charged to investigate the destruction of both the Twin Towers and World Trade Center 7.

Ryan began his critique with a precise account of how NIST's basic approach to the investigation presupposed the cause of the destruction. He went on to point out that the level of heat generated by the burning jet fuel was nowhere near intense enough to weaken the steel construction of the World Trade Center edifices, buildings constructed with girders that, he claimed, UL had earlier "certified." Ryan's original concern was that the interests of his employer were being undermined as NIST's investigators lined up to insert the appearance of fact into the fiction that the steel construction of the WTC structures was substandard. He properly pointed out that this unjustified condemnation of the quality of the construction materials would give cause, however unfounded, for many dwellers and tenants of towers constructed with UL-certified steel to doubt the structural integrity of their host buildings.

While Ryan initially drew on his professional expertise in procedures for testing the properties of structural steel, his assessment of the scope of the professional malfeasance and cover-up grew quickly. "Anyone who honestly looks at the evidence has difficulty finding anything in the official story of 9/11 that is believable," he wrote. "It's not just one or two strange twists or holes in the story, the whole thing is bogus from start to end."[161]

A major part of the movement seeking a true account of the events of 9/11 has taken up the contention of Ryan and many other specialists in related professional fields that only controlled demolitions could have destroyed the three World Trade Center towers in the ways recorded by many cameras that filmed the destruction from a variety of angles and perspectives. The sudden collapse of World Trade Center 7, which unlike the Twin Towers was not struck by an airplane, is often cited as the "smoking gun" of the debacle. Ryan grappled with the irrationalities of what he calls "Bush science." He laments the irredeemable harm being done to key institutions such as the National Institute of Standards and Technology and Underwriters Laboratories when their executives and managers allow political interference to override a commitment to empirical evidence as the necessary basis for findings and recommendations.

Rather than give into despair, Ryan opted to contribute to the citizens' investigation into 9/11 which has developed as a result of the failure of governments and the mainstream media to provide credible explanations of what happened on that fateful day. Once Ryan was satisfied that all three of the World Trade Center towers exploded to the ground through controlled demolitions, he set himself the task of investigating the networks of businesses and government agencies that had the capacity and the motives to plant explosives in the three doomed edifices. Who stood to benefit most from the economic changes that would come about because of the initiation of a Global War on Terror, based on the interpretation that those responsible for the crimes of 9/11 were zealous Islamic fanatics encouraged and trained by Osama bin Laden to destroy the West as the necessary prelude to a religious caliphate?

Like many of those who have employed the technique of following the money to investigate possible responsibility for crimes, Ryan maps elaborate networks of political and economic relationships permeating the events of 9/11. Again and again this technique leads him back to widespread involvement on the part of many suspects, Rudy Giuliani prominent among them, in what Ryan refers to as "the terrorist financing BCCI," the Bank of Credit and Commerce International.[162] This global institution was founded in the early 1970s, around the time that President Richard Nixon made the secret deal with the government of Saudi Arabia to secure the future dominance of a gusher of Saudi-American petrodollars as the world's primary reserve currency. The build-up of the BCCI especially during the US presidency of Ronald Reagan in the 1980s marked an acceleration of the rush of the national security state to infiltrate the geopolitics of oil and gas exploitation in Eurasia.[163] The other side of this decision was a corresponding move away from new investment in the industrial infrastructure of manufacturing in the United States. Indeed, the increasingly worldwide operations of the Pakistani-based BCCI heralded and facilitated the growing involvement of Anglo-America in the privatized terror economy that would become so integral to the global economy after the events of 9/11.

Prominent among the BCCI's customers were Adnan Khashoggi, Ubu Nidal, Saddam Hussein, the bin Laden corporate clan, and the Bush family of war profiteers. Pulling many of the BCCI's political strings was CIA director William Casey, the national security state's point man in the delivery of Reagan's anti-communist jihad to the Soviet-backed regime in Afghanistan. The BCCI became an essential financial link in this and other related operations. Based throughout the world, the bank's executives oiled conduits for the movement of arms, money, and drugs, facilitating the military confrontation of the US- and Pakistani-backed mujahadeen with its more secular enemies. The mujahadeen incorporated both elements of a constituency that would later divide in a civil war between the Taliban and the Northern Alliance. Both configurations of Afghanis are largely tribal in character, and both have been drawn into Anglo-American schemes for pipelines in the region.

The mujahadeen's computer base of communications was identified in Arabic as "al-Qaeda." The well-armed proxy army was composed of radical Islamic jihadists recruited from around the world. This fighting force was assembled, armed, financed, and trained by US and Saudi sponsors. Some soldiers of Islam were trained at the US military base in Fort Bragg, North Carolina. Others were prepared for armed combat in the mountainous terrain where Afghanistan borders on Pakistan. The ultimate objective of this activity was to force the Soviet Union to withdraw its army and all its other systems of support from its Afghan puppet regime. The US support of its military proxies in Afghanistan was part of a larger strategic intervention in the region to encourage pro-Islamic agitation against Soviet rule in the oil- and gas-rich region of Azerbaijan, Uzbekistan, Kazakhstan, Turkmenistan, Tajikistan, and Kygystan. The BCCI provided the financial medium for the interlinked transactions between the CIA, the Pakistani Inter-Services Intelligence Agency, Saudi theocrats and financiers, and the multinational mujahadeen.

The BCCI was at the centre of many of covert operations during a period when the national security state and its increasingly unregulated clients, patrons, and operatives engaged in transfers of nuclear technology, drug dealing, bribery, money laundering, and the planning, instigation, and engineering of seemingly random acts of violence calculated to excite and exploit public hysteria, fear, and insecurity. News reports of this type of synthetic terror have sometimes been purposely manipulated to intensify negative stereotypes aimed at whole groups of demonized peoples. The demonizing of populations targeted for displacement and destruction is a traditional tactic in preparing public opinion on the side of the belligerents to accept the expense together with complicity in the violent criminality of aggressive warfare.[164] This genre of black operation is one of several means for creating the conditions for what Naomi Klein has identified in *The Shock Doctrine* as "disaster capitalism."

The Iran-Contra scandal that broke over the presidency of Ronald Reagan in the late 1980s was deeply intertwined with the scandal that exposed some of the dark workings of the BCCI in the early 1990s. Both events provide small but significant windows into the otherwise hidden interface between high finance, corporate corruption, and the national security state. Both investigations were the last of their type until the moment of this writing in the last days of 2009. Both scandals involved much effort to depict the exposed wrongdoing as aberrations rather than as markers of how business is regularly done at the highest levels of power. Both scandals exposed a flight by elites from traditional systems of checks and balances in the name of national security. The containment of the fallout from both events is indicative of the strength of the culture of impunity that continues to put the most organized and ruthless perpetrators of international crime behind firewalls of state protection.[165]

Kevin Ryan sees the insurance company AIG, along with related enterprises such as Marsh and McLennan and Kroll Associates, as possible inheritors of the type of legacy left by BCCI. "Like BCCI," writes Ryan, "AIG developed the same fragmented and difficult to trace network of ... holding companies, affiliates, banks-within-banks, insider dealings and nominee relationships ... spread across 130 countries and 400 regulators."[166] Certainly the global insurance business was among the big beneficiaries of the events of 9/11. Moreover, the insurance business, but particularly AIG, was at the core of the financial crisis in 2008 and 2009 because of its prior expansion into new frontiers of hedging and betting on the future value of derivative instruments – such as the opaque speculative devices known as credit default swaps.

CUBA'S WAR ON TERROR

The leadership of the Cuban Revolution has had a deep and troubled history of relations with the government of the United States. This history of antagonism is reflected in the way the Cubans have constructed their own version of the War on Terror. For them, the terrorists have most often been anti-Castro Cubans who have worked with the US government to sabotage the Cuban Revolution. The most blatant example of this hostility was the full-fledged US military invasion of Cuba at the Bay of Pigs in 1961. But the violent interventions did not end there. It is widely known that Fidel Castro has faced literally dozens if not hundreds of US-engineered and US-backed assassination attempts since his government replaced the US-backed puppet regime of Fulgencio Batiste in 1959.[167] In 1962 the Joint Chiefs of Staff and other branches of the national security state responded to their failures at the Bay of Pigs by planning Operation Northwoods as a false-flag operation. The scheme's goal was to prepare public opinion for a second invasion of Cuba by orchestrating events on the ground and in the media so that Castro's government would be blamed for sponsoring acts of terrorism directed at targets within the United States. As James Bamford writes in his history of the National Security Agency: "People would be framed for bombings they did not commit; planes would be hijacked. Using phony evidence, all of it would be blamed on Castro, thus giving [General] Lemnitzer and his cabal the excuse, as well as the public and international backing, they needed to launch their war."[168] While President John F. Kennedy opted not to implement Operation Northwoods, the existence of this plan points to the kind of scenarios that have been conceived by war-games planners in the more covert branches of the military-industrial complex.

Luis Posada Corriles is for many Cuban people the personification of terrorism. In 1976 this Cuban-American CIA agent engineered the bombing of an Air Cubana passenger jet killing seventy-three innocent people. This expert in explosives is also thought to have been responsible for many other bombings, including those that rocked the tourist district in Havana in 1997. The Cuban government has sound reason to believe that more than three thousand of its citizens have been murdered and about two thousand maimed in US-engineered or US-backed terrorist incidents. Several Cuban citizens went to Florida to investigate the possibility of more terrorist attacks directed against their own brothers, sisters, children, and parents. Five of them were arrested to face a broad range of charges, including those of espionage and conspiracy to commit murder. Like the US legal proceedings surrounding the case of Poseda Corriles, the legal proceedings surrounding the Cuban Five illustrate the deep internal corruption plaguing the criminal justice system and its political masters in the United States.[169]

In the age of elite impunity, some of those who regularly commit international crimes maintain firm control over vast arsenals of weapons of mass destruction. The implications of this systematic and heavily armed lawlessness in the global community hold many parallels with the situation faced by Fidel Castro when he attacked, with about a hundred fellow patriots, the Moncada Barracks of the Cuban Army on July 26, 1953. The day of this attack, July 26, is the national holiday of the Cuban Revolution. Castro was apprehended in the aftermath of this failed attempt to begin the process of removing Batista's corrupt regime. Castro's final words in his four-hour summation at his own trial form the basis of the text *History Will Absolve Me*. In phrases that suggest the enormity of the responsibility falling on international jurists in an era when most perpetrators of international crimes go unpunished or even unidentified, Castro's summation resonates with contemporary significance: "The guilty continue at liberty and with weapons in their hands – weapons which continually threaten the lives of all citizens.

If the weight of the law does not fall upon the guilty because of cowardice or because of domination of the courts, and if then all the judges do not resign, I pity your honor. And I regret the unprecedented shame that will fall upon the Judicial Power."[170]

CHAPTER FOURTEEN

Genocide and Global Capitalism

It is not rational to say we live in a globalized world economy, that
there is a one world global market place, that financial markets
must be open and transparent from one country to another, and
to reject the inevitable conclusion in relation to matters such as
human rights and the environment.

The Right Honourable Malcolm Fraser, 2000

IMAGINING AND DESCRIBING GENOCIDE
ON THE FRONTIERS OF GLOBAL CIVILIZATION

At what point does the proliferation of mass murder grow to become the
basis of an international crime – a crime against all humanity? Why is it
that the murder of individuals often generates more serious attention from
police and prosecutors than the crime of eliminating whole national, ethnic, racial, social, or religious communities? Why do the culprits responsible for assaults on targeted groups so rarely face legal accountability for
their orders and actions? These queries were among the basic questions
underlying the research, publication, and political interventions of Raphael
Lemkin, a jurist known for his stubborn attachment to precise prescriptions
for global justice. In dispensing his remedies, Lemkin emerged as one of
the twentieth century's most brilliant and energetic champions of international law.[1] It was Lemkin who coined the term "genocide" in 1944 in a text
entitled *Axis Rule in Occupied Europe*.[2] The word results from a combination
of the Greek expression for race or tribe, *genos*, and the Latin expression
for killing, *cide*. As Lemkin saw it, "the realities of European life in the years
1933–45 called for the creation of such a term and for the formulation of a
legal concept of destruction of human groups."[3]

Lemkin was a Polish-Jewish lawyer who emigrated to the United States at
the onset of the Second World War to escape Nazi persecution in his home
country. He taught at Duke University and shepherded his proposal to treat
genocide as an international crime through the Nuremberg process and
into the early proceedings of the United Nations. His efforts twice acquired
enduring legislative form, culminating in the UN's adoption in 1948 of the
Convention on the Prevention and Punishment of the Crime of Genocide.[4]
Lemkin began his studies of international crime by focusing on the mass
slaughter of Christian Armenians by the zealots of Turkish nationhood

during the era of the First World War.[5] He paid careful attention to the trial in 1921 of Soghomon Tehlirian, a survivor of Turkey's onslaught on the Armenians. Tehlirian had murdered one of the perpetrators of the massive crime directed against his nation. Lemkin became preoccupied with the inconsistencies of a legal regime that allowed Tehlirian to be tried for murder even as the Turkish butchery directed at the Armenian population went largely unprosecuted and unpunished.

As he worked his way through the issues, Lemkin became ever more critical of the way the doctrine of national sovereignty could so easily be abused to provide protection for those guilty of the highest order of criminality. He was particularly troubled by the system of international relations going back to the Treaty of Westphalia. The doctrine that invests absolute sovereignty of governments within their territories enabled state officials to murder, maim, dispossess, disempower, and deport large numbers of their own constituents without legal consequence. Lemkin's concern with this travesty of justice led him to demand the addition of a new international crime to the same body of transnational law that had already prohibited piracy, slavery, the counterfeiting of money, and the illicit trade in women and children. "It seems inconsistent with our concepts of civilization," he wrote to the New York Times in 1946, "that selling a drug to an individual is a matter of worldly concern while gassing millions of human beings might be a problem of internal concern." He added, "It seems inconsistent with our philosophy of life that the abduction of one woman for prostitution is an international crime, while the sterilization of millions of women remains an internal affair."[6]

Lemkin's efforts to articulate and implement a transnational regime for the prevention and punishment of genocide built on the work of many others.[7] George Washington Williams had coined the term "crimes against humanity" in 1890 when he, a Black clergyman from the United States, reported the results of his first-hand exploration in King Leopold's vast personal proprietorship in the watershed of the Congo River. From his travels throughout a region that Joseph Conrad would subsequently render legendary as "the heart of darkness," Williams was able to describe and document the violent enslavement of Indigenous peoples through the industrial application of murderous and deforming atrocities.[8] It was the continuation of these atrocities that caused W.E.B Du Bois at the pan-African Congress in Brussels in 1921 to condemn in jurists' language the rampant colonialism still under way in the Belgian Congo.[9] Belgium's "colonial policy is still mainly dominated by the banks and great corporations," Du Bois alleged as he introduced his call for a restoration of the "ancient common ownership" of African lands.[10] In Europe, the British jurist Hugh H. Bellot broke new ground in introducing principles that Lemkin would later elaborate and expand upon. Bellot was prominent among the handful of intellectuals seeking new means of adjudicating the culpability of those alleged to have committed international crimes during the First World War.[11] In Poland,

Lemkin had built up his area of expertise with the help and advice of law professor Émil Stanislaus Rappaport, whose own vision of international crimes included the production of propaganda aimed at mobilizing mass support for wars of aggression.[12]

Many ideas and forces came together, therefore, at a jurists' conference in Madrid in 1933 when Lemkin proposed an expanded definition of international crimes. He called for the codification of the crime of barbarity as a way to create a blanket prohibition on the destruction of racial, religious, ethnic, and social collectivities. As part of the same initiative, he sought to institutionalize the crime of vandalism in order to punish and prevent the willful destruction of the artistic and cultural creations of persecuted peoples. Lemkin brought these principles forward just as the National Socialist Party was coming to power in Germany. An early voice of alarm on the Nazis' capacity to commit criminal acts on an enormous scale, Lemkin was one of the world's most prescient predictors of the Nazi holocaust. The terrible history surrounding the life and times of his decimated family during the reign of European fascism seemed to support Lemkin's theory that a uniformly enforced regime of universal international law would provide humanity with its best protection against any return to Hitlerian savagery. His analysis lacked the precision of that of Hannah Arendt or Aimé Césaire in making explicit the connections between the repressiveness of fascist totalitarianism and the genesis of racist imperialism as it developed in the expansion of European empires. Nevertheless, it is easy to find in Lemkin's work a subtext suggesting the parallels and linkages between the German quest for *lebensraum* and the history of European and Anglo-American empire building.

The Nazis had plenty of imperial precedent on which to draw as they developed their own approaches to enslaving, isolating, dispossessing, disempowering, dehumanizing, and, sometimes, eliminating altogether the distinct societies of those peoples lying in the way of the Third Reich's design to achieve eugenic and geopolitical pre-eminence for the German nation. As Lemkin outlined in *Axis Rule in Occupied Europe*, there were many means of promoting the elimination or subordination of targeted groups. The techniques extended from mass slaughter to the state's withdrawal of the conditions for cultural renewal, economic survival, and medical well-being. For those groups seen to be racially compatible with the German nation, the techniques of genocide stressed assimilative integration. For those deemed ineligible for assimilative blending into the imagined master race, more ruthless and direct means were deployed to eliminate the identities and gene pools of the unwanted groups. As Lemkin saw it, the techniques of genocide could include the implementation of laws designed to remove jobs, property, and access to medical care from targeted groups. They could extend to the involuntary sterilization of women or the removal of children from their biological families. They might include prohibitions on forms of pedagogy and public education emphasizing the distinct histories, languages, and cultures of those peoples whose collective identities were deemed suitable for demolition. In his effort to explain the broad scope of state policies that would qualify as genocide, Lemkin referred repeatedly to the Nazi destruction of the cultural institutions of non-Germans – for instance, to the dismantling of libraries, archives, museums, art galleries, and national theatres. The aim of these assaults was to eliminate the historical memory and cultural attachments of those peoples designated as unfit for a distinct place in the construction of the future. This form of vandalism impoverished the global community because "the contribution of any particular collectivity to world culture as a whole forms the wealth of all humanity, even while exhibiting unique characteristics."[13] With these thoughts, Lemkin anticipated many of the Fourth World ideals of the Non-Aligned Movement.

Lemkin promoted the view that, when the time comes to prosecute individuals suspected of having committed the international crime of genocide, all the world's states, together with its citizens, should share a combined stake in a universal jurisdiction. Underlying his conviction was the belief that all humanity is linked through a common connection to a universal set of attributes, interests, rights, and responsibilities. This shared complex extends to the global totality of persons but also to the worldwide totality of national, ethnic, religious, social, and political communities. The institutions and polities developed to serve the needs of these various communities tend to provide much of the organizational basis for the renewal of diverse cultures and for the creation and replication of the conditions of collective well-being. In promoting the concept of universal jurisdiction, Lemkin helped advance the vision that all human beings are members of a single political community bound in some areas of jurisdiction by a uniform rule of law.

Lemkin's advancement of an inclusive regime of international law extended ideals that had informed the quest to outlaw slavery, extend voting rights to women, and entrench the right of workers to organize and bargain collectively. His 'campaign to universalize the prevention and punishment of genocide was rooted in the notion that all human beings are connected, or ought to be connected, by adherence to a single simple code of shared morality. As a result, no one individual or group, no matter how rich or powerful, could claim an exemption from the principle that the destruction of social, political, religious, or ethnic groups constitutes the highest order of crime punishable by law. In this sense Lemkin sought to confine the scope of moral relativism. His' conception of the law of genocide as an expression of universal principles of global morality expressed understandings similar to those that animated some aspects of the World's Parliament of Religions in 1893. His conception of a class of crime that transcends the geographical and jurisdictional boundaries of state sovereignty gave added form and substance to the strain of idealism that inspired some to view both the League of Nations and the United Nations as entities holding the democratic potential to provide true global governance. Lemkin's work therefore helped to maintain and widen the tradition of universal egalitarianism leading from the Declaration of the Rights of Man and Citizen in 1789 to the Rome Statute of 1998. This statute in turn set in motion the process of ratification leading to the establishment of the International Criminal Court.

Lemkin's vision of humanity favoured the ideals of commonality over the sometimes arbitrary divisions created by national boundaries. This conception eliminates space for provincial or xenophobic attitudes that would divide the human species between those who resemble "us" and those belonging to "the Other." Lemkin's concentration on the universal elements of the human condition transcend more limited notions of unity inspiring, for instance, the pan-Indianism of Tecumseh, the pan-Africanism of Marcus Garvey, the pan-Slavism of Frantiek Palacky, the pan-Arabism of Gamal Abdel Nasser, the pan-Anglo-Americanism of Charles Dilke and Goldwin Smith, or the pan-Germanism of Bismarck and Hitler. The comprehensiveness of Lemkin's vision of universal jurisdiction lies on the frontiers of a particular vision of globalization. This global vision finds expression in the ideal that all groups and individuals can find protection from annihilation in a cohesive body of international law consistently upheld by agencies empowered by the global community to arbitrate and enforce transnational enactments in fair and uniform ways. Such a regime of world order need not favour monocultural constructions of global society. Lemkin's emphasis on the importance of protecting the unique artistic and cultural achievements of humanity's distinct branches is based on a sophisticated embrace of pluralism and diversity as gifts to posterity – on a clear understanding of global society as a community of communities and an astute appreciation of the need for vigilance and international intervention to protect all human groups together with their unique contributions to humanity's fragile commonwealth of knowledge, philosophy, art, and culture. There need not be, therefore, any contradiction between a system of governance that cultivates biocultural diversity and one that favours the adoption of some universal standards in the formulation, arbitration, and enforcement of international law. Integral to this balance is the need to affirm the basic human right to be concurrently equal yet different. Indeed, individuals and groups have a fundamental right to some measure of security and protection when they act out and express their reasonable differences.

In *Axis Rule in Occupied Europe*, Lemkin presents a definition of genocide based on his broad understanding of the wide array of actions and policies that might constitute facets of this international crime. He refers to genocide as

a coordinated plan of different actions aimed at the destruction of the essential foundations of the life of national groups, with the aim of annihilating the groups themselves. The objectives of such a plan would be the disintegration of the political and social institutions of culture, language, national feelings, religion, and the economic existence of national groups, and the destruction of personal security, liberty, health, dignity, and even the lives of the individuals belonging to such groups. Genocide is directed against the national group as an entity, and the actions involved are directed against individuals not in their individual capacity, but as members of a national group.[14]

In late 1946, Lemkin attended the first session of the UN General Assembly at Lake Success, New York. He worked with a number of delegations in the formulation and enactment of UN Resolution 96(1), which states:

Genocide is a denial of the right of existence of entire human groups, as homicide is the denial of the right to live of individual human beings; such denial of the right of existence shocks the conscience of mankind, results in great losses to humanity in the form of cultural and other contributions represented by these human groups, and is contrary to moral law and to the spirit and aims of the United Nations.

Many instances of such crimes of genocide have occurred when racial, religious, political, and other groups have been destroyed, entirely or in part.

The punishment of the crime of genocide is a matter of international concern.

The General Assembly, therefore,

Affirms that genocide is a crime under international law which the civilized world condemns, and for the commission of which principals and accomplices – whether private individuals, public officials or statesmen, and whether the crime is committed on religious, racial, political or any other grounds – are punishable.[15]

While UN Resolution 96(1) was bold in defining the crime of genocide, its drafters were far more conservative in charting how the new international law was to be enforced. With wording that would help facilitate the lawlessness of elites during the age of impunity, the text merely invited the UN's member states to enact domestic legislation and to cooperate in its enforcement. The failure to provide a global system for the protection of universal human rights begins with the superpowers' unwillingness to institute an international agency capable of arbitrating and enforcing the law of genocide with transnational consistency. In a world where the enforcement of the law of international crimes is left primarily to officials in the countries where the violations took place, there is every opening for conflicts of interest to become so deeply entrenched that they are rendered almost invisible. There are simply too many factors preventing prosecutors and judges enclosed within the domestic confines of their own nation-states from acting independently to enforce and punish the international crime of genocide. There is plenty of incentive for officials of nation states where genocide may have taken place to conspire together to prevent the development of any process that might bring to light the complicity or involvement of themselves or their peers in the commission of this most serious genre of international crime.

Many delegations contributed to the process of narrowing the definition of genocide originally articulated in 1946 in UN Resolution 96(1). With Lemkin as their guide, the initial drafters of the UN Convention called for the identification of three categories of genocide associated with its physical, biological, and cultural aspects and for the creation of an international court to prosecute genocide, a crime that they proposed to define as "the destruction of a group or preventing its preservation or development."[16] Many elements of these initial proposals were pared down or abandoned altogether as governments sought to limit their vulnerability to charges and investigative processes that might implicate their own officials. The result was a series of compromises crystallized in the adoption by the UN General Assembly in December 1948 of the Convention for the Prevention and Punishment of the Crime of Genocide. This new instrument cited the affirmation in UN Resolution 96(1) that "genocide is a crime under international law, contrary to the spirit and aims of the United Nations and condemned by the civilized world." This convention was not ratified by the United States until 1989. The key definitions outlined in the UN Convention are as follows:

Article 2
In the present Convention, genocide means any of the following acts committed with intent to destroy, in whole or in part, a national, ethnical, racial or religious group, as such:
(a) Killing members of the group;
(b) Causing serious bodily or mental harm to members of the group;
(c) Deliberately inflicting on the group conditions of life calculated to bring about its physical destruction in whole or in part;
(d) Imposing measures intended to prevent births within the group;
(e) Forcibly transferring children of the group to another group.

Article 3
The following acts shall be punishable:
(a) Genocide;
(b) Conspiracy to commit genocide;
(c) Direct and public incitement to commit genocide;
(d) Attempt to commit genocide;
(e) Complicity in genocide.

Raphael Lemkin was nominated seven times for the Nobel Peace Prize, but the honour never went to him. His importance tends to loom larger in a world rocked by illegal energy wars tied to the extreme politicization of religious fundamentalism in all three of the Abrahamic faiths. The increased anarchy of international relations has heightened the allure of Lemkin's rational approach to the elaboration and enforcement of global law within a framework of universal jurisdiction. In seeking to institute precise definitions and standardized procedures to universalize the prosecution of the most serious international crimes, Lemkin's endeavours unfolded within the same continuum of inspiration that had motivated Sir Sandford Fleming to seek a uniform global system for the keeping of Standard Time. Lemkin worked within the same continuum of modernity that saw financiers and industrialists seek to derive greater efficiencies from the transnational standardization of rules for manufacturing, measurement, communications, and the purchase, sale, and exchange of goods and services. Lemkin's agenda, however, was held back by the bias entrenched in global and local relationships of power. This structure of power has afforded far higher levels of international protection to the imperatives of profit, property, and the movement of capital than to the individual and collective rights of human beings. In conflicts between human persons and corporate persons, the legal and political advantages most often adhere to the latter.

THE EPISTEMOLOGY AND PSYCHOLOGY OF GENOCIDE

Initially the idea of genocide was closely and narrowly associated with Auschwitz and the other Nazi extermination camps. In the decades following the Second World War the tight identification of the concept of genocide with the most dramatic displays of Hitlerian horror was a natural outgrowth of the expanding realization that the Nazis had extended the methodology of mass extermination to new magnitudes of ruthlessness, speed, and industrial efficiency. "We have finally realized of what man is capable," observed the German-Jewish political theorist Hannah Arendt.[17] Gradually, however, the discussion of genocide extended beyond the Nazis' eugenic nightmare to include an array of perspectives more reflective of Lemkin's many-faceted explanation of the new category of international crime. Gradually the epistemology of genocide has been pointed at a wider spectrum of injustices affecting a broader array of victims.[18]

Two enactments of the UN Security Council contributed to the expanding range of settings, periods, episodes, perpetrators, and victims linked to the international crime of genocide. In a clear demonstration of victors' justice, the Security Council created in 1993 an International Criminal Tribunal with the goal of prosecuting individuals alleged to have committed genocide and other international crimes in the former Yugoslavia. Then in 1994 the same UN body created a second court to deal with the aftermath of the recent genocide in Rwanda.[19] The fact that the UN seriously intervened only *after* the worst of the ethnic violence had already taken place in Rwanda marks a major failure for the world organization and its most powerful members. This failure extends to the court's unwillingness to address the crimes against humanity committed by *both* sides in the Rwandan civil war. Only the crimes of Hutu *genocidaires* were prosecuted by the UN's jurists, whereas the atrocities committed by the Tutsi-dominated

Rwandan Patriotic Front were ignored even as the perpetrators of these crimes have been immunized from punishment.

The failure of the judicial proceedings extends also to the failure to trace responsibility for the genocide in Rwanda above the national level to higher echelons of decision makers in the international community. The record is very clear that the governments of the United States and Britain possessed the information and logistical capacity to stop the mass slaughter but chose not to do so.[20] As Michael Barnett has written, "The Rwandan genocide is not only about the evil that is possible. It is also about the complacency exhibited by those who have the responsibility to confront the evil."[21] But can the Anglo-American failure to intervene be attributed to complacency alone? Or were darker forces at play in Washington and London in helping to create the conditions for the installation of a Rwandan government dominated by a US-trained soldier, General Paul Kagame? By the time he became Rwanda's president in 2000, Kagame had allied the activities of the Rwandan armed forces and its network of privately backed armies in the eastern Congo with the interests of many Anglo-American mining companies devoted to extracting mineral wealth from one of the most resource-rich portions of the globe.

In spite of its failures and limitations, however, the International Criminal Court on Rwanda is the first judicial body to render the Genocide Convention as the basis of formal prosecutions and convictions. Some of these persecutions involved accusations about the systematic deployment of rape. Other precedent-setting prosecutions pointed to the manipulation of radio broadcasts to incite acts of ethnic violence. In drawing the connection between genocide and the dehumanization of targeted groups through the dissemination of propaganda, the UN tribunal explored a major frontier of international law in a era when big media cartels have become core institutions in engineering the environment of public opinion required to justify the aggressions of the military-industrial complex. The UN jurists advanced interpretations of international crime introduced by Emil Stanislaus Rappaport, Lemkin's professorial mentor in Poland.

The reach of the juridical processes extended all the way to the domestic courts of Canada and Germany. In 2007 a Hutu immigrant from Rwanda, Désiré Munyaneza, was charged under Canada's *Crimes against Humanities and War Crimes Act*.[22] This statute was enacted in 2000 with the goal of making Canada's domestic law conform with international law. Munyaneza's trial came to a close in Canada in December 2008 just as the UN tribunal based in Arusha, Tanzania, was about to sentence Théoneste Bagosora, the "the colonel of death." Bagosora was condemned to life imprisonment for his role in planning and instigating from inside the Rwandan army the Hutu onslaughts on Tutsi victims.[23] In the autumn of 2009 more arrests of alleged Hutu genocidaires took place in Germany.[24]

UN secretary general Kofi Annan announced that the UN tribunal in Arusha had "delivered the first-ever judgment on the crime of genocide by an international court"[25] in deciding in 1998 to convict Jean-Paul Akayesu. The failure of international institutions to enforce the Genocide Convention even once during the half century preceding Akayesu's conviction points to the aptness of Lisa Hijar's thesis that international law for the protection of human rights has functioned "not as law but as moral rhetoric framed in legal language."[26] The strength of this pattern is further highlighted by the propensity to confine prosecutions for international crimes to individuals belonging to constituencies that have been defeated in armed conflict. The hypocrisy inherent in this bias has had a corrosive effect on the credibility of many law-enforcement agencies the world over. In Canada, for instance, some drew attention to the double standard entailed in the Canadian government's zealous prosecution of alleged Hutu genocidaires at the same time that former US president George W. Bush, his vice president Richard Cheney, and his secretary of state Condoleezza Rice were allowed to move freely throughout the country as though they were exempt from the provisions of the Canadian *Crimes against Humanity and War Crimes Act*. Similarly, the initial focus of the International Criminal Court (ICC) in 2009 was on prosecuting African warlords, ignoring simultaneously those in the richer countries that fund, arm, and direct private armies even as they authorize state-sanctioned terror, including the international crime of torture. Thus the ICC seemingly extended the same patterns of discriminatory law enforcement that give rise to the disproportionately high rates of African-American incarceration in US jails.[27]

Accordingly, the political bias of victors' justice has consistently tainted even those very few instances when the Genocide Convention has been enforced. Although Lemkin's contribution to international jurisprudence has never been applied in uniform, equitable, and consistent ways, however, the very existence of this law has served to call attention to the criminal character of many different episodes and styles of colonization. The tendency to apply Lemkin's ideas to an expanding array of cases can be pictured as the democratization of the concept of genocide. As more and more groups and individuals have seized on the power of the idea of genocide as a judiciable genre of international crime, the subject matter of holocaust studies has expanded to go far beyond the Nazi assault on European Jewry.[28] This pattern was epitomized by the expanded mandate given a project that began in 1997 with the goal of creating a Canadian version of the Holocaust Museum in Washington, DC. The initial sponsors of this project, a Canadian media conglomerate named CanWest Global, resolved to widen the scope of this cultural institution to become the Canadian Museum for Human Rights.[29] The construction of the museum edifice began under federal auspices in Winnipeg, Manitoba, in 2009. It remains to be seen whether the museum will be balanced and fair in its representation of crimes against humanity or whether it will co-opt and twist the concept of human rights to advance a partisan agenda concocted by the project's political and corporate sponsors.

The gradual widening of how the international crime of genocide is conceived has led to a growing propensity to highlight attacks on Indigenous peoples in all parts of the world.[30] Many Indigenous societies have been extremely vulnerable to genocidal incursions because of their relative smallness and the fragility of their members' delicate attachments to the local ecologies of their Aboriginal territories. Even a small increase in the death rate can have a large impacts on miniature societies, especially when survivors struggle simultaneously with the loss of their traditional means of obtaining food, housing, clean water, and medicine. This type of material disruption is usually accompanied by all manner of dislocations preventing communities and their members from holding ground and renewing the familial, cultural, political, psychological, and spiritual facets of their personal and collective well-being. The result is often marked in the self-destruction epitomized by high rates of addiction, suicide, and domestic violence. This kind of prognosis permeates many studies focusing on the genocidal destruction of small groups, including the Herero people of South-West Africa; the Chakma, Mro, Marma, and other groups indigenous to the Chittagong Hill Tracts of Bangladesh;[31] the Aboriginal societies of West Papua;[32] the Penan of Sarawak;[33] the Nuba of Sudan;[34] the Innu of Labrador;[35] and the Yanomami of Brazil.[36]

While one stream of investigation has concentrated on assaults on very small societies, the epistemology of genocide can also be constructed to emphasize intersecting cycles of destruction pressed over long periods against broad amalgams of related peoples. This large-scale approach is probably best suited to the study of the treatment of Indigenous peoples in the Western Hemisphere since 1492 and in Australia since 1788. Together with Australia, the Western Hemisphere is the part of the world where the human environment has been most thoroughly remade in the course of imperial, national, and corporate colonization. The Columbian conquests began just as the most vicious phase of Christendom's anti-Islamic Crusades came to an end with Roman Catholic Spain's *reconquista* of the Moorish Caliphates in the Iberian Peninsula. The conquistadorial extension of power to the Western Hemisphere began in 1492 with a concerted drive to make a New World for Europeans by eliminating the Old World civilizations of Indigenous peoples. The aim of this genocidal project was to clear the way for the growth of a transplanted civilization that would draw most of its people and cultural inspiration from other lands. What process of genocide has been as invasive, long-lived and ruthlessly destructive as that which took has taken place throughout Americas since 1492?[37] Did this centuries-old process of genocide ever come to a definitive end?

The initial surge of genocidal destruction in the Americas was followed by wave upon wave of massive emigration from Europe and Africa and later from Asia. That process of overwhelming the Aboriginal population with a population derived primarily from immigrants and their descendants continues unabated to this day. The process of rendering the Indigenous peoples of a whole hemisphere as fragmented, poor, and marginalized minorities within their own Aboriginal continents can easily be characterized as a saga of vast genocidal proportions. The Reverend Jeremiah Evarts was one of those who observed long ago that the entire course of North American history was moving along a trajectory that future generations would come to characterize as genocidal. As part of his scathing critique in 1829 of President Andrew Jackson's proposed policy of Indian removal, Evarts asked rhetorically, "Who will dare to advocate the monstrous doctrine, that the people of a whole continent may be destroyed, for the benefit of the people of another continent?"[38]

The authors of a very significant article in the *Encyclopaedia Judaica* acknowledge the monumental extent of the devastation wrought on Indigenous peoples through the violent appropriation of America by European Christendom. This article is devoted to describing "the singularity of the Holocaust," always a difficult, controversial, and potentially divisive subject.[39] They write: "The catastrophic encounter of European civilization with the Indigenous peoples of the Americas is one of the most tragic meetings in all of human history. It entailed not only immense socioeconomic and geopolitical transformations for the native population but also enormous despoliation. On the grounds of the erosion of population, their collective tragedy parallels, even exceeds, that of European Jewry."[40]

A major extenuating factor in any attempt to measure the extent of genocide throughout much of the Western Hemisphere is the large amount of intermarriage that took place especially in those areas that came to be dominated by the Roman Catholic Church.[41] In most of Central and South America, the largest portion of the population is mixed-ancestry mestizo people who trace their history back both to the conquistadors and to the Indians that their conquering ancestors slaughtered and enslaved by the millions. So prolific and powerful has been the process of familial blending over more than five centuries of intercultural love and war that the majority of people in large parts of the Americas have some Indian ancestry. This pattern of mixing, however, is most weak in the portion of North America that came to be dominated by Protestant religion and the English language – much of Canada and all of the United States. In this northern portion of the Western Hemisphere very distinct legal and territorial barriers have been built up to divide and segregate Indigenous peoples from the rest of the population. The reserves and reservations of Canada and the United States stand as telling monuments of the attempt to enact a North American version of ethnic cleansing, one aimed at freeing up the huge territories outside the Aboriginal enclaves for the use, proliferation, and enrichment of non-Aboriginal settlers and corporations. The transformation of large parts of Indian Country into surveyed grids of privatized proprietorship provided great stores of new capital to stimulate and finance Anglo-America's expansionary urges.

The architects and enforcers of South African apartheid claimed, how-ever disingenuously, that their goal was to make the country's divided communities separate but equal. No such sentiments were attached, how-ever, to the system of Indian reserves and reservations in North America. With the exception of the brief reign of John Collier's Indian New Deal, the dominant expectation was that reserves and reservations would even-tually be absorbed into surrounding municipalities and systems of land tenure, in the same way that their inhabitants would eventually be cultur-ally and legally assimilated into surrounding populations. There is a deep inheritance of genocide beneath the still-prevalent expectation in much of English-speaking North America that Aboriginal societies are terminal societies. North American governments have long operated as agencies devoted to the continuation of the old civilizing mission that began with the European colonization of the Western Hemisphere. Until the 1960s and 1970s, the federal governments of Canada and the United States remained firmly attached to policies based on the principle that they could best serve their Indian wards by hurrying the demise of Aboriginal societies as culturally and legally distinct polities. These assimilationist policies easily fit Lemkin's view of genocide as a phenomenon that includes attempts to destroy the distinct cultural identities of designated groups, even though the individuals living within the communities targeted for extinction are permitted to live.

In 1945 Allan G. Harper provided a clear description of the assimi-lationist plan for bloodless genocide in his essay on the basic concepts and objectives of Canada's Indian administration. In the Pan-American journal *America Indigena*, he wrote, "The purpose of government is two-fold: (1) to train the Indian people in the habit of self-support within the economic framework of the country and (2) to lead them by degrees to abandon their aboriginal inheritance and to adopt the culture and religion of the dominant society." He continued: "The ultimate end is 'emancipation,' i.e. the admission of Indian people into full citizenship and their biological absorption."[42]

In order to illustrate the nature of the genocidal forces that have shaped North American society, it is necessary to place this subject in the context of comparisons. Throughout most of Europe, Africa, and Asia, the lan-guages one hears and the people one sees are mostly indigenous – at least to their own home continents. Immigration may be rapidly changing the face of Europe, but indigenous Europeans are still a long way from being rendered like the Indians of North America – as tiny minorities in their own Aboriginal territories. A focus on language helps to illustrate the extent of the de-aboriginalization of North America, where Aboriginal languages are rarely heard outside the larger reserves and reservations or on the airwaves of Aboriginal broadcasting.[43] These Aboriginal languages frequently lack any official recognition whatsoever from the non-Aboriginal governments that dominate the lands which Indians and Inuit once controlled. The marginalization of Aboriginal languages serves as a metaphor for many other forms of marginalization and de-aboriginalization.

It is as if a giant flip has taken place, one that has made imported cultures the primary basis for the creolized norms of local North American cultures. In the process, Aboriginal societies have been pushed so far towards the economic, political, and cultural edges of mainstream society that Indigenous peoples appear as outsiders in the territories of their ancestors. This dramatic reversal of roles is so complete that its ironies have become almost invisible to the vast majority of North Americans who do not identify themselves as Indians, Inuit, and Métis. The flip provides a striking indication that North America, like Australia, has been shaped by the pervasive and cumulative effects of a long and many-faceted genocide. This assault culminated in the emergence of the United States as a country that simultaneously embraces an idea of itself as a New World polity and as the primary recipient, embodiment, and defender of Western Civilization's heritage.[44] Similarly, the assault on Aboriginal America established the conditions for the creation of the North Atlantic Treaty Organization as a US-centred military alliance that was initially created to defend the shared heritage and interests of the North Atlantic community. NATO's conception of that North Atlantic community certainly does *not* extend in any serious and considered way to the Aboriginal societies of North America. Indeed, throughout the nineteenth century, the growth of the military apparatus of the United States, NATO's main sponsor and guide, was built up through the waging of many Indian wars aimed at consolidating control of the Imperial Republic's transcontinental empire. NATO's military intervention in Afghanistan as an initiating act of the US-led War on Terror repeated in Eurasia some of the same patterns of colonizing violence that developed during the Indian wars that characterized the westward expansion of Euro-American settlements in North America.

It would be wrong to attribute the diminished place of Aboriginal societies in North America entirely to genocide. As many demographers of Aboriginal America have pointed out, one of the major causes for the shrinking numbers of Native people from the 1500s to the early 1900s was the introduction of new diseases into the Western Hemisphere.[45] An emphasis, however, on illness and differences in immune systems can be pushed too far. This thrust of interpretation can be extended to such extremes that it is made to seem that the tragedies that befell Indigenous peoples are almost entirely attributable to bacteria and viruses, and not at all to the decisions and actions of human beings. The authors of the article in the *Encyclopaedia Judaica* on the singularity of the Holocaust can be accused of this form of excess. They write: "Students of the demographic annihilation of the Indian are agreed that its overwhelming cause was unintended disease which produced vast epidemics ... When mass deaths occurred, it was almost without exception caused by microbes not militia, unintentionally rather than by design."[46]

These comments and others like them are far too dismissive of the role of warfare in North American genocide. In the eyes of many, warfare legalizes murder even as it legitimizes hatred of the real or imagined enemy. Warfare has been strategically deployed as one of many strategies in the multi-faceted assault on the Old World civilizations of the peoples indigenous to the Western Hemisphere. The outcome of this assault was to invent America as a Promised Land for immigrants and their descendants. Who has lost most in terms of life, liberty, and happiness from the transformation of two of the world's richest continents into havens devoted to the enrichment of the most acquisitive newcomers and their privileged progeny? The transatlantic family dynasty founded by the fur-trading, opium-smuggling, and real-estate mogul John Jacob Astor epitomizes the character of an American Dream realized spectacularly by an elite few who derive the major' share of the benefits from a process that included the genocide of indigenous populations.

From the Pequot War, which cleared the way for the English settlement of Connecticut in 1637, to the Battle of Fallen Timbers in 1794, to the confrontation at Wounded Knee in 1973, warfare and genocide have been inseparably intertwined with the rise of North American capitalism. In the seventeenth and eighteenth centuries the Indigenous peoples of North America were major participants in conflicts large and small that often involved hostilities between competing European powers. Canada exists to this day because the members of a powerful Indian Confederacy strategically allied themselves with the British Empire in the civil wars of Anglo-America.[47] The Indian alliance with the imperial government of Great Britain was a factor in the federal decision pressed forward by President Andrew Jackson to remove all surviving Indians east of the Mississippi River through the coercive intervention of the US army. Throughout the nineteenth century the westward expansion of the United States was punctuated with the violence of many Indian wars. These events were instrumental in helping to shape the institutions, philosophy, and expansionary orientation of the superpower's military-industrial complex.[48] Indian wars and the Trail of Tears confirmed the imperative of conquest over adherence to the rule of law. The decision of the US Congress in 1871 to outlaw the making of further treaties with Indigenous peoples institutionalized the emergent superpower's embrace of the imperatives of force over the principles of consent in the worldwide expansion of US military, commercial, and political power.

North of the forty-ninth parallel, the building of the Canadian Pacific Railway led in 1885 to an armed intervention aimed at disarming, criminalizing, and eliminating those Métis and Cree who opposed the new order.[49] The hanging of Métis leader Louis Riel by authorities of the dominion's government made the point that western Canada would be developed as a domain where White, English-speaking Protestants would prevail over Indians and their mixed-ancestry descendants, many of whom were French-speaking Roman Catholics. In British Columbia the military force of the British Navy was coercively deployed to overpower the resistance of West Coast Indians to Crown rule.[50] Beginning in the final decades of the twentieth century, the Americanization of Canada was marked by the outbreak of confrontations resembling US Indian wars. These confrontations included those that took place in Anicinabe Park in Kenora, Ontario, in 1974, Lubicon Territory in Alberta's Oil Patch during the late 1980s,[51] Oka, Quebec, in 1990, Gustafsen Lake, BC, and Ipperwash, Ontario, in 1995, and, beginning in 2006, at the Douglas Creek Estates housing development in Caledonia, Ontario.[52]

The genocidal spirit of the Indian wars has its origins in the originating acts of the Columbian conquests. Spain's dramatic conquest of the Mexican empire of the Aztecs extended aspects of the *reconquista* of the multicultural Islamic Caliphates that thrived for a time in the Iberian Peninsula. The conquest of Mexico established a precedent in the colonization of the Americas that has never been reversed. The imperial powers set out to create a *New* Spain, a *New* Netherlands, a *New* France, a *New* England, a *New* York, a *New* Hampshire, a *New* Jersey, a *Nova* Scotia. Hence the initial waves of transatlantic colonizers set out to remake their "new found land" into extensions of the polities they had left behind in Europe. In Newfoundland itself, a Canadian province only since 1948, the island's invaders escaped the authority of government to hunt down indigenous Beothuk to the point of total extinction, total genocide.[53] To this day the expectation of extinguishment never ceased to influence the non-Aboriginal conduct of relations with Indigenous peoples. Indeed, the push to "deny and negate" rather than "recognize and affirm" the existence of Aboriginal and treaty rights remains integral to the treatment of Indigenous peoples in Canada, the United States, Australia, and many other polities to this day. This failure to adhere to bold declarations of constitutional principle is marked in the systemic failure of law-enforcement agencies to prevent and punish the actions of private individuals, corporations, municipalities, and other government agencies that violate the rights and titles of Indigenous peoples. This failure to enforce the laws of existing Aboriginal and treaty rights begins the cycle of impunity that extends up many chains of responsibility for the commission of major international crimes.

The perception has continued that Aboriginal societies are terminal polities that must eventually disappear in the course of progress. Only rarely has this expectation of obsolescence been lifted, as happened briefly when John Collier was empowered by President Franklin Roosevelt to plan and implement the Indian New Deal. The expectation that the assimilation of Aboriginal communities would lead to their extinction has tended to prevail even when officials of European empires and their successor states uttered bold pronouncements about the character of Indian treaties as sacred instruments of relationship meant to last for as long as the sun shines, the grass grows, and the waters flow. The Indian wars provided public demonstrations of the direct connection between the growing power of the new societies and the shrinking stature of the Aboriginal societies. This shift in the balance of power was briefly halted during the War of 1812, the final bout in the Anglo-America civil war whose outcome was decisively affected by the military muscle displayed by Tecumseh's Indian Confederacy. Thereafter the violent clashes on the moving frontiers of Euro-American settlements tended to confirm the view that the Aboriginal survivors were conquered people who must either disappear altogether or submit to the dominant motifs and governing authority of the triumphant civilization.

While disease and warfare constitute the lethal extremes of the viral and human onslaughts on Aboriginal groups, many of the most corrosive forces aimed at Aboriginal individuals and communities lie in the realm of bloodless genocide – genocides of the mind, of memory, of collective consciousness, of culture. They lie in the outcome of long campaigns of psychological warfare aimed at inflicting amnesia on Indigenous peoples. The colonizers' aim has been to block the continuity of local and indigenous memory and thereby remove all mental obstacles to the realization of the imperial dictate that there should be no secure and lasting place for small Aboriginal societies in the global monoculture of monopoly capitalism. The constant repetition of the message of Aboriginal inferiority by teachers, administrators, police, clergy, judges, and many other figures of authority has frequently intensified this psychological onslaught on the self-esteem, self-confidence, and self-awareness of subjugated peoples. The Darwinian clichés of racial stereotyping have frequently saturated this form of indoctrination. The psychological warfare deployed in the mental mine fields of the Columbian conquests has therefore helped to weaken the resistance of indigenous and Fourth World forces to the most intolerant advocates of Western universalism.

Malcolm X and Frantz Fanon both emphasized the importance of psychological warfare in generating crippling attitudes of self-reproach in some colonized communities. Both have emphasized the propensity of some individuals in subjugated groups to internalize the views of their oppressors. This brainwashing can plant feelings in some victims that they are deformed by the stigmas associated with their origins and ancestry. As a Black psychiatrist from Martinique who studied mental illness in Algeria, Fanon was especially alive to the injuries inflicted by the unceasing repetition of the idea that one's community is backwards and obsolete, lacks the capacity for adaptation and self-renewal, and that the only viable way for individuals to get ahead is to absorb and imitate the attitudes of the colonizing society. Fanon predicted that this pattern of self-reproach, self-doubt, and imitation would produce indigenous elites inclined to sabotage

the liberating potential of decolonization by becoming clones and caricatures of the colonial elites they replaced. Malcolm X raised similar issues
in a more personal way. In his autobiography he discussed the problem of
internalized racism through an account of his own decision to renounce
the popular practice that saw many in his community purchase expensive
chemicals for painful treatments aimed at straightening out the natural
kinks in their Afro-American hair.[54] His rejection of this expression of self-
loathing helped point the way to the decolonization inherent in the affirmation that Black Is Beautiful.

In one of his mimeographed messages to a large mailing list of Indian
activists, Louis Hall, a founding elder of the American Indian Movement and
the militant Mohawk Warriors, commented in 1976 on the reason for high
rates of Indian suicide. With his characteristic flourishes of highly racialized
language, he attributed this form of self-destructiveness to the internalization by some Indian youth of what he refers to as a "plan of genocide":

For 400 years an all out psychological warfare has been waged by the white race
against Native Americans. It has caused untold suffering among Red Indians.
Numerous suicides, among other casualties, like alcoholism and drug addiction,
have resulted from the mind warfare. Other Indians are merely dispirited, demoralized and see no future as far as surviving as Indians is concerned. They only see
Indians surviving as imitation white people and part of the white nation to be eventually absorbed until no traces remain of the Red race. They have reconciled themselves to extinction. This is the desired result of psychological warfare. This type
of warfare is every bit as deadly as the one with guns. Brainwash the Indians, make
them feel inferior, create conditions worse than death and the victims may destroy
themselves ... Not all Indians are destroyed in this way. Some will fight on and
on. As they go along, they learn to fight this insidious and subtle struggle ... Self-
destruction is not the answer.[55]

As extreme as Hall's allegations may initially appear, the issues he raises
cannot be lightly dismissed. The evidence is enormous that the idea of
progress in North America has been expressed in ways that have not been
friendly to the prospect of Indians surviving *as Indians*. Increasingly this
prejudice is directed not so much at the assimilation of individuals but at
the assimilation of the institutions of Aboriginal governance so that they
conform to the privatized motifs of capitalist business transaction.[56] As
an era of universalized capitalism replaced the mercantilism of European
empire building and then the bipolar alignments of the Cold War, the need
to adapt to the dominant structures of a single global regime of material
interaction became an imperative that was no longer restricted to particular
groups or to those who reside in particular parts of the planet. It became,
rather, a universal requirement of human survival. Hence the assimilative
pressures directed at Indigenous peoples created the Aboriginal history
of the expansionary drive to eliminate those expressions of diversity and

pluralism that blocked the creation of a single global market. The monopoly of universalized capitalism thus grew to resemble the uniformity of an agricultural monoculture. The global economy was rendered vulnerable to threats similar to those that arise when natural ecosystems are plundered to make room for the cultivation of single crops. When a contagion strikes, the commercial monocultures possess few resources of genetic diversity to draw upon in order to survive the attacks of predatory organisms.

In the post–Cold War era, the culture of monopoly capitalism began to approach dominance in virtually every theatre of social, political, and cultural relations. Indeed, the agents and agencies of capitalism broke down all major obstacles that had previously blocked the integration of the world's diverse political economies into a single system of proprietary interaction. The extent of this integration of many economies into one became very clear in the autumn of 2008. Beginning with a massive breakdown in the repayment of home mortgages, the weakness of the real economy in the United States finally burst through the illusions created by the massive frauds of fantasy accounting in the most deregulated branches of the financial sector. Thus the festering boil of illusory wealth was inflated to the breaking point by Wall Street's overzealous promotion of private indebtedness. When the infectious build-up of toxic transactions in money-like instruments known as derivatives finally burst, the resulting "contagion" disassembled global markets like a computer virus. In the journal *Foreign Affairs*, Roger C. Altman explained the political consequences of the cataclysm: "The Anglo-Saxon brand" of market-based capitalism was placed "under a cloud."[57]

CHURCH, STATE, AND INTERNATIONAL LAW IN THE PERPETRATION OR PREVENTION OF GENOCIDE

Some of those assimilative activities that Raphael Lemkin identified as integral to genocide were institutionalized and bureaucratized in administrative machineries, especially of those countries where it was taken for granted that Indigenous peoples must move aside to make room for immigrants and their descendants. Canada's Duncan Campbell Scott epitomized the class of civil servant who administered Aboriginal affairs in polities devoted to forms of capitalist expansion that depended on the appropriation of natural resources from the land's indigenous titleholders. Scott's primary reputation is as a poet who wrote and promoted various forms of Canadian literature. Like Stephen Leacock and many of his own peers, Scott's Canadian nationalism coincided with his attachment to Great Britain. It gave rise to his expectation that the continuing decentralization of the British Empire would result in the creation of a new kind of federal system. "The manifest destiny of Canada," he wrote in 1896 in the New York *Bookman*, "is to be one of the greatest powers in the Federated Empire of England."[58]

Scott's day job for over half a century was as a bureaucrat in the Canadian Indian Department, an agency of government that was frequently neglected by the elected minister formally in charge of a unit that administered the day-to-day affairs of the dominion's disenfranchised Aboriginal wards. Gradually Scott moved up in the bureaucracy's hierarchy, becoming its highest unelected official in 1913. As deputy superintendent general of his department, Scott pictured himself as the inheritor of the administrative legacy of the Sir William Johnson, the first superintendent of Indian affairs in British imperial Canada.[59] In his essay about his predecessor, Scott characterized Johnson as "the great prototype of all Indian officials."[60]

The differences between the administration of Indian affairs under Johnson and Scott were, however, enormous. While Johnson sought to polish the silver Covenant Chain by treating with his Six Nations neighbours and relatives as allies of the Crown, Scott attempted to terminate this tradition of Indian diplomacy. As he explained in 1920 to a parliamentary committee considering his proposal in Bill 14 to permit the Indian Department to remove individuals unilaterally from Canada's registry of legally recognized Indians, "I want to get rid of the Indian problem ... Our objective is to continue until there is not a single Indian in Canada that has not been absorbed into the body politic, and there is no Indian question, and no Indian Department."[61]

In Scott's era, almost every policy and program of the Department of Indian Affairs in Canada was geared to the genocidal goal of hastening the time when Aboriginal collectivities would cease to exist as legally and culturally distinct groups.[62] The system of federally funded, church-run Indian residential schools was the most ambitious component in a broad array of initiatives aimed, however ineffectively, at breaking up Aboriginal communities and absorbing Indian individuals into the body politic.[63] Several Christian denominations began establishing church-run Indian residential schools in the mid-nineteenth century as vehicles of their missionary enterprises. As the Dominion of Canada extended its influence into the vast domain it had purchased from the Hudson's Bay Company, it gradually began to fund Christian churches to deliver the Indian schooling consistently promised between 1871 and 1929 in the negotiation of eleven Crown-Aboriginal treaties, as well as in subsequent adhesions to them. While some Indian families embraced church-run schooling voluntarily, during Scott's term as deputy minister this regime of Indian education was thoroughly integrated into an increasingly repressive administrative regime aimed at terminating distinct Indian societies through the forced assimilation of their members.

The cumulative effect of about 120 of these schools over their lifetime clearly meets the criteria of Article 2(e) of the Genocide Convention.[64] That section defines genocide as "forcibly transferring the children of the group to another group." In Canada the forcible nature of the transfer was enacted in 1920 through provisions in Bill 14, the same statute that was the vehicle of Scott's attempt to empower his department to eliminate individuals from the dominion government's registry of status Indians without their consent. While Canada's parliamentarians prevented Scott from using such tactics to diminish the number of legally recognized Indians, the lawmakers did agree to enact an ambitious set of regulations and punishments aimed at enforcing compulsory attendance of many Indian children in the dominion's church-run residential schools. As wards of the federal government, Indian parents were not able to take legal action to prevent their children from being removed from their care. Nor were they in a position to protect their offspring from being abused once they entered the Indian residential schools. Indeed, the legal link between Indian parents and their children was subjected to a double jeopardy because the Crown transferred custody of the students from their parents to the principals of the institutions housing the youths.

It is virtually impossible to deny that the hammer of Canadian law, including aggressive enforcement by the Royal Canadian Mounted Police, was used to transfer Indian children from one group to another even after Canada's adherence to the UN's Genocide Convention in 1948. While the terms of Article 2(e) of the Genocide Convention were clearly met, the systematic abuses of Indian students within Indian residential schools, and the effects of these abuses on their families, communities, and Aboriginal nationalities, also touch on Articles 2(b), (c), and (d). Article 2(d) is applicable because of the forced sterilizations imposed on some girls and women in the residential schools.[65] These incidents form a small part of a far larger effort to limit the reproductive capacity of Indigenous peoples in many jurisdictions, including the United States. This phenomenon drew on the racist orientation of the eugenics movement and its renewal in some aspects of the family planning movement.[66]

Article 2(c) of the Genocide Convention speaks of "deliberately inflicting on the group conditions calculated to bring about its physical destruction in whole or in part." The unusually high rates of mortality resulting from recurring epidemics of tuberculosis constitute the primary basis for the most serious charge that calculated acts of physical destruction did take place, albeit mostly before 1948. The mortality rates were high even in comparison to the high rates of tubercular infection that plagued many Indian reserves in areas such as Saskatchewan's Qu'Appelle region.[67] Kevin Annett has estimated that tuberculosis was the primary agent in the death of about 50,000 of the 120,000 youth who he calculates attended the residential schools over the entire course of their existence.[68] Another report in the Edinburgh-based *Scotsman* refers to 80,000 survivors of "a practice that ripped an estimated 150,000 children from their communities."[69]

In April 2007 the high death rates were reported as front-page news in Toronto's *Globe and Mail*. In an article entitled "Natives Died in Droves as Ottawa Ignored Warnings," Bill Curry and Karen Howlett reported, "As many as half of the aboriginal children who attended the early years of residential schools died of tuberculosis, despite repeated warnings to the federal government that overcrowding, poor sanitation and lack of medical care created a toxic breeding ground for the rapid spread of disease." John Milloy, one of the academic experts quoted in the article, remarked that the purpose of the schools was "to eradicate Indians as a cultural group. If genocide has to do with destroying a people's culture, this is genocide, no doubt about it." Elsewhere in the article he took exception with aspects of Annett's work, arguing that the high death rates had more to do with the dominion's formula for funding the schools on a per capita basis than a deliberate effort to "sick" the students "with tuberculosis and wipe them out as a species on earth." Commenting on the sending of so many Indian youth with advanced cases of tuberculosis to a residential school in Shubenacadie, Nova Scotia, one official is quoted as complaining in 1930 to his superiors, "Evidently somebody has mistaken our residential school for a TB sanitorium ... Its very unfair to the children who are clean and well." Curry and Howlett reported the existence of many unmarked mass graves around some of the former schools.[70]

While the mortality rates remain contested and controversial, everyone who has looked closely at the health-related problems in Indian residential schools agrees that many Aboriginal students died while attending the institutions or shortly following their release from these death traps. One medical official who investigated the mortality rates at the time they were occurring arrived at the startling conclusion that the conditions feeding the epidemics were "deliberately created." In his reports of 1907 and 1909, Dr P.H. Bryce emphasized that many problems could be lessened through the implementation of relatively simple changes such as improved ventilation and sanitation, filtering entering students for contagious illness, and isolating sick individuals away from crowded dormitories. Anticipating the possibility of a time when the world's governments would be held accountable to the international community for crimes against humanity, Bryce labelled Canada's administration of the Indian residential schools as a "national crime."[71]

Duncan Campbell Scott responded by acknowledging publicly that problems existed. In his professional correspondence with a federal Indian agent in British Columbia, however, Scott seemingly justified a policy of inaction because it conformed with his preoccupation of reducing the number of registered Indians to zero. Scott is reported to have explained: "It is readily acknowledged that Indian children lose their natural resistance to illness by habiting so closely in these schools, and that they die at much higher rates than in their villages. But this alone does not justify a change in the policy of this department, which is geared towards the final solution to the Indian problem."[72]

There would be serious ramifications if it could be demonstrated conclusively that top officials in Canada's Indian Department deliberately failed to intervene to prevent the epidemics of tuberculosis from doing maximum damage in the Indian residential schools. The fact that there is some evidence to support this hypothesis highlights the problematic nature of the assertion in the *Encyclopaedia Judaica* that the reduction of the Aboriginal population through disease was "unintentional rather than by design." If some of Canada's residential schools were the site of such genocidal deployment of microorganisms, it would not be the first time in North American history that germ warfare, however rudimentary, was directed at Indigenous peoples. In at least one instance the British imperial army engaged in biological attacks on Native North Americans by giving some of them blankets from a small-pox hospital. Soldiers under the command of General Jeffrey Amherst set this dark precedent in 1763. Amherst agreed to unleash the weaponry of inculcated illness when Pontiac and the Indian confederacy he briefly personified intervened militarily to demonstrate that the British conquest of the French imperial army did not extinguish their Aboriginal title to Canada.[73]

The Canadian system of Indian residential schools continued in full force until well into the 1970s. The last of the institutions was not closed down until the 1990s. The evangelical zeal expressed in this system's religious orientation epitomized the persistence of the civilizational mission that began with the planting of Christian crosses throughout the Americas as symbols of the sovereign claims advanced by European monarchs. Like the Canadian *Indian Act*, the residential schools can be seen as markers of the nationalized colonialism that developed in those countries where Indigenous peoples were transformed into small minorities. In the United States, one scholarly observer has characterized the pedagogy of his country's Indian boarding schools as "education for extinction."[74] This genocidal approach continued to dominate the more decentralized and eclectic mix of US schools until the ideological impact of the Indian New Deal began to exert some mitigating influence. In Australia, child welfare authorities at the state and national levels developed aggressive programs aimed at removing Aboriginal children, but especially those of mixed ancestry, from their biological families so they could be socialized to "white standards." In 1997 the Australian Human Rights and Equal Opportunity Commission (AHREO) described the cumulative impact of about 100,000 such removals as genocidal. It presented detailed accounts of the abuse and exploitation experienced by Aboriginal youths in orphanages and adopted homes, where they were frequently beaten and sometimes exploited as unpaid labour or sex slaves.[75]

The insertion of the charge of genocide into the political, legal, and academic discourse of Australia had a polarizing effect.[76] The AHREO Commission's "Stolen Generation" report intensified a growing controversy that began to gather momentum in 1992, when the Australian High Court ruled that Indigenous peoples retained some collective rights in their Aboriginal territories.[77] The debates about the treatment of Indigenous peoples played a prominent role in shaping Australia's political culture during an era when many citizens sought to move beyond their country's identity as a former penal colony where a notorious "Whites Only" immigration policy had long held sway. As divisive as the debates on Aboriginal issues have sometimes been, they nevertheless provided Australians of all backgrounds with a common point of reference to evaluate the quality of their own citizenship, and to consider the relationship between history and their emerging nation's orientation to Asia, the United States, the Commonwealth, the United Nations, and the broader global community. In their efforts to understand the connections between their country's origins and its destiny, the citizens of Australia illustrate the power of Aboriginal history as an orienting beacon in the contest between the forces of change and of continuity.

In introducing the Stolen Generation report in 1997, one of its authors, Mick Dodson, demanded that the government of Prime Minister John Howard bring Australia's Aboriginal policies and legislation into conformity with the spirit and intent of the Genocide Convention. Dodson's origins lie in the Yawuru branch of Aboriginal Australia. As the social justice commissioner of AHREO, he linked the removal of Aboriginal and Torres Strait Islander children from their biological families to the larger process of stripping Indigenous peoples from the lands of their ancestors. As he expressed it, "Another phrase for genocide is extinguishment." Referring to the development of Australia on the legal principle of *terra nullius* – that before the arrival of the Europeans it was an empty land – Dodson observed, "It seems that extinguishment is a bit of a theme in this country. Extinguishment leads to extinction."[78]

Howard fended off a barrage of appeals and petitions aimed at persuading him to apologize on behalf of the whole Australian nation for the abuses heaped on the stolen generation and their families.[79] Indeed, he tapped into a strong surge of popular resentment aimed at the alleged excesses of the so-called "Black Armband" view of Australia's past.[80] As a Thatcherite politician of the right, Howard discovered he could gain political leverage by cultivating popular antagonism towards the movements emphasizing both reconciliation with Aboriginal peoples and fair treatment of immigrants and refugees. He advanced this reactionary strategy by maintaining a course that fell just short of outright endorsement of the radical anti-Aboriginal, anti-immigration policies of Pauline Hanson and her One Nation Party.[81] Howard's' encouragement and exploitation of popular resentment towards those Australians seeking to transcend the prejudices of the past culminated in his insistence that United Nations agencies had wrongfully meddled in Australia's domestic sphere. He condemned a UN report criticizing the overrepresentation of Aboriginal and Torres Strait Islander peoples in Australia's criminal justice system. He extended his anti-UN stance by refusing its officials' entry to Australia, where they intended to study the harsh and possibly illegal treatment of Asian refugees.[82]

Howard had come to dominance as the finance minister under Malcolm Fraser, Australia's prime minister from 1975 to 1983. In August 2000 'Fraser entered the political fray. He criticized the Australian government, alleging that Prime Minister Howard's "rejection of what many Australians would regard as justified criticism of Aboriginal policies by international institutions, in a way that puts jingoistic nationalism over and above the concept and ideal of human rights, is a step into the past that should not have been taken."[83] Fraser presented his remarks in a memorial lecture named after Vincent Lingiari, who, in 1966, had led the Wave Hill walk-off of Aboriginal cattle-ranch workers – a strike that highlighted the dispossessed plight of Indigenous peoples during an era when they still lacked all the protections of citizenship.[84]

Fraser returned several times to the principle that the Australian government was guilty of hypocrisy when it criticized others for violating the international law of human rights while denying the applicability of this same law to inequities within its own national sphere. Whatever the "imperfections" of the United Nations, he said, "we do not advance the cause of civilization and of security and peace by condemning the instruments of the international order." Fraser characterized the resort to unilateralism, whether by Australia or its ally, the United States, as "the greatest threat to world stability and progress." He added, "It is overwhelmingly in our interest to assist the United Nations and its instrumentalities in establishing a rule of law which can apply internationally to the great and powerful, just as the rule of law can apply to the great and powerful within Australia." He cautioned, "Governments can't have it both ways ... It is not rational to say we live in a globalized world economy, that there is a one world global market place, that financial markets must be open and transparent from one country to another, and to reject the inevitable conclusion in relation to matters such as human rights and the environment."

Fraser nodded his approval of the position advanced by Dodson and others that Australia should enter into some sort of treaty relationships with Aboriginal and Torres Strait Islander peoples similar to those already in place in Canada and New Zealand. He condemned the Australian government's aggressive and extremely expensive resort to the adversarial venue of the courts in order to avoid any admission of guilt and liability for the damage done to the stolen generations. He revealed that his growing understanding of the international crimes committed by the Australian government against Indigenous peoples had caused him to alter his position that the English common-law system was a sufficient shield for the protection of human rights in Australia. He therefore expressed the view that his country should entrench an Australian Bill of Rights in its constitution. Fraser's analysis emphasized the importance of the Universal Declaration of Human Rights, rather than the Genocide Convention. Unlike the Genocide Convention, which is framed as an element of an international criminal code, the Universal Declaration is a broad statement of principles that does not include any mention of procedures to identify and punish those who violate its provisions. In that respect Fraser did not go as far as Mick Dodson and the Australian Human Rights and Equal Opportunity Commission.

The AHREPC report emphasized that the genocidal character of Australia's Aboriginal policies could not be relegated entirely to the past. The era of the stolen generations never really ended in a country where officials of the child welfare system and the criminal justice establishment still removed Aboriginal and Torres Strait Islander youth from their biological families at disproportionately high rates. In Canada the rates of child apprehension remained even higher than those in Australia. In 2007 a report explaining the substance of a major human-rights complaint about to be mounted by the Assembly of First Nations indicated that an Aboriginal child in Canada was twenty times more likely to be removed from his or her biological family than a non-Aboriginal child.[85]

Before 1998 the government of Canada held firmly to the position that it was not accountable, legally or morally, for any wrongs done to the students of Indian residential schools or to their families and communities. The federal position held that any blame that might exist belonged exclusively to the Christian churches that administered these institutions. Then Jane Stewart, the minister of Indian affairs and northern development in the Liberal government of Prime Minister Jean Chrétien, acknowledged in a Statement of Reconciliation that the Canadian state bore some responsibility for the physical beatings and sexual abuse that had taken place far too frequently in the federally funded schools. Almost a decade later a new government in Australia sought "to turn a new page in Australia's history by righting the wrongs of the past." In February 2008 Kevin Rudd, the Labor prime minister who had replaced the defeated John Howard only weeks earlier, apologized on behalf of his government and his country to all those Aborigines who had been harmed by the Stolen Generation policies. He proclaimed, "For the indignity and degradation thus inflicted on a proud people and a proud culture, we are sorry." He asserted the determination of his government to ameliorate the destructive legacies of Australia's Aboriginal policies through an effort "to close the gap that lies between us in life expectancy, educational achievement and economic opportunity."[86]

In June 2008 Stephen Harper, the Canadian prime minister, made a similar speech in the Parliament of Canada. "The government of Canada sincerely apologizes and asks the forgiveness of the Aboriginal peoples of this country for failing them so profoundly." He explained that the "two primary objectives of the residential schools system were to remove and isolate children from their homes, families, traditions and cultures, and to assimilate them into the dominant cultures." Part of the process of trying to eliminate the cultural distinctiveness of Indigenous peoples involved prohibitions on speaking Aboriginal languages in the schools. This system for "killing the Indian in the child" gave rise to all manner of "emotional, physical and sexual abuse and neglect of helpless children." It separated them "from powerless families and communities." Harper continued, "We recognize the policy of assimilation was wrong, has caused great harm, and has no place in this country."[87]

Not surprisingly, neither Rudd nor Harper directly connected the events for which they apologized to the international crime of genocide. In taking note of this fact one pundit observed, "If there is one thing that Mr. Harper's 'apology' provided that could be considered groundbreaking or new, it's the idea that there can be crimes without criminals."[88] Dr Roland Chrisjohn, a psychiatrist from an Oneida community in Ontario, has been an unrelenting critic of the failure of the people, government and mainstream media to acknowledge that the overall operation of Indian residential schools was clearly genocidal in intent and effect.[89] He asserted that Canada's treatment of its Indian wards in the Christian institutions met all five of the UN's criteria of genocide, but especially Article 2(e). "There is absolutely no way," he argued, "that Canada can deny that they legislated the transference of children from their parents to church authorities."

Chrisjohn drew attention to the inclusion of the crime of genocide in Canada's criminal code in 1952. He noted that the original definitions given in the domestic legislation clearly match those in the UN's Convention for the Prevention and Punishment of the Crime of Genocide minus Articles 2(b) and (c). Article 2(b) refers to the "causing [of] serious bodily or mental harm to members of the group," whereas 2(e) refers to "forcibly transferring children of the group to another group." Then in 1985, just as the news about the involuntary sterilization of some Native women began to surface, the Canadian government removed Article 2(d). "It's not a coincidence," Chrisjohn announced. This removal of three-fifths of the international law from the Canadian domestic law took place because officials did not want to incorporate in federal legislation "what they were doing to First Nations people from 1948 – the crime of genocide."[90]

John Howard seems to have persuaded Stephen Harper in May 2006 to withdraw the support of the government of Canada from the United Nations Declaration on the Rights of Indigenous Peoples.[91] This international instrument grows directly from the movement of anti-imperial globalization that gathered momentum throughout the twentieth century. The declaration, which was adopted by the UN General Assembly in September 2007, continues the project of decolonization that has been embedded in the formal constitution of the United Nations since its inception in the Atlantic Charter of 1941. The UN Declaration on Indigenous Peoples' Rights extended conceptions and abstractions that are as least as old as the parliamentary investigation in the late 1830s into the conditions of "Aborigines" in British settlements. That effort, an outgrowth of the ant-slavery movement, was carried on by the London-based Aborigines' Protection Society, a forerunner of organizations such as the US-based

Cultural Survival, the Scandinavian-based International Work Group for Indigenous Affairs, or the Philippines-based Tebtebba Indigenous Peoples' International Center for Policy Research and Education. The declaration gave fresh expressions to ideas and strategies that grew from the ground-breaking work of the International Labor Organization, an entity that first adopted a focus on "native labor" as initially emphasized at the pan-African conferences organized by W.E.B, Du Bois and others during the Versailles Treaty negotiations of 1919. It drew on the principles and language injected into the discourse of international relations by Deskahe, the ambassador of the Longhouse Confederacy who, in the early 1920s, lobbied delegates at the League of Nations in Geneva to oppose the assault on the rights and titles of small nations.

The declaration stands as a monument to the vision that inspired George Manuel in his work to transcend the bipolar alignments of the Cold War and to advance instead the non-aligned ideals of biocultural diversity as a key to achieving forms of globalization more attuned to the ecological equilibrium essential to the Fourth World. Manuel's international work was instrumental in the founding in 1975 of the World Council of Indigenous Peoples. The creation of this polity, like that of the more militant AIM-based International Treaty Council, signalled a growing understanding of the role that international law and the United Nations could play as media for the continued struggle to oppose the ongoing colonization of Indigenous peoples and their Aboriginal lands.

The drafting of the declaration began formally in 1982. One of the early struggles was over the use of the term "peoples." Mindful of maintaining the legal underpinnings of their territorial integrity, many of the UN delegations, including that of Canada, insisted that they would only sanction processes dealing with "Indigenous populations." In a global organization that describes itself in its founding charter and in many of its core conventions and protocols as a confederacy of *peoples*, the perception existed that the adoption by the United Nations of the term "Indigenous peoples" might widen the constituency of polities that could claim the right to assert sovereign jurisdiction in international relations. The linguistic standoff eased considerably after the UN's sponsorship in 1993 of the International Year of the World's Indigenous Peoples. In 1995 the UN initiated the International Decade of the World's Indigenous Peoples.

The UN Declaration of 2007 specifically outlaws the "forced assimilation" projects that have been pushed ahead by the governments of many nation-states. Article 7.2 declares, "Indigenous peoples have the collective right to live in freedom, peace and security as distinct peoples and shall not be subjected to any act of genocide or any other act of violence, including the removing of children of the group to another group." The declaration looks beyond the relatively recent era when Aboriginal schooling was devoted largely to religious indoctrination. It anticipates a time when Indigenous peoples will have the right and capacity "to establish and control their educational systems and institutions" with due provision for renewing their own languages and "in a manner appropriate to their cultural methods of teaching and learning." The declaration ranges over a large array of topics, from health care to intellectual property, artistic expression, and the wrongful abuse of Indigenous peoples' land for military purposes. Not surprisingly, much of the document deals with lands and resources, including a provision proclaiming "the urgent need to respect and promote the rights of Indigenous peoples affirmed in treaties."

The declaration was passed with 143 state delegations voting for it and four delegations – those of the United States, Canada, New Zealand, and Australia – voting against it. In the final stages of the negotiations, several African governments, in spite of their own peoples' harsh experience of colonial repression, continued to have serious reservations about sanctioning the new international instrument. It was largely to address the concerns of the African delegations that decisive wording was added to Article 46. That provision affirms, "Nothing in this Declaration may be ... construed as authorizing or encouraging any action which would dismember or impair, totally or in part, the territorial integrity or political unity of sovereign and independent states."[92]

The joining together of the governments of Canada, the United States, New Zealand, and Australia to oppose the UN Declaration on Indigenous peoples' rights stands as a telling episode in the ongoing history of global inequity, international crime, and international law. Clearly, these four countries are all dominated by constituencies that are, by and large, beneficiaries of the cycles of colonization that began in 1492 and continue to this day. It seems that those who have gained the most from the expansion of the British Empire and its outgrowths are most resistant to any extension into their own countries of the same processes of decolonization that quadrupled the membership of the United Nations during its first half century.

An emphasis on the partial and unfinished character of the round of decolonization that briefly gained momentum in the 1960s helps to highlight the problems of definition that are bound to arise from the use of the term "Indigenous peoples." Throughout this text I have employed the words Indigenous peoples in the broadest way possible. Often I use the expression to refer in a general way to the many constituencies that experienced European imperialism and its Anglo-American extensions more as a force of repression than as a broadening of horizons and opportunity. The outcomes of this process of imperial domination and subjugation are marked most clearly in the human geography of wealth, well-being, and power in Canada, the United States, Australia, and New Zealand. These four predominantly English-speaking polities share a history where the expansionary thrust of European imperialism was internalized to give rise to national policies whose genocidal tendencies are evidenced in the institutionalized marginalization felt to this day by most Indigenous peoples in their own Aboriginal territories.

In all four of these predominantly English-speaking states, the forced transfer of natural resources from the shared domain of Aboriginal collectivities to the privatized ownership of newcomers, their descendants, and their corporate extensions has helped fuel the rise to global pre-eminence of what Roger C. Altman has described as "the Anglo-Saxon brand of market-based capitalism." The difficulty of the four nay-saying governments in coming to grips in the international community with their own genocidal heritages weakens their capacity to act with consistency and integrity as effective participants in the process of identifying, arbitrating, or punishing the terrible international crimes that have taken place in recent years in, for instance, Rwanda, the former Yugoslavia, Cambodia, East Timor, Sierra Leone, Sudan, Congo, Gaza, and Azerbaijan.

The continuing failure of both the Canadian and the Australian governments to embrace the UN's declaration certainly calls into question the sincerity and credibility of the apologies issued in 2008 by Prime Minister Kevin Rudd and especially by Prime Minister Stephen Harper. The latter bears the direct burden of responsibility for the Canadian government's decision in September 2007 to deny and negate, rather than recognize and affirm, the constitutional existence of Aboriginal and treaty rights in the world's main juridical venue of international relations. Rather than taking a global leadership role that would have drawn on Canada's recent achievements negotiating modern-day treaties and self-government agreements with Indigenous peoples, Harper chose to identify his country with the most retrograde and reactionary forces that continue to project the Columbian conquests into the twenty-first century.

CORPORATIONS AND GENOCIDE

The delegates to the World Council of Churches who assembled in Barbados in 1971 gave careful consideration to the genocidal consequences that sometimes arise from the industrial expansion of capitalist enterprise in new frontiers of resource extraction. As part of their program to combat racism, they addressed the conditions facing various Indian groups in South America. The delegates received expert reports on the subject from members of the Ethnology Department at the University of Berne. These social scientists concentrated on the industrial devastation inflicted on specific areas in the vast Amazonian rainforest. The installation by Texaco of a new refinery in a previously remote district of Ecuador was the subject of considerable attention. One of the experts in attendance presented evidence indicating that, as a direct result of Texaco's incursions, including road building, pollution, and the violence accompanying the rapid influx of new settlers, close to 90 per cent of the resident Kofan Indians had rapidly died off. With the view that the plight of this one group illustrated far larger processes affecting Indigenous peoples throughout the Western Hemisphere, the authors of the Barbados Declaration stated that those who actively advanced such outcomes, as well as those who remained complicit through their silence, "must be held responsible by default for crimes of ethnocide and connivance with genocide."[93] They called for the governments of nation-states to intervene to protect Indigenous peoples from "antagonistic forces," such as those industries contributing most heavily to "the expansion forces of the national frontier."[94]

The World Council of Churches gave expression within a predominantly Christian framework to some of the same urges of ecumenical exchange and cooperation that had permeated the World's Parliament of Religions during the World's Columbian Exposition in Chicago in 1893. Again the delegates grappled with the role and responsibilities of religious communities in the process of empire building and commercial exploitation. They considered the ethnographers' view that some Protestant missionaries were working closely with Texaco and other oil companies to persuade the Indians to accommodate rather than resist the exploitation of their Aboriginal lands. "A religious pretext," they indicated, "has too often justified the economic and human exploitation of the aboriginal population." After detailing a number of allegations, the ethnographers called on the churches to "suppress the practice of removing Indian children from their families for long periods in boarding schools where they are imbued with values not their own, converting them in this way into marginal individuals, incapable of living either in the larger national society or their native communities."

The ethnographers addressed the soul searching then taking place within some Christian communities. "We recognize that, recently, dissident elements within the churches are engaging in a conscious and radical self-evaluation of the evangelical process. The denunciation of the historical failure of the missionary task is now a common conclusion of such critical analyses." Those leading the discussion concluded, "to the degree that the religious missions do not assume these minimal obligations they, too, must be held responsible by default for crimes of ethnocide and connivance with genocide."[95] In supporting the position put before them, the religious leaders present at Bridgetown demonstrated once again the reality that representatives of Christian communities have often been present on both sides of the great contentions testing different interpretations of the rights and titles of the Indigenous peoples in the colonized world. In attempting to widen the scope and application of international law to defend the lives, rights, and cultures of the Indian peoples of South America, the Christian leaders carried on the tradition of lobbying for the protection of human rights embodied in the earlier work of, for instance, Bartolemé de las Casas, William Penn, Jeremiah Evarts, William Duncan, and Arthur O'Meara.

The effect of the looming Cold War on cutting short the financiers' trials at Nuremberg illustrates the powerful nature of the political forces insulating corporate directors from legal accountability for the role of their companies in perpetrating international crimes. At Nuremberg the bankers and industrialists responsible for building up the Nazi genocide machine were, with some few exceptions, not prosecuted let alone convicted. As Robert Jackson and others feared at the time, this failure to deal systematically with the criminality of the Third Reich's key business figures and the corporations they ran had the effect of entrenching the belief that the limited liability of corporate entities and their executive branches extended to a blanket immunity when they participate in perpetrating international crimes such as genocide. It contributed to shaping the kind of corporate culture that helped to steer the bloody anti-communist purges in, for instance, Indonesia towards a particularly vicious attempt to use mass murder as a means of ideological cleansing. The effort to remove ideological obstacles through the tactic of mass murder cleared the way for the conference organized by the Ford Foundation and Time-Life in Geneva in 1967. At this conference, access to Indonesia's rich resources, its cheap labour, and its large markets was put on offer to corporate delegations representing, among other enterprises, Chase Manhatten Bank, General Motors, Siemens, Goodyear, American Express, International Paper Company, and Alcoa.

There have been a number of attempts to hold corporate entities accountable for their role in the most severe crimes against humanity since the Nuremberg trials. Very serious issues were raised, for instance, about the role of Dow Chemical in producing the napalm that wrought such havoc when sprayed on the territories of the Indigenous populations of Indochina throughout the US military aggressions there. Indeed, arms manufacturers generally cannot indefinitely escape some reckoning with the issue of legal liability for the killing and maiming that is the primary purpose of the products they make. Similarly, the role of oil companies in the destruction of Aboriginal societies has been the subject of significant litigation and some media coverage. The role of Texaco and Chevron in the continued destruction of large parts of the rainforest in Ecuador, for instance, has remained the subject of court cases and political contention.[96] One of the organizations that has continued to advance some of the principles articulated in the Barbados Declaration is the Confederation of Indigenous Nationalities of Ecuador (CONAIE).[97] It would emerge at the beginning of the twenty-first century to become one of the most internationally engaged of South America's agencies of Aboriginal representation.

Much international attention has swirled around Shell Oil for backing the Nigerian dictatorship that, in 1995, executed activist Ken Saro-Wiwa and others for their role in leading the Ogoni resistance to the industrial desecration of their Aboriginal territories.[98] Similarly, U'wa activists from Columbia revisited many of the principles of the Barbados Declaration when, in 1999, they drew attention to the consequences for their people of the development schemes advanced in their territories by the Occidental Petroleum Company (OPC). Generally speaking, the ethnically and linguistically diverse Indigenous peoples of Colombia, but especially those in oil-rich areas, are subjected to terrible violence and intimidation from both sides in the ongoing brutalities of a deeply entrenched civil war. On one side are the formal and paramilitary armies of a heavily armed government that has become the third largest recipient of US military aid in the world. The Colombian government purchases many of its weapons systems from companies based in the territory of its close ally, Israel. On the other side are the Marxist forces of FARC, Latin America's oldest guerrilla army. The violence perpetrated on both sides is heavily permeated with deep and corrupt politics of oil extraction, the production and export of cocaine, and the many-faceted duplicity integral to the so-called War on Drugs.

The U'wa, together with their allies in Friends of the Earth, Rainforest Relief, and Amazon Watch, formed the U'wa Defense Working Group. This network attracted considerable attention in their peaceful protests aimed at the Fidelity Investment Company and, later, Bernstein Alliance Capital, both major shareholders in OPC.[99] This kind of transnational alliance replicated some of the tactics employed in the coalition supporting the Penan resistance to the logging of their traditional territory in Malaysia. Survival International and the European Parliament helped to internationalize this campaign. In Canada, the Lubicon Cree and the Ojibwa of northwestern Ontario stood at the centre of similar controversies. In both instances, government has aggressively intervened between corporations and those groups who have sought to hold corporations accountable for the genocidal cataclysms befalling some Aboriginal societies as a result of the industrial destruction of their indigenous political economies. Indeed, in one instance there seems to have been a concerted effort on the part of government to lift the burden of liability off a notorious corporate polluter by presenting itself as the guilty party in the near-obliteration of an Ojibwa community. In a small way this episode highlighted the lessons of the proceedings at Nuremberg, where there was major political pressure to exclude commercial corporations and their officers from prosecution for war crimes and crimes against humanity.

Between 1977 and 1979 a group known as the Anti-Mercury Ojibway Group (AMOG) responded to the polluting operations of the Reed Paper Mill at Dryden in northwestern Ontario. Reed's activities introduced toxic mercury throughout the English and Wabigoon rivers. This rich aquatic system had long been the prolific fishing domain of those Ojibwa peoples who settled in recent times at the Grassy Narrows and Whitedog reserves. AMOG was an alliance of Indian activists from these communities who joined together with a few Euro-Canadian social scientists, including Peter Usher, Hugh Brody, and Jennifer Keck.[100] AMOG sought to demonstrate how Reed's operations had overturned a whole way of life, including the physical, spiritual, and psychological equilibrium of the inhabitants of the Grassy Narrows and Whitedog communities. The effect of the loss of the fishery, AMOG argued, was no less traumatic than the loss of the buffalo for the Indigenous peoples of the North American prairies.[101] It was traumatic because, for thousands of years, the cultures and belief systems of the Aboriginal fishing societies have been deeply integrated with the life cycles of their aquatic prey. By proving in court that the loss of the fishery affected Indigenous peoples in ways that went far beyond the loss of one kind of food or the loss of employment as guides, the implication was that the polluting corporation must bear legal liability and even criminal responsibility for the immense human costs of the ecological and social collapse it helped to inflict.

This collapse was especially tragic at the federal Indian reserve of Grassy Narrows. The breakdown, involving a ghastly epidemic of all manner of self-abuse, family abuse, suicide, and homicide, is one of the most extreme and fully documented cases of social pandemonium recorded in recent North American history. In an article entitled "Choosing Your Poison," Peter Usher discussed the application of pressures to keep the key contentions of the Grassy Narrows and Whitedog people out of court and to contain the matter within an interpretive approach emphasizing government wrongdoing. His commentary highlighted particularly the complex and many-layered role in the affair of Anastasia Shkilnyk, a social scientist who moved between employment for the Canadian Department of Indian and Northern Affairs and the Grassy Narrows band as she researched her thesis for the Massachusetts Institute of Technology. According to Usher, there was a manipulative hidden agenda behind Shkilnyk's identification of the relocation of the Grassy Narrows band as the primary cause of their social breakdown. This interpretation, later published by Yale University Press as *A Poison Stronger than Love*, focused on the responsibility of the federal government, rather than that of the industrial polluter, for the breakdown of all social cohesion at Grassy Narrows. Although Shkilnyk did not totally discount the mercury poisoning as a factor in the social collapse, she minimized the loss of the fishery as "the last nail in the coffin."[102] In Shkilnyk's estimation, the poison stronger than love was alcohol, not mercury, as AMOG had worked so hard to demonstrate.

By the mid-1980s, the industrial polluter as well as the federal and provincial governments all settled out of court by agreeing to pay compensation to the damaged Indian bands. While Reed Paper admitted some blame in creating the conditions of the lethal chaos suffered by the Ojibwa, there was no legal precedent to clarify the liability or criminality of the polluters in the maiming and breakdown of Aboriginal societies. Dr Shkilnyk's involvement in the controversy casts an important light on the possible role of federal bureaucracies in such episodes. Part of the task assigned to these agencies, it seems, is to act as targets and receptacles of blame for the arguably genocidal consequences visited on Indigenous peoples by the process of breaking their connections with their Aboriginal lands and waters. The emphasis on federal wrongdoing towards their Aboriginal "clients" helps to divert attention away from corporate centres of private government.

In her controversial volume, Skilnyk observed that Grassy Narrows in the late 1970s displayed by far the most lethal combination of social maladies she had ever witnessed. She maintained that the pathologies of poverty, alienation, and internalized violence she chronicled in northwestern Ontario went far beyond the human suffering she had witnessed, for instance, in the squatter settlements of South American cities where large numbers of displaced people are annually absorbed. Of this Canadian Indian reserve she wrote, "I had never seen such hopelessness anywhere in the Third World."[103] In spite of this judgment, however, she condemned the AMOG activists and those of their ilk as "self-seeking groups" whose object was "the exploitation of Grassy Narrows people." Without addressing her own role as an influential interpreter of this appalling human tragedy, she concluded darkly, "the way in which the mercury issue was defined, managed, and politicized mirrors much of what is so wrong with our own mainstream society."[104]

An organization called Friends of the Lubicon (FOL) has worked along lines similar to those of AMOG and the alliance of environmentalists who attempted to assist the U'wa of Columbia and the Penan of Malaysia. The work, therefore, continues the quest to advance the principles outlined in the Barbados Declaration. After the Lubicon Crees in the Peace River District of northern Alberta had exhausted without resolution all the remedies available to them through the domestic courts, the FOL began to point a spotlight of attention at the role of the corporate sector in the affair. They concentrated especially on encouraging individual and corporate consumers to boycott the products of Daishowa, a Japanese pulp and paper company with a lucrative Crown licence to clear-cut trees on Lubicon hunting grounds. The FOL members put themselves at the nexus of an activist network with branches throughout North America, Europe, and, to a lesser extent, Japan. An important part of this alliance was the World Council of Churches, whose ecumenical arm in Canada was known first as Project North and then as the Aboriginal Rights Coalition. The role of this coalition of mainstream Christian churches in Canada represented a direct extension of the work leading to the formulation of the Barbados Declaration of 1971.

A UN official characterized the plight of the Lubicon Cree in 1990 as "the best-documented Aboriginal rights case in the world."[105] The reserveless Lubicons were passed over in 1899 by Crown negotiators of Treaty 8, and their effort to enter into some kind of modern-day treaty with the Crown has been frustrated by the judgments of the Alberta courts and the actions of the Alberta government. The Alberta government implemented especially draconian measures in the mid-1970s, passing legislation to close off *retroactively* the legal right of the Lubicons to freeze land transactions in their ancestral territories while their dispute was being litigated.[106] In other words, the government exercised legislative supremacy by reaching backward in time to change existing rules *after* it looked as though these rules were about to benefit an Indian group. The Lubicons spent thirteen years in Canadian courts in an effort to demonstrate that they have an Aboriginal title that has never been addressed through the procedures stipulated in the Royal Proclamation. They received considerable backing in this effort from the James Bay Crees of northern Quebec. According to the Lubicons' adviser, Fred Lennarson, most of the judges who heard the Indian group's arguments were in classic conflict-of-interest situations, having worked as lawyers for the complex of oil companies exploiting Lubicon lands.[107] The scope of this exploitation has been large. By 1983, four hundred oil wells had been drilled within a 24 kilometre radius of the Lubicons' settlement of Little Buffalo. By the end of the twentieth century, these wells had extracted somewhere in the neighbourhood of $8 billion in fossil fuel currency.[108]

According to Lennarson, the Lubicons withdrew from the process of domestic litigation only after it had been established that "there was not a single Canadian court which was prepared to hear a Lubicon Aboriginal land rights case against the federal government."[109] Beginning in the mid-1980s, therefore, the Lubicons and their far-flung network of supporters turned to the court of public opinion both domestically and internationally. One of the first oil and gas companies to exploit the Lubicons' traditional territory was Union Oil of California (Unocal). In its global operations, Unocal has been notorious for its poor environmental record and for its siding with particularly repressive regimes. For instance, Unocal invested heavily in drilling and pipeline operations in the oppressive military regime of Myanmar (Burma). In the process, the company backed the forced relocation of many Aboriginal communities, some of whose members were pressed into virtual slave labour. In Alberta, Unocal Corporation built a dangerous sour gas plant very close to the site that was under consideration in the Lubicons' negotiations to establish a reserve. By the early years of the twenty-first century, the company faced a lawsuit headed by the Alliance for Democracy and the National Lawyers Guild International Law Project for Human, Economic and Environmental Defense. This suit was aimed at revoking Unocal's corporate charter based on allegations of its "incorrigible recidivism" in breaking the laws of its host countries.[110]

Lubicon chief Bernard Ominayak and his advisers made a conscious decision to identify the dispossession of the Lubicons with more general histories of what has repeatedly happened to Indigenous peoples throughout the Americas and around the world. The Calgary Winter Olympics in 1988 provided a key venue for the initiative to raise the profile of the Lubicon land dispute to a higher international visibility. By infusing political controversy into the main cultural exposition of the Calgary Olympics, the Lubicons and their allies publicized their allegations that officials overseeing the operation of the oil and gas industry failed to respect the rule of law in their treatment of Indigenous peoples. The Lubicons invited officials in many museums in Europe and North America to refrain from lending Indian artifacts to Calgary's Glenbow Museum. The officers of the Glenbow had decided to bring together a comprehensive display of North American Indian artifacts, a large portion of which have historically been collected in Europe. Sponsored by Shell Oil, Petro-Canada, and the government of Canada, the Glenbow's project was entitled "The Spirit Sings." The Lubicons based their call for a boycott on allegations detailing the role of Shell and Petro-Canada in actively destroying the ability of the Lubicon to renew their Aboriginal way of life.

While the Lubicons' old way of life was effectively extinguished by the industrialization and alien privatization of their hunting grounds, no alternative instruments of collective survival were provided. There was no will to afford the Lubicons the resources and legal instruments they would need to make a successful transition to an alternative political economy capable of enabling the members of the community to retain their Aboriginal cohesion. The Lubicons justified the call for a boycott by presenting their view of the disparity between the positive imagery of the museum display and the negative treatment of a living Aboriginal society by the event's sponsors. The Lubicon people asked: Why should representatives of the oil and gas industry go unchallenged in displaying North America's Aboriginal heritage to enhance the prestige of their corporations, when these same corporations had been directly responsible for preventing living Indian societies from maintaining some degree of continuity with that same heritage? Why should the oil and gas industry, together with its government licensors and sponsors, benefit from celebrating the Aboriginal past when these same agencies were so deeply implicated in denying the existence of Aboriginal title as a means for the Lubicon Cree to negotiate a viable future for themselves?

In the late 1980s these arguments won a number of adherents inside and outside Indian Country. When, for instance, the Petro-Canada Corporation called on citizens to Share the Flame of the cross-Canada Olympic Torch Run, Lubicon supporters organized alternative ceremonies with the counter-slogan, Share the Shame. Following the Olympics, the Lubicons were forced to contend with the opening of a new resource frontier in their traditional territories. In 1991 the Japan-based Daishowa-Marubeni International Corporation opened the largest hardwood pulp mill in Canada 100 kilometres from the main Lubicon settlement of Little Buffalo.[111] The Lubicons' ancestral lands had been earmarked to provide a large part of the new mill's supply of trees. Responding to this latest development, the Lubicons and their supporters, some of whom constituted themselves as the Friends of the Lubicon, took their case against Daishowa into the marketplace. They called for boycotts of all those companies that used Daishowa's paper packaging.

Among the major companies who sought to avoid boycotts by shifting their business away from Daishowa were Woolworth's, A and W, Roots,

Safeway, Kentucky Fried Chicken, Pizza Pizza, Country Style Donuts, and the Body Shop. The apparent success of the Friends of the Lubicon caused Daishowa first to cease its logging operations on Lubicon lands and then to seek an injunction in 1995 preventing the activists from publicly conducting their boycott. For three years the case made its costly way through the courts, projecting as it went all the subtle silencing effects of libel chill. The ante was raised yet further when Daishowa attempted to get a ban on the publications of those lawyers and academics who have characterized Daishowa's actions as a classic example of what has come to be known as a SLAPP – a strategic lawsuit against public participation. For its attempts to silence its critics, Daishowa earned a citation from the *Multinational Monitor* as one of the "Ten Worst Corporations of 1996."[112]

With the assistance of lawyer Clayton Ruby as well as the Sierra Legal Defense Fund, the Friends of the Lubicon successfully defended themselves. In this instance the rights to freedom of speech prevailed over the asserted property rights of Daishowa. Mr Justice James MacPherson of the Ontario Court's General Division decided that "the manner in which the Friends have performed their picketing is a model of how such activities should be conducted." Moreover, he ruled that the "current state of affairs for the Lubicon Crees ... deserves the adjectives tragic, desperate and intolerable."[113] The judge did qualify his vindication of the Friends of the Lubicon by criticizing them for associating in their publicity the word "genocide" with Daishowa's relationship to the Indian group. A significant portion of the trial was devoted to testimony concerning the meaning of this most potent term. Among those who gave expert testimony was Professor Ward Churchill, author of *A Little Matter of Genocide*.[114] Another witness who spoke about his understanding of genocide was the Anglican archbishop Edward Scott. This clergyman was asked to comment on the discussions in the World Council of Churches since 1971, when the Barbados Declaration identified some frontier industrial activities with the concept of "connivance with genocide." Archbishop Scott replied: "The World Council [of Churches] took the view that people are involved within cultural contexts, and that their whole being as human beings relates to the culture. And if you start destroying the cultural aspects, then you're destroying the person. So they saw 'genocide' as more than killing the individual people or the group of people, but that which also destroyed the very core of their being and gave them meaning as human beings and as a community."[115]

Lawyer Bruce Clark faced reprimands, arrests, an involuntary psychological assessment, and a well-documented RCMP media "smear campaign" in his unorthodox efforts to represent his Aboriginal clients on a number of issues, including allegations that the Canadian judiciary were complicit in allowing the international crime of genocide. One of his clients was William Jones Ignace, the most elderly member of the Ts'peten Defenders, who was widely stigmatized as a terrorist in the Battle of Gustafsen Lake in 1995. In the subsequent trial, neither Ignace nor Clark could be persuaded to back down from their contention that the law officers judging the case were guilty of complicity in genocide for failing to acknowledge their institutionalized conflicts of interest in arbitrating Aboriginal assertions of sovereignty and jurisdiction. On its way to disbarring Clark from professional practice in 1999, the Law Society of Upper Canada conducted an investigation into a number of accusations pressed against the controversial jurist. The Law Society's report, written by Clayton Ruby and Gavin MacKenzie, indicated, "The genocide of which Mr. Clark speaks is real, and has very nearly succeeded in destroying the Native Canadian community that flourished here when European settlers arrived. No one who has seen many of our modern First Nations communities can remain untouched by this reality."[116]

The detailed consideration given at Barbados in 1971 by the World Council of Churches to the alleged role of some corporations in the genocidal destruction of Indigenous peoples has continued to resonate across the decades into the twenty-first century. The focus on corporate involvement in genocide as adopted by some branches of the Christian ecumenical movement became a significant factor in the response to the proliferation of war crimes and crimes against humanity committed in Sudan. Sudan is one of those African countries whose internal conflicts are closely bound up with the artificial character of the national boundaries its citizens have inherited from the imperial powers of Europe. These imposed national boundaries often conflict with many Aboriginal configurations of territory that have emerged from thousands of years of local relations between and among Indigenous peoples.

In 2001 the Presbyterian Church of Sudan initiated a civil action against a Calgary-based Canadian oil company, Talisman Energy.[117] The plaintiffs alleged that Talisman had aided and abetted the Sudanese government in genocide and in a host of related atrocities, including ethnic cleansing, torture, rape, slavery and the confiscation of property. The allegations arose in the context of a one-sided civil war giving rise to the violent elimination since 1983 of more than 2 million victims. The vast majority of these victims lived along the southern margins of the Sahara Desert, where many of the Indigenous peoples mix Christianity with their own local traditions of Aboriginal spirituality. The Sudanese army and its attending paramilitary forces known as the *janaweed* have attacked these Black Africans at the behest of the Khartoum-based government, one dominated by Islamic theocrats and Arab expansionists. This assault on the Indigenous peoples of southern Sudan, including the Nuer and Dinka, was executed with a full array of high-tech weaponry, such as fighter jets and heavily-armed helicopters, all purchased with revenues from oil extraction. The plaintiffs alleged that several oil companies, including Talisman, have profited from, and participated in, the violent removal of Indigenous peoples from the oil-rich lands of southern Sudan.

The Presbyterian Church of Sudan brought its civil suit before a federal court in New York. The weakness of international law enforcement in the age of impunity created the background for this resort to civil litigation in a matter set amid such blatant episodes of the most heinous kinds of international crime.[118] The failure to apprehend, try, and punish at least some of those most guilty for the atrocities can be interpreted as an international extension of the same breakdown in the US domestic sphere that was illustrated by the failures of law enforcement agencies to deal with their own many-faceted involvements in the well-documented conspiracies that led to the murder of the Martin Luther King Jr in 1968. In the age of impunity, the lawyers for the King family, as well as those seeking to represent the victims of the Sudanese genocide, attempted to sue some of the alleged culprits through the US federal courts as a substitute for the flawed or non-existent processes of criminal prosecution.

The lawyers for the Presbyterian plaintiffs invoked the *Alien Tort Claims Act* to seek damages from Talisman Energy, which had a New York office. Significantly, the ATCA was enacted in 1789 primarily as a means of assisting with the prohibition and punishment of piracy. The struggle to outlaw and prevent piracy on the high seas helped to establish the framework for the emergence of international law from what used to be referred to as the law of nations. The Talisman case could be viewed as an effort to help put some checks on forms of corporate piracy that have developed especially in those parts of the world where there are few legal restraints on exercising the imperatives of untrammeled power. The use of the ATCA as a substitute for the elaboration and uniform enforcement of international criminal law, but particularly in relation to the involvement of corporations in human rights violations, is emerging as an issue of hot contention in the United States.[119] One of the ironies of this contentiousness is reflected in the tension between the claim that corporations have the rights and protections of "natural persons" and the characterization of these same entities as "artificial persons" in their relationship to the responsibilities and liabilities generally associated with citizenship.[120] The ATCA states: "The district courts shall have original jurisdiction of any civil action by an alien for tort only, committed in violation of the law of nations or a treaty of the United States."

The lawyers for Talisman Energy sought precedents in the Nuremberg trials, noting that all the persecutions against financiers and industrialists were pressed against individuals rather than the corporations they represented. They argued that corporations "are legally incapable of violating the law of nations." In March 2003 Judge Allen G. Schwartz of the Federal District Court of Southern New York rejected the defendants "myopic reading of the complaints." Just a day before his accidental death, Judge Schwartz allowed the case to proceed in a decision that Eric Reeves welcomed as a landmark ruling. A college professor whose role in calling international attention to genocidal crimes in Sudan has been compared to that of E.D. Morel in exposing the atrocities visited by King Leopold's regime on the people of Congo,[121] Reeves described Schwartz's decision as a judicial precedent "crafted with the greatest skill, the most scrupulous care, and with superb moral intelligence."[122] In his ruling, Judge Schwartz drew on the few but highly significant Nuremberg prosecutions of industrialists in ways that reflect a broader shift in the juridical interpretation of these proceedings. In his survey of way the Nuremberg precedents have been viewed in the Talisman case and other instances of civil litigation, Gwynne Skinner wrote: "The growth of multinational corporations over the last twenty-five years, the manner in which they operate, and the lack of safeguards ensuring good corporate governance, justify and provide strong support for holding corporations liable under Nuremberg standards."[123]

In 2006 Talisman Energy was released from the adversarial grip of this litigation without any convictions. The plaintiffs were found not to have met the high standards of evidence necessary to make the company legally liable for the damages sought.[124] By this time, however, the Calgary-based company had already responded to the bad publicity and the pressures of a well-organized campaign to persuade owners of Talisman shares to divest themselves of these stocks. In 2003 Talisman had sold its Sudanese properties to an oil company based in India. This transfer of assets was part of a more general pattern whereby Asian interests, but especially those of China, have asserted increasing financial and political control over the natural resources of Africa.[125] While negotiations led to a relative state of peace in southern Sudan, the western province of Darfur became the scene of similar conflicts both in terms of the nature of the violence on the ground and in the contest to influence international public opinion. In the summer of 2008, the chief prosecutor of the International Criminal Court responded to this ongoing violence by issuing a warrant against Sudan's president, Omar Hassan al-Bashir. The ICC's prosecutor alleged that al-Bashir had directed the genocidal slaughter and displacement by government and *janaweed* forces at many non-Arab civilians.[126]

Then, in January 2009, a coalition of human rights organizations led by Investors against Genocide sought to make PetroChina, the publicly traded wing of the China National Petroleum Company, accountable for its involvement in helping to fund and facilitate the human rights violations in Darfur. The coalition sought to persuade the United Nations Global Compact, an association of business corporations chaired by UN secretary general Ban Ki-moon, to act against PetroChina. The UN Global Compact group has issued a ten-part mission statement composed of general statements affirming the ideals of human rights, labour rights, and environmental protection.[127]

In the spring of 2007 Fidel Castro published an article introducing yet another perspective on genocide. The ailing Cuban leader called attention to a new industrial threat to the ecology of biodiversity and to the prospects for the healthy survival of poor peasants throughout Latin America. In "The Internationalization of Genocide," Castro pointed to a US-led plan to divert agricultural production throughout the Western Hemisphere from the growing of food to the growing of crops for biofuels such as ethanol. Castro predicted that the plan to build up the infrastructure of the agro-energy business would take nourishment from the poor even as it would result in the further elimination of forests: "The world will see how many hungry people on this planet will cease to consume corn. What is worse, let the poor countries receive some financing to produce ethanol from corn or any other foodstuff and very soon not a single tree will be left standing to protect humanity from climate change."[128] A Cuban colleague of Castro put it even more bluntly. "What we are witnessing," asserted Osvaldo Martinez, "is the conflict between the right of human beings to eat and the 'right' of some human beings to drive powerful cars."[129]

BLOOD MINERALS AND GENOCIDE IN THE POLITICAL ECONOMY OF CENTRAL AFRICA

Many of the West's most extravagant fantasies of debasement and enrichment have been expressed through intervention in the domestic economy of Central Africa. King Leopold II's manipulation of his dubious title to the vast territory drained by the Congo River illustrates the dichotomy. Leopold's regime epitomized the gap between bold declarations of benign intent and corporate gorging on new frontiers to feed capitalism's unrelenting appetite for increased profit. During the culminating era of Victorian imperialism, Leopold succeeded in making himself the trustee of the Congo River basin on behalf of a strange association of "civilized" states. Claiming he would atone for the crimes of slavery by working to bring the advantages of trade, education, and modern medicine to the Congo's Indigenous peoples, Leopold put his African proprietorship at the service of corporate *concessionaires*. With the backing of Leopold's henchmen, these corporate privateers forced African workers to inject the necessary ingredient of labour into the lucrative flow of blood rubber. Rubber sap and, before that, elephant tusks proved to be only the beginning of the riches available for plunder in Central Africa. In the twentieth century, the Congo, but especially its eastern districts, was discovered to hold a treasure trove of rare minerals. Some of these minerals, such as niobium, cassiterite, cobalt, uranium, zinc, and manganes, acquired added value with the rise of computer technology, nuclear weaponry, aerospace industries, and modern communications systems, including vast networks of personal cell phones.

Many of the international companies seeking enrichment from Congo's vast reserves of amazingly diverse and valuable minerals worked with government partners in the military-industrial complex to install an ambitious and ruthless military dictator into the position initially created by King Leopold. On the way to his obtaining in 1965 the job as Congo's chief kleptocrat, General Joseph-Désiré Mobutu took part in the coup resulting in the arranged assassination of Patrice Emery Lumumba – the Congo's original lightening rod of national unity and indigenous self-determination. A trade unionist who had boldly embraced the spirit of pan-Africanism and the Non-Aligned Movement at Africa's first ever indigenous pan-African conference at Accra Ghana in 1958, Lumumba would emerge two years later as the Congo's first elected prime minister. He was allowed to serve his people for only a few weeks before he was removed from office and killed on the orders of officials in the United States and Belgium.[130] Once he consolidated his control of indigenous politics, General Mobutu changed his name to Mobutu Sese Seko Kuku Ngbendu waza Banga, or Sese Seko for short. The English translation of the dictator's name is "the all-powerful warrior who, because of his endurance and inflexible will to win, will go from conquest to conquest leaving fire in his wake." In 1971 Sese Seko continued his policy of African "authenticity" by reconstituting the Congo as Zaire.

Mobutu's regime provided a base of strategic operations in the mineral-rich heart of Central Africa for all sorts of interests aligned with the US-led side of the Cold War. Many of these activities included the hiring and deployment of mercenary soldiers who took part in conflicts throughout a region that was just beginning to emerge from the formal imperialism of the European powers. Many of these mercenary soldiers came from White South Africa and Rhodesia, countries ruled by governments that equated their apartheid systems of racial segregation with the imperatives of anti-communism. The expanding enterprise of Private Military Contractors – PMCs – in the twenty-first century grew from the business of providing mercenary soldiers to those governments, businesses, and crime syndicates that could afford to hire them. This history has made Central Africa the scene of an especially elaborate and busy array of contractors that continue to combine the extraction of valuable minerals and, increasingly, petroleum with the commercialized visitation of death, destruction, and all the traumas of mass displacement on the region's Indigenous peoples. The escalation of these for-profit cycles of violence has made the eastern Congo the scene of the largest-scale genocide since the Second World War. Between 1996 and 2009 the toll of premature deaths generated by invasion and military conflicts in the region was estimated to be approximately 6 million.[131] This number approaches the magnitude of the genocidal abuses inflicted during the first four decades following King Leopold's founding of the Congo Free State in 1885.[132]

This background of remote-control violence in Central Africa has made the region one of the incubators of the terror economy that would become so important in the overall world economy, especially after the events of September 11, 2001. As gruesomely demonstrated by, for instance, the recent history of oil extraction in Sudan, Nigeria, Colombia, and Guatemala, the business of removing oil, gas, and minerals from the ground is often quite closely connected to the mercenary business of murdering and/or displacing those Indigenous peoples that get in the way. The connection between these two branches of capitalist enterprise became starkly clear in the killing fields interspersed throughout the Great Lakes region of Central Africa. One of these sites of human suffering and carnage is the desolate containment camps in the northwestern quarter of Uganda, where over a million internally displaced people were corralled in the course of a government feud with hostile local warlords.

The agony experienced by many millions of common people in Central Africa is symbolized by the eerie translucent glow emanating from one of the region's most characteristic gems. The lethal mystique permeating blood diamonds exported from many of Africa's war zones has helped to crystallize public sensitivity to the web of connections linking some forms of mineral extraction with contract killing. Just as blood diamonds were closely associated with Mobutu's kleptocracy, and as blood rubber oozed forth from Leopold's crimes against humanity, so blood cell phones have become the most recent icon representing the plunder of Africa's indigenous wealth. Cell phones cannot work without electronic components made from columbite-tantalite, col-tan. The eastern Congo is one of the major world sources of industrial-grade coltan.[133]

In his testimony to a congressional subcommittee investigating in 2001 the abuses of human rights in the mineral-rich districts of Central Africa, journalist Wayne Madsen spoke of the role of "unscrupulous international mining companies" that often help stimulate "ethnic and civil turmoil" in order to turn the chaos to their own advantage. They exploit the violence in order "to fill their own coffers with conflict diamonds, gold, copper, platinum and other special minerals including one, columbite-tantilite, also know as coltan, which is a primary component of computer microchips and printed circuit boards."[134] Elsewhere Madsen has written of how the "overt and covert forces" of Central Africa's terror economy "continuously sought to fracture the [Congo] nation into warring parties ... into fiefdoms controlled by warlords who act on behalf of Western mining and oil companies."[135] Some of these warlords made a specialty of recruiting and exploiting child soldiers as well as deploying the violence of mass rape as the means of imposing the corrosive dominance of their fighting forces.

In the final decade of the twentieth century, Paul Kagame became the primary military point man for the many Anglo-American cartels involved in extracting, exporting, and transforming the mineral and oil wealth emanating from Central Africa. As a child, Kagame was forced to flee with his family members from Rwanda to neighbouring Uganda during a severe onslaught of ethnic antagonism directed at his own Tutsi population. In Uganda, Kagame befriended a fellow Tutsi, Yoweri Museveni. With the aim of acquiring political, military, and economic power in Central Africa, Museveni and Kagame became prominent commanders in the guerrilla units of the National Resistance Army. This activity culminated in a military coup that brought Museveni to presidential power in Uganda in 1986.

The new Ugandan leader extended his friend and fellow tribesman great latitude to continue to build up the Tutsi element of Uganda's armed forces. As part of this process, Kagame and some members of the military intelligence unit he commanded were sent to Cuba, where they received training in political activism and guerrilla warfare tactics. With the Cold War beginning to wind down, Museveni then sent Kagame to take part in an officers' training course at Fort Leavenworth in Kansas in 1990. In this fashion, Kagame joined the American imperium along with other elite soldiers drawn from countries the world over.[136] After this stint in the United States, Kagame was given overt and covert support by both the national security state and its favoured complex of military, mining, and oil-extraction companies active in Central Africa. Indeed, with his help, many key Anglo-American business interests were integrated into the activities of the Tutsi-dominated fighting forces that became well organized first in Uganda and then spread their military sprouts throughout the Great Lakes region into Rwanda, Burundi, and the eastern Congo. In this fashion a domain of French colonial enterprise became subject to the informal control of English-speaking polities.

Since the 1980s, therefore, Museveni, Kagame, and their corporate and government backers have been deeply engaged in making the Ugandan army the seed institution of the Tutsi-dominated Rwandan Patriotic Front (RPF). The military successes of this well-equipped and well-trained fighting unit would prove instrumental in elevating Kagame to a position of political dominance in Rwanda. On his way to becoming the Rwandan president in 2000, Kagame cooperated with Museveni in asserting direct and indirect control over a network of favoured warlords dominating many of the eastern Congo's most lucrative mining sites.

The Rwandan civil war that brought Kagame to power reached genocidal proportions in April 1994 after the RPF and its backers covertly deployed a sophisticated missile system to shoot down a plane carrying Juvenal Habyalimana and Cyprien Ntaryamira, the Hutu presidents of Rwanda and Burundi. The passengers of the doomed airplane also included members of the French pilots' families as well as government ministers and other top officials. According to Wayne Madsen, investigators from the United Nations and the French government have characterized this covert strike as an act of international terrorism. Many initially blamed the missile strike on Kagame's enemies. This well-cultivated misapprehension has helped to invest the episode with the aura of a false-flag operation.

The elimination of Habyalimana had terrible consequences for Rwanada's moderate Hutus as well as its Tutsi minority. The targeting of the presidential airplane initiated a crime spree of historic proportions that opened the way for the dramatic build-up of Kagame's and Museveni's US-backed proxy armies in Central Africa. From the initial missile attack, to the negotiation of contracts with private military companies involved in the Tutsi ascendance, to the apportionment of mining and oil leases in Africa's Great Lakes region, many of the logistical features of this classic example of privatized empire building have been coordinated by a shadowy

Washington-based "front" identified by Madsen as the International Strategic and Tactical Organization.[137]

In 1993 Canadian General Roméo Dallaire was appointed head of the small United Nations Assistance Mission sent to Rwanda to oversee the implementation of a fragile peace agreement. With Habyalimana gone, Hutu extremists, including notorious gangs of *interahamwe* thugs, began exterminating their Tutsi neighbours at an accelerating pace. Urged on by the hate speech of anti-Tutsi radio announcers and army officers, this surge of civilian violence produced almost a million victims during several months. Dallaire is very explicit about who is to blame for the "sabotage" in 1994 of his understaffed, under-resourced peace keeping mission. In *Shake Hands with the Devil* the General writes, "The [UN] Security Council under the overbearing weight of the United States had once again sold us out." [138]

Not surprisingly Dallaire's vivid eye-witness account of the genocide seems blind to the role of the RPF as a proxy army for those Anglo-American interests seeking to displace competing cartels in a part of the world once viewed as France's own *chasse garde* – its private hunting ground.[139] As a graduate of the US Marine Corps Command and Staff College in Quantico, Virginia, Dallaire's own training at a core institution of the military-industrial complex was similar to that of Kagame. The Canadian general clearly admired his fellow soldier. Dallaire reported his initial opinion of Kagame based on a meeting in 1993: "A truly impressive leader [who] perhaps deserved the sobriquet that the media had given him: the Napoleon of Africa."[140] The Western media's lionization of Kagame as Africa's Napoleon leaves unexamined the derisive irony that would be understood by many Black intellectuals of giving the RPF's military leader the name of Toussaint L'Overture's primary nemesis and executioner.

Once they achieved military mastery in Rwanda, the soldiers of the RPF pursued fleeing Hutu refugees into the Lake Kivu region of eastern Zaire. These migrants did include bands of *interahamwe* killers. As subsequent events would demonstrate, however, Kagame's military interventions beyond Rwanda's borders had more to do with the expansionary muscle flexing of his armed forces than with imposing justice on Hutu genocidaires. As part of this process of enlarging the geographic extent of Kagame's and Museveni's power base, the US military contractor, Kellogg, Brown, and Root (KBR), then a subsidiary of the massive Halliburton Company, built a military base in Rwanda near the border with the Congo.[141] There the US proxy army received training from Military Professional Resources Inc., a private military contractor based in Alexandria, Virginia. According to Madsen, KRB is also reported also to have built training camps for Kagame's forces in Ethiopia.[142] The main objective of all this military activity was to prepare African ground forces for the task of removing the spent and decrepit regime of Mobutu Sese Seko from power.

To achieve this purpose, the full force of the Ugandan and Rwandan armies was channelled into support for the insurrection led by Laurent

Kabila, a weathered veteran of Africa's Cold War conflicts who had once fought Mobutu's forces beside Che Guevara and his small band of Cuban revolutionaries. As part of the process of providing logistical support for Kabila's Alliance of Democratic Forces for the Liberation of Congo-Zaire, Bechtel Corporation provided the anti-Mobutu forces with strategically vital satellite images and infrared images. When Kabila took power in 1997, he reconstituted Mobutu's Zaire as the Democratic Republic of Congo. Bechtel was rewarded for its role in the change of government when its subsidiary, Nexant Corporation, was chosen as the main contractor to build a pipeline from Uganda to Kenya to export petroleum discovered under the waters of Lake Albert and Lake Victoria. Shell and the China Petroleum Company are also involved in the project. [143]

Once in power, Kabila did not deliver as was expected of him by Kagame, Museveni, and many of their foreign backers. Consequentially, the Rwandan and Ugandan armies intervened in 1998 to remove the new leader from office. They were opposed by the armed forces of Zimbabwe, Angola, and Namibia, which defended Kabila's government. Soldiers from Chad, Libya, and Sudan also entered conflict zones, where they joined in a multi-sided conflict involving at least twenty-five armed groups. The result of this increasingly complex conflagration is sometimes referred to as Africa's World War, a conflict that broke up the country into four distinct zones, each governed chaotically by its own combination of warlords and national armed forces. An agreement negotiated in Sun City, South Africa, in 2002 resulted in a brief easing of the hostilities, but the underlying causes of the conflict have continued to destabilize the region.

Ever since the Belgian government formally withdrew its imperial agents from Africa, the division of the Congo into smaller polities has long been a favoured expedient of neo-colonialism. This tactic was first attempted in July 1960, for instance, when 6,000 Belgian soldiers intervened to back the secession of the southern province of Katanga, the site of rich copper, gold, and uranium reserves. The external hostility to a united Congo forms one aspect a more concerted and systematic resistance on the part of the US government and the former imperial powers to any manifestations of pan-African ideas that animated, for instance, W.E.B. Du Bois, Kwame Nkruhmah, Patrice Lumumba, Malcolm X, and Bob Marley.

The rapid export of the Congo's mineral wealth continued throughout the conflict. In fact, according to a panel of experts who submitted four reports to the UN Security Council, the proliferation of violence has helped to facilitate what they referred to as "mass-scale looting."[144] The beneficiaries of this looting include many high-tech military companies, including Lockheed Martin, Halliburton, Northrup Grumman, Boeing, Raytheon, General Electric, and Bechtel. They include electronics and software giants such as Sony, Motorola, Compaq, Nokia, Alcatel, Ericsson, and Microsoft as well as metal and component producers such as Cabot Corporation, Germany's H.C. Starck, and China's Nigncxia. The list of foreign mining companies operating in the Democratic Republic of Congo is long. Prominent among them are the US-based American Mineral Fields and Leon Templesman and Son as well as South African-based AngloGold Ashanti.

A number of Canadian mining and oil companies have staked claims to some of the Congo's natural resources. These companies include Vancouver-based International Panorama Resources, First Quantum Mining, Banro Mining, and Barrick Gold. Barrick's Watsu mine in Ituri province is considered to be the richest of its kind in the world. Barrick Gold was founded in 1983 by philanthropist Peter Munk with help from arms dealer Adnan Khashoggi. One of the most prominent Saudi financiers of the Pakistan-based Bank of Credit and Commerce International, Khashoggi was deeply involved in the Iran-Contra scandal. Barrick's directors have included the former Canadian prime minister Brian Mulroney and the former CIA director and US president George H.W. Bush.

Many aviation companies have thrived in Central Africa in the strategic zone between the servicing of mining enterprises and the provision of transport to private military contractors whose business it is to procure mercenary soldiers as well as logistical support for warlords, governments, and other customers. Museveni's government retained the London branch of Hill and Knowlton to sanitize its public image in the Western media, while one of Kagame's most effective PR consultants has been Andrew Young of GoodWorks International.[145] Hill and Knowlton is the notorious PR firm that manufactured consent in 1990 for US president George H.W. Bush's First Gulf War by concocting a fraudulent tale about the killing of babies in a Kuwaiti hospital by the Iraqi army.

The rush to exploit the spoils of Central Africa has clearly been integral, therefore, to the waves of genocide that have made that region one of the laboratories for the global terror economy in the twenty-first century. Indeed, the most ruthless and life-destroying attributes of capitalist neo-colonialism are unmistakable in this part of the world – one that seemed remote from mainstream media scrutiny in the West until President Barack Obama's Kenyan ancestry helped to draw attention to the region.

Any careful assessment of the role of the military-industrial complex in the Rwandan genocide opens up the possibility that this particular international crime came about not for the reasons that General Dallaire and others have alleged. There is evidence to indicate that the victims of the killing spree of 1994 were regarded by key individuals in the national security state as mere collateral damage to be sacrificed on the altar of geopolitics. By equipping Kagame's forces to remove moderate Hutus from the levers of authority, the way was opened for the installation in Central Africa of Tutsi-dominated fighting force to serve the ambitions of a tight network of private military contractors and resource extraction firms.

The antagonism towards Tutsi people felt by Hutus and many other ethnic groups throughout the Great Lakes region has deep and substantial roots in the history of the European colonization of Central Africa. German and later Belgian officials who colonized Rwanda and Burundi beginning in the late nineteenth century developed bizarre theories about local hierarchies of peoples. These theories were informed by Victorian conceptions of anthropology that were permeated with heavy doses of Social Darwinism and scientific racism. From this intellectual and ideological mix emerged the hypothesis that Tutsi people, many of whom are taller and have fairer complexions than other African groups, were descended from a kind of conquering master race that had migrated into Central Africa from Ethiopia.

The Christian churches and imperial governors expressed their theories by imposing a system of registry on all Rwandans. Each individual was assigned an identity as either Hutu or Tutsi, often an artificial distinction in a society characterized by considerable ethnic blending. To be classified as a member of the Tutsi minority carried with it many advantages, including superior access to European education, the eligibility to apply for lucrative forms of land tenure, and preferred status in the competition for good jobs as assistants and advisers to colonial administrators. This favoritism naturally gave rise to growing resentment from the majority Hutu population. In the flawed anthropology of Social Darwinism, the Hutu were classified as members of the inferior Bantu family of tribes and peoples.[146] As Mahmood Mamdani has written in his reflections on the historical background of the Rwandan genocide, "Hutu was constructed as a subject identity alongside Tutsi as an identity of power."[147] The inflammation of this ethnic divide did not end with the formal severing of Rwanda and Burundi from Belgian control in 1962. Thereafter the government of France tried to expand its informal influence in the region by fanning and exploiting Hutu resentment towards the elite status that many Tutsis inherited from their roles of privilege in the old system of European imperialism.

It is fair to ask if the foreign backing extended to Kagame's and Museveni's well-armed and well-financed forces in Central Africa renews an old and unfortunate pattern that has cultivated Tutsi collaborators as the favoured agents and facilitators of imperial rule in the Great Lakes region. Throughout the global history of formal imperialism, the forces of colonization have often channelled preferred status and support to the expansionary policies of particular Aboriginal groups. In the seventeenth century, for instance, the commercial and evangelical agents of the French empire in North America initially identified the powerful Huron Confederacy as their key allies in pursuit of imperial goals. Alternatively, the Protestant makers of the Dutch and British empires in North America worked closely with the Mohawk Nation and their fellow Longhouse polities in building up the imperial role of New Netherlands and New York. In the course of quelling the Sepoy Mutiny of 1857, the British imperial government in India developed especially close military ties with some Sikh groups in the Punjabi region. This imperial incorporation of the Sikh military caste would provide the British armed forces with an abundant supply of well-disciplined soldiers in two world wars. Similarly the Ndebele people, a breakaway faction of Zulus, were transformed into favoured agents of imperial rule after their initial resistance to foreign domination in the South African polity that was named after, and built up by, Cecil Rhodes. Another variation on this theme calls attention to the prominent role of Ibn Saud and members of his Wahabi clan in the recent history of the Arabian Peninsula. In 1933 Saud and his entourage became the preferred local business partners of Standard Oil Company of California. This alliance was built upon after the Second World War by the US government, with enormous geopolitical consequences that continue to this day.

Accordingly, the foreign stimulation and exploitation of ethnic divisions in Central Africa represent a contemporary continuation of a very old strategy of empire building. The frequent failure of the mainstream media to identify and explain the economic factors underlying the genesis of ethnic and religious violence is often a factor in the perpetuation and intensification of that violence.[148] This failure of analysis and interpretation helps to feed deep prejudices and stereotypes that classically result in the blaming of the victims of neo-colonialism for their often poor and chaotic living conditions. At the same time, the diversion of attention away from the economic factors driving ethnic and religious conflict often results in the whitewashing of the corporate and military interests that arm and promote violence with impunity.

Such failures of interpretation can easily be connected to the biases and distortions that have made the UN's International Criminal Tribunal for Rwanda (ICTR) the site of a clear-cut example of one-sided victors' justice. This bias has so far shielded Paul Kagame and his far-flung network of Tutsi-dominated soldiers and warlords from prosecution for their role in the larger genocide that has drenched Central Africa, but especially eastern Congo, with blood. Even within Rwanda itself the evidence seems to point to many crimes against humanity for which the RPF may be responsible. According to Peter Erlinder, the ICTR's chief prosecutor, Carla Del Ponte, was removed from her position after she sought to press charges against Kagame and other high-ranking Tutsis in the Rwandan government for various crimes, including shooting down the airplane carrying Juvenal Habyalimana. From the moment she joined the ICTR, Del Ponte was critical of it for its biases and blind spots. The tribunal had become "little more than a means for the international community to absolve itself of its responsibilities for failing to act to prevent or limit the genocide," Del Ponte argued.[149] Erlinder's investigation also extended to former ICTR prosecutor, Louise Arbour, now a Canadian Supreme Court judge. Erlinder alleges that Arbour suppressed information about the identity of those who committed the terrorist act that sparked the Rwandan genocide.[150]

Gradually the important role of Kagame's Tutsi-dominated army in the Congo's genocidal debacle has come to light, causing the governments of Sweden, the Netherlands, Spain, and Germany to cut off aid to Rwanda.

In a surprise move, in January 2009 Kagame ordered the arrest of Laurent Nkunda, one of the Tutsi strong men in the Congo responsible for much bloodshed and the diversion of vast mineral wealth for export through Rwanda and Uganda. Kagame's effort to appease international public opinion by apprehending Nkunda took place as new waves of violence swept over the eastern Congo. This violence has proliferated in spite of 17,000 UN soldiers who were sent to the region. That force has proven ineffective. As General Dallaire demonstrated, UN commanders are not above taking sides or favouring the policies and geopolitical orientations of their own national armed forces. Nor are the rank-and-file soldiers in UN uniforms always above committing the very acts they are meant to prevent.[151] Meanwhile, the International Criminal Court embarked on its first prosecution at The Hague by charging, arresting, and then trying Thomas Lubunga Dyilo, a warlord identified with the Union of Congolese Patriots. At different times this member of the Hema tribe has allied himself with both Kagame's and Museveni's forces. Lubunga was accused of the crime of recruiting and deploying child soldiers under the age of fifteen.[152]

CAPITALISM, ECOLOGY, AND SURVIVAL

The emergence of the future capitalist superpower from the British Empire was based in significant measure on a disagreement over whether the Aboriginal lands and citizens of the Indian Country of North American would receive the protection of law. Would Indigenous peoples be incorporated into British North America according to the principles outlined in the Royal Proclamation of 1763 or would they be criminalized as "merciless Indian savages" and subjected to genocidal elimination? In correspondence, George Croghan discussed such matters with his patron, Sir William Johnson. The "great prototype" of Indian affairs administration and the lord of Johnson Manor was well aware that the common folk in the frontier regions of Anglo-America believed that "it was meritorious to kill [Indian] Heathens whenever they are found."[153] Frontiersmen often acted on this conviction, causing Richard White to observe of the Anglo-American frontier in the mid-1700s, "whites killed Indians with impunity."[154] The same pattern of frontier vigilantism would be re-enacted repeatedly in the Aboriginal histories of new jurisdictions like Ohio, Kentucky, Missouri, Texas, and California.[155] Darwin's theories arrived in the second half of the nineteenth century to give a patina of pseudo-scientific justification to the worldwide deregulation of imperial violence against Indigenous peoples, as if their elimination and subjugation embodied the fulfillment of natural law.

There are many ways to visit forced obsolescence and death on individuals, groups, and polities seen to be blocking the expansion of the dominant motifs of industrial production and commercial transaction. Anna Jameson has left a poignant account of the nature and implications of forced obsolescence after witnessing the remnants of Tecumseh's old Indian Confederacy at a ceremony hosted in 1837 by the British imperial government on Manitoulin Island in the Great Lakes of North America. At this event she was struck by the sophisticated artistry displayed on the embroidery gracing "dresses of mountain sheep and young buffalo skins." She compared these items "to the softness of a Cashmere shawl." Jameson observed that the dexterity and refined aesthetic sensibility displayed in these items "might have been progressively improved... had we not substituted for articles they could procure or fabricate, those which we fabricate." She added, "We have substituted guns for bows and arrow – but they cannot make guns." From these observations Jameson concluded: "For the natural progress of arts and civilization springing from within, and from their own intelligence and resources, we have substituted a sort of civilization from without, foreign to their habits, manners, organization."[156]

Karl Marx commented in more abstract language on the wholesale destruction of many indigenous ways of life and diverse forms of political economy on the moving edges of capitalist expansion. He described how "the cheapness of articles produced by machinery, and the improved means of transport and communication" result in the "ruining of handicraft production."[157] As "capital drives beyond national barriers and prejudices," it becomes unrelentingly "destructive" towards the "reproduction of old ways of life." This onslaught results in "tearing down all the barriers which hem in the development of forces of production, the expansion of needs ... and the exploitation and exchange of natural and mental forces."[158] In a series of Canadian radio addresses he delivered only months before his assassination, the civil rights leader Martin Luther King Jr explored the personal dimension of what it means to be relegated to capitalism's human trash heap through unemployment. "In our society," he asserted, "it's murder, psychologically, to deprive a man [or woman] of a job or an income. You're in substance saying to that man [or woman] that he [or she] has no right to exist. You're in a real way depriving him [or her] of life, liberty and pursuit of happiness."[159]

The history of capitalism entered a new phase with the demise of the Soviet Union in the early 1990s. The founding of the World Trade Organization in 1994 symbolized the view that the Cold War's end had eliminated all possibilities for the maintenance and elaboration of political economies that did not conform to a global regime of universalized capitalism. Added pressure was thereby placed on humanity's diverse branches to cast aside all inheritances of culture, tradition, and personality that did not adhere to the material structure of a seemingly unipolar world. For the last few years of the twentieth century, it briefly appeared that this unipolar world would be shaped even more intensely than in the past by the marriage of business and militarism as consummated in the global involvements of the United States. In this way the material, political, and psychological construction of capitalism extended its reach yet further into the realm of mind, matter, and relationship. With the failure of the major state apparatus founded in direct rhetorical opposition to capitalism's inequities, there seemed to be no remaining space for the survival of any collectivity whose members did not conform to the dominant mores of the ascendant commercial monoculture.

In much the same way that the domestication of agricultural monocultures has eliminated the habitat for the renewal of uncommodified life forms, so too have whole societies been pushed into extinction when their members could not, or would not, adapt to the requirements of monopoly capitalism. Capitalism's unrelenting assault on many kinds of barriers continued to strip diversity from our world's community of communities. Generally speaking, the tragic and preventable elements of this elimination have been downplayed. In much the same way that old machinery is discarded as the inevitable castoffs of technological improvement, so too has the removal of the conditions for the survival of many collectivities, but especially Aboriginal groups, been made to seem like necessary expedients for the smooth operation and expansion of global capitalism. The economic dimension of genocide has rarely been addressed with the seriousness it demands. The commercial factors governing the disappearance of distinct peoples have most often been treated as if they embody the inevitable outgrowth of progress or natural law, rather than the result of the priorities and decisions of powerful human beings.

The expansion of global capitalism grew from the development of laws, institutions, and networks of common understanding that have increasingly homogenized diverse regimes of proprietary interaction. Just as all national collectivities and local communities have had to grapple with the problem of how to accommodate and exploit the capitalist construction of material interaction, so too has this imperative extended in one way or another to almost every individual on Earth. The constant pressure to accommodate and exploit the unending tumult of revolutionary capitalism created tremendous anxieties and pressures in the psychology of everyday human existence. As capitalist interaction reached universal proportions, the structure of personality itself had to be bent in the unrelenting race to reduce prices, enhance commercial demand, and maximize industrial efficiencies of scale. What psychic costs have occurred from this constant reconfiguration of human mentality to serve the ideals of competition, production, consumption, and limitless technological change?

Was it a protest against the fate apparently dealt them in capitalist North America that prompted George Hunt and the other Kwakwaka'wakw performers to mount such a scandalously controversial show during Great Britain Day at the World's Columbian Exposition in Chicago in 1893? The location of the imitation Indian villages among the other "odd bits of tribes and nationalities" on the exposition's Midway Plaisance foreshadowed the treatment of many of the world's Aboriginal societies as obsolete polities whose only remaining role in the economy would be to provide quaint folkloric spectacles for the amusement of tourists.[160] From Buffalo Bill's Wild West Show to the performing Indians of Glacier National Park to the hula dancers working the resorts of Hawaii, the same pattern of trivialization and commodification of Aboriginal lifeways has been enacted again and again all over the world.

This facet of commercialization forms one aspect of a larger process that subordinates virtually all forms of cultural expression to the pre-eminent culture of capitalism. The imitation Mayan ruins located amid the cafés and amusement rides on the Midway Plaisance metaphorically signalled the fate assigned to most Aboriginal societies if the vision of progress advanced in 1893 by the planners and designers of the World's Columbian Exposition was allowed to go forward. By breaking out of the prepared script and shocking their audience, George Hunt and the other Kwakwaka'wakw performers announced their resistance to the transformation of their rich culture into a consumer item or an exotic artifact. Could the Kwakwaka'wakw and members of the other "odd bits of tribes and nationalities" along Midway Plaisance imagine where the currents of history were taking their peoples? Could they picture an era when many members of their communities would live in poverty even as sports conglomerates, automobile companies, and weapons manufacturers transformed their Aboriginal names into logos, brands, and other forms of patented intellectual property? Could they imagine an era when the shelves of self-help sections in big box bookstores would groan with multitudes of New Age publications offering Aboriginal elixirs for all sorts of ailments, even as the members of many Aboriginal societies would suffer from disproportionately high rates of illness, addictions, and other syndromes of internalized violence?

The attributes of capitalism's most fit competitors are far from those that make for the healthy maintenance of life's sacred web. The depredations of pollution and global warming converge with the rapid depletion of biocultural diversity to highlight the dramatic disparity in the criteria for survival in capitalism and survival in the ecological web of life.[161] The great predicaments of our time arise from the tensions between capitalism's prolific generation of products at the same time as it spawns genocide and the many forms of environmental destruction that, all together, perpetrate ecocide. Our economic support system is destroying the ecological equilibrium that is the real basis of life's bounty and renewal. The genocidal destruction of the indigenous political economies of Aboriginal peoples thus forms but one facet of a more pervasive process, one that ultimately menaces the survival of all humanity as well as the interdependent plant and animal communities with whom we share this Earth. Genocide, ecocide, and the possibility of collective suicide are intimately connected.

The paradox is striking. Life's regenerative forces form the deepest sources of nature's most genuine gifts to humanity. And yet the global commons that contains this gift-giving abundance is fast being appropriated, broken up, and privatized to extend capitalism's monopoly. Who is to be held accountable for the genocide and ecocide that sometimes accompanies capitalism's colonization of new districts and facets of the global biosphere? Who is to be held financially or criminally liable for the loss of the cod, the buffalo, the bees, the frogs, the old-growth forests, the coral reefs, not to mention the genocidal assaults on the Beothuk, Cree, Ogoni, Uigher, and the Indigenous peoples of the Chittagong Hill Tracts in Bangladesh? Who is to be held accountable for the loss of a young girl's smile after her leg has been blown off by a land mine?

Responsibility is diffused very broadly for the genocidal and ecocidal outgrowths that arise with the expansion of capitalism and its attending military-industrial complex. It is very difficult to hold individuals directly accountable for the demise of those corporations, individuals, and peoples that do not make it through capitalism's Darwinian filter of survival. This diffusion of responsibility arises because of the strength of the argument that it is the impersonal workings of the market, not the decisions and actions of its biggest beneficiaries, which dictate what entities live and what entities die in global capitalism's lethal theatres of commercial combat.

Although some must compete for survival, the taxpayer-supported bailouts of the some of the world's largest financial institutions in 2008 and 2009 demonstrate that, in the final analysis, politics prevails over competition at the highest levels of capitalism's money sequence. Indeed, the biggest beneficiaries of so-called free markets are in fact shielded with protective barriers to limit the legal vulnerability of corporations and their executives to the negative military, environmental, and social consequences of their quests for profit. The corporate law of limited liability stands as a metaphor for a systemic bias permeating capitalism. While some receive enormous protections from capitalism's agencies of law enforcement, the property and persons of the weak are sometimes left entirely exposed to the kleptocratic incursions of the powerful.

Government responses to the financial meltdowns of 2008–9 epitomized the propensity of capitalism's ruling oligarchs to socialize the risks and liabilities of doing business and to privatize profits. But there was opportunity as well as danger in the financial crisis. The debacle should have underlined the principle that there must be no return to legalized executive theft, disguised as laissez-faire capitalism, from corporate shareholders. The public mythology that enabled the barons of high finance to deploy Enron-style fantasy accounting to rob average citizens of the fruits of their work and small investments arose from the lies and deceits of Reaganomics, Thatcherism, and the heyday of financial deregulation under US presidents Bill Clinton and George W. Bush. In guiding the public along the road to financial disaster, the media worked overtime to obfuscate the crony capitalism of those empowered by corrupt politicians to raid the public purse as well as the savings and future earnings of ordinary men and women whose everyday transactions form the heart of the real economy.

Who can deny that the political economy of human interaction with one another and the rest of nature must be transformed to move beyond capitalism's genocidal and ecocidal propensities and promote instead the ideals of equity, human rights, self-determination, and biocultural diversity. Economist Herman E. Daly has proposed a sweeping agenda of change that is consistent with many of the ideals of the Fourth World. He has sought ways of leaving behind the preoccupation of his peers with unlimited and never-ending growth, a pure fantasy on a planet where "economics is a subsystem of a finite biosphere."[162]

The need for some kind of reckoning with the limits of growth is becoming inescapable as the reach of economic activity begins to affect the entire spectrum of ecological relationships among all life forms on Earth. Daly points to the "absurdity" of professional macroeconomics when the scale of the imagined financial castles is calculated "to grow beyond the biophysical limits of the Earth." He writes: "The closer the economy approaches the scale of the whole Earth, the more it will have to conform to the physical behavior mode of the Earth." In his estimation, the core principle of that behaviour mode "is a steady state – a system that permits qualitative development but not aggregate quantitative growth." In trying to emphasize the need to move away from models of growth that value above all else the expansion of Gross Domestic Product (GDP), Daly draws a distinction between the benefits of "development" and what he calls "throughput growth." In a metaphor that equates the main variable of economic choice with the eating decisions of a single organism, Daly writes: "Throughput growth means pushing more food through the same larger digestive tract; development means eating better food and digesting it more thoroughly." In a global context, the ushering in of a "steady state economy" would require the rich "to reduce their throughput growth to free up resources and ecological space for use by the poor, while focusing their domestic efforts on development, technical and social improvements that can be freely shared with the poor countries."[163]

The global financial crisis unfolded in the context of the larger forces of environmental corrosion menacing life's true support systems. The convergence of these human-induced breakdowns points to the need for correctives that are concurrently international, ecological, and personal. In moving to repair the damage, it will be necessary for authorities to be far more conscientious in enforcing international laws that already exist, such as those designed for the prevention and punishment of genocide. The elimination of the political economies of so many Indigenous peoples in the continuing economic colonization of their Aboriginal lands easily falls within the criteria of genocide as understood by Raphael Lemkin. It meets the criteria codified by the UN General Assembly in Resolution 96(1) in 1946. This resolution, which is referred to in the Genocide Convention of 1948, defines the international crime of genocide as "a denial of the right of existence of entire human groups, as homicide is the denial of the right to live of individual human beings."

For groups not to be denied the right of existence, they require the material, institutional, and political instruments necessary for the renewal of their polities. The outlawing of genocide can therefore be understood as one side of the same construction of international law whose other side recognizes and affirms the inherent right of all peoples to self-determination. How else can societies continue their existence in a changing world without the material, legal, and political tools to express their self-determination? How can true self-determination be expressed in the economic sphere if the survival of all people, groups, and nations on Earth is made to depend on their abject submission to the imperatives and requirements of a single global regime of monopoly capitalism?

CHAPTER FIFTEEN

From General Motors to AIG to the Bowl with One Spoon: Reading the Financial Crisis

The real destroyer of the liberties of the people is he who spreads among them bounties, donations and benefits.
Ronald Reagan, citing Plutarch, 1964

PRESIDENT BARACK OBAMA AND THE MIDDLE GROUND

The worldwide spread in 2008 of a financial contagion that began in the United States set in motion major cycles of transformation that altered forever the underlying constitution of the global economy. The core players in the financial system may continue to describe themselves as capitalists, but the speed, scope, and long-term implications of enormous government bailouts to integrated networks of banks, investment brokers, and insurance firms have highlighted the lie that global finance functions in a milieu of free and open markets. At the highest level, economic interactions are ruled by politics, patronage, and cronyism rather than by the movements of Adam Smith's imagined invisible hand.

The crisis was widely interpreted as a consequence of the overzealous deregulation of national and transnational operations of the financial sector, a phenomenon that began with the inauguration in 1981 of President Ronald Reagan. In taking control of the levers of executive authority in the United States, the world's richest and most powerful country, Reagan repeated his declarations of war on the power of government to intervene in the workings of markets. After almost three decades of applying Reaganomics to the global architecture of economic interaction, the meltdown of 2008 brought this major episode in financial history to a close. As Roger C. Altman declared in the summer of 2009 in *Foreign Affairs*, "the era of laissez-faire economics has ended." As a result of this "seismic global event ... the role of the state, together with financial and trade protectionism, is ascending."[1]

But how would the state be reconstituted in the wake of the financial meltdown? Would growth in the role of government be accompanied by a boost in the capacity of citizens to influence the actions of their respective states? Or would the opposite occur? Would the sudden pull of governments into a more activist role in the economy further subordinate their operations to the dominance of a small financial cabal whose actions are thought to have caused the financial meltdown in the first place? As Kevin Baker saw it, the bailouts set a terrible precedent that emboldened the class most responsible for transforming the US economy into an instrument for their own narrow self-aggrandizement. The very interests that "spent much of the last two decades gobbling up previously public sectors such as health care, education, and transportation" were intent on using the financial crisis "to make government their helpless junior partner."[2]

Baker's warning was part of his critical assessment of the early stages of President Barack Obama's presidency. Baker compared the Obama administration's actions to those of President Herbert Hoover during the latter's single term in office. Hoover won the US presidency just months before the crash of stock markets in 1929 began the Great Depression. Baker highlighted the notorious cronyism involved in Hoover's attempt to reverse his country's financial fortunes by distributing large amounts of federal largesse through the Reconstruction Finance Corporation. When Franklin Roosevelt defeated Hoover in 1932, the new president repeated many of the former administration's mistakes. He instituted the National Recovery Administration, for example – a polity at the core of a "flabby utopian plan that would have had business, labor and government collaborate to set prices, wages, and industry standards down to the last detail."

As Baker saw it, Obama repeated many of the mistakes of Hoover and of Roosevelt in his first New Deal by thinking he could "bring together all classes of Americans together in some big, mushy cooperative scheme." Obama suffered particularly by allowing himself to become captive to the manipulations of a small financial elite representing a constituency whose members threatened to "devour every federal dollar available to recoup their own losses, and thereby preclude the use of any monies for the rest of Barack Obama's splendid vision."

This author hopes that Obama will transcend the legacy of Hoover's "business progressivism" and President Bill Clinton's "business liberalism" to embark instead on a program more like that of Roosevelt in his "second New Deal." After his false start, Roosevelt abandoned the National Recovery Institute to unleash creative conflict between the "countervailing forces" of business, labour, and government. As an aggressive participant in the wrangling, the US executive branch helped to fashion the elements of managed capitalism. For about four decades the state's regulation of industrial relations and financial transactions resulted in major gains in terms of productivity, prosperity, equity, and the power of citizens to act as instruments of their own self-governance.

Baker casts his net of blame far beyond the administration of Barack Obama. He bemoans "the utter fecklessness of the American elite" in failing to confront the broader implications of the financial crisis. "From both the private and public sectors, across the entire political spectrum, the lack of will and new ideas has been stunning," he writes.[3] Baker's remarks failed to take notice, however, of the bold and clearly stated insights of William K. Black on the frauds and failures of law enforcement that helped to instigate and worsen the economic breakdown.[4] His generalization similarly passed over the many public interventions of Joseph Stiglitz, an eloquent public advocate of the need to incorporate the democracy of multilateralism into the international regulation of the global economy.[5]

These qualifications aside, however, I accept Baker's general assessment of the relative intellectual poverty of responses to the global financial debacle, and I offer this culminating chapter of *Earth into Property* as a corrective. In it, I explore the economic breakdown by looking at its genesis through the lens of two huge enterprises plucked from obliteration through the financial intervention by government. In the histories of General Motors and AIG, American International Group, I find very clear reflections of some of the major themes running throughout this text and its preceding volume. In particular I see the government takeover and renewal of General Motors as a potential vehicle for the future expression of principles such as those of the common good, public interest, and public service. I associate all these ideals with the totemic symbolism of the Bowl with One Spoon.

The idealism inherent in public invocations of the collective good has been demeaned, denigrated, and pushed to the margins of public discourse by the pre-eminent myths and symbols of Reaganomics. We have been indoctrinated by the mythology of a false conservatism whose proponents have preached to us for over a generation that personal consumption forms the quintessence of democratic self-determination. We have been indoctrinated to see the deregulation of business as a triumph of liberty, even as we have been blocked from channelling our social capital into building up the powers of government to express our shared rights and responsibilities as citizens. We have been encouraged to view great disparities of wealth as markers of capitalist freedom rather than as the outcome of monopolies over political power by economic elites.

What was conservative about a propaganda message aimed at covering up the workings of an elite kleptocracy enabled and facilitated by the overzealous deregulation of business? The financial crisis has exposed for the observant the gross exploitation of the imagery of conservatism by opportunists who have betrayed its deeper meanings. Much of the confusion can be traced back to Reagan's identification of the revolutionary founding of the United States as an act of conservatism. This interpretation fails to take into account the conservative philosophy of those who fought to prevent the Anglo-American secessionists from severing the British Empire.

Many of those allied with the conservative ideology of the British imperial government were Mohawk Indians, Black freedom fighters, and members of small religious communities who feared that their minority rights would be trampled by the tyranny of the majority in the new republic.[6]

Their opposition to the principles driving the rise of the future superpower must be revisited in this era when the disruptions of ecological disequilibrium merge with the unrestrained gangsterism of those who, in the name of national security, commit international crimes such as torture and mass murder with impunity. The misrepresentation of conservatism in order to give cover to the highest order of crimes against posterity must be exposed for the fraud that it is. In our troubled times conservatism contains too many vital strands of meaning, inspiration, and strategy to allow it to be severed it from the heritage of the Bowl with One Spoon. The movement to oppose the imperial rule of crony capitalism must embrace the ethos of ecological conservation within the framework of a richer, more organic, more nuanced, and more authentically based school of conservative ideology. Conservatism is too important to the future of humanity to be left as the exclusive intellectual property of the right.

The image of the Bowl with One Spoon symbolizes the need to conserve shared resources in the public interest and the common good. This symbol on the wampum depiction of treaties between First Nations draws on the Aboriginal history of Indian Country in North America to renew ancient principles in broadened global contexts. Many ideals of common citizenship and community are renewed by bringing alive the picture of our world as a common hunting territory to be shared by all its inhabitants, both human and non-human. Our collective survival depends on serving the interests and rights of posterity by protecting and cultivating the global commons. Some Six Nations Longhouse people express this conservative ideal by regularly referring to the need to make decisions with the interests of our seventh generation of descendants in mind.

Although the idea of the common good and the public interest invokes the shared rights and interests of those alive in the present, these concepts must also invoke our collective responsibility to be true to spoken and unspoken contracts connecting the dead to the unborn. This appreciation calls for the resuscitation of genuine expressions of conservatism that eschew Reaganomics, a system whose lies and contradictions were exposed in the rush to commandeer massive amounts of public funds to bailout some of the world's largest financial cartels.

According to John McMurtry, the North American auto companies received a loan whose value was about 2 percent of what Wall Street institutions received as a gift from agencies funded by the US taxpayer.[7] As the crisis worsened, it emerged that the financial services company, AIG, was patient number one in the spread of the financial contagion that deeply infected the already shaky health of the entire global economy. As the crisis worsened, the New York Federal Reserve intervened to pay off tens of billions of dollars in insurance premiums that AIG owed to financial institutions that had gotten too deeply involved in reckless transactions such as so-called credit default swaps. Much could be read into the revelation that the supposedly conservative insurance business had made itself integral to the most speculative activities in the most deregulated branches of the financial services industry. This involvement went far beyond the political economy of home mortgages and such. By the time of the financial meltdown, AIG was deeply integrated into the national security state, the military industrial complex, and the privatized terror economy through a complex array of reinsurers, subsidiaries, affiliates, partnerships, and holding companies spread across 130 countries, some of them tax havens. AIG's integration into some of the covert operations generated by the axis of influence linking Wall Street with the Pentagon may explain much of the secrecy and obfuscation in the unwinding of its insurance contracts on derivative instruments with so-called counterparties.

The crisis afflicting AIG and its many large corporate partners was closely connected to its overzealous integration of insurance with new types of derivative products and hedge funds. As the name implies, derivatives are derived from actual wealth as embodied in, for instance, currency, stocks, bonds, and the legal title to land. The development of new types of derivatives extended into the arena of the Internet transactions many old cycles of expansion integrating fresh frontiers of private property into capital's empire of accumulation. The accelerating movement of capital through expanding networks of linked computers helped to break down clear distinctions between wealth's true substance and its representation in the virtual world of cyberspace. The digitalization of virtual capital gave added power to the move away from gold-based currencies towards fiat currencies. Fiat currencies are backed by nothing more than the promises of governments to enforce their function as legal tender.

The confusion between wealth's original sources and the illusions *derived* from mere representations of its substance developed almost naturally in the transition from the age of analog to that of digital communications. In an era when digital information moves on the Internet from computer to computer without any significant erosion of quality, distinctions tend to be lost between original recordings and the copies *derived* from originals. Where are the boundaries between original sources and their digital derivatives in the empire of Internet communications?[8]

The American empire of private property was initially formed in rejection of the Royal Proclamation of 1763, an innovation of British imperialists seeking compromises with Indigenous peoples on the middle ground of cross-cultural mediation in the colonization of North America.[9] President Roosevelt's New Deal extended principles similar to those of the Royal Proclamation into new frontiers of industrial civilization. In the New Deal, laws and policies were put in place to encourage compromise between labour and management on the middle ground of industrial relations. Beginning with the Treaty of Detroit in 1950, the North American automotive industry for a time epitomized these principles of constructive compromise between capitalists and workers. These ideals could be renewed if General Motors returned to the principles of Pontiac and the Bowl with One Spoon in concentrating on the construction of public transit to advance the public interest.

The internationalization of the New Deal can be attributed largely to President Franklin Roosevelt and his wife, Eleanor Roosevelt. She outlived her husband to play a central role in the United Nations' drafting and adoption in 1948 of the Universal Declaration of Human Rights.[10] The unorthodox relationship that helped expose Franklin Roosevelt to the Bohemian culture of his avant-garde wife was similar in some regards to the unusual partnership linking Sir William Johnson to Molly Brant. Molly was Sir William's Mohawk housekeeper, lover, and mother of several of his children. She helped educate her partner, the officer in charge of the British imperial conduct of Indian Affairs, into the complex diplomacy of the Six Nations Longhouse League and the Covenant Chain.

Sir William drew on his own experiences in the negotiation of Longhouse and Covenant Chain federalism to animate a steady stream of advice counselling the British imperial government on how best to incorporate Indigenous peoples into British North America on the basis of consent and law. Johnson's advice formed the primary basis for the Aboriginal provisions in the Royal Proclamation of 1763. This seminal instrument in the constitutional history of the British Empire called for an end to wars of dispossession through an expanded regime of treaty federalism with Indigenous peoples on the moving frontiers of Anglo-American colonization.

The United States was founded in rejection of the Royal Proclamation's conservative prohibition on empire building through Indian wars. However, Franklin and Eleanor Roosevelt not only embraced some of the Royal Proclamation's core principles but extended them in their effort to empower the United Nations to outlaw all forms of territorial acquisition through military conquest. In their quest to internationalize the New Deal, the Roosevelts were moved by the same marriage of liberal idealism and conservative pragmatism that had facilitated the historic partnership between the leadership of the Longhouse League and its Red Tory allies, as epitomized by Sir William Johnson's leadership of the northern division of the British Imperial Indian Department.

The Roosevelts' internationalization of the New Deal extended to the effort to help humanity transcend the heavy burden of genocide. They did so by embracing the principles of international criminal law developed by Raphael Lemkin and others as part of the process of establishing the United Nations on the juridical foundations of the Atlantic Charter, the Genocide Convention, and the Universal Declaration of Human Rights. In rejecting the deployment of state power to assimilate Indigenous peoples, John Collier's Indian New Deal had pointed the way towards a more sophisticated international embrace of pluralism and non-alignment in the Fourth World.

If President Barack Obama is to return to the more ennobling themes of the Roosevelts' internationalization of the New Deal through an embrace of the United Nations' founding principles, the US president will have to move the United States away from its disastrous dependence on the permanent war economy. President Obama will have to shift his country away from its imperial role towards a more open embrace of the biocultural diversity of the Fourth World. Moreover, he must affirm his administration's determination to uphold the rule of law rather than continue the systemic cover-up of the criminal actions of the national security state whose corrupting effects helped to contaminate the business dealings of AIG and many of the other corporate members of the military-industrial complex. The decision to use the Federal Reserve's Maiden Lane corporations to protect and continue AIG's most dubious variety of transaction extends the age of impunity to new frontiers of commercial activity. The federal continuation of AIG's most egregious transactions mirrored the initial unwillingness of President Obama to authorize deep and objective investigations into the actions of US officials and their corporate proxies who are credibly suspected of having committed many international crimes in the name of national security and the Global War on Terror.[11]

The converging activities of the most self-serving opportunists on the capitalist side of the Cold War found expression in many of the transactions that took place in the 1980s under the umbrella of the Saudi-backed Bank of Credit and Commerce International. The corrupt and often illegal deals made within the BCCI's structures epitomized the nature of the move away from the managed capitalism that was one of the New Deal's primary legacies. The BCCI seed bed of the privatized terror economy highlighted the kleptocratic character of a regime favouring the confiscation of public wealth by elites under the cover of a false doctrine of conservatism popularized by Ronald Reagan. With the encouragement and backing of the axis of influence linking Wall Street and the Pentagon, this confiscation of public wealth by financial elites was expressed on a gigantic scale in the process of privatizing the national property of the former Soviet Union as well as that of its dependencies and breakaway republics.

The roots of AIG run far deeper in the history of the American Empire than the influence of Reagan and the expression of the dark side of his policies in the activities of the BCCI. The corporate ancestry of AIG extends all the way back to the activities in Shanghai of Cornelius V. Starr and, before him, John Jacob Astor. Astor was the New Yorker real-estate mogul who originally built his fortune by extending the transcontinental fur trade of the United States all the way to China. In moving from the export of furs to the importation of opium into China, Astor's actions anticipated how Anglo-America would secure its commercial beachhead in the world's most culturally sophisticated and heavily populated country. The Opium Wars of the first half of the nineteenth century would set in motion cycles of business deregulation whose global excesses were dramatically displayed in the financial crisis beginning in 2008.

GENERAL MOTORS IN WAR AND IN PEACE

In June 2009 President Barack Obama announced the formal demise of one of the world's largest and most iconographic corporations.[12] As "the old General Motors" was relegated to bankruptcy, the failing superpower's fledgling chief executive promised that a "new General Motors" would emerge from a process of industrial trimming, consolidation, and reorientation. The new polity would be 60 per cent owned by the US government, 12 per cent owned by the governments of Canada and Ontario, and 17.5 per cent owned by the health fund of the United Auto Workers. In the weeks and months before the announcement, federal loans and guarantees were all that kept the broken corporate vessel financially afloat. In taking control of GM's steering mechanism, the Obama administration altered GM's Board of Directors and replaced the company's CEO, Richard Wagoner, with its own appointee.

The US president claimed that he was "reluctant" to make his government the majority owner of this ailing industrial giant, which he dubbed "an emblem of the American spirit ... a pillar of our economy that has held up the dreams of millions of our people." Obama attributed the decision to nationalize the largest part of a company that had once been a leviathan of corporate capitalism to "the most severe economic crisis since the Great Depression," one that had "crippled private capital markets and forced us to take steps in our financial system – and with our auto companies – that we would not have otherwise considered."[13]

In extending the bailout of many financial institutions to GM as well as Chrysler Corporation, Obama infused the grease of public capital into the rusting machinery of a huge industrial enterprise that had once been synonymous with the dynamic mobility of American capitalism. By intervening in this way, Obama renewed old contestations even as he introduced new debates about the role of the state in creating those hierarchies of power and property that constitute the core of industrial relations.

Even more than the Ford Motor Company, which avoided bankruptcy in the financial downturn, General Motors and its wide array of automotive products came to epitomize for a time the glossy allure of life in the fast lane of market relations. By embracing so enthusiastically the culture of cars, Americans altered their orientation to space and time, refashioning their cities, town sites, rural landscapes, individual psyches, and community mores to incorporate the accelerated connectivity of motorized road travel. The mass production of relatively cheap cars gave many consumers access to modules of mobility that introduced new forms of privacy into the shared sphere of public thoroughfares. The proliferation of automobiles as a mass medium of individualized transport thus proved pivotal in helping to embed the culture of privatization yet more deeply into the twentieth century's most powerful political economy. Whole complexes of material interaction were dramatically transformed as, for instance, producers of commercial radio worked closely with marketers of fast food, builders of sprawling suburbs, and developers of shopping malls to alert car drivers and their passengers to the new array of consumer choices available to them as they sped along the expanding networks of motorized commerce.

The easy availability of affordable cars gave millions of average citizens a proprietary stake in an increasingly well-integrated system of energy extraction, industrial production, social engineering, and psychological conditioning necessary to speed the rise of the world's most elaborate military-industrial complex. Where Henry Ford made utilitarian cars broadly affordable by applying large-scale automation to manufacturing processes, the executives of General Motors conquered new frontiers of economic power by exploiting consumers' desire to express their personalities, tastes, and fantasy lives by choosing from an array of automobile brands, colours, shapes, and styles. The industrial designer Harley J. Earl was a key figure in the transition from cars as media of transport to cars as vehicles for the channelling of ego, machismo, and mojo. He was lured to GM headquarters in Detroit from his Hollywood machine shop, where he manufactured custom-made automobile bodies for rich movie stars. GM's chairman and CEO, Alfred P. Sloan, gave Earl broad latitude to infuse his Hollywood sensibilities into GM products, investing them with huge tail fins, wrap-around windows, and audacious displays of gleaming chrome.[14]

With his decision to transform the principles underlying General Motors' form of ownership and corporate organization, President Obama reoriented the relationship between his own Democratic Party and a key constituency of trade unionists. In combining the power of public capital with the principle that the health plans of the United Auto Workers would own almost one-fifth of GM and more than a half of a dramatically restructured Chrysler Corporation, he altered the conditions of a class of industrial workers that had been instrumental in electing the African-American lawyer to the world's most influential job. Would this innovation create a new middle ground of industrial compromise where the interests of automobile workers as wage labourers would merge with their newly acquired status as proprietors of a substantial portion of their own industrial enterprises? Did the partnership of workers and the state in the ownership of these troubled companies signal a fundamental shift towards some new system of post-capitalist production?[15] Would trade unions and their members benefit or lose from having representation on both sides of the table of industrial bargaining between workers and owners? How would corporate productivity, American society, and the global community as a whole be affected? Was some fundamental paradox revealed in Obama's assertion that his government would "resist" intervening in "all but the most fundamental corporate decisions" of GM, even as he promised that the company's next generation of green vehicles would open the way to an "energy independent future" for the United States?

One libertarian lobby group characterized Obama's decision to national-ize GM as a declaration of "war" against American capitalism.[16] In a similar vein, Mike Huckabee, a candidate for the Republican presidential nomi-nation in 2008, accused the US president of changing GM to advance his goal of creating a "Union of American Socialist Republics."[17] The intensity of such rhetoric continued the saga that has long rendered Detroit's most important and characteristic industry as a major flash point of ideological antagonisms between competing systems of political economy. As an out-growth of the nuances of both race relations and the politics of trade union-ism within the Democratic Party, Obama's career was itself an outgrowth of some of the very forces that made the Detroit car companies objects of controversy. These corporate spark plugs of motorized transport have been strategically placed at the juncture where the gas-powered surges in the industrial revolution were oxygenated by the rise of the United States as capitalism's great frontier, laboratory, engine, and exporter.

In their early days, the car companies of Detroit were closed to both Black workers and organized labour. This pattern was complicated in the 1920s when Henry Ford reached out to some Black churches as a source of employees. The famous industrialist hand picked some of their mem-bers in order to oppose the growing effort to organize labourers in the car industry. The prospects for an expanded role for trade unionism in the North American automobile industry widened significantly, however, after the economic cataclysm of the Great Depression opened the way to the New Deal. Franklin Roosevelt's *Wagner Act* of 1935 helped to establish a legal framework for collective bargaining and legal strikes. The United Auto Workers, part of the Congress of Industrial Organizations, emerged from this altered environment, one that undermined support for the reac-tionary policies of the conservative crafts unions that Samuel Gompers had organized under the banner of American Federation of Labor. The UAW, for instance, lowered some of the walls of discrimination that had excluded many Black workers from integration into the ranks of orga-nized labour.

In the winter of 1936–7, members of the United Auto Workers withstood a number of police raids aimed at ending their sit-down occupations of GM's facilities. The pivotal strike took place at GM's Fisher plant no. 1 in Flint, Michigan. The determination of the car workers to assert their rights, together with the refusal of federal and state officials to resort to more lethal tactics of union busting, resulted in General Motors making its first formal agreement to recognize the auto workers' union. Soon thereafter Chrysler Corporation too acknowledged the UAW as the collective bargain-ing unit of its workers. It was not until 1941, however, that the Ford Motor Corporation followed suit. The unionization of Ford culminated a process that saw public opinion gradually turn against the auto giant's resistance to organized labour, especially after 1937, when James E. Kilpatrick won the first Pulitzer Prize for photography by capturing graphic images of corporate thugs roughing up organizers who were carrying a banner on a prominent Detroit overpass proclaiming "Unionism Not Fordism."[18]

The publicity attending the "Battle of the Overpass" helped to call attention to the subversive system of spying, violence, and intimidation deployed against those seeking to advance the rights, interests, and imperatives of organized labour in Ford factories. By the late 1930s, however, questions about the role of trade unions in the industrial relations of the Detroit car companies had acquired a significance that went far beyond domestic boundaries. The award from Adolf Hitler to Henry Ford in 1938 of the Grand Cross of the Order of the German Eagle suggested just how far Fordism's father had already moved in extending his union busting priorities into the international arena.

As the machinery of combat was assembled and positioned in the run-up to the Second World War, Henry Ford stood prominently among a number of US-based industrialists and financiers who were instrumental in helping to build up in the German heartland of Central Europe a fascist bastion of capitalist opposition to those claiming that the Soviet Union represented the vanguard of international workers' rights.[19] When it came to his willingness to translate the power of his anti-Semitism into action, however, Ford stood in a class of his own. He obsessively channelled his anti-Jewish conspiracy theories in ways that directly fed the ferocity of Hitlerian attacks on organized labour.[20]

The onset of relative peace in the labour relations of Detroit's automotive companies took hold just in time for these powerhouses of industrial productivity to be remade under the federal auspices of the War Production Board. As the US government entered the Second World War, GM, Ford, and Chrysler expanded and retooled their production facilities in order to churn out huge quantities of military jeeps and trucks, tanks, machine guns, bullets, shells, airplanes, and the like. In making this transition, the Detroit car makers – along with many other of the largest corporations in the United States – embarked on activities that would render these institutions as core units in what President Dwight D. Eisenhower would later dub the military-industrial complex.

A group of corporate executives played a major role in the decision in 1944 to continue the militarization of the US economy in spite of the imminent end of the Second World War. Charles E. Wilson introduced this proposition to a federal committee looking at army ordinance. The unveiling of the concept of a permanent war economy is often attributed to the Charles E. Wilson who moved from the job of GM president to become Eisenhower's secretary of defense in 1953. The actual source of the proposal, however, was not GM's "Machine Charlie" but a different Charles E. Wilson – "Electric Charlie Wilson" – who was the CEO of General Electric.[21] In 1944 this titan of industry proposed that the leadership of the largest US companies should establish more permanent and entrenched procedures for industrial cooperation with the military and political leadership of the

United States. This alliance between business and government in engineer-ing the economy of unending war would be "a continuing program and not a creature of emergency."[22]

Wilson's advice helped to solidify the decision that military contracts would indefinitely remain the primary means for federal authorities to sub-sidize US business, but especially in the area of research and development. Some have described as "military Keynesianism" the outgrowth of this deci-sion to stimulate the further elaboration of a somewhat centralized and controlled command economy by directing the heaviest concentrations of government spending primarily at defence industries, rather than at pro-viding US citizens with, say, access to high-quality social services, free uni-versity education, or universal health care. In choosing this strategy, those directing the capitalist superpower set out on a path that would necessi-tate the constant production of real or mythological enemies that could be made to seem formidable enough to produce the necessary ingredients of fear and loathing in the minds of taxpayers called upon to underwrite the expansion and elaboration of the military-industrial complex.[23]

Especially after the entrenchment of the *National Security Act* of 1947, the institutionalization of the permanent war economy helped put in place many of the relationships of interest and power that would govern the push to universalize the genre of capitalism that had emerged from the previous history of Anglo-American expansion. The determination to make the economy of war a permanent feature of US relations with the rest of the world flowed with consistency from the rise of a country born of civil war within the British Empire and maintained through a civil war pitting proponents of a strong federal authority against secessionists seeking to maintain the political economy of their pro-slavery polity. Moreover, the entrenchment of an economy of perpetual warfare helped to project onto the global stage the outgrowth of a persistent trajectory of settler expansion directed at many foes, starting with the North American empires of France, Great Britain, and Spain. The key strategists in charge of all these European empires in North America attempted to gain and hold ground by devel-oping military and commercial alliances with select groups of Indigenous peoples. Alternatively, the makers of the New World polity of immigrants and their descendants tended to eschew this course of colonization and embrace instead the ethos of continual conquest as the most promising strategy for making the ascent from colony to superpower.[24]

The Aboriginal history of the permanent war economy draws on the long trajectories of US expansion animated by the ideals of Manifest Destiny. From the frontier violence generated in the growth of Puritan New England, to the militarism entailed in the transcontinental expansion of the United States, to the early stages of US empire building throughout the Pacific region, to the 9/11 wars, the consistency of violent frontier aggres-sions directed against Indigenous peoples accompanied the permanent war economy that became embedded at the core of US industrial relations.

To this day the entrenchment of the political economy of unending warfare remains a central feature in the internal structures and global orientation of the world's pre-eminent military superpower, one whose military budget was larger in 2008 than that of the combined total of the next forty-five highest spending countries. The United States monopolizes half of the world's military economy even as about half of the US economy is connected one way or another to fighting wars, preparing for wars, selling wars, and engaging in war's attending operations such as espionage, regime change, as well as so-called counter-intelligence and counter-insurgency.[25]

The Aboriginal history of the permanent war economy is especially integral to the history of many of the largest corporations in the United States. These streams of past experience merge with particular force in the history of those corporate conglomerates that situated their multinational operations on both sides of the conflict pitting Hitlerian capitalism against the capitalism of Roosevelt and the New Deal. The lessons learned from the deep involvement of many of the largest US corporations in mobilizing Nazi Germany for war and genocide did not evaporate into thin air after end of the Second World War. The close and privileged relations that developed between military contractors and government officials in Nazi Germany helped to establish patterns and preferences that would be renewed and built upon once the United States took over much of the arsenal of anti-communism following the failed bid of European fascists to smash the Soviet Union.

Accordingly, when Charles E. Wilson addressed the US panel on army ordinance in 1944, he spoke on behalf of one of those many US companies that had contributed to building up the military economy of Nazi Germany. Like, for instance, IBM, ITT, DuPont, Alcoa, Hearst Corporation, and Standard Oil of New Jersey, GE was an early and deep partner in the complex of transactions that had rendered the Hitlerian state and its international network of partners and allies so formidable.[26] The experiences and precedents drawn from the right-wing side of the conflict aligning the followers of Hitler, Mussolini, and Hirohito against those of Roosevelt, Churchill, and Stalin figured significantly in the formulation of the US decision to retain military Keynesianism within the framework of an economy geared to the requirements of unending warfare.

There can be no doubt that many members of the business constituency for whom Wilson spoke had preferred aligning their enterprises with the militarism of the fascist regime that had embraced the tyrannies of slave labour as one of many tactics for breaking the power of trade unions. The notorious ruthlessness of Henry's Ford's union-busting strategies was thus amplified and extended in the industrial policies of Hitlerian Germany, a regime in which the largest of the Detroit car companies played especially large and influential roles. General Motors was even more instrumental than the Ford Motor Company in building up the industrial base of Nazism. Ford and GM intermittently cooperated and competed in exploiting the supply of Jewish, Slav, and dissident slave labour procured for them by the ss Storm Troopers of Nazi corporate capitalism.[27]

At the beginning of the Second World War, the German branch plants of Ford and GM had already manufactured about 70 per cent of Germany's motorized vehicles. This pattern of industrial production was maintained and further militarized throughout the course of the Second World War. In commenting on the role of General Motors in the context of a growing controversy over the role of Swiss banks in redirecting the wealth of victims of the Nazi holocaust, Bradford Snell, a researcher employed by the US Congress, asserted: "General Motors was far more important to the Nazi war machine than Switzerland. Switzerland was just a repository for looted funds. GM was an integral part of the German war effort." He continued: "The Nazis could have invaded Poland and Russia without Switzerland. They could not have done so without GM."[28]

In Nazi-occupied Europe, GM's war production took place in the German factories of Adam Opel AG, a wholly owned subsidiary of the Detroit-based company. Along with IG Farben's backer and partner, Standard Oil of New Jersey, GM funnelled into Nazi advancements in technology the ingredients necessary for the industrial production of lead-tetraethyl. In the era, when Hitler, Roosevelt, and Stalin cast long shadows over humanity's destiny, ethyl emerged as a vital ingredient in the industrial chemistry of mechanized warfare.

Alfred P. Sloan, GM's president and chairman of the board, closely directed the role of his company on both sides of the conflict between Hitler and Roosevelt. This graduate of electrical engineering at the Massachusetts Institute of Technology pioneered many modern management techniques integral to the rise of those corporate leviathans that would come to dominate the organization of money, machines, workers, distribution, and marketing in capitalist industrialization.[29] Sloan developed and applied some of the key principles for the deployment of resources on an enormous scale that would later be built upon by Robert McNamara in his stints as president of the Ford Motor Company, US defense secretary, and World Bank president.

Like Henry Ford, GM's CEO preferred the business-friendly milieu of Hitlerian fascism to the labour-friendly trade unionism of the American New Deal. Sloan was particularly determined to resist all efforts to subordinate the industrial imperatives of his world-beating company to the power of popularly elected government. This principle, however, was becoming increasingly difficult to uphold in Roosevelt's America, a polity, Sloan lamented, where "government and not industry constitute the final authority."[30]

The antagonism that developed between the different types of capitalism in the New Deal and the Third Reich did not end after 1945, when Europe's division into Soviet and US-dominated zones epitomized the bipolarism of the Cold War. In the name of its global assault on socialist internationalism, the Washington-based national security state adopted many of the tactics, methods, and personnel of Nazi anti-communism, generating new variations on the cartelized forms of gangsterism that had thrived under Axis rule. Back in Detroit, however, the legacy of Roosevelt prevailed over that of gangster capitalism. As the car companies reverted back to producing vehicles largely for civilian consumption, their executives opted to deepen the integration of trade unions and organized labour into their systems of corporate industrial relations.

In the 1950s and 1960s the North American car factories were staffed by some of the most commercially productive, best-treated, and most highly paid industrial workers in the world. This state of affairs was part of a more general pattern where the large polarities between rich and poor in the United States were briefly narrowed. The Treaty of Detroit became a primary marker and instrument of this happy run of shared prosperity. The agreement brought to industrial relations some of the ideals of collective empowerment through an embrace of shared interests as symbolized by the Bowl with One Spoon.

The Detroit Treaty was a very different kind of agreement from those treaties negotiated with the powerful Indian nations who congregated in that area long before Henry Ford chose this strategic border zone as the capital of his industrial empire. This precedent-setting labour relations contract, negotiated in 1950 between GM and the United Auto Workers, helped to set high standards for millions of unionized workers across many fields of manufacturing in terms of workers' pay, pensions, health-care benefits, and even cost-of-living provisions. The deep integration of trade unionism into the auto industry and many other branches of US manufacturing gave rise to a period when large segments of organized labour joined the North American middle class. Although the Detroit Treaty helped improve the standard of life of millions of workers, the agreement has drawn criticism for setting standards of compensation so high that they would, in later years, drag down the future capacity of the US automobile companies to remain internationally competitive.

The Canada-US Auto Pact of 1965 helped to formalize the continental extension of this integrative approach to the making of cars through managed capitalism.[31] While Canada, Great Britain, and many other Western European countries had developed entrenched social democratic parties, no similar third-party option was allowed to coalesce in the United States. No stable electoral platform was permitted to form where voters and candidates could meet in giving top political priority to the rights and interests of organized labour. The more recent impediments put in the way of a US version of the British Labour Party or the Canadian New Democratic Party were similar to those that had prevented Eugene V. Debs from founding a viable Socialist Party earlier in the twentieth century. The legacy of the Red Scare was thus renewed in the politics of the Cold War. Gatekeepers, especially of the moderate left, were given broad encouragement to make sure that the US embrace of trade unionism was contained within the confines of the existing system of political representation. No proponents of any revolutionary departure from managed capitalism would be allowed to organize a significant break from the monopoly of the American two-party system. Competition between Republican and Democratic candidates would be maintained within the narrow and simple dichotomy epitomized by, say, the marketing war between Pepsi-Cola and Coca-Cola.

With Walter Reuther of the United Auto Workers leading the way, the largest constituency of trade unionists was integrated into the New Deal's primary agency – the Democratic Party. The tumultuous career of Teamster Union boss Jimmy Hoffa illustrated another facet of the US effort to avert class polarization by integrating trade unionism within the superpower's existing matrix of material interaction. As the don of collective bargaining for the powerful truck drivers' union, Hoffa was the target by Attorney-General Robert Kennedy and others for his allegedly criminal involvements with underworld racketeers. The violent responses of Hoffa's Mafia associates to the criminal proceedings pressed against them, extending in all likelihood to the assassination of Kennedy's brother, suggested just how much had changed since events such as the Ludlow Massacre and the Battle of the Overpass illustrated the vulnerability of organized labour to the violence of their employers' hired thugs.[32] Hoffa's complex network of backers, allies, and friends extended to the top levels of the Republican Party. This association was a major factor in President Richard Nixon's decision to grant Hoffa a pardon in 1971 on a jail sentence for jury tampering.[33]

The brief and violently terminated presidency of John F. Kennedy coincided with the years when General Motors reigned as the largest US corporation, with a growing worldwide network of branch plants, subsidiaries, and dealerships. In 1962, when its seventy-fifth million car flowed from its assembly lines, GM supplied half of the US market. The tentacles of this massive corporate octopus spread far and wide. GM engineers, for instance, created the navigation systems that the roving lunar vehicles used between 1969 and 1972 in the moon landings of NASA's Apollo missions.

The heyday of industrial creativity centred in Detroit coincided with the period when Berry Gordy's Motown records captured the artistic verve of the "Motor City." Gordy left his job on the Ford assembly line to churn out classic Motown tunes sung by the likes of Stevie Wonder, Marvin Gaye, The Jackson Five, as well as Diana Ross and the Supremes. Their soulful songs and lyrics helped fulfill Antonin Dvořák's prediction following his visit to the World's Columbian Exposition in Chicago in 1893 that "Negro melodies" would provide America with a "great and noble" school of music.[34] Like the automobile culture spawned in Detroit, the music of Motown was exported to a world of diverse peoples, many of whom shared sentiments of common affection for the populist genius that tends to permeate the best traditions of US creativity. Gordy's decision to move Motown records to Los Angeles in 1972 anticipated the decline about to afflict the once-charmed seat of automotive innovation, where so many American Dreams of self-propelled mobility found their vehicles of transport.

ECONOMIC TRANSFORMATIONS IN THE GENESIS OF "GOVERNMENT MOTORS"

The economics of the car business changed forever as the glory days of the US lunar landings came to a close. In 1973 the Arab oil embargo announced major shocks in the global systems of energy extraction, high finance, and industrial relations – and soon there proved to be far more than had immediately been apparent behind the soaring prices of black gold. Underlying the end of the era of cheap gasoline was a secret agreement between President Richard Nixon and the ruling dynasty of Saudi Arabia. In consultation with many of the other oil-exporting countries, the Saudis had obtained US consent for a quadrupling of the price of fossil fuels on the condition that suppliers would accept only US dollars as payment.

This linking of the value of the US dollar to the price of oil gave renewed viability to the world's pre-eminent unit of exchange, one that had recently been decoupled from the gold standard.[35] The reinvention of US currency essentially as Saudi-American petrodollars helped to accelerate the move of high finance away from the US manufacturing base, where the legacy of the New Deal had briefly prospered. The strengthened US business partnership with Saudi elites such as arms dealer Adnan Khashoggi helped to energize the emergent and increasingly privatized terror economy whose prototypes of transaction began to coalesce in the meteoric career of the Pakistani-based BCCI – the Bank of Credit and Commerce International.[36]

During its heyday in the late 1970s and 1980s, the worldwide operations of the Saudi-backed BCCI provided a core venue of financial interaction enabling many of the world's main national security agencies, but especially the CIA, to do business with Islamic and anti-communist proxy armies, pipeline builders, oil conglomerates, money launderers, drug cartels, extortionists, and the builders of Pakistan's arsenal of nuclear weapons.[37] Jimmy Hoffa's involvement in the interactions linking the CIA and the Mafia in the era when the Kennedy brothers and Martin Luther King were assassinated can be seen, in retrospect, to have been rudimentary compared to the deep integration of the national security state into the new syndicates of organized crime that coalesced in and around the financial dealings facilitated by the BCCI. Prominent among its customers were the US- and Saudi-backed mujahadeen, the protagonists of the anti-Soviet jihad in Afghanistan. One of the Arabic terms to emerge from the mujahadeen was *al-Qaeda*, the phrase used to describe the CIA-provided base of the jihadists' digital communications network.[38]

Between 1986 and 1994 the sporadic probes of the Iran-Contra investigations provided small but important windows into some of the changing politics of the national security state in the genesis of the terror economy.

The full extent of this terror economy would not be fully realized until the depiction of the events of September 11 as an externally planned Arab and Islamic surprise attack. To borrow some phrases from the Pulitzer Prize–winning journalist Chris Hedges, the "exotic shock" created by "dragging out" from the "the Halloween closet" the menacing imagery of "bearded Islamic extremists" translated into immediate public support for costly new Eurasian adventures.[39] Nevertheless, well before the pulverization of the three World Trade Center towers as well as the puncturing of the Pentagon's walls, the terror economy's major elements were already well developed, especially where the activities of the national security state intersected with the deep politics of Israel, Saudi Arabia, Pakistan, the Balkans, Central America, and the primary corporate beneficiaries of the permanent war economy.[40]

Much of the domestic activity in the terror economy's US homeland revolved around the highly secretive and comprehensive emergency measures plan known as Continuity of Government (cog).[41] During the presidency of Ronald Reagan, the architects of this "secret government within a government" developed a particular focus on "domestic anti-terrorism." They made elaborate provisions not only for the continuation of US governance after a nuclear attack by the Soviet Union but also in the event of "violent and widespread internal dissent or national opposition to a U.S. military invasion abroad." Among the cog's activities was the establishment and maintenance of rex 84 detainment facilities by the Federal Emergency Management Agency for deployment under conditions of martial law.[42]

As James Mann and Peter Dale Scott have documented, Donald Rumsfeld and Richard Cheney took part over more than three decades in cog's regular exercises. During Reagan's two-term presidency, these veteran operatives were extremely active among those who worked both the corporate and the government sides of the national security state in its accelerating efforts to construct the basis of a shadow government that would replace the US Constitution with a regime of centralized and unbounded executive rule. It was during this culminating period in the Cold War that many of the main protagonists and beneficiaries involved in and around the contested events of 9/11 connected with one another through the banking system at the bcci.[43]

The beginning of the career of Saudi-American petrodollars coincided with the US-backed coup in Chile. The violent elimination of the popularly elected government of Salvador Allende cleared the way for the installation of the military dictatorship of General Augusto Pinochet. His closest advisers included the radical libertarian economist Milton Friedman as well as other Chicago School disciples of Frederick Hayek. As Naomi Klein outlines in her country-by-country account of the rise of "disaster capitalism," the Chilean coup of 1973 started a more concerted phase in the worldwide push to eliminate not only socialism but also the institutional basis of managed capitalism on the middle ground of industrial compromise.

This global assault on the ability of citizens to mobilize the power of the state on behalf of human rather than corporate "persons" led not only to rapid deindustrialization in many regions and sectors but also to a huge transfer of wealth from workers to share owners. Old brand-name factories were shut down as manufacturing jobs and industrial capacities were transferred to areas with large and poor populations that could more easily be exploited. Very few human factors were allowed to get in the way of this push to maximize capitalism's "creative destruction" by eliminating most national impediments to global flows of capital.[44] One result of deindustrialization in the United States was an increase in the political and economic leverage of the arms industry, one of the few sectors there which was able to retain and even add to the number of its relatively high-paying manufacturing jobs.

Although the sheer magnitude of the Detroit-based companies and the entrenched strength of the United Auto Workers somewhat delayed the time of reckoning, the deindustrialization process gradually extended to the automobile sector in North America. The loss of market share began when a significant portion of North American car shoppers responded to increased energy prices by buying smaller, more energy efficient cars produced primarily in Japan and Western Europe. Companies such as Volkswagen, Toyota, Honda, Nissan, Suzuki, and, later, the Korean-based Hyundai capitalized on the comparative advantage they enjoyed in the changed commercial environment. They increased the scale as well as the transnational reach of their manufacturing and marketing operations even as they continued to improve the quality of their vehicles. Meanwhile, Mercedes-Benz, BMW, and Volvo made significant inroads at the high end of the North American market by incorporating sophisticated engineering into their vehicles.

The political economy of the car business continued to change as growing portions of the emerging middle classes, especially in China, India, and Brazil, sought to express their newfound economic capacities by purchasing and driving cars. In China alone, 33 million cars were added between 2008 and 2010.[45] The rising commercial strength of communities on the new frontiers of intensive industrialization created major opportunities for fresh initiatives in automotive design and manufacturing. In 2008, for instance, Ratan N. Tata, chairman of Tata Motors, introduced India's version of "the people's car," much as Henry Ford had once done with his Model T or as Adolf Hitler had done when he announced plans to manufacture his simple beetle-shaped car design for average German *Volks*. The cheapest version of the two-cylinder, 30 horse-power Nano entered the market with a price tag of about $2,500. It was equipped with engines manufactured by Bosch, a German firm that became a leader in the globalization of its industrial strategies. Tata's own systems for the production of cars, trucks, and buses involved elaborate partnerships with vehicle makers in many countries, including Spain, Italy, Thailand, Brazil, and South Korea.

This same globalized approach to production and marketing was central to the structure of the deal that, for a time, seemed like a formula for saving the German-based Opel Corporation from bankruptcy along with the rest of General Motors. A core unit of Nazi war production before 1945, Opel was at the heart of a complex deal put together by the Canadian-based Magna International and the Russian-based GAZ Corporation, with a major infusion of capital from the German government and from Russia's Sberbank. The deal was to have kept Opel factories running in Germany, Poland, Spain, and Portugal. It also was meant to keep Vauxhall products rolling off British assembly lines. The transaction seemed to open the way for the manufacturing of some Opel products in Canada and Russia.[46] Russia is widely viewed as a car market with significant potential for growth. Magna International's Franck Stronach was a key architect of the deal to reinvent GM's European wing. In the midst of his negotiations with GM, GAZ, Sberbank, and the affected governments, Stronach announced that his Canadian car-parts company would work directly with Ford Motor Company in making an electric car to compete with GM's Volt.[47]

The deal broke down in November 2009 when an improved economic climate enabled the post-bankruptcy GM to retain its ownership of the Opel and Vauxhall operations.[48] Nevertheless, the bold reach of Stronach's many-faceted plans for the growth of his business even amid the economic gloom highlighted the nature of important fault lines in industrial competitiveness in North America. As part of the system of compensation initiated in the Treaty of Detroit, members of the United Auto Workers in the United States were extended significant health-care benefits paid for by the car companies. This approach helped to establish patterns that have been broadly replicated throughout the US political economy. Unlike in Canada, the US government in 2009 had no publicly funded system of universal health care for all its citizens. It has generally been the country's employers, rather than the government, that assumed much of the cost of providing health care through a privatized system of for-profit insurance businesses. The difference between the publicly funded system in Canada and the privately administered one in the United States has historically given some Canadian companies, but especially the automotive branch plants and parts manufacturers such as Magna International, a significant competitive advantage.

In June 2009, in a speech to the American Medical Association, President Barack Obama connected the failures in the US approach to health care to larger problems in the US system of industrial relations: "Our largest companies are suffering, as well. A big part of what led General Motors and Chrysler into trouble in recent decades was the huge costs they racked up providing healthcare for their workers – costs that made them less profitable and less competitive with automakers around the world. If we do not fix our health care system, America may go the way of GM – paying more, getting less, and going broke."[49] The connections Obama drew among health care, trade unionism, and international competitiveness point to the need to attempt broad analytical connections across many fields of specialty in an era when the effects of globalization permeate relationships of all sorts. This broader perspective clearly informed the urgency of the Obama administration's effort to reform the world's most expensive system of health care, one that nevertheless failed to provide any insurance coverage for about 50 million US citizens. This institutionalized inequity was deeply rooted in the history of a country where the military Keynesianism of the permanent war economy has drawn resources away from the development of programs that might otherwise have guaranteed, for instance, health care for all US citizens. In spite of the obstacles, however, in March 2010 President Obama signed into law a major health-care reform bill extending insurance coverage dramatically.

The connection between the massive size of the US military budget and the impediments that had kept the US government from providing guaranteed health-care coverage to all its citizens gave rise to the development of popular campaigns aimed at shifting priorities. Various groups have participated in the genesis of the movement whose slogan is Health Care Not Warfare.[50] In February 2009 the Progressive Democrats of America adopted this priority by announcing:

Half the world's spending on war, and preparations for war, is currently done by the United States. That's too much. Half of our discretionary budget goes to war and preparations for war. That's too much. Now is the time to return to the dreams of our Founders, to provide for the general welfare and build a more perfect Union – rather than a future of sprawling overseas bases, thousands of nuclear weapons, and a militarized outer space ... Let's spend the money on the almost 50 million Americans without any health coverage.[51]

The transformation in the imagery of GM to that of Government Motors raises a host of questions about the role of the state in material interactions of many sorts. Should, for instance, workers be put in a situation where their access to health care depends on whether the companies they partially own can turn a profit? Is access to basic health care best understood as a privilege of those who come out on top in capitalist society or should it be seen more as a fundamental facet of human rights whose proper framework is universal rather than local or national? Is there anything to learn from Cuba, a country that has structured itself internally as well as in its orientation to the rest of the world around the principle of health care as a public good to be freely shared? When workers are compelled to use their union's health-care and pension funds to keep their jobs, as in post-bankruptcy GM and Chrysler, what role should they play in the management of those companies that they partially own? Can corporate governance and ownership be transformed to express better the principles of the Bowl with One Spoon; to balance more democratically the overlapping rights and interests of citizen owners, private shareholders, workers, managers, and consumers?

Post-bankruptcy GM and Chrysler are not the complete misfits and aberrations of industrial relations they are sometimes made out to be. As David Welch and David Kiley point out, "governments from Berlin to Beijing have been propping up their domestic industries." The authors identified thirty major car producers in the global economy. Together, these firms held the capacity to produce 90 million vehicles in 2008, whereas they sold only 55 million new units.[52] Should this excess capacity be maintained and enlarged or should the surplus industrial capabilities in the car industry be pointed at the achievement of other objectives, such as improving the infrastructure of public transit?

The spread of the global financial crisis to the car industry occurred at a pivotal point in the technological history of mass transport. Although the century of the internal combustion engine appeared to be coming to an end, it remained unclear what technology would replace it. While many deemed that mass mobility would best be delivered through the flow of electricity rather than gasoline, there was much less certainty about what infrastructures would be required and how they would be structured financially, logistically, and politically. Would the nuclear energy industry move into the vacuum to supply energy for electric cars or for the production of the chief ingredient in hydrogen-fuel-cell–powered cars? Or could sufficient renewable energy from the wind, sun, the tides, and thunder be harnessed to provide the power of propulsion to new technologies of mass transport? Should the pace and form of the move into the new technologies of industrial transport be left to market forces? Or does the sheer magnitude of the technological transformation, together with the great range of public interests and environmental variables involved in the transition, require leadership from governments and informed citizenries on a global scale?

The potential for tens of millions or even hundreds of millions of new drivers in India and China to acquire Tata Nanos or other similar low-cost vehicles helps to focus attention on the need to place limits on humanity's technological interventions into life's complex web of ecological relationships. From weaponry to cars to medicine, so powerful have our manufactured tools become that there is no way to secure a decent human future for posterity without creating systems of checks and balances to regulate interactions among technology, people, and the rest of nature. The imagery of the Bowl with One Spoon can be of service in providing an icon of the need to protect the shared public interest on a truly global scale. This imagery, along with the political will to apply its meanings, is vital in an era when the prospect of further mass destruction on a global scale is posed not only by the excesses of financial deregulation but also by the excesses of technological deregulation across many branches of industry.

The ideals of the Bowl with One Spoon point towards the need to protect and cultivate public spaces, resources, and enterprises, including in the strategic field of public transit. This emphasis could be as simple as providing increased provision for urban bicycle transport, using the bike lanes and bike parking facilities of, say, Amsterdam as a model. In China and India it would involve further development of the already good rail systems, together with a conscious decision to veer away from the enticements of privatized transport as embodied in the culture of cars. In North America it will require an enormous act of will to lessen our reliance on automobiles. This dependence was cultivated through the orchestrated political interventions of many agencies, including GM, Firestone Tires, and Standard Oil of California. These firms and others mounted a concerted drive beginning in the 1920s to undermine the effectiveness of electrified light rail transport.[53] This move to limit the extent of electric-powered public transit systems forms one part of the campaign to usher North Americans towards the convenience of mobility in privately owned vehicles, an objective that could not have been achieved without an enormous public investment in roads and highways.

The importance of the military-industrial complex in promoting the culture of cars was epitomized by the role of "Machine Charlie" Wilson in 1956 when, as President Eisenhower's secretary of defense, the former CEO of GM helped to consolidate political support for the $25 billion *Federal-Aid Highways Act*.[54] In making the case for this enormous public investment, Eisenhower was explicit about his desire to apply the military lessons he had acquired on his way to making the old headquarters of IG Farben in Frankfurt, Germany, into the headquarters of US military operations in Western Europe. In moving towards the victory of allied forces during the Second World War, General Eisenhower had to contend with the lightening fast blitzkrieg movements of enemy forces along sophisticated highway networks. Hence the primary prototype for the Interstate highway system in the United States was the autobahns built by the Third Reich. This connection continued the intense pattern of US-German interaction in the car industry epitomized by Adolph Hitler's tribute to Henry Ford's Model T in the fascist leader's own design for the Volkswagen beetle.

The history of GM's enormous successes and monumental failures has set the stage for the next phase in the life of this wounded giant of managed capitalism. President Obama invested abundant amounts of his own personal political capital as well as tens of billions of taxpayers' dollars in creating the basis for the emergence of the new GM from the selected remnants of the bankrupt entity. It was the magnitude of this commitment that caused one observer to characterize the US leader as GM's "Savior-in-Chief."[55] But where is this new departure in political economy headed? Will the ray of hope held out by the young US president lead to political redemption for GM's saviors or to yet more rude awakenings from broken American Dreams? Is it possible that the citizen and worker owners of GM could empower the enterprise to point the way towards a renaissance in public transport?[56] Such a role might well give clear expression to the ethos of a new era of public service based on a recognition of the unique capacity of democratic government to transcend private interests in order to serve the public good.

In the event of such a development, let the name of Pontiac be revived yet again in identifying the GM division devoted to upgrading public transit. It was Pontiac's genius that gave heightened constitutional meaning to images of the Bowl with One Spoon on shelled wampum belts, signifying treaty agreements among Indian nations willing to share hunting territory in common. Pontiac's teachings were taken, refined, and disseminated by Tecumseh in his inspirational campaign to elevate the sovereign personality of the Indian Confederacy in the North American interior. This prophetic oracle of the principles of the Bowl with One Spoon was instrumental in instilling sufficient unity into the Aboriginal fighting forces of the Indian Country of Canada that the Armed Forces of the United States were briefly dislodged from their control over the frontier post of Detroit during the War of 1812.[57] Detroit has been the site of repeated conflict between the American Empire and the Fourth World.

Moving on from the insights of Pontiac, Tecumseh, Gandhi, W.E.B. Du Bois, Rigoberta Menchú, George Manuel, and many other leaders in the Fourth World struggle against colonial domination, we have the option of joining together to act in accord with a vision of the world as a shared vessel of bounteous life to be enjoyed together by a global confederacy of allied peoples. Alternatively, we can continue to condemn our posterity to oblivion at worst, hell on earth at best, by accepting the tyranny of those who have tied their interests to the permanent economy of endless warfare.

The transformation of the company that was once Detroit's pride into Government Motors offers a significant opening for innovative experiments in the industrial stewardship of public property. It creates a significant venue for the infusion of new ideas into the necessary project of regulating business and technology in the public interest. This imperative requires renewed confidence in the power of the state to mediate in the public interest on the middle ground of industrial relations. In the final analysis, governments chosen by and genuinely accountable to citizens provide the best vehicle to merge the heritage of Enlightenment egalitarianism with the animating spirit of the Bowl with One Spoon.

WALL STREET, DERIVATIVES, AND THE GLOBAL ECONOMIC CONTAGION

The bankruptcy and nationalization of a downsized GM occurred in the context of a major financial constriction with worldwide reach. The crisis brought to light the political implications of many changing patterns in commercial interaction, but especially those arising from China's quick ascent towards the commanding heights of the global economy. It revealed emerging fault lines in the process of formulating policies governing the trade and currency of the European Union. It illuminated Africa's continuing marginalization, the high-stakes betting accompanying Russia's uncertain orientation to the international community, and the surprisingly high level of indigenous support for some sort of Latin American Union of Federated Socialist Republics. It exposed how a banking crisis could mow down in an instant the economic viability of a tiny country like Iceland. Moreover, the crisis drew attention to the changing composition of the oil and gas industry, in which government-owned firms such as those of Russia, China, Abu Dhabi, Brazil, Indonesia, Iran, Norway, and Nigeria have been asserting control over most of the world's proven reserves.

In the midst of the crisis in 2009, Juan Somavia, the director general of the International Labor Organization, estimated that the loss of jobs globally would be somewhere between 30 and 50 million. He calculated, moreover, that the malaise would increase the number of workers earning less that $2 a day by about 200 million. The $2 mark is the figure used by the ILO to indicate the threshold of extreme poverty. Over two billion global citizens attempt to survive daily on less than this amount. Somavia characterized as "daunting" the "political and security implications" of the economic plunge.[58] A similar sense of emergency rippled through police, military, and intelligence forces the world over. For instance, the prospect of serious disruption arising from sharp economic downturns deeply coloured the proceedings accompanying Admiral Dennis C. Blair's appointment as President Obama's director of national intelligence. In anticipating the outlines of his assignment, Blair identified the job of preparing government responses to the barrage of challenges they might face from citizens outraged by the quick disappearance of their assets as one of the main tasks of national security.[59]

The rapid spread of the "contagion" from the financial sector of the United States to so many facets of the entire global economy demonstrates the pervasive interdependency of commercial relationships in the twenty-first century. As Ian Greenberg, the chief CEO of the Montreal-based Astral Media explained, "This [crisis] is different because it's deeper than any we've seen over the years, because this one is affecting all industries. You had the tech bubble, you had the real estate meltdown, but you never saw it affecting all industries. I don't think any industry has been left out of this tsunami."[60]

The worldwide spread of severe economic problems from region to region and from sector to sector helped to illustrate the pervasive vulnerability that has emerged from the homogenization of many different political economies to form a single global system of material interaction. Our collective capacity to immunize at least some sectors and some branches of the human family from the effects of economic plague have been impaired by the steady erosion of legal, political, and ideological supports for bio-cultural diversity. Moreover, the narrowing base of biocultural diversity has diminished the pool of possible remedies, antidotes, and alternative philosophies on which to draw in the attempt to fend off global maladies, whether economic, biological, ideological, or spiritual.

Many of the voices that initially emphasized the need for global perspectives and correctives emanated from Europe, but especially from those metropolitan centres whose long advancement of imperial globalization helped to broaden and intensify the net of material interaction presently linking most branches of the human family. British prime minister Gordon Brown and French president Nicholas Sarkozy were prominent among those who called for a major reworking of the world's financial architecture to culminate in what they described as a second Bretton Woods. "We now have global financial markets," said Brown, "but what we do not have is anything other than national and regional regulation and supervision."[61] Brown and others favoured building up the International Monetary Fund as the central agency to regulate the global economy. This recommendation was accompanied by many proposals, such as calls for a return to fixed rates of exchange, the creation of a new global reserve currency, and the elimination of tax havens.

Anticipating the devaluation of its huge reserves of US dollars because of the Federal Reserve Board's rapid inflation of the US money supply, the government of China was especially anxious to institute a new unit of exchange based on the combined worth of a basket of different currencies.[62] The governments of France and Russia supported the Chinese in advocating a broadly expanded role for the system of Special Drawing Rights – SDRs – which have formed the basis of the International Monetary Fund's reserves since 1969. The quest for a new and more broadly representative unit of international exchange built on ideas introduced by John Maynard Keynes in the negotiations leading up to the Bretton Woods Agreements of 1944. In calling for the creation of an International Clearing Union (ICU) to give coherence to interlocking regimes of trade, investment, and currency creation, Keynes advocated the creation of a new form of ICU money to be known as grammor. In 1943 he refined his initial suggestion, proposing that the world conduct much of its international business in unitas.[63]

The attempt to build up a more powerful array of international mechanisms to regulate the workings of the global economy helped highlight the dramatically diminished economic clout of the United States and the fast-rising importance especially of China, India, and Brazil. The convergence of the financial crisis with the political necessity of representing a more multipolar world came together in the effort to make the political leadership of the G20 group of countries a major instrument of a more stable and sustainable regime of material interaction. The 2009 meetings of G20 leaders first in London in April and then in Pittsburgh in September provided a significant venue for the new leadership of a severely wounded Anglo-

America to attempt to manage the transition towards a more viable system of global economic governance.[64]

According to Keynesian economist Joseph Stiglitz, the so-called G192 – all member countries of the UN General Assembly – went further than the G20 in calling for a major reworking of the global financial system. "We have allowed economic globalization to outpace political globalization," he wrote. Many of the delegations that took part in the special New York summit of the G192 in June 2009 called attention to the double standard between the domestic response of the rich world to the downturn in their own countries and the imposition by international financial institutions of severe austerity measures when poorer countries face economic trauma. The trillions of taxpayers' dollars used in bailing out the banks, Stiglitz asserted, "make claims that there are insufficient funds to finance development assistance ring hollow."[65]

There are many reasons that the first major rumblings of the global financial crisis occurred on Wall Street. Its major institutions both promoted and exploited the decision to abandon the New Deal's legacy of managed capitalism. The other side of the many-faceted deindustrialization of the United States had been the elevation of the financial sector as reflected, for instance, in the change of laws allowing the merger of banking, brokerage, and insurance firms. The expectation in the axis of negotiations linking Wall Street and Washington was that the US financial sector would become the major global funnel for the transfer of wealth from workers in high-wage areas to shareholders around the world. In order to realize this agenda in the trickle *up* theory of wealth, the executive branches of the most globalized cartels and conglomerates partnered with operatives in China, Indochina, and other low-wage regions to point capitalism's creative destruction towards new frontiers of cut-rate industrialization. This massive global reorganization of the manufacturing sector was pushed forward fast and hard, with little regard for the suffering and violence felt by those whose domestic economies were shattered by fundamental alteration in the machinery devoted to Earth's transformation into property.

This strategy of deregulation in the financial sector specifically, and in the global economy more generally, was deeply tied up with the complex of relationships that made Wall Street a central symbol and site of the Cold War. Throughout this period, the financial institutions of Wall Street retained the inside edge in the particular class of business transaction that has long been a core component in the permanent war economy of the United States. But the Cold War and the wars that replaced it have also been enormously important in the generation of potent public mythologies that have enabled Wall Street institutions to brand themselves as bastions of the personal and corporate liberties associated with what Harry Truman described in 1947 as "freedom of enterprise." Attempting to equate the new turn of phrase with the more familiar principles of religious freedom and freedom of speech, Truman helped initiate the political rhetoric of the

Cold War. In 1947 at Baylor University in Waco Texas, he solemnly declared to the world and his own nation that freedom of enterprise – free enter-prise – "is part and parcel of what we call American."[66]

The cosmology of symbols and myths within which the deregulation of Wall Street institutions took place drew strongly from the politics of the real and imagined showdown between the capitalist superpower and the Soviet Empire's regime of central planning. The stark dichotomy engendered by the imagery of a free world in mortal combat with an evil empire became even more compelling in the immediate aftermath of the Soviet system's failure. In the years that followed the demise of the Soviet Empire, it was made to seem that no remaining state or ideological obstacle was powerful enough to block the triumphant push to globalize markets in a unipolar world dominated by the combined force of American capitalism, American culture, and the brute muscle of the American military-industrial complex.

The dismantling of federal regulations governing Wall Street was widely viewed among those riding the bandwagon of American triumphalism after the Cold War as part of the victory dividend for defeating the world's most heavily armed bastion of anti-capitalism. This deregulatory movement found expression in 1999, when Congress passed the *Financial Services Modernization Act* to eliminate many of the remaining prohibitions put in place by the *Glass-Steagall Act* of 1933. Like the *Securities Exchange Act* the following year, the *Glass-Steagall Act* was a seminal expression of Roosevelt's New Deal. Ferdinand Pecora's penetrating investigative work as chief coun-sel for the US Senate Committee on Banking helped prepare the way for this surge of regulation in the second New Deal. The feisty Pecora made national headlines with his aggressive interrogations highlighting the abundant conflicts of interests linking Wall Street insiders. With the goal of restraining the speculative recklessness that had caused stock markets to crash in 1929, the *Glass-Steagall Act* required the US financial sector to divide commercial banking for depositors from investment brokerage.[67]

The *Financial Services Modernization Act* opened the way to mergers of companies oriented to commercial banking, investments, and insurance. These mergers led to the formation of huge, multifunction companies that offered dramatically widened arrays of financial products and services. The high-powered merchandising in Wall Street's modernization of its global operations was supposed to offer some consolation for, and relief from, the loss of US manufacturing might. The switchover from the manufacturing of goods to a growing emphasis on money's manipulation gave only brief pause to the capitalist superpower's economic slide ever since the spigot of Saudi-American petrodollars was opened in 1973. In the three decades leading up to this fundamental alteration in the world's most important unit of exchange, the managerial and technological efficiencies of the US manufacturing sector had been the envy of much of the world. Jean-Jacques Servan-Schreiber had highlighted those efficiencies in 1967 in *Le Défi Américain*, his runaway bestseller in France.

The Congressional enactment of the *Commodity Futures Modernization Act* (CFMA) in 2000 proved to be the biggest step of all in the movement to deregulate the financial sector. This law has been described as "the most egregious example of private enterprise dictating public policy." The bill was drafted in part by officials of the Enron Corporation to create the conditions for the treatment of energy, including electricity, as a commodity to be traded on futures markets.

The CFMA's "Enron loophole" was accompanied by many similar bows to the dogma of deregulation across most fields of financial transaction.[68] Part of the law's text was drafted to make explicit the exemption of derivatives trades from the kind of transparency and rules-based protections that a brave whistle-blower named Brooksley Born had sought in 1997. As chair of the federally appointed Commodities Futures Trading Commission, Born proposed remedies to the growing abuses she saw developing in derivatives markets. Her attempt to safeguard the public interest quickly aroused the opposition of Alan Greenspan, the Federal Reserve's chairman, and Robert Rubin, President Clinton's treasury secretary.[69] With their backing, along with the muscle flexing of the power brokers at the Wall Street firm of Goldman Sachs, the CFMA brought many requirements for external auditing to a close. Washington's favoured bankers and brokers thus used their enhanced autonomy to further exclude government from all but nominal roles in the formulation and marketing of even their most speculative new products.[70]

There was a surge in the availability of "liar loans" after Washington gave Wall Street this green light to push ahead yet faster in opening up new frontiers of risk to a wider array of customers. Liar loans, known also as ninja loans, are transacted without proper checks to verify borrowers' claims about their ability to carry and repay their debts. The increase in fraud-based credit was transformed through the alchemy of derivates into "securitized" paper that was sold and resold throughout the world. As Born had warned in the events leading up to Congress's enactment of the CFMA, the derivative products of the twenty-first century turned out to possess properties that would become toxic when they swirled from the virtual world into the real economy. As the unleashed viruses reached epidemic proportions, they attacked the financial basis of those commercial interactions that facilitate the production of those goods and services that render life possible and sometimes even pleasant in industrial civilization. In this fashion the fast proliferation of derivative products would confound some of our most basic assumptions about the nature of capital as well as of the capitalist system that encompasses it.

Derivatives are not new. As their name implies, they are financial instruments *derived* from the changing value of more traditional forms of capital such as currency, bonds, real estate, and corporate shares. There is no limit on the scope of variables that derivative betting can cover. Since the parties in derivative contracts are not taking ownership of the actual assets on whose future value they wish to gamble, there is no necessity to begin transactions by handing over money or other valuable commodities. Nor is it necessarily required for the contracting parties to possess the financial resources to cover possible losses arising from their bets.

A simple example of how the generation of derivatives might begin lies in the hypothetical case of a contract being made between a buyer and a seller who agree to exchange a fixed amount of money for a commodity to be delivered at a set date in the future regardless of the market price on the delivery day. In such a transaction the contract between the parties may also become a marketable commodity. The agreement to purchase a product at a set price on a fixed future date might be sold and resold several times before the commodity that began the process is delivered. Yet another layer of derivative would develop if observers of this process start betting among themselves on whether the original contract will be fulfilled. Their bets would be derived from the original derivative, which is the contract where promises were made to complete a transaction in the future. Another layer of complexity would be added if an insurance agency decided to sell policies promising to protect the betting parties from the negative financial consequences incurred from making wrong predictions.

How far could such a pyramid scheme of bets on bets on bets be extended before the speculative excesses of its flimsy structure would cause it to collapse? A giant human experiment in speculative pyramid building was initiated with the convergence of extreme deregulation in the financial sector and the application of powerful computers to the process of modelling derivative products. Financiers, mathematical theoreticians, computer scientists, and marketers joined forces to produce a new generation of derivative by selling bets and counter-bets on a range of scenarios for the future involving intricate interactions among a vast array of variables. As these models of speculative gaming became more and more abstract, they moved increasingly far away from any basis in material reality.[71] In the final result, the attempt to incorporate these derivative models of hypothetical futures into the material interactions of the world destabilized the entire global economy.

Much of the growth in derivative trading was driven by the rise of hedge funds. The marriage of hedge funds and derivatives depended on the involvement of some parts of the insurance industry, but especially the global financial giant American International Group (AIG). The founders of the Financial Products unit of AIG did much of the early experimentation in the mid-1980s in the computerization of financial derivatives.[72] No doubt these pioneers on capitalism's proliferating digital frontiers drew on the software and mathematical theories of war games in fashioning their digital programs aimed at modelling the clashes of competing scenarios in the making of the future. Their marriage of hedging with derivative products was one small element in a sweeping reconfiguration in whole landscapes of knowledge, finance, and spying as capital was transformed into one of many different forms of digitalized information for transmission through Internet.

Once the floodgates of financial deregulation opened in 2000, AIG quickly expanded its business by developing insurance products to help those holding and trading derivatives to hedge their bets. Much of this activity took place in AIG's London office, where an agent named Joseph Cassano earned huge bonuses in merchandising the new array of risky financial instruments.[73] In making these sales, AIG was prepared to lend the imprimatur of its high credit rating to those derivative transactions that passed through its apparatus. Indeed, major credit-rating agencies such as Standard and Poor's opted to buy into the increased economic activity attending the trades rather than do due diligence to identify the abundant risks of the heavy involvement of AIG and other brand-name financial institutions in the generation of derivative products such as the now notorious credit default swaps.

In 2003 Warren Buffett famously described the proliferation of money-like instruments know as derivatives as "financial weapons of mass destruction" – as "time bombs of the parties that deal in them and the economic system." The successful hedge-fund manager explained how executives could use derivatives to cook the books by creating the appearance of profit that qualified them to obtain lucrative stock options. As the trajectory of deregulation became more and more integral to the operation of the financial sector, most of the big commissions and bonuses available to insiders involved deals connected to liar loans and to the fantasy accounting that the ballooning global market for derivatives both drove and facilitated. As Buffett noted, "the parties to derivatives have enormous incentive to cheat in accounting for them." He added, "As a general rule, contracts involving multiple reference items and distant settlement dates increase the option for the counter-parties to use fanciful assumptions."[74]

The growth of fantasy accounting connected to trades in derivatives was slowed temporarily by the downfall of both Enron and the accounting company Arthur Anderson. The demise of these entities, as well as the prosecution and conviction of some of their top executives, proved insufficient, however, to stem the contamination of Wall Street institutions and their worldwide financial networks with the dubious assumptions, practices, and products generated from mushrooming trades in derivatives. The enactment in 2002 of the *Sarbanes-Oxley Act* proved to be more about creating the optics of investor confidence than bringing the core practices of chartered accountants back to first principles of objectivity, honesty, rigour, and transparency. The *Sarbanes-Oxley Act* was the main Congressional response to the Enron fiasco and other cases where prominent executives were shown to have cooked the books of their companies in order to obtain lucrative stock options. These frauds cheated shareowners of the full capital worth of their investments.

The proliferation of all sorts of derivative products would remain the elephant in the room of the global economy. In 2008 the Swiss-based Bank for International Settlements presented the startling finding that the global pool of many different categories of derivatives had reached a monetary value of $1.14 quadrillion.[75] A quadrillion is one thousand times a trillion. This amount dwarfed the total gross domestic product of the entire world in 2008 – about $60 trillion. The entire value of all real estate on the planet is calculated to be about $75 trillion.[76] What is to be made of the comparison between the numbers that describe the magnitude of the real economy and those that have been generated by the fantasy accounting connected to derivatives? This stunning discrepancy goes far to clarify the madness inherent in all types of economic and financial calculations made without regard for the finite properties of a small planet whose capacity for ecological regeneration constitutes the only real source of genuine wealth and well-being for humanity.

After the demise of the Soviet Union, the push to universalize capitalism and to further the deregulation of its interactions led financiers to develop forms of derivative accounting. Their quest to squeeze profits from pyramid schemes in hedged betting on computer-generated scenarios of the future created audacious trajectories of expansion in the imagined process of privatizing the global commons. The figures provided by the Bank for International Settlements to describe the size of markets in derivatives was completely disproportionate to the day-to-day costs and rewards of doing business. The huge size of trading in derivatives suggested the magnitude of the hyperinflation to come from the devaluation entailed in the fast pumping up of currency supplies. It pointed to a hypothetical future that exceeded the Earth's physical capacity to host such an exploitative and unsustainable monoculture of possessive individualism.

The pictured trajectories of privatization on capitalism's future frontiers were structured in ways that would further empower a disproportionately entitled minority to derive even more wealth from the world's disentitled majority. Seen in this light, the more recent forms of derivatives intensify old processes that have been under way since the modern era of globalization began with the inception of the Columbian conquests in 1492. The beneficiaries of vampire hedge funds continue to draw blood wealth from colonial processes that began with the imperial theft of Aboriginal lands and resources as well as with the appropriation of labour through slavery and its continuing legacies. These legacies have been expressed through the global deregulation of industrial relations in order to break the power of unions and thereby facilitate the exploitation of workers.

THE ROAD TO MAIDEN LANE

As Barry Ritholtz observes in *Bailout Nation,* Ronald Reagan was the undisputed "intellectual father of the modern radical deregulatory movement."[77] It was Reagan more than any other figure who made the deregulation of business appear to many like a return to the core principles of freedom and democracy. He popularized this concept in the course of a political career where he regularly invoked the powerful symbolism of the American Revolution and the subsequent "winning of the West" as if this conquest of a continent embodied civilization's ascent over savagery. In this fashion the Great Communicator renewed in the context of the Cold War the imagery that Frederick Jackson Turner had identified in 1893 at the World's Columbian Exposition as the originating source of the sense of exceptionalism and providential mission that permeates American national identity to this day. Many forces would join together to exploit Reagan's depiction of American business as the quintessential site of the rugged individualism that Turner had first associated with those pioneers who violently eliminated and displaced Indians on the moving frontiers of American capitalism.

In the updated version of Turner's frontier thesis, the deregulation of Wall Street and its worldwide networks of agents, customers, and partners rendered conditions ripe for yet another extension of the same processes that began with the US seizure of Indian Country's wealth. Freed from the constraints of law and even the requirement to reflect some semblance of reality in the bookkeeping of profit and loss, the trail breakers on American capitalism's most extended frontiers could point their acquisitiveness towards raids on the savings and future earnings of millions of tax-paying citizens at home and around the world. Once again, the mythological invocation of a sanctified culture of cowboy freedom helped give cover to the kleptocratic workings of a system of crony capitalism based on huge inequities of entitlement.

Ronald Reagan became the ideal personification of the Turnerian mythology of the American frontier. He was the heroic leading man who stepped right out of Hollywood "Westerns" into the job of US president. In doing so he epitomized many of the paradoxes that would permeate the American Empire's subsequent rise and fall.[78] Between 1954 and 1962 this former president of the Hollywood Screen Actors Guild was the primary television spokesperson for General Electric. A corporate veteran of the military establishments on both sides of the Second World War, GE was deeply involved in the decision to continue the permanent war economy of the United States. Under the heavy influence of his GE patrons, Reagan took up the cause of those large US corporations most anxious to break free from the power of trade unions that had benefited from the New Deal's legacy. When the opportunity arose, Reagan moved quickly from the union to the executive side in the negotiations of industrial relations on the middle ground of managed American capitalism.

Already by 1964, Reagan and his patrons had put together the main elements of the potent political mythology that would move from strength to strength until the bailouts of 2008 and 2009 exposed the disastrous consequences of too much disconnection between business and the regulatory authority of government. Reagan entered national politics with a declaration that could well be used to highlight the massive contradictions that would mark the end of the ideological revolution he unleashed with his appeal to the rugged individualism and independence of the American people. The future US president could well have been condemning the actions of those Republican leaders who claimed to be his intellectual heirs even as they began pouring massive infusions of public money in 2008 into those supposedly capitalist institutions that had long cultivated an image of themselves as embodiments of laissez-faire liberty. In 1964 Reagan quoted Plutarch to warn that "the real destroyer of the liberties of the people is he who spreads among them bounties, donations and benefits."

Reagan's citation was part of a televised address supporting the unsuccessful candidacy of the Republican presidential nominee, Barry Goldwater. In his attempt to explain the essential features of Goldwater's candidacy, Reagan asked the American people rhetorically "whether we believe in our capacity for self-government or whether we abandon the American Revolution and confess that a little intellectual elite in a far distant capital can plan our lives better for us than we can plan for ourselves." Reagan cautioned that a "government invasion of public power is eventually an assault on your own business." He included in his talk an attack on "socialized medicine." The actor-politician drew together in simple, straightforward language the themes of economic liberty, self-government, deregulation, and the Cold War when he asserted: "We are faced with the most evil enemy mankind has ever known in his long climb from the swamp to the stars ... Those who ask us to trade our freedom for the soup kitchen of the welfare state are architects of a policy of accommodation."[79]

If Reagan could effectively represent GE to the United States, why could he not represent the United States to the rest of the world? In his rise to the planet's most powerful job, Reagan became the governor of California in 1966. In his inaugural address in 1981, the new US president returned to the first principles of his business libertarianism by declaring war on the principles of the Bowl with One Spoon: "Government is not the solution to our problems. Government is the problem."[80]

Reagan's core messages were conveyed through the mainstream media's giant echo chambers with such powerful effect that they transformed the political landscape for a generation. Among the many politicians who rode the waves of the ideological movement the US president did most to initiate were Margaret Thatcher, Brian Mulroney, and the emerging leadership of Eastern European anti-communism. The manipulations of the shock doctrine and disaster capitalism formed an important part of the process of stripping away the Keynesian legacy of the New Deal and Scandanavian-style social democracy in the push to remove all national and human barriers to the agenda of downsized governments and enlarged space for business. The process was significantly assisted by the zeal that Reagan inspired in his acolytes, admirers, defenders, disciples, and imitators around the world.

Both New Labour and the Democratic Party in Anglo-America bowed to many of the popular attractions of Thatcherism and Reaganomics.

President Bill Clinton's Democratic administration snuck the *Commodity Futures Modernization Act* into its last submission to Congress in the hours before it moved aside to make way for the Republican takeover of the US executive branch. In Bush's presidency, the doctrine of business deregulation was treated almost as an element of faith that drew on the evangelical fervour of the times. Just as the condemnation of atheistic communism had tended to invest the institution of private property with an aura of patriotic religiosity during the Cold War, so the defeat of the Soviet enemy seemed to confirm the triumphant wisdom of further diminishing the role of government in the conduct of business.

During the presidency of George Bush, the US executive branch aligned itself closely with the philosophy of Alan Greenspan, the Federal Reserve Board chairman appointed by Ronald Reagan in 1987. A zealous defender of the path of deregulation in most facets of business, including the global expansion of markets in derivatives, Greenspan pushed interest rates so low that personal and corporate indebtedness skyrocketed even as the federal government pushed the throttle in its own debt spending to finance massive military invasions as well as the often covert workings of the increasingly privatized terror economy.[81]

The whole machinery of debt-driven speculation began to sputter in 2007 when the massively leveraged and inflated real-estate market in the United States started to crash, exposing the false economics of a whole class of derivative known as collateralized debt obligations (CDOs). The largest body of these CDOs emerged from packages of indebtedness derived from home mortgages that Wall Street companies sold as interest-bearing assets to banks and pension funds around the world. The bursting of the housing bubble and the rapid devaluation of the attending CDOs began to expose the ephemeral quality of the whole interlocking structure of derivative betting that, by then, had become a staple of the financial sector in many countries. As news spread that some derivative products were based on what Warren Buffett had delicately described as "fanciful assumptions," the lubricant of trust easing the interaction of credit and debt within the core institutions of the financial sector was lost. The most basic interactions in the inner machinery of the world's banking system ground almost to a halt.

The provision in March 2008 of Federal Reserve funds to help JP Morgan Chase Bank purchase for pennies on the dollar the fabled old Wall Street firm of Bear Stearns signalled that some tectonic shift was under way in the failing American Empire's troubled commercial capital. The demise six months later of the 158-year-old Wall Street investment house Lehman Brothers sent shock waves throughout the world when it became the biggest US company to that point ever to go bankrupt.[82] The financial debacle continued throughout the transition from the presidency of George W. Bush to that of Barack Obama. Both administrations, together with the governments of many other countries, attempted to ease the severity of the crisis by plunging their treasuries more deeply into debt in order to inject liquidity into the seized-up machinery of capital markets.

As the crisis grew, 360 banks received capital from the US government. As part of this process, the US Treasury branch purchased preferred equity stakes in a number of financial institutions including Goldman Sachs, Morgan Stanley, JP Morgan Chase, Wells Fargo, Bank of New York Mellon, Citigroup, and State Street. The federal government initially spent $200 billion to take control of Freddie Mac and Fannie Mae, the two giant financial firms whose primary business is to extend credit for home mortgages. In acquiring ownership of these companies, however, the US government is thought have saddled taxpayers with somewhere in the vicinity of $5.5 trillion in unrecoverable debt. This transfer to taxpayers of massive liabilities not of their own making points to the hidden facets of the salvage operations attempted by public agencies in light of the failed promises issued by the false prophets of deregulation since the days of Ronald Reagan's political ascent.

In the opening rounds of the bailout, much public attention was directed at the hundreds of billions of dollars dispensed to the financial and automotive sector through the Bush administration's Troubled Asset Relief Program (TARP) and the Obama administration's Public-Private Investment Program. These amounts, however, did not properly represent the full extent of the financial commitments made by fifty agencies of the US government involved in the debacle. In his quarterly report to Congress in July 2009, Neil Barofsky, the special inspector general of TARP, reported that the taxpayers of the United States were exposed to the tune of $23.7 trillion as a result of his government's efforts to slow and reverse the financial debacle.[83]

The financial crisis led to an expansion in the power exercised by the strange amalgam of public authority and private power that meets in the Federal Reserve system of the United States. Barofsky reported that, as of July 2009, the Federal Reserve had exposed US taxpayers to at least $6.8 trillion in liabilities. The recipients of this money and the nature of the collateral offered for access to it, however, remained largely secret because of a controversial interpretation of an obscure law used to block Congress from auditing the institution with the monopoly power to create US currency and sell the attending indebtedness to the US Treasury.[84] It did emerge, however, that in taking controlling interest of the insurance giant AIG, the Federal Reserve had assumed the responsibility to pay insurance claims on US and foreign derivative contracts. The full extent of these contracts, however, can only be guessed as long as the company's books remained closed to public view.

In February 2009 Joe Nocera, a business columnist at the *New York Times*, wrote that "AIG is ground zero for the practices that led the financial system to ruin." This insurance giant, he said, could not be allowed to go bankrupt because of its central role in insuring derivatives such as credit default swaps. If AIG failed, then so would its partners that "essentially constitute the entire Western banking system ... all the European banks whose toxic assets are supposedly insured by AIG would suddenly be sitting on immense losses. Their already shaky capital structures would be destroyed." Nocera observed that "other firms used many of the same tactics as AIG but none of them on such a broad scale and with such utter recklessness." Thus "the company is being kept alive because it behaved so badly." Although "fully aware of how the scams worked," the government for "practical purposes" has to keep them going. Because of AIG's massive involvement in derivatives, it "pretty much has the world's financial system by the throat."[85]

By the summer of 2009 the Federal Reserve used about two-thirds of the approximately $180 billion it had directed at the AIG fiasco to pay back insurance claims on derivatives contracts. While public attention tended to focus on the bonuses directed to AIG officers and employees even after the company received bailout monies, the amounts involved were relatively small compared to the size of the payments to AIG's counterparties. Some of these payments were funnelled through two companies incorporated in Delaware named Maiden Lane. Thirty-three Maiden Lane is the address of one of the buildings housing the headquarters of the Federal Reserve Bank of New York. The Maiden Lane companies were established during the period when Timothy Geithner, who would become President Obama's treasury secretary, was chair of the Federal Reserve Bank of New York. Geithner participated in the selection of Black Rock Financial Management, a part of the Blackstone group, to administer the Maiden Lane polities according to Section 13(3) of the *Federal Reserve Act*.[86] Peter G. Peterson, a former chair of the Council on Foreign Relations and Geithner's predecessor as chair of the New York Fed, is a founder of the Blackstone group.

Maiden Lane II was established to pay off claims on "mortgage-backed securities." Maiden Lane III was given a far broader mandate to purchase "multi-sector collateralized debt obligations" from "certain counterparties" that took part in "credit default swaps and similar contracts" written up by AIG Financial Products Corporation.[87] The original Maiden Lane was set up to enlist taxpayers in taking over the toxic derivatives of Bear Stearns, leaving the investment bank's purchaser, JP Morgan Chase, free of this financial obligation.

Some of the Maiden Lane payments were made public and some remained secret. Among the revealed recipients were Goldman Sachs with $13 billion, Deutsche Bank and Société Général with $12 billion each, Barclay's Bank with $7.9 billion, Switzerland's UBS with $5 billion, Merrill Lynch with 6.8 billion, Bank of America with $5.2 billion, and US municipalities with $12 billion. According to Edward M. Liddy, the Federal Reserve's emergency chair and CEO of AIG, the Bank of Montreal, Wachovia, and the Royal Bank of Scotland were among the "dozens of financial counterparties" that received taxpayer-backed payments from Maiden Lane II and Maiden Lane III.[88]

In November 2009 it was revealed that President Obama's treasury secretary, Timothy Geithner, had intervened in his former role of chair of the New York Federal Reserve Bank in order to pressure AIG officials not to reveal the full details about those who received payouts through Maiden Lane III.[89] A former official of Goldman Sachs, Geithner was criticized also for agreeing to pay AIG's counterparties 100 per cent of the value of the insurance payouts on the policies they had purchased to hedge their bets in entering into derivative contracts such as the ill-fated credit default swaps.[90] AIG's old nemesis, former New York governor and attorney-general Eliot Spitzer, charged that "the AIG bailout was a way to hide an enormous second round of cash to the same group of companies that had received TARP money already." Spitzer added, "The appearance that this was an inside job is overwhelming." He characterized AIG as "a Ponzi scheme," arguing that its counterparties should have faced financial penalties for their dubious investment decisions.[91] Questions concerning the Federal Reserve's lack of transparency in taking over AIG's financial obligations became part of a more general discussion on a bill sponsored by Congressmen Ron Paul and Alan Grayson. If successful, this enactment would result in the first Congressional audit ever of the financial transactions of the Federal Reserve. One of the central issues in the movement of the *Wall Street Reform and Consumer Protection Act* through Congress in 2009 and 2010 pits those who support the US executive branch's effort to invest the Federal Reserve with yet more power to regulate the economy against those who this view this unaccountable agency as a menace to many interests in the United States and the rest of the world.

Many fundamental questions about the nature of American capitalism arise from the role of the Maiden Lane companies in taking over and continuing the transactions involving the toxic assets of Bear Stearns and AIG. To whom are the officers of the Maiden Lane companies accountable? Are the Maiden Lane entities best understood as part of the private sector or are they part of the public property of the United States? What principles of property and public policy do the Maiden Lane companies embody? What are the rules now that the US executive branch has gone into the derivatives business in such a big way by taking over legal responsibility for the most risky and secret components of Bear Stearns and AIG's international portfolios?

FROM JOHN JACOB ASTOR TO CORNELIUS V. STARR TO MAURICE GREENBERG ON THE EXPANDING FRONTIERS OF AMERICAN EMPIRE

What was the nature of this company described in the *New York Times* as "ground zero" of the financial crisis? How did AIG seize the future of the world's financial system "by the throat?" How could it be that the world's largest conglomerate specializing in a business as seemingly staid and conservative as insurance would come to epitomize risk and uncertainty? What was it about AIG that so encapsulated the inner contradictions and paradoxes of a troubled empire of capital where a major institution meant to offer financial protections against the negative consequences of unforeseen tragedies and disruptions itself became a primary centre of chaotic volatility across a broad spectrum of economic relations?

In 2000, AIG shares were collectively worth more than those of any other insurance or financial services organization listed on the New York Stock Exchange. Seven years later Forbes Magazine rated AIG as the world's sixth largest company, with operations in 130 countries and well over 100,000 employees. The company had grown from seemingly obscure origins in Shanghai, China, to become the world's largest underwriter of commercial and industrial insurance. It had long been one of Japan's most important foreign companies. It included in its unusual business portfolio ownership of 494 aircraft that the company both leased and operated in maintaining its global operations.

Over the years, AIG and its corporate ancestors had played a significant role in pushing back commercial impediments to American business raised by the Iron Curtain. It developed joint ventures with government entities in Hungary, Poland, and Romania in the 1960s. In 1975 Maurice "Hank" Greenberg, the company's CEO, helped to lead the way in returning Western businesses to commercial activity in China. He began by cultivating *guanxi* – friendly relations – that AIG had inherited from an earlier era of Asian history. Greenberg's networks of friendship led the government of the People's Republic of China to enter into a joint venture with AIG in 1980 and then, in 1992, to grant the company a precedent-setting licence to sell insurance policies directly to citizens and companies in the world's most heavily populated country. Greenberg extended his prominent role in the exercise of US foreign policy by working with his broad network of associates around the world, but especially in Asia, to help expand the membership of the World Trade Organization. This process culminated in China's entry into the WTO in 2001.[92]

Greenberg became a lawyer in 1953. He served his country in the Second World War and the Korean conflict, and he received the Bronze Star. In 1960 Greenberg began to learn the insurance trade under the tutorship of the legendary Cornelius V. Starr, who died in 1968, the year after AIG was formally incorporated and the year before it became a publicly traded company. Starr left his protégé to govern the insurance empire he had built, starting with his founding of American Asiatic Underwriters in Shanghai in 1919. From his Shanghai base, Starr spread his insurance network to Hong Kong, the Philippines, Hanoi, Saigon, Jakarta, and Kuala Lumpur. The onset of the Second World War compelled Starr to move his headquarters in 1939 to New York, where he collaborated closely with the head of the Office of Strategic Services, William J. Donovan. The OSS was the forerunner of the CIA.

Starr and "Wild Bill" Donovan worked together in the years when the OSS gave backing, for instance, to Mao Zedong's Red Army and Ho Chi Minh's Viet Minh in their military campaigns to resist the incursions of imperial Japan. Donovan and Starr concentrated their efforts to set up the Insurance Intelligence Branch of the OSS, a small unit that played a significant role in the war zones of both Europe and Asia.[93] The insurance business turned out to be a veritable gold mine of military intelligence deployed to help direct the activities of the embattled armies on both sides of the Second World War. So important to the outcome of military conflict was the information gleaned from insurers that their actions were closely monitored by intelligence agencies on both sides. As Mark Fritz wrote in the *Los Angeles Times*, "Starr's people and other insurance executives had intimate knowledge of the people involved in the global insurance industry and so they were able to track potential collaborators."[94]

After the war, Starr moved quickly to further globalize his business operations by extending his operations into Europe and Latin America. He continued to marry insurance and espionage after the OSS gave birth to the more elaborate structures of the national security state whose powers were outlined in 1947 in the *National Security Act*.[95] As Peter Dale Scott detailed in 1972 in *The War Conspiracy*, Starr's involvement with CIA officials and CIA-owned and related companies continued as US networks of business, intelligence, counter-intelligence, and military enterprise moved into spheres of imperial activity that had been opened in an earlier era of the Columbian conquests by Portuguese, French, Dutch, and British builders of empire in southeast Asia.

Beginning with John Jacob Astor's move from selling otter skins to selling opium in Shanghai, some facets of the West's imperial role in the Far East have proven surprisingly resilient. The Anglo-American push in the Opium Wars to exploit drug addictions as the thin edge of the wedge into China's rich trading corridors established patterns of power and wealth that have continued to this day. By the time Cornelius V. Starr set up shop in Shanghai in the early twentieth century, it had become a very comfortable and profitable seat of trade for men of his class, outlook, and background. Starr's insurance enterprises, which formed the basis for the founding and growth of AIG, continued the trajectory of growing US influence throughout some of Asia's more contested regions.

As this process unfolded, Starr's business operations overlapped at a number of points with the CIA's now well-documented involvement in the region's production, distribution, and export of illegal drugs. The extension of the imperialism of the Opium Wars into the geopolitics of the Cold War moved the locus of production into Indochina. The mixture of drug money, business enterprise, covert operations, and warfare in the military clashes engulfing Vietnam, Laos, and Cambodia formed the basis of a Hollywood movie, *Air America*, starring Mel Gibson. As Scott and others have documented, the political economy of the drug trade blended with the intensifying efforts to locate oil and gas in Eurasia and to secure and hold pipeline corridors for its export. The success of such enterprise depended on the gathering, interpreting, and deploying of good intelligence to give strategic coherence to the targeting of military and political interventions.[96]

Starr's career deeply influenced that of his primary heir and understudy. Between 1967 and 2005, Maurice Greenberg and his insurance company were on the frontier of the drive to globalize business in a US mould. Greenberg's acumen in creating international networks of informants and collaborators seemed especially well suited to the changing formations of capital's empire as the United States moved away from the domestic economy of manufacturing into riskier strategies for accelerating the pace of Earth's transformation into property. Greenberg was able to put AIG at the synergistic nexus of many types of enterprise. By keeping up with the application of computers to block modelling in the interrelated activities of spying, insurance sales, and derivatives development, for instance, Greenberg was able to situate AIG on strategic imperial turf during the era when the permanent war economy of the United States went from analog to digital.

A number of investigators, including New York's former attorney-general Eliot Spitzer, were drawn to probe AIG's financial manipulations, triggering Greenberg's resignation in 2005. Their probes opened windows exposing some of AIG's manipulation of offshore tax havens, reinsurance schemes, shell companies, and the like to hide profit and loss as deemed most lucrative to the counterparties in a system of shadow banking whose transactions would later form the basis of the Federal Reserve's Maiden Lane companies.[97] Two branches of AIG's network of associated enterprises were Marsh and McLennan and Kroll Associates. Kroll Associates is widely known as the "CIA of Wall Street." It operated as a kind of investigation and enforcement unit involved in the deep politics of corporate competition, property recovery, and takeover bids. Marsh and McLennan's CEO on September 11 was Jeffrey Greenberg, Maurice Greenberg's son. Kevin Ryan has investigated the many connections of Marsh and McLennan, whose offices were located near the top of the World Trade Center's North Tower, to the economic background and genesis of the Global War on Terror.[98] Where the Cold War involved opposition to the real or imagined incursions of a specific type of enemy, the Global War on Terror dramatically widened the field of possible foes. Most of the people in the world were transformed by the national security state into possible terrorists, thereby justifying the deployment of vast, intrusive, and extremely expensive investigation techniques.

This change in the constitution of the permanent war economy opened enlarged possibilities for the selling of protection and security by private companies. It widened the terrain of commercial transaction into areas of investigation, protection, and militarization that had once been guarded as the exclusive preserve of governments. In this fashion, companies such as Blackwater or Xe, Kroll Associates, Halliburton, Science Applications International Corporation, Global Risk International, DynCorp International, and many more corporate polities entered the increasingly privatized domain of the terror economy. As the political economy of fear expanded along with the Global War on Terror, new frontiers of business opened up for the insurance industry and its ruling giant, AIG. Some of the obvious and not-so-obvious connections between terrorism and insurance were highlighted in November 2002, when President George W. Bush introduced the *Terrorism Risk Insurance Act*. This legislation has twice been renewed. The initial legislation anticipated the sequence of events that took place when the financial crisis made the federal government the economic backstop and reinsurer of final resort.

While Greenberg's career expressed much of the unique character of US-driven globalization during the twentieth century's final decades, he also brought forward older traditions inherited from Starr and, before him, John Jacob Astor. These three individuals all helped point the transcontinental expansion of the United Stare towards new frontiers of proprietary acquisition. Like Greenberg, Astor based his financial dealings in New York, and he used the wealth he derived from buying furs from Indians and selling opium to the Chinese to purchase prime New York real estate. The founder of a legendary Anglo-American dynasty, Astor extended his North American fur-trade empire into the China trade by coordinating his efforts closely with those of the US Army Corps of Discovery led by Merriwether Lewis and William Clark.

Following immediately on the heals of the Louisiana Purchase, President Thomas Jefferson had ordered Lewis and Clark to find an overland route to the Pacific coast to give the United States its first claim of transcontinental sovereignty. In their movement westward, the Discovery Corps gathered vital military intelligence concerning the alliances and antagonism of the Indigenous peoples they met along the way. Once the Lewis and Clark expedition reached its destination in 1805, Astor extended the westward movement of the Discovery Corp all the way to the Heavenly Kingdom. The exploits of Astor and the other Anglo-American vanguards of the China trade helped make Shanghai the comfortable place it was for Western business when Starr set up shop there in 1919.

Like Astor and Starr, Greenberg worked closely with military and intelligence officials to expand the orbit of US business and power. William Casey, Reagan's choice to head the CIA, regularly consulted Greenberg and even sought to enlist him as his deputy.[99] Casey had worked closely with Allen Dulles in the European branch of the OSS during the era when Donovan and Starr teamed up in New York to conduct international espionage. In 1995 Greenberg was named as a possible director of the CIA. It is a widely known secret that Greenberg's work for the main US spy agency involved the effort to make the Hong Kong headquarters of AIG double as a CIA base for its China operations. The plan apparently had to be abandoned when the Chinese intelligence service learned of the initiative and wired AIG's building with the aim of advancing its own spying program.[100]

Like those who would set up and manage the Maiden Lane companies, Greenberg served as chair of the Federal Reserve Bank of New York. He also served as deputy chair of the Council on Foreign Relations, heading the committee that, in 1996, produced the document *Making Intelligence Smarter: The Future of US Intelligence.*[101] While the CEO of AIG was deeply involved in many facets of the covert and overt operations of the national security state in the 130 countries where his financial services company maintained a presence, Greenberg showered special attention on the Asian hub of his mentor's empire of business and intelligence. Greenberg and his company frequently called on the advice of his good friend and colleague Henry Kissinger. It is reported that AIG's CEO shared with the Saudi arms dealer Adnan Khashoggi a deep and sustained interest in exploiting the oil and natural gas reserves of Uzbekistan by building a pipeline through Russia's Uralskaya region.[102] Like Casey and a number of officials involved in different ways with Marsh and McLennan, Khashoggi was deeply involved in the genesis of the privatized terror economy.

Investigations into the financial transactions of Greenberg's company would cause the *Christian Science Monitor* in 2005 to question if AIG was "the New Enron."[103] As the centrality of AIG in the derivatives fiasco became increasingly clear, those searching for appropriate comparisons looked to the operations of the Bank of Credit and Commerce International. The BCCI was the notoriously corrupt financial institution that both symbolized and facilitated the move away from rules-based managed capitalism at the same time as the United States and Great Britain abandoned much of the manufacturing sector in favour of an expanded and deregulated financial sector. Rather than pursue profit by making things, many Anglo-American enterprises sought enrichment by hitching their wagons to covert operations such as regime change in Eurasia in preparation for pipeline construction. This kind of covert activity is linked with the growth of the terror economy, whose *modus operandi* includes trading on the violence and fear generated by false flag operations and blowback events. Shortly before the pulverization of the three WTC towers and the hit on the Pentagon, Chalmers Johnson labelled hostile foreign responses to the covert operations of the national security state as "blowback."[104]

Jason Mason of RGE Monitor is one of those business reporters who has looked at the resemblances between AIG and BCCI, explaining how both financial institutions could operate "virtually unregulated" all over the world by conducting many of their most dubious transactions in jurisdictions like the Cayman Islands, Luxembourg, Barbadoes, Bermuda, and the Isle of Man. "The international context of AIG makes BCCI look puny by comparison," concluded Mason.[105] As general counsel for the Federal Reserve Bank of New York, Thomas C. Baxter engineered much of the AIG bailout, including the appointment of three trustees to manage what remained of

AIG apart from the contracts taken over by the Maiden Lane companies. In describing the historical context of his work, Baxter observed that "the closest thing to a precedent arose during the collapse in 1991 of the scandal-ridden Bank of Credit and Commerce International to separate [it] from the American First Corporation, a holding company that BCCI secretly controlled and the government wanted to sell."[106]

AIG seems poised at the nexus of many forces in the crisis of global capitalism. Its leadership was deeply involved in the original experimentation, political lobbying, and large-scale marketing of financial derivatives, but especially those that radically extended old principles of insurance into computerized bets on bets on bets that form the essence of financial hedging. I find it difficult not to suspect that the enormous expansion in the buying and selling of derivatives went far beyond the hedging of bets on competing scenarios for the repayment of debt on house mortgages. To me it would be strange if this type of speculation did not extend to the hedging of derivative bets on the future course of covert operations aimed, for example, at taking control of oil reserves and strategic pipeline routes in Asia and the Middle East. What has been the role of this kind of activity in the financial crisis? How much of the underlying causes of the economic chaos has been swept from public view and thus from public accountability in the name of national security?

THE BOWL WITH ONE SPOON AND THE PUBLIC INTEREST

As Kevin Baker has explained, Barack Obama seemed in the early stages of his presidency to be captive of the same clique of Wall Street power brokers who had created the conditions of the financial crisis in the first place. This tendency is well illustrated by the Obama administration's massive commitment of federal funds to keep alive AIG's dubious pyramid schemes of derivative betting with counterparties. The US government's continuation of these schemes expresses and perpetuates some of the worst lies and contradictions of Reaganomics. It ties the leadership of the US executive branch to the legacies of a false conservatism that serves the private interests of a few rather than the public interests of the many. For conservatism to be genuine, it must serve the public interest rather than violate it.

A proud embrace by the US president of his role in nationalizing General Motors could potentially help point humanity towards higher and better ground in the conduct of more ecologically sound systems of industrial relations. By mandating GM to provide global leadership in the delivery of more efficient public transport, President Obama would send a signal of his government's determination to play an activist role in protecting and advancing the public interest. While the success of such an initiative would require much new thinking, it would also return the world's troubled superpower to the more familiar and sustainable terrain of the managed capitalism. It would create a venue for the expression of a richer and more diversified array of political economies that draw concurrently on the best streams of socialist, liberal, and conservative thought. It would help renew the conditions in a global context of the Bowl with One Spoon.

The image of the Bowl with One Spoon serves as a symbol of the public interest that emerges from the Indian Country of Canada. [107] In Canada the Anglo-American tradition of making treaties with Indigenous peoples has never been pre-empted. The Aboriginal provisions of the Royal Proclamation are being renewed in British Columbia and elsewhere in treaty negotiations with First Nations that continue until this day.[108] The higher ideals of this tradition of intercultural diplomacy have not always been well understood or respected. Nevertheless, this continuing heritage offers the world a North American example of an approach to human interaction that eschews the extremes of conquest and embraces instead a broader vision of the public interest and the public good.

From Imperial Absolutism to Reasonable Relativism, 1893–1992

> The powerful who legitimize their privileges by heredity cultivate nostalgia. History is studied as if we are visiting a museum; but this collection of mummies is a swindle. They lie to us about the past as they lie to us about the present: they mask the face of reality. They force the oppressed victims to absorb an alien, dessicated, sterile memory fabricated by the oppressor, so they will resign themselves to a life that isn't theirs as if it were the only one possible.
>
> Eduardo Galeano, *Open Veins of Latin America,* 1973

The commemorative events announcing the 500th anniversary of 1492 conveyed very different messages from those heralding the passing of the first four centuries since Christopher Columbus first planted the Christian cross of his Spanish sponsors on an island in the Bahamas. By mounting the World's Columbian Exposition in Chicago in 1893, the United States cast itself as the principal embodiment and guardian of Christopher Columbus's legacy. In this interpretive project, the memory of the Italian explorer's most transformative voyage was conflated with the imagery of the emerging urban centre of Chicago, the busy frontier metropolis on the political, commercial, and imaginative edges of America's invention and growth. The merger of Columbus's reputation as Europe's original transatlantic pioneer with imagery depicting the ongoing movement of Euro-American peoples across North America helped to bolster the idea of the United States as the lead agency on Western Civilization's richest and most active frontiers.

With a deep sense of pride in the actions of those pugnacious individuals who had pushed the frontiers of US civilization westward, Frederick Jackson Turner lent his rhetorical talents to building up the mystique associated with the Americanization of the European heritage. Turner's interpretation of the deeper meanings of the World's Columbian Exposition pointed humanity towards the possibility of futures that were very different from those first scouted by Franz Boas – the major force in designing the living ethnography exhibits dotting the course of the Midway Plaisance in Chicago in 1893.

It was Boas in his role as a professional anthropologist at Columbia University who most energetically provided a theory of social science that would counter the harsh Darwinian dictates that reinforced racist justifications for Victorian imperialism. Instead of adopting the hierarchical theories of racial evolution that dominated the academy at the time, Boas returned to the more egalitarian legacies of the Enlightenment. He proposed cultural relativism as an intellectual key that helped to open doors to more tolerant and pluralistic conceptions of how human relationships are constructed. In realizing the importance of relativity as an expedient of coexistence in an increasingly integrated global society, Boas anticipated a more general shift arising from science's changing orientation to time's passage.

Albert Einstein captured the essential character of this shift most decisively with his formulation of theories advancing the principle that relativity constitutes an essential element of our universe. His discoveries helped to foment a major crisis of consciousness in the twentieth century. If even the passage of time is relative to the movement of light in space, what other aspects of perceived reality are mirages fooling our senses? The growing acceptance of relativity called into question many orthodoxies concerning the nature and source of progress. In a society inspired by relativism, who could locate with certainty the divisions separating civilization from savagery? Who could decide definitively whose way of life was backward and thus disposable and whose cultural attributes merited cultivation and edification? Whose dictates could be relied on to relegate some peoples to the obsolescence of the past and others to elevated roles in shaping the conditions of the future?

As the claims of relativism grew, doubt was cast on ethnocentric forms of nationalism such as the theory espoused by Frederick Jackson Turner in his characterization of American history as a saga of civilization's ascent over savagery. As Turner's academic authority began to wane, that of Franz Boas increased. An early proponent of relativity's importance in understanding the substance of human relationships, Boas received his first widespread recognition in his role as a key member of the ethnography unit at the World's Columbian Exposition.

The effort to speed up the linear and ethnocentric view of progress by eliminating Indigenous peoples from the present could be advanced by means as crude as murder or as calculating as policies that stripped away the victims' right to vote, hold public office, make contracts, or seek remedies for injustice through the medium of litigation. The treatment of Indigenous peoples as the uncivilized wards of civilized states could take place at the national level, as happened, for instance, in Canada, the United States, Australia, and South Africa. Or it could occur internationally, as happened when the Indigenous peoples of the Congo Basin were made wards of the "civilized nations" under the trusteeship delegated to Belgium's King Leopold. Generally speaking, the essence of colonialism involves the treatment of Indigenous peoples as the subject of laws, policies, and relationships of power not of their own making. The transfer of land and resources from Aboriginal wards and victims to human and corporate "persons" on the expanding frontiers of imperial capital has repeatedly formed a central ritual in the ongoing colonization of mind and matter.

The term "genocide" describes the relegation of Indigenous peoples to the past by removing from them the means to survive in the present. It marks the ultimate elimination of time on Earth for those deemed unworthy to pass along their biological and cultural seeds to future generations. The political economy of genocide extends to the industrial annihilation of the great buffalo herds. It draws on the secularization of sacred Aboriginal gardens, burial grounds, and hunting territories. Spiritual places are transformed by the unrelenting materialism of capitalism into tourist destinations and natural resources. The drive for privatized wealth transforms Aboriginal grasslands and old-growth forests into chemically treated zones devoted to the agricultural replication of trees and other commodified monocultures. The political economy of genocide sometimes involves the environmental degradation brought on by the damming of free-flowing rivers and the industrial pollution of soil, air, and aquatic systems. Those looking at genocide in the future might well look backwards to our own time when industrial biotechnology has become the main medium for the unprecedented cross-species blending and merging of genetic codes in untested and potentially cataclysmic combinations.

While Indigenous peoples have been the first to face the full onslaught of industrial incursions into life's capacity to renew the ecology of biological diversity, the ecocidal and genocidal consequences do not end with the breakdown of Aboriginal communities. The effects spread out across all divisions of ethnicity, class, and even species. In this fashion the prospects for the unending renewal of healthy life are made to seem as tenuous as treaty promises that were to last for as long as the sun shines, the grass grows, and the waters flow. As social contracts break down, many global citizens begin to experience treatment once reserved for dispossessed Indians.

The World's Columbian Exposition anticipated the move of the United States into the imperial vacuum that would be left vacant once the European powers exhausted themselves during two world wars. The assembly in Chicago also gave podiums to a few critics of colonization's worst onslaughts. Among those who directly or indirectly called attention to the imperial bias of the World's Columbia Exposition was the Anishinabenini intellectual Simon Pokagan; the theosophist and future head of the Indian National Congress, Annie Besant; and some of the Hindu delegates attending the World Parliament of Religions. The anti-imperialism implicit in Franz Boas's cultural relativism may have helped to influence the ironic presentation on British Empire Day of the Kwakwaka'wakw performers as they forced their audience to examine critically their own dark stereotypes of Aboriginal cannibalism.

The hostility to empire building expressed in Chicago found many global extensions in, for instance, the Filipino nationalism promoted by the martyred novelist José Rizal or the Hawaiian nationalism that moved Queen Liliuokalani to protest the betrayal of her people through the US deployment of armed force in 1893 to oust her indigenous government. Rizal's anti-imperialism drew on his broad reading in Spain and France of anarchist idealizations of personal autonomy. Queen Liliuokalani led a monarchical regime modelled on the court of Queen Victoria. The hybrid marriage of revolutionary and conservative traditions in the genesis of Fourth World ideology is highlighted in the contrast between Rizal's sources of inspiration and the Hawaiian queen's promotion of the Aboriginal rights of her people through a system of governance closely modelled on Great Britain's constitutional monarchy.

What had been an undercurrent of support for decolonization in 1893 grew to become the dominant sentiment expressed in the process of marking the 500th anniversary of Christopher Columbus's most transformative voyage. Those who led the way in characterizing the meaning of the quincentenary of 1492 tended to emphasize the idea of "confronting Columbus."[1] Indeed, some of the most radical discussion sought to link Columbus to almost every imaginable environmental crime and human-rights abuse. This sense of self-righteous condemnation permeated the text of a broadly distributed pamphlet entitled *Rethinking Columbus.* One of its articles sought to assign to Columbus and his legacy responsibility for everything "from the ecologically devastating James Bay hydro-electric project in Quebec, to the poisonous chemical dumps in Louisiana, to the massive clear cutting of ancient forests in Central and South America." The authors added, "Columbus' exploitative spirit lives on – with a vengeance."[2]

The activities accompanying the distribution of *Rethinking Columbus* are outlined in Howard Zinn's *A People's History of the United States, 1492 to Present.* This chronicle was part of Zinn's account of the counter-Columbus movement. His decision to begin his narrative of US history with an account of Columbus's transatlantic venture was one of many scholarly initiatives aimed at examining the quincentenary of 1492 from a variety of perspectives.[3]

The transformation in thinking about the contemporary meanings of the transatlantic connections made in 1492 was not limited to academic circles. In 1992 Canada and Australia became sites of major political and juridical processes reflecting changing orientations to the ongoing consequences of the Columbian conquests. In Canada, the country's first ministers agreed to a constitutional accord affirming that the jurisdiction of Aboriginal government constitutes one of three orders of Canadian government. Although this vision of a post-colonial state was not subsequently implemented, it nevertheless introduced a new paradigm of intercultural federalism to broaden appreciation of the demands of democracy in an increasingly interdependent world.

In Australia, the High Court rejected the theory of *terra nullius*, thereby implying that Indigenous peoples retain some form of title in their

Aboriginal lands. Historian Henry Reynolds was one of the Australian scholars whose expert testimony helped the High Court arrive at its decision in the *Mabo* case. In his reflections on the progress of the movement for "reconciliation" with Indigenous peoples in Australia, Reynolds commented, "In communities right across Australia, there are people meeting, thinking, researching, talking and coming up quite often with extremely interesting and creative proposals to try and reach reconciliation there in their own communities."[4] According to historian Howard Zinn, the 500th anniversary of 1492 stimulated similar processes throughout scores of communities in the United States. He explained that "there were counter-Columbus activities all over the country, unmentioned in the press or on television. In Minnesota alone, a listing of such activities for 1992 reported dozens of workshops, meetings, films, art shows."[5]

The 500th anniversary of Columbus's colonial venture took place at a moment when it seemed possible that humanity might transcend the division of the world into warring camps. With the demise of the Soviet Union, the Cold War came to an end. As the delegates to the Bandung Conference had predicted in 1955, the bipolarism of the Cold War had replicated many features of European imperialism. The rivalry between capitalist and communist superpowers had limited the capacity of Indigenous peoples to move forward internationally along diverse trajectories of history that expressed the strength and continuity of their own Aboriginal heritages, customs, and traditions.

In defence of its permanent war economy, the US government moved quickly in the early 1990s to block the possibility that new transnational alliances of peoples' power would arise from a global outbreak of peace. In the lead up to the first Gulf War, Prescott Bush's son, US president George H.W. Bush had himself pictured in a jacket with an insignia on its back of the globe. Bush's wardrobe was the basis of a photo op designed to provide imagery for his much cited speech about the United States as the core polity in "a new world order where diverse nations are drawn together in common cause to achieve the universal aspirations of all mankind."[6] The essence of this new world order, it seemed, was for the US government to perpetuate its permanent war economy by doing military violence to any foe that threatened, or might potentially threaten, its global dominance.

In a display of "smart" bombing beamed by the Pentagon to television stations around the world, capitalism's triumphant military-industrial complex demonstrated its new capacities of technological wizardry combined with a new world order of Orwellian propaganda. The murder of innocent civilians in Iraq was cosmetically rebranded to become "collateral damage." The US Army and allied troops followed up the bombing attacks in 1991 with a hundred-hour blitzkrieg campaign that stopped short of seizing the Iraqi capital in order to topple the government of former US ally Saddam Hussein. This display of military force began a long period of controversial UN sanctions. Over the following years, these blocks on the importation of food, medicine, and other necessities dramatically diminished the length and quality of life for millions of Iraqi men, women, and children. "We've kicked the Vietnam syndrome once and for all," boasted President Bush.[7]

While the charter members of the national security state busied themselves with the identification and manufacturing of new enemies to justify the permanent war economy, other constituencies looked to the new possibilities opening up for humanity in the aftermath of the Cold War. Some of this life-affirming energy found a focus in the Earth Summit that took place in Brazil's Rio de Janeiro during the summer of 1992. One element of this many-faceted gathering of environmentalists took place at Kari-Oca. Bringing together Aboriginal delegations from many parts of the world including Siberia, West Papua, Kenya, the Philippines, Canada, Malaysia, Central and South America, and the Chittagong Hills Tracts of Bangladash, the gathering was entitled the World Conference of Indigenous Peoples on Territory, Environment, and Development.

The proceedings at Kari-Oca serve as a telling counterpoint to the World's Columbian Exposition in Chicago a century earlier. The delegates produced a document know as the Kari-Oca Declaration. Much of its content was devoted to calls for the United Nations to enforce international law in order to defend Indigenous peoples from international crimes. Special emphasis was devoted to the need to regard treaties with Indigenous peoples as instruments that deserve international recognition and respect. Some of the declaration's many provisions dealt with antagonisms that sometimes develop between Aboriginal groups and environmentalists. The delegates proclaimed, "We value the efforts of protection of biodiversity, but we reject to be part of an inert diversity which pretends to be maintained for scientific or folkloric purposes."[8] This desire to move out of the romanticized aura of "noble savagery" ran strongly throughout the proceedings. "We are not myths of the past, ruins in the jungle, or zoos," proclaimed Rigoberta Menchú, a Nobel Peace Prize winner who had drawn significant international attention to the continuing Indian wars in Guatemala in the 1980s.[9]

Marcos Terena of Brazil was elected to bring the decisions reached at the Kari-Oca gathering forward to the larger assembly of government delegations assembled at Rio. Why, asked Terena, did the apportionment of assets and liabilities from "development" so frequently disadvantage Indigenous peoples? In seeking to probe the meanings of this controversial word, Terena explained:

The models of development which you have imposed on Indigenous peoples have not brought us any benefits. On the contrary, until now, your model of development has destroyed our forests, poisoned our rivers and our air, contaminated our soils and subsoils, and robbed the rich biodiversity which we have maintained for generations. Now you have noticed this type of development cannot continue but you still have not realized that you need us. You talk of preserving the flora and fauna, of the ozone layer, of the forests. You talk about unsustainable models of production and consumption, but what you need to understand is that you have to contemplate all these things as a whole. Indigenous peoples have always considered the world in a holistic manner. We do not separate the forests, the rivers, the soil, the animals and the insects from ourselves. It is this knowledge and this practice over centuries which is real sustainable development. We have sustained our world over thousands of years and guarded the integrity of the ecosystems and the biodiversity. Isn't this what you are looking for?[10]

A decade after the Kari-Oca Declaration, Rigoberta Menchú renewed the call for procedures beyond the national level to deal with crimes against humanity, but especially those committed throughout Latin America. With the example of the processes initiated by the UN Security Council to deal with criminal responsibility for the debacles in the former Yugoslavia and Rwanda, Menchú proposed the establishment of a similar international court to deal particularly with the recent reigns of terror in the US-backed dictatorships that governed Argentina, Chile, and Guatemala. Calling the crimes of these regimes "three paradigmatic cases," Menchú emphasized the importance of preparing the legal evidence "in anticipation of the day when we have a legitimate tribunal." She declared that "the most important thing now is that the evidence of genocide not be lost."[11]

Menchú's comments echoed those of the Jewish historian Simon Dubnow. Moments before he was shot dead by Nazi soldiers in 1941, Dubnow is reported to have admonished his fellow witnesses and victims of the holocaust to "write and record."[12] In making her own plea to write and record, Menchú implicitly countered old assumptions about the place of Indians in the continuum of time. She transcended a harsh Darwinian dictate of obsolescence when, as a Mayan intellectual, she called for the collection and preservation of information on the treatment of Indigenous peoples in anticipation of the day when a genuinely independent body will be in a position to enforce the rule of law globally – especially in the hemisphere most radically transformed by the genocidal incursions of the continuing Columbian conquests.

How should we respond to Menchú's desire for some reckoning with history? Can we move forward along a path of justice without coming to terms with the crimes of the past? Can we find peace and security on the middle ground between the anti-imperial absolutism of Che and the shifting moral relativism of Obama?

Notes

INTRODUCTION

1 Karl Marx, *The Portable Karl Marx*, ed. Eugene Kamenka (New York: Viking Press, 1983), 462

2 Frantz Fanon, *The Wretched of the Earth*, trans. Constance Farrington (New York: Grove Press, 1965)

3 George Manuel and Michael Posluns, *The Fourth World: An Indian Reality* (Don Mills: Collier-Macmillan, 1974)

4 Francis Fukuyama, *The End of History and the Last Man* (New York: Avon Books, 1992)

5 Edward W. Said, *Culture and Imperialism* (New York: Random House, 1993), 328

6 Ibid., 331

7 Ibid., 336. Emphasis in original

8 Luisa Maffi, ed., *On Biocultural Diversity: Linking Language, Knowledge, and the Environment* (Washington, DC: Smithsonian Institution Press, 2001)

9 Richard Evans Schultes and Siri von Reis, eds., *Ethnobotany: Evolution of a Discipline* (Portland Oregon: Diosorides Press, 1995)

10 Che Guevara, *Global Justice: Liberation and Socialism*, ed. Mariadel Carmen Ariet Garcia (Melbourne: Ocean Press, 2002), 23

11 Earnesto "Che" Guevara, *The African Dream: The Diaries of the Revolutionary War in the Congo*, trans. Patrick Camiller (New York: Grove Press, 2000), 6

12 Earnesto "Che" Guevaro, *The Motorcycle Diaries: A Journey around Latin America*, trans. Ann Wright (London: Verso, 1995)

13 John Lee Anderson, *Che: A Revolutionary Life* (New York; Grove Press, 1997)

14 Piero Gleijeses, *Conflicting Missions: Havana, Washington, and Africa, 1959–1976* (Chapel Hill: University of North Carolina Press, 2002), 9

15 Isaac Saney, "African Stalingrad: The Cuban Revolution, Internationalism, and the End of Apartheid," *Latin American Perspectives* 33, 5 (2006): 81–117

16 Speech of Nelson Mandela at the initiation of the Southern Africa–Cuba Solidarity Conference, Johannesburg, October 6, 1995, cited in *The*

Militant 59, 39, October 23, 1995, at http://www.hartford-hwp.com/archives/43b/122.html

17 Martin Hart-Landsberg, "Learning About ALBA and the Bank of the South," *Monthly Review*, September 2009, at http://monthlyreview.org/090901hart-landsberg.php

18 Naomi Klein, "No Logo at Ten," in Naomi Klein, *No Logo, 10th Anniversary Edition* (Toronto: Vintage Canada, 2009), xx–xxi

19 Webster Griffin Tarpley, *Obama: The Postmodern Coup* (Joshua Tree, Cal.: Progressive Press, 2008), 48

20 Barack Obama, *Dreams from My Father: A Story of Race and Inheritance* (1995; New York: Three Rivers Press, 2004), vii

21 Ibid., 11–12

22 President Barack Obama, cited in Obama Administration, Press Conference at the Summit of the Americas, April 19, 2009, at http://obamacuba.blogspot.com/2009/04/obama-opening-statement-and-press.html

23 Remarks by Barack Obama to the 64th UN General Assembly, Voltairenet, September 23, 2009, at http://www.voltairenet.org/article162229.html

24 See Arthur Schlesinger Jr, *War and the American Presidency* (New York: W.W. Norton, 2004).

25 James Mann, *The Rise of the Vulcans: The History of Bush's War Cabinet* (New York: Viking, 2004)

26 Project for the New American Century, Rebuilding America's Defenses: Strategy, Forces and Resources (Washington, DC: PNAC, September 2000), download from http://www.newamericancentury.org/defensenationalsecurity.htm

27 Remarks by Barack Obama at West Point, December 1, 2009, Voltairenet, at http://www.voltairenet.org/article163179.html

28 Michel Chossudovsly, "The Destabilization of Pakistan," December 30, 2007, at http://www.globalresearch.ca/index.php?context=va&aid=7705; Part 2, January 8, 2008, at http://www.globalresearch.ca/index.php?context=va&aid=7746; Jeremy Scahill, "The Secret War on Pakistan," *The Nation*, November 23, 2009, at http://www.thenation.com/doc/20091207/scahill/print; Webster Tarpley, Obama Declares War on Pakistan, Voltairenet, December 12, 2009, at http://www.voltairenet.org/article163281.html

29 See, for instance, Ahmed Mosaddeq Nafeez, *The War on Truth: 9/11, Disinformation and the Anatomy of Terrorism* (Northampton, Mass.: Olive Branch Press, 2005); Ahmed Mosaddeq Nafeez, *The London Bombings: An Independent Inquiry* (London: Gerald Duckworth, 2006); Peter Dale Scott, *The Road to 9/11: Wealth, Empire and the Future of America* (Berkeley: University of California Press, 2007).

30 Hannah Arendt, *Eichmann in Jerusalem: A Report on the Banality of Evil* (New York: Viking, 1963)

31 Adam Hochschild, *King Leopold's Ghost: A Story of Greed, Terror and Heroism in Colonial Africa* (Boston: Houghton Mifflin, 1998)

32 Obama, *Dreams from My Father*, 103

33 David Ray Griffin, *Osama bin Laden: Dead or Alive?* (Northampton, Mass.: Olive Branch Press, 2009)

34 Chris Hedges, *Empire of Illusion: The End of Literacy and the Triumph of Spectacle* (Toronto: Knopf Canada, 2009), 89–90

35 C.B. MacPherson, *The Political Theory of Possessive Individualism: Hobbes to Locke* (London: Oxford University Press, 1962)

36 Max Weber, *The Protestant Ethic and the Spirit of Capitalism*, trans. Talcott Parsons (London: Allen and Unwin, 1930)

37 Roger Maaka and Augie Fleras, *The Politics of Indigeneity: Challenging the State in Canada and Aotearoa New Zealand* (Dunedin: Universituy of Otago Press, 2005)

38 Great Britain, *Report of the Select Committee on Aborigines (British Settlements),with Minutes of Evidence, Appendix and Index: Imperial Blue Book, 538 of 1836* (London: King's Printer, 1837)

39 Alpheus Snow, *The Questions of Aborigines in the Law and Practice of Nations* (1918; Wilmington, Del.: Scholarly Resources, 1974)

40 Frantz Fanon, *Les Damnés de la terre* (Paris: F. Maspero, 1961); Frantz Fanon, *The Wretched of the Earth*, trans. Constance Farrington (New York: Grove Press, 1965)

CHAPTER ONE

1 Ray Allen Billington, *Frederick Jackson Turner: Historian, Scholar, Teacher* (New York: Oxford University Press, 1973)

2 Robert Rydell, *All the World's a Fair: Visions of Empire at American International Expositions, 1876–1916* (Chicago: University of Chicago Press, 1984)

3 On the World's Columbian Exposition in Chicago, see Rossiter Johnson, ed., *A History of the World's Columbian Exposition Held in Chicago in 1893* (New York: D. Appleton, 1897); Stanley Applebaum, *The Chicago World's Fair of 1893: A Photographic Record* (New York: Dover Publications, 1980); Reid Badger, *The Great American Fair: The World's Columbian Exposition and American Culture* (Chicago: N. Hall, 1979); Neil Harris et al., *Grand Illusions: Chicago World's Fair of 1893* (Chicago: Chicago Historical Society, 1993); Robert Muccigrosso, *Celebrating the New World: Chicago's Columbian Exposition of 1893* (Chicago: I.R. Dee, 1993); Dennis B. Downey, *A Season of Renewal: The Columbian Exposition and Victorian America* (Westport, Conn.: Praeger, 2002); Julie K. Brown, *Photography and the World's Columbian Exposition* (Tucson: University of Arizona Press, 1994); Robert W. Rydell, John E. Finding, and Kimberly D. Pelle, *Fair America: World's Fairs in the United States* (Washington, DC: Smithsonian Institution Press, 2000); Robert W. Rydell and Nancy E. Gwinn, eds., *Fair Representations: World's Fairs and the Modern World* (Amsterdam: VU University Press, 1994); Hubert Howe Bancroft, *The Book of the Fair* (Chicago and San Francisco: The Bancroft Company, 1893); World's Columbian Exposition, *Report of the President to the Board of Directors of the World's Columbian Exposition* (Chicago: Rand McNally, 1898); Trumball White and William Ingleheart, *The World's Columbian Exposition, 1893* (Philadelphia: Historical Publishing

Company, 1893); World's Columbian Exposition, *Official Catalogue* (Chicago: Conkey, 1893).

4 Walter Prescott Webb, "The Frontier and the 400 Year Boom," in George Rogers Taylor, ed., *The Turner Thesis, Concerning the Role of the Frontier in American History* (Lexington, Mass.: D.C. Heath and Company, 1972), 132. On Turner's influence, see Wilbur R. Jacobs, *On Turner's Trail: One Hundred Years of Writing Western History* (Lawrence: University Press of Kansas, 1994); Kerwin Lee Klein, *Frontiers of Historical Imagination: Narrating the European Conquest of Native America, 1890–1990* (Berkeley: University of California Press, 1999).

5 Frederick Jackson Turner, *Reuben Gold Thwaites: A Memorial Address* (Madison: State Historical Society of Wisconsin, 1914)

6 William Cronon, *Nature's Metropolis: Chicago and the Great West* (New York: W.W. Norton, 1991)

7 Richard Moran, *Executioner's Current: Thomas Edison, George Westinghouse, and the Invention of the Electric Chair* (New York: Knopf, 2002)

8 John Patrick Barrett, *Electricity at the Columbian Exposition* (Chicago: R.R. Donnelley and Sons, 1894)

9 Chauncey W. Depew, cited in Major Benjamin Cumming Truman, *History of the World's Fair, Being a Complete Description of the World's Columbian Exposition from Its Inception* (Chicago: Chicago World's Columbian Exposition, 1893), 124, 134

10 Henry Watterson, cited ibid., 117

11 H.W. Brands, *The Reckless Decade: America in the 1890s* (Chicago: University of Chicago Press, 2002)

12 Alan Trachtenberg, *The Incorporation of America: Culture and Society in the Gilded Age*, consulting editor, Eric Foner (New York: Hill and Wang, 1982)

13 World Wide Web. http://xroads.virginia.edu/~MA96/WCE/legacy.html. See Marilyn Kern-Foxworth, *Aunt Jemima, Uncle Ben, and Rastus: Blacks in Advertising, Yesterday, Today, and Tomorrow* (Westport, Conn.: Greenwood Publishing Group, 1994)

14 Naomi Klein, *No Logo: Taking Aim at the Brand Bullies* (Toronto: Vintage Canada, 2000)

15 Eric Schlosser, *Fast Food Nation: The Dark Side of the All-American Meal* (New York: HarperCollins, 2002)

16 Steven Watts, *The Magic Kingdom: Walt Disney and the American Way of Life* (Boston: Houghton Mifflin, 1997); Richard Schickel, *The Disney Version: The Life, Times, Art, and Commerce of Walt Disney* (New York: Avon Books, 1968); Marc Eliot, *Walt Disney: Hollywood's Dark Prince* (London: André Deutsch, 1993)

17 Robert T. Handy, *A Christian America: Protestant Hopes and Historical Realities* (New York: Oxford University Press, 1991)

18 On the importance of internal tensions and contradictions in the expansionary dynamism of Western culture, see William H. McNeill, *The Rise of the West: A History of the Human Community* (Chicago: University of Chicago Press, 1963), 539, 567, 585, 588

19 Michael Hardt and Antonio Negri, *Empire* (Cambridge, Mass.: Harvard University Press, 2000)

20 See Leo Marx, *The Machine in the Garden: Technology and the Pastoral Idea in America* (New York: Oxford University Press, 1970); David E. Nye, *American Technological Sublime*, (Cambridge Mass.: MIT Press, 1994).

21 Bancroft, *The Book of the Fair*, 953–5

22 Antonin Dvorak, cited in Alec Robertson, *Dvorak* (London: J.M. Dent and Sons, 1964), 170

23 Adrienne Fried Block, "Dvorak, Beach, and American Music," in Richard Crawford, R. Allen Lott, and Carol J. Oja, eds., *A Celebration of American Music: Words and Music in Honor of H. Wiley Hitchcock* (Ann Arbor: University of Michigan Press, 1990), 256–80; Edward A. Berlin, *King of Ragtime: Scott Joplin and His Era* (New York: Oxford University Press, 1995)

24 Ida B. Wells et al., *The Reason Why the Colored American Is Not in the World's Columbian Exposition: The Afro-American's Contribution to Columbian Literature*, ed. Robert W. Rydell (Urbana: University of Illinois Press, 1999)

25 Richard Seager, *The Dawn of Religious Pluralism: Voices from the World's Parliament of Religions* (LaSalle, Ill.: Open Court, 1993); Clay Lancaster, *The Incredible World's Parliament of Religions at the Chicago Columbian Exposition* (Fontwell, Sussex: Centaur Press, 1987); John H. Barrows, ed., *The World's Parliament of Religions*, 2 vols. (Chicago, The Parliament Publishing Company, 1893); Walter R. Houghton, ed., *Neely's History of the Parliament of Religions and Religious Congresses of the World's Congress Auxiliary of the World's Columbian Exposition*, 2 vols. (Chicago: Rand McNally, 1893); Egal Feldman, "American Ecumenism: Chicago's World Parliament of Religions of 1893," *A Journal of Church and State* 9 (spring 1967): 180–99; Eric J. Ziolkowski, ed., *A Museum of Faiths: Histories and Legacies of the 1893 World's Parliament of Religions* (Atlanta: Scholars Press, 1993)

26 Washington Gladden and the Reverend D.S. Schaff, cited in Carl T. Jackson, *The Oriental Religions and American Thought: Nineteenth-Century Explorations* (Westport, Conn.: Greenwood Press, 1981), 253, 255

27 Eastern and Western Disciples, *Life of Swami Vivekananda* (Calcutta: Avaita Ashrama, 1955)

28 Raj Kumar, *Annie Besant's Rise to Power in Indian Politics, 1914–1917* (New Delhi: Concept Publishers, 1981); Anne Taylor, *Annie Besant: A Biography* (New York: Oxford University Press, 1992)

29 Edward Said, *Orientalism* (New York: Vintage, 1978); Walter D. Mignolo, *Local Histories / Global Designs: Coloniality, Subaltern Knowledges, and Border Thinking* (Princeton: Princeton University Press, 2000), 51

30 Hindu delegate, cited in Bancroft, *The Book of the Fair*, 952

31 Donald B. Smith, *Honore Jaxon: Prairie Visionary* (Regina: Coteau Books, 2007)

32 Frederick Jackson Turner, "The Significance of the Frontier in American History," reprinted in Walker D. Wyman and Clifton B. Kroeber, eds., *The Frontier in Perspective* (Madison: University of Wisconsin Press, 1965), 18

33 Ibid., 2, 1

34 Ibid., 2, 4

35 Ibid., 37–8
36 William Christie MacLeod, *The American Indian Frontier* (New York: Alfred A. Knopf, 1928)
37 Kwame Nkrumah, *Neo-Colonialism: The Last Stage of Imperialism* (London: Thomas Nelson and Sons, 1965)
38 Richard Drinnon, *Facing West: The Metaphysics of Indian Hating and Empire Building* (New York: Schocken Books, 1980)
39 Mark Kurlansky, *1968: The Year That Rocked the World* (New York: Random House, 2005)
40 Ibid.
41 See Benedict Anderson, *Under Three Flags: Anarchism and the Anti-Colonial Imagination* (London: Verso, 2007)
42 William Randolph Hearst, cited in Gray Brechin, *Imperial San Francisco: Urban Power, Earthly Ruin* (Berkeley: University of California Press, 1999), 230.
43 See, for instance, Chalmers Johnson, *Blowback: The Costs and Consequences of American Empire* (New York: Henry Holt, 2000); William Blum, *Killing Hope: U.S. Military and CIA Interventions since World War II* (Monroe, Maine: Common Courage Press, 1995); William Blum, *Rogue State: A Guide to the World's Only Superpower* (London: Zed Books, 2002); Jon Pilger, *Hidden Agendas* (London: Vintage, 1999); Christopher Hitchins, *The Trial of Henry Kissinger* (London: Verso, 2001); Saul Landau, *The Dangerous Doctrine: National Security and U.S. Foreign Policy* (Boulder, Col.: Westview Press, 1988); Gabriel Kolko, *Confronting the Third World: The United States Foreign Policy, 1945–1980* (New York: Pantheon Books, 1988)
44 Turner, "The Significance of the Frontier in American History," 2
45 *The Canadian Indian*, Sept. 15, 1893, cited in Paige Raibmon, "Theatres of Conflict: The Kwakwaka'wakw Meet Colonialism in British Columbia and the Chicago World's Fair," *Canadian Historical Review* 81, 2 (2000): 179
46 Truman, *History of the World's Fair*, 550, 565. See Curtis M. Hinsley, "The World as Marketplace: Commodification of the Exotic at the World's Columbia Exposition, Chicago, 1893," in Ivan Karp and Stevan Lavine, eds., *Exhibiting Cultures: The Poetics and Politics of Museum Display* (Washington, DC: Smithsonian Institution Press, 1991), 344–65.
47 Paul Greenhalgh, *Ephemeral Vistas: The Expositions Universelles, Great Exhibitions, and World's Fairs* (Manchester and New York: Manchester University Press and St. Martin's Press, 1988), 127–8. See also L.G. Moses, *Wild West Shows and the Images of American Indians, 1883–1933* (Albuquerque: University of New Mexico Press, 1996).
48 Michael Broyles, "Art Music from 1860 to 1920," in David Nicholls, ed., *The Cambridge History of American Music* (Cambridge: Cambridge University Press, 1998), 249–53
49 Raibmon, "Theatres of Contact," 178
50 Peter Macnair, "From Kwakiutl to Kwakwaka'wakw," in R. Bruce Morrison and C. Roderick Wilson, eds., *Native Peoples: The Canadian Experience*, 2nd ed. (Toronto: McClelland & Stewart, 1995), 586–605

51 Paul Tennant, *Aboriginal Peoples and Politics: The Indian Land Question in British Columbia, 1849–1989* (Vancouver: UBC Press, 1990)

52 Franz Boas, *The Ethnography of Franz Boas: Letters and Dairies of Franz Boas, Written on the Northwest Coast from 1886 to 1931*, ed. Ronald P. Rohner; trans. Hedy Parker (Chicago: University of Chicago Press, 1969); "Franz Boas and the Kwakiutl: Interview with Mrs. Tom Johnson," in June Helm, ed., *Pioneers of American Anthropology: The Uses of Biography* (Seattle: University of Washington Press, 1966), 214

53 Charles D'Harlez, "The Comparative Study of the World's Religions," cited in Barrows, ed., *The World's Parliament of Religions*, 1: 62

54 Franz Boas, *Race, Language, and Culture* (1940; Chicago: University of Chicago Press, 1982)

55 Jeanne Cannizzo, "George Hunt and the Invention of Kwakiutl Culture," *Canadian Review of Sociology and Anthropology* 20, 1 (1983): 44–58

56 On the idea of negotiation and compromise as a factor in the encounter between Indigenous peoples and newcomers, see Richard White, *The Middle Ground: Indians, Empires, and Republics in the Great Lakes Region, 1650–1815* (Cambridge: Cambridge University Press, 1991).

57 George Manuel and Michael Posluns, *The Fourth World: An Indian Reality* (Don Mills: Collier-Macmillan, 1974)

58 London *Sunday Times*, Aug. 20, 1893, cited in Raibmon, "Theatres of Conflict," 183

59 Lawrence Vankoughnet, cited ibid., 184

60 Lucy Maddox, *Citizen Indian:Native American Intellectuals, Race and Reform* (Ithaca: Cornell University Press, 2005), 1–4

61 Simon Pokagon's Chicago Day speech, reprinted in Frederick E. Hoxie, ed., *Talking Back to Civilization: Indian Voices from the Progressive Era* (Boston: Bedford / St Martin's Press, 2001), 31, 35

62 Adam Hoshschild, *King Leopold's Ghost: The Story of Greed, Terror, and Heroism in Colonial Africa* (Boston: Houghton Mifflin, 1999)

63 Karl E. Meyer and Shareen Blair Brysac, *Tournament of Shadows: The Great Game and the Race for Empire in Central Asia* (Washington, DC: Counterpoint, 1999), 113

64 Thomas W. Palmer, cited in Truman, *History of the World's Fair*, 19–20

CHAPTER TWO

1 See A.J. Robbie Robertson, *The Three Waves of Globalization: A History of Developing Global Consciousness* (Nova Scotia / London: Fernwood Publishing / Zed Books, 2003), 49–77; Ulrich Beck, *What Is Globalization?* (Cambridge, Mass.: Polity Press, 2000); A.G. Hopkins, ed., *Globalization in World History* (London: Pimlico, 2002); Patrick Manning, *Navigating World History: Historians Create a Global Past* (New York: Palgrave, 2003); Michael Geyer and Charles Bright, "World History in a Global Age," *American Historical Review* 100 (1995): 1034–60; David Christian, *Maps of Time: An Introduction to Big*

History (Berkeley: University of California Press, 2004); Jurgen Osterhammel and Neils P. Pettersson, *Globalization: A Short History*, trans. Dona Geyer (Princeton: Princeton University Press, 2005).

2 Joseph Needham, *Science and Civilization in China* (Cambridge: Cambridge University Press, 1954)

3 Karen Armstrong, *A History of God: The 4,000-Year Quest of Judaism, Christianity, and Islam* (New York: Ballantine Books, 1993)

4 Tzvetan Todorov, *The Conquest of America: The Question of the Other*, trans. Richard Howard (New York: Harper and Row, 1984)

5 Walter D. Mignolo, *Local Histories / Global Designs: Coloniality, Subaltern Knowledges, and Border Thinking* (Princeton: Princeton University Press, 2000); Olive Patricia Dickason, *Canada's First Nations: A History of Founding Peoples from Earliest Times*, 2nd ed. (Toronto: Oxford University Press, 1997), 5

6 *Inter Caetera*, cited in Wilcombe E. Washburn, *Red Man's Land / White Man's Law: A Study of the Past and Present Status of the American Indian* (New York: Charles Scriber's Sons, 1971), 5. See also Luis Weckmann-Munoz, "The Alexandrine Bulls of 1493: Pseudo-Asiatic Documents," in Fredi Chiapell et al., eds., *First Images of America: The Impact of the New World on the Old*, 2 vols. (Berkeley: University of California Press, 1976), 201–10; Miguel Batllori, "The Papal Division of the World and Its Consequences," in Chiapell et al., eds., *First Images of America*, 211–20; Olive Patricia Dickason, *The Myth of the Savage and the Beginnings of French Colonialism in the Americas* (Edmonton: University of Alberta Press, 1984), 126–8.

7 William H. McNeill, *The Rise of the West: A History of the Human Community* (Chicago: University of Chicago Press, 1963), 538–9, 567, 588. See also William H. McNeill and John R. McNeill, *The Human Web: A Bird's Eye View of World History* (New York: W.W. Norton, 2003).

8 Paul Kennedy, *The Rise and Fall of Great Powers: Economic Change and Military Conflict from 1500 to 2000* (London: Unwin Hyman, 2000). The quote is from Kennedy's review of Hugh Thomas, *Rivers of Gold: The Rise of the Spanish Empire from Columbus to Magellan* (New York: Random House, 2004), in the New York Times Book Review, July 25, 2004, 10.

9 Max Weber, *The Protestant Ethic and the Spirit of Capitalism* (Mineola, NY: Dover Publications, 2003)

10 Carl Ortwin Sauer, *Sixteenth Century North America: The Land and People as Seen by the Europeans* (Berkeley: University of California Press, 1971), 16–23

11 Gavin Menzies, *1421: The Year China Discovered the World* (London, New York: Bantam Books, 2003)

12 Kirkpatrick Sale, *The Conquest of Paradise: Christopher Columbus and the Columbian Legacy* (New York: A.A. Knopf, 1990)

13 John S. Badeau, Majid Fakhry, et al., *The Genius of Arab Civilization: Source of Renaissance*, 2nd ed. (Cambridge, Mass.: MIT Press, 1983)

14 Tomaz Mastnak, *Crusading Peace: Christendom, the Muslim World, and the Western Political Order* (Berkeley: University of California Press, 2002)

15 Michael Baigent and Richard Leigh, *The Inquisition* (London: Penguin, 2000)

16 Mahmood Mamdani, *Good Muslim, Bad Muslim: America, the Cold War and the Roots of Terror* (New York: Pantheon Books, 2004), 5

17 J.H. Parry, *The Age of Reconnaissance, Discovery, Exploration, and Settlement* (Berkeley: University of California Press, 1981), 29. See also J.H. Parry, *The Spanish Theory of Empire in the Sixteenth Century* (Cambridge: Cambridge University Press, 1940).

18 Giovanni Arrighi, *The Long Twentieth Century: Money, Power, and the Origin of Our Times* (London: Verso, 1994), 85–158; Gino Luzzatto, *An Economic History of Italy from the Fall of the Roman Empire to the Beginning of the Sixteenth Century* (London: Routledge, 1961); Robert L. Reynolds, "Origins of Modern Business Enterprise: Medieval Italy," *Journal of Economic History* 12 (fall 1952): 350–65; M.M. Postan, *Medieval Trade and Finance* (Cambridge: Cambridge University Press, 1973); Richard A. Goldthwaite, "The Medici Bank and the World of Florentine Capitalism," *Past and Present* 114 (Feb. 1987): 3–31; Edwin S. Hunt, "Multinational Corporations: Their Origin, Development, and Present Forms," in B.L. Isaac, ed., *Research in Economic Anthropology 8* (Greenwich, Conn.: JAI Press, 1987); Edwin S. Hunt, *The Medieval Super-Companies: A Study of the Peruzzi Company of Florence* (Cambridge: Cambridge University Press, 1994)

19 Bernal Diaz del Castillo, *Discovery and Conquest of Mexico, 1517–1521*, trans. A.P. Maudslay (New York: Farrar, Straus and Cudahy, 1956), xv, 215

20 Ronald Wright, *Stolen Continents: The "New World" through Indian Eyes since 1492* (Toronto: Viking, 1992), 160; Miguel Leon-Portilla, "Men of Maize," in Alvin M. Josephy, *America in 1492: The World of Indian Peoples before the Arrival of Columbus* (New York: Vintage, 1993), 147–75

21 Charles Gibson, *Spain in America* (New York: Harper and Rowe, 1966), 29

22 Ibid., 103

23 Eduardo Galeano, *Open Veins of Latin America: Five Centuries of the Pillage of a Continent*, trans. Cedric Belfrage (1973; New York: Monthly Review Press, 1997); Frederick S. Weaver, *Latin America in the World Economy: Mercantile Colonialism to Global Capitalism* (Boulder, Col.: Westview Press, 2000)

24 Pablo Stefani, "Bolivia: Social Conflict and Resistance in El Alto," *Green Left Weekly*, June 23, 2004

25 Fred Anderson and Andrew Cayton, *The Dominion of War: Empire and Liberty in North America, 1500–2000* (New York: Viking, 2005), 25

26 Glyn Davies, *A History of Money from Ancient Times to Present*, rev. ed. (Cardiff: University of Wales Press, 1996), 189

27 Fernand Braudel, *A History of Civilizations*, trans. Richard Mayne (New York: Penguin, 1993), 444

28 Philip Caraman, *The Lost Paradise: An Account of the Jesuits in Paraguay, 1607–1768* (London: Sidgwick, 1975); Elman R. Service, *Spanish-Guarani Relations in Early Colonial Paraguay* (Westport, Conn.: Greenwood Press, 1971)

29 David E. Stannard, *American Holocaust: Columbus and the Conquest of the New World* (New York: Oxford University Press, 1992)

30 Jared Diamond, *Guns, Germs, and Steel: The Fates of Human Societies* (New York: W.W. Norton, 1997), 375

31 See Richard White, *The Middle Ground: Indians, Empires, and Republics in the Great Lakes Region, 1650–1815* (Cambridge: Cambridge University Press, 1991).

32 See Kavalam M. Pannikar, *Asia and Western Dominance: A Survey of the Vasco da Gama Epoch of Asian History, 1498–1945* (London: Allen and Unwin, 1953).

33 John Cabot's Royal Charter, cited in Wilcombe E. Washburn, Introduction to *Handbook of North American Indians*, William C. Sturtevant, gen. ed., vol. 4: *History of Indian-White Relations* (Washington, DC: Smithsonian Institution, 1988), 6. See also Patrick McGrath, "Bristol and America, 1480–1631," in his *Westward Enterprise: English Activities in Ireland, the Atlantic, and America, 1480–1650* (Liverpool: Liverpool University Press, 1978), 81–102.

34 David Beers Quinn, *The Discovery of America, 1481–1620: From the Bristol Voyages of the Fifteenth Century to the Pilgrim Settlement at Plymouth: The Exploration, Exploitation, and Trial-and-Error Colonization of North America by the English* (New York: Alfred A. Knopf, 1974); David Beers Quinn, *Set Fair for Roanoke: Voyages and Colonies, 1584–1606* (Chapel Hill: University of North Carolina Press, 1985)

35 Kenneth R. Andrews, *Elizabethan Privateering: English Privateering during the Spanish War, 1585–1603* (Cambridge: Cambridge University Press, 1964); James G. Lydon, *Pirates, Privateers and Profits* (Upper Saddle River, NJ: Gregg, 1970)

36 Harry Kelsey, *Sir Francis Drake: The Queen's Pirate* (New Haven: Yale University Press, 1998)

37 R. Samuel Bawlf, *The Secret Voyage of Sir Francis Drake* (Vancouver: Douglas & McIntryre, 2004); Norman J. W. Thrower, ed., *Sir Francis Drake and the Famous Voyage* (Berkeley: University of California Press, 1984)

38 John Maynard Keynes, *A Treatise on Money*, vol. 2: *The Applied Theory of Money* (1930; London: Macmillan, 1965), 156

39 Janice E. Thomson, *Mercenaries, Pirates, and Sovereigns: State-Building and Extraterritorial Violence in Early Modern Europe* (Princeton: Princeton University Press, 1994), 35

40 Edmund Burke, cited ibid., 32. See also K.N. Chaudhuri, *The East India Company: A Study of an Early Joint-Stock Company, 1600–1640* (New York: Augustus M. Kelley, 1965); and K.N. Chaudhuri, *Trade and Civilization in the Indian Ocean: An Economic History from the Rise of Islam to 1750* (Cambridge: Cambridge University Press, 1985).

41 Charles R. Boxer, *The Dutch Seaborne Empire, 1600–1800* (New York: Knopf, 1965); Jonathan Israel, *Dutch Primacy in World Trade, 1585–1740* (Oxford: Clarendon Press, 1989); Simon Schama, *The Embarrassment of Riches: An Interpretation of Dutch Culture in the Golden Age* (Berkeley: University of California Press, 1988)

42 Observer writing in 1728, cited in Charles Wilson, *The Dutch Republic and the Civilization of the Seventeenth Century* (New York: McGraw-Hill, 1968), 22

43 Braudel, *A History of Civilizations*, 264

44 Charles R. Boxer, *The Portuguese Seaborne Empire, 1415–1825* (Harmondsworth, UK: Penguin Books, 1973); Niels Steensgaard, *The Asian Trade Revolution of the Seventeenth Century: The East Indian Companies and the Decline of the Caravan Trade* (Chicago: University of Chicago Press, 1974); R.J. Barendse, *The Arabian Seas: The Indian Ocean World of the Seventeenth Century (Armonk and London: Sharpe, 2002)*

45 Arrighi, *The Long Twentieth Century*, 155

46 Peggy Liss, *Atlantic Empires: The Network of Trade and Revolution, 1713–1826* (Baltimore: Johns Hopkins University Press, 1983)

47 Cornelius Goslinga, *The Dutch in the Caribbean and the Wild Coast, 1580–1680* (Assen, Netherlands: Van Gorcum, 1971); Cornelius Goslinga, *The Dutch in the Caribbean and Guiana, 1680–1791* (Assen, Netherlands, and Dover, NH: Van Gorcum, 1985)

48 Sidney W. Mintz, *Sweetness and Power: The Place of Sugar in Modern History* (New York: Viking, 1985)

49 Philip D. Curtin, *The Rise and Fall of the Plantation Complex: Essays in Atlantic History*, 2nd ed. (New York: Cambridge University Press, 1998); Arthur I. Stinchcombe, *Sugar Island Slavery in the Age of Enlightenment: The Political Economy of the Caribbean World* (Princeton: Princeton University Press, 2002); Eduardo Galeano, "King Sugar," in John Yewell, Chris Dodge, and Jan Desirey, eds., *Confronting Columbus: An Anthology* (Jefferson, NC, and London: McFarland and Co, 1992), 76–82; W.R. Aykroyd, *Sweet Malefactor: Sugar, Slavery and Human Society* (London: Heinemann, 1967)

50 Niall Ferguson, *Empire: The Rise and Demise of the British World Order and the Lessons for Global Power* (New York: Basic Books, 2002), 14

51 See Philip D. Curtin, *Cross-Cultural Trade in World History* (New York: Cambridge University Press, 1984).

52 See Donald Creighton, *The Empire of the St. Lawrence* (1937; Toronto: Macmillan, 1970).

53 Jerry Martien, *Shell Game: A True Account of Beads and Money in North America* (San Francisco: Mercury House, 1996)

54 John Steele Gordon, *An Empire of Wealth: The Epic History of American Economic Power* (New York: HarperCollins, 2004), 103–4

55 George T. Hunt, *The Wars of the Iroquois: A Study in Intertribal Trade Relations* (Madison: University of Wisconsin Press, 1940)

56 Axel Madsen, *John Jacob Astor: America's First Multimillionaire* (New York: John Wiley, 2001); John D. Haeger, *John Jacob Astor: Business and Finance in the Early Republic* (Detroit: Wayne State University Press, 1991); Kenneth W. Porter, *John Jacob Astor: Business Man*, 2 vols. (Cambridge: Harvard University Press, 1931)

57 See Gray Brechin, *Imperial San Francisco: Urban Power, Earthly Ruin* (Berkeley: University of California Press, 2001); Richard Drinnin, *Facing West: The Metaphysics of Indian-Hating and Empire-Building* (New York: Schocken Books, 1980).

58 Gareth Stedman Jones, "The History of US Imperialism," in R. Blackburn, ed., *Ideology in the Social Sciences* (New York: Vintage, 1972), 216–17

59 Henry Cabot Lodge, cited in John J. Mearsheimer, *The Tragedy of Great Power Politics* (New York: W.W. Norton, 2001), 238

60 Karl E. Meyer and Shareen Blair Brysac, *Tournament of Shadows: The Great Game and the Race for Empire in Central Asia* (Washington, DC: Counterpoint, 1999), 10

61 William N. Fenton, *The Great Law and the Longhouse: A Political History of the Iroquois Confederacy* (Norman: University of Oklahoma Press, 1998)

62 See, for instance, Cadwallader Colden, *The History of the Five Nations of Canada* (1947; Toronto: Coles, 1972); Baron de Lahontan, *New Voyages to North America by baron de Lahontan,* 2 vols., ed. R.G. Thwaites (1703; Chicago: A.C. McClurg, 1905); John Brown Childs, "Beyond Unity: The Transcommunal Roots of Coordination in the Haudenosaunee (Iroquois) Model of Cooperation and Diversity," in Roxann Prazniak and Arif Dirlik, eds., *Places and Politics in an Age of Globalization* (Lanham, Maryland: Rowan and Littlefield, 2001), 267–96.

63 Jose Barreiro, ed., *Indian Roots of American Democracy* (Ithaca, NY: Akwe: kon Press, Cornell University, 1992), 75; United States Congress Senate Select Committee on Indian Affairs, *Acknowledging the Contribution of the Iroquois Confederacy of Nations to the Development of the United States Constitution,* Report 100-565 (Washington, DC: USGPO, 1988)

64 Lewis Henry Morgan, *League of the Iroquois* (1851; New York: Corinth Books, 1962)

65 Lewis Henry Morgan, *Ancient Society, or Researches in the Lines of Human Progress from Savagergy through Barbarism to Civilization* (1877; New York: Gordon Press, 1976)

66 Lewis Henry Morgan, *The Origins of the Family, Private Property and the State in Light of the Researches of Lewis Henry Morgan* (1884; New York: International Publishers, 1972)

67 Paul A. Wallace, *The White Roots of Peace* (1946; Port Washington, NY: Ira J. Friedman, 1968)

68 Samuel Eliot Morison, *The Oxford History of the American People* (New York: Oxford University Press, 1965), 75

69 Peter Hood, *How Time Is Measured,* 2nd ed. (Oxford: Oxford University Press, 1969), 46; Eric G. Forbes, *Greenwich Observatory,* vol. 1: *Origins and Early History* (London: Taylor and Francis, 1975); Derek House, *Greenwich Time and the Longitude* (London: Philip Wilson, 1997)

70 "Corporation," in *Encyclopedia Britannica,* 9th ed. (Edinburgh: Adam and Charles Black, 1877), 6: 432

71 Sir Percival Griffiths, *A Licence to Trade: The English Chartered Companies* (London: Ernest Benn, 1974)

72 E.E. Rich, *The Hudson's Bay Company, 1670–1870,* 3 vols. (Toronto: McClelland & Stewart, 1960)

73 Charter of the Hudson's Bay Company, with some paraphrasing by the author, cited in George Cawston and A.H. Keane, *The Early Chartered Companies (A.D. 1296–1858)* (1896; New York: Burt Franklin, 1968), 157–60

74 Charles Derber, *Corporate Nation: How Corporations Are Taking Over Our Lives and What We Can Do About It* (New York: St Martin's Griffin, 1998)

75 Benedict Anderson, *Under Three Flags: Anarchism and the Anti-Colonial Imagination* (London: Verso, 2007), 9

76 Perry Miller, *Roger Williams: His Contributions to the American Tradition* (New York: Atheneum, 1965)

77 Lewis Hanke, *The Spanish Struggle for Justice in the Conquest of America* (Boston: Little, Brown, 1965); Anthony Pagden, *Spanish Imperialism and the Political Imagination* (New York: Yale University Press, 1990); L.C. Green and Olive P. Dickason, *The Law of Nations and the New World* (Edmonton: University of Alberta Press, 1989); Robert A. Williams Jr, *The American Indian in Western Legal Discourse* (New York: Oxford University Press, 1990), 96–108

78 Samuel M. Janney, *The Life of William Penn* (1851; Freeport, NY: Books for Libraries Press, 1970), 164–70, 1885–6; Edward C.O. Beatty, *William Penn as Social Philosopher* (New York: Columbia University Press, 1939)

79 Edmund Burke, *Reflections on the Revolution in France*, ed. Conor Cruise O'Brien (New York: Penguin, 1981)

80 Edmund Burke, cited in Ferguson, *Empire*, 54–5. See Peter J. Marshall, *The Impeachment of Warren Hastings* (Oxford University Press, 1965); Nicholas B. Dirks, *The Scandal of Empire: India and the Creation of Imperial Britain* (Cambridge Mass.: Belknap Press of Harvard University Press, 2006)

81 G.R. Mellor, *British Imperial Trusteeship* (London: Farber and Farber, 1951)

82 Sir Charles Metcalfe and Thomas Babington Macaulay, cited in Meyer and Brysac, *Tournament of Shadows*, 55–7

83 Paul Johnson. *The Birth of the Modern: World Society, 1815–1830* (London: Weidenfeld and Nicolson, 1991), 321–36

84 C.L.R. James, *The Black Jacobins: Toussaint L'Overture and the San Domingo Revolution*, 2nd ed., revised (New York: Vintage Books, 1963)

85 Gordon S. Brown, *Toussaint's Clause: The Founding Fathers and the Haitian Revolution* (Jackson: University of Mississippi Press, 2005)

86 Noel Mostert, *Frontiers: The Epic of South Africa's Creation and the Tragedy of the Xhosa People* (New York: Alfred A. Knopf, 1992), 802

87 Kenneth N. Bell and W.P. Morrell, eds., *Select Documents on British Colonial Policy, 1830–1860* (Oxford: Clarendon Press, 1928), 545–6

88 Great Britain, *Sessional Papers* (Commons), vol. 7: "Report of the Select Committee on Aborigines in British Settlement, 26 June, 1837" (London: King's Printer, 1837), 29–30

89 Fred Anderson, *Crucible of War: The Seven Years' War and the Fate of Empire in British North America, 1754–1766* (New York: Alfred A. Knopf, 2000)

90 David Dixon, *Never Come to Peace Again: Pontiac's Uprising and the Fate of the British Empire in North America* (Norman: University of Oklahoma Press, 2005), 247–75

91 Wilcomb E. Washburn, *The Governor and the Rebel: A History of Bacon's Rebellion in Virginia* (New York: Norton, 1972)

92 The Royal Proclamation of 1763 is published in its entirety in Ian A.L. Getty and Antoine S. Lussier, eds., *As Long as the Sun Shines and Water Flows: A Reader in Canadian Native Studies* (Vancouver: UBC Press, 1983), 29–37.

93 Thomas Jefferson, *A Summary of the Rights of British America* (Williamsburg: Clementinarind, 1774), republished in Julian P. Boyd, ed., *The Papers of Thomas Jefferson* (Princeton: Princeton University Press, 1950), 1: 121–37

94 John Locke, *Two Treatises of Government*, ed. Peter Laslette (New York: New American Library, 1965). See also Robert A. Williams Jr, *The American Indian in Western Legal Discourse* (New York: Oxford University Press, 1991), 263–300; Barbara Arneil, *John Locke and America: The Defence of English Colonialism* (Oxford: Clarendon Press, 1996).

95 Henry Clay, cited in Fred Anderson and Andrew Cayton, *The Dominion of War: Empire and Liberty in North America, 1500–2000* (New York: Viking, 2005), 226

96 C.A. Bayly, *The Birth of the Modern World, 1780–1914: Global Connections and Comparisons* (Oxford: Blackwell Publishing, 2004), 161–5

97 Richard Hofstadter, *Social Darwinism in American Thought*, rev. ed. (Boston: Beacon Press, 1955); Gertrude Himmelfarb, *Darwin and the Darwinian Revolution* (New York: W.W. Norton, 1959)

98 C.B. Macpherson, *The Political Theory of Possessive Individualism: Hobbes to Locke* (London: Oxford University Press, 1962)

99 Albert K. Weinberg, *Manifest Destiny: A Study of National Expansion in American History* (Baltimore: Johns Hopkins University Press, 1935); Anders Stephanson, *Manifest Destiny: American Expansionism and the Empire of Right* (New York: Hill and Wang, 1995)

100 Citizen Works, Corporate Scandal Sheet at http://www.citizenworks.org/enron/corp-scandal.php

101 Richard Blackwell, "Panel Alleges Black Ran 'Corporate Kleptocracy,'" *Globe and Mail*, Sept. 1, 2004, A1

102 J. Richard Finlay, "How Dubya Dropped the Ball," ibid., July 10, 2002, A11

103 Kevin Phillips, *Bad Money: Reckless Finance, Failed Politics, and the Global Crisis of American Capitalism* (New York: Viking, 2008), 107, 70

104 See Thomas Frank, *One Market under God: Extreme Capitalism, Market Populism, and the End of Economic Democracy* (New York: Doubleday, 2000).

105 Phillips, *Bad Money*, 64

106 Ibid., 64, 45

107 Ibid., 57

108 Ibid., 58–64

109 Martin Wolf, "Why Banking Is an Accident Waiting to Happen," *Financial Times*, November 27, 2007, cited in Kevin Phillips, *Bad Money*, 205

110 Alex Berenson, "The Other Legacy of Enron: The Idea That Anything Can Be Traded," *New York Times*, May 28, 2006, section 4, 1, 4

111 Barrie Zwicker, *Towers of Deception: The Media Cover-Up of 9/11* (Gabriola, BC: New Society Publishers, 2006); Webster Griffin Tarpley, *Synthetic Terror: Made in the USA* (Joshua Tree, Cal., 2006); David Ray Griffin, *The 9/11 Commission: Omissions and Distortions* (Northampton, Mass.: Olive Branch Press, 2005); David Ray Griffin, *The New Pearl Harbor Revisited: 9/11, the Cover-Up, and the Expose* (Northampton, Mass.: Olive Branch Press, 2008)

112 Jeremy Scahill, *Blackwater: The Rise of the World's Most Powerful Mercenary Army* (New York: Nation Books, 2008)

113 Reported by CBS News on September 10, 2001, at http://www.youtube.com/watch?v=xU4GdHLUHwU

114 Zbigniew Brzezinski, *The Grand Chessboard: American Primacy and Its Geostrategic Imperatives* (New York: Basic Books, 1997); Michael T. Klare, *Rising Powers, Shrinking Planet: The New Geopolitics of Energy* (New York: Metropolitan Books, 2008)

CHAPTER THREE

1 John Noble Wilford, *The Mapmakers: The Story of the Great Pioneers in Cartography from Antiquity to the Space Age* (New York: Vintage, 1981); Norman J.W. Thrower, *Maps and Civilization: Cartography in Culture and Society* (Chicago: University of Chicago Press, 1972); Alan Gurney, *Compass: A Story of Exploration and Innovation* (New York: W.W. Norton, 2004)

2 David S. Landes, *Revolution in Time: Clocks and the Making of the Modern World* (Cambridge, Mass.: Harvard University Press, 1983), 12

3 Garrick Mallery, *Picture-Writing of the American Indians*, 2 vols. (Washington, DC: Smithsonian Institution, 1893); Arlene Hirschfelder and Martha Kreipe de Montano, *The Native American Almanac: A Portrait of Native America Today* (New York: Prentice Hall, 1993), 4–7

4 Biloine Whiting Young and Melvin L. Fowler, *Cahokia: The Great Native American Metropolis* (Urbana: University of Illinois Press, 2000); Thomas E. Emerson, *Cahokia and the Archaeology of Power* (Tuscaloosa: University of Alabama Press, 1997); Rinita A. Dalan et al., *Envisioning Cahokia: A Landscape Perspective* (DeKalb: Northern Illinois University Press, 2003); Sally A. Kitt Chappell, *Cahokia: Mirror of the Cosmos* (Chicago: University of Chicago Press, 2002)

5 Anthony M. Alioto, *A History of Western Science*. 2nd ed. (Englewoods Cliff, NJ: Prentice Hall, 1993)

6 Peter Hood, *How Time Is Measured*, 2nd ed. (Oxford: Oxford University Press, 1969), 13, 22–3

7 Jeremy Rifkin, *Time Wars: The Primary Conflict in Human History* (New York: Henry Holt, 1987), 82–5

8 Malcolm M. Thomson, *The Beginning of the Long Dash: A History of Timekeeping in Canada* (Toronto: University of Toronto Press, 1978), 36

9 L.J. Burpee, *Sandford Fleming: Empire Builder* (London: Oxford University Press, 1915); Hugh Maclean, *Man of Steel: The Story of Sir Sandford Fleming* (Toronto: Ryerson Press, 1969); Lorne Green, *Chief Engineer: The Life of a Nation Builder – Sandford Fleming* (Toronto: Dundurn Press, 1993)

10 Sir Sandford Fleming, cited in Thomson, *The Beginning of the Long Dash*, 34–5

11 Hood, *How Time Is Measured*, 46; Eric G. Forbes, *Greenwich Observatory*, vol. 1: *Origins and Early History* (London: Taylor and Francis, 1975); Derek House, *Greenwich Time and the Longtitude* (London: Philip Wilson, 1997)

12 Scotland's royal astronomer, cited in Green, *Chief Engineer*, 59

13 Frances Cairncross, *The Death of Distance: How the Communications Revolution Will Change Our Lives* (Boston: Harvard Business School Press, 1997)

14 Stephen Hawking, *A Brief History of Time*, updated and expanded 10th anniversary edition (New York: Bantam, 1996), vii

15 Ibid., 147

16 Max Born, *Einstein's Theory of Relativity*, rev. ed. (New York: Dover, 1962); Gerald E. Tauber, *Albert Einstein's Theory of General Relativity* (New York: Crown Publishers, 1979); Albert Einstein, *Theory of Relativity and Other Essays* (New York: MJF Books, 1998); Amir D. Aczel, *God's Equation: Einstein, Relativity, and the Expanding Universe* (New York: Four Walls Eight Windows, 1999)

17 T.S. Kuhn, *The Structure of Scientific Revolutions* (Chicago: University of Chicago Press, 1970)

18 Herbert Marshall McLuhan, *The Mechanical Bride: Folklore of Industrial Man* (New York: The Vanguard Press, 1951), 3

19 W.V Kirk, *Relativism and Reality* ((London: Routledge, 1999); Paul O'Grady, *Relativism* (Montreal: McGill-Queen's University Press, 2002)

20 Lewis S. Feuer, *Einstein and the Generations of Science* (New York: Basic Books, 1974), 61

21 See Michel Foucault, *Madness and Civilization*, trans. Richard Howard (New York: Random House, 1965).

22 Paul M. Wood, *Biodiversity and Democracy: Rethinking Society and Nature* (Vancouver: UBC Press, 2000)

23 Wyn Craig Wade, *The Titanic: The End of a Dream* (New York: Rawson, Wade Publishers, 1979); Lawrence Beesley, *The Loss of the SS Titanic* (Boston: Houghton Mifflin, 1912)

24 George A. Codding, *The International Telecommunication Union* (Leiden: E.J. Brill, 1952)

25 Landes, *Revolution in Time*, 4

26 James Gleick, *Faster: The Acceleration of Just About Everything* (New York: Pantheon Books, 1999)

27 James Gleick, *What Just Happened: A Chronicle from the Information Age* (New York: Pantheon, 2002)

28 William Greider, *One World, Ready or Not: The Manic Logic of Global Capitalism* (New York: Touchstone, 1997), 23

29 John Bankston, *Henry Ford and the Assembly Line* (Bear, Del.: Mitchell Lane Publishers, 2004); Richard Bak, *Henry and Edsel: The Creation of the Ford Empire* (Hoboken, NJ: Wiley, 2003)

30 Landes, *Revolution in Time*, 308

31 Ron Chernow, *Titan: The Life of John D. Rockefeller* (New York: Vintage, 1999)

32 Stephem Myer III, *The Five Dollar Day* (Albany: State University of New York Press, 1981)

33 Max Wallace, *The American Axis: Henry Ford, Charles Lindbergh, and the Rise of the Third Reich* (New York: St Martin's Griffin, 2003)

34 William Dodd, cited in Wallace, *The American Axis*, 219

35 Henry R. Luce, *The Ideas of Henry Luce*, ed. John K. Jessup (New York: Atheneum, 1969); James L. Baughman, *Henry R. Luce and the Rise of American News* (Baltimore: Johns Hopkins University Press, 2001); Robert Edwin Hertzstein, *Henry R. Luce: A Political Portrait of the Man Who Created the American Century* (New York: C. Scribner's Sons, 1994).

36 Dwayne R. Winseck and Robert M. Pike, *Communication and Empire: Media, Markets, and Globalization, 1860–1930* (Durham, NC: Duke University Press, 2007)

37 Laird Goldsborough in the July 1934 edition of *Fortune*, cited in http:// members.tripod.com/~american_almanac/morgan3.htm

38 Ferdinand Lundberg, *Imperial Hearst: A Social Biography* (New York: Equinox Press, 1936); Judith Robinson, *The Hearsts: An American Dynasty* (Newark: University of Delaware Press, 1991)

39 See Alfred E. Eckes and Thomas W. Zeiler, *Globalization and the American Century* (Cambridge: Cambridge University Press, 2003); A.G. Hopkins, ed., *Globalization in World History* (New York: W.W. Norton, 2003); William G. Robbins, *Colony and Empire: The Capitalist Transformation of the American West* (Lawrence: University Press of Kansas, 1991).

40 George Seldes, *One Thousand Americans* (New York: Boni and Gaer, 1948); George Seldes, *Facts and Fascism* (New York: In Fact, 1943); George Seldes, *Lords of the Press* (New York: J. Messner, 1938)

41 W.A. Swamburg, *Luce and His Empire* (New York: Scribner's, 1972), 128

42 Henry Luce, "The American Century," *Life*, Feb. 17, 1941, 61–5

43 Donald W. White, *The American Century: The Rise and Decline of the United States as a World Power* (New Haven: Yale University Press, 1996), 9

44 Reinhold Niebuhr, *Discerning the Signs of the Time: Sermons for Today and Tomorrow* (New York: Scribner's, 1946), 11, 78

45 Henry Wallace, *The Century of the Common Man*, ed. Russell Lord (New York: Yeynal and Hitcock, 1943), 14, 17–20

46 State Department, cited in Noam Chomsky, *Hegemony or Survival: America's Quest for Global Dominance* (New York: Henry Holt, 2003), 150. See also Irvine H. Anderson, *Aramco, the United States, and Saudi Arabia: A Study of the Dynamics of Foreign Oil Policy, 1933–1950* (Princeton: Princeton University Press, 1981).

47 Paul Kleber Monod, *The Power of Kings: Monarchy and Religion in Europe, 1598–1715* (New Haven: Yale University Press, 1999)

48 Fred Kaplan, *The Wizards of Armageddon* (New York: Simon and Schuster, 1983); Richard K. Betts, *Nuclear Blackmail and Nuclear Balance* (Washington, DC: Brookings Institution Press, 1987); Arthur M. Katz, *Life after Nuclear War: The Economic and Social Impacts of Nuclear Attacks on the United States*

(Cambridge, Mass.: Ballinger, 1982); Herman Kahn, *On Thermonuclear War: Three Lectures and Several Suggestions*, 2nd ed. (New York: Free Press, 1969); Charles L. Glaser, *Analyzing Strategic Nuclear Policy* (Princeton, NJ: Princeton University Press, 1990)

49 Harry Elmer Barnes, "Hiroshima: An Assault on a Beaten Foe," *National Review*, May 10, 1958; Gar Alperovitz, *Atomic Diplomacy: Hiroshima and Potsdam* (New York: Simon and Schuster, 1965); Gar Alperovitz, *The Decision to Use the Atomic Bomb and the Architecture of an American Myth* (New York: Alfred A. Knopf, 1995); Jay Lifton and Greg Mitchell, *Hiroshima in America: A Half Century of Denial* (New York: Avon Books, 1995); Paul Boyer, *By the Bomb's Early Light: American Thought and Culture at the Dawn of the Atomic Age* (New York: Pantheon Books, 1985)

50 John F. Kennedy, cited in William Rivers Pitt with Scott Ritter, *War on Iraq: What Team Bush Doesn't Want You to Know* (New York: Context Books, 2002), 7

51 Immanuel Kant, "Idea for a Universal History," 1784, "Perpetual Peace," 1795, in Immanuel Kant, *On History*, ed. Lewis White Beck (Indianapolis: Bobbs-Merrill, 1963), 16–17

52 Senate of the State of North Carolina, 1941, cited in Ian Clark, *Reform and Resistance in the International Order* (Cambridge: Cambridge University Press, 1980), 7

53 Paul A.W. Wallace, *The White Roots of Peace* (Philadelphia: University of Pennsylvania Press, 1946)

54 See, for instance, Terence H. Qualter, *Propaganda and Psychological Warfare* (New York: Random House, 1962); Robert T. Holt and Robert W. Van de Velde, *Strategic Psychological Operations and American Foreign Policy* (Chicago: University of Chicago Press, 1960); Robert E. Summers, ed., *America's Weapons of Psychological Warfare* (New York: H.W. Wilson, 1951); Thomas C. Sorensen. *The Word War: The Story of American Propaganda* (New York: Harper and Row, 1968).

55 Arthur M. Schlesinger Jr, *The Vital Centre: The Politics of Freedom* (1949; Boston: Houghton Mifflin, 1962), 157

56 D.F. Fleming, *The Cold War and Its Origins, 1917–1960*, 2 vols. (New York: Doubleday, 1961); John Lewis Gaddis, *We Now Know: Rethinking Cold War History* (Oxford: Clarendon Press, 1997); John Lewis Gaddis, *The Long Peace: Inquiries into the History of the Cold War* (Oxford: Oxford University Press, 1987)

57 C. Wright Mills, *The Power Elite* (New York: Oxford University Press, 1956); Arthur A. Ekirch, *The Civilian and the Military* (New York: Oxford University Press, 1956); I.F. Stone, *The Hidden History of the Korean War* (New York: Monthly Review Press, 1952); Lewis Mumford, *The Pentagon of Power* (New York: Harcourt, Brace, Jovanovitch, 1970); William Appleman Williams, *From Colony to Empire: Essays in the History of American Foreign Relations* (New York: J. Wiley, 1972); William Appleman Williams, *The United States, Cuba, and Castro: An Essay on the Dynamics of Revolution and the Dissolution of Empire*

(New York: Monthly Review Press, 1962); Edmund Wilson, *The Cold War and the Income Tax: A Protest* (New York: Farrar, Strauss, 1963); David Horowitz, *The Free World Colossus: A Critique of American Foreign Policy in the Cold War*, rev. ed. (New York: Hill and Wang, 1971); Walter Lippman, *The Communist World and Ours* (New York: Little, Brown, 1958); Sidney Lens, *The Futile Crusade: Anti-Communism as an American Credo* (Chicago: Quadrangle Books, 1964); Arnold J. Toynbee, *America and the World Revolution and Other Lectures* (New York: Oxford University Press, 1962); Noam Chomsky, *American Power and the New Mandarins* (New York: Pantheon Books, 1969). For a rich discussion of revisionist writing on the opening phases of the Cold War, see Murray N. Rothbard, "Harry Elmer Barnes as Revisionist of the Cold War," in Arthur Gollard, ed., *Harry Elmer Barnes, Learned Crusader: A New History in Action* (New York: Ralph Myles Publishing, 1968), 314–38.

58 William Appleman Williams, *The Tragedy of American Diplomacy* (Cleveland: World Publishing Company, 1959); William Appleman Williams, *The Contours of American History* (Cleveland: World Publishing Company, 1961); William Appleman Williams, *Roots of the Modern American Empire* (New York: Random House, 1969); Paul Buhle and Edward Rice-Maximin, *William Appleman Williams: The Tragedy of Empire* (New York: Routledge, 1995)

59 Senator Arthur Vandenburg, cited in Gore Vidal, *Imperial America: Reflections on the United States of Amnesia* (New York: Nation Books, 2004), 97

60 A.J.P. Taylor, cited in Horowitz, *Free World Colossus*, 21

61 Vidal, *Imperial America*, 83

62 Harry Elmer Barnes, in "Revisionism and the Historical Blackout," in Barnes, ed., *Perpetual War for Perpetual Peace* (Caldwell, Id.: Caxton Printers, 1953), 4ff, 59ff

63 On the rise of US militarism, see Chalmers Johnson, *The Sorrows of Empire: Militarism, Secrecy, and the End of the Republic* (New York: Henry Holt, 2004).

64 Gabriel Kolko, *Confronting the Third World: United States Foreign Policy, 1945–1980* (New York: Pantheon Books, 1988); V.G. Kiernan, *America, The New Imperialism: From White Settlement to World Hegemony* (London: Zed Books, 1978); Stephen E. Ambrose and Douglas G. Brinkley, *Rise to Globalism: American Foreign Policy since 1938*, 8th rev. ed. (New York: Penguin Books, 1997); William Blum, *Killing Hope: US Military and CIA Interventions since World War II* (Monroe, Maine: Common Courage Press, 1995)

65 Arnold J. Toynbee, cited in D.F. Fleming, "Can Pax Americana Succeed," in Neal D. Houghton, ed., *Struggle against History: U.S. Foreign Policy in an Age of Revolution* (New York: Washington Square Press, 1968), 297

66 Harry Elmer Barnes, *Intellectual and Cultural History of the Western World*, 3rd rev. ed., 3 vols. (New York: Dover, 1965), 1324–32

67 Raymond Pearson, *The Rise and Fall of the Soviet Empire* (New York: Palgrave, 2002); General Oleg Sarin and Colonel Lev Dvoretsky, *The Soviet Union's Agression against the World, 1917–1989* (Novato, Cal.: Presidio Press, 1996); Olaf Kirkpatrick Caroe, *Soviet Empire: The Turks of Central Asia and Stalinism* (New York: St Martin's Press, 1967)

68 Mennen Williams and Dean Rusk, cited in Piero Gleijeses, *Conflicting Missions: Havana, Washington, and Africa, 1959–1976* (Chapel Hill: University of North Carolina Press, 2002), 125

69 Arthur M. Schlesinger Jr, *The Politics of Upheaval: The Age of Roosevelt* (Boston: Houghton Miflin, 1960)

70 Schlesinger Jr, *The Vital Centre*, 159

71 Ruth Benedict, *Patterns of Culture* (Boston: Houghton Mifflin, 1934); Kerwin Lee Klein, *Frontiers of Historical Imagination: Narrating the European Conquest of Native America, 1890–1990* (Berkeley: University of California Press, 1999), 173. See also Margaret Mead, *An Anthropologist at Work: Writings of Ruth Benedict* (Boston: Houghton Mifflin, 1959); Judith Schachter Modell, *Ruth Benedict: Patterns of a Life* (Philadelphia: University of Pensylvania Press, 1983); Margaret M. Caffrey, *Ruth Benedict: Stranger in This Land* (Austin: University of Texas Press, 1989).

72 Dwight D. Eisenhower's Farewell Address, published in Bruce Young, *Hotel California* (North Vancouver: The Good Earth, 1979), 213–15

73 George Creel, *How We Advertised America* (1920; New York: Arno Press, 1970)

74 Lock K. Johnson, *America's Secret Power: The CIA in a Democratic Society* (New York: Oxford University Press, 1989); William Blum, *CIA: A Forgotten History* (London: Zed Books, 1986); Fitzhugh Green, *American Propaganda Abroad* (New York: Hippocrene Books, 1988)

75 Carl Berstein, "The CIA and the Media: How America's Most Powerful Media Worked Hand in Glove with the Central Intelligence Agency and Why the Church Committee Covered It Up," *Rolling Stone*, Oct. 20, 1977, 55–67; Stuart Loory, "The CIA's Use of the Press: A Mighty 'Wurlitzer,'" *Columbia Journalism Review*, Sept./Oct. 1974, 6–18; Council on Foreign Relations, *Making Intelligence Smarter* (New York: CFR, 1996); Fred Landis, "The CIA and Reader's Digest," *Covert Action Information Bulletin*, no. 29 (winter 1988); Ashley Overbeck, "A Report on CIA Infiltration and Manipulation of the Mass Media," http://www.geocities.com/cpa_blacktown/20000318mediaoverb.htm; Alex Constantine, "Who Controls the Media," www.alexconstantine.50megs.com/the_cia_and.html; Martin E. Lee, *The Beast Reawakens* (Boston: Little Brown, 1997)

76 W.E.B. DuBois, "Negroes and the Crisis of Capitalism in the United States," *Monthly Review* 4 (April 1958): 478

77 Lewis H. Lapham, "Tentacles of Rage: The Republican Propaganda Mill, A Brief History," *Harper's Magazine*, Sept. 2004, 41; John Micklethwaite and Adrian Woolridge, *The Right Nation: Why America Is Different* (New York: Penguin Books, 2004); Thomas Frank, *What's the Matter with America? The Resistible Rise of the American Right* (London: Secker and Warburg, 2004)

78 Global Issues, Poverty: Facts and Stats at http://www.globalissues.org/TradeRelated/Facts.asp; UNICEF, Child Poverty in Perspective: An Overview of Child Well-Being in Rich Countries, Innocenti Report Card 7, 2007, at http://www.unicef-irc.org/search.php?q=child+well-being+in+rich&search.x=953&search.y=12

79 Elizabeth Gudrais, "Unequal America: Causes and Consequences of the Wide – and Growing – Divide between Rich and Poor," *Harvard Magazine,* July–Aug. 2008, at http://harvardmagazine.com/2008/07/unequal-america.html

80 David Korten, *When Corporations Rule the World* (San Francisco: Kumarian Press, 1995); Charles Derber, *People before Profit: The New Globalization in an Age of Terror, Big Money, and Economic Crisis* (New York: Picador, 2003)

81 George Orwell, "You and the Atomic Bomb," *Tribune,* Oct. 19, 1945

82 Harry Elmer Barnes, "How Nineteen Eight-Four Trends Threaten American Peace, Freedom, and Prosperity," in Barnes, *Revisionism: A Key to Peace and Other Essays* (San Francisco: Cato Institute, 1980); Murray N. Rothbard, "George Orwell and the Cold War: A Reconsideration," in Robert Mulvihill, ed., *Reflections on America, 1984: An Orwellian Symposium* (Athens and London: University of Georgia Press, 1986)

83 James Burnham, *The Managerial Revolution* (1941; Bloomington: Indiana University Press, 1966)

84 Raymond Vernon, *Sovereignty at Bay: The Multinational Spread of U.S. Enterprise* (New York: Basic Books, 1971)

85 Stuart W. Leslie, *The Cold War and American Science: The Military-Industrial Complex at MIT and Stanford* (New York: Columbia University Press, 1993)

86 Robert S. McNamara with Brian VanDeMark, *In Retrospect: The Tragedy and Lessons of Vietnam* (New York: Vintage, 1996); Robert S. McNamara, *Wilson's Ghost: Reducing the Risk of Conflict, Killing, and Catastrophe in the 21st Century* (New York: Public Affairs, 2003)

87 Ronald Steel, *Pax Americana,* rev. ed. (New York: Viking Press, 1970), 19

88 Robert J.S. Tross and Kent C. Trache, *Global Capitalism: The New Leviathan* (Albany: State University of New York Press, 1990)

89 D. Michael Warren, L. Jan Slikkerveer, and David Brokensha, eds., *The Cultural Dimension of Development: Indigenous Knowledge Systems* (London: Intermediate Technological Publications, 1995); Paul A. Olson, ed., *The Struggle for the Land: Indigenous Insight and Industrial Empire in the Semiarid World* (Lincoln: Center for Great Plains Studies and the University of Nebraska Press, 1990)

90 David R. Montgomery, *Dirt: The Erosion of Civilizations* (Berkeley: University of California Press, 2007)

91 Alex Roslin, "A Tough New Row to Hoe," *Globe and Mail,* July 19, 2008, F8

92 Robert S. McNamara, *The McNamara Years at the World Bank* (Baltimore: Johns Hopkins University Press, 1981); Catherin Gwin, *U.S. Relations with the World Bank, 1945–1992* (Washington: Brookings Institution, 1994); Bruce Rich, *Mortgaging the Earth: The World Bank, Environmental Impoverishment, and the Crisis of Development* (Boston: Beacon Press, 1994); Catherine Caufield, *Masters of Illusion: The World Bank and the Poverty of Nations* (New York: Henry Holt, 1996); Sebastian Mallaby, *The World's Banker: Story of Failed States, Financial Crises, and the Wealth and Poverty of Nations* (New York: Penguin Books, 2004);

Jill Torrie, ed., *The Global Impact of the IMF and World Bank* (Toronto: Between the Lines, 1983)

93 Robert McNamara, cited in Jean-Jacques Servan-Schreiber, *The American Challenge*, trans. Ronald Steele (London: Hamish Hamilton, 1968), 58–9

94 Richard Drinnon, *Facing West: The Metaphysics of Indian Hating and Empire Building* (Minneapolis: University of Minnesota Press, 1980)

95 Arnold J. Toynbee, "Introduction: Colonialism and the United States," in Houghton, ed., *Struggle against History*, xxxvii

96 See D.L. Hardesty, *Ecological Anthropology* (New York: John Wiley, 1977).

97 World Intellectual Property Organization, Patent Reports on Worldwide Patent Activity (2007 ed.) at http://www.wipo.int/ipstats/en/statistics/patents/patent_report_2007.html

98 Lawrence Lessing, *The Future of Ideas: The Fate of the Commons in a Connected World* (New York: Random House, 2001); Pradip N. Thomas, "Private Property or Common Resources," www.indiatogether.org (accessed May 2004)

99 John Bray, *The Communications Miracle: The Telecommunications Pioneers from Morse to the Information Superhighway* (London: Plenum Press, 1995); Kenneth Flamm, *Creating the Computer: Government, Industry, and High Technology* (Washington, DC: Brookings Institution, 1988)

100 Claude Levi-Strauss, *Race and History* (New York: United Nations Scientific and Cultural Organization, 1968), 22

101 Ellen Schrecker, ed., *Cold War Triumphalism: The Misuse of History After the Fall of Communism* (New York: New Press, distributed by W.W. Norton, 2004)

102 Condoleezza Rice, "Promoting the National Interest," *Foreign Affairs* 79, 1 (2000): 49

103 New York Stock Exchange Inc., "Facts and Figures," at http://www.nysedata.com/factbook

104 David Harvey, *The New Imperialism* (New York: Oxford University Press, 2005)

105 See Zbigniew Brzezinski, *The Grand Chessboard: American Primacy and Its Geostrategic Imperatives* (New York: Basic Books, 1997).

106 Richard Falk, *Predatory Globalization: A Critique* (Cambridge, Mass.: Polity Press, 1999)

107 Lewis Henry Morgan, *Ancient Society, or Researches in the Lines of Human Progress from Savagery through Barbarism to Civilization (1877)*, cited in Frederick Engels, *The Origins of the Family: Private Property and the State in Light of the Researches of Lewis Henry Morgan* (New York: International Publishers, 1972), 236–7

108 Tom Hayden, ed., *The Zapatista Reader* (New York: Thunder's Mouth Press/ Nation Books, 2002)

109 Naomi Klein, *Fences and Windows: Dispatches from the Front Lines of the Globalization Debate*, ed. Debra Ann Levy (Toronto: Vintage Canada, 2002); L. Langman, D. Morris, and J. Zalewski, "Globalization, Domination, and Cyberactivism," in W. Dunaway, ed., *The 21st Century World-System: Systemic Crisis and Antisystemic Resistance* (Westport, Conn.: Greenwood Press, 2002); Walden Bello, "2000: The Year of Global Protest," *International Socialism* 90 (2001): 71–6

110 Joseph S. Nye Jr, "Globalization's Democratic Deficit," in Nye, *Power in the Global Information Age: From Realism to Globalization* (London: Routledge, 2004), 201–5

111 See Arthur A. Ekirch, *Progressivism in America: A Study of the Era from Theodore Roosevelt to Woodrow Wilson* (New York: New Viewpoints, 1974); Gabriel Kolko, *The Triumph of Conservatism: A Reinterpretation of American History, 1900–1916* (Chicago: Quadrangle Books, 1967).

112 See William Greider, *One World, Ready or Not: The Manic Logic of Global Capitalism* (New York: Touchstone, 1998); Ellen Israel Rosen, *Making Sweatshops: The Globalization of the U.S. Apparel Industry* (Berkeley: University of California Press, 2002).

113 Gordon White, *Riding the Tiger: The Politics of Economic Reform in Post-Mao China* (Stanford, Cal.: Stanford University Press, 1993); World Bank, *China Engaged: Integration with the Global Economy* (Washington, DC: World Bank, 1997); Yuezhi Zhoa, *Media, Market, and Democracy in China: Between the Party Line and the Bottom Line* (Urbana: University of Illinois Press, 1998); Feng Li amd Jing Li, *Foreign Investment in China* (New York: St Martin's Press, 1999); Joseph Kahn, "China's Leaders Manage Class Conflict Carefully," *New York Times,* Jan. 25, 2004, 5; Charles Kernaghan, *Made in China: Behind the Label* (New York: National Labor Committee, 2000)

114 Leslie Sklair, *Globalization: Capitalism and Its Alternatives,* 3rd ed. (Oxford: Oxford University Press, 2002), 37

115 Carl Boggs, *The End of Politics: Corporate Power and the Decline of the Public Sphere* (New York: Guilford Press, 2000)

116 Sara Diamond, *Roads to Dominion: Right-Wing Movements and Political Power in the United States* (New York: Guilford Press, 1995); Susan Friend Harding, *The Book of Jerry Falwell: Fundamentalist Language and Politics* (Princeton: Princeton University Press, 2000); Thomas Bodheimer and Robert Gould, *Rollback: Right-Wing Power in U.S. Foreign Policy* (Boston: South End Press, 1989)

117 Mahmood Mamdani, *Good Muslim, Bad Muslim: America, the Cold War and the Roots of Terror* (New York: Pathenon Books, 2004); William Minter, *Apartheid's Contras: An Inquiry into the Roots of War in Angola and Mozambique* (Atlantic Highland, NJ: Zed Books, 1994); Michael T. Klare and Peter Kornbluh, eds., *Low-Intensity Warfare: Counter-Insurgency, Proinsurgency, and Antiterrorism in the Eighties* (New York: Pantheon, 1988); Tom Carew, *Jihad: The Secret War in Afghanistan* (Edinburgh and London: Mainstream Publishing, 2000)

118 Peter Dale Scott, *Drugs Oil and War: The United States in Afghanista, Colombia, and Indochina* (Lanham, Md: Littlefield Publishers, 2003); Alfred W. McCoy, *The Politics of Heroine: CIA Complicity in the Global Drug Trades* (New York: Lawrence Hill Books, 1991); Alfred W. McCoy, "Drug Fallout: The CIA's Forty-Year Complicity in the Narcotics Trade," *The Progressive,* Aug. 1, 1997, 24–7; Alexander Cockburn and Jeffrey S. Clair, *Whiteout: The CIA, Drugs, and the Press* (London: Verso, 1998)

119 Sean D. Naylor, "7th Cavalry Inflicts Heavy Casualties in Running Battle," *USA Today,* March 27, 2003 at http://www.usatoday.com/news/world/iraq/

2003-03-25-war-zone_x.htm; Walter C. Rodgers, *Sleeping with Custer and the Seventh Cavalry: An Embedded Reporter in Iraq* (Carbondale: Southern Illinois University Press, 2005)

120 Zeev Sternhell with Mario Sznajder and Maria Asheri, *The Birth of Fascist Ideology: From Cultural Rebellion to Political Revolution*, trans. David Maisel (Princeton: Princeton University Press, 1994), 7. See also David F. Schmitz, *Thank God They're on Our Side: The United States and Right-Wing Dictatorships, 1921–1965* (Chapel Hill: University of North Carolina Press, 1999); David F. Schmitz, *The United States and Fascist Italy, 1922-1940* (Chapel Hill: University of North Carolina Press, 1988).

121 Naomi Klein, *The Shock Doctrine: The Rise of Disaster Capitalism* (Toronto: Knopf Canada, 2007); Mark Ensalaco, *Chile under Pinochet: Recovering Truth* (Philadelphia: University of Pennsylvania Press, 2000); Hugh O'Shaughnessy, *Pinochet: The Politics of Torture* (London: Latin America Bureau, 2000); Gregory Palast, "Tinker Bell Pinochet and the Fairy Tale Miracle of Chile," *London Observer*, Nov. 22, 1998

122 Naomi Klein, "Iraq under U.S. Thumb," *Globe and Mail*, March 24, 2004; Naomi Klein, "Iraq Is Not America's to Sell," *The Guardian*, Nov. 7, 2003

123 Paul Krugman, "Privatization in Iraq Is Out of Control," *International Herald Tribune*, May 5, 2004

124 Naomi Klein, "Iraq: Privatization in Disguise," *The Nation*, April 10, 2004

125 Neil King Jr, "Bush Officials Devise a Broad Plan for Free-Market Economy in Iraq," *Wall Street Journal*, May 1, 2003

126 Naomi Klein, "Baghdad Year Zero: Pillaging Iraq in Pursuit of Neocon Utopia," *Harper's Magazine*, Sept. 2004, 43–55

127 Anthony Sampson, *The Seven Sisters and the World They Made* (London: Hodder and Stoughton, 1975)

128 Stephen C. Pelletiere, *Iraq and the International Oil System* (Westport, Conn.: Praeger, 2001); Batatu Hannah, *The Old Social Classes and the Revolutionary Movements of Iraq* (Princeton: Princeton University Press, 1978)

129 Linda McQuaig, *It's the Crude, Dude: War, Big Oil, and the Fight for the Planet* (Toronto: Doubleday, 2004)

130 Dan Priest and Mary Pat Flaherty, "Under Fire, Security Firms Form an Alliance," *Washington Post*, April 8, 2004; Nicolas Von Hoffman, "Privatization in Iraq: 'Contractors' with Guns," *New York Observer*, April 23, 2004

131 Jeremy Scahill, *Blackwater: The Rise of the World's Most Powerful Mercenary Army* (New York: Nation Books, 2008), 48

132 Ibid., 262–7

133 Ibid., 429–34; P.W. Singer, *Corporate Warriors: The Rise of the Privatized Military Industry* (Ithaca: Cornell University Press, 2003), 116–17

134 Seymour M. Hersh, *Chain of Command: The Road from 9/11 to Abu Ghraib* (New York: HarperCollins, 2004)

135 Julian Borger, "The Danger of Market Forces," *The Guardian*, May 6, 2004; Dana Priest and Joe Stephens, "The Secret War of US Interrogation," *Washington Post*, May 11, 2004; Susan Sontag, "Regarding the Torture

of Others: Notes on What Has Been Done – and Why – to Prisoners by Americans," *New York Times Magazine*, May 23, 2004, 24–9, 42

136 Naomi Klein, "The Multibillion Dollar Robbery the US Calls Reconstruction," *The Guardian*, June 26, 2004

137 Scahill, *Blackwater*, 454

138 James Bamford, "This Spy for Rent," *New York Times*, June 13, 2004, 13

139 Alfred W. McCoy, *A Question of Torture: CIA Interrogation from the Cold War to the War on Terror* (New York: Metropolitan Books, 2006)

140 Monia Mazigh, *Hope and Despair: My Struggle to Free My Husband* (Toronto: McClelland & Stewart, 2008)

141 Philippe Sands, *Lawless World: America and the Making and Breaking of Global Rules* (New York: Penguin, 2005); Philippe Sands, *Torture Team: Deception, Cruelty and the Compromise of Law* (London: Allen Lane, 2008)

142 "Guantanamo Pair's Charges Dropped," BBC News, June 5, 2007, http://news.bbc.co.uk/2/hi/americas/6720315.stm

143 Omar El Akkad, "Child Soldier Khadr Needs Protection, Dallaire Says," *Globe and Mail*, May 13, 2008

144 Romeo Dallaire, *Shake Hands with the Devil: The Failure of Humanity in Rwanda* (Toronto: Random House, 2003)

145 Advertisement cited in Scahill, *Blackwater*, 347

146 Ibid., 457

147 See Deborah D. Avant, *The Market for Force: The Consequences of Privatizing Security* (Cambridge: Cambridge University Press, 2005); Madelaine Drohan, *Making a Killing: How and Why Corporations Use Force to Do Business* (Guilford Connecticut: The Lyon's Press, 2004)

148 Benjamim DeMott, "Whitewash as Public Service: How the 9/11 Commission Report Defrauds the Nation," *Harper's Magazine*, Oct. 2004; See also David Ray Griffin, *The 9/11 Commission: Omissions and Distortions* (Northampton, Mass.: Olive Branch Press, 2005).

149 Christian Reus-Smith, *American Power and World Order* (Cambridge, Mass.: Polity Press, 2004), 42, 46–7. Emphasis in original

150 James Mann, *Rise of the Vulcans: The History of the Bush War Cabinet* (New York: Viking, 2004)

151 http://www.newamericancentury.org/publicationsreports.htm

152 Dilip Hiro, *Secrets and Lies: Operation Iraqi Freedom and After* (New York: Nation Books, 2004)

153 The White House, *The National Security Strategy of the United States of America*, released Sept. 17, 2002. See Miriam Sapiro, "The Shifting Sands of Preemptive Self-Defense," *American Journal of International Law* 97, 3 (July 2003): 599–607

154 Joseph S. Nye, *The Paradox of American Power: Why the World's Only Superpower Can't Go It Alone* (Oxford: Oxford University Press, 2002)

155 Immanuel Wallerstein, *The Decline of American Power* (New York: The New Press, 2003)

156 Kevin Phillips, *Bad Money: Reckless Finance, Failed Politics, and the Global Crisis of American Capitalism* (New York: Viking, 2008), 121

157 Ibid., 122, 139
158 "No Real Alternative to Oil: Rise in Demand Seems Unavoidable," *International Herald Tribune*, Oct. 29, 2007
159 John Authers, "The Short View: Falling Dollar," *Financial Times*, Sept. 17, 2007

CHAPTER FOUR

1 Immanuel Wallerstein, *Historical Capitalism with Capitalist Civilization* (London: Verso, 1995), p. 16
2 George Clutesi, *Potlach* (Sidney, BC: Gray's Publishing, 1969)
3 Matt Mason, *The Pirate's Dilemma: How Youth Culture Is Reinventing Capitalism* (New York: Free Press, 2008), 24
4 Charles Derber, *Corporation Nation: How Corporations Are Taking Over Our Lives and What We Can Do About It* (New York: St Martin's Griffin, 1998), 126–31
5 Andrew Nikiforuk, "Are Some Uses of Freshwater Irresponsible?" *Energy Processing Canada*, July/August 2002 at http://findarticles.com/p/articles/mi_qa5406/is_200207/ai_n21318864
6 Johan Bastin and Ismail Serageldin, cited in Maude Barlow, *Blue Gold: The Global Water Crisis and the Commodification of the World's Water Supply. A Special Report* (San Francisco: International Forum on Globalization, 1999), 17, 2
7 William Finnegan, "The Economics of Empire: Notes on the Washington Consensus," *Harper's Magazine*, May 2003, 51
8 Felipe Quispe, cited in Pablo Stefanoni, "Bolivia: Social Conflict and the Resistance in El Alto," *Green Left Weekly*, June 23, 2004; Juan Forero, " A Treasure of the Andes, Ancient Demons Included," *New York Times*, July 18, 2004, 14
9 Paul Farmer, *Pathologies of Power: Health, Human Rights, and the New War on the Poor* (Berkeley: University of California Press, 2005), xxv
10 John C. Weaver, *The Great Land Rush and the Making of the Modern World, 1650–1900* (Montreal: McGill-Queen's University Press, 2003), 352
11 Lewis Henry Morgan, *Ancient Society, or Researches in the Lines of Human Progress from Savagery through Barbarism to Civilization (1877)*, cited in Frederick Engels, *The Origins of the Family, Private Property and the State* (New York: International Publishers, 1972), 236–7
12 John K. Thornton, *Africa and Africans in the Making of the Atlantic World, 1450–1800* (Cambridge: Cambridge University Press, 1998)
13 Weaver, *The Great Land Rush*
14 Paul Johnson, *The Birth of the Modern: World Society, 1815–1830* (London: Weidenfeld and Nicolson, 1991), 209
15 Conway Zirkle, "How Maize Got to Europe," *Journal of Heredity* 43, 3 (1952): 116; Redcliffe N. Salaman, *The History and Social Influence of the Potato* (Cambridge: Cambridge University Press, 1985)
16 Francis Jennings, *The Creation of America through Revolution to Empire* (Cambridge: Cambridge University Press, 2000)

17 President Dwight Eisenhower, cited in Gore Vidal, *Imperial America: Reflections on the United States of Amnesia* (New York: Nation Books, 2004), 92

18 Jason Goodwin, *Greenback: The Almighty Dollar and the Invention of America* (New York: Henry Holt, 2003), 221–2

19 Kevin Phillips, *American Theocracy: The Peril and Politics of Radical Religion, Oil, and Borrowed Money in the 21st Century* (New York: Viking, 2006); Chris Hedges, *American Fascists: The Christian Right and the War on America* (New York: Free Press, 2006)

20 Peter Kulchyski, "Towards a Theory of Dispossession: Native Politics in Canada" (PhD thesis, York University, 1988)

21 Peter Kulchyski, *Like the Sound of the Drum: Aboriginal Cultural Politics in Denendeh and Nunavut* (Winnipeg: University of Manitoba Press, 2005), 44

22 Eugene Linden, "Lost Tribes, Lost Knowledge: When Native Cultures Disappear, So Does a Trove of Scientific and Medical Wisdom," *Time*, September 23, 1991, 44–56

23 E.O. Wilson, *The Diversity of Life* (Cambridge, Mass.: Harvard University Press, 1992); Robert Robins and Eugenius Uhlenback, *Endangered Languages* (Providence, NH: Berg, 1991); Marie Battiste and James (Sa'ke'j) Henderson, *Protecting Indigenous Knowledge and Heritage* (Saskatoon: Purich, 2000)

24 Edward S. Herman and Robert W. McChesney, *The Global Media: The New Missionaries of Global Capitalism* (London: Cassell, 1997); Robert W. McChesney, *The Problem of Media: U.S. Communication Politics in the 21st Century* (New York: Monthly Review Press, 2004); Herbert I. Schiller, *Culture Inc.: The Corporate Takeover of Public Expression* (New York: Oxford University Press, 1989); Andrew Wernick, *Promotional Culture: Advertising, Ideology and Symbolic Expression* (London: Sage Publications, 1991)

25 John Locke, *Two Treatises of Government*, ed. Peter Laslett (New York: New American Library, 1965), 328–43

26 Marshall Sahlins, *Stone Age Economics* (Chicago: Aldine-Atherton, 1972); Harvey Feit, "Hunting and the Quest for Power," in Bruce Morrison and C. Roderick Wilson, eds., *Native Peoples: The Canadian Experience* (Toronto: McClelland & Stewart, 1986); Julie Cruikshank, *The Social Life of Stories* (Vancouver: UBC Press, 1998); Paul Nadasdy, *Hunters and Bureaucrats: Power, Knowledge and Aboriginal-State Relations in the Southwestern Yukon* (Vancouver: UBC Press, 2003); Peter Kulchyski and Frank Tester, *Tammarniit: Inuit Relocation in the Eastern Arctic, 1939–1963* (Vancouver: UBC Press, 1994)

27 Elizabeth Kemf, ed., *The Law of the Mother: Protecting Indigenous Peoples in Protected Areas* (San Francisco: The Sierra Club, 1993)

28 Peter Kulchyski, "A Review of the Summary of Understandings between Nisichawayasihk Cree Nation and Manitoba Hydro with Respect to the Wuskwatim Project in Historical Context and in Relation to Similar Agreements, October 2003," at www.energymanitoba.org/ presentations/ wuskwatimfull_7.doc

29 Hugh Brody, *The Other Side of Eden: Hunter, Farmers and the Shaping of the World* (Vancouver: Douglas & McIntyre, 2000)

30 Kulchyski, *Like the Sound of a Drum,* 54

31 Noam Chomsky, *Hegemony or Survival: America's Quest for Global Dominance* (New York: Henry Holt, 2004), 52–3, 59–60

32 Evo Morales, cited in Finnegan, "The Economics of Empire," 51

33 Titus Alexander, *Unravelling Global Apartheid: An Overview of World Politics* (Cambridge: Polity Press, 1996)

34 Eduardo Galeano, *Open Veins of Latin America: Five Centuries of the Pillaging of a Continent,* ed. Cedric Belfrage (New York: Monthly Review Press, 1997), 267

35 Barlow, *Blue Gold,* 11

36 Global Issues, Poverty: Facts and Statistics at http://www.globalissues.org/ TradeRelated/Facts.asp

37 Peter Dale Scott, *Deep Politics and the Death of JFK* (Berkeley: University of California Press, 1993); Peter Dale Scott, *Drugs, Oil, and War: The United States in Afghanistan, Columbia, and Indochina* (Lanham, MD: Roman and Littlefield, 2003)

38 Carroll Quigley, *Tragedy and Hope: A History of the World in Our Time* (New York: Macmillan, 1966); Arsene de Goulevich, *Czarism and Revolution,* trans. N.J. Couriss (Hawthorne, Cal.: Omni Publications, 1962); Antony C. Sutton, *Wall Street and the Bolshevik Revolution* (Sandton: Valiant Publications, 1975); G. Edward Griffin, *The Creature from Jekyll Island: A Second Look at the Federal Reserve* (Westlake Village: American Media, 2002)

39 Thomas Homer-Dixon, "Global Capitalism Teeters on the Brink," *Globe and Mail,* March 19, 2008, A17

40 Irwin Cotler, "The Conference against Racism That Became a Racist Conference against Jews," Global Jewish Agenda, at http://www.jafi.org.il/ agenda/2001/english/wk3-22/6.asp

41 Proposed resolution, cited in Irina Filatova and R.W. Johnson, "Slavery Reparation Sneaks into the Agenda," *National Post,* August 28, 2001, A14

42 United Nations General Assembly, Report of the World Conference against Racism, Racial Discrimination, Xenophobia and Related Intolerance, Jan. 25, 2002, A/Conf. 189/12

43 David Ray Griffin and Peter Dale Scott, eds., *9/11 and American Empire: Intellectuals Speak Out,* (Northampton Mass.: Olive Branch Books, 2007); Ian Henshall, *9/11 Revealed: The New Evidence* (New York: Carroll and Graf, 2007)

44 Bernard Lewis, *Islam and the West* (New York: Oxford University Press, 1993); Samuel P. Huntington, *The Clash of Civilizations and the Making of World Order* (New York: Simon and Schuster, 1996)

45 David Frum and Richard Perle, *An End to Evil: How to Win the War on Terror* (New York: Random House, 2003)

46 Phyllis Bennis, "The Global War on Terror: What It Is, What It's Done to the World," in Phyllis Bennis, Arundhati Roy, John Berger, et al., *War with No End* (London: Verso, 2007), 11–32; Michael Scheuer, *Imperial Hubris: Why the West Is Losing the War on Terror* (Washington, DC: Brassey's, 2004)

47 M.K. Gandhi, *Satyagraha in South Africa* (Ahmedabad: Navajivan, 1928); Erik H. Erikson, *Gandhi's Truth: On the Origins of Militant Nonviolence* (New York: W.W. Norton, 1969)

48 Nelson Mandela, "Gandhi the Sacred Warrior," at http://www.tolstoyfarm. com/mandela_on_gandhi.htm

49 "Unbending Intent: Philip Glass Talks with Tricycle about How Gandhi Inspired His Life and Work," *Tricycle: The Buddhist Review*, spring 2008, 71, 73

50 Martin Luther King Jr, cited in Charles Johnson, "Blueprints of Freedom," ibid., 76

51 James Shaheen, "Heroes and Communities," ibid., 7

52 Andrew Carnegie, "The Gospel of Wealth," *North American Review* 148, June 1889, 653–65

53 Mandela, "Gandhi the Sacred Warrior"

54 Pixley ka Isaka Seme, cited in Richard Rive and Tim Couzens, *Seme: The Founder of the ANC* (Lawrenceville, NJ: Africa World Press, 1993), 12; see Peter Walshe, *The Rise of African Nationalism in South Africa: The African National Congress, 1912–1952* (Berkeley: University of California Press, 1970)

55 Pixley ka Isaka Seme, "Native Union," *Imvo Zabantsundu* 24 (Oct. 1911), at http://www.anc.org.za/ancdocs/history/early/native_union.htm

56 Deep Chand Bandhu, *History of the Indian National Congress* (Delhi: Kalpaz Publishers, 2003)

57 Presidential Address by Annie Besant at the 32nd Indian National Congress Held at Calcutta, December 26, 1917, at http://www.theosophycardiff.care-4free.net/caseindia.htm

58 African National Congress, *Africans' Claims in South Africa. A Response to the Atlantic Charter Adopted by the ANC at Bloemfontein, December 24, 1943* (Johannesburg: ANC, 1943) at http://www.anc.org.za/ancdocs/history/ claims.html

59 Ismail Vadi, *The Congress of the People and the Freedom Charter Campaign* (New Delhi: Sterling Publishers, 1995)

60 Nelson Mandela, *A Long Walk to Freedom: The Autobiography of Nelson Mandela* (New York: Little, Brown, 1994), 150

61 The ANC's Freedom Charter, 1955, at http://www.anc.org.za/ancdocs/ history/charter.html

62 William Mervin Gumede, *Thabo Mbeki and the Battle for the Soul of the ANC* (Cape Town: Zebra Press, 2005)

63 Naomi Klein, *The Shock Doctrine: The Rise of Disaster Capitalism* (Toronto: Alfred A. Knopf, 2007), 250

64 Nelson Mandela, cited in Richard Meares, "Mandela's Parting Words Bitter toward Rich Whites," *Globe and Mail*, Dec. 17, 1997, A12

65 Klein, *The Shock Doctrine*, 258–9

66 Ibid., 238

67 Ibid., 245

68 Benjamin R. Barber, *Consumed: How Markets Corrupt Children, Infantilize Adults, and Swallow Citizens* (New York: W.W. Norton, 2007), 130, 133, 128

69 Deborah Campbell, "Kick it Over: The Rise of Post-Autistic Economics," *Adbusters*, no. 55, Sept.–Oct. 2004, at http://adbusters.org/the_magazine/55/Kick_it_Over_The_Rise_of_PostAutistic_Economics.html

70 Nancy Moran, "Columnist's Erudite Call Led Conservatives from the Fringes to the White House," *Globe and Mail*, Feb. 28, 2008, R5

71 Robin D. G. Kelley, "A Poetics of Anti-Colonialism," *Monthly Review* 51, 6 (Nov. 1999); Kelley, "House Negroes on the Loose: Malcolm X and the Black Bourgeoisie," *Callaloo* 21, 2 (spring 1998): 419–35

72 Vijay Prashad, *The Darker Nations: A People's History of the Third World* (New York: The New Press, 2007), 16–30

73 Jamie Mackie, *Bandung 1955: Non-Alignment and Afro-Asian Solidarity* (Singapore: Editions Didler Millet, 2005); George McTuran Kahlin, ed., *The Asian-African Conference: Bandung, Indonesia, April 1955* (Ithaca, NY: Cornell University Press, 1956); Carlos Romulo, *The Meaning of Bandung* (Chapel Hill: University of North Carolina Press, 1956)

74 R.F. Holland, *European Decolonization, 1918–1981: An Introductory Survey* (London: Macmillan, 1985)

75 Piero Gleijeses, *Conflicting Missions: Havana, Washington, and Africa, 1959–1976* (Chapel Hill: University of North Carolina Press, 2002); Isaac Saney, "African Stalingrad: The Cuban Revolution, Internationalism. And the End of Apartheid," *Latin American Perspectives* 33, 5 (2006): 81–117

76 Angadipuram Appadorai, *The Bandung Conference* (New Delhi: Indian Council of World Affairs, 1955); G.H. Jansen, *Afro-Asia and Non-Alignment* (London: Faber and Faber, 1966); George McTuran Kahin, *The Asian-African Conference: Bandung, Indonesia, April 1955* (Ithaca: Cornell University Press, 1956)

77 Richard Wright, *The Color Curtain: A Report on the Bandung Conference* (Cleveland: World Publishing Company, 1956), cited in Mathew Quest, "The Lessons of the Bandung Conference: Richard Wright's *The Color Curtain* 40 Years Later," at www.spunk.org/library/pubs/lr/sp001716/bandung.html

78 Iraqi delegate and the Bandung resolution on Israel, cited in Erna Paris, "What Sort of People Did This?" *Globe and Mail*, Sept. 13, 2001, A19

79 H.W. Brands, *The Specter of Neutralism: The United States and the Emergence of the Third World, 1947–1960* (New York: Columbia University Press, 1989), 3. On the US response to Bandung, see Cary Fraser, "An American Dilemma: Race and Realpolitik in the American Response to the Bandung Conference, 1955," in Brenda Gayle Plummer, ed., *Window on Freedom: Race, Civil Rights, and Foreign Policy, 1945–1988* (Chapel Hill: University of North Carolina Press, 2003).

80 Achmed Sukarno, cited in Vijay Prashad, *The Darker Nations*, 34

81 Nehru, cited in Claude Markovits, *Indian Business and Nationalist Politics, 1931–1939: The Indigenous Capitalist Class and the Rise of the Congress Party* (Cambridge: Cambridge University Press, 1985), 206

82 Kwame Nkrumah, *Neo-Colonialism: The Last Stage of Imperialism* (New York: International Publishers, 1965)

83 Mahinda Rajapaksa, leader of the Opposition in Sri Lanka, 2002, cited in Antonia Finnane, "Zhou Enlai in Bandung: The Official Story with Commentary," unpublished paper

84 Ludo De Witte, *The Assassination of Lumumba*, trans. Ann Wright and Renee Fenby (London: Verso, 2002)

85 John Pilger, *The New Rulers of the World* (London: Verso, 2003), 17–47

86 Bandung Principles, cited ibid., 31

87 Leonard Mosley, *Dulles: A Biography of Eleanor, Allen, and John Foster Dulles and Their Family Network* (New York: The Dial Press/ James Wade, 1978), 384–5

88 Quest, "The Lessons of the Bandung Conference: Richard Wright's *The Color Curtain* 40 Years Later"

89 Martin Meredith, *The Fate of Africa: From the Hopes of Freedom to the Heart of Despair, A History of Fifty Years of African Independence* (New York: Public Affairs, 2005), 180

90 G.A. Nasser, "The Philosophy of the Revolution," in *Nasser Speaks: Basic Documents*, trans. E.S. Farag (London: Morssett Press, 1972), 45

91 Richard A. Clarke, *Against All Enemies: Inside America's War on Terror* (New York: Free Press, 2004), 140–8

92 Donald Petterson, *Inside Sudan: Political Islam, Conflict, and Catastrophe* (Boulder, Col.: Westview Press, 2003); Edgar O'Ballance, *Sudan, Civil War and Terrorism* (New York: St Martin's Press, 2000)

93 Peter Willetts, *The Non-Aligned Movement: The Origins of a Third World Alliance* (London and New York: Frances Pinter and Nichols Publishing, 1978); Govind Narain Srivastava, Nehru, Tito, *Nasser: Non-Alignment and the Contemporary World* (New Delhi: Indian Institute for Non-Aligned Studies, 1988)

94 www.southcentre.org/mwalimu/speeches/written/written.htm

95 Peter McFarlane, *Brotherhood to Nationhood: George Manuel and the Making of the Modern Indian Movement* (Toronto: Between the Lines, 1993)

96 Rudolph C. Ryser, "The Legacy of Grand Chief George Manuel: Neither Left nor Right, We Must Find Our Own Way to the Fourth World," www.cwis.org/manuel.html

97 Ronald Niezen, *The Origins of Indigenism: Human Rights and the Politics of Identity* (Berkeley: University of California Press, 2003); Mathias Guenther, "The Concept of Indigeneity," *Social Anthropology* 14, 1 (2006): 17–32

98 Goran Hyden, cited in Meredith, *The Fate of Africa*, 250

99 Dean McHenry, *Tanzania's Ujaama Villages: The Implementation of a Rural Development Strategy* (Berkeley: University of California Press, 1979); Dean McHenry, *Limited Choices: The Political Struggle for Socialism in Tanzania* (Boulder, Col.: Rienner, 1994); Goran Hyden, *Beyond Ujaama in Tanzania: Underdevelopment and an Uncaptured Peasantry* (London: Heinemann, 1980)

100 George Manuel and Michael Poslins, *The Fourth World: An Indian Reality* (Don Mills: Collier-Macmillan Canada, 1974), 236, 245

101 Bill Curry, Steven Chase, and Joe Friesen, "Natives Threaten Olympic Disruption," *Globe and Mail,* April 18, 2008, A1, A4

102 David E. Stannard, *American Holocaust: Columbus and the Conquest of the New World* (New York: Oxford University Press, 1992)

103 See Samir Amin, *Eurocentrism,* trans. Russell Moore (New York: Monthly Review Press, 1989).

104 International Treaty Council, *Treaty Council News: Special Issue: The Geneva Conference on Discrimination against Indigenous Populations in the Americas,* vol. 1, no. 7, 1977; Lydia van de Fliert, ed., *Indigenous Peoples and International Organizations* (Nottingham, Eng.: Spokesman, 1994); S. James Anaya, *Indigenous Peoples in International Law* (Oxford: Oxford University Press, 2000); Michael N. Barnett, *Rules for the World: International Organizations in Global Politics* (Ithaca: Cornell University Press, 2004)

105 Hannah Arendt, *The Origins of Totalitarianism,* new ed. with added preface (San Diego: Harcourt Brace, 1976)

106 Jonathan Schell, *The Unconquerable World: Power, Nonviolence, and the Will of the People* (New York: Henry Holt, 2003), 255

107 Noreena Hertz, *Silent Takeover: Global Capitalism and the Death of Democracy* (London: William Heinemann, 2001); John Gray, *False Dawn: The Delusions of Global Capitalism* (London: Granta, 1998)

108 Farmer, *Pathologies of Power,* passim

109 David Batstone, Eduardo Mendieta, Lois Ann Lorentzen, and Dwight D. Hopkins, eds., *Liberation Theologies, Postmodernity, and the Americas* (London: Routledge, 1997)

110 Hernando de Soto, *The Mystery of Capital: Why Capitalism Triumphs in the West and Fails Everywhere Else* (New York: Basic Books, 2000), 227

111 See Frederique Apffel-Marglin with PRATEC, eds., *The Spirit of Regeneration: Andean Culture Confronting Western Notions of Development* (London: Zed Books, 1998); David Lehmann, ed., *Ecology and Exchange in the Andes* (Cambridge: Cambridge University Press, 1982).

112 Schell, *The Unconquerable World,* 259

113 F.A. Hayek, *The Road to Serfdom* (Chicago: University of Chicago Press, 1944); Karl R. Popper, *The Open Society and Its Enemies,* 2 vols. (Princeton: Princeton University Press, 1963)

114 Schell, *The Unconquerable World,* 259

115 Tom Hayden, ed., *The Zapatista Reader* (New York: Thunder's Mouth Press/ Nation Books, 2002)

116 Walden Bello, *The Future in the Balance: Essays on Globalization and Resistance* (Oakland: Food First Books and Focus on the Global South, 2001)

117 Michael Hardt and Antonio Negri, *Multitude: War and Democracy in the Age of Empire* (New York: Penguin Press, 2004), xiv; Michael Hardt and Antonio Negri, *Empire* (Cambridge: Harvard University Press, 2001)

118 Hardt and Negri, *Multitude,* xviii. See also Bruce G. Trigger, *Archaelogy and the Future,* Distinguished Lecture in the Faculty of Arts, November 11, 1986 (Montreal: McGill University, 1986)

119 Hardt and Negri, *Empire*, 45

120 Rahul Mahajan, *Full Spectrum Dominance: U.S. Power in Iraq and Beyond* (New York: Seven Stories Press, 2003)

121 Chomsky, *Hegemony of Survival*, 222

122 Karl Grossman, *The Wrong Stuff: The Space Program's Nuclear Threat to the Planet* (Monroe, Maine: Common Courage Press, 1997); Gordon R. Mitchell, *Strategic Deception: Rhetoric, Science, and Politics in Missile Defense Advocacy* (East Lansing: Michigan State University Press, 2000); US Space Command, *Vision for 2020*, Feb. 1997; US Air Force Command, *Strategic Master Plan for 2004 and Beyond*, Nov. 5, 2002

123 Eduardo Galeano, *Open Veins of Latin America: Five Centuries of Pillage of a Continent*, trans. Cedric Belfrage (New York: Monthly Review Press, 19997), 175

124 "Argentina and the Fund," *Washington Post*, Aug. 3, 2004; Joseph E. Stiglitz, *Globalization and Its Discontents* (New York: W.W. Norton, 2002), 69–70

125 Linda McQuaig, *It's the Crude, Dude: War, Big Oil, and the Fight for the Planet* (Toronto: Doubleday, 2004), 95–117

126 William F. Pepper, *An Act of State: The Execution of Martin Luther King* (London: Verso, 2008), 275, 288

127 Brazilian president Fernando Henrique Cardoso, cited in Paul Knox, "Tango at the Abyss," *Globe and Mail*, Aug. 14, A11

128 MST web site at http://www.mstbrazil.org/?q=book/print/16

129 Avery Cohn, Corrina Stewart, et al., *Agroecology and the Struggle for Food Sovereignty in the Americas* (New Haven: Yale School of Forestry and Environmental Studies, 2006)

130 "Brazil Peasants Target Multinational Firms," Reuters, June 12, 2008, at http://www.flex-news-food.com/pages/17092/Brazil/Bunge/Wal-Mart/brazil-peasant-protests-target-multinational-firms.html Laura Carlsen, "Via Campesina Sets and International Agenda," August, 8, 2007, at http://americas.irc-online.org/am/4459

131 Kevin Phillips, *The Cousins' Wars: Religion, Politics, and the Triumph of Anglo-America* (New York: Basic Books, 1999)

132 Alexander Hamilton, cited in Scott Nearing and Joseph Freeman, *Dollar Diplomacy: A Study of American Imperialism* (New York: B.W. Huebsch and the Viking Press, 1926), 233

133 Arthur Meiser Schlesinger, *The Colonial Merchants and the American Revolution, 1763–1776* (1917; New York: Frederick Ungar Publishing, 1957)

134 See, for instance, Jack M. Sosin, *Whitehall and the Wilderness: The Middle West in British Colonial Policy, 1760–1775* (Lincoln: University of Nebraska Press, 1961); Lawrence Hentry Gibson, *The Coming Revolution, 1763–1775* (New York: Harper and Row, 1954); Bernard Bailyn, *The Ideological Origins of the American Revolution* (Cambridge, Mass.: Harvard University Press, 1967); Marc Egnal, *A Mighty Empire: The Origins of the American Revolution* (Ithaca: Cornell University Press, 1988); Gordon S. Wood, *The Radicalism of the American Revolution* (New York: Random House, 1991); Edward Countryman, "Indians,

the Colonial Order, and the Social Significance of the American Revolution,"
William and Mary Quarterly, third series, 53, 2 (1996): 342–62

135 Charles A. Beard, *An Economic Interpretation of the Constitution of the United States*
(New York: Macmillan Company, 1913), 324

136 Charles A. Beard, *The Open Door at Home* (New York: Macmillan Company,
1934), 38

137 Ibid., 125–6

138 William Appleman Williams, *The Contours of American History* (Cleveland: The
World Publishing Company, 1961), 487–8

139 William Appleman Williams, "The Frontier Thesis and American Foreign
Policy," *Pacific Historical Review* 24 (Nov. 1955): 395

140 Andrew J. Bacevich, *American Empire: The Realities and Consequences of U.S.
Diplomacy* (Cambridge Mass.: Harvard University Press, 2002), 25

141 105 Clarence Walworth Alvord, *The Mississippi Valley in British Politics: A Study
of the Trade, Land Speculation and Experiments in Imperialism Culminating in the
American Revolution*, 2 vols. (Cleveland: Arthur H. Clark Co., 1917)

142 George E. Lewis, *The Indiana Company, 1763–1798* (Glendale, Cal.: Arthur H.
Clark Co., 1941); Thomas Perkins Abernethy, *Western Lands and the American
Revolution* (New York: Russell and Russell, 1959); Dorothy V. Jones, *License for
Empire: Colonialism by Treaty in Early America* (Chicago: University of Chicago
Press, 1982); Shaw Livermore, *Early American Land Companies* (New York:
Commonwealth Fund, 1939); Francis Jennings, *Empire of Fortune: Crowns,
Colonies, and Tribes in the Seven Years' War in America* (New York: W.W. Norton,
1988); Robert A. Williams Jr, *The American Indian in Western Legal Discours*,
(New York: Oxford University Press, 1990)

143 Hugo Dixon, "Is the U.S. Hooked on Foreign Capital," *Wall Street Journal*,
March 6, 2003; Edward Alden, Jeremy Grant, and Victor Mallet, "Opportunity
or Threat? The U.S. Struggles to Solve the Puzzle of Its Trade with China,"
Financial Times, Nov. 4, 2003

144 Kenneth Pomeranz, *The Great Divergence: China, Europe and the Making of the
Modern Economy* (Princeton: Princeton University Press, 2000)

CHAPTER FIVE

1 Joseph Stalin, cited in "The Long Telegram" of George F. Kennan, *New York
Times*, March 20, 2005, 7

2 Leonard Schapiro, *The Communist Party of the Soviet Union*, 2nd ed. (London:
Methuen, 1985)

3 David S. Foglesong, *America's Secret War against Bolshevism: U.S. Intervention in
the Russian Civil War, 1917–1920* (Chapel Hill: University of North Carolina
Press, 1995); Betty Miller Unterberger, *The United States, Revolutionary Russia,
and the Rise of Czechoslovakia* (Chapel Hill: University of North Carolina Press,
1989)

4 Woodrow Wilson, cited in Max Boot, *The Savage Wars of Peace: Small Wars and
the Rise of American Power* (New York: Basic Books, 2002), 207

5 Antony Sutton, *Wall Street and the Bolshevik Revolution* (New Rochelle, NY: Arlington House, 1974)

6 Robert Skidelsky, *John Maynard Keynes, 1883–1946: Economist, Philosopher, Statesman* (London: Macmillan, 2003)

7 Samir Amin, *Obsolete Capitalism: Contemporary Politics and Global Disorder* (London: Zed Books, 2003), 14

8 Erich Eyck, *Bismark and the German Empire* (New York: W.W. Norton, 1964)

9 Theodore Draper, *American Communism and Soviet Russia* (New York: Viking, 1960)

10 Melvyn A. Dubofsky, *We Shall Be All: A History of the Industrial Workers of the World*, 2nd ed. ((Urbana: University of Illinois Press, 1988)

11 Shapiro, *The Communist Party of the Soviet Union*, 55–71

12 Preamble to the IWW Constitution, cited by Howard Zinn, "The Wobbly Spirit," 1965, www.thirdworldtraveler.com/Zinn/Wobblies_ZR.html

13 Allan J. Lichtman, *White Protestant Nation: The Rise of the American Conservative Movement* (Jackson, Tenn: Atlantic Monthly Press, 2008)

14 Edmund S. Morgan, *The Puritan Dilemma: The Story of John Winthrop* (Boston: Little, Brown, 1958), 8

15 Woody Guthrie, "The Ludlow Massacre," first recorded for Moe Asch in 1946; first printed in *Sing Out* 8, 3 (1959)

16 Robert K. Murray, *Red Scare: A Study of National Hysteria* (Minneapolis: University of Minnesota Press, 1955); Arthur I. Waskow, *From Race Riot to Sit-in: 1919 and the 1960s* (Garden City, NY: Anchor Books, 1966)

17 Nancy MacLean, *Behind the Mask of Chivalry: The Making of the Second Ku Klux Klan* (New York: Oxford University Press, 1994)

18 W.E.B. Du Bois, *New York Times*, Aug. 14, 1927

19 David Levering Lewis, *W.E.B. Du Bois: The Fight for Equality and the American Century, 1919–1963* (New York: Henry Holt, 2000), 30, 47–8

20 W.E.B. Du Bois, "The Class Struggle," *The Crisis*, June 1921, 55–6

21 W.E.B. Du Bois, "My Recent Journey," *The Crisis*, Dec. 1926, 64–5, cited in Lewis, *W.E.B. Du Bois*, 203–4

22 Walter Karp, *The Indispensable Enemies: The Politics of Misrule in America* (New York: Franklin Square Press, 1993); Walter Karp, *The Politics of War: The Story of Two Wars Which Altered Forever the Political Life of the American Republic* (New York: Harper and Row, 1979)

23 Lewis H. Lapham, *Gag Rule: On the Suppression of Dissent and the Stifling of Democracy* (New York: Penguin Press, 2004), 66

24 A.M. Palmer, "The Case against the 'Reds,'" *Forum*, Feb. 1920, cited in Arthur M. Schlesinger Jr, *The Crisis of the Old Order, 1919–1933* (Boston: Houghton Mifflin, 1964), 42–3

25 John Maynard Keynes, *The Economic Consequences of the Peace* (London: Macmillan, 1919)

26 Glenn Porter, *The Rise of Big Business, 1860–1920* (Wheeling, Ill.: Harlan Davidson, 2006); Paul A. Baran and Paul M. Sweezy, *Monopoly Capital: An Essay on the American Economic and Social Order* (New York: Monthly Review

Press, 1966); Arthur R. Burns, *The Decline of Competition: A Study of the Evolution of American Industry* (Westport, Conn.: Greenwood Books, 1974)

27 Cited in Schlesinger Jr, *The Crisis of the Old Order*, 18

28 John Dewey, "The Imperative Need for a New Radical Party," *Common Sense*, Sept. 1933

29 Edmund Wilson, "An Appeal to Progressives," *New Republic*, Jan. 14, 1931; Edmund Wilson, *Travels in Two Democracies* (New York: Harcourt, Brace, 1936), 321

30 Winston Churchill, *Illustrated Sunday Herald*, Feb. 8, 1920

31 "Heinreich Ford: Idol of Bavaria Fascisti Chief," *Chicago Tribune*, March 8, 1923, 2

32 Joachim Fest, *Hitler* (New York: Harcourt Brace Jovanovich, 1974)

33 See Dietrich Eckart, *Bolshevism from Moses to Lenin: A Dialogue between Adolf Hitler and Me* (1923; New York: Historical Review Press, 1998).

34 Rudolf Hess, cited in Robert Jay Lifton, *The Nazi Doctors: Medical Killing and the Psychology of Genocide* (New York: Basic Books, 1989), 31

35 Robert N. Proctor, *Racial Hygiene: Medicine under the Nazis* (Cambridge, Mass.: Harvard University Press, 1988)

36 Edwin Black, *War against the Weak: Eugenics and America's Campaign to Create a Master Race* (New York: Thunder's Mouth Press, 2004), xxi

37 Charles Davenport, cited ibid., 300

38 Ibid., 316

39 Clarence Campbell, cited ibid., 314

40 www.religioustolerance.org/fin_nazi.htm

41 http://en.wikipedia.org/wiki/I.G._Farben_Building

42 Joseph Borkin, *The Crime and Punishment of IG Farben* (New York: Free Press, 1978); Josiah Ellis Du Bois, *The Devil's Chemists: 24 Conspirators of the International Farben Cartel Who Manufactured Wars* (Boston: Beacon Press, 1952)

43 John Cornwell, *Hitler's Scientists: Science, War, and the Devil's Pact* (New York: Viking, 2003), 52–3, 369–76

44 James Stewart Martin, *All Honorable Men* (Boston: Little, Brown, 1950); Ervin Hexner, with Adelaide Walters, *International Cartels* (Westport, Conn.: Greenwood Press, 1971)

45 Paul Manning, *Martin Boorman: Nazi in Exile* (Seancus, NJ: Stuart, 1981), chapter 4; Hjalmar Schact, *Confessions of "The Old Wizard"* (Boston: Houghton Mifflin, 1956); Norman Edward Peterson, *Hjalmar Schact* (Boston: Christopher Publishing House, 1954)

46 Senator Bone and US War Department report, cited in Antony C. Sutton, *Wall Street and the Rise of Hitler* (Seal Beach, Cal.: '76 Press, 1976), chapter 2

47 Ian Kershaw, *The Hitler Myth: Image and Reality in the Third Reich* (Oxford: Oxford University Press, 1987)

48 MacLean, *Behind the Mask of Chivalry*; Robert O. Paxton, *The Anatomy of Fascism* (New York: Alfred A. Knopf, 2004), 49, 201

49 Gerard Colby, *DuPont Dynasty* (Secaucus, NJ: Stuart, 1984)

50 Jules Archer, *The Plot to Seize the White House* (New York: Hawthorne Books, 1973); George Wolfskill, *The Revolt of the Conservatives: A History of the American Liberty League* (Boston: Houghton Mifflin, 1962); George Seldes, *One Thousand Americans* (New York: Boni and Gaer, 1947)

51 Omer Bartov, *The Eastern Front, 1941–1945: German Troops and the Barbarisation of Warfare*, 2nd ed. (New York: Palgrave, 2001)

52 Walter S. Dunn Jr, *Kursk: Hitler's Gamble, 1943* (Westport, Conn.: Praeger, 1997)

53 Noam Chomsky, *Failed States: The Abuse of Power and the Assault on Democracy* (New York: Metropolitan Books, 2006), 122

54 Roland Sarti, *Fascism and the Industrial Leadership in Italy, 1919–1940: A Study in the Expansion of Private Power under Fascism* (Berkeley: University of California Press, 1971)

55 Conan Fischer, *The German Communists and the Rise of Nazism* (New York: St Martin's Press, 1991); Donna Harsch, *German Social Democracy and the Rise of Nazism* (Chapel Hill: University of North Carolina Press, 1993)

56 See Peter Hayes, *Industry and Ideology: IG Farben in the Nazi Era* (Cambridge: Cambridge University Press, 1987); Henry A. Turner, *Big Business and the Rise of Hitler* (New York: Oxford University Press, 1985).

57 Charles Linbergh, "Aviation, Race, and Geography," *Reader's Digest*, Nov. 1939, 64–7

58 Black, *War against the Weak*, 133, 298

59 Lothrop Stoddard, *The Rising Tide of Color against White Supremacy* (New York: Charles Scribner's Sons, 1926), 303–4, 259–60

60 "Berlin Hears Ford Is Backing Hitler," *New York Times*, Dec. 20, 1922

61 Albert Lee, *Henry Ford and the Jews* (New York: Stein and Day, 1980), 91

62 Henry Ford, *The International Jew: The World's Foremost Problem* (Dearborn: Dearborn Publishing, 1921)

63 Samuel Utermeyer, cited in Max Wallace, *The American Axis: Henry Ford, Charles Lindbergh, and the Rise of the Third Reich* (New York: St Martin's Griffin, 2003), 44

64 Baldur von Schirach, cited ibid., 42

65 See Albert Lee, *Henry Ford and the Jews* (New York: Stein and Day, 1980); Neil Baldwin, *Henry Ford and the Jews: The Mass Production of Hate* (New York: Public Affairs, 2001); Leo Ribuffo, "Henry Ford and the International Jew," *American Jewish History* 69 (1980): 440; James Pool, *Who Financed Hitler?* (New York: Dial Press, 1979).

66 Adolf Hitler, *Mein Kampf*, ed. Ralph Manheim (Boston: Houghton Mifflin, 1971), 639

67 Henry Ford, cited in Keith Sward, *The Legend of Henry Ford* (New York: Rinehart, 1948), 370

68 Wallace, *The American Axis*, 136–7

69 FBI file on Harry Bennett, "Nazi and Ukrainian Sabotage and Espionage Ring and Fifth Column Activities," file 61-10497-45; American Jewish Committee Archives, Casimir Palmer to Nathan Isaacs, May 11, 1937, cited in Wallace, *The American Axis*, 138

70 Wallace, *The American Axis*, 140–5; Alan Brinkley, *Voices of Protest: Huey Long, Father Coughlin, and the Great Depression* (New York: Knopf, 1982)

71 Victoria de Grazia, *Irresistible Empire: America's Advance through 20th-Century Europe* (Cambridge, Mass.: The Belknap Press of Harvard University Press, 2005), 79

72 Frederic F. Clairmont, "Volkswagen's History of Forced Labor," *Le Monde Diplomatique*, Jan. 1998, trans. Sally Blaxland, republished at www.mondediplo.com/1991/01/11volkswag

73 John Toland, *Adolf Hitler* (New York: Garden City, 1976), 702

74 James Pool, *Hilter and His Secret Partners: Contributions, Loot, and Rewards* (New York: Pocket Books, 1997), 254–5, 273–4

75 Lilian Friedberg, "Dare to Compare: Americanizing the Holocaust," *American Indian Quarterly* 24, 3 (2000): 353–80

76 Thomas J. Fleming, *The New Dealers' War: FDR and the War within World War II* (New York: Basic Books, 2001)

77 William Roger Louis, *Imperialism at Bay: The United States and Decolonization of the British Empire, 1941–1945* (Oxford: Oxford University Press, 1978)

78 Julius Stone, *The Atlantic Charter: New Worlds for Old* (Sydney: Current Book Distributors, 1945); Theodore A. Wilson, *The First Summit: Roosevelt and Churchill at Placentia Bay, 1941*, rev. ed. (Lawrence: University of Kansas Press, 1991); Douglas Brinkley and David R. Facey-Crowther, eds., *The Atlantic Charter* (New York: St Martin's Press, 1994); Elizabeth Borgwaldt, *A New Deal for the World: America's Vision for Human Rights* (Cambridge, Mass.: Belknap Press of Harvard University Press, 2005)

79 www.yale.edu/lawweb/avalon/wwii/atlantic.htm

80 J.F.C. Fuller, *A Military History of the Western World* (New York: Funk and Wagnalls, 1955), vol. 3: 453

81 www.yale.edu/lawweb/avalon/decade/decade03.htm

82 George Padmore, ed., *Colonial and Coloured Unity: A Programme of Action, History of the Pan-African Congress* (London: Hammersmith Bookshop, 1947); Brenda Gayle Plummer, *Rising Winds: Black Americans and U.S. Foreign Affairs* (Chapel Hill: University of North Carolina Press, 1996); Penny M. Von Eschen, *Race against Empire: Black Americans and Anti-colonialism* (Ithaca: Cornell University Press, 1997)

83 Nelson Mandela, *Long Walk to Freedom: The Autobiography of Nelson Mandela* (Boston: Little, Brown, 1994), 110

84 Michael H. Hogan, *A Cross of Iron: Harry S. Truman and the Origins of the National Security State, 1945–1954* (Cambridge: Cambridge University Press, 1998); David Rothkopf, *Running the World: The Inside Story of the National Security Council and the Architects of American Power* (New York: Public Affairs, 2005)

85 Skidelsky, *John Maynard Keynes, 1883–1946*, 388

86 Ron Chernow, *The House of Morgan* (New York: Atlantic Monthly Press, 1990)

87 Frank Costigliola, "The United States and the Reconstruction of Germany in the 1920s," *Business History Review* 50, 4 (1976): 477–502

88 Frank Costigliola, "The Other Side of Isolationism: The Establishment of the First World Bank, 1929–1930," *Journal of American History* 59, 3 (1972): 602–20; Henry H. Schloss, *The Bank for International Settlements* (Amsterdam: North Holland Publishing, 1958)

89 John Cornwell, *Hitler's Pope: The Secret History of Pius XII* (New York: Viking, 1999); Peter Godman, *Hitler and the Vatican: Inside the Secret Archives That Reveal the New Story of the Nazis and the Church* (New York: Free Press, 2004)

90 Lloyd George, cited in R. Palme Dutt, *World Politics, 1918–1936* (London: Victor Gollancz, 1936), 265

91 Dutt, *World Politics, 1918–1936*, 267

92 Ibid.

93 Ian Kershaw, *Making Friends with Hitler: Lord Londonderry and Britain's Road to War* (London and New York: Allen Lane, 2004)

94 Christopher Sykes, *Nancy: The Life of Lady Astor* (London: William Collins Sons, 1972)

95 Winston Churchill, *The Great Republic: A History of America*, ed. Winston S. Churchill (New York: Random House, 1999), 3

96 John Maynard Keynes cited in Robert Skidelsky, *John Maynard Keynes*, 210

97 Sutton, *Wall Street and the Rise of Hitler*; Charles Higham, *Trading with the Enemy: An Exposé of the Nazi-American Money Plot, 1933–1949* (New York: Delacorte Press, 1983); John Loftus, *The Belarus Secret: The Nazi Connection in America* (New York: Paragon House, 1989); John Loftus and Mark Aarons, *The Secret War against the Jews: How Western Espionage Betrayed the Jewish People* (New York: St Martin's Press, 1992); John Loftus and Mark Aarons, *Unholy Trinity: The Vatican, the Nazis, and the Swiss Banks* (New York: St Martin's Griffen, 1998); Berhard Schreiber, *The Men behind Hitler: A German Warning to the World* (Paris: La Hay-Mureaux, 1975); Christopher Simpson, *The Splendid Blond Beast: Money, Law and Genocide in the Twentieth Century* (New York: Grove Press, 1993)

98 Nancy Lisagor and Frank Lipsins, *A Law unto Itself: The Untold Story of the Law Firm of Sullivan and Cromwell* (New York: Paragon House, 1989)

99 Kevin Phillips, *American Dynasty: Aristocracy, Fortune, and the Politics of Deceit in the House of Bush* (New York: Viking, 2004); Webster Griffin Tarpley and Anton Chaitkin, *George Bush: The Unauthorized Biography* (Washington: Executive Intelligence Review, 1992)

100 Kathrin Lassila and Mark Alden Branch, "Whose Skull and Bones?" *Yale Alumni Magazine*, May/June 2006; Tim Giago, "Where Are They Hiding Geronimo's Skull," *Lakota Nation Journal*, winter 2000; Antony C. Sutton, *America's Secret Establishment: An Introduction to the Order of the Skull and Bones* (Billings, Mont.: Liberty House Press, 1986); Alexandra Robbins, *Secrets of the Tomb: Skull and Bones, the Ivy League and Hidden Paths of Power* (Boston: Little Brown, 2002); Peter Dale Scott, *Deep Politics and the Death of JFK* (Berkeley: University of California Press, 1993)

101 Phillips, *American Dynasty*, 199

102 Fritz Thyssen, *I Paid Hitler* (London: Hodder and Stoughton, 1941)

103 Sander A. Diamond, *The Nazi Movement in the United States, 1924–1941* (Ithaca: Cornell University Press, 1974)

104 William Dodd, cited in George Seldes, *Facts and Fascism* (New York: In Fact, 1943), 122

105 Phillips, *American Dynasty*, 262

106 Bradford C. Snell, "GM and the Nazis," *Ramparts Magazine*, June 1974, 14–16

107 Linda McQuaig, *It's the Crude, Dude: Big Oil and the Fight for the Planet* (Toronto: Doubleday, 2004); John Malcolm Blair, *The Control of Oil* (New York: Vintage, 1978)

108 Richard Sasuly, *IG Farben* (New York: Boni and Gaer, 1947), 128

109 Edwin Black, *IBM and the Holocaust: The Strategic Alliance between Nazi Germany and America's Most Powerful Corporation* (New York: Crown Publishers, 2001)

110 William L. Langer, *Our Vichy Gamble* (New York: A.A. Knopf, 1947); Anthony Sampson, *The Sovereign State of I.T.T.* (New York: Stein and Day, 1976); Anthony Sampson, *The Arms Bazaar: From Lebanon to Lockheed* (New York: Viking Press, 1977); Anthony Sampson, *The Seven Sisters: The Great Oil Companies and the World They Shaped* (New York: Viking Press, 1975)

111 General George S. Patton, cited in Leonard Mosley, *Dulles: A Biography of Eleanor, Allen, and John Foster Dulles and Their Family Network* (New York: Dail Press / James Wade, 1978), 227

112 Philip Gourevitch and Errol Morris, *Standard Operating Procedure* (New York: Penguin, 2008)

113 Eleanor Roosevelt and Teleford Taylor cited in http://www.spartacus.schoolnet.co.uk/FWWkruppA.htm

114 Ladislas Farago, *German Psychological Warfare* (New York: Putnam, 1941); Christopher Simpson, *The Science of Coercion: Communication Research and Psychological Warfare, 1945–1960* (New York: Oxford University Press, 1994)

115 Kai Bird, *The Chairman: John J. McCloy and the Making of the American Establishment* (New York: Simon and Schuster, 1992); Walter Isaacson and Evan Thomas, *The Wise Men: Six Friends and the World They Made – Acheson, Bohlen, Harriman, Kennan, Lovett, McCloy* (New York: Simon and Schuster, 1986)

116 Antony C. Sutton, *Wall Street and FDR* (New Rochelle, NY: Arlington House, 1975); Carroll Quigley, *Tragedy and Hope: A History of the World Order in Our Time* (New York: Macmillan, 1966); Lawrence H. Shoup and William Minter, *Imperial Brain Trust: The Council on Foreign Relations and United States Foreign Policy* (New York: Monthly Review, 1977); Phoebe and Kent Courtney, *America's Unelected Rulers: The Council on Foreign Relations* (New Orleans: Conservative Society of America, 1962); Gary Allen, *The Rockefeller File* (Seal Beach, Cal.: '76 Press, 1976)

117 Paul Manning, *Martin Bormann: Nazi in Exile* (Secaucus, NJ: Stuart, 1981); Paul Manning, *Hirohito: The War Years* (New York: Bantam, 1989); Herbert P. Bix, *Hirohito and the Making of Modern Japan* (New York: Harper Perennial, 2001); Timothy P. Maga, *The Judgment at Tokyo: The Japanese War Crime Trials* (Lexington: University of Kentucky Press, 2001)

118 Peter Grose, *Gentleman Spy: The Life of Allen Dulles* (Boston: Houghton Mifflin, 1994)

119 Burton Hersh, *The Old Boys: The American Elite and the Origins of the* CIA (New York: Scribner's, 1992)

120 Richard Harris Smith, *OSS* (Berkeley: University of California Press, 1972)

121 Martin E. Lee, *The Beast Reawakens* (Boston: Little, Brown, 1997); Christopher Simpson, *Blowback: America's Recruitment of Nazis and Its Effects on the Cold War* (New York: Weidenfield and Nicolson, 1988); Martin E. Lee, "The CIA's Worst-Kept Secret: Newly Declassified Files Confirm US Collaboration with Nazis," *San Francisco Bay Guardian,* May 7, 2001

122 Bradley F. Smith and Elena Agarossi, *Operation Sunrise: The Secret Surrender* (New York: Basic Books, 2004)

123 Denis Boneau, "When the CIA Financed European Intellectuals," http://www.voltairenet.org/article136478.html

124 Mike Wright, "The Disney–Von Braun Collaboration and Its Influence on Space Exploration" at http://history.msfc.nasa.gov/vonbraun/disney_article.html

125 See Roy Harvey Pearce, *Savagism and Civilization: A Study of the Indian and the American Mind* (Baltimore: John Hopkins Press, 1967)

126 References and poll results from Kevin Phillips, *American Theocracy: The Peril and Politics of Radical Religion, Oil, and Borrowed Money in the 21st Century* (New York: Viking, 2006), 251, 259, 102

127 Naomi Wolf, *The End of America: Letter of Warning to a Young Patriot* (White River Junction, Vt: Chelsea Green Publishing, 2007)

128 David Cole and James X. Dempsey, *Terrorism and the Constitution: Sacrificing Civil Liberties in the Name of National Security. Revised and Updated* (New York: New Press, 2006); H.L. Polman, *Terrorism and the Constitution: The Post 9/11 Cases* (Lanham: Rowan and Littlefield, 2008)

129 Reports of the United States Commission on National Security (USCNS) at http://www.sourcewatch.org/index.php?title=Hart-Rudman_Task_Force_on_Homeland_Security

130 Michael C. Rupert, *Crossing The Rubicon: The Decline of the American Empire at the End of the Age of Oil* (Gabriola, BC: New Society Publishers, 2004), 152–74; Jerry Mazza, "The Promis of 9/11 and Beyond," Oct. 17, 2006, Online Journal at http://onlinejournal.com/artman/publish/article_1322.shtml

131 On the history of the Twin Towers, see http://www.pbs.org/wgbh/amex/newyork/peopleevents/p_rockefellers.html

132 See http://www.kuro5hin.org/story/2001/9/12/192330/380

133 See http://whatreallyhappened.com/WRHARTICLES/fematape.html

134 See http://en.wikipedia.org/wiki/War_games_in_progress_on_September_11,_2001

135 See http://whatreallyhappened.com/WRHARTICLES/cutter.html

CHAPTER SIX

1 Francis Paul Prucha, *Atlas of American Indian Affairs* (Lincoln: University of Nebraska Press, 1990), 83–110

2 Robert M. Utley, *The Indian Frontier of the American West* (Albuquerqie: University of New Mexico Press, 1984)

3 Eric Schlosser, "The Prison Industrial Complex," *Atlantic Monthly*, Dec. 1998, 51–77; Tara Herival and Paul Wright, eds., *Prison Nation: The Warehousing of America's Poor* (New York: Routledge, 2003)

4 Charles F. Wilkinson, "Indian Tribes and the American Constitution," in Frederick E. Hoxie, ed., *Indians in American History* (Arlington Heights, Ill.: Harlan Davidson, 1988), 117–34

5 Edward Countryman, "'To Secure the Blessings of Liberty': Language, the Revolution, and American Capitalism," in Alfred F. Young, ed., *Beyond the American Revolution: Explorations in the History of American Radicalism* (DeKalb: Northern Illinois University Press, 1993), 139

6 Ray Allen Billington, *Western Expansion: A History of the American Frontier* (New York: Macmillan, 1967), 212

7 Ibid., 212–20

8 Ibid., 218

9 See Wiley Sword, *President Washington's Indian War: The Struggle for the Old Northwest, 1790–1795* (Norman: University of Oklahoma Press, 1985).

10 The Speech of the Commissioners of the United States to the Deputies of the Confederate Indian Nations Assembled at the Rapids of the Miamis River, July 31, 1793, in E.A. Cruickshank, ed., *The Correspondence of Lieutenant Governor John Graves Simcoe* (Toronto: The Ontario Historical Society, 1923), 1: 405–9

11 Northwest Ordinance, 1787, cited in Albert L. Hurtado and Peter Iverson, eds., *Major Problems in American Indian History: Documents and Essays* (Lexington, Mass.: D.C. Heath, 1994), 168–9

12 Treaty of Greenville, cited in Francis Jennings, "The Indians' Revolution," in Albert l. Hurtado and Peter Iverson, eds., *Major Problems in American Indian History* (Lexington, Mass.: D.C. Heath, 1994), 184

13 See Harvey Lewis Carter, *The Life and Times of Little Turtle: First Sagamore of the Wabash* (Urbana: University of Illinois Press, 1987).

14 Little Turtle's speech at the negotiation of the Treaty of Greenville, cited in W.C. Vanderwerth, *Indian Oratory: Famous Speeches by Noted Indian Chieftains* (Norman: University of Oklahoma Press, 1979), 59

15 General Anthony Wayne, cited in Andrew R.L. Cayton, "'Noble Actors' upon 'the Theatre of Honour,'" in Andrew R.L. Cayton and Fredrika J. Teute, eds., *Contact Points: American Frontiers from the Mohawk Valley to the Mississippi, 1750–1830* (Chapel Hill: Published for the Omohundro Institute of Early American History and Culture by the University of North Carolina Press, 1998), 266

16 Timothy Pickering, cited ibid., 258

17 Ibid., 239

18 S. James Anaya, *Indigenous Peoples in International Law* (New York: Oxford University Press, 1996)

19 Francis Jennings, *The Invasion of America: Indians, Colonialism, and the Cant of Conquest* (New York: W.W. Norton, 1976), 254–81

20 Walter Williams, "American Imperialism and the Indians," in Frederick E. Hoxie, ed., *Indians in American History* (Arlington Heights, Ill.: Harlan Davidson, 1988), 231–49

21 The portfolio was published in London in 1837 as *The Indian Tribes of North America with Biographical Sketches and Anecdotes of the Principal Chiefs.* The engravings are reproduced in James D. Horan, *The McKenney-Hall Portrait Gallery of American Indians* (New York: Crown Publishers, 1972).

22 See Anthony F.C. Wallace, "Political Organization and Land Tenure among the Northeastern Indians, 1600–1830," *Southwestern Journal of Anthropology* 13, 4 (1957): 301–21.

23 Alec R. Gilpin, *The War of 1812 in the Old Northwest* (Toronto and East Lansing: Ryerson Press and the Michigan State University Press, 1958), 73–4

24 Willard Carl Klunder, *Lewis Cass and the Politics of Moderation* (Kent, Ohio: Kent State University Press, 1996)

25 Thomas Gummersall Anderson, "Reminiscences of Capt. Thomas Gummersall Anderson, copied by the late George Coventry," Ontario Historical Society, *Papers and Records* 6 (1905): 109–35

26 See Andrew C. McLaughlin, "The Influence of Governor Cass on the Development of the Northwest," American Historical Association, *Papers*, no. 2 (1889): 67–83.

27 Lewis Cass, "Indians of North America," *North American Review* 22 (1826): 53–119; Richard Drinnon, *White Savage: The Case of John Dunn Hunter* (New York: Schocken Books, 1972)

28 Lewis Cass, *Remarks on the Policy and Practice of the United States and Great Britain in the Treatment of Indians* (from North American Review) (Boston: Frederick T. Gray, 1827), 26, 38

29 Thomas McKenney, cited in Drinnon, *White Savage*, 240

30 See Gregory Evans Dowd, *A Spirited Resistance: The North American Indian Struggle for Unity, 1745–1815* (Baltimore: Johns Hopkins Press, 1992); Benjamin Drake, *The Life of Tecumseh and His Brother the Prophet: With a Historical Sketch of the Shawnee Indians* (1858; New York: Kraus Reprint, 1969); David R. Edmunds, *Tecumseh and the Quest for Indian Leadership* (Boston: Little, Brown, 1984); Edmunds, *The Shawnee Prophet* (Lincoln: University of Nebraska Press, 1983); Robert Allen, *His Majesty's Indian Allies: British Indian Policy and the Defence of Canada, 1774–1815* (Toronto: Dundurn, 1992); John Sugden, *Tecumseh: A Life* (New York: Henry Holt, 1998); Guy St Denis, *Tecumseh's Bones* (Montreal: McGill-Queen's University Press, 2005).

31 Cass, *Remarks on the Policy and Practice of the United States and Great Britain,* 54

32 Ibid., 55

33 Ibid., 39–40

34 Ibid., 30–1

35 Ibid., 40–8

36 Ibid., 34–7

37 Ibid., 49

38 See Cass's rationalization for Indian removal in his "Removal of the Indians," *North American Review* 30 (1830): 62–121.

39 Cass, *Remarks on the Policy*, 78

40 Congressional speech of President James Monroe, cited in John A. Garraty, *The American Nation: A History of the United States* (New York: Harper and Row, 1966), 207

41 Richard Drinnon, *Facing West: The Metaphysics of Indian-Hating and Empire-Building* (New York: New American Library, 1980), 115

42 See L.F.S. Upton, "Contact and Conflict on the Atlantic and Pacific Coasts of Canada," *BC Studies* 45 (1980): 103–15; Robin Fisher, *Contact and Conflict: Indian-European in British Columbia, 1774–1890*, 2nd ed. (Vancouver: UBC Press, 1992).

43 See Stephen E. Ambrose, *Undaunted Courage: Meriwether Lewis, Thomas Jefferson, and the Opening of the American West* (New York: Simon and Schuster, 1997); James P. Ronda, *Lewis and Clark among the Indians* (Lincoln: University of Nebraska, 1984); Donald Jackson, *Thomas Jefferson and the Stony Mountains: Exploring the West from Monticello* (Urbana: University of Illinois Press, 1981).

44 See Washington Irving, *Astoria, or Anecdotes of an Enterprise Beyond the Rocky Mountains* (New York, 1850).

45 E.W. Gilbert, *The Exploration of Western America, 1800–1850: An Historical Geography* (Cambridge: Cambridge University Press, 1933), 131–3

46 Heather Divine, "Roots in the Mohawk Valley: Sir William Johnson's Legacy in the North West Company," in Jennifer S.H. Brown, W.J. Eccles, and Donald P. Heldman, eds., *The Fur Trade Revisited: Selected Papers of the Sixth North American Fur-Trade Conference, Mackinac Island, Michigan, 1991* (East Lansing/Mackinac Island: Michigan State University Press and Mackinac State Historic Parks, 1994), 223–31

47 Donald G. Creighton, *The Commercial Empire of the St. Lawrence, 1760–1850* (Toronto: Ryerson Press, 1937)

48 Barry Gough, *First across the Continent: Sir Alexander Mackenzie* (Norman: University of Oklahoma Press, 1997)

49 Alexander Mackenzie, *Voyages from Montreal on the River St. Lawrence through the Continent of America* (London, 1801)

50 D.W. Meinig, *The Great Columbia Plain: An Historical Geography, 1805–1910* (Seattle: University of Washington Press, 1968), 48–53. On the North West Company, see William McGillivray, "Some Account of the Trade Carried on by the North West Company," Public Archives of Canada, *Report for the Year 1928* (Ottawa, 1928); Marjorie Wilkins Campbell, *The North West Company* (1957; Vancouver: Douglas & McIntyre, 1983)

51 John C. Jackson, *Children of the Fur Trade: Forgotten Metis of the Pacific Northwest* (Missoula, Montana: Mountain Press Publishing, 1996)

52 John S. Galbraith, "A Note on the British Fur Trade in California," *Pacific Historical Review* 24 (1955): 253–60; Albert L. Hurtaldo, *Indian Survival on the California Frontier* (New Haven, Conn.: Yale University Press, 1988), 46–7

53 Bernard DeVoto, *The Course of Empire* (Boston: Houghton Mifflin, 1952), first paragraph of preface

54 Bernal Diaz del Castillo, *The Discovery and Conquest of Mexico, 1517–1521*, trans. A.P. Maudslay (New York: Farrar, Straus and Cudahy, 1956), 66–7, 128, 230, 318; William H. Prescott, *History of the Conquest of Mexico and History of the Conquest of Peru* (1843 and 1847; New York: Modern Library, nd), passim

55 Leslie A. Fiedler, "The Indian in Literature in English," in Wilcombe E. Washburne, vol. ed., *History of Indian-White Relations*, vol. 4: *Handbook of North American Indians* (Washington, DC: Smithsonian Institution, 1988), 573

56 See Thomas Donohoe, *The Iroquois and the Jesuits: The Story of the Labors of Catholic Missionaries among the Indians* (Buffalo, NY: Buffalo Catholic Publications, 1895), 222–9.

57 Leonard Cohen, *Beautiful Losers* (New York: Viking Press, 1966)

58 Jean Johnson, "Molly Brant, Mohawk Matron," *Ontario History* 56 (June 1964), 105–24

59 See Sylvia Van Kirk, "Thanadelthur," *The Beaver*, spring 1974, 40–5.

60 Sylvia Van Kirk, "'Women in Between': Indian Women in Fur Trade Society," in Ken S. Coates and Robin Fisher, eds., *Out of the Background: Readings on Canadian Native History*, 2nd ed. (Toronto: Copp Clark, 1996), 105

61 Reader's Digest, *Through Indian Eyes: The Untold Story of Native Peoples* (Montreal: Reader's Digest Association, 1996), 280–1

62 Harold A. Innis, *The Fur Trade in Canada: An Introduction to Canadian Economic History* (New Haven, Conn.: Yale University Press, 1930)

63 Marshall McLuhan, *Understanding Media: The Extensions of Man* (New York: McGraw-Hill, 1964), 7; Graeme Patterson, *History and Communications: Harold Innis, Marshall McLuhan, and the Interpretation of History* (Toronto: University of Toronto Press, 1990); see also McLuhan's introduction to Harold Innis, *The Bias of Communication* (Toronto: University of Toronto Press, 1973).

64 Alan Morantz, *Where Is Here? Canada's Maps and the Stories They Tell* (Toronto: Penguin, 2002), 47

65 See Sylvia Van Kirk, *Many Tender Ties: Women in Fur Trade Society, 1670–1870* (Norman: University of Oklahoma Press, 1983); Jennifer S.H. Brown, *Strangers in Blood: Fur Trade Families in Indian Country* (Vancouver: UBC Press, 1980).

66 W. Kaye Lamb, ed., *The Journals and Letters of Alexander Mackenzie* (Cambridge: Cambridge University Press, 1970), 152, cited in Van Kirk, "'Women in Between,'" 105

67 Frederick Merk, ed., *Fur Trade and Empire: George Simpson's Journal, 1824–25* (Cambridge, Mass.: Harvard University Press, 1931), 104, cited in Van Kirk, "'Women in Between,'" 106

68 See Ron Bourgeault, "Indian, Métis and the Fur Trade: Class, Sexism and Racism in the Transition from Communism to Capitalism," *Studies in Political Economy* 12 (fall 1983): 45–80.

69 Sarah Carter, *Capturing Women: The Manipulation of Cultural Imagery in Canada's Prairie West* (Montreal: McGill-Queen's University Press, 1997); Sarah Carter, *Unsettled Pasts: Reconceiving the West through Women's History* (Calgary: University of Calgary Press, 2005)

70 The Reverend Jeremiah Evarts, cited in Jeremiah Evarts, *Cherokee Removal: The "William Penn" Essays and Other Writings*, ed. Francis Paul Prucha (Knoxville: University of Tennessee Press, 1981), 19

71 Cited ibid., 195

72 Ibid., 50

73 Ibid., 49

74 Ibid., 194

75 Ibid., 51

76 Samuel M. Janney, *The Life of William Penn* (Freeport, NY: Books for Libraries Press, 1970), 164–70, 185–6

77 Benjamin West, cited in Anderson and Cayton, *The Dominion of War*, 56

78 Edward C.O. Beatty, *William Penn as Social Philosopher* (New York: Columbia University Press, 1939), 266–73

79 John Locke, *Two Treatises of Government*, ed. Peter Laslett (New York: New American Library, 1965), 327–44

80 Evarts, *Cherokee Removal*, 54–5

81 See Michael Paul Rogin, *Fathers and Children: Andrew Jackson and the Subjugation of the American Indian* (New York: Alfred A. Knopf, 1975).

82 Evarts, *Cherokee Removal*, 194 (emphasis in original)

83 Ibid., 192

84 Ibid., 80

85 Ibid., 81

86 Ibid., 72

87 Ibid., 52

88 See Catherine Bell and Michael Asch, "Challenging Assumptions: The Impact of Precedent in Aboriginal Rights Litigation," in Michael Asch, ed., *Aboriginal and Treaty Rights in Canada: Essays on Law, Equality, and Respect for Difference* (Vancouver: UBC Press, 1997), 38–74. The details and background of *Calvin's Case* are elaborated in Geoffrey S. Lester, "The Territorial Rights of the Inuit of the Northwest Territory: A Legal Argument" (2 vols., PhD thesis in jurisprudence, York University, 1981), 1: 342–55.

89 See Dorothy V. Jones, *License for Empire: Colonialism by Treaty in Early America* (Chicago: University of Chicago Press, 1982).

90 John C. Weaver, *The Great Land Rush and the Making of the Modern World, 1650–1900* (Montreal: McGill-Queen's University Press, 2003), 133–77

91 Evarts, *Cherokee Removal*, 129–30

92 Michael Ignatieff, *Virtual War: Kosovo and Beyond* (Toronto: Viking, 2000)

93 Evarts, *Cherokee Removal*, 27, 73. See Stephen E. Ambrose and Douglas G. Brinkley, *Rise to Globalism: American Foreign Policy since 1938*, 8th rev. ed. (New York: Penguin, 1997).

94 Lewis Hanke, *All Mankind Is One: A Study of the Disputation between Bartolome de Las Casas and Juan Gines de Sepulveda in 1550 on the Intellectual and Religious Capacity of the American Indians* (DeKalb: Northern Illinois University Press, 1974)

95 Albert K. Weinberg, *Manifest Destiny: A Study of Nationalist Expansion in American History* (Chicago: Quadrangle Books, 1963)

96 Evarts, *Cherokee Removal*, 194, 77, 124

97 *Worcester v. Georgia*, cited in Russel Lawrence Barsh and James Youngblood Henderson, *The Road: Indian Tribes and Political Liberty* (Berkeley: University of California Press, 1980), 56–9

98 Cited in Charles Warren, *The Supreme Court in United States History*, rev. ed., 2 vols. (Boston: Little, Brown and Company, 1932), 1: 759

99 Ronald N. Satz, *American Indian Policy in the Jacksonian Era* (Lincoln: University of Nebraska Press, 1975)

100 Angie Debo, *And Still the Waters Run: The Betrayal of the Five Civilized Tribes* (Princeton, NJ: Princeton University Press, 1940)

101 Anthony Hall, "The Red Man's Burden: Land, Law and the Lord in the Indian Affairs of Upper Canada, 1791–1858" (PhD thesis, University of Toronto, 1984), 128–82

102 Paula Mitchell Marks, *In a Barren Land: American Indian Dispossession and Survival* (New York: William Morrow, 1998), 90

103 *New York Daily Advertiser*, Jan.15, 1831, cited in Charles Warren, *The Supreme Court in United States History*, 2 vols. (Boston: Little, Brown, 1923), 1: 738

104 Chief Justice Marshall to Judge Story, Sept. 22, 1832, cited ibid, 769

105 David Dixon, *Never Come to Peace Again: Pontiac's Uprising and the Fate of the British Empire in North America* (Norman: University of Oklahoma Press, 2005), 247–55, 273–74

106 Address of the "Committee and Council of the Cherokee Nation in General Council Convened" to the People of the United States, *Cherokee Phoenix and Indians' Advocate*, July 24, 1830, cited in Jeremiah Evarts, *Cherokee Removal: The "William Penn" Essays and Other Writings*, ed. Francis Paul Prucha (Knoxville: University of Tennessee Press, 1981) 260, 262 (emphasis in original)

CHAPTER SEVEN

1 Chalmers A. Johnson, *The Sorrows of Empire: Militarism, Secrecy, and the End of the Republic* (New York: Metropolitan Books, 2004)

2 Chalmers Johnson, interview with Dan Kapelovitz, "Is Democracy Doomed?" *Hustler*, Oct. 2004

3 Zbigniew Brzezinski, *The Grand Chessboard: American Primacy and Its Geostrategic Imperatives* (New York: Basic Books, 1997)

4 Isabel Hilton, "The 800-lb Gorilla in American Foreign Policy," *The Guardian*, July 28, 2004; James Risen and Thom Shanker, "Post 9/11 Web of US Prisoners," *New York Times*, Dec. 18, 2003; Brian Urquhart, "Outlaw World," *New York Review of Books*, May 11, 2006; Allen Freeman, "EU Eyes Alleged CIA Jails," *Globe and Mail*, Nov. 8, 2005, A1

5 Kevin Phillips, *American Dynasty: Aristocracy, Fortune, and the Politics of Deceit in the House of Bush* (New York: Viking, 2004), 271–6

6 Jeremy Scahill, *Blackwater: The Rise of the World's Most Powerful Military Army* (New York: Nation Books, 2008), 67–88

7 *Market Watch*, Jan. 26, 2006; Peter Dale Scott, "10-Year Strategic Plan Revives Proposals from Oliver North," Pacific News Service, Feb. 21, 2006

8 Rosenau, Franks, and Simon all cited in Doug Saunders, "The Fourth World War," *Globe and Mail*, Sept. 6, 2003, F6–7

9 Colin G. Calloway, *One Last Winter Count: The Native American West before Lewis and Clark* (Lincoln: University of Nebraska Press, 2003)

10 Fred Anderson and Andrew Cayton, *The Dominion of War: Empire and Liberty in North America, 1500–2000* (New York: Viking, 2005), 421–3. Emphasis in original.

11 Niall Ferguson, *Colossus: The Price of America's Empire* (New York: Penguin Press, 2004), 36

12 Anderson and Cayton, *Dominion of War*, 103

13 Ibid., 1–53, 124

14 Ibid., 422

15 Reginald Horsman, *Race and Manifest Destiny: The Origins of American Racial Anglo-Saxonism* (Cambridge, Mass.: Harvard University Press, 1981), 100

16 Jack D. Forbes, "The Indian: Looking Glass into the Souls of Anglo-Americans," in Jack D. Forbes, *Tribes and Masses: Explorations in Red, White and Black* (Np: Published by the author, 1978), 47

17 Felix S. Cohen, *Handbook of Federal Indian Law* (Washington, DC: US Government Printing Office, 1942; reprinted Albuquerque: University of New Mexico Press, 1971)

18 Felix S. Cohen, "The Erosion of Indian Rights, 1950–1953: A Case Study in Bureaucracy," *The Yale Law Journal* 62, 3 (1953): 348

19 John Collier, "United States Administration as a Laboratory of Ethnic Relations," *Social Research* 12 (Sept. 1945): 265–8; John Collier and Saul K. Padover, "Institute of Ethnic Democracy," *Common Ground* 4 (autumn 1943): 3–7; John Collier, *America's Colonial Record* (London: Fabian Publications, 1947)

20 Roxanne Dunbar Ortiz, *Indians of the Americas: Human Rights and Self-Determination* (New York: Praeger, 1984), 278

21 Patricia Nelson Limerick, *The Legacy of Conquest: The Unbroken Past of the American West* (New York: W.W. Norton, 1987), 56

22 Victoria de Grazia, *Irresistible Empire: America's Advance through 20th-Century Europe* (Cambridge, Mass.: The Belknap Press, 2005); Jeremy Rifkin, *The European Dream: How Europe's Vision of the Future is Quietly Eclipsing the American Dream* (New York: Tarcher Penguin, 2004)

23 Theodore W. Allen, *The Invention of the White Race*, vol. 2: *The Origin of Racial Oppression in Anglo-America* (London: Verso, 1997), 9. See also Theodore W. Allen, *The Invention of the White Race*, vol. 1: *Racial Oppression and Social Control* (London: Verso, 1995).

24 Allen, *The Invention of the White Race*, 2: 240

25 Ibid., 203–22

26 Statute of 1723, cited ibid., 241

27 See David Roediger, *Towards the Abolition of Whiteness: Essays on Race, Politics, and Working-Class History* (London: Verso, 1994).

28 Senator Thomas Hart Benton, cited in John Mack Faragher, "'More Motley than Mackinaw:' From Ethnic Mixing to Ethnic Cleansing on the Frontier of the Lower Missouri, 1783–1833," in Andrew R.L. Cayton and Fredrika J. Teute, eds., *Contact Points: American Frontiers from the Mohawk Valley to the Mississippi, 1750–1830* (Williamsburg, Vir.: Published for the Omohundro Institute of Early American History and Culture by the University of North Carolina Press, 1998), 319–20

29 John Mack Faragher, *Daniel Boone: The Life and Legend of an American Pioneer* (New York: Henry Holt, 1992)

30 Thomas Hart Benton, cited in Marquis James, *The Life of Andrew Jackson* (Indianapolis: Bobs-Merrill, 1938), 154

31 William H. Goetzmann, *Army Exploration in the American West, 1803–1863* (New Haven, Conn.: Yale University Press, 1965); Henry Savage Jr, *Discovering America, 1700–1875* (New York: Harper and Row, 1979), 238–313

32 David Lavender, *The American Heritage History of the Great West* (New York: American Heritage Publishing,1965), 107–11

33 Thomas Hart Benton, cited in Michael Paul Rogin, *Fathers and Children: Andrew Jackson and the Subjugation of the American Indian* (1975; New Brunswick, NJ: Transaction Publishers, 1991), 129

34 Nathaniel Bacon, cited in Washburn, *Red Man's Land / White Man's Law*, 43

35 John Scott, cited in Faragher, "'More Motley than Mackinaw,'" 319

36 Thomas Hart Benton, *Letter from Col. Benton to the People of Missouri* (Washington, DC: Privately published, 1853); Thomas Hart Benton, *Thirty Years' View; or, A History of the Working of the American Government, from 1820 to 1850*, 2 vols. (New York, 1854)

37 Faragher, "'More Motley than Mackinaw,'" 321, 323

38 William Christie MacLeod, *The American Indian Frontier* (New York: Knopf, 1928), 363–9

39 Thomas D. Clark, *Frontier America: The Story of the Westward Movement* (New York: Charles Scribner's Sons, 1959), 467

40 Mark Cocker, *Rivers of Blood, Rivers of Gold: Europe's Conquest of Indigenous Peoples* (New York: Grove Press, 1998), 216

41 Brigadier-General George Crook, cited in John G. Bourke, *On the Border with Crook* (New York: Scribners, 1891), 234

42 Gary B. Nash, *Red, White, and Black: The Peoples of Early America* (Englewood Cliffs, NJ: Prentice Hall, 1974); William Loren Katz, *Black Indians: A Hidden Heritage* (New York: Atheneum, 1986)

43 Piscataway Treaty of 1700, cited in Allen, *The Invention of the White Race*, 2: 43

44 William S. Willis, "Divide and Rule: Red, White, and Black in the Southeast," *Journal of Negro History* 48, 3 (1963): 157–76

45 John K. Mahon, *The History of the Second Seminal War, 1835–1842* (Gainsville: University of Florida Press, 1967)

46 David Brion Davis, *The Problem of Slavery in the Age of Revolution, 1770–1823* (New York: Oxford University Press, 1999); David Brion Davis, *Challenging the Boundaries of Slavery* (Cambridge, Mass.: Harvard University Press, 2003)

47 W.E.B. Du Bois, "American Negroes and Africa's Rise to Freedom," *National Guardian*, Feb. 13, 1961, in W.E.B. Du Bois, *The World and Africa: An Inquiry into the Part Which Africa Has Played in World History* (New York: International Publishers, 1965), 334

48 Simon Schama, *Rough Crossings: Britain, the Slaves and the American Revolution* (New York: Viking, 2006)

49 Wilson Jeremial Moses, *Creative Conflict in African-American Thought: Frederick Douglas, Alexander Crummell, Booker T. Washington, W.E.B. Du Bois, and Marcus Garvey* (New York: Cambridge University Press, 2004); Tamba E. M'bayo, "W.E.B. Du Bois, Marcus Garvey, and Pan-Africanism," *The Historian* 66, 1 (2004): 19–44

50 Marcus Garvey, *Marcus Garvey, Man of Vision and Action: His Life, Ideology and Work*, ed. Linda S. Jimison (Indianapolis: Life Star Enterprises, 1995)

51 I.K. Sundiata, *Brothers and Strangers: Black Zion, Black Slavery, 1914–1940* (Durham, NC: Duke University Press, 2003); Monday B. Akpan, "Black Imperialism: Americo-Liberian Rule over the African Peoples of Liberia," *Canadian Journal of African Studies* 7 (1973): 217–36; David Levering Lewis, *W.E.B. Du Bois: The Fight for Equality and the American Century, 1919–1963* (New York: Henry Holt, 2000)

52 Du Bois "American Negroes and Africa's Rise to Freedom," 334

53 Michael A. Hallet, *Private Prisons in America: A Critical Race Perspective* (Urbana: University of Illinois Press, 2006); Bruce Western, *Punishment and Inequality in America* (New York: R. Sage Foundation, 2006)

54 Glenn C. Loury, ""Why Are So Many Americans in Prison? Race and the Transformation of Criminal Justice," *Boston Review*, July/August, 2007 at http://bostonreview.net/BR32.4/loury.html

55 Peter Dale Scott, *Drugs, Oil, and War: The United States in Afghanistan, Colombia, and Indochina* (Boulder: Rowman and Littlefield, 2003)

56 Philippe Sands, *Lawless World: Making and Breaking Global Rules* (London: Penguin Books, 2006), xii, 21

57 Scahill, *Blackwater*, 79–87

58 D.M.R. Esson, *The Curse of Cromwell: A History of the Ironside Conquest of Ireland, 1649–1653* (Totowa, NJ: Rowman and Littlefield, 1971), 156–87; Patrick J. Corish, "The Cromwellian Conquest, 1649–53," in T.W. Moodie, F.X. Matin, F.J. Byrne, eds., *A New History of Ireland*, vol. 3: *Early Modern Ireland, 1534–1691* (Oxford: Clarendon Press, 1978), 336–86

59 See Edward W. Said, *Orientalism* (New York: Pantheon Books, 1978).

60 For arguments for the government of Ontario in the St Catherine's Milling case, see Canada, *Reports of the Supreme Court*, vol. 13 (Ottawa: Queen's Printer, 1887), 596–97.

61 Cited in Wilcomb E. Washburn, *Red Man's Land / White Man's Law: A Study of the Past and Present Status of the American Indian* (New York: Charles Scribner's

Sons, 1971), 43. See also Wilcomb E. Washburn, *The Governor and the Rebel: A History of Bacon's Rebellion in Virginia* (Chapel Hill: University of North Carolina Press, 1957).

62 *Sublimus Bull,* 1537, cited in L.C. Green and Olive P. Dickson, eds., *The Law of Nations and the New World* (Edmonton: University of Alberta Press, 1989), 18

63 James Hennesey, *American Catholics: A History of the Roman Catholic Community in the United States* (New York: Oxford University Press, 1981)

64 W.R. Wightman, *Forever on the Fringe: Six Studies in the Development of Manitoulin Island* (Toronto: University of Toronto Press, 1982), 20–93

65 D.N. Sprague, *Canada and the Metis, 1869–1885* (Waterloo: Wilfred Laurier University Press, 1988)

66 Rene Fumoleau, *As Long as This Land Shall Last: A History of Treaty 8 and Treaty 11, 1870–1939* (Calgary: Universiy of Calgary Press, 2004); Peter Kulchyski, *Like the Sound of a Drum: Aboriginal Cultural Politics in Denendeh and Nunavut* (Winnipeg: University of Manitoba Press, 2005), 77–115

67 John Wolfe Lydekker, *The Faithful Mohawks* (Cambridge: The University Press, 1938); Peter M. Doll, *Revolution, Religion, and National Identity: Imperial Anglicanism in British North America, 1745–1795* (Madison, NJ: Fairleigh Dickinson University Press, 2000)

68 David A. Nock, *A Victorian Missionary and Canadian Indian Policy: Cultural Synthesis vs Cultural Replacement* (Waterloo: Wilfred Laurier University Press, 1988)

69 Paul Tennant, *Aboriginal Peoples and Politics: The Indian Land Question in British Columbia, 1849–1989* (Vancouver: UBC Press, 1990)

70 George A. Schultz, *An Indian Canaan: Isaac McCoy and the Vision of an Indian State* (Norman: University of Oklahoma Press, 1972)

71 Albert G. Ellis, "Recollections of the Rev. Eleazar Williams," *Wisconsin Historical Collections* 8 (1877–79): 322–52

72 Richard Drinnon, *White Savage: The Case of John Dunn Hunter* (New York: Schocken Books, 1972), 203–29

73 Fredonia's Declaration of Independence, cited ibid, 207

74 John Dunn Hunter, *Memoirs of a Captivity among the Indians of North America, from Childhood to the Age of Nineteen: With Anecdotes Descriptive of Their Manners and Customs. To Which Is Added Some Account of the Soil, Climate, and Vegetable Products of the Territory Westward of the Mississippi* (London: Longman, Hurst, Rees, Orme, Brown and Green, 1823)

75 Major John Norton, *The Journal of Major John Norton, 1816,* ed. Carl F. Klinck and James J. Talman (Toronto: Champlain Society, 1870)

76 Hunter, cited in Drinnon, *White Savage,* 40

77 Lewis Cass, "Indians of North America," *North American Review* 22 (1826): 53–119; Lewis Cass, *Remarks on the Policy and Practice of the United States and Great Britain in the Treatment of Indians* (from North American Review) (Boston: Frederick T. Gray, 1827)

78 Stephen F. Austin, cited in Drinnon, *White Savage,* 215

79 Donald Jackson, *Ma-ka-tai-me-she-kia-kiak, Black Hawk: An Autobiography* (Urbana: University of Illinois Press, 1955)

80 John Frost, *Indian Wars of the United States from the Earliest Period to the Present Time* (Auburn and Buffalo: Miller, Orton and Mulligan, 1855), 266

81 Kerwin Lee Klein, *Froniers of Historical Imagination: Narrating the European Conquest of Native America, 1890–1990* (Berkeley: University of California Press, 1999), 7

82 Theodore Roosevelt, *The Winning of the West.* 4 vols. (New York: Putnam, 1889–96)

83 Cheddi Jagan, *The West on Trial: My Fight for Guyana's Freedom* (Berlin; Seven Seas Publishers, 1966)

84 Hugh Tinker, *A New System of Slavery: The Export of Indian Labour Overseas 1820–1920* (London: Oxford University Press, 1974); Walton Look Lai, *Indentured Labor, Caribbean Sugar: Chinese and Indian Migrants to the British West Indies, 1838–1918* (Baltimore: Johns Hopkins University Press, 1993)

85 See Ronald Radosh, *American Labor and United States Foreign Policy* (New York: Random House, 1969).

86 Norman Davies, *Europe: A History* (New York: Harper Perennial, 1998); Norman Davies, *Europe East and West* (New York: Vintage, 2007)

87 John Darwin, *After Tamerlane: The Global History of Empire since 1405* (London: Allan Lane/Penguin, 2007), 51

88 Ibid, 18–19

89 See Russell Thornton, *American Indian Holocaust and Survival: A Population History since 1492* (Norman: University of Oklahoma Press, 1986).

90 See Laura Peers, *The Ojibway of Western Canada, 1780–1870* (Winnipeg: University of Manitoba Press, 1994).

91 John Leonard Taylor, "The Development of Indian Policy for the Canadian North-West, 1869–1879" (PhD thesis, Queen's University, 1975); Hugh A. Dempsey, *Big Bear: The End of Freedom* (Vancouver: Douglas & McIntyre, 1984); John L. Tobias, "Canada's Subjugation of the Plains Cree, 1779–1885," *Canadian Historical Review* 64, 4 (1983): 519–48

92 See James Treat, ed., *Native and Christian: Indigenous Voices on Religious Identity in the United States and Canada* (New York and London: Routledge, 1996); R. Pierce Beaver, *Church, State and the American Indian* (St Louis: Concordia Publishing House, 1966).

93 See Trudy Nicks, "The Iroquois and the Fur Trade in Western Canada," in Carol M. Judd and Arthur J. Ray, eds., *Old Trails and New Directions: Papers of the Third North American Fur-Trade Conference* (Toronto: University of Toronto Press, 1980).

94 John C. Ewers, "Iroquois Indians in the Far West," Montana: *The Magazine of Western History* 13, 2 (1963): 2–10; Theodore Binnema, *Common and Contested Ground: A Human and Environmental History of the Northwestern Plains* (Norman: University of Oklahoma Press, 2001)

95 Robert Ignatius Burns, *The Jesuits and the Indian Wars of the Northwest* (New Haven, Conn.: Yale University Press, 1966), 41

96 Reader's Digest, *Through Indian Eyes*, 284–8

97 John Webster Grant, *Moon of Wintertime: Missionaries and the Indians of Canada in Encounter since 1534* (Toronto: University of Toronto Press, 1992), 121

98 Thomas E. Jesset, *Chief Spokan Garry, 1811–1892: Christian, Statesman, and Friend of the White Man* (Minneapolis: T.S. Denison and Co., 1960)

99 Meinig, *The Great Columbia Plain*, 100

100 See Bernard De Voto, *Across the Wide Missouri* (Boston: Houghton, Mifflin, 1975).

101 Reginald C. Stuart, *United States Expansionism and British North America, 1775–1871* (Chapel Hill: University of North Carolina Press, 1988), 103–5

102 Bernard De Voto, *The Course of Empire* (Lincoln: University of Nebraska Press, 1983), 533

CHAPTER EIGHT

1 PBS Frontline, The Opium Kings, "Opium Throughout History," www.pbs.org/wgbh/pages/frontline/shows/heroin/etc/history.html

2 Madsen Axel, *John Jacob Astor: America's First Multimillionaire* (New York: John Wiley, 2001)

3 Peter Ward Fay, *The Opium War, 1840–1842: Barbarians in the Celestial Empire and the Early Part of the Nineteenth Century and the War by Which They Forced Her Gates Ajar* (Chapel Hill: University of North Carolina Press, 1998); Arthur Waley, *The Opium War through Chinese Eyes* (Stanford: Stanford University Press, 1979)

4 Eric Eustace Williams, *Capitalism and Slavery* (Chapel Hill: University of North Carolina Press, 1994)

5 Ch'ien Lung's letter of 1793 to King George cited at www.fordham.edu/Halsall/mod/1793qianlong.html

6 Webster Griffin Tarpley and Anton Chaitkin, *George Bush: The Unauthorized Biography* (Joshua Tree California: Progress Press, 2004), chapter 7

7 Martin Booth, *Opium a History* (New York: St Martin's Press, 1998); Barbara Hodgson, *In the Arms of Morpheus: The Tragic History of Laudanum, Morphine, and Patent Medicines* (Buffalo: Firefly, 2001)

8 Griffin Tarpley and Chaitkin, *George Bush*, chapter 7

9 R.P.T. Davenport-Hines, *The Pursuit of Oblivion: A Global History of Narcotics* (London: Weidenfeld and Nicolas, 2001); David T. Courtwright, *Forces of Habit: Drugs and the Making of the Modern World* (Cambridge: Harvard Uniiversity Press, 2001); Carl A. Trocki, *Opium, Empire, and the Global Political Economy: A Study of the Asian Opium Trade, 1750–1950* (London: Routledge, 1999); Timothy Brook and Bob Tadashi Wakabayashi, eds., *Opium Regimes: China, Britain, and Japan, 1839–1952* (Berkeley: University of California Press, 2000); Alfred W. McCoy, *The Politics of Heroin: CIA Complicity in the Global Drug*

Trade (Brooklyn: Lawrence Hill, 1991); M. Emdad-ul Haq, *Drugs in South Asia: From the Opium Trade to Present Day* (New York: St Martin's Press, 2000); Peter Dale Scott, *Drugs, Oil, and War: The United States in Afghanistan, Colombia, and Indochina* (Boulder: Rowman and Littlefield, 2003)

10 Clarence L. Ver Steeg, *Robert Morris, Revolutionary Financier* (Philadelphia: University of Pennsylvania Press, 1954)

11 Ray Allen Billington, *Westward Expansion and the History of the American Frontier*, 2nd ed. (New York: Macmillan, 1964), 251–63

12 Colin Mooers, "Introduction: The New Watchdogs," in Colin Mooers, ed., *The New Imperialists: Ideologies of Empire* (Oxford: One World, 2006), 1–8

13 David Harvey, *The New Imperialism* (Oxford: Oxford University Press, 2003)

14 Pauline Maier, "The Revolutionary Origins of the American Corporation," *The William and Mary Quarterly*, 3rd Series, vol. 50, 1 (1993): 83, 56–8; Edwin Merrick Dodd, *American Business Corporations until 1860, with Special Reference to Massachusetts* (Cambridge: Harvard University Press, 1954)

15 David F. Linowes, "The Corporation as Citizen," in A.E. Dick Howard, ed., *The United States Constitution: Roots, Rights, and Responsibilities* (Washington: Smithsonian Institution Press, 1992), 345–59

16 Gary Lawson and Guy Seidman, *The Constitution of Empire: Territorial Expansion and American Legal History* (New Haven: Yale University Press, 2004); Mira Wilkins, *The Emergence of Multinational Enterprise: American Business Abroad from the Colonial Era to 1914* (Cambridge Mass.: Harvard University Press, 1970)

17 Clarence Walworth Alvord, *The Mississippi Valley in British Politics: A Study of the Trade, Land Speculation, and Experiments in Imperialism Culminating in the American Revolution*, 2 vols. (Cleveland: Arthur H. Clark Company, 1917)

18 See Daniel R. Headrick, *The Invisible Weapon: Telecommunications and International Politics, 1851–1945* (New York: Oxford University Press, 1988).

19 See Alfred Chandler, *The Railroads: The Nation's First Big Business* (New York: Harcourt, Brace, 1965).

20 Coleen A. Dunlavy, *Politics and Industrialization: Early Railroads in the United States and Prussia* (Princeton: Princeton University Press, 1994)

21 Stuart Banner, *Anglo-American Securities Regulation: Cultural and Political Roots, 1690–1860* (Cambridge: Cambridge University Press, 1998)

22 J.W. Hurst, *The Legitimacy of the Business Corporation in the Law of the United States, 1780–1970* (Charlottesville: University of Virginia, 1970); A.A. Berle and G.C. Means, *The Modern Corporation and Private Property* (New York: Commerce Clearing House, 1932); Hebert Hovenkamp, *Enterprise and American Law, 1836–1937* (Cambridge, Mass.: Harvard University Press, 1991)

23 Naomi Lamoreaux, *The Great Merger Movement in American Business, 1895–1904* (Cambridge: Cambridge University Press, 1985); Martin J. Sklar, *The Corporate Reconstruction of American Capitalism, 1890–1916* (Cambridge: Cambridge University Press, 1988); William G. Roy, *Socializing Capital: The Rise of the Large Industrial Corporation in America* (Princeton: Princeton University Press, 1997); Olivier Zunz, *Making America Corporate, 1870–1920* (Chicago: University of Chicago Press, 1990)

24 Edward H. Spicer, *Cycles of Conquest: The Impact of Spain, Mexico, and the United States on the Indians of the Southwest, 1533–1960* (Tucson: University of Arizona Press, 1962); Albert L. Hurtado, *Indian Survival on the California Frontier* (New Haven: Yale University Press, 1988)

25 Christopher L. Miller, *Prophetic Worlds: Indians and Whites on the Columbian Plateau* (New Brunswick, NJ: Rutgers University Press, 1985). See John C. Ewers, *The Role of the Indian in National Expansion* (Washington, DC: United States Department of the Interior, National Parks Service, 1938).

26 David Howard Bain, *Empire Express: Building the First Transcontinental Railway* (New York, Viking, 1999), 3–53

27 Bernard Smith, *Imagining the Pacific: In the Wake of the Cook Voyages* (New Haven: Yale University Press, 1992)

28 Asa Whitney, cited in Bain, *Empire Express*, 29

29 *New York Herald*, June 15, 1851, cited ibid., 45

30 Edgar A. Haine, *Seven Railroads* (South Brunswick, NJ: A.S. Barnes, 1979); Ian J. Kerr, *Building the Railways of the Raj* (Oxford: Oxford University Press, 1998)

31 William Hemsley Emory, *Report on the United States and Mexican Boundary Survey*, 3 vols. (Washington: C. Wendell, 1857–59)

32 Henry Laurens, *L'expedition d'Egypte, 1798–1801* (Paris: Editions du Seuil, 1997)

33 See William McNeill, *The Pursuit of Power: Technology, Armed Force, and Society since A.D. 1000* (Chicago: University of Chicago Press, 1984).

34 William H. Goetzmann, *Army Exploration in the American West, 1803–1863* (New Haven: Yale University Press, 1965), 305. See also William H. Goetzmann, *Exploration and Empire* (New York: Knopf, 1971).

35 Bain, *Empire Express*, 50

36 Francis N. Blanchet, J.B. Bolduc, Modeste Demers, and Antoine Langlois, *Notices and Voyages of the Famed Quebec Mission to the Pacific Northwest. Being the Correspondence, Notices, etc., of Fathers Blanchet and Demers, Together with Those of Fathers Bolduc and Langlois*, trans. Carl Landerholm (Portland: Oregon Historical Society, 1956); Blanchet, *Historical Sketches of the Catholic Church in Oregon, during the Past Forty Years* (Portland: Catholic Sentinel Press, 1878); John G. Shea, *History of the Catholic Missions among the Indian Tribes of the United States, 1529–1854* (New York: T.W. Strong, 1855); John C. Jackson, *Children of the Fur Trade: Forgotten Metis of the Pacific Northwest* (Missoula, Montans: Mountain Press Publishing Company, 1995)

37 Robert Ignatius Burns, *The Jesuits and the Indian Wars of the Northwest* (New Haven: Yale University Press, 1966), 41–60

38 Cited in Francis Paul Prucha, *The Great Father: The United States Government and the American Indians*, abridged ed. (Lincoln: University of Nebraska Press, 1986), 132

39 Ibid., 134

40 Paula Mitchell Marks, *In a Barren Land: American Indian Dispossession and Survival* (New York: William Morrow, 1998), 140

41 Owhi, Peopeomoxmox, Spokan Garry, and Chief Joseph, cited ibid., 140–1

42 Burns, *The Jesuits and the Indian Wars of the Northwest*, 241

43 James Douglas, cited in Barry M. Gough, *Gunboat Frontier: British Maritime Authority and Northwest Coast Indians, 1846–90* (Vancouver: University of British Columbia Press, 1984), 59

44 Major Isaac Stevens, cited in Burns, *The Jesuits and the Indian Wars of the Northwest*, 239–40

45 John D. Unruh Jr, *The Plains Across: The Overland Immigrants and the Trans-Mississippi West, 1840–1860* (Urbana: University of Illinois Press, 1979)

46 Ibid., 240–2

47 Cole Harris, "The Fraser Canyon Encountered," in Cole Harris, ed., *The Resettlement of British Columbia: Essays on Colonialism and Geographical Change* (Vancouver: UBC Press, 1997), 109–14

48 F.W. Howay, W.N. Sage, and H.F. Angus, *British Columbia and the United States: The North Pacific Slope from Fur Trade to Aviation* (1942; New York: Russell and Russell, 1970), 159–60

49 Robert Ignatius Burns, "Roman Catholic Missions in the Northwest," in Wilcombe E. Washburn, ed., *History of Indian-White Relations*, vol. 4, *Handbook of North American Indians* (Washington, DC: Smithsonian Institution, 1988), 499

50 American Friend Service Committee, *Uncommon Controversy: Fishing Rights of the Muckleshoot, Puyallup, and Nisqually Indians. A Report Prepared for the American Friends Service Committee* (Seattle: University of Washington Press, 1972)

51 See Donald L. Parman, *Indians and the American West in the Twentieth Century* (Bloomington: Indiana University Press, 1994).

52 Kevin Phillips, *The Cousins' Wars: Religion, Politics, and the Triumph of Anglo-America* (New York: Basic Books, 1999), 598

53 Peter Carstens, *The Queen's People: A Study of Hegemony, Coercion, and Accommodation among the Okanagan of Canada* (Toronto: University of Toronto Press, 1991), 37–47

54 Burns, *The Jesuits and the Indian Wars of the Northwest*, 285

55 Enclosure in Principle Secretary of State for the Colonies, Sir Edward Bulwer Lytton, to Governor James Douglas, Sept. 2, 1858, in British Columbia Legislature, *Papers Connected with the Indian Land Question, 1850–1875* (Victoria: Government Printer, 1875), reprinted at Victoria by the Queen's Printer, 1987, 12–13

56 David R. Williams, *The Man for a New Country: Sir Matthew Baille Begbie* (Sydney, BC: Gray's Publishing, 1977)

57 Judge Begbie, cited in Sidney L. Harring, *White Man's Law: Native People in Nineteenth-Century Jurisprudence* (Toronto: University of Toronto Press, 1998), 205

58 Enclosure in Lytton to Douglas, Sept. 2, 1858, in British Columbia Legislature, *Papers Connected with the Indian Land Question, 1850–1875*, 13

59 Malcolm J. Rohrbough, *Days of Gold* (Berkeley: University of California Press, 1997)

60 John A. Garraty, *The American Nation: A History of the United States* (New York: Harper and Row, 1966), 324

61 See Edward Castillo and Robert Jackson, *Indians, Franciscans, and Spanish Colonization* (Albuquerque: University of New Mexico Press, 1995).

62 Cited in Clifford E. Trafzer and Joel R. Hyer, eds., *Exterminate Them! Written Accounts of the Murder, Rape, and Enslavement of Native Americans during California's Gold Rush* (East Lansing: Michigan State University Press, 1999), x

63 Edward Castillo, Foreword, ibid, x. See also Robert F. Heizer and Alan J. Almquist, *The Other Californians* (Berkeley: University of California Press, 1971); Albert Hurtado, *Indian Survival on the California Frontier* (New Haven: Yale University Press, 1988); Richard L. Carrico, *Strangers in a Stolen Land* (Newcastle California: Sierra Oaks Publishing, 1987).

64 *New York Times*, cited in enclosure of Lytton to Douglas, Sept. 2, 1858, in British Columbia Legislature, *Papers Connected with the Indian Land Question, 1850–1875*, 13

65 Desmond Morton, "Comparison of U.S./Canadian Military Experience on the Frontier," in James P. Tate, ed., *The Military on the Frontier: Proceedings of the 7th Military History Symposium* (Washington, DC: Office of Air Force History, 1978); Morton, "Cavalry or Police: Keeping the Peace on Two Adjacent Frontiers, 1870–1900," *Journal of Canadian Studies* 12 (spring 1977): 27–37

66 Matthew Begbie, cited in Tina Loo, *Making Law, Order, and Authority in British Columbia, 1821–1871* (Toronto: University of Toronto Press, 1994), 151

67 Cited in Barry M. Gough, *Gunboat Frontier*, 211

68 Leland Donald, *Aboriginal Slavery on the Northwest Coast of North America* (Berkeley: University of California Press, 1997)

69 Chief Nestecanna, cited in Gough, *Gunboat Frontier*, 88

70 Chris Arnett, *The Terror of the Coast: Land Alienation and Colonial War on Vancouver Island and the Gulf Islands* (Vancouver: Talonbooks, 1999)

71 Harring, *White Man's Law*, 206

72 Robert M. Utley, "Indian–United States Military Situation, 1848–1891," in Wicombe E. Washburne, ed., *History of Indian-White Relations*, vol. 4, *Handbook of North American Indian*, 163–84

73 Burns, *The Jesuits and the Indian Wars of the Northwest*, 176

74 Andrew Wolford, *Between Justice and Certainty: Treaty Making in BC* (Vancouver: UBC Press, 2005)

75 Tony Penikett, "The Haida Don't Let Go Easily," *Globe and Mail*, Sept. 9, 2003, A21

76 Office of the Treaty Commissioner, *Treaty Implementation: Fulfilling the Covenant* (Saskatoon: Office of the Treaty Commissioner, 2007)

77 Ronald Steel, *Pax Americana* (New York: Viking, 1970)

78 See the *Pax Britannica* trilogy by James (Jan) Morris. These volumes are entitled *Heaven's Command: An Imperial Progress; Pax Britannica: The Climax of Empire; Farewell the Trumpets: An Imperial Retreat* (New York: Harcourt Brace Jovanovich, 1973–80).

79 Byron Farwell, *Queen Victoria's Little Wars* (New York: W.W. Norton, 1985)

80 Paul Johnson, *The Birth of the Modern: World Society, 1815–1830* (London: Weidenfeld and Nicolson, 1991), 269. See Robert Joseph Kerner, *The Urge to the Sea: The Course of Russian History. The Role of Rivers, Portages, Ostrogs, Monasteries and Furs* (Berkeley: University of California Press, 1942).

81 Joseph W. Esherick, *The Origins of the Boxer Uprising* (Berkeley: University of California Press, 1987)

82 Ian Knight, *The Zulu War of 1879* (Oxford and New York: Osprey Publishing, 2003)

83 James Belich, *The Victorian Interpretation of Racial Conflict: The Maori, the British, and the New Zealand Wars* (Montreal: McGill-Queen's University Press, 1989)

84 David Svaldi, *Sand Creek Massacre and the Rhetoric of Extermination: A Case Study in Indian-White Relations* (Lanham: University Press of America, 1989)

85 Aziz Al-Azmeh, "After the Fact: Reading Tocqueville in Baghdad," in Mooer, ed., *The New Imperialists*, 30

86 Jan-Bart Gewald, *Herero Heroes: A Socio-Political History of the Herero People of Namibia, 1890–1923* (Athens: University of Ohio Press, 1999); Jon Bridgman and Leslie H. Worley, "Genocide of the Hereros," in Samuel Totten, William S. Parsons, and Israel W. Charny, eds., *Century of Genocide: Critical Essays and Eyewitness Accounts* (New York: Routledge, 2004), 3–40

87 Christine Bolt, *Victorian Attitudes to Race* (Toronto: University of Toronto Press, 1971)

88 Edward W. Said, "Zionism from the Standpoint of Its Victims," in Moustafa Bayoumi and Andrew Rubin, eds., *The Edward Said Reader* (New York: Vintage Books, 2000), 131–2, 135.

89 Immanuel Wallerstein, *The Modern World System, I: Capitalism Agriculture and the Origins of the World-Economy in the Sixteenth Century; II: Mercantilism and the Consolidation of the European World Economy, 1600–1750; III: The Second Era of Great Expansion of the Capitalist World Economy* (New York: Academic Press, 1974, 1980, 1988); Immanuel Wallerstein, *The Capitalist World-Economy* (Cambridge: Cambridge University Press, 1979); Immanuel Wallerstein, *Historical Capitalism* (London, Verso, 1983)

90 Edward Sleigh Hewlett, "The Chilcotin Uprising of 1864," *BC Studies*, no. 19 (autumn 1973): 50–72

91 See Jill Lepore, "Remembering American Frontiers: King Philip's War and the American Imagination," in Andrew R.L. Cayton and Fredrika J. Teute, eds., *Contact Points: American Frontiers from the Mohawk Valley to the Mississippi, 1750–1830* (Chapel Hill: Published for the Omohundro Institute of Early American History and Culture by the University of North Carolina Press, 1998), 327–60; Richard Slotkin, *Regeneration through Violence: The Mythology of the American Frontier, 1600–1860* (Middleton, Conn.: Wesleyan University Press, 1973).

92 See Robin Fisher, *Contact and Conflict: Indian-European Relations in British Columbia, 1774–1890*, 2nd ed. (Vancouver: UBC Press, 1992), 115–16.

93 Williams, *The Man for a New Country*, 116–17

94 Cited ibid., 112

95 Judge Begbie, cited ibid., 115

96 Reverend R.C. Lundin Brown, *Klatsassan, and Other Remininscences of Missionary Life in British Columbia* (London: Society for Promoting Christian Knowledge, 1873), 102

97 Sidney L. Harring, *Crow Dog's Case: American Indian Sovereignty, Tribal Law, and United States Law in the Nineteenth Century* (Cambridge: Cambridge University Press, 1995), 16–17

98 Bruce Clark, *Justice in Paradise* (Montreal: McGill-Queen's University Press, 1999)

99 Bruce Clark, "Peace through Justice Research Project," Oct. 11, 2001 (xerox copy taken from email distribution)

100 Olive Fairholm, "John Robson and Confederation," in W. George Shelton, ed., *British Columbia and Confederation* (Victoria: Published for the University of Victoria by the Morriss Printing Company, 1967), 97–124

101 "Indian Policy," *British Columbian*, May 14, 1864, cited in Loo, *Making Law, Order, and Authority in British Columbia, 1821–1871*, 151

102 Frederick Jackson Turner, "The Significance of the Frontier in American History," reprinted in Walker D. Wyman and Clifton B. Kroeber, eds., *The Frontier in Perspective* (Madison: University of Wisconsin Press, 1965), 18

103 Kenneth Carley, *The Sioux Uprising of 1862* (St Paul: Minnesota Historical Society, 1961)

104 Gareth Stedman Jones, "The History of US Imperialism," in Robin Blackburn, ed., *Ideology in Social Science* (New York: Vintage, 1973), 216–17 (emphasis in original)

105 Robin W. Winks, *Canada and the United States: The Civil War Years* (Montreal: Harvest House, 1971), 155–77; Donald F. Warner, *The Idea of Continental Union: Agitation for the Annexation of Canada to the United States, 1849–1893* (No place: University of Kentucky Press for the Mississippi Valley Historical Association, 1960)

106 Petition, cited in the Hon Elwood Evans, *The Re-Annexation of British Columbia to the United States, Right, Proper and Desirable* (Victoria: Morriss Printing Co., 1965), 45

107 Stephen E. Ambrose, *Undaunted Courage: Meriwether Lewis, Thomas Jefferson and the Opening of the American West* (New York: Simon and Schuster, 1996); Goldwin Smith, *Canada and the Canadian Question* (London: Macmillan, 1891)

108 Evans, *The Re-Annexation of British Columbia*, 16

109 John Quincy Adams, cited ibid, 42–3

110 Ibid., 16

111 Ibid., 48–9

112 William H. Nelson, *The American Tory* (Boston: Northeastern University Press, 1992)

113 Mel Smith, *Our Home or Native Land?* (Victoria: Crown Western, 1995); Tom Flanagan, *First Nations? Second Thoughts* (Montreal: McGill-Queen's University Press, 2000)

114 David Suzuki, *The Autobiography* (Vancouver: Greystone Books, 2006), 117

115 See John Collier, *Indians of the Americas* (New York: W.W. Norton and the New American Library, 1947), 9–10

116 Suzuki, *The Autobiography*, 119

117 Elizabeth May, *Paradise Won: The Struggle for South Morseby* (Toronto: McClelland & Stewart, 1990)

118 Doris Shadbolt, *Bill Reid* (Vancouver: Douglas & McIntyre, 1998)

119 Mark Hume, "These Nine Women Have Been Killed or Disappeared," *Globe and Mail*, June 22, 2006, A1

120 Amnesty International Canada, *Stolen Sisters: Discrimination and Violence against Indigenous Women in Canada* (Ottawa, 2004)

121 Renate Aebi, *The Trafficing in Children for the Purposes of Prostitution: British Columbia, Canada* (Vancouver: The Alliance for the Rights of Children, 2001)

122 www.harbour.sfu.ca/freda/articles/crime1.htm#_Toc467988254

123 Owen Lippert, ed., *Beyond the Nass Valley: National Implications of the Supreme Court's Delgamuukw Decision* (Vancouver: Fraser Institute, 2000)

124 Gisday Wa and Delgam Uukw, *The Spirit of the Land: Statements of the Gitskan and Wet'suwet'en Hereditary Chiefs in the Supreme Court of British Columbia, 1987–1990* (Gabriola: Reflections, 1992); Dara Culhane, *The Pleasure of the Crown: Anthropology, Law and First Nations* (Burnaby: Talon Books, 1998)

125 Thomas Berger, "The Nishga Indians and Aboriginal Rights," in Thomas Berger, *Fragile Freedoms: Human Rights and Dissent in Canada* (Toronto: Clark, Irwin, 1981); Daniel Raunet, *Without Surrender, without Consent: A History of Nishga Land Claims* (Vancouver: Douglas & McIntyre, 1984); Paul Tennant, *Aboriginal Peoples and Politics: The Indian Land Question in British Columbiua, 1849–1989* (Vancouver: UBC Press, 1990)

126 Bruce A. Clark, *Indian Title in Canada* (Toronto: Carswell, 1987); Bruce A. Clark, *Native Liberty, Crown Sovereignty: The Existing Aboriginal Right of Self-Government in Canada* (Montreal: McGill-Queen's Univesity Press, 1990); Clark, *Justice in Paradise*, www.sisis.nativeweb.org/clark/chron.html

127 Joseph Henry Smith, *Appeals to the Privy Council from the American Plantations* (New York: Octagon Books, 1965)

128 www.grahamdefense.org

129 Peter Matthiessen, *In the Spirit of Crazy Horse* (New York: Penguin Books, 1992)

130 Ellen Claver, cited in Rex Wyler, "Who Killed Anna Mae?" *Vancouver Sun*, Jan. 8, 2004

131 David Melmer, "John Graham to Stand Trial on 30-Year Old Murder," *Indian Country Today*, Dec. 14, 2007

132 Amy Carmichael, "Judge Who Abused Young Girls Apologizes to Victims," Canadian Press, Jan. 1, 2004; Ian Mulgrew, "Abusive Judge Wasn't Alone, Police Say," *Vancouver Sun*, June 5, 2004

133 www.switlo.com/opinion.php?selected=54

134 Janice G.E.A. Switlo, *Gustafsen Lake: Under Siege* ((Peachland, BC: TIAC Communications, 1997), 35

CHAPTER NINE

1 Joseph S. Nye, *Soft Power: The Means to Global Success in World Politics* (New York: Public Affairs, 2004); Leah Armistead, ed., *Information Operations: Warfare and the Hard Reality of Soft Power* (Washington, DC: Brassey's, 2004); Matthew Fraser, *Weapons of Mass Distraction: Soft Power and American Empire* (New York: Thomas Dunne Books, 2005)

2 Samuel P. Huntington, *The Clash of Civilizations and the Remaking of World Order* (New York: Simon and Schuster, 1996), 51

3 Thomas Jefferson, cited in William Appleman Williams, *Empire as a Way of Life* (New York: Oxford University Press, 1980), 185

4 Dorothy V. Jones, *License for Empire: Colonialism by Treaty in Early America* (Chicago: University of Chicago Press, 1982)

5 Henry M. Stanley, *The Congo and the Founding of Its Free States* (New York: Harper and Brothers, 1885)

6 See, for instance, Kent McNeil, "The Meaning of Aboriginal Title," in Michael Asch, ed., *Aboriginal and Treaty Rights in Canada: Essays in Law, Equality, and Respect for Difference* (Vancouver: UBC Press, 1997), 135–54; Michael Asch, "First Nations and the Derivation of Canada's Underlying Title: Comparing Perspectives on Legal Ideology," in Curtis Cook and Juan D. Lindau, eds., *Aboriginal Rights and Self-Government: The Canadian and Mexican Experience in North American Perspective* (Montreal: McGill-Queen's University Press, 2000), 148–67: David W. Elliott, "Aboriginal Title," in Bradford W. Morse, ed., *Aboriginal Peoples and the Law: Indian, Metis and Inuit Rights in Canada* (Ottawa: Carleton University Press, 1985), 48–121; Brian Slattery, "The Land Rights of Indigenous Canadian Peoples as Affected by the Crown's Acquisition of Their Territories" (PhD thesis, Oxford University, 1979); Michael J. Kaplan, "Issues in Land Claims: Aboriginal Title," in Imre Sutton, ed., *Irredeemable America: The Indians' Estate and Land Claims* (Albuquerque: University of New Mexico Press, 1985), 71–86; James Youngblood Henderson, "Unravelling the Riddles of Aboriginal Title," *American Indian Law Review* 5 (1977): 75–137; Howard R. Berman, "Concepts of Aboriginal Rights in the Early Legal History of the United States," *Buffalo Law Review* 27 (1978): 637–67

7 Wiley Sword, *President Washington's Indian War: The Struggle for the Old Northwest* (Norman: University of Oklahoma Press, 1985)

8 The Speech of the Commissioners of the United States to the Deputies of the Confederate Indian Nations Assembled at Rapids of the Miamis River, July 31, 1793, in E.A. Cruickshank, ed., *The Correspondence of Lieutenant Governor John Graves Simcoe* (Toronto: The Ontario Historical Society, 1923), 1: 405–9

9 See Basil Davidson, *The Black Man's Burden: Africa and the Curse of the Nation State* (New York: Times Books, 1992).

10 Robert Jackson, *Quasi-States: Sovereignty, International Relations and the Third World* (Cambridge: Cambridge University Press, 1990). See Rupert Emerson, *From Empire to Nation: The Rise of Self-Assertion of Asian and African Peoples*

(Cambridge, Mass.: Harvard University Press, 1967); David A. Kay, *The New Nations in the United Nations, 1960–1967* (New York: Columbia University Press, 1970).

11 Michael C. Howard, *Fiji: Race and Politics in an Island State* (Vancouver: UBC Press, 1991); R.S. Milne, *Politics in Ethnically Bipolar States: Guyana, Malasia, Fiji* (Vancouver: UBC Press, 1981)

12 See Martin Meredith, *Our Votes, Our Guns: Robert Mugabe and the Tragedy of Zimbabwe* (New York: Public Affairs, 2002); R.W. Johnson, "South Africa's Land Wars," *London Review of Books,* June 1, 2000, 6–7; Ronald Weitzer, *Transforming Settler States: Communal Conflict and Internal Security in Northern Ireland and Zimbabwe* (Berkeley: University of California Press, 1990).

13 US Tibet Committee, *Tibet: An Independent State under Illegal Occupation* (New York: US Tibet Committee, 1994)

14 John P. Humphrey, *Human Rights and the United Nations: A Great Adventury* (Dobbs Ferry, NY: Transnational Publishers, 1984); Rosemary Righter, *Utopia Lost: The United Nations and World Order* (New York: The Twentieth Century Fund, 1995); Adam Bartos and Christopher Hitchens, *International Territory: The United Nations 1945–1995* (London: Verso, 1994)

15 www.fordham.edu/halsall/mod/1960-un-colonialism.html

16 Edward Said, "Zionism from the Standpoint of Its Victims," in *The Edward Said Reader,* ed. Moustafa Bayoumi and Edward Rubin (New York: Vintage, 2000), 129

17 David Dixon, *Never Come to Peace Again: Pontiac's Uprising and the Fate of the British Empire in North America* (Norman: University of Oklahoma Press, 2005), 275

18 John Quincy Adams, cited in Alpheus Henry Snow, *The Question of Aborigines in the Law and Practice of Nations* (Washington, DC: Government Printing Office, 1919), 73

19 Robert Muckle, *The First Nations of British Columbia: An Anthropological Survey* (Vancouver: UBC Press, 1998)

20 Paul Tennant, *Aboriginal Peoples and Politics: The Indian Land Question in British Columbia, 1849–1989* (Vancouver: UBC Press, 1990), 47–50

21 Christopher McKee, *Treaty Talks in British Columbia: Negotiating a Mutually Beneficial Future* (Vancouver, UBC Press, 1996); ARA consulting Group Inc., *Social and Economic Impacts of Aboriginal Land Claim Settlements – A Financial and Economic Perspective* (Victoria: Queen's Printer for British Columbia, 1996); Andrew Woolford, *Between Justice and Uncertainty: Treaty Making in British Columbia* (Vancouver: UBC Press, 2004)

22 Anthony Hall, "Indian Treaties," *The Canadian Encyclopedia,* CD-ROM edition (Toronto: McClelland & Stewart, 2000)

23 Tennant, *Aboriginal Peoples and Politics,* 47–50

24 Ibid., 102–7

25 Len Marchand and Matt Hughes, *Breaking Trail: The Autobiography of Len Marchand* (Prince George: Caitlin Press, 2000)

26 Jones, *License for Empire*

27 Henry Clay, cited by Fred Anderson and Andrew Cayton, *The Dominion of War: Empire and Liberty in North America, 1500–2000* (New York: Viking, 2005), 226

28 Theodore Roosevelt, *The Winning of the West*, 4 vols. (New York and London: G.P. Putnams, 1889–96), 4: 8

29 Thomas Jefferson, cited in Richard Drinnon, *Facing West: The Metaphysics of Indian-Hating and Empire-Building* (New York: New American Library, 1980), 94

30 Judge James Ballard, cited in Michael Paul Rogin, *Fathers and Children: Andrew Jackson and the Subjugation of the American Indian* (New York: Vintage, 1976), 129

31 John Richardson, chairman, Committee of Trade at Montreal, and James Irvine, chairman, Committee of Trade at Quebec, to George Provost, Governor General over the province of Upper and Lower Canada, Oct. 14 and 24, 1812, in Library and Archives Canada, Colonial Office Records 42 (CO 42), vol. 159

32 James McGill, cited in George F.G. Stanley, "The Indians and the War of 1812," in Morris Zaslow, ed., *The Defended Border: Upper Canada and the War of 1812* (Toronto: Macmillan, 1964), 178

33 James P. Ronda, *Astoria and Empire* (Lincoln: University of Nebraska Press, 1990)

34 James Douglas to the Secretary of State for the Colonies, March 25, 1861, in British Columbia Legislature, *Papers Connected with the Indian Land Question, 1850–1875* (Victoria: Government Printer, 1875), reprinted at Victoria by the Queen's Printer, 1987, 19

35 Edward Gibbon Wakefield, *A View of the Art of Colonization in Present Reference to the British Empire* (New York: A.M. Kelley, 1969); Karl Marx, *Das Kapital*, vol. 1, chapter 33, at http://www.bibliomania.com/2/1/261/1294/frameset.html

36 Alan Ward, *A Show of Justice: Racial "Amalgamation" in Nineteenth-Century New Zealand* (Toronto: University of Toronto Press, 1973), 30–6. See Klaus E. Knorr, *British Colonial Theories* (Toronto: University of Toronto Press, 1963)

37 British Columbia Legislature, *Papers Connected with the Indian Land Question*, 5–11

38 Secretary of State for the Colonies to Governor Douglas, Oct. 19, 1861, in British Columbia Legislature, *Papers Connected with the Indian Land Question*, 20

39 Anthony Hall, "Native Limited Identities and Newcomer Metropolitanism in Upper Canada, 1814–1867," in David Keane and Colin Read, eds., *Old Ontario: Essays in Honour of J.M.S. Careless* (Toronto: Dundurn, 1990), 148–73

40 Library and Archives Canada, Indian Department Records (RG 10), vol. 245, D. Thornburn to R. Pennefather, Oct. 13, 1858

41 Great Britain, Parliament, *Sessional Papers (Commons)*, vol. 7, "Report of the Select Committee on Aborigines in British Settlement, 26 June, 1837" (London: King's Printer, 1837)

42 See G. R. Mellor, *British Imperial Trusteeship* (London: Faber and Faber, 1951).

43 The comment was made in 1879 by Gilbert Sproat, who then headed up a joint provincial and dominion investigation into the Indian land question. Sproat, cited in Robin Fisher, *Contact and Conflict: Indian-European Relations in British Columbia* (Vancouver: UBC Press, 1992), 192–3

44 To the editor of the *Victoria Standard*, from Father C.J. Grandidier, Okanagan Mission, August 28, 1874, in British Columbia Legislature, *Papers Connected with the Indian Land Question, 1875*, 146–7

45 Tennant, *Aboriginal Peoples and Politics*, 53

46 Attachment to Peter Ayessik to the Superintendent of Indian Affairs, New Westminster, July 14, 1874, in British Columbia Legislature, *Papers Connected with the Indian Land Question*, 136–8

47 Jean Barman, *The West Beyond the West: A History of British Columbia*, rev. ed. (Toronto: University of Toronto Press, 1996), 104

48 Article 13 of the Terms of Union, cited in Robert E. Cail, *Land, Man, and the Law: The Disposal of Crown Lands in British Columbia, 1871–1913* (Vancouver: UBC Press, 1974), 185

49 Cail, *Land, Man, and the Law*, 197–9; Fisher, *Contact and Conflict*, 180–7

50 Wilcomb E. Washburn, *The Governor and the Rebel: A History of Bacon's Rebellion in Virginia* (Chapel Hill: University of North Carolina Press, 1957); Stephen S. Webb, *1676: The End of American Independence* (New York: Alfred A. Knopf, 1984)

51 Roosevelt, *The Winning of the West*, Part IV, 8

52 Enclosure No. 1, Copy of a Report of a Committee of the Honourable Privy Council, approved by His Excellency the Governor General, on Nov. 4, 1874, in E.J. Langevin to the Under- Secretary of State to the Lieutenant-Governor of British Columbia, Nov. 14, 1874, in British Columbia Legislature, *Papers Connected with the Indian Land Question*, 151 (emphasis in original).

53 Enclosure No. 2 in E.J. Langevin to the Under-Secretary of State to the Lieutenant-Governor of British Columbia, Nov. 14, 1874, Memo of David Laird, Minister of the Interior, Nov. 2, 1874, ibid., 151–6

54 Provincial Archives, Victoria, David Mills to I.W. Powell, Aug. 2, 1877, cited in Wilson Duff, *The Indian History of British Columbia: The Impact of the White Man*, new ed. (Victoria: Royal British Columbia Museum, 1997), 93

55 Royal Proclamation of 1763, in Ian A.L. Getty and Antoine S. Lussier, eds., *As Long as the Sun Shines and Water Flows: A Reader in Canadian Native Studies* (Vancouver: UBC Press, 1983), 35

56 Tennant, *Aboriginal Peoples and Politics*, 215–18

57 Michael Asch, "First Nations and the Derivation of Canada's Underlying Title: Comparing Perspectives on Legal Ideology," in Curtis Cook and Juan D. Lindau, eds., *Aboriginal Rights and Self-Government: The Canadian and Mexican Experience in North American Perspective* (Montreal: McGill-Queen's University Press, 2000), 165

58 Roosevelt, *The Winning of the West*, Part IV, 7–8

59 Enclosure in Lytton to Governor Douglas, Sept. 2, 1858, in British Columbia Legislature, *Papers Connected with the Indian Land Question*, 13–14

60 Lytton to Governor Douglas, Sept. 2, 1858, ibid., 12

61 Lytton to Governor Douglas, Dec. 30, 1858, ibid., 15

62 G. Columbia to Secretary of State for the Colonies, May 27, 1871, enclosure in Joseph Howe, Secretary of State for the Provinces, to the Lieutenant-Governor of British Columbia, July 21, 1871, ibid., 97–8

63 John Webster Grant, *Moon of Wintertime: Missionaries and the Indians of Canada in Encounter since 1534* (Toronto: University of Toronto Press, 1992), 125–9

64 See A.G. Morice, *The History of the Northern Interior of British Columbia* (Fairfield, Wash.: Ye Galleon Press, 1971); David Mulhall, *Will to Power: The Missionary Career of Father Morice* (Vancouver: UBC Press, 1986).

65 Grant, *Moon of Wintertime*, 127

66 Eugene Stock, *The History of the Church Missionary Society: Its Environment, Its Men and Its Work*, 2 vols. (London: Church Missionary Society, 1899)

67 Henry Venn, *Retrospect and Prospect of the Operations of the Church Missionary Society* (London: Seeley, Jackson and Halliday, 1865)

68 Jean Usher, *William Duncan of Metlakalta: A Victorian Missionary in British Columbia*, National Museum of Man Publications in History, No. 5 (Ottawa: National Museum of Man, 1974)

69 Albert L. Hurtado, *Indian Survival on the California Frontier* (New Haven: Yale University Press, 1988), 47–71

70 David A. Nock, *A Victorian Missionary and Canadian Indian Policy: Cultural Synthesis v. Replacement* (Waterloo, Ont.: Wilfrid Laurier University Press, 1988); Celia Haig-Brown and David Nock, eds., *With Good Intentions: Euro-Canadian and Aboriginal Relations in Colonial Canada* (Vancouver: UBC Press, 2006)

71 Tennant, *Aboriginal Peoples and Politics*, 55

72 See Thomas Crosby, *Up and Down the Pacific Coast by Canoe and Mission Ship* (Toronto: Missionary Society of the Methodist Church, 1914).

73 Tennant, *Aboriginal Peoples and Politics*, 78–9

74 Brian Titley, *A Narrow Vision: Duncan Campbell Scott and the Administration of Indian Affairs in Canada* (Vancouver: UBC Press, 1986), 135–61; Robert Exell, "History of Native Claims in B.C.," *The Advocate*, vol. 48, part 6, Dec. 1990, 866–80

75 On James Teit, see http://www.abcbookworld.com/view_author.php?id=1107.

76 E. Palmer Patterson II, "Andrew Paull and the Canadian Indian Resurgence" (PhD thesis, University of Washington, 1962); Herbert Francis Dunlop, *Andy Paull: As I Knew Him and Understand His Times* (Vancouver: Standard Press, 1989)

77 Alan Morley, *Roar of the Breakers: A Biography of Peter Kelly* (Toronto: Ryerson Press, 1967)

78 S. James Anaya, *Indigenous Peoples in International Law* (Oxford: Oxford University Press, 2000); Ronald Niezen, "Recognizing Indigenism: Canadian

Unity and the International Movement of Indigenous Peoples," *Comparative Studies in Society and History* 42, 1 (2000): 119–48

79 John Womack, *Zapata and the Mexican Revolution* (New York: Vintage, 1969)

80 David Batsone, Bishop Samuel Ruiz and the Zapatistas, at http://www.aislingmagazine.com/aislingmagazine/articles/TAM19/Ruiz.html; Julia Preston, "Foes of Rebels Attack Bishop," *New York Times*, Nov. 8, 1997; Preston, "Chiapas Bishop Follows Rule," *New York Times*, Nov. 4, 1997; Jim Tuck, "Bartolome De Las Casas: Father of Liberation Theology," at http://www.mexconnect.com/mex_/history/jtuck/jtbartolome.html

81 George Manuel and Michael Posluns, *The Fourth World: An Indian Reality* (Toronto: Collier-Macmillan, 1974); Peter McFarlane, *Brotherhood to Nationhood: George Manuel and the Modern Indian Movement* (Toronto: Between the Lines, 1993)

CHAPTER TEN

1 See, for instance, the Declaration of Interdependence drafted at the Rio Conference in 1992 by members of the Rio Conference at http://www.davidsuzuki.org/About_us/Declaration_of_Interdependence.asp.

2 Charles Taylor, *Modern Social Imaginaries* (Durham, NC: Duke University Press, 2004)

3 Kevin Phillips, *The Cousins' War: Religion, Politics, and the Triumph of Anglo-America* (New York: Basic Books, 1999), xiv

4 Kevin Phillips, *Bad Money: Reckless Finance, Failed Politics, and the Global Crisis of American Capitalism* (New York: Viking, 2008), 124

5 Abraham Lincoln cited at http://showcase.netins.net/web/creative/lincoln/speeches/congress.htm

6 David Brion Davis, *The Rise and Fall of Slavery in the New World* (New York: Oxford University Press, 2006); Carl Degler, *Neither Black nor White: Slavery and Race Relations in Brazil and the United States* (Madison: University of Wisconsin Press, 1986)

7 Abraham Lincoln cited at http://showcase.netins.net/web/creative/lincoln/speeches/gettysburg.htm

8 President George W. Bush's speech of May 1, 2003, as posted on the US White House's website

9 Fred Anderson and Andrew Cayton, *The Dominion of War: Empire and Liberty in North America, 1500–2000* (New York: Viking, 2005), 423

10 Arthur C. Parker, *The Life of General Ely S. Parker: Last Grand Sachem of the Iroquois and General Grant's Military Secretary* (Buffalo: Buffalo Historical Society Publication 23, 1919) William H. Armstrong, *Warrior in Two Camps: Ely S. Parker, Union General and Seneca Chief* (Syracuse: Syracuse University Press, 1978)

11 Theda Perdue, *Slavery and the Evolution of Cherokee Society, 1540–1866* (Knoxville: University of Tennessee Press, 1979)

12 Ronald N. Satz, *American Indian Policy in the Jacksonian Era* (Lincoln: University of Nebraska Press, 1975); Grant Foreman, *Indian Removal: The Emigration of the Five Civilized Tribes of Indians* (Norman: University of Oklahoma Press, 1953)

13 Michael A. Morrison, *Slavery and the American West: The Eclipse of Manifest Destiny and the Coming of the Civil War* (Chapel Hill: University of North Carolina Press, 1997)

14 See William C. MacLeod, *The American Indian Frontier* (New York: A.A. Knopf, 1928); Lyman Abbot, "Proposals for an Indian State, 1778–1878," *Annual Report of the American Historical Association for the Year 1907* (1908), 87–104.

15 Annie H. Abel, *The Slaveholding Indians*, 3 vols.; vol. 1: *The American Indian as Slaveholder and Secessionist*; vol. 2: *The American Indian as Participant in the Civil War*; vol. 3: *The American Indian under Reconstruction* (1915–25; St Clair Shores: Scholarly Press, 1978)

16 Sequoyah's achievement begins a long, detailed history of Indian journalism outlined in James E. Murphy and Sharon M. Murphy, *Let My People Know: American Indian Journalism* (Norman: University of Oklahoma Press, 1981).

17 Marshall's decisions on the disputes between Georgia and the Cherokee are published in Joseph P. Cotton Jr, ed., *The Constitutional Decisions of John Marshall*, 2 vols. (New York: Da Capo Press, 1969), 2: 2–37, 309–20, 334–77.

18 Robert A. Johannsen, *Stephen A. Douglas* (New York: Oxford University Press, 1973)

19 Francis Paul Prucha, *The Great Father: The United States Government and the American Indians*. Abridged Edition (Lincoln: University of Nebraska Press, 1986), 136–51

20 H. Craig Miner, *The Corporation and the Indian: Tribal Sovereignty and Industrial Civilization in Indian Territory, 1865–1907* (Norman: University of Oklahoma Press, 1976)

21 See Ward Churchill, *A Little Matter of Genocide: Holocaust and Denial in the Americas, 1492 to the Present* (Winnipeg: Arbeiter Ring Publishing, 1998), 187–8, 220–2.

22 Ray Allen Billington, *Westward Expansion and the History of the American Frontier* (New York: Macmillan, 1964), 703

23 John G. Shott, *The Railway Monopoly: An Instrument of Banker Control of the American Economy* (Washington: Public Affairs Institute, 1950)

24 Richard C. Cortner, *The Iron Horse and the Constitution: The Railroads and the Fourteenth Amendment* (Westport, Conn.: Greenwood Press, 1993); David C. Korten, *When Corporations Rule the World* (West Hartford, Conn.: Kumarian Press; San Francisco: Berrett-Koehler Publishers, 1996), 59

25 Thom Hartmann, *Unequal Protection: The Rise of Corporate Dominance and the Theft of Human Rights* (New York: Rodale Books, 2002)

26 Sidney L. Harring, *Crow Dog's Case: American Indian Sovereignty, Tribal Law, and United States Law in the Nineteenth Century* (Cambridge: Cambridge University Press, 1994)

27 John R. Wunder, "No More Treaties: The Resolution of 1871 and the Alteration of Indian Rights to Their Homelands," in Wunder, ed. *The Range: Essays on the History of Western Land Management and the Environment* (Westport, Conn.: Greenwood Press, 1985), 39–56

28 Cited in Prucha, *The Great Father*, 165

29 Ibid., 164

30 Ibid., 53

31 Daniel Boorstin, *The Americans: The National Experience* (New York: Vintage, 1967), 263. See Robert M. Utley, *Frontier Regulars: The United States Army and the Indians, 1866–1891* (Albuquerque: University of New Mexico Press, 1973); Robert M. Utley, *The Indian Frontier of the American West, 1846–1890* (Albuquerque: University of New Mexico Press, 1984).

32 Theodore Roosevelt, *The Winning of the West*, 6 vols. (New York: G.P. Putnam's Sons, 1889–96)

33 David H. Burton, *Theodore Roosevelt* (New York: Twayne Publishers, 1972)

34 Angie Debo, *Geronimo: The Man, His Time, His Place* (Norman: University of Oklahoma Press, 1982), 417–19

35 Mark Cocker, *Rivers of Blood, Rivers of Gold: Europe's Conquest of Indigenous Peoples* (New York: Grove Press, 2001), 244–5

36 Brigadier-General George Crook, cited in Dan L. Thrapp, *The Conquest of Apacheria* (Norman: University of Oklahoma Press, 1967), 256

37 Britton Davis, *The Truth about Geromino*, ed. M.M. Quaife (New Haven, Conn.: Yale University Press, 1963), 80

38 Woodward Clum, *Apache Agent: The Story of John P. Clum* (Boston: Houghton Mifflin, 1936), 292

39 Lee Myers, "The Enigma of Mangas Coloradas' Death," *New Mexico Historical Review* 41 (Oct. 1966): 287–304

40 L.C. Hughes of the Tucson, Arizona, *Star*, cited in S.M. Barrett, *Geromino's Story of His Life* (1906; Bowie, Maryland: Heritage Books, no date), 124–5, note 3

41 See Cocker, *Rivers of Blood, Rivers of Gold*, 191; Marc Wortman, *The Millionaires Unit* (New York: Public Affairs, 2006); Webster G. Tarpley and Anton Chaitkin, *George Bush: The Unauthorized Biography* (Joshua Tree: Progressive Press, 2004), chapter 7

42 Odie B. Faulk, *The Geronimo Campaign* (New York: Oxford University Press, 1969)

43 Cocker, *Rivers of Blood, Rivers of Gold*, 216

44 Dan L. Thrapp, *General Crook and the Sierre Madre Adventure* (Norman: University of Oklahoma Press, 1972)

45 Edwin R. Sweeny, *Cochise: Chiricahua Apache Chief* (Norman: University of Oklahoma Press, 1991)

46 Dan L. Thrapp, *Victorio and the Mimbres Apaches* (Norman: University of Oklahoma Press, 1974)

47 Barrett, ed., *Geromino's Story of His Life*, v

48 Ibid., 46

49 William T. Hagan, "Quanah Parker," in R. David Edmunds, ed., *American Indian Leaders: Studies in Diversity* (Lincoln: University of Nebraska Press, 1980), 175–91

50 Benjamin Capps, *The Great Chiefs* (Alexandria, Va: Time-Life Books, 1975), 126

51 See Bea Medicine, "Native American Resistance to Integration: Contemporary Confrontations and Religious Revitalization," *Plains Anthropologist* 26 (1981): 277–86

52 Lieutenant-Colonel George Cook, cited in Keith Wheeler, *The Scouts* (Alexandria, Va: Time-Life Books, 1978), 116

53 Ibid., 173–6

54 Steve Coll, *Ghost Wars: The Secret History of the CIA, Afghanistan and Bin Laden, from the Soviet Invasion to September 10, 2001* (New York: Penguin Books, 2005); George Crile, *Charlie Wilson's War: The Extraordinary Story of the Largest Covert Operation in History* (New York: Atlantic Monthly Press, 2003); Gary Schroen, *First In: An Insider's Account of How the CIA Spearheaded the War on Terror in Afghanistan* (New York: Presidio Press / Ballantine Books, 2005)

55 Alvin M. Josephy Jr, *The Patriot Chiefs: A Chronicle of American Indian Resistance* (New York: Viking Press, 1969)

56 See Ray Allen Billington, *Land of Savagery Land of Promise: The European Image of the American Frontier in the Nineteenth Century* (New York: W.W. Norton, 1981); Henry Nash Smith, *Virgin Land: The American West as Symbol and Myth* (Cambridge, Mass.: Harvard University Press, 1978); David C. Cooke, *Fighting Indians of the West: Gun War on the Frontier* (New York: A Popular Library Eagle Book, 1955).

57 Richard Slotkin, *The Fatal Environment: The Myth of the Frontier in the Age of Industrialization, 1800–1890* (New York: Atheneum, 1985)

58 Walter Hildebrandt and Brian Hubner, *The Cypress Hills: The Land and Its People* (Saskatoon: Purich, 1994)

59 Garret Wilson, *Frontier Farewell: The 1870s and the End of the Old West* (Regina: University of Regina Press / Canadian Plains Research Centre, 2007), 299–367

60 Colonel Macleod and Sitting Bull, cited in C. Frank Turner, *Across the Medicine Line: The Epic Confrontation between Sitting Bull and the North-West Mounted Police* (Toronto: McClelland & Stewart, 1973), 135–6

61 Grant MacEwan, *Sitting Bull: The Years in Canada* (Edmonton: Hurtig, 1973)

62 David Mills, cited in Alexander Morris, *The Treaties of Canada with the Indians of Manitoba and the North-West Territories* (Toronto: Belfords, Clarke and Co., 1880), 283

63 See Donald B. Russell, *The Lives and Legends of Buffalo Bill* (Norman: University of Oklahoma Press, 1960); Robert M. Utley, *The Lance and the Shield: The Life and Times of Sitting Bull* (New York: Henry Holt, 1993).

64 Elizabeth Beck Kehoe, *The Ghost Dance: Ethnohistory and Revitalization* (Chicago: Holt, Rhinehart and Winston, 1989)

65 See Richard Drinnon, "The Metaphysics of Dancing Tribes," in Calvin Martin, ed., *The American Indian and the Problem of History* (New York: Oxford University Press, 1887), 106–13.

66 Ibid., 281–307; James Mooney, *The Ghost Dance Religion and Wounded Knee* (1896; New York: Dover Publications, 1973)

67 Jerry Keenan, *Encyclopedia of American Indian Wars, 1492–1890* (Santa Barbara, Cal.: ABC-CLIO Press, 1997)

68 Dee Brown, *Bury My Heart at Wounded Knee: An Indian History of the American West* (New York: Holt, Rinehart and Winston, 1970)

69 Frederick Jackson Turner, "The Significance of the Frontier in American History," in Walker Wyman and Clifton B. Kroeber, eds., *The Frontier in Perspective* (Madison: University of Wisconsin Press, 1965), 1

70 John Dunn Hunter, cited in Richard Drinnon, *White Savage: The Case of John Dunn Hunter* (New York: Schocken Books, 1972), 40

71 John G. Neihardt, *Black Elk Speaks: Being the Life Story of a Holy Man of the Oglala Sioux* (1932; Lincoln: University of Nebraska Press, 1984), 288–90

72 Daniel Francis, *The Imaginary Indian: The Image of the Indian in Canadian Culture* (Vancouver: Arsenal Pulp Press, 1993); Marilyn Burgess and Gail Gutherie Valaskakis, *Indian Princesses and Cowgirls: Stereotypes from the Frontier* (Montreal: Oboro, 1995); Robert F. Berkhofer Jr, *The White Man's Indian: Images of the American Indian from Columbus to the Present* (New York: Alfred A. Knopf, 1978); Roy Harvey Pearce, *Savagism and Civilization: A Study of the Indian in the American Mind* (Baltimore, Md: Johns Hopkins Press, 1965)

73 George Catlin, *Letters and Notes on the Manners, Customs, and Conditions of the North American Indian*, 2 vols. (1844; New York: Dover, 1973), 1: 18. Emphasis in original

74 Chief White Calf, cited in Mark David Spence, *Dispossessing the Wilderness: Indian Removal and the Making of the National Parks* (New York: Oxford University Press, 1999), 80

75 Land Cession of 1895, cited ibid.

76 Gerald A. Diettert, *Grinnell's Glacier: George Bird Grinnell and Glacier National Park* (Missoula, Mont.: Mountain Press, 1992)

77 Warren L. Hanna, *The Life and Times of James Willard Schultz (Apikuni)* (Norman: University of Oklahoma Press, 1986)

78 See, for instance, George Bird Grinnell, *Blackfoot Lodge Tales* (New York: Scribner's, 1892); James Willard Schultz, *Blackfoot Tales of Glacier National Park* (Boston: Houghton Mifflin, 1916).

79 James Willard Schultz, *My Life as an Indian* (Boston: Houghton Mifflin, 1914)

80 Grinnell's review, cited by Eugene Lee Silliman, Introduction to James Willard Schultz, *Many Srange Characters: Montana Frontier Tales* (Norman: University of Oklahoma Press, 1982), ix

81 Robert H. Keller and Michael F. Turek, *American Indians and National Parks* (Tucson: University of Arizona Press, 1998), 57

82 Grey Owl, *The Adventures of Sajo and Her Beaver People* (London: Lovat Dickson and Thompson Ltd, 1935)

83 J.B. Harkin to Roy A. Gibson, assistant deputy minister of the interior, April 25, 1937, cited in Donald B. Smith, *From the Lands of Shadows: The Making of Grey Owl* (Saskatoon: Western Producer Prairie Books, 1990), 157

84 See Lovat Dickson, *Wilderness Man: The Strange Story of Grey Owl* (Toronto: Macmillan, 1973).

85 Peter Iverson, *Carlos Montezuma and the Changing World of American Indians* (Albuquerque: University of New Mexico Press, 1982)

86 Laurence M. Hauptman, *The Iroquois and the New Deal* (Syracuse: Syracuse University Press, 1981)

87 Peter Kulchyski, "'A Considerable Unrest': F.O. Loft and the League of Indians," *Native Studies Review* 4, 1 and 2 (1988): 95–117

88 Norma Sluman and Jean Cuthand Goodwill, *John Tootoosis: A Biography* (Ottawa: Golden Dog Press, 1982)

89 E. Palmer Patterson, "Andy Paull and Canadian Indian Resurgence" (PhD thesis, University of Washington, 1962)

90 Clinton Rickard, *Fighting Tuscarora: The Autobiography of Clinton Rickard* (Syracuse: Syracuse University Press, 1994)

91 John L. Tobias, "Canada's Subjugation of the Crees, 1879–1885," *Canadian Historical Review* 64, 4 (1983): 519–48; Hugh A. Demsey, *Big Bear: The End of Freedom* (Vancouver: Douglas and McIntyre, 1984)

92 Scott M. Williams, "Tradition and Change in the Subarctic: Sami Reindeer Herding in the Modern Era," *Scandanavian Studies* 75 (June 2003)

93 Grey Owl's 1936 speech to the Empire Club of Toronto, "Grey Owl: 'After a Thing Like That a Man Doesn't Mind Missing a Meal,'" republished in *Globe and Mail*, Oct. 1, 1999, A9

94 Jim Igoe, *Conservation and Globalization: A Study of National Parks and Indigenous Communities from East Africa to South Dakota* (Belmont, Cal.: Thomson / Wadsworth, 2004)

95 Julio Cesar Centeno and Christopher Elliot, "Forest Home: The Place Where One Belongs, Yanomami of Venezuela," in Elizabeth Kemf, ed., *The Law of the Mother: Protecting Indigenous Peoples in Protected Areas* (San Francisco: Sierra Club Books, 1993), 95–103

96 Elaine Dewar, *Cloak of Green: The Links between Key Environmental Groups, Government and Big Business* (Toronto: James Lorimer, 1995)

97 Penny Dransart, "Cultural Tourism in an Interconnected World: Tensions and Aspirations in Latin America," in Claire Smith and Graeme K. Ward, eds., *Indigenous Cultures in an Interconnected World* (St Leonards, NSW, Australia: Allen and Unwin, 2000), 145–64; Valene L. Smith, "Indigenous Tourism: The Four H's," in R. Butler and T. Hinch, eds., *Tourism and Indigenous Peoples* (London: International Thomson Business Press, 1996), 283–307

98 Cocker, *Rivers of Blood, Rivers of Gold*, 259

99 Francis P. Prucha, *American Indian Policy in Crisis: Christian Reformers and the Indian, 1865–1900* (Norman: University of Oklahoma Press, 1976)

100 See Delos S. Otis, *The Dawes Act and the Allotment of Indian Lands* (Norman: University of Oklahoma Press, 1973); Terry L. Anderson, *Sovereign Nations or*

Reservations? An Economic History of American Indians (San Francisco: Pacific
Institute for Public Policy, 1995), 89–137.

101 Arrell M. Gibson, "Indian Land Transfers," in *Handbook of North American Indians*,
vol. 4: *History of Indian-White Relations*, ed. Wilcomb E. Washburn (Washington,
DC: Smithsonian Institution, 1988), 227; see Paul Wallace Gates, *History of
Public Land Law Development* (Washington, DC: US Government Printing Office,
1968); Louise E. Peffer, *The Closing of the Public Domain: Disposal and Reservation
Policies, 1900–1950* (Stanford, Cal.: Stanford University Press, 1951).

102 See Sidney Harring, *Crow Dog's Case: American Indian Sovereignty, Tribal
Law, and the United States in the Nineteenth Century* (Cambridge: Cambridge
University Press, 1994), 159.

103 William T. Hagan, *American Indians* (Chicago: University of Chicago Press,
1974), 147

104 Ibid., 146. See Leonard A. Carlson, *Indians Bureaucrats and Land: The Dawes Act
and the Decline of Indian Farming* (Westport, Conn.: Greenwood Press, 1981).

105 Donald L. Fixico, *Termination and Relocation, 1945–1960* (Albuquerque:
University of New Mexico Press, 1986). On the issue of federal trust respon-
sibilities for Indians in the United States, see Hank Adams et al., *Report on
Trust Responsibilities and the Federal-Indian Relationship, Including Treaty Review:
Final Report to the American Indian Policy Review Commission* (Washington, DC:
US Government Printing Office, 1976).

106 On the effects of termination, see Susan Hood, "Termination and the
Klamath Tribe in Oregon," *Ethnohistory* 19 (fall 1972): 379–92; Nancy O.
Lurie, "Menominee Termination: From Reservation to Colony," *Human
Organization* 31 (fall 1972): 257–70.

107 Supreme Court ruling on *Hee-Hit-Ton Indians v. the United States*, 1955, cited in
Ward Churchill, "The Tragedy and the Travesty: The Subversion of Indigenous
Sovereignty in North America," in Troy R. Johnson, ed., *Contemporary Native
American Political Issues* (Walnut Creek: Altamira Press, 1999), 28

108 Robert H. Jackson, *The Nürnberg Case as Presented by Robert H. Jackson* (New
York: Cooper Square Publishers, 1971), xv

109 Richard Drinnon, *Keeper of Concentration Camps: Dillon S. Myer and American
Racism* (Berkeley: University of California Press, 1987), xxviii

110 Jay Brian Nash, *The New Deal for the Indians: A Survey of the Workings of the
Indian Reorganization Act of 1934* (New York: Academy Press, 1938); Graham
D. Taylor, *The New Deal and American Indian Tribalism: The Administration of the
Indian Reorganization Act, 1934–45* (Lincoln: University of Nebraska Press,
1980); Lawrence M. Hauptman, *The Iroquois and the New Deal* (Syracuse, NY:
Syracuse University Press, 1981); Kenneth R. Philp, ed., *Indian Self-Rule: First-
Hand Accounts of Indian-White Relations from Roosevelt to Reagan* (Salt Lake City,
Utah: Institute of the American West, 1986)

111 Diamond Jenness, *Indians of Canada* (1932; Toronto: University of Toronto
Press, 1989), 264

112 Peter Kulchyski, "Anthropology in the Service of the State: Diamond Jenness
and Canadian Indian Policy," *Journal of Canadian Studies* 28, 2 (1993): 33–38

113 John Cooper, *Breaking the Heart of the World: Woodrow Wilson and the Fight for the
League of Nations* (Cambridge: Cambridge University Press, 2001); Thomas

Knock, *To End All Wars: Woodrow Wilson and the Quest for a New World Order* (Princeton, NJ: Princeton University Press, 1995)

114 Alan Knight, "Racism, Revolution, and *Indigenismo*: Mexico, 1910–1940," in Richard Graham, ed., *The Idea of Race in Latin America, 1870–1940* (Austin: University of Texas Press, 1990)

115 John Collier, *Indians of the Americas* (New York: W.W. Norton, 1947); John Collier, *From Every Zenith: A Memoir and Some Essays on Life and Thought* (Denver: Sage Books, 1963); John Collier, *On the Gleaming Way* (Denver: Sage Books, 1962)

116 *Jaime in Taos: The Taos Papers of Jaime de Angulo*, Gui de Angulo, comp. (San Francisco: City Lights Books, 1985)

117 Collier, *Indians of the Americas*, 26

118 Ibid., 24

119 Ibid., 23–4

120 Ibid., 25

121 Ibid., 15

122 Ibid., 28

123 Ibid., 19–20

124 See Lawrence C. Kelly, *The Assault on Assimilation: John Collier and the Origins of Indian Policy Reform* (Albuquerque: University of New Mexico Press, 1983).

125 Collier, *Indians of the Americas*, 16–17

126 See James Harold, *The End of Globalization: Lessons from the Great Depression* (Cambridge Mass.: Harvard University Press, 2002).

127 Joseph Bruner, cited in Donald A. Grinde Jr, "Nationalism, Pan-Indianism, and American Indian Resistance Movements in the United States, 1933–1973," unpublished paper given at the American Historical Association Meeting in Washington, DC, Dec. 28, 1992, 8

128 Collier, *Indians of the Americas*, 27–28

129 Ruth Benedict, *Patterns of Culture* (1934; Boston: Houghton Mifflin, 1959)

130 Lawrence C. Kelly, "Anthropology and Anthropologists in the Indian New Deal," *Journal of Behavioral Sciences* 16 (Jan. 1980): 6–24. For a critical view of the legacy of Collier's social scientists, see Guy B. Senese, *Self-Determination and the Social Education of Native Americas* (New York: Praeger, 1991).

131 See Robert A. Hecht, *Oliver LaFarge: A Biography* (Metuchen, NJ: Scarecrow Press, 1991).

132 See Dorothy R. Parker, *Singing an Indian Song: A Biography of D'Arcy McNickle* (Lincoln: University of Nebraska Press, 1992); D'Arcy McNickle, *Native American Tribalism: Indian Survivals and Renewals* (New York: Oxford University Press, 1973); D'Arcy McNickle and Harold E. Fay, *Indians and Other Americans: Two Ways of Life Meet* (New York: Harper and Row, 1959).

CHAPTER ELEVEN

1 Richard Rhodes, *The Making of the Atomic Bomb* (New York: Simon and Schuster, 1986); Jennet Conant, *Tuxedo Park: A Wall Street Tycoon and the Secret*

Palace of Science That Changed the Course of World War II (New York: Simon
and Schuster, 2002); Robert Buderi, *The Invention That Changed the World:
How a Small Group of Radar Pioneers Won the Second World War and Launched
the Technological Revolution* (New York: Simon and Schuster, 1996); Stephen
Budiansky, *Battle of Wits: The Complete Story of Code Breaking in World War II* (New
York: Free Press, 2000); Thomas Powers, *Heisenberg's War: The Secret History of
the German Bomb* (New York: Knopf, 1993) John Cornwell, *Hitler's Scientists:
Science, War, and the Devil's Pact* (New York: Viking, 2003)

2 V.I. Lenin, *Imperialism, the Highest Stage of Capitalism: A Popular Outline* (1916;
Moscow: Progress Publishers, 1966)

3 Arno J. Mayer, *Political Origins of the New Diplomacy, 1917–1918* (New York:
Vintage Books, 1970)

4 Stephen C. Schlesinger, *Act of Creation: The Founding of the United Nations*
(Boulder Col.: Westview Press, 2004)

5 Lawrence H. Shoup and William Minter, *Imperial Brain Trust: The Council on
Foreign Relations and United States Foreign Policy* (New York: Monthly Review
Press, 1977); Michael Wala, *The Council on Foreign Relations and American
Foreign Policy in the Early Cold War* (Providence: Berghahn Books, 1994)

6 Basil Davidson, *The Black Man's Burden: Africa and the Curse of the Nation State*
((New York: Times Books, 1992)

7 Gordon Brothers, *Book of the Fourth World: Reading the Native Americas Through
Their Literature* (Cambridge: Cambridge University Press, 1992)

8 Menno Boldt, *Surviving as Indians: The Challenge of Self-Government* (Toronto:
University of Toronto Press, 1993)

9 See Gideon Gottlieb, *Nation against State: A New Approach to Ethnic Conflicts and
the Decline of Sovereignty* (New York: Council on Foreign Relations, 1993).

10 Margaret MacMillan, *Paris 1919: Six Months That Changed the World* (New York:
Random House, 2003), xxx, xxviii.

11 Sally M. Weaver, "Six Nations of the Grand River, Ontario," *in Handbook
of North American Indians*, vol. 15: *Northeast*, Bruce G. Trigger, vol. ed.
(Washington: Smithsonian Institution, 1978), 525–36

12 Francis Jennings et al. eds., *The History and Culture of Iroquois Diplomacy: An
Interdisciplinary Guide to the Treaties of the Six Nations and Their League* (Syracuse,
NY: Syracuse University Press, 1985)

13 Anthony Hall, *The American Empire and the Fourth World* (Montreal: McGill-
Queen's University Press, 2005), 490–5

14 Allan Maclean to Sir Frederick Haldimand, May 18, 1783, cited in *The Valley
of the Six Nations: A Collection of Documents on the Indian Lands of the Grand River*
(Toronto: The Champlain Society and the University of Toronto Press, 1971),
36

15 W.E. Burghardt Du Bois, *The World and Africa: An Inquiry into the Part Which
Africa Has Played in World History* (1946; New York: International Publishers,
1969), 1–15

16 David Levering Lewis, *W.E.B. Du Bois: Biography of a Race, 1868–1919* (New
York: Henry Holt, 1993), 574–8

17 *Chicago Tribune,* Jan. 19, 1919, cited in Du Bois, *The World and Africa,* 8–9

18 Du Bois, *The World and Africa,* 240, 238

19 Elliot Rudwick, *W.E.B. Du Bois: Voice of the Black Protest Movement* (Urbana: University of Illinois Press, 1982), 208–35

20 Resolution of the Pan-African Congress in Paris, 1919, cited in Du Bois, *The World and Africa,* 11–12

21 Rudwick, *W.E.B. Du Bois,* 221–2

22 International Labour Office, *Indigenous Peoples: Living and Working Conditions of Aboriginal Populations in Independent Countries,* Studies and Reports, New Series, no. 35 (Geneva: International Labour Office, 1953), 582–601

23 Resolution of the Second Pan-African Congress in Paris, 1921, cited in Du Bois, *Africa and the World,* 239

24 Rolf Knight, *Indians at Work: An Informal History of Native Indian Labour in British Columbia, 1858–1930* (Vancouver: New Star Books, 1978)

25 Lieutenant Fred Loft, cited in Peter Kulchyski, "'A Considerable Unrest': F.O. Loft and the League of Indians," *Native Studies Review* 4, 1 & 2 (1988): 100–1

26 International Labour Office, *Official Bulletin,* vol. 72, Series A, no. 2, 1989, 59–70

27 See Alejandra Morgado Zacarias and Herlinda Zacarias Hernandez, "The Implementation of an International Convention in Mexico," in Marie Léger, ed., *Aboriginal Peoples: Toward Self-Government* (Montreal: Black Rose Books, 1994), 31–8.

28 Jeff Sallot, "Anti-US Protests Mar Summit of the Americas," *Globe and Mail,* Nov. 5, 2005, A17

29 Tecumseh, "Sleep No Longer, O Choctaws and Chichasaws," speech delivered in 1811, in W.C. Vanderwerth, *Indian Oratory: Famous Speeches by Noted Indian Chieftains* (Norman: University of Oklahoma Press, 1979), 63

30 Nicholas A. Robins, *Native Insurgencies and the Genocidal Impulse in the Americas* (Bloomington: Indiana University Press, 2005)

31 The word genocide was first used by Raphael Lemkin in *Axis Rule in Occupied Europe* (Concord: Rumford Press, 1944); see Robert Davis and Mark Zannis, *The Genocide Machine in Canada: The Pacification of the North* (Montreal: Black Rose Books, 1973).

32 The Honourable Madame Justice Louise Arbour, "The Genesis of International Justice: from an Impossible Marriage of Law to the Promising End of Impunity," *McGill International Review* 1 (winter 2000): 8–13; Erna Paris, *The Sun Climbs Slow: Justice in the Age of Imperial America* (Toronto: Knopf Canada, 2008)

33 Henry Wallace, *The Century of the Common Man,* ed. Russell Lord (New York; Yeynal and Hitcock, 1943), 14–17

34 Henry Luce, "The American Century," *Life,* Feb. 17, 1941, 61–5

35 John P. Humphrey, *Human Rights and the United Nations: A Great Adventure* (Dobbs Ferry, NY: Transnational Publishers, 1984), 12–13

36 Paul A.W. Wallace, *The White Roots of Peace* (Philadelphia: University of Pennsylvania Press, 1946)

37 Norma Sluman and Jean Goodwill, *John Tootoosis: A Biography of a Cree Leader* (Ottawa: Golden Dog Press, 1982), 177–85; Donald B. Smith, "Amerindians in Quebec and Canada, Half-a-Century Ago – and Today," in Laurier Turgeon, Denys Delange, and Réal Oulette, eds., *Transferts culturels et métissages Amérique/Europe, XVIe–XXe siècle, Cultural Transfer, America and Europe: 500 Years of Interculturation* (Quebec: Les Presses de l'Université Laval, 1996), 135

38 Archives Deschatelet, Ottawa, Doc ID: 276, HR 6060.C73R101-101, James Fox and Jules Sioui to Prime Minister Mackenzie King, Detroit, Sept. 15, 1945

39 Jules Sioui, *War ... Peace in Canada. The Invaders Responsible for the Death of Louis Riel* (Loretteville: The Indian Nation of North America, 1944); Jules Sioui, *What Are We Coming to Be Here? Where Are You Going? Who Is Your Master? Remember That the American Soil Is an Indian Possession* (Loretteville: The Indian Nation of North America, nd). See Fred Gaffen, *Forgotten Soldiers* (Penticton, BC, Theytus Books, 1985).

40 The North American Indian Constitution Act, Archives Deschatelet, Ottawa, Doc ID: 276, HR 6060.C73R101-101

41 E. Palmer Patterson II, "Andy Paull and the Canadian Indian Resurgence" (PhD thesis, University of Washington, 1962)

42 See Gaffen, *Forgotten Soldiers.*

43 Francis Paul Prucha, *The Great Father*, vol. 2 (Lincoln: University of Nebraska Press, 1984), 1006

44 John Collier, "The Indian in a Wartime Nation," *Annals of the American Academy of Political and Social Science*, no. 223 (Sept. 1942): 30

45 Norman Rich, *Hitler's War Aims*, 2 vols. (London: Andre Deutsch, 1973, 1974), 1: 8

46 H.D. Rosenthal, *Their Day in Court: A History of the Indian Claims Commission* (New York: Garland Publishing, 1990)

47 See Alan L. Sorkin, *American Indians and Federal Aid* (Washington: Brookings Institution, 1971), 137; Donald Fixico, *Termination and Relocation: Federal Indian Policy, 1945-1960* (Albuquerque: University of New Mexico Press, 1985), 21–44

48 Nell Jessup Newton, "Compensation, Reparations and Restitution: Indian Property Claims in the United States," *Georgia Law Review* 28 (1994): 453–79

49 Mario Ganzalez and Elizabeth Cook-Lynne, *The Politics of Hallowed Ground: Wounded Knee and the Struggle for Indian Sovereignty* (Urbana and Chicago: University of Illinois Press, 1999), 6

50 See William N. Fenton, "Ethnohistory and Its Problems," *Ethnohistory* 9 (winter 1962): 1–23. Fenton's career is honoured, described, and elaborated on in Michael K. Foster, Jack Campisi, and Miarianne Mithun, eds., *Extending the Rafters: Interdisciplinary Approaches to Iroquoian Studies* (Albany: State University of New York Press, 1984).

51 See Christine Bolt, *American Indian Policy and American Reform: Case Studies of the Campaign to Assimilate the American Indians* (London: Allen and Unwin, 1987), 189–208.

52 Vine Deloria Jr, *Custer Died for Your Sins: An Indian Manifesto* (New York: Macmillan, 1969), 83–104

53 Elizabeth Clark Rosenthal, "'Culture' and the American Indian Community," in Stuart Levine and Nancy O. Lurie, eds., *The American Indian Today* (Baltimore: Penguin, 1970), 88

54 Mahmood Mamdani, *Citizen and Subject: Contemporary Africa and the Legacy of Late Colonialism* (Princeton: Princeton University Press, 1996)

55 On institutional assimilation in Indian policy, see Menno Boldt and J. Anthony Long, "Native Indian Self-Government: Instrument of Autonomy or Assimilation," in Long and Boldt, eds., *Governments in Conflict? Provinces and Indian Nations in Canada* (Toronto: University of Toronto Press, 1988), 38–56.

56 Rupert Costo, in Kenneth R. Philp, ed., *Indian Self-Rule: First-Hand Accounts of Indian-White Relations from Roosevelt to Reagan* (Salt Lake City: Howe Brothers, 1986), 48. For a vigorous defence of the IRA, see Wilcomb E. Washburn, "A Fifty-Year Perspective on the Indian Re-Organization Act," *American Anthropologist* 86 (June 1984): 9–28.

57 Rolland Dewing, *Wounded Knee: The Meaning and Significance of the Second Incident,* 2nd ed. (New York: Irvington Publishers, 1995)

58 Ken Stern, *Loud Hawk: The U.S. Versus the American Indian Movement* (Norman: University of Oklahoma Press, 1994)

59 See Benjamin Barber, *Jihad vs. McWorld* (New York: Times Books, 1995).

60 Edwin F. Walker, "World Crops Derived from the Indians," *Southwest Museum Leaflets* 17 (Los Angeles: Southwest Museum, 1967); Alfred W. Crosby, *The Columbian Exchange: Biological and Cultural Consequences of 1492* (Westport, Conn.: Greenwood Press, 1972); Virgil J. Vogel, *American Indian Medicine* (Norman: University of Oklahoma Press, 1970); F.W. Waugh, *Iroquois Foods and Food Preparation,* Memoirs of the Canadian Geological Survey, vol. 6 (Ottawa: Department of Mines, Geological Survey, memoir 86, 1916); Arthur C. Parker, *Iroquois Uses of Maize and Other Food Plants* (Albany: New York State Museum Bulletin 144, 1910); John Bierhorst, *The Way of the Earth: Native America and the Environment* (New York: William Morrow, 1994); John Bierhorst, *Four Masterworks of American Indian Literature* (New York: Farrar, Straus and Giroux, 1974); José Barriero, ed., *Indian Roots of American Democracy* (Ithica, NY: Akwe: Kon Press, Cornell University, 1992); Jack Weatherford, *Indian Givers: How the Indians of the Americas Transformed the World* (New York: Crown Publishers, 1988); Warren Lowes, *Indian Giver: A Legacy of North American Indian Peoples* (Penticton, BC: Theytus Books, 1986)

61 See Ward Churchill, *Fantasies of the Master Race: Literature, Cinema and the Colonization of American Indians* (Monroe, Maine: Common Courage Press, 1992); Gretchen M. Bataille and Charles L.P. Silet, eds., *The Pretend Indians: Images of Native Americans in the Movies* (Ames: Iowa State University Press, 1980); Jon Tuska, *The American West in Film: Critical Approaches to the Western* (Westport, Conn.: Greenwood Press, 1985); Ralph and Natasha Friar, *The Only Good Indian ... The Hollywood Gospel* (New York: Drama Book Specialists,

1972); Michael Hilger, *The American Indian in Film* (Metuchen, NJ: Scarecrow Press, 1986); John E. O'Connor, *The Hollywood Indian: Stereotypes of Native Americans in Film* (Trenton: New Jersey State Museum, 1980); John A. Price, *Native Studies: American and Canadian Indians* (Toronto: McGraw-Hill Ryerson, 1978), 200–25; Elizabeth Bird, ed., *Dressing in Feathers: The Construction of the Indian in American Popular Culture* (Boulder, Col.: Westview Press, 1996); William Raymond Stedman, *Shadows of the Indian: Stereotypes in American Culture* (Norman: University of Oklahoma Press, 1982).

62 See, for instance, Gerald Vizenor's unflattering chapter on Dennis Banks in *The People Named Chippewa: Narrative Histories* (Minneapolis: University of Minnesota Press, 1984), 124–38.

63 See Russell Means, with Marvin J. Wolf, *Where White Men Fear to Tread: The Autobiography of Russell Means* (New York: St Martin's Press, 1995), 510–17.

64 Huge A. Dempsey, *Big Bear: The End of Freedom* (Lincoln: University of Nebraska Press, 1984); W.A. Waiser and Blair Stonechild, *Loyal Til Death: Indians and the Northwest Rebellion* (Markham: Fitzhenry and Whiteside, 1997)

65 http://www.ainc-inac.gc.ca/nr/nwltr/bae/fm03/fm01_e.html

66 Treaty Six Chiefs, "Opening Statement to National Treaty Conference," conference held in Edmonton, Alberta, April 6 to 9, 1992, photocopy, 4–5. Emphasis in original

67 Francis Jennings, *Empire of Fortune: Crown, Colonies and Tribes in the Seven Years' War in America* (New York: W.W. Norton, 1990)

68 See James Tully, *Strange Multiplicity: Constitutionalism in a Age of Diversity* (Cambridge: Cambridge University Press, 1995).

69 Max Ferrand, "The Indian Boundary Line," *American Historical Review* 10 (July 1905): 782–91

70 Sally Weaver, *Making Canadian Indian Policy: The Hidden Agenda, 1968–1970* (Toronto: University of Toronto Press, 1981)

71 Guy Laforest, Louis Balthazar, and Vincent Lemieux, eds., *Le Québec et la restructuration du Canada, 1980–1992* (Sillery, Que.: Les éditions de Septentrion, 1991); Guy Laforest, *Trudeau and the End of the Canadian Dream*, trans. Paul Leduc Brown and Michelle Weinroth (Montreal: McGill-Queen's University Press, 1995); Reg Whitaker, *A Sovereign Idea: Essays on Canada as a Democratic Community* (Montreal: McGill-Queen's University Press, 1992); Jeremy Weber, *Reimagining Canada: Language, Culture, Community, and the Canadian Constitution* (Montreal: McGill-Queen's University Press, 1994); Alan Cairns, *Charter versus Federalism: The Dilemmas of Constitutional Reform* (Montreal: McGill-Queen's University Press, 1992); Ramsay Cook, *Canada, Quebec and the Uses of Nationalism* (Toronto: McClelland & Stewart, 1986); Kenneth McRoberts, *English Canada and Québec: Avoiding the Issue* (Toronto: Robarts Centre for Canadian Studies, 1991); Robert C. Vipond, *Liberty and Community: Canadian Federalism and the Failure of the Constitution* (Albany: State University of New York Press, 1991); Charles Taylor, *Reconciling the Solitudes: Essays on Canadian Federalism and Nationalism* (Montreal: McGill-Queen's University Press, 1993)

72 On Indigenous peoples as founding peoples, see Olive Patricia Dickason, *Canada's First Nations: A History of Founding Peoples from Earliest Times*, 2nd ed. (Toronto: Oxford University Press, 1997); on Québécois nationalism, see Susan Mann Tofimenkoff, *The Dream of a Nation: A Social and Intellectual History of Quebec* (Toronto: Gage, 1983); Ramsay Cook, ed., *French-Canadian Nationalism: An Anthology* (Toronto: Macmillan, 1969); John Saywell, *The Rise of the Parti Québécois, 1967–1976* (Toronto: University of Toronto Press, 1977); Michael D. Behiels, *Prelude to the Quiet Revolution: Liberalism versus Neo-Nationalism, 1945–1960* (Montreal: McGill-Queen's University Press, 1985); Leon Dion, *Le Duel Constitutionnel Québec-Canada* (Montreal Les Éditions du Boréal, 1995).

73 Douglas E. Sanders, "The Indian Lobby," in Keith Banting and Richard Simeon, eds., *And No One Cheered: Federalism, Democracy and the Constitution Act* (Toronto: Methuen, 1983), 301–32; Michael Woodward and Bruce George, "The Canadian Indian Lobby in Westminster, 1979–1982," *Journal of Canadian Studies* 18, 3 (1983): 119–26

74 Royal Commission on Aboriginal Peoples, *Partners in Confederation: Aboriginal Peoples, Self-Government and the Constitution* (Ottawa: Minister of Supply and Services, 1993)

75 Sheila Watt-Cloutier, "Inuit, Climate Change, Sovereignty, and Security in the Canadian Artic," Inuit Circumpolar Conference, Jan. 25, 2002, www.inuit-circumpolar.com/index.php?ID=91&Lang=En

76 Richard White, *The Middle Ground: Indians, Empires, and Republics in the Great Lakes Region, 1650–1815* (Cambridge: Cambridge University Press, 1991)

77 James [sakej] Youngblood Henderson, "Empowering Treaty Federalism," *Saskatchewan Law Review* 58, 2 (1994): 241–329; Henderson, "Implementing the Treaty Order," in James [sakej] Youngblood Henderson, Richard Gosse, and Roger Carter, eds., *Continuing Poundmaker and Riel's Quest* (Saskatoon: Purich Publishing, 1994)

78 See Michael Asch, ed., *Aboriginal and Treaty Rights in Canada: Essays on Law, Equality, and Respect for Difference* (Vancouver: UBC Press, 1997).

79 Tony Hall, "What Are We? Chopped Liver? Aboriginal Affairs in the Constitutional Politics of Canada in the 1980s," in Michael Behiels, ed., *The Meech Lake Primer: Conflicting Views of the 1987 Constitutional Accord* (Ottawa: University of Ottawa Press, 1989), 424–56

80 Lillianne Ernestine Krosenbrink-Gelissen, *Sexual Equality as an Aboriginal Right: The Native Women's Association of Canada and the Constitutional Process on Aboriginal Matters*, Nijmegen Studies in Development and Cultural Change, vol. 7 (Saarbrücken, Fort Lauderdale: Verlag breitenbach Publishers, 1991). On the genesis of the Indian women's movement, see Janet Silman, *Enough Is Enough: Aboriginal Women Speak Out* (Toronto: The Women's Press, 1987).

81 Tony Hall, "Self-Government or Self-Delusion: Brian Mulroney and Aboriginal Rights," *Canadian Journal of Native Studies* 6, 1 (1986): 77–89; Tony Hall, "Closing an Incomplete Circle of Confederation: A Brief to the Joint Parliamentary Committee of the Federal Government on the 1987

Constitutional Accord," *Canadian Journal of Native Studies* 6, 2 (1986): 197–222

82 Pauline Comeau, *Elijah: No Ordinary Hero* (Vancouver: Douglas & McIntyre, 1993)

83 Tony Hall, "Aboriginal Issues and the New Political Map of Canada," in J.L. Granatstein and Kenneth McNaught, eds., *"English Canada" Speaks Out* (Toronto: Doubleday Canada, 1992), 122–40; Hall, "Treaties, Trains, and Troubled National Dreams: Reflections on the Indian Summer in Northern Ontario," in Louis A. Knafla and Susan W.S. Binnie, eds., *Law, Society, and the State: Essays in Modern Legal History* (Toronto: University of Toronto Press, 1995), 290–320

84 Kenneth McRoberts and Patrick Monahan, eds., *The Charlottetown Accord, the Referendum and the Future of Canada* (Toronto: University of Toronto Press, 1993); Curtis Cook, ed., *Constitutional Predicament: Canada after the Referendum of 1992* (Montreal: McGill-Queen's University Press, 1994)

85 A good example of this discourse of termination based on the principle of individual equality before the law is presented in Tom Flanagan, *First Nations? Second Thoughts* (Montreal: McGill-Queen's University Press, 2000).

86 Peter H. Russell, *Constitutional Odyssey: Can Canadians Become a Sovereign People*, 2nd ed. (Toronto: University of Toronto Press, 1993); Susan Delacourt, *United We Fall: The Crisis of Democracy in Canada* (Toronto: Viking, 1993)

87 Ovide Mercredi and Mary Ellen Turpel, *In the Rapids: Navigating the Future of First Nations* (Toronto: Viking, 1993)

88 Eric Robinson and Henry Bird Quinney, *The Infested Blanket: Canada's Constitution – Genocide of Canada's Indians* (Winnipeg: Queenston House, 1985)

89 American Indian National Bank, "Indian-Owned Business: An Entrepreneurial Explosion," *Indian Finance Digest*, pilot edition, 1984, 4

90 *Canadian Geographic*, Sept./Oct. 1995, 19

91 Hana Samek, *The Blackfoot Confederacy, 1880–1920: A Comparative Study of Canadian and U.S.A. Indian Policy* (Albuquerque: University of New Mexico Press, 1987), 1–35

92 Reverend Egerton Ryerson Young, cited ibid., 8

93 Roger L. Nicols, *Indians in the United States and Canada: A Comparative History* (Lincoln: University of Nebraska Press, 1998), 287–324

94 See Sarah Carter, "Demonstrating Success: The File Hills Farm Colony," *Prairie Forum* 16, 2 (1991): 157–83; Eleanor Brass, "The File Hills Ex-Pupil Colony," *Saskatchewan History* 6, 2 (1953): 66–9; Brian Titley, "W.M. Graham: Indian Agent Extraordinaire," *Prairie Forum* 8, 1 (1983): 25–41.

95 Albert Bushnell Hart, cited in Walter L. Williams, "American Imperialism and the Indians," in Frederick E. Hoxie, ed., *Indians in American History: An Introduction* (Arlington Heights, Ill.: Harlan Davidson. 1988), 247

96 John Mack Faragher, "'More Motley than Mackinaw': From Ethnic Mixing to Ethnic Cleansing on the Frontier of the Lower Missouri, 1783–1833," in Andrew R.L. Cayton and Fredrika J. Teute, eds., *Contact Points: American Frontiers from the Mohawk Valley to the Mississippi, 1750–1830* (Williamsburg,

Vir.: Published for the Omohundro Institute of Early American History and Culture by the University of North Carolina Press, 1998), 304–26

97 See, for instance, Wilcomb E. Washburn, "A Fifty-Year Perspective on the Indian Reorganization Act," *American Anthropologist* 86 (June 1984): 279–89.

98 Charles T. Loram, "The Fundamentals of Indian-White Contact in the United States and Canada," in Charles T. Loram and T.F. Mcllwraith, eds., *The North American Indian Today*, University of Toronto–Yale University Seminar Conference, Toronto, Sept. 4–16, 1939 (Toronto: University of Toronto Press, 1943), 4–5

99 See Nichols, *Indians in the United States and Canada*; Wilcombe E. Washburn, "Native American Renaissance, 1960–1995," in Bruce G. Trigger and Wilcomb E. Washburn, eds., *The Cambridge History of the Native Peoples of the Americas*, vol. 1: *North America*, Part 2 (Cambridge: Cambridge University Press, 1996), 401–73.

100 See, for instance, Canadian Society of Muslims, *Oh Canada! Whose Land, Whose Dream?* (Toronto, 1991).

101 Vine Deloria Jr, *God Is Red* (New York: Grosset and Dunlap, 1973)

102 Vine Deloria Jr, *Behind the Trail of Broken Treaties: An Indian Declaration of Independence* (New York: Delta Books, 1974), 53

103 A paraphrasing of the treaty-related provisions of the twenty points can be found in Alvin M. Josephy Jr, Joane Nagel, and Troy Johnson, eds., *Red Power: The American Indians Fight for Freedom*, 2nd ed. (Lincoln: University of Nebraska Press, 1999), 44–7

104 Paul Chaat Smith and Robert Allen Warrior, *Like a Hurricane: The Indian Movement from Alcatraz to Wounded Knee* (New York: The New Press, 1996); Troy Johnson, Duane Champagne, and Joane Nagel, "American Indian Activism and Transformation: Lessons from Alcatraz," in Troy R. Johnson, ed., *Contemporary Native American Political Issues* (Walnut Creek, Cal.: Alta Mira Press, c. 1999), 283–314

105 Jack D. Forbes, *Native Americans and Nixon: Presidential Politics and Minority Self-Determination, 1969–1972* (Albuquerque: University of New Mexico Press, 1986)

106 Richard Nixon, cited in Josephy, Nagel, and Johnson, eds., *Red Power*, 148

107 R.C. Gordon-McCutchan, *The Taos Indians and the Battle for Blue Lake* (Sante Fe: Red Crane Books, 1991)

108 Wade Davis, *One River: Explorations and Discoveries in the Amazon Rain Forest* (New York: Simon and Schuster, 1996), 92

109 Vine Deloria Jr, "Trouble in High Places: Erosion of American Indian Rights to Religious Freedom in the United States," in M.A. Jaimes, ed., *The State of Native North America: Genocide Colonization, and Resistance* (Boson: South End Press, 1992), 267–90; Lyman H. Legters, "Indian Religion, the First Amendment, and the States," in Lyman H. Legters and Fremont J. Lyden, eds., *American Indian Policy: Self-Governance and Economic Development* (Westport, Conn.: Greenwood Press, 1994), 91–102

110 Robert W. Fogel, *The Fourth Great Awakening and the Future of Egalitarianism* (Chicago: University of Chicago Press, 2000); Kevin Phillips, *American Theocracy: The Peril and Politics of Radical Religion, Oil, and Borrowed Money in the 21st Century* (New York: Viking, 2006); James A. Morone, *Hellfire Nation: The Politics of Sin in American History* (New Haven: Yale University Press, 2004)

111 Senator John Ashcroft, cited in Paul Knox, "When 'We Have No King but Jesus,'" *Globe and Mail*, Jan. 30, 2002, A17; http://www.spectacle.org/0201/ashcroft.html

112 Jay Hansford C. Vest, "Traditional Blackfeet Religion and the Sacred Badger-Two Medicine Wildlands," *Journal of Law and Religion* 6, 2 (1988): 485–6

113 Josephy, Nagel, and Johnson, eds., *Red Power*, 207–53; H. Marcus Price III, *Disputing the Dead: U.S. Law on Aboriginal Remains and Grave Goods* (Columbia: University of Missouri Press, 1991)

114 Fergus M. Bordewich, *Killing the White Man's Indian: Reinventing Native Americans at the End of the Twentieth Century* (New York: Doubleday, 1996); Joane Nagel, *American Indian Ethnic Renewal: Red Power and the Resurgence of Identity and Culture* (New York: Oxford University Press, 1996)

115 Charles M. Johnson, ed., *The Valley of the Six Nations* (Toronto: The Champlain Society and University of Toronto Press, 1964), 50–1

116 Annemarie Anrod Shimony, *Conservatism among the Iroquois at Six Nations Reserve* (Syracuse: University of Syracuse Press, 1994)

117 Ella Cork, *"The Worst of the Bargain": Concerning the Dilemmas Inherited from Their Forefathers along with the Lands by the Iroquois Nation of the Canadian Grand River Reserve* (San Jacinto, Cal.: Foundation for Social Research, 1962)

118 Geoffrey York and Loreen Pindera, *People of the Pines: The Warriors and the Legacy of Oka* (Toronto: Little, Brown, 1991)

119 Peter Edwards, *One Dead Indian: The Premier, the Police and the Ipperwash Crisis* (Toronto: McClelland & Stewart, 2003)

120 Isabel Kelsay, *Joseph Brant, 1743–1807: Man of Two Worlds* (Syracuse, NY: Syracuse University Press, 1986)

CHAPTER TWELVE

1 Eric J. Hobsbawm, *The Age of Empire, 1875–1914* (New York: Vintage, 1989)

2 Alex Callinicos, *Social Theory: A Historical Introduction* (New York: New York University Press, 1999); Richard Weikhart, *From Darwin to Hitler: Evolutionary Ethics and Racism in Germany* (New York: Palgrave Macmillan, 2004)

3 Micheline R. Ishay, *The History of Human Rights from Ancient Times to the Globalization Era* (Berkeley: University of California Press, 2008)

4 Muriel Evelyn Chamberlain, *Scramble for Africa* (New York: Longman, 1999)

5 Richard Hofstadter, *Social Darwinism and American Thought* (Philadelphia: University of Pennsylvania Press, 1944)

6 Francis J. Bremer, *John Winthrop: America's Forgotten Founding Father* (New York: Oxford University Press, 2003)

7 Irvine H. Anderson, *Biblical Interpretation and Middle East Policy: The Promised Land, America, and Israel, 1917–2002* (Gainesville: University of Florida Press, 2005); Rammy Haija, "The Armageddon Lobby: Dispensationalist Christian Zionism and the Shaping of US Policy towards Israel-Palestine," *Holy Land Studies* 5, 1 (2006): 75–95

8 Alpheus Henry Snow, *The Question of Aborigines in the Law and Practice of Nations, Including a Collection of Authorities and Documents* (1919; Northbrook, Ill.: Metro Books, 1972), 3 [originally published by the US Government Printing Office, Washington, DC); Alpheus Henry Snow, *The Administration of Dependencies: A Study of the Evolution of Federal Empire, with Special Reference to American Colonial Problems* (New York: G.P. Putnam's Sons, 1902)

9 Snow, *The Administration of Dependencies,* 138–9, 142

10 Snow, *The Question of Aborigines,* 132

11 Ibid., 23

12 Ibid., 7. Emphasis added

13 Ibid., 19

14 Ibid., 19

15 Ibid., 21

16 C.C. Eldridge, *Victorian Imperialism* (London: Hodder and Stoughton, 1978)

17 Snow, *The Question of Aborigines,* 133

18 Henry M. Stanley, *Through the Dark Continent, or, The Sources of the Nile around the Great Lakes of Equatorial Africa and Down the Livingston River to the Atlantic Ocean,* 2 vols. (New York: Harper and Brothers Publishers, 1878)

19 Snow, *The Question of Aborigines,* 136–8

20 President Cleveland to King Leopold, Sept. 11, 1885, cited ibid., 143

21 Snow, *The Question of Aborigines,* 133

22 John H. Bodley, *Victims of Progress* (Menlo Park, Cal.: Cummings Publishing, 1975), 34

23 Richard Harding Davis, cited in E.D. Morel, *The Black Man's Burden: The White Man in Africa from the Fifteenth Century to World War I* (1920; New York: Monthly Review Press, 1969), 117

24 Congolese proverb, cited ibid., 109

25 See Roger Louis and Jean Stengers, *E.D. Morel's History of the Congo Reform Movement* (Oxford: Clarendon Press, 1968); E.D. Morel, *Red Rubber* (New York: The Nassau Print, 1906).

26 Adam Hochschild, *King Leopold's Ghost: A Story of Greed, Terror, and Heroism in Colonial Africa* (Boston: Houghton Mifflin, 1998), 101–14

27 Bodley, *Victims of Progress,* 31–3; Walter E. Hardenburg, *The Putumayo, the Devil's Paradise: Travels in the Peruvian Amazon Region and an Account of the Atrocities Committed upon the Indians Therein* (London, 1912)

28 President Tyler, cited in Noam Chomsky, *Year 501: The Conquest Continues* (Montreal: Black Rose Books, 1993), 244

29 Winona LaDuke, *All Our Relations: Native Struggles for Land and Life* (Cambridge, Mass.: South End Press, 1999), 167–82

30 Helena G. Allen, *The Betrayal of Liliuokalani: Last Queen of Hawaii, 1838–1917* (Glendale California: A.H. Clarke Co., 1982)

31 Stephen Kinzer, *Overthrow: America's Century of Regime Change from Hawaii to Iraq* (New York: Times Books, 2006), 15

32 http://www.hawaii-nation.org/constitution-1887.html

33 Queen Liliuokalani, *Hawaii's Story by Hawaii's Queen* (Boston: Lothrop, Lee and Shepard Company, 1898), 177

34 Kinzer, *Overthrow*, 15

35 Lorrin Thurston, cited ibid., 23

36 Helena G. Allen, *Sanford Ballard Dole: Hawaii's Only President, 1844–1926* (Glendale, Cal.: Arthur H. Clark, 1988)

37 Liliuokalani, *Hawaii's Story by Hawaii's Queen*, 368

38 Ibid., 368–9

39 Ibid., 372

40 Ibid., 367

41 Colin G. Calloway, *Crown and Calumet: British-Indian Relations, 1783–1815* (Norman: University of Oklahoma Press, 1987)

42 Charles Dilke, *Greater Britain: A Record of Travel in English-Speaking Countries during 1866 and 1867* (London: Macmillan, 1869) 63–5, 69, at http://www.archive.org/stream/greaterbritainao1dilkgoog/greaterbritainao1dilkgoog_djvu.txt

43 See Kevin Phillips, *The Cousins' War: Religion, Politics, and the Triumph of Anglo-America* (New York: Basic Books, 1999).

44 Eduardo Galeano, *Open Veins of Latin America: Five Centuries of the Pillage of a Continent* (New York: Monthly Review Press, 1997), 173–204

45 Project for a New American Century, *Rebuilding America's Defenses: Strategies, Forces, and Resources for a New Century* (Washington, PNAC, Sept. 2000), 51; David Ray Griffin, *A New Pearl Harbor Revisited: 9/11, the Cover-Up, and the Expose* (Northampton, Mass.: Olive Branch Press, 2008)

46 William Edmund Livezey, *Mahan on Sea Power* (Norman: University of Oklahoma Press, 1981); Richard S. West Jr, *Admirals of American Empire* (Westport, Conn.: Greenwood, 1971); Robert A. Hart, *The Great White Fleet* (Boston: Little, Brown, 1965)

47 David McCullough, *The Path between the Seas: The Creation of the Panama Canal, 1870–1914* (New York: Simon and Schuster, 1977)

48 Nancy Lisagor and Frank Lipsins, *A Law unto Itself: The Untold Story of the Law Firm Sullivan and Cromwell* (New York: Paragon, 1989)

49 See John F. Thompson and Norman Beasley, *For Years to Come: A Story of International Nickel of Canada* (New York: Putnam, 1960); Alexander Dow, "Finance and Foreign Control in Canadian Base Metal Mining, 1918–1955," *Economic History Review* 37, 1 (1984): 54–67.

50 Jacob Viner, *Canada's Balance of International Indebtedness, 1900–1913: An Inductive Study of the Theory of International Trade* (Cambridge, Mass.: Harvard University Press, 1924)

51 John Richardson, chairman, Committee of Trade at Montreal, and James Irvine, chairman, Commission of Trade at Quebec, to George Provost, captain

general and governor in chief over the Province of Lower and Upper Canada, Oct. 14 and 24, 1812, Library and Archives Canada, Colonial Office Records 42 (CO 42), vol. 159

52 Inglis Ellis Co. to the Right Honourable Earl Bathurst, secretary of state for war and colonies, May 7, 1814, in Gordon Charles Davidson, *The North West Company* (Berkeley: University of California Press, 1918), app. N, 300

53 James McGill, cited in George F.G. Stanley, "The Indians in the War of 1812," in Morris Zaslow, ed., *The Defended Border: Upper Canada and the War of 1812* (Toronto: Macmillan, 1964), 178

54 W.B. Robinson to Colonel Bruce, superintendent-general of Indian affairs, Sept. 24, 1850, in Alexander Morris, *The Treaties of Canada with the Indians of Manitoba and the North-West Territories* (Toronto: Belfords, Clark and Company, 1880), 17

55 Louis A. Perez Jr, *The War of 1898: The United States and Cuba in History and Historiography* (Chapel Hill: University of North Carolina Press, 1998); Julius W. Pratt, *The Expansionists of 1898* (Glouster, Mass.: Peter Smith, 1959)

56 Kinzer, *Overthrow*, 39

57 Edward J. Marolda, *Theodore Roosevelt, The U.S. Navy, and the Spanish-American War* (New York: Palgrave, 2001)

58 Samuel Eliot Morison, *The Oxford History of the American People* (New York: Oxford University Press, 1965), 801

59 US Congress, cited ibid., 801

60 Brian McAllister Linn, *The Philippine War, 1899–1902* (Lawrence: University Press of Kansas, 2000); A.B. Feuer, *America at War: The Philippines, 1898–1913* (Westport, Conn.: Praeger, 2002)

61 Fred Anderson and Andrew Cayton, *The Dominion of War: Empire of Liberty in North America, 1500–2000* (New York: Viking, 2005), 160

62 Robert L. Beisner, *Twelve against Empire: The Anti-Imperialists* (New York: McGraw-Hill, 1968); Berkeley E. Tompkins, *Anti-Imperialism in the United States: The Great Debate, 1890–1920* (Philadelphia: University of Pennsylvania Press, 1970)

63 Mark Twain, cited in *New York Herald*, Oct. 15, 1900

64 Samuel Gompers, cited in John A. Garraty, *The American Nation: A History of the United States* (New York: Harper and Row, 1966), 634

65 Senator George Frisbie Hoar, cited ibid., 633

66 Richard Hofstadter, *Social Darwinism in American Thought*, rev. ed. (Boston: Beacon Press, 1966), 174–6

67 John W. Burgess, *Political Science and Comparative Constitutional Law*, 2 vols. (Boston and London: Ginn and Company, 1890–91), 1: 44–6

68 Pierro Gleijeses, *Conflicting Missions: Havana, Washington, and Africa, 1959–1976* (Chapel Hill: University of North Carolina Press, 2002)

69 President William McKinley, cited in Anderson and Cayton, *The Dominion of War*, 334

70 Craig Austin, *Lineage, Life and Labors of José Rizal, Philippine Patriot* (Manila: Philippine Education Company, 1913)

71 Benedict Anderson, *Under Three Flags: Anarchism and the Anti-Colonial Imagination* (London: Verso, 2007)

72 Cited in Fred Poole and Max Vanzi, *Revolution in the Philippines: The United States in a Hall of Cracked Mirrors* (New York: McGraw-Hill, 1984), 171

73 Brian McAllister Linn, *The Philippino War, 1899–1902* (Lawrence: University Press of Kansas, 2002); Stanley Karnow, *In Our Image: America's Empire in the Philippines* (New York: Ballantine, 1990); Thomas Schoonover, *Uncle Sam's War of 1898 and the Origins of Globalization* (Louisville: University Press of Kentucky, 2003)

74 Lester D. Langely, *The Banana Wars: An Inner History of the American Empire, 1900–1934* (Lexington: University of Kentucky Press, 1983)

75 Walter La Feber, *Inevitable Revolutions: The United States in Central America* (New York: W.W. Norton, 1983); Mary S. Renda, *Taking Haiti: Military Occupation and the Culture of U.S. Imperialism, 1915–1940* (Chapel Hill: University of North Carolina Press, 2001)

76 Lloyd C. Gardner, *Wilson and Revolutions, 1913–1921* (Philadelphia: Lippincott, 1976); Howard Jones, *Crucible of Power: A History of American Foreign Relations from 1897* (Wilmington, Del.: SR Books, 2001)

77 David Reynolds, *One World Divisible: A Global History since 1945* (New York: W.W. Norton, 2000), 62–3

78 Julian Burger, *Report from the Frontier: The State of the World's Indigenous Peoples* (London: Zed Books, 1987), 157

79 Ibid., 147–57; Anti-Slavery Society, *The Philippines: Authoritarian Governments, Multinationals and Ancestral Lands* (London, 1983); Marites Vitug and Glenda M. Gloria, *Under the Cresent Moon: Rebellion in Mindano* (Manila: Ateno Center for Social Policy and Public Affairs, 2000); Salah Jubair, *A Nation under Endless Tyranny* (Kuala Lumpur: I.Q. Marin, 1999); Thomas M. McKeena, *Muslim Rulers and Rebels: Everyday Politics and Armed Separatism in the Southern Philippines* (Berkeley: University of California Press, 1998)

80 Walden Bello, David Kinley, and Elaine Elinson, *Development Debacle: The World Bank in the Philippines* (San Francisco: Institute for Food and Development Policy, 1982)

81 Mansour Moaddel, *Class, Politics, and Ideology in the Iranian Revolution* (London: I.B. Tauris, 1985)

82 Eric Hobsbawm, *Age of Extremes: The Short Twentieth Century, 1914–1991* (London: Abacus, 1999), 453

83 Anthony McDermott, *Egypt from Nasser to Mubarak: A Flawed Revolution* (London: Croom Helm, 1988)

84 Eric Davis, "Ideology, Social Class, and Islamic Radicalism in Modern Egypt," in Said Amir Arjomand, ed., *From Nationalism to Revolutionary Islam* (Albany: SUNY Press, 1984), 134–57; John Esposito, *Unholy War: Terror in the Name of Islam* (New York: Oxford University Press), 26–71

85 Dilip Hiro, *The Longest War: The Iran-Iraq Military Conflict* (London: Paladin, 1990)

86 William Clark, "The Real Reason for the Upcoming War With Iraq: A Macroeconomic and Geostrategic Analysis of the Unspoken Truth," Jan. 2003, revised Jan. 2004 at http://www.ratical.org/ratville/CAH/RRiraqWar.html

87 Galeano, *Open Veins of Latin America*

88 Naomi Klein, *The Shock Doctrine: The Rise of Disaster Capitalism* (Toronto: Knopf Canada, 2007), 233–61

89 Matt Taibbi, "Inside the Great American Bubble Machine," *Rolling Stone*, July 2, 2009, at http://www.rollingstone.com/politics/story/28816321/inside_the_great_american_bubble_machine; Taibbi, "Obama's Big Sellout," *Rolling Stone*, Dec. 9, 2009, at http://www.rollingstone.com/politics/story/31234647/obamas_big_sellout

90 Ellen Meiksins Wood, "Democracy as Ideology of Empire," in Colin Mooers, ed., *The New Imperialists: Ideologies of Empire* (Oxford: Oneworld, 2006), 19, 21

91 Snow, *The Question of Aborigines*, 37

92 Sir H.H. Johnston, cited ibid., 36–7

93 Rev. Edwin W. Smith, *The Golden Stool*, cited in R.S. Rattray, *Ashanti Law and Constitution* (New York: Negro Universities Press, 1969), xi

94 A.H.M. Kirk-Green, *Lugard and the Amalgamation of Nigeria: A Documentary Record* (London: Frank Cass, 1969)

95 F.D. Lugard, *The Dual Mandate in British Tropical Africa*, 3rd ed. (Edinburgh: William Blackwood and Sons, 1926), 617

96 Mahmood Mamdani, *Citizen and Subject: Contemporary Africa and the Legacy of Late Colonialism* (Princeton: Princeton University Press, 1996), 53

97 George Padmore, *How Britain Rules Africa* (London: Wishart Books, 1936), 317

98 See Ifor L. Evans, *Native Policy in Southern Africa: An Outline* (Cambridge: Cambridge University Press, 1934).

99 *Report of the Northern Nigeria Lands*, 1910, cited in Sir Alan Burns, *History of Nigeria* (1929; London: Allen and Unwin, 1969), 274

100 Ruling on the case of *Amodu Tijani v. The Secretary, Southern Nigeria*, 1921, cited in Paul Tennant, *Aboriginal Peoples and Politics: The Indian Land Question in British Columbia, 1849–1989* (Vancouver: UBC Press, 1990), 214–15

101 Tennant, *Aboriginal Peoples and Politics*, 112

102 Hugh Shewell, "Jules Sioui and Indian Political Radicalism in Canada," *Journal of Canadian Studies* 34, 3 (1999): 211–42

103 For a fuller discussion of the relationship between Canadian Indian policy and the global movement for decolonization, see Alan C. Cairns, *Citizens Plus: Aboriginal Peoples and the Canadian State* (Vancouver: UBC Press, 2000)

104 See Rupert Emerson, *From Empire to Nation: The Rise to Self-Assertion of Asian and African Peoples* (Cambridge, Mass.: Harvard University Press, 1967).

105 W. Scott Lucas, *Divided We Stand: Britain, the U.S., and the Suez Crisis* (London: Hodder and Stoughton, 1991); Keith Kyle, *Suez* (London: Weidenfeld and Nicolson, 1991)

106 Edward W. Said, *The Politics of Dispossession: The Struggle for Palestinian Self-Determination, 1969–1994* (New York: Pantheon Books, 1994); Edward W. Said, *Orientalism* (New York: Pantheon Books, 1978)

107 Wunyabari Maloba, *Mau Mau and Kenya: An Analysis of a Peasant Revolt* (Bloomington: Indiana University Press, 1993)

108 R.F. Holland, *European Decolonization, 1918–1981: An Introductory Survey* (London: Macmillan, 1985); D.A. Low, *Eclipse of Empire* (Cambridge: Cambridge University Press, 1991); T.O. Lloyd, *The British Empire, 1558–1995*, 2nd ed. (New York: Oxford University Press, 1996); A.P. Thornton, *Imperialism in the Twentieth Century* (London: Macmillan, 1978); P.J. Cain and A.G. Hopkins, *British Imperialism: Crisis and Deconstruction, 1914–1990* (London: Longman, 1993)

109 Michael G. Schatzberg, *Mobutu or Chaos? The United States and Zaire, 1960–1990* (Philadelphia: Foreign Policy Research Institute, 1991); Comité Zaire, *Zaire: Le dossier de la récolonisation* (Paris: Editions l'Harmattan, 1978); David Gibbs, *The Political Economy of Third World Intervention: Mines, Money, and U.S. Policy in the Congo Crisis* (Chicago: University of Chicago Press, 1991); Sean Kelly, *America's Tyrant: The CIA and Mobutu of Zaire* (Washington, DC: American University Press, 1993)

110 Martin Meredith, *The Fate of Africa: From the Hopes of Freedom to the Heart of Despair. A History of Fifty Years of Independence* (New York: Public Affairs, 2005), 58–74; Patrick Manning, *Francophone Sub-Saharan Africa, 1880–1985*, 2nd ed. (Cambridge: Cambridge University Press, 1999)

111 Stephen R. Bown, *Merchant Kings: When Companies Ruled the World, 1600–1900* (Vancouver: Douglas and McIntryre, 2009), 7–102

112 See Herbert Feith and Lance Castles, *Indonesian Political Thinking, 1945–1965* (Ithaca: Cornell University Press, 1970).

113 John Pilger, *The New Rulers of the World* (London: Verso, 2003), 30

114 Harry Crouch, *The Army and Politics in Indonesia* (Ithaca, NY: Cornell University Press, 1997)

115 Paul Lashmar and James Oliver, *Britain's Secret Propaganda War, 1948–1977* (London: Sutton, 1998)

116 Gabriel Kolko, *Confronting the Third World: United States Foreign Policy, 1945–1980* (New York: Pantheon Books, 1988), 181

117 Pilger, *The New Rulers of the World*, 39–42

118 James Linen, cited ibid., 40–1

119 Ibid., 42–5

120 Gabriel Kolko, *Confronting the Third World*, 182

121 Anti-Slavery Society, *Plunder in Paradise: The Struggle of the West Papuan Peoples* (London, 1986)

122 Unnamed official, cited in Julian Burger, *Report from the Frontier: The State of the World's Indigenous Peoples* (London: Zed Books, 1987), 147

123 Clem Chartier, "Malaysia: Logging Greatest Threat to Indigenous Peoples of Sarawak," statement to the UN Working Group on Indigenous Populations, *IWGIA Newsletter*, no. 51/52, Oct./Dec. 1987; Al Gedicks, *The New Resource*

Wars: Native Struggle against Multinational Corporations (Boston: South End Press, 1993), 27–33; Marcus Colchester, *Pirates, Squatters, Poachers: The Political Ecology of the Dispossession of the Native Peoples of Sarawak*, New Series of Survival International Documents, no. 7, 1989

124 John G. Taylor, *Indonesia's Forgotten War: The Hidden History of East Timor* (London: Zed Books, 1991); Christopher Hitchens, *The Trial of Henry Kissenger* (New York: Verso, 2001), 90–107. See also Jose Ramos-Horta, *East Timor Debacle: Indonesian Intervention, Repression and Western Compliance* (Trenton, NJ: Red Sea Press, 1986).

125 Norrie MacQueen, *The Decolonization of Portuguese Africa: Metropolitan Revolution and the Dissolution of Empire* (London: Longman, 1997); Edward Gonzalez, "Cuba, the Soviet Union, and Africa," in David Albright, ed., *Communism in Africa* (Bloomington: Indiana Press, 1980), 145–67

126 Stephen Lewis, *Race against Time: Searching for Hope in AIDS-Ravaged Africa*, 2nd ed. (Toronto: Anasi, 2006)

127 Niall Ferguson, *The Cash Nexus: Money and Power in the Modern World, 1700–2000* (New York: Basic Books, 2001), 383

128 Masao Miyoshi, "A Borderless World? From Colonialism to Transnationalism and the Decline of the Nation-State," in Rob Wilson and Wimal Dissanayake, eds., *Global, Local: Cultural Production and the Transnational Imaginary* (Durham, NC: Duke University Press, 1996), 97

129 William Roger Louis and Ronald Robinson, "The Imperialism of Decolonization," *Journal of Imperial and Commonwealth History* 22 (1995): 462–511

130 Joan Ross, David McMurray, and Ted Swedenburg, "Arab Noise and Ramadan Nights: Rai, Rap, and Franco-Maghrebi Identities," in Jonathan Xavier Inda and Renato Rosaldo, eds., *The Anthropology of Globalization: A Reader* (Oxford: Blackwell Publishers, 2002)

131 See Miles Kahler, *Decolonization in Britain and France: The Domestic Consequences of International Relations* (Princeton, NJ: Princeton University Press, 1984).

132 Estanislao Oziewicz, "Bill Was Passed to Quell the Crisis over the Algerian War," *Globe and Mail*, Nov. 9, 2005, A12

133 Alain Ruscio, *Dien Bien Phu: La fin d'une allusion* (Paris: Harmattan, 1986)

134 Richard Slotkin, *The Fatal Environment: The Myth of the Frontier in the Age of Industrialization, 1800–1890* (Norman: University of Oklahoma Press, 1998)

135 The phrases are attributed to Michel Debré, prime minister of France under Charles de Gaulle.

136 Matthew Quest, "The Lessons of the Bandung Conference: A Review of Richard Wright's *The Color Curtain 40 Years Later*," http://www.spunk.org/texts/pubs/lr/spoo1716/bandung.html; Richard N. Wright, *The Color Curtain: A Report on the Bandung Conference* (1956; Jackson, Miss.: Banner Books, 1995)

137 See Tyler Storvall, *Paris Noir: African-Americans in the City of Light* (Boston: Houghtton Mifflin, 1996).

138 Nick Nesbitt, "Negritude," African Writers Index, http://www.geocities.com/africanwriters/origins.html

139 Albert Memmi, *Portrait du colonisé précédé du portrait du colonisateur* (Paris: Editions Correa, 1957); Albert Memmi, *The Colonizers and the Colonized*, trans. Howard Greenfield (New York: Orion Press, 1965)

140 Rita Maran, *Torture: The Role of Ideology in the French-Algerian War* (New York: Praeger, 1989)

141 Jean-Paul Sartre, Preface to Henri Alleg, *The Question*, trans. John Calder (London: John Calder, 1958), 11–28

142 Anthony Clayton, "France and the Algerian War, 1954–1962: Strategy, Operations, and Diplomacy," *Journal of Military History* 67, 2 (2003): 625–6

143 See Kristin Ross, *Fast Cars, Clean Bodies: Decolonization and the Reordering of French Culture* (Cambridge, Mass.: MIT Press, 1995); Felix Gilbert, *The End of the European Era, 1890 to the Present*, 3rd ed. (New York: W.W. Norton, 1984).

144 William J. Duiker, *Ho Chi Minh: A Life* (New York: Hyperion, 2000)

145 Basil Davidson, *Black Star: A View of the Life and Times of Kwame Nkrumah* (New York: Allen Lane, 1974); Denis Austin, *Politics in Ghana, 1946–1960* (Oxford: Oxford University Press, 1964)

146 Paul Lee, "The Western Conspiracy That Destroyed Nkrumah," *West Africa*, no. 4302 (Nov. 19–25, 2001): 11–17; William Blum, *Killing Hope: U.S. Military and CIA Interventions since World War II* (Montreal: Black Rose, 1998), 198–200

147 Kwame Nkrumah, *Neo-Colonialism: The Last Stage of Imperialism* (London: Thomas Nelson and Sons, 1965)

148 Leslie A. Fidler, *The Return of the Vanishing American* (New York: Stein and Day, 1968), 24–5

149 New York State Special Commission on Attica, *Attica: The Official Report of the New York State Special Commission on Attica*, (New York: Praeger Publishers, 1972), 139

150 Samuel Melville, *Letters from Attica* (New York: William Morrow and Company, 1972), 164

151 See also Harold Jacobs, ed., *Weatherman* (New York: Rampart's Press, 1970).

152 Melville, *Letters from Attica*, 77

153 Ibid., 162

154 George Jackson, *Blood in My Eye* (New York: Random House, 1972); Jackson, *Soledad Brother: The Prison Letters of George Jackson* (Chicago: Lawrence Hill Books, 1994)

155 John Bancore, cited in an interview with Arthur Topham, *The Radical* (Quesnel, BC) 3, 3 (Oct. 2000): 3

156 Ibid., 22

157 See F.W. Cheeson's letter in the *New York Times*, cited as an attachment in Lytton to Douglas, Sept. 2, 1858, in British Columbia Legislature, *Papers Connected with the Indian Land Question, 1850–1875* (Victoria: Government Printer, 1875), reprinted at Victoria by the Queen's Printer, 1987, 13

158 Arthur Manuel, "Indigenous Brief to the World Trade Organization: How the Denial of Aboriginal Title Serves as an Illegal Export Subsidy," in Jerry

Mander and Victoria Tauli-Corpuz, eds., *Paradigm Wars: Indigenous Peoples' Resistance to Globalization* (San Francisco: Sierra Books, 2006), 203–8

159 Ts'peten Defenders, Nitewatch, Part 1, You Tube, http://youtube.com/watch?v=rjoqaFg5ZjY

160 http://www.libertyforum.org/showflat.php?Cat=&Board=news_news&Number=294616217&page=&view=&sb=&o=&vc=1&t=0

161 Janice Switlo, *Gustafsen Lake: Under Siege: Exposing the Truth behind the Gustafsen Lake Stand-off* (Peachland, BC: TIAC Communications, 1997)

162 Joey Thompson, "Media Should Apologize for Gullibility on Gustafsen Lake," *The Province*, Sept. 26 1997

163 George Wool, cited in Sandra Lambertus, *Wartime Images, Peacetime Wounds: The Media and the Gustafsen Lake Standoff* (Toronto: University of Toronto Press, 2004), 165

164 Bruce Clark, *Justice in Paradise* (Montreal: McGill-Queen's University Press, 1999)

165 Personal discussions with William Jones Ignace and Lyn Crompton, one of Satiacum's lawyers in his successful application in 1987 for political refugee status in Canada

166 Arthur M. Schlesinger Jr, *Robert Kennedy and His Times* (New York: Ballantine Books, 1996)

167 Farnaz Fassihi, "Hussein's Lawyers Aim to Focus Trial on U.S. Occupation," *Wall Street Journal*, Oct. 19, 2005

168 Ramsay Clark's blurb on the jacket of John Boncore Hill (Dacajeweiah), with Sandra Bruderer, *From Attica to Gustafsen Lake: Unmasking the Secrets of the Psycho-Sexual Energy and the Struggle for Original Peoples' Title* (Chase, BC: John Pasquale Boncore, 2001)

169 United States District Court for the District of Oregon, *United States of America versus James Allen Scott Pitawanakwat*, Nov. 15 2000, Judgment 00-M-489-ST. The ruling is published in its entirety in the *Canadian Native Law Reporter*, no. 1 (2001): 340–60

170 "U.S. Judge Unfairly Challenges Canadian Law," *Vancouver Sun*, Nov. 27, 2000, A14

171 Anthony J. Hall, "Should George W. Bush Be Arrested in Calgary, Alberta, to Be Tried for International Crimes," Voltairenet.org, at http://www.voltairenet.org/article159233.html; Hall, "George Bush and Bill Clinton Do Toronto," IndyBay, at http://www.indybay.org/newsitems/2009/05/29/18599180.php; Hall, "Citizen's Arrest of George W. Bush for War Crimes: The Trial of Splitting the Sky," Global Research.ca at http://www.globalresearch.ca/index.php?context=va&aid=16377

172 John L. Tobias, "Canada's Subjugation of the Plains Cree, 1879–1885," *Canadian Historical Review* 64, 4 (1983): 519–48

173 Lewis Cass, *Remarks on the Policy and Practice of the United States and Great Britain in the Treatment of Indians* (from North American Review) (Boston: Frederick T. Gray, 1827), 55

174 Joseph Edmund Collins, *The Story of Louis Riel, Rebel Chief* (Toronto: J.S. Robertson and Brothers, 1885)

175 Transcript of the Trial of Louis Riel, 1885, in Canada, *Sessional Papers*, 1887, vol. 19, no. 12, appendix 43, p. 219

176 Ibid.

CHAPTER THIRTEEN

1 William T. Gossett, cited in Arthur Selwyn Miller, *The Modern Corporate State: Private Governments and the American Constitution* (Westport, Conn.: Greenwood Press, 1976), 19–20

2 John H. Storer, *The Web of Life: A First Book of Ecology* (1953; New York: Signet Key Book, 1956)

3 John McMurtry, *Value Wars: The Global Market versus the Life Economy* (London: Pluto Press, 2002)

4 John McMurtry, "9/11 and the 9/11 Wars: Understanding the Supreme Crimes," in David Ray Griffin and Peter Dale Scott, eds., *9/11 and American Empire: Intellectuals Speak Out* (Northampton, Mass.: Olive Branch Press, 2007), 140–2

5 Edward Winslow, cited in Anthony Pagden, *Lords of All the World: Ideologies of Empire in Spain, Britain and France, c. 1500–c. 1800* (New Haven: Yale University Press, 1995), 36

6 Fernand Braudel, *The Wheels of Commerce* (New York: Harper and Row, 1982), 100

7 Stephen R. Bown, *Merchant Kings: When Companies Rules the World, 1600–1900* (Vancouver: Douglas and McIntrye, 2009), 147–237

8 Leslie Sklair, *Globalization: Capitalism and Its Alternatives*, 3rd ed. (Oxford: Oxford University Press, 2002), 37

9 Charles Derber, *Corporation Nation: How Corporations Are Taking Over Our Lives and What We Can Do About It* (New York: St Martin's Griffin, 2000), 120

10 Cited in George Monbiot, *The Guardian*, July 24, 2001

11 Pauline Maier, "The Revolutionary Origins of the American Corporation," *William and Mary Quarterly*, 3rd series, 50, 1 (1993): 56–83

12 See Edwin Merrick Dodd, *American Business Corporations until 1860* (Cambridge, Mass.: Harvard University Press, 1934).

13 Virginia Supreme Court, cited in Richard L. Grossman and Frank T. Adams, *Taking Care of Business: Citizenship and the Charter of Incorporation* (Cambridge, Mass.: Charter Ink [a publication of the Program on Corporation, Law, and Democracy], 1995), 8–9

14 Pennsylvania Legislature, cited in Derber, *Corporation Nation*, 122–3

15 Robert Monks, "Growing Corporate Governance: From King George III to George Bush," in Brenda Sutton, ed., *The Legitimate Corporation* (Cambridge, Mass.: Basil Blackwell, 1993), 172

16 See Thorstein Veblen, *The Theory of the Leisure Class: An Economic Study of Institutions* (New York: Macmillan, 1902).

17 Ron Paul, *Mises and Austrian Economics* (Auburn, Ala: The Ludwig von Mises Institute of Auburn University, 2004)

18 http://www.ronpaul.com/on-the-issues/audit-the-federal-reserve-hr-1207/

19 Mark Pittman, Court Orders Fed to Disclose Emergency Loans, Aug. 25, 2009, at http://www.bloomberg.com/apps/news?pid=20601087&sid=a7CC61ZsieV4

20 Bob Ivy, "Mark Pittman, Reporter Who Challenged Fed Secrecy, Dies at 52," Bloomberg.com, Nov. 30, 2009, at http://www.bloomberg.com/apps/news?pid=20601109&sid=af7QohP8YdRo&pos=12

21 Sherman Alexie, review of *Deer Hunting with Jesus*, at http://www.amazon.com/Deer-Hunting-Jesus-Dispatches-Americas/dp/0307339378?ie=UTF8&s=books&qid=1210956592&sr=1-1

22 Joe Bageant, *Deer Hunting with Jesus: Dispatches from America's Class Wars* (New York: Three Rivers Press, 2008), cited excerpt from http://www.joebageant.com/joe/2008/10/the-bailout-in.html#more

23 William F. Pepper, *An Act of State: The Execution of Martin Luther King* (London: Verso, 2008), 264

24 Derber, *Corporation Nation*, 134

25 Anthony J. Hall, *The American Empire and the Fourth World* (Montreal: McGill-Queen's University Press, 2005), 346–63

26 Clarence Walworth Alvord, *The Mississippi Valley in British Politics: A Study of the Trade, Land Speculation, and Experiments in Imperialism Culminating in the American Revolution*, 2 vols. (Cleveland, Ohio: Arthur H. Clark, 1917)

27 Francis Jennings, *The Creation of America: Through Revolution to Empire* (New York: Cambridge University Press, 2000)

28 The membership of the International Peace Operation Associations includes among its members the following military and national security contractors: Blackwater Corp., Centigon Corp., EOD Technology Corp., Ayr Aviation, Ameco Corp., Armour Group, Mac International, MPRI, Evergreen Corp., Hart Security, Olive Group, Reed Inc., SOC-SMG Corp. (see http://ipoaonline.org/en/membership/memberslist.htm); Peter W. Singer, *Corporate Warriors: The Rise of the Privatized Military Industry* (Ithaca, NY: Cornell University Press, 2003).

29 Emran Qureshi and Michael A. Sells, eds., *The New Crusaders: Constructing the Muslim Enemy* (New York: Columbia University Press, 2003)

30 Kristi Essick, "Guns, Money, and Cell Phones," *The Industry Standard Magazine*, June 11, 2001

31 *New York Times*, Feb. 13, 1972, cited in Miller, *The Modern Corporate State*, 242–3

32 John C. Weaver, *The Great Land Rush and the Making of the Modern World, 1650–1900* (Montreal: McGill-Queen's University Press, 2003)

33 Jacques Leslie, *Deep Water: The Epic Struggle over Dams, Displaced People, and the Environment* (New York: Farrar, Straus, and Giroux, 2005)

34 Richard H. Bartlett, "Citizens Minus: Indians and the Right to Vote," *Saskatchewan Law Review* 44 (1979): 168; G.R. Mellor, *British Imperial Trusteeship* (London: Faber and Faber, 1951)

35 George Kennan, *US Cold War Planner* (1948), cited in John Pilger, *Hidden Agendas* (London: Vintage, 1999), 59. See George Kennan, *George F. Kennan and the Origins of Containment, 1944–1946: The Kennan-Lukas Correspondence* (Columbia: University of Missouri Press, 1997).

36 Ronald Steel, *Pax Americana* (New York: The Viking Press, 1967), cited in Noam Chomsky, *American Power and the New Mandarins* (New York: Random House, 1969), 207

37 Jean-Jacques Servan-Schreiber, *The American Challenge*, trans. Ronald Steel (London: Hamish Hamilton, 1968), 32, 21

38 Ibid., 12

39 Ibid., 19

40 Ibid., 8–9

41 Slavenka Drakulić, *Café Europa: Life after Communism* (London: Abacus, 1996), 12

42 Mark Kurlansky, *1968: The Year That Shook the World* (New York: Ballantine, 2004); William F. Pepper, *An Act of State: The Execution of Martin Luther King* (London Verso, 2003)

43 Ralph Summy and Michael E. Salla, eds., *Why the Cold War Ended: A Range of Interpretations* (Westport, Conn.: Greenwood Press, 1995)

44 Wojciech Roszkowski, *The Shadow of Yalta: A Report* (Warsaw: Warsaw Rising Museum, 2005)

45 Václav Havel, *Disturbing the Peace: A Conversation with Karel Hvizdala*, trans. Paul Wilson (New York: Vintage, 1991)

46 Peter Dale Scott, *The Road to 9/11: Wealth, Empire, and the Future of America* (Berkeley: University of California Press, 2007), 55

47 Edward Palmer Thompson, *Beyond the Cold War* (New York: Pantheon, 1982); Edward Palmer Thompson, *Double Exposure* (London: Merlin Press, 1985)

48 Nadeza Siskova, ed., *The Process of Constitutionalisation of the EU and Related Issues* (Groningen, The Netherlands: Europa Law Publishing, 2008)

49 Eric Reguly, "Global Economic Meltdown: European Union Unveils Stimulus," *Globe and Mail*, Nov. 27, 2008, B9

50 For a large archive of primary sources on the Nuremberg trials, see http://nuremberg.law.harvard.edu/php/docs_swi.php?DI=1&text=overview.

51 Radhabinod Pal, *International Military Tribunal for the Far East: Dissentient Judgment* (Calcutta: Sanyal, 1953); Radhabinod Pal, *Crimes in International Relations* (Calcutta: University of Calcutta Press, 1955); Ashis Nandy, "The Other Within: The Strange Case of Radhabinod Pal's Judgment of Culpability," in Ashis Nandy, *The Savage Freud and Other Essays on Possible and Retrievable Selves* (Princeton: Princeton University Press, 1995)

52 Robert H. Jackson, cited in Michael Marrus, "Why Nuremberg Resonates 60 Years Later," *Globe and Mail*, Nov. 21, 2005, A15. See Michael Marrus, *The Nuremberg War Crimes Trial, 1945–1946* (Boston: Bedfords Books, 1997)

53 Robert H. Jackson, *The Nurnberg Case as Presented by Robert H. Jackson* (New York: Cooper Square Publishers, 1971), xv. Emphasis added

54 Norman Rich, *Hitler's War Aims: Ideology, the Nazi State and the Course of Expansion*, 2 vols. (London: André Deutsch, 1973, 1974), 1: 8

55 Czesław Madajczyk, ed., *Generalny Plan Wschodni: Zbiór dokumentów* (Warszawa: Główna Komisja Badania Zbrodni Hitlerowskich w Polsce, 1990), cited in English in http://www.worldfuturefund.org/wffmaster/Reading/GPO/gpo%20sources.htm

56 See Zeev Sternhell with Mario Sznajder and Maia Asheri, *The Birth of Facist Ideology: From Cultural Rebellion to Political Revolution* (Princeton, NJ: Princeton University Press, 1994); Hannal Arendt, *The Birth of Totalitarianism* (New York: Harvest, 1973).

57 Henry Friedlander, *The Origins of Nazi Genocide: From Euthanasia to Final Solution* (Chapel Hill: University of North Carolina Press, 1995); Ian Downbiggin, *Keeping America Sane: Psychiatry and Eugenics in United States and Canada, 1880–1940* (Ithaca, NY: Cornell University Press, 1997); Stefan Kuhl, *The Nazi Connection: Eugenics, American Racism, and German National Socialism* (New York: Oxford University Press, 1994); Pauline Mazumbar, *Eugenics, Human Genetics and Human Failings: The Eugenics Society, Its Sources and Critics in Britain* (London: Routledge, 1992); Donal K. Pickens, *Eugenics and the Progressives* (Nashville: Vanderbuilt University Press, 1968); Stephen Tremblay, *The Right to Reproduce: A History of Coercive Sterilization* (London: Weidenfeldt and Nicolson, 1998); Edwin Black, *War against the Weak: Eugenics and America's Campaign to Create a Master Race* (New York: Four Walls, Eight Windows, 2003); Angus McLaren, *Our Own Master Race: Eugenics in Canada, 1885–1945* (Toronto: McClelland & Stewart, 1990)

58 Robert H. Jackson, cited in Edwin Black, *IBM and the Holocaust: The Strategic Alliance between Nazi Germany and America's Most Powerful Corporation* (New York: Crown Publishers, 2001), 421

59 Max Wallace, *The American Axis: Henry Ford, Charles Lindberg and the Rise of the Third Reich* (New York: St Martin's Press, 2003); Black, *IBM and the Holocaust*

60 Black, *IBM and the Holocaust*, 134

61 Karl Richard Bopp, *Hjalmar Schact: Central Banker* (Columbia: University of Missouri Press, 1939)

62 Hjalmar Schact, cited in http://www.bookrags.com/Hjalmar_Schacht

63 Ann Tusa and John Tusa, *The Nuremberg Trial* (London: Macmillan, 1983), 337–46

64 G.M. Gilbert, *Nuremberg Diary* (New York: Farrar, Straus and Company, 1947), 430

65 Benjamin B. Ferencz, "The Holocaust and the Nuremberg Trials," *UN Chronicle*, Dec. 2005

66 Philippe Sands, *Torture Team: Deception, Cruelty and Compromise of Law* (London: Allan Lane, 2008)

67 R. Michael Marrus, "The Nuremberg Doctors' Trial in Historical Context," *Bulletin of the History of Medicine* 73, 1 (1999): 106–23

68 Gordon Thomas, *Journey into Madness: The True Story of Secret* CIA *Mind Control and Medical Abuse* (New York: Bantam, 1989); Harvey M. Weinstein, *Psychiatry and the* CIA: *Victims of Mind Control* (Washington: American Psychiatric Press, 1990)

69 Eileen Welsome, *The Plutonium Files, America's Secret Medical Experiments in the Cold War* (New York: Dial, 1999); Carl Gallagher, *American Ground Zero: The Secret Nuclear War* (Cambridge, Mass.: MIT Press, 1993)

70 United Nations War Crimes Commission, *Law Reports of Trials of War Criminals: The IG Farben and Krupp Trials* (New York: H. Fertig, 1997)

71 John Alan Appleman, *Military Tribunals and International Crimes* (Westport, Conn.: Greenwood Press, 1971), 179

72 Ibid., 180–3

73 Josiah Ellis Du Bois, *The Devil's Chemists: 24 Conspirators of the International Farben Cartel Who Manufactured Wars* (Boston: Beacon Press, 1952); Telford Taylor, *Sword and Swastika: Generals and Nazis in the Third Reich* (New York: Simon and Schuster, 1952); Charles Higham, *Trading with the Enemy: An Exposé of the Nazi-American Money Plot, 1933–1949* (New York: Delacourt Press, 1983)

74 Victor H. Bernstein, *Final Judgment: The Story of Nuremberg* (New York: Boni and Gaer, 1947), 167); see Howard Watson Ambruster, *Treason's Peace: German Dyes and American Dupes* (New York: The Beechhurst Press, 1947); James Stewart Martin, *All Honorable Men* (Boston: Little, Brown, 1950); Joseph Borkin, *The Crime and Punishment of IG Farben* (New York: Free Press, 1978); Raymond G. Stokes, *Divide and Prosper: The Heirs of IG Farben under Allied Authority, 1945–1951* (Berkeley: University of California Press, 1988); Peter Hayes, *Industry and Ideology: IG Farben in the Nazi Era*, 2nd ed. (Cambridge: Cambridge University Press, 2000)

75 United Nations, *Report of the International Law Commission Covering Its Second Session*, June 5–July 29, 1950, Document A/1316, 11–14

76 Guy Womack, cited in Frank Rich, *The Greatest Story Ever Sold: The Decline and Fall of Truth from 9/11 to Katrina* (New York: The Penguin Press, 2006), 155

77 Ibid.; Physicians for Human Rights, *Break Them Down: Systematic Use of Psychological Torture by US Forces* (Cambridge, Mass.: PHR, 2005). See http://www.phrusa.org/research/torture/news_2005-05-01.html.

78 United Nations, General Assembly, 53rd session, "Implementation of Human Rights Agreements, Status of the Convention Against Torture, 17 August, 1998," Document A/53/150

79 Philippe Sands, *Lawless World: Making and Breaking Global Rules* (London: Penguin Books, 2006), appendix V, 301–5

80 Lisa Hajjar, "From Nuremberg to Guantanamo: International Law and American Power Politics," *Middle East Report*, no. 229 (winter 2003): 8–15, at http://www.merip.org/mer/mer229/229_hajjar.html

81 See Stephane Courtois et al., *The Black Book of Communism: Crimes, Terror, Repression*, trans. Jonathan Murphy and Mark Kramer (Cambridge: Harvard University Press, 1999).

82 Aleksandr Solzhenitsyn, *The Gulag Archipelago, 1918–1956: An Experiment in Literary Investigation*, trans. Thomas P. Whitney and Harry Willetts (New York: Perennial, 2002); Anne Applebaum, *Gulag: A History* (New York: Doubleday, 2003); Thomasz Kizny, *Gulag, Life and Death inside Soviet Concentration Camps, 1917–1990* (Richmond Hill, Ont.: Firefly Books, 2004)

83 John Sweeney, *The Life and Evil Times of Nicolae Ceaușescu* (London: Hutchinson, 1991)

84 Arshi Pipa, *Albanian Stalinism: Ideo-Political Aspects* (New York: Columbia University Press, 1990)

85 Jung Chang and Jon Halliday, *Mao: The Unknown Story* (New York: Knopf, 2005); Joseph Ball, "Did Mao Really Kill Millions in the Great Leap Forward," *Monthly Review*, Sept. 2006

86 Martin Luther King Jr, *Stride towards Freedom: The Montgomery Story* (New York: Ballantine Books, 1964), 73–4. See David J. Garrow, *Bearing the Cross: Martin Luther King and the Southern Christian Leadership Conference* (Norwalk, Conn.: Easton Press, 1989)

87 Philip Short, *Pol Pot: Anatomy of a Nightmare* (New York: Henry Holt and Company, 2004); Ben Kiernan, *The Pol Pot Regime: Race Power, and Genocide in Cambodia under the Khmer Rouge, 1975–1979* (New Haven: Yale University Press, 1996); S.S. Sethi, *Kampuchean Tragedy: Maoism in Action* (New Delhi: Kalamkar Prakashan, 1979); Elizabeth Becker, *When the War Was Over: Cambodia and the Khmer Rouge Revolution* (New York: Public Affairs, 1998); David P. Chandler, *Brother Number One: A Political Biography of Pol Pot* (Boulder, Col.: Westview Press, 1999)

88 Rachel Rinaldo, "Revisiting the Killing Fields: The Khmer Rouge and Globalization," April 17, 1997, at http://www.mekong.net/Cambodia/revisit.htm

89 Short, *Pol Pot*, 4

90 See E.P. Thompson, *The Poverty of Theory; or an Orrery of Errors* (London: Merlin Press, 1996).

91 Short, *Pol Pot*, 402–43

92 Ward Churchill and Jim Vander Wall, *Agents of Repression: The FBI's Secret Wars against the Black Panther Party and the American Indian Movement* (Boston: South End Press, 1988), 64–74

93 William F. Pepper, *An Act of State: The Execution of Martin Luther King* (London Verso, 2008), 147, 273

94 Ibid., 131

95 James DiEngenio and Lisa Pease, eds., *The Assassinations: Probe Magazine on JFK, MLK, RFK, and Malcolm X* (Los Angeles: Feral House, 2003)

96 Ward Churchill and Jim Vander Wall, eds., *The COINTELPRO Papers: Documents from the FBI's Secret Wars against Dissent* (Boston: South End Press, 1990)

97 Michael Linfield, *Freedom under Fire: U.S. Civil Liberties in Times of War* (Boston: South End Press, 1990)

98 Regin Schmidt, *Red Scare: The FBI and the Origins of Anticommunism in the United States, 1919–1943* (Copenhagen: University of Copenhagen Press, 2000)

99 J. Edgar Hoover, cited in Churchill and Wall, *Agents of Repression*, 58

100 Christopher Hitchins, *The Trial of Henry Kissinger* (London: Verso, 2001), 25–41

101 Teleford Taylor, cited ibid., pp. 28–9. See Teleford Taylor, *Nuremberg and Vietnam: An American Tragedy* (Chicago: Quadrangle Books, 1970)

102 David Halberstan, *The Fifties* (New York: Villard Books, 1993), 359–69

103 William Blum, *Killing Hope: U.S. Military and CIA Intervention since World War II* (Montreal: Black Rose Books, 1998), 8

104 Walter J. Rockler, Letter to the Editor, *Chicago Tribune*, May 10, 1999

105 Karl Polanyi, *The Great Transformation* (New York: Farrar and Rhinehart, 1944)

106 William Engdahl, *A Century of War: Anglo-American Oil Politics and the New World Order* (London: Pluto Press, 2004)

107 Rigoberta Menchú, *I Rigoberta Menchú, and Indian Woman in Guatemala*, ed. Elisabeth Burgos-Debray; trans. Ann Wright (London: Verso, 1984)

108 Piero Gleijeses, "Afterward," in Nick Cullather, *Secret History: The CIA's Classified Account of Its Operation in Guatemala, 1952–1954* (Stanford: Stanford University Press, 1999), xx

109 Larry Tye, *The Father of Spin: Edward L. Bernays and the Birth of Public Relations* (New York: Crown Publishers, 1998)

110 Elizabeth Fones-Wolf, *Selling Free Enterprise: The Business Assault on Labour and Liberalism, 1945–1960* (Urbana: University of Illinois Press, 1994)

111 Edward L. Bernays, "The Engineering of Consent," *Annals of the American Academy of Political and Social Science* 70, 494 (1947): 52–4

112 Stephen G. Rabe, *Eisenhower and Latin America: The Foreign Policy of Anti-Communism* (Chapel Hill: University of North Carolina Press, 1988)

113 William Blum, *Rogue State: A Guide to the World's Only Superpower* (London: Zed Books, 2002), 61–7; Mark Danner, *The Massacre at El Mozote* (London: Vintage, 1994); Penny Lernoux, *Cry of the People: The Struggle for Human Rights in Latin America – The Catholic Church in Conflict with U.S. Policy* (New York: Penguin Books, 1982)

114 UN Commission on Historical Clarification, cited in Mireya Navarro, "Guatemala Study Accuses the Army and Cites U.S. Role," *New York Times*, Feb. 26, 1999. See Larry Rohter, "Searing Indictment," *New York Times*, Feb. 27, 1999; Michael Shifter, "Can Genocide End in Forgiveness?" *Los Angeles Times*, March 10, 1999; Jose Pertierra, "For Guatemala, Words Are Not Enough," *San Diego Union-Tribune*, March 5, 1999

115 Fidel Castro, *Cold War: Warnings for a Unipolar World* (Melbourne and New York: Ocean Press, 2003), 1–2

116 Chalmers Johnson, *Blowback: The Costs and Consequences of American Empire* (New York: Henry Holt, 2000), 72–85

117 Ibid., 225

118 Sands, *Lawless World*, 23–68

119 Nathaniel Davis, *The Last Two Years of Salvador Allende* (Ithaca, NY: Cornell University Press, 1985)

120 Erna Paris, *Long Shadows: Truth, Lies and History* (Toronto: Knopf Canada, 2000), 431–5; John Dinges, *The Condor Years: How Pinochet and His Allies Brought Terrorism to Three Continents* (New York: New Press, 2004)

121 *The Guardian* , Nov. 26, 1998, 24

122 Interview with Zbigniew Brzezinski, *Le Nouvel Observateur*, Jan. 15, 1998, at http://www.globalresearch.ca/articles/BRZ110A.html

123 Peter Dale Scott, "Congress, the Bush Administration and Continuity of Government Planning," *CounterPunch*, March 31, 2008, at http://www.counterpunch.org/scott03312008.html

124 National Security Strategy document, cited in Sands, *Lawless World*, 49

125 Noam Chomsky, *9-11* (New York: Seven Stories Press, 2002), 17–18

126 Barry Zwicker, "The Shame of Noam Chomsky and the Gatekeepers of the Left," in Zwicker, *Towers of Deception: The Media Cover-Up of 9/11* (Gabriola Island, BC: New Society Publishers, 2006), 179–224

127 Thierry Meyssan, *Effroyable Imposture: 11 septembre, 2001* (Maghreb: Editions EDDIR: M.Y.B. Retani Editeur, 2002); Thierry Meyssan, *L'effroyable imposture II : manipulations et désinformations* (Monaco: Alphée, 2007)

128 Thierry Meyssan, *9/11: The Big Lie* (London: Carnot, 2002)

129 Nafeez Mossaddeq Ahmed, *The War on Freedom: How and Why America Was Attacked, September 11, 2001* (Joshua Tree, Cal.: Tree of Life Publications, 2002)

130 Paul Thompson: *The Terror Timeline* (New York, Harper, 2004)

131 http://www.youtube.com/user/azuberi123#p/a/u/1/aDnz4rCMeuY

132 http://patriotsquestion911.com/

133 http://stj911.org/

134 http://www.ae911truth.org/

135 George Orwell, *Nineteen Eighty-Four: A Novel* (New York: Plume, 2003), 65

136 "9/11: Debunking the Myths," *Popular Mechanics*, March 2005

137 David Dunbar and Brad Reagan, eds., *Debunking 9/11 Myths: Why Conspiracy Theories Can't Stand Up to the Facts* (New York: Hearst Books, 2006)

138 David Ray Griffin, *Debinking 9/11 Debunking: An Answer to Popular Mechanics and Other Defenders of the Official Conspiracy Theory*, rev. ed. (Northampton, Mass.: Olive Branch Press, 2007), 207

139 The 2009 edition of *Global Outlook*, issue no. 13, is devoted to the subject of false flag operations at http://www.globaloutlook.ca/Store/Magazines/13/issue_13.htm.

140 Edward L. Bernays, *Biography of an Idea: Memoires of Public Relations Counsel* (New York: Simon and Schuster, 1965)

141 Gray Brechin, *Imperial San Francisco: Urban Power, Earthly Ruin* (Berkeley: University of California Press, 1999), 235

142 Charles Lindbergh, "Aviation, Race, and Geography," *Reader's Digest*, Nov. 1939, 64–7

143 George Creel, *How We Advertised America: The First Telling of the Amazing Story of the Committee on Public Information That Carried the Gospel of Americanism to Every Corner of the Globe* (New York: Harper and Brothers, 1920)

144 Walter Lippmann, *Public Opinion* (New York: Harcourt, Brace and Company, 1922)

145 Edward L. Bernays, *Propaganda* (1928; Brooklyn, NY: Ig Publising, 2005), 37

146 Nancy Snow, *Information Wars: American Propaganda, Free Speech and Opinion Control since 9/11* (New York: Seven Stories Press, 2003)

147 Bob Feldman, "George Soros' Evil Empire Is Exposed," Portland Indymedia at http://portland.indymedia.org/en/2002/12/39402.shtml

148 http://www.newamericancentury.org/RebuildingAmericasDefenses.pdf

149 Philip Shenon, *The Commission: The Uncensored History of the 9/11 Investigation* (New York: Twelve, 2008)

150 James Ridgeway, *The Five Unanswered Questions about 9/11* (New York: Seven Stories Press, 2005); G. Pathasarathy, "9/11 Report: An Exercise in Escapism," *The Hindu, Business Line,* July 30, 2004, at http://www.thehindu-businessline.com/2004/07/30/stories/2004073000031000.htm; Michael Kane, "The Final Fraud: 9/11 Commission Closes Its Door to the Public; Cover-Up Complete," from TheWilderness.com at http://www.fromthewilder-ness.com/free/ww3/071204_final_fraud.shtml; David Ray Griffin, *The 9/11 Commission Report: Omissions and Distortion* (Northampton, Mass.: Olive Branch Press, 2004)

151 Bejmanin DeMott, "Whitewash as Public Service," *Harper's Magazine,* Oct. 2004, at http://www.foreignaffairs.org/19981101faessay1434/ashton-b-carter-john-deutch-philip-zelikow/catastrophic-terrorism-tackling-the-new-danger.html

152 http://www.youtube.com/watch?v=Tzrv-e37Es8

153 Eric Boehlert interviews Max Clelland, Salon.com, Nov. 21, 2003, at http://dir.salon.com/story/news/feature/2003/11/21/cleland/index.html

154 John Farmer, *The Ground Truth: The Untold Story of America under Attack on 9/11* (New York: Riverhead Books, 2009), 4; see Mark Crispin Miller's review of *The Ground Truth* at BuzzFlash.com at http://www.buzzflash.com/store/reviews/1834.

155 Philip Zelikow, cited in Susan B. Glasser, "Global Terrorism Statistics Released," *Washington Post,* April 28, 2005, A7

156 Ashton B. Carter, John Deutch, and Philip Zelikow, *Foreign Affairs,* Nov./Dec. 1998, at http://www.foreignaffairs.org/19981101faessay1434/ashton-b-carter-john-deutch-philip-zelikow/catastrophic-terrorism-tackling-the-new-danger.html; see also http://www.hks.harvard.edu/visions/publication/terrorism.htm.

157 Barrie McKenna, "The Financial Black Market: We Should Have Known Better – All of Us," *Globe and Mail,* Dec. 26, 2008, B3

158 Jacob Heilbrunn, "The Lies They Told," in *New York Times Book Review,* Nov. 15, 2009, 16

159 Remarks by Barack Obama at West Point, Dec. 1, 2009, Voltairenet at http://www.voltairenet.org/article163179.html

160 Noam Chomsky, *9-11* (New York: Seven Stories Press, 2002), 17–18

161 Kevin Ryan, "A Personal Decision," 911Review.com at http://911review.com/
articles/ryan/personaldecision.html. A full collection of Ryan's essays can be
accessed at http://911review.com/articles/ryan/index.html.

162 Ryan, "Demolition Access to the WTC Towers: Part One – Tenants,"
911Review.com, Aug. 9, 2009, at http://911review.com/articles/ryan/
demolition_access_p1.html

163 Peter Truell and Larry Gurwin, *False Profits: The Inside Story of BCCI, the World's
Most Corrupt Financial Empire* (New York: Houghton Mifflin, 1992); Tariq
Ali, *A Banker for All Seasons: Bank of Crooks and Cheats Incorporated* (London:
Seagull, 2008)

164 Andrew G. Marshall, "State-Sponsored Terror: British and American Black
Ops in Iraq," June 25, 2008, at http://www.globalresearch.ca/index.
php?context=va&aid=9447

165 Lawrence Walsh, *Firewall: The Iran-Contra Conspiracy and Cover-Up* (New York:
W.W. Norton, 1997)

166 Ryan, "Demolition Access to the WTC Towers: Part Two – Security,"
911Review.com, Aug. 22, 2009, at http://911review.com/articles/ryan/
demolition_access_p2.html

167 Fabian Escalente, *CIA Targets Fidel: Secret 1967 CIA Inspector General's Report on
Plots to Assassinate Fidel Castro* (Melbourne: Ocean Press, 1996)

168 James Bamford, *Body of Secrets: Anatomy of the Ultra-Secret National Security Agency
from the Cold War through the Dawn of a New Century* (New York: Doubleday,
2001), chapter 4

169 Rodofo Davalos Fernandez, *The United States versus the Cuban Five: A Judicial
Cover-Up* (Havana: Editorial Capitan San Luis, 2006)

170 http://www.marxists.org/history/cuba/archive/castro/1953/10/16.htm

CHAPTER FOURTEEN

1 Daniel Marc Segesser and Myriam Gessler, "Raphael Lemkin and the
International Debate on the Punishment of War Crimes (1919–1948),"
Journal of Genocide Research 7, 4 (2005): 453–68; Tanya Elder, "What You
See before Your Eyes: Document Raphael Lemkin's Life by Exploring His
Archival Papers," *Journal of Genocide Research* 7, 4 (2005): 469–99; Ryszard
Szawlowski, "Raphael Lemkin: The Polish Lawyer Who Created the Concept
of Genocide," *The Polish Quarterly of International Affairs*, no. 2 (2005): 98–133

2 Raphael Lemkin, *Axis Rule in Occupied Europe: Laws of Occupation, Analysis of
Government, Proposals for Redress* (Washington, DC: Carnegie Endowment for
International Peace, Division of International Law, 1944)

3 Raphael Lemkin, "Genocide as a Crime under International Law," *Journal of
International Law* 4, 1 (1947): 147

4 Samantha Power, *A Problem from Hell: America and the Age of Genocide* (New York:
Basic Books, 2002)

5 Vahakn N. Dadrian, *Warrant for Genocide: Key Elements of the Turko-Armenian
Conflict* (New Brunswick, NJ: Transaction Publishers, 1999)

6 Raphael Lemkin, *New York Times*, Nov. 8, 1946

7 Cenap Cakmak, "Historical Background: Evolution of the International Criminal Law, Individual Criminal Accountability and the Idea of a Permanent International Court," Human Rights and Human Welfare Background Papers www.du.edu/gsis/hrhw/working/2006/39-cakmak-2006.pdf

8 Adam Hochschild, *King Leopold's Ghost: A Story of Greed, Terror, and Heroism in Colonial Africa* (Boston: Houghton Mifflin, 1999), 102–20

9 David Levering Lewis, *W.E.B. Du Bois: The Fight for Equality and the American Century, 1919–1963* (New York: Henry Holt, 2000), 42–4

10 W.E.B. Du Bois, "To the World (Manifesto of the Second Pan-African Congress)," *The Crisis*, Nov. 1921, 6–10. See also Immanuel Geiss, *The Pan-African Movement in America, Europe and Africa* (New York: Holmes and Meier, 1974).

11 Daniel Marc Segesser, "The International Debate on the Punishment of War Crimes during the Balkans Wars and the First World War," *Peace and Change* 31, 4 (2006): 533–54

12 E. Stanislaus Rappaport, "The Problem of Inter-State Criminal Law," *Transactions of the Grotius Society*, vol. 18: Problems of Peace and War, papers read before the society in 1932, 41–64

13 Raphael Lemkin, "Acts Constituting a General (Transnational) Danger Considered as Crimes under International Law," paper given at the Madrid conference on the unification of penal law, 1933, trans. James T. Fussell, in http://www.preventgenocide.org/lemkin/

14 Lemkin, *Axis Rule in Occupied Europe*, 79

15 UN Resolution 96(1) on Genocide, Dec. 11, 1946, published in http://www.armenian-genocide.org/Affirmation.227/current_category.6/affirmation_detail.html

16 Proposed UN definition of genocide, cited in Robert Davis and Mark Zannis, *The Genocide Machine in Canada* (Montreal: Black Rose Books, 1973), 16

17 Hannah Arendt, cited in Jeremy Waldron, "What Would Hannah Say?" *The New York Review of Books*, March 15, 2007, 8

18 Barbara Harff and Ted Robert Gurr, "Victims of the State: Genocide, Politicides, and Group Repressions since 1945," *International Review of Victimology* 1, 1 (1989): 23–44; Sam Totten, William S. Parsons Jr, and Robert K. Hitchcock, "Confronting Genocide and Ethnocide of Indigenous Peoples: An Interdisciplinary Approach to Definition, Intervention, Prevention, and Adequacy," in Alexander Labhan Hinton, ed., *Annihilating Difference: The Anthropology of Genocide* (Berkeley: University of California Press, 2002), 54–91

19 René Lemarchand, "The Rwanda Genocide." in Samuel Totten, William S. Parsons, and Israel W. Charny, eds., *Century of Genocide: Eyewitness Accounts and Critical Views* (New York and London: Garland Publishing, 1997), 408–23; Roméo Dallaire, *Shake Hands with the Devil: The Failure of Humanity in Rwanda* (Toronto: Random House Canada, 2004)

20 Power, *A Problem from Hell*, 354–84

21 Michael Barnett, *Eyewitness to Genocide: The United Nations and Rwanda* (Ithaca, NY: Cornell University Press, 2002), 2

22 Graeme Hamilton, "Trial Brings Rwandan Genocide to Canada: Refugee Faces Charges under Canadian Law," *National Post*, March 17, 2007, A1, A14

23 Stephen Kinzer, *A Thousand Hills: Rwanda's Rebirth and the Man Who Dreamt It* (Hoboken, NJ: Wiley, 2008), 110; Sukhdev Chhatbar and Donna Bryson. "Rwanda Massacre Planner, Theoneste Bagosoro, Convicted of Genocide," *Huffington Post*, Jan. 3 2009, at http://www.huffingtonpost. com/2008/12/18/rwandan-massacres-planner_n_151990.html

24 Hutu Genocide Suspects Arrested in Germany, CBS News, Nov. 17, 2009, at http://www.cbsnews.com/stories/2009/11/17/world/main5683598. shtml?source=related_story

25 Kofi Annan, cited in http://69.94.11.53/default.htm

26 Lisa Hijjar, "From Nuremberg to Guantanamo: International Law and American Power Politics," *Middle East Report*, no. 229 (winter 2003), at http:// www.merip.org/mer/mer229/229_hajjar.html

27 Anthony J. Hall, "Should George W. Bush Be Arrested in Calgary, Alberta, to Be Tried for International Crimes," Voltairenet, March 9, 2009, at http:// www.voltairenet.org/article159233.html

28 Roger W. Smith, "Human Destructiveness and Politics: The Twentieth Century as an Age of Genocide," in Isidor Walliman and Michael N. Dobkowski, eds., *Genocide and the Modern Age: Etiology and Case Studies of Mass Death* (New York: Greenwood Press, 1987), 21–38

29 The Asper Foundation, *Human Rights and Holocaust Studies Program: Memorandum for Personal Responsibility* (Winnipeg: Canadian Museum for Human Rights, 2006)

30 Robert K. Hitchcock and Tara M. Twedt, "Physical and Cultural Genocide of Various Indigenous Peoples," in Totten, Charny, and Parsons, eds., *Century of Genocide*, 372–407; Elazar Barkan, "Genocides of Indigenous Peoples: Rhetoric of Human Rights," in Robert Gellately and Ben Kiernan, eds., *The Specter of Genocide: Mass Murder in Historical Perspective* (Cambridge: Cambridge University Press, 2003)

31 Anti-Slavery Society, *The Chittagong Hill Tracts. Indigenous Peoples and Development Series*, no. 2 (London: The Anti-Slavery Society, 1984); Akram H. Chowdhury, "Self-Determination, the Chittagong, and Bangladesh," in David P. Forsythe, ed., *Human Rights and Development: International Views* (New York: St Martin's Press, 1989), 292–301; Rounaq Jahan, "Genocide in Bangladesh," in Totten, Charny, and Parsons, eds., *Century of Genocide*, 291–316

32 John Wing and Peter King, *Genocide in West Papua? A Report Prepared for the West Papua Project at the Centre for Peace and Conflict Studies, University of Sydney* (Sydney: West Papua Project, 2005)

33 Wade Davis, "Death of a People: Logging in the Penan Homeland," in Marc S. Miller, ed., with the staff of Cultural Survival, *State of the Peoples: A Global Human Rights Report on Societies in Danger* (Boston: Beacon Press, 1993), 23–32

34 African Rights, *Facing Genocide: The Nuba of Sudan* (London: African Rights,1995)

35 Colin Samson, James Wilson, and Jonathan Mazower, *Canada's Tibet: The Killing of the Innu* (London: Survival for Tribal People, 1999)

36 Berwick, Dennison, *Savages: The Life and Killing of the Yanomami* (London: Hutchinson, 1992); Bruce Albert, "Gold Miners and Yanomami Indians in the Brazilian Amazon: The Hashimu Massacre," in Barbara Rose Johnston, ed., *Who Pays the Price? The Sociocultural Context of Environmental Crisis* (Washington, DC, and Covelo, Cal.: Island Press, 1994), 47–55

37 David Stannard, *American Holocaust: The Conquest of the New World* (New York: Oxford University Press, 1992); Ward Churchill, *A Little Matter of Genocide: Holocaust and Denial in the Americas, 1492 to Present* (San Francisco: City Lights, 1998)

38 Jeremiah Evarts, *Cherokee Removal: The "William Penn" Essays and Other Writings,* ed. Francis Paul Prucha (Knoxville: University of Tennessee Press, 1981), 129–30

39 David Stannard, "Uniqueness as Denial: The Politics of Genocide Scholarship," in *Is the Holocaust Unique? Perspectives on Comparative Genocide* (Boulder, Col.: Westview Press, 1996)

40 "Holocaust: Singularity of the Holocaust in Comparative Historical Context," *Encyclopaedia Judaica,* CD-ROM edition (Jerusalem; Judaica Multimedia)

41 Magnus Morner, *Race Mixture in Latin America* (New York: Little, Brown, 1967)

42 Allan G. Harper, "Canada's Indian Administration: Basic Concepts and Objectives," *America Indigena* 5, 2 (1945): 132

43 Barbara J. Boseker, "The Disappearance of American Indian Languages," *Journal of Multilingual and Multicultural Development* 15, 2 and 3 (1994): 1547–60

44 Samuel Huntington, *The Clash of Civilizations and the Making of World Order* (New York: Simon and Schuster, 1996), 46, 51, 151, 301–21

45 Russell Thornton, *American Indian Holocaust and Survival: A Population History since 1492* (Norman: University of Oklahoma Press, 1990)

46 "Holocaust: Singularity of the Holocaust in Comparative Historical Context"

47 Colin G. Calloway, *Crown and Calumet: British-Indian Relations, 1783–1815* (Norman: University of Oklahoma Press, 1987); Robert S. Allen, *His Majesty's Indian Allies: British Indian Policy in Defence of Canada, 1783–1815* (Toronto: Dundurn, 1992)

48 Bruce Vandervort, *Indian Wars of Canada, Mexico, and the United States, 1812–1900* (New York: Routledge, 2005); Daniel K. Richter, *Facing West from Indian Country: A Native History of Early America* (Cambridge, Mass.: Harvard University Press, 2001); Robert M. Utley and Wilcombe E. Washburn, *The Indian Wars* (Boston: Houghton Mifflin, 1985); Bill Yenne, *Indian Wars: The Campaign for the American West* (Yardley, Penn.: Westholme Publishers, 2005); William M. Osborn, *The Wild Frontier: Atrocities during the American-Indian War from Jamestown to Wounded Knee* (New York: Random House, 2001); John Frost, *Indian Wars of the United States* (Miller, Orton and Mulligan,1855); Robert V.

Remini, *Andrew Jackson and His Indian Wars* (New York: Viking, 2001); Lee Enoch Lawrence, *Indian Wars in North Carolina* (Raleigh, NC: Carolina Charter Tercentennary Commission, 1963); John Henry Brown, *Indian Wars and Pioneers of Texas* (Austin, Tex.: State House Press, 1988); Chester Hale Sipe, *The Indian Wars of Pennsylvania* (New York: Arno Press, 1971); Ray Hoard Glassley, *Indian Wars of the Pacific Northwest* (Portland, Maine: Binfords and Mort, 1972); Fairfax Davis Downey, *Indian Wars of the U.S. Army, 1776–1865* (Garden City, NJ: Doubleday, 1963)

49 John L. Tobias, "Canada's Subjugation of the Plains Cree, 1879–1885," *Canadian Historical Review* 64, 4 (1983): 519–48; Blair Stonechild and Bill Waiser, *Loyal till Death: Indians and the North-West Rebellion* (Calgary: Fifth House, 1997); D.N. Sprague, *Canada and the Metis, 1869–1885* (Waterloo, Ont.: Wilfrid Laurier University Press, 1988)

50 Chris Arnett, *Terror of the Coast: Land Alienation and Colonial Wars on Vancouver Island and the Gulf Islands* (Burnaby, BC: Talon Books, 1997)

51 John Goddard, *Last Stand of the Lubicon Cree* (Vancouver: Douglas and McIntyre, 1991)

52 Geoffrey York and Loreen Pindera, *People of the Pines: The Warriors and the Legacy of Oka* (Toronto: Little, Brown, 1991); Peter Edwards, *One Dead Indian: The Premier, the Police, and the Ipperwash Crisis* (Toronto: McClelland & Stewart, 2003)

53 L.F.S. Upton,, "The Extermination of the Beothuks of Newfoundland," *Canadian Historical Review* 63, 2 (1977): 133–53

54 Malcolm X with the assistance of Alex Haley, *The Autobiography of Malcolm X* (London: Hutchinson, 1966)

55 Louis Hall,"Suicide as a Weapon against Oppression," mimeographed newsletter, no. 11, June 22, 1976

56 Menno Boldt, *Surviving as Indians: The Challenge of Self-Government* (Toronto: University of Toronto Press, 1996)

57 Roger C. Altman, "The Great Crash, 2008: A Geopolitical Setback for the West," *Foreign Affairs* 88, 1 (Jan./Feb. 2009): 10

58 Duncan Campbell Scott, cited in Brian Titley, *A Narrow Vision: Duncan Campbell Scott and the Administration of Indian Affairs in Canada* (Vancouver: UBC Press, 1992), 25

59 Fintan O'Toole, *White Savage: William Johnson and the Invention of America* (New York: Farrar, Straus and Giroux, 2005)

60 Duncan Campbell Scott, "Indian Affairs, 1763–1841," in *Canada and Its Provinces* (Toronto: Glasgow, Brook and Co., 1914), vol. 4, 698

61 Duncan Campbell Scott, cited in Brian Titley, *A Narrow Vision: Duncan Campbell Scott and the Administration of Indian Affairs in Canada* (Vancouver: UBC Press, 1992), 50

62 Dean Neu and Richard Therrien, *Accounting for Genocide: Canada's Bureaucratic Assault on Aboriginal People* (Blackpoint, NS: Fernwood, 2003)

63 Suzanne Fornier and Ernie Crey, *Stolen from Our Embrace: The Abduction of Aboriginal Children and the Restoration of Aboriginal Communities* (Vancouver:

Douglas and McIntyre, 1997); Agnes Grant, *No End of Grief: Indian Residential Schools in Canada* (Winnipeg: Pemmican Publications, 1996); J.R. Miller, *Shingwauk's Vision: A History of Native Residential Schools* (Toronto: University of Toronto Press, 2000)

64 Roland D. Chrisjohn and Sherri Young, *The Circle Game: Shadows and Substance in the Indian Residential School Experience in Canada* (Penticton, BC: Theytus Books, 1997); Chrisjohn et al., "Genocide and Indian Residential Schooling: The Past Is Present," in Richard D. Wiggers and Ann L. Griffiths, eds., *Canada and International Humanitarian Law: Peace Keeping and War Crimes in the Modern Era* (Halifax: Dalhousie University Press, 2002)

65 "How Sorry Are We?" *Western Report*, March 10, 1998; Angus McLaren, *Our Own Master Race: Eugenics in Canada, 1885–1945* (Toronto: McClelland & Stewart, 1990)

66 Edwin Black, *War on the Weak: Eugenics and America's Campaign to Create a Master Race* (New York: Four Walls Eight Windows, 2003); "Sterilization Eugenics by Country Index," at http://members.aol.com/_ht_a/lillithsrealm/myhomepage/MISECIndex.html

67 Maureen Lux, "Perfect Subjects: Race, Tuberculosis, and the Qu'Appelle BCG Vaccine Trial,' *Canadian Bulletin of Medical History* 15, 2 (1998): 277–95; R.G. Ferguson, *Tuberculosis among the Indians of the Great Canadian Plains* (London: Adlard and Son, 1928); G.J. Wherrett, *The Miracle of Empty Beds: The History of Tuberculosis in Canada* (Toronto: University of Toronto Press, 1977)

68 See Kevin Annett, "The Final Solution to Our Indian Problem: Genocide and Native Residential Schools in Canada," *Kahtou*, April 2004 at http://www.kahtou.com/images/apr_tlkingstck.htm; Government of Canada, *Report of the Royal Commission on Aboriginal Peoples*, vol. 1, part 2, chapter 10, "Residential Schools," at http://www.ainc-inac.gc.ca/ch/rcap/sg/sgn10_e.html

69 Lorraine Mallinder, "Playground Bones Force Canada to Face Genocide of Indian Children, *The Scotsman*, Jan. 6, 2006, at http://news.scotsman.com/world/Playground-bones–force-Canada.4845558.jp

70 Bill Curry and Karen Howlett, "Natives Died in Droves as Ignored as Ottawa Ignored Warnings," *Globe and Mail*, April 24, 2007, A1, A14

71 P.H. Bryce, *Report on the Indian Schools of Manitoba and the Northwest Territories* (June 19, 1907). See also Library and Archives Canada, RG 10 Collection, vol. 3957, file 140-754-1, report of Dr P.H. Bryce, Nov. 5, 1909; P.H. Bryce, *The Story of a National Crime; An Appeal for Justice to the Indians of Canada: Our Allies in the Revolutionary War; Our Brothers-in-Arms in the Great War* (Ottawa: James Hope and Sons, 1922); John Milloy, *A National Crime: The Canadian Government and the Residential School System, 1879 to 1986* (Winnipeg: University of Manitoba Press, 1999)

72 Scott, cited in Annett, "The Final Solution" at http://www.kahtou.com/images/apr_tlkingstck.htm

73 Richard White, *The Middle Ground: Indians, Empires, and Republics in the Great Lakes Area* (Cambridge: Cambridge University Press, 1991), 288

74 David Wallace Adams, *Education for Extinction: American Indians and the Boarding School Experience, 1875–1928* (Lawrence: University of Kansas Press, 1995); see also Ward Churchill, *Kill the Indian, Save the Man: The Genocidal Impact of Indian Residential Schools* (San Francisco: City Lights, 2005)

75 Human Rights and Equal Opportunity Commission, *Bringing Them Home, The Report of the National Inquiry into the Separation of Aboriginal and Torres Strait Islander Children from Their Families* (1997), at http://www.austlii.edu.au/au/special/rsjproject/rsjlibrary/hreoc/stolen/stolen08.html http://www.human-rights.gov.au/social_justice/stolen_children/index.html

76 On the discourse on Australian genocide, see Dirk Moses, "Coming to Terms with Genocidal Pasts in Comparative Perspectives," *Aboriginal History* 25, 1 (2001); Paul Bartrop, "The Holocaust, the Aborigines, and the Bureaucracy of Destruction: An Australian Dimension of Genocide," *Journal of Genocide Research* 3, 1 (2001); Elazar Barkan , *The Guilt of Nations: Restitution and Negotiating Historical Injustices* (New York: W.W. Norton, 2000), 245–48; Sue Stanton, "Time for Truth: Speaking the Unspeakable – Genocide and Apartheid in the 'Lucky' Country," *Australian Humanities Review*, issue 14 (July–Sept. 1999) at http://www.lib.latrobe.edu.au/AHR/archive/Issue-July-1999/stanton.html

77 Peter H. Russell, *Recognizing Aboriginal Title: The Mabo Case and Indigenous Resistance to English-Settler Colonialism* (Toronto: University of Toronto Press, 2005); Henry Reynolds, "After Mabo, What About Sovereignty?" *Australian Humanities Review*, issue 1 (1996), at http://www.lib.latrobe.edu.au/AHR/archive/Issue-April-1996/Reynolds.html

78 *National Inquiry into the Separation of Aboriginal and Torres Strait Islander Children from Their Families*, Report launch speech by Mick Dodson, Aboriginal and Torres Strait Islander Social Justice Commissioner, Australian Reconciliation Convention, Melbourne, May 26, 1997, at http://www.hreoc.gov.au/speeches/social_justice/stolen_generation_launch.html

79 Robert Manne, "In Denial: The Stolen Generation and the Right," *The Australian Quarterly Essay* 1, 1 (2001): 1–113

80 Geoffrey Belaney, "Black Future," *Bulletin*, April 8, 1997

81 Margo Kingston, *Off the Rails: Pauline Hanson's Trip*, 2nd ed. (Sydney: Allen Unwin, 2001)

82 Amin Salkal, "Australia Wants No Guff from the United Nations," *International Herald Tribune*, Sept. 5, 2000

83 Rt Hon. Malcolm Fraser, Vincent Lingiari Memorial Lecture, Aug. 24, 2000, at http://kirra.austlii.edu.au/au/other/IndigLRes/car/2000/2408.html

84 Frank Hardy, *The Unlucky Australians* (Melbourne: Nelson, 1968)

85 Campbell Clark, "Natives to Hit Ottawa with Rights Complaint," *Globe and Mail*, Feb. 5, 2007, A1

86 Prime Minister Kevin Rudd's apology, published in Stephanie Peatling, "Rudd's Apology Revealed," *Sydney Morning Herald*, Feb. 13, 2008

87 Text of Prime Minister Stephen Harper's apology speech at http://le-enfant-terrible.blogspot.com/2008/06/text-of-canadian-pm-harpers-apology.html

88 Mike Krebs, "Sorry for Genocide," *The Dominion*, July 18, 2008, at http://www.dominionpaper.ca/articles/1928#comment_jump

89 Roland D. Chrisjohn and Sherri L. Young, *The Circle Game: Shadows and Substance in the Indian Residential School Experience* (Penticton, BC: Theytus Books, 2006)

90 Pierre Loiselle, "Like Weeds in a Garden," *The Dominion*, Oct. 12, 2006, at http://www.dominionpaper.ca/original_peoples/2006/10/12/like_weeds.html

91 Gloria Galloway, "Did Australia Demand Reversal on Natives? Ottawa Pulled Support after Howard's Visit," *Globe and Mail*, June 9, 2007, A1, A10

92 United Nations General Assembly, Human Rights Council, "United Nations Declaration of the Rights of Indigenous Peoples," Sept. 12, 2007, A61, L67

93 World Council of Churches, Declaration of Barbados, Jan. 30, 1971, cited in Craig Benjamin, *Native Americas: Akwe:kon's Journal of Indigenous Issues* 15, 4 (1998): 29

94 Roxanne Dunbar Ortiz, *Indians of the Americas: Human Rights and self-Determination* (London: Zed, 1984), 60. The Barbados Declaration and a series of papers presented at Bridgetown are published in Walter Dostal, ed., *The Situation of Indians in South America* (Geneva: World Council of Churches, 1972).

95 Ibid.

96 Brandon Yoder, "Indigenous Peoples and Oil Production in Ecuador's Oriente," *Fourth World Journal* 5, 1 (2002): 80–97

97 Barkan, *The Guilt of Nations*, 368, n4

98 Ike Okonta and Oronto Douglas, *Where Vultures Feast: Shell, Human Rights, and Oil in the Niger Delta* (San Francisco: Sierra Club Books, 2001); Ken Saro-Wiwa, *Genocide in Nigeria: The Ogoni Tragedy* (Port Harcourt, 1992); "Testimony of Dr. Owens Wiwa before the Joint Briefing of the Congressional Human Rights Caucus and the Congressional Black Caucus," Washington, DC, Jan. 30, 1996 (published electronically by the Sierra Club)

99 Rebeca Izquierdo, "The Thinking People: The U'wa Battle Oxy," *Cultural Survival Quarterly* 25, 3 (2001): 36–9

100 Peter Usher, "Choosing Your Poison: Differences of Opinion about the Destruction of a Native Community," *This Magazine* 20, 5 (Dec. 1986 / Jan. 1987): 40–4; Peter Usher et al., *The Economic and Social Impact of Mercury Pollution on the Whitedog and Grassy Narrows Indian Reserves, Ontario, Report to the Anti-Mercury Ojibway Group* (Kenora, Ont., 1979)

101 See F.G. Roe, *The North American Buffalo: A Critical Study of the Species in Its Wild State*, 2nd ed. (Toronto: University of Toronto Press, 1970), 601–70.

102 Anastasia M. Shkilnyk, *A Poison Stronger than Love: The Destruction of an Ojibway Community* (New Haven: Yale University Press, 1985), 181

103 Ibid., 4

104 Ibid., 181

105 Member of the UN Human Rights Committee, cited in Gordon Liard, "Speak No Evil," *This Magazine*, March / April 1998, 20

106 See John Goddard, *The Last Stand of the Lubicon Cree* (Vancouver: Douglas and McIntyre, 1991).

107 Fred Lennarson, letter to the editor of the *Globe and Mail*, April 30, 1998, written in response to Tom Flanagan, "Tactics of the Lubicon," ibid., April 1998

108 Liard, "Speak No Evil," 20

109 Lennarson, letter to the editor

110 John Bacher, "Activists Unite to Revoke the Charter of Unocal Corporation," *The Activist*, Aug. 2001, 14–15

111 See Larry Pratt and Ian Urquhart, *The Last Great Forest: Japanese Multinationals and Alberta's Northern Forest* (Edmonton: NeWest Press, 1994).

112 Christopher Genovali, "Diashowa Tries to Gag Critics," *Alternatives Journal* 23, 2 (spring 1997): 12

113 Mr Justice James MacPherson, cited in *Aboriginal Rights Coalition Insider*, April 17, 1998, 1

114 Ward Churchill, *A Little Matter of Genocide: Holocaust and Denial in the Americas, 1492 to Present* (Winnipeg: Arbeiter Ring Publishing, 1998)

115 Archbishop Edward Walter Scott, cited in *Aboriginal Rights Coalition Insider*, Fact Sheet no. 2 (summer 1998): 10

116 Mackenzie-Ruby report for the Law Society of Upper Canada, 1996, published in Randal N.M. Graham, *Legal Ethics: Theories, Cases and Professional Regulations* (Toronto: Edmond Montgomery Publications, 2004), 116

117 Roy Nielson, "Sudan: American Interests and Christian Ethics," *Witness Magazine*, Oct. 10, 2003, at http://www.thewitness.org/article.php?id=150

118 See Andrew Clapham, "The Complexity of International Criminal Law: Looking Beyond Individual Responsibility to the Responsibility of Organizations, Corporations and States," in Ramesh Thakur and Peter Malcontent, eds., *From Sovereign Impunity to the Responsibility of Organizations, Corporations, and States* (Tokyo: United Nations University Press, 2004), 233–52.

119 John Harker, "Intervention is Served: The US Federal Alien Tort Claims Act and the Irony of Ironies," *Cambridge Review of International Affairs* 16, 1 (2003): 154–64

120 On Talisman as an "artificial person," see Kenneth Anderson's Law of War and Just Law Theory blog, "New Talisman (Alien Tort Statute) Decision Upholding Corporate Liability," June 17, 2005, at http://kennethanderson-lawofwar.blogspot.com/2005/06/new-talisman-alien-tort-statute.html

121 Madelaine Drohan, *Making a Killing: How Corporations Used Armed Force to Do Business* (Toronto: Random House, 2003), 243–90

122 Eric Reeves, "Talisman Can't Escape the Burden of Genocidal Complicity in Sudan," March 24, 2003, at http://www.sudanreeves.org/Sections-req-viewarticle-artid-232-allpages-1-theme-Printer.html

123 Gwynne Skinner, "Nuremberg's Legacy Continues: The Nuremberg Trials' Influence on Human Rights Litigation in U.S. Courts under the Alien Tort Statute," *Albany Law Review* 71, 1 (2008): 370

124 Larry Neumeister, "Talisman Released from Genocide Case," Associated Press, Sept. 12, 2006, at http://www.boston.com/business/articles/2006/09/12/judge_dismisses_energy_co_genocide_case/

125 Chris Alden, *China in Africa: Partner, Competitor, or Hegemon?* (London: Zed, 2007)

126 Heba Aly, "Genocide in Darfur? What Genocide?" *Globe and Mail,* July 19 2008, F3

127 Susan Morgan, "PetroChina, the UN and Blood Money," *Huffington Post,* Jan. 7, 2009 at http://www.huffingtonpost.com/susan-morgan/petrochina-the-un-and-blo_b_155794.html

128 Fidel Castro Ruz, *The Internationalization of Genocide* (La Habana: Oficina de Publicaciones del Consejo de Estado, 2007), 5

129 Osvaldo Martinez, "Towards the Integration of Peoples," paper delivered at the Hemispheric Gathering for the Struggle against Free Trade and for the Integration of Peoples, Havana, Cuba, May 3, 2007

130 Ludo De Witte, *The Assassination of Lumumba,* trans. Ann Wright and Renee Fenby (London: Verso, 2001)

131 Gerard Prunier, *Africa's World War: Congo, the Rwandan Genocide and the Making of a Continental Catastrophe* (New York: Oxford University Press, 2009); Thomas Turner, *The Congo Wars: Conflict, Myth, Reality* (New York: Zed, 2007)

132 Hochschild, *King Leopold's Ghost,* 225–33

133 Robin Browne, "Blood Cell Phones Worsen Crisis in Congo," *Alternatives,* July 19, 2008 at http://www.alternatives.ca/article3968.html

134 Testimony of Wayne Madsen, US Congressional Report, serial no. 107–16, May 17, 2001, at http://www.globalresearch.ca/articles/MAD111A.html

135 Wayne Madsen, *Jaded Tasks: Brass Plates, Black Ops and Big Oil* (Tempe, Ariz.: Dandelion Books, 2004). 7 (published digitally at http://www.scribd.com/doc/8470565/Jaded-Tasks)

136 Stephen Kinzer, *A Thousand Hills: Rwanda's Rebirth and the Man Who Dreamt It* (Hoboken, NJ: John Wiley and Sons, 2008), 51, 59–65

137 Madsen, *Jaded Tasks,* 1–38

138 Dallaire, *Shake Hands with the Devil,* 373, 375

139 See Jacques-Roger Boobooh, *Le Patron de Dallaire Parle* (Paris: Editions Dubroiris, 2005).

140 Dallaire, *Shake Hands with the Devil,* 67

141 Andrew G. Marshall, "Martial Law Inc., KBR: A Halliburton Subsidiary," March 5, 2008 at http://www.globalresearch.ca/index.php?context=va&aid=8258

142 Madsen, *Jaded Tasks,* 12

143 Keith Harmon Snow and David Barouski, "Behind the Numbers: Untold Suffering in Congo," *z Mag,* March 1, 2006, at http://www.thirdworldtraveler.com/Africa/Congo_BehindNumbers.html; Keith Harmon Snow, "Darfurism, Uganda and the U.S. War on Terror," Nov. 11, 2007, at http://www.global-research.ca/index.php?context=va&aid=7311

144 See, for instance, United Nations, *Final Report of the Panel of Experts on the Illegal Exploitation of Natural Resources and Other Forms of Wealth in the Democratic Republic of Congo*, Oct. 8, 2002, s/2002/1146.

145 David Barouski, "Mining in Ituri Province of Congo," *Z Mag*, May 14, 2007, at http://www.zmag.org/znet/viewArticle/15432

146 Linda Melvern, *Conspiracy to Murder: The Rwandan Genocide* (London: Verso, 2004); John Pottier, *Re-Imagining Rwanda: Conflict, Survival, and Disinformation in the Late Twentieth Century* (Cambridge: Cambridge University Press, 2002)

147 Mahmood Mamdani, *When Victims Become Killers: Colonialism, Nativism, and the Genocide in Rwanda* (Princeton: Princeton University Press, 2001), 102

148 See Virgil Hawkins, "Stealth Conflicts: Africa's World War in the DRC and International Consciousness," at http://www.jha.ac/articles/a126.htm.

149 Carla Del Ponte with Chuck Sudetic, *Madame Prosecutor: Confrontation with Humanity's Worst Criminals and the Culture of Impunity, A Memoir* (New York: Other Press, 2009), 179

150 Peter Erlinder, "The Real Authors of the Congo Crimes: Nkunda Has Been Arrested but Who Will Arrest Kagame," Global Research.ca, Feb. 2, 2009, at http://www.globalresearch.ca/index.php?context=va&aid=12139

151 Joanne Tomkinson, "Ethnicity, Economics and the UN's Failure in East Congo," *Alertnet*, Oct. 30, 2008, at http://www.alertnet.org/db/an_art/47985/2008/09/30-164342-1.htm

152 Peter Walker and Chris McGreal, "Congo Militia Leader 'Trained Child Soldiers to Kill,'" *The Guardian*, Jan. 26, 2009, at http://www.guardian.co.uk/world/2009/jan/26/thomas-lubanga-international-criminal-court

153 Exchange between Sir William Johnson and George Croghan, cited in White, *The Middle Ground*, 345

154 Ibid., 348

155 William Christie MacLeod, *The American Indian Frontier* (New York: Alfred A. Knopf, 1928)

156 Anna Jameson, *Winter Studies and Summer Rambles in Canada*, 3 vols. (1838; Toronto: Coles, 1972), 3: 318–19

157 Karl Marx, *Capital*, vol. 1 (Moscow: Foreign Language Publishing House, 1959), 84

158 Karl Marx, *Grundrisse: Foundations of the Critique of Political Economy* (New York: Vintage, 1973), 338, 408, 410

159 Martin Luther King Jr, "Non-Violence and Social Change," in *The Lost Massey Lectures: Recovered Classics from Five Great Thinkers* (Toronto: Anansi, 2007), 200–1

160 Major Benjamin Cumming Truman, *History of the World's Fair, Being a Complete Description of the World's Columbian Exposition from Its Inception* (Chicago: Chicago World's Columbian Exposition, 1893), 550

161 Fred Magdoff, "Capitalism's Twin Crises: Economic and Environmental," *Monthly Review* 54 (Sept. 2002): 1–5; John Bellamy Foster, "Capitalism and Ecology: The Nature of the Contradiction," ibid., 6–16

162 Herman E. Daly, "Economics in a Full World," *Scientific American* 293, 3 (Sept. 2005): 100; see also Herman E. Daly and Joshua Farley, *Ecological Economics: Principles and Applications* (Washington, DC: Island Press, 2004)

163 Herman E. Daly, "Big Idea: A Steady-State Economy," *Adbusters: The Big Ideas for 2009*. Canadian edition, no pagination

CHAPTER FIFTEEN

1 Roger C. Altman, "Globalization in Retreat: Further Geopolitical Consequences of the Financial Crisis," *Foreign Affairs*, July / August 2009, 7

2 Kevin Baker, "Barack Hoover Obama: The Best and the Brightest Blow It Again," *Harper's Magazine*, July 2009, 37

3 Ibid., 34–7

4 See Bill Moyer's remarkable interview of economist William K. Black on PBS, April 3, 2009, at http://www.pbs.org/moyers/journal/04032009/watch.html; William K. Black, "Why Is Geithner Continuing Paulson's Policy of Violating the Law," at Huffington Post, Feb. 23, 2009, at http://www.huffingtonpost. com/william-k-black/why-is-geithner-continuin_b_169234.html.

5 http://www.josephstiglitz.com/

6 William H. Nelson, *The American Tory* (Boston: Northeastern University Press, 1992)

7 John McMurtry, "The Obama Crossroads: Neo-Liberal Coup or Responsible Government?" *The Canadian Charger*, July 15, 2009, at http://www. thecanadiancharger.com/page.php?id=5&a=70

8 See Harold Innis, *Empire and Communications* (Oxford: Oxford University Press, 1950).

9 Richard White, *The Middle Ground: Indians, Empires, and Republics in the Great Lakes Region, 1650–1815* (Cambridge: Cambridge University Press, 1991)

10 Allida M. Black, *Casting Her Own Shadow: Eleanor Roosevelt and the Shaping of Postwar Liberalism* (New York: Columbia University Press, 1996)

11 Jane Mayer, "The Secret History: Can Leon Panetta Move the C.I.A. Forward without Confronting Its Past," *The New Yorker*, June 22, 2009, 50–9

12 William Holstein, *Why GM Matters: Inside the Race to Transform an American Icon* (New York: Walker and Company, 2009)

13 Remarks by President Barack Obama on General Motors Restructuring, June 1, 2009, Organizing for America at http://my.barackobama.com/page/ community/post/obamaforamerica/gGGGgx

14 http://www.carofthecentury.com/top_10_milestones_by_harley_earl.htm

15 Seymour Melman, *After Capitalism: From Managerialism to Workplace Democracy* (New York: Alfred A. Knopf, 2001)

16 Americans for Limited Government, cited by John Ibbitson, "Meet the New President of General Motors," *Globe and Mail*, March 31, 2009, A13

17 Mike Huckabee, cited in John Ibbitson, "Barack Obama Is Putting the State in Charge of the Economy in the Land of Free Enterprise," *Globe and Mail*, April 4, 2009, A1

18 Sydney Fine, *Sit-Down: The General Motors Strike of 1936–37* (Ann Arbor: University of Michigan Press, 1969); John Barnard, *American Vanguard: The United Auto Workers during the Reuther Years, 1933–1970* (Detroit: Wayne State University Press, 2004)

19 Edwin Black, *Nazi Nexus: America's Corporate Connections to Hitler's Holocaust* (Washington, DC: Dialog Press, 2009)

20 Neil Baldwin, *Henry Ford and the Jews: The Mass Production of Hate* (New York: Public Affairs, 2001); Max Wallace. *The American Axis: Henry Ford, Charles Lindbergh, and the Rise of the Third Reich* (New York: St Martin's Press, 2003)

21 Ernest Haberkern, "Prophets of the Permanent War Economy," *Monthly Review Press*, 2009, at http://monthlyreview.org/090525haberkern.php

22 Charles E. Wilson, "For Common Defense: A Plea for a Continuing Program of Industrial Preparedness," *Army Ordinance* 16 (March–April 1944)

23 Seymour Melman, "From Private to State Capitalism: How the Permanent War Economy Transformed the Institutions of American Capitalism," *Journal of Economic Issues* 31 (June 1997): 311–30

24 George C. Herring. *From Colony to Superpower: U.S. Foreign Relations since 1776* (New York: Oxford University Press, 2008)

25 Center for Arms Control and Non-Proliferation at http://www.armscontrol-center.org/policy/securityspending/articles/fy09_dod_request_global/; see also Andrew J. Bacevich, *The New American Militarism: How Americans Are Seduced by War* (New York: Oxford University Press, 2005); Jon W. Western, *Selling Intervention and War: The Presidency, the Media, and the American Public* (Baltimore: Johns Hopkins Press, 2005).

26 Antony Sutton, *Wall Street and the Rise of Hitler* (Seal Beach, Cal.: '76 Press, 1976)

27 Michael Tad Allen, "The Business of Genocide: The SS, Slavery and the Concentration Camps," in Francis R. Nicosia and Jonathan Henner, eds., *Business and Industry in Nazi Germany* (Oxford, NY: Berghahn Books, 2004), 81–103

28 Bradford Snell, cited in Michael Dobbs, "Ford and GM Scrutinized for Alleged Nazi Collaboration," *Washington Post*, Nov. 30, 1998, A01 at http://www.washingtonpost.com/wp-srv/national/daily/nov98/nazicars30.htm

29 Peter F. Drucker, *Concept of the Corporation* (New York: The John Day Company, 1946); Alfred P. Sloan, *My Years with General Motors*, ed. John McDonald and Catharine Stevens (New York: Doubleday, 1990)

30 Alfred P. Sloan, cited by Black in *Nazi Nexus*, 102. See also Bradford Snell, "GM and the Nazis," in John C. Wood and Michael Wood, eds., *Alfred P. Sloan: Critical Evaluations in Business and Management* (London: Routledge, 2003)

31 Dimitry Anastakis, *Auto Pact: Creating a Borderless North American Auto Industry* (Toronto: University of Toronto Press, 2005)

32 Lamar Waldron, Thom Hartman, *Legacy of Secrecy: The Long Shadow of the JFK Assassination, Robert Kennedy, National Security, the Mafia, and the Assassinations of Martin Luther King* (Berkeley, Cal.: Counterpoint, 2008)

33 Thaddeus Russell, *Out of the Jungle: Jimmy Hoffa and the Remaking of the American Working Class* (New York: A.A. Knopf, 2001)

34 Antonin Dvorak, cited in Alec Robertson, *Dvorak* (London: J.M. Dent and Sons, 1964), 170

35 David E. Spiro, *The Hidden Hand of American Hegemony: Petrodollar Recycling and International Markets* (Ithaca, NY: Cornell University Press, 1999)

36 Bank of Credit and Commerce, History Commons at http://www.history commons.org/entity.jsp?entity=bank_of_credit_and_commerce_international

37 "The BCCI Affair: A Report to the Committee on Foreign Relations, United States Senate, by Senator John Kerry and Senator Hank Brown, December, 1992" at http://www.fas.org/irp/congress/1992_rpt/bcci/

38 Lucy Komisar, "The BCCI's Double Game: Banking on America, Banking on Jihad," in Steve Hiatt, ed., *A Game as Old as Empire: The Secret World of Economic Hit Men and the Web of Global Corruption* (San Francisco: Berrett-Koehler, 2007)

39 Chris Hedges, Massive Civil Unrest Possible Due to Economic Crisis, at http://www.socialdems.com/page.asp?pid=1559

40 Ahmed Mossededeq Nafeez, *The War on Freedom: Why America Was Attacked, September 11, 2001* (Joshua Tree, Cal.: Media Messenger Books, 2002)

41 Richard Lacayo, "Iran-Contra: The Cover-Up Begins to Crack," *Time*, June 24, 2001, at http://www.time.com/time/magazine/article/0,9171,157496,00.html; Oliver North Questioned – Rex 84 Exposed during Iran Contra at http://www.youtube.com/watch?v=UgoIL7k3elQ

42 Citations from Alfonso Chardy, "Reagan Aides and the Secret Government," *Miami Herald*, July 5, 1987, at http://www.theforbiddenknowledge.com/hardtruth/secret_white_house_plans.htm; *Geopolitical Monitor*, US FEMA Camps, at http://www.theforbiddenknowledge.com/hardtruth/secret_white_house_plans.htm

43 Peter Dale Scott, *The Road to 9/11: Wealth, Empire, and the Future of America* (Berkeley: University of California Press, 2007); James Mann, "The Armageddon Plan," *The Atlantic*, March 2004, at http://www.theatlantic.com/doc/200403/mann

44 On the "creative destruction" of capitalism, see Joseph A. Schumpeter, *Capitalism, Socialism, and Democracy* (New York: Harper, 1975), 82-5

45 Carolynne Wheeler, "Chinese Car Makers Target Foreign-Made Cachet," *Globe and Mail*, July 27, 2009, B1

46 Nadia Popova, "Canada-Russian Group Wins Opel," *Moscow Times*, June 1, 2009, at http://www.themoscowtimes.com/article/600/42/377551.htm

47 David Olive, "Car Czar Frank Stronach Opening New Opportunities," *Toronto Star*, June 14, 2009, at http://www.thestar.com/Business/article/650509

48 "Inside the Collapse of GM's Opel Deal," *Businessweek*, Nov. 10, 2009, at http://www.businessweek.com/globalbiz/content/nov2009/gb20091110_294573.htm

49 Remarks by the President at the Annual Conference of the American Medical Association, June 15, 2009, The White House Briefing Room at http://www.

whitehouse.gov/the_press_office/Remarks-by-the-President-to-the-Annual-Conference-of-the-American-Medical-Association/

50 http://www.google.ca/search?q=health+care+not+warfare+1993+timeline&hl=en&sa=X&tbs=tl:1&tbo=1&ei=XoZKSojHGZOqtgfH4OzaAw&oi=timeline_result&ct=title&resnum=11

51 Progressive Democrats of America, "Healthcare Not Warfare: Windmills not Weapons," Feb. 22, 2009, at http://www.pdamerica.org/articles/news/2009-02-22-11-24-33-news.php

52 David Welch and David Kiley, "The Tough Road Ahead for GM and Chrysler," *Businessweek*, May 27, 2009, at http://www.businessweek.com/magazine/content/09_23/b4134028500365.htm

53 Bradford Snell, "The Street Car Conspiracy: How General Motors Deliberately Destroyed Public Transit," Loveearth Network at http://www.lovearth.net/gmdeliberatelydestroyed.htm

54 Mathew Farish, "Panic, Civility and the Homeland," in Deborah Cowen and Emily Gilbert, eds., *War, Citizenship, Territory* (New York: Routledge, 2007), 105; Tom Lewis, *Divided Highways: Building the Interstate Highways, Transforming the American Way of Life* (New York: Penguin, 1999)

55 "The Decline of G.M.," *New York Times* video at http://www.youtube.com/watch?v=oxskbwkHN6U&feature=fvst

56 See Michael Moore, Goodbye GM, June, 1 2009, at http://www.huffingtonpost.com/michael-moore/goodbye-gm_b_209603.html

57 Tecumseh's speech, as described by Simon Pokagon, "The Massacre of Fort Dearborn at Chicago," *Harper's Magazine*, no. 98, 1899, 651

58 Juan Somavia, cited at International Labour Organization, Global Employment Trends, 2009, at http://www.ilo.org/wow/Newsbriefs/lang–en/WCMS_105188/index.htm

59 Chris Hedges, "America's Top Spy Warns Civil Riots," ceative-i at http://www.creative-i.info/?p=4778

60 Grant Robertson, "The Rob Interview," *Globe and Mail*, Dec. 24, 2008, B3

61 Kurt Nimmo, "EU Leaders Call for Global Currency," Axis of Logic, Oct. 18, 2008, at http://axisoflogic.com/artman/publish/article_28540.shtml

62 Todd Hirsch, "Junk the Greenback? Not So Fast," *Globe and Mail*, July 10, 2009

63 Robert Skidelsky, *John Maynard Keynes 1883–1946: Economist, Philosopher, Statesman* (London: Macmillan, 2003), 682–703

64 http://www.londonsummit.gov.uk/en/

65 Joseph Stiglitz, "One Small Step Forward," *The Guardian*, June 28, 2009, at http://www.guardian.co.uk/commentisfree/2009/jun/28/joseph-stiglitz-un-economic-crisis

66 President Harry S. Truman's Baylor University Speech, March 6, 1947, at http://www.presidency.ucsb.edu/ws/index.php?pid=12842

67 George J. Benston, *The Separation of Commercial and Investment Banking: The Glass-Steagall Act Revisited and Reconsidered* (New York: Oxford University Press, 1990)

68 Barry Ritholtz, *Bailout Nation: How Greed and Easy Money Corrupted Wall Street and Shook the World Economy* (Hoboken, NJ: Wiley, 2009), 139–40

69 Peter S. Goodman, "Taking a Hard Look at a Greenspan Legacy," *New York Times*, Oct. 8, 2009 at http://www.nytimes.com/2008/10/09/business/economy/09greenspan.html

70 Matt Taibbi, "The Great American Bubble Machine," *Rolling Stone*, July 9–23 , 2009, at http://zerohedge.blogspot.com/2009/06/goldman-sachs-engineering-every-major.html

71 Ellen Brown, "It's the Derivatives, Stupid! Why Fannie, Freddie, AIG Had to Be Bailed Out," Global Research.ca, Sept. 18, 2008, at http://www.globalresearch.ca/index.php?context=va&aid=10265

72 Robert O'Harrow Jr and Brady Dennis, "The Beautiful Machine," *Washington Post*, Dec. 29, 2008, at http://www.washingtonpost.com/wp-dyn/content/article/2008/12/28/AR2008122801916.html

73 Matt Taibbi, "The Big Takeover," *Rolling Stone*, March 19, 2009, at http://www.rollingstone.com/politics/story/26793903/the_big_takeover/print

74 Warren Buffett, Berkshire Hathaway Annual Report, 2002, at www.fintools.com/docs/Warren%20Buffet%20on%20Derivatives.pdf

75 Bank for International Settlements, Semiannual OTC derivative statistics at end-December 2008, http://www.bis.org/statistics/derstats.htm

76 Tom Foremski, "The Size of the Derivative Bubble+190k Per Person, *Silicon Valley Watcher*, Oct. 16, 2008, http://www.siliconvalleywatcher.com/mt/archives/2008/10/the_size_of_der.php

77 Ritholtz, *Bailout Nation*, 134

78 William Kleinknecht, *The Man Who Sold the World: Ronald Reagan and the Betrayal of Main Street* (New York: Nation Books, 2009)

79 Ronald Reagan, Address on Behalf of Senator Barry Goldwater, Oct. 24, 1964, at http://coursesa.matrix.msu.edu/~hst203/documents/ron.html

80 http://www.youtube.com/watch?v=x59wNGHe6iI

81 Kevin Phillips, *Bad Money: Reckless Finance, Failed Politics, and the Global Crisis of American Capitalism* (New York: Viking, 2008)

82 William D. Cohan, *House of Cards: A Tale of Hubris and Wretched Excess on Wall Street* (New York: Doubleday, 2009)

83 Office of the Special Inspector General for the Troubled Asset Relief Program, Quarterly Report to Congress, July 21, 2009, available at http://www.scribd.com/doc/17526813/July2009-Quarterly-Report-to-Congress

84 Ritholtz, *Bailout Nation*; Taibbi, "The Great American Bubble Machine"

85 Joe Nocera, "Propping Up a House of Cards," *New York Times*, Feb. 27, 2009, at http://www.nytimes.com/2009/02/28/business/28nocera.html?pagewanted=all

86 Maiden Lane LLC, Public Intelligence, July 7, 2009, at http://www.publicintelligence.net/?p=1210

87 Federal Reserve Bank of New York, Maiden Lane Transactions at http://www.newyorkfed.org/markets/maidenlane.html; Board of Governors, The Federal

Reserve System, Monthly Report on Credit and Liquidity Programs. June, 2009 at www.federalreserve.gov/newsevents/monthlyclbsreport200906.pdf

88 News Release, "AIG's Biggest Counterparties," March 15, 2009, at http://www. scribd.com/doc/13294757/AIGs-Biggest-Counterparties

89 Daniel Wagner, "Geithner Called On to Explain AIG Bailout Secrecy," Yahoo News, Jan. 9, 2010, at http://news.yahoo.com/s/ap/20100109/ ap_on_bi_ge/us_geithner_aig_hot_seat

90 Jill Schlesinger, "TARP Audit Finds Geithner Gave Away the Farm," CBC Money Watch, Nov. 17, 2009, at http://moneywatch.bnet.com/ economic-news/blog/financial-decoder/tarp-audit-finds-geithner-gave-away-the-farm/926/?tag=content;col1

91 Eliot Spitzer, "The Real AIG Scandal," Slate, March 17, 2009, at http://www. slate.com/id/2213942/; Spitzer, "Geithner's Disgrace," Slate, Nov. 23, 2009, at http://www.slate.com/id/2236460/

92 Richard Komaiko and Chris Stewart, "China's Imploding US Ally," Asia Times, Sept. 18, 2008, at http://www.atimes.com/atimes/China_Business/JI18Cb02. html; Richard Teitelbaum, "AIG's Greenberg Felled as Probes of Insurers Practices Mounted," Bloomberg.com, March 15, 2005, at http://www.bloomb-erg.com/apps/news?pid=10000103&sid=aLw6V6HBjFCU& refer=us; Michael C. Rupert, "AIG," From the Wilderness Publications, Aug. 14, 2001, at http://www.fromthewilderness.com/free/ciadrugs/part_2.html

93 Bradley F. Smith, In the Shadow of Warriors: oss and the Origins of the CIA (New York: Basic Books, 1983)

94 Mark Fritz. "The Secret (Insurance) Agent Men," Los Angeles Times, at http:// articles.latimes.com/2000/sep/22/news/mn-25118

95 Michael H. Hogan, A Cross of Iron: Harry S. Truman and the Origins of the National Security State (Cambridge: Cambridge University Press, 1998)

96 Peter Dale Scott, The War Conspiracy: The Secret Road to the Second Indochina War (Indianapolis: Bobbs Merrill, 1972); Scott, Drugs, Oil and War: The United States in Afghanistan, Colombia, and Indochina (Lanham, Md: Rowman and Littlefield, 2003)

97 "Down ... But Not Out," Time, June 13, 2009, at http://www.time.com/ time/magazine/article/0,9171,1071252-1,00.html. See the reports on AIG's activities by investigative reporter Lucy Komisar athttp://thekomisarscoop. com/2008/12/19/aigs-past-could-return-to-haunt/; http://thekomisarscoop. com/2005/03/17/the-fall-of-a-titan/; http://thekomisarscoop.com/2004/ 12/22/take-the-money-and-run-offshore/; http://thekomisarscoop.com/ 2004/11/17/cooking-the-insurance-books-a-decade-of-lax-regulation-lays-groundwork-for-scandal/http://thekomisarscoop.com/2004/11/01/ cooking-the-insurance-books/.

98 See Kevin Ryan, "Demolition Access to the WTC Towers: Part One and Part Two," and "Carlyle, Kissinger, SAIC and Halliburton: A 9/11 Convergence," Dec. 12, 2009, at 911 Review.com, articles by Kevin Ryan at http://911review. com/articles/ryan/index.html.

99 Ronald Shelp with Al Ehrbar, *Fallen Giant: The Amazing Story of Hank Greenberg and the History of* AIG (Hoboken, NJ: John Wiley and Sons, 2006), 10

100 Wayne Madsen, "AIG Is a Special Case," Sept. 23, 2008, at http://onlinejournal.com/artman/publish/article_3777.shtml

101 At http://www.fas.org/irp/cfr.html

102 "Adnan Khashoggi," Source Watch: A Project of the Centre for Media and Democracy at http://www.sourcewatch.org/index.php?title=Adnan_Khashoggi

103 Ron Scherer, "A Top Insurance Company as the New Enron," *Christian Science Monitor*, April 1, 2005, at http://www.csmonitor.com/2005/0401/p03s01-usju.html

104 Chalmers Johnson, *Blowback: The Cost and Consequences of American Empire* (New York: Metropolitan Books, 2000)

105 Jason Mason, "AIG Is a Hedge Fund and So Are Large Impaired Banks," RGE Monitor, March 6, 2009, at http://www.rge-onitor.com/globalmacro-monitor/255857/aig_is_a_hedge_fund__and_so_are_large_impaired_banks

106 Edmund L. Andrews, "3 Trustees of AIG Are Quiet, Perhaps to a Fault," *New York Times*, April 19, 2009, at http://www.nytimes.com/2009/04/20/business/20trustees.html

107 John Ralston Saul, *A Fair Country* (Toronto: Viking Canada, 2008)

108 Tom Molloy, *The World Is Our Witness: The Historic Journey of the Nisga'a into Canada* (Saskatoon: Fifth House, 2000)

EPILOGUE

1 John Yewell, Chris Dodge, and Jan DeSirey, eds., *Confronting Columbus: An Anthology* (Jefferson, NC: McFarland and Co., 1992)

2 Bill Bigelow, Barbara Miner, and Bob Peterson, "Why Rethink Columbus?" in Bill Bigelow et al., *Rethinking Columbus: Teaching about the 500th Anniversary of Columbus's Arrival in America* (Washington, DC: Rethinking Schools, 1991), 3

3 Howard Zinn, *A People's History of the United States, 1492–Present*, Twentieth Anniversary edition (New York: Perennial, 2003). See also Claudia L. Bushman, *America Discovers Columbus: How an Italian Explorer Became an American Hero* (Hanover, NH: University Press of New England, 1992); Francis Jennings, *The Founders of America* (New York: W.W. Norton, 1993); Ronald Wright, *Stolen Continents: The "New World" through Indian Eyes since 1492* (Toronto: Viking, 1992); Thomas R. Berger, *A Long and Terrible Shadow: White Values, Native Rights in the Americas, 1492–1992* (Vancouver: Douglas and McIntyre, 1991); Ron Bourgeault, Dave Broad, et al., eds., *1492–1992: Five Centuries of Imperialism and Resistance* (Winnipeg / Halifax: Society for Socialist Studies / Fernwood Publishing, 1992); Djelal Kadir, *Columbus and the Ends of the Earth* (Berkeley: University of California Press, 1992); Elizabeth Martinez, ed., *500 Years of Chicano History* (Albuquerque: Southwest Organizing Project, 1991)

4 Henry Reynolds, "A Crossroads of Conscience," in Michelle Grattan, ed., *Reconciliation: Essays on Australian Reconciliation* (Melbourne: Black Inc, 2000), 54

5 Zinn, *A People's History*, 628

6 President George W. Bush, cited in David Reynolds, *One World Divisible: A Global History since 1945* (New York: W.W. Norton, 2000), 588

7 Ibid., 589. See Majid Khadduri and Edmund Ghareeb, *War in the Gulf, 1990–1991: The Iraq-Kuwait Conflict and Its Implications* (New York: Oxford University Press, 1997); Dilip Hiro, *Desert Shield to Desert Storm: The Second Gulf War* (London: HarperCollins, 1992)

8 Teresa Aparicio, "Indigenous Peoples in Rio: The Kari-Oca World Indigenous Conference," in *IWGIA Newsletter* (International Work Group for Indigenous Affairs), no. 4, Oct. / Nov. / Dec. 1992, 59

9 Rigoberta Menchú, cited in Lydia van de Fliert, Introduction, *Indigenous Peoples and International Organizations*, ed. Lydia van de Fliert (Nottingham, UK: Spokesman, 1994), 7

10 Marcos Terena, cited in Aparicio, "Indigenous Peoples in Rio," 56

11 Rigoberta Menchú, cited in Bill Weinberg, "Rigoberta Menchú Calls for Latin America War Crimes Tribunal," *Native Americas Journal*, Aug. 29, 2001, at http://www.dialoguebetweennations.com/dbnetwork/spanish/rigoberta.htm

12 Simon Dubnow, cited in Michael R. Marrus, *The Holocaust in History* (Toronto: Key Porter Books, 2000), xiii

Acknowledgments

The appearance of *Earth into Property*, the second volume of *The Bowl with One Spoon*, follows the release in December 2009 of James Cameron's blockbuster, *Avatar*. This popularity of this film at the box office speaks of the impact of this anti-imperial extravaganza throughout the world – it can be understood as an iconographic announcement of a new ethos in world public opinion. A significant constituency is no longer willing to sanction the reckless and unaccountable activities of a rogue military-industrial complex tied to the so-called national security apparatus of the United States.

Cameron breaks new creative ground with his visual explorations of the rich web of life linking the human-like inhabitants of a distant orb in the Milky Way to the indigenous ecology of a menaced paradise. In my view this creative twist is far from ephemeral. As I emphasize throughout both volumes of *The Bowl with One Spoon*, much of the Fourth World's essence lies in the urge to protect and cultivate biological diversity among our plant and animals relatives. This imperative is deeply intertwined with the ability of human groups and individuals to sustain and renew our own forms of cultural pluralism. Hence the *biocultural* diversity celebrated as a key feature of the Fourth World emanates from the happy embrace of variety and difference as one of life's great hallmarks of regenerative vigour. The Fourth World provides a venue of decolonizing escape from the oppressive conformities of monocultural empire as globalized through the coercive power of imperial capital.

In spite of its search for simple answers, *Avatar* rates highly as a genuine cinematic contribution to the life-affirming potential of the Fourth World. It highlights a vision of the future with deep roots in the documented history of European and Euro-American colonization as outlined in *The American Empire and the Fourth World* as well as in its sequel, *Earth into Property*. While both texts form parts of *The Bowl with One Spoon*, each is written in such a way that it can be read in isolation from the other. Each volume is a self-contained work of non-fiction.

The saga of colonialism's ascent and transformation to form the world-wide basis for monopoly capitalism is well recorded. There is extensive documentary evidence to demonstrate empirically the force of this trajectory of commercialized appropriation of colonialism's expansionary machinery. This continuity of warring aggression on imperialism's moving frontiers has never ended in many parts of the world where the ownership and control of natural resources is still heavily contested. The ongoing appropriations of lands and resources from Indigenous peoples in the Western Hemisphere, but especially in the United States, should be understood as events of particular strategic importance in many essential trajectories of global change. The dispossession of Indigenous peoples in the transformation of large parts of the earth into the private property of individuals and corporations must be afforded careful consideration in any conscientious account of the historical genesis of global capitalism.

At various points as I worked on this project I have reflected on the relationship between character and circumstance in the making of history. Awareness of the complexities of interpretation looming behind this deceptively simple concept came my way as I discovered the work of Donald Creighton during my early years as a graduate student. Creighton helped draw my attention to the strategic importance of intercultural communications in the making of my country and, more generally, in the globalization of imperial capital. To this day I continue to be attached to Tory interpretations of transatlantic history as elaborated by Creighton and by others, including the Canadian philosopher George Grant. Both Creighton and J.M.S. Carless, my doctoral supervisor at the University of Toronto, were strong proponents of using good literary technique to bring the past to life. This same focus infused the publications of many of my teachers in the University of Toronto History Department, including Carl Berger, Graeme Patterson, Michael Bliss, Sylvia Van Kirk, Desmond Morton, and Robert Craig Brown. As a historian of the British Empire, A.P. Thornton helped me to see the advantages of looking across broad sweeps of time and place as I gradually moved to wider perspectives on how the present keeps being remade not only from the ingredients of the past but also from changes in popular perceptions of the past.

In writing *Earth into Property* I have endeavoured to transcend many straightjackets of academic specialization in order to attempt an interdisciplinary, intercultural portrait of globalization. I want to emphasize, however, that many of my perspectives on, and interpretations of, historical developments the world over remain grounded in my foundational studies at the University of Toronto. My understanding of world history has been informed especially by the patterns of interaction I first encountered in my investigations of the fur trade, of treaty negotiations with Indigenous peoples, and of the many involvements of North American First Nations in the imperial wars of the European powers and the civil wars of Anglo-America.

My first permanent academic post was as the history expert in the Native Studies Department at the University of Sudbury. As president of this university over most of the period between 1982 and 1989 when I was employed there, Father Laurent Larouche often imparted good advice. So too did Professor Nahum Kanhai, who stands out as a real champion and innovator of Native Studies in the tradition of the Sudbury department's justice-pursuing founder, Ed Newberry. One of the highlights of my years in Sudbury was my participation between 1983 and 1987 in four constitutional conferences on Aboriginal matters. These unprecedented meetings brought together the prime minister of Canada, the provincial and territorial premiers, and the leaders of four national organizations representing Indians, Inuit, and Métis. As the process developed, I increased my formal and informal collaboration with a number of Aboriginal organizations involved in an initiative aimed at giving more explicit constitutional definition to the affirmation of existing Aboriginal and treaty rights in Canada's "supreme law." My consultative role with these organizations tended to revolve around my friendship and fruitful working relationship with Ernie Debassige from Manitoulin Island. Ernie's formal title was elder of the Union of Ontario Indians, and he became my elder, mentor, and teacher on a vast array of topics, many of them reflected in the subject matter of *The Bowl with One Spoon*.

Canada's grappling with its constitutional affirmation of Aboriginal and treaty rights is part of an international process involving continuing cycles of colonization whose origins go back to the inception, in 1492, of the modern era of imperial globalization. The most recent examples of imperialism's reoccurring resource grabs from Indigenous peoples have been advanced in the name of the Global War on Terror. This campaign of violent state aggression has included the recycling of many of the old paradigms that reassert the imagined Manifest Destiny of Western Civilization to overwhelm militarily and culturally the imagined depravity of Aboriginal savagery.

My interest in the revision of many old paradigms of imperial propaganda drew me to devote considerable attention in *Earth into Property* to a careful distinction between facts and fiction in assessing the background, substance, and outgrowths of the 9/11 attacks. The events of that tragic day of infamy were instrumental in enabling many agencies of the military-industrial complex to shake off their aura of obsolescence in the post–Cold War era and to acquire enhanced funding, investment, prestige, and political clout. The many psychological and political obstacles preventing a proper evidence-based assessment of what really happened to originate this War on Terror have attracted attentive scholarly consideration by those responsible for the February 2010 issue of the *American Behavioral Scientist*. The authors and editors of these articles have joined forces to identify and examine various episodes of what they refer to as "State Crimes against Democracy." The appearance of this publication is a promising sign that we are moving beyond a particularly bleak period in the academy, when many in the professoriate became outright agents of, or complicit through their silence in, the fear mongering and superstition connected to an implausible official explanation of the 9/11 attacks.

The hasty implantation of a potent public myth to cover the absence of any immediate and credible forensic investigation of 9/11 helped to manufacture an initial wave of public opinion conducive to resuscitating the interests of those who had benefited most from lucrative activities on the capitalist side of the Cold War. A smattering of academics have endured campaigns of disinformation and smear to insist that the standard rules of evidence should be applied to a critical assessment of the originating acts of the 9/11 wars. Prominent among the Canadian contingent of this international network of scholarly truth seekers are Graeme MacQueen, the founder of the Peace Studies Centre and Program at McMaster University; Professor John McMurtry, a philosophy professor and fellow of the Royal Society of Canada; Michael Keefer of the University of Guelph's English Department; and Michel Chossudovsky, a University of Ottawa economist who founded and oversees Global Research.ca. Their example and encouragement have been instrumental in helping me to emphasize evidence over orthodoxy in discussing the origins of the 9/11 wars and all instances of illegal aggression that have been influential in shaping the landscape of global geopolitics during the difficult first decade of the twenty-first century.

My Canadian colleagues and I have drawn heavily on the pioneering work of Professors David Ray Griffin and Peter Dale Scott. I have benefited significantly from the opportunity to discuss many aspects of this contentious field of study with, to name only a few, Dr Kevin Barrett, Patrick Biron, Pierre Blais, Debora Blake, Carol Brouillet, Richard Gage, Noel Glynn, Ken Jenkins, David Kubiak, Annie Machon, Dr Paul McArthur, Cynthia McKinney, Micheal Pengue, Dr Paul Rae, Jeremy Rothe-Kushel, Kevin Ryan, Elizabeth Woodworth, Adnan Zuberi, Barrie Zwicker, and Splitting The Sky. I consider Splitting the Sky's controversial life, work, and studies as a proponent of decolonization and the rule of law in chapter 12 of this volume.

The University of Lethbridge, the institution that has employed me now for two decades, has contributed generously to the publication of both *The American Empire* and *Earth into Property*. When I joined the Department of Native American Studies there in 1990 I was surprised to learn that its address was also the address of the World Council of Indigenous Peoples. The international orientation of Native American Studies at my home institution provided a good environment for me to continue to broaden my research into the global extent of the complex of forces integral to both colonization and decolonization. The increasing controversy surrounding the changing imperatives of global commerce helped stimulate my urge to expand my subject area to the point where I successfully pitched to my dean in 2002 the idea of initiating a new academic unit to be known as Globalization Studies. Not all these professional transitions took place without controversy and political friction. I want to extend thanks particularly to Professors Brian Titley of the Faculty of Education and Malcolm Greenshields of the History Department for helping me to transform crises into opportunities for intellectual, professional, and institutional growth.

The University of Lethbridge contributed to the financing of this project in the name of helping the humanities and social studies to keep up with the more richly funded academic units devoted to the hard sciences and applied technology. The decision to proceed in this way was initiated by Dr Howard Tennant when he was president. Over the decade between the formulation of this plan and the publication of *Earth into Property*, Dr Tennant's original commitment to McGill-Queen's University Press has been renewed and enhanced by Dr Bill Cade and Dr Michael Mahon during their terms as president. The instrumental role of the Office of the President in helping to subsidize the costs of this publishing project has been mirrored by the contribution of the Office of the Dean of Arts and Science, as ably filled by Dr Bhagwan Dua and then by Dr Chris Nicol.

As a representative of the Faculty Association and more recently as vice-president academic of our school, Dr Andy Hakin has played a particularly constructive role in making it possible for the *Bowl with One Spoon* to come to fruition. I extend my deepest thanks to Andy and all the other colleagues at the University of Lethbridge who have played a part in bringing these two big and weighty volumes into the public domain. I want particularly to recognize the especially supportive friendship and advice of Professor Bruce MacKay of Liberal Education.

My greatest debt, however, is to my students in both Native American Studies and Globalization Studies. Over the years at Lethbridge, they have provided the atmosphere of curiosity and questioning engagement in which many of the ideas that appear in these volumes were first articulated, clarified, and refined. In particular I want to thank Joshua Blakeney for his commitment to, and engagement in, many of the concepts and agendas proposed in this text. For stimulating discussions, I want to thank my colleagues Donald B. Smith, Janet Chute, Malcolm Davidson, John Bacher, Paul Kennedy, Michael Posluns, Peter Kulchyski, Blair Stonechild, Joyce Green, Johanne Clare, and Heidi Rimke. In my work on Aboriginal issues in British Columbia I have drawn insights and leads from three veterans of the struggle there – Patricia Kelly, David Suzuki, and Miles Richardson.

With her sage advice and thoughtful interventions, Rebecca Shamai has grounded and inspired me as I grappled with the crucial final stages of this project. She introduced me to her interesting group of friends, colleagues, and associates, some of whom are, like her, judges in the Ontario Court of Justice. Prominent among these jurists are Patrick Sheppard and Mel Green, both of whom have assisted me in working through some of the key issues of interpretation addressed in this text. In this same circle of camaraderie and professional expertise I have reached out to Professor L. Jane McMillan, Canada Research Chair on Indigenous Peoples and Sustainable

Communities at St Francis Xavier University in Antigonish, Nova Scotia. I want to acknowledge, moreover, the helpful suggestions offered by Dr Xiolan Zhoa and Naomi Duguid. Whitney Smith, my old friend going back to our days in York Mills, has played a unique role in the genesis of this text, beginning with his urging me to travel to Africa in 1970. In recent years Jerry Mamid has made time for our broad-ranging discussions.

Much of the work of transforming my manuscripts into published volumes has taken place in the legendary Montreal offices of McGill-Queen's University Press. The first proponent of the *Bowl* project was Bruce G. Trigger, to whom *Earth into Property* is dedicated. I also owe a large debt of gratitude to Philip Cercone, the director. Throughout this period I have come to see Joan McGilvray, the managing editor, as the literary dean of MQUP. Design / production manager Susanne McAdam oversees and coordinates the final stages of book production.

The copy editor of both *The American Empire* and *Earth into Property* is Rosemary Shipton. She has encouraged me and guided me tirelessly throughout the lengthy process of moving concepts along from spoken ideas, to scribbling, to manuscript, to revised manuscript to published text. Rosemary wisely recruited Barney Gilmore to take on the large task of writing *Earth into Property*'s excellent index. Barney tells me it contains more than 7,000 page references. David Drummond has created the eye-catching jacket designs for both volumes of *The Bowl with One Spoon*. Even with all the help, encouragement, inspiration, and advice I have received along the way, however, responsibility for any mistakes that may have been made in bringing the *Bowl* project to publication is entirely my own.

Index

Note: the abbreviation MIC, used periodically in this index, denotes the Military Industrial Complex.